Nineteenth-Century Literature Criticism

Guide to Gale Literary Criticism Series

When you need to review criticism of literary works, these are the Gale series to use:

If the author's death date is:

You should turn to:

After Dec. 31, 1959
(or author is still living)

CONTEMPORARY LITERARY CRITICISM

for example: Jorge Luis Borges, Anthony Burgess,
William Faulkner, Mary Gordon,
Ernest Hemingway, Iris Murdoch

1900 through 1959

TWENTIETH-CENTURY LITERARY CRITICISM

for example: Willa Cather, F. Scott Fitzgerald,
Henry James, Mark Twain, Virginia Woolf

1800 through 1899

NINETEENTH-CENTURY LITERATURE CRITICISM

for example: Fedor Dostoevski, Nathaniel Hawthorne,
George Sand, William Wordsworth

1400 through 1799

LITERATURE CRITICISM FROM 1400 TO 1800
(excluding Shakespeare)

for example: Anne Bradstreet, Daniel Defoe,
Alexander Pope, François Rabelais,
Jonathan Swift, Phillis Wheatley

SHAKESPEAREAN CRITICISM

Shakespeare's plays and poetry

Antiquity through 1399

CLASSICAL AND MEDIEVAL LITERATURE CRITICISM

for example: Dante, Homer, Plato, Sophocles, Vergil,
the Beowulf Poet

Gale also publishes related criticism series:

CHILDREN'S LITERATURE REVIEW

This series covers authors of all eras who write for the preschool through high school audience.

SHORT STORY CRITICISM

This series covers the major short fiction writers of all nationalities and periods of literary history.

Volume 19

Nineteenth-Century Literature Criticism

Excerpts from Criticism of the
Works of Novelists, Poets, Playwrights,
Short Story Writers, Philosophers, and Other
Creative Writers Who Died between 1800
and 1899, from the First Published Critical
Appraisals to Current Evaluations

Janet Mullane
Robert Thomas Wilson
Editor

Gail Ann Schulte
Associate Editor

 Gale Research Inc. · DETROIT · LONDON

Contents

Preface

The nineteenth century was a time of tremendous growth in human endeavor: in science, in social history, and particularly in literature. The era saw the development of the novel, witnessed radical changes from classicism to romanticism to realism, and fostered intellectual and artistic ideas that continue to inspire authors of our own century. The importance of the writers of the nineteenth century is twofold, for they provide insight into their own time as well as into the universal nature of human experience.

The literary criticism of an era can also give us insight into the moral and intellectual atmosphere of the past because the criteria by which a work of art is judged reflect current philosophical and social attitudes. Literary criticism takes many forms: the traditional essay, the book or play review, even the parodic poem. Criticism can also be of several types: normative, descriptive, interpretive, textual, appreciative, generic. Collectively, the range of critical response helps us to understand a work of art, an author, an era.

Scope of the Series

Nineteenth-Century Literature Criticism (NCLC) is designed to serve as an introduction for the student of nineteenth-century literature to the authors of that period and to the most significant commentators on these authors. Since the analysis of this literature spans almost two hundred years, a vast amount of critical material confronts the student. For that reason, *NCLC* presents significant passages from published criticism to aid students in the location and selection of commentaries on authors who died between 1800 and 1899. The need for *NCLC* was suggested by the usefulness of the Gale series *Twentieth-Century Literary Criticism (TCLC)* and *Contemporary Literary Criticism (CLC)*, which excerpt criticism of creative writing of the twentieth century. For further information about *TCLC, CLC,* and Gale's other criticism series, users should consult the Guide to Gale Literary Criticism Series preceding the title page in this volume.

Each volume of *NCLC* is carefully compiled to include authors who represent a variety of genres and nationalities and who are currently regarded as the most important writers of their era. In addition to major authors who have attained worldwide renown, *NCLC* also presents criticism on lesser-known figures whose significant contributions to literary history are important to the study of nineteenth-century literature. These authors are important artists in their own right, and often enjoy such an immense popularity in their own countries that English-speaking readers should become more familiar with their work.

Author entries in *NCLC* are intended to be definitive overviews. In order to devote more attention to each writer, approximately ten to fifteen authors are included in each 600-page volume, compared with about forty authors in a *CLC* volume of similar size. The length of each author entry is intended to reflect the amount of attention the author has received from critics writing in English and from foreign critics in translation. Articles and books that have not been translated into English are excluded. However, since many of the major foreign studies have been translated into English and are excerpted in *NCLC,* author entries reflect the viewpoints of many nationalities. Each author entry represents a historical overview of critical reaction to the author's work: early criticism is presented to indicate initial responses, later selections represent any rise or decline in the author's literary reputation, and current analyses provide students with a modern perspective. In each entry, we have attempted to identify and include excerpts from all seminal essays of criticism.

An author may appear more than once in the series because of the great quantity of critical material available or because of a resurgence of criticism generated by events such as an author's centennial or anniversary celebration, the republication or posthumous publication of an author's works, or the publication of a newly translated work. Usually, one or more author entries in each volume of *NCLC* are devoted to individual works or groups of works by major authors who have appeared previously in the series. Only those works that have been the subjects of extensive criticism and are widely studied in literature courses are selected for this in-depth treatment. Jane Austen's *Emma*, Gustave Flaubert's *L'éducation sentimentale: Histoire d'un jeune homme (Sentimental Education: A Young Man's History)*, and Washington Irving's *The Sketch Book of Geoffrey Crayon, Gent.*, are the subjects of such entries in *NCLC,* Volume 19.

Organization of the Book

An author entry consists of the following elements: author heading, biographical and critical introduction, principal works, excerpts of criticism (each preceded by explanatory notes and followed by a bibliographical citation), and an additional bibliography for further reading.

- The *author heading* consists of the author's full name, followed by birth and death dates. The unbracketed portion of the name denotes the form under which the author most commonly wrote. If an author wrote consistently under a pseudonym, the pseudonym will be listed in the author heading and the real name given in parentheses on the first line of the biographical and critical introduction. Also located at the beginning of the introduction are any name variations under which an author wrote, including transliterated forms for authors whose languages use nonroman alphabets. Uncertainty as to a birth or death date is indicated by a question mark.

- A *portrait* of the author is included when available. Many entries also feature illustrations of materials pertinent to an author's career, including manuscript pages, letters, book illustrations, and representations of important people, places, and events in an author's life.

- The *biographical and critical introduction* contains background information that introduces the reader to an author and to the critical debate surrounding his or her work. When applicable, biographical and critical introductions are followed by references to additional entries on the author in other literary reference series published by Gale Research Inc., including *Dictionary of Literary Biography, Children's Literature Review,* and *Something about the Author.*

- The list of *principal works* is chronological by date of first book publication and identifies the genre of each work. In those instances where the first publication was in other than the English language, the title and date of the first English-language edition are given in brackets. Unless otherwise indicated, dramas are dated by the first performance, rather than first publication.

- *Criticism* is arranged chronologically in each author entry to provide a useful perspective on changes in critical evaluation over the years. All titles by the author featured in the critical entry are printed in boldface type to enable the user to ascertain without difficulty the works being discussed. Also for purposes of easier identification, the critic's name and the publication date of the essay are given at the beginning of each piece of criticism. Unsigned criticism is preceded by the title of the journal in which it appeared. When an anonymous essay is later attributed to a critic, the critic's name appears in brackets at the beginning of the excerpt and in the bibliographical citation. Publication information (such as publisher names and book prices) and parenthetical numerical references (such as footnotes or page and line references to specific editions of works) have been deleted at the editor's discretion to provide smoother reading of the text.

- Critical essays are prefaced with *explanatory notes* as an additional aid to students using *NCLC*. The explanatory notes provide several types of useful information, including the reputation of the critic, the importance of a work of criticism, a synopsis of the essay, the specific approach of the critic (biographical, psychoanalytic, structuralist, etc.), and the growth of critical controversy or changes in critical trends regarding an author's work. In some cases, these notes include cross-references to related criticism in the author's entry or in the additional bibliography. Dates in parentheses within the explanatory notes refer to the dates of other essays in the author entry.

- A complete *bibliographical citation* designed to facilitate the location of the original essay or book follows each piece of criticism.

- The *additional bibliography* appearing at the end of each author entry suggests further reading on the author. In some cases it includes essays for which the editors could not obtain reprint rights.

An appendix lists the sources from which material in the volume is reprinted. It does not, however, list every book or periodical consulted for the volume.

Cumulative Indexes

Each volume of *NCLC* includes a cumulative index listing all the authors who have appeared in *Contemporary Literary Criticism, Twentieth-Century Literary Criticism, Nineteenth-Century Literature Criticism, Literature*

Criticism from 1400 to 1800, Classical and Medieval Literature Criticism, and *Short Story Criticism,* along with cross-references to the Gale series *Children's Literature Review, Authors in the News, Contemporary Authors, Contemporary Authors Autobiography Series, Dictionary of Literary Biography, Concise Dictionary of American Literary Biography, Something about the Author, Something about the Author Autobiography Series,* and *Yesterday's Authors of Books for Children.* Readers will welcome this cumulated author index as a useful tool for locating an author within the various series. The index, which lists birth and death dates when available, will be particularly valuable for those authors who are identified with a certain period but whose death dates cause them to be placed in another, or for those authors whose careers span two periods. For example, Fedor Dostoevski is found in *NCLC,* yet Leo Tolstoy, another major nineteenth-century Russian novelist, is found in *TCLC.*

Each volume of *NCLC* also includes a cumulative nationality index to authors. Authors are listed alphabetically by nationality, followed by the volume numbers in which they appear.

New Index

An important feature now appearing in *NCLC* is a cumulative title index, an alphabetical listing of the literary works discussed in the series since its inception. Each title listing includes the corresponding volume and page numbers where criticism may be located. Foreign language titles that have been translated are followed by the titles of the translations, for example: *Die Leiden des jungen Werthers (The Sorrows of Young Werther).* Page numbers following these translated titles refer to all pages on which any form of the title, either foreign language or translated, appears. Titles of novels, dramas, nonfiction books, and poetry, short story, or essay collections are printed in italics, while all individual poems, short stories, and essays are printed in roman type within quotation marks. In cases where the same title is used by different authors, the author's surname is given in parentheses after the title, e.g., *Poems* (Wordsworth) and *Poems* (Coleridge).

Acknowledgments

No work of this scope can be accomplished without the cooperation of many people. The editors especially wish to thank the copyright holders of the excerpted criticism included in this volume, the permissions managers of many book and magazine publishing companies for assisting us in securing reprint rights, and Anthony Bogucki for assistance with copyright research. We are also grateful to the staffs of the Detroit Public Library, the Library of Congress, University of Michigan Library, and Wayne State University Library for making their resources available to us.

Suggestions Are Welcome

In response to various suggestions, several features have been added to *NCLC* since the series began, including: explanatory notes to excerpted criticism that provide important information regarding critics and their work; a cumulative author index listing authors in all Gale literary criticism series; entries devoted to criticism on a single work by a major author; more extensive illustrations; and a cumulative title index listing all the literary works discussed in the series.

The editors welcome additional comments and suggestions for expanding the coverage and enhancing the usefulness of the series.

Authors to Appear in Future Volumes

About, Edmond François 1828-1885
Aguilo I. Fuster, Maria 1825-1897
Aksakov, Konstantin 1817-1860
Aleardi, Aleardo 1812-1878
Alecsandri, Vasile 1821-1890
Alencar, José 1829-1877
Alfieri, Vittorio 1749-1803
Allingham, William 1824-1889
Almquist, Carl Jonas Love 1793-1866
Alorne, Leonor de Almeida 1750-1839
Alsop, Richard 1761-1815
Altimirano, Ignacio Manuel 1834-1893
Alvarenga, Manuel Inacio da Silva
    1749-1814
Alvares de Azevedo, Manuel Antonio
    1831-1852
Anzengruber, Ludwig 1839-1889
Arany, Janos 1817-1882
Arène, Paul 1843-1896
Aribau, Bonaventura Carlos 1798-1862
Arjona de Cubas, Manuel Maria de
    1771-1820
Arnault, Antoine Vincent 1766-1834
Arneth, Alfred von 1819-1897
Arnim, Bettina von 1785-1859
Arriaza y Superviela, Juan Bautista
    1770-1837
Asbjörnsen, Peter Christen 1812-1885
Ascasubi, Hilario 1807-1875
Atterbom, Per Daniel Amadeus
    1790-1855
Aubanel, Theodore 1829-1886
Auerbach, Berthold 1812-1882
Augier, Guillaume V.E. 1820-1889
Azeglio, Massimo D' 1798-1866
Azevedo, Guilherme de 1839-1882
Bakin (pseud. of Takizawa Okikani)
    1767-1848
Bakunin, Mikhail Aleksandrovich
    1814-1876
Baratynski, Jewgenij Abramovich
    1800-1844
Barnes, William 1801-1886
Batyushkov, Konstantin 1778-1855
Beattie, James 1735-1803
Becquer, Gustavo Adolfo 1836-1870
Bentham, Jeremy 1748-1832
Béranger, Jean-Pierre de 1780-1857
Berchet, Giovanni 1783-1851
Berzsenyi, Daniel 1776-1836
Black, William 1841-1898
Blair, Hugh 1718-1800
Blicher, Steen Steensen 1782-1848
Bocage, Manuel Maria Barbosa du
    1765-1805

Boratynsky, Yevgeny 1800-1844
Borel, Petrus 1809-1859
Boreman, Yokutiel 1825-1890
Borne, Ludwig 1786-1837
Botev, Hristo 1778-1842
Brinckman, John 1814-1870
Brown, Charles Brockden 1777-1810
Büchner, Georg 1813-1837
Campbell, James Edwin 1867-1895
Carlyle, Thomas 1795-1881
Castelo Branco, Camilo 1825-1890
Castro Alves, Antonio de 1847-1871
Chivers, Thomas Holly 1807?-1858
Claudius, Matthias 1740-1815
Clough, Arthur Hugh 1819-1861
Cobbett, William 1762-1835
Colenso, John William 1814-1883
Coleridge, Hartley 1796-1849
Collett, Camilla 1813-1895
Comte, Auguste 1798-1857
Conrad, Robert T. 1810-1858
Conscience, Hendrik 1812-1883
Cooke, Philip Pendleton 1816-1850
Corbière, Edouard 1845-1875
Crabbe, George 1754-1832
Cruz E Sousa, João da 1861-1898
Desbordes-Valmore, Marceline
    1786-1859
Deschamps, Emile 1791-1871
Deus, Joao de 1830-1896
Dickinson, Emily 1830-1886
Dinis, Julio 1839-1871
Dinsmoor, Robert 1757-1836
Du Maurier, George 1834-1896
Eminescy, Mihai 1850-1889
Engels, Friedrich 1820-1895
Espronceda, José 1808-1842
Ettinger, Solomon 1799-1855
Euchel, Issac 1756-1804
Ferguson, Samuel 1810-1886
Fernández de Lizardi, José Joaquín
    1776-1827
Fernández de Moratín, Leandro
    1760-1828
Fet, Afanasy 1820-1892
Feuillet, Octave 1821-1890
Fontane, Theodor 1819-1898
Freiligrath, Hermann Ferdinand
    1810-1876
Freytag, Gustav 1816-1895
Ganivet, Angel 1865-1898
Garrett, Almeida 1799-1854
Garshin, Vsevolod Mikhaylovich
    1855-1888
Gezelle, Guido 1830-1899

Ghalib, Asadullah Khan 1797-1869
Goldschmidt, Meir Aaron 1819-1887
Goncalves Dias, Antonio 1823-1864
Griboyedov, Aleksander Sergeyevich
    1795-1829
Grigor'yev, Appolon Aleksandrovich
    1822-1864
Groth, Klaus 1819-1899
Grun, Anastasius (pseud. of Anton
    Alexander Graf von Auersperg)
    1806-1876
Guerrazzi, Francesco Domenico
    1804-1873
Gutierrez Najera, Manuel 1859-1895
Gutzkow, Karl Ferdinand 1811-1878
Ha-Kohen, Shalom 1772-1845
Halleck, Fitz-Greene 1790-1867
Harris, George Washington 1814-1869
Hayne, Paul Hamilton 1830-1886
Hazlitt, William 1778-1830
Hebbel, Christian Friedrich 1813-1863
Hebel, Johann Peter 1760-1826
Hegel, Georg Wilhelm Friedrich
    1770-1831
Heiberg, Johann Ludvig 1813-1863
Herculano, Alexandre 1810-1866
Hertz, Henrik 1798-1870
Herwegh, Georg 1817-1875
Hoffman, Charles Fenno 1806-1884
Hooper, Johnson Jones 1815-1863
Horton, George Moses 1798-1880
Howitt, William 1792-1879
Hughes, Thomas 1822-1896
Imlay, Gilbert 1754?-1828?
Irwin, Thomas Caulfield 1823-1892
Isaacs, Jorge 1837-1895
Jacobsen, Jens Peter 1847-1885
Jippensha, Ikku 1765-1831
Kant, Immanuel 1724-1804
Karr, Jean Baptiste Alphonse
    1808-1890
Keble, John 1792-1866
Khomyakov, Alexey S. 1804-1860
Kierkegaard, Søren 1813-1855
Kinglake, Alexander W. 1809-1891
Kingsley, Charles 1819-1875
Kivi, Alexis 1834-1872
Koltsov, Alexey Vasilyevich 1809-1842
Kotzebue, August von 1761-1819
Kraszewski, Josef Ignacy 1812-1887
Kreutzwald, Friedrich Reinhold
    1803-1882
Krochmal, Nahman 1785-1840
Krudener, Valeria Barbara Julia de
    Wietinghoff 1766-1824

Lampman, Archibald 1861-1899
Lebensohn, Micah Joseph 1828-1852
Leconte de Lisle, Charles-Marie-René 1818-1894
Leontyev, Konstantin 1831-1891
Leopardi, Giacoma 1798-1837
Leskov, Nikolai 1831-1895
Lever, Charles James 1806-1872
Levisohn, Solomon 1789-1822
Lewes, George Henry 1817-1878
Leyden, John 1775-1811
Lobensohn, Micah Gregory 1775-1810
Longstreet, Augustus Baldwin 1790-1870
López de Ayola y Herrera, Adelardo 1819-1871
Lover, Samuel 1797-1868
Luzzato, Samuel David 1800-1865
Macedo, Joaquim Manuel de 1820-1882
Macha, Karel Hynek 1810-1836
Mackenzie, Henry 1745-1831
Malmon, Solomon 1754-1800
Mangan, James Clarence 1803-1849
Manzoni, Alessandro 1785-1873
Marii, Jose 1853-1895
Markovic, Svetozar 1846-1875
Martínez de La Rosa, Francisco 1787-1862
Mathews, Cornelius 1817-1889
McCulloch, Thomas 1776-1843
Merriman, Brian 1747-1805
Meyer, Conrad Ferdinand 1825-1898
Montgomery, James 1771-1854
Morton, Sarah Wentworth 1759-1846
Müller, Friedrich 1749-1825
Murger, Henri 1822-1861
Neruda, Jan 1834-1891
Nestroy, Johann 1801-1862
Newman, John Henry 1801-1890
Niccolini, Giambattista 1782-1861
Nievo, Ippolito 1831-1861
Obradovic, Dositej 1742-1811
Oehlenschlager, Adam 1779-1850

O'Neddy, Philothee (pseud. of Theophile Dondey) 1811-1875
O'Shaughnessy, Arthur William Edgar 1844-1881
Ostrovsky, Alexander 1823-1886
Paine, Thomas 1737-1809
Peacock, Thomas Love 1785-1866
Perk, Jacques 1859-1881
Pisemsky, Alexey F. 1820-1881
Pompeia, Raul D'Avila 1863-1895
Popovic, Jovan Sterija 1806-1856
Praed, Winthrop Mackworth 1802-1839
Prati, Giovanni 1814-1884
Preseren, France 1800-1849
Pringle, Thomas 1789-1834
Procter, Adelaide Ann 1825-1864
Procter, Bryan Waller 1787-1874
Pye, Henry James 1745-1813
Quental, Antero Tarquinio de 1842-1891
Quinet, Edgar 1803-1875
Quintana, Manuel José 1772-1857
Radishchev, Aleksander 1749-1802
Raftery, Anthony 1784-1835
Raimund, Ferdinand 1790-1836
Reid, Mayne 1818-1883
Renan, Ernest 1823-1892
Reuter, Fritz 1810-1874
Rogers, Samuel 1763-1855
Ruckert, Friedrich 1788-1866
Runeberg, Johan 1804-1877
Rydberg, Viktor 1828-1895
Saavedra y Ramírez de Boquedano, Angel de 1791-1865
Sacher-Mosoch, Leopold von 1836-1895
Satanov, Isaac 1732-1805
Schiller, Johann Friedrich von 1759-1805
Schlegel, Karl 1772-1829
Senoa, August 1838-1881
Shulman, Kalman 1819-1899

Sigourney, Lydia Howard Huntley 1791-1856
Silva, Jose Asuncion 1865-1896
Slaveykov, Petko 1828-1895
Smith, Richard Penn 1799-1854
Smolenskin, Peretz 1842-1885
Stagnelius, Erik Johan 1793-1823
Staring, Antonie Christiaan Wynand 1767-1840
Stendhal (pseud. of Henri Beyle) 1783-1842
Stifter, Adalbert 1805-1868
Stone, John Augustus 1801-1834
Taunay, Alfredo d'Ecragnole 1843-1899
Taylor, Bayard 1825-1878
Tennyson, Alfred, Lord 1809-1892
Terry, Lucy (Lucy Terry Prince) 1730-1821
Thompson, Daniel Pierce 1795-1868
Thompson, Samuel 1766-1816
Tiedge, Christoph August 1752-1841
Timrod, Henry 1828-1867
Tommaseo, Nicolo 1802-1874
Tompa, Mihaly 1817-1888
Topelius, Zachris 1818-1898
Turgenev, Ivan 1818-1883
Tyutchev, Fedor I. 1803-1873
Uhland, Ludvig 1787-1862
Valaoritis, Aristotelis 1824-1879
Valles, Jules 1832-1885
Verde, Cesario 1855-1886
Villaverde, Cirilio 1812-1894
Vinje, Aasmund Olavsson 1818-1870
Vorosmarty, Mihaly 1800-1855
Weisse, Christian Felix 1726-1804
Welhaven, Johan S. 1807-1873
Werner, Zacharius 1768-1823
Wescott, Edward Noyes 1846-1898
Wessely, Nattali Herz 1725-1805
Woolson, Constance Fenimore 1840-1894
Zhukovsky, Vasily 1783-1852

Jane Austen

1775-1817

English novelist.

The following entry presents criticism of Austen's novel *Emma* (1816). For additional information on Austen's career and *Emma*, see *NCLC*, Vols. 1 and 13.

Emma is often considered Austen's most accomplished novel. Its polished style and balanced structure, as well as Austen's innovative handling of point of view, have earned for this, her last completed work, a place in the history of the development of English fiction. Although Austen predicted that her protagonist, Emma Woodhouse, would be "a heroine whom no one but myself will much like," her insightful portrayal of Emma's intriguing personality has made Emma one of the most attractive figures in English fiction. In addition, in Mr. George Knightley, Austen created what many critics consider her most fully developed male character, while the novel's secondary characters have also been praised as masterfully drawn. Ranking second only to Austen's earlier novel *Pride and Prejudice* in popularity, *Emma* has consistently appealed to readers who value Austen's distinctive irony, wit, and realism.

Austen began writing while she was living at her childhood home, the Steventon Rectory in Hampshire, England. Her life at Steventon, though sheltered from the world at large, gave her an intimate knowledge of a segment of English society—the landed gentry—that was to provide the materials for most of her fiction, and by 1787 Austen had already begun to produce stories, dramas, and short novels. Her first attempts to find a publisher for her novels failed, but finally in 1811 *Sense and Sensibility* was published, followed by *Pride and Prejudice* in 1813 and *Mansfield Park* in 1814. Austen's personal records indicate that she started writing *Emma* in January 1814, but some critics argue that *Emma* is actually a reworking of her novel *The Watsons,* which she began and abandoned in 1803. By March of 1815 Austen had completed *Emma.* When in the summer of that year she met James Stanier Clarke, librarian to the Prince Regent (later George IV), Clarke reported that the prince kept a set of her novels in each of his residences; following Clarke's urging, Austen dedicated *Emma,* which was soon to be published, to the prince.

Austen once described her chosen subject matter as "pictures of domestic life in country villages," and *Emma* is no exception to this pattern. The novel centers on the experiences and emotional development of its principal character, the beautiful, intelligent, and wealthy Emma Woodhouse. Priding herself on her powers of observation and imagination, Emma disregards the worthwhile advice of her long-standing friend and confidante, Mr. George Knightley, and obstinately meddles in the lives of her friends in Highbury. She plays matchmaker to Mr. Elton, the local clergyman, and her protégée, Harriet Smith; speculates on the character and affections of Jane Fairfax, her talented and attractive but reticent neighbor; and believes herself in love with Frank Churchill, a dashing, irresponsible young newcomer to Highbury. In each instance, Emma eschews reason, allowing her actions to be guided by her distorted perceptions. The tangle of personal relationships and misunderstandings that Emma's interference has created is resolved only

with the revelations that follow the death of Frank's tyrannical aunt. Frank admits that his flirtation with Emma has been a cover for his secret engagement to Jane. Emma, who believed Harriet had transferred her affections from Mr. Elton to Frank, discovers that her friend aspires to marry Mr. Knightley and simultaneously recognizes her own love for him. Mr. Knightley, fearing that Emma is heartbroken by Frank's engagement, hastens to comfort her, and then learns that she loves him. The novel closes with the triumph of reason and balance in the marriages of Emma to Mr. Knightley, Jane to Frank, and Harriet to her first love, Robert Martin.

When *Emma* appeared in December 1815, Austen expressed in her letters her apprehension that the work would prove less popular than her other novels. However, *Emma* was widely praised and received more critical attention than any of her previous works, due in part to the fact that her new publisher, John Murray, was also the publisher of the *Quarterly Review.* Sir Walter Scott's largely favorable review of *Emma* in that influential periodical was important as the first sustained critical consideration of Austen's work. Attempting to define the place Austen's novels held in the tradition of English fiction, Scott emphasized the realism of her work, remarking on her skill in depicting "concrete and striking representation of that which is daily taking place." Other early reviewers of *Emma* for the most part followed Scott's lead, commending Austen's moral sensitivity and true-to-life portrayal of everyday events in a domestic setting, finding fault only with the limited scope of the work and its similarity to her earlier novels. For several decades following the initial appraisals of *Emma,* however, the novel received little attention except for brief comments in the private papers of such nineteenth-century literary figures as Henry Crabb Robinson, Charlotte Brontë, Cardinal John Henry Newman, and Anthony Trollope.

With the publication in 1870 of James Edward Austen-Leigh's memoir of Austen, interest in her works began to revive. While most late nineteenth-century commentary on Austen is anecdotal and non-scholarly, Richard Simpson's 1870 critique explored such important issues as Austen's ironic stance, didactic yet unsentimental approach, and growth as an artist. In the early twentieth century, Austen's achievement was celebrated by A. C. Bradley and Reginald Farrer, both of whom ranked *Emma* as her masterpiece, citing in particular her command of ironic tone and complex narrative method. Opposing the overwhelmingly laudatory estimations of critics in the first half of the twentieth century, E. N. Hayes in 1949 wrote his "Dissenting Opinion," focusing on *Emma* in much of his negative commentary on Austen's narrowness of scope and superficial values.

As Austen criticism began to proliferate in the 1950s and 1960s, scholars considered her novels in light of such topics as her use of irony, her treatment of social issues, the psychology of her characters, and her innovative narrative techniques and plot structuring. *Emma* has often been the focal point in these appraisals, and while the novel has been particularly vulnerable to critiques of Austen's limited range, it has also been examined as her most complex and characteristic work. Studies in the English novel frequently examine *Emma* as a major contribution to the genre for Austen's manipulation of point of view, her introduction of stream-of-consciousness narrative, and her creation of a balance between empathy and critical detachment in the reader's response to her principal characters. In addition, recent critics have approached *Emma* from a feminist standpoint, examining Austen's attitude toward women's education and place in society.

Viewed by many critics as Austen's masterpiece, *Emma* has inspired considerable and diverse study. To those critics who consider Austen's achievement diminished by her limited range, *Emma,* perhaps Austen's most restricted and uneventful narrative, is susceptible to strident critiques. Yet most scholars argue that the hallmarks of Austen's art—skilled characterizations, subtle wit, pervasive irony, and balanced structure—are more fully evident in *Emma* than in any of her other works, and consequently recognize it as a classic of English fiction.

JAMES STANIER CLARKE   (letter date 1815)

[*An acquaintance of Austen, Clarke was a clergyman and aspiring author and the librarian to the Prince Regent. In the following excerpt from a letter to her, Clarke praises Austen's work and suggests materials for future novels.*]

Your late Works, Madam, and in particular **Mansfield Park** reflect the highest honour on your Genius & your Principles; in every new work your mind seems to increase its energy and powers of discrimination. The Regent has read & admired all your publications.

Accept my sincere thanks for the pleasure your Volumes have given me: in the perusal of them I felt a great inclination to write & say so. And I also dear Madam wished to be allowed to ask you, to delineate in some future Work the Habits of Life and Character and enthusiasm of a Clergyman—who should pass his time between the metropolis & the Country—who should be something like Beatties Minstrel

> Silent when glad, affectionate tho' shy
> And now his look was most demurely sad
> & now he laughd aloud yet none knew why—

Neither Goldsmith—nor La Fontaine in his Tableau de Famille—have in my mind quite delineated an English Clergyman, at least of the present day—Fond of, & entirely engaged in Literature—no man's Enemy but his own. Pray dear Madam think of these things. (pp. 429-30)

> *James Stanier Clarke, in a letter to Jane Austen on November 16, 1815, in* Jane Austen's Letters to Her Sister Cassandra and Others *by Jane Austen, edited by R. W. Chapman, second edition, Oxford University Press, Oxford, 1952, pp. 429-30.*

JANE AUSTEN   (letter date 1815)

[*In this excerpt from a letter to Clarke, Austen expresses her apprehension that* Emma *will prove less popular than* Pride and Prejudice *and* Mansfield Park.]

I must make use of this opportunity to thank you, dear Sir, for the very high praise you bestow on my . . . novels. I am too vain to wish to convince you that you have praised them beyond their merits. My greatest anxiety at present is that this fourth work [*Emma*] should not disgrace what was good in the others. But on this point I will do myself the justice to declare that, whatever may be my wishes for its success, I am very strongly haunted with the idea that to those readers who have preferred **Pride and Prejudice** it will appear inferior in wit, and to those who have preferred **Mansfield Park** very inferior in good sense. . . . I am quite honoured by your thinking me capable of drawing such a clergyman as you gave the sketch of in your note of Nov. 16th. But I assure you I am *not.* The comic part of the character I might be equal to, but not the good, the enthusiastic, the literary. Such a man's conversation must at times be on subjects of science and philosophy, of which I know nothing; or at least be occasionally abundant in quotations and allusions which a woman who, like me, knows only her own mother tongue, and has read very little in that, would be totally without the power of giving. A classical education, or at any rate a very extensive acquaintance with English literature, ancient and modern, appears to me quite indispensable for the person who would do any justice to your clergyman; and I think I may boast myself to be, with all possible vanity, the most unlearned and uninformed female who ever dared to be an authoress. (pp. 442-43)

> *Jane Austen, in a letter to James Stanier Clarke on December 11, 1815, in her* Jane Austen's Letters to Her Sister Cassandra and Others, *edited by R. W. Chapman, second edition, Oxford University Press, Oxford, 1952, pp. 442-43.*

F. MORLEY   (letter date 1815)

[*Morley here praises* Emma *in a letter to Austen.*]

I have been most anxiously waiting for an introduction to *Emma*, & am infinitely obliged to you for your kind recollection of me, which will procure me the pleasure of her acquaintance some days sooner than I sh^d otherwise have had it.—I am already become intimate in the Woodhouse family, & feel that they will not amuse & interest me less than the Bennetts, Bertrams, Norriss & all their admirable predecessors.—I *can* give them no higher praise—

> *F. Morley, in a letter to Jane Austen on December 27, 1815, in* Jane Austen's Letters to Her Sister Cassandra and Others *by Jane Austen, edited by R. W. Chapman, second edition, Oxford University Press, Oxford, 1952, p. 448.*

JANE AUSTEN   (letter date 1815)

[*Responding to Morley's praise of* Emma *(see excerpt above dated 27 December 1815), Austen expresses her concern for the novel's success.*]

Accept my Thanks for the honour of your note, & for your kind disposition in favour of *Emma*. In my present state of doubt as to her reception in the World, it is particularly gratifying to me to receive so early an assurance of your Ladyship's approbation.—It encourages me to depend on the same share of general good opinion which *Emma*'s Predecessors have experienced, & to believe that I have not yet—as almost every Writer of Fancy does sooner or later—overwritten myself. (pp. 448-49)

> *Jane Austen, in a letter to F. Morley on December 31, 1815, in her* Jane Austen's Letters to Her Sister Cassandra and Others, *edited by R. W. Chapman, second edition, Oxford University Press, Oxford, 1952, pp. 448-49.*

THE CHAMPION   (essay date 1816)

[*In this excerpt from a favorable review of* Emma *that was first published on 31 March 1816 in the* Champion, *the critic admires Austen's depiction of everyday events.*]

One rare merit which [the volumes of *Emma*] possess, is an entire freedom from anything like the pretence or technicality of authorship.—Their style is easy, unaffected, and fluent. Simple elementary affections of middling life, and the little obvious peculiarities of character, are all which the authoress (for they are the work of a lady) pretends or professes to exhibit. Those who exclusively estimate the value of a work of fiction by its appeals to the more elevated feelings, and its display of the complex machinery of dark passions and imaginative sensations, will find very little to their taste, we fear, in the homely pictures of these volumes. Even of the sober pathos of domestic affliction, there is very little for the sentimental reader.—Lively sketches of comfortable home-scenes—graphic details of the localities of provincial life—pictures of worthy affections, unassuming amusements and occupations, and most spirited and racy touches of the grotesque peculiarities which diversify human character, are the claims which our authoress puts forth to popularity. She presents nature and society in very unornamented hues; and yet, so strong is the force of nature, that

we will venture to say, few can take up her work without finding a rational pleasure in the recognitions which cannot fail to flash upon them of the modes of thinking and feeling which experience every day presents in real life. Her scenes have the advantage of being of that middling stamp, which come within the observation of a very large proportion of readers. The country house is no castle or hall of honour,—but a plain mansion, with a shrubbery and large gates, such as every one knows at the top of a populous village, looked up to as the great house of the place; and when we are occasionally transported to London, our authoress has the originality to waive Grosvenor or Berkeley-squares, and set us down in humble Brunswick-square. There is a corresponding modesty in her characters. If we take her own description of them, one is "rational and unaffected," another, "straight-forward and openhearted;" and the heroine herself, who gives title to the work, is content with being "handsome, clever, and rich;"—to which we will add, lively, conceited, and rather proud, but benevolent, amiable, volatile,—and addicted to a very extraordinary occupation for a young lady, by no means *hors de combat*—being only twenty-one—viz. that of matchmaking. The scrapes and entanglements in which she involves herself in the pursuit of this dangerous amusement, are ingeniously managed, and give great life and interest to some parts of the work. (pp. 469-70)

Mr. Woodhouse, the father of Emma, is a character most ludicrously true, though, in finishing him up to the life, our authoress has frequently given him rather too much license of becoming tedious and prolix. He is a professed Valetudinarian, who drinks "a small half glass of wine, put into a tumbler of water"—lives in a complete state of vassalage to Perry, a genteel village apothecary, and grows eloquent on the comparative merits of sea-bathing at Cromer and Southend. This is a character of which the original is often to be seen in society—of weak mind, weak nerves, inoffensive selfishness, deliberate politeness, languid spirits, and amiable affections—"together," as Hamlet says, "with a plentiful lack of wit, and most weak hams." A very amusing trait is his persisting in calling a valuable governess, who has left his family to make an excellent match with one of his neighbours "*poor* Mrs. Weston,"—identifying her feelings with his, and attributing to her all the regrets he felt for the loss of her society and attentions.—This is an exact characteristic of this sort of drivelling mind. Perhaps a more ludicrous one is his gravely whispering, that a certain young man is "not quite the thing," because he has a habit of opening the doors and windows in July. Our authoress possesses a peculiar felicity in measuring a character—and has a nice eye and a facile pen for arresting and embodying oddities—a species of light satire for which the delicate tact of female minds is admirably adapted. There is a Miss Bates, a plain, goodhearted, voluble, vulgar, well-meaning woman, who has actually walked into the Book, from the coterie of some provincial town. She is one of those persons in whom the triumph of essential good qualities is abundantly conspicuous—in whom simplicity and worth, and good intention, succeed in excusing vulgarity, ignorance, and loquacity, and almost in rendering them agreeable. (p. 471)

[Her conversation] is a happy specimen of the eternal larum of disjointed small talk, which so often supplies the place of "the feast of reason and the flow of soul" in the rounds of provincial visiting. It is, however, innocent—and such women as Miss Bates are angels, compared to the Mrs. Candours and the Lady Sneerwells,—whom we sometimes find poisoning society,—and even to Mrs. Elton, the arrogant, half-bred, familiar daughter of a Bristol-trader—*euphoniæ gratia*—a merchant—whom the rejected Mr. Elton takes to himself for a wife, with 10,000£. We wish we could devote more space to Mrs. Elton, for she is an admirably drawn character—full of all the coarse outrées, and extravagant airs which are acquired in a school of vulgar affluence—of wealth struggling after taste and fashion.—She comes to her husband's home, bent upon finding every body very inferior and very rustic, and determined to overwhelm the neighbourhood with the pride of "Maple Grove," her brother-in-law's "seat" near Bristol, which she never fails, *invitâ Minervá*, to lug into the conversation of every half-hour's visit, with appropriate hints of "spacious apartments," "park palings," "every luxury," "barouche, landau," &c. Every thing has a Maple Grove hue. The shape of a room is like "the morning room at Maple Grove," the laurels grow like the laurels at Maple Grove. (p. 472)

Our authoress excels also in characters of another stamp. Mr. and Mrs. John Knightley, are a picture of an estimable pair. The husband of dignified sense and rather reserved disposition: English in his faults, English in his virtues,—warm in his affections, and very intolerant of heartlessness and frivolity of all sorts: the wife, just perhaps what a wife ought to be—a pattern of affectionate and devoted zeal for her husband and children—sufficiently sensible—not at all clever—of a small mind which the ties and duties of domestic life abundantly fill—with qualities which rather endear than adorn, and are grounded in pure and ardent feelings, rather than in superior intellect.—Such characters as these are by no means to be included in the sweeping sentence of insipidity, with which some persons are inclined to banish all unpretending goodness from the dramatis personae of a novel. . . .

We must shut up these amusing volumes, which plainly manifest the author to be a woman of good sense, knowledge of the world, discriminating perception and acute observation. . . . (p. 473)

> *A review of "Emma," in* Nineteenth-Century Fiction, *Vol. 26, No. 4, March, 1972, pp. 469-74.*

JANE AUSTEN (letter date 1816)

[*In the following letter to Clarke, Austen responds to his suggestion that she write a historical romance.*]

You are very very kind in your hints as to the sort of composition which might recommend me at present, and I am fully sensible that an historical romance, founded on the House of Saxe Cobourg, might be much more to the purpose of profit or popularity than such pictures of domestic life in country villages as I deal in. But I could no more write a romance than an epic poem. I could not sit seriously down to write a serious romance under any other motive than to save my life; and if it were indispensable for me to keep it up and never relax into laughing at myself or other people, I am sure I should be hung before I had finished the first chapter. No, I must keep to my own style and go on in my own way; and though I may never succeed again in that, I am convinced that I should totally fail in any other. (pp. 452-53)

> *Jane Austen, in a letter to James Stanier Clarke on April 1, 1816, in her* Jane Austen's Letters to Her Sister Cassandra and Others, *edited by R. W. Chapman, second edition, Oxford University Press, Oxford, 1952, pp. 452-53.*

AUGUSTAN REVIEW (essay date 1816)

[*In the following excerpt from a review of* Emma, *the critic emphasizes the lack of variety in Austen's work.*]

There is a remarkable sameness in the productions of this author. The Emma and Knightley of the work before us [*Emma*] are exactly the Elizabeth and Davey [*sic*] of *Pride and Prejudice*; the prototypes of which were the hero and heroine in *Sense and Sensibility*. Nor is there more variety in the subordinate characters, or the incidents; both are of a description that occurs every day in the rank of life to which they are allotted. Yet the author will always interest and please, and this exactly from the causes which we are persuaded are beyond all others desirable to her. From a certain elegance of mind, and acquaintance with the usages of polite society, from a just sense of duty which makes her show the performance of it, in all its bearings, to be its own reward, and from that rational view of happiness which enables her to teach her readers to look for it where it is certain to be found. "In the mild majesty of private life," in the culture of intellectual endowments, and in the exercise of the social affections, we find nothing ridiculed that ought not be ridiculed; no undue consequence annexed to things which have not consequence in themselves; and every person has his place, and his influence assigned him in the scale of society, with the propriety and good sense which the author is fond of exhibiting as the characteristics of her heroines. (p. 484)

The character of Mr. Woodhouse, a benevolent valetudinarian, is well drawn; his pleasure in having the cloth laid for supper, because it had been the fashion of his youth, checked by fear of the ill consequences that might accrue to his guests from the unwholesomeness of the meal in itself; his reluctance to leave his own fire-side, balanced by his unwillingness to deprive others of an expected gratification; his magnifying a snowy evening and the turn of a corner in a lane into real dangers, in order to enhance the imaginary pleasure of escaping them; are all well told, and conceived in the spirit that pourtrayed that most admirable character of Sir Hugh, in the novel of *Camilla*. His aversion also to matrimony, as the greatest of all charges in a family circle, and his always calling his eldest daughter and her amiable governess, who are both happily united to the men of their choice, "poor Isabella," and "poor Miss Taylor that was," is not only humorous in its general effects, but places his remaining daughter in an amiable and dutiful point of view, as sedulously devoting her time to her father, and falling into the error of making matches for others, through the laudable, and as she imagines unalterable, resolution never to grieve him by indulging a thought of one for herself. The younger part of our female readers will agree with us that perfect characters are not always the most agreeable, and will therefore pardon her for not, in this single instance, shewing herself infallible.

We may now take leave of *Emma,* on very good terms with the author; though we will venture to recommend in her next performance a little "less talk and more work." Miss Bates, with all her worthy qualities, is sometimes too loquacious and too tautologous for our patience; and our author shews so much skill in agreeably entangling the slender materials which she brings before us to excite conjecture, that we cannot but think that a greater variety of incidents would, in such hands as hers, well supply the place of some of that colloquial familiarity and minuteness to which she has hitherto perhaps too much confined herself. (pp. 485-86)

> *A review of "Emma," in* Augustan Review, *Vol. 2, No. XIII, May, 1816, pp. 484-86.*

BRITISH LADY'S MAGAZINE, AND MONTHLY MISCELLANY
(essay date 1816)

[*Reviewing* Emma *and* St. Valentine's Eve, *a novel by Amelia Opie, the critic praises Austen's realistic portrayal of her subjects, but considers* Emma *inferior to her previous works.*]

[The novels **Emma** and *St. Valentine's Eve*] both evince the truth of an observation . . . namely, that two or three novels generally exhaust the inventive faculties of authors in this line. The *St. Valentine's Eve* is every way unworthy Mrs. Opie; and **Emma** falls not only below **Pride and Prejudice** (probably the most pleasant novel of the last half dozen years), but also of **Mansfield Park**, a later production by the same author. (p. 180)

As to **Emma,** the falling off is . . . we firmly believe unavoidable, just as a die ceases after a while to yield strong impressions. The talent of this author is displayed in an accurate description of country society, consisting of the middling gentry and those who move in the sphere around them: every body must acknowledge these form no inexhaustible magazine. But, after all, **Emma** is not only readable, but pleasantly so:—the personage so termed is a young lady of sprightliness and mind rather than of talent, who is led by a somewhat too high opinion of her own penetration to arrange matches, in her mind, for all her acquaintance, and whose pleasant castle building always proves foundationless, and leaves her wondering and excusing herself until she finally stands corrected. Her succession of mistakes with respect to a simple young girl, whom she has taken under her especial protection, as to marriage, is described with great felicity; and the nature exhibited in the sketches of Harriet Smith and Robert Martin is truly pleasing. We have, however, to mention one defect which the author can avoid, which is thinking a foolish character will always entertain because it is natural. Thus a weak gabbling country spinster is made to talk in this novel with the nicest keeping; but she talks infinitely too much, or, rather, fills infinitely too many pages. (p. 181)

> *A review of "Emma," in* British Lady's Magazine, and Monthly Miscellany, *Vol. 4, No. 21, September, 1816, pp. 180-81.*

SUSAN FERRIER (letter date 1816)

[*Ferrier, the author of several didactic novels on the subject of marriage, expresses her admiration for Austen's style and depiction of character in the following excerpt.*]

I have been reading **Emma,** which is excellent; there is no story whatever, and the heroine is no better than other people; but the characters are all so true to life, and the style so piquant, that it does not require the adventitious aids of mystery and adventure.

> *Susan Ferrier, in a letter to Miss Clavering in 1816, in her* Memoir and Correspondence of Susan Ferrier, 1782-1854, *edited by John A. Doyle, J. Murray, 1898, p. 128.*

MARIA EDGEWORTH (letter date 1816)

[*Frequently compared with Austen, Edgeworth is chiefly noted for her contributions to the English novel of manners. Edgeworth's comments on the first volume of* Emma *are excerpted below.*]

[There was no story in **Emma**], except that Miss Emma found that the man whom she designed for Harriets lover was an admirer of her own—& he was affronted at being refused by Emma & Harriet wore the willow—*and smooth, thin water-gruel* is according to Emma's father's opinion a very good thing & it is very difficult to make a cook understand what you mean by smooth thin water gruel!

> *Maria Edgeworth, in an extract from a letter to Sneyd and Harriet Edgeworth in 1816, in* Maria Edgeworth: A Literary Biography *by Marilyn Butler, Oxford at the Clarendon Press, Oxford, 1972, p. 445.*

JANE AUSTEN (essay date 1816?)

[*Austen's record of the reactions of her family and friends to* Emma, *reprinted below, was probably compiled in 1816.*]

Captn. Austen.—liked it extremely, observing that though there might be more Wit in **Pride & Prejudice**—& an higher Morality in **Mansfield Park**—yet altogether, on account of it's peculiar air of Nature throughout, he preferred it to either.

Mrs F. A.—liked & admired it very much indeed, but must still prefer **Pride & Prejudice.**

Mrs J. Bridges—better than **Mansfield Park**—but not so well as **Pride & Prejudice**—pleased with the Heroine for her Originality, delighted with Mr K—& called Mrs Elton beyond praise.—dissatisfied with Jane Fairfax.

Cassandra—better than **Pride & Prejudice**—but not so well as **Mansfield Park**—

Fanny K.—not so well as either **Pride & Prejudice** or **Mansfield Park**—could not bear **Emma** herself.—Mr Knightley delightful.—Should like J. F.—if she knew more of her.—

Mr & Mrs J. A.—did not like it so well as either of the 3 others. Language different from the others; not so easily read.—

Edward—preferred it to **Mansfield Park**—*only.* —Mr K. liked by every body.

Miss Bigg—not equal to either **Pride & Prejudice**—or **Mansfield Park**—objected to the sameness of the subject (Matchmaking) all through.—Too much of Mr Elton & H. Smith. Language superior to the others.—

My Mother—thought it more entertaining than **Mansfield Park**—but not so interesting as **Pride & Prejudice**—No characters in it equal to Ly Catherine & Mr Collins.—

Miss Lloyd—thought it as *clever* as either of the others, but did not receive so much pleasure from it as from **Pride & Prejudice**—& **Mansfield Park**—

Mrs & Miss Craven—liked it very much, but not so much as the others.—

Fanny Cage—liked it very much indeed & classed it between **Pride & Prejudice**—& **Mansfield Park**—

Mr Sherrer—did not think it equal to either **Mansfield Park**—(which he liked the best of all) or **Pride & Prejudice.**—Displeased with my pictures of Clergymen.—

Miss Bigg—on reading it a second time, liked Miss Bates much better than at first, & expressed herself as liking all the people of Highbury in general, except Harriet Smith—but c^d not help still thinking *her* too silly in her Loves.

The family at Upton Gray—all very much amused with it.— Miss Bates a great favourite with Mrs Beaufoy.

Mr & Mrs Leigh Perrot—saw many beauties in it, but c^d not think it equal to *Pride & Prejudice*—Darcy & Elizth had spoilt them for anything else.—Mr K. however, an excellent Character; Emma better luck than a Matchmaker often has.—Pitied Jane Fairfax—thought Frank Churchill better treated than he deserved.—

Countess Craven—admired it very much, but did not think it equal to *Pride & Prejudice*—which she ranked as the very first of its sort.—

Mrs Guiton—thought it too natural to be interesting.

Mrs Digweed—did not like it so well as the others, in fact if she had not known the Author, could hardly have got through it.—

Miss Terry—admired it very much, particularly Mrs Elton.

Henry Sanford—very much pleased with it—delighted with Miss Bates, but thought Mrs Elton the best-drawn Character in the Book.—*Mansfield Park* however, still his favourite.

Mr. Haden—*quite* delighted with it. Admired the Character of Emma.—

Miss Isabella Herries—did not like it—objected to my exposing the sex in the character of the Heroine—convinced that I had meant Mrs & Miss Bates for some acquaintance of theirs—People whom I never heard of before.—

Miss Harriet Moore—admired it very much, but *Mansfield Park* still her favourite of all.—

Countess Morley—delighted with it.—

Mr Cockerelle—liked it so little, that Fanny w^d not send me his opinion.—

Mrs Dickson—did not much like it—thought it *very* inferior to *Pride & Prejudice*—Liked it the less, from there being a Mr. & Mrs Dixon in it.—

Mrs Brandreth—thought the 3^d vol: superior to anything I had ever written—quite beautiful!—

Mr B. Lefroy—thought that if there had been more Incident, it would be equal to any of the others.—The Characters quite as well drawn & supported as in any, & from being more everyday ones, the more entertaining.—Did not like the Heroine so well as any of the others. Miss Bates excellent, but rather too much of her. Mr & Mrs Elton admirable & John Kinghtley a sensible Man.—

Mrs B. Lefroy—rank'd *Emma* as a composition with *Sense & Sensibility*—not so *Brilliant* as *Pride & Prejudice*—nor so *equal* as *Mansfield Park*—Preferred Emma herself to all the heroines.—The Characters like all the others admirably well drawn & supported—perhaps rather less strongly marked than some, but only the more natural for that reason.—Mr Knightley Mrs Elton & Miss Bates her favourites.—Thought one or two of the conversations too long.—

Mrs Lefroy—preferred it to *Mansfield Park*—but liked *Mansfield Park* the least of all.

Mr Fowle—read only the first & last Chapters, because he had heard it was not interesting.—

Mrs Lutley Sclater—liked it very much, better than *Mansfield Park*—& thought I had "brought it all about very cleverly in the last volume."—

Mrs C. Cage wrote thus to Fanny—"A great many thanks for the loan of *Emma,* which I am delighted with. I like it better than any. Every character is thoroughly kept up. I must enjoy reading it again with Charles. Miss Bates is incomparable, but I was nearly killed with those precious treasures! They are Unique, & really with more fun than I can express. I am at Highbury all day, & I can't help feeling I have just got into a new set of acquaintance. No one writes such good sense. & so very comfortable.

Mrs Wroughton—did not like it so well as *Pride & Prejudice*— Thought the Authoress wrong, in such times as these, to draw such Clergymen as Mr Collins & Mr Elton.

Sir J. Langham—thought it much inferior to the others.—

Mr Jeffery (of the *Edinburgh Review*) was kept up by it three nights.

Miss Murden—certainly inferior to all the others.

Capt. C. Austen wrote—*Emma* arrived in time to a moment. I am delighted with her, more so I think than even with my favourite *Pride & Prejudice,* & have read it three times in the Passage."

Mrs D. Dundas—thought it very clever, but did not like it so well as either of the others. (pp. 436-39)

> Jane Austen, *"Opinions of 'Emma',"* in her The Works of Jane Austen: Minor Works, Vol. VI, *edited by R. W. Chapman, revised edition, Oxford University Press, London, 1975, pp. 436-39.*

HENRY CRABB ROBINSON   (diary date 1822)

[*A nineteenth-century English journalist, Robinson is remembered for his voluminous correspondence and diaries, which chronicle London's social and intellectual history. While he records a primarily negative impression of* Emma *in the following excerpt, he evidently revised his opinion, noting in October 1839 that he spent three days "reading Miss Austen's admirable* Emma.*"*]

In the evening read the last volume of *Emma,* a novel evincing great good sense, and an acute observation of human life, but it is not interesting. One cares little for Harriet, the kind-hearted girl who falls in love with three men in a year, and yet hers is the best conceived character after all. Emma, the heroine, is little more than a clever woman who does foolish things— makes mistakes for others, and is at last caught unawares herself. We hear rather too much about fools: the kind-hearted but weak father, the silly chattering Miss Bates, who gabbles in the style of polite conversation, and the vulgar impertinence of the Eltons. . . .

> Henry Crabb Robinson, *in a diary entry on April 20, 1822, in his* Henry Crabb Robinson on Books and Their Writers, Vol. I, *edited by Edith J. Morley, J. M. Dent and Sons Limited, 1938, p. 282.*

JOHN HENRY NEWMAN   (letter date 1837)

[*A leading figure in the Oxford Movement and an important Catholic apologist and educator, Newman wrote numerous essays, sermons, and lectures in addition to poetry and novels. In this excerpt, he comments briefly on* Emma.]

I have been reading *Emma*. Everything Miss Austen writes is clever, but I desiderate something. There is a want of *body* in the story. The action is frittered away in over-little things.

There are some beautiful things in it. Emma herself is the most interesting to me of all her heroines. I feel kind to her whenever I think of her. But Miss Austen has no romance—none at all. What vile creatures her parsons are! she has not a dream of the high Catholic ηθος ["ethos"]. That other woman, Fairfax, is a dolt—but I like Emma.

> *John Henry Newman, in a letter to Mrs. John Mozley on January 19, 1837, in his* Letters and Correspondence of John Henry Newman, Vol. II, *edited by Anne Mozley, 1890. Reprint by Longmans, Green and Co., 1920, p. 200.*

ANTHONY TROLLOPE   (essay date 1864)

[*A distinguished Victorian novelist, Trollope is best known for his* Barsetshire Chronicles, *a series of works that realistically and humorously depict English provincial life. Trollope's comments, which focus on Austen's characters in* Emma, *were jotted on the end papers of his copy of the novel in 1864.*]

Emma is undoubtedly very tedious;—thereby shewing rather the patience of readers in the authors day than any incapacity on her part to avoid the fault. The dialogues are too long and some of them are unnecessary.

But the story shews wonderful knowledge of female character, and is severe on the little foibles of women with a severity which no man would dare to use. Emma, the heroine, is treated almost mercilessly. In every passage of the book she is in fault for some folly, some vanity, some ignorance,—or indeed for some meanness. Her conduct to her friend Harriett,—her assumed experience and real ignorance of human nature—are terribly true; but nowadays we dare not make our heroines so little. Her weaknesses are all plain to us, but of her strength we are only told; and even at the last we hardly know why Mr Knightley loves her.

The humour shewn in some of the female characters in *Emma* is very good. Mrs Elton with her loud Bath-begotten vulgarity is excellent; and Miss Bates, longwinded, self-denying, ignorant, and eulogistic has become proverbial. But the men are all weak. There is nothing in *Emma* like Mr Bennett and Mr Collins the immortal heroes of *Pride and Prejudice*. Mr Woodhouse, the malade imaginaire, is absurd, and the Knightleys and Westons are simply sticks. It is as a portrait of female life among ladies in an English village 50 years ago that *Emma* is to be known and remembered.

We have here, given to us unconsciously, a picture of the clerical life of 1815 which we cannot avoid comparing with the clerical life of 1865. After a modest dinner party, when the gentlemen join the ladies, the parson of the parish, a young man, is noticed as having taken too much wine. And no one else has done so. But allusion is made to this, not because he is a clergyman, nor is he at all a debauched or fast-living clergyman. It simply suits the story that he should be a little flushed & free of speech. The same clergyman, when married, declines to dance because he objects to the partner proposed to him; and special mention is made of card parties at this clergyman's house. How must the mouths of young parsons water in these days as they read these details, if they are now ever allowed to read such books as *Emma*.

I cannot but notice Miss Austens timidity in dealing with the most touching scenes which come in her way, and in avoiding the narration of those details which a bolder artist would most eagerly have seized. In the final scene between Emma and her lover,—when the conversation has become almost pathetic,—she breaks away from the spoken dialogue, and simply tells us of her hero's success. This is a cowardice which robs the reader of much of the charm which he has promised himself—(pp. 246-47)

> *Anthony Trollope, "Trollope on 'Emma': An Unpublished Note," in* Nineteenth-Century Fiction, *Vol. IV, No. 3, December, 1949, pp. 245-47.*

[WILLIAM JOHN COURTHOPE]   (essay date 1879)

[*A professor of poetry at Oxford, Courthope is primarily remembered for his scholarly editions and studies of the works of Alexander Pope. In this excerpt from a survey of developments in the English novel, Courthope commends Austen's method of plot construction, particularly as revealed in* Emma.]

As society, under the influence of settled opinion, grew always more regular and refined, the local humours and customs, of which Fielding and Smollett had made so much use [in the novel of manners], gradually disappeared, and the interest of tales of modern life began to turn rather on the representation of character than of incident. The nicety and quickness of perception required for such a state of things gave new opportunities to female genius, and were admirably exhibited in the works of Madame D'Arblay, Miss Edgeworth, and Miss Austen. All these writers, but particularly the last, showed extraordinary power in constructing plots out of the little intricacies of everyday life, without any sacrifice of dignity or refinement.

With Sir Walter Scott and Miss Austen the art of novel writing in England reached its meridian. In making this statement, we assume that the chief excellence of this art lies in the construction of the story, since it is by this that the highest development is given to action and character. (pp. 97-8)

Emma, in point of construction, stands without a rival. The story relates the fortunes of a match-making heroine in a quiet country town. A more restricted subject or sphere cannot be imagined, yet so admirably are the involvements of the situation contrived, that the interest of the reader never flags. Many and various persons support the action; all of them present types of character with which we are familiar; but from the excellent humour, delicacy, and completeness with which they are drawn, they seem better representatives of the type than any we have observed ourselves. The dialogue is shrewd, natural, and well-bred. The whole of this well-proportioned story is comprised within four hundred pages. Contrast with it one of George Eliot's later novels, *Daniel Deronda*, for instance. (pp. 98-9)

> [*William John Courthope*], *"The Reflection of English Character in English Art," in* The Quarterly Review, *Vol. 147, No. 293, January, 1879, pp. 81-112.*

WILLIAM DEAN HOWELLS   (essay date 1900)

[*Howells was the chief progenitor of American realism and an influential American literary critic during the late nineteenth and early twentieth centuries. Although he wrote nearly three dozen novels, few of them are read today. Despite his eclipse, however, he stands as one of the major literary figures of his era; having successfully weaned American literature from the sentimental romanticism of its infancy, he earned the popular sobriquet "the*

Dean of American Letters." In the following excerpt, he discusses Austen's characters, focusing on Emma.]

The wonder of Jane Austen is that at a time when even the best fiction was overloaded with incident, and its types went staggering about under the attributes heaped upon them, she imagined getting on with only so much incident as would suffice to let her characters express their natures movingly or amusingly. She seems to have reached this really unsurpassable degree of perfection without a formulated philosophy, and merely by her clear vision of the true relation of art to life; but however she came to be what she was, she was . . . unquestionably great. . . . (p. 517)

Emma Woodhouse, in the story named after her, is one of the most boldly imagined of Jane Austen's heroines. Perhaps she is the very most so, for it took supreme courage to portray a girl, meant to win and keep the reader's fancy, with the characteristics frankly ascribed to Emma Woodhouse. We are indeed allowed to know that she is pretty; not formally, but casually, from the words of a partial friend: "Such an eye!—the true hazel eye—and so brilliant!—regular features, open countenance, with a complexion—ah, what a bloom of full health, and such a pretty height and size; such a firm and upright figure." But, before we are allowed to see her personal beauty we are made to see in her some of the qualities which are the destined source of trouble for herself and her friends. In her wish to be useful she is patronizing and a little presumptuous; her self-sufficiency early appears, and there are hints of her willingness to shape the future of others without having past enough of her own to enable her to do it judiciously. The man who afterwards marries her says of her: "She will never submit to anything requiring industry and patience, and a subjection of the fancy to the understanding. . . . Emma is spoiled by being the cleverest of her family. At ten years old she had the misfortune of being able to answer questions which puzzled her sister at seventeen. She was always quick and assured. . . . and ever since she was twelve Emma has been mistress of the house and you all.'"

An officious and self-confident girl, even if pretty, is not usually one to take the fancy, and yet Emma takes the fancy. She manages the delightful and whimsical old invalid her father, but she is devotedly and unselfishly good to him. She takes the destiny of Harriet Smith unwarrantably into her charge, but she breaks off the girl's love-affair only in the interest of a better match. She decides that Frank Churchill, the stepson of her former governess, will be in love with her, but she never dreams that Mr. Elton, whom she means for Harriet Smith, can be so. She is not above a little manœuvring for the advantage of those she wishes to serve, but the tacit insincerity of Churchill is intolerable to her. She is unfeelingly neglectful of Jane Fairfax and cruelly suspicious of her, but she generously does what she can to repair the wrong, and she takes her punishment for it meekly and contritely. She makes thoughtless and heartless fun of poor, babbling Miss Bates, but when Knightley calls her to account for it, she repents her unkindness with bitter tears. She will not be advised against her pragmatical schemes by Knightley, but she is humbly anxious for his good opinion. She is charming in the very degree of her feminine complexity, which is finally an endearing single-heartedness.

Her character is shown in an action so slight that the novel of *Emma* may be said to be hardly more than an exemplification of Emma. In the placid circumstance of English country life where she is the principal social figure the story makes its round with a few events so unexciting as to leave the reader in doubt whether anything at all has happened. Mr. Elton, a clerical snob as odious as Mr. Collins in *Pride and Prejudice,* is amusing, indignantly resents Emma's plan for supplying him with a wife in Harriet Smith, and marries a woman who has Emma's defects without their qualities. Frank Churchill keeps his engagement with Jane Fairfax a secret till all the possible mischief can come from it, and then acknowledges it just when the fact must be most mortifying and humiliating to Emma. After she has been put to shame before Knightley in every way, she finds herself beloved and honored by him and in the way to be happily married. There are, meantime, a few dances and picnics, dinners and teas; Harriet Smith is frightened by gypsies, and some hen-roosts are robbed. There is not an accident, even of the mild and beneficent type of Louisa Musgrove's in *Persuasion;* there is not an elopement, even of the *bouffe* nature of Lydia's in *Pride and Prejudice:* there is nothing at all so tragic as Catharine Morland's expulsion by General Tilney in *Northanger Abbey.* Duels and abductions, of course, there are none; for Jane Austen had put from her all the machinery of the great and little novelists of the eighteenth century, and openly mocked at it. This has not prevented its being frequently used since, and she shows herself more modern than all her predecessors and contemporaries and most of her successors, in the rejection of the major means and the employment of the minor means to produce the enduring effects of *Emma.* Among her quiet books it is almost the quietest, and so far as the novel can suggest that repose which is the ideal of art *Emma* suggests it, in an action of unsurpassed unity, consequence, and simplicity. (pp. 517-18)

William Dean Howells, "Heroines of Nineteenth-Century Fiction," in Harper's Bazaar, *Vol. XXXIII, No. 26, June 30, 1900, pp. 516-23.*

REGINALD FARRER (essay date 1917)

[*In this examination of* Emma, *excerpted from his appreciative survey of Austen's work, Farrer identifies the study of character as the central concern in the novel.*]

Emma is the very climax of Jane Austen's work; and a real appreciation of *Emma* is the final test of citizenship in her kingdom. For this is not an easy book to read; it should never be the beginner's primer, nor be published without a prefatory synopsis. Only when the story has been thoroughly assimilated, can the infinite delights and subtleties of its workmanship begin to be appreciated, as you realise the manifold complexity of the book's web, and find that every sentence, almost every epithet, has its definite reference to equally unemphasised points before and after in the development of the plot. Thus it is that, while twelve readings of *Pride and Prejudice* give you twelve periods of pleasure repeated, as many readings of *Emma* give you that pleasure, not repeated only, but squared and squared again with each perusal, till at every fresh reading you feel anew that you never understood anything like the widening sum of its delights. But, until you know the story, you are apt to find its movement dense and slow and obscure, difficult to follow, and not very obviously worth the following.

For this is *the* novel of character, and of character alone, and of one dominating character in particular. And many a rash reader, and some who are not rash, have been shut out on the threshold of Emma's Comedy by a dislike of Emma herself. Well did Jane Austen know what she was about, when she said, 'I am going to take a heroine whom nobody but myself will much like.' And, in so far as she fails to make people like

Emma, so far would her whole attempt have to be judged a failure, were it not that really the failure, like the loss, is theirs who have not taken the trouble to understand what is being attempted. Jane Austen loved tackling problems; her hardest of all, her most deliberate, and her most triumphantly solved, is Emma.

What is that problem? No one who carefully reads the first three opening paragraphs of the book can entertain a doubt, or need any prefatory synopsis; for in these the author gives us quite clear warning of what we are to see. We are to see the gradual humiliation of self-conceit, through a long self-wrought succession of disasters, serious in effect, but keyed in Comedy throughout. Emma herself, in fact, *is never to be taken seriously.* And it is only those who have not realised this who will be 'put off' by her absurdities, her snobberies, her misdirected mischievous ingenuities. Emma is simply a figure of fun. To conciliate affection for a character, not because of its charms, but in defiance of its defects, is the loftiest aim of the comic spirit; Shakespeare achieved it with his besotted old rogue of a Falstaff, and Molière with Celimène. It is with these, not with 'sympathetic' heroines, that Emma takes rank, as the culminating figure of English high-comedy. And to attain success in creating a being whom you both love and laugh at, the author must attempt a task of complicated difficulty. He must both run with the hare and hunt with the hounds, treat his creation at once objectively and subjectively, get inside it to inspire it with sympathy, and yet stay outside it to direct laughter on its comic aspects. And this is what Jane Austen does for Emma, with a consistent sublimity so demure that indeed a reader accustomed only to crude work might be pardoned for missing the point of her innumerable hints, and actually taking seriously, for example, the irony with which Emma's attitude about the Coles' dinner-party is treated, or the even more convulsing comedy of Emma's reflexions after it. But only Jane Austen is capable of such oblique glints of humour; and only in *Emma* does she weave them so densely into her kaleidoscope that the reader must be perpetually on his guard lest some specially delicious flash escape his notice, or some touch of dialogue be taken for the author's own intention.

Yet, as Emma really does behave extremely ill by Jane Fairfax, and even worse by Robert Martin, merely to laugh would not be enough, and every disapproval would justly be deepened to dislike. But, when we realise that each machination of Emma's, each imagined piece of penetration, is to be a thread in the snare woven unconsciously by herself for her own enmeshing in disaster, then the balance is rectified again, and disapproval can lighten to laughter once more. For this is another of Jane Austen's triumphs here—the way in which she keeps our sympathies poised about Emma. Always some charm of hers is brought out, to compensate some specially silly and ambitious naughtiness; and even these are but perfectly natural, in a strong-willed, strong-minded girl of only twenty-one, who has been for some four years unquestioned mistress of Hartfield, unquestioned Queen of Highbury. Accordingly, at every turn we are kept so dancing up and down with alternate rage and delight at Emma that finally, when we see her self-esteem hammered bit by bit into collapse, the nemesis would be too severe, were she to be left in the depths. By the merciful intention of the book, however, she is saved in the very nick of time by what seems like a happy accident, but is really the outcome of her own unsuspected good qualities, just as much as her disasters had been the outcome of her own most cherished follies.

In fact, Emma is intrinsically honest (it is not for nothing that she is given so unique a frankness of outlook on life); and her brave recognition of her faults, when confronted with their results, conduces largely to the relief with which we hail the solution of the tangle, and laugh out loud over 'Such a heart, such a Harriet'! The remark is typical, both of Emma and of Emma's author. For this is the ripest and kindliest of all Jane Austen's work. Here alone she can laugh at people, and still like them; elsewhere her amusement is invariably salted with either dislike or contempt. *Emma* contains no fewer than four silly people, more or less prominent in the story; but Jane Austen touches them all with a new mansuetude, and turns them out as candidates for love as well as laughter. Nor is this all that must be said for Miss Bates and Mr Woodhouse. They are actually inspired with sympathy. Specially remarkable is the treatment of Miss Bates, whose pathos depends on her lovableness, and her lovableness on her pathos, till she comes so near our hearts that Emma's abrupt brutality to her on Box Hill comes home to us with the actuality of a violent sudden slap in our own face. But then Miss Bates, though a twaddle, is by no means a fool; in her humble, quiet, unassuming happiness, she is shown throughout as an essentially wise woman. For Jane Austen's mood is in no way softened to the second-rate and pretentious, though it is typical of *Emma* that Elton's full horror is only gradually revealed in a succession of tiny touches, many of them designed to swing back sympathy to Emma; even as Emma's own bad behaviour on Box Hill is there to give Jane Fairfax a lift in our sympathy at her critical moment, while Emma's repentance afterwards is just what is wanted to win us back to Emma's side again, in time for the coming catastrophe. And even Elton's 'broad handsome face,' in which 'every feature works,' pales before that of the lady who 'was, in short, so very ready to have him.' 'He called her Augusta; how delightful!'

Jane Austen herself never calls people she is fond of by these fancy names, but reserves them for such female cads or cats as Lydia Bennet, Penelope Clay, Selina Suckling, and 'the charming Augusta Hawkins.' It is characteristic, indeed, of her methods in *Emma,* that, though the Sucklings never actually appear, we come to know them (and miss them) as intimately as if they did. Jane Austen delights in imagining whole vivid sets of people, never on the stage, yet vital in the play; but in *Emma* she indulges herself, and us, unusually lavishly, with the Sucklings at Maple Grove, the Dixons in Ireland, and the Churchills at Enscombe. As for Frank, he is among her men what Mary Crawford is among her women, a being of incomparable brilliance, moving with a dash that only the complicated wonderfulness of the whole book prevents us from lingering to appreciate. In fact, he so dims his cold pale Jane by comparison that one wonders more than ever what he saw in her. The whole Frank-Jane intrigue, indeed, on which the story hinges, is by no means its most valuable or plausible part. But Jane Fairfax is drawn in dim tones by the author's deliberate purpose. She had to be dim. It was essential that nothing should bring the secondary heroine into any competition with Emma. Accordingly Jane Fairfax is held down in a rigid dullness so conscientious that it almost defeats another of her *raisons d'être* by making Frank's affection seem incredible.

But there is very much more in it than that. Emma is to behave so extremely ill in the Dixon matter that she would quite forfeit our sympathy, unless we were a little taught to share her unregenerate feelings for the 'amiable, upright, perfect Jane Fairfax.' Accordingly we are shown Jane Fairfax always from the angle of Emma; and, despite apparently artless words of eulogy, the author is steadily working all the time to give us just that picture of Jane, as a cool, reserved, rather sly creature, which is demanded by the balance of emotion and the perspective of the picture. It is curious, indeed, how often Jane Austen repeats a favourite composition; two sympathetic figures, major and minor, set against an odious one. In practice, this always means that, while the odious is set boldly out in clear lines and brilliant colour, the minor sympathetic one becomes subordinate to the major, almost to the point of dullness. (pp. 23-7)

> Reginald Farrer, ''Jane Austen,'' in The Quarterly Review, *Vol. 228, No. 452, July, 1917, pp. 1-30.*

G. K. CHESTERTON   (essay date 1917)

[*Chesterton was one of England's most prominent and colorful men of letters during the early twentieth century. Although he is best known today as a detective novelist and essayist, he was also an eminent literary critic. Chesterton's works are characterized by their humor, frequent use of paradox, and chatty, rambling style. In the following excerpt, he counters the critical commonplace that Austen failed to deal with social and historical concerns, discussing the novelist's perceptive depiction of Emma as a representative of her class.*]

Among the many good critical tributes to the genius of Jane Austen, to the fine distinction of her humour, the sympathetic intimacy of her satire, the easy exactitude of her unpretentious style, which have appeared in celebration of her centenary, there is one criticism that is naturally recurrent; the remark that she was quite untouched by the towering politics of her time. This is intrinsically true; nevertheless it may easily be used to imply the reverse of the truth. It is true that Jane Austen did not attempt to teach any history or politics; but it is not true that we cannot learn any history or politics from Jane Austen. Any work so piercingly intelligent of its own kind, and especially any work of so wise and humane a kind, is sure to tell us much more than shallower studies covering a larger surface. (p. 502)

Negatively, of course, the historic lesson from Jane Austen is enormous. She is perhaps most typical of her time in being supremely irreligious. Her very virtues glitter with the cold sunlight of the great secular epoch between mediæval and modern mysticism. (p. 503)

But there is a positive as well as a negative way in which her greatness, like Shakespeare's, illuminates history and politics, because it illuminates everything. She understood every intricacy of the upper middle class and the minor gentry, which were to make so much of the mental life of the nineteenth and twentieth centuries. It is said that she ignored the poor and disregarded their opinions. She did, but not more than all our Governments and all our Acts of Parliaments have done. And at least she did consistently ignore them; she ignored where she was ignorant. Well it would have been for the world if others had ignored the working-class until they understood it as well as she did the middle class. She was not a student of sociology; she did not study the poor. But she did study the students—or at least the social types which were to become the students of the poor. She knew her own class, and knew it without illusions; and there is much light on later problems to be found in her delicate delineation of vanities and snobberies and patronage. She had to do with the human heart; and it is that which cometh out of the heart that defileth a nation, philanthropy, efficiency, organization, social reform. And if the

weaker brethren still wonder why we should find in Baby Week or Welfare Work a dangerous spirit, from which its best adherents find it hard to free themselves, if they doubt how such a danger can be reconciled with the personal delicacy and idealism of many of the women who work such things, if they think that fine words or even fine feelings will guarantee a respect for the personality of the poor, I really do not know that they could do better than sit down, I trust not for the first time, to the reading of *Emma.*

For all this that has happened since might well be called the Evolution of Emma. That unique and formidable institution, the English Lady, has, indeed, become much more of a public institution; that is, she has made the same mistakes on a much larger scale. The softer fastidiousness and finer pride of the more gracious eighteenth century heroine may seem to make her a shadow by comparison. It seems cruel to say that the breaking off of Harriet's humbler engagement foreshadows the indiscriminate development of Divorce for the Poor. It seems horrible to say that Emma's small matchmaking has in it the seed of the pestilence of Eugenics. But it is true. With a gentleness and justice and sympathy with good intentions, which clear her from the charge of common synicism, the great novelist does find the spring of her heroine's errors, and of many of ours. That spring is a philanthropy, and even a generosity, secretly founded on gentility. Emma Woodhouse was a wit, she was a good woman, she was an individual with a right to her own opinion; but it was because she was a lady that she acted as she did, and thought she had a right to act as she did. She is the type in fiction of a whole race of English ladies, in fact, for whom refinement is religion. Her claim to oversee and order the social things about her consisted in being refined; she would not have admitted that being rich had anything to do with it; but as a fact it had everything to do with it. If she had been very much richer, if she had had one of the great modern fortunes, if she had had the wider modern opportunities (for the rich) she would have thought it her duty to act on the wider modern scale; she would have had public spirit and political grasp. She would have dealt with a thousand Robert Martins and a thousand Harriet Smiths, and made the same muddle about all of them. That is what we mean about things like Baby Week—and if there had been a baby in the story, Miss Woodhouse would certainly have seen all its educational needs with a brilliant clearness. And we do not mean that the work is done entirely by Mrs. Pardiggle; we mean that much of it is done by Miss Woodhouse. But it is done because she *is* Miss Woodhouse and not Martha Muggins or Jemima Jones; because the Lady Bountiful is a lady first, and will bestow every bounty but freedom.

It is noted that there are few traces of the French Revolution in Miss Austen's novels; but, indeed, there have been few traces of it in Miss Austen's country. The peculiarity which has produced the situation I describe is really this: that the new sentiment of humanitarianism has come, when the old sentiment of aristocracy has not gone. Social superiors have not really lost any old privileges; they have gained new privileges, including that of being superior in philosophy and philanthropy as well as in riches and refinement. No revolution has shaken their secret security or menaced them with the awful peril of becoming no more than men. Therefore their social reform is but their social refinement grown restless. And in this old teacup comedy can be found, far more clearly appreciated than in more ambitious books about problems and politics, the psychology of this mere restlessness in the rich, when it first stirred upon its cushions. Jane Austen descibed a narrow class, but so truthfully that she has much to teach about its after adventures, when it remained narrow as a class and broadened only as a sect. (pp. 503-05)

G. K. Chesterton, *"The Evolution of Emma," in* The Living Age, *Vol. CCXCIV, No. 3816, August 25, 1917, pp. 502-05.*

ORLO WILLIAMS, M.C. (essay date 1926)

[*Williams considers Austen's antiromantic attitudes toward love and marriage in* Emma. *While conceding that the range of the novel is narrow, he states that Austen's art "is near perfection" in the work, citing in particular her use of language, her depiction of character, and her skilled structuring of the plot.*]

Emma is not a story of passion or adventure. There are those upon whom, for these very deficiencies, it can never cast its spell. They cannot take much interest in life so placid and so circumscribed, in complacent minds and minute events. They want, in reading fiction, to be swept along by a wild west wind or to be shown a vaster and more thrilling world of imagination to balance the dull incompleteness of their own. Those, on the other hand, who have once fallen under the spell of Miss Austen's art will always find that spell renewed.

Emma, the favourite of some though not of all, by its peculiar sedateness prompts one to ask the secret of its perennial fascination. Certainly the temperament which requires fiction only to be adventurous or passionate or profound or ecstatic will not enjoy *Emma.* Charlotte Brontë, we know, read it "with interest and just that degree of admiration which Miss Austen herself would have thought sensible and suitable. Anything like warmth or enthusiasm, anything energetic, poignant, heartfelt, is utterly out of place in commending these works" [see excerpt dated 1850 in *NCLC,* Vol. 1]. We understand how Charlotte Brontë felt, and respect her feelings while regretting her particular insensibility. We admit the absence from *Emma* of all that she remarks—the absence of the "stormy sisterhood" of passions and of the wildly throbbing heart. But if we speak of fascination at all, it is to claim that in judging the works of Jane Austen warmth and enthusiasm are entirely in place; as much in place as in discussing *Jane Eyre* or *Wuthering Heights,* if we are happy enough to have the discernment which can enjoy all three. (pp. 152-53)

[*Emma*] is a story which minutely draws the life of a small country district in which there is little movement but that of animals and little activity but that of husbandry, and neither in this movement nor that activity does the narrator take much interest. She deals with a little fragment of human society in which, for the women at least, talking, reading, making music and dancing were the only occupations, in which old friends called upon each other once a day, in which to walk half a mile alone was "unpleasant for a young lady," and in which a rich and well-born girl could be undisputed queen of her neighbourhood. There is a great deal of gentility here and not a little snobbishness; tears are allowed, but passionate sobs are not heard; riddles and charades exercise minds not troubled at all by the deep mysteries of human existence; and marriage, as the result of "regard," of "feeling" and of "attachments," is eagerly canvassed, while love is spoken of in a gingerly and sober fashion, as if it had normally the effects of a hot-water bottle rather than those of a volcano. Miss Austen in her character of narrator speaks of

the marriage of Miss Campbell, who by that chance, that luck which so often defies anticipation in ma-

trimonial affairs, giving attraction to what is moderate rather than to what is superior, engaged the affections of Mr. Dixon, a young man rich and agreeable, almost as soon as they were acquainted, and was eligibly and happily settled.

while Emma, considering her first agreeable flutter of heart, can reflect:

Every consideration of the subject, in short, makes me thankful that my happiness is not more deeply involved. I shall do very well again after a little while, and then it will be a good thing over, for they say everybody is in love once in their lives, and I shall have been let off easily.

This cool and philosophic tone is rather that of Lewis Carroll's Alice after she had emerged from swimming in the pool of her own tears with all the strange animals.

Yet, after all, if we consider in parenthesis this unenthusiastic attitude to the question of love and marriage, we may have to admit that Jane Austen has more than her own idiosyncrasy to support her. Young women of to-day may smile with superiority or shrug with contempt at Emma's early conversation with Harriet, in which she accepts quite calmly a prospect of well-to-do singleness.

I have none of the usual inducements of women to marry. Were I to fall in love, indeed, it would be a different thing; but I never have been in love; it is not my way, or my nature; and I do not think I ever shall. And, without love, I am sure I should be a fool to change such a situation as mine. Fortune I do not want; employment I do not want; consequence I do not want; I believe few married women are half as much mistress of their husband's house as I am of Hartfield; and never, never could I expect to be so truly beloved and important; so always first and always right in any man's eyes as I am in my father's.

She admits that, if there were any prospect of becoming a poor and garrulous old maid like Miss Bates, she would marry tomorrow; but is sure that she herself would never want occupation or interests.

If I draw less, I shall read more; if I give up music, I shall take to carpet-work. And as for objects of interest, objects for the affections, which is, in truth, the great point of inferiority, the want of which is really the great evil to be avoided in *not* marrying, I shall be very well off, with all the children of a sister I love so much to care about. There will be enough of them, in all probability, to supply every sort of sensation that declining life can need. There will be enough for every hope and every fear; and though my attachment to none can equal that of a parent, it suits my ideas of comfort better than what is warmer and blinder. My nephews and nieces: I shall often have a niece with me.

The admirable irony of Miss Austen in thus exposing, in a dialogue of which every exquisite stroke tells, the bland assurance of youth, will hardly escape any reader's notice; but, making every allowance for this, I suggest that there is a remarkable frankness and justice at the bottom of Emma's remarks. We may imagine, in these days of soul-analysis, of temperaments exposed and of repressions let loose, when it is reputed both brave and fashionable to walk about in psychological nakedness without a *cache-sexe* of any kind, that we have a great advantage over the repressed and amply breeched and petticoated society of Emma's day; but we may not often consider whether we have frankness of *thought,* if indeed our absorption in our emotions permits us any thought to be frank about.

Young people of to-day display their glands or their libidos and button up their brains; Emma did the contrary. It was the fashion of her day, which still seems to present a very admirable appearance. The result, in this particular dialogue, is a self-revelation of peculiar directness and honesty. . . . Miss Austen may have known little of the stormier passions in her own person, though quite capable of observing their effects in others, but her views upon marriage were well reflected and sensible, especially in that age.

If any error might be imputed to her it is mainly in her tendency to make her young heroines as perspicacious as she was herself. Miss Austen saw that the *great* passion of love was abnormal, but that marriage was natural, a state to be entered or rejected just as properly upon prudential as upon sentimental considerations. In fact, she made her young women reveal with more than normal young women's directness the logical premisses and conclusions of a young woman's mind. It is only since the nineteenth century that English thought on these matters has been confused by sentiment; and the fact that this dialogue of Emma's and many others in Miss Austen's novels repels the sentimentalist is, in truth, a criticism of the sentimental attitude. She left passion on one side because it was not in her nature; thus she wisely kept her artistic balance, as may be seen in this very story, where the mutual passion of Jane Fairfax and Frank Churchill is sufficiently suggested but never stressed. But where social fact is in question she is relentless truth itself. In none of her novels is this more evident than in *Emma.* I cannot think of a single sentence either of description or of reflection, nor of one line in the delightful flow of dialogue, wherein, directly or by implication, there is a sign of falsity or self-delusion. Miss Austen's pen could no more tell lies than her vision. (pp. 155-60)

[The attitude toward love and marriage reflected in *Emma*] is one of the elements of quietness in a "quiet" novel; and though the essential and justifiable enthusiasm for Jane Austen rests neither upon her sober truth nor upon the quietness of her incident, yet, just as there is a great merit in preventing feeling from obscuring fact, so there is a great deal to be said for the "quiet" view of comedy. It is temperamental, certainly, and not to be assumed at will; and it does not rise to the height of Aristophanes and Shakespeare, which is Titanic. Yet many of us, in whom the sanguine and choleric humours are not too prominent, must often feel the charm of withdrawing from the hive and watching a small corner of its life, for a moment, in detachment, and complete receptivity. Some people cannot so watch: they must moralise, as did Maeterlinck when he observed bees in a glass hive. Those, who *can,* know better than to do anything but smile, nod or shake their heads. The ordinary life of men and women, taken as a whole, is not continuously suffused by great issues or inspired by overwhelming emotions.

The part of a single individual in the sweeping movements of humanity is singularly attenuated, and he flashes to greatness only at moments. The supreme tragic or comic writers have to suggest the masses or isolate the moments; theirs is the highest talent. But the sensitive observer in direct detachment has neither to suggest nor to isolate; he has but to observe and, if an artist, to describe. Any corner of life, as much as any ant-heap, will reward such observation and justify an artist's description. If Miss Austen's corner of life does not interest you, you must turn away from it, but your departure does not condemn those who sit happily by her side. They do not sit there

all day. Other moods will bring them back again to mix in more exciting circumstance or to be charmed by more forcible spells than these. Yet, while they are with her, they will be intently absorbed, for she will show them in her little chosen perspective the curious confusion of motive which attends all human action, the strange illusions that create imaginary obstacles, the foibles and futilities which diversify every single human being, the comedies waiting upon the satisfaction of even mild desires, the conceit which makes the most trivial existence important to itself, the absurd influence of outward circumstance. And if her ground of observation is narrow, one may almost say of it, what she herself says in *Emma* of the view of Abbey Mill Farm as seen from Mr. Knightley's garden: "It was a sweet view—sweet to the eye and the mind. English verdure, English culture, English comfort, seen under a sun bright without being oppressive," though one would have to add English character to make the catalogue of beauties complete.

To observe a corner of life so clearly is no mean achievement, and to describe it so exquisitely is a great one. This is what has roused enthusiasm in the hearts of several generations. Jane Austen's range is small, but her art is near perfection. To read a work of art so beautifully and economically done as *Emma* compels joy in the heart; and those who feel this joy can hardly speak of it without a happy ring in their voice. (pp. 161-63)

One might linger in detail on the many felicities to be found in *Emma,* of description, of character-drawing and of language. The subject of language alone, once it were launched upon, would be difficult to leave, for here indeed Jane Austen has a magic. For instance, when Mr. Elton has proposed to Emma in the brougham, as it returned at a walking pace from Randalls to Hartfield, and each in their annoyance had rent to rags the other's complacency, she brings the scene of brisk comedy to an end with the magnificent paragraph:

> He was too angry to say another word; her manner too decided to invite supplication: and in this state of swelling resentment and mutually deep mortification, they had to continue together a few minutes longer, for the fears of Mr. Woodhouse had confined them to a foot-pace. If there had not been so much anger, there would have been desperate awkwardness; but their straightforward emotions left no room for the little zigzags of embarrassment. Without knowing when the carriage turned into Vicarage Lane or when it stopped, they found themselves, all at once, at the door of his house; and he was out before another syllable passed. Emma then felt it indispensable to wish him a good-night. The compliment was just returned, coldly and proudly; and, under indescribable irritation of spirits, she was then conveyed to Hartfield.

The force and propriety of this passage are absolute; nothing more violent or exclamatory could produce so sure an effect upon the reader's mind. With unstrained ease the picture is placed there for ever, graven with all the power of classical eloquence; and it could be matched a hundred times in this one book. Again, if one turns from the language to the characters, what a field there is open for admiring comment! Miss Bates has become the immortal type of the golden-hearted but inconsequent gossiping spinster of a village; Mrs. Elton, with her allusions to Maple Grove, her brother-in-law's seat, and the barouche-landau, is almost as famous a name for pert ill-breeding; while Mr. Woodhouse, with his gruel and his timorous abhorrence of novelty, is one of Miss Austen's most delicate performances, for she never lets us forget that, with all his tiresome crotchets, he has a kind heart and true gentleness of breeding. And then how neatly are Harriet Smith's vacuity of mind and John Knightley's irritability revealed in the few words that they say! Like all Miss Austen's comic characters they seem to have been born in her mind with their appropriate words in their mouths. The character of Emma has not commended itself to all readers, but for a reason which is a tribute to her creator—they feel a personal dislike for the puffed-up young woman who suffered so sadly from want of whipping. There could be no better proof of Emma's reality; and, in fact, her character is brilliantly drawn, with a power of completeness which is unsurpassed in any of Miss Austen's creations. Her merits and her stupidities are unfolded in a most ingenious fluctuating curve, and its salient points crystallised in cunning passages of dialogue which would repay a very searching analysis.

Analysis, indeed of the kind on which Mr. Percy Lubbock enlarges in his *Craft of Fiction* may very profitably be applied to Miss Austen's novels, and to none more so than to *Emma*. Many admirable writers have expatiated on her language and her well-known characters; and the familiarity of readers may be counted upon where those things are concerned; but not till after many readings, if then, is a reader likely to consider in detail the whole architecture of the story. (pp. 165-67)

[Miss Austen] has a mastery of vital rhythm, not only in her sentences, but in the whole fabric of her creations. With subtle variations, climax answers climax and repose balances repose.... As in an opera by Mozart, one bewitching theme succeeds another; our enjoyment is never strained but never relaxed. By ingenious yet easy alternations of key and measure, of piquant solos and triumphant *tutti*, our consciousness is held continuously enthralled, until the last chord has been struck. We return again, when the element of surprise is quite worn away, and again we are subjugated. It is no wonder that, having once surrendered to this enchantress, we are always in her power, listening to such bright and graceful music, so pure in form, so delicate in texture. (pp. 177-78)

> *Orlo Williams, M.C., "'Emma'," in his* Some Great
> English Novels: Studies in the Art of Fiction, *Mac-*
> *millan and Co., Limited, 1926, pp. 149-78.*

J. ISAACS (essay date 1951)

[*Isaacs regards Austen's narrative method in portions of* Emma *as stream-of-consciousness technique.*]

One of the most remarkable wielders of the [stream of consciousness] method in its primitive form, and one of the least noticed, is Jane Austen. Part of the reason for the Jane Austen revival in recent years is not the refuge her work offers, not the museum quality of her sentimental and genteel world nor its ironic treatment, but the half-perceived modernity of her technique. She has come back, as Conrad and Henry James have come back, as a modern. Almost every ingredient of the stream of consciousness technique can be found in her work: the oblique writing, prattle, soliloquy, internal monologue. There is the incessant flow of Miss Bates, which despite its direct reporting has something of the nightmare feeling of the true stream of consciousness. There is the carefully contrived total report of the conversation during the strawberry picking.

> Strawberries, and only strawberries, could now be thought or spoken of. 'The best fruit in England—everybody's favourite—always wholesome. These the finest beds and finest sorts. Delightful to gather for one's self—the only way of really enjoying them.

> Morning decidedly the best time—never tired—every sort good—hautboys infinitely superior—no comparison—the others hardly eatable—hautboys very scarce—Chili preferred—white wood finest flavour of all—price of strawberries in London—abundance about Bristol—Maple Grove—cultivation—beds when to be renewed—gardeners thinking exactly different—no general rule—gardeners never to be put out of their way—delicious fruit—only too rich to be eaten much of—inferior to cherries—currants more refreshing—only objection to gathering strawberries the stooping—glaring sun—tired to death—could bear it no longer—must go and sit in the shade.' Such, for half an hour, was the conversation.

This portrait of the collective strawberry-picker is well on the way to montage, and in Emma's agony of self-reproach and mortification Jane Austen is exactly a hundred years ahead of her time.

> The rest of the day, the following night, were hardly enough for her thoughts. She was bewildered amidst the confusion of all that had rushed on her within the last few hours. Every moment had brought a fresh surprise; and every surprise must be a matter of humiliation to her.—How to understand it all! How to understand the deceptions she had been thus practising on herself, and living under!—The blunders, the blindness of her own head and heart!

> • • • • •

> Mr. Knightley and Harriet Smith!—It was an union to distance every wonder of the kind. The attachment of Frank Churchill and Jane Fairfax became commonplace, threadbare, stale in the comparison, exciting no surprise, presenting no disparity, affording nothing to be said or thought. Mr. Knightley and Harriet Smith! Such an elevation on her side! Such a debasement on his! It was horrible to Emma to think how it must sink him in the general opinion, to foresee the smiles, the sneers, the merriment it would prompt at his expense; the mortification and disdain of his brother, the thousand inconveniences to himself. Could it be? No; it was impossible. And yet it was far, very far, from impossible.—Was it a new circumstance for a man of first-rate abilities to be captivated by very inferior powers? Was it new for one, perhaps too busy to seek, to be the prize of a girl who would seek him? Was it new for anything in this world to be unequal, inconsistent, incongruous—or for chance and circumstance (as second causes) to direct the human fate?

This is so successful, so homogeneous, that it comes as a shock when the author intrudes if only for a fleeting moment into the stream. There is also something very modern in the headlong tempo of this passage.

Brilliant as Jane Austen is, she is still one of the primitives. Her interior monologues are all individual performances, they do not impinge on each other nor contribute to the larger structure. (pp. 90-3)

> *J. Isaacs, "The Stream of Consciousness," in his*
> An Assessment of Twentieth-Century Literature, *1951.*
> *Reprint by Kennikat Press, Inc., 1968, pp. 73-102.*

MARVIN MUDRICK (essay date 1952)

[*In the following excerpt from his acclaimed study* Jane Austen: Irony as Defense and Discovery, *Mudrick discusses irony in* Emma *and examines the negative and destructive aspects of Emma's*

TO

HIS ROYAL HIGHNESS

THE PRINCE REGENT,

THIS WORK IS,

BY HIS ROYAL HIGHNESS'S PERMISSION,

MOST RESPECTFULLY

DEDICATED,

BY HIS ROYAL HIGHNESS'S

DUTIFUL

AND OBEDIENT

HUMBLE SERVANT,

THE AUTHOR.

The dedication page of Emma.

character. *Mudrick's remarks are addressed by T. B. Tomlinson (see excerpt dated 1966).*]

Emma is a throwing off of chains. The author and her characters move with a freedom and assurance unparalleled in Jane Austen's earlier work, and all the more astonishing by contrast with the uneasy stiffness of *Mansfield Park.* The new impetus is her old familiar one, but—from our first impression of *Emma*—purely assimilated to the medium as, in *Northanger Abbey* or even in *Pride and Prejudice,* it is not: the impetus is irony. In *Emma,* the sense of strain and anxiety is purged altogether. This time the author is in her novel and never out of it, never imposing upon us as in *Northanger Abbey* with her condescension or in *Pride and Prejudice* with her occasional prim moral reminders; and she is there for the comic artist's purpose only—to embody and direct our laughter.

The relaxation of an achieved technique is the very climate of *Emma.* Certainly, no other of Jane Austen's novels offers so pleasant and comfortable an atmosphere, so much the effect of an uncomplex and immediate art: wit, irony, light laughter shining in a triumph of surface. Its surface is, in fact, unmarred by a trace of self-justification, ill humor, or back-sliding into morality. The story tells itself, and nothing seems more superfluous than inquiry or deep thought about it. (p. 181)

Nowhere else is Jane Austen so relaxed, so certain, skilled, and exact in her effects. There is no excess; almost no sense of plot in this delicate ordering of a small calm world, the miniature world of the English rural gentry at the start of the nineteenth century. The ease of style and setting predisposes us to an easy response, prepares us for a mellowing, even a softening, of Jane Austen's newly reasserted irony. The characters of *Emma* seem our familiars at once, in what [George Saintsbury has] called—with a dangerous patness—"the absolute triumph of that reliance on the strictly ordinary which has been indicated as Miss Austen's title to pre-eminence in the history of the novel."

Emma herself seems one of the most attractive of all heroines: beautiful, cultivated, intelligent; solicitous of her father; inclined to snobbery and to rash judgment, but appealing even in her errors and caprices. There is more, but it does not bear out our preconception. Mr. Knightley is a man of integrity, of force, wit, and high sense, and—we suspect—rather too good for Emma; but this is just a suspicion. Frank Churchill is an elegant and engaging trifler, whose secret courtship of Jane Fairfax, the worthy girl in unworthy circumstances, comes finally to light as his only recommendation. The yielding Mrs. Weston, as Emma's sympathetic confidante, recalls to us the yielding Miss Taylor who could only have given way before her pupil's precocious wilfulness; so that with her we add to our stock of good reasons why Emma is what she is. The author provides us with five varieties of nonentity, will-less comic foils to Emma's wilfulness: Harriet, the obliging; Mr. Woodhouse, the gently querulous; Mr. Weston, the congenial; Isabella, the domestic; and Miss Bates, the interminably talkative. John Knightley sets off his brother's forthrightness by presenting the same quality with a bristly manner and a touch of misanthropy. For villains—harmless enough to be only amusing—the author gives us the Eltons: Mr. Elton, a pillar of meanly aspiring egotism; and his perfectly appropriate wife, Augusta, radiating that field of monomaniac affectation and self-deceit which no sarcasm or earthly judgment can penetrate.

These are Jane Austen's creatures in her new mild climate, and at the end she placidly disposes of them all: nobody left out, no strand left unwoven, nobody unhappy. The plot is fulfilled when the characters are placed where they wish to be: Emma with Mr. Knightley, Frank Churchill with Jane Fairfax, Mr. Elton with his Augusta, motherly Mrs. Weston with her first child; everybody at Hartfield, Donwell, Randalls, and Highbury comfortably settled.

Still, as we follow her attentively, Emma comes to appear less and less an innocuous figure in a novel of simple irony. She begins as a representative young gentlewoman of her age: snobbish, half-educated, wilful, possessive; and, certainly, her consciousness of rank accounts for a good many of her prejudices and cruelties. The fact remains that Emma has unpleasant qualities, which persist in operating and having effect. Whether we try to explain these qualities on the ground of upbringing or youth or personal impulse, we cannot blind ourselves to them. They are there, embedded in the novel.

Emma is, of course, an inveterate snob. . . . Her first thought is always of rank and family. She regards Mr. Knightley's possible attachment to Jane Fairfax as a "very shameful and degrading connection;" and although here she has other reasons, yet unknown to herself, for objecting, it is significant that her first target is Jane's family. (pp. 183-85)

Emma has neglected the genteel feminine accomplishments, and cannot endure being reminded of her neglect. Shamed by Jane's superior playing on the piano, she detests her more unjustly than ever. She sketches a fair likeness of Harriet; and the immoderate praise of her subject and Mr. Elton, though it cannot delude her, is enough to flatter her ego into silence. . . . (p. 186)

Emma is an arranger, a manager of other people's affairs. Accustomed to look after her father's every whim and to forestall his every possible discomfort, she tries to extend this duty over her circle of friends and acquaintances as well. Yet she prophesies only what she wills, and she is always wrong. She will never admit what she herself has not contrived, until the truth strikes her in the face. She is wrong about Mr. Elton's feelings toward Harriet. She quite misconceives her own feelings toward Mr. Knightley. Baffled and angered by Jane Fairfax's reserve, she creates without a shred of evidence the most outrageous slander about an affair she imagines Jane to have had with another woman's husband; and she is even ready to pass her slander on to Churchill. . . . She is wrong about Harriet's feelings toward Churchill. She complacently fabricates an entire love affair between Churchill and herself—including its decline and dissolution—with no more encouragement than the gentleman's adroit and uncommitting flirtation; yet throughout this imaginary affair she reiterates her "resolution . . . of never marrying:" for though Emma can imagine everything else, she cannot imagine her own commitment. She is wrong about Mr. Knightley's feelings toward both Harriet and herself. Even when she has recognized her own love for Mr. Knightley and heard his declaration joyfully, she finds the duty of remaining with her father superior to the claim of love:

> . . . a very short parley with her own heart produced the most solemn resolution of never quitting her father.

She is ready, then, to alter everyone's life but her father's, which is after all only a shadowy extension of her own.

Emma is occupied in altering, as she sees fit, the lives of others; and to this end any means will do. If, to save Harriet for gentility, Robert Martin must be made unhappy, he is merely another obstacle to be set aside with no more than a moment's uneasiness. . . . Even death, the death of Mrs. Churchill, is for Emma a means, serving to freshen her wholly fanciful hope for a match between Churchill and Harriet. . . . The personal, as personal, cannot engage Emma for more than a moment: her mind cannot rest upon it without making it over altogether into a means.

Emma claims the role of adviser, but denies its responsibility. She delights in bullying anyone who will yield—poor Harriet most of all, . . . yet at the last, unwilling to face Harriet after her own disastrous series of errors in her protégée's affairs, she limits her compunction and their relationship to letters. . . . Far from examining the past, Emma absolves herself of it. Even when Harriet's confession of love for Mr. Knightley has roused Emma to the pitch of self-analysis, Emma's outcry sinks easily into the luxury of an acknowledged defeat:

> She was most sorrowfully indignant; ashamed of every sensation but the one revealed to her—her affection for Mr. Knightley.—Every other part of her mind was disgusting.

the act of self-abasement that claims sin, in order to avoid the responsibility of self-knowledge.

Emma and Harriet are the most unexpected companions in all of Jane Austen's work. Nor may we pass off their intimacy—at least from Emma's side—as the effect of blind adolescent exuberance. Emma is already a worldly twenty-one; and she

is aware enough of Harriet's intellectual limitations to comment ironically on Mr. Elton's charade:

> ". . . Harriet's ready wit! All the better. A man must be very much in love indeed, to describe her so. . . ."

Emma has no intellectual ties with the unalterably sheeplike Harriet, and she can gain no material advantage from her friendship. Of course, Emma likes to manage people, and Harriet is manageable. But why Harriet, of all people; and why so tenaciously Harriet, at least until every trick has failed? (pp. 187-90)

Harriet draws her unqualified confidence as only one other person does: Mrs. Weston. Mrs. Weston has been her affectionate governess, and continued affection between them is natural enough. But Emma's regard reaches the same noteworthy excess as with Harriet. Emma has imagined herself to be falling in love with Frank Churchill; now he and Mrs. Weston, who is his stepmother, come upon her together:

> She was wanting to see him again, and especially to see him in company with Mrs. Weston, upon his behaviour to whom her opinion of him was to depend. If her were deficient there, nothing should make amends for it.

One assumes that not even imagining herself in love with him could impel Emma to forgive Churchill's possible coolness toward his stepmother.

Emma's attitude toward young men—when she is not trying to drive them into Harriet's arms—touches now and then upon the thought of a suitable marriage for herself. With Churchill she can sustain the idea of marriage just as long as it remains an idea, a neat, appropriate, socially approved arrangement. . . . The direct threat of marriage, however, she always thrusts aside, indignantly with Mr. Elton:

> ". . . I have no thoughts of matrimony at present."

after long deliberation (which has nothing to feed on but itself), with respect to Churchill:

> Her own attachment had really subsided into a mere nothing; it was not worth thinking of. . . .

even, for a time, in answer to Mr. Knightley. Meanwhile, her involvement with Harriet—until the culminating error—remains steady and strong.

The fact is that Emma prefers the company of women, more particularly of women whom she can master and direct; the fact is that this preference is intrinsic to her whole dominating and uncommitting personality. (pp. 191-92)

Emma needs to dominate, she can of course—in her class and time—most easily dominate women; and her need is urgent enough to forego even the pretense of sympathetic understanding. She feels affection only toward Harriet, Mrs. Weston, and her father: instances, not of tenderness, but rather of satisfied control. She feels affection only toward those immediately under her command, and all of them are women. Mr. Woodhouse is no exception. The effect of decayed gentlemanliness that he produces is a *tour de force* of Jane Austen's, nothing else; for Mr. Woodhouse is really an old woman, of the vacuous, mild-natured, weakly selfish sort very common to novels and (possibly) to life. He has no single masculine trait, and his only distinction lies in the transfer of sex. He is Mrs. Bates elevated to the dignity of Hartfield. (pp. 192-93)

Emma is a beautiful and clever girl, with every grace but tenderness. Without it, she exhibits the strong need to dominate, the offhand cruelty, the protective playfulness, the malice of Jane Austen, the candid Jane Austen of the letters—in which miscarriage is a joke:

> Mrs. Hall, of Sherborne, was brought to bed yesterday of a dead child, some weeks before she expected, owing to a fright. I suppose she happened unawares to look at her husband.

and death equally amusing:

> Only think of Mrs. Holder's being dead! Poor woman, she has done the only thing in the world she could possibly do to make one cease to abuse her.

recalling the more literary echo in *Emma,* on Mrs. Churchill's death:

> Goldsmith tells us, that when lovely woman stoops to folly, she has nothing to do but to die; and when she stoops to be disagreeable, it is equally to be recommended as a clearer of ill fame.

and marriage also, as—anticipating Emma on Churchill—she shrugs off the fading interest of an eligible young man:

> This is rational enough; there is less love and more sense in it than sometimes appeared before, and I am very well satisfied. It will all go on exceedingly well, and decline away in a very reasonable manner.

Emma, of course, is only an "imaginist" and twenty-one; creating her, Jane Austen is an artist and thirty-nine. In the assurance of mastery—with a quarter-century of writing behind her, a portion of fame, and a congenial subject isolated from moral qualms—Jane Austen could be freely aware of the Emma in herself, she could convert her own personal limitations into the very form of her novel. All she had to discard for the character of Emma was her own overarching artist's awareness, her unresting irony, which even in life, in her letters at least, directed and used her need to dominate, her fear of commitment: which made her coldly right where Emma is coldly wrong.

Emma is moved to play God, but without tenderness or social caution (or the artist's awareness) she falls into every conceivable mistake and misjudgment. She must feel herself to be central and centripetal, the confidante and adviser of all. Without tenderness or caution, she makes the worst of every situation: imagines evil when there is good—because Jane Fairfax is "disgustingly [reserved]" or has an "odious composure"— and good where there is nothing but an extension of self.

Mrs. Elton—for all of Emma's heartfelt aversion to her—is Emma's true companion in motive. Both must dominate every situation. Both must have admirers to confirm their position. Both are profoundly wanting in altruism and sympathy. The chief difference is that Mrs. Elton's motive lies bare, without ornament of intelligence, beauty, or rank. Mrs. Elton is "vulgar" (Emma's favorite word for her and her friends):

> ". . . A little upstart, vulgar being, with her Mr. E., and her *caro sposo,* and her resources, and all her airs of pert pretension and under-bred finery. . . ."

and Emma is "refined." Mrs. Elton has no brake of intelligence or breeding upon her egocentrism; she can rattle on and give herself away without self-consciousness. . . . Emma, though, is neither fatuous nor unperceptive. She must play the idol and the confidante, but she requires some evidence of idolatry; and she builds up a vindictive dislike of Jane Fairfax precisely because it is clear that Jane will worship or trust neither her nor anyone else.

Emma can fall back on the nonentities of her world, those vessels of neutral purpose that are always governed from the outside: Harriet, Mr. Woodhouse, Mr. Weston, Isabella, and Miss Bates. Not that they have anything to offer beyond agreeableness: Mr. Weston, happy with his son, ready to be satisfied with everyone, even Mrs. Elton; Isabella, dwindling pleasantly in hypochondria and her husband's shadow; Harriet, with her infinite pliancy; Miss Bates, spreading her obsessive good cheer. . . . (pp. 193-95)

The only character in the story who sees Emma at all clearly is Frank Churchill. He is as egoistic and calculating as she, but he beats her at her own game because he is far less self-deluded. Emma's prodigious self-deception springs at least partly from inexperience. With experience, with the especially valuable experience of pampering a cross and dictatorial old woman, Churchill has learned to be cautious, to blunt the edge of his ego with careless charm. He has learned to use people more successfully than Emma, but he is not less destructive. His playing at love with Emma is required, perhaps, in order to keep the secret of his engagement to Jane; but he takes cynical delight in tormenting the latter and mystifying the former. . . . He has no scruples, for he needs none: charm and wealth excuse everything. One wonders whether Emma—even under the vigilance of Mr. Knightley—will not be polished into the same engaging ruthlessness after several years of marriage.

Emma accepts Mr. Knightley doubtless because she loves and admires him. She has failed so discouragingly with Harriet as to give up all thought of protégées for the present; and Mr. Knightley is after all a very impressive and admirable man. He is even the most likable and most heroic of Jane Austen's heroes: unlike Darcy, he is a frank and social man; he is not a prig like Edmund Bertram, or a wary ironist like Henry Tilney. He is intelligent, perceptive, mature—but not so indivertibly as to save his judgment altogether from the effects of love. . . . That he should continue to love Emma at all, after observing her through all her misdemeanors, is in fact a tribute to the power of love; for Mr. Knightley is quite capable of recognizing and pointing out the implications of her conduct, with Harriet, with Churchill and Jane Fairfax, with Miss Bates— implications he vigorously points out to Emma herself. Success in love, though, overthrows him. As for Emma, she has been defeated. All her dreams of fruitful dominion have been at least temporarily dissipated; and, for the time being, she is willing to be dominated by a man of whom her intelligence and her snobbery can approve (though even now she accepts only on condition that he move into her father's home!). The flood of repentence has not yet subsided. Yet there is no sign that Emma's motives have changed, that there is any difference in her except her relief and temporary awareness. Later on, the story may turn back again: it is hard to think of Emma undominant for any length of time.

Emma plays God because she cannot commit herself humanly. Her compulsion operates in the absence of one quality: a quality which Emma, Frank Churchill, and Mrs. Elton—the only destructive figures in the novel—are all without. The quality is tenderness. For Emma, there is no communication of feeling. She can esteem, loathe, praise, censure, grieve, rejoice—but she cannot feel like anyone else in the world. Her ego will admit nothing but itself. Frank Churchill and Mrs. Elton fall under the same charge: but Mrs. Elton is too transparently vulgar to be effective; and Churchill, too astute to be caught playing God, keeps his own counsel, trifles, observes, and makes use of people by the less imposing and less dangerous tactic of charm. Of the three, only Emma is both foolish enough to play God and dazzling enough to blind anyone even for a short time.

The primary large irony of the novel is, then, the deceptiveness of surface. Charm is the chief warning-signal of Jane Austen's world, for it is most often the signal of wit adrift from feeling. The brilliant façades of Emma and Frank Churchill have no door. (pp. 197-201)

In *Emma,* Jane Austen has given surface the benefit of every alluring quality in the persons of the heroine and of Frank Churchill. She has given them beauty, wealth, position, and immediate circumstances most favorable to the exercise of their wills. The only results have been confusion and unhappiness, on the reduced scale appropriate to the people and the society involved.

Of course, the denouement brushes aside confusion and un-happiness, and brings Emma and Churchill into ostensibly happy marriages. *Emma* can be read as the story of a spoiled rich girl who is corrected by defeat and love, and who lives happily ever after. This is a limited vision, but it is not a false one; for Jane Austen does succeed on her primary levels in achieving her "ripest and kindliest," her most perfect love comedy. On these levels, Emma is "faultless in spite of all her faults," Frank Churchill's frivolity will be tempered by the sense and grave sweetness of his wife, even Mrs. Elton can do little harm, and everyone else is comfortably settled—with the exception of poor Mrs. Churchill, who had to die to clear the way for her nephew's marriage. The conditions are almost standard for romantic comedy: two love-affairs, one complicated by self-deception, the other by secrecy, both turning out well; no strong issue, no punishment.

Emma can be read so; but it has more to give, and not easily. Reginald Farrer, one of the few critics of Jane Austen who have taken the trouble to read her carefully, has observed [see excerpt dated 1917] that *Emma*

> is not an easy book to read; it should never be the beginner's primer, nor be published without a pre-factory synopsis. Only when the story has been thoroughly assimilated, can the infinite delights and subtleties of its workmanship begin to be appreciated, as you realize the manifold complexity of the book's web, and find that every sentence, almost every epithet, has its definite reference to equally unemphasized points before and after in the development of the plot. Thus it is that, while twelve readings of *Pride and Prejudice* give you twelve periods of pleasure repeated, as many readings of *Emma* give you that pleasure, not repeated only, but squared and squared again with each perusal, till at every fresh reading you feel anew that you never understood anything like the widening sum of its delights.

It is this multiplicity and sureness of reference that most immediately distinguishes *Emma* from the rest of Jane Austen's work: the total confident control of all her resources, without intrusion of derivativeness or fatigue or morality. The author's vision and instrument is, of course, irony: the widening sum of delights in *Emma* is, first of all, our widening recognition of the decisive pertinence with which every word, every action, and every response of Emma's establish her nature, confirm her self-deception, and prepare for her downfall. The ironic reverberations, rather than conflicting with one another or passing out of context—as they do sometimes in *Pride and Prejudice* and often in *Northanger Abbey*—remain internal and interdependent, they reinforce one another in a structure whose ap-parent lightness is less remarkable only than its compact and powerful density.

When we first observe Emma's maneuverings with Harriet, it is with the consciousness of her urge to dominate. Soon, though, this urge has become inextricable from Emma's own snobbery and her vicarious snobbery for Harriet, which drive it even farther from the possibility of caution or rational direction. Why does Emma want Harriet to marry? Harriet begins to seem a kind of proxy for Emma, a means by which Emma—too reluctant, too fearful of involvement, to consider the attempt herself—may discover what marriage is like. If Harriet is a proxy for Emma, she must serve as a defense also. Emma is outraged by Mr. Elton's proposal, not merely because she has not expected it (the basis of the simple irony here), but because Mr. Elton dares to circumvent the buffer she has so carefully set up. Harriet is to experience for her what she refuses to commit herself to, but cannot help being curious about. Yet Harriet is a very pretty girl, and being infinitely stupid and unperceptive, may be used in other uncommitting ways. Emma's interest in Harriet is not merely mistress-and-pupil, but quite emotional and particular: for a time at least—until Harriet becomes slightly resentful of the yoke after Emma's repeated blunders—Emma is in love with her: a love unphysical and inadmissible, even perhaps undefinable in such a society; and therefore safe. And in all this web of relations, by no means exhausted here, we return always to Emma's overpowering motive: her fear of commitment.

The simple irony of Emma's flirtation with Frank Churchill rises, of course, from the fact that Churchill is in love with someone else and uses Emma as a decoy. More than this, however, Churchill uses Emma so successfully only because he knows her so well. Emma is a perfect decoy for a man in love with someone else. She enjoys and invites admiration, but will draw away from any sign of serious attachment. Churchill does not use Emma merely for want of other dupes: he knows her, and exploits her with a ruthless thoroughness, not making a fool of her but revealing her as she is. "'But is it possible,'" he asks Emma blandly, later, "'that you had no suspicion?'" He knows that she neither did not could have had. She took part so eagerly in the flirtation because there she could be at once admired and unengaged, there she could smugly exchange scandal in the guise of wit, and be cynically and most delicately stroked into a pleasant (though wary) submissiveness by flattery without feeling, by assurances of her Olympian superiority.

The one quality which Mr. Knightley may regard as Emma's saving grace is her honesty. It is a very circumscribed honesty, it operates characteristically in the trough of failure and disaster, before the next rise of confidence and self-delusion; and it is another inextricable strand in the complex ironic web. Emma can recognize how badly her matchmaking schemes have turned out, and resolve never to attempt them again—but without recognizing why she attempts them at all and keeps coming back to them. . . . Most crucially, after the conventional settling of accounts, after Mr. Knightley has secured his Emma and Churchill his Jane, Emma for the first time can judge herself and Churchill as they must have seemed together in their flirtation, as they have been and are now alike:

> . . . Emma could not help saying,

> "I do suspect that in the midst of your perplexities at that time, you had very great amusement in tricking us all.—I am sure you had.—I am sure it was a consolation to you."

"Oh! no, no, no—how can you suspect me of such a thing?—I was the most miserable wretch!"

"Not quite so miserable as to be insensible to mirth. I am sure it was a source of high entertainment to you, to feel that you were taking us all in.—Perhaps I am the readier to suspect, because, to tell you the truth, I think it might have been some amusement to myself in the same situation. I think there is a little likeness between us."

He bowed.

"If not in our dispositions," she presently added, with a look of true sensibility, "there is a likeness in our destiny; the destiny which bids fair to connect us with two characters so much superior to our own."

This is honesty, and very acute. In an interlude with the man who most completely understands her, Emma recognizes and gives us the truth; and it is no mistake that Jane Austen places this clarifying exchange so close to the end of her book. Emma has finally—almost—got to know herself; but only because the knowledge is here painless and may be discarded in a little while with Mr. Knightley again, where she may resume, however self-amusedly for the present, her characteristic role:

> "Do you dare say this?" cried Mr. Knightley. "Do you dare to suppose me so great a blockhead, as not to know what a man is talking of?—What do you deserve?"
>
> "Oh! I always deserve the best treatment, because I never put up with any other. . . ."

Emma knows that she is moving toward a happy ending. Emma and Churchill are very lucky in the irony that finds them a Mr. Knightley and a Jane Fairfax to sober and direct them: this much Emma sees. So Mr. Knightley, not yet accepted by Emma, speaks bitterly of Churchill:

> ". . . Frank Churchill is, indeed, the favourite of fortune. Every thing turns out for his good.—He meets with a young woman at a watering-place, gains her affection, cannot even weary her by negligent treatment—and had he and all his family sought round the world for a perfect wife for him, they could not have found her superior.—His aunt is in the way.—His aunt dies.—He has only to speak.—His friends are eager to promote his happiness.—He has used every body ill—and they are all delighted to forgive him.—He is a fortunate man indeed!"

Still, Churchill—as Mr. Knightley knows—and Emma are lucky not by luck (except the luck of an invalid aunt's dying), but because in their social milieu charm conquers, even as it makes every cruel and thoughtless mistake; because, existing apart from and inevitably denying emotion and commitment, it nevertheless finds committed to it even the good and the wise, even when it is known and evaluated. The irony of *Emma* is multiple and its ultimate aspect is that there is no happy ending, no easy equilibrium, if we care to project confirmed exploiters like Emma and Churchill into the future of their marriages.

Emma's and Frank Churchill's society, which makes so much of surface, guarantees the triumph of surface. Even Mr. Knightley and Jane Fairfax succumb. Jane Austen, however, does not ask us to concern ourselves beyond the happy ending: she merely presents the evidence, noncommittally. (pp. 202-06)

> *Marvin Mudrick, in his* Jane Austen: Irony as Defense and Discovery, *1952. Reprint by University of California Press, 1974, 267 p.*

JOSEPH M. DUFFY, JR. (essay date 1954)

[Duffy interprets the subject of Emma *as "the awakening of a normal, intelligent young woman to the possibilities of physical love."]*

From the time of [*Emma*'s] publication, the critical reputation of this heroically lively novel has been excellent. True, there have been qualifications about various aspects of the book: early Victorian regrets over the undemocratic stratification of society; and recent suspicions about Emma's character and the possible superiority of Jane Fairfax. But all have been in agreement on the achievement of *Emma*: a landmark in novelistic structure, a masterpiece of wit, an enormously lucid delineation of a limited society. The structure has been analyzed, the wit commended, the society examined; yet inadequate attention has been given to the main line of action which is marked out by Emma herself. What the novel is "about" is the awakening of a normal, intelligent young woman to the possibilities of physical love and the direction, often chaotic, taken by her curiosity in an effort at discovery of that love. *Emma* is not simply a portrait of society having for its focal point of reference the activities of a clever and wilful girl; nor is it a portrait of that girl in her reaction against society. Society is always secondary to the career of the novel's chief performer and her subject. The theme of Emma is the passage of its heroine from innocence to experience—from dreams to consciousness; and Highbury and its environs is the arena wherein she achieves this knowledge of reality. The novel is the record of a dramatic engagement with experience that moves its protagonist relentlessly through fantasy to reality. Jane Austen's wit illuminates, through distortion, the complexities of this elaborate and disturbing ordeal. (pp. 39-40)

The novel . . . begins with this situation: Knightley loves Emma, while she cannot be said to love anyone. Emma subscribes to certain eighteenth century standards of rational conduct that compel her to make use of the machinery of reason even when she is most under the influence of her imagination. Consequently she masks the nature of her fascination with sex: she day-dreams, she plays with human dolls, she exalts the unmarried state and idealizes a brother-sister relationship between the sexes. She especially insists upon the last because it impinges upon the area of her deepest feeling and threatens her with the reality she desires but is not prepared to accept until the end of the novel.

Quite naturally Knightley is Emma's measure of manhood—he had always been a loveable and commanding fixture in her life—and the mercury of her disposition rises and falls with his approbation or disapproval of her conduct. However, Knightley's role of private idol or household god is hardly compatible with that of lover especially when a tangential kinship with the *lar* is presumed. Emma's vehement rejection of marriage for Knightley (as in her indignant dismissal of the rumor which Mrs. Weston passes on about Jane Fairfax and Knightley [Chapter 36])—or for herself (as in her exaltation of the unmarried state for a woman of property [Chapter 10]) acts both as a safeguard to her affectionate possessiveness toward Knightley and a rebuke to her own unconscious desire for such possession. Yet it is significant, for example, that early in the novel (Chapter 12) the manner in which Emma chooses to tease away Knightley's irritation over her interference in the Harriet-Martin engagement is by playfully picking up her sister's infant when she sees Knightley come in for dinner at Hartfield. She quite naturally projects herself into a role which she would like to perform and which she intuitively realizes renders her most attractive to Knightley. Their talk, as Emma holds the infant girl, is typical of the double-edged banter which they carry on with greater or less seriousness throughout the book:

> 'What a comfort it is that we think alike about our nephews and nieces! As to men and women, our opinions are sometimes very different; but with regard to these children, I observe we never disagree.
>
> 'If you were as much guided by nature in your estimate of men and women, and as little under the power of fancy and whim in your dealings with them, as you are where these children are concerned, we might always think alike.
>
> 'To be sure—our discordancies must always arise from my being in the wrong.
>
> 'Yes,' said he, smiling, 'and reason good. I was sixteen years old when you were born.
>
> 'A material difference, then,' she replied; 'and no doubt you were much my superior in judgment at that period in our lives; but does not the lapse of one-and-twenty years bring our understandings a good deal nearer?'
>
> 'Yes, a good deal *nearer*.'

The conflict in *Emma* is, as Knightley an eighteenth century thinker states it, between fancy and nature. Understanding is the rather stern custodian of fancy and the ancillary of nature which is reality. Emma thinks she is directed by her understanding when actually her fancy reels her about. Not until she makes a natural response to life (an act of the understanding that reveals as well her own nature and its longings), after a series of calamities arranged by her fancy, is the distance separating her from Knightley obliterated.

Emma acquires Harriet Smith as an article of amusement, a human toy, presumably to improve the girl through contact with the cultivated routine of life at Hartfield and to provide herself with a convenient distraction for her idleness; but actually Emma takes up Harriet in order to enjoy through her an experimental relationship with a man. The reason Emma gives for separating Harriet from Martin is that his rank is too low for the illegitimate offspring of possibly aristocratic connections. The officiousness with which Emma acts in this case needs a fuller explanation than the one she makes to herself and to others. If Harriet is a puppet through whom Emma proposes to enjoy a vicarious love affair, the object of that affair must be at least a possible husband for Emma herself. But the force of Martin's sexuality implied in his occupation is excessively disturbing to a young woman of limited experience embarking on her first experiment. Grossness, coarseness, and clownishness are the qualities Emma ascribes to the farmer although she has only observed him in passing on the streets of Highbury. These attributes are spiritually and physically antithetical to the standards of elegance, reason, and wit which Emma applies to courtship as well as to every other ritual of life.

Physical union with Martin would be unthinkable for Emma; with Elton it might be grotesque and disagreeable but not impossible. Elton, handsome, obliging, and flattering, is a more likely candidate for Emma (and, therefore, for Harriet); but Emma tires of him—though Harriet does not—before the affair runs to its climax. In every respect the experiment with Elton is a disappointment to Emma and at last a disaster. For one who had longed to test the resources of the masculine libido in pursuit of an object, Emma attains a greater degree of success with Elton than she had bargained for. . . . [His proposal to her] is the final turn of the screw in the comedy of errors: not only had Emma become directly involved where she had intended to supervise; she had become involved not so much as a young woman desired for her own sake but rather as an article of commerce, a handsome appurtenance, a high-priced fixture on which Elton might ostentatiously perch so as to be noticed by the world.

The events of the first section of *Emma* are mainly limited to Hartfield: the holiday visit of the John Knightleys and the dinners which attend the visit constitute the most significant social intercourse. But in the second and much longer part of the novel, the public aspect of Emma's encounter with experience is emphasized. Many more visits and assemblages are described; more characters are introduced; and the relationship among the principals grows more complex. This expansion of setting corresponds to the more serious and complicated nature of Emma's involvement with Frank Churchill. Frank is the agent that moves the society to activity—though the presence of the *outré* Mrs. Elton can certainly not be ignored—just as he is the agent for awakening in Emma a more varied range of feeling than she had heretofore known.

Before Frank appears in Highbury, a scene between Emma and Knightley establishes the polar extremes from which each views the young man whom they know only by report: Emma yearns toward her day-dream lover from outside Highbury and Knightley is alarmed by a portending rival who may push, besides the advantage of novelty, the claims of youth upon Emma. Knightley, whose life embodies the practice of eighteenth century enlightened benevolence, magisterially—and quite unkindly—attempts to chart for Emma the compass points of right conduct which even so young a man as Frank ought to follow. The heat of their conversation rises until Knightley announces that Frank's letters "disgust" him. Emma sums up her image of what she expects Frank to be like:

> 'My idea of him is, that he can adapt his conversation to the taste of everybody, and has the power as well as the wish of being universally agreeable. To you he will talk of farming; to me, of drawing or music; and so on to everybody, having the general information on all subjects which will enable him to follow the lead, or take the lead, just as propriety may require, and to speak extremely well on each; that is my idea of him.'

And Knightley replies with a disdainful distortion of the above picture and ends with a scarcely disguised plea to Emma;

> 'And mine,' said Mr. Knightley warmly, 'is that if he turn out anything like it, he will be the most insufferable fellow breathing! What! at three-and-twenty to be the king of his company—the great man—the practised politician, who is to read everybody's character, and make everybody's talents conduce to a display of his own superiority; to be dispensing his flatteries around, that he may make all appear like fools compared with himself! My dear Emma, your own good sense could not endure such a puppy when it came to the point.' (Chapter 18).

The situation is a tense and ironic one. Emma believes precisely what she wants to believe about Frank, and so does Knightley. That Emma predicts the appearance Frank assumes before the world, and Knightley the reality underneath the appearance, is no credit to the prescience of either. For once the "no-nonsense" facade that Knightley maintains collapses into folly.

The neolithic structure at once so formidably and so sensibly put together has no protection against the corrosive effects of unreasonable jealousy. On the other hand, Emma's blankness over the intensity of Knightley's feeling underlines her absorption in an illusion so strong that she is blind to the powerful reality which surrounds her. Self-interest motivates the sentiments of each; Emma looks forward to a rescue from reality; Knightley fears lest it turn out to be a betrayal. Not unexpectedly, the gallant and menacing stranger, when he comes, measures up to the hope of the one and to the fear of the other.

When Frank does arrive, he creates the expected tremor of satisfaction in Highbury. To say that Frank is a clever and agreeable young man is to understate the case. Frank is an archetype of all clever young men who live by their wits and their charm, whose amiability and good looks are their chief commodities, whose end in life is pleasure, and who do not flinch at swindle in order to attain this end. He is a paragon of confidence men who apparently is destined to obtain as much from the world as he chooses to demand of it. It is an ironical reward for Emma, after her handling of Harriet, to be matched against such a master performer as Frank. The only point at which she is his equal (it is her salvation) is that her egotism is as massive as his.

Frank's entry into Highbury complicates the comedy of illusion and reality of which Emma is the central performer—and chief victim. The "real" romance between Jane and Frank is concealed at Jane's expense (Jane is the bereaved and silent lover), and the flirtation between Emma and Frank occupies the attention not only of themselves but of all the interested observers of Highbury. Jane watches and is grieved; Knightley watches and is aggravated; the Westons watch and smile approval. Always a serious and fascinated student of her own psyche, Emma discovers that she is still more interesting to herself now that she has achieved an attachment. Her "love" is an idea—and an ideal—a state of mind, the titillating effects of which she analyzes, probes, and extends in economical portions. She recognizes the danger of waste or spoilage in excess of feeling. "Love" is a solipsistic game that she plays, and she imagines that it is the real thing. First she confers upon Frank "the distinguished honor which her imagination had given him, the honor, if not of being really in love with her, of being at least very near it, and saved only by her own indifference . . ." (Chapter 25). Later, at a time when Frank is on the verge of admitting his connection with Jane Fairfax and Emma wards off what she suspects is a proposal, she decides that she must be in love with him "in spite of every previous determination against it." When she is alone she muses to herself:

> 'I certainly must,' said she. 'This sensation of list-
> lessness, weariness, stupidity, this disinclination to
> sit down and employ myself, this feeling of every-
> thing's being dull and insipid about the house!—I
> must be in love; I should be the oddest creature in
> the world if I were not—for a few weeks at least.'
> (Chapter 30).

Thereupon she decides that she has exhausted the possibilities of love without having ventured into an area of excessive excitement; she "rationally" makes up her mind that the affair will go no further; and she reassures herself about Frank that though his feelings are warm they are changeable and he will not suffer too greatly from the loss. Finally, as a means of accommodating her erstwhile lover, she hits upon the notion of accommodating Harriet as well and of effecting an engagement between the two. All the while, the relationship between

Jane and Frank moves toward the crisis that brings about publication of their engagement.

The announcement of Frank's engagement and Harriet's revelation of her feelings toward Knightley follow close upon each other (Chapters 46 and 47). The double surprise leaves Emma stranded in a condition of shocked isolation amid the wreckage of her illusions. Emma cries fraud with a long, resounding wail when she learns of Frank's long-standing connection with Jane Fairfax. They have all been duped, she says, by "a system of hypocrisy and deceit, espionage and treachery" (Chapter 46). At the moment when she had supposed the problem of the still inconveniently unattached Harriet to have been solved, Emma finds out that she has been taken in by cleverness superior to her own. She cannot, however, find a scapegoat outside of herself when Harriet informs her that since she has been taught the propriety of seeking a socially superior husband, her once timid affections are now drawn upward to the region inhabited by Knightley. "'O God! that I had never seen her!'" is Emma's fervent but vain ejaculation—the desperate wish of a no longer innocent young woman. Now every vestige of fancy is effectively dislodged from her mind and she is left face to face with the significant reality—her love for Knightley. After groping about after prismatic reflections of her own imagining, she is now caught, surprised, with her hands outstretched and empty. The image Emma sees of herself is appalling; except her feeling for Knightley, "every other part of her mind was disgusting" (Chapter 47). It is a time of overwhelming moral defeat for Emma, the defeat of innocence before the unforeseen hardship of reality. Without the consolation of Clarissa's self-righteousness, she learns Clarissa's lesson: "'That the eye is a traitor, and ought ever to be mistrusted: That form is deceitful. . . .'"

As in a fairy-tale where blessings are bestowed without any reference to the merits of the recipient but according to the whimsy of an eccentric superior being, Emma is given the reward she in no way deserves. Reality now is fantastic and the way of right reason Emma plans to follow does not prepare her for Knightley's proposal. Jane Austen arranges the setting with an eye for the magical distribution of gifts: after a morning of sullen weather the clouds are dispersed and the sun appears. The interview with Knightley takes place in the garden at Hartfield amid "the exquisite sight, smell, sensation of nature, tranquil, warm, and brilliant after a storm . . ." (Chapter 49). At this late stage of the novel Emma may not be a better woman than she was at the beginning, but she is a different one. She has recognized her passion for Knightley as a force qualitatively and quantitatively quite distinct from her indulgence in vicarious courtship or from her flirtatious play with Frank. Her flirtation with Frank Churchill was an act of the will, an eccentric compound of desire and imagination. Frank's charm is vast and surrounds Emma as late as their last meeting before their respective marriages; but his shallowness is exhaustible whereas Emma is confounded by the depth of Knightley's character. Her affinity for Knightley is a movement of her nature that operates uncontrollably in subterranean regions as well as on the surface. Nevertheless when the challenge is most critical—when she believes she has lost Knightley—Emma responds most effectively: not nobly but with a fixed purpose of settling her own future. During their walk in the garden Emma resolves to hear her own fate, which is, she thinks, to lose Knightley to Harriet. Ironically the reality she now determines to face is one of her last delusions. The unexpected proposal she does hear staggers Emma, but not so much as to leave her incapable of viewing her triumph with satisfaction. The connection between Knightley and Harriet, which had shortly before seemed a logical possibility, now appears in its true perspective as so unequal and degrading a match as to be unthinkable. Emma now cherishes the ordered society against which she had conspired by recommending to Harriet both Elton and Frank Churchill.

In the sense that Emma has not only been awakened to an awareness of what life has to offer but is even close to achievement, the novel has run its course. There are the expected odds and ends of explanation by the lovers to each other: Emma of delicate self-recrimination and Knightley of gallant avowal of a long-standing love and of an equally long confidence in the eventual triumph of her understanding and principles over fancy. In addition, there is the disposal of Harriet who is given over to the persistent farmer Martin and assigned a position in society appropriate for the illegitimate offspring of neither nobility nor great wealth. And Frank Churchill succeeds in winning over all the world of Highbury by his protestations of good intent and by his fluent self-abasement. In another milieu Frank might have been a villain, but here there is an almost awesome power in the dexterity with which he manages to take away from everyone at least their good will. Even Knightley purports to find evidence of real feeling in Frank's long, skillful letter to Mrs. Weston, which was obviously written with a view to the wide circulation it receives.

In her last meeting with Frank, Emma is in high spirits and it is clear that though she favors Knightley, she is still excited by Frank's charm. She suggests to the young man that he enjoyed his masquerade in spite of its inconveniences:

> '. . . I am sure that it was a source of high entertainment to you, to feel that you were taking us all in. Perhaps I am the readier to suspect, because, to tell you the truth, I think it might have been some amusement to myself in the same situation. I think there is a little likeness between us.'

She goes on to qualify this statement by another assertion that is probably an equal mixture of hypocrisy and sincerity:

> 'If not in our dispositions,' she presently added, with a look of true sensibility, 'there is a likeness in our destiny; the destiny which bids fair to connect us with two characters so much superior to our own.' (Chapter 54).

In part Emma's ingenuousness causes her to make the first association. There is simply too much evidence of her virtue planted through the novel for her to be regarded as a person of completely ruthless behavior: her piety toward her father is in itself a singular example of devotion. In part, however, Emma makes an accurate hit. Pleasure in power, which is a form of egotism, links these two characters. In the course of the novel Emma has particularly discovered the degree of power her sex confers upon her. Her capacious love of government is faced with a new and formidable challenge through her union with Knightley. And in spite of the author's lightly satirical prediction of "perfect happiness," the question we are left with at the end of the novel is with what measure of prudence Emma, fully roused and with a knowledge of her power, undertakes the regency of her world. (pp. 43-53)

> *Joseph M. Duffy, Jr., "'Emma': The Awakening from Innocence," in ELH, Vol. 21, No. 1, March, 1954, pp. 39-53.*

JAMES GREGORY MURRAY (essay date 1954)

[*Suggesting parallels between Austen's personal and artistic philosophy and the principles of Greek classicism, Murray discusses order and balance as Austen's central moral concern in* Emma.]

To establish a connection between [Jane Austen's] art and classicism viewed as measure and balance is almost to belabor the obvious. Nor is it necessary to prove a direct relationship of study and influence. It is enough to see that Jane intuitively understood the rules, empirically approved of them, and habitually lived by them.

In Jane Austen the person we see an exemplification of the notion that the art of living is the act of living well: to live within life's limitations, to provide a proper place for both reason and sentiment, to have a rage for order, to practice self-effacement, to realize the saving truth that there may be light without heat, and to believe that the well-spring of good conduct is neither code nor class but conscience. We see in her attitude toward life an intelligent reaction to Romantic excesses. She was perfectly normal herself and was interested only in normality. Thus she appears to be concerned with life's surface and the trivialities of human relationships; but there is no need to confuse surface with normality and the lacks of highs and lows with triviality. As R. W. Chapman puts it:

> Before we infer Jane's narrowness from her silences, let us admit the possibility that she knew, better than we can, how to get the results she aimed at. The limits she imposed on herself were of her own choice.

The classic philosophies of the Greeks, idealism and stoicism, moreover, seem to combine in Jane Austen to form both an ethic and an aesthetic. The love of the beautiful and of the good life inform her works and are characterized by measure and balance. For purposes of easy assimilation, however, it is better to separate morals and aesthetics when we apply ourselves to the problem of measure and balance in a specific way to our exemplar novel, *Emma*. What Emma learns and Jane Austen teaches, for example, are moral principles which may be distinguished from, say, the structural place of Knightley (Emma's own measure and balance) or the novelist's special device (irony which puts things in right perspectives), both of which are best classified as deriving from aesthetic principles. In actual fact, however, the fusion of the matter and form in *Emma* is so nearly perfect as to render the dichotomy admittedly unnatural.

There are two kinds of measure and balance in *Emma:* what the heroine seeks to impose upon the society of Hartfield, and what Jane, through irony, brings to Emma. As for the first, [Elizabeth Jenkins has said in her *Jane Austen*] that, "when Emma said she loved things to be decided and open, she seems, by a remarkable paradox, to have dictated the tenor of the book that bears her name." We start, then, with the subject, Emma, and the object, Hartfield society. They are in one sense alike: Emma's design for order is commensurate with the pattern of a society about which [Marvin Mudrick] said, "There is no excess; almost no sense of plot in this delicate ordering of a small calm world" [see excerpt dated 1952]. In this same view of the novel, we are treated to "relations," "affinities," "mutual influences," and "conversations," all of which are characterized by a "delicacy of touch, a sense of balance, (and) a serene reasonableness" [as Legoris and Cazamian state in *A History of English Literature*].

The scene, then, is an orderly one; perhaps too orderly, too calm and balanced. For the Greeks an excess of anything, even of balance itself, is to be avoided; for Jane the excess of balance definitely points to imbalance, to an awryness which is, of course, not chaos but related to it. [Mudrick states]: "Emma deals only in measureable quantities: anything uncertain is to be dismissed, avoided. . . ." This virtue may be said to produce the imbalance in the sense that to an already ordered society she brings management. It isn't that she sees disorder and would correct it, but that she wants a more perfect order. The proper marriage for Harriet is for Emma a type of measure and balance essential to the more perfect order. But if this is indeed Emma's attitude and purpose, may we not say that she is tampering with the natural order, with at least the nonartificial if not to say fore-ordained way of things? If so, this is not a trivial matter. It is, in fact, playing the part of God. In this way, then, Emma becomes antagonistic to her well-ordered society. It now becomes woman against rather than in harmony with the world.

Employing the method of play analysis at this point, we discover harmony as the situation, Emma's desire for a more perfect union as the generating circumstance, her involvement as the rising action, her self-discovery as the climax, and—to complete the circle, for this is comedy not tragedy—the re-establishment of order as the denouement. Thus the end of the book finds each character where he wants to be and (in the natural order) ought to be. After some scramblings, then, order has been restored.

In this drama the audience focuses on two points: the character of Emma and the method of irony. It is important to notice at the outset, before the method can take effect, that Emma was not a frail creature. If she has any flaw it is vanity, but a healthy vanity. It is in Emma a flaw of strength rather than of weakness, normal rather than abnormal. (And so we are reminded that the Greeks had a way of equating beauty and health.) Now the lesson of Emma, so to speak, given this healthy, normal flaw, is palatable in proportion to Emma's ability to elicit our sympathy. This is accomplished in several ways. The fact that even the strong can rise to a fall provides a measure of balance which we appreciate. That the fallen can rise again is even more important for our psychological well-being. Finally, the fact that Emma recognizes her own faults and tries to cure them is the source of some of our admiration for her.

Emma as actress, then, the particular version of the universal, is balanced by (a) reflecting on her own mistakes, (b) seeing herself as another Mrs. Elton, and (c) by listening to the reasonable appeal supplied by Mr. Knightley. But Jane Austen will do more for her. She will provide a gentle application of irony wherever needed. Hence we have another usage of measure and balance. In a sense, irony is measure and balance: it corrects and sets aright and restores order. It puts things and people in a proper perspective. As Professor Mudrick sees it, Jane Austen's kind of irony "consists in the discrimination between impulse and pretension, between being and seeming, between—in a social setting—man as he is and man as he aspires to be...." It is gentle and firm; it both heals and provides a quiet atmosphere conducive for healing. It is at once the method of the book and what the book communicates.

Measure and balance relate to right conduct in *Emma.* As rules they are imposed by the author on the book, by the heroine on herself and her society, and by Knightley on all he surveys. Though moral, and therefore ultimately concerned with individual acts of the will, they are also related to the political world and the physical world. There is, for example, the class idea in *Emma,* which is the measure and balance of social forces seen in a hierarchical order. Such a state of being, it is to be noted, was taken seriously by Miss Austen, but not so seriously (that is, out of proportion) that one is deluded by a false scale of values derived from a real scale of position in the community. Thus there is an inner check on the outer idea of measure and balance.

Even physical nature at times concurs with the proper order of things. Mr. Woodhouse makes no objection to the bad weather during the Christmas season because inclemency is to be expected during the winter months. On the other hand, the outing at Abbey Mill Farm was particularly delightful in that "it was a sweet view—sweet to the eye and mind. English verdure, English culture, English comfort, seen under a sun bright, without being oppressive." This description amounts to a glossary of measure and balance as they are to be desired in the realm of nature.

Turning from places to people, however, we see measure and balance applied in the classic view, that is, as having to do with character and conduct. The rules are both implicit and explicit. It is a good thing for a person to manage himself and to take pride in his independence, but "the real evils of Emma's situation were the power of having rather *too much* her own way and a disposition to think a little *too well* of herself." When Emma oversteps her bounds, she is made to feel uncertain (in itself a corrective force), or at least not nearly so certain as Mr. Knightley. Emma has a good mind, stable character, and "sweet temper." Therefore, she upsets a balance by trying "to understand a bad one." The proper way for her to handle herself, Jane tells us, is illustrated by her treatment of the vexing Mr. Elton: "To restrain him as much as might be, by her own manners, she was immediately preparing to speak with exquisite calmness and gravity...."

Moreover, even as the ancients would have it, Jane Austen insists that the truly balanced person have a sense of personal responsibility. After Emma's first big mistake, Jane would have her take on more error and further pain—"if but to spare Harriet." She must learn to restrain herself under pressure, as she so well does when informed of Mr. Elton's marriage. She must perform her social duties at all times: to her father, which was a sweet duty, and to Jane Fairfax, which was disagreeable.

The person of measure and balance must know himself and his capacities if he is to make proper adjustments. For example, Emma is said to know "the limitations of her own powers too well to attempt more than she could perform with credit." This refers, of course, to piano-playing. When it shall refer to marriage-making, Emma will be truly balanced. Self-knowledge, however, may be deceptive if it be based on an examination of conscience alone. To see oneself in others is sometimes a better way to examine oneself. So Emma "silenced" by the brashness and rudeness of Mrs. Elton in the argument about whether Surrey was the garden of England doesn't teach anything to Mrs. Elton; but at least indirectly Emma learns something about her own positiveness when arguing with Mr. Knightley. And, by all means, when one is wrong, admit to it, however difficult the admission may be, even as Emma confesses to Knightley. What happens in such cases, frequently, is that one's opponent will also give in a little, as Mr. Knightley does, which is another kind of measure and balance (give a little and take a little; rights bounded by duties, etc.).

Emma never gives the impression of being lost to her vanity because she is never completely self-centered. (That her first thought is habitually and instinctively for her father's comfort is proof of this—a superb interior check and balance.) But at times she is outlandishly and outrageously definite about things of which she has no certain knowledge. At such times, to achieve proper balance, Miss Austen sees to it that Emma is caught up short, the violence of which being in proportion to the violence of Emma's original expostulation. For, it would seem, measure and balance, like gods and penal codes, demand reckonings.

A great many of these corrective measures are applied by Knightley, who seems to act as Jane Austen's spokesman. When she herself chooses to sit out the debate, she can count on him to express her own feelings. Emma gets away with very little when Knightley is about. For example, when she is gloating over her part in the marriage of Mrs. Weston, he says: "Why do you talk of success? Where is your merit? What are you proud of? You made a lucky guess; and that is all that can be said." Knightley can say such things, not only out of a knowledge of the world, but out of a specific understanding of Emma. In a sense, he sees through her and her faults (largely of imbalance): "She will never submit to anything requiring industry and patience, and a subjection of the fancy to the understanding." Again, "Emma, your infatuation about that girl blinds you." And still more, "Upon my word, Emma, to hear you abusing the reason you have is almost enough to make me think so too. Better be without reason than misapply it as you do." (One is reminded here of the chorus in *Antigone* which, though sympathetic to the girl's feeling and enthusiasm, laments the loss of reason, which to the Greeks is man's essential loss.)

Knightley balances Emma in several ways. When she is unreasonable, he corrects; when she is unkind, he reproves; when she is ultimately in need of love ("it would not be a bad thing for her to be very much in love with a *proper* object"), he rewards her with his love. Thus he may be said to be Emma's measure and balance. He is also the book's measure and balance: "My dear Emma, does not everything serve to prove more and more the *beauty of truth and sincerity* in all our dealings with each other?"—clearly a classic notion and very much Jane Austen's own.

But we must not derive the impression that because Emma stands in need of lessons in measure and balance, she does not teach them as well. She points out that balance would be upset if Harriet's charms were "wasted on the inferior society of Highbury." She reminds one of the war of the gods for the favor of men in the *Iliad* when she says that "a farmer can need none of my help, and is therefore, in one sense, as much above my nature as in every other he is below it." She repeatedly admonishes Harriet on the subject of propriety: "A woman is not to marry a man merely because she is asked, or because she is attached to her, and can write a tolerable letter." To which the reader must say, Just so, dear Emma. The irony is that you don't see that one should not marry simply because the man is marriageable in terms of money and position.

Emma has a feeling for the fitness of things—from the "unreasonableness" of "a crowd in a small room" to the impropriety of "adventuring too far, assuming too much, making light of what ought to be serious, a trick of what ought to be simple." She would also have Harriet curb her feelings lest she be in the same position as Jane Fairfax: "Poor girl. She loves him, then, *excessively*. It must have been from attachment only, that she could be led to form the engagement. Her affection must have overshadowed her judgment."

Measure and balance, then, to Emma are matters of propriety, fitness, and delicacy. She stands for a keeping of the old order lest it pass injudiciously into the new. She recognizes the limitations of things and people, and urges that we live within

them: "When a man does his best with only moderate powers, he will have the advantage over negligent superiority." This is very much like Aristotle's notion that, on the moral scale, a small jar filled is worth more than a large jar half-empty. Finally, in the best classical tradition, she realizes that the wellspring of good conduct—one both measured and balanced—is good character: "To understand, thoroughly understand her own heart, was the first endeavour." When such a person, with such a clear idea of measure and balance, is herself in need of correction, we have the final fusion, through irony, of measure and balance.

The book ends, to use an old word in its original sense, "neatly." All the lessons have been taught, the proper matches arranged, the order established and re-established. The imbalance of character and conduct has been righted. There is nothing in excess, and everything is in its place. Thus the content of the book may be said to have measure and balance: in its characters, and also in what happens to them. As for the form of the book, nothing more need be said than that irony, the ancient righter of wrongs and restorer of harmonies, dictated the shape and direction. Thus are matter and form delicately but definitely conjoined—which is the ultimate in measure and balance.

Is it going too far, then, to place Jane Austen in the company of Edith Hamilton's Greek geniuses?

> Greek art is intellectual art, the art of men who were clear and lucid thinkers, and it is therefore plain art. Artists than whom the world has never seen greater, men endowed with the spirit's best gift, found their natural method of expression in the simplicity and clarity which are the endowment of the unclouded reason. "Nothing in excess," the Greek axiom of art, is the dictum of men who would brush aside all obscuring, entangling superfluity, and see clearly, plainly, unadorned, what they wished to express. (*The Greek Way to Western Civilization*)

(pp. 161-66)

James Gregory Murray, "Measure and Balance in Jane Austen's 'Emma'," in College English, *Vol. 16, No. 3, December, 1954, pp. 160-66.*

EDGAR F. SHANNON, JR. (essay date 1956)

[*Examining the unity of subject and form in* Emma, *Shannon interprets the novel as a history of the heroine's growth to mental and emotional maturity.*]

In all her novels, Jane Austen is primarily a moral writer, striving to establish criteria of sound judgment and right conduct in human life. In *Emma* she presents her lessons so astutely and so dramatically, with such a minimum of exposition, that she places extreme demands upon the reader's perceptiveness. Yet . . . analysis of Emma's enlightenment and of the rhythmic structure of the novel discloses a valid progression of the heroine from callowness to mental and emotional maturity—a development psychologically consistent and technically consonant.

For *Emma,* Jane Austen took a heroine whom, she remarked, "no one but myself will much like." "And," as one of her ablest critics has said, "many a rash reader, and some who are not rash, have been shut out on the threshold of Emma's Comedy by a dislike of Emma herself" [see excerpt by Reginald Farrer dated 1917]. In the beginning, as every reader knows, she is spoiled and conceited. Events soon prove her to be domineering, willful, snobbish, and, at times, unfeeling.

Until the end of the morning at Box Hill, which is the emotional climax of the book and the beginning of her regeneration, she has been guilty of much that is reprehensible in both thought and deed. She has induced Harriet Smith to refuse Robert Martin's proposal of marriage because of his low social status as a farmer and has directed Harriet's aspirations toward Mr. Elton, the vicar. She has allowed Harriet a call of only fourteen minutes upon Martin's mother and sisters, whom Harriet had visited for six weeks the preceding summer. Emma has been ludicrously condescending toward the Coles. In her opinion of Miss Bates, expressed to Harriet, she has been brutally uncharitable. And though she has had "many a hint from Mr. Knightley and some from her own heart," as to her dereliction in seldom calling on Miss Bates and her mother, these promptings have not been sufficient "to counteract the persuasion of its being very disagreeable,—a waste of time—tiresome woman—and all the horror of being in danger of falling in with the second rate and third rate of Highbury." She has imagined Frank Churchill to be in love with her, has coquetted with him extravagantly, and has led even Mr. Knightley to believe her affections engaged. She has taken a dislike to Jane Fairfax, who should have been her natural friend and companion and, believing Jane to be the object of a married man's attentions, has repeated to Frank the slander she has concocted. (pp. 637-38)

Nevertheless, the novelist has endowed Emma with good qualities and has provided firm basis in her character for eventual redemption. As Mr. Knightley tells her when they are discussing their nieces and nephews, her nature is sound, and would lead her to clear judgments and right actions if her intelligence were not blinded by her imagination. Her self-assurance can be shaken by Mr. Knightley's censure of her part in Harriet's refusal of Robert Martin; and she is discontented until she can re-establish herself in his good graces. Possessing both blooming health and a "happy disposition," she is also free from personal vanity. She is devoted to her father and dutifully ministers to the poor. With discerning verisimilitude Jane Austen does not portray these two traits as unalloyed. Emma's filial piety is tinged with a sense of security in being "so truly beloved and important; so always first and always right" in her father's eyes, but her constant solicitousness toward a trying valetudinarian is distinctly a virtue—witness her arrangements for his happiness the night of the Coles's dinner and her staying behind at Donwell Abbey to go over "books of engravings, drawers of medals, cameos, corals, shells," and other collections with him, when everyone else walks out-of-doors. And Mr. Knightley speaks approvingly of "your exertions for your father's sake." Although her designs for Harriet can quickly divert her mind from philanthropy, she visits the cottagers in an exemplary spirit of charity. Toward them, as toward her sister's children, she harbors none of the illusions that obscure her vision within her own set. "Emma was very compassionate; and the distresses of the poor were as sure of relief from her personal attention and kindness, her counsel and her patience, as from her purse. She understood their ways, could allow for their ignorance and their temptations, had no romantic expectations of extraordinary virtue from those, for whom education had done so little; entered into their troubles with ready sympathy, and always gave her assistance with as much intelligence as good-will."

Emma's attitude concerning Harriet's call at the Martins' furnishes an insight into her true character behind the wrongheaded façade. She knows that Harriet must respond to Eliz-abeth Martin's call and note of invitation, but she determines to manage the matter

> in a way that, if they [the Martins] had understanding, should convince them that it was to be only a formal acquaintance. She meant to take her in the carriage, leave her at the Abbey Mill, while she drove a little farther, and call for her again so soon, as to allow no time for insidious applications or dangerous recurrences to the past, and give the most decided proof of what degree of intimacy was chosen for the future. She could think of nothing better: and though there was something in it which her own heart could not approve—something of ingratitude, merely glossed over—it must be done, or what would become of Harriet?

Thus even before the event Emma's heart, i.e., her feelings and conscience, cannot condone her plan. Its result proves unexpectedly disturbing. With Harriet back in the carriage, recounting her conversation with the Martins, Emma, though attempting to justify her actions, perceives the misery she has caused.

> Emma could not but picture it all, and feel how justly they might resent, how naturally Harriet must suffer. It was a bad business. She would have given a great deal, or endured a great deal, to have the Martins in a higher rank of life. They were so deserving, that a *little* higher should have been enough: but as it was, how could she have done otherwise?—Impossible!—She could not repent. They must be separated; but there was a great deal of pain in the process. . . .

Here, as after her instigation of Harriet's refusal of Robert Martin, Emma is not penitent—a fact that the author reiterates by using the same word, "repent," that appears twice in the previous instance. But Emma's reaction discloses sharp protest from her true inner self. Although not yet prepared to wish this latest deed undone and to mend her ways, she must seek at once the comforting and uncritical society of Mr. and Mrs. Weston: "Her mind was quite sick of Mr. Elton and the Martins. The refreshment of Randalls was absolutely necessary." Her conscience is on the verge of requiring full assent to reality, and she is exasperated when the Westons' absence from home denies her the solace she requires.

Guilty of much past error, but with just instincts and growing awareness of the complexity of human relationships, Emma begins her transformation at Box Hill. After Mr. Knightley's reproof of her cutting remark to Miss Bates, acknowledgment of her pride, both intellectual and social, overwhelms her.

> Never had she felt so agitated, mortified, grieved, at any circumstance in her life. She was most forcibly struck. The truth of his representation there was no denying. She felt it at her heart. How could she have been so brutal, so cruel to Miss Bates!—How could she have exposed herself to such ill opinion in any one she valued! And how suffer him to leave her without saying one word of gratitude, of concurrence, of common kindness! Time did not compose her. As she reflected more, she seemed but to feel it more. She never had been so depressed . . . and Emma felt the tears running down her cheeks all the way home, without being at any trouble to check them, extraordinary as they were.

The tears, which mark the turning point of Emma's development, signify an emotional as well as a mental commitment to a new mode of conduct and to the necessity of Mr. Knightley's approval. She at last recognizes that her intelligence,

A sketch of Austen by her sister, Cassandra.

wealth, and social pre-eminence require kindness, rather than contempt, toward Miss Bates. She awakens to the obligations of her position. Miss Bates shall never again have cause to reproach her: "She had been often remiss, her conscience told her so; remiss, perhaps, more in thought than fact; scornful, ungracious. But it should be so no more. In the warmth of true contrition, she would call upon her the very next morning, and it should be the beginning, on her side, of a regular, equal, kindly intercourse." This time Emma acts instead of simply making resolutions soon to be forgotten; the morrow does not, as in the past, bring any alleviation of her suffering or any tendency to disparage her guilt. Not "ashamed of the appearance of the penitence, so justly and truly hers," she calls on Miss Bates early in the morning to make amends.

The author here explicitly tells the reader of Emma's wholehearted change of attitude, illustrates it with action, and contrasts it with her former refusal to repent. Within the space of ten lines, the novelist refers both to Emma's "true contrition" and to "the penitence, so justly and truly hers." The *NED* gives "penitence for sin" as the meaning of "contrition" in this sense, and "repentance" as a synonym for "penitence." As Jane Austen's revered Dr. Johnson declares, "The completion and sum of repentance is a change of life"—exactly what Emma has begun. Her coloring at her father's undeserved praise upon her return from Miss Bates's emphasizes this change, for previously she had been quite content to accept more credit for accomplishments at the piano and the easel than she knew

to be her due. When Mr. Knightley takes her hand and seems to be on the point of carrying it to his lips, she experiences "great satisfaction" both because she is grateful for his mute commendation of her penitent act and because she is pleased by unusual gallantry from him. This gesture signals the beginning of tenderness between them.

The visit to Miss Bates produces further evidence of Emma's sincere alteration. "Her heart had been long growing kinder towards Jane"; and after Miss Bates's account of her niece's ill health, Emma invites Jane to spend the day at Hartfield, to go for an airing in the Woodhouse carriage, and to accept, from the Hartfield stores, some fine arrowroot. When Jane refuses the invitations and returns the arrowroot, Emma learns that a few days of attention cannot compensate for several months of neglect; she understands that her former coolness merits the present rebuff. Yet she has "the consolation of knowing that her intentions were good."

Having thought and acted compassionately, Emma is ready for complete redemption, but trial and expiation are still necessary. The climax of the plot—the revelation, upon the death of Mrs. Churchill, of Frank's engagement to Jane—sets the final ordeal in motion. Harriet's confession of her hopes concerning Mr. Knightley explodes one of Emma's last misconceptions and impels her to recognize her own love for him. During this interview with Harriet, where, in order to spare Harriet additional pain, Emma seeks to conceal her agitation, the controlled voice and trembling frame betoken the depth of her newly discovered emotion. In the self-examination that follows, she admits her folly:

> With insufferable vanity had she believed herself in the secret of everybody's feelings; with unpardonable arrogance proposed to arrange everybody's destiny. She was proved to have been universally mistaken; and she had not quite done nothing—for she had done mischief. She had brought evil on Harriet, on herself, and she too much feared, on Mr. Knightley.

She has finally absorbed the meaning of responsibility—that one must endure the consequences of one's acts; for now her own happiness is involved. It is the commencement of full awareness.

Ironically, Emma experiences the very fate that Mr. Knightley, near the beginning of the novel, had cherished for her: "I should like to see Emma in love, and in some doubt of a return." She is not only in doubt of Mr. Knightley's returning her love; she is virtually convinced that he loves Harriet instead. Emma, however, has progressed so far in comprehending pain and desiring to avoid giving it that, rather than hurt Mr. Knightley, she is willing to submit to what she feels certain will be an announcement of his decision to marry Harriet: "Emma could not bear to give him pain. He was wishing to confide in her—perhaps to consult her;—cost her what it would, she would listen." Appropriately, her wish to allay the distress she has caused Mr. Knightley by prohibiting an explanation of why he envies Frank leads to his declaration of love for her.

Jane Austen is too serious and deft a novelist to abandon the development of Emma's character when this climax of the love story has been reached. She does not huddle her puppets back into the box and leave the rest to the reader's indulgence and credulity. Although it is clear that Emma and Mr. Knightley will eventually marry, there are still for Emma three impediments to pure happiness: (1) her father's antipathy to marriage, (2) Harriet's disappointment and suffering, and (3) the necessity of concealing from Mr. Knightley Harriet's hopes, which she herself had unwittingly fostered. Emma's atonement has yet to be concluded. Her care for her father's comfort brings on a melancholy, sleepless night of weeping and a belief that she cannot marry. She agonizes over Harriet and over the impossibility of being entirely ingenuous with Mr. Knightley. In addition, at least three times before the end of the book, she must acknowledge and be ashamed of her calumniation of Jane Fairfax. With her own heart committed, Emma knows the pangs of love and appreciates fully the anguish Jane has endured. Although, when Emma calls, Mrs. Elton's presence prevents complete expression of her sympathy in words, her "very, very earnest" shake of Jane's hand upon arriving and her taking Jane's hand again as she departs convey the sincerity of her regard.

No longer playing God, Emma, confused and humiliated, sees no way out of the predicament in which Mr. Knightley's declaration has left her. The only scheme she allows herself—Harriet's visit to London—originates in charity and fortuitously results in Harriet's final happiness. Moreover, it is Mr. Knightley's suggestion that he and Emma live at Hartfield, not, as Mudrick asserts [see excerpt dated 1952], a condition to marriage set by Emma, which removes the obstacle of her father's comfort—"such an alternative as this had not occurred to her." Although she is relieved at the news of Harriet's engagement to Robert Martin, she gains almost as much satisfaction from the imminent end of secrecy toward Mr. Knightley as from Harriet's good fortune: "The pain of being obliged to practise concealment towards him, was very little inferior to the pain of having made Harriet unhappy."

Jane Austen's skill is patent. Emma's character develops and matures, perfectly within the credible limits of her nature as established at the outset and maintained throughout the novel. There is no sudden, unconvincing conversion, no "flood of repentance" that may be expected soon to recede. After the turning point of Emma's attitude and her genuine contrition following Box Hill, she undergoes an extended process of chastening and illumination before she attains redemption. (It is approximately four months—one third of the time span of the novel—from Box Hill to Emma's marriage at the end.) Yet the author, eschewing the temptation to overstate her theme, does not mar the portrait by converting Emma into a long-faced paragon. "Serious she was, very serious in her thankfulness" that her past folly had not prevented both herself and Harriet from eventually attaining felicity and in "her resolutions" of "humility and circumspection in future"; but she has not lost her sense of humor. She can admit that if she had been Frank Churchill, she might have found "some amusement" in "taking us all in"—and indeed how can anyone have failed to be entertained by Emma's deluded antics? She can give herself a "saucy conscious smile" that she no longer feels any sense of injury to her nephew Henry as the expectant heir to Donwell Abbey, and finds "amusement in detecting the real cause of that violent dislike of Mr. Knightley's marrying Jane Fairfax, or anybody else, which at the time she had wholly imputed to the amiable solicitude of the sister and aunt." She must laugh at Harriet's vagaries that have persuaded her she was in love with three men during the course of a few months.

This laugh at Harriet's expense is not a malicious one. It is a frank admission of Emma's former erroneous view of Harriet's attributes and claims to masculine attention. Yet it has been used to document Emma's supposedly unchanged, unfeeling contemptuousness. True, it may be said, she is penitent, she has known pain, she has performed generous acts, she has

achieved mental clarity, but after all, isn't she an unregenerate snob?

In the other major novels, Jane Austen has portrayed her heroines as victims of snobbery. In *Emma,* she has undertaken the much more difficult task of incorporating and correcting snobbery within the character of the heroine herself.... Emma's entering upon "a regular, equal, kindly intercourse" with Miss Bates heralds the purgation of her snobbish flaw; her revised attitude toward Harriet and Robert Martin evinces its completion. (pp. 639-44)

Rhythm in a novel has been defined [by E.M. Forster in his *Aspects of the Novel*] as "repetition plus variation," and Jane Austen unfolds the reorientation of Emma's character, just traced by means of a rhythmic structure of situation and incident. Perhaps taking a cue from the accepted three-volume form of the novel of her time, her repetitions appear in sequences of three (an anagogic number) or a multiple of it. There are, for instance, six major social events, each of which is extremely important to the plot or to the steps in Emma's education—the Christmas party at Randalls, the dinner at the Coles's and Emma's own dinner party, the ball at the Crown Inn, the day at Donwell Abbey, and the morning at Box Hill. The first occurs in Volume One, the second two in Volume Two, and the last three in Volume Three, thus making a progression . . . from the relative seclusion of Hartfield to an extensive involvement in society. The framework of the novel, however, does not actually depend upon such mechanical correspondence of repetition to the external divisions. . . . Emma's three experiences with mutations of love—vicarious and unwanted with Mr. Elton, flirtatious with Frank Churchill, and true with Mr. Knightley—provide the basic tripartite structure. The business with Mr. Elton culminates within Volume One; but the flirtation with Frank Churchill, though Emma realizes in Volume Two that she is not in love with him, carries over well into Volume Three; and the avowed love of Mr. Knightley occupies only a short portion of the last volume. The three climaxes, already alluded to, of emotion, plot, and story, in close sequence but expertly separated (chapters 7, 10, 13), take place in Volume Three. Hence the formal, superimposed upon the actual, structure of the novel creates a kind of counterpoint.

Three proposal scenes punctuate and symbolically enrich the significance of each of Emma's experiences with love. The novelist parallels increasing social activity with the advancing seasons conducive to it in a rural community; and when she employs the midsummer heat at Donwell Abbey and Box Hill in conjunction with the heightening emotional tension that reaches the breaking point in Emma's tears and the breach between Jane Fairfax and Frank Churchill, it is not fanciful to read overtones into the background of these proposals. On the evening of his declaration Mr. Elton is described as "spruce, black, and smiling" Black appropriately describes his clerical attire, but the color seems to have an ominous connotation as well and to prepare for Emma's subsequent aversion. His insincere, fruitless proposal vents itself not only in the confined dark of the carriage but on a bleak, snowy December night. Darkness, coldness, and confinement reflect the unpropitiousness and, for Emma, the distastefulness of the incident. Frank Churchill's proposal, prevented only, as Emma thinks, by the arrival of his father, happens indoors in February, still the barren season; and its purely imaginary nature—not a proposal at all but the prelude to a confession of his engagement to Jane Fairfax—symbolizes the sterility of Emma's relationship with Frank. In manifest contrast to these two, and especially to Mr. Elton's wine-bolstered plea, Mr. Knightley discloses his love among the shrubbery of Hartfield in the slanting sunlight of a July evening. Light, warmth, and spaciousness replace darkness, coldness, and confinement. The wind had ''changed into a softer quarter'' and the clouds had disappeared. Emma and Mr. Knightley enjoy ''the exquisite sight, smell, sensation of nature, tranquil, warm, and brilliant after a storm''—it is the understated equivalent of the fructifying natural surroundings that impel Tess and Angel Clare in Froom Vale. Mr. Knightley's confession of deep love comes at the height of fertile summer, and the marriage is solemnized in October, the harvest time of year. Emma's previous brief moments of physical contact with a man intensify the pitch of feeling during the promenade with Mr. Knightley. When Mr. Elton seized her hand in the carriage, she had been shocked and repelled; she had dwelt with pleasure upon Mr. Knightley's taking her hand and almost raising it to his lips after her visit to Miss Bates. The author need not comment in the third instance to express Emma's sensation when she finds her arm drawn through Mr. Knightley's and more than once pressed against his heart.

As to the meaning of the entire novel, the most telling use of repetition with variation involves Mr. Knightley's proposal of marriage in another way. The evening of the day after Emma discovers Harriet's aspirations toward Mr. Knightley

> was very long, and melancholy at Hartfield. The weather added what it could of gloom. A cold stormy rain set in, and nothing of July appeared but in the trees and shrubs, which the wind was despoiling, and the length of the day, which only made such cruel sights the longer visible.

> The weather affected Mr. Woodhouse, and he could only be kept tolerably comfortable by almost ceaseless attention on his daughter's side, and by exertions which had never cost her half so much before. It reminded her of their first forlorn tête-à-tête, on the evening of Mrs. Weston's wedding day; but Mr. Knightley had walked in then, soon after tea, and dissipated every melancholy fancy. Alas! such delightful proofs of Hartfield's attraction, as those sort of visits conveyed, might shortly be over.

The novelist specifically calls to mind the opening chapter of the book and invites comparison of Emma's present, though not absolute, awareness with her former state of illusion. Then she anticipated matchmaking with delight; now she sees bitterly the evils of her designs, ''and the only source whence any thing like consolation or composure could be drawn, was in the resolution of her own better conduct, and the hope that, however inferior in spirit and gaiety might be the following and every future winter of her life to the past, it would yet find her more rational, more acquainted with herself, and leave her less to regret when it were gone.'' As on the former occasion, Mr. Knightley, having just returned from London and having walked over from Donwell with direct news of Isabella's family in Brunswick Square, arrives to dispel the gloom, not, however, until the following evening and not as a friend but as a lover. When he and Emma join Mr. Woodhouse indoors, their happiness is secure. ''They sat down to tea—the same party round the same table—how often it had been collected!—and how often had her eyes fallen on the same shrubs in the lawn, and observed the same beautiful effect of the western sun!—But never in such a state of spirits, never in anything like it. . . .'' Besides the rhythm explicit in the passage itself, the western sun of the summer evening contrasts with the autumn moonlight night of the first chapter; and Emma, instead of

being engrossed with her plans for others, can think of nothing but her own joy.

The third recurrence of this tableau—Mr. Woodhouse, Emma, and Mr. Knightley sitting together at Hartfield—after Emma has achieved full awareness, is only implied; but inevitably the three must gather at the tea table on an evening during the first week in November, when the Knightleys have returned from their two weeks' wedding journey. The author avoids the ineptness of depicting this scene at the end of the book—as much as to say, ''Look, here we are again, back where we started from, but with what a change in Emma!'' Yet she provides for the thoughtful reader such a resolution of her work. In the three months since the evenings in July, Emma has completed her ordeal and penance. A marriage has recently taken place, but for Mr. Woodhouse as well as for Emma such an event is no longer the melancholy one it was exactly a year before. And Emma's having declared then that she would never accept a husband ironically emphasizes the transformation she has undergone. Mr. Knightley, who brings comfort to Mr. Woodhouse and wisdom and contentment to his daughter is, as twice formerly, present; but this time he will not have to leave them at the end of the evening. Tranquillity has replaced the stress created by Emma's misguided opinions and willful behavior. It is an artistically satisfying and realistically acceptable conclusion.

Yet some critics dissent, protesting against Emma's and Mr. Knightley's living with her father. Miss Stern, for example, exclaims, ''Oh, Miss Austen, it was *not* a good solution; it was a bad solution, an unhappy ending could we see beyond the last pages of the book.'' Jane Austen's retort is to put this very objection in the mouth of the egregious Mrs. Elton, ''Shocking plan, living together. It would never do. She knew a family near Maple Grove who had tried it, and been obliged to separate before the end of the first quarter.'' Pundits, who may not relish being classed with Mrs. Elton, might have spared themselves embarrassment if they had recollected that the author foresaw the death of Mr. Woodhouse in two years. But no matter how long he lived, they could never have erred if they had fully understood **Emma**. There is nothing ''lightly satiric'' about Jane Austen's assurance of the ''perfect happiness of the union'' between Emma and Mr. Knightley. Not merely a ''prediction,'' it is an unequivocal statement of fact, to which a close reading of the novel compels assent.

Emma, as Reginald Farrer says, ''is *the* novel of character, and of character alone, and of one dominating character in particular.'' And it is imperative that we read that character aright. The book is Jane Austen's masterpiece because she has accomplished the hazardous feat of portraying and resolving disharmony deriving entirely from within the heroine herself. She has done so with such economy, with such consummate artistry, that the surface brilliance has obscured for many the emotional depth and moral significance of the novel. Hers is no world of nonsense, but a real world of intricate human relationships. Irony is the bright instrument with which she delights, stimulates, and enlightens the reader, but with which she has practiced no ultimate deception. Far from having nothing worthwhile to say to modern men and women, through the discrepancy between appearance and reality she reminds us of human fallibility and the need for modesty, unselfishness, and compassion. She requires charity and forbearance toward the less gifted and fortunate than we. She shows the advisability of openness and sincerity, the evil of slander and of hastening to derogatory conclusions, the cruelty of inflicting mental pain, the falseness of snobbery. She demonstrates that we cannot escape the consequences of our acts, that love is not an emotion to be tampered with, and that marriage is not a game. Such truths she inculcates objectively through Emma's progress from self-deception and vanity to perception and humility. (pp. 646-50)

Edgar F. Shannon, Jr., "'Emma': Character and Construction," in PMLA, Vol. LXXI, No. 4, September, 1956, pp. 637-50.

MARK SCHORER (essay date 1959)

[*In this linguistic analysis of* Emma, *Schorer discusses Austen's use of metaphors derived from the language of business, demonstrating Emma's progression from egotism to identification with society.*]

As with most of [Austen's novels, *Emma*] has a double theme, but in no other has the structure been raised so skillfully upon it. The novel might have been called *Pride and Perception,* or *Perception and Self-Deception,* for the comedy is concerned with a heroine who must be educated out of a condition of self-deception brought on by the shutters of pride, into a condition of perception when that pride had been humbled through the exposure of the errors of judgment into which it has led her. No novel shows more clearly Jane Austen's power to take the moral measurement of the society with which she was concerned through the range of her characters.

Morality in the novel lies not in spread but in scale, in the discrimination of values on scale and the proportion that is held between values within scale. In *Emma,* the word scale has a special meaning, for its subject is a fixed social scale in need of measurement by moral scale. As the social scale is represented by the scene as a whole, by all the characters, so the chief characters establish, in addition, the moral scale. The story is the progress of the heroine on this second scale toward her position on the first. *Emma* gives us the picture of an externally balanced society which the novel itself readjusts, or puts in perspective, through the internal balance that is the root of moral, not social, judgment.

Can we permit the notion that Jane Austen is capable of making a moral judgment on that social world which she herself accepts and from which her novels emerge? . . . [The] surest way of knowing the values out of which a novel comes lies in an examination of style, more particularly, of metaphor. Jane Austen's style is, of course, remarkably non-metaphorical, if we are thinking of explicit metaphor, the stated analogy, but it is no less remarkable in the persistency with which the buried, or dead metaphors in her prose imply one consistent set of values. These are the values of commerce and property, of the counting house and the inherited estate. I will divide this set of values rather arbitrarily into five categories. First of all, of *scale* itself, all that metaphor of high and low, sink and rise, advance and decline, superior and inferior, rank and fortune, power and command; as "held below the level," "raise her expectations too high," "materially cast down," "the intimacy between her and Emma must sink." Second, of *money:* credit, value, interest, rate, reserve, secure, change and exchange, alloy, resources, gain, want, collect (for "assume"), reckon, render, account, claim, profit, loss, accrue, tax, due, pay, lose, spend, waste, fluctuate, dispense, "precious deposit," appropriate, commission, safety. Third, of *business and property:* inherit, certify, procure, solicit, entitle, business, venture, scheme, arrangement, insure, cut off, trust, charge, stock. Fourth, of *number and measure:* add, divide, multiply,

calculate, how much and how little, more and less. And fifth, of *matter:* incumbrance, weight, substance, material, as material change, or material alteration, comfort.

These terms are constantly appearing, both singly and in clusters. One or two illustrations must suffice:

> She listened, and found it well *worth* listening to. That very *dear* part of Emma, her fancy, *received* an *amusing* supply . . . it became henceforth her *prime object of interest;* and during the ten days of their stay at Hartfield it was not to be expected—she did not herself expect—that anything beyond occasional fortuitous assistance could be *afforded by her* to the lovers. They *might advance* rapidly if they would, however; they *must advance* somehow or other, whether they would or no. She hardly wished to have more leisure for them. They are people, who *the more you do* for them, *the less they will do* for themselves. Mr. and Mrs. John Knightley . . . were exciting, of course, rather *more than the usual interest.* Till this year, every long vacation since their marriage had been *divided* between Hartfield and Donwell Abbey.

This language, as a functioning element in the novel, begins to call attention to itself when we discover it in clusters where moral and material values are either juxtaposed or equated: "no material injury *accrued* either to body or mind"; "glad to have *purchased* the mortification of having loved;" "except in a moral light, as a penance, a lesson, a source of *profitable humiliation* to her own mind, she would have been thankful to be *assured* of never seeing him again . . . his welfare twenty miles off would *administer* most satisfaction."

It would seem that we are in a world of peculiarly *material* value, a world of almost instinctive material interests in its basic, intuitive response to experience. The style has created a texture, the "special feel" of that world. At the same time, on the surface of the action, this is usually a world of refined sensibility, of concern with moral propriety, and in Emma's case, presumably at least, of intelligent clarity of evaluation. A large portion of Jane Austen's comedy arises from the discrepancy that we see here, from the tension between these two kinds of value, these different *scales,* material and moral, which the characters, like the metaphors, are all the time juxtaposing and equating. But when we say that, we have moved from considerations of language alone, into the function of the language in the whole.

How do we transfer ourselves from one to the other? Notice, first of all, that in some very impressive details, the implicit stylistic values erupt every now and then into explicit evaluations in the action, explicit evaluations that are, of course, ironical illuminations of the characters in their special situations. (pp. 547-49)

Most impressive, because most central to the theme of the book, this passage:

> Emma perceived that her taste was not the only taste on which Mr. Weston depended, and felt that to be the favourite and intimate of a man who had so many intimates and confidantes, was not *the very first distinction in the scale of vanity.* She liked his open manners, but a little less of open-heartedness would have made him a higher character.

We may summarize this much as follows:

1. The language itself defines for us, and defines most clearly, that area of available experience and value from which this novel takes it rise, and on which the novel itself must place

the seal of its value. The texture of the style itself announces, therefore, the subject, and warns us, suggesting that we not be deceived by the fine sentiments and the moral scruples of the surface; that this is a material world where property and rank are major and probably as important as "character." More specifically, that this is not simply a novel of courtship and marriage, but a novel about the economic and social significance of courtship and marriage. (The basic situation in all the novels arises from the economics of marriage.) There is other evidence that Jane Austen knew marriage, in her world, to be a market; in her *Letters,* she wrote, "Single women have a dreadful propensity for being poor—which is one very strong argument in favor of matrimony."

2. The implicit textural values created by language become explicit thematic statements in important key phrases such as "the scale of vanity" and "their intimacy must sink." In such phrases we detect the novel's themes (what it has to say about its subject) and its tone, too (how Jane Austen feels about it). We are led now, from language merely, to structure, to observe the particularized dramatic expression, the actualization, of this general narrative material, this "world."

Let us consider structure from the two points of view of architectural and thematic development. The two are of course interdependent, but we may see the novel more clearly, finally, if we make the separation.

From an architectural point of view, *Emma* seems to consist of four movements, or of four intermeshing blocks, each larger than the preceding. Emma is always the focus for us, but her own stature is altered as one block gives way to the next— that is, she bulks less large in the whole action of each as one follows upon another. The first block is the "Harriet Smith" block, and here Emma's dimensions are nearly coextensive with the block itself; this gives way to the Elton's block (and that includes, of course, others); that, in turn, gives way to the Frank Churchill-Jane Fairfax block; and that, finally, to the Knightley block, where Emma is completely absorbed. John Knightley observes at one point, "Your neighborhood is increasing and you mix more with it." That is, of course, precisely what happens in the structure: an "increasing neighborhood" diminishes Emma. This development is perhaps best represented by the Cole's dinner party, where she finds herself in danger of exclusion and is herself alarmed, and it is completely dramatized in Frank Churchill's casual readiness to use—to abuse—her for his own purposes. Thus, as the plot becomes more intricate, and even as we view it through Emma's eyes, she actually plays a less and less central, or relevant part in it.

Now on these blocks of increasing size we must imagine another figure, a cone, to represent Knightley. Its point would lie somewhere near the end of the first, the Harriet block, and through each of the following blocks it would widen, until, in the final block, it would be nearly coextensive with the limits of the block itself. It is important to see that the movement from block to block is accomplished not only by new elements in the action (the arrival of Mrs. Elton; of Jane Fairfax; the death of Mrs. Churchill) but by scenes between Emma and Mr. Knightley himself, scenes in which he usually upbraids her for an error of judgment and scenes out of which she emerges with an altered awareness, a dim alteration in the first, a slightly clearer alteration in the second and third, and at last, in the fourth, as full an awareness as she is capable of. The first of these is in Chapter 8, and the subject is Harriet; the second, Chapter 18, and the subject is Frank Churchill; the

third, Chapter 33, the subject Jane Fairfax; and the last, Chapter 43, the subject Miss Bates. These scenes are debates between moral obstinacy and moral wisdom, and the first is slowly brought up to the proportion of the second. In the last scene, when Knightley takes Emma to task for her cruelty to Miss Bates, she fully recognizes and bitterly repents her fault. She *alters* at last: "could he *even* have seen into her heart," she thinks, "he would not, on this occasion, have found anything to reprove." Only then is she prepared to know that it is only Knightley that she can love, and with that the movement of awareness swells: "Every other part of her mind was disgusting." And then, before his declaration, the movement comes to rest:

> When it came to such a pitch as this, she was not able to refrain from a start, or a heavy sigh, or even from walking about the room for a few seconds; and the only source whence anything like consolation or composure could be drawn, was in the resolution of her own better conduct, and the hope that, however inferior in spirit and gaiety might be the following and every future winter of her life to the past, it would yet find her more rational, more acquainted with herself, and leave her less to regret when it were gone.

Thus we have a double movement in the architecture—the diminution of Emma in the social scene, her reduction to her proper place in the whole scale of value (which is her expiation), and the growth of Emma in the moral scheme (which is her enlargement). It is very beautiful.

Now most of this we are never told, and of Emma's diminution, not at all. We are made to experience this double development through the movement of the plot itself. This fact calls attention to Jane Austen's method, and makes us ask what her reasons were for developing it. The method consists of an alteration of narration conducted almost always through the heroine's eyes, with dramatic scenes illustrative of the narrative material. There is almost no direct statement of the significance of the material, and there is a minimum of reported action. The significance of the material comes to us through two chief sources: the dramatized scene itself, and the play of irony through the narration. Of Jane Austen's skill in making scene speak, I will say nothing, except to point out our awareness of the significance of Emma's silence—she says not a word—in the scene in Chapter 12 where her sister is praising Jane Fairfax and explaining why Jane and Emma had always seemed to everyone to be perfectly suited for an equal friendship; and that later scene, in Chapter 21, where we are made so acutely aware of the presence of the others and their several emotions, as Miss Bates blunders along on the matter of how some people had mistakenly felt that Mr. Elton might have married a certain person—well, clearly, it is Miss Woodhouse herself, who is there, again stonily silent. Now just as the dramatic values of scene are left to speak for themselves, so the moral values are left, implicit *in* the scenes, not discussed through them.

Such a method, intermingling as it does dramatic scene with narrative observations of the heroine, requires from the author a constant irony that at all times transcends the ironic habit of mind of the heroine herself. Sometimes Jane Austen achieves this simply by seeming to accept the scene as the characters pretend that it was; as, for example, following on Emma's silence when Isabella praises Jane, the narrative proceeds: "This topic was discussed very happily, and others succeeded of similar moment, and passed away with similar harmony." Sometimes she achieves it through an unobtrusive verbal pointing, as: "Poor Mr. Woodhouse was silent from consternation;

but everybody else had something to say; everybody was either surprised, or not surprised, and had some question to ask, or some comfort to offer." Could the triviality of the situation find a more effective underlining? On still other occasions, Jane Austen achieves this necessary irony simply by shifting her point of view a fraction away from the person who presumably holds it. This is shown nowhere more effectively than in the passage I have already cited, in which we begin with Emma's observation, then shift to that phrase, "the scale of vanity," which cannot possibly be hers, and then return at once to her.

> Emma perceived that her taste was not the only taste on which Mr. Weston depended, and felt that to be the favourite and intimate of a man who had so many intimates and confidantes, was not the very first distinction in the scale of vanity. She liked his open manners, but a little less of open-heartedness would have made him a higher character. General benevolence, but not general friendship, made a man what he ought to be. She could fancy such a man.

I am pressing this matter of the method of scene and the method of irony not only because it is through this method that the significance of the architectural structure of the work is brought home to us, that double movement I have described, but because it reveals an important fact about Jane Austen's relation to her audience, then and now, and because, unless we understand this relation, we cannot see as much as we should see in that thematic structure to which I will presently turn, or see at all that relationship of social and moral scale that is the heart of the book. Jane Austen was in an ambiguous situation in relation to her readers, a situation in which she was committed simultaneously to cherish and abominate her world. Within the framework of what is presumably a happy story, where everyone gets married off properly in the end, she must still make her comment, from her deepest moral evaluations, on the misery of this happiness. The texture of her style already has suggested that the world she pictures is hardly founded on the highest values. But that is not enough. She must besides develop a technique which could both reveal and conceal, that would give only as much as the reader wished to take. (That is why she can still be read in both the most frivolous and the most serious spirit.) Her problem—and perhaps this is the problem of every novelist of manners, at least if he is a satirist, who criticizes the society within which he yet wishes to remain and, indeed, whose best values are his own—her problem was to develop a novelistic technique that would at once conceal and reveal her strongest feelings, her basic observation of her heroine and her heroine's world, and that would express with sufficient clarity if one looks at that technique closely, the ultimate values here involved.

For those who do not read while they run, the range of Jane Austen's irony, from the gentlest to the most corrosive, will suggest that she was perfectly able to see with absolute clarity the defects of the world she used. I will not trouble with the mild examples, but only with the gradation at the extreme:

> "It was a delightful visit—perfect, in being much too short." And she leaned back in the corner to indulge her murmurs, or to reason them away; probably a little of both—such being the commonest process of a not ill-disposed mind.

Surely a mind that throws out observations such as these is not an entirely well-disposed one. But to go on—

> "I am persuaded that you can be as insincere as your neighbours, when it is necessary."

Still further: Emma on Miss Bates:

> ". . . and nobody is afraid of her—that is a great charm."

Consider next the bitter violence of the verb, in that comment on boarding schools, where young women are "*screwed* out of health and into vanity." And come last, to the extreme, an amazing irruption into this bland social surface of what has been called her "regulated hatred"—

> Miss Bates stood in the very worst predicament in the world for having much of the public favour; and she had no intellectual superiority to make atonement to herself, or *frighten those who might hate her into outward respect.*

Surely there is no failure . . . to judge the values of the social scale. We, in turn, are enabled to recognize these values, to judge the material, in other words, to place our evaluation upon it, not only by these oblique uses of irony, but by two other means: first, the dramatization of Emma's diminution in the community as we see more and more of it; second, by judging the real significance of her end.

The first, the dramatization of value, or moral scale, is achieved through what I have been calling "thematic structure," a structure that supports and unifies the architectural structure, the thematic integration of characters. Thematic structure exists, first of all, in the selection and disposal of characters around the heroine, and the relationship in moral traits which we are meant to observe between the heroine and the others. Emma is in many ways a charming heroine, bright and attractive and energetic, but Jane Austen never lets us forget that if she is superior to the Eltons, for example, the author (or, if you wish, Knightley) is superior to her. Emma's vanity is of no trivial kind. She is not "personally vain," Knightley tells us; "her vanity lies another way." It lies, for example, in her very charity. "Harriet would be loved as one to whom she could be useful. For Mrs. Weston there was nothing to be done; for Harriet everything." It is the vanity of giving, and brings to mind E. M. Forster's remark that, for many people indeed, it is better to receive than to give.

It is the vanity, next, of power, for through the exercise of her charity, she succeeds in the imposition of her will. It is the vanity of abstract intellect. That Emma is capable of sound judgment is evident in her recognition of the real Elton even as she is urging him upon Harriet; it is evident again in her analysis of the real relation that probably pertains between Frank Churchill and his step-mother, even as she is herself about to fall in love with him. It is evident again in some of her self-studies, when, for example, after the Elton-Harriet fiasco, she resolves, in tears, that, since it is too late to be "simpleminded and ignorant," like Harriet, she will be at least "humble and discreet." In the next chapter she reveals herself incapable of acting on her own self-judgment, and Mr. Knightley again points up the discrepancy for us.

> Emma: "He may have as strong a sense of what would be right as you can have, without being so equal, under particular circumstances, to act up to it."
>
> Knightley: "Then it would not be so strong a sense. If it failed to produce equal exertion, it could not be an equal conviction."

Emma's intellectual judgments do not relate sufficiently to her conduct; in short, she is immoral. And we are not to be surprised when, rather early in the novel, she announces her own values: "those pleasantest feelings of our nature—eager curiosity and warm prepossession." The novel shows us the disastrous moral consequences of such insufficient standards.

This is Emma in her vanity. Let us observe, now, the kind of symbolic relationships in which her vanity is placed: First, of contrast, the contrast being with Miss Bates, and none in the novel more explicit.

> Emma Woodhouse, handsome, clever and rich, with a comfortable home and happy disposition seemed to unite some of the best blessings of existence; and had lived nearly twenty-one years in the world with very little to distress her.

Ten pages later:

> Miss Bates . . . a woman neither young, handsome, rich, nor married. Miss Bates stood in the very worst predicament in the world for having much of the public favour . . . and yet she was a happy woman.

That Emma unites with "some of the best blessings of existence," some of the worst possibilities of human society, is all too soon quite evident, but nowhere more evident than when she says of Miss Bates, "so silly, so satisfied, so smiling. . . ."

The second kind of symbolic relationship is not contrasting but comparative, and is evident in Harriet and Mrs. Elton. Of Harriet we need only point out that she is a silly but harmless girl educated by Emma into exactly the same sort of miscalculations, only to be abused by Emma for her folly. The comparison with Mrs. Elton is more fully developed: Emma's judgment on the Coles, who are struggling to rise above the stigma of trade, is exactly duplicated by Mrs. Elton's judgment on a family living near Maple Grove, called Tupman: ". . . very lately settled there, and encumbered with many low connections, but giving themselves immense airs, and expecting to be on a footing with the old established families. . . . They came from Birmingham. . . . One has not great hopes for Birmingham." The analogy with Emma is detailed: Mrs. Elton, like Emma, has an almost aggressive determination to "do" for other people, and to ride over their wishes; on the "scale of vanity," she is precisely where we begin with Emma:

> a vain woman, extremely well satisfied with herself, and thinking much of her own importance; that she meant to shine and be very superior; but with manners which had been formed in a bad school; pert and familiar; that all her notions were drawn from one set of people, and one style of living; that, if not foolish, she was ignorant. . . .

And Emma makes this analysis: Emma, who herself is "amused by such a picture of another set of beings"—the Martins; who broods on the inferior society of Highbury; who makes one test only, the class test, except when she judges creations of her own, like Harriet, and even Harriet's high-born antecedents, as Emma fancies them, are apparent in her face; Emma, whose manners at one point, at any rate, are not merely pert and familiar, but coldly cruel, which even Mrs. Elton never is.

The third kind of symbolic relationship is the contrasting-comparative kind that is evident in Jane Fairfax. This is a crucial relationship in the thematic structure. We are told that they are alike in many ways—age, station, accomplishments. They are alike, furthermore, in that Emma *thinks* of Jane as complacent and reserved, whereas we *know* Emma to be both. Her reserve with Jane Fairfax is complete from the beginning, and stoney. Her complacency is nearly admitted: she "could

not quarrel with herself"; "I cannot really change for the better." What a contrast, then, in actuality. Jane, whom we see through Emma's eyes as complacent, cold, tiresome, and in some ways rather disgusting, is, really, as much an antithesis to Emma as Miss Bates, and a much more difficult antithesis for Emma ever to deal with, to really admit. She is a woman capable of rash and improper behavior, a genuine commitment to passion, a woman torn by feeling, and feeling directed at an object not entirely worthy. She is hardly prudent. In short, she is quite different from what Emma sees, and quite different from what Emma is—all too complacent and perhaps really cold—and she stands in the novel as a kind of symbolic rebuke to Emma's emotional deficiencies, just as Knightley stands as a rebuke to her moral deficiencies. That Emma has emotional deficiencies is perhaps sufficiently apparent in her attachment to her father, and in her use of that attachment. Jane Fairfax is the blurred threat to Emma's complacency, the threat that Emma herself has never brought into focus in her own life and character, and at the end of the novel still has not, and so still has not achieved it for herself, on any radical reform of her qualities. They have merely moved on the scale.

So much for the heroine and the female characters. If we look now at the men, we can consider them as variations, or gradations, on the two traits, egotism and sociability, or "Candor," which is the positive virtue sought by Mr. Knightley. These characters run from Mr. Elton, the vain social snob, all egotism; through Frank Churchill, the man whose candor conceals a treacherous egotism; through Mr. Weston, so thoroughly amiable as to be nearly without judgment, and yet an egotist himself, the egotism of parenthood; to Mr. Knightley, who is the pivot, the middleman, moderate and sound, balanced and humane, neither an egotist nor a gadabout. From him, we shade off into his brother, the dour social egotist, to Mr. Woodhouse, the destructive (though comic, of course) malingering egotist.

Emma's relationships to them are revealing: she patronizes and then scorns Elton, of course; she "loves" Frank Churchill; she is fond of Weston; toward Knightley she holds a friendly animosity; she has tolerance for John; she adores her father. These relationships or emotional responses are Jane Austen's way of dramatizing Emma, of showing us her value. We see her through them, even as we are seeing them through her. It is a process of reciprocal illumination. And so in both the men and women, we come to see her above and beyond her presentation of herself, and at the same time, of course, we come to see the community at large through them—they represent Jane Austen's social "analysis," her breakdown of a community into its major traits, its two poles. If we study the bulking up at one end or the other of the scale, we can hardly conclude that the analysis is entirely friendly.

Thus we begin to see the real accomplishment of this objective technique, how deep it can go, how much subtle work it can do, how it defines its interpretations and analysis of the material, how it separates the material (which is trivial) and the effect (which is grave). Most remarkable perhaps, how it holds together, makes one, the almost bland, comic tone, appropriate to the kind of society, too brittle for a severer tone, and a really bitter, sometimes acrid theme.

To define the theme completely we have to look closely at the real history of Emma. For all her superiority, Emma's values are really the values of the society she patronizes, and although she partially resolves her personal dilemma (her really is a "profitable humiliation"), she *retains* those qualities: complacency, a kind of social cruelty, snobbery (Harriet must sink), and even greed (little Henry, who must inherit Donwell). Emma's self-study has always been partially mistaken; will it always be correct henceforth? Except for her final moment of awareness, her others have always exempted herself from judgment; can we believe that that is never to happen again? Does the final comment not come from Knightley, when Emma says, "Poor child!... what will become of her?" and he replies, "Nothing very bad. The fate of thousands. She will be disagreeable in infancy, and correct herself as she grows older. I am losing all my bitterness against spoilt children, my dearest Emma." The modification is minor. Does Jane Austen say less? Near the end she tells us:

> Seldom, very seldom does complete truth belong to any human disclosure; seldom can it happen that something is not a little disguised, or a little mistaken; but where, as in this case, though the conduct is mistaken, the feelings are not, it may not be very material. Mr. Knightley could not impute to Emma a more relenting heart than she possessed or a heart more disposed to accept of his.

How severely does Jane Austen "chasten" Emma? "Do not physic them," says Isabella of her children; are we not left to "physic" Emma, to chasten her and her world together, with all necessary guidance from the style and the basic motives that analysis reveals in the work itself?

When we say that Emma is diminished at the end, as her world is, in a way, for us—the bright, easy society put in a real shade—we are really saying that she has been absorbed into that world, and has become inseparable from it. This observation suggests that we look again at the end of the novel. There is something apparently aimless and long-winded about it. Of *Pride and Prejudice* the author said, "The work is rather too light, bright, and sparkling; it wants shade; it wants to be stretched out here and there, with a long chapter of sense, if it could be had." In *Pride and Prejudice* and *Sense and Sensibility,* Jane Austen's heroines were superior to their world. Then, in *Mansfield Park,* her dull Fanny was completely submissive to the conventional pieties of this same world, somewhat white-washed. In *Emma,* Jane Austen seems to do what the remark about *Pride and Prejudice* aims at. Emma is finally nearly at the top of the moral scale, with Knightley, but the moral scale still has its relation to the social scale. The entire end of *Emma* is such a "shade" (even as it busily gets its characters happily married off, it is creating the shade, the moral shade, in which they will live) and the only justification for that long ending, once the Emma-Knightley arrangements have been made, is that it is needed there, as a kind of decrescendo into the social twilight that lies at the heart of the book. And so the end remains "open"—a question, in a way. It is Emma who at one point near the end exclaims, "I like everything decided and open"; everything here is at once decided and, in another sense, open.

How completely resolved are these strains of feeling? Emma and Jane, for example? Emma and Frank? How much "candor" is there? And how "happy" is this marriage, with Knightley having to move into old Mr. Woodhouse's establishment? Isn't it all, perhaps, a little superficial—not the writing but the self-avowals of the characters? A little perfunctory, as comedy may be, telling us thereby that this *is* comedy? One is reminded of the end of *Mansfield Park:*

> I purposefully abstain from dates on this occasion, that everyone may be at liberty to fix their own, aware that the cure of unconquerable passions, and the transfer

of unchanging attachments, must vary as to time in different people. I only entreat everybody to believe that exactly at the time when it was quite natural that it should be so, and not a week earlier, Edmund did cease to care about Miss Crawford, and became as anxious to marry Fanny as Fanny herself could desire.

Emma, then, is a complex study of self-importance and egotism and malice, as these are absorbed from a society whose morality and values are derived from the economics of class; and a study, further, in the mitigation of these traits, as the heroine comes into partial self-recognition, and at the same time sinks more completely into that society. Just as with Elizabeth Bennet, her individual being, as she has discovered it, will make that society better, but it will not make it different. This is moral realism, and it shows nowhere more clearly than in the very end, when the pilfering of a poultry house is given us as the qualification of "the perfect happiness of the union." The irresolution of the book gives it its richness, and its tautness and precision of structure and style give it its clarity. The two together make it great. (pp. 550-61)

> Mark Schorer, "The Humiliation of Emma Woodhouse," in The Literary Review (Fairleigh Dickinson University), *Vol. 2, No. 4, Summer, 1959, pp. 547-63.*

MALCOLM BRADBURY   (essay date 1962)

[*Bradbury deals with Austen's complex expression of social and moral values in the structure of* Emma.]

"Jane Austen" said Henry James in one of his few great misjudgments "was instinctive and charming. . . . For signal examples of what composition, distribution, arrangement can do, of how they intensify the life of a work of art, we have to go elsewhere." We do not, of course; and my purpose here is to suggest something of the complexity of the structure that Jane Austen creates to express the elaborate pattern of values contained in *Emma.* "I am going to take a heroine whom no-one but myself will much like," said Jane Austen of the novel. . . . It is presumably a moral objection she fears will be brought against Emma; and it is to be by resolving this situation—by fitting Emma in to the moral expectations which she projects outwards into the audience, as it were—that the book must work. The self-willed quality of Emma, in which her attractiveness for reader and for novelist resides, must be contained and adapted, adapted to a norm which is neither social (though it is a norm which *lives* in society) nor doctrinaire (though it is a norm pragmatic simply in the sense that it re-establishes by proof of value the best traditional decencies).

Jane Austen is concerned with two kinds of world—the social world and the moral world—and their interaction, an interaction that is intimate, but also complex. It is often complained of her that she measured life from the conventional social standards of the upper middle class about which she writes and to which she belongs, and that this limits her wider relevance and 'excludes' her from the modern novel, one of the attributes of which is a greater range in its treatment of character and value. . . . Of course it is true that class attitudes are of the greatest importance; but it is in the evaluation of these attitudes, and the building up of a scale of them for the proper conduct of the moral life, that she excels. She is nothing if not stringent. The whole structure of her inventions is recurrently that of a kind of moral assault course, an extended interview in which candidates give their qualifications, undergo a succession of tests, and are finally rewarded by the one prize that is possible and appropriate in their social context—marriage, a marriage which is aesthetically right, morally and humanly balanced, financially sound. (pp. 335-36)

What Jane Austen has to do, then, in *Emma* is to establish side by side a social world and a moral world, the latter setting up a higher level of action and judgment than the former. The social world is carefully and precisely given; it is elaborate in range, though not in class. The action takes place in Highbury, a "large and prosperous village, almost amounting to a town", sixteen miles out of London; its life is the life of the time of writing (*Emma* was published in 1816). The landscape of Highbury is a landscape of property; there is Hartfield, the home of the Woodhouses, who are "the first in consequence in Highbury"; there is Randalls, home of Mr. Weston, "a little estate"; there is Donwell Abbey "in the parish adjoining, the seat of Mr. Knightley". Emma's sister lives in London, in Brunswick Square, only relatively accessible; Highbury is a more or less self-contained social unit, and it certainly contains most of the action. Further, the upper middle-class level of Highbury life includes most of the significant characters; and this is the level we see from. (p. 336)

The constraints of a fixed society are firmly felt, and Jane Austen never tests the values that arise within this world outside the area in which they are possible (in industrial cities or in lower social brackets); there is no need to; in this agrarian and hierarchical world, subscribing by assent to a stylized system of properties and duties, she finds a context in which they can yield their full resources.

The society in which the moral action takes place is then a local, limited, stylized world, with its own operative values and its own occasions. Its social intercourse is unelaborate. When people meet they do so over dinner or at balls or in Ford's shop; encounters occur by formal arrangement; there are few accidental meetings, and so precise are the circumstances of this life that when these occur (as when Harriet meets Robert Martin in the shop) they are deeply disturbing. Persons stand out large, while the formalities make for a controlled universe, in which our own sense of propriety as readers is engaged to the degree that, when Jane Fairfax and Frank Churchill are, by a conjunction of accidents, left alone with the sleeping Miss Bates and this 'breach' goes unobserved, we alone are called on to observe it and reflect on its significance. The degree of social stability, the preciseness of social expectations, the limitations on eccentric behaviour or concealments or violent action, reinforce and make significant the moral order. They enable a concentration on the quality of the individual life. They create a high degree of consensus about behaviour—about what constitutes decent action. They provide a relatively closed and rounded world in which, once a level of adequate living has been acquired, it can be reinforced from without, for the future will be reasonably like the present.

Within these limits, though, the society throws up a broad range of values, out of which the tensions of the novel arise. . . . People define themselves by their actions, and as they act we perceive that there are in the novel superior and inferior people in moral as well as social terms. The social order yields to the moral. The morally inferior people tend in fact to be socially high, to considerable dramatic effect; Emma herself, at the beginning, is one of them and Frank Churchill another, while people of lower rank, like the Martins and the Coles, elevate themselves by their actions. In this fashion certain values emerge as positive—particularly values having to do with care and respect for others, the decent discharge of one's duties, and

the scrupulous improvement of oneself. They are values associated with, but by no means intrinsic to, an upper middle class social position. So frivolity may be despised, but accomplishments count high, since they evidence self-discipline and self-enlargement and please others—the fact that Mr. Martin reads is highly in his favour in this emergent scale, while Harriet Smith's taking a long time to choose materials at Ford's is not in hers. A friendly and social disposition is valued, but not *too* highly, since Emma's criticism of Jane Fairfax's reserve comes to tell more against Emma than it does against Jane and, what is more, it blinds her to some of the excellence of Mr. Knightley. Goodwill and a contented temper are valued, but have their associated failures—Mr. Weston is too easy-going to reasonable living, and Emma at once too indulgent over moral matters and not indulgent enough over social ones. To be "open, straight-forward and well judging", like Martin, is important, but not as important as the rewarding side of Mr. Knightley's more closed and critical temper. All this is the central area of the action, for it is what is at issue between Knightley and Emma; and yet we do come to value Emma's warmth and openness, only wanting it placed and ordered.

Birth and good manners are important, but only when there is something behind them. Elegance is admired, highly by Emma, less so by others. Mr. Elton is "self-important, presuming, familiar, ignorant and ill-bred"; the observations are Emma's, and have to be mediated by us carefully, for they show up Mr. Elton *and* Emma. This picking up of tone is most important for the book, and we are helped by alternative views—for instance, Jane Fairfax is more tolerant of Mr. Elton. Mr. Weston is a little too open-hearted for Emma—"General benevolence, and not general friendship, make a man what he ought to be. She could fancy such a man." To Harriet she commends "the habit of self-command", but responds to Harriet's "tenderness of heart"—"There is nothing to be compared to it. Warmth and tenderness of heart, with an affectionate, open manner, will beat all clearness of head in the world for attraction." But Mr. Knightley, in one of the debates in which the education of Emma—and to a lesser extent of Knightley himself—is conducted and in which a permissible range of *difference* of value is reconciled, offers a more rational and mature view; he states the case for a plan of life strictly adhered to, a sense of duty and of courtesy, and a right realization of what one owes to one's social situation and therefore one's function. This competition of values between Knightley and Emma, which is one of our main guides to the direction of the book, touches on other issues and other people, of course— an interesting example of its method being the way in which Knightley reappraises Emma's description of Churchill as "amiable":

> ". . . No, Emma; your amiable young man can be amiable only in French, not in English. He may be very 'amiable', have very good manners, and be very agreeable; but he can have no English delicacy towards the feelings of other people—nothing really amiable about him."

Other issues come into these debates, to add to the dense moral atmosphere. Thus Churchill is criticized early for being above his connections, later for being too exuberant; while he himself criticizes "civil falsehoods", but employs them. Emma admires elegance highly; she has a practical, advantage-seeking view of attractive qualities in people; she criticizes Mr. Knightley for inventing lines of conduct that are not practical. Mr. Knightley reverses this case, condemns Emma's fancy and whim, and recommends "judging by nature". In consequence,

A sketch of Box Hill, the scene of an excursion in Emma.

the moral life is in the front of the character's minds throughout; it is *linked* with class—as in the description of the estate at Donwell Abbey as belonging to "a family of such true gentility, untainted in blood *and understanding*"—but understanding is insistently prior to blood as the notion of gentility begins to take a kind of ideal shape.

And so from the very first page of the book we are conscious of a disparity between the moral and the social scale. Emma's situation is, from the start, shown to be happy—

> Emma Woodhouse, handsome, clever, and rich, with a comfortable home and a happy disposition, seemed to unite some of the best blessings of existence, and had lived nearly twenty-one years in the world with little to distress or vex her.

But the complexities of the handling are already present. There is the hint, offered through nuances of diction, that the "best blessings of existence" only *seem* to be hers; there is the point, further taken up and insisted on, that she has not been vexed but rather over-indulged. Her father is "affectionate, indulgent"; her governess has "a mildness of temper" that "had hardly allowed her to impose any restraint", and presently by an explicit statement Jane Austen converts the hints into a direct moral observation—"The real evils, indeed, of Emma's situation were the power of having rather too much of her own way, and a disposition to think a little too well of herself." (pp. 337-40)

The moral scale is centred rather particularly, throughout, upon what is reasonable and desirable in a social life whose basic unit is the family, what makes for good and open dealing between people, prospers and opens their relationships and makes them dutiful and considerate in all their public actions. Jane Austen's novels are domestic novels, novels centred on marriage; most of the commentary and moral discussion is in fact directed toward defining the conditions for a good marriage, and preparing the one good marriage which contrasts with all others in the novel and so dominates it. But marriage is a social pact and so must answer to the public dimension. The general expectations of this book are that people will make the marriages they deserve, and that the climax will be Emma's marriage, made when she has answered to her faults and resolved her dilemmas.

Whom, then, will Emma marry? This is the question on which the plot turns. This plot, simply summarised, is concerned with a girl of many fine qualities but of certain considerable errors deriving from the misuse of her own powers, who realises

these errors, perceives that they have made her make false attributions of worth to the people in her circle and, repenting, marries the man who can instruct her in an accurate reaction to the world. The first part of the plot, the Aristotelian 'beginning', takes us to Chapter 17. In this section Emma is a detached agent in someone else's destiny; this is that part of the novel concerned with Emma's attempt to intervene in the life of Harriet Smith by marrying her to Mr. Elton, and its function is to demonstrate the nature of Emma's mistakes about the world, and the dangers of detached and desultory action. By the time we reach Chapters 16 and 17, where we are presented with Emma's regrets, we have all we need in the way of moral direction for the rest of the book. Mr. Knightley's interpretation of character and event has been shown to be better than Emma's, and we have a clear sense of Emma's tendency to misread what is before her, as well as of the faults, particularly snobbery and whimsy, which make her do this. (pp. 340-41)

The second part of the novel, the 'middle', is that concerned with Emma's mistakes about the nature of Frank Churchill's and Jane's characters, and her inability to infer the truth here because of her pre-judgments. The situations are now more complicated, but Emma repeats her errors without real improvement, inventing a romance before she has even met her between Jane and Mr. Dixon, and another between Churchill and herself. Here the purpose of the action is to show how she behaves in events which increasingly come to involve not a protegé's but her own destiny, to show how she is capable of misusing herself. This part of the plot ends with a significant and crucial discovery, Emma's discovery that she is in love.

The 'end' of the book beautifully enforces the weight and meaning of the book; the waters clear, and all the significances are laid bare in a simple delaying action which enables Jane Austen to make clear all the inadequacies of her characters and the moral lesson to be learned from them. Repentance in Emma is delayed to the last and therefore most effective moment, and it comes after a train of thought in which we see Emma affected, involved, pressed into realisation of her follies. On top of understanding comes marriage, a right resolution to the plot in that it enforces the significance of true understanding. The preparation is over and by extending the novel indefinitely by a closing sentence referring to "the perfect happiness of the union" Jane Austen assures us that it is an effective understanding that Emma has come to.

These final effects are so precisely controlled and placed that it is evident that we *do* have a plot in which "composition, distribution and arrangement" are handled with the greatest finesse. It is reached through such indirect methods that one can't but wonder at the vast number of threads that need to be woven into the resolution. The most complex strategy of the novel is the device of filtering it through the eyes of a character of whom Jane Austen doesn't wholly approve, yet with whom she is strongly in sympathy. There is no unsureness about the moments of understanding and improvement that must (despite her position as heroine) come to her. The device is handled particularly by the use of Mr. Knightley as a "corrective"; but that is by no means the whole of the effect, for Mr. Knightley is not always right either. Another force exists to handle this; it resides in the values that emerge when we have taken away the irony from the treatment of events seen through Emma's eyes. For we must be careful to see that Emma is right sometimes; we must know, however, precisely when she is wrong. How well this is managed! Emma judges excessively by elegance; but though her criticism of Mrs. Elton is that she lacks elegance she perceives most of her faults. Indeed Emma is by no means consistently in error; she is clever enough to be right on nearly all the occasions where she is not giving rein to her snobbery and her prejudice—or pre-judgment. It is Mrs. Elton's snobbery that makes Emma's seem mild; and we need the scene where the two talk together to place Emma in that good light. The point then is that if Emma were judged by Jane Austen from 'outside', she would be unlikeable and highly criticized. In fact she is a violator of Jane Austen's moral scale to such a degree that it is hard at first to understand how she could have been made a heroine by her. And the fact that she *is* the heroine is the most remarkable thing about her—*Emma* is Jane Austen's *Tom Jones* in which the most devout expectation roused in the reader is the expectation that she will in some way come to grief; but we demand that her grief, like Tom Jones', will not be too painful, that repentance will occur, redemption be won and all the blessings of the prodigal son be given to her. This is what happens. The artistic problem of the book is then to make us care for Emma in such a way that we care about her fate, and like her, but that we in no way subdue our moral feelings about her faults.

And here another aspect of the tone is involved. For *Emma* is a comic novel, a novel concerned with comedy of manners in such a way as to make this the comedy of morals. There is comedy in various veins. There is the straightforward humorous treatment of Mr. Woodhouse and Miss Bates as "comic characters". This, of course, does function in the moral dimension of the book—Mr. Woodhouse's affectations are based on an indulgence to himself and it is an indulgence of the same order that has harmed Emma, while Miss Bates's absurdities make her a kind of test-case for Emma's power of responding to other people. But the significant action of the comedy in the management of the plot is to be found, for example, in the comic flavour of the scenes at the beginning where Emma, Harriet and Mr. Elton are playing at picture-making and with riddles. These scenes are treated lightly, and they are designedly about trivial events; but they are organized to show us one thing above all, that Emma is capable of misreading radically the significance of these situations. What makes them most comic to the reader is his sense of a completely different possible explanation for Mr. Elton's actions. The operative principle is, in short, an irony that works against the heroine.

This irony dominates the novel. It is contrived through the device of an omniscient narrator who is able to offer an alternative set of values, and it concerns almost always the difference between what the character sees and comes to judgment about, and other potential readings of the incident. It refers then particularly to Emma's habit of prejudging situations. It is offered by a variety of methods, such as the changes in point of view that—for example—let us, at the beginning of Chapter 20, see Jane Fairfax independently of Emma's judging eye. Its effect is not simply to set up another set of *facts* against which Emma's foolish interpretations are judged; we have to wait a while for *those*. What, at the time, we are invited to realize is not that Emma is wrong, but that she might be—that she has pre-judged. In short, then, we are drawn away from a determined interpretation or prejudice about people and events, and towards a sense of possible variety. The irony is thus in favour of empiricism; and the pattern of the book is one in which the events presented before us are capable of more complex interpretation. And because we commonly see through Emma's eyes, and because Emma doesn't see this further interpretation, it is dramatically delayed and becomes the centre of our sus-

tained interest. The devices which assure us that it is there are, among other things, the insistent and critical presence of Mr. Knightley, the occasional movements to other points of view, and the revelation of the first part that Emma has been wrong about Harriet Smith and so can be wrong again. This tension between events as they seem and events as they might be—between the pleasing Frank Churchill that Emma sees, and the temporizing and cunning Churchill that Mr. Knightley sees—is the dynamic of the book. When Churchill comes to Randalls and talks so pleasantly, pleasing everyone, we wonder, we have been prepared to wonder, whether this is because he is deeply amiable or simply cunning. Events will bear at least two interpretations. But it should be said that Emma suspects this, that her views put to Mr. Knightley are views she doubts, and that to some extent she has learned from the Harriet incident. As readers, however, skilled in plots, we are put into the position of being encouraged to entertain our suspicions longer; there is a devised relationship between reader and heroine, inherent in the ironic note.

The novel closes on a final irony. One of Emma's faults has been her external view of persons, and her willingness to interfere in the destinies of others without being prepared to involve herself. Marriages are to be made only for others. In being forced into true feelings of love, she is released and opened out; love is the final testimony, in fact, of her redemption. She concludes the book by involving herself in the essential commitment of the Austen universe, which is marriage; so she has opened out into tenderness of heart, a tenderness without weakness or sentimentality. If she has still some faults to recant, these will come in time, for the fundamental liberation has taken place; she is no longer the Sleeping Beauty.

And in this way the shape of the novel is fulfilled. It has begun by delineating a variety of contesting moral viewpoints; it ends by clarification, by offering to the reader his way through the variety. We have learned this particularly through our understanding of Emma's faults, and by learning above all how significant, how *fundamental*, they are. For Emma's aloof relation to others, her willingness to treat them as toys or counters, her over-practical view of the good quality, which she sees simply as ensuring for its possessor a good match—these become significant betrayals of human possibility. "With insufferable vanity she had believed herself in the secret of everybody's feelings; with unpardonable arrogance proposed to arrange everybody's destiny. She was proved to have been universally mistaken; and she had not quite done nothing—for she had done mischief. She had brought evil on Harriet, on herself, and, she too much feared, on Mr. Knightley . . ." The social and moral universe I described at the beginning of these comments takes on all the weight of its significance here, for it provides a context in which Emma's faults are not pecadilloes to be regarded with indulgence, but total violations of a whole worthwhile universe. Jane Austen's method is to rouse our expectations and draw on our moral stringency to such an extent that this insight becomes absolutely essential, and retribution is demanded. The agents of retribution here are Mr. Knightley and Jane Austen herself, and the retribution, once understanding has come, is genial—the lesson learned by Emma is that of how to commit herself fully and properly in the moral and social act of marriage, an act whose validity she has begun by denying and with which she begins her mature life. And what is rendered for us, then, is the moral horror of values we are awfully apt to associate with Jane Austen herself—snobbery, an excessive regard for the elegant and smart, a practical regard for goodness because it is such a *marriageable* trait. These are the values that are purged. We have been turned another way; we have learned of the duty of the individual to immerse himself in the events about him and to accept his obligations to his acquaintance finely and squarely; we have learned of the value of ''the serious spirit'', involved and totally responsible. We have been persuaded in fact of the importance of true regard for self and others, persuaded to see the full human being as full, fine, morally serious, totally responsible, entirely involved, and to consider every human action as a crucial, committing act of self-definition. (pp. 342-46)

> Malcolm Bradbury, ''Jane Austen's 'Emma','' in Critical Quarterly, *Vol. 4, No. 4, Winter, 1962, pp. 335-46.*

HOWARD S. BABB   (essay date 1962)

[*In this excerpt from his study of dialogue in Austen's fiction, Babb demonstrates that Emma's maturation in the course of the novel is reflected in changes in her speech.*]

[The change in Emma's behavior in the course of the novel] is not merely something asserted by the expository passages in the novel; it is rendered in the dialogue itself. And to see the change most accurately, we must turn . . . to some of her conversation with Mr. Knightley. . . . [He] and Emma reveal a more and more intense feeling for each other as the novel goes on, and often they do so in dialogues which exhibit Jane Austen's technique of metaphoric indirection. The prime example in *Emma* is the proposal scene, which I shall be dwelling on in a few moments. But in order to highlight what happens there, I want first to take up briefly one of the early interchanges between Emma and Mr. Knightley, using it to suggest again their typical modes.

The bit of dialogue acts as a prelude to the long quarrel between them over Harriet's refusal of Robert Martin, a refusal engineered by Emma. In the scene as a whole Jane Austen makes some use of metaphoric indirection, for Harriet, the ostensible subject of the talk, off and on becomes a vehicle by which Mr. Knightley and Emma define their attitudes toward each other. As usual, he has reason on his side, but he keeps being exasperated by her foolishness—partly because he likes her so well. And as usual, Emma adopts a calmer manner, the outward proof—so she imagines—of her superior reason, though in fact her thinking reflects her feelings only. Some of these motives and something of the scene's technique appear in its prelude, which Mr. Knightley begins with a sensible evaluation of the Harriet whom he expects to marry Robert Martin:

> ''Her character depends upon those she is with; but in good hands she will turn out a valuable woman.''

> ''I am glad you think so; and the good hands, I hope, may not be wanting.''

Probably Mr. Knightley has Robert Martin's ''good hands'' mainly in mind. But surely the phrase refers as well to Emma, the molder of Harriet. In such a context it seems most likely a reminder of Emma's responsibility, though the entire clause may also compliment Emma very discreetly by praising her friend. She assumes, of course, that he is thinking only of herself. While she pretends to remain properly objective by taking over the oblique phrasing of ''good hands,'' she actually preens herself on her ability and presses him for a franker compliment.

Mr. Knightley brings her desire into the open with characteristic bluntness, but he holds back his own feelings for Emma, deliberately citing a minimal improvement in Harriet:

> ''Come . . . you are anxious for a compliment, so I will tell you that you have improved her. You have cured her of her school-girl's giggle; she really does you credit.''

> ''Thank you. I should be mortified indeed if I did not believe I had been of some use; but it is not every body who will bestow praise where they may. *You* do not often overpower me with it.''

Stung by his refusal to cry her up, Emma at first stands on her dignity with a highly formal phrasing. But then she strikes back with the generalization about ''every body''; for just a moment the words sound like compliment to Mr. Knightley, yet they become, by her last sentence, a measure of his usual perversity. Needless to add, Emma feels convinced that the generalization proves her cool sanity, and indeed her moral superiority, to Mr. Knightley. The same assurance sustains her throughout the quarrel about Harriet that follows. The dialogue moves toward a climax when Emma, having indulged in all her fancies about Harriet's birth and personal attractions, assumes herself to be a better judge of men's taste than Mr. Knightley by proclaiming, over his objections, that ''such a girl as Harriet is exactly what every man delights in.'' But Emma is doing more here than converting her wish into law. Since she has already admitted that Harriet lacks sense, yet still makes her friend the measure of man's delight, Emma's generalization has the effect of thrusting her sensible self—and she has paraded her sense all along—beyond the reach of men. Snugly untouchable, she goes on to declare complacently, ''Were you, yourself, ever to marry, she is the very woman for you.'' It is fitting that this vision should return, after some three hundred pages, to cause Emma her greatest misery.

How much she has altered as a result of discovering her love for Mr. Knightley and how richly human he remains—both of these are unmistakable in the proposal scene. The dialogue itself compounds the technique of metaphoric indirection with ambiguity, the major dramatic technique of the novel. To be more specific: through talking about the engagement between Frank Churchill and Jane Fairfax, Mr. Knightley and Emma betray their emotion for each other; yet he suspects that her feelings relate to Frank Churchill, and she suspects that his relate to Harriet. The scene comes about because Mr. Knightley, having learned of the engagement and imagining that it must upset Emma, rushes back from London to comfort her. But Emma, not realizing that he has heard the news, fears that he wants to tell her about an engagement of his own with Harriet.

Yet Emma dreads not knowing his heart even more than knowing it. So she sets about discovering it by announcing the match between Frank Churchill and Jane Fairfax, hoping that the subject of marriage will lead him to show his intentions. Given her purpose, she tries hard to hit a purely informational tone with Mr. Knightley at first:

> ''You have some news to hear, now you are come back, that will rather surprise you.''

> ''Have I?'' said he quietly, and looking at her; ''of what nature?''

> ''Oh! the best nature in the world—a wedding.''

He interprets her tone very differently, as her attempt to remain composed in the face of losing Frank Churchill; and he reads her remark as indicating her "surprise" and mortification at having been replaced by Jane Fairfax. The reserved tone in which he himself speaks suggests to us mainly that Mr. Knightley wants to make sure of the facts and of Emma's reaction before responding more fully, and perhaps that he has no wish of encouraging her to grieve deeply over a man whom he has always distrusted. Naturally, his reserve does not help Emma understand his plans, so she pushes on in her last sentence, her tone becoming almost shrilly cheerful. She has to rejoice over "a wedding" because she must convince Mr. Knightley that she approves of them all, will not be hurt, that is, by a marriage between him and Harriet.

That Emma has indeed been trying to draw him out is implied by a tiny logical flaw at the start of the speech to follow. After learning from him that he already knows of the engagement between Jane Fairfax and Frank Churchill, Emma speculates that he was "less surprised than any of us," a phrase that clashes ever so slightly with her earlier mention of "news . . . that will rather surprise" him. More important, in what Emma now goes on to say, a complete reversal of her earlier behavior in the novel begins to make itself apparent:

> "*You* probably have been less surprised than any of us, for you have had your suspicions.—I have not forgotten that you once tried to give me a caution.— I wish I had attended to it—but—(with a sinking voice and a heavy sigh) I seem to have been doomed to blindness."

Emma both accepts the "blindness" with which she has acted and admits to the superior insight of Mr. Knightley, who has given her a "caution" about Frank Churchill's intimacy with Jane Fairfax. This self-recognition on Emma's part also has highly emotional implications, for she realizes not only that her "blindness" to Frank Churchill has been caused by her fancy, so typical, of matching him with Harriet, but that this scheme has kept her from regarding Harriet as a rival to herself for Mr. Knightley. Especially in the passionate close, Emma betrays how deeply she feels about Mr. Knightley, though her words only plead with him to sympathize as a friend with her faults. Now a supplicant, she has completely abandoned her earlier pose of haughty detachment.

And Mr. Knightley responds to her plea, even though he believes all her distress generated by the loss of Frank Churchill, the man whom he has considered his rival. There may be a touch of irony at Mr. Knightley's expense in the fact that he praises Emma's "sense" here while quite misconceiving her situation:

> "Time, my dearest Emma, time will heal the wound.— Your own excellent sense—your exertions for your father's sake—I know you will not allow yourself— . . . . The feeling of the warmest friendship—Indignation—Abominable scoundrel! . . . I am sorry for *her*. She deserves a better fate."

Yet it is typical of Mr. Knightley that, while betraying intense private emotion by his broken clauses, he should undertake to direct Emma toward her proper reaction of "sense," unselfishness, and justice to Jane Fairfax. But clearly what moves him most deeply is the sight of suffering in the woman he loves—and a lingering resentment against his former rival.

Jane Austen writes that "Emma understood him," but the statement is no more than a half-truth. Emma realizes only that Mr. Knightley thinks her attached to Frank Churchill, and she takes pains to set him right about that in several long speeches. One feature of them is Emma's running distinction between appearance and reality. The following extracts will reveal the trait, most obviously in the contrast Emma draws near the start between her "manners" toward Frank Churchill and her lack of feeling for him, and in her later contrast between the "blind" of his behavior and "his real situation":

> "Mr. Knightley . . . I am in a very extraordinary situation. I cannot let you continue in your error; and yet, perhaps, since my manners gave such an impression, I have as much reason to be ashamed of confessing that I never have been at all attached to the person we are speaking of, as it might be natural for a woman to feel in confessing exactly the reverse.— But I never have."

> "I have very little to say for my own conduct.—I was tempted by his attentions, and allowed myself to appear pleased.—An old story, probably—a common case—and no more than has happened to hundreds of my sex before; and yet it may not be the more excusable in one who sets up as I do for Understanding. . . . He never wished to attach me. It was merely a blind to conceal his real situation with another.— It was his object to blind all about him; and no one, I am sure, could be more effectually blinded than myself—except that I was *not* blinded—that it was my good fortune—that, in short, I was somehow or other safe from him."

But, if we are struck by Emma's ability to make distinctions here, what of her generalizations? Toward the close of the first extract, she certainly pretends to no more than the level of generic "woman": ". . . I have as much reason to be ashamed . . . as it might be natural for a woman to feel in confessing exactly the reverse." In the second speech, she gives up all claims to uniqueness through linking herself absolutely with "hundreds of my sex," now describing her "case" as "common," "An old story." And in the next breath—". . . it may not be the more excusable in one who sets up as I do for Understanding"—Emma does not generalize to escape responsibility, as she has done so frequently before, but to judge herself. The last lines of the speech show her private feelings welling up, half anger at Frank Churchill, half despair of Mr. Knightley. The emotions are interrelated because Emma's plotting about Frank Churchill has led her to ignore Mr. Knightley, and the interrelationship is dramatized through the shifting logic behind Emma's references to blindness. But in speaking so warmly, Emma comes too near disclosing that the source of her feeling is Mr. Knightley, and so she must break off.

She has at last convinced him, however, that she never gave her heart to Frank Churchill, and Mr. Knightley feels so cheered by the information that he immediately raises his estimate of the man somewhat. Although this turnabout has its mild irony for us, the speech as a whole attests again to the integrity of Mr. Knightley, for he will not let Frank Churchill off without further reform, nor will he forget the claims of Jane Fairfax. And he maintains this basically sensible and sensitive grip on reality when he is even more deeply moved—by a remark from Emma about the happiness of the engaged couple. Once more Mr. Knightley can take stock intelligently and firmly of the whole relationship between Frank Churchill and Jane Fairfax, but he speaks so feelingly of them because they are enjoying exactly the happiness that he has yearned to share with Emma and believes an impossibility:

> "He is a most fortunate man! . . . So early in life . . . a period when, if a man chooses a wife, he generally chooses ill. At three and twenty to have drawn such a prize!—What years of felicity that man, in all hu-

man calculation, has before him!—Assured of the love of such a woman—the disinterested love, for Jane Fairfax's character vouches for her disinterestedness; every thing in his favour,—equality of situation—I mean, as far as regards society, and all the habits and manners that are important. . . .—A man would always wish to give a woman a better home than the one he takes her from; and he who can do it, where there is no doubt of *her* regard, must, I think, be the happiest of mortals.—Frank Churchill is, indeed, the favourite of fortune. Every thing turns out for his good. . . .''

''You speak as if you envied him.''

''And I do envy him, Emma. In one respect he is the object of my envy.''

Emma is well aware, obviously, that his words reverberate with emotion. Indeed, she cannot bring herself to reply at all to his last remark, for she imagines him ''within half a sentence of Harriet.'' It is a signal irony that Emma, whom we have seen attempting all through here a clarity of vision unobscured by wishful thinking, should fall victim to this last confusion of appearance and reality.

Thus the groundwork is laid for the multiple ironies that arise when Mr. Knightley addresses himself to Emma more explicitly. For one thing, the principals work at cross purposes, Mr. Knightley trying to propose in spite of Emma's unencouraging manner, and Emma fending off what she most wants because she fears him to be thinking of Harriet:

''You will not ask me what is the point of envy.— You are determined, I see, to have no curiosity.— You are wise—but *I* cannot be wise, Emma, I must tell what you will not ask, though I may wish it unsaid the next moment.''

A further irony inheres in Mr. Knightley's transposition of the roles to which he and Emma have been assigned through most of the novel. He now presents himself as the one governed by feeling—''*I* cannot be wise,'' ''I must tell,'' ''I may wish''— and Emma as the partisan of reason—''will not ask,'' ''determined . . . to have no curiosity,'' ''wise.'' In this characterization of Emma, however, Mr. Knightley speaks a truer sense than he perhaps realizes, for she now behaves with the richest integrity. For a brief moment her dread of losing him, perhaps mixed with some antagonism toward Harriet, rules Emma, and she begs Mr. Knightley not to speak. Yet she transcends this selfishness immediately, in part through an act of will, to be sure, but mainly through being almost literally moved beyond herself by her tenderness toward Mr. Knightley, and also by some sense of justice toward Harriet:

Emma could not bear to give him pain. He was wishing to confide in her—perhaps to consult her;—cost her what it would, she would listen. She might assist his resolution, or rconcile him to it; she might give just praise to Harriet, or, by representing to him his own independence, relieve him from that state of indecision, which must be more intolerable than any alternative to such a mind as his.

Surrendering every chance for her own happiness, as she believes, Emma invites Mr. Knightley to go on. And she then learns, of course, that he loves no one but herself. Yet this fortunate result must not tempt us to undervalue what we have just witnessed: Emma shouldering her responsibilities fully in the gravest crisis that she ever endures.

The entire scene seems to me wonderfully successful in conveying—through the gestures of speech—the deep emotions of Emma and Mr. Knightley, the principles by which they act, and the moral decisions that they make. In achieving what it does, the scene invites us to question such a commentary on *Emma* and Jane Austen as [E. A. Baker's in *The History of the English Novel*]: ''Here, as always in her work, the moral, or rather the philosophy, is not ethical in the stricter sense; it has to do with manners more than with morals.'' For the dialogue shows that one's ''manners,'' one's verbal habits, cannot help dramatizing one's ''morals,'' one's ethical commitments. (pp. 194-202)

Howard S. Babb, in his Jane Austen's Novels: The Fabric of Dialogue, *Ohio State University Press, 1962, 244 p.*

CHRISTOPHER GILLIE   (essay date 1965)

[*Gillie discusses* Emma *in terms of the conflict between society and the individual.*]

Emma Woodhouse, handsome, clever, and rich, with a comfortable home and happy disposition, seemed to unite some of the blessings of existence; and had lived nearly twenty-one years in the world with very little to distress or vex her.

Emma was published in 1816. Earthly lots and destinies were much what they had been, but they had come to possess illusory finality and power of definition. In this opening sentence we are shown a character who 'seems', at her very outset, to have arrived. She is what she needs to be, and has what is to be desired. Emma has no defects which Society would call defects, nor lacks anything that Society would regard as worth regretting. Yet we are told that she '*Seemed* to unite *some* of the blessings . . .', and out of the germs of doubt in those two words, the whole novel consistently unfurls.

Emma's good fortune turns out to be golden confinement and double delusion: confinement, because its perfection precludes the idea of enlargement; delusion, because not only does it seem to render needless any effort by Emma on her own behalf, but it seems to confer the right, almost the duty, to make efforts on the behalf of others. So, her own destiny ready moulded to such advantage, Emma takes it upon herself to mould that of another.

For doing this she has the advantages of social position, natural kindness, and quick intelligence; her obvious disadvantage is her youthful inexperience of life and lack of self-knowledge— negative faults made lethal by her perfect self-confidence, based on the unquestioning deference which all her relations and friends, except Knightley, consider her due. To these disqualifications must be added another which is yet more serious inasmuch as it is so far from being obvious to her that it may be missed even by the reader, who is being 'shown the cards': she makes a common but basic confusion between literature and life.

The relationship of literature to life, especially the intrusion of literature into life and the way in which experience of the imagination can deteriorate into mere imaginary experience, are constituents of at least four of Jane Austen's six novels. In *Northanger Abbey* Catherine Morland tries to live the romance of a gothic romance and becomes entangled in real-life confusions for which she is not prepared; in *Sense and Sensibility* Marianne Dashwood, priding herself in her 'sensibility', turns her disappointment in love into a romantic catastrophe, leaving her sister—mere 'sense'—to contend with its disruptive effects on private life while she has her private sorrow to contend with as well. In **Mansfield Park** a group of young people involve their precarious and little understood personal relationships with amateur theatricals and precipitate disaster.

Emma, inexperienced in human nature, ignorant equally of the facts in other people's lives and of her own deeper feelings, tries to compose a real-life romantic novel centred on Harriet Smith, becomes a willing but unwitting puppet in a real-life farce contrived by Frank Churchill, tries to include him as a character in her novel, and finds in the end that she is on the point of bringing about a triple tragedy—that of Harriet Smith, of Jane Fairfax, and of herself.

Her initial mistake is to suppose that a person such as herself, with every external advantage, is fitted to operate other people's lives as an author operates those of his characters. Her second great error is not to perceive the interconnection between what is social and what is personal, and that in arriving at social as well as personal judgements, we commonly do no more than project our prejudices and predilections, often hidden from ourselves. She adopts Harriet Smith, who is 'the natural daughter of somebody', because Harriet's prettiness makes her a promising investment, and because her submissiveness makes her amenable to Emma's own strong will. Emma, however, chooses to see the prettiness and the submissiveness as evidences of natural refinement and aristocratic parentage, and a suitable pretext for romance. The fact that submissiveness may equally show weakness of mind and mediocrity of personality does not occur to her because of its inconvenience. Similarly, she arrives at conclusions convenient to herself about Robert Martin, the modest farmer whose engagement to Harriet she succeeds in preventing, and of the vicar, Mr Elton, whose engagement to Harriet she tries to bring about, but who, to her intense indignation, chooses instead to propose to herself:

> She thought nothing of his attachment, and was insulted by his hopes. He wanted to marry well, and having the arrogance to raise his eyes to her, pretended to be in love; but she was perfectly at ease as to his not suffering any disappointment that need be cared for. There had been no real affection either in his language or manners. Sighs and fine words had been given in abundance; but she could hardly devise any set of expressions, or fancy any tone of voice, less allied with real love. She need not trouble herself to pity him. He only wanted to aggrandize and enrich himself. . . .

All this is perfectly true: Elton's proposal to Emma is heartless. Yet, such is her ignorance of the disposition of her own heart, that she does not see how all her reflections about Elton's motives towards herself apply equally to her own motives on behalf of Harriet. She has been equally heartless in breaking the relationship between Harriet and Robert Martin; as much as the Vicar for himself has she 'only wanted' aggrandisement and enrichment for Harriet. She cannot even be excused on the ground that at least she wants these things for another, for it is evident that she is trying to live through Harriet the romance which she believes to be denied to herself, owing to the ready-made good fortune which makes her own existence so perfect.

When Harriet remonstrates with her for her willingness to become an old maid, she has her answer ready, and it is an answer that reveals so much about Emma that it constitutes a key passage in the book:

'I shall not be a poor old maid; and it is poverty only which makes celibacy contemptible to a generous public! A single woman, with a very narrow income, must be a ridiculous disagreeable old maid! . . . And the distinction is not quite so much against the candour and common sense of the world as appears at first; for a very narrow income has a tendency to contract the mind, and sour the temper. . . . This does not apply, however, to Miss Bates; she is only too good-natured and too silly to suit me; but in general, she is very much to the taste of everybody, though single and though poor. Poverty certainly has not contracted her mind: I really believe, if she had only a shilling in the world, she would be very likely to give away sixpence of it; and nobody is afraid of her: that is a great charm.'

'Dear me! but what shall you do? How shall you employ yourself when you grow old?'

'If I know myself, Harriet, mine is an active, busy mind, with a great many independent resources; and I do not perceive why I shall be more in want of employment at forty or fifty than at one-and-twenty. Women's usual occupations of eye, and hand and mind, will be as open to me then as they are now, or with no important variation. If I draw less, I shall read more; If I give up music, I shall take to carpet-work. And as for objects of interest, objects for the affections, which is in truth the great point of inferiority, the want of which is really the great evil to be avoided in *not* marrying, I shall be very well off, with all the children of a sister I love so much to care about. There will be enough of them in all probability, to supply every sort of sensation that declining life can need. There will be enough for every hope and every fear; and though my attachment to none can equal that of a parent, it suits my ideas of comfort better than what is warmer and blinder. My nephews and nieces!—I shall often have a niece with me.'

Emma contrasts her prospective self to Miss Bates. What she says about old maids and social attitudes to them shows genuine acuteness; but it strikes one that this blooming, arrogant, lively-minded girl will find it hard to grow into such a happy and beloved old maid as that simple-minded but generous and zestful old lady, so full with interest in the smallest details of her narrow life that she can never complete a sentence about any of them. Emma will always have 'occupations' for her talents, but the word is dreadful in its context, suggesting as it does that her life will be so much empty space to be carefully and precisely filled. And what of the voids that no 'Occupation' can supply? She will have nephews and nieces. One remembers that diffident sister and devoted mother, Isabella, who would find it so hard to resist the masterful, auntly incursions, and so hard not to resent them, and one ponders her husband—strong-minded, assertive, a doting father; one contemplates his rage. Emma playing with the lives of her nephews and nieces, as she is at this moment playing with the life of Harriet, is no engaging prospect. Miss Bates bores everyone with her niece, Jane Fairfax, but Miss Bates is to Jane an authentic refuge, not the moulder of fate that Emma would become.

It is part of Jane Austen's art of character creation that she erects, beside the central characters, others which provide analogy and satirical contrast to them. Miss Bates is such an oblique commentary: she does no harm and affords far more innocent pleasure to those whom she bores than Emma is likely to do to those whom she interests. A still severer commentary is the character of Mrs Elton, whom Mr Elton marries after his rebuff by Emma. Mrs Elton is vulgar, stupid and affected, whereas Emma is refined, intelligent and natural, and observes the Vicar's new wife with horrified wonderment; but she does not observe that Mrs Elton is, in her outlook and conduct, a brutal caricature of herself. Emma is quietly satisfied to be the queen of local society, but Mrs Elton arrogates to herself that position; Emma allows social distinctions to confuse her personal judgements, but Mrs Elton judges by social distinctions alone; Emma supposes that she can take over a simple, inexperienced girl and mould her life for her; but Mrs Elton supposes that her own patronage is required by Jane Fairfax, observing that she is diffident and poor, and not being capable of observing that she is reserved, proud, cultivated and talented; in short in every personal way the superior not only of herself but also of Emma, whom alone Mrs Elton regards as her equal.

Jane Fairfax is the third of the characters who act as a foil for Emma's virtues and failings. Her personal superiority to Emma is masked by her poverty, and emphasises the shallowness and unconscious cruelty of Emma's standards, and of all standards that arise from merely social discrimination. She is beautiful, and artistic to the extent of exposing Emma as a dabbler; but her poverty means that her engagement to Frank Churchill must remain a secret during the lifetime of his aunt, for fear of losing the legacy which, socially speaking, is necessary to their marriage. Churchill is not at all embarrassed, but enjoys cloaking the secret by a flirtation with Emma, and encouraging Emma's piqued, romantic speculations about Jane's circumstances. The engagement becomes precarious, and Jane's acceptance of a post as governess under Mrs Elton's patronage is narrowly averted. Emma's shrewd but flippant-toned remarks on poor old maids bear cruelly on Jane's situation. The double image of Emma as the interfering, complacent, empty-lived aunt, and Jane as the faded, diffident, impecunious governess, which at one point seems to be their likely fates, is also a tragic image of human waste, before which only a Mrs Elton could retain oblivious satisfaction.

Insensibility breeds unreality: Harriet, having been encouraged to aspire to Mr Elton, is now encouraged by Emma to aspire still further: Frank Churchill rescues her from an unpleasant encounter with some gipsies and the incident titillates Emma's imagination—it savours so well of a romantic novel. It is here, however, that she makes her climactic and most ridiculous mistake; romance and discretion alike dictate that no names should be mentioned in their discussions, with the result that while Emma supposes Harriet to be excited into gratitude and devotion to Frank on account of the gipsies, Harriet is really being drawn into love with Knightley on account of a very different service—Knightley has saved her vanity by inviting her to dance when she is left stranded at a ball. Emma believes that she knows Harriet's whole heart, but she knows it so little that she doesn't realise how little a serious embarrassment with gipsies weighs, for this young girl, against the humiliation of being left a wallflower. Sedulously, she encourages Harriet's hopes, until the Churchill-Fairfax engagement becomes public, and the moment of truth breaks.

> Harriet was standing at one of the windows. Emma turned round to look at her in consternation, and hastily said:
>
> 'Have you any idea of Mr Knightley's returning your affection?'
>
> 'Yes,' replied Harriet modestly, but not fearfully; 'I must say that I have.'

Emma's eyes were instantly withdrawn; and she sat silently meditating, in a fixed attitude, for a few minutes. A few minutes were sufficient for making her acquainted with her own heart. A mind like hers, once opening to suspicion, made rapid progress. She touched—she admitted—she acknowledged the whole truth. Why was it so much worse that Harriet should be in love with Mr Knightley, than with Frank Churchill? Why was the evil so dreadfully increased by Harriet's having some hope of return? It darted through her, with the speed of an arrow, that Mr Knightley must marry no one but herself!

This is the first time that Emma, intelligent as she is, sees and understands her own feelings, and the insight comes with the realisation that in seeking to contrive Harriet's fortune she has succeeded in contriving a scaffold for the destruction of her own happiness.

All the tragedies are averted: Emma marries Knightley; Jane marries Churchill; Harriet is taken back by Robert Martin. Jane Austen is after all, a writer of comedies. Comedies of depth, however, always provide a glimpse of the tragic alternative, and in every one of her novels this looms up before it is made to fade away. The heroines all have double standards, and usually employ them consciously: Society demands its due of deference; yet personal integrity has to be maintained. So placid, easy and secure is the surface lot of a Jane Austen heroine, that many people take her novels as sedatives; yet the heroines are tightrope walkers, and Emma is a blindfolded one, whose bandage is torn from her eyes only just in time. (pp. 117-23)

[It] is not that the personal is white and the social black; indeed, at the end of the book, the social criteria happen to be endorsed. Thus, it is conventionally suitable for Emma, the first lady of Highbury, to marry Knightley, the first gentleman; Harriet turns out to be the daughter of a tradesman and is after all not at all too good for Robert Martin; Churchill has rich maternal relations, but he is the modest Mr Weston's son for whom Jane is by no means too low. Does Jane Austen, then, after all, connive at these merely external criteria? Not at all; for what happens to be socially 'right' is achieved notwithstanding on the personal ground, and even in the teeth of what the 'Society-minded'—Emma, Mrs Elton, the invisible but powerful Mrs Churchill—try to impose. Emma is not shown to be altogether wrong in attaching value to social distinctions, for in her society they were generally involved in personal identities. She is, however, altogether wrong in failing to put the personal values first, allowing the social ones to take care of themselves— wrong both on the personal and the social counts. She is wrong not because she is superficial, stupid, or heartless, but because her social position gives her a false perspective both of personal values and of her own nature. The parable of the camel and the needle's eye applies to her; but so does Blake's proverb: 'If a fool should persist in his folly, he would grow wise.' Of the three marriages in prospect at the end of the novel, only that of Emma and Knightley has assurance of happiness, for they alone have justly assorted the personal and the social categories. (pp. 123-24)

Christopher Gillie, "The Heroine Victim," in his Character in English Literature, *Barnes & Noble, Inc., 1965, pp. 117-34.*

DAVID P. DEMAREST, JR. (essay date 1965)

[*In this excerpt, Demarest considers the theme of epistemology in* Emma, *examining the accuracy with which Austen's characters perceive their world.*]

The major theme of *Emma* is epistemological: how do we know what is real in the world around us, and how do we avoid the delusions fostered by appearance? In *Emma* Austen sets down a traditional formulation of what our faculties "half create, / and what perceive." For her the world is objective, the mind properly a measuring, not a creative instrument. We are always tempted to subjective distortion of what we see, to the delusive colorings of the imagination, but, at least theoretically, we are capable of asserting a commonsensical right reason that will allow us to understand the social reality around us. This epistemological problem is summed up in most obvious doctrinaire fashion in the chapter where we pass into Mr. Knightley's point of view as he watches Emma, Jane and Frank play at anagrams. Determined to avoid Emma's "errors of imagination," Mr. Knightley reflects on his suspicions and the problem of verifying them. He could not

> avoid observations which, unless it were like Cowper and his fire at twilight,
>
>   Myself creating what I saw,
>
> brought him yet a stronger suspicion of there being a something of private liking, of private understanding even, between Frank Churchill and Jane.

The game of detection starts: Emma watches Jane and Frank while Mr. Knightley watches them all, and the afternoon light grows dimmer, baffling the attempts at clear-eyed vision. The scene dramatizes the difficulty of perception, the patient methods requisite to accurate judgment, and—as Emma and Mr. Knightley clash in their judgments of Frank and Jane—the eternal problem of separating subjective bias from real evidence.

Minor characters are reductive mirrors of the issues outlined in this scene. The "humours" characters see everything in the extreme of their ruling passion: Mr. Weston, the sanguine, can scarcely think ill of anyone; the hypochondriac Mr. Woodhouse likes his germs and gruel; Mrs. John Knightley can no more understand anything not related to the welfare of her children than Mrs. Elton can look beyond Maple Grove and the barouche-landau. The biased privacy of every man's vision asserts itself comically each time these characters are put in a room together. From this perspective, Austen's use of minor characters in *Emma* dramatizes the universality of the problem of proper perception. And it establishes an equally important comic tone, the tolerance of this sort of satire: so goes the world; Emma may reform her wayward imagination, but men will always ride hobbyhorses, and will always provide entertainment enough for those who laugh.

It is simple Harriet Smith who is allowed to play out most fully a mock echo of the novel's detective motif. If we were to put in terms of logic what Emma learns in the course of the novel, we might say that she moves from a process of deductive reasoning—jumping to conclusions on the basis of imaginative premises—to a process of inductive reasoning—collecting and examining evidence carefully. These terms of logic are much to the point, since Austen, in setting out the uses and abuses of the rational mind, constantly employs a language of logic or law. When Emma first deals with Harriet, her language is that of the fiat: as she examines Mr. Elton's charade, she ignores the evidence before her to declare, "'The state of his mind is . . . clear and decided. . . . It is a certainty. Receive it on my judgment.'" Emma here presides; she pronounces. Later, after she has been chastened by her earlier failures, Emma admonishes Harriet to a wait-and-observe caution in what Emma assumes to be a developing interest between Harriet and Frank:

> "Consider what you are about. Perhaps it will be wisest in you to check your feelings while you can; at any rate do not let them carry you far, unless you are persuaded of his liking you. Be observant of him. Let his behavior be the guide of your sensations."

Emma sounds here as though she has learned that perception demands patient evidence-gathering. The thoughts that precede her advice to Harriet, however, mock Emma's words: "it would be safer for both, to have the judicious law of her own brain laid down with speed." The clumsy syntax of a ruling-by-decree indicates how much Emma herself still works from unexamined premises, and we feel the arbitrariness of her decision that Harriet and Frank will make a match.

The climax comes when Harriet reveals that the man she actually loves is Mr. Knightley, and when she shows how well she has learned her lessons by putting before Emma a considerable body of evidence that suggests Mr. Knightley's interest in her.

> Harriet, who had been standing in no unhappy reverie, was yet very glad to be called from it, by the now encouraging manner of such a judge. . . . [Emma] listened with much inward suffering, but with great outward patience to Harriet's detail.—Methodical, or well arranged, or very well delivered, it could not be expected to be; but it contained, when separated from all the feebleness and tautology of the narration, a substance to sink her spirit—especially with the corroborating circumstances, which her own memory brought in favour of Mr. Knightley's most improved opinion of Harriet. . . .
>
> When Harriet had closed her evidence, she appealed to her dear Miss Woodhouse, to say whether she had not good ground for hope.

(pp. 61-3)

[Here] a "simple" character has proved far more astute than Emma would have ever imagined, and, comically, far more willing to submit to the modesty of self-effacing observation than Emma herself has been. At this climactic moment in the novel both reader and heroine are forced to acknowledge again that there is not clear way to measure the value of other human beings; in fact, as we watch Emma's mistreatment of both Miss Bates and Harriet, we realize that the very foolishness in these characters that make them laughable is cautionary reason for their being treated tolerantly, considerately.

The final comic irony here is that Emma could take seriously the possibility that Mr. Knightley could be interested in Harriet. Austen has prepared a final twist: through Harriet she is able to undercut, to qualify satirically her central theme. If Emma throughout has reasoned arrogantly and deductively from biased premises, now, in this moment of anguished contrition as she hears Harriet's evidence and understands at last that she—Emma—must have Mr. Knightley, Emma jumps to the other extreme: she will believe nothing her heart tells her; she must have evidence for everything.

> In spite of all her faults, she knew she was dear to him; might she not say, very dear?—When the suggestions of hope, however, which must follow here, presented themselves, she could not presume to indulge them. . . .
>
> It must be her ardent wish that Harriet might be disappointed; and she hoped, that when able to see them together again, she might at least be able to ascertain what the chances for it were.—She should see them henceforth with the closest observance; and

wretchedly as she had hitherto misunderstood even those she was watching, she did not know how to admit that she could be blinded here.—He was expected back every day. The power of observation would be soon given—frightfully soon it appeared when he thoughts were in one course.

The epistemology of *Emma* asserts that the mind can understand an external world if reason is put to the task of detecting and evaluating objective data; Mr. Knightley, observing the game of anagrams, guarding against "creating what I saw," is a norm. Without contradicting her central theme, Austen at the end of *Emma* characteristically takes the ironic second-look: sometimes the wisdom of the heart makes the truth self-evident. (pp. 63-4)

David P. Demarest, Jr., " 'Reductio Ad Absurdum' : Jane Austen's Art of Satiric Qualification," in Six Satirists *by David P. Demarest, Jr. and others, Carnegie Institute of Technology, 1965, pp. 51-68.*

DAVID LEE MINTER (essay date 1966)

[*Identifying "the trouble with Emma" as her demand that her world be aesthetically harmonious, Minter sees the resolution of conflict between imagination and reality as a central concern in* Emma.]

Arnold Kettle's suggestion that marriage is the "subject" of *Emma* [see excerpt from a revised version of Kettle's commentary dated 1967] is helpful; for it points to the presence in *Emma* of familiar Austenean concerns—concerns, for instance, with manners and decorum, values and principles, social class and economic situation, as well as with women and the making of marriages. The suggestion, however, is also misleading not merely because *Emma*, as Lionel Trilling has noted [see Additional Bibliography], is a complex novel, but because it is, *par excellence*, a novel of nuance. Not familiar concerns per se, but familiar concerns under a certain aspect, familiar concerns made new by a controlling nuance, a defining twist, are at stake in the world of *Emma*.

In short, if *Emma* is a curiously troublesome novel, it is so because Emma Woodhouse, as Jane Austen anticipated, is a curiously troublesome character. And if *Emma* can be said to have a "subject," that subject must be Emma herself: *Emma* is Emma's book—in a way, for instance, that *Sense and Sensibility* is not Elinor's nor *Pride and Prejudice* Elizabeth's nor *Mansfield Park* Fanny's. The opening phrase ("Emma Woodhouse, handsome, clever, and rich") precisely prepares us for what follows—a full and exact portrait in which language and action so clearly focus on, so clearly define (and are defined by) Emma Woodhouse that the novel itself takes shape as a subtle process of defining and redefining what Emma is and is becoming.

Shifting focus from the subject of marriage to a complex, varied character will not itself suffice, however, to bring the troublesome aspects of *Emma* into sharp focus and fine harmony. What, we must ask, is the trouble with Emma? And in particular, what is the significance of the ironic incongruity between her active, clever, talented mind, her quick sensibility, and her prolonged, deeply misguided misunderstanding of her world and her self? Early and late Emma persists in misunderstandings—and does so despite clear warnings from Mr. Knightley and his brother about Mr. Elton; and from Mr. Knightley about Frank Churchill and Jane Fairfax.

Pride and vanity are in part responsible for Emma's troubles. For *Emma* is in part a rendering of the self-indulgence of a complexly self-involved self, and especially of the indulgence of that "very dear part of Emma, her fancy." To Arnold Kettle, for instance, Emma is "not merely spoilt and selfish" but "snobbish and proud"; and to Wayne Booth, Emma's "chief fault" is not price but a "lack of good will or tenderness" [see Additional Bibliography]. Yet, within the context of a world in which each abounds, Emma's pride and vanity, as well as her self-indulgence and lack of good will, merely raise the problem in another form: What precisely is the nature of Emma's version of these abstract traits? In a conversation with Mrs. Weston, Mr. Knightley draws an important distinction:

> . . . I do not think her personally vain. Considering how very handsome she is, she appears to be little occupied with it; her vanity lies in another way."

What then is the direction of Emma's vanity, and how do her vanity and self-indulgence differ from Mr. Woodhouse's and Miss Bates's, or from Mrs. Elton's and Frank Churchill's? Perhaps Emma's vanity and self-indulgence appear more interesting and more attractive than similar qualities in other characters simply because we see her world much as she sees it. But perhaps, on the other hand, we can discern a unique pattern in Emma's version of these traits; and perhaps in the process we can illuminate, first Emma and the secret recesses of her world, and then what Mr. Knightley calls "an anxiety, a curiosity in what one feels for Emma" and for "what will become of her."

Two "real evils," we are told, threaten Emma from the outset: "the power of having rather too much her own way, and a disposition to think too well of herself." In part these twin "evils" find expression in the ordinary tendency to want to be first and to be admired. But in short order more complex ramifications emerge to control the action of the novel. Because she demands a kind of variety and excitement life cannot supply, Emma allows her fancy and imagination to shape and distort her perception of reality; and because she demands harmony and symmetry life cannot attain, she permits herself to meddle and interfere with the lives of other people. What Emma consistently desires and frequently demands is not simply that her world admire her; it also must be as rich and vital and beautiful as she feels herself potentially to be. Emma accordingly cherishes all of the beauty of texture and structure which life can command. When it becomes necessary, however, she sets out "to superintend" the "happiness" of others. What she demands is that life follow her lead in uniting "the best blessings of existence" and in minimizing everything which seems only "to distress and vex." The crux of the matter, then, is the peculiar way in which Emma's life depends upon and is dedicated to richness and beauty in human experience. At this point Emma moves far beyond determination to be one on whom nothing in life is lost: she is also determined that life shall be—almost in each immediate moment—eminently worthy of not being lost; that it shall combine harmony, radiance, and beauty; that it shall couple perfect form within finite content.

Viewed in this manner, *Emma* becomes, in essence, a structured action in which Jane Austen renders both the nobility and the dangers, the significance and the consequences of Emma's endeavor to force an aesthetic ideal upon her world. (pp. 49-51)

Constructive, creative design and action, not perverse endeavor, are . . . characteristic of Emma's rage for perfect order. Early in the novel, shortly before Harriet comes to the fore,

Emma decides that she "must look about for a wife for Mr. Elton. There is nobody in Highbury who deserves him." Emma obviously means that there is no one in Highbury who is exactly appropriate, who deserves and is deserved by Mr. Elton. A short time later she sees a similar inappropriateness, a similar danger of waste, in Harriet's situation. Harriet's beauty and natural grace—as Emma sees it—simply "should not be wasted . . . inferior society" that is "unworthy of her." The thought of being able to make Harriet "quite perfect"—of being able to improve and reform her—and of being able to place her in a suitable situation strikes Emma as interesting, kind, and appropriate.

> She was so busy in admiring those soft blue eyes, in talking and listening, and forming all these schemes in the in-betweens, that the evening flew away at a very unusual rate. . . . With an alacrity beyond the common impulse of a spirit which yet was never indifferent to the credit of doing every thing well and attentively, with the real good-will of *a mind delighted with its own ideas,* did she then do all the honours of the meal . . . (emphasis added).

"Quick and decided in her ways, Emma lost no time": darkened only by the ominous overtones injected with the word "schemes," Emma's comprehensive design takes shape rapidly. And it too is riddled with irony. Harriet is to be made "perfect" for Mr. Elton so that a perfect marriage can follow. Terms such as "exact," "precise," and "perfect" characterize Emma's entire endeavor to make real her idea of a marriage that will be completely commensurate with (her interpretation of) the situations of both parties.

With skill and dedication Emma begins the task of making life interesting and orderly, and of making the process of putting things right rich and exciting in itself. Given her total misunderstanding of Mr. Elton's intentions and interests and character, Emma sees little trouble in preparing Mr. Elton for perfect marital bliss with Harriet. With Harriet, however, Emma's problem is more complex. She must not only begin "creating" in Harriet admiration and affection for Mr. Elton; she must also make Harriet equal to the match. The full impact of Emma's design is central to the total language and action of the novel. But the compelling core of the matter is clearly disclosed in Emma's portrait of Harriet.

> There was not want of likeness . . . and as *she meant to throw in a little improvement* to the figure, to give a little *more height,* and considerable *more elegance,* she had great confidence of its being *in every way* a pretty drawing at last, and of its filling *its destined* place with credit to them both—a standing memorial of the *beauty* of one, the skill of the other, and the *friendship* of both; with as many other *agreeable associations* as Mr. Elton's very promising attachment was very likely to add (emphases added).

Together Mrs. Weston and Mr. Knightley see what Emma has done in her portrait: she has given Harriet "the only beauty she wanted" and has "made her too tall." Emma, of course, refuses to admit what she has done in the portrait, just as she refuses to recognize what she is trying to do to life. But Jane Austen is careful to define what Emma is about. If necessary she will do violence to life in order to make the relationship between Harriet and Mr. Elton "shape itself into the proper form"; for she is determined to give love "exactly the right direction" and to send "it into the very channel where it ought to flow."

Emma's plan fails, of course. Incoercible and unyielding, life resists Emma's effort to impose her will. Here as elsewhere, irony runs deep. The more Emma endeavors to impose her will and way on the world, the more that world resists and imposes itself on her. While she seeks "to superintend" Mr. Elton's happiness, he is working to botch her whole design. (Later, in a similarly ironic way, both Frank Churchill and Harriet are arrayed against Emma.) Intoxicated by her plan, by the beauty of her idea, Emma is led to persist, despite repeated warnings, in a gross misunderstanding of her world. And when recognition comes—when reality intrudes with all its matter-of-factness and imposes itself on Emma; when she suddenly finds "her hand seized . . . her attention demanded, and Mr. Elton actually making violent love to her"—irritation and disappointment combine with remorse to plunge her into "perturbation" and "pain and humiliation."

Recognition of involvement, of having committed "the first error and the worst," and having "made every thing bend" to her own "idea," evokes a dual response, first of repentance—she'd been adventuring too far, assuming too much"—and second of resolution—she would be "humble and discreet . . . repressing imagination all the rest of her life." Emma's drive for rich and formal perfection is, of course, not easily bridled. She promptly sets about correcting the situation in which she has involved Harriet; until that had been accomplished "Emma felt . . . there could be no true peace for herself." In numerous ways, Emma proceeds to entangle herself in misunderstandings and distortions. By trying to make life commensurate with her demands, Emma unintentionally contributes handsomely to a context in which irony multiplies. Once again reality reverses the process, imposing itself on Emma, proving to her that she lives and moves in a stubbornly limited world.

Emma, however, proves less intractable. Her accommodation, not life's, provides the basis of resolution. Gradually Emma perceives and accepts what repeated encounters with reality reveal to her. Once again she learns that her attempts, however well-intentioned, to impose her will and way have led to misunderstanding and to injury; and that obstinate devotion to her own desires and designs has done more than distort perception and understanding, that it has permitted her world in general and Frank Churchill in particular to impose themselves on her. Yet neither of these insights is dominant in shaping Emma's turnabout. Only with knowledge, first, that her preoccupation with impossible demands has kept her from adequate self-knowledge, and second, that she has almost sacrificed the possible (especially her marriage to Mr. Knightley and Harriet's to Robert Martin) to the impossible, is Emma ready to accept her world. Only then can she view the real world as in its own way admirably rich and worthily ordered, however imperfectly, however unideally. And only then is she ready to accept the task of working out her life in the context of the possible.

From "her past folly" Emma acquires the only kind of "humility" that will speak to her kind of vanity and her kind of insensitivity. In light of her own folly, with new humility regarding both the beauty of her own ideas and her ability to implement them creatively rather than destructively, Emma moves to a different kind of hope.

> [The] only source whence any thing like consolation or composure could be drawn, was in the resolution of her own better conduct, and the hope that, however inferior in spirit and gaiety might be the following and every future winter of her life to the past, it would

yet find her more rational, more acquainted with herself, and leave her less to regret when it were gone.

Within the world of *Emma,* the alteration disclosed in these
lines constitutes a move toward wisdom, a move which provides the only quality Emma needs for marriage to Mr. Knightley.

The denouement of *Emma* constitutes a resolution of the conflict between Emma's demands—between her imagination, her
fancy, and her will to impose on one side; and her world, her
stubbornly incoercible, stubbornly limited world on the other.
Both that conflict and its resolution are rendered with consummate skill. But in part the beauty of the novel derives from
the beauty inherent in Emma's drive. For that drive points to
more than the vital energy of youth, even to more than profound
love of life. In calling for richness in the texture of life, in
demanding formal harmony, and in insisting that life permit
varied possibility for economical self-assertion and exertion,
Emma's struggle gives expression to perennial human aspiration and to eternal human longing.

Only the precise form that Emma's vanity and insensitivity
take allows Mr. Knightley—who "was one of the few people
who could see faults in Emma Woodhouse"—finally to see
her as "the sweetest and best of all creatures, faultless in spite
of all her faults." The cosmic irony which makes Emma's
drive for beauty self-destructive and world disruptive defies
only Emma's insistent, imprudent will to impose; it does not
deny the nobility and special relevance of the ideal. It is accordingly thematically necessary—however "unrealisitc"—that
Emma's world finally discipline her with a gentle hand. Despite
the earnest adjustment her world demands of the more Romantic aspects of her sensibility, and despite the price it exacts
for insistent conflict, that world permits, even encourages Emma
to adjust without sacrificing her own integrity and without
being totally crushed. While turning her assault back upon its
source, Emma's world does not preclude tension. To the contrary, while demanding appreciation, that world also permits
critical response to its standards and values; it permits a distinctly personal and individual sense of "style"; and it encourages the emergence of both a principled consciousness and
an ordered knowledge of self and world. In this respect, the
world of *Emma* is hopeful. More than either Fanny Price or
Elinor Dashwood, perhaps even more than Elizabeth Bennet,
Emma learns to curb, control, and direct, and yet to retain a
strong and lively imagination. By training and yet retaining
that "very dear part of [her], her fancy," Emma emerges with
an imaginative, individual sensibility, which is at the same
time humane and refined, cultured and civilized. In rendering
that adjustment, in what is perhaps her most perfectly achieved
work, Jane Austen made the only peace she thought worth
making with the Romantic mind. (pp. 55-9)

> *David Lee Minter, "Aesthetic Vision and the World
> of 'Emma'," in* Nineteenth-Century Fiction, *Vol. 21,
> No. 1, June, 1966, pp. 49-59.*

T. B. TOMLINSON (essay date 1966)

[*In this excerpt, Tomlinson suggests that Austen's ironic stance
and characterizations in* Emma *are more complex and original
than has been recognized. The critic also questions Marvin Mudrick's view of the function of irony in the novel (see excerpt dated
1952).*]

Jane Austen's work is misjudged, I think, by those who see
her as representing her times, or expressing more clearly what
others also then felt or saw. For all its settled, and at points

rather too cosy, atmosphere, it is much more creative, more
unforeseen, than that. . . . [The] ease with which Jane Austen
imagines people—as Knightley, Emma, Elizabeth Bennet, Mr
Woodhouse, etc.—who are also and at the same time much
more than just individual "characters", is practically unrivalled in English literature before the nineteenth century.
Shakespeare can do this and a great deal more beside; so perhaps, in a very different way, can Pope. But these are exceptions, and would be so in any age. Jane Austen's own originality is best described as an extraordinary turn of mind that
can make Emma, say, or Elizabeth Bennet, at once a person
to be reckoned with, manifestly alive and real throughout the
length of the novel, and at the same time an issue, a generalizing tendency, a habit of thought and action, an idea. With
her, the people in a drama and the ideas in it are indistinguish-
able. In the same way her various and varying country estates
are at the same time real and also notions, hypotheses, possibilities in the mind.

At one point late on in *Northanger Abbey* Jane Austen says:
". . . there are some situations of the human mind in which
good sense has very little power." This is a simple statement
of what I would claim is one of her main, but largely unrecognized, interests, and it points to the source of her freshness
and individuality. She is always, of course, a novelist who
pins a great deal of faith on the actual, the sensible, the rational;
and the sense of her delight in intelligently and precisely *ordering* her world so predominates as to give that impression,
by which she is commonly known, of backing unequivocally
the commonsense of an Elizabeth Bennet, an Elinor Dashwood
or an Anne Elliot. And in *Emma,* though the heroine is deluded,
the book for the most part is not.

[It] is possible, and usual, to stress too much or too exclusively
Jane Austen's dependence on a sort of sensitive rationalism.
The significance of that sentence from *Northanger Abbey* is
that it is said with no feeling of regret or impatience at the
powerlessness of good sense in "some situations of the human
mind". A clearer case still—in some ways too clear—is *Sense
and Sensibility* where, despite the many accounts of the novel
that take the sensible Elinor Dashwood as clearly and unam-
biguously her sister's superior, Marianne's impulsiveness (and
indeed Mrs Jennings's) is obviously essential to the book. Where
Elinor's "sense" is sceptical, they show an ability to commit
themselves fully, immediately and single-mindedly to a person
or situation or event. The social blunders and thoughtless-
nesses, and the disaster that follows with Willoughby, are far
from a simple condemnation of such an outlook and personality. Jane Austen is prepared to *trust* emotion here, for all the
risks involved.

Emma, however, is the most interesting case of all and the one
on which I would like to concentrate. In *Emma* Jane Austen
is finding the merely or purely "sensible" much more elusive,
and therefore still less trustworthy, or less self-sufficient, than
when she has it focused mainly in the one figure of Elinor
Dashwood. Curiously enough this results, not in any uncertainty or hesitation in the prose, but in an evident and generous
interest in the phenomena of an Emma, a Mr Woodhouse advising a little thin gruel and lightly boiled eggs, or even a Miss
Bates chattering mindlessly. Except for the Eltons and their
barouche-landau relations, Jane Austen is immediately and actively involved in almost everything she contemplates in this
novel.

This is why one's first impressions, on reading those famous
opening pages of *Emma,* are of an assured, well-placed con-

An illustration of the ball scene in Emma.

fidence. The book is tinged from the first line with an irony expectant of delusion and uncertainty in Emma's future; but to read this prose as predominantly ironic or critical or conservative would surely be to misread the tone of the whole book:

> Emma Woodhouse, handsome, clever, and rich, with
> a comfortable home and happy disposition seemed
> to unite some of the best blessings of existence; and
> had lived nearly twenty-one years in the world with
> very little to distress or vex her. . . .

The impulse here is surely forward-looking. The precision and ease of the writing obviously owe a lot to the eighteenth century (though not specifically to any of the well-known novelists except possibly Richardson), but what seems to me far more striking than any debt to the past is a sense of discovery and newness. The wandering bachelordom of Moll Flanders, Roderick Random, Humphrey Clinker, Tom Jones, adventurous though this might seem in theory, is here outdated in a few paragraphs and replaced by an entirely different, and far more interesting, sense of discovery.

Immediately, and most simply, the confidence is a confidence in the heroine herself. Jane Austen begins the novel by mixing her own account with a generous and open sharing of Emma's content and happiness: "Emma Woodhouse, handsome, clever, and rich . . ." This is, as it were, "Jane Austen" governed at

this point by something that is almost "Emma's" own confident tone and outlook. The second and third paragraphs then move into a tone of more precise, sharply factual, summary ("She was the youngest of two daughters of a most affectionate, indulgent father . . ."); but in a sentence this can change again to an alertly ironic indulgence (itself different in tone from the opening sentence) of Emma's outlook. It is almost Emma herself speaking in the special-pleading that follows the account of Miss Taylor's fondness for her: "Between *them* it was more the intimacy of sisters. . . ." The quick, assured changes of voice and outlook here are themselves a most important local sign of Jane Austen's having discovered a fresh and substantial interest that enlivens and transforms what would otherwise be a stiffly conventional social outlook. Another is the risks she is prepared and willing to take in backing—much more fully and wholeheartedly than most of her critics seem prepared to allow—her deluded heroine.

It therefore does Jane Austen no service to see *Emma* as a book that is "perfect of its kind". For one thing it isn't perfect; more importantly, this very common approach fails completely to capture the note in the prose that welcomes difficulties and disturbances. Her main endeavour, I take it, is to re-form and establish imaginatively a certain stability in social norms and personal relationships like marriage. In the act of doing this, however (of showing, for instance, how and why Knightley must marry Emma, and could not possibly marry Jane Fairfax, let alone Harriet), she discovers fresh instabilities in her society which answer to fresh instabilities that spring from her own steadying, normative outlook, and are equally important. Some of these difficulties she obviously fails to meet, or fails to meet fully. Most, however, are not merely "met" or subjugated or distanced by irony, but actively welcomed as the staple of the book's interest.

In this connexion there is one very interesting, but I think in the end crucially misleading, account of *Emma*: that in Marvin Mudrick's book, *Jane Austen: Irony as Defense and Discovery* Mudrick does demonstrate, as nobody else I know has, Jane Austen's tendency to use irony not only as a means of criticizing and shaping her "social" world, but also of warding off the impact of deeper and more unsettling "discoveries" in love and marriage. In the particular case of *Emma,* however, Mudrick thinks that she has solved these difficulties (". . . the sense of strain and anxiety is purged altogether"). I would myself dispute this sort of perfection as at all applicable to *Emma*: even the surface seems much more disturbed than Mudrick allows. More interestingly, however, I think Mudrick has distorted his own very important insight into the book by attempting to subsume it under the notion of a perfection of form.

"Irony as Form" is the title of his chapter, and its bearing is to see Jane Austen as very calmly, precisely, "noncommittally" evaluating this apparently charming girl as having no other real qualities—a certain "very circumscribed honesty" apart—than surface charm. Mudrick charts the very complex ways in which, for him, Emma's true companions are finally seen to be Frank Churchill and Mrs Elton. Mrs Elton is "too transparently vulgar to be effective" socially, but the other two seduce everybody, even Mr Knightley, by their charm; only the reader, through Jane Austen's poised art, remains immune:

> Emma's and Frank Churchill's society, which makes
> so much of surface, guarantees the triumph of surface. Even Mr Knightley and Jane Fairfax succumb.
> Jane Austen, however, does not ask us to concern

ourselves beyond the happy ending: she merely presents the evidence, noncommittally.

Well, in the first place there seems to me a clear and obvious distinction between Emma's charm, which Jane Austen (for all the criticisms that Mudrick rightly shows her to be making of it) obviously admires, and Frank Churchill's, which by comparison she sees as indeed frivolous and, despite some elements of genuineness, finally untrustworthy. There is also the simple fact that Frank Churchill's deceptions are largely deliberate, Emma's hardly ever so. As for Mrs Elton, it would seem to me more relevant to see Jane Austen's portrayal as on the edge of uncontrolled hatred than to see parallels, which are hardly more than casual, with Emma.... Mudrick has failed to read the book accurately; *Emma* is more imperfect, and Jane Austen more adventurous, than he sees. Certainly there is no sense that I can see in which she could be said to be "noncommittal".

In the place of any attempt to subsume the book under a notion of poised or noncommittal irony, I would suggest, first of all, looking at Jane Austen's active interest in situations such as those where John Knightley, having struggled to contain it at Hartfield, openly betrays his irritability at being expected to conform socially. This is more than the irritation at Mr Woodhouse's hypochondria that Mudrick, overstressing the emptiness of Emma's world and Emma's father, notes. It is often sparked off by that, but by other things as well, for instance by Mr Elton and the need to dine away from home: "I know nothing of the large parties of London, sir—I never dine with anybody."

His irritability is, in fact, an expression of something ungovernable in, probably, both the Knightleys, and Jane Austen's attention is on what this quality may do to hypotheses of containment, order, propriety.

Bulking larger in the novel is that case where chance, and some curiously submerged facets of character, make the sensible and elegantly accomplished Jane Fairfax fall in love with Frank Churchill, and furthermore return to him despite her evident distress at his public flirting with Emma, and his equally public tormenting of her over that wretched piano. Mr Knightley's condemnation of Churchill—"His letters disgust me"—is surprisingly vehement in context, and of course obviously partial since he senses Churchill as a rival for Emma; but it is also very largely right; and if one merely took Jane Austen as intent on illustrating decorum and proportion in marriage, or (which is closer to Mudrick's position) maintaining a poised irony about it, one would surely expect her to condemn this marriage of Frank and Jane as offending against every notion of judgment and good sense. Knightley is right about it, and Jane Austen herself clearly knows that there is indeed an instability in a union that must depend so much on the oddness of Jane's attraction to a shallow, irresponsible man. But Jane Austen does not condemn the marriage, or even remain uncommitted about it: we are left with the clear sense that it is more likely to succeed than fail. I think we must conclude that, for all her firmness and decision in these matters, Jane Austen takes a greater interest in deviations from rational behaviour than any simple moralist would, or any simple ironist; the possibility of instability in the Jane Fairfax-Frank Churchill marriage is not merely real to her, but as fruitful an interest as the certainty of stability and good sense (for all the struggles between them) in Knightley's marriage with Emma.

To put the same point differently: she is as interested in and as stimulated by the aberrations—I am tempted to say the suppressed turbulence—in Emma and in Mr Knightley himself as she is in their resolve and firmness of character. Mr Knightley's bluntness of manner and his irritability, particularly when these are stimulated by opposition and intransigence in Emma, are rather like the qualities of a minor Dr Johnson. He is eminently a man of sense, certainly a leader, and Emma's charmingly unguarded praise of him to Mrs Weston over the gift of the piano is thoroughly just: "I do not think it at all a likely thing for him to do. Mr Knightley does nothing mysteriously." But he is also a man whose forcefulness goes even deeper than his reasonableness: "A degradation to illegitimacy and ignorance, to be married to a respectable, intelligent, gentleman-farmer?" "Vanity working on a weak head produces every sort of mischief.... Men of sense, whatever you may choose to say, do not want silly wives." This is indeed close to the accents and mode of Johnson himself, and includes something of his unconforming energies. The outline of the long argument between Knightley and Emma from which the last two quotations come (Chapter VIII) accords entirely and predictably with Jane Austen's sense of propriety, with Knightley clearly in the right about Harriet and Robert Martin, and Emma disastrously in the wrong; but its reverberations go beyond that rational good sense of Knightley's and link him with Emma's own intransigence. Sensible though he clearly is, he is depending here on a blunt forcefulness whose roots are not entirely in the reasoning mind.

As the novel progresses, it becomes unmistakably clear that both Emma and Knightley unexpectedly diverge from the usual and the conventional, at least as much as they agree in support of it. There is one very interesting passage of hectic special-pleading from Emma where she attempts to prove to Mrs Weston that Mr Knightley is like herself in that he is a man who does not want to marry. Hearing Mrs Weston's conjecture ("In short, I have made a match between Mr Knightley and Jane Fairfax. See the consequence of keeping you company!...") she bursts out:

> "Mr Knightley and Jane Fairfax!... Dear Mrs Weston, how could you think of such a thing?—Mr Knightley!—Mr Knightley must not marry!—You would not have little Henry cut out from Donwell?—Oh, no, no, Henry must have Donwell. I cannot at all consent to Mr Knightley marrying; and I am sure it is not at all likely...."

She is of course saying this far more for her own sake (though perfectly unconscious of any selfish motive) than for little Henry whose claims are largely forgotten when, much later, Knightley proposes to her; and she is forced, by Mrs Weston's sensible logic ("I am not speaking of its prudence; merely its probability"), to rationalize helplessly:

> "But Mr Knightley does not want to marry. I am sure he has not the least idea of it. Do not put it into his head. Why should he marry?..."

But the interesting thing is that, for all the obvious self-justification and rationalizing here, Emma is not altogether off the mark about Knightley. There is something odd about a man of his stamp seeming so placidly content to live at Donwell and allow William Larkins and Mrs Hodges to regulate his domestic life for him—even down to details like the number of apples he may keep for his own use or give to a friend! ("William Larkins let me keep a larger quantity than usual this year.") The strong sense of principle that makes Knightley a leader in society and public affairs could not be half as strong as it is if it weren't at odds with—indeed partly suppressing and constricting—an almost opposite quality of impetuous and very strong feeling. Equally, there is an interesting contradiction between the strong and warm feeling he shows for Emma, and the contained bachelordom that has now lasted nearly to the age of forty. There is always a hint of some tension underlying Knightley's firm composure. It is this that makes Emma's wild comments on his not marrying partly true; and it is a related tension that underpins his qualities as a leader. In a different way, the same is true of Emma herself. For despite her extraordinary—and harmful—mistakes in judgment, she too is surely seen by Jane Austen as a leader, and this partly *because of* the impetuosity that also causes her blunders.

This is borne out by the dominance of the scene at the Box Hill picnic and the oddness or unexpectedness of Emma's role in it. Ostensibly, and certainly to the conscious mind of Emma herself reflecting on it afterwards, this scene is a condemnation of her irresponsibility and cruelty to Miss Bates. So indeed it is; but the extraordinary thing about it, and what escapes easy summaries on the level of ethics and social conduct, is the strength of the impulse that drives Emma to act as she does in those (surely perfectly ordinary) circumstances. As Mr Knightley's dismayed condemnation makes clear, it is more than mere thoughtlessness, or mere irritation at the Eltons. To put the whole situation in more modern, and perhaps too explicit, terms: there is a high charge of emotional and sexual energies and frustrations permeating the social comedy, and these focus on Emma's role in it. The "comedy" is not at all unlike, for instance, those scenes in the schoolroom and cottage early on in *Women in Love* where Ursula, Gudrun, Birkin, Gerald and Hermione confront each other in "social" terms, at the same time, however, revealing the generative and disruptive forces beneath the merely social. In *Emma,* at Box Hill, the heroine is caught in a situation where her playful match-making—comparatively innocent up to now—will no longer answer, or free her from mounting pressures and annoyances. She is therefore forced to channel her considerable energies and quickness of mind into an unexpectedly vicious attack. It is not for nothing (though wholly unconscious on Emma's part and indeed on Jane Austen's) that the object of her attack is the manifestly unmarriageable and completely innocent and harmless Miss Bates.

An account like Mudrick's would put this down as a charge against Emma's ruthlessly efficient charm, aided and abetted as she is by Churchill in this scene. In fact, of course, Emma is sincerely sorry for it, and accepts the justness of Mr Knightley's rebuke. The novel itself accepts Emma's impulse, however, even more fully than Knightley in the end does. It *is* a disruptive and destructive impulse; the comedy of the scene . . . does not attempt to disguise this. But it is also the same impulse or set of impulses as that which generates Emma's lively intelligence and through this animates the whole book.

If the book nevertheless remains clearer and firmer in outline than any later novel in English could possibly do, the clarity does not depend on previously established, rock-bottom notions of ethics or morality. In *Emma* especially, Jane Austen's clarity of mind emerges from, but is still always tinged and invigorated by, all sorts of error and confusion. Confusion bred it, at least in part.

But this is to talk as if the novel were indeed perfect, flawless. I don't want to catalogue imperfections here, but merely to state that they exist and, more importantly, that they represent certain limits to Jane Austen's originality, certain points where she is forced to retreat rather than explore further. The retreat

is observable in the way in which the irony of situation is kept up for so long; so that there are places where, since no further discovery about Emma's delusions is possible, the neatness of the irony draws attention to itself, rather than to anything it might reveal or release. This is true not merely at the end, with Emma's mistakes about Mr Knightley, but even at Box Hill where she jumps to the conclusion (surely unlikely, even given Emma's blindnesses in matchmaking!) that Frank Churchill's frivolous prescriptions for a wife might perhaps point to Harriet. In these examples the irony is needlessly insistent, and this is the more disappointing because it is clearly a failure of imagination and nerve rather than of "technique".

Something similar might be said of the social world of *Emma* considered as a whole. There is Abbey Mill Farm—quite well done, but clearly not in any sense a full-scale treatment of issues about rural communities and hence not a major extension of the Highbury horizons. There are also the Coles. The Coles are well and humanly treated by Jane Austen, but all the time it is clear that they are so because they keep their place. In the novel, they must assimilate themselves to Mr Knightley's world, not at all he to theirs. If the Coles keep their proper distance they may, the novel implies, grow into the neighbourhood and share some of its virtues; but clearly it never occurs to Jane Austen that such people, having made their money in Trade, could possibly bring anything that might add to or challenge Highbury life. By contrast the Eltons, with their pushing vulgarity, represent a threat to Knightley's and Emma's world that Jane Austen only *just* manages to contemplate steadily. By her marriage, Emma will be saved from seeing Mrs Elton taking precedence at Highbury dinners, but this is hardly a confident facing by Jane Austen of what common knowledge would have shown to be an increasing, rather than a diminishing, threat. In sum, there are moments in the novel when one feels the presence of a slightly too easy reliance on the myth of Donwell and Hartfield as all-embracing, protective.

This is related, finally, to self-protection of a much more personal kind that spoils one crucial scene at the end: Emma's acceptance of Knightley's proposal.

> She spoke then, on being so entreated. What did she say? Just what she ought, of course. A lady always does. She said enough to show there need not be despair—and to invite him to say more himself.

This is coyness taking over from confident irony. Irony alone would anyway be insufficient for this scene, but Jane Austen clearly shies away from any confident involvement in Emma's deeper feelings at this particular point. As Mudrick has very convincingly documented, this abrupt shying away from emotional involvement is typical of at any rate the earlier Jane Austen, though it is a bit unexpected if one takes *Emma* (as he does) to be much more poised and expert than earlier, or even later novels. As I have said, I think the truer view is that *Emma* is far from the perfectly poised and distanced irony Mudrick sees in it. It is taking more risks than he supposes, and its doing so is one of the things that makes it, I think, clearly her best novel. But by the same token—Jane Austen being what she is—the novel is subject to certain fits of regression. Jane Austen doesn't actually run for cover when faced with the Eltons, but her habit in treating them is to look back to established defences, rather than forward to the unknown and (at least partly) feared. With a subject that cuts much closer to the bone still—Emma's private, emotional involvement—there is at least this one moment when she had to cover up and retreat almost out of view behind the defensive, sheltering irony that marks her letters and some of her earlier work. Knightley's actual proposal is the one moment Jane Austen really fears, partly because (*pace* Mudrick) she is indeed thoroughly involved with Emma.

Personally I am very happy to leave the novel's success as largely dependent on Emma and Knightley, and on Jane Austen's close involvement with them. In most of the book, she is as open and frank as her own very engaging heroine. ("The truth is, Harriet, that my playing is just good enough to be praised, but Jane Fairfax's is much beyond it.") From the whole book it is clear that openness and frankness of this kind are very much admired by Jane Austen. There is even a self-identification (of novelist and heroine) that in most other writers would be dangerous, because likely to end in sentimentality. George Eliot is the obvious comparison here; but Jane Austen's evident liking for Emma (and through her, for Knightley) is a projection of some part of herself much wittier, much more confidently and alertly prepared for whatever blunders she or her heroine may make, than the side of George Eliot that produced Maggie Tulliver and Dorothea. To do George Eliot only common justice, her books range beyond the compass of Jane Austen's—there are simply more and greater difficulties in them for the author/heroine to meet. But Jane Austen is still doing more than prudently staying within bounds; and she is certainly doing more than regarding her foolishly adventurous heroine with a composed, ironic assurance. She is closer to admiring Emma wholeheartedly, than to exposing her weaknesses from the vantage-point of a secure and traditionally established position, when she gives her, in the penultimate chapter, the coolly demanding reply to Knightley's objection:

> "Do you dare say this?" cried Mr Knightley. "Do you dare to suppose me so great a blockhead as not to know what a man is talking of? What do you deserve?"
>
> "Oh! I always deserve the best treatment, because I never put up with any other; and, therefore, you must give me a plain, direct, answer. . . ."

It is obvious that, in the personality of Emma, the good and the less than good are mingled. This is a truism, and would apply to anybody, fictional or real. What is not so obvious is Jane Austen's intuition that good sense and worth may, in some way very hard to define outside the crisp, lively prose of the novel itself, actually draw strength from silliness, confusion, misjudgment. Jane Austen's claim—conscious or unconscious doesn't matter here—is that Emma's impulsiveness (and hence her snobbery, her mistakes with Harriet, her insults to Miss Bates) is so much a part of her engaging frankness and resolution that the two are mutually dependent: the frankness and openness spring from the same impulsiveness that constantly and at times disastrously tempts her. Indeed this is true of the book as a whole, not just of its heroine. Some narrowness and hesitations aside, Jane Austen's originality in *Emma* is to formulate, almost for the first time in English literature, the sense in which the good qualities in and of a whole society like that of Highbury may actively depend on the bad, or at least on impulses that must also result in foolishness, misjudgment, at times active cruelty. (pp. 27-37)

T. B. Tomlinson, "Jane Austen's Originality: 'Emma'," in The Critical Review, *Melbourne, No. 9, 1966, pp. 23-37.*

ARNOLD KETTLE (essay date 1967)

[*Kettle discusses Austen's treatment of the social issues inherent in interpersonal relationships, particularly marriage. He con-* *cludes that while the value of* Emma *is diminished by the inadequacies of Austen's conventional social outlook, the novel succeeds within its limited scope.*]

The subject of *Emma* is marriage. Put that way the statement seems ludicrously inadequate, for *Emma*—we instinctively feel—is not about anything that can be put into one word. And yet it is as well to begin by insisting that this novel does have a subject. There is no longer, especially after Mrs Leavis's articles [see excerpt dated 1941 in *NCLC*, Vol.1], any excuse for thinking of Jane Austen as an untutored genius or even as a kind aunt with a flair for telling stories that have somehow or other continued to charm. She was a serious and conscious writer, absorbed in her art, wrestling with its problems. Casting and recasting her material, transferring whole novels from letter to narrative form, storing her subject-matter with meticulous economy, she had the great artist's concern with form and presentation. There is nothing soft about her.

Emma is about marriage. It begins with one marriage, that of Miss Taylor, ends with three more and considers two others by the way. The subject is marriage; but not marriage in the abstract. There is nothing of the moral fable here; indeed it is impossible to conceive of the subject except in its concrete expression, which is the plot. If, then, one insists that the subject of *Emma* is important it is not in order to suggest that the novel can be read in the terms of *Jonathan Wild*, but rather to counteract the tendency to treat plot or story as self-sufficient. If it is not quite adequate to say that *Emma* is about marriage it is also not adequate to say it is about Emma.

The concrete quality of the book, that is what has to be emphasised. We have no basic doubts about *Emma.* It is there, a living organism, and it survives in the vibrations of its own being. In *Clarissa* time and again out attention is shifted in a particular direction not because it *must* be so directed but because Richardson wishes to give his reader an 'exquisite sensation'; in *Tom Jones* the happenings are too often contrived, so that we sense Fielding's presence behind the scenes, pulling a string. But *Emma* lives with the inevitable, interlocking logic of life itself; no part of it is separable from any other part. Even those episodes of the plot which seem at first mere contrivances to arouse a little suspense and keep the story going (such as the mystery of the pianoforte, Jane's letters at the post office, the confusion as to whether Harriet referred to Mr Knightley or to Frank Churchill), such passages all have a more important purpose. They reveal character, or they fail to reveal it. This latter function is subtle and important.

Jane Austen, like Henry James, is fascinated by the complexities of personal relationships. What is a character *really* like? Is Frank Churchill *really* a bounder? She conveys the doubt, not in order to trick, but in order to deepen. The more complex characters in *Emma,* like people in life, reveal themselves gradually and not without surprises. Putting aside for the moment certain minor faults which we will return to, it is not an exaggeration to say that *Emma* is as convincing as our own lives and has the same kind of concreteness.

It is for this reason that the subject of *Emma,* its generalised significance, is not easily or even usefully abstracted from the story. Just as in real life 'marriage' (except when we are considering it in a very theoretical and probably not very helpful way) is not a problem we abstract from the marriages we know, so marriage in *Emma* is thought of entirely in terms of actual and particular personal relationships. If we learn more about marriage in general from Jane Austen's novel it is because we have learned more—that is to say experienced more—about particular marriages. We do, in fact, in reading *Emma* thus enrich our experience. We become extremely closely involved in the world of Hartfield so that we experience the precise quality of, say, Mr Woodhouse's affection for his daughters, or Harriet's embarrassment at meeting the Martins in the draper's. When Emma is rude to Miss Bates on Box Hill we *feel* the flush rise to Miss Bates's cheek.

The intensity of Jane Austen's novels is inseparable from their concreteness and this intensity must be stressed because it is so different from the charming and cosy qualities with which these novels are often associated. Reading *Emma* is a delightful experience but it is not a soothing one. On the contrary our faculties are aroused, we are called upon to participate in life with an awareness, a fineness of feeling and a moral concern more intense than most of us normally bring to our everyday experiences. Everything matters in *Emma*. When Frank Churchill postpones his first visit to Randalls it matters less finely to Mr Weston than to his wife, but the reader gauges precisely the difference in the two reactions and not only appreciates them both but makes a judgment about them. We do not 'lose ourselves' in *Emma* unless we are the kind of people who lose ourselves in life. For all the closeness of our participation we remain independent.

Jane Austen does not demand . . . that our subjective involvement should prejudice our objective judgment. On the contrary a valid objective judgment is made possible just because we have been so intimately involved in the actual experience. This seems to me a very valuable state of mind. How can we presume to pass judgment on the Emma Woodhouses of the world unless we have known them, and how can we valuably know them without brining to bear our critical intelligence?

Because the critical intelligence is everywhere involved, because we are asked continuously, though not crudely, to judge what we are seeing, the prevailing interest in *Emma* is not one of mere 'aesthetic' delight but a moral interest. And because Jane Austen is the least theoretical of novelists, the least interested in Life as opposed to living, her ability to involve us intensely in her scene and people is absolutely inseparable from her moral concern. The moral is never spread on top; it is bound up always in the quality of feeling evoked.

Even when a moral conclusion is stated explicitly, as Mr Knightley states it after the Box Hill incident or while he reads Frank Churchill's letter of explanation, its force will depend not on its abstract 'correctness' but on the emotional conviction it carries, involving of course our already acquired confidence in Mr Knightley's judgment and character. Some of Mr Knightley's remarks, out of their context, might seem quite intolerably sententious.

> 'My Emma, does not everything serve to prove more and more the beauty of truth and sincerity in all our dealings with one another?'

The sentiment, abstracted, might serve for the conclusion of one of Hannah More's moral tales. In fact, in the novel, it is a moment of great beauty, backed as it is (even out of context the 'my Emma' may reveal something of the quality) by a depth of feeling totally convincing.

How does Jane Austen succeed in thus combining intensity with precision, emotional involvement with objective judgment? Part of the answer lies, I think, in her almost complete lack of idealism, the delicate and unpretentious materialism of her outlook. Her judgment is based never on some high-falutin irrelevancy but always on the actual facts and aspirations of her scene and people. The clarity of her social observation (the Highbury world is scrupulously seen and analysed down to the exact incomes of its inmates) is matched by the precision of her social judgments and all her judgments are, in the broadest sense, social. Human happiness not abstract principle is her concern. Such precision—it is both her incomparable strength and her ultimate limitation—is unimaginable except in an extraordinarily stable corner of society. The precision of her standards emerges in her style. Each word—'elegance,' 'humour,' 'temper,' 'ease'—has a precise unambiguous meaning based on a social usage at once subtle and stable. Emma is considering her first view of Mrs Elton:

> She did not really like her. She would not be in a hurry to find fault, but she suspected that there was no elegance;—ease, but no elegance—she was almost sure that for a young woman, a stranger, a bride, there was too much ease. Her person was rather good; her face not unpretty; but neither feature, nor air, nor voice, nor manner, were elegant. Emma thought at least it would turn out so.

The exquisite clarity, the sureness of touch, of Jane Austen's prose cannot be recaptured because in a different and quickly changing society the same sureness of values cannot exist.

But to emphasise the stability and, inevitably too, the narrowness of Jane Austen's society may lead us to a rather narrow and mechanical view of the novels. *Emma* is *not* a period-piece. It is *not* what is sometimes called a 'comedy of manners.' We read it not just to illuminate the past, but also the present. And we must here face in both its crudity and its importance the question: exactly what relevance and helpfulness does *Emma* have for us today? In what sense does a novel dealing (admittedly with great skill and realism) with a society and its standards dead and gone for ever have value in our very different world today? The question itself—stated in such terms—is not satisfactory. If *Emma* today captures our imagination and engages our sympathies (as in fact it does) then either it has some genuine value for us or else there is something wrong with the way we give our sympathy and our values are pretty useless.

Put this way, it is clear that anyone who enjoys *Emma* and then remarks 'but of course it has no relevance today' is in fact debasing the novel, looking at it not as the living work of art which he has just enjoyed, but as something he does not even think it is—a mere dead picture of a past society. Such an attitude is fatal both to art and to life. The more helpful approach is to enquire why it is that this novel does in fact still have the power to move us today. (pp.86-90)

The question has, I hope, been partly answered already. An extension of human sympathy and understanding is never irrelevant and the world of *Emma* is not presented to us (at any rate in its detail) with complacency. Emma faced with what she had done to Harriet, the whole humiliating horror of it, or Emma finding—the words are not minced—that, save for her feeling for Mr Knightley 'every other part of her mind was disgusting': these are not insights calculated to decrease one's moral awareness. And in none of the issues of conduct arising in the novel is Jane Austen morally neutral. The intensity with which everything matters to us in *Emma* is the product of this lack of complacency, this passionate concern of Jane Austen for human values. Emma is the heroine of this novel only in the sense that she is its principal character and that it is through her consciousness that the situations are revealed; she is no heroine in the conventional sense. She is not merely spoilt and selfish, she is snobbish and proud, and her snobbery leads her to inflict suffering that might ruin happiness. She has, until her experience and her feeling for Mr Knightley brings her to a fuller, more humane understanding, an attitude to marriage typical of the ruling class. She sees human relationships in terms of class snobbery and property qualifications: Harriet, for the sake of social position, she would cheerfully hand over to the wretched Elton and does in fact reduce to a humiliating misery; her chief concern about Mr Knightley is that his estate should be preserved for little Henry. It is only through her own intimate experiences (which we share) that she comes to a more critical and more fully human view. (p. 90)

Sufficient has perhaps been said to suggest that what gives *Emma* its power to move us is the realism and depth of feeling behind Jane Austen's attitudes. She examines with a scrupulous yet passionate and critical precision the actual problems of her world. That this world is narrow cannot be denied. How far its narrowness matters is an important question.

Its *smallness* does not matter at all. There is no means of measuring importance by size. What is valuable in a work of art are the depth and truth of the experience it communicates, and such qualities cannot be identified with the breadth of the panorama. We may find out more about life in a railway carriage between Crewe and Manchester than in making a tour round the world. A conversation between two women in the butcher's queue may tell us more about a world war than a volume of despatches from the front. And when Emma says to Mr Knightley: 'Nobody, who has not been in the interior of a family, can say what the difficulties of any individual of that family may be,' she is dropping a valuable hint about Jane Austen's method. The silliest of all criticisms of Jane Austen is the one which blames her for not writing about the battle of Waterloo and the French Revolution. She wrote about what she understood and no artist can do more.

But did she understand enough? The question is not a silly one, for it must be recognised that her world was not merely small but narrow. Her novels are sometimes referred to as miniatures, but the analogy is not apt. We do not get from *Emma* a condensed and refined sense of a larger entity. Neither is it a symbolic work suggesting references far beyond its surface meaning. The limitations of the Hartfield world which are indeed those of Surrey in about 1814 are likely therefore to be reflected in the total impact of the novel.

The limitation and the narrowness of the Hartfield world are the limitations of class society. And the one important criticism of Jane Austen . . . is that her vision is limited by her unquestioning acceptance of class society. That she did not write about the French Revolution or the Industrial Revolution is as irrelevant as that she did not write about the Holy Roman Empire; they were not her subjects. But Hartfield is her subject and no sensitive contemporary reader can fail to sense here an inadequacy. . . . It is necessary to insist, at this point, that the question at issue is not Jane Austen's failure to suggest a *solution* to the problem of class divisions but her apparent failure to notice the *existence* of the problem.

The values and standards of the Hartfield world are based on the assumption that it is right and proper for a minority of the community to live at the expense of the majority. No amount of sophistry can get away from this fact and to discuss the moral concern of Jane Austen without facing it would be hypocrisy. It is perfectly true that, within the assumptions of aristocratic society, the values recommended in *Emma* are sensitive enough. Snobbery, smugness, condescension, lack of consideration, unkindness of any description, are held up to our disdain. But the fundamental condescension, the basic unkindness which permits the sensitive values of *Emma* to be applicable only to one person in ten or twenty, is this not left unscathed? Is there not here a complacency which renders the hundred little incomplacencies almost irrelevant?

Now this charge, that the value of *Emma* is seriously limited by the class basis of Jane Austen's standards, cannot be ignored or written off as a non-literary issue. If the basic interest of the novel is indeed a moral interest, and if in the course of it we are called upon to re-examine and pass judgment on various aspects of human behaviour, then it can scarcely be considered irrelevant to face the question that the standards we are called upon to admire may be inseparably linked with a particular form of social organisation.

That the question is altogether irrelevant will be held, of course, by the steadily decreasing army of aesthetes. Those who try to divorce the values of art from those of life and consequently morality will not admit that the delight we find in reading *Emma* has in fact a moral basis. It is a position, I think, peculiarly hard to defend in the case of a Jane Austen novel, because of the obvious preoccupation of the novelist with social morality. If *Emma* is *not* concerned with the social values involved in and involving personal relationships (and especially marriage) it is difficult to imagine what it *is* about.

That the question though relevant is trivial will be held by those readers who consider class society either good or inevitable. Clearly to those who think aristocracy today a morally defensible form of society, and are prepared to accept (with whatever modifications and protestations of innocence) the inevitability of a cultural *élite* whose superior standards depend on a privileged social position based on the exploitation of their inferiors, clearly such readers will not feel that Jane Austen's acceptance of class society weakens or limits her moral perspicacity. The suspicion that the true elegance which Emma so values could not exist in Hartfield without the condemnation to servility and poverty of hundreds of unnamed (though not necessarily unpitied) human beings will not trouble their minds as they admire the civilised sensibility of Jane Austen's social standards. The position of such readers cannot of course be objected to on logical grounds so long as all its implications are accepted.

At the other extreme of critical attitudes will be found those readers whose sense of the limitations of Jane Austen's social consciousness makes it impossible for them to value the book at all. How can I feel sympathy, such a reader will say, for characters whom I see to be, for all their charm and politeness, parasites and exploiters? How can I feel that the problems of such a society have a relevance to me? Now if art were a matter of abstract morality it would be impossible to argue against this puritan attitude; but in truth it misses the most essential thing of all about *Emma,* that it is a warm and living work of art. To reject *Emma* outright is to reject the humanity in *Emma,* either to dismiss the delight and involvement that we feel as we read it as an unfortunate aberration, or else to render ourselves immune to its humanity by imposing upon it an attitude narrower than itself.

More sophisticated than this philistine attitude to the problem is that which will hold that *Emma* does indeed reflect the class basis and limitations of Jane Austen's attitudes, but that this really does not matter very much or seriously affect its value.

This is a view, plausible at first sight, held by a surprisingly large number of readers who want to have their novel and yet eat it. Yes indeed, such a reader will say, the moral basis of Jane Austen's novels is, for us, warped by her acceptance of class society; her standards obviously can't apply in a democratic society where the Emmas and Knightleys would have to work for their living like anyone else. But, after all, we must remember when Jane Austen was writing; we must approach the novels with sympathy in their historical context. Jane Austen, a genteel bourgeoise of the turn of the eighteenth century, could scarcely be expected to analyse class society in modern terms. We must make a certain allowance, reading the book with a willing suspension of our own ideas and prejudices.

This represents a view of literature which, behind an apparently historical approach, debases and nullifies the effects of art. It invites us to read *Emma* not as a living, vital novel, relevant to our own lives and problems, but as a dead historical 'document.' A work of art which has to be read in such a way is not a work of art. The very concept of 'making allowances' of this sort for an artist is both insulting and mechanical. It has something of the puritan's contempt for those who have not seen the light, but it lacks the puritan's moral courage, for it is accompanied by a determination not to be done out of what cannot be approved. The final result is generally to come to terms with the aesthetes. For if *Emma* is morally undesirable and yet Art, the Art can have little to do with morality and some new, necessarily idealist, criteria must be found.

It is important, I believe, to realise the weakness of this pseudo-historical view of *Emma*. If, in whatever century she happened to live, Jane Austen were indeed nothing but a genteel bourgeoise 'reflecting' the views of her day, she would not be a great artist and she could not have written *Emma*. The truth is that in so far as *Emma* does reveal her as a conventional member of her class, blindly accepting its position and ideology, the value of *Emma* is indeed limited, not just relatively, but objectively and always. But the truth is also that this is not the principal or most important revelation of *Emma*.

The limitation must not be ignored or glossed over. There can be no doubt that there *is* an inadequacy here, an element of complacency that does to some extent limit the value of *Emma*. The nature of the inadequacy is fairly illustrated by this description of Emma's visit, with Harriet, to a sick cottager.

> They were now approaching the cottage, and all idle topics were superseded. Emma was very compassionate; and the distresses of the poor were as sure of relief from her personal attention and kindness her counsel and her patience, as from her purse. She understood their ways, could allow for their ignorance and their temptations, had no romantic expectations or extraordinary virtue from those, for whom education had done so little, entered into their troubles with ready sympathy, and always gave her assistance with as much intelligence as good-will. In the present instance, it was sickness and poverty together which she came to visit; and after remaining there as long as she could give comfort or advice, she quitted the cottage with such an impression of the scene as made her say to Harriet, as they walked away——
>
> 'These are the sights, Harriet, to do one good. How trifling they make every thing else appear!—I feel now as if I could think of nothing but these poor creatures all the rest of the day; and yet who can say how soon it may all vanish from my mind?'

'Very true,' said Harriet. 'Poor creatures! one can think of nothing else.'

'And really, I do not think the impression will soon be over,' said Emma, as she crossed the low hedge and tottering doorstep which ended the narrow, slippery path through the cottage garden, and brought them into the lane again. 'I do not think it will,' stopping to look once more at all the outward wretchedness of the place, and recall the still greater within.

'Oh! dear no,' said her companion. They walked on. The lane made a slight bend; and when that bend was passed, Mr Elton was immediately in sight; and so near as to give Emma time only to say farther,

'Ah! Harriet, here comes a very sudden trial of our stability in good thoughts. Well (smiling), I hope it may be allowed that if compassion has produced exertion and relief to the sufferers, it has done all that is truly important. If we feel for the wretched, enough to do all we can for them, the rest is empty sympathy, only distressing to ourselves.'

Harriet could just answer, 'Oh! dear, yes,' before the gentleman joined them.

Now there can be no doubt about the quality of the feeling here. Harriet's silly responses underline most potently the doubt that Emma herself feels as to the adequacy of her own actions. There can be no point in this passage (for it has no inevitable bearing on the plot) save to give a sense of the darker side of the moon, the aspect of Hartfield that will not be dealt with. And it does indeed to a great extent answer the doubt in the reader's mind that an essential side of the Hartfield world is being conveniently ignored. But the doubt is not entirely answered. After all, the important question is not whether Emma recognises the existence of the poor at Hartfield, but whether she recognises that her own position depends on their existence. 'Comfort or advice' moreover remain the positives in Emma's attitudes and one's doubts as to their sufficiency are in fact, like Emma's, swept away by the arrival of Mr Elton and the plot. The essential moral issue is shelved; and it is, in general, the supreme merit of Jane Austen, that essential moral issues are *not* shelved.

But that the inadequacy is not crippling the passage just quoted will also suggest. That final remark of Emma's is very significant. The parenthesised 'smiling' and the idiocy of Harriet's comment have the effect of throwing into doubt the whole aristocratic philosophy that Emma is expounded and that doubt, though it does not balance the shelving of the problem, does at least extenuate it. We are not wholly lulled.

Against the element of complacency other forces, too, are at work. We should not look merely to the few specific references to the poor to confirm our sense that the inadequacies of Jane Austen's social philosophy are overtopped by other, more positive vibrations. Among these positive forces are . . . her highly critical concern over the fate of women in her society, a concern which involves a reconsideration of its basic values. Positive also are her materialism and her unpretentiousness. If aristocracy is implicitly defended it is at least on rational grounds; no bogus philosophical sanctions are called in to preserve the *status quo* from reasonable examination. And no claim is made, explicit or implicit, that we are being presented with a revelation of a fundamental truth. Hartfield is offered to us as Hartfield, not as Life.

And this is ultimately, I think, the strength of *Emma*; this rejection of Life in favour of living, the actual, concrete problems of behaviour and sensibility in an actual, concrete society. It is Jane Austen's sensitive vitality, her genuine concern (based on so large an honesty) for human feelings in a concrete situation, that captures our imagination. It is this concern that gives her such delicate and precise insight into the problems of personal relationships (how will a group of individuals living together best get on, best find happiness?). And the concern does not stop at what, among the ruling class at Hartfield, is pleasant and easily solved.

It gives us glimpses of something Mr Woodhouse never dreamed of—the world outside the Hartfield world and yet inseparably bound up with it: the world Jane Fairfax saw in her vision of offices and into which Harriet in spite of (no, *because of*) Emma's patronage, was so nearly plunged: the world for which Jane Austen had no answer. It is this vital and unsentimental concern which defeats, to such a very large extent, the limitations. So that when we think back on *Emma* we do not think principally of the narrow inadequacies of Hartfield society but of the delight we have known in growing more intimately and wisely sensitive to the way men and women in a particular, given situation, work out their problems of living. (pp. 93-8)

> *Arnold Kettle, "The Nineteenth Century: Jane Austen, 'Emma'," in his* An Introduction to the English Novel: To George Eliot, Vol. I, *second edition, Hutchinson University Library, 1967, pp. 86-89.*

LAURENCE LERNER (essay date 1967)

[*In the following excerpt, Lerner discusses* Emma *as a comedy that turns upon the protagonist's ambitions as a matchmaker.*]

If any work belongs unequivocally to any genre, *Emma* is a comedy. And it is . . . about self-deception. Before drawing any conclusions, let us pause to examine it.

Perhaps we can designate its theme even more narrowly: we can say it is about match-making. On her first appearance in the book, Emma comes before us as a match-maker. She claims the credit for having brought Mr Weston and Miss Taylor together. Since all her other attempts are so disastrous, we are perhaps inclined to agree with Mr Knightley's scepticism about this one: 'Your making the match, as you call it, means only your planning it, your saying to yourself one idle day, "I think it would be a very good thing for Miss Taylor if Mr Weston were to marry".' But as the story proceeds Emma is very much more active than this, and she mismatches almost every couple of social standing in Highbury. And when the story is over, and everybody, despite Emma's efforts, has married the right person, and she has seen the error of her ways, there is still a furtive delight to be taken in the birth of Mrs Weston's daughter. Emma

> had been decided in wishing for a Miss Weston. She would not acknowledge that it was with any view of making a match for her, hereafter, with either of Isabella's sons; but she was convinced that a daughter would suit both father and mother best.

If the story of Anne Elliott could be called *Persuasion,* that of Emma Woodhouse has a fair claim to being named *The Matchmaker*.

Match-making is a way of managing the lives of others: it is a comic version of the exercise of power. Comic, because to be married is not, after all, a calamity. The scheming of Emma

is a parallel to the scheming of Iago, but Iago's aims are calamitous, so the effect can no longer be comic. Emma makes innumerable mistakes in the course of the book, but her principal mismatchings are three: Harriet and Mr Elton, herself and Frank Churchill, Harriet and Frank Churchill.

The Harriet-Mr Elton match forms a kind of prelude: it is over, and Emma has repented, before the end of Book I. The comedy of course lies in the contrast between what we know and what Emma sees: this incongruity is clearest on a second reading, but the perceptive reader may enjoy a good deal of the joke immediately. Noticing that Mr Elton is really courting Emma and not Harriet, we admire the skill with which Jane Austen has happened to make him do so in terms that Emma can misinterpret; and we delight both in the author's technical skill, and in our superiority to Emma's limited insight.

> 'I think your manners to him encouraging. I speak as a friend, Emma. You had better look about you, and ascertain what you do, and what you mean to do.'

> 'I thank you; but I assure you, you are quite mistaken. Mr Elton and I are very good friends, and nothing more;' and she walked on, amusing herself in the consideration of the blunders which often arise from a partial knowledge of the circumstances, of the mistakes which people of high pretensions to judgement are for ever falling into; and not very well pleased with her brother for imagining her blind and ignorant, and in want of counsel.

Every detail of Emma's reflection on her brother-in-law is turned against her by the reader. Emma has high pretensions to judgment, and is mistaken; and Emma's self-deception causes us just the same amusement that John Knightley here causes her.

This first mistake leads to a first awakening:

> It was foolish, it was wrong, to take so active a part in bringing any two people together. It was adventuring too far, assuming too much, making light of what ought to be serious—a trick of what ought to be simple. She was quite concerned and ashamed, and resolved to do such things no more.

In itself, this passage contains no direct suggestion that Emma's repentance is partial or insincere; though the re-reader may observe that it has none of the force and eloquence of her later awakening:

> With insufferable vanity had she believed herself in the secret of everybody's feelings; with unpardonable arrogance proposed to arrange everyone's destiny. She was proved to have been universally mistaken; and she had not quite done nothing—for she had done mischief. She had brought evil on Harriet, on herself, and, she too much feared, on Mr Knightley.

Perhaps the only hint in the earlier passage of such a contrast is the (presumably) limiting 'quite' of 'quite concerned and ashamed'; and perhaps it would be richer if it did hint more directly. But it is not long, as we read on, before we realise that this first self-discovery of Emma's is very partial. She has not learned to cease managing others: she has merely decided to tread more carefully in future. The point is neatly (too neatly?) made as we juxtapose in memory Mr Knightley's remark 'You have been no friend to Harriet Smith, Emma,' with Emma's own 'I have been but half a friend to her. She has but half awakened.'

Now come Emma's two serious mistakes: both of them involving Frank Churchill. Though one follows the other (she obviously cannot marry him to Harriet until she had refused him herself), they are closely interrelated. The second goes ingenuously wrong: believing she is encouraging Harriet to think seriously of Frank Churchill, she is in fact encouraging her to think of Mr. Knightley. It is by discovering this mistake that she discovers her own love for Mr. Knightley. For a while Emma believes she has awoken to the truth too late, and has nothing left to her but a Stoic dignity in self-knowledge; but we are by then sufficiently adjusted to the comic tone to feel confident, even on a first reading, that all will come well. It is not until after this that Emma discovers her earlier mistake: that the affection which Frank Churchill had felt for her, and that she had refused to respond to, had never existed. And in depicting this situation Jane Austen used her gayest and most complex irony:

> There was nothing to denote him unworthy of the distinguished honour which her imagination had given him; the honour, if not of being in love with her, of being at least very near it, and saved only by her own indifference—(for still her resolution held of never marrying)—the honour, in short, of being marked out for her by all their joint acquaintance.

The joke here consists in the exquisite skill with which Emma is drawing distinctions of feeling within a non-existent situation. Once we know that Frank Churchill feels none of the interest she credits him with, we can see that hers is a parody of skill, a discrimination among shadows.

Emma's shadow-scrupulousness grows even nicer as she proceeds:

> 'I do not find myself making any use of the word *sacrifice,*' said she. 'In not one of all my clever replies, my delicate negatives, is there any allusion to making a sacrifice. I do suspect that he is not really necessary to my happiness. So much the better. I certainly will not persuade myself to feel more than I do. I am quite enough in love. I should be very sorry to be more.

By now she is talking about her own feelings. This is not because she has ceased to manipulate Frank's: on the contrary, she is now so confident that she knows the exact shade of his, that she can transfer her attention to deciding what her own proper reaction should be. It is not difficult for us to realise that she is in a shadow world: the whole basis of her discrimination is wrong, and we must at least suspect that her own feelings are no more genuine than those she attributes to Frank Churchill. Once we see what her feelings are, as her love for Mr Knightley awakens, this suspicion is confirmed. Emma is not in all this romancing discovering anything about her own true emotions: she is dealing only in the conveniently postulated emotions that the match-maker thinks he perceives. She is manipulating herself.

All is now prepared for the awakening that forms the climax of the book. Emma's explosion of self-knowledge is convincing because it has been prepared for both technically and psychologically. Technically, in being anticipated by her half-awakening at the end of Book I; psychologically because Emma's egoism is never closed, never impenetrable, like that of Mrs Elton. Jane Austen is very careful in the way she plays off Emma against Mrs Elton:

> 'Well,' said she, 'and you soon silenced Mr Cole I suppose.'

> 'Yes, very soon. He gave me a quiet hint; I told him he was mistaken; he asked my pardon, and said no more. Cole does not want to be wiser and wittier than his neighbours.'

> 'In that respect how unlike dear Mrs Elton, who wants to be wiser and wittier than all the world.'

—and how unlike dear Miss Woodhouse! At this point there is a clear irony at Emma's expense, and a reminder by Jane Austen that she is like Mrs Elton, whom she detests. For Mrs Elton too is a manipulator; she too enjoys arranging the lives of others, and does it entirely to satisfy her own ego, not out of a true interest in them. Emma must go to Bath: 'a line from me would bring you a little host of acquaintance.' When Mr Knightley has guests at his home, she insists 'Oh leave all that to me—Only give me a carte blanche—I am Lady Patroness, you know.' Most mischievous, Jane Fairfax must accept the place as a governess that she has found for her; no refusal will be tolerated; she insists 'on being authorised to write an acquiescence by the morrow's post.' It is Emma's behaviour written larger, in grosser letters.

But though Jane Austen insists on the resemblance, she also insists on the difference. There is no doubt that the letters are grosser, and, in case there was, Jane Austen is careful to follow this conversation by one between Emma and Jane Fairfax, in which Jane announces that she wishes to slip home, and Emma insists on offering her carriage—will not take no for an answer, until Jane says

> 'I am fatigued; but it is not the sort of fatigue—quick walking will refresh me. Miss Woodhouse, we all know at times what it is to be wearied in spirits. Mine, I confess, are exhausted. The kindness you can show me will be to let me have my own way, and only say that I am gone when it is necessary.'

> Emma had not another word to oppose. She saw it all; and entering into her feelings, promoted her quitting the house immediately, and watched her safely off with the zeal of a friend.

Mrs Elton's insistence is so fresh in memory, that we cannot help noticing the difference: Mrs Elton would not have left off at that point, and so could never have deserved such a phrase as 'the zeal of a friend.' (pp. 97-101)

Emma is a very warm and a very sharp book: that is, it arouses a good deal of the response appropriate to tragedy, and that appropriate to satire. Yet it remains unequivocally a comedy. The treatment of Mrs Elton is pure satire, but Emma, as I have said, is carefully distinguished from Mrs Elton. There is a good deal of satire lurking elsewhere, too. We must be careful not to get too cross with old Mr Woodhouse (when, for instance, he does poor Mrs Bates out of her sweetbread and asparagus), or we shall begin to react to him as to a figure of satire. Perhaps the ideal reader of *Emma* has not got an aged parent. This may be good for us: to keep the book as comedy, we have to surpass John Knightley in forbearance. There is much less danger of taking any of the book as tragic, and yet there is a good deal of sympathy and even grief in it. For three-quarters of the story, there is no one character on whom our sympathy can focus: it floats loosely. Emma may engage our emotions completely after her awakening, but until then identification with her is impossible. The ironic gaze is so persistent (and most of the ironies scored off Emma are by no means to her credit), that we must feel detached. Jane Fairfax and Mr Knightley, the two best characters morally, are firmly seen from the outside: to take us inside Jane Fairfax's thoughts would not only let the secret of the plot out, it would also undermine Emma's position as heroine. As for Frank Churchill, our strong moral disapproval is played off against the delight we take—and he takes—and despite herself Jane Austen takes—in his skilful managing. Somehow or other he manages to see Jane every day without anyone suspecting that he has arranged it. He is a much better Iago than Emma; and the joke on her, of course, is that when she thinks she is managing she is really being managed.

Since for three-quarters of the book there is no one person whose point of view we share and with whom we also sympathise totally, and since the book is infused with a warmth, a joy in human relationships, the pressure that builds up towards our final identification with Emma is very strong. It comes out in odd and surprising places before then—Mrs Weston, Mr Knightley, even Miss Bates, may suddenly at a chapter's end become the focus for an impulse of delight that is warmer than mere amusement. (pp. 101-02)

Emma is a full and rich and human book, all the responses it arouses dig deep into warmth and anger, grief and fear. But in no situation does any of these emotions take charge. The author's eye is fixed so steadily on the contrast between what is and what is believed, that however powerfully we are moved by one or other half, we remain aware of the whole as a balanced situation. The harm and grief are never violent enough to run away with our attention. The richer that human material, the harder it will be for the author to maintain the judicious, amused balance of comedy: to be amusing is always easier when one is merely amusing. Perhaps *Emma* is as profound as pure comedy can be. (p. 102)

> Laurence Lerner, "The Truthtellers: 'Emma', or 'The Match-maker'," in his The Truthtellers: Jane Austen, George Eliot, D. H. Lawrence, Schocken Books, 1967, pp. 96-102.

J. F. BURROWS (essay date 1968)

[*In the following excerpt from his book-length explication of* Emma, *Burrows examines Austen's use of a subtly fluctuating narrative perspective, focusing on the validity of George Knightley's perceptions.*]

In *Emma*, as elsewhere, Jane Austen's art is in continual if unobtrusive motion. Hence it is not merely futile but positively misleading to rely on those fixed points of reference that can often simplify a critic's task. When the narrator's function varies subtly as occasion requires, the narrator cannot be regarded as consistently 'reliable' or, conversely, as consistently the voice of Emma's prejudices. When Mr Knightley is one fallible creature among others, he cannot be regarded as his author's spokesman and chief guardian of her values. When Emma's relationships with her fellows are incessantly in flux, she cannot be set against one character or beside another in large, stable contrasts and comparisons. When Emma's own moods vary with dazzling rapidity, it is idle to single out a passage for 'close reading' and to declare triumphantly that *this* is the real Emma. And when even the meaning supposedly enshrined in words like "reason," "imagination," "amiable," and "elegant" varies significantly as the novel proceeds, there can be no easy generalizing about Jane Austen's moral values. If these ideas hold good, it does not follow that *Emma* is without shape or meaning. It only follows that, instead of imposing an assumed meaning, a predetermined shape, upon the novel, we must let the novel work its effect on us. (p. 9)

[Certain] problems associated with Mr Knightley must be faced at once. There is a moment late in the novel when, after reading John Knightley's reply to the news that his brother is to marry her, Emma remarks that:

> "He writes like a sensible man. . . . I honour his sincerity. It is very plain that he considers the good fortune of the engagement as all on my side, but that he is not without hope of my growing, in time, as worthy of your affection, as you think me already. Had he said any thing to bear a different construction, I should not have believed him."
>
> "My Emma, he means no such thing. He only means—"
>
> "He and I should differ very little in our estimation of the two,"—interrupted she, with a sort of serious smile—"much less, perhaps, than he is aware of, if we could enter without ceremony or reserve on the subject."
>
> "Emma, my dear Emma—"

Heedless of Mr Knightley's fond disclaimers and never pausing to remark Emma's capacity to speak so humbly and sincerely, those critics who most condemn the girl can join for once with her devotees. For she is offering, in effect, a paradigm of the novel as it is usually read. As it is usually read, *Emma* is concerned with its heroine's gradual progress to a point where she is no longer quite unworthy of the honour done her by Mr Knightley, spokesman for and apotheosis of Jane Austen's own values.

Few critics go so far as Professor Shorer who, in referring to 'the author (or, if you wish, Knightley)', obliterates all distinction between the character and his creator [see excerpt dated 1959]. But more conservative opinion still makes no doubt of Mr Knightley's authority. Thus, for Professor Shannon, as representative as he is succinct, the novel is essentially concerned with 'Emma's progress from self-deception and vanity to perception and humility;' and 'the judicious Mr. Knightley, admired by all critics, is the yardstick against which Emma's conversion must be measured' [see excerpt dated 1956].

Like any literary yard-stick, this one gives different measurements in different hands. For most critics, Emma achieves true contrition. For a few devotees, perhaps, she has little to repent. And for a few determined ironists, her progress is illusory, her penitence transient, and her marriage doomed to fail. Thus the ultimate irony detected by Professor Mudrick is that 'there is no happy ending, no easy equilibrium, if we care to project confirmed exploiters like Emma and Churchill into the future of their marriages' [see excerpt dated 1952].

These differences as to the extent of Emma's progress are compounded by differences as to its exact nature. Is the long opposition between Mr Knightley and his protégée to be seen as an opposition between maturity and immaturity? Humility and arrogance? Altruism and self-concern? True freedom and petty licence? Reality and illusion? Reason and imagination? And yet, in all these variants, the area of discussion is really very limited: in all of them, Mr Knightley still sets the terms by which the opposition itself is to be defined and its resolution interpreted.

Mr Knightley's attitude to Frank Churchill gives rise, for some critics, to moments of doubt, which are customarily resolved in comments on Jane Austen's awareness of human imperfection and which are not allowed to prejudice Mr Knightley's office as moral standard. So long as these and wider doubts are set aside, so long as Mr Knightley's obvious personal merits are used for raising him to the author's pedestal, so long as the reader believes himself possessed of an unfailing lodestone as he makes his way through the ironies of the novel—for so long as this, it is hard to accept that *Emma* fully deserves its reputation as a masterpiece. If Mr Knightley is his author's spokesman, Jane Austen's position is known to us, in all its essentials, by the end of the fifth chapter. In the four hundred pages that ensue before the predictable ending releases us at last, we are, it seems, to find what solace we can in the continuing infallibility—made so *human* by those little fallibilities—of Mr Knightley, in the charming but protracted follies of Emma, in the elaborate mystification about Frank Churchill, and in the satiric portrayal of sundry lesser worthies.

Only Professor Wright, I believe, has tried to grasp the nettle [in his *Jane Austen's Novels: A Study in Structure*]. In a statement whose implications he does not pursue, he suggests that it is time to re-open the whole question of Mr Knightley's authority:

> Are we then to suppose that Emma is meant merely to exhibit the foibles of the world against a constant standard of values exemplified by Mr Knightley? Not at all: for then we should have seen him as the central figure, and the novel would have been a didactic treatise. Instead, Emma Woodhouse is the centre of attention and attraction.

It is one thing to juggle terms like 'masterpiece' and to point to certain hypothetical advantages of questioning Mr Knightley's authority, quite another to show that it can in fact be questioned without distorting the text. Even in the passage with which we began the passage where Emma comments on John Knightley's letter, there is at least one encouraging sign. In calling John Knightley "a sensible man," Emma repeats the phrase that marks his brother's first entry into the novel, a phrase that some critics have taken as an ultimate truth. The adjective is one that Jane Austen uses frequently, sometimes as pertaining to "sensibility" (as that fluid concept was understood in the eighteenth century), sometimes in the more modern sense dismissed in Johnson's *Dictionary:* '8. In low conversation it has sometimes the sense of reasonable; judicious; wise.' The older sense, I think, has no place here. In the 'low' modern sense, John Knightley may well be "sensible" to suppose that Emma is not yet worthy of the brother he so admires. But, notwithstanding Emma's magnanimity in using the word of him, he carries frankness to the point of churlishness by being unremittingly "sensible" on such an occasion as this. It might be objected that this is carrying guilt by association to monstrous lengths, that Mr Knightley ought not to be condemned merely because an everyday phrase that is used of him—albeit in an emphatic context—is also used, four hundred pages later, of his too trenchant brother. But, whatever its exact meaning, "a sensible man" is not just an everyday phrase. In *Emma* itself, . . . it is used repeatedly, as are such variants as "men of sense;" and their increasing force culminates in an impressive dramatic irony. If Jane Austen's other novels are admitted as relevant comment, the matter grows more interesting still. It is no surprise to discover that the absurd Collins is not " 'a sensible man' " or that Mr Bennet has " 'great hopes of finding him quite the reverse' " (*Pride and Prejudice*). But that ambiguous creature, Henry Crawford, is described by the narrator as "a man of sense" (*Mansfield Park*). And even William Walter Elliot is admitted into the company. Suspicious as she is of his essential character, his cousin Anne is satisfied on this point:

> Though they had now been acquainted a month, she could not be satisfied that she really knew his character. That he was a sensible man, an agreeable man,— that he talked well, professed good opinions, seemed to judge properly and as a man of principle,—this was all clear enough. He certainly knew what was right, nor could she fix on any one article of moral duty evidently transgressed; but yet she would have been afraid to answer for his conduct. She distrusted the past, if not the present.

(Persuasion)

My object is certainly not to suggest that Mr Knightley is another William Walter! It seems clear, however, that when he is first introduced as "a sensible man about seven or eight-and-thirty," we ought not to leap to premature conclusions about his character, let alone his authority.

Nor is it true that Mr Knightley's jealousy of Frank Churchill is his only lapse from perfection. He himself is eventually to admit having misjudged Harriet Smith; to concede that, in spite of his earlier doubts, Emma has done Harriet good; and, above all, to acknowledge that his "interference" with Emma " 'was quite as likely to do harm as good' " and, indeed, that " 'I do not believe I did you any good'." [Lest] his concessions be dismissed at once as blurred by his fondness for Emma, there is the fact that, when he and Emma are to marry, at least some of his neighbours think *he* has the better of the bargain.

As a final token that the question at issue may be worth re-opening, there is a striking but neglected passage a little earlier in the novel, following immediately on Emma's acceptance of Mr Knightley's proposal of marriage, and uttered by the impersonal narrator: "This one half hour had given to each the same precious certainty of being beloved, had cleared from each the same degree of ignorance, jealousy, or distrust.—On his side, there had been a long-standing jealousy. . . ". Distracted perhaps by this last sentence, even those who have taken some account of Mr Knightley's jealousy can hardly have attended to the phrase, "the same degree of ignorance, jealousy, or distrust," or to the page of commentary that follows it. And yet that phrase, firmly if not patently supported by the commentary, puts the whole history of Emma and Mr Knightley in an uncommon light.

The question of Mr Knightley's authority, then, is easier to reopen than it may prove to close. . . . [Let] us be clear about what is entailed. It is not a matter of writing a revolutionary 'character-sketch' of Mr Knightley, somehow finding—or inventing—grounds for declaring him a knave, fool, or prig. It is a matter of accepting him as a leading but not oracular participant in the interplay of speech and action that makes up the novel, a matter of heeding his words but not bowing to them. When he is regarded in this way, one is freed from his dominance and enabled to look not merely at him but at the whole novel in an altered light. In that light, . . . *Emma* appears more subtly amusing, more richly meaningful, and more thoroughly dramatic. (pp. 9-13)

> *J. F. Burrows, in his* Jane Austen's 'Emma', *Sydney University Press, 1968, 132 p.*

DAVID LODGE (essay date 1971)

[*Lodge offers a general discussion of theme and technique in* Emma.]

On first reading, *Emma* is a comedy of mysteries and puzzles (it is no coincidence that riddles, anagrams, and conundrums figure so prominently in the action) which challenge the reader's perspicacity quite as much as the heroine's. To be sure, put on our guard from the very first page against too close an identification with Emma's hopes and expectations, we may anticipate her realization of the true state of affairs—we may guess that Mr. Elton's attentions are directed not at Harriet but at herself long before his declaration; and we may suspect, before Emma is told, that there is some secret between Jane Fairfax and Frank Churchill. Indeed, one of the marks of Jane Austen's skill is that it does not matter, as regards the effectiveness of the narrative, at what point we anticipate Emma's discoveries, if at all: the book is protected against failure for any reader, however naïve, however sophisticated. But only an uncannily knowing reader could predict the fate of every character from the outset. On first reading we must to a large extent share the heroine's bafflement, curiosity, and suspense as to the course of events. When Frank Churchill facetiously announces to the company gathered on Box Hill, 'I am ordered by Miss Woodhouse . . . to say, that she desires to know what you are all thinking of', he is in a sense stating what the novel, on first reading, is all about.

On second reading we do know what everybody is thinking of, and *Emma* becomes a comedy of ironies. From a position of privileged wisdom, we watch Emma entangle herself deeper and deeper in mistakes and misunderstandings, unwittingly preparing her own discomfiture and disappointment, while all the other characters are to some extent living in a similar world of illusion. Even Mr. Knightley does not escape unscathed, for we know that his legitimate disapproval of Emma's conduct derives some of its animus from unnecessary jealousy on Frank Churchill's account. The miracle is, that the second reading does not cancel out the first, nor exhaust the interest of subsequent readings. As Reginald Farrer said [see excerpt dated 1917]:

> While twelve readings of *Pride and Prejudice* give you twelve periods of pleasure repeated, as many readings of *Emma* give you that pleasure, not repeated only, but squared and squared again with each perusal, till at every fresh reading you feel anew that you never understood anything like the widening sum of its delights.

Thus while every sentence of description and dialogue reverberates with ironic significance on second reading, there is no passage which is not sufficiently interesting, amusing, and character-revealing to seem quite in place on first reading. Conversely, the ironic mode does not totally dominate the second reading because 'our attention is so diversified by the thick web of linguistic nuance that we do not concentrate single-mindedly on the ironic results of the mystification'. We are unlikely to exhaust the subtleties of *Emma* even on a second reading, and we can never, therefore, assume a position of entirely detached superiority towards the heroine. Becoming aware at each re-reading of what we 'missed' before, we are compelled to acknowledge, like Emma herself, the fallibility of our human understanding. This is perhaps one reason why Jane Austen's prediction when she began *Emma*—'I am going to take a heroine whom no one but myself will much like' has so often been falsified.

Of course, we must like Emma Woodhouse if the novel is to work; and of course Jane Austen's prediction was really a definition of the artistic problem she set herself: how to make us care for Emma in spite of her faults, but without glossing over those faults. Emma can be snobbish, cruel, selfish, and calculating in the field of personal relations—the way she ex-

ploits and manipulates poor Harriet in the matter of Robert Martin's suit is only one of many examples. (pp. viii-x)

Emma does . . . learn from her mistakes; but this alone would not be enough to make her acceptable, from the outset, as a heroine. How does Jane Austen make us like her? First of all, by narrating the story very largely from her point of view. We see most of the action through Emma's eyes and this naturally has the effect of making us identify with her interests and of mitigating the errors of her vision—since we *experience* those errors with her, and to some extent share them. Indeed, so powerful is the pull of sympathy exerted by this narrative method, that checks and balances have to be introduced in the form of discreet authorial comments and well-timed interventions from Mr. Knightley. Knightley is the nearest thing to a paragon of virtue in the novel, but Jane Austen has carefully prevented any *female* character from filling the same role and thus putting her heroine in the shade. Jane Fairfax is the only serious contender—indeed a more conventional lady novelist of the period would have made her the heroine; but the intrigue in which Jane is involved, as well as contributing to the mystery of the plot, conveniently makes her a passive and enigmatic, if not indeed a quite negative character. Mrs. Weston is a worthy woman, but since her story, in a sense, reaches its happy conclusion on the first page of the novel, she does not engage our interest very deeply. Beside the other women—the silly Harriet, the vulgar Mrs. Elton, the chattering Miss Bates, and all the other old women in the story (amongst whom Mr. Woodhouse should perhaps be counted)—Emma can only shine. And it must be acknowledged that Jane Austen has given her positive and attractive qualitiees. She is endlessly patient with her tiresome father. She has a cheerful and resilient temperament, and is not given to self-pity. And she is, quite simply, intelligent. She finishes her sentences (always a criterion of worth in Jane Austen); she has a fine sense of humour; her errors are the result not of stupidity, but of a quick mind that is not sufficiently extended by her limited and banal society, so that she is tempted to *invent* interest for herself. She is, to use her own word, 'an imaginist'. There is an interesting parallel to be drawn here between Emma and her creator, if we accept D. W. Harding's plausible suggestion that Jane Austen herself was as much provoked by her own milieu as attached to it, and that writing novels was a way of 'finding some mode of existence for her critical attitudes'.

We misrepresent the novel if we suppose that the authorial voice is always judicially detached from Emma. There are many passages where the attitudes and verbal styles of the author and the character are so close that it is impossible to drive a wedge between them. Emma surely shares much of the credit for such witty lines as 'Mr. Knightley seemed to be trying not to smile; and succeeded without difficulty, upon Mrs. Elton's beginning to talk to him'. Or consider the scene where it is Emma's painful duty to explain to Harriet the misunderstanding about Mr. Elton's intentions. The artless pathos of the girl's response 'really for the time convinced that Harriet was the superior creature of the two—and that to resemble Harriet would be more for her own welfare and happiness than all that genius or intelligence could do'. The next paragraph continues:

> It was rather too late in the day to set about being simple-minded and ignorant; but she left her with every previous resolution confirmed of being humble and discreet, and repressing imagination all the rest of her life.

The dry candour of the first part of this sentence, checking the over-emotional response, is deeply characteristic of Jane Austen; but again it is difficult to say whether this is an authorial observation or a wry reflection of Emma herself. The effect, anyway, is to confirm the solidarity of author and heroine in a commitment to *intelligent* virtue.

Some repression of Emma's imagination is necessary to this aim because there is a great moral difference between making literary fictions, as Jane Austen does, and imposing fictional patterns on real people, as Emma does. Furthermore, Emma's fictions are sentimental and self-indulgent, derived from inferior literary models: her fond belief that Harriet is of distinguished parentage, and that Jane Fairfax is amorously involved with Mr. Dixon, are good examples of this. When Emma finally achieves maturity and self-knowledge, and is rewarded by Knightley's declaration of love, the moment is marked by an emphatic rejection of sentimental romance:

> for as to any of that heroism of sentiment which might have prompted her to entreat him to transfer his affection from herself to Harriet, as infinitely the most worthy of the two—or even the more simple sublimity of resolving to refuse him at once and for ever, without vouchsafing any motive, because he could not marry them both, Emma had it not.

The ironic invocation of literary stereotypes is one of the ways by which Jane Austen reinforces the realism of her own fiction. 'Realism' is a notoriously slippery word, but one that applies to *Emma* in almost any sense. Ian Watt [in his *The Rise of the Novel*], for instance, distinguishes between 'realism of presentation' and 'realism of assessment': qualities, exemplified by Richardson and Fielding respectively, which are in a sense mutually antagonistic, since the illusion of life discourages detached judgement and vice versa. Yet *Emma* surely embraces and reconciles both these effects. It is rich in that faultless observation of motive and behaviour and speech habits for which Jane Austen has always been justly admired, making her characters as interesting to us as are our own acquaintances, and in much the same way—simply as human beings. This illusion of life depends upon the events of the novel seeming to follow each other in a natural and casual sequence, yet we can see that they have also been carefully patterned to lead Emma through a series of errors and instructive recognitions. The small, close-knit society of Highbury makes it natural that there should be a good deal of mutual entertaining, but it also enables Jane Austen to bring her principal characters all together at various crucial moments—Mr. Weston's dinner party, the ball at the Crown, the expeditions to Donwell and Box Hill—where the illusions and deceptions of these human beings are subjected to intense social (and therefore highly dramatic) pressure. The rendering of so much of the action through Emma's eyes intensifies the realism of presentation, but the quiet authority of the author's voice guarantees realism of assessment. Perhaps we read *Emma* first mainly for the presentation, and subsequently mainly for the assessment, but, as I said earlier, one reading does not cancel out the other. Under analysis *Emma* reveals an amazing multiplicity of ends and means, all perfectly adjusted and harmonized.

Consider, for example, Jane Austen's handling of the most serious crisis in her heroine's history. At the nadir of Emma's fortunes, when she is stricken with guilt for having insulted Miss Bates and incurred Mr. Knightley's reproof, when she has discovered the truth about Jane Fairfax and Frank Churchill, with all its embarrassing reflections on her own conduct towards them, and when she has belatedly recognized her own

An illustration of the strawberry picking party at Donwell Abbey.

love for Mr. Knightley but believes he is going to propose to Harriet, whose pretensions to such a match she has herself encouraged—at the point when all these circumstances converge to bring Emma's morale to its lowest ebb, we get this piece of description:

> The evening of this day was very long, and melancholy, at Hartfield. The weather added what it could of gloom. A cold stormy rain set in, and nothing of July appeared but in the trees and shrubs, which the wind was despoiling, and the length of the day, which only made such cruel sights the longer visible.
>
> (pp. x-xiv)

Jane Austen is, of course, exploiting the pathetic fallacy here—but so stealthily that we are not distracted from the reality of the moment by a conscious recognition of her artistry. This artistry does more than establish a general consonance between the heroine's mood and the weather. The words, 'the length of the day, which only made such cruel sights the longer visible' provide a delicately appropriate analogy for Emma's state of mind because the circumstances of her life, her very fixed social position in a small and inward-looking community (a fact frequently underlined in the course of the narrative) mean that she can expect no release from her disappointment and regret but is condemned to live with them indefinitely. Emma's situation, in short, can only make *such cruel sights* as Harriet's marriage to Mr. Knightley *the longer visible;* and this is stated explicitly a few lines later:

> The prospect before her now, was threatening to a degree that could not be entirely dispelled—that might not be even partially brightened. If all took place that might take place among the circle of her friends, Hartfield must be comparatively deserted; and she left to cheer her father with the spirits only of ruined happiness.

The words *prospect, threatening,* and *brightened* in this passage are drawn from the vocabulary of weather description and thus, together with the echo of the 'despoiled' vegetation in 'ruined happiness', link it to the earlier one. And the whole scene recalls to Emma the very first scene of the novel when, 'the wedding over and the bride-people gone, her father and herself were left alone to dine together with no prospect of a third to cheer a long evening'. On that occasion Mr. Knightley had provided an unexpected and welcome third; But there are several reasons why he cannot be looked for now.

To her credit, however, Emma does not collapse under the pressure of these distressing thoughts. The chapter ends:

> the only source whence any thing like composure could be drawn, was in the resolution of her own better conduct, and the hope that, however inferior in spirit and gaiety might be the following and every winter of her life to the past, it would yet find her more rational, more acquainted with herself, and leave her less to regret when it were gone.

The pessimistic strain of seasonal imagery is sustained in 'every winter of her life', which has the effect of making Emma's future appear as one long winter. But the importance of this passage is that it describes Emma's first really disinterested effort at moral reform, inasmuch as she hopes to gain nothing except self-respect from her good resolution. In fact, she is rewarded the very next day, of which we get this description at the beginning of the next chapter:

> The weather continued much the same all the following morning; and the same loneliness, and the same melancholy, seemed to reign at Hartfield—but in the afternoon it cleared; the wind changed into a softer quarter; and the clouds were carried off; the sun appeared; it was summer again. With all the eagerness which such a transition gives, Emma resolved to be out of doors as soon as possible.

Walking in the garden, Emma is joined by Mr. Knightley, who in due course makes his most welcome proposal. The change in the weather is thus a natural circumstance which brings the couple together, giving them the time and the privacy to disentangle their misconceptions and reach an understanding; but it is also effectively symbolic. 'It was summer again.' The restoration of weather appropriate to the season intimates the restoration of happiness to Emma, and of comedy to the novel. (pp. xiv-xvi)

> *David Lodge, in an introduction to* Emma *by Jane Austen, edited by David Lodge, Oxford University Press, London, 1971, pp. vii-xvi.*

ALISON G. SULLOWAY (essay date 1976)

[*Calling* Emma *a "secretly subversive, secretly Romantic work," Sulloway examines Austen's portrayal of women in a repressive society within the context of the ideas expressed in* A Vindication of the Rights of Woman, *a work by Austen's contemporary, the English feminist Mary Wollstonecraft.*]

[Despite] Austen's usually detached and ironic tone, some of her themes, in *Emma* and elsewhere, were the common property of Romantic writers: The taint of corruption emanating from the cities, the prevailing decadence and injustice which characterized the wealthy and propertied classes, the strangling noose of hypocrisy, and the need for greater egalitarianism between members of conflicting classes. In each of the six novels, the heroine eventually turns on some supporter, male or female, of the privileges accruing to masculinity, wealth, caste, or property, and vehemently condemns such privileges. *Emma* performs this function of overt condemnation several times.

These frank outbursts, completely devoid of irony, are almost always long speeches delivered with clarity and passion combined, in the manner of [Mary Wollstonecraft's *A Vindication of the Rights of Woman*]. In each case, the heroine is vainly trying to shake off a self-destroying code and to substitute for it a code of integrity and autonomy quite foreign to everybody else's assumptions about her needs and capacities as a woman, a code for which she has no living models, no theoretical paradigms, and no social or familial support. As Wollstonecraft remarks: "there are some loop-holes out of which a man may creep, and dare to think and act for himself; but for a woman it is an herculean task, because she has difficulties peculiar to her sex to overcome, which require almost superhuman powers." During these impassioned speeches, Austen's heroines are painfully undergoing the "herculean task" of judging, thinking, weighing events, and deciding issues for themselves, but these articulations of intelligent protest almost invariably fail to elicit intelligent responses.

Both Austen and Wollstonecraft equally deplore frivolous women with nothing but sex or marriage on their minds and clever women who manipulate other people as a revenge for their impotence. Over and over Austen insists, as Wollstonecraft does in this remark, "that the illegitimate power which [women] obtain by degrading themselves is a curse." But both writers observe, as John Stuart Mill was later to do, that these defects are not endemic to women; they are the logical issue of women's stunted education. And the Austenian heroines' overt criticisms of the way society is run indicate how dearly Austen cared for women and their good conduct, and how unproductive of good conduct she thought their humiliations to be. *Emma,* particularly, is a study of "the artificial character" which gentlewomen "are made to assume . . . from their infancy," and the serious lack, for women, of "various employments and pursuits which engage [men's] attention, and give character to the opening [male] mind." But except for *Pride and Prejudice,* where Elizabeth Bennet and Darcy both play Pygmalion to one another's Galatea and then shift roles, the novels describe only the growing maturity of the herones; nobody else's attitude toward *them* matures, for as Joseph Wiesenfarth commented, these novels demonstrate the "hard truth . . . that Pygmalion is always male."

The heroines' unmasked protests are followed or immediately preceded by authorial comments slyly supporting what the heroine has just demanded: to be accepted as a rational adult rather than as a perpetual "overgrown child." And it is these flashes of open protest, as they dramatically punctuate the prevailing light wit and irony, that lend the Austenian canon its muted, yet pervasive, sense of Romantic timeliness, even of troubled modernity. The insistence of Austen and Wollstonecraft that

women's distressed condition is the subject for serious literature may well be analogous to Wordsworth's insistence that
peasants, leech-gatherers, and shepherds are worthy of serious
attention, and the same urges may be at work in all three
writers.

As a matter of fact, Austen's preoccupation with human growth
as it is shaped by education and experience, fortuitous or otherwise, is quite Romantic. Just as *The Prelude* and the *Bio-
graphia Literaria* implicitly discuss the great modern question
as to what extent temperament—and therefore success—is born
or made, natured or nutured, so do Austen's novels. But Austen's irony about feminine possibilities, and her heroines' outbursts, echo Wollstonecraft's profound concern with women's
"false system of education," and her novels all ask, as Wollstonecraft does in these questions, how women can "attain the
vigour necessary to throw off their factitious character" and
where they can "find strength to recur to reason and rise superior to a system of oppression, that blasts the fair promise
of spring?" Austen's shallow, vicious, or boring women may
be amusing, but their conduct mutely argues that "the *knowledge* of the sexes should be the same," and that "women,
considered not only as moral but as rational creatures, ought
to endeavour to acquire human virtues . . . by the *same* means
as men, instead of being educated like a fanciful kind of *half*
being." Austen's comments about the feeble education bestowed upon Catherine Morland, the Dashwood sisters, the
Bennett sisters, the Bertram sisters, and Emma herself, all
inform us how similar were Austen's and Wollstonecraft's
commitment to rational feminine education. Wollstonecraft argues that only a free and unfettered "play of the mind" leads
to that precious quality which she called "true grace and beauty."
Austen's heroines all seek what Austen herself called "play
of Mind," and the tension in the novels derives partly from
the heroines' struggles to achieve or to maintain "true grace
and beauty" while searching for other human beings with whom
to engage in "play of Mind."

The genre of fiction, with its voices, its countervoices, and its
various types of authorial comments, was crucially helpful to
Austen; her ironic, neoclassical "play of Mind" could simultaneously muffle and reveal her own brand of Romanticism—
the celebration of a new human archetype, the gentlewoman
struggling for responsible autonomy. As Ian Watt argues [in
his *The Rise of the Novel*], "Romanticism . . . was characterised by . . . individualism and . . . originality which had found
its first literary expression in the novel." Emma Woodhouse
is one of the most original comic heroines, a macrocosmic
Lady Catherine de Bourgh, whose excesses are the issue of
her pampered sex, her pampered caste, and her vain efforts to
create a function for her intellect. Even the vicious Lady Catherine makes two remarks about matters which preoccupied
Austen herself; Lady Catherine questions the habit of "en-
tailing estates from the female line" and the habit of fathers
in assuming that daughters "are never of so much consequence
as sons."

It is the nature of original people to strip emperors of their
clothing and to cause hostility in those who have benefitted
from things as they have always been. Emma condemns the
double standard time and again, and her excesses, if not exactly
Promethean or Byronic, suggest a strangled yearning to transcend her own fettered condition and to control and manipulate
fiction—at least verbally. That this imperious creative urge is
locked in the body of a young woman perpetually confined not
only in the geographically and socially hermetic village of

Highbury, but also in the sexually hermetic province called
womanhood, is one of the sharpest ironies in the novel. For
despite her intelligence, Emma mimics Wollstonecraft's models
of psychically amputated women who are "habitual" slaves
"to first impressions" that "give a sexual character to the
mind." Emma's wealth leaves her with greater leisure than
she has been trained to use actively, although active work is
what her intelligence and her shaping imagination require, and
her analytical mind has nothing more to feed itself upon than
curiosity about who will marry whom. Austen's feminine decorum and her overt desire to amuse her readers will not allow
her to cry out for her heroines as Charlotte Brontë does for
hers, and George Eliot does for hers, but Emma's alternating
struggles either to escape or tolerate her frustrations form one
of the subjects of the novel.

Austen was quite aware that nobody but herself would appreciate her heroine, and the opening lines suggest that in the
world of comedy as in the world of tragedy, nothing is quite
what it *seems:* "Emma Woodhouse, handsome, clever, and
rich, with a comfortable home and happy disposition, seemed
to unite some of the best blessings of existence." Emma is a
model of one of Wollstonecraft's rich women who are both
slaves and despots. Both conditions "prevent the cultivation
of the female understanding" because exactly the "same obstacles are thrown in the way of the rich, and the same consequences ensue," that is, "the pleasure of commanding flattering sycophants, and many other complicated low calculations
of doting self-love."

Emma is doubly deprived of the opportunity to exercise her
obvious *metier,* the creation of legitimate fiction: her wealth
makes her the idol of a shallow society, and her sex makes
her the idol of her shallow father. To be sure, Knightley is
always suggesting that she *occupy* her mind, but the idea that
she ought to originate anything—that in fact she is already
doing so, in however destructive a fashion—never occurs either
to him or to her. Wollstonecraft describes the psychic plight
of women like Emma: "By fits and starts, they are warm in
many pursuits; yet this warmth, never concentrated into perseverance, soon exhausts itself"; and for this reason, "women,
in general, as well as the rich of both sexes, have acquired all
the follies and vices of civilization, and missed the useful
fruit." Wollstonecraft even offers a paradigm of Emma's insolent behavior to Miss Bates during a Box Hill scene: "I have
seen [a rich, idle woman] insult a worthy old gentlewoman,
whom unexpected misfortunes had made dependent on her
ostentatious bounty, and who in better days had claims on her
gratitude." But Wollstonecraft prepares for this ugly incident,
just as Austen does, by describing the "disorderly kind of
education" women receive: "What they learn is rather by
snatches; and as learning is with them in general only a secondary thing"—as it is perforce with Emma—"if they have
natural sagacity"—as Emma has—"it is turned too soon on
life and manners," in just the untrained type of floundering
that represents Emma's attempts at intellectual achievement.

Knightley, of course, is aware that something is wrong with
Emma, but for all his patent good will, he is not aware that
her condescending control and manipulation of Harriet Smith
is a parody of what Wollstonecraft analyzes as the male "condescension of protectorship," a condescension which Knightley invariably practices against Emma. He is particularly obtuse when she is trying to get him to see how trapped she is
in Highbury. Once when she is describing how Frank Weston-
Churchill might be dependent upon his rich guardian, and

Knightley denies that Frank is so constrained, Emma bursts out: "That's easily said, and easily felt by you, who have always been your own master. You are the worst judge in the world, Mr. Knightley, of the difficulties of dependency." Upon another occasion, Knightley also fails to respond to Emma's sense of imprisonment, although she jokingly points out to him, without rancor, how differently the double standard compels the two of them to live: "But you, (turning to Mr. Knightley) who know how very, very seldom I am ever two hours from Hartfield, why you should foresee such a series of dissipation for me, I cannot imagine. And as for my dear little boys, I must say that if aunt Emma has not time for them, I do not think they would fare much better with uncle Knightley, who is absent from home about five hours where she is absent one—and who, when he is at home, is reading to himself or settling his accounts." Knightley offers the primary classical response of the conventional mind when it is confronted with accurate but unwelcome ideas: "Mr. Knightley seemed to be trying not to smile; and succeeded without difficulty, upon Mrs. Elton's beginning to talk to him." And earlier on, Emma had clearly implied to her confidante, Mrs. Weston, her personal frustrations with the double standard: "A young *woman,* if she fall into bad hands, may be teazed, and kept at a distance from those she wants to be with; but one cannot comprehend a young *man's* being under such restraint, as not to be able to spend a week with his father, if he likes it." Austen herself supplies the italics in Emma's voice. And when Emma asks Mr. Knightley to admit "how very, very seldom (she is) ever two hours from Hartfield," the repetition of the sly little adverb, *very,* is unobtrusive, but it is the sort of deliberate nuance for which Austen is famous.

Although Emma is usually playful about her entrapment, she cannot bear to hear her relatives discuss the journeys have have taken: "I must beg you not to talk of the sea. It makes me envious and miserable;—I who have never seen it! South End is prohibited, if you please." As usual, Wollstonecraft provides an exemplary description for predicaments such as Emma's: "Confined, then, in cages, like the feathered race, [wealthy women] have nothing to do but plume themselves, and stalk with mock majesty from perch to perch. It is true they are provided with food and raiment, for which they neither toil nor spin, but . . . liberty, and virtue are given in exchange."

Benign as Knightley is compared to all the destructive Austenian male flirts, whose paradigms also appear frequently in *A Vindication of the Rights of Woman,* he is nevertheless too pratical, too provincial, too much of a Tory, too used to laying down the social and moral law in Highbury and commanding instant respect and obedience to realize that he is one of the abettors of Emma's unhappiness. He invariably objects, not only to Emma's vicious or silly behavior, but with a special and revealing violence to all Emma's attempts to theorize about what is wrong with her and why, and what is wrong with women and why. And Knightley's suspicious violence represents the secondary technique of conventional people when they are confronted with unwelcome truths which threaten to topple their positions of complete control. For Knightley sees the role of definer and theorizer of social and moral matters as his, and his alone in Highbury, by reason of his sex, his wealth, his middle age, and the place that Donwell Abbey has bequeathed him in the county scheme of things. At one time or another he defines every character in the novel: his brother, his sister-in-law, the pathetic Bates family, Emma's father, Emma's governess and the man she marries, Frank Weston-Churchill, Jane Fairfax, the Eltons, Harriet Smith and Robert

Martin, and of course, endlessly, Emma herself. His quarrels with Emma are battles not only about her misdeeds, but also about her repeated struggles to define her pedicament for herself. After Emma's vicious separation of Harriet Smith and Robert Martin, Knightley tells her that not only has she done wrong, as indeed she has, but that she can never think rationally, since she is sixteen years younger than he and "a pretty young woman and a spoiled child."

Knightley blames Emma for relishing a "delightful inferiority" in her captive and manipulated friend, Harriet Smith, but he, too, relishes Emma's delightful inferiority to himself. Wollstonecraft describes how women can recognize men who distrust them endemically. Such men gloat over women in oxymorons; women are full of "fair defects" and "aimable weaknesses." Knightley's oxymoronic cadences describe Emma as "the sweetest and best of all creatures, in spite of all her faults," and his final benediction upon her informs her that he has become used to "doating" on her, "faults and all," ever since she was "thirteen at least." His roles are those of father, professor, priest, and permanent guardian of a slowly maturing woman. But what maturing person can complete the process of maturation with a man who insists that he shall forever perform the role of surrogate father and rule-giver? Austen leaves the impression that Emma will eventually be able "to act," as Wollstonecraft describes this feminine predicament, "with as much propriety by this reflected light as can be expected when reason is taken at secondhand," but what other chance does she have? Her predicament allows her to meet only two marriageable men, one already secretly engaged, the other, a man who loves her precisely because "she touch'd the brink of all we hate."

But Emma is not the only spinster in this novel whose sex destines her to a servile role. In fact, all four spinsters function as foils for one another. Harriet and Miss Bates are warped by poverty, by ignorance, and by the sycophantic servility which their dependence has induced in them. Emma's treatment of them both, morally inexcusable as it is, represents an almost animal flinching, as though she cannot bear to recognize the covert similarities in their relationship to their society and her relationship to Knightley.

Emma's rejection of Jane Fairfax, ungenerous as it is, also represents her subliminal awareness that something is wrong for both of them. Emma is jealous of Jane's professionalism and repelled by the single *milieu* in which society will allow Jane its practice. As Jane herself bitterly remarks, it will be easy enough for her to find a job as nursery governess; she need simply repair to "offices for the sale—not quite of human flesh—but of human intellect." But just as Knightley thinks that Emma has nothing to complain of, Mrs. Elton thinks that Jane has nothing to complain of. Yet Emma sadly says of Jane: "She is a sort of elegant creature that one cannot keep one's eyes from. I am always watching her to admire; and I do pity her from my heart." This speech represents one of Emma's frequent moods of depression which combine penitence with justice or even tenderness for others. The pity is Austen's as well as Emma's and it is not condescending.

The opening scene in *Emma* is suffused in "gentle sorrow." Emma's talented mother has long been dead, and Miss Taylor, Emma's intelligent, yet meek, passive governess, has just been married. Emma is now suffering from a loneliness that is all the more painful because it is a sophisticated suffering which nobody but herself recognizes. For with all Emma's blessings, "natural and domestic, she was now in great danger of suffering from intellectual solitude. She dearly loved her father, but he was no companion for her. He could not meet her in conversation, rational or playful.'' Rationality and playful wit are two treasures in Austen's pantheon of virtues. Thus, the pervasive melancholy of this first scene warns us that Austen is preparing us not only for Emma's despotism and her self-congratulatory complacence, but also for her enslavement and her muted sufferings in an irrational, humorless society. For the first three pages Austen describes a lonely, bereft young woman, close to tears, a young woman whose family and friends ''afforded her no equals.'' Miss Taylor's marriage to Mr. Weston creates for Emma a most ''melancholy change,'' and she sits by the fire, alone, except for her father, who is nodding in a postprandial sleep. She asks herself: ''How was she to bear the change—?'' She sighs ''in mournful thought,'' musing sadly over ''what she had lost,'' and she continues to ''sigh over it and wish for impossible things, till her father awoke and made it necessary to be cheerful.'' The sensible Knightley now comes to comfort the sad pair, father and daughter, but his courteous yet imperious speech patterns and his entrance almost immediately after Austen's description of what Emma lacks, both indicate that he does not represent the equal partner she so badly needs for maturity. Wollstonecraft frequently says that young people need their peers to grow, and Emma has no peers.

It was Emma's destiny to imitate her own creator, whose witty letters from youth to middle age informus that she, too, often sighed over her own fate and wished for impossible things. But Emma, unlike her creator, seems to have no women writers as models, and thus, instead of turning her fantasies about her neighbors into professional fiction, she tries to fasten her forbidden fictions upon them and to force them to reenact in the flesh the sexual dramas she has created for them.

But Emma's mind is not all fantasy; she often sees more than is comfortable for those she criticizes. She once informed Knightley that he was ''very fond of bending little minds,'' including hers, and that he lacked any ''idea of what is requisite in situations directly opposite to [his] own.'' But despite her tart assessment of his unconscious fault, she is capable of greater justice toward him, in some respects, than he is toward her. ''She did not always feel so absolutely satisfied with herself, so entirely convinced that her opinions were right and her adversary's wrong, as Mr. Knightley.'' After all their quarrels, he would sit in punitive silence, walk away from her ''in more complete self-approbation than he left for her,'' or tell her that she was talking nonsense. But her own ''fair defects and aimiable weaknesses'' allow her always to praise ''the real liberality of mind which she was . . . used to acknowledge in him; for with all the high opinion of himself, which she had often laid to his charge, she had never before . . . supposed it could make him unjust to the merits of another.''

At times, Emma's rueful penitence about her transgressions indicates the insoluble conflict in which she is locked. After she had admitted to herself and to Harriet that she has behaved shamefully, she finds herself ''in the humour to value simplicity and modesty to the utmost''; she even goes so far as to tell herself that ''Harriet was the superior creature of the two— and that to resemble her would be more for her own welfare and happiness than all that genius or intelligence could do.'' Emma concludes that it is ''rather too late in the day to set about being simple-minded and ignorant; but she left [Harriet] with every previous resolution confirmed of being humble and discreet, and repressing imagination all the rest of her life.''

Despite Emma's ''genius or intelligence,'' she is now briefly considering how to become that ''factitious,'' passive, ignorant kind of woman whom Wollstonecraft deplored so often, and of whom Isabella Knightley, Emma's sister, is an amusing paradigm. Just two pages before the description of Emma's decision to practice self-demolition, Austen herself has gently but inexorably indicated that she does not think too highly of this solution to the problem between the sexes. Austen's description of Isabella is full of the Austenian informative yet concealing irony: ''poor Isabella, passing her life with those she doated on, full of their merits, blind to their faults, and always innocently busy, might have been the model of right feminine happiness.'' Austen's use of the conditional verb, ''might have been,'' implies that Isabella might not have seemed such a model to everybody. Austen's verb ''doated on,'' and her comment that Isabella is blind to the faults of ''those she doated on,'' reminds us that Knightley eventually says to Emma: ''I could not thing about you so much without doating on you, faults and all.''

In this same authorial comment, the unobtrusive phrase, ''blind to all their faults,'' also indicates an important Austenian motif. Many Austenian characters are the unconscious practitioners of ''that favouring blindness'' which allows them to believe what they want, despite all evidence to the contrary. Mr. Woodhouse thinks that Emma will never marry. Isabella thinks that her bad-tempered husband and noisy children are perfect. Emma's father and governess think that she is perfect, while Knightley thinks her a ''fair defect of nature.'' Mr. Weston thinks that his son, Frank, wants to pay the courteous bride-visit, and is unavoidably detained. Mrs. Elton believes that she is highly respected in Highbury. Jane Fairfax thinks the selfish Frank is worth marrying. And Emma herself is the victim not only of her own ''favouring blindness'' toward herself, in certain moods, but of Knightley's equally ''favouring blindness'' toward her genuine needs and wrongs. Ironically, Emma's mood-swings about herself—as victim and tyrant, totally good or sinfully evil—are more correct than anybody else's more rigid view that she is totally one or the other.

For lack of any viable solution to her problem, Emma thinks of it in terms of two fierce and punitive dichotomies: she can be brilliant and imaginative, but only destructively, or she can strive for humble passivity, discretion, and ignorance in imitation of those for whom she can rationally entertain little respect. To the extent that she might manage this ''factitious'' character, she will mutilate herself as thoroughly as she had damaged others. Even the participle, ''*repressing* imagination,'' is ominous; Austen's pantheon of virtues includes all types of intelligence, such as wit, intellectual energy, and taste; it also includes strong and lively feelings coupled with sensible decorum, but never virtue by means of ''repression.'' Again, Wollstonecraft offers the archetype for Emma's plight: ''Destructive, however, as riches and inherited honours are to the human character, women are more debased and cramped, if possible, by them than men, because men may still in some degree unfold their faculties by becoming soldiers and statesmen.'' And, one might add, by becoming gentlemen farmers of a handsome and productive estate.

Under these conditions, it is no wonder that Emma, bidden as her creator was, to turn a smiling face upon the society which takes her ''repressions'' for granted, demonstrates all the paradigmatic symptoms of a damaged human being. Knightley assumes that under his care she is to be permanently in *statu pupillare;* her retreats into fantasy, her rejection of her own intellectual and imaginative talents in response to her society's contempt for them, her anxiety in the presence of the intellectually successful Jane Fairfax, and her extreme mood-swings during which she first tries to imitate Knightley's own "complete self-approbation" and then Harriet Smith's pathological self-hatred, all indicate a woman unnerved by forces both within and without which she can find no acceptable means either to "repress" or to direct. She cannot love and she cannot work, for to do one decisively is to shut the door forever upon the possibility of doing the other. And Emma is so constituted that she must do both; her fondness for her nieces and nephews and her obsession with marriage indicate that she craves love, and her obsession with storytelling indicates that she craves work that shapes and transcends experience, and not mere amateur copy work.

Knightley, as always, sees the surface problem, and as always, he offers a kind, yet insufficient remedy. He sees that Emma has trouble concentrating, yet he dismisses her fantasies and her curiously adult awareness that she is buried alive as mere inability to subject "the fancy to the understanding." He says that "she is spoiled by being the cleverest of her family," and that "she had the misfortune of being able to answer questions which puzzled her sister at seventeen. She was always quick and assured: Isabella slow and diffident." He sees how serious for Emma was the loss of her mother, but he sees the dead mother as someone who would have dominated Emma in a parental way, as he is trying to do: "In her mother she lost the only person able to cope with her. She inherits her mother's talents, and must have been under subjection to her." How much good is this man going to be able to do for Emma, a man who considers her cleverness a "misfortune" and her talents almost a crime that require "subjection"? He sees only one solution to her predicament, the classic one: "It would not be a bad thing for her to be very much in love with a proper object." But if she is to become a "proper object" to him, she must turn herself into his type of "factitious" child-wife; a woman, he says, who is "fit for a wife" must be capable "on the very material point of submitting" her "own will" to that of her husband's, and "doing as [she] were bid." As he remarks with his exasperating benevolent smile, that other sort of wife he can eagerly recommend. (pp. 321-29)

The climax of the moral tension between Emma and Knightley takes place late in the novel; the climax of the intellectual and theoretical quarrel between them takes place very early, as though Emma thereafter realized that feudalists, even the finest of them, have closed minds, and that therefore one cannot reason with them. The moral tension represents Emma's obvious transgressions. The intellectual and theoretical quality in the quarrels are Emma's contribution entirely; it represents the toughness, the indomitability of Emma's mind, and the sad truth of her first premise, however wrong some of her second and third premises are. During these battles, Knightley is urging Emma to accept his benevolent feudalism, and she is urging him to listen, at least, to her subversive modernism.

The particular obvious and painful truth that Knightley hurls at Emma is the irreparable damage she has done to Harriet Smith and Robert Martin. The general and less obvious truth, then, as now, emerges in the impassioned yet rational cadences astonishingly reminiscent of Wollstonecraft. Emma cries out: "till it appears that men are much more philosophic on the subject of beauty than they are generally supposed; till they do fall in love with well-informed minds instead of handsome faces, a girl with such loveliness as Harriet has . . . the power

of choosing [a husband] from among many." Harriet, says Emma, is a young woman with a "very humble opinion of herself, and a great readiness to be pleased with other people. I am very much mistaken if your sex in general would not think such beauty, and such temper, the highest claim a woman could possess." One is instantly reminded of Austen's own ironic comment in *Northanger Abbey*: "where people wish to attach, they should always be ignorant. To come with a well-informed mind is to come with an inability of administering to the vanity of others. . . . A woman especially, if she have the misfortune of knowing any thing, should conceal it as well as she can." Austen then comments: "I will only add in justice to men, that though to the larger and more trifling part of the sex, imbecility in females is a great enhancement of their personal charms, there is a portion of [men] too reasonable and too well informed themselves to desire any thing more in woman than ignorance." Wollstonecraft also delivers the charge that most men "look for beauty and the simper of good humoured docility," and that with all of "their superior powers and advantages," they still fail "to turn from the person [of a woman] to the mind." In the discussions of the double standard, Wollstonecraft also uses the subordinate syntax: "The passions of men have thus placed women on thrones, and till mankind become more reasonable, it is to be feared that women will avail themselves of the power which they attain with the least exertion . . . yes, they will smile." The intimate connection between weak marriages and patriarchal capitalism troubles Austen, although she has no radical suggestions. Wollstonecraft abhors primogeniture: "But till hereditary possessions are spread abroad, how can we expect men to be proud of virtue? And till they are, women will govern them by the most direct means"—the proffering of sexual attraction as bait. And the most interesting similarity in theme and syntax between Austen and Wollstonecraft is this comment: "till women are more rationally educated, the progress of human virtue and improvement in knowledge must receive continual checks."

To be sure that Emma's arguments will receive credence, Austen herself echoes Emma's antipathy for the double standard. Austen is discussing a marriage that has taken place before the novel opens. In choosing a wife, the wealthy Mr. Dixon ignores Jane Fairfax, a woman of no wealth and position, but of "decided superiority in both beauty and acquirements" to the plain, dull, but rich woman whom he marries. Austen ironically remarks upon "that chance, that luck which so often defies anticipation in matrimonial affairs, giving attraction to what is moderate rather than to what is superior." Austen means that Dixon prefers nonentity to intelligence in a wife.

Austen is not trying to say that Knightley is as second-rate as Dixon. She is too fair to the serious impediments in the training of both sexes not to value Knightley's surface kindness, his responsible and practical management of his estate, his respect for the sturdy yeoman farmer, Robert Martin, and his courtesies, however self-conscious and ponderous, to the poor and the despised. All these virtues she knew would automativally predispose most of her readers to him, for he is the archetypal English squire, with all of his virtues and all of his blindness. For the most part, his blindness and his belief that the privileges of defining everybody is his alone are not unduly destructive. It is only when he meets a counter-definer whom he loves and therefore wishes to subdue, that he becomes as morally destructive as he is morally salutory. Angus Wilson is one of the few critics who seriously questions Knightley as a husband for Emma: "Mr. Knightley, so much admired by modern critics, seems to me to be pompous, condescending, and a bore. His manliness consists in the looming spectre of a Victorian *pa-terfamilias,* authoritative on every subject, lecturing, always . . . in the right . . . what sort of a husband will he make for Emma's untutored, high intelligence? What will she do all day while he is busy, healthily walking about in all weathers? What has he learned but to treat her as 'the little woman,' 'my Emma,' who has made him think better of spoiled children?"

But let us allow Austen herself to comment upon women in marriage to her lively, imginative, intelligent, witty, novel-writing niece, Fanny Knight. Austen writes with almost delirious joy in Fanny's great variety of attractions and talents, and with equal anxiety about Fanny's problematical future: "You are inimitable, irresistable . . . the delight of my Life . . . such entertaining Letters. . . . Such a lovely display of what Imagination does.—You are worth your weight in Gold. . . . I cannot express to you what I have felt in reading your history of yourself, how full of Pity & Concern & Admiration & Amusement I have been. . . . It is very, very gratifying to me to know you so intimately." Austen concludes this paean of praise with the sad little comment: "Oh! what a loss it will be when you are married. You are too agreeable in your single state, too agreeable as a Niece. I shall hate you when your delicious play of Mind is all settled down into conjugal & maternal affections." (pp. 330-31)

Again and again, Austen's letters comment upon the various types of insolence to which she and her family were subjected, from the most subtle condescension to the most gross. Her comments are couched in every voice: ironic, farcical, rueful, indignant, saddened. *Emma* must have offered her a welcome opportunity to produce a secretly subversive, secretly Romantic work in which the most attractive kind of man, but still, withal, an utterly traditional man, clashes with a perverse yet brilliant version of the exhilarating Fanny Knight or Austen herself. The conventions of the novel then required a happy ending at the altar, as rigidly as Shakespeare's comedies required a comic circle of felicity in the last scene; and our hearts do yearn to accept the fairy-tale ending in which "the wishes, the hopes, the confidence, the predictions of the small band of true friends who witnessed the ceremony, were fully answered in the perfect happiness of the union." But the persistent accumulative evidence with which the novelist supplies us suggests otherwise. (p. 332)

Alison G. Sulloway, "Emma Woodhouse and 'A Vindication of the Rights of Woman'," in The Wordsworth Circle, *Vol. VII, No. 4, Autumn, 1976, pp. 320-32.*

SUSAN MORGAN (essay date 1980)

[*In her* In the Meantime: Character and Perception in Jane Austen's Fiction, *from which the following excerpt is drawn,* Morgan *argues that "Austen's subject is the problem of perception and that to recognize this provides a unified interpretation of her work and illuminates it in areas until now considered obscure." Here, Morgan considers the positive role of the imagination in* Emma.]

Emma is not a book about mature understanding replacing immature fancy. Nor is it about a girl's fear of involvement in life being overcome. It is about the powers of the individual mind, the powers of sympathy and imagination, and about how these powers can find their proper objects in the world outside the mind. The heroine insists that life be interesting and tries to make it so. She makes the child's demand that she be entertained. But the source of that demand is her imagination.

Emma's demand is valid; the largeness of her claims on life gives her greatness, in spite of her faults. The claim of the novel is that life is interesting, that fact can be as delightful as fiction, that imagination need not be in conflict with reality.

At the end of the novel Emma marries Mr. Knightley and is assured of happiness. For Mr. Knightley, who sees her lovingly and clearly, she is "faultless in spite of all her faults." But Emma can no longer think of herself as first because there is someone else in the world. And that someone else is not Mr. Knightley. It is Jane Fairfax. Jane must leave Highbury without ever satisfying that wish to know her which the author has so deliberately created. *Emma* celebrates the joys of close family connections, well-known scenes, "very old friends." It is a story in which the ideal of a lover has turned out to be a relative and neighbor since childhood, in which the idyll of perfect happiness is to be lived without leaving home. But Highbury is not a closed world. And Jane is our promise that there are interesting people yet to become acquainted with. Austen can send her heroine out from the proven delights of her own mind into the world of other people because she has provided someone worth making that journey for.

What Emma learns by the end of the story has been present for the reader throughout in the narrative technique. The leap which takes writer and reader into the minds of chracters is impossible in life but common in novels. Austen is the first writer in English fiction to make this privileged perspective a major technique. She uses "free indirect speech" to see into a character and to see from that character's point of view. Certainly, as [Wayne] Booth has pointed out [see Additional Bibliography], seeing into Emma provides sympathy for her as well as knowledge of her faults:

> By showing most of the story through Emma's eyes, the author insures that we will travel with Emma rather than stand against her . . . the sustained inner view leads the reader to hope for good fortune for the character with whom he travels, quite independently of the qualities revealed.

This inside view has become necessary because of Austen's sense of difficulties of perception, her conviction that there is a space between an inner and outer view. What people or characters in books say and do is not enough to know them by. There are, of course, acts that by themselves condemn the doers. But villains are rare and easily judged. Austen concerns herself with the more difficult and more subtle problem of how to understand those around us and ourselves. Morality in *Emma,* as in all Austen's novels, is not a code, or norm, or principle, which one can live and die by. Instead, it is a way of seeing which includes within its definition some sort of candor or affection. Judgment is seldom conclusive, never infallible. So we understand best and judge best when aided by sympathy and imagination. Austen lets us understand Emma by allowing us, for a little while, to live in her mind.

Austen called Emma a character "whom no one but myself will much like," but it is clear that the joy and pleasure of the book depend upon caring about Emma. Certainly, the external events are not gripping. There are no abductions or seductions, no rapes or near rapes, no murders or stray babies, no stirring adventures, no dark deeds, no characters beneath contempt or even above reproach. There are a few gypsies who wander in and scare Harriet, but they seem a little silly in the environs of Highbury and are soon dispatched. In fact, they remind us that it is not Harriet's rescue from them but her rescue on the dance floor which actually matters. Not only does nothing out of the way happen—very little happens at all. There are some dinners, a couple of parties, one secret engatement, and even a few marriages. We do learn by hearsay of trips, a death, and a birth. In *Emma* the lack of large-scale events is a prominent fact. This is characteristic of Austen. Nonetheless, *Emma* is an extreme case. Less happens in this novel than in any of her others. It is the only one set all in one place, and Emma the only heroine who is never away from home.

Emma is also extreme in the decency of its characters. Austen was never directly interested in villains, but in all her other novels there is at least one man and one woman who are wicked. We do hear about Mrs. Churchill, and the Eltons are both crude and cruel. But they do not compare, at least in their actions, to Isabella Thorpe and General Tilney, Wickham and Lady Catherine de Bourgh, Willoughby and Lucy Steele, Henry Crawford and Mrs. Norris, or Mr. Elliot and Mrs. Clay. Some of these people do horrible things. The Eltons are probably capable of meanness beyond their public cruelty to Harriet or their excruciating officiousness to Jane Fairfax. And Mrs. Churchill could have swooped down like Lady Catherine if Austen had wished to advance her story by external conflict, by having the not-so-nice people get in the way of the nice. But Highbury is an idyll, and its evil characters are ineffectual.

The only character whose actions provide obstacles to the deserved happiness of others is Emma herself. Her snobbery damages Robert Martin as Lady Catherine had tried to damage Elizabeth Bennet, and she flirts as self-indulgently as Mary Crawford. We side with Elizabeth and Fanny, and with farmer Martin and Jane. Still, by what Booth calls that "stroke of good fortune," Emma is the heroine. We don't turn a page to see Robert Martin get his girl or even to see Mr. Knightley get his, but just to see more of Emma.

Emma's power to interest the reader is inseparable from her power to interest herself. Emma will always love herself. In thinking of what she learns it is clear that the aim is not to relinquish her self-love. It is almost the end of the story when Emma makes that wonderful remark to Mr. Knightley that "I always deserve the best treatment, because I never put up with any other." Emma's love of herself is part of what makes her creative and part of why she asks so much of her world. . . . In *Emma* loving oneself is the necessary condition for morality and imagination. This had already been true for heroes. Austen has transformed the idea of the heroine in English fiction by making it true of Emma.

When Mr. Knightley tells her that Robert Martin has at last got Harriet, Emma is relieved and grateful that her interference had in the end not been irretrievable. She vows humility and circumspection: "Serious she was, very serious in her thankfulness, and in her resolutions; and yet there was no preventing a laugh, sometimes in the very midst of them." Without that laugh Emma's joy in her world would have shrunk. For Harriet's fluctuating heart is comical. Emma is not too reformed to appreciate that. Early in the novel, after the pain of telling Harriet Mr. Elton's true intentions, Emma had made a similar resolution, of "being humble and discreet, and repressing imagination all the rest of her life." But Emma has done no such thing. For imagination, like tenderness, belongs to the strong people. To repress it would be to repress the power of the self to reach out and make significant "all those little matters on which the daily happiness of private life depends." (pp. 38-43)

Susan Morgan, in her In the Meantime: Character and Perception in Jane Austen's Fiction, *University of Chicago Press, 1980, 210 p.*

LeROY W. SMITH (essay date 1983)

[*In this excerpt from his book-length study of Austen and feminist issues, Smith interprets the theme of* Emma *as the growth of its principal characters from stereotypical gender-defined roles to states of "self-knowledge" and "wholeness."*]

Emma is Austen's most artful, ironic and objective treatment of the 'drama of woman'. Emma Woodhouse embarks on a 'flight from womanhood'. She resists taking her place in the adult female world because she sees that a woman's place is one of dependence and assumed inferiority. She spurns the 'feminine' role, as signified by her rejecting marriage and asserting her independence of others' control. Although in the traditional critical view her behaviour is wilful and eccentric and any criticism of the social environment is little more than incidental, the special nature of Emma's behaviour, as well as the attention that Austen also gives in the novel to the inequality of the sexes, the indignity of marriage and the plight of single women, raises doubt that her primary purpose is to illustrate individual idiosyncrasy or immaturity. (p. 131)

[Were] Emma's career to follow the traditional pattern, we would watch her struggle to overcome the active forces within her in the process of accepting a passive, dependent role. But Emma, endowed with energy, spirit, imagination and intelligence, and encouraged by uniquely favourable circumstances, refuses to surrender her autonomy, to become 'feminine'. She rejects the idea that a woman must charm a masculine heart. In a society where one's freedom and identity depend upon the possession of power, she adopts the prerogatives of the privileged male as her own. Her attempt to turn the tables may explain Austen's labelling her a heroine whom no one would much like but herself.

Does Emma's 'flight from womanhood' produce a constructive change in her life? Emma may be her own mistress, but she is bound by a false, crippling code. Although she is free not to marry, she is not free to marry as she pleases; and although she rejects the woman's role handed to her, she is not free, apparently, to be whatever it is within her nature to be. If, finally, she acquiesces to patriarchal rule or if her self-assertion, like that of the 'corrupted' children of *Mansfield Park,* follows the lure of a false freedom, then the outcome will be tragic. But neither the tone nor the events justify such a conclusion. Emma's 'flight from womanhood' turns to pursuit and ends in achievement of a true freedom and equality. (pp. 131-32)

Emma seeks to separate herself from the conditions that produce women's dependence and subordination and from the women who can not escape them. She will not accede to the role of passive, complaisant female. . . . Emma perceives that subordinates must please but not the powerful. Miss Bates's behaviour reflects the self-abasement and the self-reduction of the female who attempts to overcome the spectre of non-being by denying the self. Emma's revultion may explain her scorn, and her wish to be among the wielders of power rather than among its victims may contribute to her cruel treatment of Miss Bates at Box Hill.

One potential source of danger to her independence, Emma believes, is the emotion of love. Paradoxically, although she sees that to have a loving relationship is the most important thing in marriage, she fears the power of love to overcome one's self-control.

It moves individuals to action and behaviour which contradict reason and cause a loss of will; it raises the threat of one's being undervalued, of being taken as a fluttery, dependent creature, a 'female', rather than as a person of intellect and dignity; and it may direct one contrary to one's best intentions. If love is dangerous for a man, with his advantages, how much worse for a vulnerable female, as the predicament of Jane Fairfax illustrates. Not having experienced love, Emma is pleased by the idea that she is safe from emotional involvement. (pp. 133-34)

In place of the conditions that restrict women, Emma seeks to create those that would give her control of her life. But her revolt initially is misdirected by her assimilation of patriarchal values. In order to be listened to and have her opinion approved, she replaces 'feminine' docility with 'masculine' self-assertion. In reaction to the contingency of women's lives, she sets out to be 'a manager of destinies'. Emma's treatment of Harriet Smith, who fits the stereotype of the 'feminine' woman, is patronising and condescending, as a male mentor's would be. She manipulates Harriet freely, although 'for her own good', and she manages the task of finding her a suitable husband with all the concern for security and suitability of a patriarchal father: 'This is an attachment which a woman may well feel pride in creating. This is a connection which offers nothing but good. It will give you every thing that you want—consideration, independence, a proper home—it will fix you in the centre of all your real friends. . . .'

Knightley attributes Emma's lack of outstanding attainment in the common female accomplishments to insufficient industry and patience. In fact, she is more attracted by the 'masculine' activities of self-assertion and command. She competes with the Knightley brothers to prove the superiority of her judgement, a 'masculine' attribute. . . . Her distorting fancy bends facts to fit her ideas and fuels her pride in her 'masculine' ability to rule wisely.

But Austen is as sensitive to what may be the drawbacks of exercising control over one's life as she is to the need for it. While events remind the reader of the likely fate of the dependent female, Emma discovers the hazards of an independent life. The 'masculine' behaviour that she copies is as restrictive as the 'feminine' behaviour that she repudiates and poses as great a threat to selfhood. It produces the same sense of isolation and of unsatisfactory relationships. Emma finds that she is in danger of moving beyond reach of what she most desires. It also encourages an egotism that blinds her to the real existence of others and stimulates in her the 'masculine' treatment of women that had repelled her. Like other characters in Austen's fiction who combat male oppression by strength of will, good fortune and the mastery of 'masculine' behaviour patterns, she risks a dangerous dehumanisation. (pp. 135-36)

In sum, Emma's flight from womanhood is self-defeating in a variety of ways: (1) it falsifies her perception of reality; (2) her identification with the behaviour of the oppressor forces her to live vicariously and restricts the growth of meaningful personal relationships; and (3) her adoption of the masculine role limits her ability to recognise and pursue her deepest personal needs and interests. Emma's behaviour becomes aggressive and dogmatic, selfish and self-absorbed. She acts unfeelingly and insolently and sets a bad example for others. She misinterprets what she sees and makes judgements from in-

complete knowledge. She imagines that the games she invents are real and slides into self-deception. Through the arrogance of believing herself in the secret of the feelings of others and proposing to arrange their destinies, she performs actual mischief. Her vulnerability continues, rather than decreases, because she becomes susceptible to flattery, blinds herself to the needs and liabilities of her sex, seems unaware of the existence of others, and becomes involved, for unflattering reasons, where she had intended to supervise. Although Emma seeks to escape the female's confined existence, she does not escape the stamp of the female stereotype in the eyes of others, such as Philip Elton and Frank Churchill. She fails to recognise the world's independence from her control and her dependence on the world. She is ignorant of the true nature of love and of her own emotional and sexual needs. She finds her vaunted isolation frustrating, and she feels the weight of loneliness and melancholy. Unable to acquire the control over her life that she expected, she discovers her own incompleteness. (p. 139)

In resisting the pressure to conform to a 'feminine' stereotype, Emma embraces the 'masculine' stereotype. Then the false self that she has created encounters the social realities of the patriarchal order. But Emma is not defeated by this collision, as some critics believe. She moves to a centre that balances feminine and masculine personal qualities in a unified whole.

Emma Woodhouse's situation is similar to Emma Bovary's in that they confront the possibility of finding no course of action suited to their consciousness of themselves as individuals or of finding no single human being who can comprehend what is happening to them. But in *Emma* the potential for tragedy is muted. Emma Woodhouse has the money which is the key to escaping subjection; her keen intelligence can not be permanently diverted from the truth; she has the courage and the desire to accept actuality and genuinely wants to change; she is not fixed by nature or nurture in a single pattern but can grow in response to new influences; and, finally, she finds the single human being who can understand and appreciate her uniqueness. The issue is decided by the triumph of Emma's core gender identity over the fantasy of being a male and by the learning experience—psychological, emotional and cognitive—that both she and Knightley undergo.

Indisputably, *Emma* is a novel about education, in the course of which Emma Woodhouse acquires self-knowledge. At that point agreement almost ends. To resolve the major issues— the value for Emma of her education, Knightley's nature and role, the outcome of events and the final relationship between Emma and Knightley—one must recognise that *Emma* also is a novel about the need for openness and equality between individuals, as shown in the relationship between men and women. Austen insists that the happiness of the individual requires both self-knowledge, represented by the discovery and integration within the self of the range of possibilities of human behaviour, and concord between the sexes, represented by the integration of two selves, male and female, through the dissolution of artificial social and psychological barriers. The two subjects are complementary and interdependent: achievement of openness and equality requires self-knowledge, but without hope of the former a full and true self-knowledge is difficult to attain. To these two subjects one should add a third of only slightly less prominence: *Emma* is a novel about the responsibility of those who possess power to protect, rather than to oppress, those without it. Finally, one must recognise that the movement towards self-knowledge and mutuality involves Knightley as well as Emma. The self-knowledge gained by either will produce only frustration and despair unless matched by that gained by the other. Emma and Knightley both seek openness and equality, but they do not initially recognise this intention or pursue it wisely. (pp. 142-43)

Truth and sincerity are the guarantors of openness and equality in personal relationships. Emma and Knightley become lovers, finally, because they can be friends. Nowhere else is Austen so insistent that her heroine's marriage is one of equals. 'The perfect happiness of the union', the novel's final phrase, describes a personal integration as well as a wedding.

However, before this union can occur, both Knightley and Emma must overcome the ingrained patriarchal attitudes which prompt Emma to emulate the privileged male and which lead Knightley . . . to assume a superiority because of his sex. Emma must mature, which means that she must free herself from fear of a woman's life; but, equally important, Knightley must accept her maturing, which means that he must learn to treat her not as a child or stereotypically but as an equal. Both must learn to accept the world with its faults: Emma, by discovering the self-defeating effects of her elaborate defence, and Knightley, by learning to tolerate fallibility in others through a discovery of his own failings. (p. 146)

Emma and Knightley experience a liberating move towards wholeness. Blessed equally with energy and vitality, they have ignored, repressed or turned away from properties of their human nature which the society has stigmatised as 'feminine', especially the emotional properties associated with tenderness, giving and sacrifice. However, they finally overcome the psychological barrier of personality stereotypes and acknowledge the range of 'masculine' and 'feminine' impulses that each possesses. By uniting their formerly divided selves, they establish the basis for mutuality and reciprocity in their marriage relationship.

The marriage of Emma and Knightley is based on the spirit of equality and mutual respect that will permit 'truth and sincerity' to rule. It is a marriage that holds the fullest promise of life, one in which the female is openly admired and shares decisions and in which there is mutual trust and a healthy sense of companionship. It is a marriage in which each recognises the human reality of the other, accepts the other's individuality and independence, and feels right and secure enough in their relationship to want to give rather than to receive. Mutual good will governs their actions, as in the decision to reside at Hartfield. Abandoning her flight from womanhood, Emma finds in Knightley a companion for herself and a partner in the duties and cares she will eventually face. (pp. 154-55)

LeRoy W. Smith, in his Jane Austen and the Drama of Woman, *St. Martin's Press, 1983, 206 p.*

FAY WELDON   (essay date 1984)

[*Weldon is an English novelist, dramatist, and short story writer known for her works dealing with the problems of women in contemporary society. Her* Letters to Alice on First Reading Jane Austen, *from which the following excerpt is taken, is a series of fictional letters written in the persona of Aunt Faye, a novelist, to her niece, a "punk" college student required to read Austen's works. Aiming to "make an Austen convert" out of the reluctant Alice, Aunt Faye points out pertinent biographical and historical issues and evaluates Austen's artistry. Her enthusiastic comments on the continuing relevance and appeal of* Emma *are excerpted below.*]

You complain about **Emma.** You say you have read the first third. I will admit there is a middle section of **Emma** which drags, rather.

Let me give you a quick run-down of the plot—the peg upon which Jane Austen hangs her novels. Plots, I assure you, are nothing but pegs. They stand in a row in the writer's mind. You can use one or another for your purposes, it makes some difference, but not much, which one it is. The plot of **Emma** is not quite so flimsy as that of **Pride and Prejudice**: it can support altogether more character, and more observation, and more meaning: and more boredom on the part of the grudging and hasty reader—in whose ranks I still include you. . . . (pp. 78-9)

Emma opens with a paragraph which sends shivers of pleasure down my spine: it glitters with sheer competence: with the animation of the writer who has discovered power: who is at ease in the pathways of the City of Invention. Here is Emma, exciting envy in the heart of the reader and also, one suspects, the writer—and now, she declares, Emma will be undone; and I, the writer, and you, the reader, will share in this experience:

> Emma Woodhouse, handsome, clever and rich, with
> a comfortable home and happy disposition, seemed
> to unite some of the best blessings of existence: and
> had lived nearly twenty-one years in the world with
> very little to distress or vex her. . . .

It's the word 'seemed', fourteen in, which sets the whole book up. It will take four hundred pages to resolve. You have five variations there—handsome, clever, rich, comfortable home, happy disposition—five to the power of five, which you can relate in various combinations of the 'blessings of existence'.

It is so simple, you see, and so wonderfully full of promise, which bypasses the conscious mind of the reader, gets us instantly into the City of Invention, and off we go.

I frequently find myself saying to unpublished and resentful writers who do not understand the reason for their rejection, 'but you must think of your *readers*', and they think I am telling them to write for a market, but I am not. I am trying to explain that writing must be in some way a shared experience between reader and writer: the House of Imagination built with doors for guests to enter in, and pegs for their coats, and windows for them to look out of: it is no use being a recluse. You will die of hypothermia and malnutrition if you live alone in your house, however beautifully constructed it is. It must be a welcoming place, or exciting, if dangerous, or educative, if unpleasant, or intensely pleasurable.

Emma lives with her (to me, but not Emma) irritating, difficult, hypochondriacal father, Mr Woodhouse, in the village of Hartfield. Her mother died in her infancy: she has a married sister, Isabella. She has £30,000 of her own. She was brought up by a governess, who presently marries, thanks to Emma's matchmaking, and leaves Emma lonely. She is conceited. There is a fairly obvious suitor in the village, a Mr Knightley; but Emma sees him in the role of friend, not lover. (Lover in the old sense of suitor, Alice. Fornication was simply not in the minds of decent and self-controlled people. . . .) Another possible lover is approaching over the horizon—a Frank Churchill— brought up, like her own brother, Edward, in rather grander circumstances that the ones into which he was born. Emma has befriended Harriet Smith; Harriet Smith is a beautiful but misbegotten girl. 'The misfortune of your birth ought to make you particularly careful of your associates,' Emma warns her. Illegitimate! Harriet is on the verge of marrying Robert Martin, farmer, but Emma, believing Harriet could do better in the marriage stakes, turns the foolish girl against poor Mr Martin. Mr Knightley reproaches her for this. Emma means Harriet to marry Mr Elton, the handsome curate, and mistakes his courtesy to Harriet for passion. Mr Knightley reproaches her. Jane Fairfax appears as a foil to Emma—more talented, more clever, and more serious than her, and doomed to be misunderstood, and ever so slightly disliked. (I wonder sometimes if Jane Fairfax is not more of a self-portrait of Jane Austen than Elizabeth Bennet—the bright, lovable, wayward heroine of *Pride and Prejudice,* as is so often supposed.) Emma is unkind to Miss Bates. Mr Knightley reproaches her. Mr Elton takes a detestable wife. In and out the relationships intertwine. (pp. 79-80)

I believe that Jane Austen, from the internal evidence of *Emma,* was at that time driven to distraction by her mother and Cassandra, and to boredom by the manner of her life, and not quite having the courage to go to the kind of parties where Madame de Staël would appear, and developing a fatal illness, and humiliated by living in a corner house in the village by courtesy of her brother, who lived up in the big house, when the Prince Regent had a set of her books in each of his houses. I think she wrote on, gritting her teeth, wrapping her misery into herself, taking refuge in the world of invention, instead of going there with a clear mind and heart, travelling freely in and out, unable quite to get the coat properly off the peg. She kept tugging and it wouldn't come; and that is why you have no trouble with the first third of the book and then stopped reading. She was having trouble too.

She did get it off the hook. Harriet develops aspirations to Mr Knightley which shocks Emma into realizing her own love for him. Harriet's origins are discovered to be even lower than at first thought, so she can be safely married to Robert Martin. The odious Mr Woodhouse is talked into liking the idea of Mr Knightley and Emma marrying. The intimacy between Emma and Harriet changes into a calmer sort of goodwill. Well, it would have to, wouldn't it, if Emma is going to be Mrs Knightley. Some have doubted that the marriage of Emma to Mr Knightley is indeed a happy ending, but I am content to let Jane Austen know her own characters best.

We return, very much, in all this, to the 'breeding must out' preoccupation of the times. Emma befriends Harriet, who was born into such sorry circumstances, and tries to teach and improve her, whilst taking pleasure in her simple gaiety (even then, it seems, the gentry looked a little askance at their own refinement, envying the common herd their general energy and lack of inhibition—as our modern-day cultural spokesman will love to go to football matches, and middle-class young ape the language of the streets, and music critics attempt to take the Beatles seriously, and in general invent art forms which require an untutored imagination rather than a dangerously desiccated expertise)—but Harriet was in the end a disappointment to Emma. Mr Knightley, who knew everything, knew it would be so.

Harriet may have been well born (there were funds for her education, so presumably at least one of her parents had money) but she was not virtuously born; she had better make do with a yeoman farmer for a husband. Seven out of ten for genes, take away three for unfortunate beginnings, add one for a good sound education, another two for prettiness and charm, and take away two for a general lack of soundness and you end up with five out of ten—the same marks as Robert Martin, yeoman farmer, began and ended with; it was therefore a good match.

The delight of *Emma*—which I trust by now you have taken up again—is in the violent seesawing of marks out of ten, especially in Harriet's case, which the author awards. Emma herself hovers between seven and eight, losing marks for folly and wilfulness, gaining them for being good to her dreadful father, Mr Woodhouse, losing them (and quite right too) for being so obnoxious to Miss Bates, gaining them again for putting up with grief without making a fuss (unlike Harriet)—and finally making it through to nine out of ten, and thus being allowed to marry Mr Knightley—a steady nine out of ten throughout. And he would have had a ten out of ten, like Mr Darcy, had he been nobly born and about to be a Marquis any minute. (pp. 81-82)

• • • • •

[I] listened to John Tydeman's admirable dramatization of *Emma,* wonderfully produced (in radio they call directors producers) by Richard Imeson, and almost changed my mind about the tediousness of several of its chapters, and rejoiced again at the picnic at Box Hill, where everyone went to be happy and no one was: it was far too hot; and Mrs Elton bullied Jane Fairfax, and Emma was so dreadfully unkind to Miss Bates. Emma let her tongue run away from her; she preferred for an instance the satisfaction of an irritated, witty remark to the satisfaction of being good and kind; allowed a brusque pattern of words to interrupt the delicate intertwining of human response, and

Knightley's proposal to Emma.

thus earned Mr Knightley's reproaches and her own remorse. And such a little thing! Frank Churchill says everyone must say three boring things. Miss Bates, desirous of compliment, offers to do it. Emma says, in effect, but we have a difficulty here. What, only three! Miss Bates, when do you ever stop?, and Miss Bates, stricken and publicly humiliated says, I must learn to hold my tongue.

All our lives, on whatever scale they are lived, however studded with events, sexual obsession, divorce, cancer, the making and breaking of fortunes, public recognition or approbation, reduce themselves at times, like some rich sauce over a low flame, to these little, powerful, painful simmerings, where small events loom impassively large. A picnic on Box Hill on a summer's day, when everything goes wrong; to be remembered, in real life in the future, after a fashion, but never quite, as it were, head-on. The mind slips away, hastily gets round, somehow, like a car going into rapid reverse, grating its gears, when it encounters these small, scraping memories, which do not count as Major Life Events (to use the terminology of the times), do not merit Working Through, but are simply there, and one wishes they weren't. Social lapses; most embarrassing moments; carcinogenic rubbings in the mind. Long years with a psychoanalyst will smooth them over, listening to *Emma* on the radio will do pretty well, sharing this fictional understanding, not just with *Emma*'s writer, but with all her readers as well. A package tour to the City of Invention!

Alice, does it not seem to you most extraordinary: the amazing phenomenon of shared fantasy. I can never get used to it. I suppose half a million people listened to *Emma* this afternoon; of those a few hundred thousand would already know the book; a few thousand, with me, would be willing and wishing Emma *not* to say that she did say, while knowing that indeed she would say it:

> Miss Bates: 'I shall be sure to say three dull things as soon as ever I open my mouth, shan't I?' (looking round with the most good-humoured dependence on everybody's assent). 'Do you not all think I shall?'
>
> Emma could not resist.
>
> Emma: 'Ah, ma'am, but there may be a difficulty. Pardon me, but you will be limited as to number—only three at once!'

Alice, Emma lives!

Or let me put it another way, if that makes you shuffle and feel uneasy. (There are more ways of killing a cat, and making a Jane Austen convert, than you would suppose.) All over the country irons were held in suspension, and car exhaust bandages held motionless and lady gardeners stayed their gardening gloves, and cars slowed, as Emma spoke, as that other world intruded into this. (pp. 91-2)

> *Fay Weldon, "Emma Lives!" and "'I Never Read Much',"* in her Letters to Alice on First Reading Jane Austen, *1984. Reprint by Harcourt Brace Jovanovich, 1986, pp. 74-83, 88-94.*

ADDITIONAL BIBLIOGRAPHY

Barfoot, C. C. "*Emma:* A Woman's Destiny." In his *The Thread of Connection: Aspects of Fate in the Novels of Jane Austen and Others,* pp. 62-84. *Costerus,* n.s. Vol. XXXII. Amsterdam: Rodopi, 1982.

A consideration of the terms "destiny" and "fate" and Austen's attitude toward these forces in *Emma.*

Booth, Wayne C. "Control of Distance in Jane Austen's *Emma.*" In his *The Rhetoric of Fiction,* pp. 243-66. Chicago: University of Chicago Press, 1961.

Demonstrates the way in which Austen ensures the reader's sympathetic identification with Emma by establishing her as the central consciousness of the novel, and yet, at the same time, corrects the reader's perceptions through the use of such rhetorical devices as authorial intervention, irony, and the commentary of reliable characters.

Chandler, Alice. "'A Pair of Fine Eyes': Jane Austen's Treatment of Sex." *Studies in the Novel* VII, No. 1 (Spring 1975): 88-103.

Includes a discussion of the riddle about "Kitty, a fair but frozen maid," referred to in Chapter IX of *Emma.*

Corsa, Helen Storm. "A Fair but Frozen Maid: A Study of Jane Austen's *Emma.*" *Literature and Psychology* XIX, No. 2 (1969): 101-23.

Examines Emma's character in psychological terms.

Craig, G. Armour. "Jane Austen's *Emma:* The Truths and Disguises of Human Disclosure." In *In Defense of Reading: A Reader's Approach to Literary Criticism,* edited by Reuben A. Brower and Richard Poirier, pp. 235-55. New York: E. P. Dutton & Co., 1962.

Argues that in *Emma* Austen was primarily concerned with "the play of mind against mind."

Craik, W. A. "*Emma.*" In her *Jane Austen: The Six Novels,* pp. 125-65. London: Methuen & Co., 1966.

Discusses *Emma*'s place in Austen's oeuvre.

Davies, J. M. Q. "*Emma* as Charade and the Education of the Reader." *Philological Quarterly* 65, No. 2 (Spring 1986): 231-42.

Considers Austen's didacticism in *Emma.*

De Rose, Peter L., and McGuire, S. W. *A Concordance to the Works of Jane Austen.* 3 vols. New York: Garland Publishing, 1982.

A concordance keyed to the R. W. Chapman edition of Austen's works.

Drew, Elizabeth. "Jane Austen: *Emma.*" In her *The Novel: A Modern Guide to Fifteen English Masterpieces,* pp. 95-110. New York: Dell Publishing Co., A Laurel Edition, 1963.

A general introduction to the novel focusing on Austen's "method of social comedy."

Dry, Helen. "Syntax and Point of View in Jane Austen's *Emma.*" *Studies in Romanticism* 16, No. 1 (Winter 1977): 87-99.

Examines the correlation between linguistic constructions and point of view in *Emma.*

Duckworth, Alistair M. "*Emma* and the Dangers of Individualism." In his *The Improvement of the Estate: A Study of Jane Austen's Novels,* pp. 145-78. Baltimore: Johns Hopkins Press, 1971.

Concentrates on the novel's setting and Emma's standing in her society.

Edge, Charles. "*Emma:* A Technique of Characterization." In *The Classic British Novel,* edited by Howard M. Harper, Jr. and Charles Edge, pp. 51-64. Athens: University of Georgia Press, 1972.

Examines Austen's use of comparison and contrast in *Emma.* Edge analyzes the novel in terms of teacher and student, ruler and subject, and health and ill health.

Forster, E. M. "People (Continued)." In his *Aspects of the Novel,* pp. 65-82. New York: Harcourt, Brace and Co., A Harvest Book, 1954.

Cites examples from *Emma* in his discussion of "flat" and "round" characters.

Gilson, David. *A Bibliography of Jane Austen*. Oxford: Clarendon Press, 1982, 877 p.
A comprehensive bibliography of primary and secondary materials published through 1975.

Hagan, John. "The Closure of *Emma*." *Studies in English Literature, 1500-1900* XV, No. 4 (Autumn 1975): 545-61.
A study of the final chapters of the novel. Hagan finds the conclusion of *Emma* central to a complete appreciation of Austen's realism.

Halperin, John, ed. *Jane Austen: Bicentenary Essays*. Cambridge: Cambridge University Press, 1975, 334 p.
A collection of essays on assorted topics in Austen criticism. The volume includes three studies devoted to discussion of *Emma*.

Hellstrom, Ward. "Francophobia in *Emma*." *Studies in English Literature, 1500-1900* V, No. 4 (Autumn 1965): 607-17.
Suggests that Austen's attitudes toward contemporary political, philosophical, and economic problems are revealed in *Emma*.

Jefferson, Douglas. *Jane Austen's "Emma": A Landmark in English Fiction*. Text and Context, edited by Arnold Kettle and A. K. Thorlby. London: Sussex University Press, 1977, 89 p.
Examines various aspects of the novel, including its plot, characters, and style.

Kirkham, Margaret. *Jane Austen, Feminism and Fiction*. Sussex: Harvester Press, 1983, 187 p.
A study of Austen's achievement in the context of the feminist issues of her day. Kirkham maintains that in her portrayal of women in *Emma* Austen subverts literary stereotypes and corrects Romantic misconceptions.

Lawry, J. S. "'Decided and Open': Structure in *Emma*." *Nineteenth-Century Fiction* 24, No. 1 (June 1969): 1-15.
Traces the interrelationship of the novel's structure and its theme of misguided imagination.

Leavis, F. R. "The Great Tradition." In his *The Great Tradition*, pp. 9-41. Garden City, N.Y.: Doubleday & Co., Anchor Books, 1954.
Comments briefly on the relationship between *Emma*'s formal perfection and Austen's moral preoccupations.

Liddell, Robert. "*Emma*." In his *The Novels of Jane Austen*, pp. 90-117. London: Longmans, 1963.
A general study of *Emma* touching on such topics as characterization, setting, and suspense in the plot.

Lodge, David, ed. *Jane Austen, "Emma": A Casebook*. Casebook Series, edited by A. E. Dyson. London: Macmillan & Co., 1968, 256 p.
Reprints early appraisals of the novel in addition to important essays by Arnold Kettle, Marvin Mudrick, Lionel Trilling, R. E. Hughes, Wayne Booth, and W. J. Harvey.

Marie, Beatrice. "*Emma* and the Democracy of Desire." *Studies in the Novel* 17, No. 1 (Spring 1985): 1-13.
Explores the numerous triangular relationships in the novel.

Martin, W. R. "*Emma*: A Definition of Virtue." *English Studies in Africa* 3, No. 1 (March 1960): 21-30.
Proposes that *Emma* is similar to a morality play and that the novel demonstrates the true meaning of virtue.

Merrett, Robert James. "The Concept of Mind in *Emma*." *English Studies in Canada* VI, No. 1 (Spring 1980): 39-55.
Examines how the eighteenth-century philosophical debate about the relationship between imagination and reason influenced Austen's composition of *Emma*.

Moler, Kenneth L. "*Emma* and the 'Formula of Romance'." In his *Jane Austen's Art of Allusion*, pp. 155-86. Lincoln: University of Nebraska Press, 1968.

Explores parallels between *Emma* and contemporary romantic novels and satires on the romantic novel.

Nardin, Jane. "Egotism and Propriety in *Emma*." In her *Those Elegant Decorums: The Concept of Propriety in Jane Austen's Novels*, pp. 109-28. Albany: State University of New York Press, 1973.
Traces the changes in Emma's ideal of "true propriety."

——. "Charity in *Emma*." *Studies in the Novel* VII, No. I (Spring 1975): 61-72.
Views Emma's charitable activities as one aspect of a central issue in the novel—the proper relationship between different social classes.

Parrish, Stephen M., ed. *Emma*, by Jane Austen. A Norton Critical Edition. New York: W. W. Norton & Co., 1972, 460 p.
An authoritative text of the novel, including background materials, letters, and excerpts from contemporary reviews and modern criticism.

Penrith, Mary C. "Plain and Contorted Speech in *Emma*." In *An English Miscellany Presented to W. S. Mackie*, edited by Brian S. Lee, pp. 149-62. Cape Town: Oxford University Press, 1977.
Analyzes the direct speech of various characters in the novel. According to Penrith, there is a correlation in *Emma* "between linguistic varieties and the moral values of the speakers."

Pickrel, Paul. "Lionel Trilling and *Emma*: A Reconsideration." *Nineteenth-Century Fiction* 40, No. 3 (December 1985): 297-311.
Questions the validity of Trilling's influential reading of the novel (see entry below).

Rosmarin, Adena. "'Misreading' *Emma*: The Powers and Perfidies of Interpretive History." *ELH* 51, No. 2 (Summer 1984): 315-42.
Suggests that the standard mimetic interpretations of *Emma* are intrinsically flawed and offers an affective model for reading the novel.

Roth, Barry. *An Annotated Bibliography of Jane Austen Studies: 1973-83*. Charlottesville: University Press of Virginia, 1985, 359 p.
An annotated guide to Austen criticism that supplements Gilson's bibliography (see entry above).

Southam, B. C., ed. *Jane Austen: The Critical Heritage*. Critical Heritage Series, edited by B. C. Southam. London: Routledge & Kegan Paul, 1968, 276 p.
Contains excerpts from nineteenth-century critical commentary on *Emma*.

Stovel, Bruce. "Comic Symmetry in Jane Austen's *Emma*." *Dalhousie Review* 57, No. 3 (Autumn 1977): 453-65.
Contends that the structure of *Emma* is "essentially comic."

Swingle, L. J. "The Perfect Happiness of the Union: Jane Austen's *Emma* and English Romanticism." *The Wordsworth Circle* VII, No. 4 (Autumn 1976): 312-19.
Asserts that in *Emma* Austen dealt with many of the concerns of the English Romantics.

Tanner, Tony. "The Match-Maker: *Emma*." In his *Jane Austen*, pp. 176-207. London: Macmillan, 1986.
Attempts to account for Emma's appeal to readers.

Tave, Stuart M. "The Imagination of Emma Woodhouse." In his *Some Words of Jane Austen*, pp. 205-55. Chicago: University of Chicago Press, 1973.
A study of *Emma* focusing on Austen's treatment of the theme of imagination.

Ten Harmsel, Henrietta. "*Emma*." In her *Jane Austen: A Study in Fictional Conventions*, pp. 130-63. Studies in English Literature, vol. IV. London: Mouton & Co., 1964.
An analysis of *Emma* in which the critic investigates how Austen adapted and transformed the conventions of eighteenth-century fiction.

Trilling, Lionel. "Emma and the Legend of Jane Austen." In his *Beyond Culture: Essays on Literature and Learning*, pp. 28-49. New York: Harcourt Brace Jovanovich, 1965.

An influential, appreciative essay in which Trilling considers *Emma*
as a pastoral idyll, compares the novel to Austen's other works,
and examines Emma's character.

White, Edward M. "*Emma* and the Parodic Point of View." *Nineteenth-Century Fiction* 18, No. 1 (June 1963): 55-63.
Notes ways in which Austen's characteristically parodic view of
life shaped the novel.

Williams, Michael. "*Emma:* Mystery and Imagination." In his *Jane
Austen: Six Novels and Their Methods,* pp. 117-53. London: Macmillan, 1986.
An exploration of the novel focusing on Austen's method of creating uncertainty and mystery.

Robert Browning

1812-1889

English poet and dramatist.

One of the most prominent poets of the Victorian era, Browning is chiefly remembered for his unparalleled mastery of the dramatic monologue and for the remarkable diversity and scope of his works. In "Fra Lippo Lippi," "Andrea del Sarto," "The Bishop Orders His Tomb at San Praxed's," and many other well-known poems, as well as in his masterpiece, *The Ring and the Book,* Browning advanced the art of the dramatic monologue to new levels of technical and psychological sophistication. At the same time, his works reflect a versatility of approach and a cosmopolitan range of knowledge that anticipate the eclectic and international character of modern literature. As a highly individual force in the history of English poetry, Browning also made significant innovations in language and versification. For all of these reasons, Browning ranks as an important figure in English literature, one who had a profound influence on numerous twentieth-century poets, including such key figures as Ezra Pound and T. S. Eliot.

Browning was born in the borough of Camberwell in southeast London, where he grew up in a setting of relative affluence. His father, Robert Browning, was a well-read, broad-minded man who worked as a clerk for the Bank of England; his mother, Sarah Anne Wiedemann, was a strict Congregationalist who sought to pass her faith on to her son. Biographers have suggested that his father's cultivated literary tastes—the elder Browning had an extensive library—and his mother's religious devotion had an important influence on Browning's character and writings. Although Browning's home provided an intellectually rich environment, his formal education has been described as erratic. Encouraged to take advantage of his father's collection of books, he read widely as a boy, acquiring an abundant, if unsystematic, knowledge of a wide range of different literatures. He displayed a premature aptitude for poetry, composing his first verses at the age of six, and at ten was sent to nearby Peckam School, where he remained for four years. Because he had not been raised as an Anglican, Browning was barred from attending the major English universities at Oxford and Cambridge, but in 1828 he entered recently founded London University. He broke off his studies after less than a year, however, determined to pursue a career as a poet. Due to the income provided him by his parents, with whom he continued to live until 1846, Browning was able to devote his entire energies to his art.

Browning was an extremely prolific writer who produced works throughout his long life. His literary career proper began in 1833 with the anonymous publication of *Pauline: A Fragment of a Confession.* Because the poem was cast in the form of a self-revelation made to a fictional character named Pauline, many of its first readers interpreted the sentiments expressed as Browning's own. Biographers now speculate that the negative reaction of these readers to what they believed were Browning's thoughts and feelings led the poet to distance himself from the characters and emotions portrayed in his subsequent writings by adopting the relatively objective framework offered by dramatic forms of expression. Browning's next work, published in 1835 under the title *Paracelsus,* exemplifies this trend. Based on the life of the Renaissance chemist of the same name, *Paracelsus* is a dramatic monologue detailing a person-

ality that readers could not have confused with Browning's own. The critical reception of *Paracelsus* was largely positive, but *Sordello,* another poem based on a Renaissance subject, met with widespread derision when it appeared in 1840, becoming, according to the critic Philip Drew, a "byword for incomprehensibility." In an effort to regain some measure of the critical respect that *Sordello* had lost him, Browning initiated in 1841 a series of poems and dramas entitled *Bells and Pomegranates.* Published in pamphlet form, *Bells and Pomegranates*—the last volume of which appeared in 1846—unfortunately did little to repair the damage done to Browning's reputation by *Sordello.*

Despite the overall lack of favorable attention accorded them, Browning's works had illustrious admirers, including Elizabeth Barrett, who was a respected and popular poet when in 1844 she praised Browning in one of her works and received a grateful letter from him in response. The two met the following year, fell in love, and in 1846, ignoring the disapproval of her father, eloped to Italy, where—except for brief intervals—they spent the remainder of their life together. In Italy, Browning continued to write, publishing the theologically oriented *Christmas-Eve and Easter-Day* in 1850 and the important collection *Men and Women* in 1855. The latter work contains many of his best-known love poems and dramatic monologues, including "One Word More," "Love Among the Ruins," "Fra

Lippo Lippi,'' and ''Andrea del Sarto.'' Although public success still eluded Browning, his works attracted increasing respect from critics, and following Elizabeth's death in 1861, he returned to England, where after a brief period of literary inactivity he began writing again. The appearance in 1864 of the collection *Dramatis Personae,* which contained such important poems as ''Rabbi Ben Ezra,'' ''Caliban upon Setebos,'' and ''Abt Vogler,'' finally brought Browning his first sizable outpouring of critical and popular admiration. In 1868-69 he published *The Ring and the Book,* a series of twelve dramatic monologues spoken by different characters and based upon the record of an Italian murder case that he had discovered in Florence. Tremendously and immediately popular, *The Ring and the Book* firmly established Browning's reputation in Victorian England. From 1868 on, Browning and Alfred, Lord Tennyson were generally regarded as England's greatest living poets. He remained highly productive, and while much of the poetry he produced between 1869 and his death is not now regarded as his finest, the publication of his *Dramatic Idyls* and other works brought him worldwide fame. In 1880 the Browning Society was established in London for the purpose of paying tribute to and studying his poems, and near the end of his life he was the recipient of various other honors, including a degree from Oxford University and an audience with Queen Victoria. Following his death in 1889 while staying in Venice, he was buried in the Poets' Corner of Westminster Abbey.

Scholars agree that Browning's place in English literature is based to a great extent on his contribution to the poetic genre of the dramatic monologue, the form he adopted for a large proportion of his works. With his topical eclecticism, striking use of language, and stylistic creativity, his ground-breaking accomplishments in this genre constitute the basis of his reputation. Literary historians define the dramatic monologue as a poem in which the speaker's character is gradually disclosed in a dramatic situation through his or her own words. In ''Fra Lippo Lippi,'' for example, the hypocritical nature of the narrator becomes increasingly apparent to the reader as the poem progresses. As the monk speaks, he reveals aspects of his personality of which even he is unaware, while the voice of the poet seems to be absent from the poem altogether. Whether he chose a historical or an imaginary figure, a reliable or an unreliable narrator, Browning evolved the techniques of exposing a character's personality to an unprecedented degree of subtlety and psychological depth. As few previous poets had done, he explored the makeup of the mind, scrutinizing the interior lives of his creations. His characters vary from sophisticated theologians and artists to simple peasant children, spanning a range of personalities from the pure and innocent to the borderline psychotic. A considerable percentage of his men and women, however, display his overriding interest in thwarted or twisted personalities whose lives are scarred by jealousy, lust, or avarice. In addition to its psychological depth, critics concur that one of the chief strengths of Browning's work is its sheer abundance and variety in terms of subject matter, time, place, and character. His often difficult subjects usually demand intellectual effort from the reader and reflect the enormous breadth of his interests in science, history, art, and music. His primary source of inspiration was Renaissance Italy; its mixture of powerful religion and worldly grandeur, the egotism and brilliance of its leaders, scientists, and artists, and the flourishing of art it brought forth provided him with many of his themes and characters. Nevertheless, his settings range from the Middle Ages to his own era, reflecting a diverse assortment of cultures. Browning's poetic diction also shows

the influence of many cultures and fields of interest. He introduced a very large and varied vocabulary into his works, using not only colloquial and traditionally unpoetic language, but also obscure and specialized terms drawn from the past or from contemporary science. Rough syntax, contractions, and the rejection of the vague imagery of romantic poetry in favor of more exact and blunt forms of expression also characterize his writings. Like his use of language, Browning's approach to versification was frequently unconventional. In assessing this facet of his poetry, scholars emphasize the variety of his invention—his use of uncommon rhymes and his metrical and stanzaic flexibility.

The critical history of Browning's works initially shows a pattern of slow recognition followed by enormous popularity and even adulation in the two decades prior to his death. His reputation subsequently underwent a decline, but gradually recovered with the appearance in the 1930s, 1940s, and 1950s of important biographical and critical studies by William C. DeVane and other scholars. Browning's early reviewers often complained about the obscurity, incomprehensibility, and awkward language of his works. The long-standing popular impression that his poetry was intellectually difficult and even unintelligible owed its source in large part to *Sordello.* Although Browning spent nearly twenty-five years following the publication of *Sordello* trying to escape from the charge of obscurity, when he did achieve fame with *Dramatis Personae* and *The Ring and the Book,* it was sizable. His late Victorian audience considered Browning a great, profound philosophical thinker and teacher who had chosen poetry as his medium of expression. Scholars point out that if his contemporaries often continued after he became popular to regard his poetry as rough-hewn, unnecessarily challenging, and obscure, they found its difficulties justified by what they considered the depth and profundity of his religious faith and optimism. While modern critics generally agree that the Victorians were mistaken in their conception of Browning as primarily and unhesitatingly optimistic in his outlook on life, the prevailing image of the poet as philosophically sanguine is widely believed to have contributed to the reaction against his works beginning at the turn of the century. In 1900, for example, George Santayana attacked Browning in an essay entitled ''The Poetry of Barbarism,'' setting the tone for an era that found his mind superficial, his poetic skills crude, and his language verbose. Describing the reasons for Browning's poor reputation throughout much of the first half of the twentieth century, DeVane stated that the poet's outlook on life ''seemed incredibly false to generations harried by war and a vast social unrest.'' Despite this critical disfavor, scholars now recognize that Browning's works had a significant impact on early twentieth-century poets in both England and America. Commentators cite in particular the influence of Browning's diction on the poetic language of Ezra Pound and the effect of his dramatic monologues on the pivotal works of T. S. Eliot. In addition to their considerable influence, the value of Browning's works in their own right continues to be reassessed, with critics focusing less on the philosophical aspects of his writings and more on his strengths as a genuinely original artist. While his reputation has never again been as high as it was during his lifetime, few scholars would deny his importance or influence. For his contribution to the development of the dramatic monologue, as well as for his prophetic eclecticism, linguistic originality, and stylistic ingenuity, Browning remains a seminal figure in English poetry.

PRINCIPAL WORKS

Pauline: A Fragment of a Confession   (poetry)   1833
Paracelsus   (poetry)   1835

Strafford   (drama)   1837
Sordello   (poetry)   1840
*Pippa Passes   (drama)   1841
*Dramatic Lyrics   (poetry)   1842
*King Victor and King Charles   (drama)   1842
*A Blot in the 'Scutcheon   (drama)   1843
*The Return of the Druses   (drama)   1843
*Columbe's Birthday   (drama)   1844
*Dramatic Romances and Lyrics   (poetry)   1845
*Luria. A Soul's Tragedy   (dramas)   1846
Christmas-Eve and Easter-Day   (poetry)   1850
Men and Women   (poetry)   1855
Dramatis Personae   (poetry)   1864
The Ring and the Book. 4 vols.   (poetry)   1868-69
*Balaustion's Adventure, Including a Transcript from
      Euripedes*   (poetry)   1871
Prince Hohenstiel-Schwangau, Saviour of Society   (poetry)
      1871
Fifine at the Fair   (poetry)   1872
Red Cotton Night-Cap Country; or, Turf and Towers
      (poetry)   1873
*Aristophanes' Apology, Including a Transcript from
      Euripedes, Being the Last Adventure of Balaustion*
      (poetry)   1875
The Inn Album   (poetry)   1875
Pacchiarotto, and Other Poems   (poetry)   1876
La Saisiaz. Two Poets of Croisic   (poetry)   1878
Dramatic Idyls   (poetry)   1879
Dramatic Idyls, second series   (poetry)   1880
Jocoseria   (poetry)   1883
Ferishtah's Fancies   (poetry)   1884
*Parleyings with Certain People of Importance in Their Day,
      to Wit: Bernard de Mandeville, Daniel Bartoli,
      Christopher Smart, George Budd Doddington, Francis
      Furini, Gerard de Lairesse, and Charles Avison*
      (poetry)   1887
**An Essay on Percy Bysshe Shelley   (essay)   1888
Asolando: Fancies and Facts   (poetry)   1889
The Works of Robert Browning. 10 vols.   (poetry, dramas,
      and translation)   1912
The Complete Poetical Works of Robert Browning   (poetry)
      1915
The Complete Works of Robert Browning. 5 vols. to date.
      (poetry, dramas, and essay)   1969-
The Brownings' Correspondence. 4 vols. to date.   (letters)
      1984-

*This work was included in the series *Bells and Pomegranates,* published from 1841 to 1846. Dramatic works in this series are chronologized by date of publication rather than first performance.

**This work was first published in 1852 as an introductory essay in
  Letters of Percy Bysshe Shelley.

———

THE ATLAS   (essay date 1833)

[*In this excerpt from a review first published in the* Atlas *on 14
April 1833, the anonymous critic briefly discusses the strengths
and weaknesses of* Pauline.]

In this little poem, a poetical spirit struggles against some
mechanical difficulties that often give to the lines a prosaic
character. The metrical construction is occasionally faulty, and

the language is often plain where the image with which the
poet is labouring is mystical.

Pauline is metaphysical throughout, or is intended to be so.
The author is in the confessional, and acknowledges to his
mistress the strange thoughts and fancies with which his past
life has been crowded. This is not always accomplished with
becoming dignity. He does not always speak of his agonies in
language worthy of one who evidently understood them so well;
he sometimes runs slip-shod through his afflictions. But there
are many passages in the piece of considerable beauty, and a
few of such positive excellence that we augur very favorably
of the genius that produced them. (pp. 36-7)

> *From an extract in* Browning: The Critical Heritage,
> *edited by Boyd Litzinger and Donald Smalley, Barnes
> & Noble, Inc., 1970, pp. 36-7.*

[WILLIAM MAGINN]   (essay date 1833)

[*Maginn was one of the most prominent journalists in England
during the first half of the nineteenth century; his articles range
from burlesques in verse to literary criticism and contain a rich
blend of farcical humor, classical allusions, and political commentary. In December 1833, Maginn briefly reviewed* Pauline,
ridiculing both the author and the work in a Fraser's Magazine
*article entitled "The Poets of the Day: Batch the Third." His
comments are excerpted below.*]

'Non dubito quin titulus,' &c., quotes the author of ***Pauline*** . . .
from Cornelius Agrippa; which we, shearing the sentence of
its lengthy continuation, translate thus: 'We are under no kind
of doubt about the title to be given to you, my poet;' you being,
beyond all question, as mad as Cassandra, without any of the
power to prophesy like her, or to construct a connected sentence
like any body else . . . we designate you 'The Mad Poet of the
Batch;' as being mad not in one direction only, but in all. A
little lunacy, like a little knowledge, would be a dangerous
thing.

> [*William Maginn*], *in an extract in* Browning: The
> Critical Heritage, *edited by Boyd Litzinger and Don-
> ald Smalley, Barnes & Noble, Inc., 1970, p. 38.*

JOHN STUART MILL   (essay date 1833)

[*An English essayist and critic, Mill is regarded as one of the
greatest philosophers and political economists of the nineteenth
century. Mill was recognized at an early age as a leading advocate
of the utilitarian philosophy of Jeremy Bentham, but during the
1830s he gradually diverged from Bentham's utilitarianism and
acknowledged the importance of intuition and feelings, attempting
to reconcile them with his rational philosophy. Today, he is considered a key figure in the transition from the rationalism of the
Enlightenment to the renewed emphasis on mysticism and the
emotions of the Romantic era. The excerpt below is taken from
notations that Mill wrote in 1833 as he read* Pauline. *In addition
to influencing Browning, who read them and was deeply affected
by Mill's censure, the notes have become, according to the critic
Philip Drew, "the most famous of all critical accounts of Browning's work."*]

With considerable poetic powers, the writer [of ***Pauline***] seems
to me possessed with a more intense and morbid self-consciousness than I ever knew in any sane human being. I should
think it a sincere confession, though of a most unlovable state,
if the Pauline were not evidently a mere phantom. All about
her is full of inconsistency—he neither loves her nor fancies
he loves her, yet insists upon *talking* love to her. If she *existed*

and loved him, he treats her most ungenerously and unfeelingly. All his aspirings and yearnings and regrets point to other things, never to her; then he *pays her off* toward the end by a piece of flummery, amounting to the modest request that she will love him and live with him and give herself up to him *without* his *loving her—moyennant quoi* he will think her and call her everything that is handsome, and he promises her that she shall find it mighty pleasant. Then he leaves off by saying he knows he shall have changed his mind by tomorrow, and despite 'these intents which seem so fair', but that having been thus visited once no doubt he will be again—and is therefore 'in perfect joy', bad luck to him! as the Irish say. A cento of most beautiful passages might be made from this poem, and the psychological history of himself is powerful and truthful—*truth-like* certainly, all but the last stage. *That,* he evidently has not yet got into. The self-seeking and self-worshipping state is well described—beyond that, I should think the writer had made, as yet, only the next step, viz. into despising his own state. I even question whether part even of that self-disdain is not *assumed*. He is evidently *dissatisfied,* and feels part of the badness of his state; he does not write as if it were purged out of him. If he once could muster a hearty hatred of his selfishness it would *go;* as it is, he feels only the *lack* of *good,* not the positive evil. He feels not remorse, but only disappointment; a mind in that state can only be regenerated by some new passion, and I know not what to wish for him but that he may meet with a *real* Pauline.

Meanwhile he should not attempt to show how a person may be *recovered* from this morbid state—for *he* is hardly convalescent, and 'what should we speak of but that which we know?' (pp. 176-77)

> *John Stuart Mill, ''Pauline,'' in* Robert Browning: A Collection of Critical Essays, *edited by Philip Drew, Houghton Mifflin Company, 1966, pp. 176-77.*

THE SPECTATOR   (essay date 1835)

[*In the following excerpt from an essay originally published in the 15 August 1835 issue of the* Spectator, *the anonymous critic focuses on the formal shortcomings of* Paracelsus.]

The defect in the structure of this poem [*Paracelsus*] is palpable: there is neither action nor incident, scarcely even a story to excite the attention of the reader. Of this the author seems to be in some sort conscious; stating that he has endeavoured to write a poem, not a drama, and to reverse the method usually adopted by writers whose aim it is to set forth any phœnomenon of the mind or of the passions by the operations of persons and events; and that instead of having recourse to an external machinery of incidents to create and evolve the crisis he desired to produce, he has ventured to display somewhat minutely the mood itself in its rise and progress, and has suffered the agency by which it is influenced and determined to be generally discernible in its effects alone. But admitting all this to have been designed, the design may still be very injudicious: for the form of dialogue precludes those descriptions and digressions by which the author in a narrative poem can vary his subjects and 'interchange delights'; whilst the fundamental plan renders the whole piece a virtual soliloquy, each person of the drama *speaking up* to Paracelsus, in order to elicit his feelings, thoughts, or opinions. For these reasons, we conceive that such a poem contains in its structure the elements of tediousness, which no execution could obviate; and, unfortunately, the execution of *Paracelsus* is not of a nature to overcome difficulties. Evidences

of mental power, perhaps of poetical talent, are visible throughout; but there is no nice conception and development of character, nothing peculiar or striking in the thoughts, whilst the language in which they are clothed gives them an air of mystical or dreamy vagueness. (pp. 39-40)

> *From an extract in* Browning: The Critical Heritage, *edited by Boyd Litzinger and Donald Smalley, Barnes & Noble, Inc., 1970, pp. 39-40.*

[JOHN FORSTER]   (essay date 1836)

[*Forster was an English biographer, historian, critic, and journalist who is best known for his* The Life of Charles Dickens, *which is considered one of the finest biographies of a literary figure in the English language. Here, he responds positively to* Paracelsus, *ranking Browning among the foremost poets of the age and praising his powers as a dramatic poet. Forster's remarks were originally published in the* New Monthly Magazine *in March 1836.*]

[*Paracelsus*] is the simple and unaffected title of a small volume which was published some half-dozen months ago, and which opens a deeper vein of thought, of feeling, and of passion, than any poet has attempted for years. Without the slightest hesitation we name Mr. Robert Browning at once with Shelley, Coleridge, Wordsworth. He has entitled himself to a place among the acknowledged poets of the age. This opinion will possibly startle many persons; but it is most sincere. It is no practice of ours to think nothing of an author because all the world have not pronounced in his favour, any more than we would care to offer him our sympathy and concern on the score of the world's indifference. A man of genius . . . needs neither the one nor the other. He who is conscious of great powers can satisfy himself by their unwearied exercise alone. His day will come. He need never be afraid that truth and nature will wear out, or that Time will not eventually claim for its own all that is the handywork of Nature. Mr. Browning is a man of genius, he has in himself all the elements of a great poet, philosophical as well dramatic,—

> The youngest he
> That sits in shadow of Apollo's tree

—but he sits there, and with as much right to his place as the greatest of the men that are around him have to theirs. For the reception that his book has met with he was doubtless already well prepared,—as well for the wondering ignorance that has scouted it, as for the condescending patronage which has sought to bring it forward, as one brings forward a bashful child to make a doubtful display of its wit and learning. 'We hope the best; put a good face on the matter; but are sadly afraid the thing cannot answer.' We tell Mr. Browning, on the other hand, what we do not think *he* needs to be told, that the thing WILL answer. He has written a book that will live—he has scattered the seeds of much thought among his countrymen— he has communicated an impulse and increased activity to reason and inquiry, as well as a pure and high delight to every cultivated mind;—and this in the little and scantily-noticed volume of *Paracelsus*! (pp. 45-6)

Mr. Browning has the power of a great dramatic poet; we never think of Mr. Browning while we read his poem; we are not identified with him, but with the persons into whom he has flung his genius. The objections to a dialogue of the French school do not apply. We get beyond conjecture and reasoning, beyond a general impression of the situation of the speakers, beyond general reflections on their passions, and hints as to their rise, continuance, and fall. We are upon the scene our-selves,—we hear, feel, and see,—we are face to face with the actors,—we are a party to the tears that are shed, to the feelings and passions that are undergone, to the 'flushed cheek and intensely sparkling eye.' The same unrelaxing activity of thought and of emotion, by which the results of the poem are meant to be produced, is made to affect the reader in its progress; and he is as certain of the immediate presence of all that is going on, as in life he would be certain of any thing that made him laugh or weep. *In the agitation of the feelings, sight is given to the imagination.* This is an essential dramatic test, in which Mr. Browning is never found wanting. (p. 47)

> [*John Forster*], *in an extract in* Browning: The Crit-ical Heritage, *edited by Boyd Litzinger and Donald Smalley, Barnes & Noble, Inc., 1970, pp. 45-7.*

THE DUBLIN REVIEW   (essay date 1840)

> [*This anonymous critic expresses disappointment in* Sordello, *finding fault with the construction, syntax, versification, language, and style of the poem.*]

[*Sordello*] is a work by the author of **Paracelsus,** and one not likely to exalt his reputation, or to produce any adipose ten-dency in the exchequer of his respectable publisher. The title page is brief, not defining its character. This brevity may be studied, to enhance curiosity, or forced, from the difficulty of selecting the most appropriate description of the production issued. We have noted down several definitions, out of many that have struck us in the perusal, as being fitted to characterise it; such as "Sordello a conundrum," from the difficulty of making out the meaning or object of the author. "Sordello, couplets illustrative of the interrogative system;" from the pro-fuse use made of the contorted marks of interrogation, which are spread in great numbers through the pages, standing like so many Scarrons, Popes and Æsops, but not contributing their wit, melody, or wisdom. "Sordello, or exercises for the asth-matics," from the wheezy, spasmodic, sobbing nature of the verse. These are but a few specimens which the perusal has suggested to us; but as the determination, seeing their conflict-ing pretensions, is difficult, we must imitate a late chancellor, and postpone our final judgment.

We remember perusing the **Paracelsus** with some gratification, as a work of promise, which, despite its many defects, led us to hope that ultimately, we should be able to hail the author as one deserving of taking his seat among the crowned poets of the age, and whose productions would hereafter contribute fresh stores of beauty, strength, philosophic insight, and har-monious thought, apparelled in majestic and melodious num-bers, to the literature of our country. The play of **Strafford** somewhat checked that expectation. Although in it there was no insignificant dexterity in the construction, the language oc-casionally exhibited power and richness, and somewhat of an artistic eye, there was a meanness in the working out of his conceptions, a want of dignity and appropriateness in the dia-logue, and an offensive and vicious style, apparently grounded on some conceited theory, at utter variance with all the canons of taste and propriety.

Our perusal of **Sordello** has not renewed our early anticipation. The faults of Mr. Browning are here exaggerated and profusely displayed, to the destruction of all interest, comprehension of the narrative, sympathy with the author, or approbation of his intellectual pretensions. The story is most elliptically con-structed, full of breaks and leaps; the syntax of quite an unusual

character, a mass of perplexity and obscurity; the versification is harsh and knotty; the language, instead of being throughout "English undefiled," is larded with many fantastic and arbi-trary inversions, and the whole set together in a ricketty, hys-terical, capricious style, producing the most startling and re-pulsive effect. All this makes us fear that the defects, which we had previously fancied were ascribable to immaturity, are the result of some obstinate system which has now obtained too strong a control over the writer, ever to let him stand up a free man, to discourse of noble and regenerating themes in a mode worthy of such, or of the sublime and responsible avocation of a poet. If the critical aphorism of Coleridge be true, that the poem to which we *return* with the greatest plea-sure, possesses the genuine power and claims the name of *true poetry,* then is **Sordello** certainly condemned; for it is as im-possible to *return* to, as to read it for the first time even with pleasure. (pp. 551-53)

[Mr. Browning] has given indication of powers, that if faith-fully, diligently, and loftily cultivated, might place him in an honourable and benificent position. The world of the beautiful is not exhausted, the number of poets is not yet made up; there are thousands of manifestations of the good, the true, the lovely, the eternal in man, yet to be revealed. He may yet give the world assurance that he is one who has been appointed to this high calling which he aims at; If he *aspire rightly,* he will *attain.* We hope that he will do so; but let him take this warning from us, in the only quotation we shall make from his **Sordello**—

> Change no old standards of perfection; vex
> With no strange forms *created to perplex.*
>
> (p. 553)

> *A review of "Sordello," in* The Dublin Review, *Vol. VIII, No. XV, second quarter, 1840, pp. 551-53.*

THE ATHENAEUM   (essay date 1841)

> [*An anonymous critic here reviews* Pippa Passes, *applauding the moral lessons of the work while disapproving of Browning's de-liberate obscurity.*]

Mr. Browning is one of those authors, whom, for the sake of an air of originality, and an apparent disposition to *think,* as a motive for writing,—we have taken more than common pains to understand, or than it may perhaps turn out that he is worth. Our faith in him, however, is not yet extinct,—but our patience *is.* More familiarized as we are, now, with his manner—having conquered that rudiment to the right reading of his produc-tions—we yet find his texts nearly as obscure as ever—getting, nevertheless, a glimpse, every now and then, at meanings which it might have been well worth his while to put into English. We have already warned Mr. Browning, that no amount of genius can fling any lights from under the bushel of his affec-tations. Shakespeare himself would, in all probability, have been lost to the world, if he had written in the dead languages. On the present occasion, Mr. Browning's conundrums begin with his very title-page. **Bells and Pomegranates** is the general title given (it is reasonable to suppose Mr. Browning knows why, but certainly we have not yet found out—indeed we "give it up") to an intended "Series of Dramatical Pieces," of which this is the first; and **Pippa Passes** is a very pretty exercise of the reader's ingenuity, which we believe, however, on reading the poem, we may venture to say we have succeeded in solving. A curious part of the matter is, that these "Dramatical Pieces" are produced in a cheap form . . . to meet and help the large demand—the "sort of pit-audience"—which Mr. Browning anticipates for them! How many men does Mr. Browning think there are in the world who have time to read this little poem of his? and of these, what proportion does he suppose will waste it, in searching after treasures that he thus unnecessarily and deliberately conceals? "Of course," he says, "such a work as this must go on no longer than it is liked;"—and, therefore, we are speaking of it, now, with that reverence and forbearance which one is accustomed to exercise towards the dead. Still-born, itself, it is also, no doubt, the last of its race—that is, if their being maintained by the public is a positive condition of their being begotten. Yet it has its limbs and lineaments of beauty, and exhibits the traces of an immortal spirit.

The idea of this little drama is, in itself, we think, remarkably beautiful, and well worth working out in language suited to its own simple and healthy moral. One of the daughters of labour, Pippa, a young girl employed in the silk-mills of Asolo, in the Trevisan, rises from her bed, on new-year's morning,—her single holiday of all the year: and, as she pursues the long, but willing, labours of her toilet, the map of its boundless enjoyments unfolds before her imagination. Then, among the light-hearted girl's thoughts, come those which *must* intrude upon the speculations of the poor—the contrasts with her own lowly lot presented by the more fortunate forms of life which she sees everywhere around her. Her neighbours of the little town of Asolo pass in review before her, with their several circumstances of what, to the outward eye, is advantage; and a touch of the envy and ill will, from which even the humble cannot be wholly exempt, mingles with her purer fancies, and dims the brightness of her holiday morning. But, in the breast of this joyous-hearted girl, these feelings soon take a healthier tone,—resolving themselves into reliance upon providence, contentment with her lot, which has in it this *one* chartered day—now only beginning—and a sense that she is a child of God as well as all the others, and has a certain value in the sum of creation, like the rest:—and so, she breaks away out into the sunshine, merry as a May-day queen. . . . And then, the poem, which has no unity of action,—is held together by the single unity of its moral, and is dramatic only because it is written in dialogue-form—introduces us, by a series of changes, into the interiors of certain of those dwellings which the envious thoughts of Pippa had failed to pierce: and we are present at scenes of passion or intrigue, which the trappings, that had dazzled her eye, serve to hide. One of these, between the wife of a rich miser and her paramour,—on the night which conceals the murder of the husband, by the guilty pair, but just as the day is about to dawn upon it—is written with such power of passion and of painting (with a voluptuousness of colour and incident, however, which Mr. Browning may find it convenient to subdue, for an English public) as marks a master-hand,—and makes it really a matter of lamentation, that he should persist in thinking it necessary for a poet to adopt the tricks of a conjuror, or fancy that among the true spells of the former are the mock ones of the latter's mystical words. Into this scene of guilt and passion,—as into all the others to which we are introduced,—breaks the clear voice of a girl, singing in the young sunshine. By each and all of them, "Pippa passes,"—carolling away her one untiring burthen of gladness,—carrying everywhere her moral that "God's in his heaven," and the world beneath his eye—scattering sophisms and startling crime. Before this one natural and important truth, taught to a cheerful and lowly heart, the artificialities of life severally dissolve, and its criminals grow pale. Surely, there is something very fine in this! Not only have we the trite, but valuable, moral that happiness is more evenly distributed than it seems, enforced in a new form,—but also that other and less popularly

understood one, which it were well the poor should learn,—and still better that the rich should ponder,—that the meanest of them all has his appointed value in God's scheme,—and a higher part may be cast to him who has to play it in rags, than to the puppet of the drama who enacts king, and walks the stage in purple. This despised little silk-weaver, like a messenger from God, knocks at the hearts of all these persons who seem to her so privileged,—and the proudest of them all opens to her. Again, we say, this is very fine;—and Mr. Browning is unjust both to himself and others, when he subjects it to the almost certainty of being lost. Why should an author, who can think such living thoughts as these, persist in making mummies of them?—and why should we, ere we could disengage this high and beautiful truth, have had to go through the tedious and disagreeable process of unwrapping?

> *"Anthology for 1841," in* The Athenaeum, *No. 737, December 11, 1841, p. 952.*

CHARLES DICKENS   (letter date 1842)

[*Dickens, a nineteenth-century English novelist, short story writer, and dramatist, is one of the greatest and most popular novelists in world literature. His works display his comic gifts, his deep social concerns, and his extraordinary talent for characterization. In the excerpt below, taken from a letter to John Forster, Dickens expresses deep admiration for* A Blot in the 'Scutcheon, *emphasizing its affective power.*]

Browning's play [*A Blot in the 'Scutcheon*] has thrown me into a perfect passion of sorrow. To say there is anything in its subject save what is lovely, true, deeply affecting, full of the best emotion, the most earnest feeling, and the most true and tender a source of interest, is to say that there is no light in the sun, and no heat in the blood. It is full of genius, natural and great thoughts, profound and yet simple and beautiful in its vigour. I know of nothing that is so affecting, nothing in any books I have ever read, as Mildred's recurrence to that 'I was so young—I had no mother.' I know no love like it, no passion like it, no moulding of a splendid thing after its conception, like it. And I swear it is a tragedy that *must* be played; and must be played, moreover, by Macready. There are some things I would have changed if I could (they are very slight, mostly broken lines), and I assuredly would have the old servant begin his tale upon the scene; and be taken by the throat, or drawn upon, by his master, in its commencement. But the tragedy I never shall forget, or less vividly remember than I do now. And if you tell Browning that I have seen it, tell him that I believe from my soul there is no man living (and not many dead) who could produce such a work.

> *Charles Dickens, in an extract from a letter to John Forster on November 25, 1842, in* Browning: The Critical Heritage, *edited by Boyd Litzinger and Donald Smalley, Barnes & Noble, Inc., 1970, p. 92.*

E. B. BARRETT   (letter date 1845)

[*Barrett began corresponding with Browning in January 1845, meeting him in person for the first time in May of that year. In the interim, she made the following critique of his writing in a letter to Thomas Westwood, noting that Browning's "Sphinxine" obscurity hindered widespread appreciation of his work. For additional commentary by Barrett, see excerpt dated 21 July 1845.*]

The sin of Sphinxine literature I admit. Have I not struggled hard to renounce it? Do I not, day by day? Do you know that

I have been told that *I* have written things harder to interpret than Browning himself?—only I cannot, cannot believe it—he is so very hard. Tell me honestly . . . if anything like the Sphinxineness of Browning, you discover in me; take me as far back as "The Seraphim" volume and answer! As for Browning, the fault is certainly great, and the disadvantage scarcely calculable, it is so great. He cuts his language into bits, and one has to join them together, as young children do their dissected maps, in order to make any meaning at all, and to study hard before one can do it. Not that I grudge the study [or] the time. The depth and power of the significance (when it is apprehended) glorifies the puzzle. With you and me it is so; but with the majority of readers, even of readers of poetry, it is not and cannot be so.

The consequence is, that he is not read except in a peculiar circle very strait and narrow. He will not die, because the principle of life is in him, but he will not live the warm summer life which is permitted to many of very inferior faculty, because he does not come out into the sun. (pp. 254-55)

> *E. B. Barrett, in a letter to Mr. Westwood in April, 1845, in* The Letters of Elizabeth Barrett Browning, *Vol. I, edited by Frederic G. Kenyon, Smith, Elder, & Co., 1897, pp. 254-55.*

ELIZABETH BARRETT BARRETT (letter date 1845)

[*Browning published several poems in* Hood's Magazine *in 1844-45, subsequently including them in* Dramatic Romances and Lyrics. *Barrett discusses these verses in the letter to Browning excerpted below, praising various qualities of the works yet stressing Browning's need to establish a more fluid rhythm in his poems. For additional commentary by Barrett, see excerpt dated April 1845.*]

[The *Hood* poems have delighted me; **"The Tomb at San Praxed's"**] is of course the finest and most powerful . . . and indeed full of the power of life . . . and of death. It has impressed me very much. Then the [**"Boy and the Angel,"**] with all its beauty and significance!—and the **"Garden Fancies"** . . . some of the stanzas about the name of the flower, with such exquisite music in them, and grace of every kind— and with that beautiful and musical use of the word 'meandering,' which I never remember having seen used in relation to *sound* before. It does to mate with your '*simmering* quiet' in *Sordello,* which brings the summer air into the room as sure as you read it. Then I like your burial of the pedant so much!— you have quite the damp smell of funguses and the sense of creeping things through and through it. And the **"Laboratory"** is hideous as you meant to make it:—only I object a little to your tendency . . . which is almost a habit, and is very observable in this poem I think, . . . of making lines difficult for the reader to read . . . see the opening lines of this poem. Not that music is required everywhere, nor in *them* certainly, but that the uncertainty of rhythm throws the reader's mind off the *rail* . . . and interrupts his progress with you and your influence with him. Where we have not direct pleasure from rhythm, and where no peculiar impression is to be produced by the changes in it, we should be encouraged by the poet to *forget it altogether;* should we not? I am quite wrong perhaps—but you see how I do not conceal my wrongnesses where they mix themselves up with my sincere impressions. And how could it be that no one within my hearing ever spoke of these poems? Because it is true that I never saw one of them—never!—except **"Claret and Tokay,"** which is inferior to all; and that I was quite unaware of your having printed so much with Hood—or at all, except this **"Claret and Tokay,"** and this [**"Flight of the Duchess"**]! The world is very deaf and dumb, I think— but in the end, we need not be afraid of its not learning its lesson. (pp. 134-35)

> *Elizabeth Barrett Barrett, in a letter to Robert Browning on July 21, 1845, in* The Letters of Robert Browning and Elizabeth Barrett Barrett: 1845-1846, *Vol. I, Harper & Brothers, Publishers, 1899, pp. 133-35.*

[GEORGE HENRY LEWES] (essay date 1847)

[*Lewes was one of the most versatile men of letters of the Victorian era. Critics often cite his influence on the novelist George Eliot, to whom he was a companion and mentor, as his principal contribution to English letters, but they also credit him with critical acumen in his literary commentary, most notably in his dramatic criticism. Lewes regarded Browning as an original voice in poetry who yet lacked the intellectual depth and prosodic sensitivity necessary for poetic distinction. He expresses this opinion in the excerpt below, which is taken from a review of* Bells and Pomegranates.]

[Robert Browning] is assuredly not a great poet; he is not even a distinguished poet, whose works will be gathered into future collections; but he is nevertheless a man who stands out in relief from his contemporaries—he is a writer of whom one must speak with the respect due to originality. In an age more favourable to the production of poetry, he might have been conspicuous; for he is endowed with some portion of the great faculty which we may metaphorically call the 'eye to see.' Deficient in some of the great requisites of his art, he has that one primary requisite: the power of seeing for himself and writing in his own language. Robert Browning is Robert Browning—call him sublime or call him feeble, take any view you will of his poems, you must still admit that he is one standing up to speak to mankind in his speech, not theirs— what he thinks, not what they think. We do not say that there are no traces of other poets in his works: he is of his age, and no man can pretend to escape its influence; he has studied poetry, and no man can at all times separate in his mind the acquired from the generated; but we do say emphatically that he is, in our strict and narrow sense of the term, no imitator, but an original thinker and an original writer.

Unfortunately, this high praise demands some qualification, and we are forced to add, that he is neither a deep thinker nor a musical writer. So that, although his originality has created for him an eminent position amongst a race of imitators, he has never yet been able to charm the public—he has never produced anything like "Mariana at the Moated Grange," "Locksley Hall," "Ulysses," "Œnone," "Godiva," or the "Miller's Daughter," (we mention those least resembling each other,) with which Tennyson has built himself a name. Nor do we anticipate that he will ever do so. He has now been some years before the public, and in various characters. His first poem, which (unlucky circumstance!) is still regarded as his best, was *Paracelsus.* We well remember its appearance, and the attention it drew on the new poet, who, being young, was held destined to achieve great things. As a first work, it was assuredly remarkable. It had good thoughts, clear imagery, genuine original speech, touches of simple pathos, caprices of fancy, and a power of composition which made one hope that more experience and practice would ripen him into a distinguished poet. There were two objections, which occurred to us at the time. We did not lay much stress upon them, as the author was evidently young. Age and practice, we thought, would certainly remove them. They were the sort of faults most likely to be found in youthful works—viz., a great mistake in the choice of subject, and an abruptness, harshness, and inelegance of versification. It was pardonable in a young man to make a quack his hero; it looked a paradox, tempting to wilful and skilful ingenuity. On the other hand, it also betokened, or seemed to betoken, a want of proper earnestness and rectitude of mind—a love rather of the extraordinary than of the true. Paracelsus was not the hero a young man should have chosen; and yet one felt that he was just the hero a young man would choose. It seems to us that what this betokened has come to pass, and that in his subsequent works we have, if not the *same* fault, yet a fault which springs, we take it, from the same source. His conceptions are either false or feeble. In the work which succeeded *Paracelsus* [i.e., *Strafford*], we noted a repetition of the very error itself—viz., in the attempt to idealize into a hero that great but desperate Strafford, the 'wicked earl,' as he was called, and as his actions prove him. Meanwhile the other fault—that, namely, of harshness and abruptness—was carried almost to a ridiculous extent; the language was spasmodic, and tortured almost into the style of Alfred Jingle, Esq., in *Pickwick,* as the *Edinburgh Reviewer* remarked at the time. Next, after an interval of two or three years, if our memory serves us, came *Sordello.* What the merit or demerit of conception in that poem may be, no one can presume to say: for except the author himself and the printer's reader (in the course of duty), no earthly being ever toiled through that work. Walking on a new-ploughed field of damp clayey soil, would be skating compared to it. Even his staunchest admirers could say nothing to *Sordello.* Great as is the relish for the obscure and the involved in some minds, there was no one found to listen to these Sybilline incoherences. Other dealers in the obscure have at least charmed the ear with a drowsy music, but Sordello's music was too grating and cacophonous to admit of the least repose. Whether Browning is to this day convinced of his mistake we know not, but to our ever-renewed surprise we often see *Sordello* advertised. That he has not burnt every copy he could by any means lay hands on, is to be explained only upon the principle which makes a mother cherish more fondly the reprobate or the cripple of her family.

This much, at any rate, is significant; he has ventured on no such experiment on the public patience since *Sordello.* The subsequent poems here collected, as *Bells and Pomegranates,* are always readable, if not often musical, and are not insults to our ears. But, as we hinted, the old objections still remain. He has not yet learned to take due pains with his subject, nor to write clearly and musically. It appears as if he sat down to write poetry without the least preparation; that the first subject which presented itself was accepted, as if any canvass was good enough to be embroidered upon. And respecting his versification, it appears as if he consulted his own ease more than the reader's; and if by any arbitrary distribution of accents he could make the verse satisfy his own ear, it must necessarily satisfy the ear of another. At the same time, he occasionally pours forth a strain of real melody, and always exhibits great powers of rhyming. One of the most evenly written of his pieces happens to be a great favourite of ours ["**The Lost Leader**"]. . . . (pp. 495-97)

There are some expressions . . . to which one might object, but the whole poem exhibits a strength, solidity, and sobriety uncommon in contemporary writing. There is no affectation of thought in it; there is none of the pretension which usually mars such poems. The feeling is true, and is manly in its sorrow; and if poets ever listened to the advice so liberally

offered them by critics, we would counsel Robert Browning to spare us his caprices, and give us more such writing. He is still young, but he is old enough to have outlived the tendency which urges inexperienced poets into a fantastic and unreal region, simply because they have not sufficiently penetrated into the world of reality. For as Jean Paul, in his *Vorschule der Œsthetik,* admirably says, 'the novelty of their feelings makes them suppose that the objects which excite them are also novel; and they believe that through the former they produce the latter. Hence they plunge either into the unknown and unnamed, in foreign lands and times; or, still more willingly, occupy themselves with the lyrical: for, in the Lyric, there is no other nature to be represented than that which the Lyrist brings with him.' This period Browning has outlived; and from him now, if ever, we ought to expect works that are the transcript of real experience.

But will he pardon us if we say, that we would more gladly meet him on the next occasion as a writer of prose? It may seem a strange compliment to pay a man who comes before us as a poet; yet a compliment it is. We could say the same to few of his rivals: mediocre as is their poetry, their prose we suspect would be detestable. By dint of assiduous study, 'a reasonable good ear in music,' and a fluent rhyming faculty, they produce verses which, if they do not touch the heart, nor stir the soul, do nevertheless, in some measure, gratify the ear. But if we pause for a moment to consider the *material* for their works, we shall find it so weak, vapid, common-place, or false, that to think of it in prose is alarming. They do not seem to have thought enough and seen enough to be able to be reasonable in prose. This is not the case with Browning. His works have many defects, but they have not that; they show a clear, open mind, prone to reflection; they show that he thinks for himself, and such a man is worth hearing. But he would be better worth hearing in prose than in verse, because, as Göthe said of the rhymers of his day, it is a pity to hear men attempt to *sing* what they can only *speak*. . . . Browning is certainly not a born singer, and what is more, he has not caught the echo of another's music—he wants the melody and grace of which verse should be made. The sense of Beauty is not keen in him; and thoughts, however noble, conceptions, however grand, will not supply the place of beauty. (pp. 498-99)

The exigences of prose would be beneficial to him, by curbing his capricious flights, and making him pay more attention to the ground plan than he now does. (p. 499)

[George Henry Lewes], ''Robert Browning and the Poetry of the Age,'' in The British Quarterly Review, *Vol. VI, November, 1847, pp. 490-509.*

[GEORGE ELIOT] (essay date 1856)

[*Eliot is considered one of the foremost English novelists of the nineteenth century. Her novels, including* Middlemarch *and* The Mill on the Floss, *explore psychological and moral issues while providing intimate pictures of everyday life informed by a profound insight into human character. In the following excerpt from a review of* Men and Women, *Eliot assesses the strengths and weaknesses of Browning's poems, faulting their ''want of music'' but praising such qualities as their originality and energy.*]

Turning from the ordinary literature of the day to such a writer as Browning, is like turning from Flotow's music, made up of well-pieced shreds and patches, to the distinct individuality of Chopin's Studies or Schubert's Songs. Here, at least, is a man who has something of his own to tell us, and who can tell it impressively, if not with faultless art. There is nothing sickly or dreamy in him: he has a clear eye, a vigorous grasp, and courage to utter what he sees and handles. His robust energy is informed by a subtle, penetrating spirit, and this blending of opposite qualities gives his mind a rough piquancy that reminds one of a russet apple. His keen glance pierces into all the secrets of human character, but, being as thoroughly alive to the outward as to the inward, he reveals those secrets, not by a process of dissection, but by dramatic painting. We fancy his own description of a poet applies to himself:—

> He stood and watched the cobbler at his trade,
> The man who slices lemons into drink,
> The coffee-roaster's brazier, and the boys
> That volunteer to help him at the winch.
> He glanced o'er books on stalls with half an eye,
> And fly-leaf ballads on the vendor's string,
> And broad-edge bold-print posters by the wall.
> *He took such cognizance of men and things,*
> *If any beat a horse, you felt he saw;*
> *If any cursed a woman, he took note;*
> *Yet stared at nobody,—they stared at him,*
> *And found, less to their pleasure than surprise,*
> *He seemed to know them and expect as much.*

Browning has no soothing strains, no chants, no lullabys; he rarely gives voice to our melancholy, still less to our gaiety; he sets our thoughts at work rather than our emotions. But though eminently a thinker, he is as far as possible from prosaic; his mode of presentation is always concrete, artistic, and, where it is most felicitous, dramatic. Take, for example, **"Fra Lippo Lippi,"** a poem at once original and perfect in its kind. The artist-monk, Fra Lippo, is supposed to be detected by the night-watch roaming the streets of Florence, and while sharing the wine with which he makes amends to the Dogberrys for the roughness of his tongue, he pours forth the story of his life and his art with the racy conversational vigour of a brawny genius under the influence of the Care-dispeller. (p. 291)

Extracts cannot do justice to the fine dramatic touches by which Fra Lippo is made present to us, while he throws out [his] instinctive Art-criticism. And extracts from **"Bishop Blougram's Apology,"** an equally remarkable poem of what we may call the dramatic-psychological kind, would be still more ineffective. "Sylvester Blougram, styled *in partibus Episcopus*," is talking

> Over the glass's edge when dinner's done,
> And body gets its sop and holds its noise
> And leaves soul free a little,

with "Gigadibs the literary man," to whom he is bent on proving by the most exasperatingly ingenious sophistry, that the theory of life on which he grounds his choice of being a bishop, though a doubting one is wiser in the moderation of its ideal, with the certainty of attainment, than the Gigadibs theory, which aspires after the highest and attains nothing. The way in which Blougram's motives are dug up from below the roots, and laid bare to the very last fibre, not by a process of hostile exposure, not by invective or sarcasm, but by making himself exhibit them with a self-complacent sense of supreme acuteness, and even with a crushing force of worldly common sense, has the effect of masterly satire. . . . Belonging to the same order of subtle yet vigorous writing are the **"Epistle of Karshish, the Arab physician,"** **"Cleon,"** and **"How it strikes a Contemporary."** **"In a Balcony"** is so fine, that we regret

it is not a complete drama instead of being merely the suggestion of a drama. One passage especially tempts us to extract.

> All women love great men
> If young or old—it is in all the tales—
> Young beauties love old poets who can love—
> Why should not he the poems in my soul,
> The love, the passionate faith, the sacrifice,
> The constancy? I throw them at his feet.
> Who cares to see the fountain's very shape
> And whether it be a Triton's or a Nymph's
> That pours the foam, makes rainbows all around?
> You could not praise indeed the empty conch;
> *But I'll pour floods of love and hide myself.*

These lines are less rugged than is usual with Browning's blank verse; but generally, the greatest deficiency we feel in his poetry is its want of music. The worst poems in his new volumes are, in our opinion, his lyrical efforts; for in these, where he engrosses us less by his thought, we are more sensible of his obscurity and his want of melody. His lyrics, instead of tripping along with easy grace, or rolling with a torrent-like grandeur, seem to be struggling painfully under a burthen too heavy for them; and many of them have the disagreeable puzzling effect of a charade, rather than the touching or animating influence of song. We have said that he is never prosaic; and it is remarkable that in his blank verse, though it is often colloquial, we are never shocked by the sense of a sudden lapse into prose. Wordsworth is, on the whole, a far more musical poet than Browning, yet we remember no line in Browning so prosaic as many of Wordsworth's, which in some of his finest poems have the effect of bricks built into a rock. But we must also say that though Browning never flounders helplessly on the plain, he rarely soars above a certain tableland—a footing between the level of prose and the topmost heights of poetry. He does not take possession of our souls and set them aglow, as the greatest poets do. We admire his power, we are not subdued by it. Language with him does not seem spontaneously to link itself into song, as sounds link themselves into melody in the mind of the creative musician; he rather seems by his commanding powers to compel language into verse. He has *chosen* verse as his medium; but of our greatest poets we feel that they had no choice: Verse chose them. Still we are grateful that Browning chose this medium: we would rather have **"Fra Lippo Lippi"** than an essay on Realism in Art; we would rather have **"The Statue and the Bust"** than a three-volumed novel with the same moral; we would rather have **"Holy-Cross Day"** than "Strictures on the Society for the Emancipation of the Jews." (pp. 294-96)

> [*George Eliot*], "*Belles Lettres*," in The Westminster Review, n.s. Vol. IX, January, 1856, pp. 290-312.

THOMAS CARLYLE (letter date 1856)

[*A noted nineteenth-century essayist, historian, critic, and social commentator, Carlyle was a central figure of the Victorian age in England and Scotland. Advocating a Christian work ethic and stressing the importance of order, piety, and spiritual fulfillment in his writings, he exerted a powerful moral influence in an era of rapidly shifting values. The following excerpt is taken from a letter of advice that Carlyle wrote to Browning. Although he hails him as perhaps the most promising poet of his generation, Carlyle also stresses the threat that Browning's "unintelligibility" poses to his art and reputation.*]

It is certain there is an excellent opulence of intellect in [*Men and Women*]: intellect in the big ingot shape and down to the smallest current coin;—I shall look far, I believe, to find such a pair of eyes as I see busy there inspecting human life this long while. The keenest just insight into men and things;—and all that goes along with really good insight: a fresh valiant manful character, equipped with rugged humour, with just love, just contempt, well carried and bestowed;—in fine a most extraordinary power of expression; such I must call it, whether it be 'expressive' enough, or not. Rhythm there is too, endless poetic fancy, symbolical help to express; and if not melody always or often (for that would mean finish and perfection), there is what the Germans call *Takt*,—fine dancing, if to the music only of drums.

Such a faculty of talent, 'genius' if you like the name better, seems to me worth cultivating, worth sacrificing oneself to tame and subdue into perfection;—none more so, that I know, of men now alive. Nay, in a private way, I admit to myself that here apparently is the finest poetic genius, finest possibility of such, we have got vouchsafed us in this generation, and that it will be a terrible pity if we spill it in the process of elaboration. Said genius, too, I perceive, has really grown, in all ways, since I saw it last; I hope it will continue growing, tho' the difficulties are neither few nor small!

Well! but what is the shadow side of the picture, then? For in that too I ought to be equally honest. My friend, it is what they call 'unintelligibility!' That is a fact: you are dreadfully difficult to understand; and that is really a sin. Admit the accusation: I testify to it; I found most of your pieces too hard of interpretation, and more than one (chiefly of the short kind) I had to read as a very enigma. I did make them all out,—all with about two insignificant exceptions;—but I do not know if many readers have got so far. Consider that case; it is actually flagrant!

Now I do not mean to say the cure is easy, or the sin a mere perversity. God knows I too understand very well what it is to be 'unintelligible' so-called. It is the effort of a man with very much to say, endeavouring to get it said in a not sordid or unworthy way, to men who are at home chiefly in the sordid, the prosaic, inane and unworthy. I see you pitching big crags into the dirty bottomless morass, trying to found your marble work,—Oh, it is a tragic condition withal!—But yet you must mend it, and alter. A writing man is there to be understood: let him lay that entirely to heart, and conform to it patiently; the sooner the better!

I do not at this point any longer forbid you verse, as probably I once did. I perceive it has grown to be your dialect, it comes more naturally than prose;—and in prose too a man can be 'unintelligible' if he like!... Continue to write in verse, if you find it handier, And what more? Aye, what, what! Well, the sum of my ideas is: If you took up some one great subject, and tasked all your powers upon it for a long while, vowing to Heaven that you would be plain to mean capacities, then—!—But I have done, done. Good be with you always, dear Browning; and high victory to sore fight! (pp. 198-200)

> *Thomas Carlyle, in an extract from a letter to Robert Browning on April 25, 1856, in* Browning: The Critical Heritage, *edited by Boyd Litzinger and Donald Smalley, Barnes & Noble, Inc., 1970, pp. 198-200.*

RICHELIEU (essay date 1868)

[*In this excerpted review of* The Ring and the Book, *the pseudonymous critic defends Browning against his detractors, claiming that here as elsewhere the poet is speaking as a "messenger of truth" to his age. These comments were originally published in the 28 November 1868 issue of* Vanity Fair.]

In a few days Mr. Browning will publish another of those great and supposed enigmatical poems at which all Vanity Fair stands aghast—not exactly with terror, but with the half-amused, half-puzzled look of the honest country folk who hear for the first time in their lives a Frenchman or a German speaking in his own language. Once more the critics in plush will be heard echoing and re-echoing the verdict of the critics in kid gloves, and while the moustache is gracefully twirled, or the cigar held in suspense, *The Ring and the Book* will be turned over with a patronising air, and in all the sincerity of supercilious wonderment plaintively pronounced 'monstwously cwude in style, and altogether puzzling "to a fella", you know!' There is no help for this sort of thing. It is not Mr. Browning's fortune to stand on a level with the criticism of the present generation. His voice is 'the voice of one crying in the wilderness', and they who dwell in kings' houses will not go out to hear him, and are little likely to be influenced by his teaching.

By particular favour I have seen enough of Mr. Browning's new poem to be quite prepared for a repetition of the old verdict of *Vanity Fair* upon his choice of a subject and his treatment of it; yet I shall venture to speak of this book as one of the most striking lessons ever read by poet or philosopher in the ears of an evil generation. The story is a pitiful one—more pitiful than Hood's "Bridge of Sighs," if that be possible. A young girl of Rome, in those old times which Mr. Browning loves to paint—yet not so remote from the present as his middle-aged dramas—is married to an Italian count, shortly after which she and her father and mother are found murdered by him—nay, he is taken red-handed almost in the very act of butchery, and is eventually executed for the crime. This is the substance of the story found by Mr. Browning in an old 'Book'. How he treats it is to be gathered from his opening apologue of the *Ring*. Some alloy must be mingled with your virgin gold to make it workable, but the goldsmith having finished his design (the 'lilied loveliness' of the ring) the gold is set free from its baser companionship by the last touch of the workman's art. Once more it is pure gold, 'prime nature with an added artistry'. And so understood, the antique goldsmith's ring serves, in the fore-front of the poem, as a symbol or speaking emblem of the poet's method. Say he has a divine message. How shall he utter it? The story of Guido Franceschini and the babe-like woman he made his bride is the answer.

It is not, therefore, to relate this story with such embellishments as his poetic instinct and sense of artistic beauty might suggest, that Mr. Browning has written. There is a deeply-felt purpose in his work of art, and to accomplish that purpose he has mixed the gold with 'gold's alloy.' We are first told of the tragedy in all its naked ghastliness. Then what 'half Rome' said of it, and what the 'other half.' The motives of the different actors in the drama, and all the little incomplete incidents which go to make up its completeness, are thus vividly realised. We pass them all over, to remark on Mr. Browning's aim, or what may be called the gist of his message in the character of Seer. The handwriting on the wall seems to be this, 'Can evil be done and evil not come of it?' Or this, to vary the expression, 'Is the world ruled by man's cunning devices, or by God's laws?' Or, again, this, 'Can a lie be told, and not make itself manifest, sooner or later, as the work of him who is the father of lies?' Yet, *The Ring and the Book* is not a sermon. It is deeply, intensely, human. It is nevertheless, and for that very reason, a burning protest against the atheistic belief that men and women are the creatures of circumstances. It asserts a Presence in the world, before which every lie, spoken or acted, must wither up, and possibly—nay, most certainly—bring destruction upon those who trust in it.

We picture Dante walking, with sad wide-open eyes, through Purgatory and Hades before he reached the shore of the river across which the loving eyes of Beatrice beamed upon him, and he once more took comfort. So through Vanity Fair and its devious ways, crowded with spectres of men and women as mournful to seeing eyes as those which grieved the heart of the Mantuan bard, we follow the steps of the poet who has been entrusted with this message, and who has already given utterance to it in many like parables. All criticism of Mr. Browning's verse which does not recognise this central fact of his relationship to the age as a messenger of truth seems to me worthless. It is true the good folk in Vanity Fair do not like this sort of thing, and it may be there are times when none of us like it. Belshazzar at high festival has no relish for the mystical handwriting on the wall. It is not always pleasant to be in earnest, and, like Mr. Tennyson's ''Lotus Eaters'', we rather enjoy floating down the stream; or like the crew in his glorious ''Voyage'', we have aims of our own in which it is vexatious to be disturbed. The answer to this objection is that we are not troubled every day, or even every other day, with a great poet's earnest expression of feeling, or with his sense of the living truth of things. No fear that there will not always be space enough in the Fair for vain shows, or, let us say, for harmless mirth and pleasantry. Now and then we may surely pause a moment in the round of ambition or pleasure to hear the Voice of Truth, and to lay up a gracious remembrance for less festive occasions. This, at least, is the kind of appeal which Mr. Browning's new poem makes to the world, be it received how it may. (pp. 284-86)

> *Richelieu, in an extract in* Browning: The Critical Heritage, *edited by Boyd Litzinger and Donald Smalley, Barnes & Noble, Inc., 1970, pp. 284-87.*

WALTER BAGEHOT (essay date 1869)

[*Bagehot was a prominent nineteenth-century English economist, journalist, and critic. In the following excerpt, he discusses Browning's reputation in relation to that of Alfred, Lord Tennyson and commends the first volume of* The Ring and the Book, *focusing on the psychological and narrative aspects of the work. These remarks were originally published in the January 1869 issue of* Tinsley's Magazine.]

The position of Robert Browning in the limited roll of contemporary poets is a very peculiar one. By his disciples and admirers—and they are a select, if not a numerous, body— Browning is considered to be, beyond all comparison, the master of modern English poetry; by the majority of intelligent book-readers—those who actually form their opinions from books, and not at second-hand, from the columns of weekly reviews—he is regarded as a man of vast intellectual power, who allows a certain capricious tendency towards mysticism or indirectness of phrase to run away with him; while by nearly all those who catch up the floating echoes of social literary judgment, he is held to be the leader of the *Festus* school, a man intentionally obscure, a writer whom people who value easy literary digestion ought piously to avoid. Among men capable of forming an independent, unbiassed, and valuable opinion in such matters, the relative question, and the decision arrived at with regard to this question may generally be taken to be a pretty clear indication of the critic's personal idiosyn-

crasy. So clearly is this recognised to be the case, that one never thinks of weighing the arguments on both sides to discover upon which side the value of testimony hangs. If you deem Browning to be the first of living English poets, good. No one can gainsay you. Had Providence altered, by a hair's-breadth, the disposition of your intellectual sympathies, you would have been a worshipper of Tennyson. In either case, your judgment, being honestly in accordance with certain natural sympathies, is not to be controverted by argument. We have, thank goodness, no empirical or academical rules by which any man's poetry may be tested or his position as a poet declared. The weakness of trying to measure the value of poetry by measuring the length of its lines, is confined to a few incapable critics; it is never shared by the public. It is true that if you confine the question to the music of poetry, you get the Browningites into a corner. Browning has an astonishing power both in versification and in the ring and clatter of words (witness his legend of the Piper of Hamelin), but he has none of the subtle modulation of Tennyson's sweet and gracious lines; in fact, the two men are not rivals; each is 'like a star, and dwells apart.' Whether you prefer the powerful intellectual vigour of Browning, or the calm, wise tenderness of Tennyson, does not much matter. In either case you have within you that receptive, reciprocative sympathy for which you ought to thank God.

We gather from some stray hints in this the first volume of **The Ring and the Book,** that Mr. Browning is well aware that he is not popular with the British public. Here are some lines (which at first sight look remarkably like a conundrum) referring to his relations with the public, and the reflex action of admitted public bewilderment:

> Such, British Public, ye who like me not
> (God love you!)—whom I yet have laboured for,
> Perchance more careful whoso runs may read
> Than erst when all, it seemed, could read who ran,—
> Perchance more careless whoso reads may praise
> Than late when he who praised and read and wrote
> Was apt to find himself the self-same me,—
> Such labour, &c.

But Mr. Browning's occasional obscurity—or shall we say carelessness of explanation?—is not the only reason why he lacks that popularity which so great a poet ought to have in his own country. Mr. Browning has lived the greater part of his literary life in Italy. The colouring of his mind and the colouring of his work are alike Italian. It is Italian life that he has so skilfully analysed; it is Italian scenery and accessories which form the background for his vivid dramatic pictures. If Mr. Browning had studied England and English character as faithfully and successfully as he has studied Italy and Italian character, his position as an English poet would have been other than it now is. So different is the material on which he has chosen to expend his poetical labour from all that we see around us, that we cannot regard the result otherwise than as a mere artistic product. Behind our admiration of such a poem as the *Morte d'Arthur, Maud,* or *In Memoriam,* there lies the distinct consciousness that the poet who speaks to us is one of ourselves, breathing the same atmosphere of inarticulate longing and tender hope, of unrest, and indignation, and wonder over the things that are. We are inclined to believe, however, that no poet ever lived who so accurately reflected the spirit of his time as Mr. Tennyson has done—it is his individual gift. And there is this further consideration, that genius has a wonderful selective faculty, a sort of divine instinct, which leads its possessor, in the face of prudential or other arguments, to select this or that material, this or that scene. Perhaps Mr. Browning has lived in Italy and written of things Italian because they best suited the bent of his dramatic, intense, colour-loving spirit. *Pippa Passes* could never have been written in England. It is easier to believe this than that Mr. Browning has paid the heavy price of a restricted audience for the merely personal pleasure of living in a more comprehensible climate, under brighter skies, and among more picturesque and less conventional people than England offered him.

The selective faculty of which we have spoken is almost invariably exercised unconsciously, and no doubt it was so in the choice Mr. Browning has made of a subject for his latest poem. It is impossible to think of one better fitted to draw out the special characteristics of his genius. *The Ring and the Book* is founded on the report of a trial for murder which took place at Rome in 1698. An Italian nobleman was accused of having, aided by four hired accomplices, murdered his wife (who had fled from his house) and the two old people with whom she was then living. The five were found guilty, and executed. But around and about the story hangs an atmosphere of mystery, which gives ample scope for the poet's imaginings. Who was the guilty one, the husband or the wife? What occult springs of human passion thus bubbled up through the crust of social quiet, and startled people with their colour of blood? Here, surely, is room for that play of psychical theory and suggestion which Browning loves. It is to be noted that nearly all the characterisation of Browning's most dramatic efforts is mental. There is little of the outside action with which most poets describe passion. He never deals in 'body-colour.' Even when glimpses of the glowing scenery of the South appear in his poems, they are only used in so far as they tint the mind of the speaker, colouring it transparently as the electric light colours a fountain. Browning's *dramatis personae* are disembodied souls that love, and quarrel, and fight in a spiritual world over which he, as master-magician, presides. True, they tell you of their solid appearance, and of the solid appearance of the world in which they move; they describe these coloured husks and shells in bright, vivacious touches; yet all the while you know that the action, and passion, and incidents coming before you are psychical, not physical. Hence Browning is at once intensely subjective and intensely dramatic—a curious combination. He does not display the acute emotional analysis of Tennyson, but he exhibits a wonderful intellectual analysis which produces as valuable results in another way. Put before him a psychological conundrum, and he will turn off a dozen solutions in a minute. Nothing can equal his suggestiveness in accounting for mental phenomena. No one obvious explanation of anything ever occurs to him. There is a recurrent 'or' continually in his mind. He has always at command a dozen lines of rail tapering down to the same point on the horizon. When the young wife in the present poem is first struck by her husband, she prays that she may be allowed to live long enough to confess and be absolved; and lo! in spite of her grievous wounds, she still lingers on the margin of life. Whereupon the chronicler is ready with his divers theories of the miracle:

> Whether it was that, all her sad life long,
> Never before successful in a prayer,
> This prayer rose with authority too dread,—
> Or whether, because earth was hell to her,
> By compensation, when the blackness broke
> She got one glimpse of quiet and the cool blue,
> To show her for a moment such things were,—
> Or else—as the Augustinian Brother thinks,
> The friar who took confession from her lip—
> When a probationary soul that moves

> From nobleness to nobleness, as she,
> Over the rough way of the world, succumbs,
> Bloodies its last thorn with unflinching foot,
> The angels love to do their work betimes,
> Stanch some wounds here, nor leave so much for God.

This fertility of psychological explanation is the *raison d'être* of *The Ring and the Book*. The raw material of the original story is a profound problem, two solutions of which the poet here gives us, with a promise of others in the volumes to come. Out of these various theories, the product of various methods or capacities of observation, we are to extract the truth of the mystery. Perhaps the position of the poet and the aim of the poem will be more clearly understood by our having recourse to Mr. Browning's metaphor of the making of a ring:

> That trick is, the artificer melts up wax
> With honey, so to speak; he mingles gold
> With gold's alloy, and, duly tempering both,
> Effects a manageable mass, then works.
> But his work ended, once the thing a ring,
> O, there's repristination! Just a spirit
> O' the proper fiery acid o'er its face,
> And forth the alloy unfastened flies in fume;
> While, self-sufficient now, the shape remains,
> The rondure brave, the lilied loveliness,
> Gold as it was, is, shall be evermore.

As with the ring, so with the book—'this square old yellow book', which contains the legal history of the trial, the bare, outward facts of the case, the pleadings on both sides, the statements of witnesses. The poet takes up the pure gold of absolute fact, and mingles with it the gold's alloy of human interpretation, of human theories of causality, of his own dramatic readings of the possibilities of the case. He blends his imaginings with this hard mass of circumstance to make it pliable, and by and by you shall see a complete and perfect work of art evolved—a story intelligible and compact, with all the side-lights of human weakness and inconsistency bearing down upon and lessening the shadow of mystery which now hangs around it. . . . (pp. 300-04)

Were *The Ring and the Book* to go no further than this first volume, we should be disposed to say that Mr. Browning had never written anything more powerful than the tragic story which is there conceived and developed. Doubtless its extreme severity will repel many readers. There is in it not a trace of that lyrical joyousness which runs through the varied scenes of *Pippa Passes* like a thread of silver. The air around Pompilia Comparini is too heavy for singing. Over the unhappy young wife's head there is no clear blue to which she may turn and listen for the song of a lark, but a lurid atmosphere of wrong, and hate, and suspicion. There is no room for music in the book. The harsh throats of 'Half-Rome' can only croak lies; the other half of Rome is struck with awe over the fate of the young wife, and wonders where the angels were to permit it. Here and there we find a touch of humour—it were not a poem of Browning's else—but it is that bitter humour which loves to gibe reflectively in a churchyard. There is not even in the poem the sad sweetness of unhappy love. There is no love in it. Pompilia had never a voice in her choice of a husband; and his regards were fixed upon her dowry. There was not even a young cavalier in the question, to suggest what *might* have been to the sad and weary wife. She accepted the services of the priest with gratitude, as she would have received the aid of a toothless peasant; and as for him—no hint of love is present to blot the white escutcheon of his noble self-sacrifice. So tragic is the tragedy that even the customary clown's scenes can find no place in it. But, on the other hand, no writer so carefully avoids *ad captandam* appeals to the emotions as Mr. Browning does. He does not pile up sorrow upon sorrow, and beseech you to weep. On the contrary, here, as elsewhere, the tragedy is related in an off-hand matter-of-fact way by men who do not perceive the drift of what they are saying. The narrators are too near, are too much taken up with minute points of detail, to see or comprehend the majesty of suffering they are unconsciously revealing. They are like the stone-cutters who, with augur, measure, and chisel, mechanically cut out of the block of marble the figure that the artist has modelled in clay. They are themselves only instruments, and are not supposed to have, like a Greek chorus, a divine knowledge of the emotional aspects of everything that is going on. In the very process of narration they are unconsciously exhibiting their own little failings, their odd notions of things, the particular range of their sympathies; but they never appeal to the reader and bid him be sorrowful over the sad story. They are in Rome, not in England; and they live amid all the bustle, and wonder, and stir of the morning which announced the tragedy that had taken place in Pietro's house.

Nor can one fail to be struck by the manner in which the poet has kept himself in hand in this matter. We will say that in writing the section entitled "Half-Rome" he was describing the views and opinions, directly opposed to his own, of a man or section of men whom he must hold in abhorrence or contempt. How great, therefore, was the temptation to exaggerate this or that mean interpretation so as to make the speaker illogically at variance with himself and doubly contemptible! But the object of the book is not to point a moral of this obvious kind. It was necessary that, mean as were the suspicions and impressions of 'Half-Rome,' they should be reasonable, humanly possible of belief, with that appearance of truth which would commend them to a certain class. Mr. Browning has not permitted himself to take sides in the matter. In both cases he hints the presence of 'a hidden germ of failure' which shall baffle the honest feeling for truth:

> Some prepossession such as starts amiss,
> By but a hair's-breadth at the shoulder-blade,
> The arm o' the feeler, dip he ne'er so brave;
> And so leads waveringly, lets fall wide
> O' the mark his finger meant to find, and fix
> Truth at the bottom, that deceptive speck.

Here, for the present, at least, we must leave *The Ring and the Book*. The advent of a fresh work of genius is not a thing to be passed over, in these times, with silence; and we have only done our duty to our readers in calling their attention to this powerful and elaborate work of art, written by one of the few strong men of our time. (pp. 304-06)

> *Walter Bagehot, in an extract in* Browning: The Critical Heritage, *edited by Boyd Litzinger and Donald Smalley, Barnes & Noble, Inc., 1970, pp. 300-06.*

[R. W. BUCHANAN]   (essay date 1869)

> [*Buchanan here reviews volumes 2-4 of* The Ring and the Book, *hailing the completed work as "the most precious and profound spiritual treasure that England has produced since the days of Shakespeare."*]

At last, the *opus magnum* of our generation lies before the world—the "ring is rounded"; and we are left in doubt which to admire most, the supremely precious gold of the material or the wondrous beauty of the workmanship. The fascination of the work is still so strong upon us, our eyes are still so spell-bound by the immortal features of Pompilia (which shine through the troubled mists of the story with almost insufferable beauty), that we feel it difficult to write calmly and without exaggeration; yet we must record at once our conviction, not merely that *The Ring and the Book* is beyond all parallel the supremest poetical achievement of our time, but that it is the most precious and profound spiritual treasure that England has produced since the days of Shakespeare. Its intellectual greatness is as nothing compared with its transcendent spiritual teaching. Day after day it grows into the soul of the reader, until all the outlines of thought are brightened and every mystery of the world becomes more and more softened into human emotion. Once and for ever must critics dismiss the old stale charge that Browning is a mere intellectual giant, difficult of comprehension, hard of assimilation. This great book *is* difficult of comprehension, *is* hard of assimilation; not because it is obscure—every fibre of the thought is clear as day; not because it is intellectual,—and it is intellectual in the highest sense,—but because the capacity to comprehend such a book must be spiritual; because, although a child's brain might grasp the general features of the picture, only a purified nature could absorb and feel its profoundest meanings. The man who tosses it aside because it is "difficult" is simply adopting a subterfuge to hide his moral littleness, not his mental incapacity. It would be unsafe to predict anything concerning a production so many-sided; but we quite believe that its true public lies outside the literary circle, that men of inferior capacity will grow by the aid of it, and that feeble women, once fairly initiated into the mystery, will cling to it as a succour passing all succour save that which is purely religious. Is it not here that we find the supremacy of Shakespeare's greatness? (p. 399)

We should be grossly exaggerating if we were to aver that Mr. Browning is likely to take equal rank with the supreme genius of the world; only a gallery of pictures like the Shakespearean group could enable him to do that; and, moreover, his very position as an educated modern must necessarily limit his field of workmanship. What we wish to convey is, that Mr. Browning exhibits—to a great extent in all his writings, but particularly in this great work—a wealth of nature and a perfection of spiritual insight which we have been accustomed to find in the pages of Shakespeare, and in those pages only. His fantastic intellectual feats, his verbosity, his power of quaint versification, are quite other matters. The one great and patent fact is, that, with a faculty in our own time at least unparalleled, he manages to create beings of thoroughly human fibre; he is just without judgment, without pre-occupation, to every being so created; and he succeeds, without a single didactic note, in stirring the soul of the spectator with the concentrated emotion and spiritual exaltation which heighten the soul's stature in the finest moments of life itself.

As we have said above, the face which follows us through every path of the story is that of Pompilia, with its changeful and moon-like beauty, its intensely human pain, its heavenly purity and glamour. We have seen no such face elsewhere. It has something of Imogen, of Cordelia, of Juliet; it has something of Dante's Beatrice; but it is unlike all of those—not dearer, but more startling, from the newness of its beauty. From the first moment when the spokesman for the "Other Half Rome" introduces her—

> Little Pompilia, with the patient brow
> And lamentable smile on those poor lips,
> And under the white hospital array
> A flower-like body—

to the moment when the good old Pope, revolving the whole history in his mind, calls her tenderly

> My rose, I gather for the gaze of God.

—from the first to the last, Pompilia haunts the poem with a look of ever-deepening light. Her wretched birth, her miserable life, her cruel murder, gather around her like clouds, only to disperse vapour-like, and reveal again the heavenly whiteness. There is not the slightest attempt to picture her as saintly; she is a poor child, whose saintliness comes of her suffering. So subtle is the spell she has upon us, that we quite forget the horrible pain of her story. Instead of suffering, we are full of exquisite pleasure—boundless in its amount, ineffable in its quality. When, on her sorry death-bed, she is prattling about her child, we weep indeed; not for sorrow—how should sorrow demand such tears?—but for the "pity of it, the pity of it, Iago!" . . .

Very noticeable, in her monologue, is the way she touches on the most delicate subjects, fearlessly laying bare the strangest secrecies of matrimonial life, and with so perfect an unconsciousness, so delicate a purity, that these passages are among the sweetest in the poem. But we must leave her to her immortality. She is perfect every way; not a tint of the flesh, not a tone of the soul, escapes us as we read and see.

Only less fine—less fine because he is a man, less fine because his soul's probation is perhaps less perfect—is the priest, Giuseppe Caponsacchi. "Ever with Caponsacchi!" cries Pompilia on her death-bed,

> O lover of my life, O soldier-saint!

And our hearts are with him too. He lives before us, with that strong face of his, noticeable for the proud upper lip and brilliant eyes, softened into grave melancholy and listening awe. What a man had he been, shining at ladies' feasts, and composing sonnets and "pieces for music," all in the pale of the Church! In him, as we see him, the animal is somewhat strong, and, prisoned in, pricks the intellect with gall. Little recks he of Madonna until that night at the theatre,

> When I saw enter, stand, and seat herself,
> A lady, young, tall, beautiful, and sad.

Slowly and strangely the sad face grows upon his heart, until that moment when it turns to him appealingly for succour, and when, fearless of any criticism save that of God, he devotes his soul to its service. . . . The whole monologue of Caponsacchi is a piece of supreme poetry, steeped in lyrical light. The writer's emotion quite overpowers him, and here, as elsewhere, he must sing. In all literature, perhaps, there is nothing finer than the priest's description of his journey towards Rome with Pompilia, that night she flies from the horror of Guido's house. Every incident lives before us: the first part of the journey, when Pompilia sits spell-bound, and the priest's eyes are fascinated upon her,— . . . the breaking dawn,—her first words,—then her sudden query—

> "Have you a mother?" "She died, I was born."
> "A sister then?" "No sister." "Who was it—
> What woman were you used to serve this way,
> Be kind to, till I called you and you came?"

—every look, thought, is conjured up out of the great heart of the lover, until that dark moment when the cat-eyed Guido overtakes them. What we miss in the psychology Pompilia herself supplies. It is saying little to say that we have read nothing finer. We know nothing whatever of like quality.

In a former review we gave a sketch of the general design of the work, explaining that, of the twelve books into which it is divided, ten were to be dramatic monologues, spoken by various persons concerned in or criticizing the Italian tragedy; and the remaining two a prologue and epilogue, spoken in the person of the poet himself. The complete work, therefore, is noticeable for variety of power and extraordinary boldness of design. All the monologues are good in their way, the only ones we could well spare being those of the two counsel, for and against Guido. These, of course, are extraordinarily clever; but cleverness is a poor quality for a man like Robert Browning to parade. The noblest portions of the book are "Giuseppe Caponsacchi," "Pompilia," and "The Pope." The last-named monologue is wonderfully grand—a fitting organ-peal to close such a book of mighty music; and it rather jars upon us, therefore, that we afterwards hear again the guilty scream of Guido. It seems to us, indeed, if we are bound to find fault at all, that we could have well dispensed with about a fourth of the whole work—the two legal speeches and Guido's last speech. To the two former we object on artistic grounds; to the latter, we object merely on account of its extreme and discordant pain. Yet in Guido's speech occurs one of the noblest touches in the whole work—where Guido, on the point of leaving his cell for the place of execution, exclaims—

> Abate,—Cardinal,—Christ,—Maria,—God.
> Pompilia, will you let them murder me?—

thus investing her at the last moment with almost God-like power and pity, in spite of the hatred which overcomes him,—hatred similar in kind, but different in degree, to that which Iscariot may be supposed to have felt for the Master. Nor let us forget to record that the poet, in his bright beneficence, has the lyric note even for Guido. We are made to feel that the "damnable blot" on his soul is only temporary, that the sharp axe will be a rod of mercy, and that the poor, petulant, vicious little Count will brighten betimes, and be saved through the purification of the very passions which have doomed him on earth. No writer that we know, except Shakespeare, could, without clumsy art and sentimental psychology, have made us feel so subtly the divine light issuing at last out of the selfish and utterly ignoble nature of Guido Franceschini.

Fault-finders will discover plenty to carp at in a work so colossal. For ourselves, we are too much moved to think of trifles, and are content to bow in homage, again and again, to what seems to us the highest existing product of modern thought and culture. (p. 400)

> [*R. W. Buchanan*], *in a review of "The Ring and the Book," in* The Athenaeum, *No. 2160, March 20, 1869, pp. 399-400.*

[ROBERT LOUIS STEVENSON]　(essay date 1875)

[*Stevenson was a Scottish novelist and essayist who wrote some of the nineteenth century's most beloved novels, including* Treasure Island, Doctor Jekyll and Mr. Hyde, *and* Kidnapped. *His novels are considered classics for their fast-paced action, strong plots, and well-drawn characters. In this excerpt from a review of* The Inn Album, *Stevenson charges Browning with indiscriminate productivity, suggesting that careless composing habits have helped swell the writer's output. These comments were originally published in the 11 December 1875 issue of* Vanity Fair.]

Mr. Browning intends apparently to finish a laborious life in an access or paroxysm of indiscriminate production. He floods acres of paper with brackets and inverted commas. He showers octavos on the public with a facility and grace like that of a conjuror scattering shoulder-knots and comfits out of a confederate's hat. What! we exclaim, all this monstrous quantity of verse out of no more of a poet than can be buttoned into one single-breasted waistcoat!

And yet the prodigy is not really so marvellous as it seems at first, and the problem resolves itself somewhat after the same fashion as the old school question of the lever—what you gain in power you lose in time. The more octavos the looser stuff. It smacks of a paradox, but is none the less true, that all this incredible effusion of writing-ink is not a sign of passionate industry, as you might suppose, but a phase of sheer and incurable idleness. Even this notice, slight as it is, would give us a deal less trouble if we let it run to twice the length. Compression is the mark of careful workmanship, and it takes less real power out of a man and gives fewer headaches to write a folio full of scimble-scamble, skirmishing literature than to fashion a dozen sonnets into perfect shape.

The Press is utterly silent nowadays about Mr. Browning's ragged, renegade versification, for the good reason that they have said their say even unto satiety, and Wisdom cannot be always crying at the street corner. If Mr. Browning will not hearken to her accents, he must just go his own way until a dart strikes through his liver. And yet it is not without a considerable pang that we leave a brilliant spirit like his to 'take directly up the way to destruction'; that we see a man who has now and again written fine and shapely verses pour out before us year after year—nay, we had almost said month after month— his periodic quantity of devilled prose. It is a pity to let the public into literary secrets; but a word in their ear is due to them. Mr. Browning's verse is a thing infinitely more easy to write than anything like careful prose. It is simply the result of a clever man 'giving way.' And he has a trick of his own when he wishes to cloak and dissemble the ill-success of his own lines before his heavenly Father and his earthly brethren, which we here denounce with the delight of all virtuous men in virtuous actions.

Suppose you were conducting an orchestra, and had arrived at a particular juncture in the piece where you knew, from previous rehearsals, a false note was on the cards; and suppose, with an ingenuity worthy of the Evil One, you calculated your time to a nicety, and, just at the moment when the ear-piercing discord was to be expected, you upset your music-stand with a prodigious crash? Well, it could not be said that you had really spared the sensibilities of the audience, and yet you would have saved your orchestra some disgrace. Nay, there would not be wanting persons to describe you as a specially dashing conductor, all passion and eccentricity, and burning in a white heat for art.

Now this is purely and simply what is done by Mr. Browning. When he finds a line shambling out from underneath him in a loose mass of unaccented syllables; when he finds it, like an ill-made blanc-mange, subside into a squash or quagmire instead of standing on its own basis with a certain sort of dignity or strength—quick, says Mr. B., break it up into an unexpected parenthesis, choke off the reader with a dash, leave him clinging at the verse's end to a projecting conjunction, cut a somersault before him, flick off his hat with your toe in true Mabille fashion; in short, do what you will so you bewilder him and the limping verse will get away to cover undetected.

So it will, for a while; and for a while sheer idleness may pass itself off under the *alias* of eccentricity. But at last the public

will begin to put their heads together and wag their solemn beards. 'This man,' they will say, 'gives himself out for more than ordinarily handsome. It may be so; but why does he always come before us in an Indian war-paint and cutting fantastic capers? Let him wash the red off his nose and the green off his ears; let him uncurl his legs from about his neck, and sit down quietly for a moment in this easy-chair, and then we shall see what he is, and tell him candidly whether he is Apollo or Quasimodo.'

Only Mr. Browning is such a wag and so volatile that you will require to get up very early in the morning to find him sitting honestly on a chair. He is always upside down or outside in. . . . (pp. 410-11)

[Mr. Browning's new book, ***The Inn Album***,] is as clever as any that went before it, and has the strange merit of being interesting. It bears a remarkable resemblance to some of Balzac's shorter tales, and might very well have been a transcript in verse from the author of *Le Colonel Chabert* or *La Duchesse de Langeais*. It has the same purely human import and the same fundamental cruelty that we find in the great world of the *Comédie humaine*. Only, alas! it is done so much more carelessly! Old Balzac, wrestling with obdurate language, honestly determined to tell his tale as well as lay in him, would steam like a tea-urn on cold nights in an agony of intellectual effort. And perhaps if Mr. Browning had had one or two such vigils over the ***Inn Album***, it would have happened to him to re-write the better part of it in some form more worthy of an admirable conception; and it would not have occurred to us, when his heroine dies towards the end, to lose five minutes of our brief life ere we could find out the how or the why of this deplorable catastrophe. It was only after a close examination of what went before, a sort of coroner's inquest in our own mind, that we were enabled to give a verdict of *felo-de-se*. And this at the climax of the story! O fie, Mr. Browning!

We are weary of finding fault with one who is perhaps too old to improve, and is certainly far too strong and caustic to be lightly quarrelled with. It goes against the grain to cavil at a man to whom we owe so many happy hours and so much occasion for intellectual gymnastic. We really do not like to play the little critic snarling at the heels of a great poet.

And, indeed, there is no more fault to find. Three out of the four characters who take part in this little tragedy (and the fourth is a mere outline) are firmly conceived and brilliantly drawn. Mr. Browning's power of ventriloquism—for he is more of a mimic than a dramatist—has rarely been seen to more advantage.

Most men will own some kinship to the wicked lord, as he indulges in useless repentance in the bright summer morning. These bright summer mornings, with their birds and their dewdrops, and their confounded affectation of innocence, are certainly the very moment for remorse; and all the worse, if, like his lordship in ***The Inn Album***, you have not been to bed the night before. Not less natural in its own way is his shameful conduct in the parlour, when he grows more and more Satanic as he finds those around him more virtuous. To have been really repentant half an hour before, is so bad for the moral tone half an hour after! (p. 412)

[*Robert Louis Stevenson*], *in an extract in* Browning: The Critical Heritage, *edited by Boyd Litzinger and Donald Smalley, Barnes & Noble, Inc., 1970, pp. 410-12.*

THE SATURDAY REVIEW, LONDON   (essay date 1876)

[*In reviewing* Pacchiarotto, *this anonymous writer vigorously objects to the "scurrilous attack" that Browning mounted against his critics in the poem.*]

Mr. Browning's unparalleled and increasing rapidity of production is, as might be expected, attended by an additional redundance of the peculiarities which appear admirable only to himself. The present volume [*Pacchiarotto, and Other Poems*] abounds in proofs of the sensitiveness with which he repels the imputation of that obscurity and harshness which might seem to be natural results of excessive volubility. If the immunity from criticism which Mr. Browning claims were conceded in personal deference to his genius, it would still be a legitimate cause for regret that he should of late seldom have taken time to embody in intelligible forms the conclusions of a subtle and imaginative intellect. In the present volume he challenges all who presume to form and express an independent judgment of his poems in language so unprovoked, so unreasonable, and so coarse that it would be almost an act of cowardice not to answer his defiance. Like some other men of genius, and like a multitude of writers who have no pretence to genius, Mr. Browning, while he professes to denounce criticism, really objects only to censure. He may perhaps be indifferent to praise, but it is improbable that he should dislike it. The plea to the jurisdiction is only filed as a precaution against an adverse judgment. There are competent and incompetent critics; but it is a monstrous pretension to deny the right of criticism to students who have perhaps proved the accuracy of their taste by a keen enjoyment of the best poetry of all countries, and even by their appreciation of Mr. Browning's works before he wrote the *Inn Album* and [**"Of Pacchiarotto, and How He Worked in Distemper"**]. The claim of a poet to live in regions inaccessible to ordinary men is a fantastic and modern affectation suggested rather by suspected weakness than by conscious strength. It would not have occurred to Chaucer or to Shakespeare that he was a demigod, and still less that it was not his business to deal with mankind. A speaker who is too much above his audience is not a master of his business; and he stands self-condemned if he boasts of being unintelligible to the most competent judges of his subject and his art. A thoughtful and scholarly critic would regret that involuntary contempt for a feeble and passionate protest should even seem to apply to a great writer who would on other occasions command his respect. Unsavoury topics, and careless or perverse treatment, cannot be justified by vehement and exaggerated boasts. Murders, criminal trials, and the hanging, beheading, and torturing of murderers, may advantageously be excluded from literature.

The first poem in the present volume records the follies of one Pacchiarotto, who, according to Mr. Browning's judgment, was a bad painter, and who, if the narrative may be trusted, was a half-witted adventurer. Mr. Browning's minute familiarity with the obscure traditions of Italian art enables him to state that Pacchiarotto is sometimes confounded with Pacchia, who seems to have been a better painter. Indeed Pacchia "decked (as we know, My Kirkup!) San Bernardino"; and perhaps there may be a few amateurs who share the knowledge of the favoured Mr. Kirkup. Pacchiarotto, on the other hand, painted on the walls of a grotto, at a place called Stalloreggi, certain figures of kings, popes, peasants, and other typical characters, and then proceeded to make them speeches. Afterwards he transferred his eloquence to a political club at Siena; and, being turned out of it, after a gratuitously offensive episode, he re-turned to his business of painting. It is not easy to understand why so dull and unmeaning a story should have been told in a vivacious kind of doggerel. At the end of the tale Mr. Browning suddenly diverges into a facetious and somewhat scurrilous attack on profane commentators on his poetry:—

> I have told with simplicity
> My tale, dropped those harsh analytics,
> And tried to content you, my critics,
> Who greeted my early uprising!
> I knew you through all the disguising,
> Droll dogs, as I jumped up, cried Heyday
> This Monday is—what else but May-day
> And these in the drabs, blues, and yellows
> Are surely the privileged fellows.
> So, salt-box and bones, tongs and bellows!
> (I threw up the window) "Your pleasure?"

The drabs, blues, and yellows, or the *Quarterly* and *Edinburgh*, representing literary journals and criticism in general, are then addressed as chimney-sweeps. They are requested to strike up the drum and triangle to prove that "I break rule as bad as Beethoven," "Schumann's self was no worse contrapuntist." In other words, every defect which can be imputed to the poet represents some mysterious and unattainable excellence. Mr. Browning then warns the critics that his housemaid Xantippe will empty slop-pails over them if they stay; and he gracefully apostrophizes them as "Quilp Hop o'my Thumb there," and as "Banjo-Byron who twangs the strum-strum there." All this poor stuff is evidently intended to be humorous and satirical. But he has not yet done with the objects of his implacable resentment. They have, it seems, for forty years troubled his repose, and yet he has never discharged upon them the arrow of his scorn—

> Because, though high up in a chamber
> Where none of your kidney may clamber,
> Your hullabaloo would approach me.

Do they wish to teach him grammar? He is master of language:—

> Was it "clearness of words which convey thought?"
> Ay, if words never needed enswathe aught
> But ignorance, impudence, envy,
> And malice—what word-swathe would then vie
> With yours for a clearness crystalline?
> But had you to put in one small line
> Some thought big and bouncing—as noddle
> Of goose born to cackle and waddle
> And bite at man's heel as goose-wont is,
> Never felt plague its puny *os frontis*—
> You'd know as you hissed, spat, and sputtered
> Clear "quack-quack" is easily uttered.

Mr. Browning, in his dreary and laboured jocosity, has apparently confounded geese with ducks; but it is a graver mistake to suppose that clearness is inseparable from malignity, frivolity, and baseness. If poets wish to put into a line not so vulgar a meaning as "a big and bouncing thought," but a pregnant condensation of wisdom, such as Dante, and, in his happier moods, Mr. Browning himself, has sometimes included in a verse, they must put it in so that it can be found there; and not leave it out, while they mistake their own uncommunicated reflections for products of creative art. Mr. Browning's frequent and growing obscurity resembles a cypher of which the key is withheld. The poet is evidently thinking of something casually associated in his mind with expressions that convey no meaning to the most intelligent reader, unless he by accident finds the clue. Sometimes the reference is to a curious fragment of knowledge which rests in the poet's memory; but more often he has grudged the labour, or has been

Elizabeth Barrett Browning in 1858.

wanting in the skill, to give expression to a complicated thought. The indolence which is inseparable from habitual rapidity of composition is the most frequent cause of a flagrant and undeniable defect. The puerile vanity of professing to live in an upper chamber where critics cannot clamber would be more pardonable in an inferior writer. The rough vituperation addressed to critics by no means indicates the transcendent superiority which it is intended to assert. Mr. Browning may be well assured that in **"Pacchiarotto"** there is as little wisdom as poetry.

Another and less objectionable apology is contained in a supposed speech of Shakespeare's at the "Mermaid." It would be well if poets would desist from writing about their poetry; but Horace and Milton and many other poets have set an example which is only avoided by the greatest and proudest masters of the art. At the same time there is no reason why a poet should not sometimes give expression to his own personal feelings. Shakespeare himself described in his Sonnets his sorrows, his affections, and his aspirations with as single-minded a devotion to his immediate subject as if he had been dealing with Lear, or Hamlet, or Falstaff. He had apparently no morbid repugnance to being understood, or even to becoming the subject of discussion; but it is difficult to believe that he could ever have written a poem about what the world thought of his plays. At the "Mermaid" he is represented as indulging in an inverted egotism, not less trivial than Byron's obtrusive pre-

sentation of himself. He is anxious to convince his friends that in reading his works they have learned nothing of himself:—

> Which of you did I enable
> 　Once to slip inside my breast
> There to catalogue and label
> 　What I like least, what love best,
> Hope and fear, believe and doubt of,
> 　Seek and shun, respect—deride?
> Who has right to make a rout of
> 　Rarities he found inside?

The same theme is further pursued in two little poems called **"House"** and **"Shop."** The disclosure of privacy when the front of a house had been thrown down by an earthquake, and the prying curiosity of the profane world of critics, suggest to Mr. Browning a rebuke which, even if it is just, might be conveyed in more elegant language, if not in musical verse:—

> Outside should suffice for evidence:
> 　And whoso desires to penetrate
> Deeper must dive by the spirit-sense—
> 　No optics like yours, at any rate!

> "Hoity toity! A street to explore,
> 　Your house the exception! *'With this same key
> Shakespeare unlocked his heart,'* once more."
> 　Did Shakespeare? If so, the less Shakespeare he.

In the next allegory the poet is symbolized as a shopkeeper dealing in jewels and other commodities, but scarcely condescending to notice his customers:—

> Howe'er your choice fell, straight you took
> 　Your purchase, prompt your money rang
> On counter,—scarce the man forsook
> 　His study of the "Times," just swang
> 　Till-ward his hand that stopped the clang.

When business hours are over, the dealer, it seems, finds occupations which are probably remote from the business of the day. If Mr. Browning's reiterated protests are directed against vulgar intruders who pry into the private lives of poets or of other eminent persons, his indignation is of course just, though it is strange that it should occupy so large a share of his thoughts. It is not generally known that even the humbler hangers-on of literature have meddled with Mr. Browning's personal character or circumstances. Criticism stands wholly apart from domestic relations and from the habits and private tastes of authors. The casually exposed room, the shop when the shutters are closed, attract no passing glance or thought. The personal equation which may properly be regarded in an estimate of artistic faculty is derived exclusively from data furnished by the writer himself. It would be impertinent to inquire whether Mr. Browning in his private capacity prefers English or foreign associations; but it is a legitimate observation that for artistic purposes he almost always selects Italian subjects and Southern imagery. There can be no doubt that Mr. Browning has a perfect command of idiomatic English; but critics may reasonably find fault with the habitual harshness of his omission of the definite article. The awkward inversion of "Shall I sonnet sing you about myself" produces a sensation as of teeth set on edge, wholly unconnected with any wish that "sonnet" should or should not be sung. The imperious demand on the faith of readers who are suspected of deficient deference is finally resumed in the Epilogue at the end of the volume. Sceptics and schismatics are assured that, if the strong drink furnished by the poet is not sweet enough for their taste, they are fools and hypocrites. They pretend indeed to admire Shakespeare and Milton, but Mr. Browning says that they never really read those poets. After much more scolding, he again informs them that his own poetic wine is of the finest quality, and, above all, it satisfies himself:—

> Wine, pulse in might from me!
> It may never emerge in must from vat,
> Never fill cask nor furnish can,
> Never end sweet, which strong began—
> God's gift to gladden the heart of man;
> But spirit's at proof, I promise that!
> No sparing of juice spoils what should be
> Fit brewage—mine for me.

It is a whimsical fancy of a genuine poet to write verses in the hope of frightening and insulting readers into admiration and reverence. Even the present volume, of which so unnecessarily large a space is wasted on self-laudation, furnishes much better arguments for the faith which is unsuccessfully propagated with violence and menace in **"Pacchiarotto"** and in the Epilogue. The ballad of Hervé Riel, here republished, proves, like the famous [**"How They Brought the Good News from Ghent to Aix"**], the rare versatility of power which would have enabled Mr. Browning, if he had thought fit, to be the most popular and spirit-stirring among lyrical poets of action. It is only of deliberate choice that he has not been distinguished by transparent clearness of language and thought. A poem called **"Fears and Scruples,"** in Mr. Browning's more usual style, is a characteristic satire on biblical and theological criticism. The repugnance of the religious mind to disturbing doctrines, and the triumph with which the embarrassed believer at last turns on his unwelcome teachers, are represented in Mr. Browning's happiest manner. It is to be regretted that a fine poem should be disfigured by the vulgar levity of addressing the troublesome rationalist as "You brute, you." **"St. Martin's Summer,"** **"Bifurcation,"** and **"Numpholeptos,"** are poems of a kind which has long been familiar to Mr. Browning's admirers; they all consist of imaginative puzzles to be wholly or partially solved by the willing labour of sympathizing and grateful students. The less ambitious can scarcely fail to penetrate the mysteries of **"Bifurcation,"** and they may then proceed to **"St. Martin's Summer." "Numpholeptos"** will reward the diligence of pertinacious ingenuity, if in no other way, at least as the occasion of an interminable controversy as to the meaning which it probably contains, though it can scarcely be said to convey it. It would probably be regarded as unpardonable presumption to suggest to Mr. Browning that "nymph" is more euphonious as well as more familiar than "numph." **"Cenciaja"** is a painful result of the irresistible attraction which the Roman Newgate Calendar exercises on Mr. Browning as a poet. In Shelley's *Cenci*, the Pope refuses Beatrice a reprieve because crimes against parents were at the time rife in Rome. "Paolo Santa Croce," says the Pope, "murdered his mother also yester eve." The incident has in its place a dramatic fitness as a motive or pretext for the Pope's decision. Unfortunately it occurred to Mr. Browning that two murders, a malignant Cardinal, an obsequious judge, and an unjust execution, would furnish a delightful commentary on the text of Shelley. To critics in their lower abode it seems that the story of the Cenci is in itself sufficiently disagreeable, and that Paolo Santa Croce and the villains whom he left behind might profitably have been left in the obscurity which they have hitherto adorned. The story is, as Mr. Browning truly observes, "no great things." That it is new, and true besides, is no reason for telling a tale of the prison and the scaffold. Shelley selected the repulsive subject of Cenci, amongst other reasons, because his morbid hatred of his own father extended itself in imagination to fathers in general. The appendix about Paolo Santa Croce has not even the excuse of a perverted moral. **"A Forgiveness"** is an elab-

orate study of murder and adultery in a Spanish Court two or three centuries ago. A statesman discovers the infidelity of his wife, and, after compelling her for three years to live with him on ceremonial terms, at the end of the period puts her to death with a poisoned dagger. The story is told in the form of confession to a monk, himself the unlawful lover, who had taken refuge in the cloister. The elaborate analysis of the injured husband's feelings is in Mr. Browning's most effective manner. Like many of his former poems, it suggests to profane and audacious critics a feeling of regret that modern times, English customs, and ordinary human motives have rarely presented themselves to his imagination as susceptible of poetic treatment. (pp. 205-06)

> *"Browning's 'Pacchiarotto',"* in The Saturday Review, *London, Vol. 42, No. 1085, August 12, 1876, pp. 205-06.*

GERARD MANLEY HOPKINS, S. J.   (letter date 1881)

[*Hopkins, whose poetry is distinguished by his striking diction and pioneering use of meter, is considered a major English poet. Although his work was almost completely unknown in the nineteenth century, he is now firmly established as an outstanding innovator and a major force in the development of modern poetry. In the excerpt below, Hopkins shares his impressions of Browning's poetry with R. W. Dixon, with whom he had earlier discussed the writer's work.*]

[Browning] has got a great deal of what came in with Kingsley and the Broad Church school, a way of talking (and making his people talk) with the air and spirit of a man bouncing up from table with his mouth full of bread and cheese and saying that he meant to stand no blasted nonsense. There is a whole volume of Kingsley's essays which is all a kind of munch and a not standing of any blasted nonsense from cover to cover. Do you know what I mean? The **"Flight of the Duchess,"** with the repetition of 'My friend,' is in this vein. Now this is *one* mood or vein of human nature, but they would have it all and look at all human nature through it. And Tennyson in his later works has been 'carried away with their dissimulation.' The effect of this style is a frigid bluster. A true humanity of spirit, neither mawkish on the one hand nor blustering on the other, is the most precious of all qualities in style, and this I prize in your poems, as I do in Bridges'. After all it is the breadth of his human nature that we admire in Shakespeare.

I read some, not much, of the *Ring and the Book,* but as the tale was not edifying and one of our people, who had been reviewing it, said that further on it was coarser, I did not see, without a particular object, sufficient reason for going on with it. So far as I read I was greatly struck with the skill in which he displayed the facts from different points of view: this is masterly, and to do it through three volumes more shews a great body of genius. I remember a good case of 'the impotent collection of particulars' of which you speak in the description of the market place at Florence where he found the book of the trial: it is a pointless photograph of still life, such as I remember in Balzac, minute upholstery description; only that in Balzac, who besides is writing prose, all tells and is given with a reserve and simplicity of style which Browning has not got. Indeed I hold with the oldfashioned criticism that Browning is not really a poet, that he has all the gifts but the one needful and the pearls without the string; rather one should say raw nuggets and rough diamonds. I suppose him to resemble Ben Jonson, only that Ben Jonson has more real poetry. (pp. 74-5)

Gerard Manley Hopkins, S. J., in a letter to Richard Watson Dixon on October 12, 1881, in The Correspondence of Gerard Manley Hopkins and Richard Watson Dixon, *edited by Claude Colleer Abbott, Oxford University Press, London, 1935, pp. 71-6.*

EDWARD DOWDEN   (essay date 1887)

[*Dowden was an important nineteenth-century Irish critic who is best known for his Shakespearean criticism. In the excerpt below, first published in June 1887 in the* Fortnightly Review, *Dowden commends Browning's poetry as an antidote to the spiritual maladies affecting his contemporaries.*]

If Mr. Arnold is the poet of our times who as poet could least resist *la maladie du siècle* in its subtler forms, he whose energy of heart and soul most absolutely rejects and repels its influence is Mr. Browning. To him this world appears to be a palæstra in which we are trained and tested for other lives to come; it is a gymnasium for athletes. Action, passion, knowledge, beauty, science, art—these are names of some of the means and instruments of our training and education. The vice of vices, according to his ethical creed, is languor of heart, lethargy or faintness of spirit, with the dimness of vision and feebleness of hand attending such moral enervation. Which of us does not suffer now and again from a touch of spiritual paralysis? Mr. Browning's poetry, to describe it in a word, is a galvanic battery for the use of spiritual paralytics. At first the shock and the tingling frightened patients away; now they crowd to the physician and celebrate the cure. Which of us does not need at times that virtue should pass into him from a stronger human soul? To touch the singing robes of the author of **"Rabbi Ben Ezra"** and **"Prospice"** and **"The Grammarian's Funeral,"** is to feel an influx of new strength. We gain from Mr. Browning, each in his degree, some of that moral ardour and spiritual faith and vigour of human sympathy which make interesting to him all the commonplace, confused, and ugly portions of life, those portions of life which, grating too harshly on Mr. Matthew Arnold's sensitiveness, disturb his self-possession and trouble his lucidity, causing him often, in his verse, to turn away from this vulgar, distracting world to quietism and solitude, or a refined self-culture that lacks the most masculine qualities of discipline. To preserve those spiritual truths which are most precious to him Mr. Browning does not retreat, like the singer of *In Memoriam,* into the citadel of the heart; rather, an armed combatant, he makes a sortie into the world of worldlings and unbelievers, and from among errors and falsehoods and basenesses and crimes, he captures new truths for the soul. It is not in calm meditation or a mystical quiet that the clearest perception of divine things come to him; it is rather through the struggle of the will, through the strife of passion, and as much through foiled desire and defeated endeavour as through attainment and success. For asceticism, in the sense of that word which signifies a maiming and marring of our complete humanity, Mr. Browning's doctrine of life leaves no place; but if asceticism mean heroic exercise, the *askesis* of the athlete, the whole of human existence, as he conceives, is designed as a school of strenuous and joyous asceticism. 'Our human impulses towards knowledge, towards beauty, towards love,' it has been well said, 'are reverenced by him as the signs and tokens of a world not included in that which meets the senses.' Therefore, he must needs welcome the whole fulness of earthly beauty, as in itself good, but chiefly precious because it is a pledge and promise of beauty not partial and earthly, but in its heavenly plenitude. And how dare he seek to narrow or enfeeble the affections, when in all their errors and their never-satisfied aspirations, he discovers evidence of an infinite love, from which they proceed and towards which they tend? Nor would he stifle any high ambition, for it is a wing to the spirit lifting man towards heights of knowledge or passion or power which rise unseen beyond the things of sense, heights on which man hereafter may attain the true fulfilment of his destiny. (pp. 499-500)

Edward Dowden, in an extract in Browning: The Critical Heritage, *edited by Boyd Litzinger and Donald Smalley, Barnes & Noble, Inc., 1970, pp. 499-500.*

[HENRY JAMES]   (essay date 1890)

[*James was an American-born English novelist, short story writer, critic, and essayist of the late nineteenth and early twentieth centuries. He is regarded as one of the greatest novelists of the English language and is also admired as a lucid and insightful critic. James published the following impressionistic reflections on the significance of Browning's burial in Poets' Corner, Westminster Abbey, in the* Speaker *in 1890.*]

[The writers buried in Poets' Corner] are a company in possession, with a high standard of distinction, of immortality, as it were; for there is something serenely inexpugnable even in the position of the interlopers. As they look out, in the rich dusk, from the cold eyes of statues and the careful identity of tablets, they seem, with their converging faces, to scrutinize decorously the claims of each new recumbent glory, to ask each other how he is to be judged as an accession. How difficult to banish the idea that Robert Browning would have enjoyed prefiguring and playing with the mystifications, the reservations, even perhaps the slight buzz of scandal, in the Poets' Corner, to which his own obsequies might give rise! Would not his great relish, in so characteristic an interview with his crucible, have been his perception of the bewildering modernness, to much of the society, of the new candidate for a niche? That is the interest and the fascination, from what may be termed the inside point of view, of Mr Browning's having received, in this direction of becoming a classic, the only official assistance that is ever conferred upon English writers.

It is as classics on one ground and another—some members of it perhaps on that of not being anything less—that the numerous assembly in the Abbey holds together, and it is as a tremendous and incomparable modern that the author of **Men and Women** takes his place in it. He introduces to his predecessors a kind of contemporary individualism which surely for many a year they had not been reminded of with any such force. The tradition of the poetic character as something high, detached and simple, which may be assumed to have prevailed among them for a good while, is one that Browning has broken at every turn; so that we can imagine his new associates to stand about him, till they have got used to him, with rather a sense of failing measures. A good many oddities and a good many great writers have been entombed in the Abbey; but none of the odd ones have been so great and none of the great ones so odd. There are plenty of poets whose right to the title may be contested, but there is no poetic head of equal power—crowned and recrowned by almost importunate hands—from which so many people would withhold the distinctive wreath. All this will give the marble phantoms at the base of the great pillars and the definite personalities of the honorary slabs something to puzzle out until, by the quick operation of time, the mere fact of his lying there among the classified and protected makes even Robert Browning lose a portion of the bristling surface of his actuality.

For the rest, judging from the outside and with his contemporaries, we of the public can only feel that his very modernness—by which we mean the all-touching, all-trying spirit of his work, permeated with accumulations and playing with knowledge—achieves a kind of conquest, or at least of extension, of the rigid pale. We cannot enter here upon any account either of that or of any other element of his genius, though surely no literary figure of our day seems to sit more unconsciously for the painter. The very imperfections of this original are fascinating, for they never present themselves as weaknesses; they are boldnesses and overgrowths, rich roughnesses and humours, and the patient critic need not despair of digging to the primary soil from which so many disparities and contradictions spring. He may finally even put his finger on some explanation of the great mystery, the imperfect conquest of the poetic form by a genius in which the poetic passion had such volume and range. He may successfully say how it was that a poet without a lyre—for that is practically Browning's deficiency: he had the scroll, but not often the sounding strings—was nevertheless, in his best hours, wonderfully rich in the magic of his art, a magnificent master of poetic emotion. He will justify on behalf of a multitude of devotees the great position assigned to a writer of verse of which the nature or the fortune has been (in proportion to its value and quantity) to be treated rarely as quotable. He will do all this and a great deal more besides; but we need not wait for it to feel that something of our latest sympathies, our latest and most restless selves, passed the other day into the high part—the show-part, to speak vulgarly—of our literature. To speak of Mr Browning only as he was in the last twenty years of his life, how quick such an imagination as his would have been to recognize all the latent or mystical suitabilities that, in the last resort, might link to the great Valhalla by the Thames a figure that had become so conspicuously a figure of London! He had grown to be intimately and inveterately of the London world; he was so familiar and recurrent, so responsible to all its solicitations, that, given the endless incarnations he stands for today, he would have been missed from the congregation of worthies whose memorials are the special pride of the Londoner. Just as his great sign to those who knew him was that he was a force of health, of temperament, of tone, so what he takes into the Abbey is an immense expression of life—of life rendered with large liberty and free experiment, with an unprejudiced intellectual eagerness to put himself in other people's place, to participate in complications and consequences; a restlessness of psychological research that might well alarm any pale company for their formal orthodoxies.

But the illustrious whom he rejoins may be reassured, as they will not fail to discover: in so far as they are representative it will clear itself up that, in spite of a surface unsuggestive of marble and a reckless individualism of form, he is quite as representative as any of them. For the great value of Browning is that at bottom, in all the deep spiritual and human essentials, he is unmistakably in the great tradition—is, with all his Italianisms and cosmopolitanisms, all his victimization by societies organized to talk about him, a magnificent example of the best and least dilettantish English spirit. That constitutes indeed the main chance for his eventual critic, who will have to solve the refreshing problem of how, if subtleties be not what the English spirit most delights in, the author of, for instance, **"Any Wife to any Husband"** made them his perpetual pasture, and yet remained typically of his race. He was indeed a wonderful mixture of the universal and the alembicated. But he played with the curious and the special, they never submerged him, and it was a sign of his robustness that he could

play to the end. His voice sounds loudest, and also clearest, for the things that, as a race, we like best—the fascination of faith, the acceptance of life, the respect for its mysteries, the endurance of its charges, the vitality of the will, the validity of character, the beauty of action, the seriousness, above all, of the great human passion. If Browning had spoken for us in no other way, he ought to have been made sure of, tamed and chained as a classic, on account of the extraordinary beauty of his treatment of the special relation between man and woman. It is a complete and splendid picture of the matter, which somehow places it at the same time in the region of conduct and responsibility. But when we talk of Robert Browning's speaking 'for us' we go to the end of our privilege, we say all. With a sense of security, perhaps even a certain complacency, we leave our sophisticated modern conscience, and perhaps even our heterogeneous modern vocabulary, in his charge among the illustrious. There will possibly be moments in which these things will seem to us to have widened the allowance, made the high abode more comfortable, for some of those who are yet to enter it. (pp. 12-16)

[*Henry James*], *"Browning in Westminster Abbey,"* in Robert Browning: A Collection of Critical Essays, edited by Philip Drew, Houghton Mifflin Company, 1966, pp. 11-16.

WILLIAM BUTLER YEATS   (essay date 1890)

[*Yeats was an Irish poet, playwright, and essayist of the late nineteenth and early twentieth centuries. The leading figure of the Irish Renaissance, he was also an active critic of his contemporaries' work. Yeats records his general impressions of Browning's poetry in the excerpt below, originally published in the* Boston Pilot *on 22 February 1890.*]

Our newspapers and popular preachers seem all to have fastened on Browning's optimism as the one thing about him specially to be commended, and to have magnified it into a central mood. I was talking recently with a great friend of Browning's, who insisted that this way of taking him as a kind of sermon-maker was quite false, that he was only an optimist because he was an artist who chose hopefulness as his method of expression, and that he could be pessimistic when the mood seized him. I think, though going rather too far, there is a good deal of truth in this: thought and speculation were to Browning means of dramatic expression much more than aims in themselves. He did speak out his own thoughts sometimes though—dramatized Robert Browning. I like to think of the great reverie of the Pope in *The Ring and the Book,* with all its serenity and quietism, as something that came straight from Browning's own mind, and gave his own final judgment on many things. But nearly always he evades giving a direct statement by what he called his dramatic method. It is hard to know when he is speaking or when it is only one of his *dramatis personae.* An acquaintance of mine said once to him, "Mr. Browning, you are a mystic." "Yes," he answered, "but how did you find it out?"

To Browning thought was mainly interesting as an expression of life. In life in all its phases he seems to have had the most absorbing interest; no man of our day has perhaps approached him there. In a thinker like Herbert Spencer one finds, I imagine, Browning's opposite. Spencer probably cares little for life, except as an expression of thought. He lives in boarding houses surrounded by endless clatter and chatter, but has proved himself equal to the occasion. He has had two buttons, or things like buttons, designed by an artist and made exactly to fit his ears. When the clatter and chatter grows too great, he simply thrusts in the buttons and is at once deaf as a post. Eager lion hunters may gather round in vain; he smiles and says, "Yes, yes," but all the time his mind is far off, thinking those abstract generalizations of his. To Robert Browning the world was simply a great boarding house in which people come and go in a confused kind of way. The clatter and chatter to him was life, was joy itself. Sometimes the noise and restlessness got too much into his poetry, and the expression became confused and the verse splintered and broken. (pp. 97-9)

> *William Butler Yeats, "Browning," in his* Letters to the New Island, *edited by Horace Reynolds, Cambridge, Mass.: Harvard University Press, 1934, pp. 97-104.*

OSCAR WILDE   (essay date 1890)

[*Wilde was an Anglo-Irish dramatist, novelist, poet, critic, essayist, and short story writer who is identified with the nineteenth-century "art for art's sake" movement. In the excerpt below, Wilde assesses Browning's literary stature, focusing his critique on the poet's language and method of characterization.*]

Taken as a whole, [Browning] was great. He did not belong to the Olympians, and had all the incompleteness of the Titan. He did not survey, and it was but rarely that he could sing. His work is marred by struggle, violence, and effort, and he passed not from emotion to form, but from thought to chaos. Still, he was great. He has been called a thinker, and was certainly a man who was always thinking, and always aloud; but it was not thought that fascinated him, but rather the processes by which thought moves. It was the machine he loved, not what the machine makes. The method by which the fool arrives at his folly was so dear to him as the ultimate wisdom of the wise. So much, indeed, did the subtle mechanism of mind fascinate him that he despised language, or looked upon it as an incomplete instrument of expression. Rhyme, that exquisite echo which in the Muse's hollow hill creates and answers its own voice; rhyme, which in the hands of a real artist becomes not merely a material element of metrical beauty, but a spiritual element of thought and passion also, waking a new mood, it may be, or stirring a fresh train of ideas, or opening by mere sweetness and suggestion of sound some golden door at which the Imagination itself had knocked in vain; rhyme, which can turn man's utterance to the speech of gods; rhyme, the one chord we have added to the Greek lyre, became in Robert Browning's hands a grotesque, misshapen thing, which made him at times masquerade in poetry as a low comedian, and ride Pegasus too often with his tongue in his cheek. There are moments when he wounds us by monstrous music. Nay, if he can only get his music by breaking the strings of his lute, he breaks them, and they snap in discord, and no Athenian tettix, making melody from tremulous wings, lights on the ivory horn to make the movement perfect or the interval less harsh. Yet, he was great: and though he turned language into ignoble clay, he made from it men and women that live. He is the most Shakespearian creature since Shakespeare. If Shakespeare could sing with myriad lips, Browning could stammer through a thousand mouths. Even now, as I am speaking, and speaking not against him but for him, there glides through the room the pageant of his persons. There, creeps Fra Lippo Lippi with his cheeks still burning from some girl's hot kiss. There, stands dread Saul with the lordly male-sapphires gleaming in his turban. Mildred Tresham is there, and the Spanish monk, yellow with hatred, and Blougram, and the Rabbi Ben Ezra,

and the Bishop of St. Praxed's. The spawn of Setebos gibbers in the corner, and Sebald, hearing Pippa pass by, looks on Ottima's haggard face, and loathes her and his own sin and himself. Pale as the white satin of his doublet, the melancholy king watches with dreamy treacherous eyes too loyal Strafford pass to his doom, and Andrea shudders as he hears the cousin's whistle in the garden, and bids his perfect wife go down. Yes, Browning was great. And as what will he be remembered? As a poet? Ah, not as a poet! He will be remembered as a writer of fiction, as the most supreme writer of fiction, it may be, that we have ever had. His sense of dramatic situation was unrivalled, and, if he could not answer his own problems, he could at least put problems forth. Considered from the point of view of a creator of character he ranks next to him who made Hamlet. Had he been articulate he might have sat beside him. The only man living who can touch the hem of his garment is George Meredith. Meredith is a prose-Browning, and so is Browning. He used poetry as a medium for writing in prose. (pp. 126-27)

> *Oscar Wilde, "The True Function and Value of Criticism," in* The Nineteenth Century, *Vol. XXVIII, No. CLXI, July, 1890, pp. 123-47.*

GEORGE SANTAYANA   (essay date 1900)

[*Santayana, who was a Spanish-born philosopher, poet, novelist, and literary critic, made an influential attack on Browning in his 1900 essay "The Poetry of Barbarism." In the following excerpt from that work, Santayana elaborates on his contention that Browning's genius was essentially barbaric in character by underscoring the irrationality and vulgarity of his approach to religious, philosophical, and artistic concerns.*]

If we would do justice to Browning's work as a human document, and at the same time perceive its relation to the rational ideals of the imagination and to that poetry which passes into religion, we must keep, as in the case of Whitman, two things in mind. One is the genuineness of the achievement, the sterling quality of the vision and inspiration; these are their own justification when we approach them from below and regard them as manifesting a more direct or impassioned grasp of experience than is given to mildly blatant, convention-ridden minds. The other thing to remember is the short distance to which this comprehension is carried, its failure to approach any finality, or to achieve a recognition even of the traditional ideals of poetry and religion.

In the case of Walt Whitman such a failure will be generally felt; it is obvious that both his music and his philosophy are those of a barbarian, nay, almost of a savage. Accordingly there is need of dwelling rather on the veracity and simple dignity of his thought and art, on their expression of an order of ideas latent in all better experience. But in the case of Browning it is the success that is obvious to most people. Apart from a certain superficial grotesqueness to which we are soon accustomed, he easily arouses and engages the reader by the pithiness of his phrase, the volume of his passion, the vigour of his moral judgment, the liveliness of his historical fancy. It is obvious that we are in the presence of a great writer, of a great imaginative force, of a master in the expression of emotion. What is perhaps not so obvious, but no less true, is that we are in the presence of a barbaric genius, of a truncated imagination, of a thought and an art inchoate and ill-digested, of a volcanic eruption that tosses itself quite blindly and ineffectually into the sky.

The points of comparison by which this becomes clear are perhaps not in every one's mind, although they are merely the elements of traditional culture, æsthetic and moral. Yet even without reference to ultimate ideals, one may notice in Browning many superficial signs of that deepest of all failures, the failure in rationality and the indifference to perfection. Such a sign is the turgid style, weighty without nobility, pointed without naturalness or precision. Another sign is the "realism" of the personages, who, quite like men and women in actual life, are always displaying traits of character and never attaining character as a whole. Other hints might be found in the structure of the poems, where the dramatic substance does not achieve a dramatic form; in the metaphysical discussion, with its confused prolixity and absence of result; in the moral ideal, where all energies figure without their ultimate purposes; in the religion, which breaks off the expression of this life in the middle, and finds in that suspense an argument for immortality. In all this, and much more that might be recalled, a person coming to Browning with the habits of a cultivated mind might see evidence of some profound incapacity in the poet; but more careful reflection is necessary to understand the nature of this incapacity, its cause, and the peculiar accent which its presence gives to those ideas and impulses which Browning stimulates in us.

There is the more reason for developing this criticism (which might seem needlessly hostile and which time and posterity will doubtless make in their own quiet and decisive fashion) in that Browning did not keep within the sphere of drama and analysis, where he was strong, but allowed his own temperament and opinions to vitiate his representation of life, so that he sometimes turned the expression of a violent passion into the last word of what he thought a religion. He had a didactic vein, a habit of judging the spectacle he evoked and of loading the passions he depicted with his visible sympathy or scorn.

Now a chief support of Browning's popularity is that he is, for many, an initiator into the deeper mysteries of passion, a means of escaping from the moral poverty of their own lives and of feeling the rhythm and compulsion of the general striving. He figures, therefore, distinctly as a prophet, as a bearer of glad tidings, and it is easy for those who hail him as such to imagine that, knowing the labour of life so well, he must know something also of its fruits, and that in giving us the feeling of existence, he is also giving us its meaning. There is serious danger that a mind gathering from his pages the raw materials of truth, the unthreshed harvest of reality, may take him for a philosopher, for a rationaliser of what he describes. Awakening may be mistaken for enlightenment, and the galvanising of torpid sensations and impulses for wisdom.

Against such fatuity reason should raise her voice. The vital and historic forces that produce illusions of this sort in large groups of men are indeed beyond the control of criticism. The ideas of passion are more vivid than those of memory, until they become memories in turn. They must be allowed to fight out their desperate battle against the laws of Nature and reason. But it is worth while in the meantime, for the sake of the truth and of a just philosophy, to meet the varying though perpetual charlatanism of the world with a steady protest. As soon as Browning is proposed to us as a leader, as soon as we are asked to be not the occasional patrons of his art, but the pupils of his philosophy, we have a right to express the radical dissatisfaction which we must feel, if we are rational, with his whole attitude and temper of mind.

The great dramatists have seldom dealt with perfectly virtuous characters. The great poets have seldom represented mythologies that would bear scientific criticism. But by an instinct which constituted their greatness they have cast these mixed materials furnished by life into forms congenial to the specific principles of their art, and by this transformation they have made acceptable in the æsthetic sphere things that in the sphere of reality were evil or imperfect: in a word, their works have been beautiful as works of art. . . . When we read the maxims of Iago, Falstaff, or Hamlet, we are delighted if the thought strikes us as true, but we are not less delighted if it strikes us as false. These characters are not presented to us in order to enlarge our capacities of passion nor in order to justify themselves as processes of redemption; they are there, clothed in poetry and imbedded in plot, to entertain us with their imaginable feelings and their interesting errors. The poet, without being especially a philosopher, stands by virtue of his superlative genius on the plane of universal reason, far above the passionate experience which he overlooks and on which he reflects; and he raises us for the moment to his own level, to send us back again, if not better endowed for practical life, at least not unacquainted with speculation.

With Browning the case is essentially different. When his heroes are blinded by passion and warped by circumstance, as they almost always are, he does not describe the fact from the vantage-ground of the intellect and invite us to look at it from that point of view. On the contrary, his art is all self-expression or satire. For the most part his hero, like Whitman's, is himself; not appearing, as in the case of the American bard, *in puris naturalibus,* but masked in all sorts of historical and romantic finery. Sometimes, however, the personage, like Guido in *The Ring and the Book* or the "frustrate ghosts" of other poems, is merely a Marsyas, shown flayed and quivering to the greater glory of the poet's ideal Apollo. The impulsive utterances and the crudities of most of the speakers are passionately adopted by the poet as his own. He thus perverts what might have been a triumph of imagination into a failure of reason.

This circumstance has much to do with the fact that Browning, in spite of his extraordinary gift for expressing emotion, has hardly produced works purely and unconditionally delightful. They not only portray passion, which is interesting, but they betray it, which is odious. His art was still in the service of the will. He had not attained, in studying the beauty of things, that detachment of the phenomenon, that love of the form for its own sake, which is the secret of contemplative satisfaction. Therefore, the lamentable accidents of his personality and opinions, in themselves no worse than those of other mortals, passed into his art. He did not seek to elude them: he had no free speculative faculty to dominate them by. Or, to put the same thing differently, he was too much in earnest in his fictions, he threw himself too unreservedly into his creations. His imagination, like the imagination we have in dreams, was merely a vent for personal preoccupations. His art was inspired by purposes less simple and universal than the ends of imagination itself. His play of mind consequently could not be free or pure. The creative impulse could not reach its goal or manifest in any notable degree its own organic ideal.

We may illustrate these assertions by considering Browning's treatment of the passion of love, a passion to which he gives great prominence and in which he finds the highest significance.

Love is depicted by Browning with truth, with vehemence, and with the constant conviction that it is the supreme thing in life. The great variety of occasions in which it appears in his pages and the different degrees of elaboration it receives, leave it always of the same quality—the quality of passion. It never sinks into sensuality; in spite of its frequent extreme crudeness, it is always, in Browning's hands, a passion of the imagination, it is always love. On the other hand it never rises into contemplation: mingled as it may be with friendship, with religion, or with various forms of natural tenderness, it always remains a passion; it always remains a personal impulse, a hypnotisation, with another person for its object or its cause. Kept within these limits it is represented, in a series of powerful sketches, which are for most readers the gems of the Browning gallery, as the last word of experience, the highest phase of human life.

> The woman yonder, there's no use in life
> But just to obtain her! Heap earth's woes in one
> And bear them—make a pile of all earth's joys
> And spurn them, as they help or help not this;
> Only, obtain her!. . .

In the piece called **"In a Gondola"** the lady says to her lover:—

> Heart to heart
> And lips to lips! Yet once more, ere we part,
> Clasp me and make me thine, as mine thou art.

And he, after being surprised and stabbed in her arms, replies:—

> It was ordained to be so, sweet!—and best
> Comes now, beneath thine eyes, upon thy breast:
> Still kiss me! Care not for the cowards; care
> Only to put aside thy beauteous hair
> My blood will hurt! The Three I do not scorn
> To death, because they never lived, but I
> Have lived indeed, and so—(yet one more kiss)—
>   can die.

We are not allowed to regard these expressions as the cries of souls blinded by the agony of passion and lust. Browning unmistakably adopts them as expressing his own highest intuitions. He so much admires the strength of this weakness that he does not admit that it is a weakness at all. It is with the strut of self-satisfaction, with the sensation, almost, of muscular Christianity, that he boasts of it through the mouth of one of his heroes, who is explaining to his mistress the motive of his faithful services as a minister of the queen:—

> She thinks there was more cause
> In love of power, high fame, pure loyalty?
> Perhaps she fancies men wear out their lives
> Chasing such shades. . . .
> I worked because I want you with my soul.

(pp. 161-67)

[This] method of understanding . . . [contrasts with] that adopted by the real masters of passion and imagination. They began with that crude emotion with which Browning ends; they lived it down, they exalted it by thought, they extracted the pure gold of it in a long purgation of discipline and suffering. The fierce paroxysm which for him is heaven, was for them the proof that heaven cannot be found on earth, that the value of experience is not in experience itself but in the ideals which it reveals. The intense, voluminous emotion, the sudden, overwhelming self-surrender in which he rests was for them the starting-point of a life of rational worship, of an austere and impersonal religion, by which the fire of love, kindled for a moment by the sight of some creature, was put, as it were, into a censer, to burn incense before every image of the Highest Good. Thus love ceased to be a passion and became the energy of contemplation: it diffused over the universe, natural and ideal, that light of tenderness and that faculty of worship which the passion of love often is first to quicken in a man's breast.

Of this art, recommended by Plato and practised in the Christian Church by all adepts of the spiritual life, Browning knew absolutely nothing. About the object of love he had no misgivings. What could the object be except somebody or other? The important thing was to love intensely and to love often. He remained in the phenomenal sphere: he was a lover of experience; the ideal did not exist for him. No conception could be farther from his thought than the essential conception of any rational philosophy, namely, that feeling is to be treated as raw material for thought, and that the destiny of emotion is to pass into objects which shall contain all its value while losing all its formlessness. This transformation of sense and emotion into objects agreeable to the intellect, into clear ideas and beautiful things, is the natural work of reason; when it has been accomplished very imperfectly, or not at all, we have a barbarous mind, a mind full of chaotic sensations, objectless passions, and undigested ideas. Such a mind Browning's was, to a degree remarkable in one with so rich a heritage of civilisation. (pp. 167-68)

The irrationality of the passions which Browning glorifies, making them the crown of life, is so gross that at times he cannot help perceiving it.

> How perplexed
> Grows belief! Well, this cold clay clod
> Was man's heart:
> Crumble it, and what comes next? Is it God?

Yes, he will tell us. These passions and follies, however desperate in themselves and however vain for the individual, are excellent as parts of the dispensation of Providence:—

> Be hate that fruit or love that fruit,
> It forwards the general deed of man,
> And each of the many helps to recruit
> The life of the race by a general plan,
>   Each living his own to boot.

If we doubt, then, the value of our own experience, even perhaps of our experience of love, we may appeal to the interdependence of goods and evils in the world to assure ourselves that, in view of its consequences elsewhere, this experience was great and important after all. We need not stop to consider this supposed solution, which bristles with contradictions; it would not satisfy Browning himself, if he did not back it up with something more to his purpose, something nearer to warm and transitive feeling. The compensation for our defeats, the answer to our doubts, is not to be found merely in a proof of the essential necessity and perfection of the universe; that would be cold comfort, especially to so uncontemplative a mind. No: that answer, and compensation are to come very soon and very vividly to every private bosom. There is another life, a series of other lives, for this to happen in. Death will come, and—

> I shall thereupon
> Take rest, ere I be gone
> Once more on my adventure brave and new,
>   Fearless and unperplexed,
>   When I wage battle next,
> What weapons to select, what armour to endue.
>
> For sudden the worst turns the best to the brave,
>   The black minute's at end,
> And the element's rage, the fiend-voices that rave
>   Shall dwindle, shall blend,
> Shall change, shall become first a peace out of pain,
>   Then a light, then thy breast,
> O thou soul of my soul! I shall clasp thee again
>   And with God be the rest!

Into this conception of continued life Browning has put, as a collection of further passages might easily show, all the items furnished by fancy or tradition which at the moment satisfied his imagination—new adventures, reunion with friends, and even, after a severe strain and for a short while, a little peace and quiet. The gist of the matter is that we are to live indefinitely, that all our faults can be turned to good, all our unfinished business settled, and that therefore there is time for anything we like in this world and for all we need in the other. It is in spirit the direct opposite of the philosophic maxim of regarding the end, of taking care to leave a finished life and a perfect character behind us. It is the opposite, also, of the religious *memento mori,* of the warning that the time is short before we go to our account. According to Browning, there is no account: we have an infinite credit. With an unconscious and characteristic mixture of heathen instinct with Christian doctrine, he thinks of the other world as heaven, but of the life to be led there as of the life of Nature. (pp. 169-71)

Browning has no idea of an intelligible good which the phases of life might approach and with reference to which they might constitute a progress. His notion is simply that the game of life, the exhilaration of action, is inexhaustible. You may set up your tenpins again after you have bowled them over, and you may keep up the sport for ever. The point is to bring them down as often as possible with a master-stroke and a big bang. That will tend to invigorate in you that self-confidence which in this system passes for faith. But it is unmeaning to call such an exercise heaven, or to talk of being "with God" in such a life, in any sense in which we are not with God already and under all circumstances. Our destiny would rather be, as Browning himself expresses it in a phrase which Attila or Alaric might have composed, "bound dizzily to the wheel of change to slake the thirst of God."

Such an optimism and such a doctrine of immortality can give no justification to experience which it does not already have in its detached parts. Indeed, those dogmas are not the basis of Browning's attitude, not conditions of his satisfaction in living, but rather overflowings of that satisfaction. The present life is presumably a fair average of the whole series of "adventures brave and new" which fall to each man's share; were it not found delightful in itself, there would be no motive for imagining and asserting that it is reproduced *in infinitum.* So too if we did not think that the evil in experience is actually utilised and visibly swallowed up in its good effects, we should hardly venture to think that God could have regarded as a good something which has evil for its condition and which is for that reason profoundly sad and equivocal. But Browning's philosophy of life and habit of imagination do not require the support of any metaphysical theory. His temperament is perfectly self-sufficient and primary; what doctrines he has are suggested by it and are too loose to give it more than a hesitant expression; they are quite powerless to give it any justification which it might lack on its face.

It is the temperament, then, that speaks; we may brush aside as unsubstantial, and even as distorting, the web of arguments and theories which it has spun out of itself. And what does the temperament say? That life is an adventure, not a discipline; that the exercise of energy is the absolute good, irrespective of motives or of consequences. These are the maxims of a frank barbarism; nothing could express better the lust of life, the dogged unwillingness to learn from experience, the contempt for rationality, the carelessness about perfection, the admiration for mere force, in which barbarism always betrays

itself. The vague religion which seeks to justify this attitude is really only another outburst of the same irrational impulse.

In Browning this religion takes the name of Christianity, and identifies itself with one or two Christian ideas arbitrarily selected; but at heart it has far more affinity to the worship of Thor or of Odin than to the religion of the Cross. The zest of life becomes a cosmic emotion; we lump the whole together and cry, "Hurrah for the Universe!" A faith which is thus a pure matter of lustiness and inebriation rises and falls, attracts or repels, with the ebb and flow of the mood from which it springs. It is invincible because unseizable; it is as safe from refutation as it is rebellious to embodiment. But it cannot enlighten or correct the passions on which it feeds. Like a servile priest, it flatters them in the name of Heaven. It cloaks irrationality in sanctimony; and its admiration for every bluff folly, being thus justified by a theory, becomes a positive fanaticism, eager to defend any wayward impulse.

Such barbarism of temper and thought could hardly, in a man of Browning's independence and spontaneity, be without its counterpart in his art. . . . His limitations as a poet are the counterpart of his limitations as a moralist and theologian; only in the poet they are not so regrettable. Philosophy and religion are nothing if not ultimate; it is their business to deal with general principles and final aims. Now it is in the conception of things fundamental and ultimate that Browning is weak; he is strong in the conception of things immediate. The pulse of the emotion, the bobbing up of the thought, the streaming of the reverie—these he can note down with picturesque force or imagine with admirable fecundity.

Yet the limits of such excellence are narrow, for no man can safely go far without the guidance of reason. His long poems have no structure—for that name cannot be given to the singular mechanical division of *The Ring and the Book.* Even his short poems have no completeness, no limpidity. They are little torsos made broken so as to stimulate the reader to the restoration of their missing legs and arms. What is admirable in them is pregnancy of phrase, vividness of passion and sentiment, heaped-up scraps of observation, occasional flashes of light, occasional beauties of versification,—all like

> the quick sharp scratch
> And blue spurt of a lighted match.

There is never anything largely composed in the spirit of pure beauty, nothing devotedly finished, nothing simple and truly just. The poet's mind cannot reach equilibrium; at best he oscillates between opposed extravagances; his final word is still a *boutade,* still an explosion. He has no sustained nobility of style. He affects with the reader a confidential and vulgar manner, so as to be more sincere and to feel more at home. Even in the poems where the effort at impersonality is most successful, the dramatic disguise is usually thrown off in a preface, epilogue or parenthesis. The author likes to remind us of himself by some confidential wink or genial poke in the ribs, by some little interlarded sneer. We get in these tricks of manner a taste of that essential vulgarity, that indifference to purity and distinction, which is latent but pervasive in all the products of this mind. The same disdain of perfection which appears in his ethics appears here in his verse, and impairs its beauty by allowing it to remain too often obscure, affected, and grotesque. (pp. 171-74)

[Browning's] favourite subject-matter is . . . the stream of thought and feeling in the mind; he is the poet of soliloquy. Nature and life as they really are, rather than as they may appear to the ignorant and passionate participant in them, lie beyond his range. Even in his best dramas, like *A Blot in the 'Scutcheon* or *Columbe's Birthday,* the interest remains in the experience of the several persons as they explain it to us. The same is the case in *The Ring and the Book,* the conception of which, in twelve monstrous soliloquies, is a striking evidence of the poet's predilection for this form.

The method is, to penetrate by sympathy rather than to portray by intelligence. The most authoritative insight is not the poet's or the spectator's, aroused and enlightened by the spectacle, but the various heroes' own, in their moment of intensest passion. We therefore miss the tragic relief and exaltation, and come away instead with the uncomfortable feeling that an obstinate folly is apparently the most glorious and choiceworthy thing in the world. This is evidently the poet's own illusion, and those who do not happen to share it must feel that if life were really as irrational as he thinks it, it would be not only profoundly discouraging, which it often is, but profoundly disgusting, which it surely is not; for at least it reveals the ideal which it fails to attain.

This ideal Browning never disentangles. For him the crude experience is the only end, the endless struggle the only ideal, and the perturbed "Soul" the only organon of truth. The arrest of his intelligence at this point, before it has envisaged any rational object, explains the arrest of his dramatic art at soliloquy. His immersion in the forms of self-consciousness prevents him from dramatising the real relations of men and their thinkings to one another, to Nature, and to destiny. For in order to do so he would have had to view his characters from above (as Cervantes did, for instance), and to see them not merely as they appeared to themselves, but as they appear to reason. This higher attitude, however, was not only beyond Browning's scope, it was positively contrary to his inspiration. Had he reached it, he would no longer have seen the universe through the "Soul," but through the intellect, and he would not have been able to cry, "How the world is made for each one of us!" On the contrary, the "Soul" would have figured only in its true conditions, in all its ignorance and dependence, and also in its essential teachableness, a point against which Browning's barbaric wilfulness particularly rebelled. Rooted in his persuasion that the soul is essentially omnipotent and that to live hard can never be to live wrong, he remained fascinated by the march and method of self-consciousness, and never allowed himself to be weaned from that romantic fatuity by the energy of rational imagination, which prompts us not to regard our ideas as mere filling of a dream, but rather to build on them the conception of permanent objects and overruling principles, such as Nature, society, and the other ideals of reason. A full-grown imagination deals with these things, which do not obey the laws of psychological progression, and cannot be described by the methods of soliloquy.

We thus see that Browning's sphere . . . [was] elementary. It lay far below the spheres of social and historical reality in which Shakespeare moved; far below the comprehensive and cosmic sphere of every great epic poet. Browning did not even reach the intellectual plane of such contemporary poets as Tennyson and Matthew Arnold, who, whatever may be thought of their powers, did not study consciousness for itself, but for the sake of its meaning and of the objects which it revealed. The best things that come into a man's consciousness are the things that take him out of it—the rational things that are independent of his personal perception and of his personal existence. These he approaches with his reason, and they, in the same measure, endow him with their immortality. But precisely these things—the objects of science and of the constructive imagination—Browning always saw askance, in the outskirts of his field of vision, for his eye was fixed and riveted on the soliloquising Soul. And this Soul being, to his apprehension, irrational, did not give itself over to those permanent objects which might otherwise have occupied it, but ruminated on its own accidental emotions, on its love-affairs, and on its hopes of going on so ruminating for ever.

The pathology of the human mind—for the normal, too, is pathological when it is not referred to the ideal—the pathology of the human mind is a very interesting subject, demanding great gifts and great ingenuity in its treatment. Browning ministers to this interest, and possesses this ingenuity and these gifts. More than any other poet he keeps a kind of speculation alive in the now large body of sentimental, eager-minded people, who no longer can find in a definite religion a form and language for their imaginative life. That this service is greatly appreciated speaks well for the ineradicable tendency in man to study himself and his destiny. We do not deny the achievement when we point out its nature and limitations. It does not cease to be something because it is taken to be more than it is. (pp. 175-77)

George Santayana, "The Poetry of Barbarism," in his Essays in Literary Criticism of George Santayana, *edited by Irving Singer, Charles Scribner's Sons, 1956, pp. 149-78.*

G. K. CHESTERTON (essay date 1903)

[*Chesterton was one of England's most prominent and colorful men of letters during the early twentieth century. Although he is best known today as a detective novelist and essayist, he was also an eminent literary critic. In the following commentary, Chesterton defends Browning against his detractors, underscoring his innovativeness with respect to poetic form and attempting to vindicate the grotesque elements in his work. Chesterton's remarks are addressed by Havelock Ellis (see excerpt below dated 1903).*]

Mr. William Sharp, in his *Life* of Browning, quotes the remarks of another critic to the following effect: "The poet's processes of thought are scientific in their precision and analysis; the sudden conclusion that he imposes upon them is transcendental and inept."

This is a very fair but a very curious example of the way in which Browning is treated. For what is the state of affairs? A man publishes a series of poems, vigorous, perplexing, and unique. The critics read them, and they decide that he has failed as a poet, but that he is a remarkable philosopher and logician. They then proceed to examine his philosophy, and show with great triumph that it is unphilosophical, and to examine his logic and show with great triumph that it is not logical, but "transcendental and inept." In other words, Browning is first denounced for being a logician and not a poet, and then denounced for insisting on being a poet when they have decided that he is to be a logician. It is just as if a man were to say first that a garden was so neglected that it was only fit for a boys' playground, and then complain of the unsuitability in a boys' playground of rockeries and flower-beds.

As we find, after this manner, that Browning does not act satisfactorily as that which we have decided that he shall be—a logician—it might possibly be worth while to make another attempt to see whether he may not, after all, be more valid than we thought as to what he himself professed to be—a poet. (pp. 133-34)

No criticism of Browning's poems can be vital, none in the face of the poems themselves can be even intelligible which is not based upon the fact that he was successfully or otherwise a conscious and deliberate artist. . . . Browning knew perfectly well what he was doing; and if the reader does not like his art, at least the author did. The general sentiment expressed in the statement that he did not care about form is simply the most ridiculous criticism that could be conceived. It would be far nearer the truth to say that he cared more for form than any other English poet who ever lived. He was always weaving and modelling and inventing new forms. Among all his two hundred to three hundred poems it would scarcely be an exaggeration to say that there are half as many different metres as there are different poems. (p. 136)

[If] we study Browning honestly, nothing will strike us more than that he really created a large number of quite novel and quite admirable artistic forms. It is too often forgotten what and how excellent these were. *The Ring and the Book,* for example, is an illuminating departure in literary method—the method of telling the same story several times and trusting to the variety of human character to turn it into several different and equally interesting stories. *Pippa Passes,* to take another example, is a new and most fruitful form, a series of detached dramas connected only by the presence of one fugitive and isolated figure. The invention of these things is not merely like the writing of a good poem—it is something like the invention of the sonnet or the Gothic arch. The poet who makes them does not merely create himself—he creates other poets. It is so in a degree long past enumeration with regard to Browning's smaller poems. . . . A hundred instances might . . . be given. Milton's "Sonnet on his Blindness," or Keats' "Ode on a Grecian Urn," are both thoroughly original, but still we can point to other such sonnets and other such odes. But can any one mention any poem of exactly the same structural and literary type as **"Fears and Scruples,"** as **"The Householder,"** as **"House"** or **"Shop,"** as **"Nationality in Drinks,"** as **"Sibrandus Schafnaburgensis,"** as **"My Star,"** as **"A Portrait,"** as any of *Ferishtah's Fancies,* as any of the **"Bad Dreams."**

The thing which ought to be said about Browning by those who do not enjoy him is simply that they do not like his form; that they have studied the form, and think it a bad form. If more people said things of this sort, the world of criticism would gain almost unspeakably in clarity and common honesty. Browning put himself before the world as a good poet. Let those who think he failed call him a bad poet, and there will be an end of the matter. (pp. 137-38)

Browning has suffered far more injustice from his admirers than from his opponents, for his admirers have for the most part got hold of the matter, so to speak, by the wrong end. They believe that what is ordinarily called the grotesque style of Browning was a kind of necessity boldly adopted by a great genius in order to express novel and profound ideas. But this is an entire mistake. What is called ugliness was to Browning not in the least a necessary evil, but a quite unnecessary luxury, which he enjoyed for its own sake. For reasons that we shall see presently in discussing the philosophical use of the grotesque, it did so happen that Browning's grotesque style was very suitable for the expression of his peculiar moral and metaphysical view. But the whole mass of poems will be misunderstood if we do not realise first of all that he had a love of the grotesque of the nature of art for art's sake. Here, for

example, is a short distinct poem merely descriptive of one of those elfish German jugs in which it is to be presumed Tokay had been served to him. This is the whole poem, and a very good poem too—

> Up jumped Tokay on our table,
> Like a pigmy castle-warder,
> Dwarfish to see, but stout and able,
> Arms and accoutrements all in order;
> And fierce he looked North, then wheeling South
> Blew with his bugle a challenge to Drouth,
> Cocked his flap-hat with the tosspot-feather,
> Twisted his thumb in his red moustache,
> Jingled his huge brass spurs together,
> Tightened his waist with its Buda sash,
> And then, with an impudence nought could abash,
> Shrugged his hump-shoulder, to tell the beholder,
> For twenty such knaves he would laugh but the bolder:
> And so, with his sword-hilt gallantly jutting,
> And dexter-hand on his haunch abutting,
> Went the little man, Sir Ausbruch, strutting!

I suppose there are Browning students in existence who would think that this poem contained something pregnant about the Temperance question, or was a marvellously subtle analysis of the romantic movement in Germany. But surely to most of us it is sufficiently apparent that Browning was simply fashioning a ridiculous knick-knack, exactly as if he were actually moulding one of these preposterous German jugs. Now before studying the real character of this Browningesque style, there is one general truth to be recognised about Browning's work. It is this—that it is absolutely necessary to remember that Browning had, like every other poet, his simple and indisputable failures, and that it is one thing to speak of the badness of his artistic failures, and quite another thing to speak of the badness of his artistic aim. Browning's style may be a good style, and yet exhibit many examples of a thoroughly bad use of it. (pp. 139-41)

[It] is only just to Browning that his more uncouth effusions should not be treated as masterpieces by which he must stand or fall, but treated simply as his failures. It is really true that such a line as

> Irks fear the crop-full bird, frets doubt the maw-crammed
>   beast?

is a very ugly and a very bad line. But it is quite equally true that Tennyson's

> And that good man, the clergyman, has told me words of
>   peace,

is a very ugly and a very bad line. But people do not say that this proves that Tennyson was a mere crabbed controversialist and metaphysician. They say that it is a bad example of Tennyson's form; they do not say that it is a good example of Tennyson's indifference to form. Upon the whole, Browning exhibits far fewer instances of this failure in his own style than any other of the great poets, with the exception of one or two like Spenser and Keats, who seem to have a mysterious incapacity for writing bad poetry. (pp. 141-42)

[The] essential issue about Browning as an artist is not whether he, in common with Byron, Wordsworth, Shelley, Tennyson, and Swinburne, sometimes wrote bad poetry, but whether in any other style except Browning's you could have achieved the precise artistic effect which is achieved by such incomparable lyrics as **"The Patriot"** or **"The Laboratory."** The answer must be in the negative, and in that answer lies the whole justification of Browning as an artist.

The question now arises, therefore, what was his conception of his functions as an artist? We have already agreed that his artistic originality concerned itself chiefly with the serious use of the grotesque. It becomes necessary, therefore, to ask what is the serious use of the grotesque, and what relation does the grotesque bear to the eternal and fundamental elements in life?

One of the most curious things to notice about popular æsthetic criticism is the number of phrases it will be found to use which are intended to express an æsthetic failure, and which express merely an æsthetic variety. Thus, for instance, the traveller will often hear the advice from local lovers of the picturesque, "The scenery round such and such a place has no interest; it is quite flat." To disparage scenery as quite flat is, of course, like disparaging a swan as quite white, or an Italian sky as quite blue. Flatness is a sublime quality in certain landscapes, just as rockiness is a sublime quality in others. In the same way there are a great number of phrases commonly used in order to disparage such writers as Browning which do not in fact disparage, but merely describe them. One of the most distinguished of Browning's biographers and critics says of him, for example, "He has never meant to be rugged, but has become so in striving after strength." To say that Browning never tried to be rugged is like saying that Edgar Allan Poe never tried to be gloomy, or that Mr. W. S. Gilbert never tried to be extravagant. The whole issue depends upon whether we realise the simple and essential fact that ruggedness is a mode of art like gloominess or extravagance. Some poems ought to be rugged, just as some poems ought to be smooth. . . . [To] say that Browning's poems, artistically considered, are fine although they are rugged, is quite as absurd as to say that a rock, artistically considered, is fine although it is rugged. Ruggedness being an essential quality in the universe, there is that in man which responds to it as to the striking of any other chord of the eternal harmonies. As the children of nature, we are akin not only to the stars and flowers, but also to the toadstools and the monstrous tropical birds. And it is to be repeated as the essential of the question that on this side of our nature we do emphatically love the form of the toadstools, and not merely some complicated botanical and moral lessons which the philosopher may draw from them. For example, just as there is such a thing as a poetical metre being beautifully light or beautifully grave and haunting, so there is such a thing as a poetical metre being beautifully rugged. In the old ballads, for instance, every person of literary taste will be struck by a certain attractiveness in the bold, varying, irregular verse—

> He is either himsel' a devil frae hell,
> Or else his mother a witch maun be;
> I wadna have ridden that wan water
> For a' the gowd in Christentie,

is quite as pleasing to the ear in its own way as

> There's a bower of roses by Bendermeer stream,
> And the nightingale sings in it all the night long,

is in another way. Browning had an unrivalled ear for this particular kind of staccato music. The absurd notion that he had no sense of melody in verse is only possible to people who think that there is no melody in verse which is not an imitation of Swinburne. (pp. 143-46)

This, then, roughly is the main fact to remember about Browning's poetical method, or about any one's poetical method— that the question is not whether that method is the best in the world, but the question whether there are not certain things which can only be conveyed by that method. It is perfectly true, for instance, that a really lofty and lucid line of Tennyson, such as—

> Thou wert the highest, yet most human too,

and

> We needs must love the highest when we see it,

would really be made the worse for being translated into Browning. It would probably become

> High's human; man loves best, best visible,

and would lose its peculiar clarity and dignity and courtly plainness. But it is quite equally true that any really characteristic fragment of Browning, if it were only the tempestuous scolding of the organist in **"Master Hugues of Saxe-Gotha"**—

> Hallo, you sacristan, show us a light there!
>   Down it dips, gone like a rocket.
> What, you want, do you, to come unawares,
> Sweeping the church up for first morning-prayers,
> And find a poor devil has ended his cares
> At the foot of your rotten-runged rat-riddled stairs?
>   Do I carry the moon in my pocket?

—it is quite equally true that this outrageous gallop of rhymes ending with a frantic astronomical image would lose in energy and spirit if it were written in a conventional and classical style, and ran—

> What must I deem then that thou dreamest to find
> Disjected bones adrift upon the stair
> Thou sweepest clean, or that thou deemest that I
> Pouch in my wallet the vice regal sun?

Is it not obvious that this statelier version might be excellent poetry of its kind, and yet would be bad exactly in so far as it was good; that it would lose all the swing, the rush, the energy of the preposterous and grotesque original? In fact, we may see how unmanageable is this classical treatment of the essentially absurd in Tennyson himself. The humorous passages in *The Princess,* though often really humorous in themselves, always appear forced and feeble because they have to be restrained by a certain metrical dignity, and the mere idea of such restraint is incompatible with humour. If Browning had written the passage which opens *The Princess,* descriptive of the "larking" of the villagers in the magnate's park, he would have spared us nothing; he would not have spared us the shrill uneducated voices and the unburied bottles of ginger beer. He would have crammed the poem with uncouth similes; he would have changed the metre a hundred times; he would have broken into doggerel and into rhapsody; but he would have left, when all is said and done, as he leaves in that paltry fragment of the grumbling organist, the impression of a certain eternal human energy. Energy and joy, the father and the mother of the grotesque, would have ruled the poem. We should have felt of that rowdy gathering little but the sensation of which Mr. Henley writes—

> Praise the generous gods for giving,
>   In this world of sin and strife,
> With some little time for living,
>   Unto each the joy of life,

the thought that every wise man has when looking at a Bank Holiday crowd at Margate.

To ask why Browning enjoyed this perverse and fantastic style most would be to go very deep into his spirit indeed, probably a great deal deeper than it is possible to go. But it is worth while to suggest tentatively the general function of the grotesque in art generally and in his art in particular. There is one very curious idea into which we have been hypnotised by the more eloquent poets, and that is that nature in the sense of what is ordinarily called the country is a thing entirely stately and beautiful as those terms are commonly understood. The whole world of the fantastic, all things top-heavy, lop-sided, and non-sensical are conceived as the work of man, gargoyles, German jugs, Chinese pots, political caricatures, burlesque epics, the pictures of Mr. Aubrey Beardsley and the puns of Robert Browning. But in truth a part, and a very large part, of the sanity and power of nature lies in the fact that out of her comes all this instinct of caricature. . . . Men who live in the heart of nature, farmers and peasants, know that nature means cows and pigs, and creatures more humorous than can be found in a whole sketch-book of Callot. And the element of the grotesque in art, like the element of the grotesque in nature, means, in the main, energy, the energy which takes its own forms and goes its own way. Browning's verse, in so far as it is grotesque, is not complex or artificial; it is natural and in the legitimate tradition of nature. The verse sprawls like the trees, dances like the dust; it is ragged like the thunder-cloud, it is top-heavy, like the toadstool. Energy which disregards the standard of classical art is in nature as it is in Browning. The same sense of the uproarious force in things which makes Browning dwell on the oddity of a fungus or a jellyfish makes him dwell on the oddity of a philosophical idea. Here, for example, we have a random instance from **"The Englishman in Italy"** of the way in which Browning, when he was most Browning, regarded physical nature.

> And pitch down his basket before us,
>   All trembling alive
> With pink and gray jellies, your sea-fruit;
>   You touch the strange lumps,
> And mouths gape there, eyes open, all manner
>   Of horns and of humps,
> Which only the fisher looks grave at.

Nature might mean flowers to Wordsworth and grass to Walt Whitman, but to Browning it really meant such things as these, the monstrosities and living mysteries of the sea. And just as these strange things meant to Browning energy in the physical world, so strange thoughts and strange images meant to him energy in the mental world. When, in one of his later poems, the professional mystic is seeking in a supreme moment of sincerity to explain that small things may be filled with God as well as great, he uses the very same kind of image, the image of a shapeless sea-beast, to embody that noble conception.

> The Name comes close behind a stomach-cyst,
> The simplest of creations, just a sac
> That's mouth, heart, legs, and belly at once, yet lives
> And feels, and could do neither, we conclude,
> If simplified still further one degree.
>
>   **("Sludge")**

These bulbous, indescribable sea-goblins are the first thing on which the eye of the poet lights in looking on a landscape, and the last in the significance of which he trusts in demonstrating the mercy of the Everlasting. (pp. 146-51)

But when it is clearly understood that Browning's love of the fantastic in style was a perfectly serious artistic love, when we understand that he enjoyed working in that style, as a Chinese potter might enjoy making dragons, or a mediæval mason making devils, there yet remains something definite which must be laid to his account as a fault. He certainly had a capacity for becoming perfectly childish in his indulgence in ingenuities that have nothing to do with poetry at all, such as puns, and

rhymes, and grammatical structures that only just fit into each other like a Chinese puzzle. Probably it was only one of the marks of his singular vitality, curiosity, and interest in details. He was certainly one of those somewhat rare men who are fierily ambitious both in large things and in small. He prided himself on having written *The Ring and the Book,* and he also prided himself on knowing good wine when he tasted it. He prided himself on re-establishing optimism on a new foundation, and it is to be presumed, though it is somewhat difficult to imagine, that he prided himself on such rhymes as the following in **"Pacchiarotto"**:—

> The wolf, fox, bear, and monkey
> By piping advice in one key—
> That his pipe should play a prelude
> To something heaven-tinged not hell-hued,
> Something not harsh but docile,
> Man-liquid, not man-fossil.

This writing, considered as writing, can only be regarded as a kind of joke, and most probably Browning considered it so himself. It has nothing at all to do with that powerful and symbolic use of the grotesque which may be found in such admirable passages as this from **"Holy Cross Day"**:—

> Give your first groan—compunction's at work;
> And soft! from a Jew you mount to a Turk.
> Lo! Micah—the self-same beard on chin,
> He was four times already converted in!

This is the serious use of the grotesque. Through it passion and philosophy are as well expressed as through any other medium. But the rhyming frenzy of Browning has no particular relation even to the poems in which it occurs. It is not a dance to any measure; it can only be called the horse-play of literature. It may be noted, for example, as a rather curious fact that the ingenious rhymes are generally only mathematical triumphs, not triumphs of any kind of assonance. **"The Pied Piper of Hamelin,"** a poem written for children, and bound in general to be lucid and readable, ends with a rhyme which it is physically impossible for any one to say:—

> And, whether they pipe us free, fróm rats or fróm mice,
> If we've promised them aught, let us keep our promise.

This queer trait in Browning, his inability to keep a kind of demented ingenuity even out of poems in which it was quite inappropriate, is a thing which must be recognised, and recognised all the more because as a whole he was a very perfect artist, and a particularly perfect artist in the use of the grotesque. (pp. 152-53)

In the case of what is called Browning's obscurity, the question is somewhat more difficult to handle. Many people have supposed Browning to be profound because he was obscure, and many other people, hardly less mistaken, have supposed him to be obscure because he was profound. He was frequently profound, he was occasionally obscure, but as a matter of fact the two have little or nothing to do with each other. Browning's dark and elliptical mode of speech, like his love of the grotesque, was simply a characteristic of his, a trick of his temperament, and had little or nothing to do with whether what he was expressing was profound or superficial. Suppose, for example, that a person well read in English poetry but unacquainted with Browning's style were earnestly invited to consider the following verse:—

> Hobbs hints blue—straight he turtle eats.
>   Nobbs prints blue—claret crowns his cup.
> Nokes outdares Stokes in azure feats—
>   Both gorge. Who fished the murex up?
> What porridge had John Keats?

The individual so confronted would say without hesitation that it must indeed be an abstruse and indescribable thought which could only be conveyed by remarks so completely disconnected. But the point of the matter is that the thought contained in this amazing verse is not abstruse or philosophical at all, but is a perfectly ordinary and straightforward comment, which any one might have made upon an obvious fact of life. The whole verse of course begins to explain itself, if we know the meaning of the word "murex," which is the name of a sea-shell, out of which was made the celebrated blue dye of Tyre. The poet takes this blue dye as a simile for a new fashion in literature, and points out that Hobbs, Nobbs, etc., obtain fame and comfort by merely using the dye from the shell; and adds the perfectly natural comment:—

> . . . Who fished the murex up?
> What porridge had John Keats?

So that the verse is not subtle, and was not meant to be subtle, but is a perfectly casual piece of sentiment at the end of a light poem. Browning is not obscure because he has such deep things to say, any more than he is grotesque because he has such new things to say. He is both of these things primarily because he likes to express himself in a particular manner. The manner is as natural to him as a man's physical voice, and it is abrupt, sketchy, allusive, and full of gaps. Here comes in the fundamental difference between Browning and such a writer as George Meredith, with whom the Philistine satirist would so often in the matter of complexity class him. The works of George Meredith are, as it were, obscure even when we know what they mean. They deal with nameless emotions, fugitive sensations, subconscious certainties and uncertainties, and it really requires a somewhat curious and unfamiliar mode of speech to indicate the presence of these. But the great part of Browning's actual sentiments, and almost all the finest and most literary of them, are perfectly plain and popular and eternal sentiments. Meredith is really a singer producing strange notes and cadences difficult to follow because of the delicate rhythm of the song he sings. Browning is simply a great demagogue, with an impediment in his speech. Or rather, to speak more strictly, Browning is a man whose excitement for the glory of the obvious is so great that his speech becomes disjointed and precipitate: he becomes eccentric through his advocacy of the ordinary, and goes mad for the love of sanity. (pp. 154-56)

Many, who could understand that ruggedness might be an artistic quality, would decisively, and in most cases rightly, deny that obscurity could under any conceivable circumstances be an artistic quality. But here again Browning's work requires a somewhat more cautious and sympathetic analysis. There is a certain kind of fascination, a strictly artistic fascination, which arises from a matter being hinted at in such a way as to leave a certain tormenting uncertainty even at the end. It is well sometimes to half understand a poem in the same manner that we half understand the world. One of the deepest and strangest of all human moods, is the mood which will suddenly strike us perhaps in a garden at night, or deep in sloping meadows, the feeling that every flower and leaf has just uttered something stupendously direct and important, and that we have by a prodigy of imbecility not heard or understood it. There is a certain poetic value, and that a genuine one, in this sense of having missed the full meaning of things. There is beauty, not only in wisdom, but in this dazed and dramatic ignorance.

But in truth it is very difficult to keep pace with all the strange and unclassified artistic merits of Browning. He was always trying experiments; sometimes he failed, producing clumsy and irritating metres, top-heavy and over-concentrated thought. Far more often he triumphed, producing a crowd of boldly designed poems, every one of which taken separately might have founded an artistic school. But whether successful or unsuccessful, he never ceased from his fierce hunt after poetic novelty. He never became a conservative. The last book he published in his lifetime, *Parleyings with Certain People of Importance in their Day,* was a new poem, and more revolutionary than *Paracelsus.* This is the true light in which to regard Browning as an artist. He had determined to leave no spot of the cosmos unadorned by his poetry which he could find it possible to adorn. An admirable example can be found in that splendid poem **"Childe Roland to the Dark Tower Came."** It is the hint of an entirely new and curious type of poetry, the poetry of the shabby and hungry aspect of the earth itself. Daring poets who wished to escape from conventional gardens and orchards had long been in the habit of celebrating the poetry of rugged and gloomy landscapes, but Browning is not content with this. He insists upon celebrating the poetry of mean landscapes. That sense of scrubbiness in nature, as of a man unshaved, had never been conveyed with this enthusiasm and primeval gusto before.

> If there pushed any ragged thistle-stalk
>   Above its mates, the head was chopped; the bents
>   Were jealous else. What made those holes and rents
> In the dock's harsh swarth leaves, bruised as to baulk
> All hope of greenness? 'tis a brute must walk
>   Pashing their life out, with a brute's intents.

This is a perfect realisation of that eerie sentiment which comes upon us, not so often among mountains and water-falls, as it does on some half-starved common at twilight, or in walking down some grey mean street. It is the song of the beauty of refuse; and Browning was the first to sing it. Oddly enough it has been one of the poems about which most of those pedantic and trivial questions have been asked, which are asked invariably by those who treat Browning as a science instead of a poet, "What does the poem of **"Childe Roland"** mean?" The only genuine answer to this is, "What does anything mean?" Does the earth mean nothing? Do grey skies and wastes covered with thistles mean nothing? Does an old horse turned out to graze mean nothing? If it does, there is but one further truth to be added—that everything means nothing. (pp. 157-59)

> *G. K. Chesterton, in his* Robert Browning, *The Macmillan Company, 1903, 207 p.*

HAVELOCK ELLIS (essay date 1903)

[*Ellis was a pioneering sex psychologist and a respected English man of letters. His most famous work is his seven-volume* The Psychology of Sex, *a study containing frankly stated case histories of sex-related psychological abnormalities that was greatly responsible for changing British and American attitudes toward the previously forbidden subject of sexuality. Ellis reassesses Browning's literary stature in the following excerpt. In the first part of the article, he evaluates—and generally deflates—Browning's reputation for erudition, psychological insight, and moral leadership; in the second part, Ellis challenges Chesterton's defense of Browning's use of the grotesque (see excerpt above dated 1903).*]

To the philosophic spectator of literary criticism—if such there be—the spectacle presented by Browning's critics must be puzzling. They are all clearly anxious, even eager, to admire Browning, they are all certain that there is something to admire; but as to what that something is, the most various opinions prevail. If one attempts to sum up the estimates of critics it would, on the whole, appear that Browning is an artist and poet of the very first order, who has discovered new forms of poetic art and opened up new horizons of poetic energy; that he is, in addition, a writer who merits our admiration on account of his extraordinary erudition and scholarship; that, moreover, we have to recognise in him a psychologist of the highest order; that, further, he was a philosophic, or, at all events, theological moralist, with a new message to humanity; that he was, finally, one of the supreme amateurs of the world, in the higher sense of that much-abused word.

Everyone who is anxious, and even eager, to admire Browning and to place him justly—as indeed we all are—cannot fail to find here an amply satisfying conception. A man who combined the varying qualities of a Shakespeare, a Herbert Spencer, a St. Paul, and a Leonardo must certainly be regarded as a unique personality. Yet even on this calm acclivity to which the critics of Browning have so skilfully conducted us, it is inevitable that, however sympathetic we may remain, certain reflections should arise. It may not be altogether useless to give expression to these reflections in order.

For the moment, indeed, we may put aside the first point, in regarding Browning as poet and artist. We may assume, as a working hypothesis, that he was, even essentially, a poet and artist, while for the present not attempting to determine the precise quality or degree of his poetic art.

First, then, there is that erudition and scholarship to which the critic of Browning never fails to direct our admiring attention. It can scarcely be claimed that erudition is more than a subsidiary aid to the psychologist, the moralist, or even the amateur, and, indeed, it is in connection with Browning as poet that this vision of immense learning is evoked. Here, it must first be pointed out that, in reality, every poet—every poet, that is, who goes beyond the simple swallow-flights of personal lyric song—is learned. Learning is a necessary part of a poet's stock-in-trade, of his raw material. Homer, when we rightly understand his relation to his time, appears as a very learned poet; Shakespeare was appallingly learned. Keats was learned. The truly notable point about the learning of Browning is not its existence, nor even its extent, still less its accuracy—he was in no proper sense a scholar, and never professed to be—but the fact that it was united with an extremely retentive memory. Homer and Shakespeare and Keats do not impress us by their learning; to repeat a famous simile, in their learning they were like workers in the diamond mines of Golconda: they only sought for jewels; Browning's absorbant memory was like a sponge that sucked up diamonds and mud alike, and with the native energy of his temperament, he sponged them out alike. His learning was thus more conspicuous; we need not too hastily conclude that it was greater or more admirable. (pp. 121-22)

The point may be easily yielded; but Browning's position as a great psychologist remains unaffected by any considerations as to the precise quantity and quality of his learning. It is claimed that Browning's special distinction is the invention of the dramatic lyric, and the distinctive character of this literary species lies in its psychological insight, its casuistical skill, its ability to present in all ramifications the mental attitude of a person quite other than the dramatic lyrist himself. **"Bishop Blougram's Apology"** is commonly regarded as one of the most accomplished examples of this species. It so happens that we can go behind Bishop Blougram; Browning stated definitely that in Blougram he had in mind Cardinal Wiseman, and that, moreover, he was not moved by any hostile motive; he was really writing an "apology" for Cardinal Wiseman.

In the absence of any intimate personal knowledge of Wiseman—in the absence of knowledge which it is fairly certain that Browning shared—we must fall back on the biography of Wiseman, which presents us with a completely intelligible and, so far as can be judged, veracious portrait of a man whose sincerity was beyond question, and who bears scarcely any resemblance to Blougram. Browning's psychological defence of Wiseman, has, therefore, no real relation to the man he is defending; it is even without that kind of value which belongs to a felicitous caricature. As a psychological analysis it breaks down altogether; its value must be estimated on an artistic basis. It is not difficult to see why the claim of Browning the psychologist cannot be maintained. As Mr. Chesterton, the latest and one of the most discriminating of his critics, quite truly observes, Browning was not an "intellectual." He had not that sensitive, supple, receptive temperament—such as Renan possessed in so high a degree—which enables a man to put aside for the time his own convictions and his own point of view, to shift his standpoint, to enter imagining into another man's skin. Browning's defective psychological insight is reflected in his defective critical insight. The attraction he felt for insignificant formalities in art has always been noted, but it is usual to slur over the fact that, in many cases, certainly, Browning himself by no means regarded them as insignificant. His critical estimates were, even in his own day, already passing out of date. In two of the happiest and most effective of his poems it is easy to read between the lines that he regarded Andrea del Sarto as a painter who narrowly escaped reaching the highest summits of art, and Fra Lippo Lippi as the painter of mere feminine prettiness. Browning's dramatic lyric is really a distorted personal lyric, and the distinction involves an important difference. We are not really being led into the intimate recesses of another man's soul, we are simply being told how one Robert Browning—a sturdy, conventional English gentleman, endowed with an extraordinarily vigorous mind, and very pronounced views on morality and religion—would feel if by some mysterious fate he had himself become a scamp, a coward or a humbug. Browning evidently delighted in inviting difficult exercises of this kind, and was justified, for they constituted a gymnastics peculiarly suited to his athletic mind. But they have no very close connection with psychology and not much with casuistry.

The critic of Browning becomes indifferent alike to his erudition and his psychology when he turns to Browning the moralist and theologian. The profound sincerity of Browning's moral and theological convictions cannot be questioned. They were all the more fundamental, and not the less genuine, because they were temperamental. Indeed, one may almost say they were inherited. Little as Browning had in common with his father, the thorough-going eighteenth century optimism which his father had imbibed from Pope, and the Nineteenth Century Liberal Nonconformity which he had added to it, were accepted intact by his son, whose native energy of character merely made the optimism more aggressive—so aggressive, indeed, that it sometimes almost persuades us of the beauty of pessimism—and the Liberal Nonconformity more comprehensive, as his restless mental fertility played around them. But in essentials they never moved very far from the starting point. "Merely man, and nothing more"—but for Browning a "man" was a sturdy, conventional British, Liberal Nonconformist, middle-class gentleman. Thus Browning represented admirably one aspect of the religious thought of his time, just as Tennyson, with his more gracious, but perhaps less radical, Broad Church Anglicanism, represented another. But let us turn to one of the great masters—to Shakespeare. Here also we find, as well as a great poet, a moralist grappling with the problems of life and of death. But we always find Shakespeare above or below the plane on which the definitely circumscribed groups of believers are fixed. It is a curious fact, all the more notable since it is clearly not due to any trimming caution, that Shakespeare never offends the most sensitive free-thinker, the most devout Catholic. It can scarcely be said of Browning. Whether we are able to enter the little chapel at Camberwell, or whether we only listen outside, we cannot fail to feel the stimulating magnetism of this strident preacher's voice, with its unfailing theological optimism. But it is not thus that we approach Gœthe or Shakespeare. (p. 122)

• • • • •

But, after all, what have scholarship, psychology, theology, to do with literature? It is with Browning the poet and artist that the critic is finally and centrally concerned. That Browning possessed the fundamental temperament of the poet, and that he strenuously strove to be an artist, may fairly be taken as facts that are beyond argument. It is when an attempt is made to define his precise position and to estimate its significance that the difficulty comes in. Mr. Chesterton has truly said that the general characteristic of Browning's form at its point of greatest originality is its flashes and dexterous use of the grotesque, more especially as used to express sublime emotion, and that the indulging source and meaning of this grotesqueness is energy. In other words, Browning is the poet of energy artistically expressing itself in the grotesque. This seems admirable. Then Mr. Chesterton goes on bravely to argue that grotesque energy is a form of art which has been reached at the highest moments of human inspiration. But here we pause, and, once again, we begin to reflect. Certainly, energy is very fundamental in Browning; it was ingrained in the nervous texture of the man, in his loud voice, his emphatic gestures: "I was ever a fighter." And the man is reflected in his work. He cannot easily talk without shouting, or walk without running; if the humour should take him to dance it could surely be nothing less athletic than a bolero. He presents in a supreme degree the quality which Coleridge termed Nimiety, the quality of *Too-muchness*, and certainly a man of this temperament is naturally attracted to the grotesque. The man of exuberant energy craves to come in touch with the material aspect of things; he wants to handle strange, rough, unfamiliar shapes. The grotesque, one may point out, always gives the impression of unconquered material, of matter not yet subdued by spirits, it must always be unfamiliar. This last characteristic was clearly realised by Browning himself, and he describes those strange and quaintly-shaped sea creatures "which only the fishes looks grave at." To the man who truly knows them they are not grotesque. Many persons can probably remember when as children they first heard a violin; the player may have been a master; but the impression produced by the unfamiliar sound of the instrument was exquisitely grotesque.

When we really understand a grotesque thing, when it has become luminous to intelligence, it is no more grotesque than is any ordinary "two-legged bird without feathers" to his fellow men. It will be seen that we have struck on the reason why it is that to exalt unduly the poetry of the grotesque reveals a certain mental confusion, a certain defect of critical insight. The searching inquisitive artist is interested in the grotesque; Leonardo, as his note-books show, was eagerly interested in the grotesque, but there is nothing grotesque in the art of Leonardo; he treated the grotesque as crude material of art, and in passing through his searching brain it ceased to be grotesque.

The poet of energy, however, delights in exercising his energy in the manipulation of the crude material of art; he loves to pile up the raw strange chunks, with all the sharp points sticking out, into fantastic edifices. He strives to embody the maximum amount of natural material in his art. No doubt there was a real organic reason why Browning adopted this method: it was the method that suited him best. Mr. Chesterton observes that Browning was a poet who stuttered. There is real insight in this remark. A person who stutters is expending an immense amount of articulatory energy, but he has forgotten the less obvious but equally essential necessity for harmonious breathing. His failure is strictly analogous to that of the young violinist who puts so much energy into his bow-hand that he forgets his string-hand. Browning's poetry is a stutter, an idealised stutter, in its perpetual emphasis, its strenuous combative energy, possessing so Titanic a quality as to induce even the critic who has acutely pointed out this characteristic to place Browning in the front rank of the world's poets and artists.

Yet let us turn to the great artists, whose mastery is universally acknowledged; whatever the form of their art may have been the grotesque has fallen away to an altogether subordinate place; there are no heavy chunks of unworked material, no sharp points sticking out; even energy is no more visible, being absorbed in securing the perfect adjustment of each part to the whole; string-hand and bow-hand are working together in absolute harmony. "I was ever a fighter,"—that saying was never heard from the lips of any supreme artist. Look at some fragment of sculpture by a Greek, or by Rodin, and it seems as light as foam and almost as translucent; listen to some piece of music by Mozart, its felicity is divine, but there is nothing in it; stand in the room that holds the Meninas of Velasquez, and you seem to see a vision that has come miraculously, effortlessly, which in another moment may cease to be. Or take the art we are here immediately concerned with, and on whatever scale of magnitude you please. Shakespeare or Verlaine; we no longer hear the strenuous, insistent voice of the stutterer, we seem only conscious of a breath, on which the meaning aerially floats. It is idle to argue that *Hudibras* may be placed beside the *Canterbury Tales*, and the *Alchemist* beside *Lear*. Browning belongs to the same circle in the Paradise of Art as Butler and Ben Jonson; as an artist his ambitions were greater than Butler's, his achievements scarcely less; as a personality and a poet he is not unworthy to be named with Ben Jonson. We do him an injustice by comparing him to Chaucer or Shakespeare; with the divine masters he can never be, but his place in our literature remains a noble and assured place. (p. 147)

Havelock Ellis, "Browning's Place in Literature," *in* The Weekly Critical Review, *Vol. II, Nos. 32 and 33, August 27 and September 3, 1903, pp. 121-22, 147.*

PERCY LUBBOCK   (essay date 1912)

[Lubbock was an early twentieth-century editor, critic, historian, and biographer. His most renowned critical work, The Craft of Fiction, *is a detailed analysis of the works of Leo Tolstoy, Gustave Flaubert, and Henry James. Lubbock discusses Browning's failure as a dramatist in the excerpt below, which was drawn from an essay originally published in the* Quarterly Review *in 1912.]*

If the faults of [Browning's] plays were the faults of immaturity, they would not be worth lingering over; for a youthful poet is a youthful poet, and though he may tell us about youth . . . , he will not necessarily tell us much about himself individually.

But Browning, at any rate after *Pauline,* was never youthful in this sense; he had entered into complete control of himself and his manner in more than time to be able to sit down at four-and-twenty and produce a fully elaborated play 'on commission'; writing blank verse as unmistakably his own, for its fearless attack, its resilience, its sound texture, as the verse of *The Ring and the Book.* And more than this, his plays have a decorative economy which is perhaps the quality we should least expect in the first flowering of so exuberant a genius as his. *Colombe's Birthday,* for example, whatever else may be said of it, is an admirable piece of decoration, fitted securely into its frame, entangled with no more material than it needs, and worked out with a freshness and sweetness which make it one of the most lovable of all his productions. If some of the plays do not trace themselves so surely, there is the same lucidity of design in two such touching motives of irony as *King Victor and King Charles* and *A Soul's Tragedy.* With these before us we cannot say that Browning had not mastered the dramatic form in so far as that demands the orderly and gradual figuration of an idea. The notion that he could never tell a story without turning it upside down at the start and forgetting to right it again, was doubtless born (and no unnatural birth) of our struggles, early and late, to understand the story of *Sordello*; but beyond *Sordello* it has little or no application. It is true that in the more complicated situations of plays like *Strafford* or *The Return of the Druses,* the curve is not so firmly followed as in those just mentioned; while in one, *A Blot in the 'Scutcheon,* the sombre beauty of the treatment only exposes pitilessly the hapless absurdity of the plot. Yet with every reservation made, it is not in the shaping or the handling of these plays that we shall find Browning by temperament at cross-purposes with drama.

That which surely, whether consciously or no, turned him from the set play-form to the dramatic monologue with which he had started, was his lack of power to grasp a character, as opposed to his immense and varied power to grasp a mood. It is not for nothing that in most of his plays the unity of time is so closely observed, the action being often practically continuous, or at most contained within a limited number of hours. This device does not, of course, in true drama, meet the difficulty of the writer who sees his personages only in the light of the particular situation, but it disguises it. Character is character and mood is mood, however short or long the exposure; and tragic drama absolutely demands the figure in the round, even though we may immediately be concerned with but one aspect of it. To say that Browning's plays are undramatic by reason of their allusive quickness and the difficulty of following it without time for reflection, is beside the point; for there is nothing essential in such ineffectiveness as would be abolished by a sharpening, however unexpected, of our wits. The point would rather be that, whereas the language, the arrangement, the apparatus, are all sturdily dramatic, the figures themselves, so nimble and lively and intelligent as they are, are embodied only by the exigencies of the moment, seem struck into life by the momentary embarrassment or felicity, and so cannot hold our attention as lives to be lived. Such a contention as this naturally could not be made good except with elaborate examination and quotation from the works themselves, impossible here; but it will be borne out if we feel that the pleasure they have given in the reading has been essentially the pleasure of watching moment break in on moment, each caught up so responsively by these finely-tuned intelligences; the dissatisfaction at the end of it all, hardly to be avoided, being due to the fact that we have been more conscious of this play of events on them, the agile interlacing of action and reaction, than of

An oil painting of Browning in 1860, by Michele Gordigiani.

the men and women, the human stuff in whose interest the scene was set. It is delightful to wonder what Colombe, Luitolfo (in *A Soul's Tragedy*), Luria, will do, they are so certain to do something rare and surprising and poignant. What they were before, what they will be presently, in what sense they have developed, are questions which are allowed to drop, and which, when it is all over, reappear still unanswered. (pp. 44-5)

[Browning] cannot be surpassed for certainty and swiftness of touch [in character analysis, yet,] when it comes to the synthetic grasp of the myriad fragments, he fails us. There is not a case which, as it arises, he cannot instantly take possession of. A single hint, and he is off along the line it suggests and back again with a dozen of its implications. But his own interest in the question at issue is so keen that it positively weakens his sense of its dramatic value. The particular dilemma presents itself to him less as a matter involved in certain lives and brought about by certain circumstances than as one to be instantly confronted and resolved. All the wits of all the people concerned dart forward to the work; the resolution is exquisitely accomplished, and the maze of fine feelings and perceptions, intricate as it often becomes, never cheats the attention it asks for, but proves to have been traced with perfect lucidity. And if again and again we feel that what the action lacks is not beauty or order, but simply weight—if we enjoy watching these spiritual intrigues disentangled and forget all about the human beings who are doing it—that is because Browning himself has seen the innumerable ways in which they would act and react upon each other so much more clearly than he has seen their own substance. He was, indeed, later to show a power of character-drawing beyond anything to be found in the plays: Guido and Pompilia and Caponsacchi are characters conceived and held in the fullest sense; and it might seem that the lack of any figures to put beside them from the plays is merely a mark of immaturity. Already, however, in *Paracelsus,* and again in *Pippa Passes,* Browning had shown that he worked more happily in a mixed manner—a loose structure approaching the device of the monologue, or a simple juxtaposition of scenes, unified by a lyrical embroidery running round and through them. The different problems thus arising . . . were more suited to his hand; and after *Luria* he never wrote another play.

All this does not for a moment mean that he was not in a more restricted sense a dramatic poet, or that he was ever interested in his intrigue to the point of forgetting that he was speaking 'in character'. His handling of these cases is not abstract; it is always in sharp concrete terms of human beings. We touch here upon a not unknown confusion of criticism in dealing with dramatic and creative genius. It is sometimes suggested, for example, that Shakespeare's amazing power of creating character is expressed by saying that he utterly identifies himself with every one of his own inventions, himself slipping through our fingers . . . and defying our definition of his own qualities. It is rather Browning who identifies himself with his characters, with the double result that his drama is incomplete, and that no poet has written his own temperament more legibly over all his work. The creative writer is, in fact, creative exactly in so far as he refrains from merging himself in his productions. He keeps outside them; it is his detachment from them that enables him to seize them so firmly; they are far more to him than mere agents in the particular matter he is exhibiting. It is when he tries to portray himself, or rather such a character as lies nearest to his own sympathies, that the result is apt to be unsatisfying. It was not because Browning failed to feel with his characters, but exactly because he felt with them too promptly and easily, that his drama wants body. He became them so thoroughly that he could not see them. It will be noted, then, how right was the instinct which led him once for all away from the play to the dramatic monologue, the dramatic idyl, the dramatic lyric. This was the field in which everything that was fine and just in his plays could be utilised, and where that which in them was shortcoming became the appropriate and the harmonious. (pp. 46-7)

> *Percy Lubbock, "Robert Browning," in* Robert Browning: A Collection of Critical Essays, *edited by Philip Drew, Houghton Mifflin Company, 1966, pp. 36-57.*

FRANK HARRIS   (essay date 1915)

[*Harris was a highly controversial English editor, critic, and biographer. As a commentator he is noted for his* Contemporary Portraits, *containing essays marked by his characteristically vigorous style and patronizing tone. In the following excerpt from* Contemporary Portraits, *Harris compares Browning the poet with Browning the man.*]

[Browning] is often spoken of as the least inspired of poets. To my mind he owed more to verse and the inspiration of reflection than any man of genius I ever met. His belief as shown in the **"Rabbi Ben Ezra"** and other poems is uncompromising, definite, clear, authoritative as the utterance of a Jewish prophet. But when you probed the man in quiet conversation, you found no such certainty.

His beliefs were really a mere echo of his childhood's faith, and his optimism was of health and sound heart rather than of

insight. He was not one of those who had gone round the world and returned to his native place; he had always lingered in the vicinity of home without seeking to justify his preference. His was a bookish mind, and apart from books not eventfully original. He had spent many years in Italy without knowing the Italian, and had lived on the crater-edge of socialist unrest almost without noticing it. Unfortunately for his fame he had always had a competence, enough to live on comfortably and so had never to struggle with the necessities and learn their lesson. Had he ever gone hungry and been forced to eat "the bitter-salt bread" of humiliation that Dante spoke of he might have become a world-poet. As it was he accepted all the pitiable conventions of London society because he was used to them, just as he donned the dress. I have heard him tell a fairly good story; I never heard him say anything original. In fact, if I had not known his poetry I should have met him and talked to him many times without ever imagining that he was a man of any distinction of mind. (pp. 224-25)

> *Frank Harris, "Robert Browning," in his* Contemporary Portraits, *1915. Reprint by Brentano's Publishers, 1920, pp. 219-27.*

EZRA POUND   (poem date 1920)

[*An American poet, translator, essayist, and critic, Pound was "the principal inventor of modern poetry," according to Archibald MacLeish. Considered one of the most innovative and creative artists of his generation, he is chiefly renowned for his poetic masterpiece, the* Cantos, *which he revised and enlarged throughout much of his life. Pound also influenced modern poetry considerably through his encouragement and editorial and financial support of such writers as William Butler Yeats, T. S. Eliot, James Joyce, and William Carlos Williams. Pound, who acknowledged Browning as an important influence on his work, published the following tribute to him in a 1920 collection of poems entitled* Homage to Robert Browning.]

MESMERISM

"And a cat's in the water-butt."—ROBERT BROWNING

Aye you're a man that! ye old mesmerizer
Tyin' your meanin' in seventy swadelin's,
One must of needs be a hang'd early riser
To catch you at worm turning. Holy Odd's bodykins!

"Cat's i' the water butt!" Thought's in your verse-barrel,
Tell us this thing rather, then we'll believe you,
You, Master Bob Browning, spite your apparel
Jump to your sense and give praise as we'd lief do.

You wheeze as a head-cold long-tonsilled Calliope,
But God! what a sight you ha' got o' our in'ards,
Mad as a hatter but surely no Myope,
Broad as all ocean and leanin' man-kin'ards.

Heart that was big as the bowels of Vesuvius,
Words that were wing'd as her sparks in eruption,
Eagled and thundered as Jupiter Pluvius,
Sound in your wind past all signs o' corruption.

Here's to you, Old Hippety-Hop o' the accents,
True to the Truth's sake and crafty dissector,
You grabbed at the gold sure; had no need to pack cents
Into your versicles.

        Clear sight's elector!

> *Ezra Pound, "Mesmerism," in his* Personae: The Collected Shorter Poems of Ezra Pound, *1952. Reprint by New Directions Books, 1971, p. 13.*

WILLIAM CLYDE DeVANE, JR. (essay date 1927)

[*A leading Browning scholar, DeVane interpreted* Parleyings with Certain People *as a mental autobiography featuring Browning's reflections on his early intellectual mentors. The critic discusses the "Parleying with Gerard de Lairesse" in the excerpt below, using Browning's response to the seventeenth-century Dutch painter's ideas to elucidate his aesthetic practices and values. For additional commentary by DeVane, see excerpt dated 1947.*]

[To Lairesse's *The Art of Painting in All its Branches*] Browning acknowledges no small indebtedness. He loved Lairesse, he says in the [**"Parleying With Gerard de Lairesse"**],

> Because of that prodigious book he wrote
> On Artistry's Ideal.

And he read the book again and again, delighting in both the text and the prints, so that in his later years he still remembered the work. In the very copy which he had read as a child he wrote in 1874:

> I read this book more often and with greater delight
> when I was a child than any other: and still remember
> the main of it most gratefully for the good I seem to
> have got from the prints and wonderful text.

The work thus singled out as the favorite book of such a voracious reader as the boy Browning attains at once a position of great significance in his education.

Deeply interested as he was in Lairesse's prodigious book, Browning the boy determined to "pay due homage" to the artist by making an expedition to see some of his pictures. (pp. 215-16)

But Browning's pilgrimage which was to have paid his homage to the painter whose book he loved so well, resulted in nothing but disappointment. Perhaps he had hoped too much from the wonderful book. At any rate he has to admit, in the *"Parleying"*:

> So my youth's piety obtained success
> Of all-too dubious sort: for though it irk
> To tell the issue, few or none would guess
> From extant lines and colors, De Lairesse,
> Your faculty . . .

So while he is eternally grateful for the service done him by the prodigious book, he is more than dubious about the value of the artist's own pictures:

> I lack
> Somehow the heart to wish your practice back
> Which boasted hand's achievement in a score
> Of veritable pictures, less or more,
> Still to be seen: myself have seen them . . .

Thus we learn that gratitude led Browning to see in all some score of Lairesse's pictures during his lifetime; but we see no less definitely that the poet's early disappointment in the painter's artistry persisted. (p. 217)

Perhaps the most salient characteristic of Lairesse, both as a painter and as an instructor, is his insistence upon the beauty and perfection of the classic antique, contrasted with the sordidness and "deformed ugliness" of the modern subject. This one idea informs the whole of Lairesse's work. . . . [He] took for his great master Poussin, who in the paraphernalia of the pseudo-classical school—tombs, temples, statuary, satyrs, and gods—could tell a story better than any other painter. Lairesse too tells stories. There is scarcely a picture of his which does not attempt to portray some fable from Ovid, or some tale from classical history. His genius exercises itself upon such subjects

as the metamorphosis of Dryope into a tree as she plucks the lotos twig, or Apollo pursuing Daphne until she is fixed to the earth, or Jupiter wooing the hapless Calistro. Lairesse seldom condescends to treat a subject that is later than Ovid, for he believes strongly in the superiority of the ancient over the modern subject:

> But let us reflect on two arts, noble and ignoble or
> *antique* and *modern,* and see how much they differ
> both in objects and execution. *The antique is unlim-*
> *ited,* that is, it can handle *history,* sacred as well as
> profane, *fables* and *emblems* both moral and spiritual;
> under which three heads it comprehends, *all that ever*
> *was, is, and shall be; the past, present,* and *to come;*
> *and that, after an excellent manner, which never*
> *alters, but remains always the same: The modern,*
> *contrarily, is so far from being free, that it is limited*
> *within certain narrow bounds; and is of small power;*
> *for it may or can represent no more than what is*
> *present, and that too in a manner which is always*
> *changing: What is past and to come is without its*
> *power; as also histories, fables and emblems, as well*
> *poetical and philosophic as moral.* Hence we may
> judge what the *modern* art of painting is, and why it
> cannot be called *noble;* much less of any harmony
> with the *antique.*

This then is Lairesse: he abjures the modern and the realistic, and clings to the emblematic and allegorical. He must embellish his flat Holland with god and goddess, nymph and satyr. He must find sepulchre and temple and statuary until it is indeed "Holland turned Dreamland." Browning in characterizing him has caught his spirit; nothing is simple:

> The rose? No rose unless it disentwine
> From Venus' wreath the while she bends to kiss
> Her deathly love . . .

Nor does Browning exaggerate when he tells how Lairesse shows the sky traversed by flying shapes, and the earth stocked with brood of monsters—centaurs and satyrs—not omitting, on the other hand, the shapes of gods and goddesses. For the painter, in his discussion of the theory of his art, drew constantly for his illustrations upon the great body of fable and history that a diligent study of the Latin writers had stored in his mind.

But as Browning had turned, as a boy, from the actual paintings of Lairesse, he was to turn, in his more mature years, from Lairesse's theories of art. He tells us in the *"Parleying"* that

> Bearded experience bears not to be duped
> Like boyish fancy . . .

The poet cannot be satisfied with unreal fancies spun from ancient and fabulous lore. The sense of actuality is too strong in him. This difference in point of view between the seventeenth-century painter and the nineteenth-century poet is, indeed, the crux of the whole *"Parleying."* Browning, who sees things without the embellishments of fancy, can in his later days scarcely comprehend Lairesse's fanciful vision. He addresses Lairesse:

> . . . make it plain to me,
> Who, bee-like, sate sense with the simply true,
> Nor seek to heighten that sufficiency . . .

Browning was too much captivated by his love of realism to be able to follow any longer Lairesse's fancies.

But in one essential respect Browning did not reject Lairesse. One part of the painter's teaching had been so thoroughly assimilated by the poet in those early days of their acquaintance that it had become an integral part of his own thought. This was the conception of what was beautiful, and what was horrible, in landscape.

Landscape was, in Lairesse, the least fanciful of his creations. He would, it is true, sprinkle his canvases or his descriptions of pictures with many strange figures, but he never failed to fill in an appropriate background of landscape. He has a certain very definite conception of what is appropriate material for the artist and what is not. In fact, Lairesse has a very typical favorite landscape; and while he strongly recommends diversity, it is after all diversity within rather narrow limits. He admires

> . . . woods with vistos, wherein the eye may lose itself; rocks, rivers, and water-falls, green fields, &c. delightful to the eye. Herein lies the stress of a landscape. . . . However, this variety consists not only in the difference or irregularity of the objects, as trees, hills, fountains, and the like, but in the diversity of each of them; for instance, bending and strait trees, large and small hills, . . . green and russet lands, &c. The same diversity is to be observed in colouring, according to the seasons of the year; that lovers may not be cloyed by producing, with the cockoo, always the same thing; as stir and motion, crooked and mis-shapen bodies of trees, waving branches, barren grounds, blue mountains, or beasts, birds, huntings and the like; or, contrarily, always repose and quietness . . .

Lairesse was especially fond of urging his readers to suit the action to the time of day in their pictures, or the time of day to the action. . . . [In *The Art of Painting,* he] carefully lists the times of day, with the actions appropriate to them, so that his followers may not make any mistakes. To give examples of some of these:

> "Day-break."
>
> This first-born time of the day favours the enterprizes of great generals in besieging or storming a town; no time more proper for it, by the example of *Joshua* in taking *Jericho.* This rule, though not without exception, has been observed by all nations . . . It is also the proper time for hunting; as in the representation of a *Diana, Cephalus, Adonis,* or any such subject. . . .
>
> "The Morning."
>
> This time principally rejoices nature; even inanimate things are sensible of it: the glittering light takes the tops of high mountains, and causes, both in buildings and landscape, great shades, appearing very delightful. This light, at breaking out, gives uncommon sweetness when the objects shine in the water; as also a certain freshness mixed with vapours, which bind the parts of things so well together, as entirely to please the eye of the knowing.
>
> At this time the *Heathens* offered their sacrifices; . . . the *Children of Israel* had . . . their *morning oblations* . . . The *Jews* retain those customs to this day; as also did the ancient *Christians* . . . The *Persians* moreover honoured the morning by their offerings . . .

So he goes through "The Light between Morning and Noon," "Noon," "The Afternoon," and "The Evening." (pp. 219-22)

Reading *The Art of Painting* over and over until he knew it almost by heart, as we have seen that Browning did as a boy,

he unconsciously took over the artist's conceptions of the beautiful and the appropriate in landscape. They became part of the very warp and weft of Browning's intellectual character. To such an extent is this true that we may observe that whenever, in the poet's works, the necessity for description is upon him, he seems to revert naturally to Lairesse's judgment concerning what is "painter-like" or "unpainter-like." Like Lairesse he has a feeling for the appropriate scenery for the particular time of day. His love for the Alpine and the wild savors often of Byron, rather than of Lairesse. Nevertheless, the Dutch painter seems to have left his mark. So generally dispersed through *The Art of Painting* are Lairesse's landscapes that it is impossible to select any one long description for quotation; but perhaps the reader has caught sufficiently the spirit of Lairesse's scenes to enable him to observe the resemblance between his landscapes and Browning's. In ***Pauline,*** for example, in describing morning, noon, and night in that perfect land to which the lovers are to fly, Browning leans naturally toward the artist's conception of what a landscape ought to be:

> Night, and one single ridge of narrow path
> Between the sullen river and the woods
> Waving and muttering, for the moonless night
> Has shaped them into images of life,
> . . . No, we will pass to morning—
> Morning, the rocks and valleys and old woods.
> How the sun brightens in the mist, and here,
> Half in the air, like creatures of the place,
> Trusting the element, living on high boughs
> That swing in the wind—look at the silver spray
> Flung from the foam-sheet of the cataract
> Amid the broken rocks! Shall we stay here
> With the wild hawks? No, ere the hot noon come,
> Dive we down—safe! See this our new retreat
> Walled in with a sloped mound of matted shrubs,
> Dark, tangled, old and green, still sloping down
> To a small pool whose waters lie asleep
> Amid the trailing boughs turned water-plants:
> And tall trees overarch to keep us in,
> Breaking the sunbeams into emerald shafts,
> And in the dreamy water one small group
> Of two or three strange trees are got together
> Wondering at all around, as strange beasts herd
> Together far from their own land: all wildness,
> No turf nor moss, for boughs and plants pave all
> And tongues of bank go shelving in the lymph,
> Where the pale-throated snake reclines his head,
> And old gray stones lie making eddies there,
> The wild-mice cross them dry-shod. Deeper in!
> Shut thy soft eyes—now look—still deeper in!
> This is the very heart of the woods all round
> Mountain-like heaped above us; yet even here
> One pond of water gleams; far off the river
> Sweeps like a sea, barred out from land; but one—
> One thin clear sheet has overleaped and wound
> Into this silent depth, which gained, it lies
> Still, as but let by sufferance; the trees bend
> O'er it as wild men watch a sleeping girl,
> And through their roots long creeping plants outstretch
> Their twined hair, steeped and sparkling; farther on,
> Tall rushes and thick flag-knots have combined
> To narrow it; so, at length, a silver thread,
> It winds, all noiselessly through the deep wood
> Till through a cleft-way, through the moss and stone,
> It joins its parent-river with a shout . . .

This is the longest unbroken description of landscape in Browning, with the exception of the present "Parleying"; and it is decidedly typical. The same details recur to some extent in ***Paracelsus,*** in ***Sordello,*** in **"By the Fireside,"** in **"Love Among the Ruins,"** and many other poems. They combine with the description of the actual country of the Saleve in *La Saisiaz*; and when Browning comes to parley with Gerard de Lairesse, they occur in full purity and directness once more. These countries of Browning's mind are not mere Lairesse; their scenery is richer and more luxuriant. But Lairesse was nevertheless the starting-point for the poet's imagination, and that Browning recognized this fact is clear from the space given to landscape in the "Parleying." Moreover, the descriptions in the poem, avowedly modelled upon those of Lairesse, reveal how closely Browning has followed the blind painter's conception of the beautiful in landscape, throughout his life.

The same thing, it may be said in passing, is true concerning what Browning conceived to be ugly and repulsive in landscape. Lairesse's discussion of things that were unpainter-like had made a profound impression upon him:

> . . . All these, I say, may claim the title of painter-like: but a piece with deformed trees, widely branched and leaved, and disorderly spreading from east towards west, crooked bodied, old and rent, full of knots and hollowness; also rugged grounds without roads or ways, sharp hills, and monstrous mountains filling the off-scape, rough or ruined buildings with their parts lying up and down in confusion; likewise muddy brooks, a gloomy sky, abounding with heavy clouds; the field furnished with lean cattle and vagabonds of gypsies: such a piece, I say, is not to be called a fine landscape. Can any one, without reason, assert him to be a painter-like object, who appears as a lame and dirty beggar, cloathed in rags, splay-footed, bound about the head with a nasty clout, having a skin as yellow as a backed pudding, killing vermin; or in fine, any such paltry figure?

Whenever Browning had occasion to describe a desolate and wild country, as in **"Childe Roland,"** such scenes as this sketched by Lairesse in his *Art of Painting* supplied the details. (pp. 223-26)

In spite of the fact that Browning revolted against much that Lairesse had taught him, he still has, in the "Parleying," words of high praise for the painter:

> Beyond
> The ugly actual, lo, on every side
> Imagination's limitless domain
> Displayed a wealth of wondrous sounds and sights
> Ripe to be realized by poet's brain
> Acting on painter's brush! . . .

The fact that his praise of the painter's procedure says much that might be construed as a description of his own poetic art, leads to the conclusion that Browning was indebted to the artist for other things than his conceptions of landscape:

> Faustus' robe,
> And Fortunatus' cap were gifts of price:
> But—oh, your piece of sober sound advice
> That artists should descry abundant worth
> In trivial commonplace . . .

Town and country are to be transformed by the imagination of the artist, a recommendation in which Browning finds much virtue.

But there is nevertheless a decided difference between Lairesse's treatment of the trivial commonplace, and Browning's. Lairesse uses it only as a starting-point, until by his method "Holland becomes Dreamland." He puts his visions in place of reality. Browning takes the trivial commonplace and turns on it the light of his imaginative insight, in an attempt to find the deeper reality. So while his appreciation of Lairesse's pow-

ers of imagination is great, he must differ with him on the question of what is the proper use of those powers. To Browning, fancy can never approach in value to realism. It is one of the axioms of his artistic creed. That of course is the reason for his love of "Art's spring-birth so dim and dewy." He saw the Greek art as a form that had taught its lesson concerning the dignity and beauty of the human body to the world, yet which now had nothing more to offer. The early Christian painters, setting aside the Greek forms which had stagnated, perceived the value of realism. They introduced a subtler kind of painting—a realistic depiction of man that revealed the soul within the body. So Browning describes their advance over the Greeks:

> On which I conclude, that the early painters,
>   To cries of "Greek Art and what more wish you?"—
> Replied, "To become now self-acquainters,
>   And paint man, man, whatever the issue!
> Make new hopes shine through the flesh they fray,
>   New fears aggrandize the rags and tatters:
> To bring the invisible full into play!
>   Let the visible go to the dogs—what matters?"

That is, they want to see beyond the obvious to the essential truth; it is the invisible which is important.

To Browning, Fra Lippo Lippi is the exponent of this realism which descries abundant worth in trivial commonplace because it sees beyond the externals. When Lippi painted his realistic and familiar figures on the wall, it will be remembered, the monks "closed in a circle and praised loud," until they were reminded that realism was not the function of art. . . . So they rubbed out Lippi's pictures and told him it was art's decline. Yet Lippi goes on enunciating his belief concerning the true function of art:

> God's works—paint any one, and count it crime
> To let a truth slip. Don't object, "His works
> Are here already; nature is complete:
> Suppose you reproduce her—(which you can't)
> There's no advantage! You must beat her, then."
> For, don't you mark? we're made so that we love
> First when we see them painted, things we have passed
> Perhaps a hundred times nor cared to see,
> And so they are better, painted—better to us,
> Which is the same thing. Art was given for that;
> God uses us to help each other so,
> Lending our minds out. Have you noticed, now,
> Your cullion's hanging face? A bit of chalk,
> And trust me but you should, though! How much more
> If I drew higher things with the same truth!

Thus Lippi is to Browning the first of the realists in art. Man as he is, is the subject; paint him as he is, and the soul will shine through the flesh. This was a discovery indeed, and Browning continually celebrates the great advance made by the realists in art. They made the contribution of artistic insight.

But Browning had gone further. Not only did he celebrate this progress in artistic insight in the field of art; he also applied the principle to his own poetry. He showed a growing tendency to deal with modern subjects in a realistic fashion. Contemporary figures, such as Bishop Blougram, Mr. Sludge, Hohenstiel-Schwangau, and the characters in **Red Cotton Night-Cap Country** and **The Inn Album,** become increasingly frequent in Browning's poems as the years go on.

So, looking back on Lairesse and his theories, Browning sees how far he has advanced over the old painter. He himself has taken the same step in poetry that constituted Fra Lippo Lippi's advance over the Greeks and their followers. So his "Parleying'' is largely occupied with a comparison of the two attitudes. He defines the difference between his method and that of Lairesse precisely as Fra Lippo Lippi had defined his advance in realism, thirty-two years earlier:

> If we no longer see as you of old,
> 'T is we see deeper. Progress for the bold!
> You saw the body, 't is the soul we see,

he says to Lairesse. Naturally Browning feels that this difference indicates a gain. But another question arises. Has he—have the realists—suffered a corresponding loss? Are the powers of fancy and of imaginative insight mutually exclusive? Relatively, Browning prefers the latter gift; but according to his doctrine of progress man ought not to lose, in the course of his development, any good thing.

> Not one of man's acquists
> Ought he resignedly to lose, methinks . . .

Thus the question becomes a vital one:

> How were it could I mingle false with true,
> Boast, with the sights I see, your vision too?
> Advantage would it prove or detriment
> If I saw double? Could I gaze intent
> On Dryope plucking the blossoms red,
> As you, whereat her lote-tree writhed and bled,
> Yet lose no gain, no hard fast wide-awake
> Having and holding nature for the sake
> Of nature only—nymph and lote-tree thus
> Gained by the loss of fruit not fabulous,
> Apple of English homesteads . . .

In order to test the general question, Browning next puts a specific one. He recalls with delight a walk which Lairesse had described in his book, an imaginary walk in which he pointed out to his pupils what was painter-like and what un-painter-like, in the open air. Can he, Browning, take such a walk, using the ''freakish brain'' to supplement nature? He is sure he can:

> . . . we poets go not back at all:
> What you did we could do—from great to small
> Sinking assuredly . . .

So he challenges Lairesse to a contest, in which he is to match Lairesse's famous walk with one of his own. The issue is not only the superiority of the newer imaginative insight over the old fancy. Browning claims for the moderns the gift of keener insight; it remains to prove that they are still gifted with the power of fancy:

> Try now! Bear witness while you walk with me,
> I see as you: if we loose arms, stop pace,
> 'T is that you stand still, I conclude the race
> Without your company.

Then follows a long descriptive passage, comprising a series of scenes which are avowedly modelled on Lairesse. Browning describes several scenes, going through the day and choosing for each time of day an action and setting which Lairesse would consider appropriate.

But even in his attempt at reproducing such a walk as Lairesse's, Browning achieves a different result. The landscapes and the actions described are to be sure word-pictures that Lairesse might well have envied. But there is in them a strong suggestion of Browning. To mention the minor difference first, Browning unconsciously draws for his material upon the ancient Greek sources rather than upon Ovid. But much more important is the fact that the treatment of the material is typical of Browning. Instead of crowding his canvas with figures as

Lairesse does, Browning has, in every case save one, just one or two figures; and in that one case there are two outstanding figures, each backed by his army. Still more important, Browning manages to infuse into his descriptions something of his own psychological method. The best example of this is the description of noon, in which he tells a story of a satyr and a nymph such as Lairesse might have told, but into which he weaves a subtlety of interpretation such as Lairesse never dreamed of. His habit of imaginative insight made him discontented with mere picture, and led him to enter dramatically into the passions of his characters.

The result of the contest between Browning and Lairesse is of course a foregone conclusion. The decision is left to the reader, but there can be but one judgment. Browning proves completely that he can outdo Lairesse in Lairesse's own chosen field. The point is that Browning believes that, relatively speaking, that sort of thing is not worth doing. He loved men and women, as he said, better than he loved nature; and in dealing with men and women he could not be content with mere narrative and pictorial representation. He had put that sort of thing aside with his boyhood. Consequently he feels that people who are still content to do that sort of thing are in the earlier stage of development out of which he has grown. (pp. 226-32)

Almost alone of the poets of the latter half of the nineteenth century, Browning chose subjects for his poetry from the life that he saw about him. The Pre-Raphaelites avowedly sought the past for their inspiration. The popular fame of Tennyson rested upon the *Idylls* and other poems that went to the past for their origins. Matthew Arnold was writing *Empedocles* and *Merope*. By comparison with these men Browning's debt to the Middle Ages, and even to Greece, seems small indeed. And as he grew older, he turned more and more to modern subjects. So, filled with his conviction of the value of the realistic treatment of modern subjects, Browning finds in Lairesse, with his fanciful treatment of ancient fables, an apt analogy to modern conditions. He addresses the artist:

> Fancy's rainbow-birth
> Conceived mid clouds in Greece, could glance along
> Your passage o'er Dutch veritable earth,
> As with ourselves, who see, familiar throng
> About our pacings men and women worth
> Nowise a glance—so poets apprehend—
> Since naught avails portraying them in verse:
> While painters turn upon the heel, intend
> To spare their work the critic's ready curse
> Due to the daily and undignified.

Although Browning seems here to include himself among the poets whom he censures, his next lines indicate definitely what his position is:

> I who myself contentedly abide
> Awake, nor want the wings of dream,—who tramp
> Earth's common surface, rough, smooth, dry or damp,
> —I understand alternatives, no less
> —Conceive your soul's leap, Gerard de Lairesse!

He understands both attitudes; but for himself, he does no want the wings of dream.

His criticism, in its coupling of poets and painters, seems to be directed at the Pre-Raphaelite Brotherhood and its followers. In reading his lines one thinks almost immediately of the Rossettis, Morris, Burne-Jones, Millais, Madox Brown, Holman-Hunt, and Swinburne. (pp. 232-34)

There occurs, some two hundred and fifty lines later, a more specific criticism of contemporary practice and a more definite objection on Browning's part. Here too Lairesse suggests the grounds of criticism, for the passage deals with the choice of subjects from *classical* lore:

> Wherefore glozed
> The poets—"Dream afresh old godlike shapes,
> Recapture ancient fable that escapes,
> Push back reality, repeople earth
> With vanished falseness, recognize no worth
> In fact new-born unless 't is rendered back
> Pallid by fancy, as the western rack
> Of fading cloud bequeaths the lake some gleam
> Of its gone glory!"
>
> Let things be—not seem,
> I counsel rather,—do, and nowise dream!
> Earth's young significance is all to learn:
> The dead Greek lore lies buried in the urn
> Where who seeks fire finds ashes. Ghost,
> forsooth!
> What was the best Greece babbled of as truth?

Here the reference is plainly pointed toward poets who were dealing with Greek themes, for there are three mentions of Hellenism within as many lines. (pp. 234-35)

[It] is certain that [Browning] could not have made such a criticism without having in mind the leading Hellenist of the age, Matthew Arnold. Partly because the two men were friends, and partly because Browning himself had shared Arnold's interest in Greek themes, the reference in the lines quoted above lacks the animus that would serve to identify Arnold without question, by its personalities. Nevertheless, Arnold's admitted position as the leading Hellenist of the time makes the criticism point very clearly to him. (p. 235)

[The] whole passage in which Browning deals with the Hellenists is almost a direct answer to Arnold's dictum on the very same subject, in his famous "Preface to Poems," 1853. . . . Throughout the "Preface" Arnold had upheld the desirability of dreaming afresh "old godlike shapes." A few passages will show how clearly the issue was joined between him and the Browning of 1887:

> "The Poet," it is said, and by an intelligent critic, "the Poet who would really fix the public attention must leave the exhausted past, and draw his subjects from matters of present import, and *therefore* both of interest and novelty."
>
> Now this view I believe to be completely false. It is worth examining, inasmuch as it is a fair sample of a class of critical dicta everywhere current at the present day, having a philosophical form and air, but no real basis in fact; and which are calculated to vitiate the judgment of readers of poetry, while they exert, so far as they are adopted, a misleading influence on the practice of those who write it.
>
> • • • • •
>
> A great human action of a thousand years ago is more interesting to it [the elementary part of our nature, our passions] than a smaller human action of to-day, even though upon the representation of this last the most consummate skill may have been expended, and though it has the advantage of appealing by its modern language, familiar manners, and contemporary allusions, to all our transient feelings and interests. . . .

[Thus] Arnold is on the opposite side from Browning on this question of the proper subject for poetry. (pp. 236-37)

The question arises, Why should Browning, once so vitally interested in Hellenism that he pictured himself spending his old age reading the ancient Greeks, have turned finally against these things that he had loved? The answer to this question is to be found in Browning's general philosophy. It is another case of Browning's shutting his eyes to the evidence of his intellect and the dictates of his own tastes. As he grew older one idea grew more and more fixed in his mind, and the necessity for insisting upon it more and more vital. It was the idea of progress in all human things. Whatever was inconsistent with that axiom Browning was ready to cast ruthlessly away. He shut his eyes on the achievements of Greece in order to point clearly the progress of man. When Matthew Arnold and other Hellenists proclaimed the Greek civilization the greatest mankind had yet evolved, Browning's whole nature revolted. If their statement was true, where was progress? He had preferred the early Christian painters, in all their crudity, to the perfect work of the Greeks. This preference, incidentally, upheld his theory of progress. He himself had developed a realistic method in poetry, and that again seemed to him a sign of advance. But he carried the idea to its ultimate conclusions: the meanest modern subject was superior to the noblest of Greek themes. In this way the **"Parleying With Gerard de Lairesse"** joins the current of Browning's general philosophy. He proves to his own satisfaction that the moderns have developed a deeper insight into the soul of man; and this, to Browning, was the highest virtue of poetry. That his beloved Greeks should go by the board was unfortunate but necessary. He was once more rigidly applying his favorite idea that

> The first of the new, in our race's story,
> Beats the last of the old. . . .
>
> (p. 238)

> *William Clyde DeVane, Jr., in his* Browning's Parleyings: The Autobiography of a Mind, *Yale University Press, 1927, 306 p.*

STOCKTON AXSON (lecture date 1929)

[*Axson delivered a series of lectures on Browning in March 1929 entitled "Browning: His Times, His Art, His Philosophy." The following excerpt from that series is focused on Browning's relation to the Victorian era. After discussing the poet's differences from his contemporaries, Axson explores Browning's philosophy, praising it as a brave assault on the spiritual problems of the Victorian age.*]

It would be inaccurate to say that there is no "Victorianism" in Browning—there is a great deal—but compared with Tennyson, Dickens, Ruskin, even Carlyle, Thackeray and George Eliot, the Victorianism in Browning is oblique, evasive, indirect, almost ineluctable; not obvious, patent, easily demonstrable as it is in Tennyson. When we are seeking the representative poet of the Victorian Age we turn to Tennyson rather than to Browning. Though Tennyson was somewhat of a recluse, and though Browning was a "man of the world", a "mixer", a most sociable person, mingling, after his wife's death and his temporary withdrawal from Italy, with all sorts and conditions of men and women in England, especially in London, it was Tennyson rather than Browning who fused in poetry most of the obvious things about which English men and women were talking: their politics, their social problems, their religious faith and misgivings, their every-day conceptions of what English people are, should be, or fail to be, their English patriotism and insularity. (pp. 145-46)

In short, Tennyson in the reign of Victoria, like Pope in the age of Anne and the Early Georges, could say better than anybody else the things that many were thinking. Browning, on the other hand, was perplexing most English people of his age, as the Apostle Paul (to whom Browning bore many resemblances) puzzled the fisherman apostle Peter with, as Peter writes, "some things hard to be understood." Tennyson spoke the language of his own time, Browning, the language of a later time. Tennyson was a contemporary; Browning a progenitor. In short, Browning, like many another great man, was a generation or two ahead of his era. (pp. 146-47)

Browning himself had checked, practically halted, his own popularity by overloading much of his poetry with learning too erudite or philosophy too original and involved for the tastes of the Early Victorians. His second important poem, *Paracelsus,* published in 1835, when he was twenty-three years old, had attracted considerable attention from the discerning in England. It came in a "flat" period of English poetry—an eddy, a calm. The great early nineteenth century poetic epoch (the Wordsworth-Byron era) was ended—these earlier poets were either dead (like Coleridge, Scott, Byron, Shelley and Keats), or too old to write with fresh inspiration (Wordsworth and Southey). Tennyson had begun, and the discerning saw that in him a delicately accomplished artist had arrived—but whether the artist would ever discover anything important to say remained to be seen. In *Paracelsus* there was obviously a poet with a great deal to say, and he was saying it in an original and impressive manner. (p. 151)

Then, as if deliberately, Browning set to work to nip his budding fame: by writing a series of plays that did not prove "playable," and by perpetrating such a baffling piece of obscurity as the long poem *Sordello*—a poem which with all its fascinations (and they are many) is still difficult reading. . . . If *Sordello* is difficult now for us who are familiar with Browning's habits of mind and art, his vast learning, introversions of speech, allusions, evasiveness, long parentheses, and all his other idiosyncrasies of matter and manner, including his strange combination of alternating prolixity and condensation, it is not remarkable that the Early Victorians, unaccustomed to his manner and methods, found the poem hopelessly unintelligible. Even the intellectually elect were baffled by it. It was to be a long time before the author of *Sordello* could win popular favor from the Victorians, but he went doggedly his own way, saying that he had never proposed to write poetry as a substitute for a lazy man's after-dinner cigar or game of dominoes.

This apparent discrepancy between Browning and his age (the discrepancy is only apparent) was due to many things, among them: Browning's attitude toward the public, his attitude toward himself, his attitude toward his art, and his attitude toward what we now call "questions of the day"—the political, economic and social questions which absorbed so much of the thought of thinking people in the first decades of Queen Victoria's reign—the pregnant age of political, economic, industrial and social reform—questions which gave much of the character and color to the work of Tennyson, Ruskin, Dickens, Charles Reade, Charles Kingsley, Matthew Arnold and Mrs. Browning herself—but not Browning.

His attitude toward the public and himself may be dealt with in one category. Browning was so original in his thought and in his manner of expressing his thought that he needed an interpreter, and he declined to be his own interpreter. . . . [He] declined to meet the public on the public's terms; declined to persuade them to understand and like his poetry; declined to

lead them gradually to his own mountain tops of thought, feeling and expression; they must climb for themselves without assistance from him. There was his poetry—people could like it or leave it—Browning would not be exalted by their favor or vexed by their neglect. In one respect—in one only—Browning was like his Andrea del Sarto: Andrea, in the poem, tells his wife:

> I, painting from myself and to myself,
> Know what I do, am unmoved by men's blame
> Or their praise either.

So it was with Browning: writing from himself and to himself he pursued his way serenely. Not even his poet-wife . . . could intrude upon his creative moods. (pp. 152-54)

Sometimes when Browning was requested to say what he meant in a designated passage, he would smilingly refer the questioner to the Browning Society. He had a similar attitude of aloofness toward his poetry—in marked contrast with Tennyson's coddling of *his* poetry. When the Browning Society discovered that Browning did not possess printed copies of at least some of his own poems, the Society presented to him a complete set of the [works of Robert Browning] accompanied by a letter recommending them to his attention, as books which contained some good reading matter. Once a lady read to him some lines of poetry, and Browning "slapped his thigh [a characteristic gesture] and said, 'By Jove, that's fine'". He was enlightened and edified when the lady informed him that the author of the lines was one Robert Browning.

The most eccentric feature of all this is that Browning himself was not at all eccentric—on the contrary a normal sort of person—so normal that . . . many who met him for the first time found it difficult to believe that he was a poet: in dress and manner and conversation he seemed more like a banker or a prosperous merchant. Nevertheless, the fact remains that, after the select success of the early poem *Paracelsus*, Browning for more than thirty years lost favor instead of augmenting it by writing as he pleased instead of studying the public demand and striving to supply it. I do not know that any moral is to be drawn from this. Another and even greater poet, William Shakespeare, studied carefully the popular taste, and met it, and succeeded. But Shakespeare had to make a living by writing, while Robert Browning, a man of independent, moderately comfortable means, could afford to do what he pleased as he pleased to do it.

Not different from this was Browning's attitude toward his art. He wrote nine plays, but none of them has been a really popular success on the stage—notwithstanding extravagant claims to the contrary by some Browning enthusiasts who seem to mistake artistic success for stage success—the latter being a quite tangible thing, ascertainable by statistics of "runs" and box office receipts.

This raises the question . . . why the most dramatic English poet since the age of the Elizabethans did not fit his genius better to a practical stage. One simple answer has already been given, his refusal to study and meet popular demand. Another answer is that he found his true vein, his best medium, in monologue rather than in dialogue. In the dramatic monologue he has few predecessors, shoals of successors, no equals. One of his volumes is called *Dramatic Lyrics*—and that name is emblematic of the character of much of Browning's work— lyric poetry externalized, impersonalized, dramatized. Oscar Wilde said in his *De Profundis,* "I took the drama, the most objective form known to art, and made of it as personal a mode of expression as the lyric or sonnet.'' Browning might have reversed that statement: I took the lyric, the most subjective form known to art, and made of it as impersonal a mode of expression as the drama. (pp. 154-56)

It is possible, as has been remarked by another, that Browning unconsciously put more of his own personal traits (his reckless courage and his chivalry) into Caponsacchi, the hero-priest of *The Ring and the Book,* than into any other of his characters. But his ideal of poetic creation was the impersonalism of Shakespeare, the dramatic projection of natures and personalities other than his own. Almost truculently, he defied the public to find him, Robert Browning, in his poems. We find this defiance categorically in the poem "House." Only rarely does he deliberately express himself, his personality, in his poems: as in the Epilogue to *Asolando; Prospice*; the exquisite concluding lines of the first book of *The Ring and the Book,* the address to his dead wife, beginning

> O lyric Love, half angel and half bird
> And all a wonder and a wild desire;

and in the concluding poem of the volume *Men and Women,* the poem addressed to his living wife, "One Word More," surely one of the devoutest love poems in the language. . . . Add to these things, his first published poem, *Pauline,* and a few of his later poems (notably *La Saisiaz*) and we practically exhaust the personal poems of Browning. The rest, the great mass of them, express frequently passionate convictions and often subtle arguments, but not the personality of Robert Browning. He is a curious combination of intense attachment to ideas and austere detachment from self-revelation. Such, briefly summarized, is his attitude toward his art, an attitude which accentuates his aloofness from his time. Certainly his art is not "Victorian," is distinctly "modern"—twentieth century. One of our "new" American poets (one of the modernists), once said to me, "Browning was the first of us—the first to dramatize a mood."

Finally, there is Browning's attitude toward questions of his day—the problems of the era of reform, the new democracy. He, the most insistent questioner in nineteenth century English poetry, applied few questions to the engrossing matters of political and social reform. He was primarily interested in other things.

Typical Victorian literature was socialized literature, from Carlyle through Kipling. But this dominant note is virtually absent from Browning's poetry. His is an almost unique case of an author, vividly interested in everything about him and yet silent about contemporary actualities. When the creative mood overtook him, he was less responsive to people in their social and political relationships than to people as individuals. . . . His biographer, Mrs. Orr, says: "His politics were, so far as they went, the practical aspect of his religion. Their cardinal doctrine was the liberty of individual growth" [see Additional Bibliography]. That statement, which has the truth of finality, is strikingly illustrated by a comparison of Browning's sonnet "Why I am a Liberal" (published 1885) with several untitled poems by Tennyson (published 1842) on the subject of British liberalism founded in constitutional development. There is one of these stanzas by Tennyson which a pre-eminent student of constitutional law who rose to be President of the United States never wearied of quoting in support of his position as a conservative progressive—believing that it expressed the essence of political wisdom under orderly (not radical) change:

> A land of settled government,
>   A land of just and old renown,
>   Where Freedom slowly broadens down
> From precedent to precedent.

But what devotee of politics, theoretical or practical, would find any pointed political wisdom in Browning's answer to a questionnaire circulated among prominent men of England in 1885, asking why they were Liberals? The answer is not in terms of politics but in terms of God and the Soul of man—the subjects which most occupied his thinking. In a prefatory note to a reprint of *Sordello* in 1863 he had said that "the stress" was "on the incidents in the development of a soul; little else is worth study."

Victorian literature, in general, by no means neglected "soul." But most of it, that was typical, stressed also the political and social idea: Dickens the Reformer; Carlyle the inquirer into the workings of democracy; Ruskin, with the long shelf of volumes in which he faced about from art to consider questions in economics and social arrangement; Tennyson the inspired interpreter of English liberalism; George Eliot, author of *Felix Holt the Radical*; Charles Kingsley; Charles Reade; Frederick Denison Maurice; and many others, including Mrs. Browning herself.

The contemporary popularity of the poetry of Elizabeth Barrett Browning and the unpopularity of her husband's poetry throw light on Victorianism and the Brownings. Mrs. Browning was intensely interested in "questions of the day." . . . Her *Aurora Leigh, Casa Guidi Windows, Poems Before Congress* and "The Cry of the Children" are altogether "contemporary" with political and social reform. Consider, for example, "The Cry of the Children" (published 1841). It is the cry of Dickens for reform, of Ruskin against machinery, of Carlyle against the subjugation of the poor, of Dickens' and Tennyson's sentiment—true Victorian sentiment, which in this hard-boiled twentieth century we have come to call sentimentality. It is typically "Victorian" in both its political-social subject and in its treatment of the subject.

None of her husband's poetry is either. In 1841 (before he was married) he had written *Pippa Passes,* a poem about a little mill girl. But there is nothing in this charming dramatic poem about Pippa's economic subjection. It is about her joy as she wanders singing through the village of Asolo on her one holiday in all the year, and the way her singing reaches the hearts, the "souls" of a number of different people, each in a crisis, and turns the destiny of each. It was a new poetic form—not quite dramatic, not quite lyric, a blend of the two—not quite like anything that had been written before, either in matter or manner. It was not "obvious" to people in 1841. But "The Cry of the Children" by Mrs. Browning was entirely obvious to all who were thinking about industrial reforms. It said precisely what many were thinking. Mrs. Browning did not write to "hit the popular taste" any more than did Carlyle. But she was a product of the era which Carlyle, and after him Ruskin, almost created. Robert Browning, "writing from himself and to himself" was not quite of that era. So in 1844-1860 Mrs. Browning was a famous poet, mentioned for the laureateship after the death of Wordsworth in 1850, while Robert Browning was her husband—who also wrote verses. (pp. 156-60)

In talking about Browning and the Victorian Age I have been chiefly occupied with statements of what is *non*-Victorian in the poetry of Browning. Yet, as Percy Hutchison says: "Robert Browning, while in small degree reflecting the purely social aspect of his time and thereby differing essentially from Tennyson, 'dates' even more indelibly than does Tennyson. For the very fount of Browning's compositions was the intellectual rebellion, the aroused intellectual curiosity of his day." The new science and a new philosophy springing out of the new science led some Victorians to doubt and despair, but led Browning to a fresh fervent reaffirmation of God, the Immortality of the Soul, the Freedom of the Will, and an optimism that is gorgeous. Much that was bravest and best in the mental life of the Victorians got its boldest and most dynamic expression in Browning's poetry. Of all Victorians he was the bonniest fighter and certainly the greatest poet: facing the spiritual problems of the Victorian era, and either arguing them out with tenacious logic, or fighting out the issue with the faith and courage of Paul who met the wild beasts at Ephesus. (pp. 162-63)

· · · · ·

It is an inexcusably superficial view which finds an easy-going optimism in Browning's poetry. Lines separated from the body of his poetry may seem chirping and a bit too chirper, such as the familiar lines of Pippa

> God's in his heaven—
> All's right with the world.

Taken *in esse,* it must be remembered that the lines are dramatic, not personal, part of a gladsome song that a little simple-hearted factory girl sings in her joyous rambles on her one holiday of all the year. Taken *in posse,* as an expression of Browning's own faith, they are the conclusion, not the postulate, of a prolonged philosophical process. And whether evil is a negation, an absence of good, as cold is an absence of heat, rest an absence of motion, silence an absence of sound (as Browning's Abt Vogler sees it), it is none the less something to be overcome, and that by valiant fighting. Indolence may be only absence of activity but the indolent man has to make as strong an effort to overcome it as if it were a positive entity. (pp. 186-87)

Browning, speaking through the Pope in *The Ring and the Book* envisages evil as spiritual death, and continual struggle the means whereby evil may be eliminated. In practical living what difference does it make whether the concept of evil is, in the abstract, negative or positive? The conflict is real whether the conflict is with a personal devil or a phantasmagoria such as Shakespeare faced when he wrote *King Lear.*

To assume that Browning reasoned and battled in ignorance or wilful dismissal of the pinch of evil is to disregard Browning's reiterated language, the language not only of his poetry but also of his private correspondence. In a letter dated May 11, 1876, Browning wrote: "I see ever more reason to hold by . . . hope, and that by no means in ignorance of what has been advanced to the contrary." The road to sound optimism is no bower of roses, honeysuckle and sweet jasmine; it is a granite, steep, cobble-strewn trail beset with many difficulties and precipices and crevasses, and a misstep may pitch the pilgrim into perdition.

Browning loved the road precisely because it was not smooth, precisely because he relished a good fight and the glow of fighting. "Am I no a bonny fighter?" exclaims Stevenson's Alan Breck, in the flush of contest. Browning said similar things many times in more recondite language than Alan's.

> It is by no breath,
> Turn of eye, wave of hand, that salvation joins issue with
>   death,

exclaims David in Browning's poem **"Saul,"** that is to say by no easy gesture, by no *fiat lux.* Steadily as Milton himself does this nineteenth century optimist Browning welcome battle and scorn easeful ways. (pp. 187-88)

Out of his own heart, mind and experience, he wrote the Epilogue to *Asolando,* speaking for the last time, not as dramatic poet, but as Robert Browning himself; here is the third stanza:

> One who never turned his back, but marched breast forward,
> Never doubted clouds would break,
> Never dreamed, though right were worsted, wrong would
>   triumph,
> Held we fell to rise, are baffled to fight better,
> Sleep to wake. . . .

So much for Browning's optimistic attitude, the optimism of a fighter by temperament; the only sort of optimism that is worth while, the optimism which clearly recognizes that this is a tough old world, in which, among all busy-ness, none is busier than the devil, whether the devil be a person, a principle or a negation. (pp. 189-90)

With regard to the antinomy of God and Nature which perplexed Tennyson, Browning was abrupt, though not always brief. He swept away (in so far as he himself was concerned) the whole idea of beneficent nature, and, apparently without a struggle, abandoned search in Nature for evidence of a loving God. In Nature he saw overwhelming evidence of a God of Power and Knowledge, but no evidence of a God of Love. The evidence of God's love is in man, not in nature—man ready to sacrifice himself for the object of his love. The reasoning is subtle, retraversed in many poems, well condensed in "Saul." Reduced to a sentence, it comes simply to this, that postulating God . . . as infinite in power and wisdom and as creator of man, it is illogical to assume that he could have put into man a faculty which he himself does not possess, the faculty of enduring, and often sacrificial love. In other words, Browning reasons back from man to God: the created could not possess a faculty which the Creator had not himself to give his creature.

Browning faces the antinomy of knowledge and faith, with an assertion, like Tennyson's, of the incapacity of knowledge to solve the problem which many people account the most vital of all, man's relationship to God and the individual spirit's survival of death. He was probably more intimately acquainted than was any other English poet of his day with Victorian science. Having the insatiable curiosity of the men of the Renaissance (about whom he knew so much) he was vividly curious about the new science—read widely, even dabbled a little in experimentation. But he was entirely skeptical about the qualifications of science to solve problems of the human spirit. In the poem *La Saisiaz* he questions even the color of grass. We say "green," but comes one who says "red." "Color-blind" we say, but how do we know that? Suppose his is the normal vision, ours the abnormal. Suppose only he and one other inhabited the world—how could the color of grass be determined? Is truth ascertainable by a majority vote? The opinion of today's minority may be the majority opinion tomorrow. It has been so in history. Truth, the truth which saves, comes not through the intellect, but through love, says this most intellectual of the poets. (pp. 190-91)

Progression was Browning's measure of vitality. Not what man is but what man is becoming enlisted his interest. The developmental idea of the new science stirred his dynamic imagination, and led him to philosophical conclusions which lie at the heart of his thinking. These conclusions were often paradoxical: for instance, his comfort in imperfection. Imperfection is a condition of vital development: where there is growth, there is something to be attained; where there is something to be attained there is obviously something yet unobtained; where there is something unobtained there is incompleteness; where there is incompleteness, there is imperfection; or, to state the paradox in a syllogism:

> the only perfect thing is a thing completed;
> but the only completed thing is a dead thing;
> therefore, the only perfect thing is something dead.

That is argued out in the poem, **"Dis Aliter Visum."**

His paradox of failure is close akin: failure also is a negation, a discrepancy between infinite purpose and finite powers. Because of man's alliance with the infinite he is constantly striving for something beyond his grasp:

> Only I discern
> Infinite passion, and the pain
> Of finite hearts that yearn,

he says in **"Two in the Campagna."** In the *consciousness* of failure, the paradoxical Browning saw the measure of success. Real success is to strive nobly; real failure is not to strive; it is only "apparent failure" when the thing done is less than the thing envisioned; dissatisfaction with the result is only the evidence of the loftiness of the purpose. (pp. 191-92)

Tennyson and Browning accepted the new ideas of science because as thinking men they did not see how they could reject them. But that which Tennyson accepted wistfully, Browning accepted joyously. To his way of thinking the new ideas strengthened rather than weakened the Christian faith. In Paul's epistles Browning had read of the Christian life as a battle, in metaphors which Paul took largely from active struggles: war and fighting wild beasts and athletic contests. And now, in the new science, Browning seemed to learn that this is the law of vitality: struggle, with crown and palm for him who has the courage and endurance to keep fighting. Browning glorified the strenuous life, the life of hopeful fighting. There are several Browning poems (among them **The Inn Album** and **"Apparent Failure"**) in which Browning glimpses hope that God in his mercy will forgive and redeem criminals led by their strenuous activity into wild sins. But repeatedly, in one dramatic form or another, he abandons hope for the slothful, listless, idle, shallow, timid. (p. 193)

[The] poem *La Saisiaz* is one of the most significant in the Browning corpus . . . because it is the last long confessional poem in which he frankly speaks, not dramatically, but as Robert Browning, and utters his own conclusions about the mystery of life and death. . . . Carefully he goes over his old arguments, so familiar to readers of Browning. But bit by bit he abandons arguments and falls back on two intuitions which to him were certainties, God and his own soul. Good and evil, life and death, dissolution and immortality—he reasons about them again, as he had so often reasoned about them. And then he explicitly disavows purpose to solve the problem of evil and God's superintendence in philosophical terms, saying

> I shall "vindicate no ways of God's to man," . . . .
> Traversed heart must tell its story uncommented on.

And again:

> Question, answer, presuppose
> Two points: that the thing itself which questions, answers—is,
> it knows

> . . . . .

> God then, call that—soul and both—the only facts for me.

Do we get the point? Robert Browning, now sixty-eight years old, confronted by the crashing fact of death, definitely re-

hearsed his old arguments and retreated to intuitive faith for the only answer for him, Robert Browning. Alexander Pope, the shallow logician, had undertaken to "vindicate the ways of God to man." John Milton, the learned theologian, had undertaken in a philosophical poem, *Paradise Lost,* to "justify the ways of God to men." But Robert Browning, Pope's superior as a logician, Milton's equal in theology and learning, will neither "vindicate" nor "justify" the mystery of Providence. He accepts, and in his acceptance, he is reassured. Browning concludes his long years of scrutiny, not in a theodicy, but in a reaffirmation of his personal faith in God and the indestructibility of the soul. Not what God means in this vast universe, but what God means to him, Robert Browning, and to all believing souls, is the sum and substance of it all.

A lame and impotent conclusion of the long years of inquiry by the most inquiring mind in nineteenth century English poetry? Perhaps so, if you think science and logic can prove anything about the reality of God and the human spirit. Not so, if you believe they can prove nothing whatever. (pp. 195-97)

People sometimes complain that . . . Browning wrote so much about things morbid and ugly. Browning loved the beautiful and often wrote of it. But a world garlanded in orange-blossoms is not all the world. And Browning, the all-curious, wanted to see all of it. He wanted to proclaim the beauty of life while facing its ugliness. It requires courage to do that. In the dim and hushed solemnity of the cathedral, under its vaulted arches, splashed with prismatic colors from its stained-glass windows, when the organ is pealing and the surpliced choir lifts on high the anthem, with the incense in our nostrils, before our adoring eyes the symbols of sacrificial cross and victorious crown, amid the bowed worshippers and the sonorous ritual—here it is not hard to believe in God. But can we leave the cathedral and go into the alley, see the cripple in his rags, the lazar in his sores, hear the harlot's curses, and the drunkard's ravings—can we do this and still believe in God? If we cannot, we don't believe in Him very much. Browning really did believe in God. Not an absentee God, remote, concealed somewhere behind his tent of blue sky, but an always present God. Not an inert God, but a vitalizing God. And he believed that in strenuous living of the life of the spirit, in sympathetic living with his fellow men, he was linking himself with God's own spirit.

Browning's spirit is more important than his reasoning. His arguments may not convince the reason, but his courage is infectious. The reasons he gives for his optimism are the least important things about his optimism. His arguments are only the corollary of his instinct, and instinct is personal. Not God in the universe, but God in the spirit of the individual is Browning's real theme. His spirit tingled with the spirit of God. And for us his spirit is a challenge, to turn failure into victory, doubt into faith, weakness into strength. It is a challenge to be brave, to keep on fighting, believing, hoping, recuperating. He was glad because he believed that he and you and I are engaged in a great adventure, the outcome of which depends chiefly upon our courage for the adventure. (pp. 198-99)

> *Stockton Axson, "Browning: His Times, His Art, His Philosophy," in* The Rice Institute Pamphlet, *Vol. XVII, No. 4, October, 1931, pp. 145-99.*

H. B. CHARLTON   (essay date 1939)

[*Charlton links Browning's failure as a dramatist to his individualistic philosophy, observing that it undermined a crucial aspect of the playwright's art: the ability to represent and appeal to communal values.*]

[Browning] looked out on life and saw it as an aggregation of separate human souls seeking their relation to God. He never saw, never felt the real existence of the something or other besides God and yet not ourselves which gives its vital force to a community. He was a nonconformist, in the complete sense that he had no notion of a church; he was a liberal, but the current liberal creed of nationalism only appealed to him when it exhibited itself in the fate of a few individual Italians. A theatre audience was just a fortuitous assembly of folks as individual as Robert Browning: but he expected them to have his own imaginative alertness, and forgot that a conventional, corporate language is indispensable to communication. Even worse, he used an art which by its nature must represent, or must excite expectation of the representation of, the corporate forces which condition the issues of that life which men live in concourse with each other; and he was constitutionally blind to such forces.

Sometimes Browning's blindness to these and similar inevitable institutions is so flagrant that it is ludicrous, ludicrous that is, if the scene before our eyes represents, as does a stage, the semblance of a world which has shaped itself by means of such institutions and conventions, a world in which civilisation progresses and safeguards itself by such organisations as it has found to be necessary. Take *Pippa Passes,* for instance. One of its scenes turns on the patriot Luigi's escape from the police. But another scene, the Sebald-Ottima episode, involves a murder: yet not once is there a suggestion that the police may be interested; and the culprits want the corpse out of the way because it is aesthetically an eyesore, not because there is a corporate institution, moral or legal, called the law. Indeed Ottima gaily announces that she will show Sebald over the silk-mills which are now his: evidently there is not even a system of organised inheritance, nothing but the individualist's state of nature where possession is ten points of the law and might is right—except of course that from the poet's point of view there is the primal dispensation, the individual soul and God, its maker.

It was unfortunate that for his first two formal plays Browning chose political themes, unfortunate even though he lived in the Carlylean age which looked on history in the main as the achievements of great individuals. Like Carlyle with Cromwell, in the Commonwealth puritans Browning found figures who towered majestically as moral individuals: almost inevitably, therefore, he found in the royalism of their opponents little beyond an aesthetic or a personal preference for a particular way of life. But these are points of view which distort the political struggle between royalist and parliamentarian. Principles as political motives disappear from a panorama which represents nothing but the personal animosities and preferences of people accidentally living in the same time and place. Ideals are invoked and familiar ideas are named, such, for instance, as this or that conception of sovereignty; but the cry is nothing but a catchword, and the response to it by its professed devotees is unpredictable and unintelligible. Parliaments are dissolved, wars declared, and trials ordered in the background, but they rumble behind the scene as the mere whims of the characters concerned, never projecting themselves as the powers which sway the patterns of corporate political life. The prevailing anarchy in larger motive naturally affects the consistency of personal characterisation: and Strafford's devotion to a worthless king, who is also almost a contemptible human individual, remains a mere vagary of individual incalculability.

King Victor and King Charles is also political in its story, but entirely unpolitical in its essential theme. Nominally the tale tells how King Victor, having got his country into a political mess, astutely determines to abdicate in favour of a politically feckless son who can bear the brunt of the political clean-up, and then give way again to his father. But the play proceeds just as if the issue was no more than a temporary transfer of a small private estate; and the interest is nothing but the effect of unexpected responsibility on a more or less insignificant individual. The vaster issue of kingship, and even the merely public consequences of dynastic adjustments clamour in our minds for an expression which is denied to them by Browning's stage. Such stultifying of expectation frustrates the effect of the dénouement. King Charles has grown in moral stature through addicting himself to political responsibility: but in the end, the very powers which have been alleged to be the means of his growth, he puts aside easily in response to a sentimental plea from his father. It may be theatrically effective, but it is dramatic suicide. Even so Charles' actions are not so completely out of an intelligible scheme of characterisation as is the *volte face* of Charles' wife, Polyxena. She it was who revealed to him the call of the larger life:

> Pause here upon this strip of time
> Allotted you out of eternity!
> Crowns are from God: you in his name hold yours.
> Your life's no least thing, were it fit your life
> Should be abjured along with rule; but now
> Keep both. Your duty is to live and rule. . . .

But in a trice her action unsays all she has so nobly uttered. She connives at Charles' surrender and presumably, when after it Charles tells her "I love you now indeed," she has gained the highest reward which is to be won in the dispensation of Browning's dramas. There are only four characters in the play; and only one of them moves with an impression of psychological truth, D'Ormea, faintly prefiguring Ogniben [in *A Soul's Tragedy*], and, like Ogniben, a man whose political machinations have taught him one of the forms of worldly wisdom which gives a semblance of reality to dramatic characters. But apart from D'Ormea, *King Victor and King Charles* must be reckoned as one of Browning's most signal failures.

In two other plays the ghost of a political subject haunts the theme, *The Return of the Druses* and *Luria.* But Browning is more skilful in covering his unconcern with it. Instead of merely neglecting it, he gives sufficient recognition to its existence to secure a tacit agreement, for the moment, that it shall merely provide the back cloth with its pattern. He proceeds then in both cases to switch the whole interest on to the personal fate of the hero, and to allow this to have no direct and controlling influence on the communities of which the heroes were apparently the shaping factors. In the one play, the Druses, and in the other Florence follow their destiny independently of the death of Djabal and of Luria. The island of Rhodes and the Florence of Luria are merely decorative historic scenarios for the two plays; they are not integral elements in the drama, which is the tragedy of Djabal, and the tragedy of Luria. (pp. 45-9)

In many ways *A Blot in the 'Scutcheon* seems by its plot and its theme to be the most suitable of Browning's dramas for the normal needs of a stage-play. There is much good "theatre" in it, incidents and scenes of the kind traditionally effective, no episodic complication or elaboration, no blurring of its main figures by merging them in accessory crowds, no mystification of them by suggestions of obscure conflicting motives. Yet the play failed, and must fail. The actions of the characters are in a dramatic sense incredible because they are unintelligible; they are unintelligible because they are arbitrary. Their arbitrariness is another outcome of the disadvantages for drama inherent in the Browning way of seeing life. To the individualist, freedom of will must tend to absoluteness, and a man's actions will appear almost completely as his own choice. Yet what for him are the noblest impulses may seem but whims to others, and his highest sanctions may appear as the distorted apprehensions of a moral anarch. Mildred's purity, Mertoun's humility, and Thorold's honour are notions of right which are clearly prompted by an impulse for goodness; but each of them, to justify itself as an authoritative sanction, presupposes conditions incompatible one with the other, to the utter confusion of any comprehensive system in which right remains right and wrong is indubitably wrong.

To give a semblance of order to this moral chaos, Browning resorts to honour as the code which will provide an unequivocal standard of moral compulsion for his audience, and therefore, a sense of natural obligation for his characters, the dramatic inevitable which Aristotle called necessity. The issue of the action must be what it is because honour compels it.

But the device is a failure. Honour has not the impressive finality of Nemesis in the ultimate arbitrament of human destiny. It is so ephemeral in its imperatives, so casual in its confusion of time and eternity. (pp. 49-50)

There have, of course, been dramatists who have built their tragic schemes on such themes as the conflict of Love and Honour. But their success has depended almost entirely on the extent to which the term ''honour'' could be replaced by the word ''virtue,'' taking virtue to mean that quality which best becomes a man in the eyes of the men amongst whom he lives. (p. 51)

If Browning had had the dramatic skill to represent life in *A Blot in the 'Scutcheon* as a moral system governed by honour as its mainspring, his characters might have exhibited such consistency amongst themselves as the fellow-creatures in a purely imaginary moral culture will perforce exhibit. But even so much collectivism in comprehension defeats him. He lacked the right sort of historic sense. This may seem an absurd judgment of a poet who, as in **"The Bishop Orders His Tomb,"** or in **"My Last Duchess,"** conveys more of the spirit of the Renaissance than did all the historians: but these are poems in which he divines individual responses to particular circumstances. It is the converse, the form of an epoch and its pressure on men at large which fails to catch his imagination. His plays range in the period of their action from the fourteenth to the nineteenth century. But their cultural back-cloth is fundamentally the same. There are attempts in *A Blot in the 'Scutcheon* to give a sense of the baronial medievalism which is the material counterpart of the spiritual temper of Earl Tresham. But his eighteenth century castle is as unreal as is Walpole's *Otranto* or his Strawberry Hill. Its ''cross-bow shafts,'' ''the bow-hand or the arrow-hand's great meed,'' ''unhand me, peasant,'' the falcons, hawks and hawkers and the whole paraphernalia of the first scene, with ''many retainers crowded at the window of a lodge in view of the entrance to the mansion,'' and amongst them, Gerard, duly installed as the Warrener, and their talk of poursuivants, of silk and silver varlets, of ribbon-ties and rosettes, of white-staff and of the traditional retainer who

> Fairly had fretted flesh and bone away
> In cares that this was right, nor that was wrong,
> Such a point decorous, and such by rule—
> He knew such niceties, no herald more—

all this is mere stage canvas. The temper of the world of the play will spring most forcibly from the intellectual idiom of its characters: and the painted cloth at the back reveals the artificiality of the factitious moral values incorporated in the play instead of lending reality to them. The exposure is the greater since two of the characters, Gwendolen and Austen, are allowed not only an intellectual idiom as modern and current as the others, but, instead of the others' prescribed standards of conduct, they display a simple humane wisdom which makes them appear the only real and natural people in the play. Unfortunately the plot does not permit them to control the story, or common sense would have turned a series of funerals into a happy marriage-feast.

As the play stands, it is a shapeless medley of confused moral gestures; and the one set up as the symbol of highest good, Thorold's unswerving sense of honour, proves insufficient even to himself. He would put aside, he declares in the moment of his firm resolve, he would put aside all the stern verdicts consecrated by ancestral honour, and forgive everything, merely for a single homely word, one human glance from his sister, were it not that she is planning an even deadlier sin, and one entirely beyond the scope of formal moral heraldry; she is proposing to marry merely to make a husband provide a private bawdy house for a lover and herself. If here honour has been replaced by a simple, universal and intelligible sentiment of common decency, both are mathematically nullified by Thorold's final words, as he tells us what has brought on the tragedy. ''Haste and anger have undone us.'' In other words, there has been much ado about nothing: at least, all that was propounded as momentous was in reality extraneous and irrelevant. The real tragedy has not been presented.

So it is always when Browning, adopting the dramatic form, has of necessity to desert his assessment of individuals as individuals. Indeed, for the individual, since nothing matters but God and himself, there *is* no tragedy in the traditional sense. To the overhearer of each man's monologue there may seem as much moral anarchy as there is in **"The Statue and the Bust,"** but that for his moment is an irrelevant consideration, and since the theme is merely one of personal and therefore of comparative assessment—*de te fabula*. At best, it may rise to the judgment of a disinterested, though experienced and responsible spectator, the summary of an onlooker concerned for the triumph of virtue, as, for instance, the pope in *The Ring and the Book*. But, exercising such an office, he speaks neither as the voice of society nor as the interpreter of it: he is nominally and actually God's vice-gerent. (pp. 51-3)

> *H. B. Charlton, ''Browning as Dramatist,'' in Bulletin of The John Rylands Library, Vol. 23, No. 1, April, 1939, pp. 33-67.*

BERNARD GROOM   (essay date 1939)

[*In this detailed discussion of Browning's diction, Groom sheds light on such aspects of the poet's style as his use of compounds, rare words, specialized language, and alliteration.*]

Browning will never win admirers by the manifest attractions of his style. On the other hand, its merits are evident enough for those who choose to look, and one great merit, that of being 'varied in discourse' was justly ascribed to Browning in the well-known lines of Landor. Browning's happy effects are not the result of mere luck, as has sometimes been suggested. An analysis of his dramatic monologues shows him to have possessed the poet's instinct of long self-preparation for new and original achievement, and many of the features of his style are, as we shall see, due to the exigencies of his favourite form. The clue to an understanding of Browning's technique is to regard his early work as a progress towards, and his later work as a decline from, the art of the dramatic monologue as he practises it in his best years—that is, during the period which begins about the time of his marriage and ends shortly after his wife's death.

Browning, of course, knew that his attitude towards poetry was unusual. In the last year of his life he wrote a letter to Professor Knight in which, as his biographer, Mrs. Sutherland Orr, remarks, 'he states the view of the position and function of poetry, in one brief phrase which might form the text to an exhaustive treatise':—'It is certainly the right order of things: Philosophy first, and Poetry, which is its highest outcome, afterward—and much harm has been done by reversing the natural process' [see Additional Bibliography]. This doctrine is in marked conflict with the theory that words and thought come simultaneously into the mind of the poet, that the poet knows what he wants to express by expressing it. Besides holding this theory of expression, Browning was a confirmed word-collector. As soon as he had chosen poetry as his vocation, he read through Johnson's *Dictionary*, and throughout his career he not only coined words, but adopted and adapted them freely from various languages. He had no fastidious shyness of influences: his inner life was so robust that he delighted to rub shoulders with the outer world—the world of ideas and words, no less than the world of men and women. Hence his work reflects many aspects of the language of his time: it is a magazine of colloquial phrases, it is rich in learned and artistic terms, and it contains no less a wealth of words associated with poetry in general and Victorian poetry in particular. (pp. 117-18)

Although the language of Browning varies much in different poems, some use of 'poetic' words is a fairly constant feature of his style. . . . The following is a short list, which could be easily increased, of 'poetic' words used in different parts of his work: *abysm, aëry, besprent, bosky, burthen, cinct, clomb, drear, dreriment, empery, hests, marge, marish, murk, pens* (feathers), *ope, steed, thrid, syllable* (verb). None of these words would cause the least surprise if met with in *Endymion* or *Hyperion*, and many of them are used by Tennyson. But in the effect which they produce the difference is great. Keats and Tennyson choose them for their atmosphere and associations, but to Browning they are more often than not the merest makeshifts. *Ope*, for example, occurs again and again; but it is simply a strange monosyllable in a context of ordinary English. When Tennyson writes:

> The circle widens till it lip the marge,

he gives an unhurried rhythm to the line which invites the reader to savour the words one by one, and the rare concluding word is in harmony with the rest; but when Browning uses the same word in **"Instans Tyrannus"**:

> Say rather, from marge to blue marge
> The whole sky grew his targe,

he seems to be clipping the final syllable partly in his haste, partly to fit the rhyme. . . . These examples are typical. Browning rarely uses what the dictionary calls a 'poetic' word to produce a poetic effect. He shows no more respect to one word than to another; he appears impatient of the finer tones of diction.

The variety of Browning's language is illustrated by his compound words, many of them new, formed by means of affixes. He has the Victorian taste for compound adverbs of which the first element is the prepositional prefix *a-*, as in *adrift*. Such words in the verse of the time usually have a romantic grace or charm. Some of Browning's also have this quality, but a great many are wholly different, being formed in a mood of jest or mockery. The following is a varied specimen list: *a-bloom, a-blush, a-bubble, a-chuckle, a-clatter, a-crackle, a-crumble, a-flare, a-flaunt, a-flicker, a-flutter, a-glimmer, a-grime, a-heap, a-seethe, a-simmer, a-smoke, a-spread, a-straddle, a-tangle, a-waft, a-whirl, a-wing*. A similarly mixed list might be compiled from the compounds formed with the prefix *be-*, though probably there would be a preponderance of jocular formations. Some affixes naturally lend themselves to a particular tone or style. For instance, Browning's compound verbs beginning with *en-* are mostly serious or romantic; even taken out of their context they suggest something of the pre-Raphaelite flavour, e.g. *enarm, enchase, encircle, enhaloed, enisled, enmesh, enwreathe*. His compounds ending with the suffix *-ry* are, as might be expected, of a very different quality: *archbishopry, cousinry, dupery, enginery, gossipry, serpentry, stitchery, varletry;* perhaps the most serious formation in this group is *artistry*, of which Browning is perhaps the inventor. The use of adjectives ending with the suffix *-some* is characteristic of his style, e.g. *lightsome, toothsome, playsome, pranksome*. Such words agree with his prevailing colloquial tone; so do others of a similar type, e.g. *beseemingness(es), darlingness, uncomfortableness*. Many compounds he uses are rare or obsolescent, e.g. *lathen* (of lath), *grieffull, blinkard, plenitudinous, morbify, immerd, dissheathe, celestiality*. Such lists do something to suggest the vast range of the vocabulary which is needed when a mind so rapid, subtle, and original expresses itself in metrical form.

To do justice to Browning's style it is necessary to consider the special objects which he had in view. His most finished and elaborate works are the dramatic monologues of his middle period, and though it is of the essence of these poems that each is a highly individual work, yet they possess certain general qualities in common. For one thing, it is part of his plan to devise a situation in which the speaker should be able to unburden his mind with absolute freedom. Several of the speakers even pause to reflect on this frankness. For instance, Karshish in [**"An Epistle of Karshish"**] apologizes for troubling his correspondent with private matters:

> I half resolve to tell thee, yet I blush,
> What set me off a-writing first of all. . . .

Caliban, at the end of his monologue, laments his indiscretion in talking so freely:

> There scuds His raven that has told Him all!
> It was fool's play, this prattling!

To suit the frankness of these self-revelations, Browning cultivates the utmost informality of style. His handling of colloquial idiom in little pieces like **"The Lost Mistress"** and **"Confessions"** is one of his finest achievements, and he shows the same skill on a larger scale in the best of the monologues. (pp. 118-21)

Having mastered the colloquial style in verse, it was characteristic of him to go too far and become too colloquial. He had a bent towards the jocose, the disparaging, and the satirical, and in his later work he gave the impulse free play. This, of course, was partly due to his choice of imperfect and flawed characters as the main subjects of his poetry; but it was due as well to his own explosive vigour. His impatient energy impels him to give a ludicrous turn to the plainest statement. The line

How both knelt down, prayed blessing on bent head

might have been written by Browning about the time of his *Pauline*, or he might have composed it when in the rare mood of **"The Guardian-Angel"**, but it is much more like him to write (as in fact he does):

How both *flopped* down, prayed blessing on bent *pate,*

Again, other men might have written the line:

Pitted against a pair of juveniles,

but the version of Browning is, of course:

Pitted against a *brace* of juveniles.

The mood of satire, whether gay or grave, is so common that it colours Browning's whole style: in no other poet of the century is to be found so large a store of contemptuous or disparaging words. Thus besides *pate* for 'head', he finds many occasions for *noddle;* for 'speak' he frequently uses *prate;* for 'bow' he will substitute *lout;* for 'child', *bantling;* for 'move', *budge;* for 'wrath', *bile;* for 'bear' (verb), *spawn;* for 'go' or 'march', *trundle.* 'Daub his phyz' is quite Browningesque, so is 'we drub Self-knowledge rather, into frowzy pate'. He searches out odd words of this abusive class, finding (for instance) *letch, chouse, shag-rag,* and sometimes he enforces the effect by alliteration, as in the line:

And nuns a-maundering here and mumping there.

Many of these examples have been drawn from Browning's later work: his style has less equilibrium after about 1864, the date of **Dramatis Personae**; but even in **Men and Women,** where his writing is most balanced, the note of exuberant mockery begins to be heard—for instance, in **"Holy-Cross Day"**.

Verbal reminiscences from other poets are fairly common in Browning's work, and though they do not by themselves give a full idea of his style, they suggest what its tendencies are. His early work shows some traces of romantic diction, as in the line:

That under-current soft and *argentine*

where the last word might have been borrowed from Keats; and there is a well-known echo of Keats's manner in the song 'Heap cassia' in **Paracelsus**. Reminiscences of the fine passages in other poets do not disappear from Browning's later writing, but as the dramatic character of his work increases they come to be chosen more and more for a dramatic purpose, like the quotations of Bishop Blougram in his reflections on Shakespeare. . . . Browning's non-dramatic echoes of other men's words are . . . [more original]. The tendency towards abuse and disparagement which we noticed before is evident again here. Numberless English writers have shown their familiarity with Shakespeare's language, and Browning is among them, but it is not so much the highways of his poetry which he seems to know, as its bypaths and even its underworld. The phrases which he echoes from *Hamlet* are of this kind: 'to be round with you', 'Provençal roses', 'chop-fallen', 'imposthume',

Pages from the manuscript of The Ring and the Book.

'squeak and gibber'. From *Othello* he remembers 'clink the cannikin' ('let me the canakin clink'), 'prove a haggard': the phrase 'nor cog nor cozen' is perhaps a variation of 'cogging, cozening slave'. From *Macbeth* he remembers 'lily-livered'. 'Mewls' is presumably from *As You Like It,* and 'clapperclaw-ing' from *The Merry Wives of Windsor.* 'Just-lugged bear' sounds like a variant of 'head-lugged bear' in *King Lear,* and 'treads close on kibe' is Shakespearian, but not from any one passage. From Milton, as might be imagined, he does not borrow much, but one word at least is a highly characteristic choice, viz. *scrannel.* . . . Of Bunyan, a spiritual fighter like himself, he was a close reader, and Bunyan provides him with several phrases. The allusion to Apollyon in **"Childe Roland to the Dark Tower Came"** is, of course, from *The Pilgrim's Progress,* and the description of Christian's fight with Apollyon who 'stradled quite over the whole breadth of the way' leaves a trace in the phrase 'a-straddle across its length' in **"Ned Bratts"**, which is a poem on two of Bunyan's converts. . . . To illustrate Browning's verbal reminiscences I have drawn on only a few of his poems, but further examples would emphasize the same points.

One element in the design of Browning's dramatic monologues is, as I have said, the unfettered freedom of the speaker's self-revelation. Another element, equally important, is the historical background which, to answer its purpose, must seem both real and accurate. Further, it is often a background of special significance. Browning loves to choose some moment of crisis, some period when great issues hang in the balance. [**"An Epistle of Karshish"**] and **"Cleon"**, the moment is one in which Christianity has just opened upon an unbelieving world: **"A Death in the Desert"** is dated a short time later. The Renaissance is one of his favourite periods: **"The Bishop orders his Tomb at St. Praxed's"**, **"My Last Duchess"**, **"Andrea del Sarto"** are all Renaissance poems, and **"A Grammarian's Funeral"** is headed 'Shortly after the revival of learning in Europe'. Even in **"Bishop Blougram's Apology"**, a more or less precise date is essential to the conception:

> Had I been born three hundred years ago
> They'd say, 'What's strange? Blougram of course believes;'
> And, seventy years since, 'disbelieves of course'.
> But now, 'He may believe; and yet, and yet
> How can he?'

Sometimes, though not so often, Browning is equally explicit about place, heading the poems 'Rome' or 'Ferrara', or making it plain from the context that the scene is London, Florence, or elsewhere. The illusion of historical accuracy is necessary to the effect which he seeks to produce. But, binding himself in one way, he leaves himself free in another—the main character is either little known or wholly imaginary. Hence the detailed picture which he draws violates no familiar facts. On one occasion when he breaks this rule, namely in his portrait of Napoleon III, he secures some measure of freedom by calling the ex-Emperor 'Prince Hohenstiel-Schwangau', but even this dialogue receives the precise and significant date, 1871.

In this scheme of producing the appearance of historical exactness, without sacrificing the poet's freedom of invention, diction plays an important part. Browning cares nothing for an atmosphere of vague romantic beauty, nothing for verbal melody or suggestion on their own account. He surveys remote lands and remote ages through a pellucid atmosphere: distance lends no enchantment to the view. . . . His scheme demands the accumulation of many small exact details of time, place, and circumstance. Hence the care bestowed on local colour,

hence the frequent naturalization of foreign words, hence too the wealth of technical terms. His method is well displayed in his poem on the dying Bishop of St. Praxed's with his passion for architecture. The speaker's tastes are illustrated by the number and precision of his technical terms: '*onion-stone*' ('cipollino'), '*antique-black*' ('nero antico'), *lapis lazuli, gritstone, mortcloth, tabernacle, vizor, bas-relief, entablature, tavertine.* The first seven words in this list are not used elsewhere by Browning—a proof of his careful differentiation of one poem from another. A similar effect is produced in [**"An Epistle of Karshish"**] with its fitting display of medical terms: *snakestone, gum-tragacanth, sublimate* (noun), *tertian, viscid*: these words also are not used again in Browning's poetry. One wonders what other poet could have given such clear-cut reality to an imaginary letter from an Arab physician of the First Century. It is more difficult to differentiate the language of a speaker who is not presented in his professional capacity or under any one aspect. Yet Browning succeeds here also. Bishop Blougram, for instance, is revealed less as a prelate than as a cultivated man of the world. Such a man, talking rapidly and intimately, will sometimes coin a word on the spur of the moment, sometimes use a rare word which he has perhaps never thought of before. It is thus that the bishop does in fact speak; *decrassify* here makes its first appearance not only in Browning's work but apparently in the English language as well; *entourage, demirep, eventuality, experimentalise, excitation, fictile* occur in this dialogue and nowhere else in Browning. For the poet's peculiar method, great learning was necessary, and Browning's learning is generally to be trusted, though there are a few phantom allusions, like the 'Emperor Aldabrod' of **"The Heretic's Tragedy"**. It is true of Browning as of Milton that to appreciate him to the full is one of the rewards of consummated scholarship. His best work is strong enough to carry off some effect of strangeness in the language. Thus *loric* was not a word before Browning used it in his Roman poem **"Protus"**, but it suits the context and it dispels the intervening centuries better than 'breast-plate'. It is of course not the case in poetry that the end justifies the means. The technical terms which Browning uses for a special dramatic purpose do not in his hands immediately turn into poetry, like the technical terms of Milton in the line:

> Cornice, or frieze with bossy sculptures graven.

Nor can the language of the arts have the same universal appeal as the common language of men. On that ground at least a cuckoo's cry is better described as a 'twofold shout' than as a 'minor third'. Opinions on the merits of the second phrase will naturally differ. For my part I cannot help liking it any more than I can help liking the 'commiserating sevenths' of **"A Toccata of Galuppi's"**; but that is a purely personal view.

No poetry is safe in ignoring altogether the ideal of simplicity. It is characteristic of Browning that he so seldom approaches the plain dignity of Biblical English. His diction is centrifugal: his restless activity impels him to avoid the norm; for him, as for Abt Vogler, the C Major of this life is a resting-place which invites sleep. Nor is he the man to use moderation. Some of his work, especially that of his later life, reads like a parody of his own method. The lines in **"A Grammarian's Funeral"**:

> He settled *Hoti's* business—let it be!—
> Properly based *Oun*—

produce a slight shock when first read, but, when familiar, they may give a kind of pleasure; so much can scarcely be said of:

> *Amo -as -avi -atum -are -ans,*
> Up to *-aturus*, person, tense, and mood.

Nor is it clear why Count Guido Franceschini, who is not a physician, should call a pain in his shoulder-blade 'an ailing in this omoplat'. On the matter of technical terms in verse no two persons can possibly feel in the same way, a fact which in itself tells against them. For my own part, I can see why Browning in his character of dramatic realist should allude to the Pope's *cheirograph* in *The Ring and the Book*, that being the correct term for 'one of three forms in which the will of the Papal See is expressed in writing'. I can also see some ground for the allusion to *tarocs* (i.e. playing-cards) in Caponsacchi's autobiographical sketch. But to form a nonce-word *baioc* from 'bajocco', the name of a small Italian coin, is simply unfair to the reader. Browning's declared principles in diction are cosmopolitan. He is naturally amused at 'the sturdy Briton who, Ben Jonson informs us, wrote ''The Life of the Emperor Anthony Pie''—whom we now acquiesce in as Antoninus Pius', but a little more insularity would have done nothing but good to Browning himself. Why, for instance, should he coin *ampollosity* from the Italian 'ampolloso' rather than *ampullosity*, from the Latin 'ampullosus'? The mere fact that he was writing a poem on Italian life is hardly reason enough. His refusal to latinize Greek names in the traditional manner, using instead such forms as *Olumpos, Phaidra, Phoibos, Sophokles, Klutaimnestra* is a small thing in itself, but it is significant of his attitude towards English usage. In his translation of the *Agamemnon* he aimed, as he tells us, at producing 'the very turn of each phrase in as Greek a fashion as English will bear'. He applies this principle to his diction in *Aristophanes' Apology*, giving us such expressions as: *dikast and heliast, kordax-step, peplosed and kothorned, choinix, barbiton, exomion* and *chaunoprokt*. (pp. 121-28)

The purpose of Browning's rare words is often clear enough. Many in *Sordello*, for instance, have the same object as those in the best poems of *Men and Women*: they contribute to the local or historical colour. But one wonders why he so often chooses the unfamiliar form of a word which is itself sufficiently unfamiliar; for Browning is clearly not a Milton or a Tennyson to weigh the musical value of a single letter. Why, for instance, in *Sordello,* should he write *valvassor* for 'vavasour', *truchman* for 'dragoman', *plectre* for 'plectrum', *trifoly* for 'trefoil', *orpine* for 'orpiment'? Possibly the pre-Raphaelites had an inkling of the answer, for some of these words have the medieval flavour which they liked, and Browning's early work helped to form their style. Throughout his career Browning had a taste for obscure and obsolete words and forms of words. For 'frantic' he will write *frenetic;* for 'restive', *restif;* for 'swart', *swarth;* for 'snigger', *snicker;* for 'spit', *spawl;* for 'canter' or 'curvet', *tittup.* It is just like him to introduce the word *cue-owl,* a word used by himself and Mrs. Browning, but unknown, it seems, to the world at large. The strain which he puts on the use of rare words sometimes amounts to inaccuracy. In one of his poems, *catafalk,* which properly means 'a stage or platform erected to receive a coffin', is used for 'a kind of open hearse or funeral car'; in the same poem *encoulure,* a French word for 'the neck of an animal' is used to mean 'the mane' (of a horse). Browning frequently forms or uses participles analogous to Milton's *increate* from 'increatus', a practice common among writers of the sixteenth and early seventeenth centuries. Examples are: *exenterate, miscreate, saturate, contaminate, extravasate, unimplicate, undesecrate, consecrate, decollate, excommunicate, affiliate,* to which may be added *attent* from 'attentus', and *porporate* from the Italian 'porporato'. Some of Browning's Latinisms seem to belong to the age of Burton or Browne rather than to the nineteenth century: for instance *benefic, crepitant, strepitant,*

mollitious. The words in these last two lists, though queer and crabbed, at least bear the marks of scholarship, but occasionally Browning, like Spenser, incurs the reproach of 'writing no language'. (pp. 130-31)

Browning liked the vigorous effect of accumulated epithets; he also liked the emphasis of alliteration. In poems of his middle period, it is not uncommon to meet these two effects in combination: for instance in Fra Lippo Lippi's description of himself in his own painting,

> Mazed, motionless, and moon-struck,

and in the account which Karshish gives of his meeting with Lazarus:

> Out there came
> A moon made like a face with certain spots
> Multiform, manifold, and menacing.

Browning's taste for alliteration grew with years; and in some of his later work, when he wrote with a flowing pen and gave free play to his satirical mood, an effect is produced which is curious in itself and interesting to students of our early poetry. From the time of *The Ring and the Book* onwards, one meets with line after line, passage after passage, in which alliteration enforces the emphasis on certain key-words with remarkable vigour. I will quote a few examples from the large number which I have noticed:

> Proves a *p*lague-*p*rodigy to God and man.

> Look at my *l*awyers, *l*acked they grace of *l*aw,
> *L*atin or *l*ogic?

> Out with you! *Tr*undle, log!
> If you cannot *tr*amp and *tr*udge like a man, *tr*y all-fours like a dog!

> *fl*at thus I lie nor *fl*inch!
> O God, the *f*eel of the *f*ang *f*urrowing my shoulder!—see!
> It *g*rinds—it *g*rates the bone.

In these passages alliteration seems to be struggling to become the master-principle of the metre as it was in our ancient poetry, and when one meets a succession of lines like the following, one feels that the spirit and manner of a long-forgotten past have mysteriously revived in this mid-Victorian writer:

> I tried chaff, *f*ound I *f*amished on such *f*are,
> So *m*ade this *m*ad rush at the *m*ill-house door,
> Buried my head up to the ears in dew,
> *Br*owsed on the *b*est: for which you *br*ain me, Sirs!

Alliteration has played a part in the verse of many English poets since the Elizabethan age, but for a parallel to this regular use of it upon three stressed words in the line we must go back to the alliterative poets before Wyatt and Surrey. In the tone of the passages which I have quoted, we hear something of the voice of Langland: he, like Browning, was a poet of headlong energy and unvarnished speech. But, for my own part, I am reminded even more clearly of the West Midland author of *Patience*, that poet of many moods, the tender, the humorous, the denunciatory. (pp. 132-33)

I have dwelt freely on what I presume to call the 'faults' of Browning's diction, yet it is clear that he was a great though irregular master of English. His influence on the language has been small in proportion to his powers. As we have seen, he is possibly the inventor of the word *artistry*, and a few of his phrases are current, e.g. 'the first fine careless rapture', 'the little more, and how much it is! And the little less, and what worlds away'; but his contribution to the language is much smaller than Tennyson's. In his lifetime, the influence of his style was not wide, but it was apparent in the work of two or three outstanding men. The pre-Raphaelites caught something of the spirit of his early style. It is possible that D. G. Rossetti learned from Browning his idiom of the possessive noun + metaphor, e.g. 'her neck's rose-misted marble' (Browning), 'her eyes' o'erhanging heaven' (Rossetti). Certain features in the style of G. M. Hopkins are evidently borrowed from Browning, e.g. the accumulation of compound epithets, the asyntactic compound epithet (in which Hopkins is bolder than his master) and perhaps the use of emphatic monosyllables in a compact series. Browning's most profitable example to later poets lay in his use of colloquial English for the impassioned lyric. As G. K. Chesterton excellently puts it: 'He substituted the street with the green blind for the faded garden of Watteau, and the "blue spirit of a lighted match" for the monotony of the evening star.' In this respect Hardy is Browning's disciple, and from Hardy the example has spread far and wide into modern verse. That Browning's dramatic monologues have been little imitated is natural, for each piece has its distinct style, and to write a series of such poems would demand a combination of powers such as Browning alone possessed. Few writers have ever paid less regard to critics; he almost seems, like the fourteenth-century poets with whom I have compared him, to belong to a pre-critical age. 'Tennyson', he noted, 'reads the *Quarterly* and does as they bid him with the most solemn face in the world—out goes this, in goes that, all is changed and ranged. Oh me!' Browning could not have been what he was without his sturdy independence; yet his best admirers cannot help wishing that he had heeded—if not the criticism of living men—at least the silent and searching criticism which is operative in the spirit of the English language. (pp. 134-35)

> Bernard Groom, "Browning," in his On the Diction of Tennyson, Browning and Arnold, *Oxford at the Clarendon Press*, 1939, pp. 117-35.

WILLIAM O. RAYMOND (essay date 1940)

[*Raymond examines Browning's dualistic approach to love and reason as it is reflected in the casuistry of "Bishop Blougram's Apology" and* Fifine at the Fair.]

A study of Browning's casuists *per se* may seem to lie quite apart from a consideration of his vital contribution to English poetry. In that conflict between imagination and intellect which was acute in Browning, his casuistic writings represent in the main the nadir of his poetic faculty. The dramatic and poetical unities of such masterpieces as **"The Bishop Orders his Tomb at Saint Praxed's Church"** and **"My Last Duchess,"** where character and incident, thought and emotion are adequately fused, are replaced by psychological analysis in which the understanding takes the bit in its teeth and makes the abstract play of the mind an end in itself. . . .

[The] casuistic poems of Browning are an integral product of his genius, and a knowledge of them is essential to the grasp of it. Viewed, not in isolation, but in relation to the central ideas and interests of his poetry, these frequently crabbed writings have a value out-reaching their intrinsic content. (p. 641)

It is . . . through their relation to Browning's philosophy of life that the casuistic poems are of special import. One phase of this—the cleavage between man's faculties of love and reason—they illustrate in a pre-eminent degree. In an attempt to vindicate his ethical convictions and to establish a firm basis for his religious faith, Browning is driven to place all stress on love, and by contrast to debase reason. The universal problems of sin and suffering and the particular doubts and difficulties of his age seem to him insoluble from the point of view of reason. His distrust of the capacities of man's mind is of a thorough-going character. He does not merely hold that knowledge is relative and limited. Reason is for ever baffled in its search for truth, and its quest ends in the *cul-de-sac* of deception and illusion. Its futile groping is, to use the poet's figure in **The Ring and the Book,** like an arm thrust into water, deflected by the medium through which it passes and falling wide of what it seeks to grasp.

But Browning's emotional gnosticism is as unqualified as his intellectual agnosticism. He cuts the Gordian knot by exalting the heart above the head and by regarding love as infallible in its intuitive perception of truth.

> Wholly distrust thy knowledge then, and trust
> As wholly love allied to ignorance!
> There lies thy truth and safety.

In **"Saul,"** love in man's heart is an *a priori* evidence to David of the existence of a God of love. Thence there follow as corollaries Immortality, and a prophetic vision of a scheme of redemption in the Incarnation and Atonement of Christ. Once convinced of the importance of reason, Browning makes it, in a left-handed way, support his concept of the supreme worth of man's moral struggle. Truth is concealed from the eyes of the intellect in order that the venture and trial of faith may be the more heroic.

Browning's sceptical attitude towards reason in the interests of his ethics and religious belief has often been represented as individual and unique. But it is, rather, a specialized form of that way of retreat from apparently insuperable problems adopted by many of the great Victorians. Newman and Tennyson exhibit it as markedly as Browning. Arnold dallied with it in "Dover Beach." He too felt the lure of that escape to the Ages of Faith which by blinding the eyes of reason would regain security of belief. Yet he could not foreswear allegiance to "the high, white star of Truth." "The Victorian Compromise," manifest in other spheres, is nowhere else more strikingly illustrated than in the endeavour to withdraw religion from the realm of knowledge in order to obtain spiritual peace, though at a costly price. (pp. 642-43)

This *reductio ad absurdum* of reason is paralleled in scientific works of the decade. In *Omphalos: An Attempt to untie the Geological Knot*, Philip Gosse, an able entomologist, gravely argued that God had planted fossils in the earth as a sort of gargantuan pious fraud. The divine purpose of the imposture, according to Gosse, was to give opportunity for faith to rise above the apparent confutation of the cosmology of *Genesis* in the testimony of the fossils. Men must still believe in the scientific accuracy of the Biblical account of creation, despite the contradictory evidence of the senses and reason. God consequently becomes, as Kingsley put it in criticising *Omphalos*, a *Deus quidam deceptor,* and the end justifies the means. Such shifts and straits of casuistry are a measure of the intellectual perplexities of the epoch. If Browning is at times enmeshed in their toils, his position can only be fairly estimated and sympathetically judged in the light of the historical background of his day.

I have dwelt on Browning's intellectual scepticism, because of its intimate connection with his casuistic poems. For a nescient theory of knowledge is the very soil in which casuistry breeds. If reason, self-tricked and deluded, is always involved in a "vile juggle," casuistry must be constantly attendant upon it and, indeed, inherent in its nature. Browning escapes the fogs of sophistry when he invokes the sunlight of love to dispel the mists that becloud the mind. The emotions of the heart are in intuitive touch with truth. But when the poet descends to the arena of reason, he is unavoidably entrapped in casuistry. Hence it becomes an interesting question, how far his hand is dyed by the medium in which he works. To what extent is he above his casuists, and to what extent is he at one with them? The arguments through which Bishop Blougram strives to justify his religious position have more than a superficial likeness to those used by Browning in his later poems to defend his own faith. Even that subtle sophist Don Juan, seems, at times, equipped with some of the choicest weapons from the poet's arsenal. It is difficult to avoid the conclusion that Browning's casuists are never really routed from the standpoint of reason. Here the poet's negative attitude towards knowledge sprains him. "Wisdom is justified of her children," and however gifted a man's intellect, he must have faith in reason in order to vindicate the ways of reason. It is only by recourse to the sovereign principle and virtue of love that Browning triumphs over casuistry. He carries the case to a higher tribunal, but he does not defeat the sophist on the latter's chosen ground. (pp. 644-45)

I turn now to the particular consideration of the casuistry of **"Bishop Blougram's Apology"** in its relation to the basic dualism of the poet's thought,—a gulf between love and reason involving a profound distrust of the latter faculty. I have drawn attention to the fact that an agnostic rejection of knowledge is the seedling of casuistry; and raised the question, how far is Browning himself caught in the sophistry he is probing? I have also pointed out that the Victorian Compromise, through which belief was preserved at the expense of reason by confining religion to the sphere of faith and the intuitions of the heart, overleaps the boundaries of denominational allegiance. The Roman Catholic, Newman; the Broad Church Anglican, Tennyson; the Dissenter, Browning, in whose veins ran the blood of Puritan ancestors,—adopt a position, in this regard, fundamentally akin. There is, consequently, in the realm of reason, an intrinsic bond of sympathy, conscious or unconscious, between Browning and the creation of his brain, Bishop Blougram. It was, undoubtedly, a recognition that the poet's renunciation of reason in the interests of faith was not far removed from the Roman Catholic credo, which led Wiseman, when reviewing **"Bishop Blougram's Apology"** in the *Rambler*, to write:

> Though much of the matter is extremely offensive to Catholics, yet beneath the surface there is an undercurrent of thought that is by no means inconsistent with our religion; and if Mr. Browning is a man of will and action, and not a mere dreamer and talker, *we should never feel surprise at his conversion.*

There are two main threads of casuistry running through the arguments of Bishop Blougram. The first is primarily ethical, in its bearing on the conduct of life. The second is primarily intellectual, in its bearing on the issues of faith and doubt. The Bishop bases part of his defence on the contrast between the futility of abstract idealism and the success of a prudent and practical adaptation of one's talent and outlook to the environment and capacities of a workaday world. Browning, himself, had a keen sense of the necessity of making a fruitful use of the means and possibilities of man's earthly lot. "All poetry," he once wrote to Ruskin, "is the problem of putting the infinite into the finite." In **Pauline, Paracelsus,** and **Sor-**

dello, he grappled with this problem in the sphere of life. The heroes of these poems are men of genius, and the crux of their difficulties lies in reconciling the inexhaustible cravings of the spirit with the conditions and limitations of a finite world. Browning wrestles with this moral paradox as strenuously as Jacob with the angel and, in the main, successfully. He does not, like Bishop Blougram, conclude that the urgency of working within the cabin confines of earthly experience justifies an acceptance of worldly standards. A man should not spurn the actual, but neither should he be content with it. He must constantly strive to press beyond it and to lift it up towards the light of the ideal. The ethical convictions of Browning are the core of his philosophy, and on moral grounds, *per se,* he is rarely, if ever, entangled in casuistry.

When, however, we turn to that argument of Bishop Blougram which is primarily intellectual, revolving about the issues of belief and doubt, the poet's position is on a different footing. The Bishop declares that he casts in his lot with the adherents of faith on account of its utilitarian value. He then goes on to suggest that the inability of reason to attain religious truth or to solve the problems of the universe may be preordained in order that men may rely entirely on faith. Difficulties of belief from the standpoint of intellect are like breaks in the mountain path of life, but, the Bishop speculates:

> What if the breaks themselves should prove at last
> The most consummate of contrivances
> To train a man's eye, teach him what is faith?
> And so we stumble at truth's very test!

If this comparison were simply an illustration of the relativity of human knowledge which leaves scope for faith, it would not, in itself, involve an agnostic attitude towards reason. But Bishop Blougram pushes his argument further. He widens the chasm between belief and reason in two directions. The maximum of belief is represented by an absolute form of it in Roman Catholicism, the maximum of agnosticism by a complete intellectual scepticism. The broader and deeper the abyss between belief and reason, the greater is the challenge to faith, and the more signal its triumph when it leaps the gulf. "Let doubt occasion still more faith!" exclaims the Bishop, and again:

> With me, faith means perpetual unbelief
> Kept quiet like the snake 'neath Michael's foot
> Who stands calm just because he feels it writhe.

On this ground the poet, with Newman in his mind, makes Blougram defend the most preposterous of churchly miracles,—the liquefaction of the blood of St. Januarius at Naples, and the motion of the eyes of the Madonna in the Roman States. The extreme irrationality of these miracles is but a foil for the unqualified exhibition of faith in its unreasoning acceptance of the supernatural.

Although Browning would scout the crass materialism of such miracles, it is indisputable that his agnostic abnegation of knowledge entangles him, personally as well as dramatically, in the casuistry of **"Bishop Blougram's Apology."** This is especially evident in his later writings, where his rejection of reason is drastic, and all worth is centered in faith motivated by love as a solvent of life's problems. He, too, along with Bishop Blougram, tries to turn his rationalistic scepticism to moral advantage, by making the incapacity of reason a challenge to the daring venture of faith in the blackness of night environing the intellect. He, too, fixes a great gulf between the intuitions of the heart and what are regarded as the phantoms of the mind. It is, therefore, not surprising to find that Bishop

Blougram is, at times, the mouthpiece of Browning's inmost religious convictions. The Bishop's argument that a searing vision of God's omnipresence would blind man on earth, and that the existence of evil is necessary if the world is to be a place of probation and testing, is a familiar tenet of the poet's ethics. In the *apologia* for Christianity put on Blougram's lips, the correspondence of dramatic and personal thought is still more striking. Who can doubt that Browning is voicing his own belief when the Bishop asserts:

> It is the idea, the feeling and the love,
> God means mankind should strive for and show forth
> Whatever be the process to that end,—
> And not historic knowledge, logic sound,
> And metaphysical acumen, sure!
> "What think ye of Christ," friend? when all's done and said,
> Like you this Christianity or not?
> It may be false, but will you wish it true?
> Has it your vote to be so if it can?

The elements of truth in these words are apt to cloak the "Achilles' heel" of the statement, but the criticism of "historic knowledge, logic sound" in connection with the evidences of Christianity, is based on that distrust of reason which is the root of casuistry. And Browning is as deeply involved in this sophistry as his Roman Catholic prelate. In his later writings, where his intellectual agnosticism is most pronounced, he becomes extremely sceptical of any approach to religious truth through the exercise of reason. In laying exclusive stress on love, he is inclined to regard the revelation of Christianity, not merely as historically unproven, but as embodying a narrative of events absolutely inconceivable from the point of view of intellect.

As a result of his rationalistic scepticism, Browning is unable to refute the casuist on the battle-ground of reason. But in **"Bishop Blougram's Apology,"** as elsewhere, he rises above casuistry through recourse to the cardinal virtue of love, in whose light doubts dissolve as mists in the sun. The Bishop is an adherent of belief, but he is not himself a believer at heart. His decision to embrace Roman Catholicism is based on utilitarian grounds. Faith has positive value; it works; it provides practical results in the sphere of life. Over against such prudential motives, Browning places the intuitive witness of the heart to the validity of the fundamental truths of religion. The existence of a loving and self-sacrificing God, which is the core of Christian revelation, is attested by evidences deeper than rational proof. Its guaranty lies in faith inspired by love in the soul of the individual, in transfigured lives, in the spiritual experience of humanity. Bishop Blougram acknowledges that Luther's fire of religious conviction is far superior to his own cold, formal, and calculating acceptance of belief as an instrument of worldly policy.

> Believe—and our whole argument breaks up,
> Enthusiasm's the best thing, I repeat;
> . . . . . .
> Why, to be Luther—that's a life to lead,
> Incomparably better than my own.

In such lines the poet voices his own ideals. (pp. 648-52)

By transferring the argument of **"Bishop Blougram's Apology"** to his own chosen ground, the poet wins what may be called a Pyrrhic victory. He triumphs, yet surrenders the outposts of intellect to the casuist. In the realm of love the hollowness of the Bishop's sophistry is exposed, but in the realm of knowledge, Browning is, in a sense, fighting with his own shadow.

The dialectics of Blougram are never pierced by the sword of reason. (pp. 652-53)

Fifine at the Fair is the greatest of Browning's casuistic monologues. It . . . plumbs the intricacies of casuistry in masterly fashion. (p. 661)

The monologist in *Fifine* is the arch-voluptuary Don Juan. But his personality undergoes a sea-change in the poet's hands. Milton's Satan in *Paradise Regained* is not more unlike Satan in *Paradise Lost* than Browning's Don Juan is unlike the Don Juan of Molière and Byron. The indulgence of the passions of sense, which is the principal motif of the traditions and legends that cluster about Don Juan, is a mere point of departure in *Fifine*. The liaison with the gypsy is kept in the background. It is not the experience of sensuality, but the intellectual sophistry through which a libertine may strive to extenuate his philandering, that is the central theme of the poem. (pp. 661-62)

Numerous threads of casuistry are woven into the complex fabric of *Fifine*. The first and most important of these is intimately blended with the general setting of the monologue. Fifine and her gypsy tribe are Bohemians. They symbolize a roving, independent type of life free from the tramels of form and convention. In a left-handed way they represent the principle of liberty. Their freedom is linked by Browning with those instincts of the human spirit which chafe at the barriers of the finite moulds and orthodox institutions of society. If the spirit cannot satisfy its aspirations through legitimate channels, it may seek to escape even at the risk of violating the conventional precepts of morality. This innate craving of the human spirit for liberty is the basis of Don Juan's sophistical argument that this momentary defection from constancy to his wife Elvire is justified. Even though Don Juan has a peerless wife, there must be some enticement to gratify "expectancy's old fume and fret." The crystallization of any relationship, however precious, involves a limitation and confinement of the spirit. As Don Juan carefully explains, his fleeting passion for Fifine cannot be compared in worth or depth with his habitual love for Elvire. But his indulgence in a passing fancy for the gypsy banishes ennui, quickens "novel hopes and fears," and combats the tediousness and monotony of life.

A second favourite casuistic argument of Don Juan is equally inwrought in the fabric of *Fifine*. It is based on the contention that, since human life is a state of probation, experiment and practice with evil are necessary to the understanding and evaluation of good. The probationary character of life is vividly exemplified by the symbolism of the sea. Similes and metaphors linked with the sea are pervasive in *Fifine*, and many of them are of great poetic beauty. In the body of the poem, the imagery of the swimmer struggling with the instability and treacherousness of the sea is used as an illustration of man's dealing with the false and shifting appearances of life, through which he learns to value the truth and permanence residing in the heaven above him. In another illustration drawn from man's experience with the sea, companionship with Elvire is compared to a voyage in a safe and superior ship, while intercourse with Fifine is like embarking in a mere cockle-shell. The navigation of "the rakish craft" will be perilous, since the course is uncharted and the helmsman must steer "through divers rocks and shoals." But, Don Juan argues, it is on that account a better test of expert seamanship, and gives the mariner a more intimate knowledge of the forces of wind and wave.

Despite the importance of the imagery of the sea, it is far from exhausting the store of simile and metaphor with which the poet endows Don Juan, as his supple brain plays about the crux of the interrelationships between good and evil, truth and falsehood, in a fallible and imperfect world. As an absolute idealist, Browning believes that the existence of evil and falsehood has to be reconciled with the divine plan for the universe. Therefore by penetrating beneath their appearances to reality they must be made to yield their ultimate contribution to goodness and truth. By giving a casuistic twist to this conviction, Don Juan argues that a man must be actually involved in the toils of evil and falsehood before he can appreciate what goodness and truth are. Through intercourse with Fifine he professes to show that elemental flame may spring from straw and rottenness as well as from gums and spice. His temporary commerce with one of the baser forms of evil will finally teach him

> That, through the outward sign, the inward grace allures,
> And sparks from heaven transpire earth's coarsest covertures,
> All by demonstrating the value of Fifine!

Finally, Don Juan stresses the illusory character of life, and from this conjures a score of casuistic arguments. Fifine and her tribe are actors, but their frank acknowledgment that they play parts has the grace of sincerity. The mimicry of the circus performers is "honest cheating." The rest of humanity are actors on the stage of life, but they do not openly avow their roles. They deal with illusion and falsehood, yet pretend that they are in direct contact with truth. At this juncture, Don Juan's illustrations drawn from the practice and love of miming become comprehensive in their range. The Pornic Fair widens into the Venetian carnival and that, in turn, to the pageantry and masquerade of life. While listening to the music of Schumann's "Carnival," Don Juan imagines himself ensconced on a pinnacle in the vicinity of St. Mark's Church, whence he gazes on the masqueraders far below in the streets of Venice. The scene as viewed from this dizzy height appears monstrous and incomprehensible. But when he descends from his "pinnacled-pre-eminence" to the streets and mingles with the revellers, incongruities diminish, and nearness to the masks enables him to discern some traces of the elemental humanity beneath each of them. This imagery is used to emphasize the distinction between an absolute point of view which might be that of the spirit world, and a relative point of view which must be that of our mortal condition. In this earthly sphere, men can only struggle towards truth by traffic with the evil and falsehood environing them, till they learn to pierce through such semblances to essential reality. In the long run "evil proves good, wrong right, and 'howling' childishness." Consequently, Don Juan maintains, we should accept worldly standards, come to close grips with life, and not criticize it from the standpoint of an abstract idealism.

> I found
> Somehow the proper goal for wisdom was the ground
> And not the sky,—so slid sagaciously betimes
> Down heaven's baluster-rope, to reach the mob of mimes
> And mummers.

The casuistry of *Fifine at the Fair* is so protean that it is difficult to determine at what points Browning is personally entangled in its sophistry and at what points he is above it. In no other monologue is there such a range of casuistic argument. The vistas of *Fifine* are as shifting and kaleidoscopic as the seascapes introduced by way of illustration. The protagonists of the poem are often symbolic. As I have formerly written:

> Frequently in *Fifine*, the gypsy ceases to be a material
> woman and becomes representative of life itself, with
> its siren arts, confusing the soul through the dazzling

fence of sophistry pointed with truth and beguiling it into disloyalty to its own past.

Yet in *Fifine at the Fair,* as elsewhere in the casuistic monologues . . . , it is clear that the poet's intellectual agnosticism ensnares him. The general picture of life drawn in *Fifine* is not merely that of a sphere of being in which man's knowledge is relative and imperfect, but of a state in which truth is hidden from the mind, and basic elements of falsehood and illusion are engrained in the very faculty of human reason. What men deem to be the gold of knowledge is in reality but lacquered ignorance. It is impossible to escape the conviction, if such a point of view be accepted, that the mind of man must ever be haunted by casuistry, since it works with deceptive materials and its conclusions always fall wide of the truth.

It is noteworthy that in *Fifine at the Fair,* as in **"Bishop Blougram's Apology"** and other monologues, Browning invokes the testimony and assurance of love in order to rout casuistry. The defeat of knowledge forces him to turn elsewhere for an explanation of life's mystery. The heart is appealed to in order to controvert the evidence of the head.

> knowledge means
> Ever-renewed assurance by defeat
> That victory is somehow still to reach,
> But love is victory, the prize itself:
> Love—trust to!

In the Epilogue to *Fifine,* the final apostrophe to love has a peculiar depth and poignancy. It is linked with Browning's passionate conviction of the supremacy of love as revealed in the enduring tie between his own spirit and that of his wife. The waters of this monologue . . . have been troubled by the poet's brooding on what he regarded as a momentary lack of constancy to the memory of Mrs. Browning. But in the Epilogue, he leaves the dark house of sophistry where he has been lingering, and closes the most intellectually sceptical of his poems with the triumphant ejaculation put on the lips of his wife: " 'I end with—Love is all and Death is nought!' quoth She."

The general relation of Browning's philosophy of life to his casuistic monologues may now be summed up. The poet on his intellectual side—particularly in his later verse—has much of the temper of a casuist. This is due, as has been stressed, to his lack of faith in reason. Such an attitude is not purely individualistic. A distrust of knowledge is reflected in the writings of many of the great Victorian men of letters, and might almost be said to be inwrought in the spirit of the age. Yet on his emotional side, Browning is untroubled by the sophistries that beset the intellect. The intuitions of the heart are undimmed by the mists of falsehood and illusion darkening the mind. Hence love is the solvent of casuistry, since its perception of truth and contact with reality are instinctive and unerring. (pp. 662-66)

William O. Raymond, "Browning's Casuists," in Studies in Philology, Vol. XXXVII, No. 4, October, 1940, pp. 641-66.

F. E. L. PRIESTLEY   (essay date 1946)

[*Priestley provides a reading of "Bishop Blougram's Apology" that emphasizes Gigadib's role in shaping Blougram's comments. According to Priestley, the bishop does not always express his own beliefs in the monologue, often deliberately arguing from Gigadibs's skeptical premises in order to systematically expose their weaknesses.*]

[In general, the critics of **"Bishop Blougram's Apology"**] have paid too little attention to the significance of the title, and far too little attention to Gigadibs. The whole monologue is an *apology* in the sense of a piece of apologetics; its whole course is dictated by Gigadibs. In no other monologue of Browning's is the *muta persona* so important; in no other monologue is Browning so careful to keep us aware of the presence of the auditor. Every word of the Bishop's is uttered with a full understanding of the character of his guest, and of what his guest is thinking.

Consider for a moment who Gigadibs is, and why he is in the Bishop's presence. Gigadibs is a thirty year old journalist, ambitious for "success" (if his name means anything, success in terms of a gig and "dibs"). His contributions to *Blackwood's* have so far attracted no attention; his scholarly work, as yet unprinted, consists of "two points in Hamlet's soul unseized by the Germans yet"; his one success is an imitation of Dickens, a piece of sensational journalism with a second-hand literary flavour. His mind is that of the ordinary third-rate journalist; the Bishop calls him "You . . . the rough and ready man who write apace, Read somewhat seldom, think perhaps even less"; he is on the alert for the sensational, the dramatic antithesis, "the honest thief, the tender murderer, the superstitious atheist"; he needs simple labels, neat summary phrases, "man of sense and learning too, The able to think yet act, the this, the that," to embody these dramatic journalistic contrasts. Phrases, indeed, serve him instead of thought; he has never pursued thoughts far enough to reach solid ground; his opinions are "loose cards, Flung daily down, and not the same way twice."

In his own estimation, however, Gigadibs is no ordinary figure. He is an artist-soul, with the artist's nobility of aim and stern integrity; "clever to a fault"; proud of his scepticism, since to him unbelief is a sign of honest thinking; proud of his vague aspirations, of his insistence on being himself, "imperial, plain and true," proud of his rigid certainty that "truth is truth."

He has come to interview the Bishop with a purpose perfectly evident to Blougram from the start. To Gigadibs, it is a self-evident proposition that intelligence and religious faith are incompatible. Consequently, Blougram must be either an imbecile or a hypocrite, a fool or a knave. And he is obviously no fool. Gigadibs is confident that, if granted an interview, he, the shrewd journalist, the trained ferret, can surely penetrate the pretence, and expose the impostor; through his skilful questioning, Blougram can be led to make "The Eccentric Confidence," to admit, at least by implication, that "he's quite above their humbug in his heart." (pp. 139-40)

Gigadibs has arrived, has spoken his home truths, has challenged Blougram to say what he can for his way of life, assuming always that his own way of life is the only one compatible with truth, honesty, and a lofty morality. Blougram is far from ready to admit that his own is the vulnerable position. He is not defending, but attacking. He has no great hope of changing Gigadibs' prejudices; he can perhaps make him realize that even the Gigadibsian philosophy, beautiful as it is in its simplicity, is not uniquely coherent and reasonable. Being a skilled apologist, he recognizes the necessity for attacking on his opponent's ground; since Gigadibs would scornfully reject all the Bishop's premises, the arguments must proceed from premises acceptable to the sceptic. Throughout, Blougram uses the apologetic method, stating Gigadibs' objections fairly and strongly, then replying to them. The stages in the argument are quite clear in the Bishop's mind as he drives Gigadibs systematically from one position to another, at every point anticipating the movements of his hearer's thought.

The Bishop is so much master of the situation, so much superior to his opponent, that he permits himself flourishes, or scores a point with insulting ease. The whole performance is shot through with irony, and Blougram enjoys it. He enjoys particularly giving Gigadibs the impression that he is about to hear what he has come to hear. ("These hot long ceremonies of our church Cost us a little—oh, they pay the price, You take me—amply pay it!" Is this a bit of the "truth that peeps Over the glasses' edge?" Or does "price" hold two possible meanings?) Gigadibs' naive conviction that a few glasses of wine will lead an intelligent prelate into indiscreet utterance, and the sigh of the eager face across the table, waiting for the wine to work and the eccentric confidence to flow, offer Blougram tempting opportunities. He opens and closes the interview on the same theme: he begins by explaining, to Gigadibs' embarrassment, the sort of confidence Gigadibs expects, and ends by a challenge to Gigadibs to publish what he has learned. The full irony of the challenge is apparent only to those who stop to consider exactly what Gigadibs has learned in the course of the conversation. That will appear if we follow the conversation step by step.

As it opens, Blougram is examining Gigadibs' charges against him, his grounds for despising him. These are: first, that the Bishop's official position implies the possession of a religious faith which in Gigadibs' opinion is impossible to an intelligent man; and secondly, that the Bishop is less ascetic and otherworldly than a bishop, in Gigadibs' opinion, ought to be. If these charges were being made by a pious ascetic, they would be coherent; but they are proceeding from a sceptic and secularist, from one who denies the validity of the religious ideal and the utility of the ascetic ideal. Blougram at once proceeds to the attack. When Gigadibs condemns Blougram's way of life, what is his criterion? What is the ideal way of life by which he is measuring Blougram's? Gigadibs has not thought the matter out; he is sure only that he would like to be something distinguished (Blougram offers an anti-climactic trio of possibilities) and that the chief quality to be sought is integrity, which of course the Bishop lacks. Even as Pope, Blougram could not, thinks Gigadibs, realize the majestic ideal of being himself, "imperial, plain and true."

At this point, a less skilful apologist would have at once challenged Gigadibs' assumption of the unworthiness of the Bishop's way of life. But Blougram is patient and shrewd. The only approach to Gigadibs is through premises he will accept. By way of preliminary groundwork, then, the Bishop establishes the basic premise that a plan of life must relate to life as it is, not to an "abstract intellectual plan of life," but to the life "a man, who is man and nothing more, may lead." This is a premise which Gigadibs must accept. As a sceptic, he cannot admit other-worldly criteria; any admission that man is more than man, the natural being, makes his whole case against Blougram collapse. Measured by his own this-worldly criterion, then, is Gigadibs' plan of life superior to the Bishop's? If mundane values are the only ones we can accept, whose life is the better fitted to realize those values? This question, framed playfully in the "cabin" analogy, confronts Gigadibs at the outset with the basic problem of values, and tends to force him into a recognition of the inconsistency of his own axiology. If no other values than the simply material must guide our plan of life, then why is not the life of a bishop a choice one, since it brings the good things of this world (apart from any other good things)? Why will not Gigadibs be a bishop too?

Gigadibs' answer comes rapidly: he can't believe in any revelation called divine; that is, believe "fixedly And absolutely and exclusively. . . ."

[Before] considering the nature of faith, the Bishop proposes to start from Gigadibs' premise of the necessity of total unbelief ("I mean to meet you on your own premise") and examine its consequences.

Since they are both agreed that the primary concern of man is to find the fittest, most coherent way of life, Blougram raises the question, how can we make unbelief bear fruit to us? Gigadibs has challenged the utility of belief; now he must show the utility of unbelief. But first, again by way of applying Gigadibs' own logic to his argument, since he will not accept anything but complete and perfect belief, can he accept anything but complete and perfect unbelief? and how can he be certain of complete unbelief? This argument, combined perhaps with the warmth and evident sincerity of Blougram's assertion of the possibility of a divine purpose, leads Gigadibs to abandon his position of positive unbelief for the agnostic "chess-board."

Blougram is now ready for the next stage in the argument. "We'll proceed a step." The problem of belief or unbelief is not a simple matter of choice between equally tenable propositions of a theoretic nature. "Belief or unbelief Bears upon life, determines its whole course." Every act implies a faith; every effort a man makes implies faith in the value of what he strives for. The only consistent course for the thorough unbeliever is to keep his bed, to "abstain from healthy acts that prove you man." Even on the basis of material values, if Gigadibs wishes to exclude all other, the Bishop can show success in gaining the world's estimation, and its good things. If the sensitive artistic idealism of Gigadibs is repelled by the blunt way in which Blougram proclaims the goodness of worldly power and comforts, he must remember that consistent materialism admits only material values, naturalism only natural values, and draw his own conclusions. At this point he is ready to concede that "it's best believing if we may." He is next asked to concede, still on his own premises of unbelief, that "if once we choose belief, . . . We can't be too decisive in our faith . . . To suit the world which gives us the good things." Success in life (that is, in material terms of riches, honour, pleasure, work, repose) does not come to the indifferent; whatever a man chooses to pursue, we do not call him a fool "so long as he's consistent with his choice." The choice once made is irrevocable. Blougram's own choice, viewed (in accordance with the agreed premise of unbelief) from the merely material point of view, has given his life a singleness and continuity of purpose, and has brought the material returns. Gigadibs would object here that the Bishop's taste is gross; that were he made of "better elements" he would not call this sort of life successful. Again Blougram draws his attention to the logical inconsistency. Gigadibs is denying the validity of the ascetic ideal, and condemning the Bishop for not following it; he is proclaiming that the Bishop cannot be genuinely religious, yet blaming him for not being so. "Grant I'm a beast," says Blougram, "why, beasts must lead beasts' lives." Gigadibs is trying to have it both ways. Again the "cabin" is brought out to remind him that the discussion is concerned with living life as it is, not as it might be.

But the Bishop is by no means willing to grant that he is a beast; the patronizing assumption of moral superiority by Gi-

gadibs is not patently justified. Gigadibs feels himself nobler simply because he is thoroughly convinced that Blougram is fool or hypocrite, and that he "pines among his million imbeciles" uneasily conscious of the piercing eyes of the Gigadibsian experts. . . .

Why may not the simple truth be that Blougram actually believes what he professes to believe?

But even granted that Blougram's life is not one of which Gigadibs can approve, what is his ideal? The direct question disconcerts Gigadibs; it is one thing to be complacently aware of lofty, if vague, aspirations; to define them is another matter involving more rigorous thinking. The Bishop waits in vain, then offers suggestions. Suppose that Gigadibs aspires to be a Napoleon, a man of action, and granted that he has the requisite qualities ("A large concession, clever as you are," says Blougram), then, remembering that we are still accepting the Gigadibsian premise of unbelief ("We can't believe, you know— We're still at that admission, recollect!"), what guiding principle will justify the life? What possible admirable worldly end can explain such a career? "What's the vague good o' the world, for which you dare With comfort to yourself blow millions up?" If this life is all, Napoleon wins a "dozen noisy years" and "ugly thoughts," while if "doubt may be wrong— there's judgment, life to come!" On either basis, Napoleon's life offers no admirable pattern. If not the man of action, then perhaps the great artist offers an ideal. Should we try to be Shakespeares? What aims in life did Shakespeare pursue? On the material level, he sought the kind of comfort which has come much more abundantly to Blougram: "We want the same things, Shakespeare and myself, And what I want, I have." *If this life's all,* then Blougram beats Shakespeare. With this *reductio ad absurdum* the attack on Gigadibs' first premise, the assumption of unbelief, is closed. Gigadibs is forced to recognize something beyond this life and its purely temporal and material values.

The discussion can now be moved on to an important new stage. "Believe—and our whole argument breaks up." Gigadibs has been forced by argument from his own premises to abandon them and accept the one basic premise of Blougram's position. He has been brought to acknowledge the use of faith, and as Blougram says, "We're back on Christian ground." What remains now is to proceed from that premise to Blougram's conclusion. The procedure is clearly to examine the nature of faith. Both are now agreed that "enthusiasm's the best thing," that "fire and life Are all, dead matter's nothing," and that faith has power to "penetrate our life with such a gloss As fire lends wood and iron"; but fire in itself may be good or ill, enthusiasm may be well or ill directed. Moreover, how can we command it? "Paint a fire, it will not therefore burn." Gigadibs, having granted the value of enthusiasm, is inclined to restrict his approval to enthusiasm like Luther's, enthusiasm "on the denying side." But "ice makes no conflagration." Moreover, there is a limit to denying; after Luther comes Strauss, and once the denying has taught the world that it owes not a farthing (or a duty) to the Church or to St. Paul, what has been gained except the comfort (perhaps temporary) of him who denies? He may feel a Gigadibsian satisfaction at being himself, "imperial, plain and true," but the consequences of following the inner light of doubt may not be all good.

"But," objects Gigadibs, still convinced of the Bishop's secret scepticism, "imperfect faith is no more available to do faith's work than unbelief like mine. Whole faith, or none!" This is the objection Blougram has been waiting for, and, indeed, leading up to. It is time to attack Gigadibs' definition of faith, as he had promised to do earlier. ("Well, I do not believe— If you'll accept no faith that is not fixed, Absolute and exclusive, as you say. You're wrong—I mean to prove it in due time.") Faith is to be distinguished from empirical knowledge; "it is the idea, the feeling and the love, God means mankind should strive for and show forth Whatever be the process to that end." Faith is not solely an act of the intellect; it is a free act of will: "If you desire faith—then you've faith enough: What else seeks God—nay, what else seek ourselves?" "What matter though I doubt at every pore, Head-doubts, heart-doubts . . . If finally I have a life to show?" Gigadibs is demanding, not faith, but factual knowledge verifiable by the senses; like Thomas, he cannot believe until he has seen with his eyes and felt with his hands. (pp. 140-44)

If Gigadibs thinks that there have been times, or that there are places, in which belief as he defines it has ever prevailed, he is wrong. No intellectual acceptance of religious doctrines has ever been qualitatively the same as the acceptance of empirically observed experience. No "ragamuffin-saint Believes God watches him continually, As he believes in fire that it will burn, Or rain that it will drench him." The two sorts of knowledge, even as knowledge, are not alike, and can never be equally immediate. It is not part of the divine scheme that they should be so. "Some think, Creation's meant to show him forth: I say it's meant to hide him all it can. . . . Under a vertical sun, the exposed brain . . . less certainly would wither up at once Than mind, confronted with the truth of him."

It follows that the criteria to be applied to empirical knowledge are not applicable to the substance of faith. The demand to "decrassify" faith, to "experimentalize on sacred things," since it eventually means the rejection of all that cannot be empirically verified, must end in "Fichte's clever cut at God himself."

Gigadibs is still inclined to object to "leaving growths of lies unpruned," so Blougram again introduces the "cabin" analogy, to remind his hearer again that the Gigadibsian logic cannot be free to argue from diverse premises: the Bishop cannot be condemned for rejecting an empirical view of faith and in the same breath be condemned for accepting an empirical view of life. The "cabin" and the following "traveller" analogy, besides offering a logical objection, also put forward the characteristic Browning argument of the goodness and significance of this life. Whether this denial of asceticism is an important part of the Bishop's own belief does not, at this point, matter; it serves here to drive Gigadibs into asserting once and for all whether he recognizes absolute values. Presented with this clear-cut issue, Gigadibs meets it by maintaining the value of truth, and the necessity of acting up to it.

Now the attack can be pressed home: Gigadibs, who has accused the Bishop of failure to fit his life to his professed ideals, has now announced the transcendental rule by which *his* life is governed. Does he consistently live by the dictates of reason (as he would define reason) in search of truth (as he would define truth)? If he applies to natural religion the test he has used to demolish the revealed, what is left that checks his will? His behaviour is obviously not unrestrainedly amoral; upon what empirically rational grounds does he base his system of morality? Why is he chaste, for example? After all, he rejects the religious ideal of chastity, and as for a natural law, what authority can it preserve against the analysis of the anthropologist? Natural morality can show no more validity than super-

natural. Is Gigadibs chaste, then, from an instinctive feeling that self-restraint is good, and indulgence evil? If so, then his whole pretence of following "reason" breaks down with the introduction of an element which belongs not to his scheme of things, but to the Bishop's. Does he restrain himself from mere timid conformity to convention, because "your fellow-flock Open great eyes at you and even butt?" Conformity to convention can be justified on a utilitarian basis of weighing pleasures against pains, but what then becomes of the lofty pursuit of truth?

With this final challenge, Blougram has finished his argument. It is time to dismiss Gigadibs, and again the Bishop recalls why he has come. He is again aware of the ironic fact that the very worldly position which Gigadibs affects to despise him for valuing is all that makes him important in the journalist's eyes. The real lover of power, rank, luxury, and high worldly place is this same ambitious Gigadibs who is feeling so patronizingly superior. Once more the Bishop is moved to retaliate. Since it is power and social position that Gigadibs admires, it is only fitting to return his condescension with interest by reminding him of his own insignificance. The final insult is to offer the episcopal influence in the publishing world; the implications are that Gigadibs needs (or wants) the money, and that his writing is not good enough to be accepted on its own merits. The irony of the invitation to publish "The Outward-Bound" is effective and complicated. It carries a reminder of the journalist's insignificance, and it also draws attention to Gigadibs' original purpose of "exposing" the Bishop. He is now free to publish to the eager world the startling revelations that the Bishop, though not necessarily granting the good things of his world preeminence, does not despise them and actually enjoys good food, works of art, and a position of eminence; and that he, like most theologians, distinguishes between faith and knowledge, recognizing the activity of the will in belief. It would take more than the Dickens touch to give these revelations the sensational quality Gigadibs had anticipated. And so Gigadibs departs, still detesting Blougram perhaps, still eager to defame him, but at least not despising him as an opponent. There is a deliberate ambiguity, of course, in the Bishop's use of the word "despising."

Blougram, we are told, "believed, say, half he spoke." The rest was shaped "for argumentatory purposes." It should by now be evident enough which half Blougram believed. Quite clearly, the arguments from Gigadibsian premises are not, and are not intended to be, his own beliefs. The "arbitrary accidental thoughts That crossed his mind, amusing because new," are obviously the analogies of the "cabin" and the "traveller"; these are ingenious, are brought in more than once, and represent stages in the argument necessary for the attack on Gigadibs' assumptions. Blougram's own beliefs are indicated by the deeper tone, the heightened poetry of the expression in certain passages; they all deal with the affirmation of faith and the power of faith. His deeper religious thoughts and feelings he did not utter, partly because they are not readily expressed, partly because their expression would have meant nothing to Gigadibs. His purpose was not to make a fruitless exposition of his own point of view for the scoffer's benefit, but to show the scoffer upon what crumbling ground his scoffing rested. After Gigadibs has seen the shallowness of his own thinking, then he can start the process of trying to reach firmer ground ("So, let him sit with me this many a year!").

But Blougram has been more successful than he had expected. Gigadibs, seized with a "sudden healthy vehemence," renounces his ambitions of power and place, of literary eminence, and sails for Australia. He has presumably found an ideal, and is proposing to follow it. Moreover, he is, apparently, intent on the study of the Gospels. He has in fact turned away from precisely those things in Blougram's career which he formerly valued, and is seeking that which he formerly despised; he who doubted above all the possibility of the life of faith is now pursuing it. The victory, unexpected to be sure in its scope, is Blougram's. (pp. 145-47)

F. E. L. Priestley, "Blougram's Apologetics," in University of Toronto Quarterly, Vol. XV, No. 2, January, 1946, pp. 139-47.

WILLIAM C. DeVANE (essay date 1947)

[In the excerpt below, DeVane identifies the Perseus-Andromeda myth as an important element in Browning's life and work, tracing the mythic pattern in his relationship with Elizabeth Barrett Browning and in such works as The Ring and the Book and Parleyings with Certain People. For additional commentary by DeVane, see excerpt dated 1927.]

In Browning circles, the year 1946 was one of jubilation. There were ceremonies in London and Florence, abroad, and at home the autumnal but vigorous Browning Societies of such cultural centers as Boston, New York, and Los Angeles were in high celebration, for on September 12, one hundred years ago, Robert Browning, the poet, snatched Elizabeth Barrett, considerably more renowned than himself in her day, from her parental home in Wimpole Street, married her before a handful of witnesses in Marylebone Church, and carried her off to the sun-drenched shores of Italy. (p. 33)

The episode . . . catches neatly in its totality the character of the hero of the affair, "that infinitely respectable rebel," Robert Browning. It was an event that could have happened in quite the way it did only in the benign and domestic reign of Queen Victoria. A half century earlier, a Shelley or a Byron would have dispensed with the services of the church and the clergy, and a century later the romance would probably have been the fifth or sixth on each side. But here was a marriage made in heaven, or as we say colloquially, "for keeps." The success of the marriage has become proverbial, a legend to posterity. That Browning was at all times conscious of the full implications of his deed, and had in prophetic fashion anticipated and shaped the event itself will be seen from what follows. My present comments fall into three parts, which might be called anticipations of romance, the reality of marriage, and the afterglow of romance.

It ought to be clearly understood that Browning was ready for his moment when it came to him in his thirty-fifth year. He had long dreamed how the event should happen, and had constructed or found a private myth by which the event was to be controlled and shaped. Browning's private myth is a singularly revealing one, reflecting perfectly his romantic, dramatic, and strong-minded character. This myth was the legend of Andromeda. (pp. 33-4)

Readers of Browning's letters and biography will remember that the young poet always wrote at a desk over which there hung a copy of Caravaggio's picture of Andromeda, "the perfect picture," as he called it. As he wrote his first poem,

Pauline, in the winter of 1832-33, he glanced up at the picture, and recorded what he saw in verse:

Andromeda!
And she is with me: years roll, I shall change,
But change can touch her not—so beautiful
With her fixed eyes, earnest and still, and hair
Lifted and spread by the salt-sweeping breeze,
And one red beam, all the storm leaves in heaven,
Resting upon her eyes and hair, such hair,
As she awaits the snake on the wet beach
By the dark rock and the white wave just breaking
At her feet; quite naked and alone; a thing
I doubt not, nor fear for, secure some god
To save will come in thunder from the stars.

The years rolled, but Browning did not change as much as he imagined he would. Two years before the end of his career, that is, in 1887, in the **"Parleying with Francis Furini,"** he employed for the last time the myth of Andromeda. . . . The emphasis in the [**"Parleying with Francis Furini"**] is upon the nakedness of Andromeda and the goodness of the flesh, but the setting is the same; the blackness, with the single beam of light, the sea and the wind. A little further in the poem the myth of Andromeda is applied differently; this time Andromeda represents Browning's own faith, standing precariously upon the rock of consciousness amidst the growing darkness of the sky and the waters waste and wild, and awaiting destruction from the monsters of new scientific thought, or rescue from heaven.

Early and late, then, Browning uses the Andromeda myth to express his faith. But these brackets must by no means be thought to be empty. In one form or another, the Andromeda pattern may be traced all through the poet's life and works. In the Forties, Count Gismond was the Perseus to rescue the maligned lady of the romance; the ancient Gipsy rescued the Duchess in **"The Flight of the Duchess;"** in **"My Last Duchess"** no god came to the rescue of outraged innocence. That was an exception, and the lady of **"The Glove"** fared better in spite of the established story to the contrary. But Browning had good reason to make the Perseus of this latter story attractive and young, for the poem was written in 1845 under the eye of Miss Barrett. It was a short step from writing these things and thinking habitually in these terms, to performing them in actual life, so we are not surprised when in 1846 Browning plays the part of Perseus to Miss Barrett's Andromeda, with only the part of the dragon left over for the unfortunate and misunderstood Mr. Barrett. Such a stroke as that might well confirm a man's belief in his role for life. In Browning's Italian days, the Perseus-Andromeda pattern finds a more subtle expression—all the obvious rescues have been accomplished—but after Mrs. Browning's death, the pattern becomes prominent again in retrospect. This is especially true in *The Ring and the Book,* where Browning is striving to build his masterpiece on a huge scale, and to make it a masterpiece peculiarly his own. Here we see Pompilia-Mrs. Browning-Andromeda rescued from the dragon Guido by Caponsacchi-Browning-Perseus, first; and later when truth or justice is endangered, Pope Innocent, the Vicegerent of God, is the rescuer.

But this is to anticipate those middle years of Browning's life, mainly spent in Italy, when his romance turned into the reality of marriage. The fine poetic flowering of these years is given to us in *Men and Women,* published in 1855, nine years after his marriage and his flight to Italy, and it is the thinking and feeling of those two superb volumes that I wish to examine at this point. For it is in *Men and Women* that Browning ceases to be the romantic young man, and turns his heart and intelligence to the scrutiny of the relationship in marriage of man to woman and woman to man. Here the poet is not the romantic dreamer, but the observer and the recorder, and assuredly the moralist. (pp. 35-7)

[As Browning] walked about Florence he thought of many things—of the kind of poetry he could write, and only he; of the great artists of earlier times, the musicians and painters, and their relations to their women, of the true function of the poet, and, above all, of the intimate relation between man and woman in the blessed state of matrimony. There was no rebellion towards his wife in him, but rather a profound gratitude and wonder at his own good fortune. In the poem **"By the Fireside,"** he watched her as she sat

> Reading by fire-light, that great brow
> And the spirit-small hand propping it. . . .

And to himself he said:

> . . . If I tread
> This path back, is it not in pride
> To think how little I dreamed it led
> To an age so blest that, by its side,
> Youth seems the waste instead?

For art's sake, the poet transfers the perfect meeting of lovers' spirits in this poem to a forest scene, high in the Apennines. It really just took place in London's dreary Wimpole Street. For that high rare communion of hearts he is everlastingly grateful—

> You might have turned and tried a man,
>   Set him a space to weary and wear,
> And prove which suited more your plan,
>   His best of hope or his worst despair,
> Yet end as he began.
>
> But you spared me this, like the heart you are,
>   And filled my empty heart at a word.
> If two lines join, there is oft a scar,
>   They are one and one, with a shadowy third;
> One near one is too far.
>
> A moment after, and hands unseen
>   Were hanging the night around as fast;
> But we knew that a bar was broken between
>   Life and life: we were mixed at last
> In spite of the mortal screen.
>
> The forests had done it; there they stood;
>   We caught for a moment the powers at play:
> They had mingled us so, for once and good,
>   Their work was done—we might go or stay,
> They relapsed to their ancient mood.

(pp. 38-9)

[This is but one of the] poems in *Men and Women*, volumes which give us the anatomy of married love. Look for a moment at the titles of the poems: **"Love among the Ruins," "A Lovers' Quarrel," "A Woman's Last Word," "Any Wife to Any Husband," "A Serenade at the Villa," "The Statue and the Bust," "Love in a Life," "Life in a Love," "The Last Ride Together," "Andrea del Sarto," "In Three Days," "In a Year," "Women and Roses," "The Guardian Angel," "One Way of Love," "Another Way of Love," "Misconceptions," "One Word More."** . . . Not since John Donne had any such intimate revelation of married love been given us. In the full scope we see love triumphant, and love rejected; love eager and young, and love satiated; love a strong support, and love betrayed; love making heroes of men, and love enslaving and corrupting them. The poet's theme is love in all its guises. If

at one end of the human scale, love is a foretaste of heaven, at the other end it can be a foretaste of hell. From the whole we gradually ascertain the unforgivable sin against love—the sin that is committed by the lovers of the **"Statue and the Bust."** For those lovers, profoundly committed in their hearts to their love for each other, never dare to take the illicit step which would unite them. Indecision, respect for convention, and cowardice are the qualities of their failure. . . . These lovers are really lost souls:

> So! While these wait the trump of doom,
> How do their spirits pass, I wonder,
> Nights and days in the narrow room?
>
> Still, I suppose, they sit and ponder
> What a gift life was, ages ago,
> Six steps out of the chapel yonder.
>
> Only they see not God, I know,
> Nor all that chivalry of his,
> The soldier-saints who, row on row,
>
> Burn upward each to his point of bliss—

(pp. 40-1)

The golden time of Browning's life and genius comes to an end in 1861, for in that year Mrs. Browning died. From that time to the end of his life, his comments upon love are the remembrance of things past. We now enter his third phase in these matters, and it is a phase in which he reverts to his first or Andromeda phase, with experience and memory added. Earlier in this essay I mentioned the large pattern of *The Ring and the Book*, of 1868, where Browning attempted to build his masterpiece on an epic scale, and to make it a work in technique and substance peculiarly his own. In *The Ring and the Book*, we see Pompilia rescued from the dragon Guido by Caponsacchi in the first instance; and later when truth or ultimate justice is endangered, Pope Innocent comes to save it.

But to point to these large patterns in *The Ring and the Book* is to give the barest indication of the manner in which the myth of Andromeda (with which Mrs. Browning is now completely identified) has penetrated and shaped the conscious thinking and the deeper unconscious feeling in the poet's greatest single achievement. I wish now to look at the prevalence, or rather the all-pervasiveness, of the Andromeda legend through certain books of *The Ring and the Book*—including with the Andromeda myth its Christian cognate, the legend of St. George and the dragon. In those books of *The Ring and the Book* where the speakers give favorable judgments upon Pompilia and Caponsacchi, I have counted at least thirty references to the Andromeda and its cognate myth, not counting such facts as this— that Browning, for all his accuracy and care in consulting the Astronomer Royal upon the condition of the moon on the night of Pompilia's flight, April 29-30, 1697, at the last moment changed the date, but not the moon, so that the flight would fall on April 23, St. George's Day. By the light or cynical speakers in *The Ring and the Book*, the flight of Pompilia and Caponsacchi is usually referred to in the terms of the story of Helen and Paris, "De Raptu Helenae"; and Guido's pursuit is likened humorously to Vulcan pursuing Mars to get back his Venus. But it is not too much to say that whenever Browning is representing, favorably to Pompilia and Caponsacchi—and that is a great deal of the time—the great scene at the inn at Castelnuovo where the real conflict between the opposing forces takes place, he habitually and consistently thinks of it in the terms of the Andromeda situation, with Caponsacchi as Perseus, Pompilia as the manacled victim, and Guido as the dragon. Moreover, the scene is generally set as nearly as possible with the colors he imagined in the Andromeda scene. Caponsacchi thus pictures Pompilia in that moment at the inn:

> She started up, stood erect, face to face
> With the husband: back he fell, was buttressed there
> By the window all aflame with morning-red,
> He the black figure, the opprobrious blur
> Against all peace and joy and light and life.

And Pompilia speaking of the same scene describes Guido as "the serpent towering and triumphant." When the Pope thinks of Pompilia in the clutches of Guido, he uses a figure appropriate to Andromeda's plight:

> Such denizens o' the cave now cluster round
> And heat the furnace sevenfold: time indeed
> A bolt from heaven should cleave roof and clear place,
> Transfix and show the world, suspiring flame,
> The main offender, scar and brand the rest
> Hurrying, each miscreant to his hole: then flood
> And purify the scene with outside day—
> Which yet, in the absolutest drench of dark,
> Ne'er wants a witness, some stray beauty-beam
> To the despair of hell.

When Browning himself describes the same situation—Pompilia in the power of Guido and his family—he says:

>   . . . these I saw,
> In recrudescency of baffled hate,
> Prepare to wring the uttermost revenge
> From body and soul thus left them: all was sure,
> Fire laid and cauldron set, the obscene ring traced,
> The victim stripped and prostrate: what of God?
> The cleaving of a cloud, a cry, a crash,
> Quenched lay their cauldron, cowered i' the dust the crew,
> As, in a glory of armour like Saint George,
> Out again sprang the young good beauteous priest
> Bearing away the lady in his arms. . . .

Indeed, so steadily is the Perseus-St. George legend used in *The Ring and the Book* that we may know what to think of each speaker by the treatment he accords the myth, and by what version of the myth he employs. The speaker in "The Other Half-Rome," favorable to Pompilia, gives the legend a Christian character, but he only faintly realizes his figure. When he has sketched the miraculous rescue of Pompilia by Caponsacchi, he turns upon his auditor:

> How do you say? It were improbable;
> So is the legend of my patron-saint.

In Caponsacchi's monologue the scene of Andromeda's distress before the rescuer comes is set again and again—in the box at the theatre with Guido lurking in the background, and in the window of her house, for example—and always in the same terms of darkness and light. Of course, Caponsacchi was only a partially effective Perseus or St. George, and being modest, cannot refer to himself in such terms, except ironically, as he does here when he is addressing the judges:

> I rise in your esteem, sagacious Sirs,
> Stand up a renderer of reasons, not
> The officious priest would personate Saint George
> For a mock Princess in undragoned days.

But there is nothing, or very little, to keep Pompilia in her monologue from speaking of Caponsacchi as Perseus or St. George, and she constantly refers to him as such. One of the legends in the tapestries in her house, she recalls, had as its subject "the slim young man with wings at head, and wings at feet, and sword threatening a monster." And, of course, though she cannot call herself Andromeda, she constantly rec-

ognizes herself in the role of the helpless and innocent victim, and Caponsacchi as the heaven-sent rescuer.

The characters of evil import in *The Ring and the Book* use the same essential myth, but use it in a debased form or for a base purpose. Thus Guido uses it when in his defense he gives an account of one of his ancestors who met death in the region where Perseus and St. George had performed their exploits:

> One of us Franceschini fell long since
> I' the Holy Land, betrayed, tradition runs,
> To Paynims by the feigning of a girl
> He rushed to free from ravisher, and found
> Lay safe enough with friends in ambuscade
> Who flayed him while she clapped her hands and laughed:
> Let me end, falling by a like device.

The keen intelligence of Guido sees the matter clearly, whatever he may make of it, but the dim mind of Bottinius, the lawyer for Pompilia's cause, can only arrive at this approximation of the Andromeda myth in his defense of Pompilia's conduct in arranging for her flight:

> Methinks I view some ancient bas-relief.
> There stands Hesione thrust out by Troy,
> Her father's hand has chained her to a crag,
> Her mother's from the virgin plucked the vest,
> At a safe distance both distressful watch,
> While near and nearer comes the snorting orc.
> I look that, white and perfect to the end,
> She wait till Jove despatch some demigod;
> Not that,—impatient of celestial club
> Alcmena's son should brandish at the beast,—
> She daub, disguise her dainty limbs with pitch,
> And so elude the purblind monster! Ay,
> The trick succeeds, but 'tis an ugly trick,
> Where needs have been no trick! . . .
> Trick, I maintain, had no alternative.
> The heavens were bound with brass,—Jove far at feast . . .
> With the unblamed Aethiop,—Hercules spun wool
> I' the lap of Omphale, while Virtue shrieked—
> The brute came paddling all the faster. You
> Of Troy, who stood at distance, where's the aid
> You offered in the extremity? . . .
>   He,
> He only, Caponsacchi 'mid a crowd,
> Caught Virtue up, carried Pompilia off. . . .
>   . . . what you take for pitch
> Is nothing worse, belike, than black and blue,
> Mere evanescent proof that hardy hands
> Did yeoman's service, cared not where the gripe
> Was more than duly energetic . . .

All this is sufficiently far from that other admirer of Euripides who thought in his youth that "if Virtue feeble were, Heaven itself would stoop to her," but it is characteristic of Browning and will serve. It must not be imagined that Browning dropped the Perseus-Andromeda conception of life after *The Ring and the Book*. Perhaps the most direct and poignant use of the theme of rescue in all the poet's writings occurs in *Balaustion's Adventure*, two years later, where Browning gives us a transcript of Euripides' *Alcestis*. There, it will be remembered, Heracles rescues the lady from death itself. Both overtly and covertly the poem is bound to the memory of the poet's dead wife. But this is only one instance among a dozen. In the **"Parleying with Francis Furini"** at the end of his life, as we have seen, Browning made another frank avowal of his myth, and utilized it this time as an explanation of his religious faith. How closely Mrs. Browning had become a part of that total faith one may easily see.

By the time that Browning was writing his **"Parleying with Francis Furini,"** in 1887, the bright world of his youth had taken on a sombre hue. In the death of Mrs. Browning he had suffered an irreparable loss, and after 1861, for all his dining out and being lionized, he was often a lonely man. In the realm of his faith, too, the shocks had come. The fierce assaults of the Higher Criticism upon the literal authority of the Bible had undermined and doomed the evangelical position in which Browning had been bred. Science, moreover, had shaken his faith in his dearly loved doctrine of progress, or at least had changed that conception from the triumphal march of an earlier notion to the long, slow evolution of man with many setbacks and retrogressions. Economically and industrially, too, the lines of the graph no longer strained to the upper right-hand corner. There was distress in imperial England, and there were wars and rumors of wars in the air. There was not much to comfort the serious observer in 1887. The bright morning of the Forties had turned into an ominous twilight.

The murky atmosphere of this later time is faithfully reflected in Browning's last use of the Andromeda myth. In the **"Parleying with Francis Furini"** the maiden is once more chained to the rock amidst the dark waters. Here in the dusk she symbolizes the poet's faith in the destiny of man and the providence of God. There is an air of desperation in the scene, for as yet no God has come in thunder from the stars to effect a rescue, and the sea beast comes apace.

And Elizabeth Barrett Browning, dead now for twenty-six years, has become

> Perhaps but a memory, after all!
> —Of what came once when a woman leant
> To feel for my brow where her kiss might fall.
>
> (pp. 41-6)

> *William C. DeVane, "The Virgin and the Dragon," in* The Yale Review, *Vol. XXXVII, No. 1, September, 1947, pp. 33-46.*

E. D. H. JOHNSON   (essay date 1952)

[Johnson portrays Browning as a thoroughgoing intuitionist whose rejection of rationalism led him to oppose conventional values in such areas as religion, love, and art.]

By his constant advocacy of intuitive over rational knowledge, Browning took over the anti-intellectualism of the Romantics and pushed it in the direction of pure primitivism. Along with Carlyle, although much more subtly, Browning endorsed the unconscious as the true wellspring of being. Pippa is only the first of a long line of innocents, including, to name only a few, the duke's last duchess, the maligned lady of **"Count Gismond,"** Brother Lawrance, the Pied Piper, and the resurrected Lazarus of **"An Epistle of Karshish."** In Browning's world, the prophets and artists, the lovers and doers of great deeds are never primarily remarkable for intellectual power. Their supremacy is the result of a genius for experiencing life intuitively. They possess a phenomenal capacity for passionate emotion, combined with a childlike reliance on instinct. These qualities put them in conflict with conventionalized modes of social conduct. Whether it be Fra Lippo, or Rabbi Ben Ezra, or David in **"Saul,"** or the Grammarian, or Childe Roland, Browning's heroes are always the children of their intuitions.

In their capacity for instinctive action Browning's heroes are akin to Tennyson's visionaries. The moments of recognition come to both in the same mysterious and unpredictable ways.

Thus, Childe Roland, reaching his journey's end, knows in a blinding flash what is expected of him. Abt Vogler and David improvise their rhapsodies in states of trance-like exaltation. More especially, true love is love at first sight. Such instantaneous perceptions of elective affinity occur, among other poems, in **"Count Gismond," "Christina," "The Statue and the Bust," "Evelyn Hope."**

His belief that the intuitions operate through the instrumentality of the emotions rather than the intellect led Browning to a frank

Browning in 1889.

celebration of man's physical nature, very foreign to Victorian reticence in such matters. Remembering the Prior's pretty niece, Fra Lippo says: "If you get simple beauty and nought else, You get about the best thing God invents." Such an admission is unthinkable in Tennyson, for whom the essential philosophic problem was to league mind and spirit into effective opposition against the bodily appetites. To Browning, on the other hand, flesh and the spirit seemed natural allies against the insidious distortions of the intellect. So Fra Lippo in his defense of the street-urchin's apprenticeship to life exclaims: "Why, soul and sense of him grow sharp alike." Browning's constant assertion of the soul's interrelationship with the body on an instinctual plane permits him to make claims of the latter which would not otherwise have been admissible. Indeed, two of the most forthright statements that fleshly and spiritual well-being are bound up together come from the mouths of holy men. The Apostle John in **"A Death in the Desert"** says:

> But see the double way wherein we are led,
> How the soul learns diversely from the flesh!
> With flesh, that hath so little time to stay,
> And yields mere basement for the soul's emprise,
> Expect prompt teaching.

And in the words of Rabbi Ben Ezra:

> Let us not always say
> "Spite of this flesh today
> I strove, made head, gained ground upon the whole!"
> As the bird wings and sings,
> Let us cry "All good things
> Are ours, nor soul helps flesh more, now, than flesh helps soul!"

The vitalism inherent in Browning's emphasis on man's intuitive as opposed to his ratiocinative faculties further explains the poet's acceptance of the real and demonstrable, and, conversely, his distrust of make-believe. The characters in his poems whom we are asked to admire are all exceptionally clear-sighted in their confrontation of actuality. They see through the false shows at which society connives, preferring to meet life on its own terms rather than to indulge in fanciful self-delusion. Although Browning's lovers are usually unhappy, there is never any question of escape into a Tennysonian dream world. In his hopeless predicament the lover of **"In a Gondola"** three times falls to imagining ideal situations which would allow his mistress and himself to be together, and as often rejects the wish for the fact:

> Rescue me thou, the only real!
> And scare away this mad ideal
> That came, nor motions to depart!
> Thanks! Now, stay ever as thou art!

Finally, worldly criteria for success lose their validity in Browning's poetry. The poet's so-called philosophy of imperfection, with its lesson that "a man's reach should exceed his grasp," has anti-social implications. This belief holds that an individual's first and highest obligation is to fulfill his own being regardless of consequences. A lifetime of devotion to settling "*Hoti's* business," properly basing *Oun*, and providing "us the doctrine of the enclitic *De*" entitles the grammarian to a final resting-place on the heights. . . . And Childe Roland's ultimate intuition is that success in his quest means just to die bravely.

Once the intuitional psychology at the heart of Browning's thinking is fully understood, all the major thematic concerns in his poetry become meaningful as deriving therefrom. Among Victorian poets he is the great champion of individualism. If self-realization is the purpose of life, then it follows that any agency which thwarts that process is inimical to the best interests of human nature. And since formalized systems of thought operating through social institutions have always tended to repress freedom of belief and action, Browning's most characteristic poems have to do with the conflict between the individual and his environment. There is a wisdom of the mind and a wisdom of the heart; and the two are always at odd, since the one teaches compliance with the ways of the world while the other inculcates non-conformity. Thus, where his political and religious convictions or his beliefs about love and art are concerned, each man must make a choice between intellectual subservience to customary values and emancipation from all such restrictions.

In insisting on the integrity of the individual soul, Browning allies himself on one side with the Romantic poets, and on the other with the Pre-Raphaelites. He differs from both, however, in his concept of the artist's responsibilities. Whereas Byron delivered frontal assaults on contemporary manners and morals and Rossetti inclined to ignore his milieu, Browning adopted an oblique approach to his age. By dramatizing individual case histories, he stepped before his readers in such a variety of poetic guises that it was impossible to identify him with any single role. Furthermore, since he made his attacks piecemeal through anatomizing characters each of whom embodied but a single aspect of contemporary thought, he could be sure of enlisting on his side all those who did not share this particular foible, and so of forestalling unified opposition. It is only when the widely diversified types in Browning's catalogue are grouped according to family resemblance that one begins to comprehend the scope and consistency of the poet's opposition to existing values, and hence the extent of his alienation from Victorian society. (pp. 92-6)

Browning's most forcible condemnations of rationalism . . . come in those poems which deal with the problems of religious belief. In *Christmas-Eve and Easter-Day,* the poet had worked out the grounds of his own highly individualistic faith. It sprang from a purely intuitive conviction of the necessity for a loving God. **"Saul"** and **"Rabbi Ben Ezra"** give full expression to this religious optimism; but the modern reader may well take greater interest in those works which dramatize alternative positions and show the poet dealing with the sceptical tendencies in contemporary thought. Among the best things to be found in *Men and Women* and *Dramatis Personae* is a series of monologues surveying the principal intellectual traditions which have militated against the Christian revelation.

A uniform tone of nostalgia pervades **"An Epistle, containing the Strange Medical Experience of Karish, the Arab Physician;" "Cleon"**; and **"Caliban upon Setebos; or, Natural Theology in the Island."** The speaker in each poem, instinctively realizing the spiritual limitations of the system of thought to which he is committed, is driven against his will to postulate a Christian deity. Yet wistful longing never actualizes itself in terms of faith, because it is smothered under the weight of inherited prejudice. Karshish stands for the scientific mentality wholly at a loss to cope with the mystery of Lazarus' resurrection. Cleon, living in the end of the Hellenistic era, finds such meager consolation as he can in the synthesizing temper of a decadent culture. In the superficial view Caliban appears to belong among Browning's primitives; actually he is man materialized to the point where he can only construct God in his own capricious and spiteful image. The historical or literary guise under which these issues are presented suggests the devious operation of Browning's critical intent. The poet was not really interested in the historical process, as Carlyle or Ruskin tried to be; nor did he have Tennyson's genius for reanimating myth. Karshish, Cleon, and Caliban are representative Victorians in fancy dress. As time passed, Browning inclined more and more to put aside the cloak of historical remoteness and to address himself to the psychoanalysis of contemporary types. **"Bishop Blougram's Apology"** and **"Mr. Sludge, 'The Medium,'"** for example, bring the charge of spiritual sterility directly home to Victorian society. (pp. 97-8)

Browning's intuitionism announces itself most ardently when he writes about love, this being a subject which he handles with greater candor and penetration than any other poet of the early and mid-Victorian periods. It is not hard to understand why he should have thought the experience of love so important. Through the emotions which it releases man reaches heights of intensity, both physical and spiritual, such as are achievable in no other way. Romantic love, however, is little subject to discipline; and the Victorians in their regard for social stability endeavored to safeguard themselves against its disruptive power behind an elaborate system of conventions. A double standard of conduct was in force for the sexes, and the family stood as the central support of the entire social fabric. To the authority of these ideals Tennyson's poetry bears constant testimony. Browning, on the other hand, challenges the sexual morality of the Victorians at nearly every point. His interest is in the fulfillment of passion, rather than in the preservation of domestic proprieties. In no way are his convictions less conformable to accepted theories than in his refusal to recognize any basis for social inequality between men and women. His adoration of Elizabeth Barrett no doubt explains a good deal in this connection; but while Browning yielded to no other Victorian in his idealization of womanhood, his thinking had very little in common with the contemporary concept of the womanly woman. Only Meredith's heroines challenge Browning's in the qualities of fortitude, loyalty, idealism, intelligence, and insight. The Euripides of [*Aristophanes' Apology*] is speaking for his creator when he says: "Mere puppets, once, I now make womankind, / For thinking, saying, doing, match the male." Browning, like Meredith, finds that the woman is usually right. With a few exceptions, his love lyrics fall into two classes. In the first the speaker is a man who has been rejected and who humbly accepts responsibility for failure, attributing it to some inadequacy in his own nature. In the second it is the woman who has been cast off. She too is humble; but we are made to feel that she suffers not because of any innate unworthiness, but rather because of some flaw in her lover. (pp. 100-01)

Browning holds that undue reliance on the intellect with its ulterior motivations makes for failure in affairs of the heart. The feminine nature is wiser than the masculine in its instinctive response to emotional impulse. In a number of poems love is destroyed through the man's determination to establish his mental superiority over the woman. This is the theme of **"Mesmerism,"** for example, as well as of **"A Woman's Last Word."** . . . Since in the poet's thinking the intellectual faculties are self-corrupting and prone to infection by the uses of the world, another group of poems, written from the female point of view, lays blame for the man's infidelity on the temptations held out by society. Examples in this vein are **"Any Wife to Any Husband,"** and the group of highly sophisticated lyrics, **"James Lee's Wife."** (pp. 102-03)

Browning's conviction that the passionate intensity of romantic love is incompatible with conventionalized social morality leads him to glorify the one at the expense of the other. That perennial theme, the world well lost for love, is so appealing that Victorian readers in their sentimentality were apparently willing to overlook its frequent anti-social corollary in Browning's poetry, where the decision to give all for love more often than not involves some course of action at variance with established codes of conduct. Too extreme, perhaps, is the example of **"Porphyria's Lover"** where the demented narrator has committed murder and in this way made the final choice for a mistress.

> Too weak, for all her heart's endeavour,
> To set its struggling passion free
> 　　From pride, and vainer ties dissever,
> And give herself to me for ever.

In **"The Flight of the Duchess,"** however, we are compelled to sympathize with the duchess in her flight from the staidly formalistic home of her husband to join the gypsies; and the prevaricating speaker in **"Too Late"** seems most manly when he reconstructs the lost opportunity to take his beloved away from her husband, by force if necessary. **"In a Gondola"** presents a more fatal but equally persuasive picture of adultery as the solution to loveless marriage. And the inescapable implication of **"Respectability"** is that the illicit affair there described has gained its intensity and seriousness from being carried on outside the pale of social conventions. . . . (pp. 103-04)

If we turn now to Browning's aesthetics, it is immediately apparent from such poems as **"Youth and Art"** and **"The Statue and the Bust"** that for this poet art could never supplant life. No position is more consistently maintained throughout his writing than the one deriving from the assumption that all enduring artistic expression is incidental to the experience which inspires it. Poems otherwise so different as **"The Last Ride Together," "In a Balcony," "Cleon," "Old Pictures in Florence," "Transcendentalism: A Poem in Twelve Books" "James Lee's Wife,"** and **"One Word More"** reiterate the author's vitalism. Art exists simply as one form of creative endeavor to educe life's meaning. The test of an artist's genius lies in his ability to move his audience to action. The Pied Piper, Fra Lippo Lippi, and the David of **"Saul"** have this faculty in common. The rats and children of Hamelin Town jubilantly follow wherever the piper's music leads. Fra Lippo is going to have to repaint his fresco of St. Laurence at Prato since the faithful are obliterating its details in their devout rage. The mounting ecstasy of David's song lifts from Saul's spirit the gloom which has incapacitated him.

On first glance, Browning's artistic theories seem to accord fully with his age in its endorsement of the Ruskinian arguments that the highest art results from the perception of moral truth and promotes virtuous conduct. The poet's application of these propositions, however, is again suggestive of a double awareness. Just as the religious or political man must take a stand with regard to institutionalism and the lover with regard to conventional morality, so the artist is threatened by the tyranny of tradition. As it impinges on the life of the imagination, traditionalism has a dual authority. Its influence may be largely intellectual, regimenting instinct to a lifeless formalism. This way leads to art for art's sake. Or, in its more popular aspect, tradition may inform the artist's desire to communicate and so make of him a virtuoso. Whether he inhabit an ivory tower or the market place, the artist who subordinates his native talent to traditional modes has, in Browning's opinion, betrayed his birthright. (pp. 109-10)

In *An Essay on Shelley,* written in 1852 to preface a spurious collection of that poet's letters, Browning distinguished between two kinds of objective poet or "fashioner." Concerning the creative impulse of the first kind, the question to be asked is: "Did a soul's delight in its own extended sphere of vision set it, for the gratification of an insuppressible power, on labor, as other men are set on rest?" For the second class, the question is rephrased as follows: "Or did a sense of duty or of love lead it to communicate its own sensations to mankind? Did an irresistible sympathy with men compel it to bring down and suit its own provision of knowledge and beauty to their narrow scope?" **"Pictor Ignotus"** and **"Andrea del Sarto"** seem to exemplify the corrupt extremes of these two types. The unknown painter has become the morbidly self-conscious victim of his "soul's delight in its own extended sphere of vision," while Andrea in his desire to communicate has sacrificed originality and compelled his talent "to bring down and suit its own provision of knowledge and beauty" to the "narrow scope" of a vulgar audience. *An Essay on Shelley,* however, goes on to propose another kind of poet whose response to experience is primarily subjective. This is the seer, described by Browning as follows:

> He, gifted like the objective poet with the fuller perception of nature and man, is impelled to embody the thing he perceives not so much with reference to the many below as to the one above him, the supreme. Intelligence which apprehends all things in their absolute truth,—an ultimate view ever aspired to, if but partially attained, by the poet's own soul. . . . Not with the combination of humanity in action, but with the primal elements of humanity, he has to do; and he digs where he stands,—preferring to seek them in his own soul as the nearest reflex of the absolute Mind, according to the intuitions of which he desires to perceive and speak. . . . He is rather a seer, accordingly, than a fashioner, and what he produces will be less a work than an effluence.
>
> (pp. 112-13)

[The general tone of Browning's] remarks strongly suggests that in his concept of the seer he was proposing a higher orientation for the poetic impulse than would result from conforming to the demands either of the individual ego or of society at large. And certainly in Browning's own poetry devoted to the arts and their practice it is the seer who emerges as the supreme type of artist, embodying in transmuted form the two aspects of the fashioner and merging them under the authority of a transcendent vision adequate to the opposing impulses which inhere in a double awareness.

Although *Christmas-Eve and Easter-Day* is largely a defense of Browning's particular brand of Christianity, the philosophic implications of religion and art were so closely allied in his thinking that the poem is also a declaration of his aesthetic creed. **"Christmas-Eve"** considers among other things the discrepancy between the ideal and the actual in this life—all that is signified by Abt Vogler's statement: "On earth the broken arcs; in heaven, a perfect round." The ideal, as it exists in God, is unattainable on earth; but this knowledge does not exonerate humanity from attempting the impossible; for in the effort lies the hope of spiritual salvation. Hence Andrea del Sarto's saddened perception: "Ah, but a man's reach should exceed his grasp, Or what's a heaven for?" The artist, endowed with special intuitions, is better equipped than other men to apprehend the spirit world. His senses are more keenly responsive to beauty and his mind probes deeper into the laws of cause and effect; but the faculty on which before all others

he relies is imaginative insight. Possession of this attribute to an unequalled degree made Shakespeare a poet apart. But, as Browning proceeds to expound in **"Easter-Day,"** the artist's unique gifts impose on him the highest possible responsibility. Perceiving the divine plan, he must place his genius at God's disposal. Thus, although the creative impulse has its source within the individual consciousness, its operation must not be expended on self-expression, but rather on elucidation of the heavenly will. (pp. 113-14)

"How It Strikes a Contemporary" exemplifies this concept of the artist in his capacity as God's "recording chief-inquisitor." The protagonist of the poem is a solitary figure, alert to every incident in the life around him, yet mysteriously alien to his environment, his whole loyalty absorbed by the "King" to whom he writes his nightly missive. Of the poet-seer Browning also says that his writing will "be less a work than an effluence." **"Saul"** and **"Abt Vogler"** illustrate the true nature of artistic inspiration. David in the former poem, at the approach of the final ecstatic vision of Christ, flings away the harp which has formalized his earlier utterances: "Then truth came upon me. No harp more—no song more!" And in contrast to the musician who labors over the mannered fugues of Hugues of Saxe-Gotha, Abt Vogler is a master of extemporization. Vogler, furthermore, is playing in an empty church solely for his own pleasure when the inspiration descends. His mystic communion with God is thus achieved as a private revelation. And although his improvisations can never be recaptured on earth, he is consoled by the knowledge that they have reached the One to whom they were addressed. . . . (p. 115)

But Abt Vogler remains something of an exception in Browning's gallery of artists. Even the seer's field of activity is this world and the life which he shares with other men. God is manifest through his handiwork, and all that mortals can know of his being comes in rightly interpretating the phenomena which condition earthly existence. It is on these phenomena that the imagination must exercise itself, avoiding all willful delusions prompted by the intellect. Any work of the imagination which fails to take cognizance of the facts of human experience is necessarily for Browning either false or imperfect. Thus, in **"Old Pictures in Florence"** he chooses Christian in preference to Greek art because of the classic artist's unrealistic refusal to "paint man man." Similarly, the speaker in the eighth lyric of **"James Lee's Wife"** has learned from Leonardo that their is more true beauty in the work-worn hand of a peasant than in any academic dream of perfection that "lived long ago or was never born." (p. 116)

The fullest expression of the poet's aesthetic philosophy is to be found in **"Fra Lippo Lippi."** The circumstances under which we encounter Fra Lippo are significant in themselves; for he has just been apprehended as a potential law-breaker. We learn that he has fled the confinement of his patron's house because it is carnival time and he is unable to resist the lure of the streets. The irrepressible gaiety of life is implicit in the jigging refrain that keeps running through the painter's mind:

> Flower o' the broom,
> Take away love, and our earth is a tomb!

With this preparation, it is not surprising to find that Fra Lippo has rejected the institutional repression of the Church, and especially that he has thrown over traditional forms of ecclesiastical art as exemplified in the work of such artists as Fra Angelico and Lorenzo Monaco. Fra Lippo is one of Browning's incorruptible innocents. He paints by instinct; and what he paints is the world of his perceptions, not an intellectualized abstraction of it: "The world and life's too big to pass for a dream." But underlying the intensity of his response to human experience is the innate perception of a higher reality made manifest, if at all, through the appearances of this world. The artist cannot do better than reproduce with as great fidelity as possible his individual sense of the observed fact; in so doing he records his own gratitude for the privilege of living, and in the process opens the eyes of others to the meaning of life. . . . (pp. 116-17)

E. D. H. Johnson, "Authority and the Rebellious Heart," in his The Alien Vision of Victorian Poetry, *Princeton University Press, 1952, pp. 91-136.*

G. ROBERT STANGE (essay date 1954)

[*Stange discusses Browning's influence on modern poetry, crediting him with contributing significantly to the movement toward dramatic treatment, simplicity of diction, and economy of thought and imagery evidenced in the works of Ezra Pound, T. S. Eliot, and other twentieth-century poets. Stange's remarks were originally published in the* Pacific Spectator *in 1954.*]

It is necessary to begin [our discussion of Browning's influence on the twentieth century] with some dangerous generalisations about the poetry of our time. Let us agree first that the distinguished English and American poets of this century have been concerned with technique to an unusual extent; they have continually examined and theorised upon the instruments and resources of their craft. In respect to technique modern poetry displays three main characteristics. The leading poets emphasise the necessity of a dramatic treatment, with the objectification that that term implies; Pound sought the novelist's method of dispassionate, presentation; Eliot spoke notoriously of his "objective correlative" to a personal emotion; Yeats laboured to create a poetic mask, to write poetry that was "hard and cold as the dawn".

Another striking technical quality of modern verse is its simplicity of diction. Pound said that his apprenticeship was an attempt "to find and use modern speech". And as Eliot put it, the influences to which both he and Pound responded were those which insisted upon "the importance of *verse as speech*". In their manifesto the Imagists too demanded the language of common speech and the *exact* rather than the decorative word. This search for simplicity and naturalness does not carry over, as the average reader would be quick to point out, to total poetic expression. In creating a structure of thought and imagery—and this would be a third notable characteristic—most modern poets try to achieve extreme economy, to use an elliptical method which leaves the task of supplying transitions to the reader himself. This technique is familiar to anyone who knows Eliot or Pound or the later Yeats, but it has been most neatly described by an older poet who lectured a puzzled reader as follows:

> I *know* that I don't make out my conception by my language. . . . You would have me paint it all plain out, which can't be; but by various artifices I try to make shift with touches and bits of outlines which *succeed* if they bear the conception from me to you. You ought, I think, to keep pace with the thought tripping from ledge to ledge of my "glaciers", as you call them; not stand poking your alpenstock into the holes and demonstrating that no foot could have stood there; suppose it sprang over there?

The impatient poet who speaks here is Robert Browning; his chastened reader is John Ruskin.

Each of these salient characteristics of modern verse is at the heart of Browning's contribution to English poetry. The growth of his poetic powers from his first published work, ***Pauline: A Fragment of a Confession,*** on up to ***Men and Women,*** to their culmination in ***The Ring and the Book,*** might almost be described as the achievement of a dramatic method in poetry. It could be said that in developing the form of the dramatic monologue Browning performed in his own career the kind of redirection of poetic interest that, repeated by twentieth-century poets, was defined as a revolution in taste. The hero of the young Browning was Shelley, whom he apostrophised as the "Sun-treader" and defined as the model of the subjective poet. In his ***Essay on Shelley*** Browning remarked that the subjective poet does not "deal with the doings of men (the result of which dealing, in its pure form . . . is what we call dramatic poetry)", but that his study is himself, and he selects as subjects those silent scenes "in which he can best hear the beating of his individual heart". (pp. 185-86)

As Browning matured he advanced toward dramatic—what he called *objective*—poetry, and though he never lost his admiration for Shelley, he was increasingly influenced by the later Shakespeare and by Donne. Certainly the soliloquies of Shakespeare and the dramatic poems of Donne are the two main sources of the monologue form displayed in such poems as **"My Last Duchess"**, **"The Bishop Orders His Tomb"**, and **"Andrea del Sarto"**.

In Shakespeare's soliloquies Browning found the technique of concise revelation through speech. Particularly in the later plays the soliloquies are in sharp contrast to the lengthy self-analysis and lyrical effusions which mark Browning's earliest poetry. A good example of Shakespeare's method is Edmund's soliloquy in Act I scene 2, of *King Lear.* (*Lear* was Browning's favourite Shakesperean play.) Edmund reveals himself unwittingly, not through statement, but through the connotations of his language:

> Thou, Nature, art my goddess. To thy law
> My services are bound. Wherefore should I
> Stand in the plague of custom, and permit
> The curiosity of nations to deprive me,
> For that I am some twelve or fourteen moonshines
> Lag of a brother? Why bastard? wherefore base?
> When my dimensions are as well compact,
> My mind as generous, and my shape as true
> As honest madam's issue?

The character speaks the truth as he sees it; the dramatist's method of exposure is indirect, ironic. Only by penetrating the tone of speech and attitude, the rhythm of the language, the casuistic use of words (as, for example, Nature) do we perceive Edmund's villainy. This is the technique of objectification, the command of the nuances of revelatory language, that Browning learned from Shakespeare, and that modern poets were to learn from both masters.

The Shakespearean soliloquy, however, involves no suggested interlocutor, no precise localisation of scene or time. The character is perceived within a known plot situation, but there is no emphasis on realistic historical moment, on nation, or milieu; these specifying features Browning supplied in creating his compressed form of drama. Some of the characteristics of the nineteenth-century dramatic monologue can, however, be found in the poetry of Donne. The dramatic poems of *Songs and Sonnets* and some of the elegies are set in a particular time and place, and in addition to the speaker, one or more subsidiary characters are suggested who help to define the situation or to reveal a conflict of attitudes. Browning, as well as his modern successors, might also have learned from Donne the use of natural speech rhythms, of idiomatic language, of concentration on psychological complexity and strong feeling. The moment in these poems of Donne's is usually one of crisis. Browning frequently followed Donne in conceiving a dramatic monologue as a passionate outburst that consummates a long train of action, in beginning his poems with shocking abruptness, in revealing the details of his setting so indirectly that the reader cannot perceive it as a whole until he has finished reading the poem.

Browning's continued and clearly expressed admiration for Donne should interest a generation that believes Donne was "discovered" in the twentieth century. Browning was attracted to Shakespearean and metaphysical poetry because he found in it those very features which were to excite the poets of our time. He, like

> Donne, I suppose, was such another
> Who found no substitute for sense,
> To seize and clutch and penetrate.

The description is T. S. Eliot's.

But a general interest in dramatic poetry, and the particular achievement of a monologue form flexible enough to accommodate a wide range of psychological and historical interests, are obviously the basis of Browning's appeal to modern poets. The dramatic monologue, it can justly be said, has become the dominant form of twentieth-century poetry. And it has become so, not accidentally, but as a result of Browning's practice. (pp. 186-88)

[Ezra Pound regarded] Browning as a poetic model: "Above all, I stem from Browning. Why deny one's father?" He defined his programme for the reform of English poetry as having two aims: the first, which he claimed to have derived from Browning, was the elimination from poetry of all superfluous language; the second was based on Flaubert's ideal of the *mot juste,* and of *presentation ou constatation*—a procedure which is related to the practice of dramatic poetry. (pp. 189-90)

Early in his career Pound seems to have set out to school himself in objectivity—an exercise for which the dramatic monologue was well suited. Some of the early poems are evident imitations of Browning or variations on his themes: "Fifine," "Paracelsus in Excelsis," "Scriptor Ignotus (Ferrara 1715)." Though the more interesting of the early monologues are in Pound's own poetic language, he uses the form much as Browning did. His dramatic poems are sometimes the means of objectifying his speculations on the nature of art, and almost always attempts to apprehend the spirit of a past age through a created character. (p. 190)

The most complete realisation of the possibilities of Browning's method is to be found in one of Pound's major poems, "Near Périgord."... As in Browning's Renaissance studies we find a suggested auditor, an objective tone, startling leaps of thought, strange juxtapositions of ideas or images, even a fascination with varying approaches to the same set of facts, with the blurred distinction between "truth" and fiction. ...

The subject of Browning's influence on Pound's *Cantos* can hardly be discussed without lengthy exegesis of the work itself. One might begin an investigation by observing that the *Cantos* have been interpreted as an enormous dramatic monologue. The flux and reflux of this complicated work can be regarded as a series of extraordinarily compressed self-revelations de-

livered by a host of historical personages—a kind of many-voiced monologue. (p. 191)

The fact need not be emphasised that Eliot, the self-styled pupil of Pound, ... practiced the dramatic monologue form for nearly twenty years. "Prufrock," "Portrait of a Lady," "Gerontion," "Journey of the Magi," *The Waste Land* itself, are, if not in the precise manner of Browning, variations on the form he created. Browning's monologues are designed to proceed from one fragment of narrative or thought to another; the complete poem achieves a coalescence of these fragments into a consistent psychological whole displayed in a real action. Eliot, in his early monologues at least, substitutes for this narrative and ideological base the flow of fragmented images which by opposition, analogy, and repetition produce a vision of character in its moral *ambiance*. (p. 193)

Eliot several times remarked that Browning had nothing to teach him about poetic diction. Perhaps one example will be sufficient to show that the younger poet has not been entirely deaf to the language of the "old mesmeriser." Here are some lines from Eliot's "Fragment of an Agon:"

> When you're alone in the middle of the night
>   and you wake in a sweat and a hell of a fright
> When you're alone in the middle of the bed and
>   you wake like someone hit you on the head
> You've had a cream of a nightmare dream and
>   you've got the hoo-ha's coming to you.

This is slightly reminiscent of the verse of W. S. Gilbert, but I think it is more like this passage from Browning:

> If at night when doors are shut,
>   And the wood-worms picks,
>   And the death-watch ticks,
> And the bar has a flag of smut,
>   And a cat's in the water-butt—
>
> And the socket floats and flares,
>   And the house-beams groan,
>   And a foot unknown
> Is surmised on the garret-stairs,
> And the locks slip unawares—

The influences I have discussed so far have operated on the techniques of dramatic poetry, and to a lesser extent on the creation of poetic diction. It is in such matters that Browning's inspiration has been most strongly felt. At first sight it would seem that very little common ground could be perceived between the poetic attitude and subject matter of Browning and those of the distinguished moderns. Modern poetry ... has been marked by a tendency to pessimism, by the antirationalist bias of most modern thought, and by what can only be called a neo-classical approach to the nature of art. Now in spite of certain contradictory evidence (a few passages in *La Saisiaz* and elsewhere), it is difficult to prove that Browning's poetry displays a leaning toward pessimism. And in spite of the extraordinary discipline and devotion he brought to the practice of his art, he cannot be aligned with classic tradition. Browning's positions in both these respects have been rejected by most modern poets and by many readers. The "thought content" of his work, his "philosophy," is at a very low ebb of respectability. The picture of Browning as thinker does not appeal to the modern imagination, and the poems of his that are now most generally admired are those that contain the least philosophy.

And Browning was not, even as Victorian poets go, a very consistent thinker. In his crafty dissection of the truth he preferred leaps of logic, sudden pounces and illuminations, to consecutive reasoning. He explicitly suggested (primarily in *The Ring and the Book*) that the process of ratiocination could not carry one far toward perceiving the truth of a human situation. In this sense—and this connexion must be made very tentatively—he anticipated that distrust of abstract reason which is so marked a characteristic of the modern mind. What Browning substituted for a reasoning *about* man or history was a profound instinct for life, a magnificent sympathy for the rich energies, whether confused, disciplined, or misdirected, which inform the vital gestures of men and women. His subject was emotion, emotionally perceived. The object of his scrutiny was man in history, and he showed us not so much how men *thought* in certain epochs as how they *felt*, and how that feeling makes for the continuity of the human story.

No modern poet can equal Browning on this ground. Again, though, the course he marked out has been followed. Pound said the primary purpose of his "assaults on Provence" was to use the region as subject matter, "trying to do as R. B. had with Renaissance Italy." In one of his essays on Pound, Eliot praises his treatment of the Middle Ages: "If one can really penetrate the life of another age, one is penetrating the life of one's own." Pound, he feels, sees his subjects as "contemporary with himself, that is to say, he has grasped certain things in Provence and Italy which are permanent in human nature." Eliot's comment applies to Browning as well as to Pound. It may be used to combat those supercilious critics who disparage Browning for having made all his historical figures contemporary to himself. The criticism is irrelevant. To the extent that Browning realised his conceptions he made his personages contemporary to us all, to the extent that he brought his characters to life he endowed them with his own emotional energy. Pound, as a practising poet, could recognise such a virtue where an *avant-garde* critic would fail to perceive it. Like Browning, Pound did not attempt an objectivity devoid of feeling. In answer to the question, "Do you agree that the great poet is never emotional?" Pound answered, in part, "The only kind of emotion worthy of a poet is the inspirational emotion which energizes and strengthens, and which is very remote from the everyday emotion of sloppiness and sentiment. . . ." The comment is, once more, appropriate to Browning. (pp. 194-96)

> *G. Robert Stange, "Browning and Modern Poetry,"*
> *in* Browning's Mind and Art, *edited by Clarence*
> *Tracy, Oliver and Boyd, 1968, pp. 184-97.*

ROBERT LANGBAUM (essay date 1957)

[Langbaum is considered an important Browning critic, having provided influential commentary on the dramatic monologues in his study The Poetry of Experience, *excerpted below. Langbaum here focuses on the reader's response to Browning's monologues, asserting that, as evidenced in "My Last Duchess," "Bishop Blougram's Apology," and other poems, sympathy and suspension of moral judgment on the part of the reader are integral to the dramatic monologue form.]*

When we have said all the objective things about Browning's **"My Last Duchess,"** we will not have arrived at the meaning until we point out what can only be substantiated by an appeal to effect—that moral judgment does not figure importantly in our response to the duke, that we even identify ourselves with him. But how is such an effect produced in a poem about a cruel Italian duke of the Renaissance who out of unreasonable jealousy has had his last duchess put to death, and is now about to contract a second marriage for the sake of dowry? Certainly, no summary or paraphrase would indicate that condemnation

is not our principal response. The difference must be laid to form, to that extra quantity which makes the difference in artistic discourse between content and meaning.

The objective fact that the poem is made up entirely of the duke's utterance has of course much to do with the final meaning, and it is important to say that the poem is in form a monologue. But much more remains to be said about the way in which the content is laid out, before we can come near accounting for the whole meaning. It is important that the duke tells the story of his kind and generous last duchess to, of all people, the envoy from his prospective duchess. It is important that he tells his story while showing off to the envoy the artistic merits of a portrait of the last duchess. It is above all important that the duke carries off his outrageous indiscretion, proceeding triumphantly in the end downstairs to conclude arrangements for the dowry. All this is important not only as content but also as form, because it establishes a relation between the duke on the one hand, and the portrait and the envoy on the other, which determines the reader's relation to the duke and therefore to the poem—which determines, in other words, the poem's meaning.

The utter outrageousness of the duke's behaviour makes condemnation the least interesting response, certainly not the response that can account for the poem's success. What interests us more than the duke's wickedness is his immense attractiveness. His conviction of matchless superiority, his intelligence and bland amorality, his poise, his taste for art, his manners—high-handed aristocratic manners that break the ordinary rules and assert the duke's superiority when he is being most solicitous of the envoy, waiving their difference of rank ("Nay, we'll go / Together down, sir"); these qualities overwhelm the envoy, causing him apparently to suspend judgment of the duke, for he raises no demur. The reader is no less overwhelmed. We suspend moral judgment because we prefer to participate in the duke's power and freedom, in his hard core of character fiercely loyal to itself. Moral judgment is in fact important as the thing to be suspended, as a measure of the price we pay for the privilege of appreciating to the full this extraordinary man.

It is because the duke determines the arrangement and relative subordination of the parts that the poem means what it does. The duchess's goodness shines through the duke's utterance; he makes no attempt to conceal it, so preoccupied is he with his own standard of judgment and so oblivious of the world's. Thus the duchess's case is subordinated to the duke's, the novelty and complexity of which engages our attention. We are busy trying to understand the man who can combine the connoisseur's pride in the lady's beauty with a pride that caused him to murder the lady rather than tell her in what way she displeased him, for in that

> would be some stooping; and I choose
> Never to stoop.

The duke's paradoxical nature is fully revealed when, having boasted how at his command the duchess's life was extinguished, he turns back to the portrait to admire of all things its life-likeness:

> There she stands
> As if alive.

This occurs ten lines from the end, and we might suppose we have by now taken the duke's measure. But the next ten lines produce a series of shocks that outstrip each time our understanding of the duke, and keep us panting after revelation with no opportunity to consolidate our impression of him for moral judgment. For it is at this point that we learn to whom he has been talking; and he goes on to talk about dowry, even allowing himself to murmur the hypocritical assurance that the new bride's self and not the dowry is of course his object. It seems to me that one side of the duke's nature is here stretched as far as it will go; the dazzling figure threatens to decline into paltriness admitting moral judgment, when Browning retrieves it with two brilliant strokes. First, there is the lordly waiving of rank's privilege as the duke and the envoy are about to proceed downstairs, and then there is the perfect all-revealing gesture of the last two and a half lines when the duke stops to show off yet another object in his collection:

> Notice Neptune, though,
> Taming a sea-horse, thought a rarity,
> Which Claus of Innsbruck cast in bronze for me!

The lines bring all the parts of the poem into final combination, with just the relative values that constitute the poem's meaning. The nobleman does not hurry on his way to business, the connoisseur cannot resist showing off yet another precious object, the possessive egotist counts up his possessions even as he moves toward the acquirement of a new possession, a well-dowered bride; and most important, the last duchess is seen in final perspective. She takes her place as one of a line of objects in an art collection; her sad story becomes the *Cicerone's* anecdote lending piquancy to the portrait. The duke has taken from her what he wants, her beauty, and thrown the life away; and we watch with awe as he proceeds to take what he wants from the envoy and by implication from the new duchess. He carries all before him by sheer force of will so undeflected by ordinary compunctions as even, I think, to call into question—the question rushes into place behind the startling illumination of the last lines, and lingers as the poem's haunting afternote—the duke's sanity.

The duke reveals all this about himself, grows to his full stature, because we allow him to have his way with us; we subordinate all other considerations to the business of understanding him. If we allowed indignation, or pity for the duchess, to take over when the duke moves from his account of the murder to admire the life-likeness of the portrait, the poem could hold no further surprises for us; it could not even go on to reinforce our judgment as to the duke's wickedness, since the duke does not grow in wickedness after the account of the murder. He grows in strength of character, and in the arrogance and poise which enable him to continue command of the situation after his confession of murder has threatened to turn it against him. To take the full measure of the duke's distinction we must be less concerned to condemn than to appreciate the triumphant transition by which he ignores clean out of existence any judgment of his story that the envoy might have presumed to invent. We must be concerned to appreciate the exquisite timing of the duke's delay over Neptune, to appreciate its fidelity to the duke's own inner rhythm as he tries once more the envoy's already sorely tried patience, and as he teases the reader too by delaying for a lordly whim the poem's conclusion. This willingness of the reader to understand the duke, even to sympathize with him as a necessary condition of reading the poem, is the key to the poem's form. It alone is responsible for a meaning not inherent in the content itself but determined peculiarly by the treatment.

I have chosen **"My Last Duchess"** to illustrate the working of sympathy, just because the duke's egregious villainy makes especially apparent the split between moral judgment and our actual feeling for him. The poem carries to the limit an effect peculiarly the genius of the dramatic monologue—I mean the effect created by the tension between sympathy and moral judgment. Although we seldom meet again such an unmitigated villain as the duke, it is safe to say that most successful dramatic monologues deal with speakers who are in some way reprehensible.

Browning delighted in making a case for the apparently immoral position; and the dramatic monologue, since it requires sympathy for the speaker as a condition of reading the poem, is an excellent vehicle for the "impossible" case. Mr Sludge and Bishop Blougram in matters of the spirit, Prince Hohenstiel-Schwangau in politics, and in love Don Juan of *Fifine*, are all Machiavellians who defend themselves by an amoral casuistry. The combination of villain and aesthete creates an especially strong tension, and Browning exploits the combination not only in **"My Last Duchess"** but again in **"The Bishop Orders His Tomb,"** where the dying Renaissance bishop reveals his venality and shocking perversion of Christianity together with his undeniable taste for magnificence. . . . (pp. 82-6)

To the extent that these poems are successful, we admire the speaker for his power of intellect (as in **"Blougram"**) or for his aesthetic passion and sheer passion for living (as in **"The Bishop Orders His Tomb"**). *Hohenstiel-Schwangau* and *Fifine* are not successful because no outline of character emerges from the intricacy of the argument, there is no one to sympathize with and we are therefore not convinced even though the arguments are every bit as good as in the successful poems. Arguments cannot make the case in the dramatic monologue but only passion, power, strength of will and intellect, just those existential virtues which are independent of logical and moral correctness and are therefore best made out through sympathy and when clearly separated from, even opposed to, the other virtues. (p. 86)

The past . . . [is also] a means for achieving another extraordinary point of view [in the dramatic monologue]. Since the past is understood in the same way that we understand the speaker of the dramatic monologue, the dramatic monologue is an excellent instrument for projecting an historical point of view. For the modern sense of the past involves, on the one hand, a sympathy for the past, a willingness to understand it in its own terms as different from the present; and on the other hand it involves a critical awareness of our own modernity. In the same way, we understand the speaker of the dramatic monologue by sympathizing with him, and yet by remaining aware of the moral judgment we have suspended for the sake of understanding. The combination of sympathy and judgment makes the dramatic monologue suitable for expressing all kinds of extraordinary points of view, whether moral, emotional or historical—since sympathy frees us for the widest possible range of experience, while the critical reservation keeps us aware of how far we are departing. The extraordinary point of view is characteristic of all the best dramatic monologues, the pursuit of experience in all its remotest extensions being the genius of the form.

We are dealing, in other words, with empiricism in literature. The pursuit of all experience corresponds to the scientific pursuit of all knowledge; while the sympathy that is a condition of the dramatic monologue corresponds to the scientific attitude of mind, the willingness to understand everything for its own sake and without consideration of practical or moral value. We might even say that the dramatic monologue takes toward its material the literary equivalent of the scientific attitude—the equivalent being, where men and women are the subject of investigation, the historicizing and psychologizing of judgment.

Certainly the Italian Renaissance setting of **"My Last Duchess"** helps us to suspend moral judgment of the duke, since we partly at least take an historical view; we accept the combination of villainy with taste and manners as a phenomenon of the Renaissance and of the old aristocratic order generally. The extraordinary combination pleases us the way it would the historian, since it impresses upon us the difference of the past from the present. We cannot, however, entirely historicize our moral judgment in this poem, because the duke's crime is too egregious to support historical generalization. More important, therefore, for the suspension of moral judgment is our psychologizing attitude—our willingness to take up the duke's view of events purely for the sake of understanding him, the more outrageous his view the more illuminating for us the psychological revelation.

In **"The Bishop Orders His Tomb,"** however, our judgment is mainly historicized, because the bishop's sins are not extraordinary but the universally human venalities couched, significantly for the historian, in the predilections of the Italian Renaissance. Thus, the bishop gives vent to materialism and snobbery by planning a bigger and better tomb than his clerical rival's. This poem can be read as a portrait of the age, our moral judgment of the bishop depending upon our moral judgment of the age. . . . What matters . . . is that Browning has presented an historical image the validity of which we can all agree upon, even if our moral judgments differ as they do about the past itself.

In the same way, our understanding of the duke in **"My Last Duchess"** has a primary validity which is not disturbed by our differing moral judgments after we have finished reading the poem—it being characteristically the style of the dramatic monologue to present its material empirically, as a fact existing before and apart from moral judgment which remains always secondary and problematical. Even where the speaker is specifically concerned with a moral question, he arrives at his answer empirically, as a necessary outcome of conditions within the poem and not through appeal to an outside moral code. Since these conditions are always psychological and sometimes historical as well—since the answer is determined, in other words, by the speaker's nature and the time he inhabits—the moral meaning is of limited application but enjoys within the limiting conditions of the poem a validity which no subsequent differences in judgment can disturb.

Take as an example Browning's dramatic monologues in defence of Christianity. Although the poet has undoubtedly an axe to grind, he maintains a distinction between the undeniable fact of the speaker's response to the conditions of the poem and the general Christian formulation which the reader may or may not draw for himself. The speaker starts with a blank slate as regards Christianity, and is brought by the conditions of the poems to a perception of need for the kind of answer provided by Christianity. Nevertheless, the perception is not expressed in the vocabulary of Christian dogma and the speaker does not himself arrive at a Christian formulation.

The speakers of the two epistolary monologues, **"Karshish"** and **"Cleon,"** are first-century pagans brought by the historical moment and their own psychological requirements to perceive the need for a God of Love (**"Karshish"**) and a promise of personal immortality (**"Cleon"**). But they arrive at the perception through secular concepts, and are prevented by these same concepts from embracing the Christian answer that lies before them. Karshish is an Arab physician travelling in Judea who reports the case of the risen Lazarus as a medical curiosity, regarding Jesus as some master physician with the cure for a disease that simulates death. He is ashamed, writing to his medical teacher, of the story's mystical suggestions and purposely mixes it up with, and even tries to subordinate it to, reports of cures and medicinal herbs. Yet it is clear throughout that the story haunts him, and he has already apologized for taking up so much space with it when he interrupts himself in a magnificent final outburst that reveals the story's impact upon his deepest feelings:

> The very God! think, Abib; dost thou think?
> So, the All-Great, were the All-Loving too—.

Nevertheless, he returns in the last line to the scientific judgment, calling Lazarus a madman and using to characterize the story the same words he has used to characterize other medical curiosities: "it is strange."

Cleon is a Greek of the last period; master of poetry, painting, sculpture, music, philosophy, he sums up within himself the whole Greek cultural accomplishment. Yet writing to a Greek Tyrant who possesses all that Greek material culture can afford, he encourages the Tyrant's despair by describing his own. The fruits of culture—self-consciousness and the increased capacity for joy—are curses, he says, since they only heighten our awareness that we must die without ever having tasted the joy our refinement has taught us to conceive. He demonstrates conclusively, in the manner of the Greek dialectic, that life without hope of immortality is unbearable. "It is so horrible," he says,

> I dare at times imagine to my need
> Some future state revealed to us by Zeus,
> Unlimited in capability
> For joy, as this is in desire for joy,
> —To seek which, the joy-hunger forces us.

He despairs because Zeus has not revealed this. Nevertheless, he dismisses in a hasty postscript the pretensions of "one called Paulus," "a mere barbarian Jew," to have "access to a secret shut from us."

The need for Christianity stands as empiric fact in these poems, just because it appears in spite of intellectual and cultural objections. (pp. 96-9)

In **"Bishop Blougram's Apology,"** the case is complicated by the inappropriateness of the speaker and his argument to the Christian principles being defended. Blougram, we are told in an epilogue, "said true things, but called them by wrong names." A Roman Catholic bishop, he has achieved by way of the Church the good things of this world and he points to his success as a sign that he has made the right choice. For his relatively unsuccessful opponent, the agnostic literary man, Gigadibs, the bishop is guilty of hypocrisy, a vice Gigadibs cannot be accused of since he has made no commitments. Since the bishop admits to religious doubt (Gigadibs lives "a life of doubt diversified by faith," the bishop "one of faith diversified by doubt"), Gigadibs can even take pride in a superior respect for religion, he for one not having compromised with belief. Thus, we have the paradox of the compromising worldly Christian against the uncompromising unworldly infidel—a conception demonstrating again Browning's idea that the proofs do not much matter, that there are many proofs better and worse for the same Truth. For if Blougram is right with the wrong reasons, Gigadibs with admirable reasons or at least sentiments is quite wrong.

The point of the poem is that Blougram makes his case, even if on inappropriate grounds. He knows his argument is not the best ("he believed," according to the epilogue, "say, half he spoke"), for the grounds are his opponent's; it is Blougram's achievement that he makes Gigadibs see what the agnostic's proper grounds are. He is doing what Browning does in all the dramatic monologues on religion—making the empiricist argument, starting without any assumptions as to faith and transcendental values. Granting that belief and unbelief are equally problematical, Blougram proceeds to show that even in terms of this world only belief bears fruit while unbelief does not. This is indicated by Blougram's material success, but also by the fact that his moral behaviour, however imperfect, is at least in the direction of his professed principles; whereas Gigadibs' equally moral behaviour is inconsistent with his principles. Who, then, is the hypocrite? "I live my life here;" says Blougram, "yours you dare not live."

But the fact remains—and this is the dramatic ambiguity matching the intellectual—that the bishop is no better than his argument, though he can conceive a better argument and a better kind of person. He cannot convert Gigadibs because his argument, for all its suggestion of a Truth higher than itself, must be understood dramatically as rationalizing a selfish worldly existence. What Gigadibs apparently does learn is that he is no better than the bishop, that he has been the same kind of person after the same kind of rewards only not succeeding so well, and that he has been as intellectually and morally dishonest with his sentimental liberalism as the bishop with his casuistry. All this is suggested indirectly by the last few lines of the epilogue, where we are told that Gigadibs has gone off as a settler to Australia. Rid of false intellectual baggage (the bishop's as well as his own), he will presumably start again from the beginning, "inducing" the Truth for himself. "I hope," says Browning,

> By this time he has tested his first plough,
> And studied his last chapter of St John.

St John, note, who makes the empiricist argument in **"A Death in the Desert,"** and whose Gospel Browning admired because of its philosophical rather than thaumaturgic treatment of Christianity. (pp. 100-02)

["**Blougram**" makes its] case empirically because in non-Christian terms. [It] might be considered as setting forth the rhetorical method of the more dramatic poems, a method for being taken seriously as intelligent and modern when broaching religion to the skeptical post-Enlightenment mind. The reader is assumed to be Gigadibs (it is because the bishop is so intelligent that Gigadibs finds it difficult to understand how he can believe), and the poet makes for his benefit a kind of "minimum argument," taking off from his grounds and obtruding no dogmatic assertions. (p. 102)

[We have seen that] the tension between what is known through sympathy and what is only hypothesized through judgment generates the effect characteristic of the dramatic monologue.

Since sympathy is the primary law of the dramatic monologue, how does judgment get established at all? How does the poet make clear what we are to think of the speaker and his statement? Sometimes it is not clear. . . . Readers still try to decide whether Browning is for or against Bishop Blougram. (p. 106)

I have tried to indicate that more is involved in our judgment of the bishop than the simple alternatives of *for* and *against*. As the bishop himself says of the modern interest in character, which interest is precisely the material of the dramatic monologue:

> Our interest's on the dangerous edge of things.
> The honest thief, the tender murderer,
> The superstitious atheist, demirep
> That loves and saves her soul in new French books—
> We watch while these in equilibrium keep
> The giddy line midway: one step aside,
> They're classed and done with. I, then, keep the line
> Before your sages,—just the men to shrink
> From the gross weights, coarse scales and labels broad
> You offer their refinement. Fool or knave?
> Why needs a bishop be a fool or knave
> When there's a thousand diamond weights between?

There is judgment all right among modern empiricists, but it follows understanding and remains tentative and subordinate to it. In trying to take into account as many facts as possible and to be as supple and complex as the facts themselves, judgment cuts across the conventional categories, often dealing in paradoxes—the honest thief, the tender murderer. Above all, it brings no ready-made yardstick; but allows the case to establish itself in all its particularity, and to be judged according to criteria generated by its particularity.

In other words, judgment is largely psychologized and historicized. We adopt a man's point of view and the point of view of his age in order to judge him—which makes the judgment relative, limited in applicability to the particular conditions of the case. This is the kind of judgment we get in the dramatic monologue, which is for this reason an appropriate form for an empiricist and relativist age, an age which has come to consider value as an evolving thing dependent upon the changing individual and social requirements of the historical process. For such an age judgment can never be final, it has changed and will change again; it must be perpetually checked against fact, which comes before judgment and remains always more certain. (pp. 107-08)

> *Robert Langbaum, "The Dramatic Monologue: Sympathy versus Judgment," in his* The Poetry of Experience: The Dramatic Monologue in Modern Literary Tradition, *Random House, 1957, pp. 75-108.*

J. HILLIS MILLER   (essay date 1963)

[*Miller is associated with the "Yale critics," a group that includes Harold Bloom, Paul de Man, and Geoffrey Hartman. Throughout his career, Miller has successfully applied several critical methods to literature, among them New Criticism, the existential phenomenology of Georges Poulet, and deconstructionism. In the excerpt below, Miller examines Browning's conception of his role as an artist, basing his remarks upon an investigation of Browning's philosophy concerning the relationship between the universe, God, and the poet.*]

Browning rejects any notion of radical discontinuity in a person or in the universe as a whole. His model for both is organic growth. Though there may be startling changes, the flower and the fruit are already present in the seed, and any stage of the universe contains all its past and all its future too. Each stage grows out of all that have preceded and yet goes beyond them in complexity and fineness of development. (p. 111)

The creation slowly grows closer and closer to the goal which attracts it from the future: the divine perfection. The gap between the transcendent God and the immanent God will endure as long as time itself, for the creation is like an arrow aimed truly toward an infinitely distant goal, and each new stage in "that eternal circle life pursues" has a new "tendency to God" (*Paracelsus*).

Along its eternal circle life crawls from point to point. As in De Quincey's world, so in Browning's, it is impossible to leap over the intervening grades and reach God at once. This is bad enough, but in fact the situation is even worse, for Browning pictures God himself as continually going beyond his own infinity to reach an infinity of a higher power. Browning's universe is expanding, but his deity too is an expanding God, and makes a perpetual "progress through eternity." There seems no chance for the creation ever to catch up. It is like an arrow speeding toward an infinitely distant target which is receding with infinite speed:

> . . . where dwells enjoyment there is [God];
> With still a flying point of bliss remote,
> A happiness in store afar, a sphere
> Of distant glory in full view; thus climbs
> Pleasure its heights for ever and for ever.

Browning remains faithful to this intuition of the relation between the creator and the creation, and many years after *Paracelsus* devised a brilliant and definitive metaphor to describe it. In this figure the creation is seen not as an eternal circle, but rather as a curve one of those mathematical lines, like the tangent curve, which approaches closer and closer to a straight line, its asymptote, which it will touch only at infinity. This is a better image than that of the eternal circle, for the eternal circle suggests an impossible attempt by the creation to return to its beginning after an infinite procession through time, while the image of the curve and asymptote is closer to Browning's idea of an indefinitely prolonged approach of the creation toward God:

> As still to its asymptote speedeth the curve,
>
> So approximates Man—Thee, who, reachable not,
>   Hast formed him to yearningly follow Thy whole
> Sole and single omniscience!

The curve gets closer, but never touches the asymptote it yearningly follows. There is always a gap between the creation and God.

In that gap stands the poet.

The poet faces in two directions, upward toward the transcendent God, and downward toward God as incarnated in the creation. He must go through the whole universe with loving care, re-creating all its forms. He must also try to reach closer to God through this process. "A poet's affair," says Browning, "is with God, to whom he is accountable, and of whom is his reward." What this means we can learn from **"How It Strikes a Contemporary,"** a charming poem in which Browning describes the true poet, a somewhat shabby man in a "scrutinizing hat" who walks through the town as a seemingly casual spectator. In reality he is "scenting the world, looking it full in face." His sharp eyes are ferreting out the heart-secrets of all its men and women. He is the town's "recording chief-inquisitor," and at night he goes home and reports everything he has seen to God. The poet, as God tells him in the poem, stands between God and man: "Too far above my people,—beneath me!" Like David, in **"Saul,"** the poet must be able to say:

I have gone the whole round of creation: I saw and I spoke:
I, a work of God's hand for that purpose, received in my brain
And pronounced on the rest of his handwork—returned him again
His creation's approval or censure: I spoke as I saw:
I report, as a man may of God's work. . . .

The poet must turn away from God, and set himself the task of making a complete inventory of God's creatures, plunging into their inner lives one by one and wresting their secrets. He must make clear the meaning of all these lives by reproducing them, for, as Fra Lippo Lippi boasts, we only begin to see the beauty and wonder of the world around us when it has been imitated in art. The poet can look at all possible lives from a point of view which is both detached and engaged. Therefore he is able to see the meaning which is hidden from people who are actually living their own narrow lives. This is valuable in part to other men, who are brought by art to see what is there all along but invisible to them. But the poet's ultimate responsibility is to God. Going through the whole world, he reports its nature to God. The poet is God's spy. Only because he has a commission from God has he the right and the power to go the whole round of the creation. He is the avenue by which the world is returned to its maker. The poet cannot go to heaven directly, but only with the whole creation. So Browning always affirmed the necessity of beginning at the bottom, recapitulating the whole ladder of creation, before trying to advance another rung. . . . (pp. 111-13)

Browning remains true to this conception of the task of the poet, and makes it the basis of his fullest treatment of the subject in his essay on Shelley. In that essay he distinguishes between the objective poet, like Shakespeare, who turns toward the world, to imitate "the inexhaustible variety of existence," and the subjective poet, like Shelley, who is "impelled to embody the thing he perceives, not so much with reference to the many below as to the one above him, the supreme Intelligence which apprehends all things in their absolute truth,—an ultimate view ever aspired to, if but partially attained, by the poet's own soul." Browning imagines an ideal poet who will perfectly fulfill both functions, though he admits that such a poet has not yet appeared. Both faculties operate to some degree in all poets, for each poet must start with the material world and spiritualize that by lifting it one step higher towards God. Poets must face first toward the world, and then toward the deity: "For it is with this world, as starting point and basis alike, that we shall always have to concern ourselves: the world is not to be learned and thrown aside, but reverted to and relearned. The spiritual comprehension may be infinitely subtilized, but the raw material it operates upon must remain."

An eloquent passage in this essay gives Browning's definitive picture of the progress of poetry. . . . There is one kind of poet who merely systematizes and makes generally comprehensible what is already known of the world. There comes a time when this view of the creation becomes stagnant and dead, "the shadow of a reality." Then will be the time for another sort of poet, a poet who is both destructive and constructive. First he will break the old picture of reality into pieces. This will allow him to get at new substance and see things no one else has seen. The new material will spontaneously take shape in the imagination of a later subjective poet. Finally, that new structure will reveal its resonance with God himself, its correspondence to the deity at a higher level than any so far achieved. The poets, working together, objective and subjective faculties alternating, will have gone with the whole creation one step closer to God, and "one more degree will be apparent for a poet to climb in that mighty ladder, of which, however cloud-involved and undefined may glimmer the topmost step, the world dares no longer doubt that its gradations ascend.'' (pp. 114-15)

The first step in the fulfillment of this grandiose scheme is the imitation of all the multitudinous forms of life. The poet must seek in the world itself the new substance which will ultimately be recombined under a higher ''harmonizing law.'' His first business is a patient investigation of this world, our perpetual ''starting point and basis.'' What is the method of this vast inventory of creation?

Browning has the inexhaustible plenitude of created forms inside his own soul, but only in a latent state. He needs the outside world, where these forms, or some of them, already exist, in order to realize himself. This mirrorlike relation between Browning and the world is the basis of his theory of intuitive comprehension. There is no otherness, no mystery, in his world. Every person is immediately comprehensible to him because each man lives a life Browning himself might have lived. The validity of his poetry rests on his assumption that he can spontaneously put himself in the place of Guido, or Caponsacchi, or Miranda (in *Red Cotton Night-Cap Country*), or Chatterton (in the **''Essay on Chatterton''**), and tell us how they felt and why they acted as they did. If someone should try to show him that he has misinterpreted the facts, Browning will reply that his inner sense cannot be wrong, that he knows Guido, Miranda, and the rest as well as he knows himself. Only because he contains all forms of life inside himself has he the power to go outside himself and enter into the life of all people and things.

There is another motive for Browning's passionate desire to place himself in the interior of other lives and find out their secrets. He assumes that God exists behind every thing or person, and delights himself in the unique flavor of each life. To reach the real truth behind a person, a flower, or an historical event is to reach not only the particular secret of a particular existence, but always and everywhere to encounter the divine truth itself. (pp. 115-16)

Every least object, and every least human being, carries a spark of the divine sun in his breast, and if we can really pierce to the center of any one of them we shall reach God himself. Fire under dead ashes, gold under dross, truth hidden behind a surface of lies—Browning devises numerous ways to express this notion. It first appears, appropriately enough, in *Paracelsus*. The idea that God will be found at the center of the soul is an important part of the mystic tradition to which the Swiss alchemist belonged, and it was this tradition which was revived in the eighteenth century by writers like Saint-Martin, Hamann, Von Baader, and Steffens. From these writers it is only a step to Blake and Shelley, and so to Browning, who begins with the double tradition of Protestantism and romanticism, both of which contain this idea of the divine truth at the center of each soul, baffled and hidden by a carnal mesh of lies:

> Truth is within ourselves; it takes no rise
> From outward things, whate'er you may believe.
> There is an inmost centre in us all,
> Where truth abides in fulness; and around,
> Wall upon wall, the gross flesh hems it in,
> This perfect, clear perception—which is truth.

Browning cannot, in isolation, find the tiny point at the center of his own soul where he coincides with God. His only recourse is to bring into existence his inner potentialities one after another by plunging into the lives of other people, in hopes that

he may reach the divine spark in that way. His task as poet is to reach and express the infinite enclosed in the finite: ''From the given point evolve the infinite.'' He can free his own infinite depths if he can attain them in what is outside himself.

How does Browning take this plunge into the secret life of another man or woman?

There are two ways to know another thing or person: to make oneself passive and receptive, like an objective scientist, and let the thing reveal itself by displaying itself, or to fight one's way to its center, assaulting its secret places and taking it by storm. Browning's is the second way.

Browning repeatedly describes the poet's knowledge of others in terms of the physical penetration of some object which is hidden or closed in on itself, like a fruit or a shut-up flower. The poet knows the world through his senses and his intuitive power, and these permit him to plunge ''through rind to pith'' of each thing he appropriates. (pp. 117-18)

Browning's problem is double. He has to batter his way to the secret center of the life of others, and he also has to express that experience in words. By naming things and people by the right words Browning breaks through rind to pith. . . .

The first principle of Browning's poetry is his attempt to make the words of the poem participate in the reality they describe, for he seeks to capture the ''stuff / O' the very stuff, life of life, and self of self.'' He wants his words to be thick and substantial, and to carry the solid stuff of reality. He wants, as he said in a striking phrase, ''word pregnant with thing.'' To read a poem by Browning should be a powerful sensuous experience, a tasting and feeling, not a thinking. The poem should go down like thick strong raw wine, ''strained, turbid still, from the viscous blood / Of the snaky bough.'' It must make the same kind of assault on the reader that the poet has made on reality to seize its pith. (p. 118)

Browning wants to make the movement, sound, and texture of his verse an imitation of the vital matter of its subject, whether that subject is animate or inanimate, molten lava, flower, bird, beast, fish, or man. He thinks of matter, in whatever form, as something dense, heavy, rough, and strong-flavored, and there is for him a basic similarity between all forms of life—they are all strong solid substance inhabited by a vital energy. There are everywhere two things: the thick weight of matter, and within it an imprisoned vitality which seethes irresistibly out. The particular forms, however finely developed, are still rooted in the primal mud, and the means of expressing one are not unrelated to the means of expressing the other. It is by imitation of the roughness of a thing that one has most chance to get inside it. Things are not made of smooth appearances, but of the dense inner core which is best approached through heavy language.

Grotesque metaphors, ugly words heavy with consonants, stuttering alliteration, strong active verbs, breathless rhythms, onomatopoeia, images of rank smells, rough textures, and of things fleshy, viscous, sticky, nubbly, slimy, shaggy, sharp, crawling, thorny, or prickly—all these work together in Browning's verse to create an effect of unparalleled thickness, harshness, and roughness. These elements are so constantly combined that it is difficult to demonstrate one of them in isolation, but their simultaneous effect gives Browning's verse its special flavor, and could be said to be the most important thing about it. They are the chief means by which he expresses his sense of what reality is like. No other poetry can be at once so ugly, so "rough, rude, robustious," and so full of a joyous vitality.

Sometimes Browning achieves his effect by a direct appeal to the kinesthetic sense. The words invite us to imitate with our bodies what they describe, or to react to the poem as if it were a physical stimulus:

> As he uttered a kind of cough-preludious
> That woke my sympathetic spasm . . .

> . . . the pig-of-lead-like pressure
> Of the preaching man's immense stupidity. . . .
>
> (pp. 119-20)

Sometimes the chief means is onomatopoeia—language at the level of interjection, exclamation, the sound of the word echoing the reality, often an affirmation of the body's organic life:

> Fee, faw, fum! bubble and squeak!

> . . . the thump-thump and shriek-shriek
> Of the train. . . .
>
> (p. 120)

Sometimes it is the use of words clotted with consonants, for bunched consonants seem to have power to express not only unformed chaos, but also the sharp texture of particular things:

> . . . slimy rubbish, odds and ends and orts . . .

> And one sharp tree—'t is a cypress—stands,
> By the many hundred years red-rusted,
> Rough iron-spiked, ripe fruit-o'ercrusted. . . .

Sometimes, as in the last quotation, it is the use of verbs of violent action, whether in their primary form or in the form of participles which have become part of the substance of what they modify: . . .

> If there pushed any ragged thistle-stalk
> Above its mates, the head was chopped; the bents
> Were jealous else. What made those holes and rents
> In the dock's harsh swarth leaves, bruised as to baulk
> All hope of greenness? 't is a brute must walk
> Pashing their life out, with a brute's intents.

Sometimes the chief device giving strength and substance to the line is alliteration, often of explosive consonants:

> Here's John the Smith's rough-hammered head. Great eye,
> Gross jaw and griped lips do what granite can
> To give you the crown-grasper. What a man!. . .

> No, the balled fist broke like thunderbolt,
> Battered till brain flew!

> The barrel of blasphemy broached once, who bungs?

Sometimes the chief effect is produced by the quick heavy, often syncopated, rhythm, the heartbeat of the verse helping the reader to participate in the substance of the thing or person and the pace of its life. The rhythm of Browning's poems is internal, vegetative. It is not the mind speaking, but the depths of corporeal vitality, the organic pulsation of life. Browning manages, better than any other poet, to convey the bump, bump, bump of blood coursing through the veins, the breathless rush of excited bodily life, the vital pulse of the visceral level of existence, the sense of rapid motion. No other poetry is more robust in tempo:

> I sprang to the stirrup, and Joris, and he;
> I galloped, Dirck galloped, we galloped all three . . .
> Noon strikes,—here sweeps the procession! our Lady borne
>   smiling and smart
> With a pink gauze gown all spangles, and seven swords stuck
>   in her heart!
> *Bang-whang-whang* goes the drum, *tootle-te-tootle* the fife;
> No keeping one's haunches still: it's the greatest pleasure in
>   life.

Sometimes the effect is produced by a cascade of grotesque metaphors. In Browning's world anything can be a metaphor for anything else, and often he gets an effect of uncouth vitality by piling up a heap of idiosyncratic things, each living violently its imprisoned life:

> Higgledy piggledy, packed we lie,
> Rats in a hamper, swine in a stye,
> Wasps in a bottle, frogs in a sieve,
> Worms in a carcase, fleas in a sleeve.

Sometimes, however, it is a more subtle use of metaphor. Browning tends to qualify his description of external events with metaphors taken from the human body. This humanizing of dead objects is so pervasive in Browning's verse that it is easy not to notice it. His anthropomorphizing of the landscape is not achieved by a strenuous act of the imagination which transfers bodily processes to mountains or rivers. Everything in the world is already humanized for Browning, as soon as he sees it, and can be experienced as intimately as if it were his own body. The best proof of this is the casual and habitual way in which body-words are applied to the external world:

> Oh, those mountains, their infinite movement!
>   Still moving with you;
> For, ever some new head and breast of them
>   Thrust into view
> To observe the intruder; you see it
>   If quickly you turn
> And, before they escape you, surprise them.

"Childe Roland to the Dark Tower Came" is a masterpiece of this kind of empathy. The effect of this weird poem comes not so much from the grotesque ugliness and scurfy "penury" of the landscape, as from the fact that the reader is continually coaxed by the language to experience this ghastly scene as if it were his own body which had got into this sad state:

> Now blotches rankling, coloured gay and grim,
>   Now patches where some leanness of the soil's
>   Broke into moss or substances like boils;
> Then came some palsied oak, a cleft in him
> Like a distorted mouth that splits its rim
>   Gaping at death, and dies while it recoils.

Kinesthesia, onomatopoeia, "consonanted" words, verbs of violent action, alliteration, visceral rhythm, grotesque metaphors, pathetic fallacy—by whatever means, Browning's aim is to get to the inmost center of the other life, and working out from it, to express that life as it is lived, not as it appears from the outside to a detached spectator. This power of what Hazlitt called "gusto" is surely one of Browning's chief qualities as a poet. His ability to convey the "thingness" of things, in his own special apprehension of it, belongs not at all to the realm of ideas, and yet is at one the most obvious thing about his verse, and, it may be, the most profound. (pp. 120-23)

J. Hillis Miller, "Robert Browning," in his The Disappearance of God: Five Nineteenth-Century Writers, *Cambridge, Mass.: The Belknap Press of Harvard University Press, 1963, pp. 81-156.*

RICHARD D. ALTICK AND JAMES F. LOUCKS II   (essay date 1968)

[*In the following excerpt from their study* Browning's Roman Murder Story: A Reading of "The Ring and the Book," *Altick and Loucks provide a detailed analysis of Browning's masterpiece. According to the critics, the poet fashioned a three-part series of monologue "triads" in* The Ring and the Book *to illustrate his central theme, identified by Altick and Loucks as the "elemental conflict of intuitive truth* vs. *reasoned falsehood."*]

Some of Browning's most thoughtful and sympathetic critics have asserted that *The Ring and the Book* lacks form. Henry James, for one, lamented the poem's "great loose and uncontrolled composition, [its] great heavy-hanging cluster of related but unreconciled parts" [see Additional Bibliography]. What is ordinarily regarded as the "Gothic" structure of the poem seems at odds with the Jamesian ideal of artistic shape, but it is by no means as devoid of organization and control as the popular connotation of "Gothic" suggests. Not least among the poem's many wonders, indeed, is its superb architecture. Given its basic movement—the coalescence of partial truths into a transcendent Truth—the succession of the twelve books must be regarded as completely logical. (p. 37)

Encircled by the "ring" of Books 1 and . . . 12, Books 2-11 contain the alleged facts of the Franceschini case as set forth and interpreted by nine speakers. The chief key to the poem's structure lies in the three triads (plus one additional monologue in which Guido reappears) into which these ten internal books are divided. The first triad (2-4) involves chiefly an exposition of the externalities, the events of the case; the second (5-7) shifts emphasis to character, and the third (8-10) to theme (the poem's great issues, such as truth, deceit, language, and religion). Thus there is a continuous upward progress toward a revelation of the ultimate significance of event and character.

In the first triad, designated as "Rome and rumour," three speakers, identified only as "Half-Rome," "the Other Half-Rome," and "Tertium Quid," voice opinions of the kind which, as one learns from the so-called "anonymous pamphlets" included in the Old Yellow Book, were current in the city as the murder case swept to its climax; these are the divergent views of the spectators. Here in particular, though the demonstration continues throughout the poem, Browning displays the principal reasons why men ordinarily are incapable of discerning, much less of expressing, the whole truth about any episode of human experience. Their vision is clouded by the "idols of the mind" which Bacon enumerated in the *Novum Organum* as the sources of human error. In the second triad, hearsay gives way to the inside testimonies of the three protagonists, Guido, Caponsacchi, and Pompilia. In the third, we move from the principals first to their professional advocates and then to the Pope, who in effect adjudicates the lawyers' conflicting claims. In the last of the monologues (Book 11), given additional prominence by its separation from the scheme of triads, Guido speaks again. Every one of the nine speakers asserts or implies that his own version of events and motives is the true one.

The poem's symmetry derives mainly from the patterning of the individual triads. At the base corners of each triangle are speakers who represent extreme opposites in point of view and line of argument, yet who also have some kind of affinity, such as equal social position or similarity of personal experience. At the apex of each triangle is a speaker who is superior to the other two in authority, either social or moral, and who speaks either in extension of the previous arguments or in opposition to them. In the first triad the two prejudiced witnesses, the diametrically opposed two Halves of Rome, give way to the "quality," the socially and (on the surface) intellectually superior Tertium Quid, who substitutes a posture of judiciousness and disinterestedness for the relatively unconcealed bias of his predecessors. In the next triad Guido and Caponsacchi, the first two speakers, though antagonists in the drama, are linked in that both are men of experience in human weakness: Guido has succumbed to his inner propensity to evil, while Caponsacchi, after a severe test of his priestly vows, has triumphed over it. Above them presides the saintly Pompilia, the quiet, self-effacing center of all the controversy and the very embodiment of innocence, who places in due moral perspective the characters of the two men. In the third triad it is the rival lawyers who provide the base. Both betray the causes they have been retained to defend, and in so doing reveal the extent of their ignorance—or deliberate neglect—of the true issues involved, which transcend the largely irrelevant questions they labor in their respective pleadings. Far above them broods the aged Pope Innocent XII, whose use of the intuitive powers available to all who abjure selfish interests in their search for truth is commentary enough on the blindness of the lawyers and their kind. Books 4, 7, and 10, the apex monologues, therefore are the pivotal arguments, each serving to illuminate the meaning of the two monologues that have immediately preceded it. They are emblematic—Tertium Quid, of compromising intellect; Pompilia, of uncompromised innocence; and the Pope, of uncompromising justice and surpassing insight. Together they embody Browning's opinions on the central moral themes of the poem. (pp. 38-40)

Despite the implication of the name Browning gives him, the first speaker, Half-Rome, represents the heavily dominant portion of public opinion. Meeting by chance an acquaintance outside the church of San Lorenzo, in which the bodies of the murdered Comparini are lying exposed to the gaze of sensation seekers, Half-Rome, buttonholing him with a fixity reminiscent of the Ancient Mariner, treats him to what purports to be an authoritative account of the events that resulted in the slaughter. It is (not least because it is the first detailed version we read) a fairly plausible story, redounding to Guido's credit. The speaker undoubtedly believes what he says. But in a surprise ending, he reveals that he is the very antithesis of a detached observer. Because, like Guido, he "keeps" a wife to whose window a certain man is in the habit of repairing, he uses the Franceschini story (and a casually displayed knife?) to convey a wholesome warning to the suitor through his auditor, who happens to be the suitor's cousin. Thus his disqualifying bias is revealed: it is inevitable that, having a marital situation analogous to Guido's, he should be Guido's partisan. His version of truth is invalidated by prejudice born of personal identification and sympathy.

The Other Half-Rome would appear to be a foil to Half-Rome, not only in name but in his prejudices and sympathies. A bachelor, he is understandably little concerned with the honor of husbands; his sympathies are with Pompilia, whom he envisions as a pure hapless flower of a girl lying on her deathbed, yet alive as if by miracle. (pp. 41-2)

[But the] Other Half-Rome, though plainly siding with Pompilia, is not the simple-minded, thoroughgoing sentimentalist implied in his opening lines. The bulk of his monlogue is in fact an apparently judicious weighing of evidence on both sides, one which anticipates in form and technique the following speech of Tertium Quid, thus presaging the theme of the safe "middle course" which will reappear in a number of subsequent books. This judicious temper persists down to the last lines, where it vanishes as he reveals that, like his predecessor, he is interested personally in the case, not because it happens to mirror his own situation—it obviously does not because he is nursing a long-standing grievance against the accused himself. He cannot forgive an insult (whether real or imagined we are not told) by Guido, who was co-heir of an estate administered by the speaker. Guido's objection to the Other Half-Rome's performance of that trust has become a stain upon his honor fully as malign as that which Half-Rome has represented Guido to have suffered through his wife's elopement with the priest. In effect, then, the emotional distance between the first two speakers is not so great as the substance and the manner of their diverging arguments would lead us to believe; and both of them, for reasons that are unlike yet related, are prevented from seeing the truth, even though they purport to reveal it.

For the apex monologue of the first triad the scene shifts from the pavements of Rome to an aristocratic drawing room, where a *soirée*, well populated by ecclesiastics, is in progress. . . . [The] speaker here is a supercilious logic chopper whom Browning appropriately names "Tertium Quid": "neither this nor that / Half-Rome aforesaid; something bred of both: / One and one breed the inevitable three.". . . . Tertium Quid's predecessors, relatively simple in their approach to the Franceschini case, were candid in their respective views of the rights and wrongs. Tertium Quid's approach, on the contrary, is sophisticated and studiedly ambiguous: he sweepingly, scornfully rejects the emotional treatment favored by "reasonless unreasoning Rome.". . . . Instead of the shadowy bypaths of the mob, he takes the high road of the intellect:

> You get a reasoned statement of the case,
> Eventual verdict of the curious few
> Who care to sift a business to the bran
> Nor coarsely bolt it like the simpler sort.
> Here, after ignorance, instruction speaks;
> Here, clarity of candour, history's soul,
> The critical mind, in short: no gossip-guess. . . .

[Tertium Quid's] elaborate pretense of judiciousness and "candour" is only window-dressing to conceal a thoroughgoing partisanship for Guido, one born of both personal and class sympathies. His actual prejudice is the more culpable because it is everywhere disavowed. And his own remark, in the middle of his speech, that "Guido lacks not an apologist," is a monumental understatement. . . . [Through] Tertium Quid, who is entirely Browning's invention, the poet discredits logic and its rhetorical uses by having him adopt it to defend Guido. The end being morally repugnant—for Browning has made it clear in the beginning of the poem that the Count is a villain—Browning requires us to find equally repugnant the means by which it is achieved, a one-man debate in which pivotal points are developed by sophistry and casuistry. It was not the only time in his career that he sought to bring rational processes

A cartoon by Max Beerbohm entitled "Mr. Robert Browning, Taking Tea with the Browning Society."
Reproduced by permission of Eva Reichmann.

into disrepute by representing them as sophistry and associating them with an unacceptable moral position. (pp. 42-5)

Book 4, marked throughout by Tertium Quid's self-interested pose of disinterestedness, provides a thematic climax to the first triad, in which it is demonstrated how events can be progressively misconstrued and truth *not* arrived at. Prejudice born of identification with a participant, as in Book 2, or of personal grudge, as in Book 3, beclouds the issues. But even less effective a means to truth than bias, Browning would say—in fact, a more insidious enemy of truth—is that adopted by Tertium Quid, the one who trumpets most loudly and often about his devotion to truth. Cold reason (or the posture thereof), he demonstrates, can be as crippling as conscious bias, not least when it is deliberately employed for self-advancement. (p. 46)

In the next triad (books 5-7) hearsay evidence and attributed motives are supplanted by the testimony of the participants themselves—a development which encourages us, falsely as it turns out, to believe that the full truth of all disputed matters is now in prospect. Guido speaks first. (pp. 46-7)

His whole performance . . . [is] a shrewd *mélange* of casuistry, nervous jokes, flattery, false humility, emotional outbursts, and appeals to class sympathy. Despite the show of passion and pathos, his version of the story is, even more than that of Tertium Quid, one of the mind—calculated, intellectualized. (p. 48)

Of all Guido's strategic devices, the one which most conclusively removes him from the reader's sympathy, whatever effect it may be presumed to have on his auditors, is his recurrent likening of himself to Christ. . . . On being offered a reviving potion after his torture, he is both sarcastically surprised and obsequiously delighted to find that it is good Velletri wine, "not vinegar and gall" or (later) a "cup of bitterness" which "knocks at my clenched teeth." He alludes to his family's resemblances to "our Lord" in saintliness and sacrificial poverty, to his "crown of punishments," to the indignity of being spat upon; he makes ready analogies between his conduct and that of the church, the spouse of Christ. He portrays himself as the good shepherd, a role, sanctified by Scripture and the custom of early Christian art, which would inferentially cast Pompilia, the lost lamb "Who once was good and pure . . . / And lay in my bosom," as a sinner. He recalls how, after the court's decision sending Pompilia to the care of the Convertite nuns and Caponsacchi to Civita Vecchia, he traveled the road back to Arezzo as if it were the road to Calvary, "station by station," each with its reminder of his agony. He handily converts the Comparini's reputed lot at Arezzo to a "stiff crucifixion by my dais," they being by implication, the thieves and he the Christ. His return home after prosecuting Pompilia and Caponsacchi was suggestive of Christ's being laid in the sepulcher—a relatively plausible analogy, considering what was undoubtedly the tomblike atmosphere of the Franceschini palace. (His sympathizer Half-Rome has called it "the dark house" and specifically a sepulcher.) But there was no rest, no glory, even there, for he had to endure a descent into the hell of gibes and jests:

> [I] found myself in my horrible house once more,
> And after a colloquy . . . no word assists!
> With the mother and the brothers, stiffened me
> Strait out from head to foot as dead man does,
> And, thus prepared for life as he for hell,
> Marched to the public Square and met the world.
>
>   (pp. 49-50)

Guido's justification of the murder of his wife Pompilia is simple and, taken at face value, persuasive: by his account he had been much sinned against, though never sinning. He was constantly victimized by hypocritical institutions, especially church and marriage, and misled by bad advice. Furthermore, even as a dishonored husband, he acted with dignity, courage, and restraint (all this in a land where tempers flare easily over violations of domestic honor and where cuckolds are publicly scorned). It is not surprising, therefore, that Guido's argument is chiefly devoted to the careful rehearsal of his manifold provocations and temptations, together with his saintly, nay, Christlike forbearance.

Of Guido may be said what used to be observed of Milton's Satan: as a dramatic character he almost steals the show. He is at once a symbol of monstrous, unmitigated evil and an engaging comic figure; and Browning's triumph lies in his making this dual nature credible. The enormity of Guido's pretending to the role of a latter-day Christ, the sulphurous terms in which he is denounced by the sympathetic speakers, and his horrifying self-revelation in his second appearance (Book 11) leave no doubt that he is the devil incarnate. On the other hand, he is also portrayed, in at least as great detail, as (in present-day terminology) a comic anti-hero. Strikingly unhandsome, indeed contemptible in appearance and manner, this inexpert schemer is also mean, cowardly, failure-prone. Many of the situations in which he figures have their comic side: the penuriousness of his family, his inability to make headway in the church, his Boccaccian May-December marriage, his Byronic pursuit of his escaped wife and her friend the priest across the Italian countryside, his discomfiture at Castelnuovo, his climactic ill-luck when his flight to Arezzo after the murders is foiled by "the one scrupulous fellow in all Rome." The farcical nature of all this . . . is constantly underscored by the ridicule heaped upon him by the onlookers. And though the two roles of devil and comedian are diametrically opposed, Browning firmly connects them by describing Guido in a variety of metaphors drawn from the whole intervening moral spectrum, terms which range from lamb to wolf, from patient ox to furious bull, from swan to snake, from cuckold to Antichrist. Altogether, the portrait, so masterly in its reconciling of incongruities, reflects a side of Browning's judgment of life which is seldom sufficiently recognized: if, as the story of Pompilia and Caponsacchi shows, the hand of God may be seen in the humble, unregarded events of everyday life, it is equally true that the Prince of Darkness may lurk there, so disguised as to be not fearful but comic. As a satanic character, Guido is the most human in literature, and, by that very fact, one of the most terrible.

Hard upon his final obsequious, forgiving words to his judges comes Caponsacchi's angry speech before the same tribunal, those "blind guides," as he calls them, "who must needs lead eyes that see! / Fools, alike ignorant of man and God!" He had been in their presence earlier, after his arrest at Castelnuovo. Brought back now as *amicus curiae*, he bitterly recalls their imperfectly concealed amusement at the scrape this spirited young priest had got himself into. While they smiled their indulgent smiles, Guido had been free to murder the "young, tall, beautiful, strange and sad" girl who was his wife and Caponsacchi's spiritual savior. As she lies dying in St. Anna's hospital, Caponsacchi recounts how her intolerable situation at Arezzo afforded him—a handsome worldly scion of the church, a "coxcomb and fribble" who was destined for great things if he played his cards right—the means by which he could serve God and redeem his soul. (pp. 52-3)

In lines as reverberant with true passion as Guido's were filled with craft, he interprets his experience of self-sacrifice in religious terms: he was not only St. George slaying the dragon, but his namesake Joseph escorting a Madonna-like figure to safety from a murderous Herod. In the religious phraseology and imagery which color the latter portion of his narrative, their spontaneity contrasting with Guido's calculating use of biblical allusion, is foreshadowed the Pope's eventual interpretation of the priest's and Pompilia's experience as possessing divine significance. Caponsacchi's newly purified and heightened instinct assures him that the experience has been wholly different from that which any of the four preceding speakers were capable of imagining. The "revelation" has, in fact, been of ineffable importance and so cannot be adequately expressed in temporal terms. . . . Nevertheless the meaning of this experience, insofar as he is able to define it, is limited; he can realize it only in terms of his individual awakening. God, through Pompilia, has touched an errant human being and revealed the transcendent claim of spirit over flesh, a claim to which the response is virtuous conduct and, if need be, decisive action. He has learned

> To live, and see her learn, and learn by her,
> Out of the low obscure and petty world—
> Or only see one purpose and one will
> Evolve themselves i' the world, change wrong
> to right:
> To have to do with nothing but the true,
> The good, the eternal—and these, not alone
> In the main current of the general life,
> But small experiences of every day,
> Concerns of the particular hearth and home:
> To learn not only by a comet's rush
> But a rose's birth,—not by the grandeur, God—
> But the comfort, Christ.

In his view, the miracle—not the least miraculous portion of which has been his discovery that sublimity may reveal itself in simple circumstances—involves him and Pompilia alone. Through moral struggle, specifically the determination to redeem his soul from the temptations of an easy life in the church by serving God through one of his imperiled children, he has won divine grace.

Among the chief actors in this drama, Caponsacchi occupies the middle ground between the devils and the angels. His resemblances to Guido, though largely fortuitous, are significant. Both men are from noble families; one is, the other has been, a cleric whose ambiguous standing—each on a different level—is the one certain thing about his recent life. Although cast as adversaries through the agency of fate, both have sought personal salvation—again on very different levels and for different reasons—through Pompilia. Caponsacchi regards the advent of Pompilia as an act of healing administered to his sick and worldly soul, just as Guido under Paolo's persuasion had earlier regarded marriage to Pompilia as the salvation of his ailing worldly interests. And although both argue from opposite rhetorical positions (Guido from studied humility, Caponsacchi from righteous indignation) both have a nice sense of personal honor. Caponsacchi is, then, *l'homme moyen sensuel*, a fact perhaps most emphatically revealed in his having frequented "a certain haunt of doubtful fame" across from Guido's palace—an allegation made by Half-Rome and regretfully accepted by the Pope. Nor does his transformation into a chivalric hero, illustrating Browning's vital principle of moral growth, remove him from the middle ground in the spectrum of the poem's characters. His instinct as a man still provides for uncompromising retribution. Urging frightful eternal punish-

ment for Guido, in a Dantesque vision he sees Pompilia's vengeful husband slithering on the edge of creation, there to meet an earlier outcast, Judas:

> Kiss him the kiss, Iscariot! Pay that back,
> That smatch o' the slaver blistering on your lip—
> By the better trick, the insult he spared Christ—
> Lure him the lure o' the letters, Aretine!
> Lick him o'er slimy-smooth with jelly-filth
> O' the verse-and-prose pollution in love's guise!
> The cockatrice is with the basilisk!
> There let them grapple, denizens o' the dark,
> Foes or friends, but indissolubly bound,
> In their one spot out of the ken of God
> Or care of man, for ever and ever more!

(pp. 53-6)

Caponsacchi . . . in his masculine dignity and his righteous sense of outrage, his energy, and his chivalric mien, represents the church militant in the manner of Spenser's Red Cross Knight. A fallible human he may be, but it is through such men that the Gospel is extended into the lives of ordinary mortals who must apprehend divine truth through experience rather than through the intellect. It is his action, after all, which is the pivot of the whole drama. (p. 56)

If Caponsacchi is the Red Cross Knight, [Pompilia] is Una. If he is the church militant, she is the great exemplar of Christian morality. Where he is vigorous and active, she is wrapped in innocent passivity; where he denounces the evil embodied in men like Guido, she finds it impossible to conceive of that evil, let alone recognize and least of all cope with it.

Pompilia reveals herself as a victim of villainy which most often took the form of a deceit, though she does not call it by so harsh or particular a name. All she knows is that her whole life, down to the escape from Arezzo, was a series of visitations of falseness, of unreal episodes which she endured as if in a dream. To her, as to the Neoplatonists of whom she has never heard, evil is not a positive force but simply the absence of good—a blank rather than a palpable blackness. She bears no enmity toward Guido, who was, to her, no villain; whatever fault there was in their relationship, she implies (for she is too unsophisticated to put the notion into words), lay in man's fallen condition, or in the nature of a universe in which reality is constantly masked by appearance. In the course of her monologue the true, unbelievable measure of her inability to believe in malign motives is found in her concurrence, time after time, in the apologies of Guido's partisans and in Guido's own self-exculpation. He sinned, but out of ignorance or misapplied desire to do good: the same forgiveness she applies to the Comparini.

Her fatal experience of evil therefore left her soul unblemished. Indeed, the very improbability inherent in her remaining pure is part of Browning's design: she is the antithesis of fallen Eve. In her, Browning illustrates both the power for good inherent in the pure spirit—she was the divinely chosen means by which Caponsacchi's eyes were opened to true moral and religious values—and the mystic affinity that leads good instinctively to recognize and cling to good. Her instantaneous sense of Caponsacchi's worth, contrasted with her comprehensive ignorance of the evil that environed her, shows how deep may call unto deep and goodness evoke response where evil fails. (pp. 57-8)

In this second triad as compared with the first, the relationship among the books is inverted. It is the first book of the three, not the last, that portrays cunning reason at work, albeit behind a façade of emotion. Against this background of Guido's slippery self-defense, the twin speeches of Caponsacchi and Pompilia, ennobled by their sincerity, unconscious pathos, and self-abnegation, vindicate the pure natural instinct—not the debased and misapplied instinct invoked by Tertium Quid in his apologia for Guido and then by Guido himself—as the way to such a degree of spiritual truth as is accessible to human beings. If we come closer to truth in their books, it is because in them cold rationality has no place and the heart in communion with God speaks. Intuition as a means of vision is not clouded by personal prejudice, as in the two Halves of Rome. Instead, the value of its function when undefiled is shown by the selfless experience of Caponsacchi, who sacrificed his churchly career for Pompilia (and found his soul in the process), and of Pompilia, who sacrificed her fame among men for her unborn child and for the possibly redeemable soul of her husband. But, like Caponsacchi, Pompilia cannot grasp the broader significance of what she has been through; hence, as her monologue concludes this movement of the poem, the ultimate truth is still to seek. (pp. 58-9)

In . . . the third triad of books (8-10), truth is subjected to the inquiry not of casual bystanders nor of participants but of representatives of august institutions [the law and the church]. The first two of these representatives, like the judges before whom Caponsacchi has appeared, have eyes and see not; as individual men they devote themselves to the manipulation of language and logic and the narrow self-seeking that to Browning invalidate human law as a means to truth. (p. 59)

[The two] lawyers, whose mission, as Browning wryly puts it, is to "teach our common sense its helplessness," live in a mental world in which the uncontested facts of the Franceschini case are regarded merely as inconvenient, but easily superable, embarrassments to their sophistical and rhetorical flights. Their pleadings are a "leash of quibbles strung to look like law," a "spiritual display, / Proud apparition buoyed by winged words / Hovering above its birth-place in the brain": nothing so dull as an attempt to separate the rights from the wrongs of the case and thus serve the ends of truth and justice. (p. 60)

[The defense counsel] Arcangeli faces virtually insuperable difficulties. All he can do in the circumstances is offer arguments in extenuation or mitigation, but he excels in these. To be sure, he deliberately jettisons some of his strongest points (for instance, the alleged illegality of a nobleman's confession made under torture) for the sporting sake of increasing the odds against him. But he valiantly pursues the argument that vindication of one's marital honor is justified by the laws of nature, man, and God. Since the legitimacy of the end is not questioned, any means by which it can be attained is lawful. This is the argument the historic Arcangeli used, and some of the applications, ludicrous as they may strike us, cannot be attributed to Browning; they are found, advanced in all seriousness, among the pleadings in the Old Yellow book. But Browning, a talented hand at intellectual comedy, improved on some and invented still others, with the result that Arcangeli cuts a ridiculous figure as he prepares Guido's defense against Bottini's [the prosecuting attorney] anticipated attack. His personality is wholly comic; his argument too, though based on the precepts of classical forensics, is comic in its machinery if not in its conclusions. It is the ingenuity, not the cogency or the morality of his arguments that evokes admiration. He cites authority for *honoris causa* ranging from the bees (at least, he says, of the "nobler sort") to the church fathers. In a master stroke he uses the accomplices' confession that, when Guido failed to pay

them, they had planned to kill him on the way back to Arezzo, as a stone to kill two birds. On the one hand it is proof that Guido's murder of Pompilia and the Comparini was motivated only by lofty desire to preserve honor, money being furthest from his mind at this time; and on the other hand it is proof that the thugs were mercenaries who killed without malicious intent and therefore were guiltless of murder. (pp. 63-4)

But these intellectual gymnastics hardly promote the discovery of truth. Arcangeli's purpose is solely to win his case. He hungers for the applause Rome has for a brilliant lawyer who gets his client off despite heavy odds; he relishes the prospect of Bottini's discomfiture as his fumbling stupidity is exposed to general laughter; and he looks forward to a stiff fee, including the pearls, once Violante's, that will make a necklace to adorn his wife's bosom. (p. 64)

If the truth of the Franceschini affair is rendered more remote by the professional vanity of Guido's lawyer, it is totally obscured by the rhetorical extravagances of the prosecuting attorney. Physically and temperamentally Bottini is Arcangeli's opposite. The well-fed Arcangeli scorns him as a "lean-gutted hectic rascal," and we discover him to be, in addition, a pompous courtroom Chanticleer. . . . [An] enthusiastic Latinist, he venerates the language primarily as a repository of hothouse flowers of speech and story. Classic myth and models of oratorical splendor are to him what lamb fry is to his opponent; and as he gorges himself at the Ovidian-Ciceronian feast, hapless truth is sacrificed before his preposterous declamation.

A bachelor, Bottini finds a somewhat arid substitute for familial affections in his vaunted devotion to the maternal figure of the law—a loyalty which provides an instructive counterpart to Guido's earlier sycophantic eulogies of law and her faithful servants and at the same time a dissent from Arcangeli's unlawyerlike opinion that law does not adequately serve man's needs. This filial allegiance poses a serious problem for Bottini, one that is as formidable to him as the existence of Guido's confession is to Arcangeli. His venerated Lex Mater, passing judgment on the adultery suit after the episode at Castelnuovo, has already decided that Pompilia is not without blame. Since he obviously cannot question that decision, he must make the best of it in Pompilia's behalf by simultaneously acknowledging her possible guilt and asserting her relative blamelessness—or maintaining that whatever sins she committed were motivated by ignorance, fear, and feminine weakness.

It is a most agreeable challenge. Stimulated by the latter excuse, the prurience which is soon revealed as a dominant element in his character leads him to turn what should be "The last speech against Guido and his gang, / With special end to prove Pompilia pure" into what amounts to a prosecution of the injured wife for chronic inchastity. . . . Bottini welcomes every charge that Guido's partisans have made against her, with emphasis on her alleged sexual intrigues, and when these prove to offer insufficient scope for his powers of rebuttal he devises more outrageous ones of his own. His way with these charges, whether real or invented, is masterly. First he denies them, *pro forma;* then he takes them up, almost lovingly, and—for the sake, he says, of argument—treats them as if true. Having done so, with particular recourse to the *reductio ad absurdum,* he concludes that each allegation is false, or exaggerated, or simply ridiculous. But while such a procedure may win tactical victories, in the long run it leads to strategic disaster, for each initial concession does such damage to Pompilia's reputation that no amount of subsequent sophistry can repair it. After all the fireworks have died away, the image of Pompilia which persists is not that of an innocent victim of a vicious husband's cruelty but that of a splendid wanton. (pp. 64-7)

Browning uses [the two laywers] to resume, extend, and expose the idea first embodied in Tertium Quid's monologue. Like him, they are not disinterested seekers after truth. To them intellectual analysis and pleading are means to an end, and the end is not truth but some form of private gain. Nor have they any personal concern for their clients; Guido and Pompilia are merely pawns in a court case, straw figures without a life of their own. In such a manner does Browning further discredit reason as the way to truth. The lawyers' cynical misuse of its powers reduces the search for truth to nothing more than an intellectual frivolity. (p. 67)

In Book 10, the climax of the third triad of books as it is the philosophical climax of the entire poem, Pope Innocent XII conducts his wintry rumination over the court records brought before him by Guido's appeal from the death sentence. . . . Like both lawyers, he immediately consults precedent, now in a ponderous history of the Papacy. For guidance as he meditates Guido's fate he reviews the protracted ancient controversy over whether a ninth-century Pope, one Formosus, was a true vicar of Christ or an impostor. Is this apparently senile Pope . . . to be nothing more than a superficially spiritualized version of the lawyers, appealing to dubious authority and equally incapable of perceiving the true issues underlying the Franceschini case? His humility as he presently closes the volume of history suggests otherwise; he may, after all, possess a degree of wisdom denied the rest. "Which of the judgments was infallible? / Which of my predecessors spoke for God?" The Pope emerges as that rarity, a man ready to admit that he lacks the delusion of certainty. Nor does he pretend to the sort of judiciousness to which Tertium Quid, however speciously, laid claim, because he is to pronounce on a profound moral issue in which disinterestedness can have no place.

Instead, he applies to the rights and wrongs of the Franceschini affair the peculiarly incisive intuition he has acquired through longevity, further sharpened by the imminence of death. More than one Browning commentator has called him "a Protestant Pope." He claims no special access to truth by virtue of his office, but his humble awareness that the whole truth is withheld from men enables him fully to discern whatever portion is vouchsafed from heaven. In addition, he is the first to recognize that the question of Guido's guilt and Pompilia's and Caponsacchi's innocence cannot be resolved by natural or human law, as the lawyers tried for the most part to do, or by cold ratiocination. Hence, he proceeds to apply God's law as he understands it; and this means reviewing the case with a mind inspired and guided by the highest and noblest emotions of which man is capable. (pp. 67-9)

The Pope's soliloquy bears to the speeches of the two lawyers the same relationship that Tertium Quid's bore to those of the two Halves of Rome. But the import of this triad is inverted. Tertium Quid sought, he said, to resolve the contradictions of the two opposing factions of emotion-heated public opinion by applying calm, judicious reason; but far from achieving truth, he merely rationalized society's bias in favor of Guido. The Pope resolves the more blatant contradictions of the lawyers, those professional sophists, by applying emotion, but emotion of a sort infinitely more pure and exalted, and therefore more efficacious, than any known in the Roman streets, salons, or law offices. His truth-finding faculty is of the same nature as Pompilia's and Caponsacchi's, but while theirs was necessarily limited by their youth and their involvement with each other,

his is rendered more penetrating by age and self-abnegation and more comprehensive by the absence of earthly passion. The Pope sees the Roman murder case as Browning wishes us to see it—as a kind of morality play, with characters representing the forces of good and evil, truth and error, in conflict; and with implications far exceeding the mere guilt, innocence, or fate of several individual human beings.

When Guido speaks again, in Book 11 (which lies outside the triads but is indispensable to the climactic argument of the poem), he promptly substantiates the Pope's judgment. Revealing his true bestial self, he argues that, having fallen from his niche in the hierarchy of being, he deserves to be free to act according to the ethic of his present station. Stripped of his title and family name, he is the archetypal "natural man," a creature to whom the earthly life, dedicated to feral rapacity and crass self-indulgence, is all. Here the Guidonian amorality, glimpsed from time to time in Book 5, is fully seen for what it is, not merely the aberration of a single human being but a disease to which the whole race is susceptible. Because Browning has taken pains to depict Guido, in the midst of his diabolic nature, as being at the same time an all too recognizable specimen of the common run of humanity, clothing his cynicism and Godlessness in plausible common sense, the point is clear enough. Guido is a mirror of what all men have it within themselves to be unless they are redeemed by Christianity and thenceforward remain firm in the faith. By offering a final picture of depravity, his speech provides a black background against which the remembered radiance of Pompilia's and Caponsacchi's purity becomes all the brighter, as well as an immediate proof of the Pope's conviction that in this world evil is always present to challenge the children of God. (pp. 69-70)

Guido's consummate hypocrisy is unmistakable in the passages in which he resumes from his earlier monologue his insistence that his fate is analogous to Christ's. In his recollection of the legal ordeal through which he has passed—

> This path, twixt crosses leading to a skull
> [Matt. 27:33]

> Paced by me barefoot, bloodied by my palms
> From the entry to the end

—the spears of "affront, failure, failure and affront" were thrust into his side. He imagines himself nailed to the cross and mocked by the Pope:

> "Save yourself!"   [Matt. 27:39-40]
> The Pope subjoins—"Confess and be absolved!
> So shall my credit countervail your shame,
> And the world see I have not lost the knack
> Of trying all the spirits,—yours, my son,   [1 John 4:1]
> Wants but a fiery washing to emerge
> In clarity! Come, cleanse you, ease the ache
> Of these old bones, refresh our bowels, boy!"
> [Phil. 1:20]

And when he speaks of his belated resolve to act decisively regardless of the cost—a resolve that brought death to the Comparini—he uses imagery reminiscent of the Last Supper:

> I, like the rest [his accomplices], wrote "poison"
>   on my bread;
> But broke and ate:—said "those that use the sword
> Shall perish by the same;" then stabbed my foe.
> [Matt. 26:52]

In this horrific inversion of the Eucharist, Guido portrays himself as breaking the bread of death which is to be distributed to the Comparini and to that suddenly militant wife who at Castelnuovo challenged him at sword-point.

In this monologue . . . Browning adds one more dimension to his study of truth. What is claimed to be truth, it now appears, varies not only from man to man: within a single man it changes with the passing of time, and even in the course of a single hour's tirade. Guido's accents and manner are alternatively those of Christ and Satan. Assertions, denials, contradictions tumble over one another in frantic confusion; and a close comparison with his earlier speech reveals how often he now suppresses or evades the charges he cited and met then. All these differences render terribly ironic his repeated claim that he is changeless and unchangeable. At bottom, however, the truth of Guido's inner character reveals itself as indeed constant: from the moment of birth he has been, as the Pope decided, a man of unmitigated evil, whom no amount of beneficent opportunity and example could swerve from his black course. (pp. 72-3)

It is too sentimental and melodramatic to suppose, as some have done, that Browning implies that Guido, in [his desperate plea to Pompilia's spirit], has come to a last-second realization of her spiritual nobility and therefore, the scales of evil torn from his eyes, stands a chance of being saved. Browning's intention can be read clearly enough in his preview of Book 11:

> While life was graspable and gainable, free
> To bird-like buzz her wings round Guido's brow,
> Not much truth stiffened out the web of words
> He wove to catch her: when away she flew
> And death came, death's breath rivelled up the lies,
> Left bare the metal thread, the fibre fine
> Of truth, i' the spinning: the true words come last.

The ultimate desperate attempt he makes to save his life is the final measure of the man. The "truth" revealed is not so much in the words themselves as in what they tell of the speaker—the utter evil of a man who does not hesitate, in the shadow of death, to beg aid from the very one he has despised and wrought upon.

What remains is by way of epilogue, the closing of the ring. Book 12 is short and miscellaneous—a tension-relaxing montage which draws together loose threads of plot, allows several characters to reappear, and in its last pages recapitulates the meaning of all that has gone before. The book almost inevitably is anticlimactic in part, a fact suggested at the outset by the fine image of the rise and fall of a rocket, emblematizing the spectacular but ephemeral blaze of a deed that enabled God's truth momentarily to appear in the heavens above a dark, uncomprehending world. Anticlimactic too are the episodes which, we learn, followed the scene in Guido's cell. His execution was the occasion of a true Roman holiday. . . . And in the midst of the festive spirit, circumstances and Guido's penchant for role-playing extended into one more scene the ironies of the parallel between his story and that of Christ. For Guido's progress through the streets to the place of execution was implicitly a *via crucis,* and the site of the execution itself, the Place of the People, was a Calvary where, with his accomplices dangling "on either side" as the Pope had ordered, Guido "harangued the multitude beneath," begging 'forgiveness on the part of God.'". . . [After his execution bets] were paid; Arcangeli briskly prepared for new cases ("Serve them hot and hot!") which failed to materialize, his prospective clients being fed up with the law's caprices; and Bottini, having, as he is confident, vindicated Pompilia's fame, reports that he

has accepted a brief from the Convertite nuns who wish to brand her a harlot in order to receive her estate. . . . (pp. 73-5)

In the letter announcing this felicitous turn of events Bottini encloses a portion torn from a newly printed sermon preached by Pompilia's Augustinian confessor—a "longwinded" paragraph, so he says, for whose language and substance he has only impatient contempt. But the fragmentary sermon contains a summary interpretation of the late happenings in Rome which actually is more succinct and to that extent more eloquent than the Pope's own. Finally Browning adds his own short homily on art as "the one way possible / Of speaking truth, to mouths like mine, at least," and the ring is closed. From the chaotic, ambiguous materials of the Old Yellow Book—the asseverations and lies, the half-truths, sophistries, evasions, rumors, and sudden fugitive veracities—the indirectness of Browning's art has fashioned a circle of transcendent, universal truth.

Thus *The Ring and the Book,* while it lacks the sort of unity that is supplied by a continuous development of plot and the presence of a central, controlling intelligence, has an adequately solid and symmetrical structure imposed on it by its philosophical preoccupations. We know how the story ends as early as Book 1; Browning goes out of his way to avoid any suggestion of suspense in the ordinary meaning of the term. Even in Book 10 the question of whether the Pope will or will not reject Guido's appeal, which might supply dramatic tension, is answered almost at the outset. We do not learn until the climax in Books 10 and 11, however, what the story means. The manifold conflicts of truth and error, of good and evil are developed gradually, and it is only when we stand back to regard the completed poem from a certain distance that we realize how carefully Browning has interwoven and balanced his themes. In particular, we observe how, in successive books, the two opposing faculties, intellect and intuition, are placed in ever-changing contrast. In each book, from Half-Rome to the Pope, one or the other is exemplified, but never twice in the same form, and usually with an admixture of the other. The two Halves of Rome, Tertium Quid, Guido in his first monologue, and the two lawyers illustrate the operation of error in the world, either through emotion debased by self-interest or through casuistry. But they are interrupted by the books of Caponsacchi and Pompilia, whose perceptions, though imperfect, are accurate as far as their scope allows, and they are crowned by the book of the Pope, toward whose monologue those of the spiritual lovers had been pointing. The elemental conflict of intuitive truth *vs.* reasoned falsehood has been sustained throughout. (pp. 75-6)

> *Richard D. Altick and James F. Loucks II, in their* Browning's Roman Murder Story: A Reading of "The Ring and the Book," *University of Chicago Press, 1968, 376 p.*

ISOBEL ARMSTRONG (essay date 1969)

[*Armstrong defends the grotesque elements in Browning's style, maintaining that they are deliberately employed and effective devices for involving the reader in the process of extracting meaning from Browning's poetry.*]

Since Walter Bagehot called Browning's art 'grotesque' this has become an indispensable word in the discussion of Browning's style—there are so many things which are immediately and strikingly ugly. Few poets create such an unease in the reader and few readers will feel that the poet is at ease with his language. The wrenching of metrical patterns, the heterogeneous vocabulary compounded of aggressive colloquialisms and highly literary fragments of poetic diction, these together have an eccentricity which it is appropriate to call grotesque. Effects are exaggerated to the point of extravaganza, whether it is the constant present tense or the habit of straining the syntax by omitting articles, relatives, verbs and auxiliaries. Ways of articulating the words are thrown out so that the language is left to hit one with the raw immediacy and obviousness of a sensation. And Browning's devices for doing this *are* obvious: the violence of his expletives and exclamations, the preference for extended simile and for strings of brute physical adjectives and compounds rather than metaphor, create a sort of verbal melodrama. Who, after all, says 'Grr'? And 'Zooks!' is excessive even in the context of Fra Lippo Lippi's muscular aestheticism. Hopkins's description of Browning's style as a man talking loudly while chewing a mouthful of bread and cheese [see excerpt dated 1881] admirably captures the insistent, almost wilful, delight in inchoateness. There is a deliberate disowning of order, a refusal to structure language. This, I think, springs from a belief that experience cannot be structured and a scepticism about the capacity of language to express the true structure of our experience which I shall discuss. Meanwhile, it is enough to point out the centrifugal movement of Browning's poems; they throw words outwards, leaving a litter of linguistic wreckage for the reader to reconstruct, a wreckage which has a curious way of demanding more attention than it seems to deserve, even though one is tempted to call it the result of simple carelessness. (pp. 93-4)

It is primarily for his use of language that Browning has been described variously as a 'barbarian' [see excerpt by George Santayana dated 1900], a 'semantic stutterer', or, more frankly, as a 'vulgar' poet. J. Hillis Miller in *The Disappearance of God*, sees him as a kind of swamp poet wallowing in an almost pre-verbal state, a view which seems oddly to contradict the patently constructed and willed nature of Browning's style. I would argue that the sheer artifice of the style cannot be ignored; there is a good case for regarding Browning's style rather as one regards a convention with its own decorums, a convention which is capable of being handled skilfully or unskilfully. A literary convention requires an audience to be in collusion, as it were, with a selective and special way of using language or with a special range of stances and postures. One thinks of the conventions of poetic diction or of courtly love. I believe that Browning's melodramatic grotesque style requires the same kind of complicity and differs from a convention only in the extent, but not in the nature, of the complicity required. A style would scarcely make its effect if one were not conscious of its *being* a style, and in the case of the grotesque the violence and distortion of the manner draw particular attention to themselves and make really heavy demands on the reader. But they can establish a kind of decorum, even though this is a decorum of violation which is particularly prone to failure. The attention which this style draws to its theatrical excess is correspondingly large when the manner is misjudged. When Browning's style fails it does so not because it is grotesque—he does not always stop being vulgar even at his most successful—but because he loses control of the grotesque. When he is in control he can achieve a curious and complicated relationship with the reader and a style which creates rich and surprising effects, an odd mixture of brashness and subtlety. (pp. 94-5)

A good deal of the brashness of manner in Browning's poetry is caused by his strenuous attempts to alert the reader to his self-consciously projected rôle, a rôle projected half-ironically, sometimes with a full awareness of the efforts being made. Some writers have attributed this to his failure to find a proper poetic voice, to his uneasiness about and distrust of the reactions of his public, or to a lurking consciousness of the inadequacies of his own identity. These diagnoses are partly correct, I think, but there is a sort of tough confidence about his way of forcing himself on a reader, cajoling him, making him participate and involve himself, which suggests a more assured intention; I think they are devices to push the reader into a much more active and reciprocal response to the poem than he is used to. This is where the union of subtlety with brashness becomes important, for the rapid shifts, displacements and lacunae of Browning's style are so disorientating that they demand a real effort of reconstruction and synthesis from the reader before the meaning is extracted from the poem. In his impressive discussion, ''Two Styles in the Verse of Robert Browning,'' Robert Preyer argues that this style mimes 'the disorder, incompleteness, and puzzlement that clings to human activity', and constantly represents the ways 'by which we seek to complete and comprehend actions'. I would agree that no poet could have been more aware, sadly, exasperatedly, of the fluid, messy, almost runny, nature of experience which continually evades the hard and resistant formulations of language, the 'abysmal bottom-growth, ambiguous thing / Unbroken of a branch, palpitating . . .' described in [**"Parleying with Charles Avison"**]. On the other hand, I am not sure that Browning carries us to the brink of communication, or beyond communication, by confronting us with experiences which are 'logically unorderable' and 'incommunicable', for this seems to me a way of saying in a brilliant and courteous fashion that Browning simply could not communicate.

Certainly Browning was thoroughly sceptical about the power of language, the 'poet's word-mesh' as he calls it in [**"Charles Avison"**], to capture the half-wet 'liquidity', the evanescent 'mercury' of perceptual life and of the consciousness itself, but he does not retreat into nescience. On the contrary, his best poetry marvellously renders the structure of experience as a fluid, unfinished *process* on which we continually try to impose a shape, an order. Browning's poetry is unique in its attempt to force the reader to go through these unfinished processes and, indeed, to *create* them and their meaning as he reads. Like music (which towards the end of his life, he began to prefer to language as a way of getting at the subtlety of experience) Browning's poems are really incomplete until they have been created, synthesised and interpreted in a reader's mind. A Tennyson poem is a burnished, meticulously finished object, demanding no more completion than it possesses; a Browning poem is organised so that the untidy, living immediacy of experience can be gone through and shaped as it is experienced. (pp. 96-7)

The following passage from Book One of *Sordello* produces the typical shocks of Browning's style. It describes the castle of Goito where the young poet Sordello grows up in isolation. The castle is made implicitly analogous with the labyrinthine complexities of Sordello's consciousness. The font here stands apparently for the source of his creative power—tainted and suspect as the unexpanded hint, 'contrived for sin', the mysterious dimness and garish eroticism suggest. It might be appropriate to call this kind of writing, as Bagehot did, distorted, but it is a controlled distortion, a controlled heterogeneity.

> Pass within.
> A maze of corridors contrived for sin,
> Dusk winding-stairs, dim galleries got past,

You gain the inmost chambers, gain at last
A maple-panelled room: that haze which seems
Floating about the panel, if there gleams
A sunbeam over it, will turn to gold
And in light-graven characters unfold
The Arab's wisdom everywhere; what shade
Marred them a moment, those slim pillars made,
Cut like a company of palms to prop
The roof, each kissing top entwined with top,
Leaning together; in the carver's mind
Some knot of bacchanals, flushed cheek combined
With straining forehead, shoulders purpled, hair
Diffused between, who in a goat-skin bear
A vintage; graceful sister-palms! But quick
To the main wonder, now. A vault, see; thick
Black shade about the ceiling, though fine slits
Across the buttress suffer light by fits
Upon a marvel in the midst. Nay, stoop—
A dullish grey-streaked cumbrous font, a group
Round it,—each side of it, where'er one sees,—
Upholds it; shrinking Caryatides
Of just-tinged marble like Eve's lilied flesh
Beneath her maker's finger when the fresh
First pulse of life shot brightening the snow.

The whole passage is a thoroughly good piece of theatre. The imperatives and exclamations are used very much as gestures insisting not only upon the immediacy of the reader's experience but also upon making him conscious of having it. They are in the nature of a public agreement made with the reader that he will assent to the mannered excess—Browning is never a private poet speaking to himself. Morbid excess is the norm in the strained and violent heterogeneity of the diction and the imagery, oriental, classical and biblical. The pillars, compared first with oriental palms, then with bacchanals, are eliminated from rather than illuminated by the simile and are buried lavishly in the things they are compared with. In the last biblical simile, not content with a conventional image, Browning galvanises the usual comparison by turning it upside down. Flesh is usually compared with marble, not marble with flesh, lilies and snow! The language seems to be modelled on the language which Sordello himself 're-wrought'. There is the odd juxtaposition of the archaic-sounding 'got past' (an attempt at an English ablative absolute) with the more colloquial 'You gain'. An extended, virtually metaphorical meaning is given to 'marred', where the verb means something like 'covered up'. In the bacchanal simile the shards of poetic diction—'purpled', 'diffused'—might be at home in an eighteenth century poem, but they are alongside the hectic 'flushed cheek' and 'straining forehead', which would certainly not. The collision emphasises rather than diminishes the orgiastic quality of the simile. The metre likewise is handled with violence so that the basic pattern of the pentameter couplet is rarely allowed to emerge. No sentence ends where the line ends and heavy pauses chop the line into irregular fragments. The language is so consciously manipulated that the final effect is of a kind of baroque virtuosity and display. Browning is so distanced from his set piece that one could never accuse him of a confused and romantic indulgence in it.

The extravagance of this passage leads one to expect a good deal of metaphoric language, but it is infrequent, or weak when it occurs. Browning relies on rather frenetic verbs of motion and on piling up adjectives. The explanation for this, I think, is that verbs and adjectives do direct attention to the raw immediacy, the 'thisness' of an experience, whereas metaphor can direct one away from it. (pp. 100-02)

Until one examines Browning's syntax it is not easy to account for the union of violence and complexity in this passage. The huge sentences are fractured into discrete units in such a way that the relationship each unit bears to another is concealed or ambiguous. The grammar, assisted by the breaks in the lines, constantly creates and dispels *illusions* of meaning and relationship and requires a continuous reorientation and adjustment to its direction. The second half of the first sentence, describing the gradual illumination of the maple-panelled room, is a good example. Two clauses intervene before the main verb picks up the sentence and the second clause, with its indefinite pronoun 'it'—'if there gleams / A sunbeam over it'—might refer either to the haze or to the panel or to both and floats ambiguously between them, like the sunbeam itself, making the part of the sentence before the verb merge and mingle. The same shifting process is at work in 'A dullish grey-streaked cumbrous font, a group . . .' where the line-break encourages a reading of the font and the group as joint subjects. But then follows 'Round it' in the next line and then a dislocating parenthesis and the font re-arranges itself as a subordinate part of the sentence. It could even be said that the font plays a double function, first as a subject (for one reads it momentarily as a subject) and then, like a palimpsest, imposes itself as a free-floating appositional phrase. The different ways of describing the phrases testify to the hallucinatory effect of these sentences.

I have already said that this truncated syntax and the shifts and lacunae created by it are an important element in Browning's grotesque style; *Sordello* provides a good deal of evidence for regarding syntax as crucially significant. Of course, the grammar here is mimetic in that it could be said to enact the experience syntactically of feeling one's way through a maze; on the other hand, the language of *Sordello* works like this most of the time and when there is no such dramatic necessity for it to do so. It forces one to be aware of the elementary process of perceiving, which is usually automatic. The processes of discovering a meaning and of discovering what it is like to discover are as important as the meaning itself. In Book Two Browning actually describes Sordello's audience (referred to rather haughtily as the 'crowd') being forced to 'clutch / And reconstruct' his language—'painfully it tacks / Thought to thought. . .'. The explanation he gives is that Sordello's experience is not orderable by the conventional structure of language. Sordello apprehends experience in 'perceptions whole', that is, with a kind of all-at-onceness, grasping everything instantaneously. Perception, he explains, is quite alien to 'thought' which makes language its vehicle and is never more than a representation of perception, a translation into entirely different terms. Thought is sequential; it breaks experiences down and spreads them out, replacing 'the whole / By parts, the simultaneous and the sole / By the successive and the many'. Language would obviously have to defy itself if it were required to convey the immediacy and the irreducible all-at-onceness of Sordello's perceptions; and in despair he attempted to exploit the sequential nature of language while forcing his audience to be aware that the nature of experience is different from the order of language. This explicit preoccupation with the nature of experience and perception would account (I am identifying Browning with Sordello here and the evidence is the style of the poem itself) for the particularly shifting, amorphous grammar of this poem—but there is a sense in which the important things that go on in all Browning's poems happen outside it as the reader is forced through the processes of inference and discovery.

On the other hand, compelled though he is to exploit sequence, language nevertheless comes very close indeed to defying itself in Browning's poetry. The 'parts', the 'successive and the many', cannot achieve simultaneity, the wholeness and indivisible flux of experience, but they can suggest syntactic equivalents of it. This is what Browning seems to be trying to do in *Sordello* and in a more modified way elsewhere in his poetry. In the passage above, for instance, the prolific colons coil up sentences within one another in circular fashion. Everything is done to obscure the grammatical precedence that one part of a sentence takes over another—destroying precedence stands as the equivalent of destroying sequence. Parentheses and disjunctions, inversions and omissions, these are the obvious ways in which this is achieved. Not so obvious is the way in which participles create self-contained, free-floating units all on a grammatical level with one another (the bacchanal simile) or prepositions stand in for verbs so that groups of phrases are run together with an effect of grammatical foreshortening (the Eve simile). Most important of all, though the word order is arranged to convey the successive order of the visual experience, the grammatical relationships perpetually strain against this visual order and cut across it. The description of the font, to which I have already referred, is an example. The first sentence is another.

> A maze of corridors contrived for sin,
> Dusk winding-stairs, dim galleries got past,
> You gain the inmost chambers, gain at last
> A maple-panelled room:

The initial participle phrases seem to mark off a succession of experiences, suggesting . . . and then . . . and then . . . , but these are telescoped when 'got past' collects them all together. When in the third line the main verb asserts itself and the tense shifts from past to present the first two lines are firmly collapsed into subordinate parts of the sentence. Grammatically speaking, you might say, the experience is over before you've begun. The same process is at work in the following co-ordinate clauses—'you gain . . . gain . . .' The co-ordinate clauses, grammatically static and parallel, seem to be trying to bond together successive actions, or successive actions seem to be asserting themselves against a grammatical equation. 'Room', leaping to another stage in the journey through the castle, is not a synonymous amplification of 'chambers' as the clausal parallelism leads one to expect. How different if Browning had written 'rooms'. It is as if two kinds of order are made to react upon one another, a 'logical' or perceptual order and a grammatical order. This goes on, of course, whenever we read, but here, by encouraging and deviating from the reader's expectations and forcing him to correct the false analogies suggested to him, Browning intensifies the process until it becomes virtually the meaning of the passage.

This syntax requires a drastic reduction of the ways of putting a sentence together and can be monotonous. But in this passage the complexity of response created by the attempt at all-at-onceness makes one feel that the poem is enriched rather than impoverished by Browning's grammar. The syntactical surprises, inducing the sense and process of discovery, co-operate with the general flamboyance of the style. This is another way, like the attitudinising gestures I began by discussing, of making the reader absolutely conscious of the demands being made on him and of encouraging through this consciousness an assent to the need to discover an order in the poem. (pp. 102-05)

Isobel Armstrong, "Browning and the 'Grotesque' Style," in The Major Victorian Poets: Reconsiderations, *edited by Isobel Armstrong, Routledge & Kegan Paul, 1969, pp. 93-123.*

HAROLD BLOOM   (essay date 1979)

[*Bloom, an American critic and editor, is best known as the formulator of "revisionism," a controversial theory of literary creation based on the concept that all poets are subject to the influence of earlier poets and that, to develop individual voices, they attempt to overcome this influence through a deliberate process of "creative correction," which Bloom calls "misreading." In the following excerpt, the critic considers the difficulties and rewards of reading Browning's poetry, which he characterizes as a complex rhetorical field in which "every self is a picnic of selves, every text a tropological entrapment."*]

Of all the problematic elements in Browning's poetry, what increasingly seems the central challenge to a reader is the peculiar nature of Browning's rhetorical stance. No poet has evidenced more than Browning so intense a will-to-power over the interpretation of his own poems. The reader rides through the Browning country with the poet always bouncing along at his side compulsively overinterpreting everything, very much in the manner of his own Childe Roland, who thus usurps the reader's share. Browning as self-interpreter has to be both welcomed and resisted, and he makes the resistance very difficult. Such resistance, though, may be Browning's greatest gift to his attentive reader. The Sublime, as Longinus formulated it, exists to compel readers to forsake easy pleasures in favor of more strenuous satisfactions, and Browning, like his master Shelley, crucially extends the possibilities of a modern Sublime.

One of the greatest achievements of English or Wordsworthian Romanticism was an uneasily transitional Sublime, which retained just enough of a Miltonic aura of theophany without committing itself to biblical doctrine. This uneasy or skeptical sublimity, which Browning had learned to love by reading Shelley, was not available to Browning nor to the central poets after him, whether we take these to have been Pound and Eliot, or else Yeats and Stevens. Browning's quite nihilistic Sublime, founded upon the abyss of a figurative language always declaring its own status as figuration, became a major influence upon all four of these poets, and goes on working on contemporary poetry, though frequently in hidden ways.

To read Browning well we need to cope with his poetry's heightened rhetorical self-awareness, its constant consciousness that it *is* rhetoric, a personal system of tropes, as well as a persuasive rhetoric, an art that must play at transcendence. Browning is read very badly when that apparent and deeply moving transcendence is too easily accepted, as Browning in his social or public self tended to accept it. But Browning teaches his more strenuous readers not only the Sublime necessities of defense against his poems' self-interpretations, but also a healthy suspicion that poet and reader alike are rhetorical systems of many selves, rather than any single or separate self. Here I think is the true center in reading Browning. The problems of rhetoric—of our being incapable of knowing what is literal and what is figurative where all, in a sense, is figurative—and of psychology—is there a self that is not trope or an effect of verbal persuasion?—begin to be seen as one dilemma.

If Browning did not share this dilemma with all poets and their readers, then he would not be representative or even intelligible. However, his particular strength, which insures his permanent place in the canon, is that he appropriated the dilemma for his time with a singular possessiveness. An informed reader, brooding upon the rhetorical limits of interpretability, and upon the labyrinthine evasions of self-identity, will think very quickly of Browning when these problematic matters rise in the context of English poetic tradition. Browning's strength, like Milton's or Wordsworth's, is finally a strength of usurpation, in which a vast literary space is made to vacate its prior occupancy so as to permit a new formulation of the unresolvable dilemmas that themselves constitute poetry.

A number of the traditional issues that vex Browning criticism can be reoriented if we see them as burdens of rhetorical stance, when that stance itself determines Browning's psychopoetics. The dramatic monologue is revealed to be neither dramatic nor a monologue but rather a barely disguised High Romantic crisis lyric, in which antithetical voices contend for an illusory because only momentary mastery. The frequently grotesque diction appears a reaction formation away from Shelleyan verbal harmony, which means that the grotesquerie becomes a pure irony, a bitter digression away from meaning itself. The violent thematicism of Browning, including his exuberance in declaring a highly personalized evangelical belief in Christ, becomes something dangerously close to a thematics of violence, in which fervor of declaration far surpasses in importance the supposed spiritual content of the declaration. The notorious optimism begins to look rather acosmic and atemporal, so that the hope celebrated is much less Pauline than it is Gnostic. The faith demystifies as a Gnostic elitist knowledge of Browning's own divine spark, which turns out to be prior to and higher than the natural creation. Most bewilderingly, the love that Browning exalts becomes suspect, not because of its manifest Oedipal intensity, but because something in it is very close to a solipsistic transport, to a wholly self-delighting joy. He is a great lover—but primarily of himself, or rather of his multitude of antithetical selves.

The Browning I describe is hardly recognizable from much if not most of the criticism devoted to him, but few other poets have inspired so much inadequate criticism. Only Whitman and Dickinson among the major nineteenth-century poets seem to me as badly misrepresented as Browning has been. The prime fault of course is Browning's own, and so I return to his will-to-power over the interpretation of his own texts.

Hans Jonas remarks of the Gnostics that they delighted in "the intoxication of unprecedentedness," a poetic intoxication in which Browning, Whitman, and Dickinson share. Borges, with Gnostic irony, has pointed to Browning as one of the precursors of Kafka, an insight worthy of exploration. Against the Bible and Plato, the Gnostics refused the dialectics of sublimation and substitution, the Christian and Classical wisdom of the Second Chance. Like the Gnostics, Browning is interested in evasion rather than substitution, and does not wish to learn even the Wordsworthian version of the wisdom of the Second Chance. The "sober coloring" of a belated vision had no deep appeal to Browning, though he exemplifies it beautifully in the character and section of *The Ring and the Book* called "The Pope." The fire celebrated in the "Prologue" to his final volume, *Asolando: Fancies and Facts,* is the Gnostic fire of the First Chance, now "lost from the naked world." Browning appeals to "the purged ear," and a Voice rather clearly his own, at its most stentorian, proclaims: "God is it who transcends." 'God' here is an hyperbole for poetic strength, which is Browning's violent and obsessive subject, whether in the overtly Shelleyan long poems that began his career or in the ostensibly dramatic romances, monologues, and lyrics of his more profoundly Shelleyan maturity. (pp. 1-4)

Browning's splendidly outrageous aggressivity is not so much latent as it is concealed in his more characteristic poems. Even in the charming and good-natured self-idealization of **"Fra**

Lippo Lippi,"** where Browning loves his monologist as himself, the appetite for a literal immortality is unabated. Poetic divination, in Browning, returns to its primal function, to keep the poet always alive: "Oh, oh, It makes me mad to see what men shall do / And we in our graves!" One of the Browning-selves evidently means **"Cleon"** to show how hopeless the Arnoldian or post-Christian aesthetic dilemma is, but a stronger Browning-self gets to work, and expresses a yet more poignant dilemma:

> Say rather that my fate is deadlier still,
> In this, that every day my sense of joy
> Grows more acute, my soul (intensified
> By power and insight) more enlarged, more keen;
> While every day my hairs fall more and more,
> My hand shakes, and the heavy years increase—
> The horror quickening still from year to year,
> The consummation coming past escape
> When I shall know most, and yet least enjoy—
> When all my works wherein I prove my worth,
> Being present still to mock me in men's mouths,
> Alive still, in the praise of such as thou,
> I, I the feeling, thinking, acting man,
> The man who loved his life so over-much,
> Sleep in my urn. It is so horrible. . . .

The rhetorical consciousness here characteristically makes us doubt the self-persuasiveness of this superb passage, since Cleon-Browning's death-in-life is livelier still than his life-in-death. His fate may be deadly, but the tropes are madly vigorous, even the "horror" *quickening,* and the "consummation" carrying its full range of significations, as it must, for what poet can fail to love his own life "so over-much"? The separate selves dance in the exuberant Browning when the reader juxtaposes to **"Cleon"** the now underpraised **"Rabbi Ben Ezra,"** where another poet, not imaginary, proclaims the life-affirming force of his supposedly normative Judaism:

> Thoughts hardly to be packed
>   Into a narrow act,
> Fancies that broke through language and escaped
>   All I could never be,
>   All, men ignored in me,
> This, I was worth in God, whose wheel the pitcher shaped.
>   Ay, note that Potter's wheel,
>   That metaphor! and feel
> Why time spins fast, why passive lies our clay,—
>   Thou, to whom fools propound,
>   When the wine makes its round,
>
> 'Since life fleets, all is change; the Past gone, seize to-day!'
>   Fool! All that is, at all,
>   Lasts ever, past recall;
> Earth changes, but thy soul and God stand sure:
>   What entered into thee,
>   *That* was, is, and shall be:
> Time's wheel runs back or stops: Potter and clay endure.

"That metaphor" is normative and prophetic, but the poem's burden is Gnostic rather than Pharasaic. The "figured flame which blends, transcends" all the stars is one with the Gnostic *pneuma* or "spark" that preceded nature. Browning's vision, and hardly the historical Ibn Ezra's, sees man as "a god though in the germ." What Browning "shall know, being old" is what he always knew, his own "*That* was, is, and shall be." Not the Old Adam nor Christ as the New Adam is the paradigm, but what we might call the Old Browning, the Gnostic primal Anthropos or preexistent Adam. (pp. 5-7)

Browning does all he can to evade what Yeats (following Nietzsche) named as the *antithetical* quest in Shelley, the drive beyond nature to a nihilistic annihilation that is the poetic will's ultimate revenge against time's ''it was.'' But the evasion was only half-hearted:

> For I intend to get to God,
>   For 'tis to God I speed so fast,
> For in God's breast, my own abode,
>   Those shoals of dazzling glory, passed,
> I lay my spirit down at last.
>   I lie where I have always lain,
> God smiles as he has always smiled. . . .

True that this is Johannes Agricola the Antinomian, chanting in his madhouse cell, but no reader would dispute such exuberance if he substituted the Gnostic alien god, the Abyss, for the ''God'' of these lines. Make the substitution and Johannes Agricola may be permitted to speak for another Browning-self or soul-side, and for the entire *antithetical* tradition.

Much of Tennyson's astonishing power was due to the Laureate's not knowing what it was that his daemon or antithetical self was writing about, but Browning was so daemonic that something in him always did know. Naming that something becomes the quest of Browning's capable reader, a quest unfulfillable in the Browning country where every self is a picnic of selves, every text a tropological entrapment. Browning's St John, in **"A Death in the Desert,"** gives us two passages whose juxtaposition helps us define his reader's quest for meaning:

> Therefore, I say, to test man, the proofs shift,
> Nor may he grasp that fact like other fact,
> And straightway in his life acknowledge it,
> As, say, the inevitable bliss of fire.
> Sigh ye, 'It had been easier once than now'?
> To give you answer I am left alive;
> Look at me who was present from the first!
>
> . . .
>
> Is this indeed a burthen for late days,
> and may I help to bear it with you all,
> Using my weakness which becomes your strength?

Browning's visionary is arguing against Cerinthus and other early Gnostics, but the argument is more Gnostic than Christian (which may have been Browning's shrewd unconscious reading of the Fourth Gospel). To be present from the first, at the origins, is to have priority over nature and history, and involves denying one's own belatedness, which is thus equated with weakness, while a return to earliness is strength. To do the deed and judge it at the same time is to impose interpretation, one's will-to-power over both text and the text of life. Browning is most uncanny as a poet when two or more of his selves contend within a poem to interpret that poem, a struggle that brings forth his greatest yet most problematic achievements, including **"A Toccata of Galuppi's," "By the Fireside," "Master Hugues of Saxe-Gotha," "Love Among the Ruins," "The Heretic's Tragedy," "Andrea del Sarto," "Abt Vogler," "Caliban Upon Setebos," "Numpholeptos," "Pan and Luna," "Flute-Music, with an Accompaniment,"** and **"'Childe Roland' to the Dark Tower Came."** These dozen poems alone would establish Browning's permanent importance, but I have space here only to glance briefly again at **"Childe Roland,"** which is a text that never lets go of a reader once it has found you. The poem may well be the definitive proof-text for the modern Sublime, more uncanny than Kafka, stronger than Yeats at his most uncompromising. (pp. 7-9)

The ogreless Dark Tower, where the quester must confront himself and his dead precursors, to ''fail'' at least as heroically as they have failed before him, is a composite trope for poetry if not for the Sublime poem itself. Indeed, the figuration is so suggestive that the Dark Tower can be read as the mental dilemma or *aporia* that Browning's reader faces in the poem. The Dark Tower is the black hole in the Browning cosmos, where Power and Love become one only through a supremely negative moment, in which loss of the self and loss of the fullness of the present pay the high price of achieved vision:

> What in the midst lay but the Tower itself?
>   The round squat turret, blind as the fool's heart,
>   Built of brown stone, without a counterpart
> In the whole world. The tempest's mocking elf
> Points to the shipman thus the unseen shelf
>   He strikes on, only when the timbers start.
>
> Not see? because of night perhaps?—why day
>   Came back for that! before it left
>   The dying sunset kindled through a cleft:
> The hills, like giants at a hunting, lay,
> Chin upon hand, to see the game at bay,—
>   'Now stab and end the creature—to the heft!'
>
> Not hear? when noise was everywhere! it tolled
>   Increasing like a bell. Names in my ears
>   Of all the lost adventurers my peers,—
> How such a one was strong, and such was bold,
> And such was fortunate, yet each of old
>   Lost, lost! one moment knelled the woe of years.

After a life spent training for the vision of the Dark Tower, you do not see it until burningly it comes on you all at once. How do we interpret the shock of ''This was the place!'' when we have learned to resist every one of Roland's earlier interpretations? Is it that we, like Roland, have overprepared the event, in Pound's fine phrasing? Roland is overtrained, which means that he suffers an acute consciousness of belatedness. We are overanxious not to be gulled by his reductiveness, which means that we suffer an acute consciousness that we have selves of our own to defend. In the Sublime agon between Roland and the reader, Browning stands aside, even at the very end, not because he is an ''objective'' as opposed to antithetical poet, but because he respects the *aporia* of the Dark Tower. Poetry is part of what the Gnostics called the Kenoma or cosmic and temporal emptiness, and not part of the Pleroma, the fullness of presence that is acosmic and atemporal. The Pleroma is always absent, for it inheres in the Abyss, the true, alien God who is cut off from nature and history.

The name of that alien God in Roland's country is Shelley's trumpet of a prophecy, which enters by way of another precursor, the boy-poet Chatterton, whose poetry provides the slug-horn that is sounded:

> There they stood, ranged along the hillside, met
>   To view the last of me, a living frame
>   For one more picture ! in a sheet of flame
> I saw them and I knew them all. And yet
> Dauntless the slug-horn to my lips I set,
>   And blew. 'Childe Roland to the Dark Tower came.'

The picture is Browning's, the frame or context is given by the living but contradictory presence, where there can be no presence, of the precursors: Shelley, Chatterton, Keats, Tasso, who lived and died in Yeats's Condition of Fire, Roland's ''sheet of flame.'' Browning as man and poet died old, but his anxiety seems to have been that his poethood *could* have died young, when he forswore the atheist Shelley in order to win back the approving love of his evangelical mother. Roland's equivocal triumph achieves the Sublime, and helps guarantee Browning's poetic survival.

Roland sees and knows, like Keats's intelligences which are at once atoms of perception and God. What he sees and knows are the heroic precursors who are met to see *him*, but who cannot know him, as presumably his readers can. Roland's knowledge ought to daunt him, and yet against it he sets the trumpet of his prophecy. His will is thus set in revenge against time's: "It was," but we do not know the content of his prophecy. After a full stop, and not a colon, comes the poem's final statement, which is at once its Shakespearean title and epigraph. Either the entire poem begins again, in a closed cycle like Blake's "The Mental Traveller," or else Roland proclaims his story's inevitable lack of closure. What seems clear is that Roland is not performing his own poem, in direct contrast to Shelley at the close of the "Ode to the West Wind," where the words to be scattered among mankind are the text of the "Ode."

It is after all the many-selved Browning who is undaunted by belatedness, by the dilemmas of poetic language, and by his own struggle for authority as against both precursors and readers. Poetic self-confidence delights us when we are persuaded that it can sustain itself, that it has usurped imaginative space and has forced its way into the canon. Again we are in the Sublime of Longinus, as the reader becomes one with the power he apprehends. The danger of sublimity is that the pit of the bathetic suddenly can open anywhere, and Browning (who wrote much too much) sometimes pulls us down with him. This hardly matters, where we are given so large a company of splendid self-deceivers and even more splendid deceivers of others, of all but the wariest readers. (pp. 9-12)

> *Harold Bloom, "Introduction: Reading Browning,"* in Robert Browning: A Collection of Critical Essays, *edited by Harold Bloom and Adrienne Munich, Prentice-Hall, Inc., 1979, pp. 1-12.*

NINA AUERBACH (essay date 1984)

[*Auerbach argues that Browning disagreed with his wife's poetics, ultimately appropriating material from her poem* Aurora Leigh *and "butcher[ing]" it in* The Ring and the Book.]

Before their marriage, Robert Browning described [his and Elizabeth Barrett's] contrasting poetic voices with characteristic deference to Elizabeth's: "you *do* what I always wanted, hoped to do, and only seem now likely to do for the first time. You speak out, *you*,—I only make men & women speak—give you truth broken into prismatic hues, and fear the pure white light, even if it is in me." In fact, in the "married" poems this essay considers, the two voices were more closely allied than this often-quoted letter suggests. Elizabeth, if anything, seems to move toward Robert. In *Casa Guidi Windows*, the poet's "I" announces itself boldly and often—"I love all who love truth," she proclaims unabashedly—but in *Aurora Leigh* she forfeits her own voice, for the epic authority is herself a dramatic character. The glorious free-spirited Aurora has little in common with the frail, family-beleaguered Elizabeth Barrett, who lived as the broken daughter her creature escaped becoming.

Aurora Leigh seizes possession of the truth via its author's abdication of the right to speak out directly: Elizabeth Barrett Browning grants her heroine an authority she herself never claims. In *Men and Women* and *The Ring and the Book,* Robert Browning abandons whatever attempt he once had made to "speak out": both volumes are a cacophony of obscure voices from an exotic past, "tell[ing] a truth / Obliquely" as they contradict each other. Both Robert and Elizabeth claim "the truth," but neither dares utter it directly. Their methods in this period are more similar than different. The truths they tell are very different indeed.

Aurora's boast, at the center of her poem, has thrilled women readers from her day to our own:

> Never flinch,
> But still, unscrupulously epic, catch
> Upon the burning lava of a song
> The full-veined, heaving, double-breasted Age:
> That, when the next shall come, the men of that
> May touch the impress with reverent hand, and say
> "Behold,—behold the paps we all have sucked!
> This bosom seems to beat still, or at least
> It sets ours beating: this is living art,
> Which thus presents and thus records true life."

Through its heroine, *Aurora Leigh* celebrates its epic self audaciously as a grand female body who takes contemporaneity into herself. Nineteenth-century epics abounded in giant female personifications, though few of them had such moist and palpable breasts: Coleridge's Life-in-Death, Byron's Catherine the Great and her controlling female avatars in *Don Juan*, Keats's Moneta, Shelley's Asia, Tennyson's Vivien, Emily Brontë's A.G.A., Swinburne's Atalanta, and on a slighter scale Robert Browning's Pippa, are all grand women who in some sense, like Britannia herself, personify their age. But its vaunted contemporaneity sets *Aurora Leigh* apart from other nineteenth-century attempts at epic. The younger Romantics and their Victorian followers set their long poems in a remote and mythic past; *Aurora Leigh* turns scornfully away from work that "trundles back . . . five hundred years, / Past moat and drawbridge, onto a castle-court." It decrees that the "sole work [of poets] is to represent the age, / Their age, not Charlemagne's."

In scorning the past and claiming its time, *Aurora Leigh* scorns virtually all present poetry. Taking as its inspiration novels like *Jane Eyre*, which also glorifies the imperious "I" of a heroine with an irrefutably topical career, it seizes the age male bards have shunned. The epic present is personified as a full-breasted woman because, among poets, only insurgent women dare to claim it, just as in *Casa Guidi Windows* and *Poems Before Congress,* only a woman dare embody the revitalized Italy male politicians fear and betray. . . . Aurora's denunciation of poets who "flinch from modern varnish," withdrawing into "Roland with his knights at Roncesvalles" may even be a furtive swipe at Robert's great dark "'**Childe Roland to the Dark Tower Came'**," though Elizabeth does allow her husband his lizards and toads:

> I do distrust the poet who discerns
> No character or glory in his times,
> And trundles back his soul five hundred years,
> Past moat and drawbridge, into a castle-court,
> To sing—oh, not of lizard or of toad
> Alive i' the ditch there,—'twere excusable,
> . . . . . .
> [But] dead must be, for the greater part,
> The poems made on their chivalric bones.
>
>   (pp. 163-64)

In "**Old Pictures in Florence,**" one of the few nondramatic monologues in *Men and Women,* the "I"—is Robert Browning speaking out at last?—embraces and restores the dead things Aurora Leigh kicks away. Musing "that Old and New are fellows,'' the speaker champions a past that is constantly obliterated:

> Their ghosts now stand, as I said before,
> Watching each fresco flaked and rasped,
> Blocked up, knocked out, or whitewashed o'er
> —No getting again what the church has grasped
> The works on the wall must take their chance.

Aurora's ''full-veined, heaving, double-breasted Age'' is supplanted by a past of crumbling plaster, each square of which once blazoned a vision as ephemeral as the long-dead men and women themselves. The truth in *Men and Women* expresses itself through the poet's trick of animating ghosts. The past is its terrain, specifically the male past, despite a few interpolated utterances by nameless women (''**A Woman's Last Word,**'' ''**Any Wife to Any Husband**''). . . . Women may gaze celestially, but the past Browning animates throngs with male artists, seers, and spiritual questers of all sorts, engaged not in Aurora's triumphant appropriation but in the thwarting process of missing their moment. (pp. 164-65)

In Keats's terms, Elizabeth Barrett Browning's epic celebrates the egotistical sublime, even if the ego is not directly the poet's own, while Robert's volume displays the virtuosity of the chameleon poet. From the first page, *Aurora Leigh* assaults us with a torrent of ''I''s and ''my''s. At the end, the power of the ''I'' is, if possible, intensified, for Aurora's godly lover, blinded and abased, permits her to ''Shine out for two.'' Robert's speakers never claim such paramount authority. The vociferousness and copiousness of the volume allows them to elbow each other aside; the robust 'Zooks!'' of Fra Lippo Lippi means more to us with the ''dust and ashes'' of Galuppi's toccata echoing in our ears. The delicate orchestration of the volume prevents any single speaker from achieving full authority, while it gives each the authority to undermine the claims of the rest.

Moreover, the form of the dramatic monologue undermines by its very nature the claims of the epic. Robert Langbaum's influential study emphasizes what we would now call reader response to the dramatic monologue as it suspends us tantalizingly between sympathy and judgment [see excerpt dated 1957]. On the face of it, though, the dramatic monologue makes fewer demands on the reader than the epic does. The epic concerns itself with our acquiescence. If, after reading *Paradise Lost,* we do not feel that the ways of God have been justified, the Bard has failed, though the poem may have succeeded wonderfully. If, after reading *Aurora Leigh,* we fail to accept Aurora as the capacious spirit of her turbulent Age, the poem has insufficiently captivated us. In dramatic monologues, the speakers turn their designs away from us, directing their insistence to a generally skeptical listener. We hear and observe the speaker not in full face, but at an angle, through a glass darkly, relieved of the full force of his or her obsessed attention. Unlike the epic bard, the speaker is at no great pains to persuade us.

The unbelieving auditor, not the pressure of truth, dictates the dramatic monologue. The unseen authoritarian husband in ''**A Woman's Last Word**'' orchestrates his wife's utter, and utterly disingenuous, collapse; the ham-handed torch-waving guard dictates for that moment who Fra Lippo Lippi is, just as Lucrezia's scorn generates Andrea's self-scorn, or Saul's soul-sickness, David's prophetic self-glorification. Not only are the selves of these speakers denied absolute authority, but they are in the process of continual and convoluted formation according to the auditors' unspoken demands. ''So free we seem, so

fettered fast we are,'' sighs Andrea for all these luxuriantly loquacious speakers. He is, in Browning's world, right, but God does not lay down the fetters: they arise from the constraints imposed by those unsympathetic others who dictate to the malleable self what it should be. The dramatic monologue celebrates self-creation, but it is a self-creation enforced by the power of skepticism over the insecurity of being. Other listeners would probably dictate other poems. In its essence, the dramatic monologue asks of us neither sympathy nor judgment. Rather, it strikes home to us the impurity of our own tale telling, the ways in which our own truth has been adjusted, not to a remote and acquiescent audience, but to our intimates who do not believe us.

Browning's dramatic monologues, then, are an oblique defense of the ''prismatic hues'' of his poetic truth, exposing the fatuousness of accusations like F. J. Furnivall's, in 1881:

> The interest of [Browning's ''**Essay on Shelley**''] lay in the fact that Browning's ''utterances'' here are *his*, and not those of any one of the ''so many imaginary persons'' behind whom he insists on so often hiding himself, and whose necks I for one should continually like to wring, whose bodies I would fain kick out of the way, in order to get face to face with the poet himself, and hear his own voice speaking his own thoughts, man to man, soul to soul. Straight speaking, straight hitting, suit me best.

For Browning, there is no single ''face to face'' revelation, but only faces, each one of which imprints a different soul, and thus a different truth, on its interlocutor.

For Elizabeth, on the other hand, face to face revelations were an absolute experience of epiphany and salvation. As Dolores Rosenblum puts it, ''Looking into the mirror face of a mother-sister marks Aurora's discovery of an integrated self and a poetics.'' The spiritual authorities Elizabeth holds dearest dissolve mockingly in Robert's *Men and Women* to a pageant of distorted refractions. We are not seen by others with the grandiosity we see in ourselves, Robert's volume reminds us. The self is embarrassingly adjustable, contemporaneity embarrassingly obtuse. (pp. 166-67)

So far, in looking at *Men and Women* in conjunction with *Aurora Leigh,* we find, as in our own arms race, explosive material each poet is afraid to use. The vision in each book could be lethal to the other one, so they sit side by side, never quite in contact. Perhaps Robert speaks for both poets when he defines the nervous truce of ''**A Woman's Last Word**'':

> What so false as truth is,
>   False to thee?
> Where the serpent's tooth is,
>   Shun the tree—
>
> Where the apple reddens
>   Never pry—
> Lest we lose our Edens,
>   Eve and I!

Once the worst had happened—Elizabeth's death and the loss of his Italian exile—Robert freed himself to transplant her material and her legend into his own poetic territory. During her life, she had regarded his fascination for the Old Yellow Book with some horror . . . ; when he melded its violence and intrigue into *The Ring and the Book,* he must at last have known she was dead. To be safe, though, he killed her again. His absorption of Elizabeth's iconography—particularly the glorification of Marian Erle in *Aurora Leigh* as a holy twin of the supreme woman poet who personifies her age—resurrects his sainted wife in order to butcher her in the person of Pompilia. His most radical butchery is spiritual. *The Ring and the Book* erodes Elizabeth Barrett Browning's cherished systems of salvation, a devastation over which he makes her preside in the attenuated person of "Lyric Love."

Lyric Love has little in common with the vibrantly physical poet evoked in Book V of *Aurora Leigh*. Since she is "half angel and half bird," she has no breasts and little blood to speak of; since "heaven [is her] home," she has evaporated helplessly out of her age, passing from cynosure to spectator, forced to gaze on a bloody past she cannot affect. *Aurora Leigh* dismissed the 'ghosts" *Men and Women* restored. Now, Elizabeth herself is relegated to ghostliness, while Robert reanimates the seventeenth century in all its confused vitality. The woman who claimed to embody her age has been pushed into a past more remote than Italy's, forced to become the Muse of a tale she never would have told.

Moreover, Elizabeth Barrett Browning's most cherished material is part of the base metal out of which Robert forges his ring. *Aurora Leigh* celebrates the choric power of female community: its triumphant achievement is not Aurora's marriage to the diminished Romney, but her union with the victimized seamstress, Marian Erle. In the best tradition of fairy tale princes, the wealthy Romney had reached down to "save" Marian from her abased class and gender, only to be rejected twice; Aurora does save her not by elevating her, but by recognizing and ratifying her absolute truth. Together, Aurora and Marian exemplify the mystic interdependence of the female victim and queen, an interdependence which . . . is a resonant presence in Victorian iconography. *The Ring and the Book* mutes this vibrant union to the solitary whisper of the moribund Pompilia, whose truth is heard only by the pure of heart and the dying. This pale, isolated heroine drains from female truth its clarion authority.

In *Aurora Leigh,* both Aurora and Marian tell stories that have an instantaneous impact. Aurora's stories—her poems, and the poem we are reading—are validated by their immediate success; her age crowns her truth. Marian's two stories have a similar authoritative impact on their sole hearer, Aurora herself. When they first meet, she tells the initially skeptical Aurora the sad story of her life. Most of Robert Browning's auditors would remain skeptical, thus squeezing Marian's tale into that embarrassed compound of lies and semi-truths that constitutes the dramatic monologue. Aurora, on the other hand, is instantly converted, authenticating Marian's history by blending it into her own. . . . (pp. 168-69)

Later, a chastened Aurora and a Marian purified by humiliation meet again in Paris. This time, Marian's wildly implausible tale of abduction, rape, and miraculous motherhood needs no validation: Aurora allows her to tell it at length, in her own voice. Its truth is instantaneously apparent. Without hesitation or attempts at confirmation, Aurora writes to a powerful friend:

> 'Dear Lord Howe,
> You'll find a story on another leaf
> Of Marian Erle,—what noble friend of yours
> She trusted once, through what flagitious means,
> To what disastrous ends;—the story's true.'

The truth of Marian's stories echoes and reinforces the truth Aurora claims for herself as the self-crowning Bard of her own life history. The embodiments of truth know each other instantly in *Aurora Leigh,* as the good people do in Dickens' novels, because their very beings are illuminated. Thus, when

Marian finds her mission in motherhood, we must not doubt that God has taken her shape:

> For Romney, angels are less tender-wise
> Than God and mothers: even *you* would think
> What *we* think never. He is ours, the child;
> And we would sooner vex a soul in heaven
> By coupling with it the dead body's thought,
> Than, in my child, see other than . . . my child.
> We only never call him fatherless
> Who has God and his mother.

Even the best of men are excluded from this God-endowed authority of true womanhood: God obligingly abdicates his conventional fatherhood to legitimize a mother's self-completeness. As Marian is to her child, so is Aurora to her poem. Both women are the only begetters, the sole, self-consecrating authorities in a world with no other legitimate storytellers. Their affinity with God irradiates their spiritual power. In *The Ring and the Book,* Pompilia's intimacy with God assures that she will be silenced for a hundred and seventy years.

In recasting his wife's epic into his own, Robert Browning compressed these two powerful women into a single, dying young girl; he also modulated the elation of inspiration into the agony of sanctification. Pompilia's large eyes, her fineness of perception, her aesthetic and pictorial instinct, all look back to Aurora Leigh, as well as to Elizabeth Barrett Browning; the ordeal of her victimization is Marian Erle's. But Pompilia's truth rests in her martyrdom, not in the story she barely articulates. The inspired utterances of Aurora and Marian become the Christ-like wounds displayed involuntarily by a saint whose seal of purity is her illiteracy. (pp. 169-70)

It is impossible to imagine seventeenth-century Rome personified as a giant, heaving-breasted Pompilia; the spirit of the age is embodied in the men who shout and dissemble and display themselves as she lies dying. The authenticity of Pompilia's truth lies in her very removal from the turbulent contemporary life Aurora Leigh embodied. The spiritual authority of Elizabeth Barrett Browning's women is thrust to the margins of the social and political life Barrett Browning's poetry of the 1850s celebrated.

It may be Robert Browning's ultimate victory over his celebrated wife that he robs Pompilia of a public voice. Aurora Leigh's glory was more Bardic than moral, a glory she shared with the poet Marian. Robert Browning is at pains to bless Pompilia, his own victim / queen, with illiteracy, though the Old Yellow Book proves that the historical Pompilia could both read and write. Pompilia herself uses illiteracy as a badge of distinction opposed to her falsifying weight of name. Aurora Leigh's writing exalted her as the spirit of her age, while Pompilia's inability to write exalts her by isolating her from that age:

> How happy those are who know how to write!
> Such could write what their son should read in time,
> Had they a whole day to live out like me.
> Also my name is not a common name,
> "Pompilia," and may help to keep apart
> A little the thing I am from what girls are.

"The thing I am" removes her utterly from the life of her culture, almost from humanity itself; like Lyric Love, "half angel and half bird," Pompilia forfeits human privileges. The Pope's soliloquy authorizes her by blessing her most un-Aurora

The Poets' Corner of Westminster Abbey, where Browning was buried. The Bettmann Archive/BBC Hulton.

Leigh-like silence: after apotheosizing her as "perfect in whiteness," the Pope muses:

> It was not given Pompilia to know much,
> Speak much, to write a book, to move mankind,
> Be memorized by who records my time.

Because she is neither the author nor the spirit of her age, Pompilia shines as the "one prize" in the secret ruminations of the lone, dying Pope.

Her silence is rewarded with a fittingly secret benediction: like Pompilia, the Pope speaks in soliloquy. The purity of both is immunized from the ambiguous entanglements of the dramatic monologue. Pompilia is spoken about incessantly in street and court, but she speaks only to an indeterminate audience in the privacy of her deathbed, and her death is more speaking than her words. (pp. 170-71)

Since the trial does in fact vindicate Pompilia's innocence, *The Ring and the Book* might well have ended with general recognition of the dead saint. Instead, it ends in a tangle of dark and unregenerate activities with the bitter refrain, "Let God be true, and every man a liar." The lawyer who had "sainted" her plans to indict her as a "person of dishonest life," allowing the Convertite nuns to claim her property; and these presumably are the very nuns who heard her deathbed soliloquy. Far from

being instantaneously converted, as Aurora Leigh was by Marian Erle's tales, the Convertites repudiate her truth and proceed on their hale if unglorified way. (pp. 171-72)

Like Marian Erle before her, Pompilia exalts the absolute and divine power of her motherhood, claiming kinship with a mother God who expunges male violence:

> Let us leave God alone!
> Why should I doubt He will explain in time
> What I feel now, but fail to find the words?
> My babe nor was, nor is, nor yet shall be
> Count Guido Franceschini's child at all—
> Only his mother's, born of love not hate!

Pompilia asserts her divinely sanctioned self-sufficiency only to have the poem destroy it. Even the fitfully omniscient narrator corrects her and puts her in her place:

> Well, proving of such perfect parentage,
> Our Gaetano, *born of love and hate,*
> Did the babe live or die?—one fain would find!
> What were his fancies if he grew a man?
> Was he proud,—a true scion of the stock,—
> Of bearing blason, shall make bright my Book—
> Shield, Azure, on a Triple Mountain, Or,
> A Palm-tree, Proper, whereunto is tied
> A Greyhound, Rampant, striving in the slips?
> Or did he love his mother, the base-born,
> And fight i' the ranks, unnoticed by the world?

Browning's narrator is unyielding: Pompilia is allowed no mitigation of her invisibility and silence. Gaetano's inheritance from her is not glory, but the distinction of being consistently unnoticed. Elsewhere . . . , Professor U. C. Knoepflmacher explores ways in which, under Elizabeth's influence, Robert Browning gives a voice to the martyred women his earlier poems had silenced. This is so, but *The Ring and the Book* is ruthless in insisting that if the saving poet had not descended to give Pompilia his own versatile voice, she would have been forever unheard. Elizabeth Barrett Browning's "unscrupulously epic" claims for absolute authority in her age are in *The Ring and the Book* suppressed with loving brutality. The story of Pompilia, who is perfect in whiteness and exemplifies truth, suggests that a woman speaks with purity only by dying unheard.

Having survived a poet who made epic claims for herself, Robert Browning perpetuated her voice by turning it into his own; he "married" Elizabeth Barrett one more time when he appropriated her after her death, weaving her declarations into the corrosive fabric of his dramatic monologues. (pp. 172-73)

Robert Browning had a man's last word. Characteristically, his final tribute to Elizabeth twisted the promise that was, in **"A Woman's Last Word,"** a wife's:

> Teach me, only teach. Love!
> As I ought
> I will speak thy speech, Love.
> Think thy thought.

Robert Browning ended up by speaking his wife's speech and thinking her thought, but in muting them to a dying whisper among dramatic monologues, he drained them of authority. Initially, he had praised Elizabeth enviously for her capacity to "speak out"; finally, he spoke out for her, making her voice one of many testimonies to the superior survival power of a poet who could "make men & women speak." In his crowning work, he added his wife to the chorus of his creations. (p. 173)

> *Nina Auerbach, "Robert Browning's Last Word,"*
> in Victorian Poetry, *Vol. 22, No. 2, Summer, 1984,*
> *pp. 161-73.*

ADDITIONAL BIBLIOGRAPHY

Armstrong, Isobel, ed. *The Major Victorian Poets: Reconsideratons.* Lincoln: University of Nebraska Press, 1969, 323 p.
    A collection of essays that includes critical revaluations of *Sordello* and *The Ring and the Book.*

Bloom, Harold. "Testing the Map: Browning's 'Childe Roland'." In his *A Map of Misreading*, pp. 106-22. New York: Oxford University Press, 1975.
    Explicates "'Childe Roland to the Dark Tower Came'" in light of his theory of creative misreading.

———, and Munich, Adrienne, eds. *Robert Browning: A Collection of Critical Essays.* Twentieth Century Views, edited by Maynard Mack. Englewood Cliffs, N.J.: Prentice-Hall, A Spectrum Book, 1979, 207 p.
    Includes commentary by such noted critics as John Hollander, Harold Bloom, and Robert Langbaum.

Broughton, Leslie Nathan; Northup, Clark Sutherland; and Pearsall, Robert. *Robert Browning: A Bibliography, 1830-1950.* Cornell Studies in English, edited by Charles W. Jones, Francis E. Mineka, and William M. Sale, Jr., vol. XXXIX. Ithaca, N.Y.: Cornell University Press, 1953, 446 p.

Considered a primary reference tool in Browning studies. The authors supply detailed, comprehensive information concerning writings by and about Browning for the period indicated.

Brown, E. K. "The First Person in 'Caliban upon Setebos'." *Modern Language Notes* LXVI, No. 6 (June 1951): 392-95.
    Argues that Caliban's use of the first and third person in his speech reflects his inner conflict "between fear and guile on the one hand, and impudence and self-love on the other."

Bush, Douglas. "Browning." In his *Mythology and the Romantic Tradition in English Poetry*, pp. 358-85. The Norton Library. New York: W. W. Norton & Co., 1963.
    Discusses Browning's treatment of classical myths and themes in *Balaustion's Adventure, Aristophanes' Apology,* and other works.

Collins, Thomas J. *Robert Browning's Moral-Aesthetic Theory, 1833-1855.* Lincoln: University of Nebraska Press, 1967, 164 p.
    Attempts to "present a unified and coherent analysis of the progressive development of Robert Browning's ideas concerning the nature and purpose of art, and the role of the artist, between 1833 and 1855."

Cook, A. K. *A Commentary upon Browning's "The Ring and the Book."* 1920. Reprint. Hamden, Conn.: Archon Books, 1966, 343 p.
    Explains numerous allusions in *The Ring and the Book* and sheds light on the sources, composition, text, and historical details of the poem.

Cook, Eleanor. *Browning's Lyrics: An Exploration.* Toronto: University of Toronto Press, 1974, 317 p.
    A detailed examination of Browning's lyric poetry. Cook includes studies of Browning's imagery and poetics as part of her exploration of the lyrics.

Crowell, Norton B. *The Triple Soul: Browning's Theory of Knowledge.* Albuquerque: University of New Mexico Press, 1963, 235 p.
    Investigates—and generally defends—Browning's theory of knowledge. In opposition to many critics, Crowell denies that Browning was anti-intellectual, asserting that he valued the mind as an integral part of the "triple soul of man: body, mind, and spirit."

Davies, Hugh Sykes. *Browning and the Modern Novel.* Hull, England: University of Hull Publications, 1962, 28 p.
    Considers Browning's contribution to the modern novel.

DeVane, William Clyde. *A Browning Handbook.* 2d ed. New York: Appleton-Century-Crofts, 1955, 594 p.
    Generally regarded as an invaluable aid to Browning studies. DeVane devotes a section of his *Handbook* to each of Browning's publications, describing the work and providing information on such topics as composition and publication dates and contemporary reaction to the volume.

Drew, Philip. *The Poetry of Browning: A Critical Introduction.* London: Methuen & Co., 1970, 471 p.
    Lays the groundwork for appreciating Browning's poetry by challenging misconceptions concerning his work and by underscoring the distinctively Victorian qualities of his verse. Specifically, Drew refutes the notion that Browning wrote in the Romantic tradition, and he also contests the poet's reputation for deliberate obscurity and "heedless optimism."

———, ed. *Robert Browning: A Collection of Critical Essays.* Boston: Houghton Mifflin Co., 1966, 278 p.
    Provides a wide variety of commentary on Browning. Both nineteenth- and twentieth-century criticism is included in the collection, which contains general studies of the author as well as essays on individual poems.

DuBois, Arthur E. "Robert Browning, Dramatist." *Studies in Philology* XXXIII, No. 4 (October 1936): 626-55.
    A highly regarded essay assessing Browning's importance as a dramatist in terms of his involvement with ironic drama.

Elton, Oliver. *The Brownings.* 1924. Reprint. New York: Haskell House Publishers, 1971, 96 p.

A literary survey giving extensive consideration to Robert Browning's writing career.

Fairchild, Hoxie N. "Browning the Simple-Hearted Casuist." *University of Toronto Quarterly* XVIII, No. 3 (April 1949): 234-40.
Focuses on the tension between mind and heart in Browning's poetry. According to Fairchild, Browning ultimately sides with the heart, indicating his preference by employing a device here labeled as "the giveaway."

Fuson, Benjamin Willis. *Browning and His Predecessors in the Dramatic Monolog.* State University of Iowa Humanistic Studies, edited by Franklin H. Potter, vol. VIII. Iowa City: State University of Iowa, 1948, 96 p.
Refutes the notion that Browning invented the dramatic monologue, citing a long history of such compositions in English literature.

Gosse, Edmund. *Robert Browning: Personalia.* London: T. Fisher Unwin, 1890, 96 p.
Features a reprint of "The Early Career of Robert Browning, 1812-1846," a literary and biographical sketch based on interviews that Gosse conducted with Browning.

Greer, Louise. *Browning and America.* Chapel Hill: University of North Carolina Press, 1952, 355 p.
Covers such subjects as Browning's associations with Americans and the progress of his popularity and critical reputation in the United States.

Griffin, W. Hall, and Minchin, Harry Christopher. *The Life of Robert Browning.* New York: Macmillan Co., 1912, 342 p.
Long considered the standard biography of Browning.

Hair, Donald S. *Browning's Experiments with Genre.* University of Toronto Department of English Studies and Texts, no. 19. Toronto: University of Toronto Press, 1972, 204 p.
Studies Browning's experimentation with the structure, conventions, and techniques of such genres as the drama and lyric, dramatic, and narrative poetry.

Hassett, Constance W. *The Elusive Self in the Poetry of Robert Browning.* Athens: Ohio State University Press, 1982, 175 p.
Identifies self-assessment as a dominant theme in Browning's work.

Honan, Park. *Browning's Characters: A Study in Poetic Technique.* 1961. Reprint. Hamden, Conn.: Archon Books, 1969, 327 p.
Examines Browning's poems and dramas in the context of character portrayal, maintaining that such an investigation reveals the "complexity, intensity, and unity of his best dramatic verse."

Irvine, William, and Honan, Park. *The Book, the Ring and the Poet: A Biography of Robert Browning.* New York: McGraw-Hill Book Co., 1974, 607 p.
A modern life of Browning written by two nineteenth-century literature scholars.

James, Henry. "The Novel in 'The Ring and the Book'." In his *Notes on Novelists, with Some Other Notes,* pp. 385-411. New York: Charles Scribner's Sons, 1914.
Speculates on constructing a novel from the materials in *The Ring and the Book.*

Jones, Henry. *Browning as a Philosophical and Religious Teacher.* 2d ed. Glasgow: James Maclehose & Sons, 1896, 349 p.
An influential explication of Browning's philosophy including discussions of his optimism and his approach to the problem of evil.

Khattab, Ezzat Abdulmajeed. *The Critical Reception of Browning's "The Ring and the Book," 1868-1889 and 1951-1968.* Salzburg Studies in English Literature: Romantic Reassessment, edited by James Hogg, vol. 66. Salzburg: Institut für Englische Sprache und Literatur, Univesität Salzburg, 1977, 214 p.
Surveys and compares the response of Victorian and modern critics to *The Ring and the Book.*

King, Roma A., Jr. *The Bow and the Lyre: The Art of Robert Browning.* Ann Arbor: University of Michigan Press, Ann Arbor Paperbacks, 1964, 162 p.
Explores the characteristics of Browning's artistry. King bases many of his conclusions on his readings of five "representative" works: "Andrea del Sarto," "Fra Lippo Lippi," "The Bishop Orders His Tomb at San Praxed's," "Bishop Blougram's Apology," and "Saul."

Litzinger, Boyd. *Time's Revenges: Browning's Reputation as a Thinker, 1889-1962.* Knoxville: University of Tennessee Press, 1964, 192 p.
Traces the critical reaction to Browning's thought during the years 1889 to 1962.

―――, and Knickerbocker, K. L., eds. *The Browning Critics.* Lexington: University of Kentucky Press, 1965, 426 p.
Reprints essays by George Saintsbury, Paul Elmer More, Kenneth Knickerbocker, and others.

―――, and Smalley, Donald, eds. *Browning: The Critical Heritage.* The Critical Heritage Series, edited by B. C. Southam. New York: Barnes and Noble, 1970, 550 p.
Reprints selected nineteenth-century critical commentary on Browning's work.

Lounsbury, Thomas R. *The Early Literary Career of Robert Browning.* London: T. Fisher Unwin, 1912, 205 p.
A series of lectures exploring Browning's contemporary critical reputation. Lounsbury focuses on the reception given to *Pauline, Paracelsus, Strafford, Sordello,* and *Bells and Pomegranates.*

Lucas, F. L. "Browning." In his *Eight Victorian Poets,* pp. 23-38. Cambridge: Cambridge University Press, 1930.
Assesses Browning's artistry, frequently comparing it with that of Alfred, Lord Tennyson.

Miller, Betty. *Robert Browning: A Portrait.* London: John Murray, 1952, 302 p.
A biographical study noted for its provocative interpretations of Browning's life and works.

Muir, Edwin. "Robert Browning." In his *Essays on Literature and Society,* pp. 103-09. London: Hogarth Press, 1949.
A general assessment that includes commentary on Browning's optimism.

Orr, Mrs. Sutherland. *Life and Letters of Robert Browning.* Rev. ed. Boston: Houghton, Mifflin and Co., 1908, 431 p.
Considered an important early biography. This edition of the *Life,* which was originally published in 1891, includes material revised and rewritten by Frederic G. Kenyon.

―――. *A Handbook to the Works of Robert Browning.* 6th ed. 1892. Reprint. New York: Kraus Reprint Co., 1969, 420 p.
An early reference book on Browning, largely descriptive in nature.

Peterson, William S. *Robert and Elizabeth Barrett Browning: An Annotated Bibliography, 1951-1970.* New York: Browning Institute, 1974, 209 p.
Lists and describes select biographical, critical, reference, and bibliographic works on the Brownings.

Phelps, William Lyon. *Robert Browning: How to Know Him.* Indianapolis: Bobbs-Merrill Co., 1915, 381 p.
A general biographical and critical study.

Porter, Katherine H. *Through a Glass Darkly: Spiritualism in the Browning Circle.* Lawrence: University of Kansas Press, 1958, 160 p.
Investigates the Brownings' involvement in spiritualism.

Pottle, Frederick A. *Shelley and Browning: A Myth and Some Facts.* 1923. Reprint. Hamden, Conn.: Archon Books, 1965, 94 p.
A detailed examination of Percy Bysshe Shelley's influence on Browning's early life and works.

Pound, Ezra. *Literary Essays of Ezra Pound.* Edited by T. S. Eliot. New York: A New Directions Book, 1968, 464 p.

Contains scattered references to Browning, including a passage in the essay "T. S. Eliot" praising the dramatic monologue form used in *Men and Women* as the "most vital form" in Victorian poetry.

Ruskin, John. "The Mountain Glory." In his *Modern Painters*. Vol. IV, *Of Mountain Beauty,* pp. 365-406. London: George Allen, 1897.
Includes a section in which Ruskin praises Browning's insight into the spirit of the Renaissance, particularly as revealed in "The Bishop Orders His Tomb at San Praxed's."

Ryals, Clyde de L. *Browning's Later Poetry, 1871-1889.* Ithaca, N.Y.: Cornell University Press, 1975, 262 p.
Underscores the artistic integrity of Browning's later works, focusing on his commitment to discovering new formal methods for expressing his vision of reality.

————. *Becoming Browning: The Poems and Plays of Robert Browning: 1833-1846.* Columbus: Ohio State University Press, 1983, 292 p.
Examines Browning's early work in light of his "philosophy of becoming," described by the critic as a set of beliefs centered on the principles of change and progress.

Rys, Ernest. *Browning and His Poetry.* Poetry and Life Series, edited by William Henry Hudson. London: George G. Harrap & Co., 1918, 127 p.
An introductory biographical and critical study of the poet.

Shaw, W. David. *The Dialectical Temper: The Rhetorical Art of Robert Browning.* Ithaca, N.Y.: Cornell University Press, 1968, 328 p.
Focuses on the dialectical temper of Browning's poetic rhetoric.

Swinburne, Algernon Charles. Letter to John Nichol. In his *The Swinburne Letters: 1854-1869,* Vol. I, edited by Cecil Y. Lang, pp. 100-01. New Haven: Yale University Press, 1959.
Acknowledges the excellence of "Mr. Sludge," "The Medium," and "Caliban upon Setebos." On previous occasions Swinburne had denounced Browning's poetry.

Thomas, Donald. *Robert Browning: A Life within Life.* New York: Viking Press, 1982, 334 p.
A modern biography offering particular insight into Browning's "inner world."

Tracy, Clarence, ed. *Browning's Mind and Art.* Edinburgh: Oliver and Boyd, 1968, 224 p.
A collection of essays that includes discussions of Browning's themes, literary techniques, and influences.

Victorian Poetry, An Issue Commemorative of the Centennial of the Publication of "The Ring and the Book" VI, Nos. 3-4 (Autumn-Winter 1969): 215-375.
Contains eleven essays on *The Ring and the Book,* including articles by such noted Browning critics as Park Honan, Isobel Armstrong, and William O. Raymond.

Thomas Campbell

1777-1844

Scottish poet, critic, journalist, biographer, and historian.

Campbell was a minor poet of the early nineteenth century. Chiefly remembered for his lyric poetry, he is today best known as the author of several of the most stirring martial odes in English, "Hohenlinden," "Ye Mariners of England," and "The Battle of the Baltic." During his lifetime, however, Campbell was renowned for his narrative poem "The Pleasures of Hope." While the popularity of this work declined after his death, certain lines are still widely quoted, including "'Tis distance lends enchantment to the view" and "Like angel-visits, few and far between."

The youngest of eleven children, Campbell was born in Glasgow, Scotland, to Margaret and Alexander Campbell. Shortly before his birth, his father's trading business was interrupted by the American Revolution, and the once-prosperous family suffered a severe financial setback. Campbell attended grammar school in Glasgow and later, from 1791 to 1796, Glasgow University, where he composed poetry, practiced debate, and excelled at Greek translation, often winning school prizes; his appreciation for classical writers, which is considered a major influence on the style of his work, dates from this period. In 1797, Campbell moved to Edinburgh. There, he began taking on miscellaneous editorial and journalistic projects, and he also entered what is considered his greatest period of creative activity, publishing *The Pleasures of Hope, with Other Poems* in 1799 to widespread acclaim. Following the appearance of this work, Campbell traveled in Germany and Denmark, settling in London shortly after his return. In 1803, he married his second cousin, Matilda Sinclair. With the births, in 1804 and 1805, of two sons, Campbell suffered financial difficulties, which were offset in part by the grant of a small government pension and by his constant production of articles for magazines, newspapers, and encyclopedias. He also started working on a long-term project, the anthology *Specimens of the British Poets,* and continued to write poetry, publishing the widely praised collection *Gertrude of Wyoming,* which solidified his reputation, in 1809.

The completion of *Gertrude of Wyoming* marked the close of what most critics consider Campbell's major creative period. After this point, he focused primarily on lectures, editing, and journalism. In 1812, he gave the first in a series of public lectures in London on the theory and history of poetry; the series was so successful that he repeated it in London and later in Liverpool and Birmingham. He also continued working on *Specimens of the British Poets,* which appeared in 1819. In this anthology, Campbell included selections from British poetry, biographical and critical sketches of many of the authors, and an introductory "Essay on English Poetry." While contemporary reviewers praised Campbell's discriminating and perceptive critical judgments, they faulted *Specimens of the British Poets* for its uneven quality and lack of careful scholarship, and it has received little subsequent attention. Following its publication, Campbell's career took a new direction. He served as editor of the *New Monthly Magazine* from 1820 to 1830 and of the *Metropolitan* from 1831 to 1832. In addition to his editorial responsibilities, he worked on many independent

projects, one of the most important of which was his organization of the Polish Association in 1832; a group formed to aid Polish exiles, the Association testified to his lifelong enthusiasm for liberty. Campbell published a variety of works in the 1830s and 1840s, among them biographies of the Italian poet Petrarch and the tragic actress Sarah Kemble Siddons, a collection of letters describing his travels in Algiers, and his final volume of poems, *The Pilgrim of Glencoe.* However, none of these proved popular with either critics or the public. Campbell's last years were marked by poor health, and in 1843 he left London for Boulogne, searching for a milder climate; he died there in 1844.

Of Campbell's diverse body of works, just two of his long poems—"The Pleasures of Hope" and "Gertrude of Wyoming"—and a few of his short lyric poems have received much critical attention. "The Pleasures of Hope," a discursive didactic poem written in heroic couplets, consists of a series of scenes that illustrate different aspects of hope: Part I depicts such temporal concerns of human life as domestic matters and social and political issues, while Part II, which is considered more abstract, addresses the hope for immortality. Campbell experimented with a range of themes and styles in this poem, and critics often cite the influence of John Milton's *Paradise Lost,* Mark Akenside's *The Pleasures of Imagination,* Samuel

Rogers's *The Pleasures of Memory*, and the works of Alexander Pope. With its moral platitudes, emphasis on taste and polish, and formal, mechanical couplets, "The Pleasures of Hope" is frequently linked to the eighteenth-century neo-classical tradition of didactic poetry. Indeed, many commentators have suggested that these qualities, which earned Campbell the acclaim of his contemporaries, were also responsible for the decline in the poem's popularity after his death: its regular and conventional lines lacked the intensity, passion, and spontaneity that characterized the developing Romantic movement. Campbell's second narrative poem, "Gertrude of Wyoming," describes the Mohawk Indians' destruction in 1778 of a settlement in the Wyoming valley of the Susquehanna River in Pennsylvania. Focusing on one family of settlers, the story is divided into three parts that cover the childhood, marriage, and death of the title character. Certain flaws were routinely noted by early reviewers, who criticized the poem's confusing story line, historical and scientific inaccuracies, and often convoluted and inverted phrasing, which they attributed to the rigid rhyme scheme imposed by Campbell's use of the Spenserian stanza and to his penchant for excessive revision. While acknowledging these faults, many critics ascribed the poem's polished style to Campbell's scrupulous revision and praised its taste, delicacy, tenderness, and pathos.

Campbell's lyric poems are now considered his finest works. He wrote in several forms, including ballads, odes, and songs, and on a variety of topics—nature, patriotism, war, politics, liberty, and Scottish history. Two of his best-known poems, "Lochiel's Warning" and "Lord Ullin's Daughter," are based on Scottish legend. "Lochiel's Warning" recounts a dialogue between the Highland chieftain Lochiel and an omniscient wizard, who attempts to dissuade the heroic but stubborn Lochiel from engaging in a hopeless battle, while the ballad "Lord Ullin's Daughter," a traditional story based on Highland legend, describes the attempt of a woman and her lover to undertake a dangerous crossing by boat in a storm while pursued by her father. Both poems have been praised for their vivid descriptions, energetic rhythms, and simple yet effective poetic technique. This last aspect of Campbell's poetry inspired the critic Lafcadio Hearn to comment: "When *he is most simple*, he is most haunting; and the simplicity is of the delusive kind,—the kind that you think anybody can do when you first read it, yet which can really be done but very few times in the course of a century." The same simplicity characterizes Campbell's martial odes. Although each covers a different subject—"Hohenlinden" details the Austrian defeat by the French in the 1800 battle at the village of Hohenlinden, "Ye Mariners of England" is a sustained apostrophe to the English navy, and "The Battle of the Baltic" celebrates the English victory over the Danish in the 1801 Battle of Copenhagen—these poems share many characteristics. Their energetic and vigorous movement, clear and authentic description of events, evocation of intense emotions, and appeal to patriotic feelings are often attributed to Campbell's skillful handling of meter and rhyme scheme, as well as to his use of sound effects. These qualities make Campbell's war odes, in the opinion of many scholars, his greatest poems.

Campbell's popular and critical reputation has changed dramatically since his lifetime. "The Pleasures of Hope," published when Campbell was only twenty-two years old, was immediately successful, and reviewers routinely hailed the work as evidence of great promise. With the appearance ten years later of "Gertrude of Wyoming," Campbell's contemporary position as one of the greatest poets of his era was secured.

Yet his later works never fulfilled this early promise, and the high reputation that he sustained throughout his life was based almost solely on his first narrative poems. By the end of the nineteenth century, critical approbation had shifted from Campbell's long poems to his lyrics, especially his war odes, and this focus has continued to the present day. Most scholars now recognize certain defects and merits in Campbell's works: they typically fault his habit of excessive revision and lack of spontaneity and profound thought or emotion, while generally applauding the clarity, simplicity, energy, and elegance of his best poems, particularly those celebrating freedom and patriotism. Although he is not a popular author today, Campbell continues to command critical respect because, in the words of Georg Brandes, "in his best verse there is a spirit, a swinging march time, and a fire, that entitle him, if only for the sake of half-a-dozen short pieces, to a place among great poets."

PRINCIPAL WORKS

The Pleasures of Hope, with Other Poems   (poetry)   1799
Poems   (poetry)   1803
Annals of Great Britain from the Ascension of George IIId. to the Peace of Amiens   (history)   1807
**Gertrude of Wyoming: A Pennsylvanian Tale, and Other Poems*   (poetry)   1809
Specimens of the British Poets, with Biographical and Critical Notices, and an "Essay on English Poetry" 7 vols. [editor]   (poetry and essays)   1819
***Theodric: A Domestic Tale, and Other Poems*   (poetry) 1824
Poland   (poctry)   1831
Life of Mrs. Siddons   (biography)   1834
Letters from the South. 2 vols.   (letters)   1837; also published as *The Journal of a Residence in Algiers,* 1842
Life of Petrarch   (biography)   1841
The Pilgrim of Glencoe, and Other Poems   (poetry)   1842
The Poetical Works of Thomas Campbell   (poetry)   1851
The Complete Poetical Works of Thomas Campbell (poetry)   1907

*This collection includes the poems "Hohenlinden" and "Lochiel's Warning."

**This collection includes the poems "The Battle of the Baltic," "Lord Ullin's Daughter," and "Ye Mariners of England."

***This collection includes the poem "The Last Man."

THE BRITISH CRITIC   (essay date 1799)

[*In this review of* The Pleasures of Hope, *the anonymous critic praises the title poem's style, versification, and polish, yet denounces Campbell's youthful liberal political principles.*]

So uncommon a degree of merit appears in the first and principal of these Poems [in *The Pleasures of Hope*], that we cannot let it pass without particular notice. This distinction is, from us, the more valuable, because the author is apparently tainted with principles which we cannot ever approve. But he is very young. Report says so, and many circumstances confirm it; and if the generous zeal for liberty runs a little wild in a youthful and very ardent mind, there is great hope that maturer age will correct this, as well as other luxuriances of early life, and reduce it within the limits of right reason. Let him continue to abhor Despotism, properly so called. Greybeards as we are, we will hate it with him, as much as he can desire. But let him hate it under republican forms, as much as under unlimited monarchies. Let him lament the fate of Poland. Who that deserves the name of a free-man, will not lament it? But when he sees things in their true light, he will hardly idolize Kosciusko. Let him, among the Pleasures of Hope, reckon that of seeing the extension of just government and rational freedom among men; but let him beware of the cant of Condorcer and Godwin, into which, if he does not completely fall in some passages of this Poem, he at least approaches so near to it, as to authorize the suspicion, that as yet his mind has not attained sufficient vigour to reject it.

The Pleasures of Hope are surely as good a subject for a rising poet, as can well be chosen. It is the very essence of genius (as is not forgotten in this Poem) to form ideal scenes of future gratification; which, if not at all destined to be realized, confer, for the time, an actual happiness by anticipation; and thus snatch from fate even more than it designs to give. This subject is treated by Mr. Campbell with much genius, and, in general, with good judgment; certainly with a very singular splendour and felicity of versification. There is, however, a material distinction to be made between the first part and the second. There is no comparison between the polish and perfection of the two; the clearness of the style, and of the transitions (most essential points of good writing) and every thing that raises the writer of the first far above the generality of his contemporaries. We should conceive the second part to be an after-thought. Perceiving that he had omitted the most material object of Hope, the hope of a future life, the author wrote perhaps the second part for the sake of leading the reader to it. But he bestowed less care, and exercised less judgment in performing this second task; possibly from weariness, possibly from a pardonable, though injudicious impatience, to lay the composition before the public. (pp. 21-2)

When poetry is wrought up to a high degree of polish, there is always some danger, particularly in the present times, lest affectation should insinuate itself instead of refinement. This appears to us the leading fault of the second part of the **"Pleasures of Hope."** It is affected, and tainted with false refinement, in the thoughts, as well as many expressions. Yet still the poet frequently appears in his true garb; as in this line;

> Delirious Anguish on his fiery wing.

To substantiate the charge of affectation, by an induction of proofs, would lead us into a long detail; and we say it not to injure the Poems, which we admire, but to put the author on his guard when he shall correct it. He has taste enough to see what we mean, when he takes himself to task. We regret still more his admiration of that barbarous and unnatural play, the Robbers of Schiller; the very extract from which, as given in his Notes, is detestable in every point of view. To part with commendation, according to the general tenor of this critique, we will cite the author's description of the sublimest hopes of man.

> Unfading Hope! when life's last embers burn,
> When foul to foul, and dust to dust return!
> Heav'n to thy charge resigns the awful hour!
> Oh!, then, thy kingdom comes! Immortal Power!
> What though each spark of earth-born rapture fly
> The quivering lip, pale cheek, and closing eye!
> Bright to the soul thy seraph hands convey
> The morning dreams of life's eternal day—
> Then, then, the triumph and the trance begin!
> And all the Phoenix spirit burns within!

> Cease, every joy, to glimmer on my mind,
> But leave—oh! leave—the light of Hope behind!
> What though my winged hours of bliss have been,
> Like angel visits, few and far between;
> Her musing mood shall every pang appease,
> And charm—when pleasures lose the power to please!

The line, "Like angel visits, few and far between," is exquisite, and so are many parts of that quotation. We shall conclude, by an earnest exhortation to the writer, to cultivate his great talent for poetry; but, from no temptation, and on no account, to omit that strict and severe criticism on himself, which alone can keep his genius within the limits of correct taste, and enable him to give laws to future critics, as well as to satisfy the present.

The remaining Poems in this book are short. They are not destitute of merit, but by no means so remarkable in any respect as the passages which we have, and some which we have not cited, from **"The Pleasures of Hope."** (pp. 25-6)

> *A review of "The Pleasures of Hope, with Other Poems," in* The British Critic, *Vol. XIV, July, 1799, pp. 21-6.*

[ALEXANDER HAMILTON]   (essay date 1799)

[*Hamilton reviews* The Pleasures of Hope, *claiming that Campbell shows great promise as a poet.*]

[In reviewing **"The Pleasures of Hope,"** it] would be unreasonable to expect, in a poem on this subject, the same exactness and method which occur in the *Pleasures of Memory,* or perhaps the *Pleasures of Imagination.* All that can be done, in delineating the effects of the passion here described, is to form pleasing groupes, and to combine them by natural transitions. In one transition, we think, the present author has been too abrupt: namely, in passing from the subject which introduces the Episode, to the Sorrows of Conrad and his daughter. The characteristic style of the poem is *the pathetic,* though in some passages it rises into a higher tone. (p. 422)

Though there seems to be no settled mode of arrangement adopted in disposing of the successive pictures which constitute the poem, yet there is an evident climax followed out. The 'march-worn soldier' entering the field of battle is the first description; to which succeeds an allusion to the situation of the celebrated Commodore Byron; who, actuated by the influence of anticipation, encountered so many difficulties with exemplary fortitude. A domestic scene is then naturally introduced, in which the influence of Hope on parental affection is well pourtrayed. (pp. 422-23)

From scenes or private life, the writer then passes to a nobler subject, viz. the prospect of the amelioration of the human race, and of their progress in science, liberty, and virtue. He has selected the partition of Poland, to illustrate a period at which every well-wisher to mankind entertained sanguine hopes of the emancipation of millions of the human species; and he concludes with a poetical prophecy that the day of Polish freedom may be yet expected. In all his allusions to politics, Mr. Campbell takes no notice of the French Revolution; a circumstance which at least argues that he regards the revolution of Poland and that of France in a different light. In fact, we are by no means inclined to suppose, from the tenor of Mr. C.'s writings, that his admiration of Brutus and Kosciusko have tinged his mind with improper principles; and from his silence on the subject of French Liberty, we argue his disapprobation of its horrors and excesses. In his allusion to the partition of Poland, he describes the last fatal contest of the oppressors and the oppressed, the capture of the city of Prague, and the massacre of the Poles at the bridge which crosses the Vistula. . . . (p. 424)

From this pathetic allusion to modern politics, the poet passes by an easy transition to another, equally interesting. The picture of the Negroe, hunting on his native plains,

> With fires proportion'd to his native sky,
> Strength in his arm and lightning in his eye,

is finely contrasted with the fetter'd and degraded slave. This subject, though almost exhausted, seems to have presented itself to the poet's mind in new and glowing colours.

The concluding lines on this topic introduce a simile which, we think, is entirely original, and beautiful:

> The widow'd Indian, when her Lord expires,
> Mounts the dread pile, and braves the funeral fires!
> So falls the heart at thraldom's bitter sigh!
> So Virtue dies, the Spouse of Liberty!

The second part of the poem is shorter than the first, but still more pleasing. The allusion to the solitude of Adam, before the creation of his helpmate, is very poetical; and the anticipation of the lover, while musing on the future happiness which he is to enjoy in the society of

> The kind, fair friend, by Nature mark'd his own,

is a pleasing picture of the domestic life. The writer's versification and manner in that passage, particularly, remind us of the simplicity of Goldsmith, although this young Bard seems not to have made that writer his model. Much, however, as we might commend the beginning of the second part, we think that the author has violated the climax which he seems to have intended, in pursuing the reflections as they succeed each other according to their importance. The scenes of domestic life ought to have been all thrown into one place; and thence he should have proceeded to the political topics introduced in his poem.

The last of Mr. Campbell's 'Pleasures,' judiciously reserved, are those which he deduces from the Hopes of immortality; and in these passages, the poem rises into a tone of unvaried sublimity, suited to the sacred nature of the subject.

The conclusion is in the true style of a Grand Finale, and the idea is bold and impressive:

> Eternal Hope! when yonder spheres sublime,
> Peal'd their first notes to sound the march of time!
> Thy joyous youth began—but not to fade.
> When all the sister planets have decay'd,
> When wrapt in fire the realms of Ether glow,
> And Heav'n's last thunder shakes the world below;
> Thou, undismay'd, shalt o'er the ruin smile,
> And light thy torch at Nature's funeral pile!

To characterize this performance in a few words, we think that it is an highly promising poem, although marked with some defects. It has no incident; no story to embellish it; nor is the plan regularly followed up: but we deem it entitled to rank among the productions of our superior Bards of the present day, as it unquestionably contains many striking proofs of the juvenile author's capacity for genuine and sublime poetry.

The minor pieces are chiefly songs and translations: the latter are not inelegant, and the former possess a simplicity which,

when united to melody, must produce a pleasing effect. (pp. 425-26)

> *[Alexander Hamilton], "Campbell's 'Pleasures of Hope'," in* The Monthly Review, *London, Vol. XXIX, August, 1799, pp. 422-26.*

[FRANCIS JEFFREY]   (essay date 1809)

[Jeffrey was a founder and editor of the Edinburgh Review, *one of the most influential magazines in early nineteenth-century England. A liberal Whig, Jeffrey often allowed his political beliefs to color his critical opinions. In the following excerpt from a review of* Gertrude of Wyoming, *Jeffrey praises Campbell as a talented poet, but cautions him against excessively revising his work. For additional commentary by this critic, see excerpt dated 1819.]*

We rejoice once more to see a polished and pathetic poem **["Gertrude of Wyoming"]**, in the old style of English pathos and poetry. This is of the pitch of the "Castle of Indolence," and the finer parts of Spencer; with more feeling, in many places, than the first, and more condensation and diligent finishing than the latter. If the true tone of nature be not everywhere maintained, it gives place, at least, to art only, and not to affectation—and, least of all, to affectation of singularity or rudeness. (p. 1)

The descriptive stanzas in the beginning, which set out with an invocation to Wyoming, though in some places a little obscure and overlaboured, are, to our taste, very soft and beautiful.

> On Susquehana's side, fair Wyoming!
> Although the wild-flower on thy ruin'd wall
> And roofless homes a sad remembrance bring
> Of what thy gentle people did befall,
> Yet thou wert once the loveliest land of all
> That see the Atlantic wave their morn restore.
> Sweet land! may I thy lost delights recall,
> And paint thy Gertrude in her bowers of yore,
> Whose beauty was the love of Pensylvania's shore!
>
> (p. 6)

[The beauties of this poem] consist chiefly in the feeling and tenderness of the whole delineation, and the taste and delicacy with which all the subordinate parts are made to contribute to the general effect. Before dismissing it, however, we must say a little of its faults, which are sufficiently obvious and undeniable. In the first place, the narrative is extremely obscure and imperfect, and has greater blanks in it than could be tolerated even in lyric poetry. We hear absolutely nothing of Henry, from the day the Indian first brings him from the back country, till he returns from Europe fifteen years thereafter. It is likewise a great oversight in Mr Campbell to separate his lovers, when only *twelve* years of age,—a period at which it is utterly inconceivable that any permanent attachment could have been formed. The greatest fault, however, of the work, is the occasional constraint and obscurity of the diction, proceeding apparently from too laborious an effort at emphasis or condensation. The metal seems in several places to have been so much overworked, as to have lost not only its ductility, but its lustre; and, while there are passages which can scarcely be at all understood after the most careful consideration, there are others which have an air so elaborate and artificial, as to destroy all appearance of nature in the sentiment. (p. 16)

[Of the smaller pieces which fill up *Gertrude of Wyoming,* the] greater part of them have been printed before; and there are probably few readers of English poetry who are not already familiar with the **"Lochiel"** and the **"Hohenlinden"**—the one by far the most spirited and poetical denunciation of woe since the days of Cassandra; the other the only representation of a modern battle, which possesses either interest or sublimity. The song to the **"Mariners of England,"** is also very generally known. It is a splendid instance of the most magnificent diction adapted to a familiar and even trivial metre. (p. 17)

"The Battle of the Baltic," though we think it has been printed before, is much less known. Though written in a strange, and we think an unfortunate metre, it has great force and grandeur, both of conception and expression—that sort of force and grandeur which results from the simple and concise expression of great events and natural emotions, altogether unassisted by any splendour or amplification of expression. The characteristic merit, indeed, both of this piece and of **"Hohenlinden,"** is, that, by the forcible delineation of one or two great circumstances, they give a clear and more energetic representation of events as complicated as they are impressive,—and thus impress the mind of the reader with all the terror and sublimity of the subject, while they rescue him from the fatigue and perplexity of its details. Nothing, in our judgment, can be more impressive than the following very short and simple description of the British fleet bearing up to close action.

> As they drifted on their path,
> There was silence deep as death;
> And the boldest held his breath,
> For a time—

The description of the battle itself (though it begins with a tremendous line) is in the same spirit of homely sublimity; and worth a thousand stanzas of thunder, shrieks, shouts, tridents, and heroes. (pp. 17-18)

We close this volume, on the whole, with feelings of regret for its shortness, and of admiration for the genius of its author. There are but two noble sorts of poetry,—the pathetic and the sublime; and we think he has given very extraordinary proofs of his talents for both. There is something, too, we will venture to add, in the style of many of his conceptions, which irresistibly impresses us with the conviction, that he can do much greater things than he has hitherto accomplished; and leads us to regard him, even yet, as a poet of still greater promise than performance. It seems to us, as if the natural force and boldness of his ideas were habitually checked by a certain fastidious timidity, and an anxiety about the minor graces of correct and chastened composition. Certain it is, at least, that his greatest and most lofty flights have been made in those smaller pieces, about which, it is natural to think, he must have felt least solicitude; and that he has succeeded most splendidly where he must have been most free from the fear of failure. We wish any praises or exhortations of ours had the power to give him confidence in his own great talents; and hope earnestly, that he will now meet with such encouragement, as may set him above all restraints that proceed from apprehension, and induce him to give free scope to that genius, of which we are persuaded that the world has hitherto seen rather the grace than the richness. (p. 19)

> [Francis Jeffrey], "Campbell's 'Gertrude of Wyoming'," in The Edinburgh Review, Vol. XIV, No. XXVII, April, 1809, pp. 1-19.

[SIR WALTER SCOTT]   (essay date 1809)

[*Scott was a Scottish novelist, poet, historian, biographer, and critic of the Romantic period who is best known for his novels,*

which were great popular successes. In this excerpt from a review of Gertrude of Wyoming, *Scott faults the title poem's disconnected narrative and, while he finds much to admire in the volume, advises Campbell to labor less at revisions.*]

We open [**Gertrude of Wyoming**] with no ordinary impression of the delicacy and importance of the task which it imposes on us, and the difficulty of discharging it at once with justice to the author and to that public at whose bar we as well as Mr. Campbell must be considered to stand. It is not our least embarrassment that in some respects Mr. Campbell may be considered as his own rival; and in aspiring to extensive popularity has certainly no impediment to encounter more formidable than the extent of his own reputation. To decide on the merit of **"Gertrude of Wyoming"** as the work of a poet hitherto undistinguished, would be comparatively easy. But we are unavoidably forced upon comparing it with Mr. Campbell's former pieces, and while our judgment is embroiled by the predilections, prejudices, and preferences, which the recollection of them has imprinted upon our imagination; there are other peculiar circumstances which enhance expectation, and increase proportionally the difficulty of affording it complete gratification.

"The Pleasures of Hope," a poem dear to every reader of poetry, bore, amidst many beauties, the marks of a juvenile composition, and received from the public the indulgence due to a promise of future excellence. Some license was also allowed for the didactic nature of the subject, which, prescribing no fixed plan, left the poet free to indulge his fancy in excursions as irregular as they are elegant and animated. It is a consequence of both these circumstances that the poem presents in some degree the appearance of an unfinished picture. In gazing with pleasure on its insulated groupes and figures, the reflection will often intrude, that an artist matured in taste and experience would have methodised his subject, filled up the intermediate spaces, and brought to perfection a sketch of so much promise. The public readily made every allowance that could be claimed on the score of youth—a seeming generosity often conferred on the first essays of poets, painters, and orators, but for which a claim of repayment with usurious interest is regularly preferred against them upon their next appearance. But the hope of improvement was, in Mr. Campbell's case, hardly necessary to augment the expectation raised by the actual excellence of his first poem. The beauties of an highly polished versification, that animated and vigorous tone of moral feeling, that turn of expression, which united the sweetness of Goldsmith with the strength of Johnson, a structure of language alike remote from servile imitation of our more classical poets, and from the babbling and jingling simplicity of ruder minstrels; new, but not singular; elegant, but not trite; justified the admirers of the **"Pleasures of Hope"** in elevating its author to a pre-eminent situation among living poets. Neither did Mr. Campbell suffer the admiration excited by his first essay to subside or be forgotten. From time to time we were favoured with exquisite lyrical effusions calculated rather to stimulate than to gratify the public appetite. The splendid poems of **"Hohenlinden"** and **"Lochiel"** manifesting high powers of imagination, and other short performances replete either with animation or tenderness, seemed to declare their author destined to attain the very summit of the modern Parnassus. By some this pre-eminence was already adjudged to him, while others only adjourned their suffrage until a more daring, extended, and sustained flight should make good the promises of his juvenile work and of his shorter detached poems.

It has for a considerable time been known that a new poem of some length was in Mr. Campbell's contemplation, and when it was whispered that he who sung the doubtful conflict of Hohenlinden and the carnage of Culloden, had chosen for his theme the devastation of Wyoming, expectation was raised to its height. Desire was not too suddenly quenched; and it is only after a long period of suspense that the work has been given to the public. But it is no easy matter to satisfy the vague and indefinite expectation which suspense of this nature seldom fails to excite. Each reader is apt to form an idea of the subject, the narrative, and the stile of execution; so that the real poem is tried and censured not upon its own merits, but for differing from the preconceived dream of the critic's imagination. . . . Perhaps therefore it is a natural consequence of over-strained hope, that the immediate reception of **"Gertrude of Wyoming"** should be less eminently favourable than the intrinsic merit of the poem and the acknowledged genius of the author appeared to insure; and perhaps too we may be able in the course of our investigation to point out other reasons which may for a season impede the popularity of a poem containing passages both of tenderness and sublimity, which may decline comparison with few in the English language.

The tale of **"Gertrude of Wyoming"** is abundantly simple. It refers to the desolation of a beautiful track of country situated on both sides of the Susquehannah, and inhabited by colonists whose primæval simplicity and hospitality recalled the idea of the golden age. In 1778, Wyoming, this favoured and happy spot, was completely laid waste by an incursion of Indians and civilized savages under a leader named Brandt. The pretext was the adherence of the inhabitants to the provincial confederacy; but the lust of rapine and cruelty which distinguished the invaders was such as to add double horrors even to civil conflict.

We do not condemn this choice of a subject in itself eminently fitted for poetry; yet feeling as Englishmen, we cannot suppress a hope that Mr. Campbell will in his subsequent poems chuse a theme more honourable to our national character, than one in which Britain was disgraced by the atrocities of her pretended adherents. We do not love to have our feelings unnecessarily put in arms against the cause of our country. The historian must do his duty when such painful subjects occur; but the poet who may chuse his theme through the whole unbounded range of truth and fiction may well excuse himself from selecting a subject dishonourable to his own land.

Although the calamity was general, and overwhelmed the whole settlement of Wyoming, Mr. Campbell has judiciously selected a single groupe as the subject of his picture; yet we have room to regret that in some passages at least he has not extended his canvass to exhibit, in the back ground, that general scene of tumult and horror which might have added force to the striking picture which he has drawn of individual misery. (pp. 241-44)

[Albert], the judge and patriarch of the infant settlement, is an Englishman; Gertrude, the heroine of the poem, is his only child. . . .

An Indian, of a tribe friendly to the settlers, approaches their cottage one morning, leading in his hand an English boy. . . .

The swarthy warrior tells Albert of a frontier fort occupied by the British which had been stormed and destroyed by a party of Hurons, the allies of France. . . . All had been massacred, excepting the widow of the commander of the garrison and her son, a boy of ten or twelve years old. The former, exhausted with fatigue and grief, dies in the arms of the friendly Indians,

and bequeathes to their chief the task of conducting her son to Albert's care, with a token to express that he was the son of Julia Waldegrave. Albert instantly recognises the boy as the offspring of two old and dear friends. A flood of kindly recollections, and the bitter contrast between the promise of their early days and the dismal fate which finally awaited the parents of Waldegrave, rush at once on the mind of the old man, and extort a pathetic lamentation. The deportment of the Indian warrior forms an admirable contrast to Albert's indulgence of grief, and the stanzas in which it is described rank among the finest in the poem. (p. 246)

Part II. opens with a description of Albert's abode, situated between two woods near a river, which, after dashing over a thundering cascade, chose that spot to expand itself into a quiet and pellucid sheet of living water. Beautiful in itself, the scene was graced by the presence of Gertrude, yet more beautiful, an 'enthusiast of the woods,' alive to all the charms of the romantic scenery by which she was surrounded, and whose sentimental benevolence extended itself even to England, which she knew only by her father's report. And here commences the great defect of the story. We totally lose sight of the orphan Waldegrave, whose arrival makes the only incident in the first canto, and of whose departure from Wyoming we have not been apprised. Neither are we in the least prepared to anticipate such an event, excepting by a line in which Julia expresses a hope that her orphan would be conveyed to 'England's shore'— an inuendo which really escaped us in the first, and even in the second, perusal of the poem, and which, at any rate, by no means implies that her wish was actually fulfilled. The unaccountable disappearance of this character, to whom we had naturally assigned an important part in the narrative, is not less extraordinary than that Gertrude, in extending her kind wishes and affectionate thoughts towards friends in Britain whom she never knew, and only loved because they might possibly possess

> Her mother's looks—perhaps her likeness strong,

omits all mention or recollection of the interesting little orphan of whom every reader has destined her the bride from the first moment of his introduction. Of him, however, nothing is said, and we are left to conjecture whether he has gone to Britain and been forgotten by her youthful playfellow, or whether he remains an unnoticed and undistinguished inmate of her father's mansion. We have next a splendid, though somewhat confused, description of a 'deep untrodden grot', where, as it is beautifully expressed,

> ————————rocks sublime
> To human art a sportive semblance wore;
> And yellow lichens coloured all the clime,
> Like moon-light battlements and towers decay'd by time.

To this grotto, embosomed in all the splendid luxuriance of transatlantic vegetation, Gertrude was wont to retire 'with Shakespeare's self to speak and smile alone', and here she is surprized by the arrival of a youth in a Spanish garb, leading in his hand his steed, who is abruptly announced as

> The stranger guest of many a distant land.

We were at least as much startled as Gertrude by this unexpected intruder, and are compelled to acknowledge that the suspense in which we were kept for a few stanzas is rather puzzling than pleasing. We became sensible that we had somehow lost the thread of the story, and while hurriedly endeavouring to recover it, became necessarily insensible to the beauties of the poetry. The stranger inquires for the mansion of

Albert, is of course hospitably received, and tells of the wonders which he had seen, in Switzerland, in France, in Italy, and in California, whence he last arrived. At length Albert inquires after the orphan Waldegrave, who (as his question for the first time apprizes the reader) had been sent to his relations in England at the age of twelve, after three years residence in the earthly paradise of Wyoming. The quick eye of Gertrude discovers the mysterious stranger to be "Waldegrave's self of Waldegrave come to tell,' and all is rapturous recognition. And here, amidst many beauties, we are again pressed by the leading error of the narrative, for this same Waldegrave—who, for no purpose that we can learn, has been wandering over half the world—of whom the reader knows so little, who appears to have been entirely forgotten during the space of one third of the poem, and whom even Gertrude did not think worthy of commemoration in orisons which called for blessings on friends she had never known—this same Waldegrave, of whose infantine affection for Gertrude we no where receive the slightest hint, with even more than the composure of a fine gentleman returned from the grand tour, coolly assures her and Albert at their first interview, that she 'shall be his own with all her truth and charms.' This extraordinary and unceremonious appropriation is submitted to by Gertrude and her father with the most unresisting and astonishing complacency. It is in vain to bid us suppose that a tender and interesting attachment had united this youthful couple during Waldegrave's residence at Wyoming. This is like the reference of Bayes to a conversation held by his personages behind the scenes; it is requiring the reader to guess what the author has not told him, and consequently what he is not obliged to know. This inherent defect in the narrative might have been supplied at the expense of two or three stanzas descriptive of the growing attachment between the children, and apprizing us of Waldegrave's departure for England. The omission is the more provoking as we are satisfied of Mr. Campbell's powers to trace the progress of their infant love, and the train of little incidents and employments which gave it opportunity to grow with their growth, and strengthen with their strength; in short, to rival the exquisite picture of juvenile affection presented in *Thalaba*. (pp. 247-49)

The approach of civil war in America, and the attachment of Waldegrave to the provincial cause, are briefly touched upon, as are the boding apprehensions of Gertrude, too soon to be fatally realized. One evening, while danger was yet deemed remote, an Indian worn with fatigue and age rushes hastily into Albert's cottage, and is with difficulty recognized to be the Oneyda chief Outalissi, who had guided Waldegrave to Wyoming. After an indulgence of former recollections, rather too long to be altogether consistent with the pressing nature of his errand, the Indian informs the domestic circle that the savages led by Brandt had extirpated his whole tribe on account of their friendship to the Americans, and were approaching to wreak their vengeance by laying waste the settlement of Wyoming.

> Scarce had he utter'd,—when Heav'n's verge extreme
> Reverberates the bomb's descending star,—
> And sounds that mingled laugh,—and shout,—and scream,
> To freeze the blood, in one discordant jar,
> Rung to the pealing thunderbolts of war.
> Whoop after whoop with rack the ear assail'd;
> As if unearthly fiends had burst their bar;
> While rapidly the marksman's shot prevail'd;
> And aye, as if for death, some lonely trumpet wail'd.—
> Then look'd they to the hills, where fire o'erhung
> The bandit groupes, in one Vesuvian glare;
> Or swept, far seen, the tow'r, whose clock, unrung,
> Told legible that midnight of despair.

These sounds of tumult and desolation are mingled with the more cheering notes of the drums and military music of a body of provincialists, who arrive, it would seem, to protect the inhabitants of Wyoming. The description of this band, composed of the descendants of various climes, and arrayed by 'torch and trumpet', evinces the same high tone of military poetry which glows through the stanzas on the battle of Hohenlinden. We are, however, again compelled to own some disappointment arising from the indistinctness of the narrative. The provincialists appear prepared to fight in defence of the Pensylvanian Arcadia. Outalissi chaunts his battle song, and Albert invokes, amid the blaze of neighbouring villages, the protection of the God of Hosts on the defenders of their native country; Waldegrave too assumes the sword and plume; yet, without any reason assigned, these preparations for battle terminate in a retreat to a neighbouring fort, and we are left to conjecture the motive for flight in a band so energetic and so amply provided. The destruction too of Wyoming might have claimed a more lengthened detail than is afforded by the lines which we have quoted, and the main interest in the fate of Albert and his family would have been increased rather than diminished by a glance at those numerous groupes who must necessarily have accompanied the flight, or remained to perish with their dwellings. But of these we learn no more than if Waldegrave and Julia had, like our first parents, been the sole inhabitants of this terrestrial paradise. Covered by the friendly battalion, they reach in safety the fort which was to afford them shelter; and in the few accurate yet beautiful lines which characterize its situation and appearance, the poet has happily compelled into his service even the terms of modern fortification, and evinced a complete conquest over those technical expressions which probably any other bard would have avoided as fit only for the disciples of Cohorn or Vauban.

> Past was the flight, and welcome seem'd the tow'r,
> That, like a giant standard-bearer, frown'd
> Defiance on the roving Indian pow'r.
> Beneath, each bold and promontory mound
> With embrasure emboss'd, and armour crown'd,
> And arrowy frize, and wedged ravelin,
> Wove like a diadem its tracery round
> The lofty summit of that mountain green;
> Here stood secure the group, and ey'd a distant scene.

Here while surveying in fancied security the progress of the devastation, Albert and Gertrude fall pierced by the bullets of the lurking marksmen of the enemy. A death-speech, affecting, yet somewhat too long, exhausts the last efforts of the expiring Gertrude; and as her husband kneels by the bodies in ineffable despair, the following exquisite description of Outalissi's sympathy gives an originality and wildness to the scene of woe at once appropriate to America, and distinct from the manners of every other country.

> Then mournfully the parting bugle bid
> Its farewell o'er the grave of worth and truth;
> Prone to the dust afflicted Waldegrave hid
> His face on earth;—him watch'd in gloomy ruth,
> His woodland guide; but words had none to sooth
> The grief that knew not consolation's name:
> Casting his Indian mantle o'er the youth,
> He watch'd, beneath its folds, each burst that came
> Convulsive, ague-like, across his shuddering frame!

We have gazed with delight on the savage witnessing the death of Wolfe with awe and sorrow acting upon habits of stubborn apathy; and we have perused the striking passage in Spenser whose Talus 'an iron man ymade in iron mould' is described as having nevertheless an inly feeling of sympathy with the anguish of Britomarte; yet neither the painter nor the poet has, in our apprehension, presented so perfect and powerful an image of sympathetic sorrow in a heart unwont to receive such a guest, as appears in the mute distress of the Oneyda warrior bending over his despairing foster-son. (pp. 250-52)

[The] merits and defects of "**Gertrude of Wyoming**" . . . have this marked singularity, that the latter intrude upon us at the very first reading, whereas, after repeated perusals, we perceive beauties which had previously escaped our notice. We have indeed rather paradoxically been induced to ascribe the most obvious faults to the same cause which has undoubtedly produced many of the excellencies of the poem,—to the anxious and assiduous attention, which the author has evidently bestowed upon it before publication. It might be expected that the public would regard with indulgence those imperfections which arise from the poet's diffidence of his own splendid powers, and too great deference to the voice of criticism. In some respects, however, public taste, like a fine lady, 'stoops to the forward and the bold;' and the modest and anxious adventurer is defrauded of the palm, merely that his judges may enjoy the childish superiority of condemning an overlaboured attempt to give them pleasure. (pp. 254-55)

We have hitherto only considered the labour bestowed upon "**Gertrude of Wyoming**" as an impediment to the flow of popularity which has in the present day attended poems of a ruder structure. But the public taste, although guided in some degree by caprice, is also to a certain extent correctly grounded upon critical doctrine; and the truth is, that an author cannot work upon a beautiful poem beyond a certain point, without doing it real and irreparable injury in more respects than one.

It is in the first place impossible to make numerous and minute alterations, to alter the position of stanzas, to countermarch and invert the component parts of sentences, without leaving marks of their original array. . . . There are in "**Gertrude**" passages of a construction so studiously involved, that nothing but the deepest consideration could have enabled the author to knit the Gordian knot by which his meaning is fettered, and which unfortunately requires similar exertion of intellect ere it can be disentangled. An ordinary reader is sometimes unable and always unwilling to make such an effort, and hence the volume is resigned and condemned in a moment of splenetic impatience. Some of the introductory stanzas have their beauties thus obscured, and afford rather a conjectural than a certain meaning. We allude to the second in particular. Similar indistinctness occurs in the construction of the following sentence:

> But high in amphitheatre above
> His arms the everlasting aloe threw:
> *Breathed but an air of heaven,* and all the grove
> Instinct as if with living spirit grew.

The idea here is beautiful, but it is only on reflection that we discover that the words in italics mean not that the aloe breathed an air of heaven, but that the grove grew instinct with living spirit so soon as the slightest air of heaven breathed on it. Sometimes passages, of which the tone is simple and natural, are defaced by affected inversion, as in Gertrude's exclamation:

> Yet say! for friendly hearts from whence we came
> Of us does oft remembrance intervene?

Again, in altering and retouching, inverting and condensing his stanzas, an author will sometimes halt between his first and

his latter meaning, and deviate into defects both of sense and grammar. Thus in the Oneyda's first song we have—

> Sleep, wearied one! and in the dreaming land
> Shouldst thou the spirit of thy mother greet,
> O say *to-morrow* that the white man's hand
> *Hath plucked* the thorns of sorrow from thy feet.

Lastly, and above all, in the irksome task of repeated revision and reconsideration, the poet loses, if we may use the phrase, the impulse of inspiration; his fancy, at first so ardent, becomes palled and flattened, and no longer excites a correspondent glow of expression. In this state of mind he may correct faults, but he will never add beauties; and so much do we prefer the stamp of originality to tame correctness, that were there not a medium which ought to be aimed at, we would rather take the *prima cura* with all its errors and with all its beauties, than the over-amended edition in which both are obliterated. (pp. 255-57)

Then occur the doubtful and damping questions, whether the faded inspiration was genuine, whether the verses corresponded in any degree to its dictates, or have power to communicate to others a portion of the impulse which produced them. Then comes the dread of malignant criticism; and last, but not least tormenting, the advice of literary friends, each suggesting doubts and alterations, till the spirit is corrected out of the poem, as a sprightly boy is sometimes lectured and flogged for venial indiscretions into a stupid and inanimate dunce. The beautiful poem of "**Lochiel**," which Mr. Campbell has appended to the present volume, as if to illustrate our argument, exhibits marks of this injudicious alteration. Let us only take the last lines, where in the original edition the champion declares that even in the moment of general route and destruction,

> Though my perishing ranks should be strew'd in their
>   gore,
> Like ocean weeds heap'd on the surf-beaten shore,
> Lochiel, untainted by flight or by chains,
> While the kindling of life in his bosom remains,
> Shall victor exult, or in death be laid low,
> With his back to the field, and his feet to the foe!
> And, leaving in battle no blot on his name,
> Look proudly to heav'n from the death-bed of fame.

The whole of this individual, vigorous, and marked picture of the Highland chieftain lying breathless amid his broken and slaughtered clan—a picture so strong, that we even mark the very posture and features of the hero—is humbled and tamed, abridged and corrected, into the following vague and inexpressive couplet:

> Lochiel——————————
> Shall victor exult in the battle's acclaim,
> Or look to yon heav'n from the death-bed of fame.

If the pruning knife has been applied with similar severity to the beauties of "**Gertrude of Wyoming**," the hatchet of the Mohawk Brandt himself was not more fatally relentless and indiscriminate in its operations.

The book contains, besides "**Gertrude of Wyoming**," several of Mr. Campbell's smaller pieces. "**Lochiel**" in particular and "**Hohenlinden**" are introduced, although they made part of the author's last quarto volume. We cannot be offended at meeting our favourites any where; yet when we connect the circumstance last mentioned, with the reflection that "**Lochiel**" has been unnecessarily altered and abridged, we are not thoroughly satisfied with their insertion in the present volume. Two beautiful war odes, entitled the "**Mariners of England**," and the "**Battle of the Baltic**," afford pleasing instances of that short and impetuous lyric sally in which Mr. Campbell excels all his contemporaries. Two ballads, **"Glenara,"** and **"Lord Ullin's Daughter,"** the former approaching the rude yet forcible simplicity of the ancient minstrels, the latter upon a more refined plan, conclude the volume. They were new to us, and are models in their several stiles of composition. (pp. 257-58)

> [*Sir Walter Scott*], *" 'Gertrude of Wyoming','' in* The Quarterly Review, *Vol. I, No. II, May, 1809, pp. 241-58.*

HENRY CRABB ROBINSON   (diary date 1812)

[*A nineteenth-century English journalist, Robinson is remembered for his voluminous correspondence and diaries, which chronicle London's social and intellectual history. In the following excerpt, Robinson recounts a conversation in which William Wordsworth expressed contempt for Campbell's poetry.*]

Wordsworth spoke with great contempt of Campbell as a poet, and illustrated his want of truth and poetic sense in his imagery by a close analysis of a celebrated passage in **"The Pleasures of Hope,"** 'Where Andes, giant of the Western star,' etc. [Part I, 11. 56-9], showing the whole to be a mere jumble of discordant images, meaning, in fact, nothing, nor conveying very distinct impression, it being first uncertain who or what is the giant, and who or what is the star. Then the giant is made to hold a meteor-standard and to sit on a throne of clouds and look (it is not apparent for what) on half the world. Gray's line, speaking of the bard's beard, which 'streamed like a meteor to the troubled air,' Wordsworth also considered as ridiculous, and both passages he represented to be unmeaningly stolen from a fine line by Milton, in which a spear is for its brightness only compared to a meteor. (p. 90)

> *Henry Crabb Robinson, in an extract from a diary entry on May 31, 1812, in his* Henry Crabb Robinson on Books and Their Writers, Vol. 1, *edited by Edith J. Morley, J. M. Dent and Sons Limited, 1938, pp. 89-92.*

WASHINGTON IRVING   (essay date 1815)

[*Irving is considered both the first American man of letters and the creator of the American short story. In this appreciative assessment of Campbell's poetry, Irving especially admires "Gertrude of Wyoming," praising Campbell's choice of an American subject. Irving also addresses the issue of Campbell's "scrupulous spirit of revision."*]

"Hohenlinden," "Lochiel," the **"Mariners of England,"** and the **"Battle of the Baltic."** are sufficient of themselves, were other evidence wanting, to establish [Campbell's] title to the sacred name of Poet. The two last-mentioned poems we consider as two of the noblest national songs we have ever seen. They contain sublime imagery and lofty sentiments, delivered with a "gallant swelling spirit," but totally free from that hyperbole and national rhodomontade which generally disgrace this species of poetry. In the beginning of 1809, he published his second volume of poems, containing **"Gertrude of Wyoming"** and several smaller effusions; since which time he has produced nothing of consequence, excepting the uncommonly spirited and affecting little tale of **"O'Connor's Child, or Love lies bleeding."** (p. 242)

That Mr. Campbell has by any means attained to the summit of his fame, we cannot suffer ourselves for a moment to believe. We rather look upon the works he has already produced as specimens of pure and virgin gold from a mine whose treasures are yet to be explored. It is true, the very reputation Mr. Campbell has acquired, may operate as a disadvantage to his future efforts. Public expectation is a pitiless taskmaster, and exorbitant in its demands. He who has once awakened it, must go on in a proggressive ratio, surpassing what he has hitherto done, or the public will be disappointed. Under such circumstances an author of common sensibility takes up his pen with fear and trembling. A consciousness that much is expected from him deprives him of that ease of mind and boldness of imagination, which are necessary to fine writing, and he too often fails from a too great anxiety to excel. He is like some youthful soldier, who, having distinguished himself by a gallant and brilliant achievement, is ever afterward fearful of entering on a new enterprise, lest he should tarnish the laurels he has won.

We are satisfied that Mr. Campbell feels this very diffidence and solicitude from the uncommon pains he bestows upon his writings. These are scrupulously revised, modelled, and retouched over and over, before they are suffered to go out of his hands, and even then, are slowly and reluctantly yielded up to the press. This elaborate care may, at times, be carried to an excess, so as to produce fastidiousness of style, and an air of too much art and labour. It occasionally imparts to the muse the precise demeanour and studied attire of the prude, rather than the negligent and bewitching graces of the woodland nymph. A too minute attention to finishing is likewise injurious to the force and sublimity of a poem. The vivid images which are struck off, at a single heat, in those glowing moments of inspiration, "when the soul is lifted to heaven," are too often softened down, and cautiously tamed, in the cold hour of correction. As an instance of the critical severity which Mr. Campbell excercises over his productions, we will mention a fact within our knowledge, concerning his **"Battle of the Baltic."** This ode, as published, consists but of five stanzas; these were all that his scrupulous taste permitted him to cull out of a large number, which we have seen in manuscript. The rest, though full of poetic fire and imagery, were timidly consigned by him to oblivion.

But though this scrupulous spirit of revision may chance to refine away some of the bold touches of his pencil, and to injure some of its negligent graces, it is not without its eminent advantages. While it tends to produce a terseness of language, and a remarkable delicacy and sweetness of versification, it enables him likewise to impart to his productions a vigorous conciseness of style, a graphical correctness of imagery, and a philosophical condensation of idea, rarely found in the popular poets of the day. (pp. 242-43)

Great ... as are the intrinsic merits of Mr. Campbell, we are led to estimate them the more highly when we consider them as beaming forth, like the pure lights of heaven, among the meteor exhalations and false fires with which our literary atmosphere abounds. In an age when we are overwhelmed by an abundance of eccentric poetry, and when we are confounded by a host of ingenious poets of vitiated tastes and frantic fancies, it is really cheering and consolatory to behold a writer of Mr. Campbell's genius, studiously attentive to please, according to the established laws of criticism, as all our good old orthodox writers have pleased before; without setting up a standard, and endeavouring to establish a new sect, and inculcate some new and lawless doctrine of his own.

Before concluding this sketch, we cannot help pointing to one circumstance, which we confess has awakened a feeling of good will toward Mr. Campbell; though in mentioning it we shall do little more, perhaps, than betray our own national egotism. He is, we believe, the only British poet of eminence that has laid the story of a considerable poem, in the bosom of our country. We allude to his "**Gertrude of Wyoming,**" which describes the pastoral simplicity and innocence, and the subsequent woes of one of our little patriarchal hamlets, during the troubles of our revolution.

We have so long been accustomed to experience little else than contumely, misrepresentation, and very witless ridicule, from the British press; and we have had such repeated proofs of the extreme ignorance and absurd errors that prevail in Great Britain respecting our country and its inhabitants, that, we confess, we were both surprised and gratified to meet with a poet, sufficiently unprejudiced to conceive an idea of moral excellence and natural beauty on this side of the Atlantic. Indeed, even this simple show of liberality has drawn on the poet the censures of many narrow-minded writers, with whom liberality to this country is a crime. We are sorry to see such pitiful manifestations of hostility toward us. (pp. 244-45)

The sweet strains of Mr. Campbell's muse break upon us as gladly as would the pastoral pipe of the shepherd, amid the savage solitude of one of our trackless wildernesses. We are delighted to witness the air of captivating romance and rural beauty our native fields and wild woods can assume under the plastic pencil of a master; and while wandering with the poet among the shady groves of Wyoming, or along the banks of the Susquehanna, almost fancy ourselves transported to the side of some classic stream, in the "hollow breast of Appenine." (p. 247)

Having made such particular mention of "**Gertrude of Wyoming,**" we will barely add one or two circumstances connected with it, strongly illustrative of the character of the literary author. The story of the poem, though extremely simple, is not sufficiently developed; some of the facts, particularly in the first part, are rapidly passed over, and left rather obscure; from which many have inconsiderately pronounced the whole a hasty sketch, without perceiving the elaborate delicacy with which the parts are finished. This defect is to be attributed entirely to the self-diffidence of Mr. Campbell. It is his misfortune that he is too distrustful of himself; and too ready to listen to the opinions of inferior minds, rather than boldly to follow the dictates of his own pure taste and the impulses of his exalted imagination, which, if left to themselves, would never falter or go wrong. Thus we are told, that when his "**Gertrude**" first came from under his pen, it was full and complete; but in an evil hour he read it to some of his critical friends. Every one knows that when a man's critical judgment is consulted, he feels himself in credit bound to find fault. Various parts of the poem were of course objected to, and various alterations recommended.

With a fatal diffidence, which, while we admire we cannot but lament, Mr. Campbell struck out those parts entirely; and obliterated, in a moment, the fruit of hours of inspiration and days of labour. But when he attempted to bind together and new model the elegant, but mangled, limbs of this virgin poem, his shy imagination revolted from the task. The glow of feeling was chilled, the creative powers of invention were exhausted; the parts, therefore, were slightly and imperfectly thrown together, with a spiritless pen, and hence arose that apparent want of development which occurs in some parts of the story.

Indeed, we do not think the unobtrusive, and, if we may be allowed the word, occult merits of this poem are calculated to strike popular attention, during the present passion for dashing verse and extravagant incident. It is mortifying to an author to observe, that those accomplishments which it has cost him the greatest pains to acquire, and which he regards with a proud eye, as the exquisite proofs of his skill, are totally lost upon the generality of readers; who are commonly captivated by those glaring qualities to which he attaches but little value. Most people are judges of exhibitions of force and activity of body, but it requires a certain refinement of taste and a practised eye, to estimate that gracefulness which is the achievement of labour, and consummation of art. So, in writing, whatever is bold, glowing, and garish, strikes the attention of the most careless, and is generally felt and acknowledged; but comparatively few can appreciate that modest delineation of nature, that tenderness of sentiment, propriety of language, and gracefulness of composition, that bespeak the polished and accomplished writer. Such, however, as possess this delicacy of taste and feeling, will often return to dwell, with cherishing fondness, on the "**Gertrude**" of Mr. Campbell. Like all his other writings, it presents virtue in its most touching and captivating forms: whether gently exercised in the "bosom scenes of life," or sublimely exerted in its extraordinary and turbulent situations. No writer can surpass Mr. C. in the vestal purity and amiable morality of his muse. While he possesses the power of firing the imagination, and filling it with sublime and awful images, he excels also in those eloquent appeals to the feelings, and those elevated flights of thought, by which, while the fancy is exalted, the heart is made better.

It is now some time since he has produced any poem. Of late he has been employed in preparing a work for the press, containing critical and biographical notices of British poets from the reign of Edward III. to the present time. However much we may be gratified by such a work, from so competent a judge, still we cannot but regret that he should stoop from the brilliant track of poetic invention, in which he is so well calculated to soar, and descend into the lower regions of literature to mingle with droning critics and mousing commentators. His task should be to produce poetry, not to criticise it; for, in our minds, he does more for his own fame, and for the interests of literature, who furnishes one fine verse, than he who points out a thousand beauties, or detects a thousand faults.

We hope, therefore, soon to behold Mr. Campbell emerging from those dusty labours, and breaking forth in the full lustre of original genius. He owes it to his own reputation; he owes it to his own talents; he owes it to the literature of his country. Poetry has generally flowed in an abundant stream in Great Britain; but it is too apt to stray among rocks and weeds, to expand into brawling shallows, or waste itself in turbid and ungovernable torrents. We have, however, marked a narrow, but pure and steady, channel, continuing down from the earliest ages, through a line of real poets, who seem to have been sent from heaven to keep the vagrnt stream from running at utter waste and random. Of this chosen number we consider Mr. Campbell; and we are happy at having this opportunity of rendering our feeble tribute of applause to a writer whom we consider an ornament to the age, an honour to his country, and one whom his country "should delight to honour." (pp. 247-50)

Washington Irving, "A Biographical Sketch of Thomas Campbell," in The Analectic Magazine, *n.s. Vol. V, March, 1815, pp. 234-50.*

WILLIAM HAZLITT (essay date 1818)

[*One of the most important commentators of the Romantic age, Hazlitt was an English critic and journalist. He is best known for his descriptive criticism in which he stressed that no motives beyond judgment and analysis are necessary on the part of the critic. In the following examination of Campbell's poetry, Hazlitt argues that, by fearing criticism, Campbell "starves his genius to death."*]

Campbell's **"Pleasures of Hope"** is [a work] . . . in which a painful attention is paid to the expression in proportion as there is little to express, and the decomposition of prose is substituted for the composition of poetry. How much the sense and keeping in the ideas are sacrificed to a jingle of words and epigrammatic turn of expression, may be seen in such lines as the following:—one of the characters, an old invalid, wishes to end his days under

> Some hamlet shade, to yield his sickly form
> Health in the breeze, and shelter in the storm.

Now the antithesis here totally fails: for it is the breeze, and not the tree, or as it is quaintly expressed, *hamlet shade,* that affords health, though it is the tree that affords shelter in or from the storm. Instances of the same sort of *curiosa infelicitas* are not rare in this author. His verses on the Battle of Hohenlinden [**"Hohenlinden"**] have considerable spirit and animation. His **"Gertrude of Wyoming"** is his principal performance. It is a kind of historical paraphrase of Mr. Wordsworth's poem of "Ruth". It shows little power, or power enervated by extreme fastidiousness. It is

> ——Of outward show
> Elaborate; of inward less exact.

There are painters who trust more to the setting of their pictures than to the truth of the likeness. Mr. Campbell always seems to me to be thinking how his poetry will look when it comes to be hot-pressed on superfine wove paper, to have a disproportionate eye to points and commas, and dread of errors of the press. He is so afraid of doing wrong, of making the smallest mistake, that he does little or nothing. Lest he should wander irretrievably from the right path, he stands still. He writes according to established etiquette. He offers the Muses no violence. If he lights upon a good thought, he immediately drops it for fear of spoiling a good thing. When he launches a sentiment that you think will float him triumphantly for once to the bottom of the stanza, he stops short at the end of the first or second line, and stands shivering on the brink of beauty, afraid to trust himself to the fathomless abyss. *Tutus nimium, timidusque procellarum.* His very circumspection betrays him. The poet, as well as the woman, that deliberates, is undone. He is much like a man whose heart fails him just as he is going up in a balloon, and who breaks his neck by flinging himself out of it when it is too late. Mr. Campbell too often maims and mangles his ideas before they are full formed, to fit them to the Procrustes' bed of criticism; or strangles his intellectual offspring in the birth, lest they should come to an untimely end in the *Edinburgh Review.* He plays the hypercritic on himself, and starves his genius to death from a needless apprehension of a plethora. No writer who thinks habitually of the critics, either to tremble at their censures or set them at defiance, can write well. It is the business of reviewers to watch poets, not of poets to watch reviewers.—There is one admirable simile in this poem, of the European child brought by the sooty Indian in his hand, 'like morning brought by night'. The love scenes in **"Gertrude of Wyoming"** breathe a balmy voluptuousness of sentiment; but they are generally broken off in the middle; they are like the scent of a bank of violets, faint and rich, which the gale suddenly conveys in a different direction. Mr. Campbell is careful of his own repu-

tation, and economical of the pleasures of his readers. He treats them as the fox in the fable treated his guest the stork; or, to use his own expression, his fine things are

> Like angels' visits, few, and far between.

There is another fault in this poem, which is the mechanical structure of the fable. The most striking events occur in the shape of antitheses. The story is cut into the form of a parallelogram. There is the same systematic alternation of good and evil, of violence and repose, that there is of light and shade in a picture. The Indian, who is the chief agent in the interest of the poem, vanishes and returns after long intervals, like the periodical revolutions of the planets. He unexpectedly appears just in the nick of time, after years of absence, and without any known reason but the convenience of the author and the astonishment of the reader; as if nature were a machine constructed on a principal of complete contrast, to produce a theatrical effect. *Nec Deus intersit, nisi dignus vindice nodus.* Mr. Campbell's savage never appears but upon great occasions, and then his punctuality is preternatural and alarming. He is the most wonderful instance on record of poetical *reliability.* The most dreadful mischiefs happen at the most mortifying moments; and when your expectations are wound up to the highest pitch, you are sure to have them knocked on the head by a premeditated and remorseless stroke of the poet's pen. This is done so often for the convenience of the author, that in the end it ceases to be for the satisfaction of the reader. (pp. 228-32)

> William Hazlitt, "On the Living Poets," in his Lectures on the English Poets, 1818. Reprint by Humphrey Milford, 1924, pp. 220-56.

[FRANCIS JEFFREY]   (essay date 1819)

[*In the following excerpt from a review of* Specimens of the British Poets, *Jeffrey delineates both the merits and shortcomings of the work. For additional commentary by this critic, see excerpt dated 1809.*]

We would rather see Mr Campbell as a poet, than as a commentator on poetry:—because we would rather have a solid addition to the sum of our treasures, than the finest or most judicious account of their actual amount. But we are very glad to see him in any way:—and think the work which he has now given us very excellent and delightful.

The most common fault that is found with it, we think, is, that there is so little of it original,—and that out of seven volumes, with Mr Campbell's name on the outside, there should hardly be two little ones of his writing. In making this complaint, however, people seem to forget, that the work is entitled *Specimens of British Poetry*; and that the learned Editor did not undertake to *write,* but only to select and introduce the citations of which it was to consist. Still, however, there is some little room for complaint: and the work *is* somewhat deficient, even upon this strict view of its objects, and of the promises which the title must in fairness be allowed to hold out. There is no doubt a very pleasing **"Essay on English Poetry,"**—and there are biographical and critical notices of many of its principal authors. But these two compartments of the work are somewhat inartificially blended,—and the latter, and most important, rather unduly anticipated and invaded, in order to enlarge the former. The only biography or criticism which we have upon Dryden, for example, is contained in the Preliminary Essay;—and a considerable part even of the specimens of Shirley, are to be found in the same quarter. These, however, are licenses, or lyrical transitions, which must be allowed, we suppose, to a poetical editor—and to which we should not therefore very much object. If the whole that we have a right to look for is in the book, we are very little disposed to quarrel with the author about its arrangement, or the part of the book in which he has chosen to place it. But we really think that we have not got all that we were naturally led to expect—and that the learned author still owes us an arrear, which we hope he will handsomely pay up in the next edition.

When a great poet and a man of distinguished talents announces a large selection of English poetry, 'with biographical and critical notices,' we naturally expect such notices of all, or almost all the authors of whose works he thinks it worth while to favour us with specimens. The biography sometimes may be unattainable—and it may still more frequently be uninteresting—but the criticism must always be valuable; and, indeed, is obviously that which must be looked to as constituting the chief value of any such publication. There is no author so obscure, if at all entitled to a place in this register, of whom it would not be desirable to know the opinion of such a man as Mr Campbell—and none so mature and settled in fame, upon whose beauties and defects, and poetical character in general, the public would not have much to learn from such an authority. Now, there are many authors, and some of no mean note, of whom he has not condescended to say one word, either in the **"Essay,"** or in the notices prefixed to their citations. Of Jonathan Swift, for example, all that is here recorded is, 'Born 1667—died 1744;' and Otway is despatched in the same summary manner—'Born 1651—died 1685.' Marlowe is commemorated in a single page, and Butler in half of one. All this is rather capricious:—But this is not all. Sometimes the notices are entirely biographical, and sometimes entirely critical. We humbly conceive they ought always to have been of both descriptions. At all events, we think we ought in every case to have had some criticism,—since this could always have been had, and could scarcely have failed to be valuable. Mr C., we think, has been a little lazy.

If he were like most authors, or even like most critics, we could easily have pardoned this; for we very seldom find any work too short. It is the singular goodness of his criticisms that makes us regret their fewness; for nothing, we think, can be more fair, judicious and discriminating, and at the same time more fine, delicate and original, than the greater part of the discussions with which he has here presented us. It is very rare to find so much sensibility to the beauties of poetry, united with so much toleration for its faults; and so exact a perception of the merits of every particular style, interfering so little with a just estimate of all. Poets, to be sure, are on the whole, we think, very indulgent judges of poetry; and that not so much, we verily believe, from any partiality to their own vocation, or desire to exalt their fraternity, as from their being more constantly alive to those impulses which it is the business of poetry to excite, and more quick to catch and to follow out those associations on which its efficacy chiefly depends. (pp. 462-64)

But though a poet is thus likely to be a gentler critic of poetry than another, and, by having a finer sense of its beauties, to be better qualified for the most pleasing and important part of his office, there is another requisite in which we should be afraid he would generally be found wanting, especially in a work of the large and comprehensive nature of that now before us—we mean, in absolute fairness and impartiality towards the different schools or styles of poetry which he may have occasion to estimate and compare. (p. 464)

With [these] impressions of the almost inevitable partiality of poetical judgments in general, we could not recollect that Mr Campbell was himself a Master in a distinct school of poetry, and distinguished by a very peculiar and fastidious style of composition, without being apprehensive that the effects of this bias would be very apparent in his work, and that, with all his talent and discernment, he would now and then be guilty of great, though unintended injustice, to some of those whose manner was most opposite to his own. We are happy to say that those apprehensions have proved entirely groundless; and that nothing in the volumes before us is more admirable, or to us more surprising, than the perfect candour and undeviating fairness with which the learned author passes judgment on all the different authors who come before him;—the quick and true perception he has of the most opposite and almost contradictory beauties—the good-natured and liberal allowance he makes for the disadvantages of each age and individual—and the temperance and brevity and firmness with which he reproves the excessive severity of critics less entitled to be severe. No one indeed, we will venture to affirm, ever placed himself in the seat of judgement with more of a judicial temper—though, to soften invidious comparisons, we must beg leave just to add, that being called on to pass judgment only on the dead, whose faults were no longer corrigible, and had already been expiated by appropriate pains, his temper was less tried, and his severities less provoked than in the case of living offenders—and that the very number and variety of the errors that called for animadversion, in the course of his wide survey, made each individual case appear comparatively insignificant, and mitigated the sentence of individual condemnation.

It is to this last circumstance of the large and comprehensive range which he was obliged to take, and the great extent and variety of the society in which he was compelled to mingle, that we are inclined to ascribe, not only the general mildness and indulgence of his judgments, but his happy emancipation from those narrow and limitary maxims by which we have already said that poets are so peculiarly apt to be entangled. As a large and familiar intercourse with men of different habits and dispositions never fails, in characters of any force or generosity, to dispel the prejudices with which we at first regard them, and to lower our estimate of our own superior happiness and wisdom, so, a very ample and extensive course of reading in any department of letters, tends naturally to enlarge our narrow principles of judgment, and not only to cast down the idols before which we had formerly abased ourselves, but to disclose to us the might and the majesty of much that we had mistaken and condemned.

In this point of view, we think such a work as is now before us, likely to be of great use to ordinary readers of poetry—not only as unlocking to them innumerable new springs of enjoyment and admiration, but as having a tendency to correct and liberalize their judgments of their old favourites, and to strengthen and enliven all those faculties by which they derive pleasure from such studies. Nor would the benefit, if it once extended so far, by any means stop here. The character of our poetry depends not a little on the taste of our poetical readers. . . . Present popularity, whatever disappointed writers may say, is, after all, the only safe presage of future glory;—and it is really as unlikely that good poetry should be produced in any quantity where it is not relished, as that cloth should be manufactured and thrust into the market, of a pattern and fashion for which there was no demand. A shallow and uninstructed taste is indeed the most flexible and inconstant—and is tossed about by every breath of doctrine, and every wind of authority; so as neither to desire any permanent delight from the same works, nor to assure any permanent fame to their authors;—while a taste that is formed upon a wide and large survey of enduring models, not only affords a secure basis for all future judgments, but must compel, whenever it is general in any society, a salutary conformity to its great principles from all who depend on its suffrage.—To accomplish such an object, the general study of a work like this certainly is not enough;—But it would form an excellent preparation for more extensive reading—and would, of itself, do much to open the eyes of many self-satisfied persons, and startle them into a sense of their own ignorance, and the poverty and paltriness of many of their ephemeral favourites. Considered as a nation, we are yet but very imperfectly recovered from that strange and ungrateful forgetfulness of our older poets which began with the Restoration, and continued almost unbroken till after the middle of the last century. (pp. 465-67)

There was great room therefore,—and, we will even say, great occasion, for such a work as this of Mr Campbell's, in the present state of our literature;—and we are persuaded, that all who care about poetry, and are not already acquainted with the authors of whom it treats—and even all who are—cannot possibly do better than read it fairly through, from the first page to the last—without skipping the extracts which they know, or those which may not at first seem very attractive. There is no reader, we will venture to say, who will rise from the perusal even of these partial and scanty fragments, without a fresh and deep sense of the matchless richness, variety, and originality of English poetry: while the juxtaposition and arrangement of the pieces not only gives room for endless comparisons and contrasts,—but displays, as it were in miniature, the whole of its wonderful progress, and sets before us, as in a great gallery of pictures, the whole course and history of the art, from its first rude and infant beginnings, to its maturity, and perhaps its decline. While it has all the grandeur and instruction that belongs to such a gallery, it is free from the perplexity and distraction which is generally complained of in such exhibitions; as each piece is necessarily considered separately and in succession, and the mind cannot wander, like the eye, through the splendid labyrinth in which it is enchanted. (pp. 467-68)

[In] order to give any tolerable idea of the poetry which was . . . to be represented, it was necessary that the specimens to be exhibited should be of some compass and extent. We have heard their length complained of—but we think with very little justice. Considering the extent of the works from which they are taken, they are almost all but inconsiderable fragments; and where the original was of an Epic or Tragic character, greater abridgement would have been mere mutilation,—and would have given only such a specimen of the whole, as a brick might do of a building. From the earlier and less familiar authors, we rather think the citations are too short; and, even from those that are more generally known, we do not well see how they could have been shorter, with any safety to the professed object and only use of the publication. That object, we conceive, was to give specimens of English poetry, from its earliest to its latest periods; and it would be a strange rule to have followed, in making such a selection, to leave out the best and most popular. The work certainly neither is, nor professes to be, a collection from obscure and forgotten authors—but specimens of all who have merit enough to deserve our

remembrance;—and if some few have such redundant merit or good fortune, as to be in the hands and the minds of all the world, it was necessary, even then, to give some extracts from them,—that the series might be complete, and that there might be room for comparison with others, and for tracing the progress of the art in the strains of their models and their imitators.

In one instance, and one only, Mr C. has declined doing this duty, and left the place of one great luminary to be filled up by recollections that he must have presumed would be universal. He has given but two pages to Shakespeare—and not a line from any of his plays. Perhaps he has done rightly:—a knowledge of Shakespeare may be safely presumed, we believe, in every reader; and, if he had begun to cite his Beauties, there is no saying where he would have ended. . . . Mr C. has complied perhaps too far with the popular prejudice, in confining his citations from Milton, to the *Comus* and the smaller pieces, and leaving the *Paradise Lost* to the memory of his readers. But though we do not think the extracts by any means too long on the whole, we are certainly of opinion, that some are too long and others too short; and that many, especially in the latter case, are not very well selected. There is far too little of Marlowe for instance, and too much of Shirley, and even of Massinger. We should have liked more of Warner, Fairfax, Phineas Fletcher, and Henry More—all poets of no scanty dimensions—and could have spared several pages of Butler, Mason, Whitehead, Roberts, Meston, and Amhurst Selden. We do not think the specimens from Burns very well selected; nor those from Prior—nor can we see any good reason for quoting the whole L"Castle of Indolence," and nothing else, for Thomson—and the whole Rape of the Lock, and nothing else, for Pope. (pp. 469-70)

The "**Essay on English Poetry**" is very cleverly, and, in many places, very finely written—but it is not equal, and it is not complete. There is a good deal of the poet's waywardness even in Mr C.'s prose. His historical Muse is as disdainful of drudgery and plain work as any of her more tuneful sisters;—and so we have things begun and abandoned—passages of great eloquence and beauty followed up by others not a little careless and disorderly—a large outline rather meagerly filled up, but with some morsels of exquisite finishing scattered irregularly up and down its expanse—little fragments of detail and controversy—and abrupt and impatient conclusions. Altogether, however, the work is very spirited; and abounds with the indications of a powerful and fine understanding, and of a delicate and original taste. (p. 472)

But we must now break away at once from this delightful occupation; and take our final farewell of a work, in which, what is original, is scarcely less valuable than what is republished, and in which the genius of a living Poet has shed a fresh grace over the fading glories of so many of his departed brothers. (p. 496)

> [*Francis Jeffrey*], *"Campbell's 'British Poetry',"* in The Edinburgh Review, *Vol. XXXI, No. 62, March, 1819, pp. 462-97.*

LEIGH HUNT (essay date 1821)

[*An English poet and essayist, Hunt is remembered as a literary critic who encouraged and influenced several Romantic poets, especially John Keats and Percy Bysshe Shelley. Here, Hunt focuses on "The Pleasures of Hope" and "Gertrude of Wyoming," attributing Campbell's inhibition and lack of spontaneity to his "'precise' education." Hunt's remarks originally appeared in* the Examiner *on 21 August 1821.]*

The writer of a sketch of Mr. Campbell's life in the Magazines is inclined to attribute the best part of his poetry to his assiduous study at college; and to doubt whether he would have made so great an impression on the public "had he not received *precisely* that education which he did." We are inclined to suspect, on the other hand, that Mr. Campbell's "precise" education was far from being the best thing in the world for a man of imagination and feeling. We cannot but think we see in it the main cause why he has not impressed the public still more, and ventured to entertain it oftener. Doubtless, it must have found in him something liable to be thus controlled. He had not the oily richness in him which enabled Thomson to slip through the cold hands of critics and professors, and tumble into the sunnier waters. But we will venture to say that if he had gained fewer prizes at college, or been less studious of Latin and lecturers, he would have given way more effectively to his poetical impulses, and not have reminded us so often of the critic and rhetorician. There was an inauspicious look in the title of his first production, the **"Pleasures of Hope."** It seemed written not only because Mr. Rogers's *Pleasures of Memory* had been welcomed into the critical circles, but because it was the next thing to writing a prose theme upon the *Utility of Expectation.* A youth might have been seduced into this by the force of imitation; but on reading the poem, it is impossible not to be struck with the willing union of the author's genius and his rhetoric. When we took it up the other day, we had not read it for many years, and found we had done it injustice; but the rhetoric keeps a perverse pace with the poetry. The writer is eternally balancing his sentences, rounding his periods, epigrammatizing his paragraphs; and yet all the while he exhibits so much imagination and sensibility that one longs to have rescued his too delicate wings from the clippings and stintings of the school, and set him free to wander about the universe. Rhyme, with him, becomes a real chain. He gives the finest glances about him, and afar off, like a bird; spreads his pinions as if to sweep to his object; and is pulled back by his string into a chirp and a flutter. He always seems daunted and anxious. His versification is of the most received fashion; his boldest imaginings recoil into the coldest and most customary personifications. If he could have given up his pretty finishing commonplaces, his sensibility would sometimes have wanted nothing of vigour as well as tenderness:

> Yes, at the dead of night by Lonna's steep,
> The seaman's cry was heard along the deep;
> There on his funeral waters, dark and wild,
> The dying father blest his darling child:
> Oh! Mercy shield her innocence, he cried.
> *Spent on the prayer his bursting heart,* and died.

The following passage contains most of his beauties and defects:

> Yet there, perhaps, may darker scenes obtrude,
> Than Fancy fashions in her wildest mood;
> There shall he pause, with horrent brow, to rate
> What millions died—that Cæsar might be great!
> Or learn the fate that bleeding thousands bore
> March'd by their Charles to Dnieper's swampy shore;
> First in his wounds, and shivering in the blast,
> The Swedish soldier sunk—and groan'd his last!
> File after file the stormy showers benumb,
> Freeze every standard-sheet, and hush the drum!
> Horseman and horse confess'd the bitter pang,
> And arms and warriors fell with hollow clang!

> Yet ere he sunk in nature's last repose,
> Ere life's warm torrent to the fountain froze,
> The dying man to Sweden turn'd his eye,
> Thought of his home, and clos'd it with a sigh!
> Imperial Pride look'd sullen on his plight,
> And Charles beheld—nor shudder'd at the sight!

Here is an event of so deep and natural an interest that the author might surely have had faith enough in it to leave out his turns, his hyphens, and his Latinities. The dying man thinking of his home, which is well borrowed from Virgil—the aweful circumstance of the drum's hushing, and those three common words "the bitter pang," are in the finest taste; but the horse and horseman must *confess* this pang, because confess is Latin and critical. *Horrent brow* is another unseasonable classicality, which cannot possibly affect the reader like common words; and the antithesis, instead of the sentiment, is visibly put before us in the pause of the last line. In the concluding paragraph of the poem, Mr. Campbell has ventured upon giving one solitary pause in the middle of his couplet. It has a fine effect, and the whole passage is deservedly admired; yet the last couplet, in our opinion, spoils the awful generalization of the rest by introducing Hope again in her own allegorical person, which turns it into a sort of vignette.

We should not have said so much of this early poem, had the line been more strongly marked between the powers that produced it, and those of his later ones.

The **"Gertrude of Wyoming,"** however, is a higher thing, and has stuff in it that should have made it still better. The author here takes heart, and seems resolved to return to Spenser and the uncritical side of poetry; but his heart fails him. He only hampers himself with Spenser's stanza, and is worried the more with classical inversions and gentilities. He does not like that his hero should wear a common hat and boots; so he spoils a beautiful situation after the following critical fashion:

> A steed, whose rein hung loosely o'er his arm,
> He led dismounted; ere his leisure pace,
> Amid the brown leaves, could her ear alarm,
> Close he had come, and worshipped for a space
> Those downcast features:—she her lovely face
> Uplift on one whose lineament and frame
> Were youth and manhood's intermingled grace:
> *Iberian seem'd his boot*—his *robe* the same,
> And well the Spanish plume his lofty looks became.

This is surely arrant trifling, and makes us think of the very things it would have us forget. Yet how pretty is his worshipping a space "those downcast features!" We are in love, and always have been, with his Gertrude—being very faithful in our varieties of attachment. We have admired ever since the year 1809 her lady-like inhabitation of the American forests, albeit she is not quite robust enough for a wood-nymph. She is still and will for ever be found there, in spite of the author's report of her death, and as long as gentle creatures, who cannot help being ladies, long to realize such dreams with their lovers. We like her laughing and crying over Shakespeare in her favourite valley—the "early fox" who "appeared in momentary view"—

> The stock-dove plaining through its gloom profound,

the aloes with "their everlasting arms," and last not least, the nuptial hour "ineffable,"

> While, here and there, a solitary star
> Flush'd in the darkening firmament of June.

Lines like these we repeat in our summer loiterings, as we would remember an air of Sacchini or Pæsiello. We like too what everybody likes too, the high-hearted Indian savage,

> The stoic of the woods—the man without a tear—

not omitting the picture of his bringing the little white boy with him, which the critics objected to,

> —Like Morning brought by Night.

As to the passage which precedes the wild descant into which be bursts out, when the prostrate Waldegrave after the death of his bride is observed convulsively shivering with anguish under the cloak that has been thrown over him, our eyes dazzle whenever we read it, and we are glad to pick a quarrel with the author for ever producing anything inferior. He certainly has the faculties of a real poet; and it is not the fault of the *poets* of his country that he has not become a greater.

Mr. Campbell's favourite authors appear to be Virgil and Racine; which may serve to shew both the natural and artificial bent of his genius. He has imagination and tenderness, but he has also a great notion of criticism; so he leans to those poets, ancient and modern, who have at once a genius from nature, and the most regular passports for the reputation of it from art. He forgets that what the critics most approve of in the long run, as distinguished from the more intuitive preferences of the uncritical lovers of poetry, obtains the approbation because it flatters their egotism with the nearest likeness to their own faculty. Mr. Campbell's own criticism would be perhaps worse than it is in this respect, if it were really anything else but ingenious and elegant writing. But there is a constant struggle in him between the poetical and the critical, which he doubtless takes for a friendly one; and in his prose he is always slipping from an exercise foreign to his nature into mere grace and fancy. After reading the "Essay" prefixed to his [*Specimens of the British Poets*], we recollected nothing but three things, which are characteristic enough—first, that he seemed disagreeably mystified at the great praises bestowed on our old dramatists by certain living writers!—second, that he allows Shakspeare to put us wherever he pleases in a first act, but protests against a repetition of the illegality in a second—and third, that he has written a considerable number of beautiful similes. (pp. 161-65)

> *Leigh Hunt, "Sketches of the Living Poets: No. 3, Mr. Campbell," in his* Leigh Hunt's Literary Criticism, *edited by Lawrence Huston Houtchens and Carolyn Washburn Houtchens, Columbia University Press, 1956, pp. 159-65.*

THE UNITED STATES LITERARY GAZETTE   (essay date 1825)

[*In the following excerpt from a review of* Theodric, *the critic ranks Campbell as a "second class" poet and faults his work as imitative.*]

Mr Campbell's fortune as a poet has been singular. The fame of other poets fluctuated during their whole lives, and their niches in the Temple were assigned to them by posterity; but he seems many years ago to have attained a station, from which no subsequent performances have removed him; and he is now arrived at an age which renders it improbable that he will produce any work to alter the judgment of the public. He has always been, and from the nature of things always must be, a popular poet, but, as it has been decided, a poet of the second class. There are passages in all his works which appeal directly to feelings inherent in human nature,—passages which will awaken responses in the breast of every reader.

His first work, "**The Pleasures of Hope**," was, according to the notions of the leaders of the public taste in its day, a work of high promise. But better and more exalted views of poetical excellence have since been opened. No man can now elevate himself by the most elaborate imitations, and Mr Campbell unhappily belongs to the class of imitators. We do not know but we may shock the prejudices of some of our readers by this assertion, nor do we mean to make it without some qualification. His lyric poetry is his own, pure and unmingled, and noble; but his longer works—those to which his odes are but appendages—all discover mannerism and imitation strongly marked. This will not do now, and cannot do hereafter. The master poets of the age have broken down the barriers of prejudice; they have moulded anew the public taste, and stamped it with an original impress. No revival of an obsolete school of poetry, no direct imitation of a new one, can now win the applause of the public, though it may exact the approval of critics.

Campbell was happy in the time at which "**The Pleasures of Hope**" was published; a few years later, and it would have been praised by critics and neglected by readers, if indeed his good sense would not then have entirely suppressed it. . . .

As to [*Theodric*], we do not think it will increase the fame of Campbell; neither do we think it will shake his well established reputation. It comes too late to effect this; but had it appeared immediately after "**The Pleasures of Hope**," it would have needed something better than "**Gertrude of Wyoming**," highly polished as that is, to have placed him on his former level in public estimation.

"**Theodric**" is a short tale, and, as it seems to us, carelessly told. It opens with a description of Alpine scenery, *conveyed* from Wordsworth, and sadly marred in the *transversion*. The poet imagines himself standing by the tomb of a Swiss maiden, whose story is told him by his companion: that she fell in love with a colonel in the Austrian army from the enthusiastic descriptions of her brother, who was a cornet in his troop; and learning that he was about to marry another woman, she died of love; that the colonel having one day scolded a little, because his wife stayed too long on a visit, she died of grief thereupon just about the same time. What became of the colonel and cornet afterwards, our author says not. Now any man who is conversant with the Lake poets, must know, that a fine superstructure of poetry might have been built on such a plan as this. We ourselves, admirers as we are of another school than his, did believe that Mr Campbell could have worked up this simple tale powerfully; but he has failed. The style is a strange medley—some passages are of the versification of Mr Campbell's earlier works, some of that of Lord Byron's, and now and then a dash of Crabbe's; and we could not feel affected by the incidents, however much we tried. (p. 343)

[We think that "**Theodric**" is] the work of one who draws sometimes from one and sometimes from another, without relying upon his own collected and concocted resources. Like all the works of its author, it has passages of tranquil beauty. The following description is of this kind:

> ————and to know her well
> Prolonged, exalted, bound, enchantment's spell;
> For with affections warm, intense, refined,
> She mixed such calm and holy strength of mind,
> That, like Heaven's image in the smiling brook,
> Celestial peace was pictured in her look.

Hers was the brow, in trials unperplexed,
That cheered the sad, and tranquillized the vexed;
She studied not the meanest to eclipse,
And yet the wisest listened to her lips;
She sang not, knew not Music's magic skill,
But yet her voice had tones that swayed the will.

There are lines in which the author's wish to snatch, like some of his contemporaries, "a grace beyond the reach of art," has betrayed him into a meanness of expression that sorts but oddly with the others around them. Such, for instance, as these:—

His ecstacy, it may be guessed, was much.

But how our fates from unmomentous things
May rise, like rivers, out of little springs.

The boy was half beside himself.

Of the smaller poems contained in this volume, none are equal to some which Campbell has heretofore written; several of them were first published in the *New Monthly Magazine.* Some of the contributors to that Magazine are, however, better poets than its editor, if we may suppose that the poetry there published, and not republished here, was the work of others. The love songs are about as good as love songs commonly are. They are more true to nature than Moore's, and the feeling which they express is much more like the love of ordinary mortals, than that which is expressed in Byron's. "**The Ritter Bann**" has been sufficiently ridiculed, so we will not join in the chorus. "**Reullura**" is as tame as the "**Ritter**." The Song— "**Men of England**" is more in the style of Campbell's best efforts than any thing else in the volume, and is worthy of a place not far below "**The Battle of the Baltic**." . . .

Perhaps ["**The Last Man**"] ode—if ode it be—exhibits as much power and originality as any thing in the volume; but it is difficult to forget, while reading it, some poems of modern date, which we cannot but think that Mr Campbell remembered while writing it. (p. 344)

A review of "Theodric: A Domestic Tale, and Other Poems," in The United States Literary Gazette, *Vol. I, No. 21, February 15, 1825, pp. 343-44.*

PIERCE PUNGENT (essay date 1830)

[*In this satiric attack on Campbell's literary career, the pseudonymous critic examines how his "puerile dandyism of mind" adversely affected his talents as a poet and as editor of the* New Monthly Magazine.]

When we sit down to dip our pen into black ink, upon the subject of Mr. Thomas Campbell, we involuntarily find ourselves in danger of making the affair a funeral oration, or at least a solemn sermon, taking for our text, in reference to the subject thereof, the lamentations of the old gentleman of the land of Uz, who sat in sackcloth and among the ashes,—to wit, "O that it were with him as it has been in years past, when his lamp burned bright," and so forth; but as we are ourselves conscious of being in imminent danger of falling asleep during any body's "long speaking" in the sermonising style, we shall proceed, without any further moralising, to open up the innermost intents of our subject.

We do not mean to inflict upon our respected friends, the public, much of our critical tediousness regarding the merits of the poetry which Mr. Campbell has been pleased to bestow upon the world. Small allowance has he given us, indeed, of the fruits of that muse of which so much was expected after the publication of the *Pleasures of Hope*; and of what we have had, the public has long since formed its opinion. It seems to be decided at least, that what beauties belong to his poems are not of a very profound or recondite sort, so as to make them, like Wordsworth's, a subject of controversial discussion; nor do they seem to have been charged with any peculiar or specific faults beyond the ordinary ones of a due sprinkling of mediocrity and common-place. We can, therefore, pretend to have little to say of *them* that is very new at this time of day; but as Mr. Campbell has been much before the public (that is, as much as he possibly could,) during a residence in the metropolis of about some forty years, and has, in various ways besides that of his poetical character, acted as a public man, we have sundry small matters to advert to which concern him in this latter character, which we shall do with all brevity of speech, and much considerate indulgence to himself.

And in the first place, we cannot help lamenting, in our charity, that, for the sake of Mr. Campbell's reputation, he did not die immediately after the publication of his *Gertrude of Wyoming* and his National Odes. Had he had such good fortune, we should have had the imaginations of the whole world in his favour, fancying what he *might* have done, had he lived, to enhance to extravagance the value of what he had *then* done, which would have placed him in a niche tolerably high among the poets of our country. But, alas! how different the sacred character of a dead *poet* to that of a living, struggling, elbowing, envying, and envied, public man—encountering the tear and wear of public literary life, and turning his back upon the Muses, and the wholesome though barren hills of Scotland, for the sake of the temporary friendship of lords and fine people, and a place in society which is hard to win and harder to keep, and which really humbles, instead the dark *closses* of Edinburgh, until he had seen more of the strong characteristics of common life in his own country, and come more in contact with those scenes and feelings of which a poet can make so much—had he been "badgered about," as the Americans elegantly say, through the world after a different manner—or had he actually played Strap, as he once wished, and gone shaving good-naturedly over the Continent, sleeping in haylofts and *cabarets,* and seeing what he could see, and hearing what he could hear, sometimes rejoicing in a plentiful bellyful of lentils and *soap maigre,* but oftener hungry and thirsty in a poetical way, yet always moving on for the benefit of the lusty muse and of posterity; he would not be the *dilettanti* gentlemanly Scotch cockney that he at present is, nor should we now be at all likely to be sitting down to cut him *up,* as we are about to do, from a conscientious zeal for common truth and justice all over the earth.

And yet we are almost inclined to retract the high eulogium that we were ready to have hypothetically passed upon Mr. Campbell, when we reflect that he has from the first manifested that constant hankering after the conventional honours of small gentility, so unworthy the ambition either of a genuine poet or a manly public character, of whom his country would be really proud, if it could at all, consistently with its rough apprehensions of what is worthy of fair admiration. It is this puerile dandyism of mind that is the great defect in Mr. Campbell's character, which has been at the root of that change in the man which has caused so thorough a disappointment of the poet, from the promise which seemed to be held out in his early productions. And then, like all small minds, he has early suffered himself to be spoiled by flattery. He began to write at the time when the good-natured public chose to laud highly such small-beer poets as Hector Macneil. No wonder then, that, upon the appearance of the *Pleasures of Hope,* the public thought that, in the Glasgow youth they had got a poet who was to outshine and eclipse, perhaps, all mankind; and feeling a pleasure in the "Hope," which was then naturally indulged, gave him glory and praise far beyond his actual deserts, and raised about him an outcry which has gone far to turn the poor gentleman's head, and which even yet has by no means passed away.

It is upon this point, then, that we reluctantly take up our lamentation over the declining character of Mr. Thomas Campbell. Had he had the eyesight of a respectable mind, he would have seen, even from the green age of eighteen, that it was but a poor transition for a poet, with all a poet's feelings and lofty aims, to step from the bare yet inspiring hills of Scotland, bleak and hungry though they be, into the heart of the fat and sweat of a large city, and to the premature enjoyment of partial and prophetic adulation. In truth, it was an experiment likely to prove dangerous to a man of more talent than ever Mr. Campbell could, after all, pretend to, for a young man with all the natural upsetting spirit of an ordinary Scotchman, and much of the Highland pride of the Campbells, to step so suddenly as he did, at least in a complimentary way, from the homely low-roofed house of a decent clean-looking carle, dressed in snuff-brown as his father was, and living in the third flat of some wooden building of the old Saltmarket of Glasgow, into the sickly and perfumed atmosphere of the drawing-rooms in London; where the poet who has the meanness to covet this sort of thing soon dwindles into a merely fine gentleman, if he be able to keep it up, or, if not, into a contemptible foil or servile dependent. But if this be really his taste and the object of his noble ambition, how pleasantly he learns to talk gentility like a lady's-maid, and to watch the looks of literary countesses and patronising coxcombs—bestowing his anxieties upon the tie of his cravat, or the polite *tournure* of his phraseology, until all the enthusiasm of the poet is spent, like the last gleam of a perfumed rushlight; and their being, of course, little original pith of character, the genuine freedom and remaining manliness of nature is soon polished away into namby-pamby inanity and fastidious nothingness.

Now, to speak in the most cautious terms, and with the utmost chastity of expression, the simple and naked truth, never has there been exhibited before the audience of the world a more perfect example of this degrading paltryness of aim, and perniciously small ambition, than is commended to all men's observation in the general career of Mr. Thomas Campbell. While he was writing as a boy in his Ossianic Balaam about the blue mists and blackeyed maidens of his poor but intellectual country, in his bug-invaded garret in the Saltmarket of Glasgow, we applaud him. For being turned out of his lodgings in Bun's Wynd in Edinburgh, merely because he kicked up a row in the middle of the night, and fought with the bed-posts in defence of the Muses, we quarrel not with him. For tramping through France and the *Low Countries,* without a shoe to his foot, in honour of the blessed Nine, and for the sake of seeing *life,* we had honoured him. But for a man that had any thing in him, to degrade himself by turning gentleman's gentleman, for the effeminate pleasure of talking small literature to frowsy old spinsters, fusty demireps, and snuffy women of quality in boudoirs, is a thing that we cannot excuse. This, however lamentable, is but too true; and it is well known to every little dog of literature, that from the day that Mr. Campbell set his foot on a Turkey carpet, he has done no good. The Asiatic curtains and Florentine blinds of great houses have completely *blinded him* to all a poet should see. Curry and hock (no higher)

have quite turned his stomach against all that is wholesome and strengthening in the nutrition and sense of human things; and silk stockings, French perfumery, and wax lights, have totally deprived him of all pluck, so that any good fillibegged Scotchman, coming from off the heath of the original country of the Cambells, might blow him over with the wind of his mouth by a single puff of fresh Highland breath—such as might be required to bring the first squeak from the drone of a Celtic bagpipe.

But the proof—the proof of all this, if any one is so ignorant or so blinded by the dust and fluster of undiscriminating popularity as to require such a thing at this time of day—the proof is not only ample to every one of the great and little things that Mr. Campbell has been doing for the last twenty years, but furnishes grave charges against him, both in reference to his own reputation, and to the effects of that influence which his engagements with the literary slop-sellers of New Burlington Street have given him over a portion of our current literature. We do not say much of his lectures on English poetry. Few people are much either impressed or instructed by such laborious and dry preachments, for they are what any moderately instructed individual could have accomplished. They, no doubt, furnish the empty tribe of critical talkers, the pretty blues and greens of simpering literature, with the necessary aliment of ready-made wishy-washy opinions to mouth and mince withal; and in this respect, taken along with his more influential works, they may have had more weight, for aught we know, than such affairs usually carry into general reading society. But, notwithstanding the absurd praises of them in the *Edinburgh Review,* with any people who knew any thing, they only served to shew more clearly that sweet-lipped shallowness, and graceful fastidiousnes of nothing, which "burst upon the world" so deftly shortly after in the pretty pages of the *New Monthly,* and has been simpering away to us now and then since the establishment of that great work, in the still small voice and dry dribblets of Mr. Campbell's most costive poetry.

We are now, therefore, brought to speak upon that important head of our discourse which regards the lights and shadows of that great work, the *New Monthly Magazine,* founded by Mr. Thomas Campbell. (pp. 563-67)

What is the *New Monthly* like, in the estimation of all rational people? It is like one of Stultze's coats without a man in it: super-super drapery, with nothing below; cut, and smoothed down, and stuffed out, and needled, and squared, and rounded, to fit the fantastic shapings of fashion, until you are sick of lookings at a *thing* so empty and so aimless. It is the semblance of an egg without wholesome salt, and from which the yolk is carefully extracted, that you may have all the insipidity without the nourishment. It is the sauce without the fish, or any bread to eat with it. It is a man without a nose to his face, or any feature that you may know him by—whose very eyebrows have been shaved away, that nature may be quite forgotten, and to make room for a plaster of paint and artificial colouring. It is the humble attendant on a drawing-room, whose tongue has been clipped, for fear it should say a word that might be offensive to ears polite, and who only whistles like a bird a few elaborate sweet strains of gently soothing nothingness which have been carefully taught it by certain cringing pseudo-exquisites and foreigners; for assuredly the *thing* is neither English nor Scotch, neither fish, flesh, nor fowl, nor even good savoury red herring.

Is not every body sick of the *New Monthly* who have any relish for what has any thing whatever in it? Are not even its contributors sick of it, and heartily ashamed of themselves and their everlasting, weary elaboration at nothing? Are they not, trained as they are in the straining school of the great wishy-washy Bookseller, tired of the slavery of being obliged to work up constant messes of whipt syllabub for the weakly stomachs of those who cannot bear the substantial ailment of sense and truth? Do not its perfumed patrons themselves, for whose exclusive use it has been created and sustained by that tasteful individual Mr. Thomas Campbell,—do not they yawn over it from month to month, turning over its boring leaves with hopeless *ennui,* looking in vain for something that strikes or stirs, and dawdling dismally over its affected sketches and inane caricatures? Is not its ambitious dulness only equalled by the empty weariness of those showy *soirées,* which Mr. Campbell has so much affected all his life, to his own infinite loss and real degradation—while an example has been set to a passive public of a taste and manner which has been working like a poison in our floating literature? Has it not been the *New Monthly* that has set the standing example of that heartless, and pithless drawing-room book-making which has of late deluged the literary world, and which, along with the vile taste of its putling criticisms, threatened to overwhelm, by the mere number of the books published in the same style and connexion, the whole field of current British bibliography.

And what criticisms (criticisms!) have been put forth to the world in that elegant-ish, dandy-ish, washy-ish periodical, under the cover of the name of Thomas Campbell! Barefaced puffery we can understand and appreciate. Penny-a-line newspaper work does not get into drawing-rooms, and creeps forth generally in a tone of conscious humility. But the coxcombic strut, the ignorant pretence and shallow senselessness, of some of Colburn's and Campbell's writers, would really make a dog sick; while their zeal for *taste,* which they do not understand, and for *gentility,* which never could own them, is only equalled by their obtuseness towards real merit, and their heartlessness towards the fair claims of manly authorship. That such a crew as they are, with few exceptions, composed of,—such a pretending coterie of literary dandies and quacks,—should have so long sickened the world with their profitless brain-spinning, is a lamentable proof of the influence of mere fashion, when it can enlist for its prophet and leader such an effeminate *literateur* as Mr. Campbell, and of how the opinionless world will consent for a time to be book-ridden to any thing by the magic of any name which it, at the time, delighteth to honour.

Every one feels that Mr. Campbell has not only, as we said, disappointed the world as a poet, but that in trying his strength with it in the character of a public man, he has failed egregiously as to the attainment of his own views, and, as far as his influence went, has done a real injury to the current literature of his adopted country, England. Placed by his early and high reputation at the head of one of the most influential third-rate organs of public opinion, he has been the example and the apostle of a school of taste which is distinguished by nothing so much as its sensitive cowardice to every thing like freedom of thought or manliness of language; while its great aim has been to please drawing-room critics merely, by empty elegance and fastidious affectation. The serious charge against Mr. Campbell then is, that the effeminacy of his taste and the puerility of his ambition have not only spoiled and frittered away the powers he possessed as a poet, but made him, in his sphere, the example and the patron of that wretched school of silk-stocking stultification, the dandies of which have so long

and so pompously been striving to keep each other in countenance, but which is unworthy of an intellectual nation, and which must ultimately be hooted out of the world by those who have hitherto been contented to laugh at it and despise it, without taking the trouble to raise their voices to cough it down.

But more than that,—is it not to the lofty airs and simpering tone of sweet-mouthed gentility assumed by the Campbell coterie, that we are in a great measure to attribute that bastard ambition which has so much infected our men of books and of pretended talent of late, namely, to be thought fine gentlemen and persons of fashion about town; who affect immensely to talk the language of high life, and babble about their intimacy with lords and great people? Has not, at least, Mr. Thomas Campbell taken the lead in this sort of thing, forgetting both the natural respect and place of aristocratic station, but also the just pride of true talent, the claims of which upon the admiration of the world are of a far different and really loftier character? We all know how infectious this ignoble affectation is, and that one prominent man has it in his power either to encourage, by his example and the airs he gives himself, this paltry pride, or by exhibiting, in his own person, the manly plainness of true talent, to discountenance an affectation so injurious to all proper pride, and so destructive to that independence in circumstances which is so desirable for the proper cultivation of genius. But we must restrain ourselves upon this subject. (pp. 567-69)

The days are long gone by since [Mr. Campbell] was a rising poet, and since he struggled with some vigour in the office of the *Statesman* newspaper, and elsewhere, in the uphill toil of ''Life in London.'' But these were the days before he came to be a man of *fine taste,* and was without controversy a fine poet. As a poet, he has, we are sorry to say, been long since dead. As a public character, he is still alive for a blessing to the *New Monthly,* and the Literary Union, and such affairs. Much good may he do them! (p. 571)

> Pierce Pungent, ''Literary Characters,'' in Fraser's Magazine for Town & Country, *Vol. I, No. V, June, 1830, pp. 563-71.*

HENRY T. TUCKERMAN (essay date 1851)

[*In the following excerpt from a review of Beattie's* Life and Letters of Thomas Campbell (*see Additional Bibliography*), *Tuckerman defends Campbell against his detractors, particularly praising the honesty and spontaneity of his poetry.*]

[Of] all the modern poets of Great Britain, the one whose memory we could have least suffered to be desecrated was Campbell; and we rejoice to have known him as the bard of Hope and not as Tom Campbell, especially as his correspondence exhibits his eminent title to poetical character as well as talent, and repudiates the shallow gossip which drew such superficial portraits of him in later years. We find, in these letters, that Campbell the man was worthy of Campbell the poet; and that the ideal we had cherished of the author of ''**Gertrude**'' and ''**Hohenlinden**'' was essentially true to nature. The manner in which he has been dealt with, even by literary men, and especially by social detractors, is only another illustration of the humiliating truth that ''Folly loves the martyrdom of Fame.'' (p. 213)

There is no instance, perhaps, in the annals of literature, of so instantaneous and complete a recognition of the advent of a poet as followed the appearance of the ''**Pleasures of Hope.**''

It introduced him at once to fame and society; and it did this by virtue of the eloquent utterance it gave to feelings that then latently glowed in every noble heart. Like a bugle whose echoes speak the morning cheer that exhilarates the frame of the newly-roused hunter, it caught up, rendered musical and prolonged the strains of pity, hope and faith, rife, though seldom audible, in the world.

It is essential to poetry of this nature that the sensibilities should be acted upon by some actual scene, person, or event; and accordingly we find that every successful composition of Campbell has a personal basis; to this, indeed, we may ascribe that spirit of reality which constitutes the distinction between forced and spontaneous verse; his muse, when herself, is awake, magnetic and spirited; the sense of beauty, or the enthusiasm of love and freedom being naturally excited, utter themselves in fervid strains. Thus the apostrophe to Poland, and the protest against skepticism, the appeal to the disappointed lover, the description of mutual happiness—and, in fact, all the animated episodes in the **"Pleasures of Hope,"** grew directly out of the events of the day or the immediate experience of the poet. **"Lochiel's Warning"** embodies a traditionary vein of local feeling derived from the land of his nativity; the **"Exile of Erin"** consecrates the woes of a poor fellow with whom he sympathised on the banks of the Elbe; the **"Beech Tree's Petition"** was suggested by an interview with two ladies in the garden where it grew; the **"Lines on a Scene in Bavaria,"** are a literal transcript from memory; **"Ye Mariners of England"** expresses feelings awakened by the poet's own escape from a privateer. It is a singular coincidence that the draft of this famous naval ode was found among his papers, seized on his return from Germany on the suspicion that his visit had a treasonable design. In the freshness of youth he witnessed a battle, a retreat, and the field upon which the night-camp of an army was pitched; and the vivid emotions thus induced, he eloquently breathed in **"Hohenlinden"** and **"The Soldier's Dream."** His dramatic tastes are finely reflected in the address to John Kemble [**"Valedictory Stanzas to Kemble"**], and his classical in the ode to the Greeks [**"Song of the Greeks"**]. We also trace the relation between the very nature of the man and whatever appealed to the sense of the heroic or the beautiful in his letters. The State Trials excited his deepest youthful sympathy; it is natural that to him the memorable experience of life was to hear Neukomm play the organ and stand with Mrs. Siddons before the Apollo Belvidere. The **"Turkish Lady"** was written while his mind was full of a project to visit the East: and his subsequent intentions of joining his brother in America, with whom he kept up a regular correspondence, accounts for his choice of "The Valley of Wyoming" as the scene of **"Gertrude."** (pp. 215-16)

We know of few specimens of English verse comparable to the best of Campbell's for effective rhythm; contrast the spirit-stirring flow of the **"Song of the Greeks"** with the organ-like cadence of **"Hohenlinden,"** or the pathetic melody of **"Lord Ulliu's Daughter"** with the deep flowing emphasis of the **"Battle of the Baltic."** It is remarkable that this fine musical adaptation belongs to all his genuine pieces;—we mean those naturally inspired; while his muse is never whipped into service as in **"Glencoe"** and **"Theodric,"** without betraying the fact in her stiff or wayward movement. This only proves how real a poet Campbell was.

We demur, however, to the opinion frequently advanced, that his poetic fire died out long before his life. One of his noblest compositions, lofty and inspiring in sentiment, and grandly musical in rhythm, is **"Hallowed Ground:"** and one of his most striking pieces, **"The Last Man,"** both of which were late productions.

The personality so characteristic of genuine feeling is not only evident to the obvious inspiration, but in the verbal execution of his conception. Thus he constantly impersonates insensible objects. It is the bugles that sing truce, and he that lays himself beneath the willow; the glow of evening is like, not the cheek and brow of woman, but of her we love. Throughout the intensity of the feeling personfies the object described, and gives human attributes to inanimate things—exactly as in the artless language of infancy and the oratory of an uncivilized people. Such is the instinct of nature; it is what separates verse from prose, the diction of fancy and emotion from that of affairs and science.

If any one is preeminently entitled to the name of Poet, in its most obvious sense, it is he who so emphatically represents in verse a natural sentiment that his expression of it is seized upon by the common voice and becomes its popular utterance. This direct, sympathetic, intelligent and recognized phase of the art has been the most signficant and effective from the days of Job and Homer to those of Tasso and Campbell. The vivid rhetorical embodiment of a genuine feeling prevalent at the time or characteristic of humanity—is the most obvious and the most natural province of the bard. The ballads of antiquity, the troubadour songs and the primitive national lyric evince how instinctive is this development of poetry. The philosophic combinations of the dramas, the descriptive traits of the pastoral and the formal range of the epic are results of subsequent culture and more premeditated skill. This is also true of the refinements of sentiment, the mystical fancies and the vague expression which German literature and the influences of Wordsworth, Shelley and Coleridge have grafted upon modern English verse. If we were to adopt a vernacular poet from the brilliant constellation of the last and present century, as representing legitimately natural and popular feeling, with true lyric energy—such as finds inevitable response and needs no advocacy or criticism to uphold or elucidate it—we should name Campbell. He wrote from the intensity of his own sympathies with freedom, truth and love; his expression, therefore, is truly poetic in its spirit; while in rhetorical finish and aptness he had the very best culture—that of German literature. Thus simply furnished with inspiration and with a style, both derived from the most genuine resources—the one from nature and the other from the highest art—he gave melodious and vigorous utterance not to a peculiar vein of imagination like Shelley, nor a mystical attachment to nature like Wordsworth, nor an egotistic personality like Byron—but to a love of freedom and truth that political events had caused to glow with unwonted fervor in the bosoms of his noblest contemporaries; and to the native sentiment of domestic and social life—rendered more dear and sacred by their recent unhallowed desecration. It was not by ingenuity, egotism, or artifice that he thus chanted,—but honestly, earnestly—from the impulse of youthful ardor and tenderness moulded by scholarship. It is now the fashion to admire verse more intricate, sentiment less defined, ideas of a metaphysical cast and a rhythm less modulated by simple and grand cadences; yet to a manly intellect, to a heart yet alive with fresh, brave, unperverted instincts—the intelligible, glowing and noble tone of Campbell's verse is yet fraught with cheerful augury. It has outlived, in current literature, and in individual remembrance, the diffuse metrical tales of Scott and Southey; finds a more prolonged response from its general adaptation, than the ever-recurring keynote of Byron, and lingers on the lips and in the hearts of those who only muse over the more elaborate pages of minstrels, whose golden ore is either beaten out to intangible thinness or largely mixed with the alloy of less precious metal. Indeed nothing evinces a greater want of just appreciation in regard to the art or gift of poetry than the frequent complaints of such a poet as Campbell because of the limited quantity of his verse. It would be as rational to expect the height of animal spirits, the exquisite sensation of convalescence, the rapture of an exalted mood, the perfect content of gratified love, the tension of profound thought, or any other state, the very law of which is rarity, to become permanent. Campbell's best verse was born of emotion,—not from idle reverie or verbal experiment; that emotion was heroic or tender, sympathetic or devotional;—the exception to the every day, the common-place and the mechanical; accordingly in its very nature, it was "like angels' visits" and no more to be summoned at will, than the glow of affection or the spirit of prayer. That idleness had nothing to do with the want of productiveness of his muse, so absurdly insisted on, during his life, is evident from his letters. He was always busy—but unfortunately, for the most part, in tasks of literary drudgery undertaken for subsistence; and deserves laudation instead of censure, for having respected the divine art he loved too much to degrade it into the service of hackneyed necessity.... Instead of lazily reposing on laurels early-won, he was eminently true to the faith and independence that make beautiful the dreams of his youth;—devoted to his kindred and friends with self-denying generosity, sympathising to the last in the cause of freedom, cognizant every where and always of the intrinsic worth of the primal sentiments whose beauty he so fondly sung; and never forgetful of the duty and the privileges of amity, courage and fame. Such is the evidence of the unstudied epistles now first collected.... (pp. 216-17)

Henry T. Tuckerman, "Thomas Campbell," in The Southern Literary Messenger, *Vol. XVII, No. 4, April, 1851, pp. 212-18.*

D. M. MOIR (essay date 1856)

[*Moir provides a highly favorable survey of Campbell's poetry.*]

No poet ever made a more brilliant *entrée* than Thomas Campbell did, in **"The Pleasures of Hope,"** written at twenty-one. In fact, it was regarded as completely a marvel of genius, and at once deservedly placed its author among the immortals; for if language is capable of embalming thought, and that thought consists of pictures steeped in the richest hues of imagination, and of sentiments which, in their splendour and directness, may be regarded as "mottoes of the heart," the poem could not possibly ever be forgotten, provided the lines of any other writer were destined to be held in remembrance. With a daring hand the young poet essayed every string of the lyre, and they each responded in tones of sublimity, or of beauty and pathos. The poem was evidently the product of fine genius and intense labour; for nothing so uniformly fine, so sustained in excellence, was ever produced without intense labour; yet so exquisite is the art, that the words seem to have dropped into their places, and the melody, "like one sweetly played in tune," flows on apparently without effort—now wailing through the depths of tenderness, and now rising into the cloud-lands of imagination with the roll of thunder. That traces of juvenility should have been here and there discernible in an effort otherwise so high and so sustained, is not to be wondered at; but, even in these exuberances, genius and taste were ever predominant, while the diction, chaste and polished, was yet instinct

with spirit. An energetic eloquence, which occasionally supplied the place of inspiration, and an art which could lead Beauty in flowery chains, without depriving her step of the air and the graces of Nature, made up for all other deficiencies.

When we look on **"The Pleasures of Hope"** as a work achieved while the author yet stood on the threshold of manhood, it is almost impossible to speak of it in terms of exaggerated praise; and whether taking it in parts, or as a whole, I do not think I overrate its merits in preferring it to any didactic poem of equal length in the English language. No poet, at such an age, ever produced such an exquisite specimen of poetical mastery—that is, of fine conception and of high art combined; but if time matures talent, and the faculties ought to strengthen by exercise, Campbell cannot be said to have redeemed the pledge given by this earliest of his efforts. How could he? With the exception of a few redundancies of diction, he left himself little to improve on, either in matter or manner; for sentiments tender, energetic, impassioned, eloquent, and majestic, are conveyed to the reader in the tones of a music for ever varied—sinking or swelling like the harmonies of an Æolian lyre—yet ever delightful; and these are illustrated by pictures from romance, history, or domestic life, replete with power and beauty. What could possibly excel, in pathos and natural truth, the mother's heart-yearnings over her cradled child?—the episode of the Wanderer leaning over the gate by "the blossomed beanfield, and the sloping green," coveting the repose and comfort of

Illustration of a woman tending a watch fire for a sailor, from "The Pleasures of Hope."

the hamlet-home beside him?—the allusion to the melancholy fortunes of the Suicide?—the parting of the Convict with his Daughter?—or in power, "The Descent of Brama?"—the apostrophe to the wrongs of Poland? and the allusion to the consummation of all things, with which the poem magnificently concludes? It is like a long fit of inspiration—a chequered melody of transcendent excellence, passage after passage presenting only an ever-varying and varied tissue of whatever is beautiful and sublime in the soul of man, and the aspects of nature. No ungraceful expressions, no trite observations, no hackneyed similes, no unnatural sentiments, no metaphysical scepticisms break in to mar the delightful reverie. The heart is lapped in Elysium, the rugged is softened down, and the repulsive hid from view; nature is mantled in the enchanting hues of the poet's imagination, and life seems but a tender tale set to music. (pp. 141-43)

If any composition could combine more energy of sentiment with versification as magnificent, it is to be found in the **"Lochiel's Warning"** of the same author. (p. 143)

Campbell has . . . concentrated in [this] short poem as much vigour of conception, grandeur of description, and originality of illustrative imagery, as would, in ordinary hands, have been deemed adequate to replenish volumes. It is throughout sterling ore, thrice refined from all alloy in the furnace of taste. (p. 144)

It was asserted by the late Lord Jeffrey, that the great writers of this age are nothing more remarkable than the very fearlessness of their borrowing. We could point out a cento of brilliant things in Campbell—who forms certainly no exception to this general charge—for which he has been indebted to a discriminating taste and a retentive memory, but then, as with Coleridge, he has conjoined a distinctness, an originality, and a superiority of view quite his own, together with that polish which is the peculiar charm of all his writings. He might admire excellencies in others, and imitate what he admired; but, beyond that, Campbell had a distinct path of his own, along "a wild unploughed, untrodden shore." He possessed the invention of true genius; and sought for and owned no prototype in **"Lochiel's Warning,"** in **"Hohenlinden,"** in **"The Battle of the Baltic,"** in **"Reullura,"** in **"The Last Man,"** or in **"O'Connor's Child,"** the diamond of his casket of gems.

In this last-named poem Campbell opened up a vein of thought and imagery, to which nothing in our preceding literature has the remotest resemblance, excepting, perhaps, the lyrical tales of Crabbe—"The Hall of Justice," and "Sir Eustace Grey." The resemblance, however, if there be any, is very slight; and it is highly problematical if Campbell had them at all in his eye during the composition of this the most thoroughly inspired of all his writings. (p. 145)

The greatest effort of Campbell's genius, however, was his **"Gertrude of Wyoming;"** nor is it likely ever to be excelled in its own peculiar style of excellence. It is superior to **"The Pleasures of Hope"** in the only one thing in which that poem could be surpassed—purity of diction; while in pathos, and in imaginative power, it is no whit inferior. The beauties of Gertrude, however, are of that unobtrusive kind, that, for the most part, they must be sought for. Its imagery is so select as to afford only indices to trains of thought. It "touches a spring, and lo! what myriads rise!" If we add to this, that, as a story, Gertrude is particularly defective, the circumstances will be made palpable which have operated against the popularity of a composition so thoroughly exquisite. The verisification of the poem is intricately elaborate, the diction fastidiously select,

and the incidents, as I have just hinted, less brought out than left to be imagined; as, for instance, where, in one stanza, Henry Waldegrave is the infantine companion of Gertrude, and, in the next, we are told of his arrival from foreign travel, ere we are dimily apprised that he had ever set out from home. Weighed, however, with the real excellencies of the poem, these and other minor blemishes—as inaccuracies in natural history—are "mere spots in the sun," and are amply counterbalanced by the Elysian description of Wyoming. . . . Campbell did not work like Wordsworth, or Crabbe, or Southey, by touches repeated and repeated, till the minims make up a whole, but by sweeping lines and bold master-strokes. The following few words, for instance, convey a whole and almost boundless prospect to the mind:—

> At evening Alleghany views,
> Through ridges burning in her western beam,
> Lake after lake interminably gleam.
>
> (pp. 148-49)

Of Campbell's highest lyrics it would be impossible to speak in terms of exaggerated praise; and in them more especially he has succeeded in engrafting the fresh wildness of the romantic school on the polished elegance of the classic. Whether we regard originality of conception, artistic skill, brilliancy of execution, vividness of illustration, moral pathos, or that impassioned energy which makes description subservient to feeling and sentiment, it would be difficult, from the far-off days of Pindar and Tyrtæus, down to those of Collins and Gray, to point to anything finer or grander, or, to use the phrase of Sir Philip Sidney, that more "rouses the heart like the sound of a trumpet," than his **"Mariners of England,"** his **"Battle of the Baltic,"** his **"Lines on Alexandria,"** his **"Hohenlinden,"** and his **"Lochiel's Warning;"** while, for mellow pathos, for picturesque touches of nature, for phrases of magical power, and words or single lines that, within themselves, concentrate landscapes, he has lent a charm all his own to **"The Exile of Erin,"** the **"Lines in Argyleshire,"** **"The Soldier's Dream,"** **"The Turkish Lady,"** **"The Grave of a Suicide,"** **"The Last Man,"** **"Lord Ullin's Daughter,"** **"Glenara,"** **"Wild Flowers,"** and **"The Rainbow."**

Campbell, like Coleridge, left utterly unfilfilled the promise of his youth; for he did few things worthy of his fame after **"Gertrude,"** and that was published when he was just thirty-two. His magnificent May had no corresponding September; his **"Theodric"** and **"Pilgrims of Glencoe"** were the mere lees of his genius, and utterly unworthy—more especially the last—of his former self. Pity they ever saw the light; and better for him had it been—knowing he had done what he had—to have hung up his harp, and silently lingered out his life in a secure consciousness of poetic immortality. (pp. 150-51)

The writings of Thomas Campbell are distinguished by their elegance and their perspicuousness, by their straightforward manliness and their high tone of moral sentiment. They abound with original imagery, with lofty aspirations after the true and beautiful, and with ideas that, from their prominent beauty, may be almost said to be tangible. Taste, however—the perfect equipoise of his fine faculties—was the source of that mastery which controlled and harmonised all. Hence he had concentration; for his poetry was like a weeded garden, and every blossom that "dedicated its beauty to the sun" was placed in the situation most appropriate to its perfection. His nervous manliness never degenerated into coarseness; and judgment ever pruned the wings of his imagination and fancy. His delicacy was free from affectation, and his enthusiasm never "o'erstepped the modesty of nature." Even when impelled by the whirlwind of inspiration, the helm obeyed his hand, and the bark ploughed on, amid the roaring of the waves, towards the haven of her destination. Few poets combined, in an equal degree, such felicity of conception with such perfect handling—such vigour of thought with such delicacy of expression; yet this delicacy was as free from mawkishness as his sentiment from metaphysical obscurity—the rock on which so many have foundered. He could not rest self-satisfied until he had placed each object in its fairest point of view—until he had harmonised all his separate materials with his general design. While in the selection of his topics he was fastidious, in his treatment of them he was alike daring and original—presenting us either with new and striking images, or with familiar ones unexpectedly placed in a novel aspect; and whatever these were, he laboured until he had imparted to them all the graces of thought and language. His usual success resulted from bold generalisations; but, when occasions offered, he descended to the minute with an elegance quite apart from tedious trifling. His genius is characterised by bursts of abrupt lyrical enthusiasm; it is like his own "Andes, giant of the western star," his "wolf's long howl from Oonalaska's shore," his "aye as if for death a lonely trumpet wailed," his panther "howling amid that wilderness of fire," his "storks that to the boundless forest shriek," his "pyramid of fire," his "death-song of an Indian chief." He took not to by-lanes, as many have done, for singularity's sake, when the fair broad highway was before him. He preferred the classical to the quaint, the obvious to the obscure; and the general sympathies of mankind to an "audience fit though few," which none, I presume, ever did, who could not help it. In the management of his subject he either grappled with it, as Hercules did with the Lernæan hydra; or tenderly blent all its elements into harmonious beauty, as if encircling it with the fabled cestus of Cytheræa. (pp. 152-53)

> *D. M. Moir, "Lecture III," in his* Sketches of the Poetical Literature of the Past Half-Century, *third edition, William Blackwood and Sons, 1856, pp. 117-61.*

GEORG BRANDES (essay date 1875)

[*Brandes, a Danish literary critic and biographer, was the principal leader of the intellectual movement that helped to bring an end to Scandinavian cultural isolation. He believed that literature reflects the spirit and problems of its time and that it must be understood within its social and aesthetic context. Brandes's major critical work,* Hovedstromninger i det 19de aarhundredes litteratur, *from which the following excerpt was drawn, won him admiration for his ability to view literary movements within the broader context of all European literature. Here, Brandes assigns Campbell to the naturalistic school in English poetry and praises his works for their lyricism and expression of liberty. Brandes's commentary was originally published in Danish in 1875.*]

The poet Thomas Campbell, descended from an ancient Highland family, and born and brought up in Scotland, was, like Scott, an ardent Scottish patriot; he also felt warm sympathy for Ireland, and, like Moore, sang her national memories and sorrows; but he combined love of the two subordinate countries with an ardent and martial British patriotism.

He was, however, not only a national poet in the sense in which Wordsworth was one, but also, from his youth to his death, an enthusiastic lover of liberty. His epic poems and his ballads are not superior to corresponding productions of Wordsworth's; but he had true lyric genius. He is the Tyrtæus or

Petöfi of the Naturalistic School. To him the cause of his country and the cause of liberty are one and the same thing, and in his best verse there is a spirit, a swinging march time, and a fire, that entitle him, if only for the sake of half-a-dozen short pieces, to a place among great poets.

His poem "**The Battle of the Baltic**" is, naturally, little calculated to make a favourable impression on Danes. His pride in the victory Nelson won over a force so much weaker than his own, but which the poem magnifies into the same size as England's, is the very extravagance of patriotism. But, side by side with this poem, and written at the same time, we have "**Ye Mariners of England**," a masterpiece, in the rhythm of which we seem to hear the gale rattling among English sails. Here the true son of the Queen of the Sea, singing of the British sailor, celebrates his mother's praises.

Notice the rushing, sweeping force and exultation compressed into the last four lines of this stanza:—

> Ye Mariners of England!
> That guard our native seas;
> Whose flag has braved a thousand years
> The battle and the breeze!
> Your glorious standard launch again
> To match another foe!
> And sweep through the deep,
> While the stormy winds do blow;
> While the battle rages loud and long,
> And the stormy winds do blow.

And observe the expression of pride in England's sovereignty of the sea:—

> Britannia needs no bulwarks,
> No towers along the steep;
> Her march is o'er the mountain-waves,
> Her home is on the deep.
> With thunders from her native oak,
> She quells the floods below,—
> As they roar on the shore,
> When the stormy winds do blow;
> When the battle rages loud and long,
> And the stormy winds do blow.
>
> (pp. 189-90)

It is the same with Campbell as with all the other authors of the group to which he belonged—his poetic faculty is based upon the freshness of his receptivity to natural impressions. He has written a poem to the rainbow ["**To the Rainbow**"] which, in spite of a rather prosaic and argumentative introduction, is a little masterpiece of simplicity and fancy. He begins by imagining the feelings of "the world's grey fathers" when they came forth to watch its first appearance:—

> And when its yellow lustre smiled
>   O'er mountains yet untrod,
> Each mother held aloft her child
>   To bless the bow of God.
>
> Methinks, thy jubilee to keep,
>   The first made anthem rang
> On earth delivered from the deep,
>   And the first poet sang.
>
> Nor ever shall the Muse's eye
>   Unraptured greet thy beam:
> Theme of primeval prophecy,
>   Be still the poet's theme!
>   .   .   .   .   .   .
> How glorious is thy girdle cast
>   O'er mountain, tower, and town,
> Or mirrored in the ocean vast,
>   A thousand fathoms down!

> As fresh in yon horizon dark,
>   As young thy beauties seem,
> As when the eagle from the ark
>   First sported in thy beam.

And one of his latest poems, "**The Dead Eagle,**" written at Oran in Africa, bears witness to the same, unenfeebled, receptivity to all the phenomena of nature as this early one. In the later work we are conscious of a joy in natural strength and power which is characteristically English. "True," the poet writes:

> True the carr'd aëronaut can mount as high;
> But what's the triumph of his volant art?
> A rash intrusion on the realms of air.
> His helmless vehicle, a silken toy,
> A bubble bursting in the thunder-cloud;
> His course has no volition, and he drifts
> The passive plaything of the winds. Not such
> Was this proud bird: he clove the adverse storm
> And cuff'd it with his wings. He stopp'd his flight
> As easily as the Arab reins his steed,
> And stood at pleasure 'neath heaven's zenith, like
> A lamp suspended from its azure dome,
> Whilst underneath him the world's mountains lay
> Like molehills, and her streams like lucid threads. . . .

There is wealth of imagination in this as well as wealth of observation.

But Campbell is greatest in his poetry of freedom, in poems like "**Men of England,**" "**Stanzas on the Battle of Navarino,**" "**Lines on Poland,**" "**The Power of Russia,**" and such noble, profound expressions of spiritual freedom as that entitled "**Hallowed Ground.**" In such productions as these he plainly shows his spiritual superiority to the poets of the Lake School, who, like him, wrote glorious verse in honour of the nations who were struggling for their independence. The Lake poets honoured the struggle only when it was against the tyranny of Napoleon, England's enemy. Campbell makes no difference of this kind; in the name of freedom he often exhorts and even rebukes England, whereas to the other poets she is freedom's very hearth and home.

Note, in "**Men of England,**" the warmth with which he insists that the records of valour in war are as nothing compared with the glowing love of liberty in the breasts of living men, and that the glory of the martyrs of freedom is worth a hundred Agincourts.

Campbell's joy at the liberation of Greece is as genuine as his grief over the fall of Poland; but the poem on Poland is more ardent, in its indignation, its hope, its lament that "England has not heart to throw the gauntlet down." And the verses on the power of Russia display as clear an understanding of the danger to civilisation which lies in the success of Russia, and of the real significance of the defeat of Poland, as if a statesman had turned poet.

> Were this some common strife of States embroil'd;—
> Britannia on the spoiler and the spoil'd
> Might calmly look, and, asking time to breathe,
> Still honourably wear her olive wreath.
> But this is Darkness combating with Light;
> Earth's adverse Principles for empire fight.

These are weighty words; and not less pregnant is the line:

> The Polish eagle's fall is big with fate to man.

The poem "**Hallowed Ground**" is, in its bold simplicity, a plain protest against all superstition, whatever name it bears,

and a manly confession of faith in the gospel of liberty as proclaimed by the eighteenth century. What is hallowed ground? asks Campbell:

> What's hallow'd ground? Has earth a clod
> Its Maker meant not should be trod
> By man, the image of his God,
>   Erect and free,
> Unscourg'd by superstition's rod
>   To bow the knee?

> That's hallow'd ground—where, mourn'd and miss'd,
> The lips repose our love has kiss'd;—
> But where's their memory's mansion? Is't
>   Yon churchyard's bowers?
> No! in ourselves their souls exist,
>   A part of ours.

> A kiss can consecrate the ground
> Where mated hearts are mutual bound;
> The spot where love's first links were wound,
>   That ne'er were riven,
> Is hallow'd down to earth's profound,
>   And up to heaven!

And, though the ashes of those who have served mankind may be scattered to the winds, they themselves, he says, live on in men's hearts as in consecrated ground; until the high-priesthood of Peace, Independence, Truth, shall make earth at last *all hallowed ground*.

Campbell cannot be numbered among the greatest poets of the Naturalistic School; but in his lyrics there is a simple, powerful, and melodious pathos which reminds us of the old Greek elegiac poets. Although Scotch by birth, his sympathies were with Ireland, and his spirit was British. Although, like the poets of the Lake School, ardently patriotic, he was distinctly the lover and champion of liberty, and of liberty as a divinity, not as an idol. (pp. 190-94)

> *Georg Brandes, "The British Spirit of Freedom," in his* Naturalism in Nineteenth Century English Literature, *Russell & Russell, 1957, pp. 189-94.*

LITTELL'S LIVING AGE   (essay date 1889)

[*In this survey of Campbell's poetry, the critic delineates the reasons for both his contemporary success and the subsequent decline in his reputation.*]

From the publication of "**Gertrude of Wyoming**" in 1809, almost up to the date of his death in 1844, Campbell was regarded in literary circles and by the general public as the greatest English poet of the nineteenth century with the possible exception of Lord Byron. What should we say now to his claim to this high position, and what chance would he have of being placed in the same category as Wordsworth or Coleridge, Shelley or Keats? While these poets, whose reputation could not compare with that of Campbell in the first quarter of the century, have steadily grown in favor, there are now few critics, I imagine, who would deny that the star of Campbell is on the wane. He is still reckoned as a standard author, but it is only by a few of his short lyrics, and not by his didactic and narrative poems, that he is likely to be ultimately remembered. To do Campbell justice, he himself seems to have felt that his popularity was out of proportion to his actual poetic qualities. "He alluded," we are told, "with genuine simplicity to his own feelings, on receiving praise and honor as a poet: You did not do all this to Burns; you neglected *him*—a real genius—a wonder; and you bestow all this on me, who am nothing, compared to him.'' A study, at the present day, of Campbell's life and writings certainly tends to confirm the truth of this piece of self-criticism. (p. 474)

It is difficult, at the present day, to understand the cause of the general outburst of admiration, which, ninety years ago, greeted that appearance of **"The Pleasures of Hope."** We can still recognize that its lines are rhythmical and melodious; its sentiments pleasing; and that there are certain felicitous expressions in the poem which have become, as they deserved to become, proverbial. But it has none, or little, of the spontaneous singing power and true poetical *afflatus* of the inspired bard; its dry, didactic, sententious moral platitudes are expressed in the regular, formal, mechanical couplets of the eighteenth-century school. It may be regarded as the last effort of the old style of poetry, of which Pope was the typical representative, against the inroads of the ''new poets,'' who, headed by Wordsworth and Coleridge, were now about to make their influence felt in literature; and it is significant that the dates of the publication of *Lyrical Ballads* and **"The Pleasures of Hope"** almost coincided. When we read the carefully balanced, laboriously polished passages of Campbell's poem, with its rhetorical tropes and florid imagery, we feel the appropriateness of the name given him by his youthful fellow-collegians—''the Pope of Glasgow;'' and we see that Byron was right when he said that Campbell's defence of Pope (in his later **"Essay on English Poetry"**) was made in ''his *own cause* too.'' Campbell was, in fact, a belated Pope, with a dash of nineteenth-century romanticism, and a larger share of Scotch national sentiment. Though, at the date of the commencement of his literary career, the star of the reformers was soon to be in the ascendant, the critics and general reading public were still almost universally attached to the traditions of the old-fashioned style; and so it happened that, while Wordsworth's *Lyrical Ballads* were assailed by a storm of ridicule and contempt, Campbell's **"Pleasures of Hope"** met with instantaneous success. Its connection with Akenside's *Pleasures of Imagination*, and Rogers's *Pleasures of Memory* was of course obvious, and was probably a point in its favor with the critics. Campbell's literary kinship with Rogers, for whom he felt strong personal admiration, was always gratefully acknowledged by him, and he is said to have expressed the opinion that *The Pleasures of Memory* is ''a much more perfect poem'' than **"The Pleasures of Hope."** But the idea of literary ''perfection'' varies from age to age; and correctness, regularity, and freedom from literary blemishes are, after all, but negative and second-rate qualities; so that to say of a poem, as was said of **"The Pleasures of Hope,"** that ''there is in it not a vulgar line—no, not a vulgar word,'' would nowadays be regarded as not necessarily and altogether a compliment. (p. 476)

Though not received with such universal favor as **"The Pleasures of Hope,"** owing to the strong influence then exercised by party politics on contemporary literature, **"Gertrude of Wyoming"** is certainly marked by higher poetical qualities than those discernible in its more staid and formal predecessor; it has less correctness, perhaps, but it has more freshness, more tenderness, and more truth. (p. 477)

[Campbell had an unconscious] recognition of the fact that his poetical qualities belonged, not to the first, but to the second order of merit; and that, as he was not gifted with the supreme imaginative and creative genius of a great poet, he must do his best to supply this want by the exercise of the faculties he *did* possess—a quick fancy, a fine sense of melody, and a power of delicate artistic finish.

Although Campbell was only thirty-two at the date of the publication of **"Gertrude of Wyoming,"** this poem was the last work of any value which he published. So far was he from fulfilling the ambitious prognostications of his friends, that the ten years' period of poetical composition through which he had just passed was already sufficient to exhaust his powers; and though, during the remainder of his long life, his reputation continued to stand high, this was solely on the strength of his early productions, for his later work was marked by increasing feebleness and want of spirit. (p. 478)

[He] published in 1824 the short narrative poem of **"Theodric,"** which was received coldly by his friends and was severely criticised by the reviewers, while Campbell himself, with strange want of insight, felt convinced that it would hereafter be recognized as a work of high merit. At the present day **"Theodric"** probably seldom finds a reader, being certainly as flat and unprofitable a piece of verse as was ever produced by any one who bore the name of poet. If the style of **"The Pleasures of Hope"** is to be attributed to Pope's influence, **"Theodric,"** with its feeble attempt at the familiar-poetic tone, must be regarded as an imitation of Crabbe, who has been not inaptly described as ''Pope in worsted stockings.'' But Campbell was not even successful in this unambitious effort; for **"Theodric"** has merely the tameness of Crabbe, without his natural simplicity and domestic pathos. (p. 479)

Campbell's last published volume of poetry was *The Pilgrim of Glencoe.* . . . [**"The Pilgrim of Glencoe"**] is a narrative poem, of about the same length as **"Theodric,"** but even more feeble in its construction and imagery: and its publication seems to have attracted little attention or interest. Already at this time it was evident to Campbell's friends that his physical, no less than his poetical, powers were rapidly on the decrease. (p. 480)

The chief characteristics of Campbell's poetical style are grace and melody of versification, a just sense of proportion, and the gift of expressing his conceptions in terse, lucid, and felicitous language. ''Chaste'' is perhaps the term which is most applicable, and has most often been applied, to his poems; they are so polished and refined, and yet (in the best instances) so simple withal, as to offer to the eye of the critic no conspicuous blemish or mannerism, being unmarked by any strong trace of their author's distinctive personality. In this respect Campbell bears a close affinity to his friend and exemplar, Rogers; and it will be remembered that when the other poets of that day were burlesqued and parodied in *Rejected Addresses*, the authors of *The Pleasures of Memory* and **"The Pleasures of Hope"** were left untouched, as affording no special mark for the aim of the caricaturist. This ''chasteness,'' in the sense of classic faultlessness, was, as I have said, much more appreciated in the opening years of this century than it is now; and the high estimate in which Campbell's poetry was once held seems to us almost unaccountable. ''I consider Campbell,'' said Goethe, ''as more *classical* than my favorite Byron, and far above any modern English poet whose works have fallen in my way. . . . In Campbell's poems there is strength combined with great natural simplicity of style, and a power of exciting high emotions, independently of brilliant epithets or meretricious ornaments.'' So the world of letters thought once; it does not think so now; nor is there anything to lead us to suppose that there will ever be a reaction of opinion in this direction.

In most of the qualities which are now held to be indispensable to the born poet, Campbell was wholly or largely deficient. He had no deep and lasting passion for poetry, nor any true sense of the feelings without which poetry could hardly exist.

With the possible exception of one or two stanzas in **"Gertrude of Wyoming,"** it is questionable if love is anywhere forcibly described in Campbell's writings, though he treats the subject with much grace and elegance in such lyrics as those commencing "When Love first came to earth," and "How delicious is the winning of a kiss at love's beginning." The stanzas which he addressed to his future bride at the time of his courtship are, as his biographer remarks, "wanting in that quick pulse which beats through intensity of amatory feeling." They sound rather like one of Shenstone's or Cowley's less successful efforts:—

> O cherub Content! at thy moss-covered shrine
> I would offer my vows if Matilda were mine;
> Could I call her my own, whom enraptured I see,
> I would breathe not a vow but to friendship and thee.

In the presence of such lines as these, we can well believe what Mr. Redding tells us, that "it is doubtful whether Campbell ever experienced love in its intensity; whether a subdued feeling of attachment, an almost feminine tenderness of regard, did not with him occupy the place of strong amatory passion" [see Additional Bibliography]; and that there is consequently in his works "an artificial rather than a natural dealing with the attachment to the sex." And as with love, so too with the aspects of external nature. Campbell's descriptions of natural scenery are chiefly expressive of the unemotional eighteenth-century feeling, and have none of the intense and passionate sympathy with nature which marked his more poetical contemporaries. He could sing deftly enough of woods and meadows and waterfalls; but it is not difficult for the reader to see that the poet's affection for wild nature was of a rather lukewarm and conventional sort. "I do not mean to think of poetry any more," he wrote to a friend in 1808; "I mean to try to make money, and keep a good house over my head at Sydenham." It may be supposed that this practical prudence, if not compatible with the rarer poetic instincts, might yet have gone hand in hand with that strength of mental power which one would expect to find in a writer of Campbell's eminence. But it was not so; for though his works abound in happy phrases and elegant turns of expression, you may search them in vain for any real richness or originality of thought.

Even his elaborate style of writing, the "perfection" of which elicited such praise from contemporary critics, has peculiar faults of its won, and did not by any means attain all that it aimed at within its limited scope. His best passages are sometimes marred by a strange inversion of the natural order of the words, owing presumably to over-refinement of workmanship, as in the following lines from **"Gertrude of Wyoming:"**—

> Hushed were his Gertrude's lips; but still their bland
> And beautiful expression seem'd to melt
> With love that could not die! and still his hand
> She presses to the heart *no more that felt.*
> Ah, heart! where once each fond affection dwelt,
> And features *yet* that spoke a soul more fair.

It is still more extraordinary that so fastidious and careful a writer as Campbell, whose painful slowness of composition gave Theodore Hook his joke that the poet had been "safely delivered of a couplet this morning," should have been betrayed by his ignorance of natural history into certain not very important, yet none the less egregious blunders concerning the fauna and flora introduced into his tales. In **"The Pleasures of Hope,"** and **"Gertrude of Wyoming,"** we find the tiger stealing along the banks of Lake Erie, and the panther domiciled in the woods of Ohio, while the flamingo disports itself on

Pennsylvanian waters, and the tropical aloe and palm flourish in the same northern latitude. These errors were pointed out to Campbell by his friends, in order that he might rectify them in later editions; but to revise his work when once printed was always an uncongenial task to him, and in defiance of the botanist and zoologist the anomalies were therefore allowed to remain in the text. Another and more pardonable error into which Campbell was led, in his chief narrative poem, by trusting to a work entitled the *History of the Destruction of Wyoming in 1778,* was brought home to him in a very strange and unexpected manner. Following the authority just mentioned, he had denounced as the treacherous destroyer of Wyoming a Mohawk chief named Brandt—"the monster Brandt" he called him in the poem—and it might well have been supposed that, right or wrong, this poetical account of so distant an event would have passed unchallenged. But it was not so; for some fifteen years after the publication of **"Gertrude of Wyoming,"** Campbell was surprised by a visit from Brandt's son, no Mohawk in appearance, but "a fine young man of gentlemanly manners," and a lieutenant in the English service, who had come to adduce proof of his father's innocence. It appeared that Brandt, so far from being the "monster" he was represented, had been a civilized and philanthropic Indian who had accustomed his tribesmen to peaceful habits, had built a church, and translated one of the Gospels into the Mohawk language! Campbell, being thus placed in the awkward predicament of libelling a Red Indian, was compelled to do penance in the notes of subsequent editions, but even here he could not be induced to introduce alterations into the text.

Campbell may justly claim the merit of having written many verses which at once caught the public ear and passed into the national storehouse of proverbial expressions. His "distance lends enchantment to the view," his "coming events," his "angel visits," his "meteor flag of England," and other familiar phrases, have furnished material for public and private quotation to innumerable speakers and writers for several decades. In one or two cases, however, these apothegms were not really original in Campbell's mouth; the most popular of all, for instance, being found in almost the same words in Blair's poem "The Grave," in Burns, and in Norris, whose line,—

> Like angel's visits short and bright,

seems to have been the original form of the conception.

It is pleasant to turn from the defects which justice compels us to note in much of Campbell's poetry to his undeniable merits. If not a great poem, **"Gertrude of Wyoming"** is in many ways a beautiful and pleasing one, tender and pathetic in tone, and full of graceful imagery and vivid description. In the melody and dreamy sweetness of its Spenserian stanzas, it at times recalls, if it does not rival "The Castle of Indolence," which seems to have been its model in rhythm and versification; yet Campbell's true masterpiece is not to be sought in **"Gertrude of Wyoming,"** but rather in his incomparable odes and ballads. The martial ode is a species of poetry in which, as far as we can judge, it is not always the greatest poet who fares most successfully; the most stirring productions of this century being those of Campbell, Scott, Wolfe, and Macaulay. The palm is certainly carried off by Campbell's famous trio, **"Hohenlinden," "The Battle of the Baltic,"** and **"Ye Mariners of England;"** although the last-named of these was of course derivative only, being based on the old song, "Ye Gentlemen of England," of which Campbell was an admirer. Whatever may be the fate of the rest of his poetry, Campbell's name will undoubtedly live in these splendid and spirited odes.

Finally, it may be said that Campbell, though by no means an original genius, was a good and worthy singer, who in his best efforts rose to high excellence, maintaining in the bulk of his poems a respectable standard. A distinguished critic of the present day has divided the poets of the highest calibre into two classes—gods and giants—such as Shakespeare and Milton on the one hand, Ben Jonson and Dryden on the other. Campbell's place is very far below either of these classes; he is but a mortal of ordinary stature, yet endowed with a genuine portion of the poetical talent. Chance, interest, the good-will of powerful friends, and his seizure of the golden moment at a critical literary juncture, combined to raise him in his lifetime to a pinnacle of fame far above his real desert; now, when a reaction has set in, and his poems can be judged in a cooler and more critical spirit, he is likely to be valued far less highly, and perhaps for a time to be under-valued. But when all his writings shall have been unsparingly sifted, and purged of the dross that at present encumbers them, at least enough gold will remain, if only in his martial odes, to secure him an honorable remembrance and a niche in the Poets' Corner. (pp. 480-82)

"Thomas Campbell," in Littell's Living Age, *Vol. LXV, No. 2330, February 23, 1889, pp. 474-82.*

LAFCADIO HEARN   (lecture date 1904?)

[*Considered one of America's leading impressionistic critics of the late nineteenth century, Hearn produced a large body of work that testifies to his love of the exotic and the beautiful. His lectures on American and European literature are exceptional for their divergence from the conventions of Victorian criticism. In the following excerpt, Hearn praises Campbell's accomplishments in his short poems, especially admiring his language and use of sound and color. Hearn's commentary was originally delivered as a lecture sometime in the ten years prior to his death in 1904.*]

[Campbell was one of the few men who became] famous through the writing of war-songs,—especially national war-songs. It is upon this kind of composition, indeed, that his fame chiefly rests; but although fame is more or less necessarily based upon popularity, there is something to be said for a merit beyond fame, with which popularity has nothing to do. It is the men of letters alone who are capable of making the best estimate of the high esteem; and these have generally agreed *to put the lyric poems of Campbell*—nearly all of them—*among the best things.* And I doubt very much whether they would accord the palm to his war-songs. I do not mean to say that Prof. Saintsbury has praised his war-songs too much: the professor was only speaking of their excellence as compared with other war-songs. We may very justly doubt whether songs of war can be said to occupy, as to subject, even a second place in lyric poetry; and some of Campbell's poems which are not war-songs at all, take more than a second place. What I am going to speak of now are his lyrical poems of another kind.

The whole of them might be put in about twenty pages. Campbell's longer compositions are not very great: his strength is not in epic, but in short narrative poetry, in lyric and ballad,—and . . . the ballad is properly related to lyrical poetry. *There are about fifteen pieces of such compositions in which Campbell is so individual and so precious* that he cannot be compared with anybody else. When *he is most simple,* he is most haunting; and the simplicity is of the delusive kind,—the kind that you think anybody can do when you first read it, yet which

can really be done but very few times in the course of a century. Most of us make our early acquaintance with Campbell through the little ballad called **"Lord Ullin's Daughter"** . . . :

> A chieftain, to the Highlands bound,
>   Cries, "Boatman, do not tarry!
> And I'll give thee a silver pound
>   To row us o'er the ferry."

That may look very easy to write, but it is not; and much less easy is such a stanza as that in which we read the words:—

> And in the scowl of heaven each face
>   Grew dark as they were speaking.

Only the best of artists would hve used such a word as "scowl" in that verse to describe the darkening of the day before a terrible storm. For "scowl" means much more than frown—it means a *threatening* frown, the look that comes before the attack. And do you not remember the stanza:—

> And fast before her father's men
>   Three days we've fled together,
> For should he find us in the glen,
>   My blood would stain the heather.

A shallow critic might imagine that the word "heather" had been chosen only because of the difficulty of finding a rhyme for "together;"—there are very few rhymes for this word in English, "feather," "weather," are almost the only others, except "tether." You will find in the ballad of "The Blessed Damozel" the way Rossetti attacked this rhyme—not without criticism. But in the case of the Scotch poem, of which the scenes are laid in a country all covered with heather, the same plant . . . from which the word "heather" is derived or, at least, its near relation (the plant of a heath), the use of the rhyme is masterly. You can take any stanza of that little ballad to pieces like the works of a fine watch,—and wonder at their workmanship and restore them to their original places without finding a flaw. Now you cannot do that with many poems.

I think the poem about the parrot [**"The Parrot"**] is less familiar . . . ; and in any case it is worth studying:

> The deep affections of the breast,
>   That Heaven to living things imparts,
> Are not exclusively possess'd
>   By human hearts.
>
> A parrot, from the Spanish Main,
>   Full young, and early caged, came o'er
> With bright wings, to the bleak domain
>   Of Mulla's shore.
>
> To spicy groves where he had won
>   His plumage of resplendent hue,
> His native fruits, and skies, and sun,
>   He bade adieu.
>
> For these he changed the smoke of turf,
>   A heathery land and misty sky,
> And turn'd on rocks and raging surf
>   His golden eye.
>
> But, petted, in our climate cold
>   He lived and chatter'd many a day:
> Until with age, from green and gold
>   His wings grew grey.
>
> At last, when, blind and seeming dumb,
>   He scolded, laugh'd, and spoke no more,
> A Spanish stranger chanced to come
>   To Mulla's shore;

> He hail'd the bird in Spanish speech;
>   The bird in Spanish speech replied,
> Flapp'd round his cage with joyous screech,
>   Dropt down, and died.

The little poem will probably never die—every word in it is exactly the right word, the best word, and the story founded upon fact, was worthy of the art. (pp. 640-43)

Perhaps anybody could tell such a story touchingly; but I doubt very much whether any other poet could have done it as Campbell did. And notice how very briefly he does [it] . . ., never wasting a word. A smaller poet could have made twenty pages with that story;—a greater poet could not have told it in less pages than Campbell and it gains immensely by the compression.

Do you know **"The Soldier's Dream"**? It is European only in the sense that it describes a few things which are local rather than general,—such as the bleating of goats on the mountain tops. Leave out the goats and one or two unimportant touches of the same thought, and you have a poem describing the heart of the soldier in all countries. I think this has been translated into Japanese. What a splendid subject it is!—a soldier in a foreign land dreams of home after the battle and before the dawn that must bring another battle. Of course a soldier has no business to think of home when he is awake. He knows better than to do that. But no man is master of his heart in the time of sleep; it is the illusion of dreams that brings him back to the village of his fathers. And, sleeping there surrounded by blood and death, with great fires burning to frighten away the wolves that come to eat the corpses, he sees his children playing and his home, and hears the sweet singing of the peasants working in the fields. I have no doubt that many a Japanese soldier in China a year ago had just such an experience; and the Scotch poet is describing something that we all know—touching a common chord of tenderness. Like a good artist he makes no comment about the emotion—the poem abruptly breaks off with the awakening; and leaves the thrill of the dream and the pain of the awakening to haunt our minds. It is quite as short a composition as **"The Parrot."**

Less familiar I imagine is the poem about **"The Last Man."** It is longer, more ambitious, and less successful, but there is great power in it, and it is upon a most curious subject. Only Byron, I think, among English poets attempted the same subject;—and it would be interesting to compare Byron's "Darkness" with Campbell's **"Last Man."** Both are original—so original that all we can think of comparing is the pictorial part of the poems, the ghastly landscape. . . . In Campbell's day very little was known about the force of the laws regulating the life and death of suns and planets; and poets were free to imagine what they liked about the thing, without being afraid of scientific criticism. So Byron could describe the going out of the sun—which no mortal man will ever live to see; and Campbell could represent facts, nearly as inconsistent with natural laws. Nevertheless it is well that both poems could be written—though it is certain that nobody will dare to write in the same way again;—

> All worldy shapes shall melt in gloom,
>   The Sun himself must die,
> Before this mortal shall assume
>   Its Immortality!
> I saw a vision in my sleep,
> That gave my spirit strength to sweep
>   Adown the gulf of Time!
> I saw the last of human mould,
> That shall Creation's death behold,
>   As Adam saw her prime!

(pp. 644-46)

The verse of Campbell has a certain magical quality that, like the colour of a morning mist, makes everything seen through it beautiful. It is not only because he was a great *natural* poet that he could make such verse;—it is also in part because he was really an English scholar. What most surprises us is the manner in which he combines polysyllables of Latin origin (or, as we might call them, Latinisms)—with the plainest Anglo-Saxon. Even in his simplest poems we sometimes find him doing this with extraordinary skill. . . . Take, for example, these little stanzas from Campbell's poem about **"Napoleon and the British Sailor"** . . . :

> He hid it in a cave: he wrought
>   The live-long day laborious; lurking
> Until he launch'd a tiny boat
>   By mighty working.
>
> Heaven help us! 'twas a thing beyond
>   Description wretched: such a wherry
> Perhaps ne'er ventured on a pond,
>   Or cross'd a ferry:—
>
> For ploughing in the salt-sea field,
>   A thing to make the boldest shudder;
> Untarr'd, uncompass'd, and unkeel'd,
>   No sail—no rudder.
>
> From neighb'ring woods he interlaced
>   His sorry skiff with wattled willows;
> And thus equipp'd he would have faced
>   The foaming billows.

You know the story how a sailor, a prisoner in France, made a little boat for himself out of a barrel and tried to escape for which action the penalty was death. But when he told Napoleon that he wanted only to see his mother, Napoleon sent him to England in a war-ship and gave him a present besides. Now look at these verses, in illustration of what I mean. . . . Only [the words "laborious," "description," and "ventured"] are of Latin origin: the rest is the purest Anglo-Saxon. In the third stanza the third line is composed entirely of false Latinisms—words of English or Latin origin compounded with a prefix of Latin origin—but not really Latin words, though they give a like effect. There are two Latin words in the succeeding stanza—"interlaced" and "equipped"—at least the second of them came from the Latin through the French. When Campbell uses Latinisms he does so always for the purpose of gaining two things—increased melody of rhythm and increased force of expression. Two such words "serene" and "attitude" are magnificently used in the following lines.

> With folded arms Napoleon stood,
>   Serene alike in peace and danger;
> And, in his wonted attitude,
>   Address'd the stranger.

But it is in the **"Battle of Hohenlinden,"** that the scholarly effect of this Latinism in construction can best be seen. The measure is very unusual, and before Campbell's time was not often used in English poetry. The last word of every fourth line taken by itself is a perfect dactyl. You cannot analyze the verse,—cannot scan it, so as to get the dactyl: it is very irregular, purposely irregular. But the dactylic effect is there and it has the strength of Latin verse rather than English. It is the splendid sound of these lines which accounts for the fact that almost every English boy knows by heart such lines as

> Far flash'd the red artillery;
>
> And charge with all thy chivalry;
>
> To join the dreadful revelry;

Of Iser, rolling rapidly.

By the way there is a good story about some student of Cambridge or Oxford, who, having drunk too much wine, fell downstairs in the night. The proctor called out, "Who is there?"—And the student wittily answered by quoting the last line of the first stanza of Campbell's poem, which (so far as sound goes) might also be written:

O I, Sir!—rolling rapidly.

As I said everybody knows that poem. But everybody does not know the grand **"Ode to Winter"** which can be compared with nothing else of its time except the very best work of Gray and does not suffer by the comparison. Let me quote one stanza only—for the sake of illustrating the effects of the sound:—

> But howling Winter fled afar,
> To hills that prop the polar star,
> And loves on deer-borne car to ride
> With barren Darkness by his side,
> Round the shore where loud Lofoden
> 　Whirls to death the roaring whale,
> Round the hall where Runic Odin
> 　Howls his war-song to the gale;
> Save when adown the ravaged globe
> 　He travels on his native storm,
> Deflowering Nature's grassy robe,
> 　And trampling on her faded form:—
> Till light's returning lord assume
> 　The shaft that drives him to his polar field,
> Of power to pierce his raven plume
> 　And crystal-cover'd shield.

The effects of sound in this poem are chiefly given by pure English words, containing the vowel o and a in various combinations—the o's predominate. But the effect made is greatly helped by some Latin words, such as "assume." (pp. 648-51)

I have told you about the particular mastery of sound characterizing Campbell's verse; but I have not yet said anything about his colour. As a matter of fact Campbell seldom exerted himself merely to produce effects of colour. He uses colour sparingly. . . . But sometimes, in love poems, or tender meditative verse, Campbell makes his language as chromatically rich as any poet before or since his time. Let us take some verses from the address **"To the Evening Star"** as an example. This is a kind of love poem, which you will find in most of the good anthologies.

> Gem of the crimson-colour'd Even,
> 　Companion of retiring day,
> Why at the closing gates of heaven,
> 　Beloved star, dost thou delay?
>
> So fair thy pensile beauty burns,
> 　When soft the tear of twilight flows;
> So due thy plighted love returns
> 　To chambers brighter than the rose:
>
> To Peace, to Pleasure, and to Love,
> 　So kind a star thou seem'st to be,
> Sure some enamour'd orb above
> 　Descends and burns to meet with thee.
>
> Shine on her chosen green resort,
> 　Whose trees the sunward summit crown,
> And wanton flowers, that well may court
> 　An angel's feet to tread them down.
>
> Shine on her sweetly scented road,
> 　Thou star of evening's purple dome,
> That lead'st the nightingale abroad,
> 　And guid'st the pilgrim to his home.

And thereafter having described the bower of his sweetheart, he tells us about herself—about her rosy cheek—

> Where, winnow'd by the gentle air,
> 　Her silken tresses darkly flow,
> And fall upon her brow so fair,
> 　Like shadows on the mountain snow.

Except Tennyson, I do not think that any English poet has given us such delicious touches of light and colour in a simple poem of this kind.

Here we have colour enough—crimson, and roses, and brilliant greens, and purples,—not to speak of a beautiful figure with dark hair and snowy skin. But, the artist must note that all these colours give us the idea of *transparency*. The crimson sunset is so described that we see what is shining through it; the lucidity of jewels enhances most delicately the tints of them. If you try to take the poem, detail by detail, perhaps you will see where the charm is. In very truth it is not in any one detail, but in the effect left upon the mind by all of them. Ask yourself why do you find pleasure in the life and colour of a beautiful summer evening. The reading of this poem produces the effect of the same quality of pleasure. Every word is indeed a gem, chosen by a great jewel smith. Please remark the beautiful use of the word "pensile" in the second stanza. It signifies hanging or suspended—gives us the notion of a lamp hanging aloft. But it so nearly resembles the equally soft word "pensive"—meaning melancholy or thoughtful, and especially thoughtful, that its sudden appearance in the line creates in our mind the sense of both words.

If I have given you some idea of the value of Campbell's shorter poems, I hope that you will try to study them for yourselves. But, bear in mind that his longer poems are not worthy of the same attention; you could employ your time with better reading. Better reading, however, than the shorter poems there is not, and that is what I have been attempting to prove. (pp. 651-53)

> *Lafcadio Hearn, "Notes on Thomas Campbell," in his* On Poets, *R. Tanabe, T. Ochiai, and I. Nishizaki, eds., The Hokuseido Press, 1934, pp. 640-53.*

ARTHUR SYMONS (essay date 1909)

[*Symons was a critic, poet, dramatist, short story writer, and editor who first gained notoriety in the 1890s as an English decadent. Eventually, he established himself as one of the most important critics of the modern era. Symons provided his English contemporaries with an appropriate vocabulary with which to define the aesthetic of symbolism in his book* The Symbolist Movement in Literature; *furthermore, he laid the foundation for much of modern poetic theory by discerning the importance of the symbol as a vehicle by which a "hitherto unknown reality was suddenly revealed." In the following largely negative appraisal of Campbell's work, Symons attempts to determine which of his poems will retain lasting significance.*]

Campbell shares with Longfellow the position of the favourite poet in elementary schools, where verse is learnt by heart as an exercise. There his good poems and his bad poems are equally appreciated: **"Lord Ullin's Daughter"** neither more nor less than **"Hohenlinden,"** and **"The Harper"** than the **"Battle of the Baltic."** In his own lifetime Byron could say, meaning what he said: 'We are all wrong except Rogers, Crabbe, and Campbell.' It could be said, without apparent extravagance, by Campbell's not too considerate biographer, Cyrus Redding, that one of his long poems, **"Gertrude of Wyoming,"** 'combines in itself the best characteristics of the classic and romantic styles, in that just medium which forms the truest principle for modern poetry'; and of the other equally famous long poem, **"The Pleasures of Hope,"** that it belonged to 'that species of poetical composition which can alone be expected to attain in the eyes of true taste a classical and healthy longevity ' [see Additional Bibliography]. He was blamed for his too conscious and too deliberate art, for 'the smell of the lamp' which clung about his verse. To-day his audience is found on the lower benches of day-schools; that audience has been faithful to him for at least two generations; but it has never heard of **"Gertrude of Wyoming"** or of **"The Pleasures of Hope,"** in which Campbell's contemporaries saw 'intimations' for him 'of immortality.'

The problem is curious, and there are complications in it; for, while all the bookish and ambitious verse has been forgotten, some of the simple verse which has remained popular is not less worthless, while some of it, a very little, has qualities more or less unique in English poetry. How are we to explain these compromises and caprices of posterity?

Campbell lived his whole life at a great distance from reality, always believing what he wanted to belive and denying what he did not want to believe. He was not a dreamer who could transpose the worlds and be content in either; he was fitful, essentially unreal, a faint-hearted evader of reality. In a conversation which might have come direct out of "The Egoist," he is seen defending Mrs. Siddons against a criticism whose justice he does not actually dispute, by saying pettishly: 'I won't admit her want of excellence in anything. She is an old friend of mine.' Himself a persistent critic of his own work, he forgave no other critic, and refused to correct an error which had been discovered by any one but himself. He despised his own **"Hohenlinden,"** which he called a 'damned drum and trumpet thing,' and only printed to please Scott. The famous false rhyme in the last stanza—'sepulchre' for what should be sounded 'sepulchry'—he neither admitted nor denied, neither blamed nor defended. We see him wondering whether such a word as 'sepulchry' ever existed, half wishing that it did, yet refusing to adopt it, and concluding weakly that the word as it is 'reads well alone, if we forget that there should be a concinnity with the preceding lines.' He was fastidious without taste, full of alarmed susceptibility; so that when he was editing Colburn's *New Monthly* he disliked his best contributor, the one who brought him most that was new, Hazlitt, and was with difficulty persuaded to accept the epical essay on the prize-fight.

The truth is that Campbell was a sentimental egoist, the Sir Willoughby Patterne of poets. His incapability of realising things as they are, until the realisation was forced upon him by some crisis, explains that unreality, that vague rosy tinge, which we find in almost all of his poetry which professes to deal with actual life. . . . He regarded, we are told, 'poetical composition as a labour,' and the inclination for it 'came upon him only at rare intervals.' It may be that 'his slowness of composition was,' as he says of Carew, 'evidently that sort of care in the poet which saves trouble to his reader.' But not only did he write with labour; poetry was never to him a means of self-expression.

It was the age when poets set themselves tasks in verse, and to Campbell as a young man Rogers' *Pleasures of Memory*, itself descended from Akenside's *Pleasures of Imagination*, presented itself as a model of what should be attempted. He found it easy, in **"The Pleasures of Hope,"** to surpass his models, but, though one of its lines is continually on our lips to-day,

> 'T is distance lends enchantment to the view,

the smooth meandering of verse, with its Micawber-like cheerfulness, becomes drearier and more dismal as we read; and when we have reached

> Come, bright Improvement, on the car of Time,
> And rule the spacious world from clime to clime,

we begin to wonder by what cottage-side poetry has gone to live in the land. With Wordsworth, perhaps, whose *Lyrical Ballads* have just been published, to the derision of a polite public which applauds **"The Pleasures of Hope!"**

Tastes change, they say, and tastes do change, though taste does not. But there is one touchstone which may be applied, apart from all technical qualities, all rules of metre or fashions of speech, whenever verse has a plain thing to say. The verse which takes what has already been finely and adequately said in prose, and makes of it something inferior in mere directness and expressiveness of statement, cannot be good verse. This is what Campbell found in the Bible: 'And the king was much moved, and went up to the chamber over the gate, and wept: and as he went, thus he said: "O my son Absalom, my son, my son Absalom! would God I had died for thee, O Absalom, my son, my son!" ' And this is what Campbell made of it in **"The Pleasures of Hope"**:—

> "My Absalom!" the voice of Nature cried,
> "O that for thee thy father could have died!
> For bloody was the deed, and rashly done,
> That slew my Absalom!—my son!—my son!"

In this poem one seems to catch the last gasp of the eighteenth century; in **"Gertrude of Wyoming,"** published ten years later, we are in the century of *Childe Harold* and the romantic tales. **"Gertrude"** is a tepid romance, such as scholgirls may dream after reading books of improving travel; a thing all feminine and foppish, written by the man, 'dressed sprucely,' whom Byron calls up for us: 'A blue coat becomes him—so does his new wig.' The blue coat and the new wig are never far away from these Pennsylvanian forests, with their panthers, palm-trees, and flamingoes of the tropics. Unreality is in every languid line.

> So finished he the rhyme (howe'er uncouth)
> That true to nature's fervid feelings ran
> (And song is but the eloquence of truth)

says Campbell, vaguely; and I suppose he believed himself to have been 'true to nature's fervid feelings' in his record of the respectable loves of Gertrude and Waldegrave. 'Never insensible to female beauty,' says the commentator, Cyrus Redding, 'and fond of the society of women, it was singular that Campbell, the poet of sentiment and imagery, should have written little or nothing breathing of ardent affection.' Campbell's was, in his own affected phrase,

> The heart that vibrates to a feeling tone;

and here as elsewhere one can imagine him to have been genuinely touched by what, in his way of telling it, fails to touch us. When people read **"Gertrude of Wyoming"** they had acquired a taste for poetical narratives; since Rousseau, the virtues of forest folk were esteemed; and the poem, no doubt, responded to some occasion in the public mind. I have tried to find a single line of genuine poetry in its thin trickle of verse, but I have found none. There is in it a little more of what used to be called 'fancy' than in the much later, wholly unsuccessful **"Theodric;"** but it is not appreciably nearer to poetry. 'The pearly dew of sensibility,' which Hazlitt discovered in its recesses, has not, as he thought it would, 'distilled and collected, like the diamond in the mine'; nor does 'the structure of his fame,' according to the singular metaphor, 'rest on the crystal columns of a polished imagination.'

Yet other props and embellishments must be knocked away from the structure of Campbell's fame before we can distinguish what is really permanent in it. There is, first of all, the series of romantic ballads. In **"Lord Ullin's Daughter"** and the rest Campbell writes with a methodical building up of circumstantial emotion which in the end becomes ludicrous, from its 'more than usual order.' Few escape absurdity, but I doubt whether any parodist has ever equalled the quite serious conclusion of **"The Ritter Bann"**:—

> Such was the throb and mutual sob
> Of the Knight embracing Jane.

Here and there, in a homelier story, Campbell seems to be trying to imitate Wordsworth, as in the foolish **"Child and Hind"** and the less foolish **"Napoleon and the British Sailor"**; and once, in **"The Parrot of Mull: A Domestic Anecdote,"** he seems to have almost caught the knack, and the piece might take its place, not unworthily, among Wordsworth's second-rate work in that kind.

Another sort of work which Campbell attempted with much immediate success, and for which he is still remembered in the schoolroom, is a kind of pathetic ballad which appeals almost indecently to the emotions: I mean such pieces as **"The Exile of Erin," "The Harper," "The Wounded Hussar."** There is emotion in them, but the emotion, when it is not childish, is genteel. I scarcely know whether the misfortunes of 'poor dog Tray' or of the 'wounded hussar' are to be taken the less seriously; the latter, perhaps, by just the degree in which it aims at a more serious effect. 'And dim was that eye, once expressively beaming': it is of the soldier he speaks, not of the dog. But it is in a better poem, **"The Exile of Erin,"** that we see most clearly the difference and the cause of the difference between Campbell's failures and successes in precisely what he could do best in the expression of patriotic feeling. **"The Exile of Erin"** is one of those many poems, written, often, by men who would have died for the convictions expressed in them, but written with so hackneyed and commonplace a putting of that passion into words that the thing comes to us lifeless, and stirs in us no more of a thrill than the casual street-singer's "Home, Sweet Home," drawled out for pence and a supper.

Conviction, it should always be remembered, personal sincerity, though it is an important ingredient in the making of a patriotic or national poem, is but one ingredient among many; and there is one of these which is even more important: poetical impulse, which is a very different thing from personal impulse. I have no doubt that the personal impulse of **"The Exile of Erin"** was at least as sincere as that of **"Hohenlinden"**; I should say it was probably much more deeply felt; but here the poetical energy lags behind the energy of conviction; the effort to be patriotic and to draw an affecting moral is undisguised; the result is a piece of artistic insincerity. In **"Hohenlinden"** some wandering spark has alighted; the wind has carried it, and one knows not from whence; only, a whole beacon is ablaze.

"Hohenlinden" is a poem made wholly out of very obvious materials, and made within very narrow limits, to which it owes its intensity. Campbell had precisely that mastery of the obvious which makes remembered lines, such as 'Distance lends enchantment to the view,' or 'Coming events cast their shadows before,' which we remember as we remember truisms, almost ashamed at doing so. They contain no poetic suggestion, they are no vital form of poetic speech; but they make statements to which verse lends a certain emphasis by its limiting form or enclosure. Very often Campbell uses this steady emphasis when no emphasis is needed, as in this kind of verse, for instance:—

> I mark his proud but ravaged form,
>   As stern he wraps his mantle round,
>   And bids, on winter's bleakest ground,
> Defiance to the storm.

This is merely meant for the picture of the friendless man, not a Byronic Corsair; and here the emphasis is above all a defect of the visual sense: he cannot see simply with the mind's eye. In such poems as the powerful and unpoetical **"Last Man"** the emphasis is like a conscious rigidity of bearing on parade, a military earnestness of rhetoric. The lines march with feet keeping time with the drill-master; and the wonder and terror which should shake in the heart of the poem are frozen at the source. In the genuine success of **"Hohenlinden"** every line is a separate emphasis, but all the emphasis is required by the subject, is in its place. The thud and brief repeated monotony of the metre give the very sound of cannonading; each line is like a crackle of musketry. What is obvious in it, even, comes well into a poem which depends on elements so simple for its success; indeed, its existence.

The one fixed passion in Campbell's shifting soul seems to have been the passion for liberty. . . . He was the patriot of all oppressed countries, and his love for his own country was only part of that wider human enthusiasm. His love of England was quickened, or brought to poetic heat, by a love of the sea, and by a curiously vivid appreciation of the life and beauty of warships. In his controversy with Bowles, as to the place of nature and of art in poetry, his most effective argument was drawn from a warship. 'Those who have ever witnessed the spectacle of the launching of a ship of the line will perhaps forgive me for adding this to the examples of the sublime objects of artificial life. Of that spectacle I can never forget the impression, and of having witnessed it reflected from the faces of ten thousand spectators. . . . It was not a vulgar joy, but an affecting national solemnity.' Something of this 'mental transport,' as he elsewhere describes it, this sense of the beauty and grandeur of the actual circumstances of sea-fighting, came, along with the patriotic fervour, into his two naval odes, **"Ye Mariners of England"** and **"The Battle of the Baltic,"** his two really great poems. **"Ye Mariners of England"** has a finer poetic substance than **"Hohenlinden"** and a more original metrical scheme, here, as there, curiously well adapted to its subject. The heavy pauses and loud rushes: 'And sweep through the deep,' with its checked flow and onset; 'When the stormy winds do blow,' twice repeated, with a vehement motion, and an exultation as of wind and water: conscious art has here, for once, caught hands with a fiercer impulse, and wrought better than it knew. Even here, however, the impulse is on the wane before the last stanza is over; and that last stanza has been made for logic's sake rather than for any more intimate need.

And even in **"The Battle of the Baltic,"** where Campbell reaches his highest height, there are flaws, weaknesses, trifling perhaps, but evident here and there; touches of false poetising, like the line in the last stanza: 'And the mermaid's song condoles.' But the manliness, haughty solemnity, the blithe courage and confidence of the poem, and also the invention of the metre (an afterthought, as we know, introduced when the poem was cut down from twenty-seven stanzas of six lines each into eight stanzas of nine) are things unique in English. The structure, with its long line moving slowly to the pause, at which the three heavily weighted, yet, as it were, proudly prancing syllables fall over and are matched by the three syllables which make the last line, the whole rhythmical scheme, unlike anything that had been done before, has left its mark upon whatever in that line has been done finely since: upon Browning in "Hervé Riel," upon Tennyson in "The Revenge." And if any one thinks that this kind of masterpiece is hardly more than the natural outcome of a fervid patriotic impulse, let him turn to others of Campbell's poems full of an even lustier spirit of patriotism, to poems as bad as the **"Stanzas on the Threatened Invasion,"** ... or as comparatively good as **"Men of England,"** and he will see just how far the personal impulse will carry a poet of uncertain technique in the absence of adequate poetic impulse and adequate poetic technique.

In much of Campbell's work there is a kind of shallow elegance, a turn of phrase which is neat, but hardly worth doing at all if it is done no better. Read the little complimentary verses to ladies, and think of Lovelace; read **"The Beech-Tree's Petition,"** with its nice feeling and words without atmosphere, and think of Marvell's garden-verses, in which every line has perfume and radiance. The work is so neat, so rounded and polished; like waxen flowers under glass shades; no nearer to nature or art.

In the **"Valedictory Stanzas to Kemble"** there is a definition of 'taste,' which shows us something of Campbell's theory and aim in art:—

> Taste, like the silent dial's power,
>   That, when supernal light is given,
> Can measure inspiration's hour,
>   And tell its height in heaven.

And he defines the mind of the actor as 'at one ennobled and correct.' Always labouring to be 'at once ennobled and correct,' Campbell is never visited by any poetic inspiration, except in those few poems in which he has not been more sincere, or chosen better, than usual, but has been more lucky, and able to carry an uncertain technique further. That, and not emotion, or sincerity, or anything else, is what distinguishes what is good from what is bad in his work, even in those poems which have given our literature its greatest war-songs. (pp. 191-200)

> *Arthur Symons, "Thomas Campbell (1775-1844),"*
> *in his* The Romantic Movement in English Poetry,
> *Archibald Constable & Co., Ltd., 1909, pp. 191-200.*

W. J. COURTHOPE (essay date 1910)

[*Courthope was an English educator, poet, literary critic, and biographer whose most notable work is his six volume* A History of English Poetry. *Described by Stuart P. Sherman as a confirmed classicist in poetical theory, he reacted against Romantic theory and practice and advocated a return to the heroic couplet and the satiric poetry characteristic of the age of Alexander Pope, whose collected works he edited. In the following excerpt, drawn from* A History of English Poetry, *Courthope discusses the predominant sentiments in Campbell's verse and also examines his work in relation to English poetic traditions of the eighteenth and nineteenth centuries.*]

The expansion of imaginative taste at the opening of the nineteenth century is vividly reflected in the character of Campbell's poetry. He himself was by instinct and conviction a literary Conservative. Byron, noting this tendency in his poetry, ranks him in his "triangular *Gradus ad Parnassum*," on the same plane with Moore—both of them being placed below Rogers, and all three below Walter Scott, but above Southey, Wordsworth, and Coleridge. Campbell, in his **"Essay on English Poetry,"** undertook the defence of Pope against Bowles; nevertheless he was far from attempting a servile reproduction of the style of the poet whom he acknowledged as his master, and for this "liberalism" he is blamed, theoretically, by Byron, who says:

> With regard to poetry in general I am convinced, the more I think of it, that he [Moore] and *all* of us—Scott, Southey, Wordsworth, Moore, Campbell—are all in the wrong, one as much as another; that we are upon a wrong revolutionary poetical system, or systems, not worth a damn in itself, and from which none but Rogers and Crabbe are free.

Two sentiments predominate in Campbell's verse, a fervent love of his native soil, and an enthusiasm for political liberty; and with these is mixed a strong element of religious feeling. His patriotism is as ardent as that of Scott, but it is not associated with the passionate love of wild nature, historic tradition, and romantic adventure, which inspired the author of *Guy Mannering* and *The Lay of the Last Minstrel*. His love of country shows itself rather in a preference for the tender affections and memories of home life. He muses before the ruined home of his ancestors in Argyllshire: Gertrude of Wyoming dreams over the

> Land of my father's love, my mother's birth,
> The home of kindred I have never seen:

the exile of Erin "revisits in dreams" its "sea-beaten shore"; and the soldier, sleeping on a foreign battle-field, tells how—also in dreams—returning

> To the home of my fathers that welcomed me back.

> I flew to the pleasant fields, traversed so oft,
>   In life's morning march when my bosom was young;
> I heard my own mountain-goats bleating aloft,
>   And knew the sweet strain that the corn-reapers sung.

But in the glowing atmosphere of contemporary battle and victory this softness is often exchanged for the lofty lyric march of poems like **"The Battle of the Baltic"** and **"Ye Mariners of England;"** while the political Whig traditions of the Campbell clan are expanded into that sympathy with the cause of national independence which, after the first Reform Bill, became one of the features of English Liberalism. The uprising of Poland, celebrated by Campbell in the first of his famous poems, **"The Pleasures of Hope,"** continued to be sung by him as late as 1831. Inspirations of liberty in Ireland, Germany, Spain, Greece, by turns awoke an answering chord in his imagination. Even in India the commercial misdoings of the English inspired him (doubtless moved by traditional Whig antipathy to Warren Hastings) with a somewhat visionary forecast:

> To pour redress on India's injured realm,
> The oppressor to dethrone, the proud to whelm;
> To chase Destruction from her plundered shore,
> With arts and arms that triumphed once before,
> The tenth Avatar comes! at Heaven's command
> Shall Seriswattee wave her hallowed wand!
> And Camdeo bright, and Ganesa sublime,
> Shall bless with joy their own propitious clime!

The religious note prevailing in his poetry indicates antagonism to the materialist tendencies of Physical Science, a feeling shared by Wordsworth and Keats. It is sounded in **"The Rainbow"**:—

> When Science from Creation's face
> Enchantment's veil withdraws,
> What lovely visions yield their place
> To cold material laws!—

and is strikingly emphasised both in the fine passage, first inserted in the second edition of **"The Pleasures of Hope,"** beginning "Oh deep enchanting prelude to repose," and in **"The Last Man."** . . . (pp. 103-04)

To a man of genius, imbued with the spirit of classical literature, there was no difficulty in expanding the metrical tradition of the eighteenth century, refined as it had been, in the earlier half of that period, by colloquial usage, so as to make it a fitting vehicle of expression for simple elementary emotions of this kind. Campbell had always an admirable instinct of what was appropriate in poetry. His fastidious taste and judgment make what he says of Parnell generally applicable to himself: "His poetry is like a flower that has been trained and planted by the skill of the gardener, but which preserves in its cultured state the natural fragrance of its wilder air." The careful study of "correct" expression, which marks him for a disciple in the school of Pope, Parnell, and Goldsmith, bore fruit in the considerable number of his lines which have become part of the quotable stock of our national poetry. "'Tis distance lends enchantment to the view": "Like angels' visits, few and far between": "The torrent's smoothness ere it dash below": "Coming events cast their shadows before": "The sentinel stars set their watch in the sky"; with other phrases of the same kind, are "familiar in our mouths as household words," and bear testimony to Campbell's gift for combining brilliant imagery with epigrammatic diction.

This faculty was not reached by him at a bound. **"The Pleasures of Hope,"** in the first edition, reads like the work of a clever schoolboy, seeking to imitate the elegant sentimentalism of Rogers and the sonorous pomp of Darwin. The following is a characteristic specimen of its thought and language:

> Hark! the wild maniac sings, to chide the gale,
> That wafts so slow her lover's distant sail;
> She, sad spectatress, on the wintry shore,
> Watched the rude surge his shroudless corse that bore,
> Knew the pale form, and, shrieking in amaze,
> Clasped her cold hands, and fixed her maddening gaze:
> Poor widowed wretch! 'twas there she wept in vain,
> Till memory fled her agonising brain;
> But Mercy gave, to charm the sense of woe,
> Ideal peace, that truth could ne'er bestow;
> Warm on her heart the joys of Fancy beam,
> And aimless Hope delights her darkest dream.

To rank the delusions of madness among the conscious Pleasures of Hope shows a feebleness of thought which is unfortunately apparent in Campbell's other illustrations of his theme. Nor, though two of the often-quoted lines mentioned above occur in **"The Pleasures of Hope,"** can the style of this youthful poem compare for a moment, in point of correct expression, with the pregnant art of Pope, when writing up to his true level, or with the chaste simplicity of Goldsmith. Campbell is often satisfied with the selection of words, which fail clearly to express his meaning, and leave the thought vague and obscure, *e.g.*:

> And mark the wretch whose wanderings never knew
> The world's regard, that soothes though half-untrue,
> Whose erring heart the lash of sorrow bore,
> But found not pity when it erred no more—

or which altogether misrepresent it, as:

> Yes! there are hearts, prophetic HOPE may trust,
> That slumber yet in *uncreated* dust;

(where he means, not that the dust is uncreated, but that there are hearts not yet created out of dust) and:

> Chide not his peace, proud Reason! nor destroy
> The shadowy forms of uncreated joy,

(where "uncreated" is used for "unsubstantial")

> That *urge* the lingering tide of life, and pour
> Spontaneous slumber on his midnight hour;

(where "urge" is apparently only used because "quicken" would not suit the metre). (pp. 104-06)

"The Pleasures of Hope," in its frequent use of Abstraction and Personification, exhibits all the features of the didactic poetry of the eighteenth century; but in his later poems, notably **"Ye Mariners of England," "Hohenlinden,"** and **"The Battle of the Baltic,"** Campbell discards these mannerisms and develops a style of his own that reflects the best and purest social idiom of the age. It would be hard to find any short poem in the English language that contains so many elements of the sublime as **"Hohenlinden."** In eight stanzas the poet, by a series of master-strokes, has called up a living picture of conflict between two vast armies. It is a typical description of the soldiers' battles of the early French Revolution, in which individual leadership disappears amidst the rush of national passions, and the successive acts of the bloody drama are indicated by images rather than of the changing aspects of Nature than of the deliberate purposes of Man. The grand view in the opening stanza of the tranquil snow-clad waste traversed by the dark and rapid river; the sudden burst of the drum-beat on the stillness of the night; the muster of the horsemen, "by torch and trumpet fast arrayed"; the thunder of heaven mingling in the dark with the roar of the artillery; the gradual change of the prevailing hue in the landscape from snow-white to blood-red; the confused shouts of the combatants shrouded "in their sulphurous canopy," impenetrable to the rays of the rising sun; the fiery exhortation to the chivalry of Munich for a supreme effort; and at last the solemn silence of the field of conflict strown with the bodies of the dead;—all these details, presented in words of which the picturesque colour is intensified by the swiftness of the metrical motion, combine to form a poetical battle-piece unequalled in the literature of the world.

Scarcely less skill in the selection and combination of metrical words is shown in **"The Battle of the Baltic,"** a composition in which patriotic emotion lifts the imagination of poet and reader into a still loftier atmosphere. Fine judgment, a quality in Campbell no less conspicuous than poetic impulse, is shown in the changes made in the structure of this poem. As at first written it consisted of twenty-seven stanzas, of which the following is a sample:

> Of Nelson and the North
> Sing the day,
> When, their haughty powers to vex,
> He engaged the Danish decks,
> And with twenty floating wrecks
> Crowned the fray.

When his poem was completed, Campbell perceived that, while it contained many fine lines, it was defective alike in the unbalanced form of the stanza and in its multiplicity of prosaic and superfluous details. He accordingly retrenched his imagery, while he amplified his metrical architecture, by prefixing four alternately rhyming lines to the two first lines of the stanza, as originally built, and running these two together in the fifth. (pp. 107-08)

Campbell's lyrics are much the best part of his poetry. He carried on the movement inaugurated by Collins and Gray, the latter of whom he resembles in the skill with which he confines romantic feeling within classic form. But while Gray had to think out his romance in the midst of uncongenial surroundings, and sometimes exhibits in his style a certain stiffness and formality, Campbell imposes form on his romantic matter with an easy freedom that suggests how much of his inspiration was derived from the exciting air of the revolutionary era. The swift movement of his rhythms, and his bold mixture of polysyllabic Latin words with picturesque monosyllables—

> The might of England flushed
> To anticipate the scene—
>
> Again! again! again!
> And the havoc did not slack,
> Till a feeble cheer the Dane
> To our cheering sent us back:
> Their shots along the deep slowly boom;
> Then ceased—and all is wail,
> As they strike the shattered sail,
> Or, in conflagration pale,
> Light the gloom—

are admirable. Other romantic features in his poetry are, doubtless, the product of a tendency in the public taste which had now for almost a generation favoured the revival of the ballad style originated by Percy's *Reliques*. But he may justly claim to have been the first to direct the new movement into popular channels. He anticipated Scott in his choice of Highland subjects of romance (*e.g.* his **"Lines Written on Revisiting a Scene in Argyleshire,"** **"Lochiel,"** and **"Lord Ullin's Daughter"**), Byron and Moore in the rolling anapaestic metres which he made the vehicle for his sentiment (e. g. **"The Wounded Hussar"** and **"The Soldier's Dream"**). Though **"O'Connor's Child"** shows plainly the influence of Scott's style, Campbell's verse is always stamped with a character peculiarly its own, free from the introspective self-portraiture which the Romanticists, who derived their inspiration from Rousseau, were bringing into fashion. While there is, as I have said, a glimpse of such a tendency in **"Lines Written on Leaving a Scene in Bavaria,"** the reflection and versification of that fine poem are much more akin to Gray's style in his *Ode on a Distant Prospect of Eton College*, than to any autobiographic composition of Wordsworth or Byron.

Campbell had no gift for narrative. **"Gertrude of Wyoming"** in respect of its representation of action and character is third-rate, and, even in its descriptive passages, the author's preference for classical generalisation is reflected in the conventionality of his landscape. As Byron said of the poem: "It has no more locality in common with Pennsylvania than with Penmanmaur." **"Theodric"** is an attempt to breathe the spirit of romance into a rather tame story of real life: in **"The Pilgrim of Glencoe,"** on the other hand, a romantic situation of past times is described in verse modelled on the prosaic realism of Crabbe's *Tales*. Neither experiment is inspired by Campbell's natural genius: both are equally unsuccessful. (pp. 110-12)

> *W. J. Courthope, "The New Whigs and Their Influence on Poetry and Criticism," in his* A History of English Poetry: The Romantic Movement in English Poetry, Effects of the French Revolution, Vol. VI, *Macmillan and Co., Limited, 1910, pp. 84-123.*

GEORGE SAINTSBURY (essay date 1923)

[*Saintsbury was an English literary historian and critic of the late nineteenth and early twentieth centuries. A prolific writer, Saintsbury composed several histories of English and European literature as well as numerous critical works on individual authors, styles, and periods. Here, Saintsbury briefly examines meter in Campbell's poetry.*]

[Campbell's] couplet-poems, from the respectable **"Pleasures of Hope"** to the illegible **"Theodric"** and the unread **"Pilgrim of Glencoe,"** may be classed, from one point of view, with those of Rogers. The Spenserians of **"Gertrude of Wyoming"** are among the least successful effects in that great metre made by any poet who has elsewhere done really good things. But his lyrics are in quite a different case. When the deadening hand of the long poem—for Campbell seems to have been not merely a slow, but a positively lazy writer—and the obsession of regular metres was off him, he became another man. . . . The anapæsts of **"Lochiel"** furnish forth some splendid and famous lines, but they have not always shaken off the rocking-horse movement, which is less, though sometimes, present, in the beautiful but much less well-known lines **"Written on Visiting a Scene in Argyllshire,"** and, after the first splendid stanza, infests the **"Soldier's Dream,"** while it has **"The Wounded Hussar"** for an almost unrescued prey. Many of the minor poems are not uninteresting prosodically; but, after all, Campbell's three most famous things are, as is not always the case, his best prosodic tests.

"Hohenlinden" comes out triumphantly. In fact the prosody is more than half this battle—the close-knit triplets with the similar but separated refrain-fourth line, the imperfect rhymes on almost though not quite assonanced word-values, are prosodic or nothing. **"The Battle of the Baltic"** is more ambitious, and at its best even finer; but its structure is more artificial, and the artifice does not always "come off." The tapering of the anapæstic scheme to the single foot line at the end is very bold indeed, and perhaps issues a perilous invitation to burlesque; but it is not easy to conceive anything better suited to the subject. While **"Ye Mariners of England"** shows that Campbell had more than something of the special skill of his countryman, Burns, at catching up and perfecting old song-snatches. (pp. 90-1)

> *George Saintsbury, "The First Romantic Group,"* in his *A History of English Prosody from the Twelfth Century to the Present Day: From Blake to Mr. Swinburne, Vol. III, second edition, 1923. Reprint by Russell & Russell, 1961, pp. 47-92.*

EDMUND BLUNDEN (essay date 1928)

[*Blunden was associated with the Georgians, an early twentieth-century group of English poets who reacted against the prevalent contemporary mood of disillusionment and the rise of artistic modernism by seeking to return to the pastoral, nineteenth-century poetic traditions associated with William Wordsworth. As a literary critic and essayist, he often wrote about the lesser-known figures of the Romantic era as well as about the pleasures of English country life. In the following examination of Campbell's poetry, Blunden highlights his political acumen.*]

What is the cause that the new generation of poets so scrupulously avoids all themes of politics and international movements? Scarcely anywhere do we hear a voice above a whisper discoursing in verse of the destiny of nations, or the work of the leaders of Europe, America and Asia. (p. 703)

Reflections like these have occurred during occasional readings of Thomas Campbell, the Bard of Hope—and greater than that—who shares with his contemporaries the powerful art of political poetry, and who looks over province and capital, frontier and campaigning area with large survey. There is a preconception of "The Dynasts" in the doomful thought and beat of **"Hohenlinden,"** in the baffling alliance of jubilee and regret sounding on through the **"Battle of the Baltic"**; Campbell's spirit might well have hovered with Hardy's "Chorus of Intelligences" over those astounding fields of Europe in the hour of Napoleon. It is as a poet of battle that Campbell is best known, and even modern war experience finds itself identified in his stern pictures, with their intimation of concealed and pitiless forces; yet this division of his work belongs to a general faculty for reviewing, anticipating and expressing European topics. It is strange that a notion of Campbell as a flimsy, mock-heroic figure should have got abroad in view of that faculty and its impressive embodiments in his poetry.

We find him, true to the habit of the nineteenth century, "preserving a continued dread of the progress of Russia, and her designs upon liberties and happiness of the Continent"; in 1832 this far-drawn anxiety, amplified by reports of Russian atrocities in Poland, culminated in a weighty poem called **"The Power of Russia."** Some of its daring declarations are prophetic with a peculiar accuracy of the feelings of many persons during the last few years, and might have served more than one leader-writer to point his warning moral:

> But Russia's limbs (so blinded statesmen speak)
>   Are crude, and too colossal to cohere.
> O, lamentable weakness! reckoning weak
>   The stripling Titan, strengthening year by year.
> What implement lacks he for war's career,
>   That grows on earth, or in its floods and mines,
> (Eighth sharer of the inhabitable sphere)
>   Whom Persia bows to, China ill confines,
>   And India's homage waits, when Albion's star declines!. . .

[Campbell's] heart was with Poland, from the time when, in his juvenile and too famous metaphor:

> Freedom shriek'd—as Kosciusko fell!

to his latest days; for Poland he gave his eloquence and his means, founding an association to foster its cause in London. . . . For Poland he wrote in strain of rapture worthy of a love affair:

> Great Poland's spirit is a deathless spark
> That's fann'd by Heaven to mock the Tyrant's rage:
> She, like the eagle, will renew her age,
>   And fresh historic plumes of Fame put on,—
>   Another Athens after Marathon,—
> Where eloquence shall fulmine, arts refine,
> Bright as her arms that now in battle shine.
>   Come—should the heavenly shock my life destroy,
>   And shut its flood-gates with excess of joy;
> Come but the day when Poland's fight is won—
> And on my grave-stone shine the morrow's sun.

That is only a phrase in his extraordinary melody, which, as it loads Poland with praises, dauntlessly insults those who did not assist her; with this kind of inspiration our modern poetry has no acquaintance at all. No one seems prepared to make his own country's ballads, let alone those of other countries, in matters of government; we hand over such agenda to the machinery of the League of Nations.

Besides the foreign policy of Britain, the honour of Poland, the "cold phosphoric eyes" of Germany, the ravenings of the Russian bear and similar Continental issues, the public spirit of Campbell discovered poetic occasions in the calamities of the Irish revolutionaries, the self-sacrifice of the Spanish patriots who rose against Napoleon, the struggles of the Greeks, the colonization of New South Wales, and the spread of industrialism along the Clyde. The poem in which he claimed a generous sympathy for the refugee Irishmen who had been concerned in the rebellion of 1798, though by no means shaped out by his finer powers of imagination, had the picturesque pathos and simple musical form to catch the taste of the many; it was the **"Exile of Erin."** . . . Campbell wrote much more splendidly, but without attracting anything like the same widespread audience, as he watched an emigrant ship leaving for Australia. This poem . . . is another prophetic adventure; how far it is found correct may be judged by the simple citation of such passages as—

> Our very speech, methinks, in after-time,
> Shall catch th' Ionian blandness of thy clime.

But the whole utterance is borne proudly forward on the surge of a puissant emotion:

> Delightful land, in wildness ev'n benign,
> The glorious past is ours, the future thine!
>   As in a cradled Hercules, we trace
>   The lines of empire in thine infant face.
> What nations in thy wide horizon's span
> Shall teem on tracts untrodden yet by man!
>   What spacious cities with their spires shall gleam.

The poet pictures the marble symmetries, the colonnaded aisles, the pavements and the statues, the organs "yielding tempests of sweet sound," and all the other noble works of Australasian endeavour; but it is his greater distinction that he predicts with unalloyed and delightful satisfaction the later generations of Australians to whom England shall be nothing but a name, but their own country's names, "to us uncouthly wild," the keys to all sweet thoughts and poetry. (pp. 703-06)

> *Edmund Blunden, "Campbell's Political Poetry,"*
> in The English Review, *Vol. XLVI, No. 6, June,*
> *1928, pp. 703-06.*

W. MACNEILE DIXON   (lecture date 1928)

[*Dixon argues that, for his lyrical verse, Campbell deserves inclusion among the ranks of important English poets.*]

Among Glasgow poets Thomas Campbell is by far the most famous. . . . He lives still, nor is it likely he will ever cease to live. Let us ask, not was he worthy the honours which fell to his lot in life, but is he deserving of that far greater honour, not readily to be yielded, a seat among the immortals?

It seems, if we ponder it, a strange thing, and to many men will always remain a mystery, why a mere verbal dexterity, or what appears to them a mere verbal dexterity, should be so highly valued, why a few lines of verse, a dozen or two maybe, should suffice to carry their author's name, when vast multitudes are wholly forgotten, safely down the stream of time, and secure for it everlasting remembrance. So the world, however, has decreed, and the present is not the hour to question its decrees. Let us allow that Campbell has obtained from that incorruptible jury, posterity, a verdict in his favour, that his fame is secure. Let us ask only, is it justified? We know that he was a harsh judge of his own compositions, never satisfied; that he often discarded what had cost him weary hours to produce. We know, too, that he had ever before his eyes "the pure lines of an Ionian horizon,'' the standard set by the masters of Greek literature. To have always in mind the highest kind of excellence is a great thing in any art. To be yourself the severest critic of your work is a second great thing. To despise easy success is a third. Campbell wrote comparatively little. It was not, I think, that, as Scott suggested, ''he feared the shadow of his own reputation.'' It was rather that he had a close acquaintance with the noblest literature of the past, and that his mind and hand were checked by it. He had a fear of the world's best, and there can be no more wholesome type of alarm. How desirable if to-day we could convert it into a widespread panic! In general the works whose value is known only to their authors and concealed from their readers are composed without reference to such a standard, never submitted to comparison with the great classics. Browning says somewhere:

> Aeschylus' bronze-throat, eagle-bark for blood
> Has somewhat spoilt my taste for twitterings.

Campbell's taste, formed in the select society of the best, protected him against twitterings, and against the dreadful facility, which betrays so many writers. It was wholly in his favour that his education had burnt into his mind the knowledge that ''all excellent things are as difficult as they are rare.'' Campbell never, even in youth, sowed wild oats in his verse. No one, indeed, could in a fever of enthusiasm describe him as faultless. I do not refer to his scientific inaccuracies. In some of his longer poems—**''The Pleasures of Hope''** and **''Gertrude of Wyoming''**—he strews them lavishly. He introduces tigers to the shores of Lake Erie, hyænas into South America, and panthers into Ohio. Flamingoes, aloes and palm trees find themselves where, it appears—I should never myself have discovered it—Nature never placed them. These, and errors such as these, may perhaps be regarded as covered by a poet's licence. They occur, however, in poems with which we need not occupy ourselves. Time has settled their account. He said all he had to say in them, but unfortunately had nothing to say. They are not without their felicities, their catching phrases, once much admired. Who has not heard of ''angel's visits, few and far between,'' or quoted

> 'Tis distance lends enchantment to the view?

Fine things, you maintain. Yes, but these fine things cannot save them. As poems their day is done. They are out of sight and clean forgotten. We must look elsewhere for Campbell's claims to immortality. What remains? A handful of lyrics, a few hundred lines of verse. Too slender a foundation, it might be argued, for an enduring monument. In this matter, however, it is never quantity but always quality which tells, and quality alone. (pp. 12-14)

A handful of lyrics, then, will suffice—they have often sufficed to defy the blotting finger of time—to make their author's name a household word. And if we examine the collection of our lyrical poetry, which has been accepted as the best, if we examine the *Golden Treasury,* the little book so familiar to all of us, we shall find, perhaps to our surprise, that Campbell occupies as large a place there as Gray or Scott, nearly as large a place as Keats or Burns themselves, poets whose names are writ in marble, in more lasting material than marble, in the hearts of their countrymen. It may be answered, ''Yes, but he is without inwardness, the things of the deepest significance in human life he leaves untouched.'' The same criticism was directed by Carlyle against Scott. But can there be a greater folly than to depreciate a talent because it is not another talent, or to ask from a man more than he has to give? Certainly it was not in Campbell's power, it was not in his nature to attempt

a justification of the ways of God to man, to deal with the larger hopes and fears, the profounder thoughts and experiences of our strange and uneasy existence. Again, we hear that he was a rhetorician rather than a poet. But I distrust the categories of the critics. I recall the old debate, ''Was Virgil an orator or a poet?'' Virgil! ''The chastest poet and the royalest that to the memory of man is known.'' Distinctions, indeed, we may and must draw, and admit that the grand subjects, the grand style were beyond Campbell, that it was not within his province to add:

> The light that never was on sea or land.

He knew it well enough, and spoke with depreciation of his own ''drum and trumpet lines,'' as if they were of small account. But patriotic and heroic poetry are not to be so lightly dismissed. ''Certainly I must confess my own barbarousness''; said Sir Philip Sidney, ''I never heard the old song of Percy and Douglas that I found not my heart moved more than with a trumpet.'' Such poetry is not to be dismissed till love of country, till delight in heroes and the heroic perish out of the world, and of such calamities we need have no fear. Campbell, it may also be urged, dealt only with simple and customary themes. I cannot think it a grievous fault. For what is literature after all but the books people like to read? And what is enduring literature but the books generation after generation continues to read? And how simple they are. How simple is all great art. The glittering summits of obscurity are easy to attain. Show me unintelligible poetry and I will show you poetry that may be praised by superior persons, but is never read. There is nothing more difficult, as Horace knew, than to make a commonplace your own, to put into the mouths of your countrymen the words they cannot find for themselves, the very words they desire to use. Campbell found those words, not once but often, and it is his glory. It is, perhaps, his peculiar glory that he wrote the only martial lyrics in our language that have gained universal currency—**''The Mariners of England''** and **''The Battle of the Baltic.''** It has been said of England, and by an English poet:

> Thy story, thy glory,
> The very fame of thee,
> It rose not, it grows not,
> It comes not, save by sea.

The sea, inconstant to others, has been her constant ally, her nursing mother and guardian; her sailors are her greatest pride. Yet it was left to a Scottish poet to write the poetry no Englishman had written, of the sea and English sailors; to celebrate Nelson, the best-beloved, almost worshipped hero of the navy and the nation. An achievement surely most surprising and most enviable.

That is not, however, Campbell's sole achievement. In that inimitable ballad **''Lord Ullin's Daughter,''** or, better still, in **''Hohenlinden''**—to take a single example of his lucid and admirable art—we have verses of which any poet, whatever his rank, might with pride have claimed the authorship, which ''not even a god, though he worked hard,'' could easily improve. How many poets in our day, and we have them in plenty, have produced anything so perfect in its kind? How immediately it arrests the attention, how economical the phrasing, how vivid the language, how complete the picture it presents! Such is its art that the difficulties overcome are not apparent. It appears an easy thing. Not until we approach a like undertaking do we appreciate its accomplishment. Then its truly formidable character reveals itself; then, and hardly till then, do we realise that poetry worthy the name is so difficult as to be well-nigh impossible. You think that statement an exaggeration? Well, take up again the book to which I have already made reference—*The Golden Treasury of English Lyrics*. It is, let me remind you, the harvest of more than three hundred years, the harvest of our whole literary history from the sixteenth to the present century; the history, too, of a people by the world's consent illustrious in poetry, so illustrious that no other people can with confidence be placed above it. Yet how slender is the book in which the lyrical verse, the golden grain of those centuries is garnered. During those centuries a legion of poets has been at work, and has added—if you will permit me a curious calculation—has added, the whole choir of our poets in session—how much shall we say? At most forty or fifty lines annually to the national treasury. That is the consummation of all their lyrical labours, all their toil. For the rest, it may have pleased their contemporaries, it pleases no longer. So unwilling is Fame to confer an unfading laurel. A depressing thought, perhaps; yet in that book, slender as it is, Campbell has his not inconsiderable sheaf. And if some critics in these days think but poorly of him, there are others whom we may regard as at least of equal authority, Goethe and Byron and Scott, who were of a contrary opinion. We are far too inclined to suppose that our estimate, the judgment of our own day, is the last word on a writer, that ours is the casting vote which determines finally his position in the hierarchy of letters. It is a mere arrogance. I sometimes wonder what the judgment of our predecessors, of Milton or of Wordsworth, would be upon the poetry of to-day, or what will be the verdict of later years upon the works and judgments of the present. I wonder and tremble. Campbell, however, is not dependent upon the suffrages of this generation. He has already taken his place at the table with the makers of our literature. Those among them who were acquainted with his writings received him into their company, and that is enough.

In classical times, at the oracle of Delphi, a strange and signal honour was, we are told, accorded to the poet Pindar, the "Theban eagle," the lyrist of unequalled splendour, who praised in song the athletes and heroes of his country. At the offering of the sacrifice the priest proclaimed aloud that the god himself desired the society of the poet's shade. We dare not, indeed, compare our poet with so far-shining a genius as Pindar, but may we not claim that he had Pindar's love of eminence and conspicuous achievements, and something at least of his authentic fire? And may we not also, in the name of Apollo, patron of the arts, echo the ancient words, and say, "Let Campbell, the poet, come in to supper with the god?" (pp. 15-20)

> *W. Macneile Dixon, in his* Thomas Campbell: An Oration, *Jackson, Wylie and Co., 1928, 20 p.*

S. K. RATCLIFFE (essay date 1944)

[*Ratcliffe assesses Campbell's place in literature on the centenary of his death.*]

Thomas Campbell died just one hundred years ago—on June 15th, 1844. . . . During the first quarter of the nineteenth century his standing was above that of all contemporary poets save only Scott and Byron. Certain lyrics of his bear the mark of immortality, and, conspicuously, he was the poet-citizen of his day. . . .

"The Pleasures of Hope" had placed him, at twenty-two, in the front rank. Such acclaim seems today astonishing; but in 1799 there were no young poets visible to the relatively large

public then calling for them; the *Lyrical Ballads* were unnoticed. . . .

There would seem to be little room for difference of opinion about the bulk of Campbell's poetry. Who among us can find pleasure in "The Pleasures of Hope," although single lines will aways be in the common speech? It is not a good reflective poem. It is derivative, poor in structure and not without passages of rhetorical nonsense. "Gertrude of Wyoming" (a lovely title, though the poet did not know how the accent fell in America) is stamped upon by George Saintsbury, who was a warm admirer of Campbell's best, as the clumsiest caricature of the Spenserian stanza [see excerpt dated 1923]. That judgment is mistaken. Uninspired the verse is, but not clumsy. Gertrude's story is a sentimental tragedy, too condensed to be clear. Welcomed with rapture in 1809, it can have very few responsive readers today. Jeffrey, by the way, was not wrong in telling Campbell that his excessive care for finish and polish was fatal [see excerpt dated 1809]. He was incapable of passing an untidy line, and yet he could allow absurd errors, such as the tigers on Lake Erie's shore, to stand uncorrected.

The group of famous short poems takes us into a wholly different world. "Lochiel's Warning" and "Lord Ullin's Daughter" belong, of course, to their time, but they will not be forgotten. It is arguable that Campbell touched his highest moment in "The Last Man," and one thing, assuredly, was done in that poem; it proved that no beat is more perfectly suited to the cadence and the noble monosyllables of our English tongue than that of the measure so often and rightly employed between Smart's *Song to David*, Cowper's *Castaway*, and Hodgson's *Song of Honour*.

There remain the three incomparable battle-pieces. It is curious that the British people, profuse in lyric expression and ever at war, should own so small a quantity of first-rate battle verse. Copenhagen 140 years ago is not for us a proud memory, but Campbell's Baltic [in "The Battle of the Baltic"] is undeniable; "Ye Mariners of England" is the anthem of an island race, and all anthologists have recognised the uniqueness of "Hohenlinden." They have not minded the visual rhyme in its final word, and in 1800 no one could forecast the ironic sound of "Wave, Munich, all thy banners wave!" The poem, it may be noted, was rejected by the *Greenock Advertiser* as not being up to the editor's standard. It could perhaps be cited in support of Goethe's view that the classic note was clearer in Campbell than in any other English poet of the half-century.

> *S. K. Ratcliffe, "A Poet of Battle," in* The Spectator, *Vol. 172, No. 6051, June 16, 1944, p. 545.*

PETER S. MACAULAY (essay date 1969)

[*Macaulay analyzes the merits and defects of "The Pleasures of Hope," arguing that the poem reveals Campbell to be a "minor poet of genuine talent."*]

[It] might be interesting to consider to what extent Campbell's decline is deserved. With this aim in mind I propose to examine "Pleasures of Hope", the work which established the poet's reputation in 1799.

The title, content and style of this long poem situate it in the tradition of Mark Akenside's *Pleasures of Imagination* and Samuel Rogers' *Pleasures of Memory*, published in 1744 and 1793 respectively. Campbell was twenty-two years of age when his poem appeared; and in many ways it is indeed a young man's poem. The handling of the didactic couplet is correct and polished, but the diction is too often imitative, and the influence of Pope, Goldsmith, Gray, Cowper, Thomson and others is encountered throughout. Convention is adhered to at the expense of poetic originality. Critics have objected to its seemingly haphazard construction and the apparent lack of any consistent unifying principle. Yet there are reasons for believing that the usual charges of diffuseness of thought and feebleness of expression might be founded upon too cavalier a reading of the **"Pleasures of Hope"**. It was immensely popular in its day, and consequently it has suffered the hard doom of popularity; but its defects should not be allowed to eclipse its genuine merits. (pp. 39-40)

The poetry is most successful in the various illustrations and episodes which enliven a long poem otherwise deficient in vitality. Throughout the **"Pleasures of Hope"** moments of poetic brilliance alternate with depressions of varying depth and length. This suggests that Campbell is a highly talented poet, but one who is unable to sustain his genius for any length of time. There is too much of what Henry James called *remplissage*, which may be due in part to the writer's inability to discriminate between true poetry and vacuous rhetoric, and in part to his misguided devotion to his eighteenth-century predecessors in this kind of moral verse. Campbell's tendency to correct rather than to select is the root of most of his defects as a poet.

There is some graceful and harmonious writing amid the rhetoric at the beginning of the **"Pleasures of Hope"**, but the poet finds his feet only when he comes to describe the sailor returning from the perils of the sea. Evocativeness and an economical vividness are two of Campbell's greatest strengths:

> Cold on his midnight watch the breezes blow,
> From wastes that slumber in eternal snow;
> And waft, across the waves' tumultuous roar,
> The wolf's long howl from Oonalaska's shore.

Both qualities owe much to the aural effect of the lines. There is a progression from the short sounds of the vowels in the first two lines through the lengthened sounds in the third, culminating in the prolonged melancholy vowels of 'the wolf's long howl' (which reappears in **"Theodric"** . . .) and 'Oonalaska's shore'. The judicious alliterative pattern in three lines prepares us for the effect of the final line, which is constructed, however, on the device of assonance rather than alliteration. This linking of sound to sense is a gift which Campbell never loses and seldom abuses. He makes us see as well as hear; and he makes us feel not only the cruelty of the elements but also the desolate condition of the sailor. Not one word is ill-chosen or superfluous.

The sailor's return home is pictured in a conventional vignette of domestic felicity which contrasts sharply with the scene of his midnight watch. This is followed by another presentation of the 'social pleasures' of a 'humble bower'. Such lines could have been written by almost any poet of the eighteenth century, and Gray and Goldsmith are hardly even below the surface of the description of the sleeping child who

> lisps with holy look his evening prayer,
> Or gazing, mutely pensive, sits to hear
> The mournful ballad warbled in his ear.

Campbell lacks the social awareness and urgent realism of a poet such as Crabbe: *The Village*, for instance, is devoid of fatuous idealism and conventional drawing-room optimism. He lacks the naturalness and sincerity of Burns, who could present

a more genuine concept of rustic piety in *The Cotter's Saturday Night*.

After a high-flown apostrophe to Hope and a description of the 'march-worn soldier' consoled by his hope of victory, there is a passage on the interesting adventures of the 'hardy Byron', wandering in South America, 'pale, but intrepid, sad, but unsubdued'. Hope goes hand in hand with Genius. The endeavours of Newton, Franklin, Herschel, Linnaeus and Plato illustrate that it is Hope which stimulates progress in the various sciences. Benjamin Franklin's contribution is expressed in a striking metaphor: he it was who grasped 'the lightning's fiery wing'. These episodic or illustrative passages seem to be fragmented because of the processional manner in which they occur: but this presentation is, in fact, the most suitable to Campbell's purpose of demonstrating the power and influence of Hope. These pictures show different aspects of Hope: consequently, we misunderstand the intention of the poet if we regard them as digressions without a definite theme running through them. They are related to each other and to the central idea of the poem.

The poem drags itself along through a section typical of Campbell at his worst—and this is indeed appalling. The lines are diffuse and ornate—one might almost say ornamental—and they slacken the poetic tension. They spring from poverty of inspiration and dereliction of taste, which Campbell tries to disguise by bombastic versifying.

The depression ends and the poetry begins with the melancholy description of the mad girl waiting forlornly on the seashore for her drowned lover. The scene has affinities with that of the sailor listening to the wolf's long howl. Once again there is bleakness and desolation and the solitary human being; once again the lengthened sounds and the relentless rhythm heighten the effect, so that the sound indeed seems an echo to the sense.

> She, sad spectatress, on the wintry shore,
> Watch'd the rude surge his shroudless corse that bore,
> Knew the pale form, and, shrieking in amaze,
> Clasp'd her colds hands, and fix'd her maddening gaze.

These lines come perilously close to melodrama since the control is less satisfying than in the other passage and the inversion in the second line is immoderate. Yet there is a clarity of visualization and a strong sense of tragedy, both of which contrast effectively with the earlier idyllic scenes of domestic happiness. The misery of the crazed girl is symbolically highlighted by the fire which she makes on the shore; the images of coldness and death are thrown into relief; the cry of the bird is answered by the shrieking of the solitary girl.

> Oft when yon moon has climb'd the midnight sky,
> And the lone sea-bird wakes its wildest cry;
> Piled on the steep her blazing faggots burn
> To hail the bark that never can return.

The relevance of this scene is that it illustrates another facet of Hope—the 'aimless Hope' which consoles the mad girl's 'darkest dreams'.

Less tragic than the maniac is the friendless wanderer, who is 'scorn'd by the world and left without a home', and for whom Hope is half-mingled with his prayer. He need not abandon the prospect of a brighter future so long as he can hope.

A subject dear to the heart of the young Whig poet is the hope of social progress through the spread of liberty and truth. It is possible that Campbell was influenced by the volume of Southey's minor poems that appeared in 1797. There is a similarity in the humanitarian tone of his revolutionary zeal, and even in some of the themes of the individual poems. As a consequence of 'bright Improvement' the murderous rites of the savage and the 'dismal song' of the Indian will give way to the dancing of shepherds and the homely tolling of the curfew. Both Campbell and Southey preferred at times to ignore the blood-drenched tyranny which followed the French Revolution. The pastoral utopianism, in which Campbell was to wallow ten years later in **"Gertrude of Wyoming"**, is absurd because of its hackneyed naïveté; it is the same attitude of mind that informs the domestic idylls. There is an improvement, however, when the reign of Mercy, Truth and Freedom is described:

> Wher'er degraded Nature bleeds and pines,
> From Guinea's coast to Sibir's dreary mines,
> Truth shall pervade th' unfathom'd darkness there,
> And light the dreadful features of despair.

Truth, Mercy and Freedom are the daughters of Hope. In the celebrated lines on Poland there is a genuine sympathy in the portrayal of Koskiusko, with his 'trusty warriors, few, but undismay'd'. Poetry of war reveals Campbell at his best; as a war poet he has few rivals in English. He abandons the lame platitudes and pulpy sentimentality which disfigure so much of his work. (pp. 40-3)

Much of the second Part of the **"Pleasures of Hope"** is too unclear, both in thought and in expression, to be used in a defence of Campbell. The theme is less sustained and less organically developed, and the transitions are not well made. The verse is uneven in quality, ranging from the graceful and powerful to the pedestrian and inflated. It is with reference to this second Part that the complaint of Hazlitt is justified: 'A painful attention is paid to the expression in proportion as there is little to express, and the decomposition of prose is substituted for the composition of poetry' [see excerpt dated 1818]. Nevertheless, Campbell's judicious use of contrast may still be observed, as well as his sensitivity to the value of sound. Few lines are more delicately beautiful than these, few further from mere rural elegance:

> And when the sun's last splendour lights the deep,
> The woods and waves, and murmuring winds asleep,
> When fairy harps th' Hesperian planet hail,
> And the lone cuckoo sighs along the vale . . .

The last line is quintessentially romantic. The gentle alliterations and unobtrusive assonances are exquisitely suggestive; and the auditory qualities are transmuted into and blended with pictorial vividness. This was what Goldsmith meant when he described poetry as a species of painting with words. Yet there is no dissolution of sense into sound, no obsessive cultivation of word-music for its own sake.

Immediately there is an abrupt contrast, and the gentle pastoral note is drowned by the elemental roar and howl of winter. A harsher aspect of Nature is described: the polar spirits sweeping the darkening world, the boundless snows covering the withered heath, the dim sun which 'scarce wanders through the storm'. Another contrast comes in the lines that follow: the warmth of family life as opposed to the 'ice-chain'd waters slumbering on the shore', thrown into relief by the insistence on the cruel harshness of winter. The blazing fire provides a counterpart to the fire made by the mad girl in the first Part, but this time the flames symbolize peace and happiness. The family read together in order to pass the long nights. They read about harrowing misfortunes and adventures: Falconer's poem *The Shipwreck,* Schiller's tragedy *The Robbers,* and the story of the dreadful fate of the army of Charles XII, trapped at

Pultawa by the murderous winter. Once again there is a foreshadowing of the magnificent war poetry Campbell was to write.

> File after file the stormy showers benumb,
> Freeze every standard-sheet, and hush the drum!
> Horseman and horse confess'd the bitter pang,
> And arms and warriors fell with hollow clang!

But such inspiration is short-lived. After an inadequate transition, the poet refers to the legend that on certain evenings of the year St. Columba stands on top of the churches of Iona to count 'every wave-worn isle and mountain hoar' in case any have been sunk by witchcraft or the power of the Devil.

From this point on, the deterioration is marked. Too great a diversity of topics is subsumed under the general heading of Hope, and the style becomes more inflamed than before. Near the conclusion, however, there is a measure of restraint. Life is worthless if Science has explored the Universe only 'to waft us home the message of despair':

> Then melt, ye elements, that form'd in vain
> This troubled pulse and visionary brain!
> Fade, ye wild flowers, memorials of my doom,
> And sink, ye stars, that light us to the tomb!

But Hope will survive the consummation of the world,

> When all the sister planets have decay'd;
> When wrapt in fire the realms of ether glow,
> And heaven's last thunder shakes the world below;
> Thou, undismay'd, shalt o'er the ruins smile,
> And light thy torch at Nature's funeral pile.

As a person, Campbell was anxious, fretful, unsure of himself; and symptoms of his temperament frequently mar his work. His extreme fastidiousness gave him a misguided passion for revising and polishing whatever he wrote, a passion which emasculated his poetry. Naturalness and vigour were replaced by correctness and formality, and sometimes by falseness and bombast. (pp. 43-5)

There are other faults. Campbell seems to be at a distance from his subject; there is little genuine involvement except in those passages dealing with freedom and with battle. As Edward Dowden said of Byron's poetry, 'true passion mingles with pseudo-passion'. It is difficult to escape the impression that the **"Pleasures of Hope"** is almost an exercise in the themes and styles of eighteenth-century English poetry. (p. 45)

The stylistic and tonal range of the **"Pleasures of Hope"** may have contributed to the notion that the poem lacks unity. Thematically and structurally it is based upon the various aspects of Hope; and since it consists of variations upon this sustained idea, its unity is more or less intact. Once this is recognized, the range of Campbell's writing may be more reasonably assessed. The passages already quoted are vivid evocations of different scenes, moods and events, Campbell's particular aptitude being for the solitary and the martial. Much of the **"Pleasures of Hope"** is verbose and turgid, but in his true poetic moments his style is economical at the same time that it is suggestive. Already we can see the impressive seriousness of **"The Last Man"**, the pathos of **"The Harper"** and the **"Exile of Erin"**, the tenderness of **"The Beech Tree's Petition"**, and the fragile beauty of **"To the Rainbow"**. Within the **"Pleasures of Hope"** itself, there is a considerable range of styles and poetic techniques, this variety being emphasized by the skilful use of contrast.

Illustration of a child's evening prayers, from "The Pleasures of Hope."

Whatever its defects, the **"Pleasures of Hope"** contains passages which not only point forwards to the best qualities of Campbell's later works, but which show him to be a minor poet of genuine talent. And poetic talent is not so commonly found that we can afford to overlook any sign of it: not even in 'Little Tommy'. (p. 46)

> *Peter S. Macaulay, "Thomas Campbell: A Revaluation," in* English Studies, *Netherlands, Vol. L, 1969, pp. 39-46.*

MARY RUTH MILLER   (essay date 1978)

[*In this excerpt from the concluding chapter of her biographical and critical study of Campbell, Miller stresses the historical importance of his work.*]

Campbell himself now is almost a "Name Unknown." His sun has set, leaving still a "shadowy tint" that, viewed from today's distance, lends little "enchantment." Yet as a minor classic poet and humanitarian with a large audience in his day, both at home and abroad, he holds a place in the great tradition of humanism in which each new generation defines its values and determines its quality of life. Through his widely quoted poems and his educational and philanthropic endeavors, he

helped to free the hearts and minds of his era; therefore, to humanists of our time he offers the values of active hope.

Few poets have become famous so early or profited so much from early success as did Campbell. Many commentators have noted his good fortune in timing the appearance of **"The Pleasures of Hope"** in 1799 both to reflect and to help set the mood of his readers. True to his eighteenth-century heritage, he spoke as a social voice rather than as a private one, and his lyricism conflicted with his didacticism. Yet many of the ideas he expressed were romantic, and he aided the triumph of the romantic movement. The dynamism of individual yearning and striving at whatever the cost to achieve the heroic ideals that are the glory of the human race—this is the romantic quest theme of many of Campbell's poems and the same one which motivated the founders of the United States. Additional romantic characteristics of Campbell include his rebellion against tyranny, sympathy with exiles, love of the wild in nature, interest in the past, concern for the common man, and delight in children. The tension between his powerful feelings and the classical restraint and polish he thought necessary for their expression was Campbell's major problem in his poetry. Few of his poems seem genuinely spontaneous.

Other tensions imperfectly resolved plagued Campbell throughout his life: creative poetry versus prose editorial work, ambition versus fulfillment, desire versus discipline, fame versus fear of its loss, and Scotland versus England. Scotland, from which he uprooted himself, signified family, friends, early training, stress on industry, and the Presbyterianism he rejected; England represented metropolitanism, gradual loss of individuality in the masses of London, financial success, indolence, and feelings of suppressed guilt. A lack of self-confidence in his writing is evident in his constant submission of his poems to his friends for critical comment.

These internal struggles contributed to the conflicing judgments of him by others. Even now, appraisals of him vary widely. In his day, when the criticism of literature often turned on political affiliations, Campbell's strong Whig partisanship frequently provoked greater censure than the actual faults of his work deserved or else higher praise than its merits were due. Contributing to the varying opinions was Campbell's position as a transitional figure in a time of changing poetic tastes. His efforts to maintain his social voice instead of freeing himself from restraint caused Scott, according to Washington Irving, to say of him: "'What a pity it is . . . that Campbell does not write more and oftener, and give full sweep to his genius. He has wings that would bear him to the skies; and he does now and then spread them grandly, but folds them up again and resumes his perch, as if he was afraid to launch away. He don't know or won't trust his own strength.'" Another of his conflicts is that "'Campbell is, in a manner, a bugbear to himself. The brightness of his early success is a detriment to all his further efforts. *He is afraid of the shadow that his own fame casts before him.*'"

Unfortunately, Campbell's friends and literary critics expected more of him than his talent, health, self-discipline, or time permitted him to accomplish. Because of their disappointed hopes, they were sharper than they might otherwise have been in their judgments. He was more unlucky than most authors in having *soi-disant* friends who sought to line their pockets by publishing in the periodicals posthumous remembrances of him depicting his weaknesses in his declining years. Many of these articles have colored later opinions. (pp. 143-44)

[Campbell's poems] vary greatly in merit, and an individual poem may be unequal within itself. Attributes of his poetry include good taste, elegance, perspicuity, vivid imagery, good metaphors, occasionally excellent choice of language, variations of verse forms, and experiments with a new music. His best lyrics are marked by energy, simplicity, and beauty. On the other side, faults too often found are lack of clarity in narration, weaknesses in point of view and structure, inversions, overuse of apostrophe, excessive use of poetic diction, platitudes, and high-flown rhetoric. Often he loses the effectiveness of immediacy by writing in the past tense for remembered time.

Campbell's poetry is based on thought as well as feeling, for he spoke to the thinking, concerned people of his day; however, the thought is often only the obvious, conveyed with appropriate sound effects. In playing the role of poet as prophet, he could criticize his own country for what he considered its failures to place human values above diplomatic maneuvers and economic gain. Yet he had strong pride in his nationality. Thus, in the highest sense, he was a patriot who tried to make not only his country but the world a better place to live. Sincerity is the characteristic tone of his work.

In his poetry, he treated archetypal themes and characters that have inspired literature for ages of humankind: search, transformation, prophecy and fulfillment; the hero, the wise old man, the fatal woman, the earth-mother. The human drama of his day and the actors therein were his subjects, as were the myths and legends of his forebears. Despite his objective point of view, there is also more of Campbell himself in his poetry than some of his critics have noticed. (p. 145)

Campbell is a link in the chain of English poetry, with bonds to his predecessors and connections with his successors. Other poets whose letters or works admit Campbell's influence at least in their youth include Crabbe, Byron, Shelley, Tennyson, Browning, Elizabeth Barrett Browning, Peacock, Hopkins, Swinburne, Carlyle (who tried some early verse), Emerson, and Whittier. Arnold, in his essay "On the Study of Celtic Literature," paid tribute to his style; and Goethe, in a letter appended by Beattie, spoke of his classicism and the "strength," "great natural simplicity of style," and "power of exciting high emotions" of his poetry. Coleridge, who did not think Campbell would survive much beyond his day, was himself one of the giants who overshadowed Campbell, even before he (Coleridge) died in 1834.

Aside from his appreciation of good prose and his practice of it in *Specimens of the British Poets,* Campbell is remembered today for his poetry of freedom, patriotism, and human worth. Many of his lines have become proverbial quotations. (pp. 145-46)

Flaws are all too evident in Campbell's poems, most of which now seem old-fashioned "period pieces": yet even the faults themselves can have historical value in revealing the past channels of English poetry and the changing responses of readers and critics. Since Campbell's day, definitions of poetry, patriotism, and freedom all have altered. As he himself said, "Nature will have her course," and versifiers do become obsolete. Nowadays those readers whose tastes respond only to the modern will relegate Campbell to the rare book shelves, but other students who appreciate their literary heritage will find their reading of a genuine poet popular at the turn of the nineteenth century rewarding, especially those poems in which

Campbell treats well the universal themes of human experience. (p. 146)

> *Mary Ruth Miller, in her* Thomas Campbell, *Twayne Publishers, 1978, 166 p.*

ADDITIONAL BIBLIOGRAPHY

Beattie, William. *Life and Letters of Thomas Campbell.* 2d ed. 3 vols. London: Hall, Virtue & Co., 1850.
    An early, comprehensive biography. Beattie makes extensive use of Campbell's correspondence.

Campbell, Lewis. Introduction to *Poems of Thomas Campbell,* by Thomas Campbell, pp. xiii-xli. London: MacMillan & Co., 1904.
    A biographical and critical study that investigates the fluctuations in Campbell's literary reputation. Lewis Campbell was the author's second cousin.

Duffy, Charles. "Thomas Campbell and America." *American Literature* 13, No. 4 (January 1942): 346-55.
    Notes that Campbell frequently thought of emigrating to America and examines the American reception of the poet's work.

Graham, Walter. "Byron and Campbell: A Parallel." *Notes and Queries* X, No. 197 (21 January 1922): 45-6.
    Presents evidence that Campbell borrowed heavily from Lord Byron's *Childe Harold* in writing "Lines on the View from St. Leonard's."

Hadden, J. Cuthbert. *Thomas Campbell.* Famous Scots Series. Edinburgh: Oliphant Anderson & Ferrier, 1899, 158 p.
    A biography that includes critical discussion of Campbell's work and commentary on his place among English poets.

Hall, S. C. "Thomas Campbell." In his *A Book of Memories of Great Men and Women of the Age, from Personal Acquaintance,* 2d ed., pp. 346-59. London: Virtue and Co., 1877.
    Personal reminiscences of Campbell by one of his associates at the *New Monthly Magazine.*

"Campbell and Washington Irving." *International Weekly Miscellany of Literature, Art, & Science* I, No. 8 (19 August 1850): 230-31.
    Reprints a portion of a letter that Irving wrote to Campbell's American publishers concerning the poet's work.

Jordan, Hoover H. "Thomas Campbell." In *The English Romantic Poets & Essayists: A Review of Research and Criticism,* rev. ed., edited by Carolyn Washburn Houtchens and Lawrence Huston Houtchens, pp. 183-96. New York: New York University Press for the Modern Language Association of America, 1968.
    Contains bibliographic information on works by and about Campbell.

"Recollections of Thomas Campbell and David M. Moir." *The Leisure Hour,* No. 1367 (9 March 1878): 156-59.
    Describes Campbell's appearance at a printers' festival in Edinburgh in 1837. The critic also briefly comments on Campbell's work.

Redding, Cyrus. *Literary Reminiscences and Memoirs of Thomas Campbell.* 2 vols. London: Charles J. Skeet, Publisher, 1860.
    An anecdotal biography in which Redding examines Campbell's poetry and his interest in educational and political reform.

Richards, George. "Thomas Campbell and Shelley's *Queen Mab.*" *American Notes and Queries* X, No. 1 (September 1971): 5-6.
    Notes the influence of "The Pleasures of Hope" on Percy Bysshe Shelley's *Queen Mab.*

"Thomas Campbell: A Criticism." *Rose-Belford's Canadian Monthly and National Review* n.s. I (August 1878): 187-97.
    Praises Campbell's humanistic values and considers his works in relation to those of his contemporaries and the "subjective" poets of the late nineteenth century.

Shumway, Daniel B. "Thomas Campbell and Germany." In *Schelling Anniversary Papers,* pp. 233-61. New York: Century Co., 1923.
> Assesses the impact of Campbell's interest in German literature on his work.

Stillinger, Jack. "Whittier's Early Imitation of Thomas Campbell." *Philological Quarterly* XXXVIII, No. 4 (October 1959): 502-04.
> Describes Campbell's "The Exile of Erin" as the model for John Greenleaf Whittier's poem "The Exile's Departure."

Sypher, Francis Jacques. "Swinburne's Debt to Campbell in 'A Forsaken Garden'." *Victorian Poetry* 12, No. 1 (Spring 1974): 74-8.
> Cites Campbell's poem "Lines Written on Visiting a Scene in Argyleshire" as a source for Algernon Charles Swinburne's poem "A Forsaken Garden."

"Thomas Campbell." *The Times Literary Supplement,* No. 2211 (17 June 1944): 295.
> A brief discussion of Campbell's poetry on the centennial of his death.

Turner, Albert Morton. "Wordsworth's Influence on Thomas Campbell." *PMLA* XXXVIII, No. 2 (June 1923): 253-66.
> A detailed examination of Wordsworthian influence in Campbell's poetry.

"Thomas Campbell (1777-1844): Critical Essay." In *The World's Best Literature,* edited by John W. Cunliffe and Ashley H. Thorndike, pp. 3159-63. The Warner Library, University Edition, vol. 5. New York: Knickerbocker Press, for The Warner Library Co., 1917.
> Combines biographical information with a discussion of the popular reception of Campbell's works.

Bankim Chandra Chatterji

1838-1894

(Also transliterated as Bankimcandra, Bankimchandra, Bankimcandrer, Bankim-Candra, Bankim-Chandra; also Chatterje, Chatterjea, Chatterjee, Cattopadhyay, Chattopadhyay, Chattopadhyaya) Indian novelist, essayist, sketch writer, and poet.

Chatterji exerted a vast influence on Indian literature and culture. Considered the first novelist to write successfully in the Bengali language, he played a crucial role in the development of modern Indian fiction, and he is also credited with helping to inspire the nationalist movement that eventually led to his country's emergence as a sovereign nation. Although the literary shortcomings of his works have become apparent over time, his originality and the seminal nature of his achievement are universally recognized. Today, Chatterji is firmly established as one of the pioneering figures in modern Indian literary history.

The son of orthodox Brahmins, Chatterji was born in Kanthalpara, Bengal, close to the city of Calcutta. He attended an English school at Midnapore starting in 1844, and, at the age of eleven, entered into an arranged marriage with a five-year-old girl. He subsequently studied at Hooghly College, where he began to compose poetry, occasionally publishing his pieces in *Sambad Prabhakar*, a weekly newspaper that served as an important literary outlet for young Bengali authors. Chatterji's earliest book, a minor volume of verse entitled *Lalita, Purakalik galpa, Tatha manas*, appeared in 1856, but it failed to attract widespread attention and for the most part he confined his efforts to prose thereafter. In 1858 he was one of the first students to receive a degree from newly founded Calcutta University; following his graduation he became a deputy magistrate in the Indian civil service. Although Chatterji published an English-language novel, *Rajmohan's Wife*, in 1864, critics generally consider his 1865 novel *Durgesnandini* (*Durgesa Nandini; or, The Chieftain's Daughter*) his first important contribution to Bengali letters.

Published to broad critical acclaim and great popularity, *Durgesa Nandini* represented a milestone in Indian fiction. The critic J. C. Ghosh remarked that "for the reader of 1865 it was a source of unprecedented delight. It was the first Bengali novel in the modern European style, and the first work of creative imagination in Bengali prose. It . . . had a sense of form, and a human interest, not found in our literature before." Scholars note that previous attempts by Bengali writers in the novel genre had largely been failures lacking the sustained narrative, depth of characterization, and consistent authorial perspective typical of the Western literary form. A historical romance, *Durgesa Nandini* is set in the sixteenth century during the conflict between the Moguls and the Pathans. Although not historically accurate and relatively crude in conception by the standards of Chatterji's later works, the novel made, according to V. S. Naravane, "a deep impression on Bengali readers partly because nothing like it had been written in that language before." Indeed, the distinguished Indian author Rabindranath Tagore compared the appearance of *Durgesa Nandini* with the "coming of dawn after a long night."

Following the enormous success of *Durgesa Nandini*, Chatterji published thirteen more novels over the next twenty-two years,

becoming the most popular and important Indian writer of his era. Approximately half of his novels are based on historical themes; the others range from moralistic works dealing with such social issues as widow remarriage and extramarital love to tales of contemporary Bengali life told simply for their intrinsic interest. Among Chatterji's most important novels is *Ananda math* (*The Abbey of Bliss*), which deals with Indian patriots fighting against the British during the 1773 Sannyasi rebellion in North Bengal. As an expression of Indian patriotism, *The Abbey of Bliss* had a profound effect upon the attitudes of Chatterji's generation toward their own country. The song "Vande Mataram," which Chatterji composed and inserted in the novel, was adopted as a hymn by the Indian nationalist movement and has consistently held a status in India comparable to that of a national anthem. Thus, in addition to his importance as the founder of the Bengali novel, Chatterji is credited with helping to shape the national self-image of India. Scholars point out that he not only espoused patriotism directly in the plots of *The Abbey of Bliss* and other novels, but also, by writing sympathetically about India's past and by portraying in realistic detail the daily lives of its people, inspired pride in Indian civilization for its own sake. Literary and cultural historians therefore honor Chatterji for his role in enabling his compatriots to recognize the elemental strengths and values of their own culture—a realization that ultimately led to the rise of nationalism, the end of British rule, and India's independence as a sovereign state.

Throughout nearly his entire literary career Chatterji retained his job as a deputy magistrate, enjoying frequent promotions in rank. In addition to his novels, he published various collections of essays and sketches on culture, literature, and religion. In such works as *Kamalakanter daptar* and *Samya (Bankim on Equality)*, he addressed social issues in contemporary Bengali life, satirizing injustice and pretension. In *Krishna charitra*, a lengthy treatise on the god Krishna, he sought to reform and revive the spirit of Hinduism. Like his novels, Chatterji's essays and sketches are considered significant for their influence on the emerging spirit of Indian nationalism. In addition to the composition of his own works, one of Chatterji's most notable achievements was his founding in 1872 of the powerful journal *Bangadarshan,* which he edited until 1876. *Bangadarshan,* according to Tagore, took "the Bengali heart by storm," and Chatterji became, as editor, what S. K. Bose described as "the fountainhead of the neo-Bengali literary renaissance of the 19th century." Chatterji guided and encouraged the rising generation of Bengali writers, directing in the process the course of modern Indian literature. Although his tenure at *Bangadarshan* lasted only four years, critics view his accomplishments there as seminal. For not only his own works, therefore, but also for his stewardship of Bengali letters during a crucial period of its history, Chatterji was regarded in his own day and continues to be seen as a dominant force in nineteenth-century Indian literature and culture. Shortly before his death in April 1894, he was made a Companion of the Indian Empire, one of the highest honors bestowed upon Indians by the British government.

The critical history of Chatterji's works reflects his distinctive role as a literary pioneer. Scholars note that in his own day the unprecedented nature of his achievement left little room for comparative criticism—as the first true Bengali novelist, there was almost no basis for evaluation of his works. After the publication of *Durgesa Nandini*, Chatterji enjoyed widespread influence and popularity; lauded both for his genuine originality and for his skill as a storyteller, he was revered in his own country for his part in revitalizing Bengali literature and also praised in the West for his vivid depictions of life on the subcontinent. During his lifetime, commentary often focused on the novelty of his works, emphasizing their cultural significance and profound effect on contemporary readers. His reputation since his death has also reflected his position as an innovator. Literary historians assert that as the first works of their kind in the Bengali language, Chatterji's writings inevitably display flaws that later writers were able to avoid only because of his trailblazing achievements. Thus, while modern critics commonly condemn his relatively shallow characterizations, often improbable plots, and overuse of such devices as coincidence and disguise, they recognize also that the limitations of his art scarcely detract from the remarkable nature of his accomplishments. Among the most frequent topics of discussion in recent criticism of his works are his use of language—specifically his introduction of the vernacular into what had been a highly formalized style of writing—and his attitudes toward the major social and political issues of his day. In summarizing Chatterji's importance, T. W. Clark wrote: "When he died, prose in Bengal was firmly established as a literary mode, and the reading public, which not many years before had complained that there was hardly anything worth reading in their own language, had a library of books and articles which they read avidly and with pride and enjoyment."

PRINCIPAL WORKS

Lalita, Purakalik galpa, Tatha manas (poetry) 1856
Durgesnandini (novel) 1865
  [*Durgesa Nandini; or, The Chieftain's Daughter*, 1880]
Kapalkundala (novel) 1866
  [*Kopal-Kundala*, 1885]
Mrinalini (novel) 1869
Indira (novel) 1873
  [*Indira, and Other Stories*, 1918]
Vishavriksha (novel) 1873
  [*The Poison Tree*, 1884]
Lokarahasya (essays) 1874
Yugalanguriya (novel) 1874
  [*The Two Rings*, 1897]
Chandrasekhar (novel) 1875
  [*Chandra Shekhar*, 1904]
Kamalakanter daptar (sketches) 1875
Radharani (novel) 1875
  [*Radharani*, 1910]
Vijnan rahasya (essays) 1875
Vivida samalochana (essays) 1876
Rajani (novel) 1877
  [*Rajani*, 1928]
Krishnakanter will (novel) 1878
  [*Krishna Kanta's Will*, 1895]
Pravanda pustak (essays) 1879
Samya (essay) 1879
  [*Bankim on Equality*, 1974]
Ananda math (novel) 1882
  [*The Abbey of Bliss*, 1904]
Rajsingha (novel) 1882
Devi chaudhurani (novel) 1884
  [*Devi Chaudhurani*, 1946]
Kamalakanta (essays) 1885
Krishna charitra (essays) 1886
Sitaram (novel) 1887
  [*Sitaram*, 1903]
Dharmatattwa (essays) 1888
  [*Essentials of Dharma*, 1977]
Bankimcandrer granthabali. 5 vols. (novels, essays, sketches, and poetry) 1904-15
*Rajmohan's Wife (novel) 1935
The Complete Works of Bankimchandra Chattopadhyaya. 3 vols. (novels, essays, sketches, and poetry) 1968-69

*This work was first published serially in the periodical *Indian Field* in 1864.

THE CALCUTTA REVIEW (essay date 1887)

[*In this excerpt from a brief review of a book about Chatterji, the anonymous critic summarizes the author's sizable influence on Indian literature and culture, describing also the nondidactic character of his fiction.*]

Babu Bankim Chandra Chatterji is the first Bengali author of the day—the man of most literary influence in the country. He is now a great power, a great educating power—and we will take leave to doubt whether *he* or our *schools and colleges* shape modern Bengali childhood and youth more effectively or decisively. All Bengali literature of the day is his in some form or other, and almost all the Bengali books that Bengalis now read for pleasure or for profit, are books written by him. He is the man of most *national* importance in the country just now, and it is, therefore, of the greatest *national* importance that his works should be appreciated and rightly understood. His novels, however, which are most widely read, are not novels of the didactic type of Miss Edgeworth's tales or Brontë's fictions. They are the spontaneous effusions of a poet and artist, who, though never immoral, and always very sublimely moral, never moralises. He creates worlds as poets create them. And poets, as we all know, create worlds after the fashion of the Greatest Poet, the God of all the Worlds. God's worlds are not moral abstractions, but luxuriant manifestations of all that *is*, or *can* exist—matter and mind, good and evil, light and darkness, purity and impurity, and what not. And so are also the little worlds that are created by God's little worshippers on earth, them that men call poets among themselves. And so are also the little worlds that our Bankim Chandra has created. They are not the moralist's worlds, for then they would not be *worlds*, but only critiques upon God's world, such as, perhaps, are the worlds created by most of the modern poets of Europe, the Cowpers and Wordsworths—not the Marlowes, Shakspeares and Byrons. They are man's worlds. (pp. xxiv-xxv)

> A review of "Bankim Chandra," in The Calcutta Review, *Vol. LXXXIV, No. 167, January, 1887, pp. xxiv-xxv.*

ROMESH CHUNDER DUTT   (essay date 1895)

[*Dutt was a Bengali novelist, lawyer, and civil servant who became a professor of Indian history at London University. In the following excerpt, he provides a contemporary account of Chatterji's rise to literary fame and power.*]

Bankim Chandra is in prose what Madhu Sudan is in verse,—the founder of a new style, the exponent of a new idea. In creative imagination, in gorgeous description, in power to conceive and in skill to describe, Madhu Sudan and Bankim Chandra stand apart from the other writers of the century; they are the first, the second is nowhere. And if the poet's conceptions are more lofty and more sublime, the novelist's creations are more varied, have more of human interest, and appeal more touchingly to our softer emotions. The palm must be given to the poet who has bodied forth beings of heaven and earth and the lower regions in gorgeous verse which sprang into existence like an echo to his ideas; but the reader, after he has traversed the universe on the wings of the mighty poet, will descend with a sense of pleasure to the homely scenes of the novelist, peopled with figures and faces so true and life-like, so sparkling and animated, so rich in their variety and beauty, that they seem to be a world by themselves, created by the will of the great enchanter. (p. 221)

In 1864, appeared [Bankim Chandra's] first historical novel *Durges-Nandini,* and the literary world in Bengal was taken by surprise, as it had been three years before, on the publication of [Madhu Sudan's] *Meghanad.* The boldness of the conception, the skill and grace of the execution, and the variety and richness and surpassing freshness of the figures which live and move and act in this wonderful work, indicated a creative genius of the highest order. Nothing so bold and original had been attempted in Bengali prose, nothing so powerful and so life-like had been executed in Bengali fiction. The venerable Vidyasagar had published his greatest work, *Sitar Banabas,* only two years before, and the work was an adaptation of a

Sanscrit drama into Bengali prose. Within two years a new epoch seemed to have dawned on the horizon of Bengali prose literature,—an epoch of original works of the imagination, the like of which Bengal had not known before.

Bankim Chandra did not escape the ridicule which greets every new endeavour. Critics and disappointed writers poured forth their rage on the devoted head of the young author, his style, his conceptions, his story, were all condemned, and he was put down as a denationalized writer, an imitator of European models. But censure and invectives pass off, and a work of real genius stands unmoved like a rock rising above the waves. And after thirty years, the reading public of Bengal acknowledge *Durges-Nandini* to be one of the greatest works in Bengali literature. (pp. 222-23)

Having won his spurs by his first endeavour, Bankim Chandra did not let the grass grow under his feet. The weird and wild story of *Kapala Kundala* is perhaps a more wonderful creation of the writer's fancy than even his first great work. And *Mrinalini* which followed, although less sustained than its predecessors, is enlivened by some characters which only a true poet can conceive.

Eight years had now elapsed since the publication of *Durges-Nandini,* and in 1872, Bankim Chandra formed the idea of issuing a first class literary magazine in Bengali. The *Banga Darsan* was accordingly started, and under the editorship of Bankim Chandra, this new magazine rapidly rose in popularity and in fame.

The literary activity of Bankim knew no bounds. Turning aside from his favorite historical romances, Bankim Chandra began to publish in the *Banga Darsan* a social tale which soon attracted thousands of readers. [*Bishabriksha*] is the first and most powerful of Bankim Chandra's social novels. Beside this story, continued in the magazine from month to month, other articles animated by wit or replete with information of the most varied kind, and all written in Bankim Chandra's matchless style, soon made the *Banga Darsan* the most popular as it was the most ably written journal of the day. Bankim Chandra now became the sole king of the literary world as Iswar Chandra Gupta had been in an early part of the century, and his long rule continued for over twenty years till the day of his death. During this period Bankim Chandra had no equal and no rival. Madhu Sudan and Dina Bandhu died in 1873. Akhay Kumar and Vidyasagar had practically retired from literary work. Hem Chandra's greatest and best works had already appeared, and the sound of his harp was now rarely heard. And the younger generation of writers and poets looked up with veneration to the great author of *Durges Nandini* and [*Bishabriksha*], and submitted to his literary sway. Many of them wrote in the *Banga Darsan,* many profited by his example, advice and help, all owned him as their king.

Novels, social and historical, now came out in rapid succession from the fertile pen of the great writer, and his style, always rich and harmonious, became more and more simple and perfect with age. His *Debi Chaudhurani* and *Ananda Matha* and [*Krishnakanter Will*] and other novels, his lighter tales sparkling with the richest humour, and his social, historical and critical essays instinct with thought, found thousands of readers all over Bengal. Whatever he touched glowed with the light of his genius. For a generation the reading world feasted on his unceasing productions; Bengali ladies in their zenana bought every new work of Bankim Chandra as it issued from the press, and young men in schools and colleges knew his latest utterances by heart.

In his later years, he began to write on religious subjects. His great work on Krishna is written on the same lines as the thoughtful English work *Ecce Homo,* and created a profound sensation in Bengal. Krishna, not as a deity but as a man, as the great Yadava chief who tried to avert war by his wise counsels and ever helped the cause of virtue,—this was the theme of his work. And he proved to the perplexity of his orthodox countrymen that the story of the amours of Krishna finds no mention in the earliest works in Sanscrit literature, and is the mischievous fabrication of later poets. He also took up the study of the Vedas, and felt himself instinctively drawn to the Hindu revival of the present generation, not to the noisy revival of ceremonials and forms and hurtful rules, but to the revival of the purer deeper and more catholic monotheism of the Hindus which alone can unite and strengthen the nation. (pp. 224-30)

> *Romesh Chunder Dutt, "Bankim Chandra Chatter-*
> *jea and His Novels," in his* The Literature of Bengal,
> *revised edition, Thacker Spink & Co., 1895, pp. 221-*
> *36.*

THE NATION, NEW YORK　(essay date 1896)

[*In the following excerpt from an anonymous review of* Krishna Kanta's Will, *the critic discusses the novel as a representative example of both the positive and negative characteristics of Chatterji's fiction.*]

Bankim Chandra Chatterjee has been acknowledged by all his contemporaries as the most distinguished of the modern Bengali novelists. . . . *Krishna Kanta's Will* . . . is an excellent type of the author's strength and weakness. To Western minds, the plot may seem somewhat weak, not from lack of striking incident, for there are a murder, the forgery and theft of a will, and other complications, but because of the descriptive matter which checks the progress of the story as a story. The characters defined are few and simple, and the scene is laid entirely in a small Bengal village. The human passion of which the novel treats is the usual theme of Western novelists, love. The hero, a handsome young Bengali, and the nephew of a rich Zamindar, who has been happily married in childhood to an adoring child-wife, falls violently in love with that most unhappy outcome of Hindu civilization, a girl widow. With considerable skill, the author represents the deplorable position of the Hindu widow, Rohini, and the moral effect of her enforced degradation upon her. At the bidding of the child-wife of Gobind Lal, she tries to drown herself, but she is recued by Gobind himself, and eventually, after Gobind has made a strenuous effort to throw off his infatuation and has been disinherited by old Krishna Kanta for his supposed infidelity to his wife, he leaves the new-made heiress and goes to live with Rohini. The child-wife's father resolves on revenge, Gobind Lal is aroused to a fury of jealousy, and murders Rohini, and the child-wife herself pines away.

This is a tragic tale indeed, but one that brings home the curses of Bengali, and indeed of Hindu, civilization—child marriage and the cruel lot of widows. Incidentally, there are in this novel some charming descriptions of Bengal scenery and some curious illustrations, of the wide difference between the European and the Asiatic fashion of looking at things.

> *A review of "Krishna Kanta's Will," in* The Nation,
> *New York, Vol. LXII, No. 1603, March 19, 1896,*
> *p. 244.*

THE ATHENAEUM　(essay date 1896)

[*In this excerpt from a review of* Krishna Kanta's Will, *the anonymous critic praises various aspects of the novel, including its realistic portrayal of Bengali life and its freedom from extraneous material.*]

[The introduction to *Krishna Kanta's Will*] gives an interesting sketch of its able and enlightened author, whose official deserts had won for him a title of honour and the badge of a C.I.E. [Companion of the Indian Empire] before his death last year at the age of fifty-seven. Eleven years ago his *Poison Tree* . . . obtained ready praise from many discerning critics as a work of real genius. [*Krishna Kanta's Will*] . . . may fairly be recommended both to readers of the former work and to those who have yet to make the author's acquaintance. It is to be regretted that the translator should have deemed it necessary to retain so many Bengali words and phrases for which English equivalents might have been found. The average reader will resent a practice for which there is no sufficient excuse, even though he is here supplied with a copious glossary and occasional notes. If he has the courage to surmount this obstacle, he will find himself well rewarded with a series of strangely interesting and often startling glimpses into the inner life of a comfortable landowner's household in Bengal. The story of *Krishna Kanta's Will* glides on with a certain purpose, but with little method, through a succession of scenes and incidents full of dramatic meaning and pathetic charm, lit up at times by a playful humour, or darkened by a cloud of crime or a gust of wild passion. It deals in a series of dramatic episodes with the doings of a number of persons connected by birth, marriage, or social ties with the old Hindu zemindar who gives his name to the book. Leaving his plot to take care of itself, the author leads us through a variety of scenes and incidents and character-sketches, amid which the central figures of his story take gradual shape and prominence. From the plots and perfidies of Hara Lal down to the closing chapters of this remarkable book, we may trace a certain logical sequence of events and motives, leading to Gobind Lal's desertion of his child-wife, to the tragical death of his mistress Rohini, and his lifelong penance for the wrong done to his noble-hearted Bhramar. These 250 pages of open print seem to express the very life and heart of human nature as studied in rural Bengal by a Bengali Baboo of wide sympathies and clear-seeing genius. Each of the characters in this striking tragi-comedy portrays itself in speech and action with lifelike clearness and individual truth. Among the heroines of fiction Bhramar herself, with her pretty, child-like talk and ways, her loving loyalty, her sorrows, her patience, and her early death, deserves, we think, to hold a foremost and abiding place in our affections. There is no padding in the book: only a few bits of apt description, a few touches of poetic colour, which furnish an effective background to the story itself.

> *A review of "Krishna Kanta's Will," in* The Ath-
> *enaeum, Vol. 108, No. 3593, September 5, 1896, p.*
> *319.*

R. W. FRAZER　(essay date 1898)

[*Frazer offers an English perspective on Chatterji's works and place in the history of Indian literature.*]

[The *Krishna Charitra* is] the work through which the name of Bankim Chandra Chatterji will probably remain famed in the memory of his own country-people.

It is the crowning work of all his labours. It inculcates, with all the purity of style of which the novelist was so perfect a master, a pure and devout revival of Hinduism, founded on monotheistic principles. The object was to show that the character of Krishna was, in the ancient writings, an ideal perfect man, and that the commonly-received legends of his immorality and amours were the accretions of later and more depraved times. Bankim Chandra Chatterji is the first great creative genius modern India has produced. For the Western reader his novels are a revelation of the inward spirit of Indian life and thought.

As a creative artist he soars to heights unattained by Tulsi Dās, the first true dramatic genius India saw. To claim him solely as a product of Western influence would be to neglect the heritage he held ready to his hand from the poetry of his own country. He is, nevertheless, the first clear type of what a fusion between East and West may yet produce, and the type is one reproduced in his successor, Romesh Chandra Dutt, and in a varied manner by others, such as Kasinath Trimbak Telang, in Bombay. It is names such as Ram Mohun Roy, Keshab Chandar Sen, Bankim Chandra Chatterji, Toru Dutt, and Telang that would live in the future as the memorial of England's fostering care, if all the material evidences of Western civilisation were swept from off the land.

To those who would know something of the life, thoughts, feelings, and religions of the Indian people, no better instructor can be found than Bankim Chandra Chatterji. The English reader must not be surprised if, in the novels of the greatest novelist India has seen, there is much of Eastern form, much of poetic fancy and spiritual mysticism alien to a Western craving for objective realism. Bankim Chandra Chatterji, with all the insight of Eastern poetic genius, with all the artistic delicacy of touch so easily attained by the subtle deftness of a high-caste native of India, or a Pierre Loti, weaves a fine-spun drama of life, fashioning his characters and painting their surroundings with the same gentle touch, as though his fingers worked amid the frail petals of some flower, or moved along the lines of fine silk, to frame therewith a texture as unsubstantial as the dreamy fancies with which all life is woven, as warp and woof. So the *Kopala Kundala* opens with a band of pilgrims travelling by boat to the sacred place of pilgrimage, where the holy River Ganges pours its sin-destroying waters into the boundless ocean. The frail boat, with its weight of sin, is being swept by the rushing flood out towards the sea. . . . In its unguided course the boat, by chance, touches land, and the hero, Nobo Kumar, volunteers to wander along the sandy shore in search of firewood. The tide rises, the boat is swept away, and Nobo Kumar is left to gaze after it in despair. The sandy waste is the abode of an ascetic worshipper of Kāli, who is waited on by the heroine, "Kopala Kundala," destined as a sacrifice to the fierce goddess. The ascetic sage is clothed in tiger skins; he is seated on a corpse, and wears a necklace of rudra seeds and human bones; his hair is matted and unshorn. The wild scene is depicted with all the dreamy, poetic repose which saturates the whole life of the East. The ocean is spread in front; across it speeds an English trading ship, with its sails spread out like the wings of some large bird; the blue waters gleam like gold beneath the setting sun; far out, in the endless expanse, the waves break in foam; along the glittering sands there runs a white streak of surf like to a garland of white flowers. The two scenes—one the lonely pilgrim and the near-seated, hideous, human-sacrificing ascetic, the other of the vastness and stillness of the sea—seem to picture forth the emptiness of man's imaginings and efforts amid the impassive

immensity of the universe. Over all, the murmuring roll of the ocean, echoed as it is in the poet's words, seems as though it bore to the senses the wailing moan of a soul lost in time and space. (pp. 419-22)

The novel throughout moves steadily to its purpose. There is no over-elaboration, no undue working after effect; everywhere there are signs of the work of an artist whose hand falters not as he chisels out his lines with classic grace. The force that moves the whole with emotion, and gives to it its subtle spell, is the mystic form of Eastern thought that clearly shows the new forms that lie ready for inspiring a new school of fiction with fresh life. Outside the *Mariage de Loti* there is nothing comparable to the *Kopala Kundala* in the history of Western fiction, although the novelist himself, and many of his native admirers, see grounds for comparing the works of Bankim Bābu with those of Sir Walter Scott, probably because they are outwardly historical.

A novel far surpassing *Kopala Kundala* in realistic interest is the same novelist's *Poison Tree*. This novel has its own artistic merits, but its chief value, for English readers, lies in the life-like pictures it presents of modern Indian life and thought. With subdued satire the interested efforts of would-be social reformers are shown to be founded often on motives of self-interest, dishonesty, or immorality. The evil results which too often follow the breaking-away from the strict seclusion and moral restraints of Hindu family life under the influence of Western education are indicated plainly. These modern movements are depicted as often leading the native more towards agnosticism and impatience of control than towards the implanting of a vigorous individuality, founded on a heightening of religious feelings, and wider views of the necessity of self-control and altruistic motives of action. It is a danger which grows graver daily; it is a movement which must be expected in the history of a nation's advance from bondage to freedom, and one to be resolutely met with a firm faith in the eternal elements underlying all enlightenment and social progress, and not with a hopelessness of a pessimistic despair. . . . The satire is perfect, the characters satirised true to life. (pp. 423-25)

R. W. Frazer, "The Fusing Point of Old and New," in his A Literary History of India, *T. Fisher Unwin, 1898, pp. 384-447.*

SIR RABINDRANATH TAGORE   (essay date 1911)

[*Tagore is considered India's greatest lyric poet and the pioneer of modernism in Bengali prose literature. In the following excerpt, he describes the popular enthusiasm generated by the serial publication of Chatterji's works in his journal,* Bangadarshan. *Tagore's remarks were first published in 1911 under the title* Jivansmriti *in the periodical* Pravasi.]

Bankim's *Bangadarsan* [took] the Bengali heart by storm. It was bad enough to have to wait till the next monthly number was out, but to be kept waiting further till my elders had done with it was simply intolerable! Now he who will may swallow at a mouthful the whole of *Chandrashekhar* or *Bishabriksha* but the process of longing and anticipating, month after month; of spreading over the long intervals the concentrated joy of each short reading, revolving every instalment over and over in the mind while watching and waiting for the next; the combination of satisfaction with unsatisfied craving, of burning curiosity with its appeasement; these long drawn out delights of going through the original serial none will ever taste again. (pp. 115-16)

Sir Rabindranath Tagore, ''Home Studies,'' in his
My Reminiscences, *translated by Surendranath Ta-*
gore, The Macmillan Company, 1917, pp. 111-16.

JAYANTA KUMAR DAS GUPTA (essay date 1937)

[*Das Gupta reviews numerous aspects of Chatterji's writings,*
including his social and philosophical ideas, principal thematic
concerns, style, method of plot construction, and portrayal of
character.]

Baṅkimcandra was something more than a mere story-teller
and in his novels there are various aspects of his thought, which
deserve more than cursory attention. Long before his death he
was recognised as a great force in the country. A contemporary
journal observed [see excerpt dated 1887], ''Babu Bankim
Chandra Chatterji is the first Bengali author of the day. He is
now a great power, a great educating power and we all take
leave to doubt whether he or our schools and colleges shape
modern Bengali childhood and youth more effectively and decisively. . . . He is the man of most national importance in the
country just now.'' This encomium he well deserved.

The world that Baṅkimcandra has created is peopled with a
variety of man and women. But he regards them all from one
standpoint. Baṅkimcandra always hopes for the best. In life
there are clouds and sunshine, laughter and tears, smiles and
sighs. But he asks with the poet, ''If Winter comes, can Spring
be far behind?'' He believes in fate, yet he is no disbeliever
in the possibilities of human effort, he does not allow his
characters to wait for opportunities to turn up; he makes them
create opportunities for themselves. Chance plays a strong part
in the lives of many of his characters, but mere chance is not
everything. The characters have their own initiative also. At
times chains of circumstance enmesh them, but they find some
way of escape out of their difficulties. Those that cannot do
so are sacrificed on the cruel altar of destiny, or by whatever
name one may choose to call it.

Cynicism finds no place in his writings. The morbidity which
disfigures the writings of many modern Bengali novelists is
conspicuously absent in Baṅkimcandra's writings. His was a
healthy and vigorous mind, keenly alert to all that was happening round him and enthusiastic about everything conducive
to human welfare. He was no pessimist brooding over human
follies and foibles. Nor was it his intention to try to fashion a
new world of imagination, where men and women could take
shelter from the everyday affairs of the world. He believed that
virtue would triumph over vice, that true love would find a
way, that wrong-doers would be punished and that in sacrifice
and service to others there was happiness.

He did not regard human beings as perfect; they to him were
mere men and women, possessing the merits and defects of
their species. He has not singled out one particular man or
woman as the epitome of all virtues or the embodiment of all
vices. Man to him is no divinity. Neither is woman a heavenly
creature. If she has her gracious qualities, she has also her
inevitable shortcomings. Out of varied human qualities Baṅkimcandra made his men and women. Can we say that they
are flawless and perfect? Can it be said about them that they
are ideal characters? About some of them this much can be
said that they come near the mark which might be regarded as
the starting point of human perfection. But even then there is
something of the world about them. Without something which
betokens their affinity with the rest of mankind, they would
be lifeless and cold like marble statues or images made from

some solid piece of rock. It is not lifeless creatures or imaginary
beings with whom Baṅkimcandra has peopled his works of
fiction. In his writings one finds men and women of flesh and
blood, men and women such as it is possible to meet in real
life. If there is a certain amount of romantic glamour around
some of them, it is not due to any attempt at an air of unreality.
The characters in a novel ought to have some relation to actual
life. The novelist deals with human passions. He cannot certainly make it his business to create life which never is nor
can ever be. It was to real life that Baṅkimcandra went for his
materials, yet he was no realist in the sense that some of the
modern novelists are.

He portrayed life with history as the background in some of
his novels. But the historical interest rarely dominated the art
of the novelist. He was an accomplished scholar and could
describe historical times with picturesque taste and accuracy.
But he fully realised the difference between fiction and history.
Therefore those who expect to find merely a fastidious antiquarian with a profound reverence for the past only and an
intense relish for historical research will be somewhat disappointed in him. (pp. 128-30)

He differed from Rameścandra Datta in whose novels history
comes first and life occupies a secondary position. Rameścandra had the mind of the historian, Baṅkimcandra the mind of
the artist. To the former the characters were part of history,
to the latter history was part of human life. Baṅkimcandra
regarded history as something quite important and deplored the
fact that Bengal had no real history. But he made no fetish of
history in his novels. He saw that the best way to inspire a
taste for history in the minds of those for whom he was writing
would be the presentation of historical incidents and persons
combined with men and women from his own imagination. It
was that method which critics like to call ''uniting the really
historical with the imaginary.'' In the atmosphere of history
he never lost the perspective of the novelist. Full freedom was
therefore allowed by him to the characters to develop themselves. Rameścandra's novels give one the impression that they
are mere history in the garb of novels and that the characters
in them are secondary things. The historian in him superseded
the novelist, while Baṅkimcandra could keep himself above
the temptation of merely recording historical events. The gift
of story-telling and an intimate knowledge of more than one
epoch of history are two of the necessary qualifications of the
historical novelist. Baṅkimcandra possessed both these requisites. (pp. 131-32)

As love is the central pivot on which the main plot rests in
most of Baṅkimcandra's novels, we may appropriately enquire
what his ideas on this matter were. He has not propounded a
love-philosophy in the sense that Plato and Shelley may be
said to have done. Of portraits of love at different stages of
human life, he has given many examples. There is not a single
novel of his in which there is not love of some kind or other,
be it the love of a man for a woman, the love of the wife for
the husband, the love of the young man for the maiden or *vice*
versa, the love of the patriot for the country, the love of the
idealist for certain ideals. Of love between man and woman
Baṅkimcandra was a very good delineator. He had here a high
standard. To him love which arose out of the appreciation of
the qualities of a person was of more value than love which
grew out of the appreciation of mere beauty.

Although Baṅkimcandra has depicted love as the natural outcome of men and women coming into contact with one another,
or arising from other causes such as early companionship,

sudden meeting, pity, sympathy, gratitude, he did not think it improper to deal with sex-complications. He was no purist in the sense that in his treatment of love he was handicapped by any stereotyped proprieties. He believed in the primary instincts of human nature. That men and women are susceptible to love or attraction for each other under certain circumstances he fully recognised. Rohini was a young widow. She was infatuated with Gobindalāl who lowered himself by a liaison with her. It was against all moral and social laws and both had to pay a heavy price for it. Kundanandinī fell in love with Nagendran-āth, who in his turn had fallen in love with her. It is interesting to note here that in two of Baṅkimcandra's novels in which there are actual sex-complications a young widow is the central figure. In Baṅkimcandra's time the girl-widow was a person who might well be the centre of romance, hedged round as she was with many social conventions. She constituted a serious practical problem for Hindu society. Baṅkimcandra found in her a likely character for the novel. Since then Bengali society has broadened to some extent and writers have other materials from which they can draw their plots and characters.

Baṅkimcandra kept love above the call of the flesh. Yet it was best appreciated by him in the daily life of men and women. Although his ideal was married love and love which culminated in marriage even when it had existed in premarital days, love could exist without marriage, as is shown in the cases of Āyesā and Pratāp. Pratāp's self-sacrifice made the man greater than his love and in Āyesā's self-control the real woman in her came out more fully than the mere lover. But when love exists without marriage in Baṅkimcandra's novels it is generally onesided. True it is that Śaibalinī and Pratāp loved each other, but Jagat did not reciprocate Ayeśā's feelings. Nor did Labaṅga make it quite clear if she loved Amarnāth.

One of the most characteristic points in Baṅkimcandra's novels is his success with women-characters. . . . His knowledge of the psychology of woman helped him to depict her sympathetically and his deep-rooted respect and innate reverence for womankind made him think of woman as "full of forgiveness, kindness and affection, the greatest success of God's creation." Some of his women embody the best ideals of womanhood and indeed some of them are too faultless. He did not think of women as merely dressed-up dolls. The heroine-like character of Draupadī attracted him more than the bashful and tender heroines in older Indian literature. So he depicted brave and self-reliant women, women who could be depended upon and could take risks in life and was successful with characters like Śānti, Bimalā and Nirmal.

He valued the proper education of women. Though his women were not college-ladies or girls educated in schools, many of them were accomplished. Tilottamā used to read Sanskrit poetry and romance, Bhramar and Dalanī read poetry, Śānti was educated with boys at a pandit's school, Bhabānī Pāṭhak supervised Praphullā's education in difficult subjects for several years. Baṅkimcandra brought many of his women out of the seclusion of the inner apartments and made them see what the world outside really was. But he regarded the home as the best place for them and not the outer world.

He realised that women were subjected to excessive social tyranny. Some of his women felt that they were under too much social subjection. Bimalā said, "How are they to introduce themselves to others who live in secrecy? Since the day God forbade women to utter the names of their husbands he also closed the way of their introducing themselves." . . . The customary Indian contempt for women was criticised by Baṅ-

kimcandra in the remark that Foster made to Dalanī: "The people of your country have no respect for the words of women."

Baṅkimcandra went so far as to disregard even the conventional ideas regarding the parentage of some of his women. Bimalā was not of pure birth, neither was Tilottamā's mother. But Bimalā's love for Bīrendra was in no way inferior to that of any other woman in Baṅkimcandra's novels. What he most insisted upon was purity in the character of women. "There is nothing more virtuous in a woman then chastity," was his firm opinion. In society woman holds an important position and so far as her relation to it is concerned she is bound by certain accepted notions. . . . A wife must be above all suspicions. But Baṅkimcandra was equally emphatic in insisting on purity in men as well. For a single act of folly in his youth Amarnāth was branded with hot iron as a thief. Debendra, Nagendra, Gobindalāl suffered for lack of moral restraint.

It is natural that a writer, who preached high ideals of wifehood . . . , should regard marriage as a great and sacred institution. In *Kapālkundalā* the priest says, "Marriage is woman's only step to religion; even the Mother of the world is wedded to Śiva." But Baṅkimcandra was not blind to the causes that often lead to married misery. . . . Social disparities often cause troubles and stand as barriers against happy married life as in the case of Kulīn Manoramā and Śrotriya Paśupati. Baṅkimcandra looked with disfavour upon anything that might disrupt the foundations of society, and that was the reason why he did not favour widow remarriage, though he had sympathy for the young widow. But he was definitely opposed to evils like childmarriage. Therefore some of his heroines were made to wait for the men they loved.

Baṅkimcandra's men can be grouped as heroes, lovers, idealists, thinkers, scholars, though the divisions overlap occasionally. He made his conception of the relation between literature and morality clear in one of his essays: "Poets are the teachers of the world, but they do not teach by propounding morality." Here by poets he meant literary artists in general. In the portrayal of his men these ideals actuated him and he laid stress on qualities like honesty, sincerity, strength of character and steadfastness of purpose. Although he has exalted physical prowess, to him moral force was superior to mere physical strength. Bīrendra would not purchase his freedom at the price of his independence. Pratāp died fighting bravely, but what raises him in our estimation as a man is not his skill with weapons but his strength of mind. Amarnāth did not find in life the happiness that was his due, but his sacrifice of his own happiness for the sake of one, whom he had once loved, makes him superior to many of those who win battles.

Baṅkimcandra was not fond of weak men who loll in luxury and lead a life of ease and comfort. He believed in work, in action which meant more to him than meditation or silent thinking. He held the ideal of the *anāsakta karma* of the Gītā rather than the ideal of renunciation or asceticism. Therefore even after they had taken the vows of ascetic life Abhirām and Rāmānanda engaged themselves with affairs in which they could be of help to others. They did not seek deliverance from the bonds of life by becoming ascetics. It was by serving others that they sought their salvation. In one of his essays Baṅkimcandra says that there are two types of people—those that are inclined to the sensual and those that are inclined to the spiritual. Both were wrong in his opinion. But the life of a *sannyasī* was in some cases the inevitable consequence of the career of men who were failures in life. Gobindalal became a *sannyasī*. Nagandranāth wanted to retire from the life of a householder when sick of the world. He was thus shirking his duty. Out of pity for these weak characters Baṅkimcandra prescribed such a life for them.

A question that often confronts serious students of the novels of Baṅkimcandra is, "Why are some of his men such miserable failures?" He had no word of praise for the idle, inactive, ease-loving, ambitionless Bengali, the product of climatic conditions in Bengal. Yet, it was with this material that he had to build some of his works. . . . One of the reasons why some of his men were unsuccessful was that the living types before Baṅkimcandra were regarded by him as poor. He lived in stirring times in the intellectual history of Bengal. Did he not find in the life of his days sufficient materials for convincing men-characters in his novels? He himself said that literature is the reflection of national character. It is very likely that he saw too many weaknesses and shortcomings in his contemporaries.

To him the Bengalis were a class of people, who had learnt craftiness from the fox, sycophancy and love of begging from the dog, cowardice from the sheep, imitativeness from the monkey and noisiness from the ass. The author who wrote, "He who is a Christian to the Missionary, a Brahmo to Keśabcandra, a Hindu to his father and an atheist to a beggar Brāhman, is a Babu. He who drinks water at home, wine at a friend's house, is abused at a public woman's residence and receives a push by the neck from his European master, is a Babu. He who hates oil at his bath, his own fingers at meals and his mother-tongue during conversation is a Babu," could not possibly depict many successful men as his opinions about the people he saw around him were far from high.

Rabindranāth is right in thinking that Baṅkimcandra has been most successful where he has portrayed the modern Bengali. In depicting characters of his own rank as Baṅkimcandra did in those novels where modern Bengal life is the subject-matter he could draw from a finished model. Rabindranāth further says that where Baṅkimcandra tried to picture the old type he has had to invent a great deal. A novelist has the advantage of imagination in supplying the leading features of characters belonging to classes and times other than his own. But Baṅkimcandra himself says that the human heart remains the same in every country and age. Some of his characters do not belong to any typical time. The same is true of other great writers also. (pp. 139-48)

Baṅkimcandra did not create many good caricatures. The best examples are Gajapati, Tārācaraṇ, Hīralāl, Debendra, the village post-master in *Kṛṣṇakānter Uil*, henpecked Rāmsaday, Rāmrām's elderly wife, but some of these are very incomplete sketches. They are not such enduring characters like Mrs. Gamp, Micawber, Pickwick and Mr. Collins. Baṅkimcandra lacked to some extent what is known as "fantastic humour" and which Dickens had in plenty. He had his villains but they are not devilish creatures like Iago, Fagin and Bill Sykes. He could not create an unscrupulous adventuress like Becky Sharp. Though Rohiṇī is something of an adventuress she is inferior to Becky. Neither was Baṅkimcandra able to depict military adventurers like Quentin Durward and D'Artagnan, Gurgan Khan might have been developed into such a character but the novelist did not proceed very far and left Gurgan a mere third rate figure. Similarly he lost another opportunity by merely referring to Dyce Sombre who was the type of those military adventurers, who made India the scene of their activities in the eighteenth century.

In discussing Baṅkimcandra's style, we have to bear in mind that before his time the learned, pedantic and verbose style was in vogue. Longwinded sentences some of which occupy as much as half a page were common in the writings of Rāmmohan Rāy and in periodicals like *Tattvabodhinī Patrikā*. The style of Akṣaykumar Datta and Iśvarcandra Vidyāsāgar was not at all suited to prose-fiction. It is fortunate that Baṅkimcandra did not take as a model the prose style of Iśvarcandra Gupta under whose influence he came in early life. Pyārīcād and Kālīprasanna had, it is true, written in a more colloquial style, but they did not command a big following. Moreover Baṅkimcandra considered the style of Hutom Pyācā poor and the style of Ālāl inappropriate for serious and dignified subjects. He was of opinion that the chief qualities required in good style are simplicity and clarity, but if the colloquial style did not for any reason serve one's purpose, there was no harm in taking recourse to a more difficult style. Therefore he adopted a middle course. In his writings there is a combination of the learned and the simpler styles. But he did not fully escape the influence of earlier writers. The opening chapter of *Durgeśnandinī* is classical in tone. . . . (pp. 149-50)

Throughout this novel and in fact his other earlier novels there are innumerable borrowings from Sanskrit, especially in the purely descriptive parts. But even when the scenes are not descriptive, he adopted a style which is not at all simple. (p.151)

From the time of the appearance of *Biṣabṛkṣa* onwards a change in Baṅkimcandra's style is noticed. The language becomes more easy and natural. There is a distinct tendency towards the avoidance of conceits and metaphors. The descriptive parts are in chaste and elegant language and there is no unnecessary piling up of compounds. There is no pompous and heavy air as the paragraphs follow one another. The monotony in style of some of the earlier novels is entirely absent. There is more directness and simplicity than is found in the first few novels. (p. 152)

Baṅkimcandra followed some of the literary conventions which formed part of the usual stock-in-trade of older Bengali writers. The descriptions of the arrival of Praphulla as a bride and the women's gathering in *Indirā* are two of the best examples of the handling of the conventional style in his novels. In his descriptions of feminine beauty also, he was conventional to some extent in his earlier novels. He was rather diffuse in his descriptions of Ayeṣā, Tilottamā, Manoramā and Mati Bibi. But gradually he eschewed this elaborate process which he had imbibed from the study of Sanskrit, and substituted brief descriptions instead and was very sparing with words while speaking of Kunda, Dalanī, Śrī, Ramā, Rajanī and Sāgar. The contrast with his earlier style is easily noticed in such cases. It is no longer the style of *Kapālkuṇḍalā* or *Mṛṇālinī*.

Baṅkimcandra tried to write now and then colloquial Bengali, but there is here a considerable mixture of the colloquial and the literary forms. It is, of course, vain to expect in him that thorough-going colloquial style for purposes of narration and description such as we find in modern Bengali writers under the influences of Rabīndranāth. (pp. 154-55)

Baṅkimcandra has made some attempts to make some of his characters talk in the colloquial style. But even in this he is not consistent and one gets the queerest jumble of literary and colloquial forms. . . . His habit of writing the literary form breaks through even his reported conversation. It is only the lighter type of conversation that is done in the colloquial, but where the subject is heroic or serious or where the person is of importance, the style is as literary as it is in the descriptions.

Baṅkimcandra was afraid to let himself go for fear of being thought low class, and was continually mixing up the colloquial and the literary in a way that is sometimes ludicrous. The result is a colloquial style which is never spoken or used in any part of Bengal.

We may turn now to Baṅkimcandra's management of the plots of his novels. . . . Baṅkimcandra generally divided his novels into several parts ranging from two as in the case of *Durgeś-nandinī* and *Kṛṣṇakānter Uil* to eight as in the case of *Rājsiṁha*. This he did in order to preserve a coherence in the plot and not to lose a sense of proportion. But there are some novels in which the story runs merely through different chapters and is not divided into parts at all.

The technique of a novelist requires that he should be economical in plot-construction and the plot should be carefully wound up. Unless this is done, there is a feebleness at the end of the story and it is marred by a sense of dullness. Both in *Kṛṣṇa-kānter Uil* and *Sītārām* Baṅkimcandra added appendices and this surely was not an artistic way of concluding a story. The plot of *Kṛṣṇakānter Uil* would not have suffered in the least from the disappearance of Gobindalāl and in *Sītārām* the readers ought to have been left to guess the fate of the hero instead of the local gossip that Baṅkimcandra indulged in.

Stevenson laid down a rather hard rule for the novelist and the story-teller when he said, "The right kind of thing should fall out in the right kind of place; the right kind of thing should follow; and not only the characters talk aptly and think naturally, but all the circumstances in a tale answer to one another like notes in music." This means that the plot of a novel should be artistically compact. Sometimes useless length spoils the plot. The fault of the first part of *Debī Caudhurānī* is that it is too long. The whole thing could have been condensed within a shorter space. The entire episode about the intrigues in Agra and Delhi in *Kapālkuṇḍalā* might have been considerably shortened. The intrigues have little to do with the main plot, but the novelist quite unnecessarily devotes several chapters to this part. In *Candraśekhar* again, one whole part is allotted to the depiction of the mental and physical agonies of Śaibalinī. The fact that many of Baṅkimcandra's novels first appeared in a serial form may have tempted him to drag them out to an unnecessary length. He himself felt it necessary to rewrite some of his novels after they had been published in a serial form and in others he made considerable alterations. (pp. 155-57)

In some of his novels Baṅkimcandra set himself to please his readers by a happy ending of the story, and in trying to do so he sometimes spoiled the beauty of the plot. The plot of *Mṛṇāl-inī* is rather thin and only the depiction of some of the characters redeems it from being mediocre. The plot of *Rajanī* is somewhat sordid. Labaṅgalatā's character loses its charms because the novelist was intent on seeing Rajanī married to Śacīndra, and so he made Labaṅga play upon Amarnāth's early love for her. In *Debī Caudhurānī* Baṅkimcandra had to reunite Praphulla to her husband in spite of her years of leadership of Bhabānī Pāṭhak's gang of robbers. There is a sense of making too much fuss which ultimately leads to nothing. The propagandist made the novelist ineffectual.

It is really in the handling of the tragic plot that Baṅkimcandra showed most skill. The tragedies of Āyeṣā and Osmān, of Kunda and Nagendra, the tragedy of Zebunnisa and Mabārak, of Sītārām and Śrī, the tragedy of Bhramar and Gobindalāl, appealed more to the novelist's imagination than those themes to which he could give a happy ending. He made Nagendranāth

and Sūryamukhī happy at last. But at what cost? Kunda had to kill herself and Sūryamukhī had to suffer intensely. Baṅkimcandra made Śaibalinī go back to Candraśekhar. But it was a merely patched-up affair. The novelist had to enlist the aid of the *yoga* or psychic force in making Śaibalinī love her husband. It was certainly not a normal course. The novelist shows much more skill in *Kapālkuṇḍalā* where the heroine is not in love with the man to whom she was married. They could not continue to live in that way for a long time and the inevitable crash came. There is a definite reason why Baṅkimcandra preferred a tragic plot above others. He thought that the best qualities in human nature showed themselves when a person was placed in unhappy circumstances. So to him Desdemona was a greater character than either Śakuntalā or Mirāndā. (pp. 157-59)

According to modern standards of classification, the novels of Baṅkimcandra may be classified as novels of character, novels of action and dramatic novels. In all these categories the plot has a distinct rôle—in some principal and in some secondary. In modern Bengali novels the plot does not play an important part as many of these are full of ideas and questionings. In Rabīndranāth's *Gorā* or Śaratcandra's *Śrīkānta* the plot is so slender that it is merely a peg to hang the novelist's ideas on. The plot is a medley of detached events. Baṅkimcandra wrote years before many of these ideas were in the air and his pre-eminence over modern Bengali novelists in the matter of plot-construction will readily be acknowledged. Judged on the whole, his novels furnish coherent plots, unity in the story and are true to the facts of life, though as a novelist he was a pioneer.

Baṅkimcandra's influence on Bengali life and literature has been far-reaching. . . . It would not be too much to say that every Bengali novelist in the second half of the nineteenth century was in a sense his disciple. His versatility enabled him to make his mark felt in more than one branch of Bengali literature and Bengali thought. He introduced serious literary journalism and criticism and the high standards that he maintained therein should still serve as lessons to those who desire to win laurels in these branches of literature. He first taught the Bengalis the vast possibilities of Bengali literature by his own novels and miscellaneous works and gave an impetus to the cultivation of *belles lettres* in Bengal. He made it possible for educated Bengalis to realise that their life and literature were inseparably bound up, the one with the other. He suggested to them the idea of applying themselves to the improvement of literature if they wanted to achieve anything in the way of national progess. In that respect he was a nation-builder.

He dominated an age by the sheer strength of his outstanding genius and forceful personality, and his contemporaries looked up to him as one who set new fashions, as one whose opinions carried considerable weight, as one who should be imitated in his literary methods, as one whose works served as models and standards of excellence. (pp. 160-62)

The Bengali novel in Baṅkimcandra's hands assumed a fully developed form. His novels were neither imitations of Arabian or Persian tales, nor of the tales of classical Indian writers like Viṣṇuśarmā, Somadeva Bhaṭṭa, Bāṇa, Daṇḍin and Subandhu. Baṅkimcandra's novels certainly have more affinity with the works of European novelists like Scott, Dumas, Hugo and Lytton. Baṅkimcandra infused fresh life and breath into forgotten periods of history and made them live again. He created in the minds of many people a new interest for old forgotten things and gave an incentive to the reconsideration of periods of history, which had still then no substantial meaning for the reading public in Bengal. To the modern world many of his novels bring a glimpse of the distant past. Out of the dry bones of history he created men and women, many of whom people now love to recognise as their own kith and kin. But he was not simply content with writing of the past. The sphere of his imagination was not restricted to a narrow circle; he was not oblivious of the currents and cross-currents of life around him. Those permanent traits of human nature, which are found in all ages and all climes were the principal materials of his novels.

Though essentially a man of his time, he did not find his sole subject-matter in the shortcomings and weaknesses of his contemporaries. Like Thackeray he did not allow himself to be obsessed by Vanity Fair nor did the social iniquities of his time engage his chief attention as they did in the case of Dickens. The darkest corners of the human mind found in him a keen observer, though he was not like Dostoievsky primarily concerned with the psychology of crime. Science attracted him, but he discussed no scientific theories in his novels. He did not attempt to portray anything in the nature of a Utopia since life in his days was less complicated and full of problems than it is now. The sombre tragedy of human life attracted him, but the helplessness of man struggling against fate did not deaden his feelings. He could see the "eternal spirit of the chainless mind" rising above the dull drudgery of human life and be happy in the faith that this indomitable spirit would conquer where the frail flesh often failed.

His lofty idealism never allowed him to play for cheap popularity or tawdry fame. A stern and uncompromising fighter, he worked against heavy odds, but difficulties did not deter him, nor could discouragement chill his unbounded enthusiasm, or embitter his feelings. To-day in Bengal and as a matter of fact in other parts of India there are many repercussions of the thoughts and ideas of the West; problems that vitally affect life, many new ways of looking at things are engaging the attention of our best minds. At such a time it is fitting that we men of the new age acknowledge our vast debt to him, who enlarged the horizon of Bengali literature, enriched the language, and opened a new vista not only for his contemporaries, but also for future generations. (pp. 162-64)

Jayanta Kumar Das Gupta, in his A Critical Study of the Life and Novels of Bankimcandra, *The Calcutta University, 1937, 186 p.*

J. C. GHOSH (essay date 1948)

[*Assessing Chatterji's place in Bengali literature, Ghosh acknowledges the author's historical importance, but focuses on his flaws, terming him a "very mediocre novelist."*]

Bankim has been the most widely read author of the last fifty years, and has received the highest praise from his readers and critics both as a novelist and a stylist. His popularity and influence have spread over the whole of India, and he is permanently enthroned as a classic. The time is ripe for a proper critical inquiry into his work, one that will take full note of his shortcomings and will not be a reiteration of the customary eulogy. Such an inquiry will not only enable us to understand him better than has been possible so far; it will give us an idea of the shortcomings of his imitators and followers, and indeed of the entire school of Bengali fiction of which until recently he was the sole inspiration and model. While it is our duty to praise him as the creator of the Bengali novel, it is equally our duty to indicate the false values he bequeathed to it. The truth

about Bankim, as the present writer sees it, is that he is a very mediocre novelist. If any further apology be needed for speaking freely of his faults, it will be found in the good reason that they do not affect the importance of the part he played in the development of the novel. His faults, again, are in a large measure traceable to the age in which he lived, to its bad standards and lack of standards. Not only were there no novels worth the name when he began to write, there was not even a well-established prose style. He had to create his own standards, or to import them from the English novels he had read. His defects are the birth-pangs of the Bengali novel, and in speaking of them the present writer does not forget the unfavourable conditions in which he worked.

Eight of Bankim's novels have an historical background and make use of historical persons and events, but none of them can be called an historical novel. The reason for this does not lie, as has been commonly supposed, in Bankim's variations from historical facts or even in his distortions of them. As a rule he is fairly true to facts, and his variations and distortions are neither many nor serious. Typical examples are found in *Ānanda-math* where Bankim makes Birbhum the scene of battles which actually took place in north Bengal, and calls by the name of Major Wood a British officer whose real name was Captain Edwards. In the preface to the third edition of *Ānanda-math,* after referring to these inaccuracies, Bankim justifies himself by saying: 'I do not consider these discrepancies fatal. A novel is a novel, not a history.' The justification was not really necessary, and Bankim might have spared us the truism about a novel being a novel. Accuracy is desirable, but no one would cavil at inaccuracies so trivial as these. No one with any literary sense would suppose that a faithful reproduction of facts would by itself make an historical novel. No historical novelist worth the name would interpret his art so narrowly as to forget the elementary principle that a novel is not a history.

One would have liked to think that in statements like these Bankim was expressing a wide view of the novel, but the unfortunate truth is that he was expressing a narrow view of history. The first chapter of the third part of *Sitārām* opens thus: 'Bhusnā was occupied. Sitārām was victorious in the battle. Torāb Khà met his death at Mrinmay's hands. These are historical matters, consequently of little importance to us, and we shall not spend our time in describing them in detail. A novelist should concern himself with inner matters, not with history.' No further evidence need be given of Bankim's unintelligent and unimaginative attitude to history. As history is a record of human actions, it provides excellent examples of those 'inner matters' with which a novelist should concern himself; and that is precisely the reason why many of the world's greatest novelists and dramatists have gone to history for their material. Bankim should also have known that to revive the past is almost as miraculous a performance as to revive the dead, and is the highest performance of which a novelist is capable. He himself went to history for more than half of his novels—one wonders why, if he really thought that historical matters were of little interest to a novelist.

In view of the use he made of history, however, one could safely surmise that he would have done better to have left it alone. The 'history' in his novels is just so much adventitious, unreal, and dead matter. Nowhere, not even in *Rājsiṃha* which he expressly called an historical novel, does he show the least awareness that there is such a thing as the life or spirit of history, let alone make any attempt to capture it. The characters are not the historical persons whose names they bear; they are undefined figures who, but for the context of events in which they appear, might be anybody or nobody. Baṅkim is equally disappointing about the incidents. He shows no curiosity about the political, economic, or social forces that brought them about, and is content to regard them as mere incidents. Quite often he records them in the manner of a schoolboy jotting down history notes. 'Bhusnā was occupied. Sitārām was victorious in the battle. Torāb Khā met his death at Mrinmay's hands.' Baṅkim, as we said above, is usually true to facts, but the bare bones of facts are all that he gives. The living breath of history escapes him, and that is why he is no historical novelist. His works are not even good period pieces, and have no value whatsoever as pictures of the manners and customs of the past. He was influenced by Scott, and was a romantic like him, and yet he could be peculiarly insensitive to the picturesque in history. *Kapāl-kundalā* is an instance. In *Rāj-siṃha*, another story of Mogul times, he had a rare opportunity for a pageant of superb magnificence, but could not fully rise to it. *Rājsiṃha* is more historical than the other novels, though Nirmalkumāri, a fictitious character, has a place in the centre of the stage.

In the other novels the historical matter merely pads out the main story or supplies a vague background. In *Chandrasekhar* the story of Mir Kāsim and Dalani has been most artificially hitched to the story of Saivalini and her husband and lover, and the historical part of *Kapāl-kundalā* is utterly irrelevant to its main story. The historical matter of *Mrinālini*, viz. the conquest of Bengal by the Muslims, clashes with the romantic story of the heroine's search for her husband. The heroine is conceived after the Rādhā of the Vaisnava Pads, and some of those Pads are actually sung by her companion Girijāyā. The Pads belong to the sixteenth century or later, while the Muslim conquest of Bengal took place in the twelfth century. There is nothing so flagrantly anachronistic in *Durges-nandini*, though it is hard to believe that the hero would have been admitted into the harem of a Muslim nawab and been nursed by the nawab's daughter.

Baṅkim is happier when he writes about the life around him, but he also has serious limitations as a social novelist. His outlook is confined to the upper middle class to which he himself belonged, and of which he was one of the greatest representatives of his age. He hardly seems to have been aware of the existence of the working class apart from domestic servants, and these he generally represents as the stock caricatures, witty and pert, of conventional comedy. Hirā, the maid-servant in *Visavriksa*, is reserved for serious treatment, but that is because the story of her seduction is designed to point a *bourgeois* moral. On those rare occasions when Baṅkim notices the lower middle class (as in the description of the domestic life of Sānti and of Praphulla and her mother), he transforms the stark realities of their poverty into dream-pictures of happiness. In his attitude to his own class, as to the other classes, Baṅkim is always the typical *bourgeois*, smug, sentimental, didactic, and conservative, and the world he creates is as narrow as it is false. All his men except Govindalāl are pasteboard, and his women, though more convincing than his men, are not altogether real. Saivalini, Rohini, and Suryamukhi, for example, are three women who spring straight from life. And are intensely real to start with, but they too end on a false note. Saivalini goes mad in repentance, Rohini pursues a cheap intrigue, and Suryamukhi drowns herself in sentimental slush. They remain true to their own nature, and live their own life, up to the middle of the story, but in the end their integrity is sacrificed to the author's propagandist purpose. The other women are creatures of propaganda from beginning to end.

The propaganda is for the conventional moral, the ready-made value, which Baṅkim unquestioningly accepts and enthusiastically upholds. As is to be expected, he is a champion of the institution of marriage, and the simple-minded zeal with which he extols the conjugal virtues, particularly in women, is responsible for many of the absurdities and falsities one finds in his novels. The heroine of *Devi Chaudhurāni* is one of Baṅkim's model wives, designed to illustrate the ultimate dependence of women on their husbands. She relinquishes her noble mission, and her queenly power and place, in order to share the life of a husband who has two more wives and is a ninny into the bargain. Saivalini, the errant wife in *Chandrasekhar*, receives examplary punishment for having left her husband and gone in search of Pratāp, the man she loves. She is repulsed by Pratāp, and expiates her sin in hellish torment of soul resulting in insanity. The fact that her husband never loved her does not mitigate the sentence Baṅkim passes on her, any more than does the other fact that she and Pratāp had loved each other in their childhood and adolescence. There is no suggestion of any physical relationship between her and her lover, but even so she must pay dearly for the dangerous thoughts she had harboured. The artistic possibilities that there were in the conflict between Saivalini's love for Pratāp and her duty to her husband are not properly explored, because the artist in Baṅkim is overshadowed by the moralist.

Lavaṅga-latā in *Rajani* is another of Baṅkim's model wives. She is a young girl who has been married to an old man with a family by another wife, but is nevertheless the happiest and most devoted of wives. The young Amarnāth loves her and is caught hiding is her room. Lavaṅga-latā vindicates her wifely virtue with sadistic fervour by having the word 'Thief' branded on Amarnāth's back with a hot iron. In the years that follow Amarnāth gains her esteem by performing many good deeds, and at the end of the story comes to take final leave of her. The following is a fair summary of the conversation that takes place between them:

> 'Are you really going away from Calcutta?' Lavaṅga asked.
>
> 'Yes,' I answered.
>
> 'And why?' she asked.
>
> 'Why should I not?' I returned, 'I have no one to ask me not to go.'
>
> 'If I ask you not to go?'
>
> 'What am I to you that you should dissuade me?'
>
> 'What are you to me? I do not know. Perhaps in this world you are nobody. But if there is another world——'
>
> Lavaṅga stopped short and did not complete the sentence. I waited a little and then said, 'If there is another world, what then?'
>
> 'I am a woman, naturally weak. What would you gain by putting my strength to the test? I can only say that I sincerely wish you well.'
>
> 'I fully believe that. But there is one thing I have never been able to understand. Why did you brand this mark of infamy on my person?'
>
> 'You committed a wicked deed. I too out of childish frivolity committed a great wrong. I only pray you will forgive me.'

'I have forgiven you before you asked. And indeed there is no question of forgiveness. It served me right, I deserved that punishment. Now I am going away, never to return, never again to see you. But if ever in the future you heard of me, would you feel any affection for me?'

'I am afraid it would be sinful of me if I felt any love for you.'

'I beg your pardon. I no longer ask for your love. But in your heart, deep and vast as the ocean, is there no room, be it ever so small, for me?'

'No, none at all. I have not the least affection for the man who fell in love with me without being my husband. I shall not harbour even such affection for him as one entertains for a pet bird.'

Sentiments so prim and proper could not but endear Baṅkim to his middle-class readers, particularly the husbands. He has one or more love-stories to tell in every novel, but takes care that they uphold, and even glorify, the social conventions. He is a moralist rather than an objective artist, and it does not take us long to learn that his good people are those who observe the social proprieties and his bad people are those who do not. The narrow and naïve world of his novels is no doubt a reflection of the Bengali society of his time, but it is also a product of the ideas he himself held on social questions; all the more so because he is not a realist who records life impersonally as he finds it, but is a romantic who transforms life according to his ideals. He lived in an age of social reformation when progessive people like Iswar-chandra Vidyāsāgar were deeply moved by the unhappy condition of widows, and fought for the legalization of widow-marriage; and yet his own attitude towards widows is most unsympathetic. Kunda in *Visavriksa* and Rohini in *Krsnakānter Will* are young widows whose natural craving for love and happiness is cruelly punished. Kunda commits suicide and Rohini is shot. Another instance of Baṅkim's reactionary conservatism is his unquestioning acceptance of polygamy in *Devi Chaudhurāni* and *Sitārām.* The antiquated ideas he held on social questions could not but restrict his artistic possibilities. He shows no interest in the complexities of human relationships, or in the subtleties and profundities of human character, and his main object is to hold before us models of the conventional virtues and vices. Pratāp is one of his ideal characters, raised to unnatural perfection for our admiration and edification. He loves Saivalini, but with a pure, silent love, and repulses her out of respect for the seventh commandment. Finally he courts death on realizing that Saivalini will not cease to love him so long as he is alive. His dying speech is one of those pieces of grandiloquence Baṅkim offers his readers a a special treat:

> What would you understand, you ascetic [Pratāp is speaking to Rāmānanda Swāmi]? Who is there in this world who can comprehend this love of mine? Who can realize how much I have loved Saivalini for the last fifteen years? I am not attached to her with a sinful heart, my love is another name for a desire for self-sacrifice. Day and night have I felt this love in my veins, in my blood, and in my bones. No one ever knew of it, no one would ever have known of it. Why did you raise this matter at the time of my death? I knew that this love would bring forth no good, and that is why I have sought death. My mind has been tainted, and a change may come over Saivalini's mind too. There was no oher way but for me to die, so I have courted death. You are wise and versed in the sāstras [sacred books], tell me what is

the atonement for my sin. Am I guilty in the eyes of God? If I am, would not my death atone for my guilt?

At the opposite end from Pratāp stand such characters as Hirā, the servant-maid who took the wrong turning, and Devendra, the young rake who seduces her. They are monsters of vice as Pratāp is a monster of virtue, and the consequence of their vice has been painted in the most lurid colours to serve us as warning.

Baṅkim is at his best in his less ambitious novels such as *Indirā.* Their light domestic theme does not call for any great insight into social or human problems, and gives Baṅkim ample scope for his powers of familiar observation and genial comment. He cannot see far or deep, but he knows his men and women well from the outside, and he can chat about them agreeably. Irrespective of the historical, social, or political significance of his theme, his interest always narrows down to domestic matters, and all his novels are in essence domestic novels.

The political novels show no understanding of political issues, and their patriotism, though genuine, is of the romantic, sentimental, and wishful sort that evaporates in high-sounding talk and theatrical action. They are, besides, heavily doped with love and mysticism. This is best illustrated by *Ānanda-math,* the greatest of Baṅkim's political novels and the gospel of Indian nationalists for nearly half a century. The revolutionary patriots of that novel are *sannyāsis* (holy men) who have turned bandits for the deliverance of their country. They live in a *maṭh* (monastery) in the depths of a forest and worship quaint, mystic images. They have taken the vow of celibacy, and it is the breaking of that vow, not any defect in their political idea or organization, that brings about their ruin and the ruin of their cause. Baṅkim presents them with great seriousness, not realizing what nincompoops he has made of them. They are halfbaked monks who play with the idea of revolution and are defeated in the end. Their revolution is bogged up in love, and both love and revolution are bogged up in mysticism. Baṅkim was an anti-revolutionary, as we know from the preface to the first edition of *Ānanda-math:* 'Social revolution is very often nothing but self-immolation. A revolutionary is a self-killer.' Why then he should have chosen the Sannyasi Rebellion of 1772 as his subject is not clear, unless it be to blunt its revolutionary issue with such things as love and mysticism. In any case the mixing up of such incongruous and irrelevant elements as revolution, love, and mysticism has produced a very unsatisfactory novel.

The worst feature of *Ānanda-math,* as of *Devi Chaudhurāni* and *Sitārām,* is the dead mass of mystical-didactic verbiage with which it is loaded. We are told that those novels contain Baṅkim's exposition of the doctrine of disinterestedness of the *Gitā,* but the exposition is trite, obtrusive, and altogether inartistic. It is not being forgotten that many of Baṅkim's limitations are the limitations of his age, that the sentimental, unrealistic, and semi-religious character of his political thought is largely due to the absence of a properly developed nationalist movement in the seventies and eighties. The anti-Muslim prejudice Baṅkim displays in many novels is accounted for by Muslim tyranny and misrule in pre-British times, but it is also an expression of communal hatred. A Hindu first and foremost, he writes with the bitterness of his persecuted race. In *Ānanda-math, Mrinālini, Sitārām,* and other novels his patriotism takes the form of glorifying Hindus who defy Muslim power. He conceives of freedom as freedom for Hindus alone, and lacks the wider vision, not altogether unknown in that age, of Hindus and Muslims united in a common nationhood. In *Ānanda-math* he hails British rule with enthusiasm and gratitude for having put an end to Muslim oppression and anarchy, but conveniently forgets the responsibility of the East India Company for the terrible famine of 1769-70 which is the background of that novel. As a matter of fact the responsibility of the Company was greater than that of the Muslim nawab who was then the nominal ruler of Bengal. In *Ānanda-math* and elsewhere he takes the view that Hinduism has decayed through the exclusive attention it has in the past paid to spiritual knowledge, and that the British have been providentially sent to India to impart that knowledge of the physical sciences without which true spirituality cannot thrive. The view is too idealistic and ignores the economic and political aspects of British rule, but there is nevertheless an element of truth in it. It runs through the synthesis between the East and the West made by Indian thinkers from Rāmmohan Rāy to Rabindranath Tagore.

Considered purely as works of art, Bankim's novels suffer from a fundamental indiscipline arising from his inordinate sentimentality. He has it in him to write with the utmost simplicity and precision, yet he fills his pages with the cheapest rhetoric, with the most absurd ostentations and affectations. Some of his descriptions of the physical appearance of his heroines would shame the most artificial of Sanskrit rhetoricians. Those who know him in the original are only too familiar with the purple passages, almost comically gushing and effusive, which he turns out with complete self-satisfaction when he wishes to write well. A good instance is the apostrophe to Pratāp at the end of *Chandrasekhar.*

> Then go, Pratāp, go to the eternal abode. Go where there is no trouble in the subjugation of the senses, where there is no evil fascination in beauty, where there is no sin in love. Go where beauty is infinite, love is infinite, happiness is infinite, and where there is infinite virtue in happiness. Go where one feels another's sorrow, where one safeguards another's virtue, sings another's praise, and where one does not have to sacrifice one's life for another. Go to that land of supreme glory. Even if you had a hundred thousand Saivalinis at your feet there, you would not care to love them.

He falsifies his characters and situations by over-dramatizing them (as in the scene in *Durges-nandini* where Āyesā declares her love for Jagat Siṃha), and his moralizings are responsible for many a dusty page. His tender and moving scenes (such as the reunion of Nagendra and Suryamukhi in *Visavriksa* and the encounters between Praphulla and Vrajeswar in *Devi Chaudhurāni*) are orgies of shoddy and tawdry sentimentality, and he has a fondness for cheap showmanship (e.g. beautiful women flourishing daggers, and bold men performing impossible feats of heroism) and crude melodrama. Kapāl-kundalā in the novel of that name is a Miranda-like girl who has grown up in the loneliness of the sea and the forest, and is out of her element in the world of men and women to which she is brought after her marriage with Navakumār. So she agrees to renounce her husband when Lutufunnisā, his first wife, asks her to do so. 'Kapāl-kundalā again pondered. Her mind's eye swept all over the world, but could not see any familiar face there. She gazed into her own heart, but she could not see Navakumār there. Then why should she stand in the way of Lutufunnisā's happiness?' Here was an excellent idea, and it would have provided the fittest ending of the story. But Bankim has spoilt it by bringing in the crude melodramatic elements of the Kāpālik's revenge and Navakumār's suspicions of Kapāl-kundalā's chastity. Nothing can be more gruesome than the last chapter where Kapāl-kundalā is taken to the cremation ground to be killed by the Kāpālik and Navakumār. The following passage from that chapter is a good example of Bankim's characteristic love of exaggeration.

> On the cremation ground could be heard now and again the hideous howl of corpse-devouring animals. . . . Navakumār took Kapāl-kundalā by the hand and led her across the cremation ground to bathe her. Bones pierced their feet. Navakumār trod on a pot of water and broke it. Near it lay a corpse—wretched corpse! no one had cremated it—and both of them touched it with their feet. Kapāl-kundalā went round it, Navakumār trampled it beneath his feet. Wild corpse-devouring animals were roaming around. At the approach of the human beings they yelled loudly, some came to attack, while others ran away howling.

These faults, however serious, might have been overlooked in a novelist who had the art of story-telling. But many of Bankim's plots violate the elementary laws of probability and naturalness. Suryamukhi turns Kunda, a girl of sixteen, out on the streets on the merest suspicion of her immorality and without asking for an explanation. Kunda takes poison, but dies in a perfectly normal state of body and mind and without any suggestion of physical pain. With a gun in his hand Govindalāl makes a long and flowery speech (the sort Bankim specially delights in writing) before shooting Rohini. Things happen in Bankim's novel is as in fairy-tales, and we are not to ask questions. A timely storm rises in obedience to the author's will and brings about the crisis of *Devi Chaudhurāni.* A timely tidal wave does the same in *Kapāl-kundalā.* Then there are the *sannyāsis, bhairavis,* and other holy men and women whose miraculous powers enable them to do whatever the author wants and who make novel-writing the easiest job on earth. Saivalini's insanity is cured miraculously by one such holy man, and Rajani's blindness by another. To give other instances of Bankim's happy-go-lucky technique: Chād Sāh Fakir gets wind of Gangārām's treachery in the most unlikely circumstances, and Hem-chandra and Byomkes are brought together by the long arm of coincidence in a city that is being ravaged by invaders.

Bankim's characters have but little freedom of action because of the importance he assigns to chance. Fate rules the lives of his men and women, and the world they inhabit is as primitive as that of Greek traagedy. This does not mean, though, that there is any exploration of the primary values in Bankim's novels as there is in Greek tragedy or Shakespearian tragedy. How primitive this world is may also be seen from the important issues that depend on dreams, waking visions, and astrological predictions. A goddess asks Kalyāni in a dream to renounce her life, and Kapāl-kundalā is led by a vision of the goddess Kāli on her way back after here meeting with Lutufunnisā. There is nothing in the dreams and visions to interest the psychologist or the psycho-analyst, and at best they represent the popular idea that coming events cast their shadows before. Kunda sees Nagendra in a dream before she meets him. In the same dream she sees her dead mother who warns her against Nagendra. In the next few years she is married to Nagendra and great unhappiness follows. Her mother re-appears in a dream, reprimands her for not having heeded her warning, and advises her to put an end to her life. Thereupon Kunda takes poison. The astrological predictions are equally naïve. The heroine of *Sitārām* has been separated from her husband because of the prediction that she will cause the death of some one dear to her. The main theme of the novel hinges on this, but in the end she causes the death, not of her husband, but of her brother. There is no tragic irony in this capricious working of fate, no appeal to our pity and terror in this tragic waste of the heroine's life. Even more pointless and fatuous is the use that has been made of the prediction in *Mrinālini*. The historical part of that novel turns on the prophecy that traders from the West will conquer Bengal from the Muslims. Hem-chandra is a western Indian prince who is a trader by caste, and he takes up arms to fulfil the prophecy. He fails, and we are left to infer that the prophecy will come true six centuries later, when the East India Company will conquer Bengal. (pp. 153-64)

J. C. Ghosh, "Calcutta Period," in his Bengali Literature, 1948. Reprint by Curzon Press, 1976, pp. 98-168.

SUKUMAR SEN   (essay date 1960)

[*In the following excerpt from his wide-ranging study of Bengali literature, Sen surveys Chatterji's works and outlines his role in the development of Bengali letters.*]

[Chatterji] did for Bengali fiction what Michael Madhusūdan Dutt had done for Bengali poetry, that is, he brought in imagination. Chatterji was more fortunate than Dutt as he did not have to set up his own diction from the very start. The prose style was already standardized; what Chatterji did was to break its monotony, shear off its ponderous verbosity and give it a twist of informality and intimacy. Chatterji's own style grew up as he went on writing.

Chatterji, following the discipline of Īśvarcandra Gupta, began his literary career as a writer of verse. Fortunately he was not slow to feel that poetry was not his *metier*. He then turned to fiction. His first attempt was a novelette in Bengali submitted for a declared prize. The prize did not come to him and the novelette was never published. His first fiction to appear in print was *Rajmohan's Wife*. . . . It is written in English and is probably a translation of the novelette submitted for the prize. *Durgeśnandinī* (Daughter of the Feudal Lord), his first Bengali romance, was published next. . . . Bhudev Mukherji's tale (*Aṅgurīyavinimay*) supplied the nucleus of the plot which was modelled somewhat after Scott's *Ivanhoe*. The high style of Vidyasagar is followed and the influence of the contemporary predilection for low humour and buffoonery is admitted in the superfluous character of the idiotic brahman. But the tale was something that was undoubtedly new and entirely delightful. The pseudo-historical background was a justification for a pure love romance intended for readers who knew only married love.

The next novel *Kapālkundalā* is one of the best romances written by Chatterji. The theme is lyrical and gripping and, in spite of the melodrama and the dual story, the execution is skilful. The heroine, named after the mendicant woman in Bhavabhūti's *Mālatīmādhava*, is modelled partly after Kālidāsa's Śakuntalā and partly after Shakespeare's Miranda. The diction matches the lyrical nature of the main story.

The next romance *Mrnālinī* indicates an amateurishness and a definite falling off from the standard. It is a love romance against a historical background sadly neglected and confused. The main characters are inchoate and undeveloped, and the story unconvincing. The parallel story of Paśupati and Manoramā could have been better developed into a separate novel. It is not unlikely that *Mrnālinī* was actually written before *Kapālkundalā*.

After this Chatterji was not content to continue only as a writer of prose romances, but appeared also as a writer with the definite mission of stimulating the intellect of the Bengali speaking people through literary campaign and of bringing about a cultural revival thereby. With this end in view he brought out the monthly *Baṅgadarśan* (Mirror of Bengal) in 1872. In the pages of this magazine all his writings except the very last two works first came out. These writings include novels, stories, humorous sketches, historical and miscellaneous essays, informative articles, religious discourses, literary criticisms and reviews.

With the exception of two stories and a novelette, Chatterji's fiction is domestic romance with a moral underlining and a social motive. *Viṣavṛkṣa (The Poison Tree)* was his first novel to appear serially in *Baṅgadarśan*. The theme is a dometic tragedy brought about by widow-remarriage. . . . In this novel the Bengalee reader for the first time received glowing glimpses of the middle class domestic life. Chatterji's narrative skill had full play in [*The Poison Tree*]. Nevertheless it marks a setback for Chatterji as a novelist as here he begins to assert himself as a teacher of morality and does not remain satisfied as an interpreter of life. It also makes him out as a non-progressive reformer. Chatterji was one of the first two graduates of the newly founded Calcutta University. He, however, held orthodox views on some vital social problems and did not support widow-remarriage.

Candraśekhar suffers markedly from the impact of two parallel plots which have little common ground. The scene is once again shifted back to the eighteenth century. But the novel is not historical. It has however one remarkable feature; it is the only novel of Chatterji that depicts the full development of a character, viz. the heroine Śaivalinī. The plot has suffered from the author's weakness for the occult.

The next novel *Rajanī* followed the autobiographical technique of Wilkie Collins' [*The*] *Woman in White*. The title role is modelled after Bulwer Lytton's Nydia in *Last Days of Pompeii*. In this romance of a blind girl Chatterji is at his best as a literary artist. Characterization is uniformly good and the style easy and unaffected.

In *Krsnakānter Uil (Krishnakanta's Will)* Chatterji added some amount of feeling to imagination, and as a result it approaches nearest to the western novel. The plot is somewhat akin to that of *The Poison Tree*. The story opens with an episode of domestic intrigue leading to the infatuation of a married man for a young widow with better looks than his wife and ends with the ruin it brought upon the family. The lesson is that the self-sacrifice of a loyal wife can ultimately save the soul of a man, and that purely carnal love can only lead to ruin.

The only novel of Chatterji's that can claim full recognition as historical fiction is *Rājsimha*. . . . But the historical environment of the plot is often marred by the introduction of unhistorical episodes and of characters that have little historical bearing. Nevertheless, the story is very interestingly told.

Ānandamaṭh (The Mission House of the Ānandas) is a political novel without a sufficient plot. It definitely marks the decline of Chatterji's power as a novelist. The plot of the meagre story is based on the Sannyasi rebellion that occurred in North Bengal in 1773. Chatterji gave it a politico-religious twist. He made his characters selfless patriots, inspired by the teachings of the *Gītā*, who fought against odds with the British whom they looked upon as the arch enemy of the country, responsible for the terrible famine of the preceding year. The author as an administrative officer of the government could not but show that this estimate of the British rule in India was wrong, and he attributed the failure of the Ānandas to their own weaknesses rather than the superior forces and ingenuity of the British. But

Chatterji was not overmuch fond of the British rule not only as a true son of India but also on personal grounds. He was also not insensible to the national movement which was slowly gathering force. *Ānandamaṭh* was his vengeance as well as his tribute. As fiction it cannot be called an outstanding work. But as the book that interpreted and illustrated the gospel of patriotism and gave Bengal the song **"Bande-mātaram"** (I Worship Mother) which became the mantra of nationalism, *Ānandamaṭh* is the most vital work of Bankim Chandra Chatterji. Incidentally it gave tremendous impetus to the various patriotic and national activities culminating in the terrorist movement initiated in Bengal in the first decade of the twentieth century.

In the mean time Chatterji was gradually missing art for propaganda. A revival of orthodox Hinduism based on a pseudo-scientific explanation of the *Bhagavadgītā* and other texts, a reactionary movement counteracting progressive thought and Brahmo monotheism, and deriving indirect support from Theosophy, made the novelist almost a complete convert. *Devī Caudhurānī* fully reveals him as such. The story is romantic and interesting and is delightfully told, no doubt. Some episodes are charmingly realistic. But the development of the central figure from the poor and neglected first wife of a well-to-do brahman young man to a female Robin Hood following the cult of Krishna the detached Master of the *Bhagavadgītā*, is unconvincing and unwarranted.

Chatterji's last novel *Sītārām* has for its theme the insurgency of a Hindu chief of lower central Bengal against the impotent Muslim rule. The central figure is well delineated but other figures are either too idealistic or impalpable. The plot is neither well conceived nor well woven, and the style is uneven and somewhat slipshod.

After the novels, the humorous sketches are the outstanding productions of Chatterji. *Kamalākānter Daptar* [enlarged as *Kamālakānta*] . . . contains half humorous and half serious sketches somewhat after DeQuincey's *Confessions of an English Opium-Eater*. It shows the writer at his best. Chatterji's serious essays are collected in two volumes. The topics range from positivism to literary criticism and from history to popular science. In two of his longest essays Chatterji took great pains to interpret the basic ideas of Mill's Utilitarianism and Compte's Positivistic Humanism. His analysis of the economic condition of agrarian Bengal is acute, and one could wish that he had maintained this interest in the life of the people. But unfortunately that element of his mental make-up which was attracted by the mysterious and the occult was gradually getting the upper hand. He lost his interest in Utilitarianism and in the problems of the Bengal peasantry and took to the study of the Sankhya philosophy and the *Gītā*. The closing years of his life were almost entirely devoted to the study of the *Gītā* and the problems of Krishnaism. The result of this enquiry is embodied in the two volumes, *Dharmatattva* (Essence of Religion) and *Kṛṣṇacaritra* (Life and Character of Krishna). The last work is a monument of Chatterji's power of critical analysis and of the clarity of his historical perspective.

Bankim Chandra Chatterji was a superb story-teller, and a master of romance. He is also a great novelist in spite of the fact that his outlook on life was neither deep nor critical, nor was his canvas wide. But he was something more than a great novelist. He was a pathfinder and a pathmaker. Chatterji represented the English-educated Bengalee with a tolerably peaceful home life, sufficient wherewithal and some prestige, as the bearer of the torch of western enlightenment. The only problem of life that stirred his literary impulse, and that too lightly, was domestic unhappiness of what now appears to have been the most superficial kind. The rosy glow of romance that pervades his novels was indeed symbolic of the easier life and the spacious days of the late Victorian Bengal. The readers of his novels felt that glow and they feel it even now. No Bengali writer before or since has enjoyed such spontaneous and universal popularity as Chatterji. His novels have been translated in almost all the major languages of India, and have helped to stimulate literary impulses in those languages. (pp. 232-38)

Sukumar Sen, "Prose Fiction and Bankim Chandra Chatterji," in his History of Bengali Literature, *Sahitya Akademi, 1960, pp. 229-44.*

HUMAYUN KABIR   (lecture date 1967)

[*In the following excerpt from a 1967 lecture, Kabir emphasizes the seminal nature of Chatterji's achievement as a novelist and also summarizes the primary strengths and defects of his fiction.*]

Bankim has two claims on the student of the Bengali novel. He was a pioneer and indicated the possibility of writing first rate fiction out of the substance of middle class Bengali life. Simultaneously, he brought the Bengali novel to a stage of development where it could attract the talents of the most promising literary men of Bengal. His main credit therefore is that he started the Bengali novel and indicated the lines of its future development. Aware of the narrow conventions which curbed contemporary Bengali society, he resorted to history in search of exciting events and incidents. Lacking in historical imagination, he could not however recapture the spirit of bygone ages. A product of the new education which was transforming Indian economy and creating a new middle class, Bankim remained essentially middle class in all his attitudes and opinions. His historical characters are in the ultimate analysis middle class men and women with the dress and trappings of kings and queens and lords and ladies. There is no truly heroic character in his historical novels and the real heroes and heroines are representatives of the middle class.

The same fact may be put in another way by saying that though Bankim dealt with many historical characters, his novels are essentially novels of social manners. Where the content and the theme remained unreconciled, we get historically improbable scenes in novels like **Durgesh Nandini** or **Sitaram**. Where theme and content coincided in his social novels, the results are far more satisfactory. Even in these, his conventional attitude and conformity to middle class morality prevented the free flowering of character. Even romantic characters like Devi Chaudhurani or Shri were ultimately absorbed by middle class morality. The most romantic of them all, Kapal Kundala, could find escape only in death. Really strong characters like Saibalini or Rohini asserted themselves against Bankim's conventional outlook but in the end Bankim the moralist triumphed over Bankim the novelist and either drove them mad or killed them.

With all his limitations, Bankim had both vision and design, qualities that are essential for a novelist. They give a certain clarity and strength to all his writings and charge them with an inner life. He was conscious of the challenge of the West and was willing to accommodate it without renouncing national identity. He shared in the nascent renaissance in Bengal and accepted many Western values. Like his other contemporaries he also failed to achieve a synthesis in all aspects of life. Whenever he was faced with a choice, he turned to the past traditions of his own country. This rooted him in Indian tradition and accounts for his energy and vitality.

Bankim's novels at times share the characteristics of European tragedy. The essence of tragedy lies in the futility of human effort where even the noblest succumb to circumstance. Man however achieves dignity by defying irrevocable fate. Bankim was attracted by this characteristic of European tragedy. He could not however accept it without reserve as it conflicted with the Hindu outlook in which virtue must triumph over evil. Bankim sought to overcome the conflict by his stress on situation rather than action. In *Kapal Kundala* and subsequent novels, we miss the inner conflict of tragedy but are compensated by a sense of the futility of human effort and the epic sublimity of supernatural forces. In *Sitaram,* Shri's wifely love itself becomes a cause of the hero's downfall. This is one reason why some critics say that Bankim wrote no novel according to modern concepts. His novels are in essence romantic tragedies but they deviate from the European tradition in one important respect. In European tragedy there is dignity even in defeat and utter ruin. In Bankim, the good is always peeping from behind and must in the end triumph. He sought human fulfilment through acceptance of the empirical and was in this respect influenced by Europe. Simultaneously he sought to base the empirical on a total realisation of knowledge, love and action, an impulse he derived from his Indian heritage. The European outlook is forward looking where it is better to travel than to arrive. For it, all experience is an arch whose margin fades for ever as we move. For India, novelty is not enough and must be based on a deeper understanding or intuition of the whole. It is to Bankim's credit that he was able to effect a partial reconciliation between these contrary views. For this and also for his skill as a story-teller, Bankim in spite of many blemishes remains the first great novelist of modern India, and the first writer in Bengali who established the novel on a firm foundation. (pp. 26-8)

> *Humayun Kabir, "Bankimchandra and the Birth of the Bengali Novel," in his* The Bengali Novel, *Firma K. L. Mukhopadhyay, 1968, pp. 1-28.*

SUNIL KUMAR BANERJEE (essay date 1968)

[*In this excerpt from the conclusion to his study of Chatterji's literary art, Banerjee discusses the design of the author's novels, providing a series of broad generalizations about such topics as his handling of plot and structure, portrayal of war, and use of history.*]

The craft of Bankim Chandra's fiction was conditioned by the personality of the man. His very physiognomy bore the stamp of dignity, determination, and of greatness. His sinewy body, broad forehead, the massive cast of his chiselled face indicated a remarkable combination of mental powers and physical strength. Intellect seemed to radiate from his eyes that were peculiarly sparkling. He moved about with a feeling of self-assurance, bordering on pride and arrogance. Such a man naturally left the impress of his distinctive personal character on all the activities of his life. His novels are informed with that spirit.

Something like a process of natural evolution is observed in the development of Bankim's faculties. . . . His career as a novelist began with the publication of *Durgesnandini* in 1865. The last work that he saw through the press was the enlarged edition of *Rajsingha;* it came out in August, 1893, eight months before his death in April, 1894. During this long period of twenty-nine years, his genius passed through some definite stages. His early ventures were mainly romances in which there was some mark of diffidence. But the man who is supposed to be a writer of romances, was really at his weakest in that field. *Durgestnandini* and *Mrinalini,* the only two pure specimens of this type, are rather tentative and inchoate. At the same time his latent powers were manifesting themselves in other directions. *Kapal-kundala* that came in between the two, indicated a shift from the pattern of the pure romance.

The inauguration of the *Vangadarsan* was in itself a significant event in Bankim's career. Of his fourteen novels the seven published in the periodical were *Vishavriksha, Indira, Yugalanguriya, Chandrasekhar, Rajani, Radharani,* and part of *Krishnakanter Will.* And the post-*Vangadarsan* period might be appropriately described as marking the third and final stage in the process of this development. Through these stages the growth of the author's technical potential was both towards range and extent as well as depth and volume. His later works came to be distinguished by a concentrated radiance rare in fictional literature. The increasing massiveness and profundity of design reached a point of perfection in the most imposing last work, *Rajsingha.*

Bankim Chandra was specially conscious of the design of his novels as he was conscious of his individual self. That age itself was characterised by two things: clearness of vision and awareness of one's own identity. The spirit of the age was conducive to concreteness in thinking, and a definite contour may be found in the plan and purpose of the stalwarts like Vidyasagar and Madhusudan. As a novelist, Bankim Chandra profited immensely from the favourable *zeitgeist.* He discarded the structures of his predecessors as amorphous and unorganised. For the real design of the novel he went over to the West, but in the great task of reconstructing the Bengali novel, he imitated no masters. He had the strength and judgement to give to a foreign model a thoroughly indigenous form. Madhusudan, his worthy contemporary, gave a masterly exhibition of the same powers in the field of poetry. The eulogy of one on the other may be applicable to both:

> To Homer and Milton, as well as to Valmiki, he (Madhusudan) is largely indebted in many ways, but he has assimilated and made his own most of the ideas which he has taken.

This design is almost always characterised by symmetry. All the constituent elements of a Bankim novel find their concrete shape and fulfilment in their mutual actions and reactions. Each detail is expanded in exact proportion to its bearing on the fundamental unity; the mass of one story is made to counterpoise that of another. The novelist seems to be guided by the primary motive of bringing about a synthesis of the different strands and sub-strands where they exist.

Bankim Chandra was perhaps one of our first litterateurs to assimilate the newly developed laws of science and apply its principles of balance and harmony to the design of fiction. The direct influence of the nineteenth century scientific thought might be noticed in the organic character of his novels, the rhythmic flow of the narrative, the overall symmetry of their design. Only *Mrinalini,* a romance, and *Devi Chaudhurani,* a thematic novel, seem not to have felt the balancing effect of science. Occasional waverings in the other two thematic novels are eclipsed by the brilliance of the total effect. In *Kapal-kundala* symmetry has been achieved within a very small compass. In *Rajsingha,* on the other hand, it spreads itself over an extensive canvas. This last is a work of magnificent proportions, and yet the beauty and harmony of its titanic dimension, like those of a rock-cut temple of South India, stand out in bold relief.

Plot is the essence of the design. Like a magician, Bankim would raise up a structure for the representation of a theme in hand. It became simple or complex according to the nature of the subject. He was quite at home in both the varieties, but his novels show that his inclination was towards complicated patterns. . . . The little vignettes like **Yugalanguriya, Radharani,** as well as **Indira,** stand at one end of the scale. They move for a while in a straight line and then end in a blaze. Complication as such is absent also in **Ananda Math** and **Devi Chaudhurani** as the story in them moves almost in a straight line. There is a sub-plot, and consequently a curved course of action, both in **Durgesnandini** and **Mrinalini;** apparently the complex pattern in the former is better managed.

The plot-structure of **Kapalkundala, Krishnakanter Will,** and **Sitaram** is to be called complex, although a subtle use of craft has tended to round off their corners. Of these three, the plot of **Krishnakanter Will** is simpler, but its spareness of narrative and leanness of structure are more than compensated by the dexterous twists and turns of technique. The sub-plot in **Kapalkundala** gives it a real curve: it is harmonised with the main plot and passion movement is generated by their interaction. **Sitaram** has more threads in its pattern. There are repeated juxtapositions of complicating agencies in it that make the story wind continually about almost all through.

But the wizardry of Bankim Chandra's craftsmanship is best revealed in the plot management of **Chandrasekhar, Vishavriksha, Rajani,** and **Rajsingha.** The pattern is most complicated in all of them. **Vishavriksha** and **Rajani** form a subsection among them as their structures are relatively close-knit. In each there are four main characters that are interconnected. In both, again, one character appears to be comparatively passive: the wife of Nagendra in **Vishavriksha,** and the husband of Labanga in **Rajani.** They wear their passivity with a difference, and yet they all contribute significantly to the development of plot.

In **Chandrasekhar** and **Rajsingha,** however, the compactness of **Vishavriksha** and **Rajani** is substituted for a more elaborate deployment of incidents and characters. They seem to possess the most amazing accumulation of events and episodes, and even the sub-actions have almost gained the stature of separate plots. A bigger and a smaller plot coalesce in each into an organic whole, Chandrasekhar, Saibalini, Lawrence Forster, Protap, and Sundari from the main part which is supplemented by the other part formed by Mir Kasem, Dalani, and Gurgan. Rajsingha, Chanchal, Aurangzeb, Nirmal, and Maniklal on the one hand, and Zebunnesa, Mobarak, and Daria on the other constitute the corresponding elements in **Rajsingha.** The arrangement in **Vishavriksha** and **Rajani** is a triangle on a triangle, that in **Chandrasekhar** and **Rajsingha** is a plot within a plot. In the main plot, again, a double triangular complication occurs. For example, the two triangles in **Chandrasekhar** in the primary strand, are Chandrasekhar-Saibalini-Forster, and Chandrasekhar-Saibalini-Protap. It seems as the pattern becomes progressively intricate, the novelist's grip over the technique tightens, the design becomes more symmetrical.

Bankim is dramatic in the striking and impressive way of presentation of the story, and in the perfect balancing of the characters with the plots of his novels. In most of them marked stages like Acts along with rising and falling actions, are observed. The events that make up the plot have the unity and

progression of a play. . . . It seems Bankim had the proper drama psychosis, the refined sensibility necessary for the portrayal of the higher emotions. He displayed that faculty in the treatment of the novels which came to be instinct with energy, passion, and movement. Perhaps in the last analysis, these qualities permeated the very atmosphere of the age in which he was nurtured. Vidyasagar, his eminent contemporary, exhibited dramatic qualities in his life and character.

The opening lines of the first novel, **Durgesnandini,** are symptomatic of Bankim's general technique. Historical facts are sifted and arranged with the object of producing a telling effect. Even in the professedly historical novel of **Rajsingha,** the narrative is started with human materials to spotlight the emotional content. In **Vishavriksha, Rajani,** and **Krishnakanter Will,** the striking turns come from the subtle use of craft. In **Chandrasekhar** and **Sitaram,** dramatic elements occur in an increasing proportion. And in **Durgesnandini, Kapalkundala,** and **Mrinalini,** impressiveness has been sought to be achieved through the technique of suspense and coincidence. These are artificial devices, but they seldom make, as they do in Ramesh Chandra, dramatic verisimilitude a casualty.

Economy of narrative and movement of story are marked features of the novels of Bankim Chandra. These are, again, concomitants of the dramatic art. He rarely gave way to details that were superfluous and detrimental to the unity of design. The artist in him was always alert, awake, and even domineering. His intellectualism chastened and subdued the romantic leanings of his early years. That accounts for the comparative absence of the lyrical strain in his novels. **Indira, Yugalanguriya,** and **Radharani** are rather exceptions in an essentially objective temperament; his sense of economy and movement served as a counterblast to his imaginative flight. . . . He revised most of his novels time and again with the twofold objective of effecting economy and coherence. Even in **Indira** and **Rajsingha,** the two novels rewritten on a bigger scale, there is carcely one chapter too many or irrelevant. The then Victorian tradition of a voluminous, slow-moving novel was not consistent with his genius.

A passion for beauty and proportion made him punctuate his narratives with pause and paragraphs. These technical devices increased the vigour of the story and at the same time accelerated its movement. Of the innumerable examples in this line, one of the earliest is the passage on time in **Durgesnandini.** Bankim had a subtle ear for the formal embellishments of pause and repose, which he found wanting in Madhusudan. Naturally he would have no word of appreciation for Scott's epicurean predilections for chewing the cud of historical memories. Conciseness and austerity seem to be the definition of his genius. He was almost constitutionally unfit for prolixity and long-windedness: it seems they were his *bete noire.* Hence it is that *longueurs* are conspicuous by their absence in his narratives. He was in his best form when presenting rapid and brilliant dioramas of attractive aspects of history and arresting moments of life.

Forster remarks that "it is on her massiveness that George Eliot depends—she has no nicety of style." But Bankim had a more comprehensive grasp of craft: he could wield the broad sword and the rapier with equal ease. **Kapalkundala** and **Krishnakanter Will** have patterns of delicate chiaroscuro and yet there is dimension and weight in their structures. Massiveness is a quality which is peculiar to the novels of Bankim Chandra. It is blazoned on the early works, and is more and more pronounced in the succeeding titles. In the latest ones specially, there is a broad sweep which we generally associate with some Russian novels. The accumulating grandeur and sonority of his fictional work attain culmination in the epic fragment of *Rajsingha*. But it is significant that these solid and heavy designs are often inwrought with fine threads of gold. Sometimes in the same novel, sometimes in novels of different genres. Bankim harmonised massiveness with nicety of style. Modern authors in this field prefer spinning delicate cobwebs of psychological analysis. Massiveness has been lost *ipso facto*. The difference between the structures of Bankim's first venture, *Durgesnandini,* and Mrs. Woolf's perfect specimen, *Mrs. Dalloway,* is one of kind.

Scenes of war in Bankim Chandra contribute to the massiveness of his design. They recur in some form or other in seven of his eleven major novels. It seems he was eager to have them, and whenever the opportunity came, he jumped into the arena with the zest of his own heroes. The scenes are in subdued colours in *Mrinalini, Chandrasekhar,* and *Devi Chaudhurani.* They are surcharged with the din and bustle of the actual field of battle in *Durgesnandini, Ananda Math, Sitaram,* and *Rajsingha.* Ramesh Chandra's art is generally too weak to infuse life and vitality into his war scenes. The Scott of *Marmion* and *Ivanhoe* comes nearer; he has Bankim's gusto but perhaps not the gathered radiance of his pictures. It is apparent the Indian author had a flair in this direction. His narratives attained a solidity and a magnitude by their comprehensiveness. They are rich with all the details of varieties of engagements, and the stratagems and manoeuvres associated with them. We hear the rattling of swords, the volleys of cannons, the very reverberation of war. The novelist presents graphic spectacles of engagements on bridges, in forests and mountain passes, in front of mounted guns battering soldiers drawn up in a needle-column array. The impression is that the novelist himself has turned a commander: he is in charge of the superintendence, direction, and control of the whole situation.

Enveloping actions of history generally form a part of Bankim's technical paraphernalia. Like scenes of striking engagements, these had no small share in building up the massiveness of the design of his novels. In those stirring days, people felt a renascent urge for doing mighty things; this desire might have prompted Bankim to connect the personages of his novels with events of history. An attraction for the recorded facts of the great world is very nearly a constant factor in these works. Nine out of fourteen of them have been set in a historical frame or fringe. The five outside the pale are three of the technically important ones, *Indira, Radharani,* and *Rajani,* and two of the passion-oriented patterns, *Vishavriksha* and *Krishnakanter Will.*

History is used in different proportions in the plot structure of the nine novels with related enveloping actions. Characters placed within the framework of the events of our country, to a great extent come to acquire concreteness, dramatic verisimilitude, as well as dimensional attributes. It is interesting to note that Bankim's first novel, *Durgesnandini,* and his last, *Rajsingha,* have both the enveloping action of history; in the latter, history has been used as a cementing factor between incidents and characters. Even a veneering of it in *Yugalanguriya* has had its effect in elevating the tone of the design. It is similarly more than a mere colourful frill in *Kapalkundala* and *Devi Chaudhurani.* The most resplendent example of the enveloping action of history is furnished by *Chandrasekhar, Sitaram,* and, of course, by *Rajsingha.*

Bankim's attitude of mind was essentially objective and scientific. But there was a strong undercurrent of traditionalism within him, which often broke through the upper crust of intellectualism and left its mark upon the design of his novels. This dual personality of the man was responsible for a rather liberal use of supermen, dreams, omens, astrology, etc. within the rigorously framed plots. Generally these were absorbed into the system, but sometimes they appeared by the force of will of the author and caused imbalance to the pattern.

Except in *Indira, Radharani,* and *Rajsingha,* the superman is a constant factor in some form or another. His character is changed in some of the novels, but the reader is at no pains to discover his identity. The most effective use of him is perhaps made as a Kapalik in *Kapalkundala,* and the next best is Chandrachur Tarkalankar in *Sitaram.* In *Vishavriksha,* the role of the Brahmachari is felicitous, though insignificant in the context of the plot. Another pleasant specimen is the hero converted into a Sannyasi at the end of *Krishnakanter Will.* The brief role of the Acharya as priest in *Yugalanguriya* is good, but not big enough for a comment.

But elsewhere his presence has not been exactly conducive to the beauty and proportion of the structure. The Acharyas in *Durgesnandini* and *Mrinalini* are patently fortuitous elements. Ramananda Swami in *Chandrasekhar* is evidently requisitioned for a special purpose, to deliver a funeral oration on the death of Protap. The Sannyasi in *Rajani* is but a thinly-disguised magician: he works miracles, and miracles do not obey the laws of probability. And not very much different is the activity of Bhawani Pathak in *Devi Chaudhurani* and the Physician in *Ananda Math.* (pp. 156-64)

Omens and dreams, however, have been managed with greater skill. The tragic emotion in *Kapalkundala* has been intensified by portents and premonitions. . . . Kunda's vision in *Vishavriksha* is an excellent piece of dramatic foreshadowing. Saibalini's dreams in *Chandrasekhar* have had their effect upon the passion movement of the narrative. Ramesh Chandra's attempts in this direction lack strength and originality, and are a study in contrast. Bimala's dream in *Vanga Bijeta,* for example, seems to be a pale imitation of Calphurnia's in *Julius Caesar.*

Astrology has been harnessed to still better advantage. In *Yugalanguriya,* it supplies an element of complication. The marriage of the hero and the heroine is postponed on account of it, the story develops along new lines, the comedy scintillates with the playful hide and seek of two young lovers. The complication created by astrological calculations in *Sitaram* has greater dramatic potency. It has tended to deepen the tragic note of the whole novel. It stands as an insuperable barrier between Sri and her husband, Sitaram, until she reaches the prime of her youth and beauty. Her aloofness, rendered necessary by astrological prognostications, causes a series of spiralling and curved movements of the story. Bankim plays the conjurer with astrology in *Sitaram.* (p. 164)

Sunil Kumar Banerjee, in his Bankim Chandra: A Study of His Craft, *Firma K. L. Mukhopadhyay, 1968, 204 p.*

T. W. CLARK   (essay date 1970)

[*Clark outlines Chatterji's distinctive contribution to Bengali literature, focusing on the role of history in his novels; his major themes; his religious beliefs; his reliance on various artistic devices; and his use of language.*]

[Bankimcandra Chatterji] wrote fourteen novels in all, though two were so short as to be more like short stories. He also wrote a book of sketches entitled *Kamalākānter Daptar,* . . . and though it is not a novel or even primarily narrative, it does contain some fictional narrative, part of which is very good indeed. The many other prose works of Bankim will not be examined here as they fall outside the scope of our present inquiry. He contributed to his own and other magazines a large number of articles on social, religious, historical and educational topics, and wrote two long dissertations on religious and philosophical themes. He attempted poetry also, but with little distinction. His novels however represent his most important contribution to Bengali literature. In point of time Bankim was the first Bengali novelist. What had gone before was preparatory stuff, at best the novel in embryo. Bankim's novels were really novels. (p. 61)

[The appearance of Bankim's novels] created a furore of excitement, first in Calcutta, and later in other parts of India. Contemporary and later critics bear clear testimony to his great and immediate popularity. An article in the *Calcutta Review* of 1873 contains the following sentence: 'This novel [*Biṣabṛkṣa*] was to be found in the *baithakkhana* [sitting room] of every Bengali Babu throughout the whole of last year.' Tagore in his autobiographies describes the impatient eagerness with which he and others waited for the next instalment. The first quotation is from *Jībansmṛti* [see excerpt by Rabindranath Tagore dated 1911], the second from *Chelebelā.*

> Then came Bankim's *Bangadarśan,* taking the Bengali heart by storm. It was bad enough to have to wait till the next monthly number was out, but to be kept waiting further till my elders had done with it was simply intolerable. Now he who will may swallow at a mouthful the whole of *Chandraśekhar* or *Bishabriksha,* but the process of longing and anticipating, month after month; or spreading over the long intervals the concentrated joy of each short reading, revolving every instalment over and over in the mind while watching and waiting for the next: the combination of satisfaction with unsatisfied craving, of burning curiosity with its appeasement; these long-drawn-out delights of going through the original serial none will ever taste again.

> *Bangadarśan* was like a comet in the sky. Sūryamukhī and Kundanandini [from *Biṣabṛkṣa*] went to and fro in every house as if they were members of the family. The whole country was on edge with anxiety to know what had happened now, and what was going to happen next. When *Bangadarśan* arrived nobody in our part of Calcutta had their afternoon nap that day.

Modern opinion is well represented by Sukumar Sen. 'No Bengali writer before or since has enjoyed such spontaneous and universal popularity as Chatterji. His novels have been translated into almost all the major languages of India, and have helped to stimulate literary impulses in those languages' [see excerpt dated 1960]. Whatever conclusion posterity may reach about the intrinsic merits of his work, no critic may safely ignore the extraordinary enthusiasm his novels created in his own and subsequent generations.

Durgeśnandinī, the first of the fourteen, is a historical novel. In his prefatory note the author described it as *itibṛttamūlak upanyās* (novel based on history). Like Bhūdeb Mukherji before him, Bankim drew his inspiration from the material made popular by Tod's *Annals and Antiquities of Rajasthan.* The hero in *Durgeśnandinī* is a Rajput in the service of the Moghul

emperor, and the co-hero a Paṭhān general in the service of the Paṭhān sultan of Bengal. It is a tale of warlike deeds and courage with a double love interest, one between Jagat Siṃha, the Rajput hero, and the daughter of a Hindu chieftain, the other a triangular affair involving Jagat Siṃha, Osmān, the Paṭhān general, and Āyeṣā, daughter of the sultan. *Durgeś-nandinī* differs in one significant respect from *Angurīyavinimay:* the action is placed in Bengal and the heroine is a Bengali princess, an innovation which did not fail to stir the emotions of its Bengali readers. Like Mukherji also, Bankim includes in his characters a holy man, Abhirām Svāmī, the first of a number of such semi-supernatural beings he was to employ. Contemporary critics were quick to suggest a resemblance between *Durgeśnandinī* and some of Scott's novels. They claimed that the unreturned love of the Muslim princess, Āyeṣā, for Jagat Siṃha, is similar to Rebecca's love for Ivanhoe. Be that as it may, Bankim according to his own statement had not read *Ivanhoe* at the time.

Bankim's third novel, *Mṛnālinī,* was described in the prefaces to the first and second editions as *aitihāsik upanyās* (historical novel). The action takes place in Bengal at the time of Lakṣman Sen during the first Muslim invasion of Bengal. Against this background is set a love affair between a prince of Magadha and a merchant's daughter from Mathurā. They are in fact man and wife, but had become separated in the confusion of the times. The story for this pair ends happily, but the secondary love affair, also to do with a man and his separated wife, ends in *satī.* Other historical novels followed: *Candraśekhar,* set in the British period when Mīr Kasim was Navāb; *Rājsiṃha,* a story of the time of Aurangzeb; *Ānandamaṭh,* probably Bankim's most famous novel, set in the British period and having as its main subject the revolt of the Sannyāsīs; *Debīcaudhurāṇī* also set in the British period and portraying from a somewhat romantic angle the banditry which was prevalent in the late eighteenth century; and finally *Sītārām,* set in Bengal in the early eighteenth century before the British assumption of power.

Two general features in Bankim's novels are noteworthy. The first is the shifting of the scene in some of them from Rajputana, Maharastra and Delhi to Bengal, with Bengali heroes and heroines in certain of the leading roles. Thus heroism came to Bengal, at first vicariously it is true, but soon it began to naturalize its domicile there, and this was not without effect on the political stirrings that were beginning to be felt at this time. The second feature, also of consequence politically, is the shift of Bankim's sympathy with regard to the communal problem during his career as a novelist. In *Durgeśnandinī,* Osmān, though a Muslim, is presented as a hero, noble of sentiment and brave in action. In the later novels, Bankim's attitude towards Muslims is hostile. In *Ānandamaṭh* and *Sītārām* particularly they are *par excellence* the enemy. They are portrayed as cowardly and cruel, rapacious and tyrannical. The heroes are Hindu, the villains Muslim. Patriotism was unequivocally identified with Hinduism. The hymn **"Bande Mātaram"**, the marching song of the Santāns in *Ānandamaṭh,* became the first rallying song of Hindu patriots, and, as Arobindo Ghoṣ later called it, the *mantra* of Nationalism.

It would be unjust to Bankim I feel, to leave the present brief consideration of his historical novels without examination of his mature opinion on the nature of the historical novel and in particular of the relation between the novel and history. He called *Durgeśnandinī* and *Mṛnālinī,* written at the beginning of his career, historical novels, but later he changed his mind and requested that they should not be so regarded. His views are set out in the preface to the fourth edition of *Rājsimha,* which he wrote only a few years before his death and several years after the publication of his last novel, *Sītārām.* 'I have never written a historical novel before [i.e. before *Rājsimha*]. *Durgŝnandin,̄ Candraśekhar* and *Sītārām* cannot be called historical novels. This [i.e. *Rājsimha*] is the first historical novel I have written. Hitherto no author has been successful in writing a historical novel. It goes without saying that I have not been successful either.' In the preface to *Debīcaudhurānī,* there is something of an emotional note in his plea. 'I shall be obliged, reader, if you will please not regard *Ānandamath* and *Debīcaudhurānī* as historical novels.' The reasons for this curious change of opinion are, so far as I am aware, nowhere fully expounded, but references in various places make it possible for us to detect in part at any rate the direction of his thinking. 'Since the publication of *Ānandamath* many people have asked me to tell them whether the book is founded on history or not.' It is possible that he found these questions embarrassing, not, I think, because he could not answer them, but because his readers seemed to be too ready to take all that he wrote in these novels as historical truth, thereby raising doubts in his mind as to whether the novel could be a suitable vehicle for history. 'Occasionally', he wrote, 'the purposes of history can be accomplished in a novel. The novelist is not always bound by the chains of truth. He can when he wants to resort to the use of his imagination to achieve the effects he desires; for this reason the novel cannot always take the place of history. . . . To ensure that my novel is a novel I have had to introduce many matters which are imaginary. . . . There is no need for everything in a novel to be historical.' And then finally, 'A novel is a novel; it is not history.' Bankim wrote a number of essays on historiology and urged that the study of history was essential if India was to develop politically. Great nations, he said, had great historians. Much of India's weakness could be ascribed to the fact that it had had no sense of history and that in consequence it had lost all connection with, and knowledge of, the greatness of its past. There is no need here to examine the logic of these arguments, but it is important to know that Bankim was convinced by them. He felt that India needed history, scientific history, not history so mixed up with mythology, as it had been in the past, that no one could tell the true from the fanciful. It is therefore feasible that his disclaimers about the historical status of some of his novels were based on a conviction that history cannot consort with fiction without diminution of its value as history. Hence *Durgeśnandinī* and the rest, except *Rājsimha,* were to be classified as novels, but not as historical novels, or even as novels based on history.

An author has a right to be heard when he is discussing his own work, but when every consideration has been paid to the problem Bankim was trying to solve, one cannot but feel that if the degree of historicity which he implies a historical novel must possess is accepted, there could be no historical novels. On the same argument Shakespeare's historical plays should not be called historical. A novel which has a historical setting may not be reliable as a source of accurate historical information, but it can have a place in literature as a novel, and there seems no harm in calling it a historical novel. *Durgeśnandinī* and the other six novels which have the same type of historical background must be called historical novels. It is hard to know how else to classify them. This conclusion is at any rate convenient, even though Bankim would not concede that it is correct. If it is accepted, then seven of Bankim's fourteen novels are historical novels. One, *Rājsimha,* deals with the early Muslim period; two, *Durgeśnandinī* and *Mrnāl-* *inī,* with Rajput and other heroes in the period of established Muslim power; and four, *Candraśekhar, Ānandamath, Debīcaudhurānī* and *Sītārām,* with eighteenth-century history before and after the coming of the British.

The remaining seven of Bankim's novels cannot be so easily classified. They do not form a single homogeneous group. In some the story is told for its own sake, in others it is told for an ulterior didactic purpose. Like some of his predecessors, Bankim wrote about the society in which he lived; but his approach, unlike theirs, was seldom that of a satirist. He tended to treat human relationships and social problems seriously, as problems to be solved. Satire was only an occasional weapon. He was capable of caustic and humorous condemnation, but he indulged it sparingly. Hīrālāl in *Rajanī* is said to be a caricature of a certain journalist, a high-talking, wine-drinking, very westernized Babu. Amarnāth in the same novel, who is presented as typical of his class, is chided for being self-centred. He is shown as totally unconcerned with the pressing problems of the day, such as the marriage of widows, kulin polygamy, juvenile marriage, the improvement of social conditions and the emancipation of women. The list, which is Bankim's, is interesting. A current scandal is referred to in the preface to *Indirā.* The method is characteristic.

> I have been criticized because I have expanded *Indirā* and also put up its price. If a man is promoted by favour of government or society he puts up his fees. The standard bribe for a police officer is one rupee, but when he becomes an inspector the rate goes up to two rupees. He has been promoted, so has his fee. Poor *Indirā* is entitled to say, ''I have become a big book, so why should not my price go up?''

All Bankim's novels, including the historical novels, have a love theme as their principal human interest. The nature of the theme varies. In *Rādhārānī,* the heroine chooses her own mate, and pursues him to the happy conclusion of marriage. The blind Rajanī falls in love and after numerous difficulties is happily married; and, to add greater happiness to her married life, Bankim arranges somewhat miraculously for her sight to be restored by a holy man. Another aspect of the love theme is the temporary separation or alienation of husband and wife. In *Indirā,* the hero and heroine had married young and been separated. The husband has forgotten what his wife looks like, but she recognizes him when they meet in Calcutta, and is able with the help of friends to arrange a happy reunion. Nāgendranāth and his wife Sūryamukhī, in the tragic story [*Bisabrksa*], are finally brought together again. The ending however is not always happy: the love of Nabakumār and Kapālkundalā ends in a fatal accident just when the difficulties which have beset the path of their married love are beginning to be resolved; and there is the sad plight of Pratāp and Śaibalinī, in *Candraśekhar.* They are childhood sweethearts but cannot marry because their relationship falls under the interdiction imposed by the Hindu law of affinity. Two of Bankim's lovers are widows. One of them, Kundanandinī, in [*Bisabrksa*], marries the hero and temporarily estranges him from his lawful wife, Sūrymukhī; but the estrangement does not last and the unfortunate Kundanandinī poisons herself. The other widow is Rohinī in *Krsnakānter Uil.* She lures the hero Gobindalāl away from his wife, but toward the end of a tortuous story he murders her. Polygamy also features in his marital pictures. Brajeśvar of *Debīcaudhurānī* and Sītārām of the novel which bears his name both had three legal wives. In neither case is any condemnation of multiple marriage implied, though in *Rajanī* Bankim does express disapproval of multiple marriages of the type entered into by kulin brahmins.

In certain cases Bankim's attitude to the love theme is that of a story teller. He is in them primarily concerned with his lovers as men and women and with the evolution of the action in which they participate. Yet in some of his later novels Bankim had a didactic purpose. His subject was the sanctity of orthodox Hindu marriage and in particular the nobility of wives who saw their highest duty in devotion and service to their husbands. *Debīcaudhuranī* is brought to an unconvincing end because Bankim was determined that Praphulla should be made to conform to his image of the perfect wife. She surrenders the excitement and benefits of her Robin Hood-like career to return to her husband, who at best is a colourless person. He had allowed her to be driven away from home by his father, who is a coward and a despicable rogue. Nor does it stop here. In the final paragraph she is apotheosized and invoked as the divine embodiment of Hindu wifehood. 'Come, come, Praphulla! Stand once more in the world of men and let us behold you. Stand in the society of this world and proclaim yourself, ''I am not new; I am from everlasting. I am the divine word. However often I come to you you forget me; yet I am here once more—From age to age I am born to save the good, to destroy the wicked, and establish true religion.'''

The social life of Bankim's novels is pitched at different levels, according to the status of his principal characters. He himself came of a middle-class family, and it is only when dealing with characters of this class that he is at home and that his descriptions are realistic and convincing.

Of the domestic and social life of princes and the very wealthy he knew little from first-hand experience, and what he says of them is from the outside. The best part of *Kṛṣṇakānter Uil,* which Bankim said was his favourite among the novels, is not its unhappy story and the vagaries of its main characters, but the picture it presents of middle class life in a Bengal village. Life in a Calcutta home is sketched in some detail in *Indirā.* Yet interested as he was in the problems thrown up by contemporary social life, Bankim had not an eye for the details of human behaviour and social situations the faithful delineation of which constitutes the greatest charm of at least two Bengali novelists of a later generation. He was a story teller rather than an observer of men and of their ways with one another.

Bankim's religious beliefs cannot be described adequately by reference to his novels alone. He studied the subject deeply in later life, but his conclusions are to be found in his essays *Dharmatattva* and *Kṛṣṇacarit,* which lie outside the purview of the present inquiry. Nevertheless it is clear from his novels that his position is that of an orthodox Hindu. He took his stand with the defenders of the ancient faith. He has nothing to say of Christianity and Islam as religions, though believers in these faiths occur frequently as characters in his stories, particularly Muslims. In the early novel *Kapālkundalā,* one of the characters is a kapālik, a sect whose unsavoury, esoteric rites included sexual orgies and human sacrifice; but though he speaks of these rites with distaste and makes the kapālik an unpleasant character, the teacher in Bankim had not yet come uppermost, and he does not attempt to develop his views on Tantricism. Of the Brāhmo Samāj too he says very little, though it was probably at its most powerful in the Calcutta of his day. He preached two deities, Kṛṣṇa and Śakti, the latter under different names, Caṇḍī, Kālī and Durgā. Bankim's Kṛṣṇa is not the deity of Caitanya; he is the heroic, kingly deity of the *Gītā.* Kālī and Caṇḍī respectively are the divine supporters and inspirers of the Hindu armies in *Ānandamaṭh* and *Sītārām.*

Bankim attempts to make a unity of Kṛṣṇa and Śakti in *Ānandamaṭh.* The Santāns are Vaiṣṇavas, but they also worship Kālī. Their marching song, **"Bande Mātaram,"** invokes the female goddess as the Mother. Presumably the purpose behind this attempted synthesis was to bring together the two main sects in Hinduism, the Vaiṣṇavas and the Śāktas (or Śaivas), by supplying them with a unified concept of the deity. In practice the attempt did not succeed, and its theological justification was not convincing; but the enthusiasm with which *Ānandamaṭh* was received owed much to the attempt it made to justify Hinduism and promote the pride of Hindus in their creed. Judged as a novel, *Ānandamaṭh* is faultily conceived and constructed, but as a prophetic utterance it was the most powerful word spoken in Bengal in the nineteenth century.

Bankim's art as a novelist owes certain debts to some British writers. Similarities to Scott are discernible, though they can be overstated, as has been indicated earlier. Both tell a good fast-moving story, and both are emotionally attracted to heroism in men and self-sacrifice in beautiful women. Hero worship and admiration for good women, particularly good wives, lie near the heart of most of Bankim's stories, and constitute an important legacy to Bengali literature and thought. Contemporary readers were quick to notice similarities between Bankim's novels and Scott's. They were soon to call him the 'Scott of Bengal', though the bestowing of this title may also have been occasioned by a desire to give their distinguished compatriot status among the writers of the world. In his preface to *Rajanī,* Bankim admitted that in writing that novel he was indebted to two other British authors. 'In that excellent novel by Lord Lytton, *The Last Days of Pompeii,* there is a blind flower girl named Nydia. . . . The character of Rajanī is built on this foundation.' And later on in the same preface he wrote, 'It is not common in the construction of a popular novel to make the hero and heroine speak for themselves, but it is not new. It was done first by Wilkie Collins in his *Woman in White.*' He goes on to say, with a naïveté I find hard to understand, that one of the advantages of letting the characters speak for themselves is that the author cannot be held responsible for any peculiar or unnatural things they may say. Can an author so easily shrug off the responsibilities of creation? In *Indirā* the narrative is the first person, the speaker being the heroine herself. This device had been used before him by both Defoe and Dickens whom Bankim had possibly read. There is no doubt that he gave much thought to the structure of his novels, and it is no detraction from his originality that he read the novels of British writers as part of that discipline and borrowed from them what seemed suitable to his purposes.

Certain other devices however which he may have borrowed Bankim clearly overworks. The first is that of the holy man. This character was first introduced into fiction by Bhūdeb Mukherji, and he on the whole handled him with discretion. Bankim used him excessively. No fewer than five of his novels have one. Furthermore he tended to use the holy man as a *deus ex machina* to intervene in the natural sequence of events when they seemed to have got out of hand, thereby casting doubts on the ability of the author to control the course of the action he himself had set in train. Divine or semi-divine intervention in the lives of men had had a long history before Bankim, particularly in the mythological ballads known as *maṅgalkāvya,* but there it could be justified as it involved no violation of the reader's willingness to believe. In a novel which deals with men and women in real life situations such intervention runs the danger of making the action seem incredible. Another type of *deus ex machina* by which Bankim strained the credibility of his plot is the frequent introduction of chance accidents. The evolution of the story in *Debīcaudhurānī,* to cite the most notable instance, is almost entirely directed by accidents. One might have been acceptable, as accidents do happen in everyday life, but four is too many; and in any case two of them go far beyond what is probable. They belong to the realm of romance, not to that of the realistic novel. Praphulla, the heroine, as the result of a fortunate but not incredible accident, finds herself alone in a forest at night. She wanders on blindly and eventually comes to a derelict house which she enters in search of shelter. There she finds an old man who is dying. She ministers to him, and before he dies he bequeaths all his possessions to her. They include a large hoard of gold coins. Having money but no food, she goes out to look for a village market. On the way she meets the leader of a band of robbers, who discovers the whereabouts of her fortune, but instead of appropriating it, he arranges for her to undergo a course of instruction in Sanskrit usually reserved for young brahmins. On completing the course she takes over from him as a sort of female Robin Hood. Success attends all her campaigns until the forces of government are massed against her and she is surrounded. At this moment a cyclonic storm descends on the area and the police party is scattered. A third device which Bankim overworks is that of disguise. He probably inherited it from the popular literature of the past, and within reason it is unexceptionable; but he uses it in no fewer than seven novels, and in some more than once.

> With regard to language also something needs to be said. Nowadays writers and students of language fall into two classes. The first of these is of the opinion that Bengali grammar should in every respect conform to that of Sanskrit. The other group, which includes a very large number of excellent Sanskrit scholars, thinks that what has now passed into current use should continue to be used even if it violates the rules of Sanskrit grammar. I myself incline to the views of the second group, but I am not prepared to support them in all cases and without reservation.

This passage forms part of the last paragraph in the preface to the fourth edition of *Rājsiṃha,* which has already been referred to in other connections. It was written only a year or two before his death, and may therefore be presumed to be a statement of his mature opinion. The two types of language which the protagonist groups support are *sādhu bhāṣā* and *calit bhāṣā.* Bankim's position, according to his own declaration, falls somewhere between the two extremes. He inclines towards *calit bhāṣā* but has reservations, and his inability to commit himself wholly to it is reflected in the language he used. It is neither one nor the other; and his choice which is neither *sādhu* nor *calit* is important in the history of written Bengali. It is no longer defensible to analyse Bengali prose into these two categories, as though the language of all prose composition were either *sādhu bhāṣā* or *calit bhāṣā.* Bankim took up an intermediate position; and many followed his precept without copying his practice, with the result that by the end of the century there were not two types of language, but many.

In the course of his career Bankim's style changed. To begin with he was nearer the Sanskritic extreme, but later he moved more and more in the direction of the colloquial; yet to the end he disliked and refused to adopt the fully colloquial style and vocabulary of *Hutom Pyācār Nakśa.* The first paragraph of his first novel is very Sanskritized. It is a short paragraph but it contains five Sanskrit compounds (samās), one having four constitutents. Moreover he used a number of Sanskrit loan words for which acceptable Bengali equivalents were available.

The first four lines contain no fewer than six of them. The proportion of Sanskrit words and compounds diminished with the years, and the vocabulary of his later novels is less heavy as a result. Bankim however was not able to bring himself to use the shorter verb and pronoun forms, which corresponded to those of the spoken language. In consequence his conversational passages are never natural: they are done in book language and so cannot be spoken. The otherwise excellent conversational opening in *Debīcaudhurānī* is perhaps the best example of the difficulty he was in but could not resolve. In it he lapses into short forms, but not often. The short forms in 'yeman adṛṣṭa *kare esechili*!' (what an unfortunate life you were born to!) are so right in the context; whereas 'upas *kariyā* kay din *bācibi*?' (how long do you expect to live if you eat nothing?), strikes an artificial note. One could wish that Bankim had followed the example of Pyāricād Mitra, who used the short verbs and pronouns in his conversations and the long ones in his narrative and descriptive passages, as did some of the greatest successors of Bankim in the art of novel writing.

To say so little about Bankim's style and language is to be unfair to him. He was a great writer, and his works represent a high-water mark in the history of Bengali prose. In his maturer compositions his sentences have a pleasant and easy flow. He has power, clarity and the feel of the artist for the right word; and in spite of some conservatism in his approach to the language problem, his work represents a great advance on the turgid and often difficult compositions of the orthodox school, many of whom still regarded Bengali as 'barbaric vernacular'.

It is far easier to find faults in Bankim's novels, than it is to give adequate expression to the extent of his achievement and the services he rendered to Bengali literature. When he died, prose in Bengali was firmly established as a literary mode, and the reading public, which not many years before had complained that there was hardly anything worth reading in their own language, had a library of books and articles which they read avidly and with pride and enjoyment. (pp. 61-74)

> *T. W. Clark, "Bengali Prose Fiction Up To Bankimcandra," in* The Novel in India: Its Birth and Development, *edited by T. W. Clark, George Allen & Unwin Ltd., 1970, pp. 21-74.*

S. K. BOSE (essay date 1974)

[*Bose details the salient features of Chatterji's novels, providing also a brief survey of the author's principal works of nonfiction.*]

Bankim has been described as "the great novelist of India during the 19th century", or more appropriately perhaps as "the first great creative genius of modern India" [see excerpt by R. W. Frazer dated 1898]. He was indeed the maker of a literature. He breathed into his neglected mother tongue the finest spirit of a master mind and put it on a footing of unquestioned elegance and dignity. In a way he resembled the English romantics who broke away from the dry 18th century tradition to create a new world of beauty and romance. Bankim too freed literature from various kinds of shackles and drawbacks to make it instinct with a new creative spirit. In the process he brought language down from the plane of pedantry to the plane of the people, so that it might serve them as a medium of instruction as well as of entertainment, without, however, losing its grace, elegance and dignity.

Bankim's primary claim to recognition rests, of course, on his novels. Indeed it was he who created the Bengali novel in its present form. Before his advent Bengali literature had no novels in the true sense of the term—it had only tales, translations and adaptations. The nearest approximation to novels were the sketches. . . . *Alaler Gharer Dulal* had most of the characteristics of a full-fledged novel, but it lacked the depth, dimension and discernment which ordinarily characterise a novel. It was left to Bankim to create novel as a literary form in Bengali. His maiden offering, *Durgeshnandini*, itself became a landmark in the development of Bengali novel, even though it was not artistically a very mature work. But it held out definite promise which found full flowering in his very next fiction, *Kapalkundala.*

What indeed were the characteristics of Bankim's novels? It is generally admitted that the form of his novel is West-inspired. "He created in India a school of fiction on the Western model". That he had a deep acquaintance with the Western masters of fiction, like Sir Walter Scott, Lord Lytton and others, is obvious. It is also apparent that in his youthful days his inherent urge for artistic self-expression derived strength and support from his study of the Western literature. This is one point on which some of his Indian critics are sore with him. They think that Bankim has dished up Western stuff in an Indian garb.

But a deeper analysis will show that the content of his novels is very much Eastern. Even in his early fictions like *Durgeshnandini* and *Kapalkundala*, where he is a pure artist unburdened with a message, he paints characters like Tilottama having all the qualities of an Indian virgin girl, loving but bashful, sweet and selfless in love and devotion. Similarly *Kapalkundala* is covered with the weird aura typical of the mysterious East. The values he upholds through his characters and situations in respect of human relations generally and in domestic matters particularly are Eastern values. At places he introduces poetic justice only to bring out the triumph of the good and the suffering of the sinful. Many of his critics regretfully feel that he brought Rohini's life to an inglorious end only to punish the sinning woman. Shaibalini too has to atone painfully for her love out of wedlock for Pratap; Bankim's preoccupation with the Indian values of morality and conduct are palpable. At the same time modern trends also left a deep impress upon his works. For instance, he brought in sentiments which were contrary to the then prevailing social mores, namely, premarital love, which had no social sanction those days. Similarly widow remarriage, the most burning question of the day, is the central theme of two of his novels. These were the reflections of the tensions and strains consequent upon the passing out of the old order and the advent of the new at the momentous juncture of which stood Bankim and his works. He borrowed a Western form no doubt but made it thoroughly instinct with Indian spirit.

Any categorisation of Bankim's novels is bound to be overlapping. Most of them have some common characteristics which are basic to them. Depending on emphasis, however, they can be put into four broad groups—romantic, historical, social and novels with a purpose. But, once again, the basic traits of these four broad categories of fiction overlap. Essentially he was a romanticist—even his social novels have not escaped the romantic touch. A romance deals with life no doubt but, at the same time, seeks to transfigure it, emphasising its beauty and passion, its heroic and imaginative aspects. In a novel, art tends towards the actual conditions of life; in a romance, it lifts life itself to a higher plane. From this point of view, his *Durgeshnandini, Kapalkundala, Mrinalini, Chandrashekhar, Anandamath, Devi Chaudhurani, Sitaram*—all are romantic.

They are no doubt built round real life, mostly against the background of the historical times, but they so transfigure life itself that it becomes a beautiful or a tragic dream, depending on the trend of the story.

Skillful plot construction, mastery of character drawing, sparkling flow of narration, splendour of description—these are some of the characteristics his novels have in abundance. The romantic quality of his novels is enchanting. But some of his fictions, *Chandrashekhar* and *Sitaram,* for instance, suffer from a surfeit of romance. Also in the wide sweep of his imagination, Bankim did not hesitate to take the help of miracle and accident. They sometimes detract from the artistic effect of his works. Even then it must be said that Bankim had a remarkable capacity for plot construction. In most, though not all, cases he fitted accidents and miracles easily and skillfully into the story without jarring upon the readers' artistic sensibility. Above all Bankim's story-telling is spell-binding.

As a novelist, Bankim belonged to the 19th century tradition. Novel as a form of art has travelled long distances from that tradition to the present day. The ideas and techniques of novels have completely changed. The modern fiction is analytical, psychological; it tends to probe deeper and deeper into the human psyche instead of going in for charming tales or entrancing narratives. Naturally the 19th century character of Bankim's fictions may not be set up to the modern liking. Even then Bankim's works continue to be greatly popular, even as classics are popular. They have a basic core of beauty and charm, an elegance and grandeur, which age cannot wither. These qualities are above the changing fashions in literary taste and will continue to claim admiring attention.

It is also interesting to note that Bankim himself turned towards a type of fiction which might be said to have marked the faint beginnings of the psychological fiction in Bengali literature. His *Rajani,* wherein the *dramatis personae* speak subjectively, and his *Indira,* wherein the heroine speaks in her own person, employ just the methods which turn from events in the physical world towards changes in the psychical.

Bankim's passion for history burns bright throughout his novels, earning him the appellation "the Sir Walter Scott of Bengal". Historical novels must deal with historical personages and situations. But must they conform strictly to the facts and details of history? There is a difference of opinion on this point. Generally it may be said that a historical novel must broadly conform to history, but at the same time the writer's imagination must not be denied a free play. Not that history should be tampered with. But the writer should have sufficient freedom to enliven the dry bones of history.

Generally speaking Bankim did not make a fetish of history. Romesh Chandra Dutt, an eminent historian and Bankim's disciple in fiction-writing, gave historical accuracy the first place in his novels. But not so Bankim, who, in most of his fictions, took the barest cue from history to build his own human story thereon. Sometimes he linked up his story with a larger historical background. In *Kapalkundala,* for instance, the historical episode linking Lutf Unnisa with Nobokumar on the one hand and the Mughal court in Agra on the other might seem irrelevant, but he fitted it in the plot very skilfully to create an additional interest in the story. Many of his novels can thus be called semi-historical. Aware of this self-imposed limitation on borrowing from history, he hesitated to call any of his novels historical except *Rajsinha*—he called it his first and only historical novel. Perhaps he was a little too unkind towards his first child, *Durgeshnandini,* which has all the qualities of an historical novel.

The story of *Rajsinha* is a part of the history of the conflicts Aurangzeb had with the Rajput chiefs. *Rajsinha* broadly conforms to history. Nowhere are the facts of history coloured or discoloured either by imaginative exuberance or by prejudice. (pp. 53-6)

Originating from a simple incident of feminine freak, the conflict takes the dimension of a large-scale warfare between the Rajputs and the Mughals in which the latter meet with repeated discomfitures. The novel gives a magnificent description of the course of the war and the movement of the entire Mughal army including the Emperor who, owing to Rajsinha's superior war strategy, are locked up in an insurmountable mountain pass. The novel is a succession of dazzling events coming with a thrilling rapidity and keeps the readers spell-bound. Here Bankim's story-telling is at its best, his narrative art at its grandest. The characters are most fascinatingly drawn. Apart from Chanchalkumari and Rajsinha, those of Nirmalkumari and Maniklal and of Mobarak and Zebunnisa are some of the finest on Bankim's portrait gallery. As a work of art, it is one of Bankim's best.

Another important fiction, *Chandrashekhar* has again got an historical background—the conflict between Nawab Mir Kashim of Bengal and the English. Bankim seems to have been particularly interested in those twilight periods of history which depict the progressive decline of the Muslim rule and the gradual advent of the English in India. Various aspects of the chaos and anarchy coming in the wake of that tremendous power vacuum occur again and again in his fictions. . . . But in *Chandrashekhar,* as in some of his other fictions, history is less important than the human story. Here Bankim links up the turmoil in the life of three individuals with the bigger turmoil on the political front, that is, the conflict between the Nawab and the English. (p. 57)

We have in Bankim's works some fine male characters. They are however drawn in rather simple outline without much of a variety or complexity in them. From that point of view his male side characters are more interesting, with all their traits, good or bad. Bankim, however, poured out all the warmth and fervour of his imagination on his female characters. They are most impressive. The dynamic force that goes into his skilful plot construction flows mostly from his female characters. Among them we have the loving but frustrated housewife, Surjamukhi, the wily widow Rohini, so unlike the mutely suffering Kundanandini, the resourceful Bimala who avenged her husband's murder on Katlu Khan and Shaibalini who is ever restless in her burning passion for Pratap. There are other such characters also.

Bankim's novels are, by and large, fine works of art, and as a novelist he occupies a position of pre-eminence. But apart from these, a large body of non-fiction writing flowed from his pen in profusion which constituted his contribution to thought. It is in itself remarkable enough to earn him an undying place in the literature of intellection. In this group fall the innumerable essays and reviews he contributed to the *Bangadarshan* or wrote otherwise, essays and dissertations on history, sociology, religion, archaeology, literature and even science. These were in addition to his two monumental works, *Krishnacharitra* and *Dharmatattwa,* and of course *Kamalakanta* which is a class by itself and stands apart.

It is a tribute to Bankim's intellectual keenness that as early as in the seventies of the last century he had grasped the intricacies of Western science and taken pains to elucidate the same on the pages of the *Bangadarshan* in simple but forceful Bengali so as to make them intelligible to the people at large. These essays compiled under the title *Vijnan Rahasya* deal with various topics like the solar system, the antiquity of man, motion and sound and so on. Bankim deeply deplored the lack of cultivation of science in India. With all his religious inclination, he was an advocate of materialism to the extent that he considered scientific culture essential to the country's rejuvenation. He said: "If you serve science, science will serve you, if you are devoted to science, science will be devoted to you. But if you ignore science it will become your mortal . . .". He realised that the power and prosperity of modern Europe was due to science. As regards India, he felt that the British had got hold over it because of their scientific superiority. Indeed with the help of their scientific knowledge the British were only emasculating the Indians. Bankim, therefore, welcomed a spell of British rule, so that some scientific spirit, some Western materialism, might be injected into the Indians who had become too other worldly. In his *Dharmatattwa,* the preceptor recommends a study of the natural and social sciences under the tutelage of the West before one could realise God through religious pursuits. Bankim was attempting something like a bridge-building between science and religion.

In another group of essays he deals with literary subjects like Uttararamcharit, Shakuntala, Miranda, Desdemona and so on. His book reviews themselves were excellent pieces of literary criticism which brought out his erudition as well as discernment. Some of these represent an early effort in the study of comparative literature.

The group of essays in which he deals with the social and historical subjects are most important. They are his own solutions to the various contemporary problems including that of national revival. With him the first premise of a nation's progress is its own history. "A nation without history is destined to suffer infinitely", he says. His greatest regret was that India had no tradition of history. If Europeans go on bird shooting, it is recorded in history. But we Indians had no sense of history, he felt. A nation that is ignorant of its past cannot be great. His utmost effort, therefore, was to reconstruct his country's past out of the materials available at that time. (pp. 58-9)

In an essay entitled *Bharat Kalanka,* he tried to show that a sense of nationality and craving for independence were lacking among the ancient Indians who had no collective consciousness for political action or political good. Indeed they appear to have been indifferent to the question whether the ruler was a son of the soil or an outsider. In the entire range of ancient Indian literature and holy texts, there are many virtues depicted in glowing terms but not nationalism as we understand it. Independence and nationality are England's two gifts to India for which Bankim is beholden to the British people. This brings us to another essay, **"Bharatvarsher Swadhinata Ebang Paradhinata"** (India's Independence and Slavery), wherein he objectively analyses the merits and demerits of the British rule in India compared to the Hindu period of history. With a frankness not ordinarily expected of a government official, he points out the various disabilities India suffered from under a ruler who did not belong to this country and was an absentee king. He refers in particular to the Home Charges which India had to pay for England's benefit and to the system of judicial discrimination under which an Indian was not entitled to trying an Englishman (this injustice was sought to be remedied through the Ilbert Bill). But Bankim does not fail to notice that in ancient India the caste system and Brahminocracy enforced greater discrimination on the people. (pp. 59-60)

In another group of writings Bankim emerges as a propounder of socio-economic views which were certainly radical by the contemporary standard. In a masterly essay, "**Bangadesher Krishak**" (Bengal's Peasantry), he strongly repudiated the claim that the country was prospering under the British rule. He propounds the thesis that the prosperity of the country was not the prosperity of the upper echelons of the society but of the people as a whole, notably the poor peasantry who constitute the vast majority of the population. (p. 60)

Bankim's *Kamalakanta* is a unique piece of literary composition. It is laughter and lyricism, patriotism and politics, all rolled into one. It defies traditional literary classification. Its nearest approximation is perhaps De Quincey's *The Confessions of an English Opium-Eater*. Kamalakanta, the hero of the book, is nothing if not a confirmed opium-eater. But unlike in De Quincey's book he does not need opium to cure his rheumatism or toothache. Opium is a part of his existence. It is his romantic passport to the world of fancy and thought. In many ways, *Kamalakanta* is more romantic than *The Confessions*. Here Bankim's imagination has its fullest play soaring high, unfettered by the artificial restraints imposed by a formal composition.

Kamalakanta, the central figure of the book, is a fascinating character. He is a half-crazy, mysterious opium-eater, who is a poet, philosopher, sociologist, politician, patriot and a confirmed idler. He subsists upon the free milk supplied to him by a milkwoman, Prasanna by name, out of sheer pity for the penniless Brahmin, and also enjoys the patronage of a local zamindar, Nasiram Babu. All the earthly possession Kamalakanta has is a *daptar* or a bundle of papers containing his ravings and fantasies which is supposed to be a sure antidote to insomnia. It seems that Bankim had thoughts and ideas which he could not afford to express through his novels and dissertations but called for a semi-romantic and semi-satirical expression through an unconventional and out-of-the-way character like Kamalakanta who is Bankim himself in an informal garb. There may be difference of opinion about Bankim's other works but not about *Kamalakanta*.

The book is divided into three parts: the first part, *Kamalakanter Daptar*, is a collection of personal essays, some written in a light vein and some, in serious; the second part is "**Kamalakanter Patra**", a collection of letters supposed to have been written by Kamalakanta to the editor of the *Bangadarshan*, all sparkling with beautiful humour and jokes; and the third part, "**Kamalakanter Jabanbandi**", is Kamalakanta's deposition in a court of law in a cow-theft case and one of Bankim's masterly creations. (p. 63)

Kamalakanta . . . is a rhapsodic composition keyed to a high pitch of imagination. It contains humour of the most sparkling type, satire on the follies and foibles of the age, progressive ideas on the socio-polity and social justice and above all a magnificent outburst of patriotism raised to the level of religious fervour. Kamalakanta is the first conscious patriot of Bengali literature, he is also its first socialist philosopher. (p. 68)

S. K. Bose, in his Bankim Chandra Chatterji, *Publications Division, Ministry of Information and Broadcasting, 1974, 152 p.*

V. S. NARAVANE   (essay date 1985)

[*Naravane offers a general evaluation of both the major limitations and pioneering strengths of Chatterji's fiction, discussing also the quality of his ideas and their seminal influence on Indian culture.*]

[Let us] make a critical assessment of the entire range of Bankim Chandra's fiction. The defects of his novels are so glaring that even an admirer of Bankim cannot overlook them. His treatment of the historical context is often slipshod. One need not expect strict adherence to historical facts because, as he himself once said in reply to a critic, "a novel is a novel, not a history book". Nevertheless a historical novelist is expected to make a thorough study of the period in which he places his story. Bankim does not seem to have done this. Apart from factual errors, he does not convey even the spirit and flavour of Mughal or Rajput history. In some of his novels, the historical and the romantic aspects are very poorly integrated; the romantic subplot seems to have hardly any connection with the clash of political forces. Bankim's style is often rhetorical and mawkish. Many of his characters appear crude and unconvincing—bandit queens and other lovely women with daggers, militant ascetics, swashbuckling heroes who fight duels and perform impossible feats. Moreover, chance and fortuitous events are sometimes brought into Bankim's novels to provide solutions which might otherwise have been difficult. To mention only one example, a cyclonic storm suddenly sweeps Kapalakundala into the swirling river at a crucial moment when she was unable to decide whether or not she should return home with her husband.

But when all these limitations are conceded, Bankim still emerges from his creative work as a pioneer in a literary genre which held immense possibilities for the future. Though Ishwar Chandra Vidyasagar and some others had laid the foundations of a modern prose style, it was Bankim who first demonstrated the effectiveness of this style in fiction. In the words of a historian of Bengali literature, "Bankim's defects were the birth pangs of the Bengali novel" [see excerpt by J. C. Ghosh dated 1948]. He introduced the techniques of the English novel into India while remaining firmly rooted to his national tradition. His imagination ranged over a wide field and in his novels he has touched upon every important aspect of Indian life political, social, economic, religious, even educational. Bankim did not write for superficial entertainment. His novels are marked by sincerity of purpose. Even those who disagree with his ideas must recognise that Bankim, through his novels, kindled patriotic fervour in the hearts of thousands of readers. We get in his works not only glimpses of the life and culture of India but also of the variety and beauty of the landscape, flora and fauna with which nature has so lavishly endowed this country. Bankim Chandra's sensitiveness to the beauty and peace of nature can be seen in many wonderful passages, particularly those in which he describes the forest, the sea and the river. (pp. 23-4)

We have . . . looked at Bankim Chandra Chatterji as a literary artist. We saw that, in spite of many limitations, he brought about a revolution in Bengali literature, introduced a new prose style and a new, modern approach to fiction. When we consider him in the role of a thinker, we again see the same situation. In some ways his ideas seem retrograde; and yet his vision of national freedom had a deep influence on the nationalist movement.

Sometimes one is tempted to draw a sharp line of division between 'progressive' and 'reactionary' thinkers. Some historians of modern India have tried to present a contrast between progressives and reformers like Rammohan Roy and Keshav Chandra Sen, and 'revivalists' and 'reactionaries' like Bankim Chandra and Dayananda Saraswati. Such generalizations can be misleading. Although they were revivalists in the sense that they derived their inspiration from the ancient Hindu scriptures, Dayananda and Bankim also expressed ideas which were considered revolutionary in their age.

To make a fair assessment of Bankim's role as a thinker, a few specific questions can be asked. Was his attitude towards modern western influences negative, and did he glorify uncritically everything that ancient India has bequeathed? Was he a defender of the *status quo* in social affairs, and did he oppose social reforms? Was he communal and anti-Muslim in his outlook on Indian history? The first question can be answered quite easily. It was simply not possible for anyone of Bankim's intellectual calibre to reject the West entirely. . . . [He] was deeply influenced by western rationalism, utilitarianism and positivism and of course English literature, particularly essay, biography and fiction. On many points he conceded that India had much to learn from the West. For instance, he asserted that the very concept of patriotism was something which the west had evolved. He believed strongly that, in evaluating religion, the rational and historical outlook of the west should be combined with devotion and faith. His caricatures of western ways were aimed only at those Indians who had lost their moorings and whose imitation of the west was part of their flattery of western rulers.

On the question of social reform, it must be admitted that Bankim was, on the whole, cautious, even half-hearted in endorsing measures which involved a radical departure from old conventions. While Ishwar Chandra Vidyasagar and his fellow reformers were waging a struggle against orthodoxy and trying to eradicate social evils like child marriage and the oppression of widows, Bankim was extremely reluctant to support legal measures to ban child marriage and permit widow remarriage. Nor did he raise his voice against the inequities of the caste system. It may seem surprising that Bankim, so much ahead of his time in the literary field, and so radical in his political visions, should take up [a] retrograde position on questions of social reform. However, it is not altogether unusual for social conservatism to go hand in hand with forward looking approaches in other spheres. A generation after Bankim Chandra, Lokamanya Tilak also expressed extremely radical views in politics while leaning towards Brahmanical orthodoxy on other issues.

From Bankim Chandra's novels and religious writings some people gathered the impression that he was against Islam and thought in terms of a 'Hindu India'. A careful reading of his works does not bear out this charge. He undoubtedly derived inspiration from Hinduism. He does not seem to have gone deeply into other faiths. Rammohan Roy was steeped in Islamic theology. Keshav Chandra had a profound knowledge of Christian history and doctrine. Unlike them, Bankim Chandra was satisfied with his Hindu heritage. But nowhere has he written anything disrespectful of Islam. His references to some of the enlightened Muslim kings—particularly Akbar—are appreciative. In some of his novels Muslim characters emerge in a more favourable light than Hindu characters. Muslim saints and *fakirs* are referred to in respectful terms. To glorify the heroism of Rajput or Maratha leaders against decadent Muslim rulers cannot be taken as hostility towards Muslims.

In conclusion, it would be appropriate to [emphasize] those features of Bankim Chandra's art and thought which made him such an important figure in the history of India in the nineteenth century. One of the things that we notice markedly in his novels and essays is his closeness to the actual life of the common people in the villages. At a time when most writers confined their attention to the upper classes, Bankim introduced in his novels peasants both Hindu and Muslim, wandering singers, artisans, and many other people representing rural India. Although his heroes and heroines are drawn from the upper classes and the aristocracy, they are shown in intimate contact with ordinary people. In his political novels Bankim shows at least a vague awareness of the fact that the struggle for freedom must draw into its orbit the masses in the countryside and should not remain limited to city intellectuals.

Bankim was among the first influential writers in modern times to think in terms of India as a whole. His interest was not limited to Bengal. He draws his characters from, and places his actions in, other parts of India, such as Bihar, Orissa, Assam, Rajasthan, Gujarat, Maharashtra and Punjab. The Mother who symbolizes India is the common mother of all Indians, wherever they may live and to whichever creed or social class they may belong.

Yet another point that we notice in Bankim's writings is his strong faith in education as the key to national progress and eventually national freedom. His emphasis on education was part of his rationalist-humanist outlook. Introduction of modern education was, in his view, one of the positive features of British rule in India. Bankim felt that the removal of social ills was possible only through education. On this point he differed from reformers like Ishwar Chandra Vidyasagar. On questions such as abolition of polygamy and child-marriage, the reformers had a two-fold approach. In the first place, they appealed to *Dharmashastras* and tried to show that the scriptures did not support these customs which were later accretions. Secondly, they said that the State must step in and enact laws which would make such practices illegal. Bankim Chandra felt that an appeal to ancient texts would not be effective against customs and institutions based on *lokachara* (popular conventions). Nor was government interference the answer. Only through education could people be persuaded to re-examine and ultimately reject beliefs and practices that are irrational and unjust. Incidentally, Bankim was one of the first to realize that only the mother-tongue can be a natural medium of instruction at lower levels of education.

Above all, Bankim's writings are permeated by a spirit of patriotism which no other writer before him had been able to express as effectively as he did. His intense love for India comes out through everything he wrote. At a time when the country was politically subjugated and economically undeveloped, Bankim retained his faith in the latent power of the Indian spirit. Through his immortal song, **"Vande Mataram,"** and through the examples of heroism and self-sacrifice which he portrayed in his novels, Bankim Chandra tried to kindle among his countrymen a sense of pride in their country, a sense of self-confidence and dignity. Two decades later, Swami Vivekananda also exhorted Indians to realize the immense latent strength of their motherland, to have faith in her future. These two great Indians of the nineteenth century, Swami Vivekananda and Bankim Chandra Chatterji, brought the vital message of vigorous, positive thinking and dynamic action. Swami Vivekananda did this through his speeches and discourses, Bankim through his powerful pen. They prepared the psychological background for that epic struggle which India was destined to wage a generation later. (pp. 27-9)

V. S. Naravane, "Bankim Chandra Chatterji: His Life, Work and Influence," in Indian Horizons, *Vol. XXXIV, Nos. 3-4, 1985, pp. 8-29.*

ADDITIONAL BIBLIOGRAPHY

Chatterjee, Enakshi. "Bankim Chandra Chatterji—His Impact on Bengal and India." *Indian & Foreign Review* 15, No. 18 (1 July 1978): 19-20.
> Briefly outlines the importance of Chatterji and his works to the development of Indian nationalism and culture.

Clark, T. W. "The Role of Bankimcandra in the Development of Nationalism." In *Historians of India, Pakistan and Ceylon,* edited by C. H. Philips, pp. 429-45. Historical Writing on the Peoples of Asia. London: Oxford University Press, 1961.
> Explores Chatterji's contribution to the evolution of Indian nationalism.

Das, Matilal. *Bankim Chandra, Prophet of the Indian Renaissance: His Life and Art.* Calcutta: Gopaldas Majumdar, 1938, 189 p.
> A laudatory tribute to Chatterji and his works.

Haldar, M. K. Introduction to *Renaissance and Reaction in Nineteenth Century Bengal,* by Bankim Chandra Chattopadhyay, translated by M. K. Haldar, pp. 1-146. Calcutta: Minerva Associates Publications, 1977.
> A lengthy biocritical introduction to Haldar's translation of Chatterji's *Samya.*

Kripalani, Krishna. *Modern Indian Literature: A Panoramic Glimpse.* Bombay: Nirmala Sadanand Publishers, 1968, 131 p.
> Contains a brief summary of Chatterji's importance to Indian literature.

Rangarajan, V. *"Vande Mataram."* Madras: Sister Nivedita Academy, 1977, 55 p.
> Examines the history of Chatterji's song "Vande Mataram"—its composition, role in the growth of Indian nationalism, and cultural significance for the country as a whole.

Marcus (Andrew Hislop) Clarke

1846-1881

Australian novelist, short story and sketch writer, essayist, and dramatist.

Clarke is chiefly remembered for *His Natural Life,* a novel depicting Australian penal conditions during the colonial period of the nineteenth century. One of the first works of fiction written in Australia to gain critical attention abroad, the novel recreates in gruesome detail the dehumanizing nature of what was euphemistically referred to in Clarke's day as the ''System.'' While Clarke wrote a number of other works, none of these have generated such extensive critical commentary as *His Natural Life.* Critics have acknowledged the ambitious themes of the novel: colonial displacement, social and spiritual alienation, and humankind's capacity for good and evil. However, commentators also agree that *His Natural Life* is flawed in important respects, citing in particular its melodramatic plot and sensational journalistic style. Nevertheless, the graphic force of *His Natural Life* continues to elicit critical admiration, and many scholars believe that although the work eludes unequivocal classification as a masterpiece, it exhibits, in the words of one reviewer, a ''core of greatness.''

Clarke was born in London and raised by his father, a well-to-do barrister. At the age of twelve, Clarke was sent to Highgate School, where he displayed literary talent and an interest in the classics. Clarke's father died when his son was sixteen, leaving a much smaller inheritance than expected. Forced to support himself, Clarke emigrated to Australia, where, with the help of an uncle already established in the country, he hoped to take advantage of greater opportunities for earning a living. Some critics have linked this early dislocation to Clarke's later treatment of the themes of alienation and displacement in *His Natural Life* and other works. Clarke arrived in Victoria, Australia, in 1863, and tried banking and then sheep farming at an outback station. Neither occupation suited his restless nature, though exposure to the outback scenery and way of life influenced him and provided him with material he later used in his fiction. The stories contained in the collection *Holiday Peak,* for example, were largely inspired by Clarke's experience in the bush. The outback setting, established by Clarke, became an important element in the later, more critically acclaimed short stories of Henry Lawson.

While working in the outback, Clarke began writing sketches for various Australian periodicals. These sketches were well received, and, as a result, he was asked to become theater critic and leader-writer for the Melbourne *Argus* in 1867. Clarke's literary interests and his abilities as a conversationalist made him welcome in Melbourne, the center for a growing coterie of writers and poets. Known for his colorful, bohemian lifestyle, he became one of the leaders of this society. At this time, Clarke ventured into magazine publishing. In 1868 he acquired the *Colonial Monthly,* in which he serialized his first novel, *Long Odds,* and the following year he founded the comic weekly *Humbug.* Both magazines went bankrupt, and these failures, combined with his marriage to actress Marian Dunn in 1869 and the births of their six children, placed Clarke in financial difficulties that haunted him for the rest of his life. Critics note that much of Clarke's literary output during his

last years was determined by his relationship with creditors and moneylenders; always in debt, Clarke squandered his talents on inconsequential dramatic works and novels of little substance.

In 1870 Clarke was appointed secretary to the trustees of the public library in Melbourne, where he researched records of the early settlement of Australia. One outcome of this research was his story collection *Old Tales of a Young Country,* which appeared in 1871. He also convinced the owners of the *Australian Journal* that a trip to Tasmania for research into convict records would produce a popular ''sensation novel'' for the newspaper, and the result, *His Natural Life,* was serialized in the *Journal* from 1870 to 1872. The novel received a lukewarm reception in its serialized form. Clarke made major revisions, and when it was published as a book in 1874, *His Natural Life* met with critical acclaim. Its meager sales did not alleviate Clarke's financial problems, however, and he declared bankruptcy in 1874. He had hopes of becoming head librarian, but monetary embarrassments and his publication of a series of essays and a play offensive to religious and political leaders kept him from the post. This disappointment, along with overwork and the stress of another bankruptcy, contributed to his illness and death in 1881.

Though Clarke was a prolific writer, few of his works other than *His Natural Life* are singled out for major critical comment. There has been some interest in his short stories and essays, but most critics dismiss his theatrical pieces and other novels as undistinguished. The plot of *His Natural Life* centers on an Englishman, Richard Devine, who is blamed for a murder he did not commit and transported as a convict to Australia. A series of coincidences begin aboard the transport ship, and Devine, now known as Rufus Dawes, becomes involved with the real murderer and with the Reverend North, who withholds information about the crime that might have saved Dawes from his fate. In a multiplication of brutal incidents, Dawes is subjected to the worst punishments meted out to recalcitrant prisoners: he is flogged, placed in irons, and tortured on a suspended frame, forms of discipline not unknown in the prison settlements of nineteenth-century Australia and employed for even minor infractions. Mistaken identity, amnesia, and narrowly missed opportunities for vindication also play a part in Dawes's tragic story. His one ray of hope during this ordeal is his love for the prison commander's wife, Sylvia Frere. They escape from prison and die in each other's arms during a shipwreck, finally free from the bondage of their misfortunes.

In the years immediately following Clarke's death, *His Natural Life* became so popular that in 1884 Arthur Patchett Martin was able to describe it as "the one standard Australian work of fiction." Martin was not completely enthusiastic about the novel, however, and his mixed reaction to it has typified the history of critical response to the work. While many critics have on the one hand praised its powerful subject matter and vivid characterization, they have also objected to the massive convolutions of its plot and sub-plot. In addition, reviewers have consistently faulted the novel's sentimental and melodramatic elements, pointing out that Clarke misses no opportunity to manipulate the reader with emotion-laden detail and that the plot sometimes lacks all semblance of realism. Commentators have remarked that Clarke's style enhances this unbelievability, for his journalistic training caused him to heighten and intensify passages to highlight dramatic incident: where he intended drama and pathos, melodrama and sentimentality emerge. Recent critics of *His Natural Life*, however, have focused on those elements of the novel—particularly character, imagery, and theme—that are unspoiled by the story's melodrama and sentimentality. Commentators have noted that the character of Reverend North is realized with great psychological penetration, and that there are structural patterns of prison and animal imagery in the novel that illuminate conflicting themes of degradation and regeneration. The novel has also been interpreted as an imaginative rendering of alienation resulting from the Australian colonial experience. Although today critics still agree that *His Natural Life* suffers from Clarke's heavy-handed use of melodrama, its powerful themes of colonial dislocation and inhumanity are of continuing interest. As John Colmer states, "The strength of the novel lies in its tribute to man's capacity to endure: this makes it a very Australian work. It also lies in its profound image of colonial society and of the alienated individual."

PRINCIPAL WORKS

Long Odds   (novel)   1869
The Peripatetic Philosopher   (essays)   1869
Old Tales of a Young Country   (short stories)   1871
Holiday Peak, and Other Tales   (short stories and sketches)   1873
His Natural Life   (novel)   1874; also published as *For the Term of His Natural Life*, 1882
'Twixt Shadow and Shine   (novel)   1875

Four Stories High   (short stories and sketches)   1877
The Future Australian Race   (essay)   1877
Civilization without Delusion   (essay)   1880
The Mystery of Major Molineux, and Human Repetends (short stories)   1881
The Marcus Clarke Memorial Volume   (short stories, sketches, essays, and poetry)   1884
Sensational Tales   (short stories)   1886
The Austral Edition of the Selected Works of Marcus Clarke (short stories, sketches, essays, and poetry)   1890
Chidiock Tichbourne; or, The Catholic Conspiracy (novel)   1893
A Colonial City: High and Low Life—Selected Journalism of Marcus Clarke   (essays and sketches)   1972
Marcus Clarke   (novel, short stories, and essays)   1976

*This work was originally published in the periodical the *Australian Journal* in 1874-75.

THE SPECTATOR   (essay date 1875)

[*In the following excerpt, the critic reviews* His Natural Life.]

We can hardly recommend ordinary readers of fiction to get and peruse the terrible and tragic story of an innocent convict's life, which Mr. Marcus Clarke has here told for us, with a grim fidelity to the natural history of convict ships and penal settlements which is as revolting as it is unquestionably powerful. From the first chapter [of *His Natural Life*], in which the "Malabar" sets sail with her crew of wretched malefactors for Hobart Town, to the last, in which the innocent convict escapes from his torture-prison only to find his fate in the foundering of the "Lady Franklin," Mr. Marcus Clarke paints for us with a frightful realism, which makes it impossible not to see vividly the scenes he describes, the incidents of a society in which crime and vice, crowded together in foul decomposing masses, fester and ferment on the one side, and coarse authority, petrified by routine into hardness and indifference, or brutal and insolent courage, proud of its unflinching nerve in the presence of cowering guilt, tyrannises and tramples on the other side. Mr. Clarke's familiarity with all the most humble details of the life of a penal settlement is far too minute, and his power of reproducing them far too graphic, to render this powerful book fit for general perusal. (p. 1426)

Mr. Clarke's power is greater in painting the moral incidents and physical scenery of the life he deals with, than in painting individual character. His hero is never clear to us, from beginning to end. There are evidences here and there, especially in the delineation of the child Sylvia, and of John Rex's mistress, Sarah Purfoy, as she is at first called, also in the outline of Captain Maurice Frere, the false, bold miscreant who is the evil genius of the story, and in the striking picture of the drinking chaplain's agony of soul when he finds how his own vice paralyses his power to save the prisoners committed to his charge from the wickedest cruelty and oppression, that Mr. Clarke might, if he took pains, draw individual character as vigorously as he draws both physical and moral scenery. But in this story, at all events, he has not done so. He has put in a considerable number of clever superficial sketches, both of criminals and their superiors. One has a distinct superficial image in one's mind of good, conventional Captain Vickers, and vain, silly Mrs. Vickers, with a genuine woman's courage in her none the less; as well as of their wilful, loving, little daughter Sylvia; of swindling John Rex, and brazen, unscrupulous Sarah Purfoy; of the hideous giant, Gabbett, and the cunning, dwarfish Vetch; of the brutal tyrant, Burgess, and the puling parson, Meekin; of Frere, with his insolence, falsehood, and presence of mind, and of North, with his shame and his culture, his religious passion and his despair. But the deeper the picture goes,—except, *perhaps,* in the drinking chaplain's case,—the vaguer it becomes. As Sylvia grows up from the child into the woman, we see her less and less clearly. "Good Mr. Dawes," and violent, bitter, hardened Mr. Dawes, are never made to us quite the same person, and neither of them is really understood by the reader. The value of the book is not in its studies of character, but in its physical and moral scenery. The general effects are wonderfully vivid; the studies of human nature, often striking at first, become less so as more touches are added. Nothing grimmer, or more likely to dwell on the imagination, than this fearful picture of tyrants and slaves, of devils ruling and devils rebelling, was ever painted. (p. 1427)

> *"An Australian Novelist," in* The Spectator, *Vol. 48, No. 2472, November 13, 1875, pp. 1426-28.*

ARTHUR PATCHETT MARTIN (essay date 1884)

[*In the following excerpt, Martin praises Clarke's* His Natural Life *for its style and narrative power, but finds the novel artistically flawed by its unsympathetic depiction of the protagonist and its lack of humor.*]

His Natural Life is as yet the one standard Australian work of fiction. Originally published in an obscure Melbourne periodical, it has been honoured by republication in England and America, and by translation into more than one European language. The testimony of competent literary critics as to its power and ability is great and ever growing. The present Lord Lytton declared that it so fascinated him that he could not lay it down until he had finished it, and Lord Rosebery has I believe recently expressed, during his visit to Melbourne, the opinion that he considers it a greater novel than *Oliver Twist.*

As a description of physical suffering and moral degradation, nothing can surpass the appalling realism of such chapters of *His Natural Life* as those headed "One Hundred Lashes," "The Valley of the Shadow of Death," "Breaking a Man's Spirit," "The Longest Straw." Nor can it be denied that his Australian novel is worthy to rank with the most powerful of English or French sensational stories; it has in fact this great advantage over any even by such masters of their craft as Wilkie Collins or Charles Reade—its underlying basis of fact and reality. But in my opinion grave exception must be taken to *His Natural Life* as a work of art. In reading it we are filled to overflowing with a sense of the repulsive cruelty to which the wretched Rufus Dawes is subjected; but though we are disgusted with his heartless gaolers, our sympathy is not profoundly touched by the story. We may be repelled by the brutality with which the cruelly-wronged hero is treated, but we shed few or no tears over his bitter sufferings. This criticism is not offered in any carping spirit, but as a protest against the cynicism of the whole work. We feel that the author looks on at the barbarity of Maurice Frere, or the laceration of Rufus Dawes, with an even pulse, that his blood is not ablaze with indignation nor his heart melted into pity. The showman gives no sign that he has anything in common with his puppets. This is as far removed as may be from that Shakespearian impar-

tiality of mind which alone leads to the just portrayal of human life, but which betokens no lack of human sympathy; for indeed that wondrous "touch of nature," begot only of intense fellow-feeling, runs through and vivifies every page of the writings of the world's great story-telling from Homer to Tourguenieff.

If we compare the most telling chapters of *His Natural Life* with those passages in such a book as *Uncle Tom's Cabin,* which have touched all human hearts, we are conscious of the limitations of the Australian novelist's art. Feeling this, I hesitate to class his work with *Oliver Twist,* and with other novels that are perhaps from a mere literary standpoint its inferiors. For with all its excellences of style, and admitting the power with which isolated incidents are related, and the skill with which they are woven into the general plot, *His Natural Life* is not a supreme work of fiction, for it is without humour and without pathos. Only in one or two of his short stories did the talented author show that he could touch the springs of our tears, and, though he was essentially a man of wit, he rarely moves us to genuine laughter. (pp. 102-04)

> *Arthur Patchett Martin, "An Australian Novelist," in* Temple Bar, *Vol. 71, May, 1884, pp. 96-110.*

FRANCIS ADAMS (essay date 1892)

[*In the following excerpt, Adams provides a British response to Clarke's major and minor works.*]

Clarke's work as a writer covers a far broader range than is known to those who have only read his one sustained effort—his novel, *For the Term of His Natural Life.* True, there is not much which is important enough to bear transplantation to England, but there is a considerable body of it which is still of great value and use to Australians, and a slim volume of selections should also take its place here as a worthy supplement to his masterpiece. To begin with, his work as a journalist is, together with the earlier potion of that of Mr. Brunton Stephens, the sole product, so far, of the Australian press which is of any use for young Australian journalists, and when one reflects that it is the journalists who stand almost entirely for the conscious culture of the whole Antipodean community, one realises the need there is for putting before them at least the best possible examples of what has been done by their predecessors. There is nothing now being written in Australia that can compare with the series of newspaper articles which Clarke gave out, at different periods and in different places, under the names of "The Peripatetic Philosopher" and "The Wicked World." Whenever he had the chance to do more serious work he took it, and some of his contributions to the local monthlies of the hour are still the pleasantest reading. They stand quite alone. Work like **"Abel Jansen Tasman,"** which appeared in the fourth number of the *Melbourne Review,* is a model of its kind. I can only hope the young writers of Australia will yet practically demonstrate some appreciation of the fact.

Clarke also did some short stories in the style of Edgar Allan Poe, and, at least, two of them, **"The Dual Existence"** and **"The Golden Island,"** are worthy of a more permanent preservation. Of his efforts at applying the predetermined pathos of Dickens to colonial subjects (such are his sketches, **"Pretty Dick," "Bullock Town,"** and others), it is not possible to speak highly. It seems sufficient to remember that Mr. O. W. Holmes says the first is "a *very* touching story, *very* well told;" but alas! the fashions of this world change, and fewer tears are shed over the demise of Paul Dombey than in the days of our fathers, even as in their days young men and maidens had lost the knack of a convulsive sympathy with the trials and triumphs of the prudently chaste Pamela. A discreet silence may also be maintained concerning his verse, though he never was so uncritical as for a moment to claim any actual inspiration for it, and he wrote two delicious parodies in the typical styles of his two friends, Gordon and Kendall, which must be counted to him for a certain sort of righteousness. (pp. 355-56)

I am not going to attempt here a detailed examination of *His Natural Life*. I am merely advancing Clarke's claims as an Australian writer to be taken seriously by his English audience, and, when I have filled out the picture of the man's work as a whole, and have reached the finest product of it, have little more to do than to praise it in general terms, and recommend readers to judge of it themselves for themselves. Clarke's debt to Balzac is a large one, a far larger one than can appear to any one who has not studied the work of the Australian writer as a whole. Clarke had enough of the infallible instinct of genius to see what was really wanting in him, if he was to attempt the achievement of anything satisfactory. He never did anything concentrated and sustained before this book: he never did anything at all in the same style afterwards. It is true that circumstances were unfavourable, but power of this calibre, if it is an organic part of a man, and not a mere phase of his development, cannot be suppressed by, at any rate, such toil and trouble as Clarke had to endure. Rising from a course of Balzac, thoroughly imbued with the literary method of the man, he wrote the first draft of the story. Then the influence passed, and he was left facing the unequal results of his work. A certain classical sense (and what is the classical sense in all literature, art, and science but the sense of proportion, of outline?) saved him from Balzac's pedantry, if he was unable to fathom Balzac's profundity, and he applied not only the *limae labor* to the book, but (what is so much more difficult still) set upon "loading all the rifts of his subject with ore," to the best of his ability. In neither operation was he wholly successful. That was not possible to him; but he was successful enough to end with having produced one of the few remarkable English novels of his time—one of the few which have won for a man a place, however small, in the crowded fane of our literature. (p. 359)

Francis Adams, "Two Australian Writers," in The Fortnightly Review, *Vol. LVIII, No. CCCIX, September 1, 1892, pp. 352-65.*

DESMOND BYRNE (essay date 1896)

[*In the following excerpt, Byrne notes Clarke's accomplished characterization in* His Natural Life.]

The strength of *His Natural Life* lies not so much in the ingenuity and dramatic quality of its plot, as in the number of striking personalities among its leading characters. That of Rufus Dawes, curiously, is distinct only at intervals. It represents, for the most part, a hopeless sufferer passing through a series of punishments which become almost monotonous in their unvaried severity.

But what could be more luminous than the portrait of Sarah Purfoy, the clever, self-possessed adventuress with the single redeeming quality of an invincible love for her worthless and villainous convict-husband? or that of Frere, the swaggering, red-whiskered, coarsely good-humoured convict-driver, glorying in his knowledge of the heights and depths of criminal ingenuity and vice, and frankly ignorant of all else?

How naturally from such a person comes that savagely humorous dissertation upon the treatment of prisoners! "There is a sort of satisfaction to me, by George! in keeping the scoundrels in order. I like to see the fellows' eyes glint at you as you walk past 'em. Gad! they'd tear me to pieces if they dared, some of 'em."

Frere is a triumph of consistent literary portraiture. He is generally understood to have been a study from life. But as the official whose name has sometimes been associated with the character was a considerably more humane disciplinarian than the persecutor of Rufus Dawes, it must be assumed that Clarke aimed only at the representation of a type.

Brutes like Frere and his vindictive associates, Burgess and Troke, there undoubtedly were on the settlements, but the average official has probably a better representative in Major Vickers, the Commandant. Vickers is not an unkind man, but does not trust himself to do anything unprovided for in the "regulations," for which he has an abject respect. "It is not for me to find fault with the system," he says; "but I have sometimes wondered if kindness would not succeed better than the chain-gang and the cat." But he never gives intelligence, much less kindness, a fair trial.

Sylvia Vickers is the only complete picture of a good woman to be found in any of the author's stories. Taken in childhood by her parents to the penal settlements, and separated there for years from youthful society, familiarised with the constant aspects of crime and suffering, and habitually in the society of her elders, she early develops into a quaint, matter-of-fact little creature, such as might well disconcert a peacock like the Reverend Meekin.

To Frere, whose knowledge of other women has been mainly immoral, her innocence and wilfulness, and her instinctive dislike of him, serve as a strong attraction. Though he becomes her husband by means of a cruel fraud, he never fully gains her trust, and the estrangement so tragically sealed in the last chapter of the novel comes almost as a relief to the sympathetic reader of her sad history. Sylvia Vickers, despite the gloomy environment of her youth, is throughout an intensely womanly woman, the delicate conception of whose character surely places her creator far above the rank of the cynics in literature.

Not the least of the elements which combine to make *His Natural Life* one of the most remarkable novels of the century is the occasional skilful varying of its painful realism with a colouring of romance, as in the relations between Dawes and Sylvia: his absorbing devotion when she is so strangely made dependent upon him at the deserted settlement; his long-continued confidence that she will effect his vindication and deliverance; and, finally, the dominant motive of securing her safety against North with which he escapes from the gaol at Norfolk Island, and joins her in the doomed schooner on its last voyage to Van Diemen's Land.

What Oliver Wendell Holmes called "the Robinson Crusoe touches" in the story—including the experiences of the marooned party at Macquarie Harbour, and those of Rex in his escape through the Devil's Blowhole—also help to leave with the reader of the novel an ineffaceable memory. (pp. 85-9)

Desmond Byrne, "Marcus Clarke," in his Australian Writers, *Richard Bentley and Son, 1896, pp. 29-89.*

A. G. STEPHENS (essay date 1941)

[*In the following excerpt, Stephens evaluates Clarke's strengths and weaknesses as a writer through a consideration of* His Natural Life *and his short stories and sketches.*]

Seeing that Marcus Clarke was in many ways so lovable and sympathetic a man—he would strip himself of everything for a man in need—it is singular that his shorter stories and sketches so rarely show warm enthusiasm, simple emotion. For the most part they sparkle coldly, illumined by the head but hardly ever heated by the heart. Yet the pages in *His Natural Life,* for example, which tell how Tommy and Bill 'did it,' have a true, natural pathos which Clarke must have felt keenly; and throughout the novel there is ever and again a glow of genuine humanity. But Clarke's other work, with rare exceptions, has no humanity whatever. He writes as cleverly as Thackeray, and often in Thackeray's vein, but there is seldom a glimpse of Thackeray's heart. Clarke was usually content to pile epithet and epigram upon the surface of things, without attempting to sound the human depths. And when, perhaps understanding his deficiencies, he deliberately tried to move his readers by pathetic arts, he failed more dismally than Dickens at his most mawkish moments. For Dickens at least was sincere, though in the attempt to reach 'effects' corresponding with his emotion he strained his art to breaking-point, and his work was false. Dickens has tried to cheat his readers, but it is nearly certain that he also cheated himself. In that grotesque and laboured sketch of **"Pretty Dick,"** which almost moves his dull editor to rears, Clarke has never cheated himself. The anti-climax shrieks throughout; and he was far too good a workman not to have heard it. It is the story of a child lost in the bush, elaborated with portentous art, as if the writer were saying, 'Now I will write a pathetic tale. I will wring out your tears, and play upon your emotions; your entrails shall be rent with compassion, and you will say, "Oh, the fine writer! the great writer!"' And always the tale is mechanical; the psychology unnatural. From the Dickensy beginning—

> A hot day. A very hot day on the plains. A very hot day up in the ranges, too. The Australian sun had got up suddenly with a savage swoop. . . . He even went down at night with a red face as much as to say, 'Take care, I shall be hotter than ever to-morrow!'

to the careful ending—such an ending from the Clarke of the Moorhouse controversy!

> Pretty Dick was lying on his face, with his hand on his arm. God had taken him home—

all is hard-ground artificiality. Clarke *must* have known his failure. And he sent it for print, with his tongue in his cheek at the full audience of Mackinnons!

Naturally Clarke, failing in emotion, wrote no poetry. Clever verses, of course, such as any man with a little penskill can accomplish; and the only two worth preserving, **"Ten Years Ago"** and **"For an Album,"** are attractively touched with sentiment in the Thackerayan manner. Clarke's verse translations have no virtue.

When Clarke was at his best he had a peg to hang his thoughts on. Some of his fresh presentations of old Australian stories are well done. He has taken a dull record and sown it with flashes of wit and phrase, as Dumas sowed the work of his collaborators, till the whole page shines and glitters. And he brings usually a shrewd, critical head to aid his commentary. Discussing Mitchel's, the Irish patriot convict's, escape from Tasmania, he points out that the imputed chivalry was very hollow:

> A word, however, about the manner of escape. It is hard to say that Mitchel broke his parole, but I am afraid that at best his escape was due to a melodramatic quibble. He certainly gave up his 'ticket-of-

leave' before his attempted escape, but he made all the *arrangements* for escape by virtue of the liberty which that ticket-of-leave afforded him. His parole obtained him interviews with Smyth, freedom to plot, money, horses, and arms. To march like a stage hero into a police-office, and with hand on pistol (purchased by virtue of the parole) disdainfully to ask an unarmed police magistrate to take him into custody, was not an honest withdrawal of his plighted word. To fulfil the terms of his contract with the Government, he should have placed himself in the hands of the constable in the condition he had been in when the parole was granted him—namely, unarmed, a prisoner, with bars and stone walls around him, and no fleet horse waiting at the door to carry him to safety, or bold companions at his side ready to withstand attempt at capture. Poor Smith O'Brien, eating his heart out in his cell at Marie Island, better understood the promise of a gentleman. I am willing to believe, however, that Mitchel—perpetually posing as a hero—was blinded by the melodramatic heroics of the proceeding to a true comprehension of its merits.

That is a gloss on the text of the escape, which John Farrell, in *his* recent recital of the facts, omitted to give.

One inclines to believe, then, that much of the force of *His Natural Life* must have lain *perdu* in the records on which Clarke based his story. But Clarke had a fine faculty of dramatic insight and dramatic expression. Given the ore he could refine it; given the situation, the scene, the men, he could bring all the contours and contrasts into prominence. His style is an admirable journalist's style, but not always good from the point of literature. It is full of light, but lacks colour and harmony. The clean, staccato sentences grow monotonous; they want a varied rhythm and sweep. In *His Natural Life* Clarke has often tried to get these things, and often succeeded. His brain was highly receptive and impressible, and seems to have largely reflected the motion and hue of the medium in which it had just previously been merged. Some passages of Clarke seem modelled on Balzac; some on Hugo; some on Disraeli, Thackeray, and Dickens. He took his literary property where he found it; and his contemporaries called him a not too scrupulous borrower. Perhaps he followed the Thackerayan model more closely than any other, since in mental vision he was nearly kin with Thackeray. But he lacked Thackeray's breadth and depth. It is sufficient that he is himself, and that the book which concentrates himself can never in Australia be forgotten. (pp. 38-41)

> *A. G. Stephens, "Marcus Clarke," in his* A. G. Stephens: His Life and Work, *edited by Vance Palmer, Robertson & Mullens Ltd., 1941, pp. 38-41.*

LESLIE REES (essay date 1942)

[*In the following excerpt, Rees examines the publication history of both the serial and book versions of* His Natural Life *and discusses the merit of each.*]

Three score years and ten are named as the human span; they are seldom the span of a book. How many authors there are who outlast the memory of their would-be immortal works! But Marcus Clarke's *For the Term of His Natural Life* (actually, Clarke called it *His Natural Life,* and was never aware of the use of the longer and more telling title) belongs to the select company of Victorian-period exceptions, for it is a little over seventy years since the novel began to be published in Melbourne. In that time, vast numbers have been spellbound by the superb adventurous tale that *His Natural Life* undoubtedly is. Yet, among all its readers, how many are aware, not only that the book has two distinct versions, but that these versions are to-day in active competition on the shelves of booksellers, appearing in popular editions under the one title?

It is not merely that the longer version has nearly twice the number of words of the version most generally known abroad. The difference is more than one of abridgment. There are important structural variations, even changes in the names and motives of characters.

For instance, in the long treatment, Richard Devine, *alias* Rufus Dawes, is transported for the alleged murder of his Dutch father-in-law, and keeps silence through his long and terrible convict life for the very thin reasons that he might have disgraced his rich, quarrelsome father and brought pain to the Dutch wife whom he does not in any case love. In the short version, Dawes is transported for the alleged murder of a man who is really his own father, but who is not married to his beloved mother; while the choleric gentleman is in the unwitting position of his step-father. When Dawes is convicted and sent to Tasmania, it is for his mother's sake he holds his tongue.

The short version ends tragically with shipwreck. Sylvia and Rufus are drowned together, but, "as they clasped hands, their freed souls, recognising each the loveliness of the other, rushed trembling together." The long version uses the name Dora instead of Sylvia; she dies in the storm, but Rufus, together with Dora's child, Dorcas, is rescued, and goes on to a new chapter of happier experiences in Victoria.

Once again he changes his name. He finds gold and becomes rich. Dorcas grows up as his daughter. A fantastic re-telling of the Eureka rebellion is introduced. Peter Lalor, still alive at the time of the book's writing, comes in as Peter McGrath, though in the first serial publication Clarke seems, cynically and rather crudely, to have called him Peter Brawler. The most startling historical licence is taken wityh the identity of Vern, the flamboyant, blather-skiting German who was prominent at Eureka. According to Clarke, Vern is not a German at all, but honest Arthur Devine, the English newphew of Dawes, in disguise. It is but consistent with Marcus Clarke's overweening love of coincidence and tidy pattern that this Arthur and Dorcas should marry and the trio return to Europe, where Dawes is romantically but improbably reunited with his patiently-waiting Dutch spouse.

To tell how these two considerably different stories both got into print and remained there, we must go back to the Melbourne of the 'sixties. Among literary coteries was to be found a young Englishman-about-town, mercurial, brilliant, worldly, the nephew of a County Court judge. His name was Marcus Andrew Hislop Clarke. At 23, he had already been sacked from a bank for requesting "a few weeks' leave of absence," had unsuccessfully tried jackerooing on a station, been sacked from the *Argus* for reviewing, as theatrical critic, an entertainment that did not take place, become well-known as a casual contributor to journals, owned and run a magazine (the *Colonial Monthly*), his aim being "the making of a new and truly Australian literature," helped to found the Yorick Club, where he met Gordon and Kendall, married an actress, written plays and suffered a breakdown requiring rest and change of air for its cure.

How was the penniless young Clarke to afford a holiday? His fertile brain soon cooked up a plan. Tasmania had been suggested as the place to go. Clarke persuaded the owners of *The*

Australian Journal to commission from him an exciting adventure serial of convict days, he to go to Tasmania and study prison records for his facts. The proprietors supplied enough cash to send him away, and he returned with the documentary and topographical material for the major portion of *His Natural Life*.

In February, 1870, the following appeared in *The Australian Journal:*

NOTICE TO READERS AND THE PUBLIC.
In conformity with our announcement in the December part, that the new year would develop new attractions in the management, we have now the pleasure to announce that, in our next issue, will be commenced and continued in each succeeding part an entirely
ORIGINAL TALE
entitled
His Natural Life, by Marcus Clarke
(Author of *Long Odds*, "Lower Bohemia," "Philosophic Humbugs," etc., etc), with appropriate illustrations.
As from the wide reputation of this popular writer, a considerable increase of circulation cannot fail to be achieved, early orders should be given to ensure copies. Also, in our next will be commenced a thrilling tale of a Maiden's Peril among the American Indians . . .

Sure enough, the March issue of the "family newspaper of literature and science" started off with a large engraving of the Bell Inn, Holborn, and the first six chapters of *His Natural Life*, virtually as they appear in the longer version to-day. (pp. 99-101)

[By] the end of a couple of years the whole remarkable tale of *His Natural Life* had been told. Did its publication have the expected beneficial influence on circulation? On the contrary, sales of the *Journal* are said to have fallen away during that time to about half.

It is one of the ironies of literary history that this story, which in book-form has sold hundreds of thousands of copies in America, England and Australia, and been translated into several languages, should not have struck a high popularity from the beginning. . . . Ida Leeson found a clue to this cause in the note printed by the *Journal* when *His Natural Life* was being serialized in 1886. The earlier, temporary loss of circulation, it was stated, was "principally ascribed to a popular distrust of local talent." From other evidence of Clarke's time, indeed from popular attitudes to Australian literature even to-day, one scarcely hesitates in accepting this explanation.

But to tell of the book-publication. Clarke, apparently feeling some doubt about *His Natural Life,* maybe because of the *Journal's* weakened grip on its readers, sought the advice of Sir Charles Gavan Duffy, who had lately been Premier of Victoria. Duffy read the serial parts, pronounced the story "powerful," but advised alteration. "The hero," he said, "underwent a lifelong torture without any credible or even intelligible motive, and on the whole was a *mauvais sujet* himself. To win the readers' sympathy, all this must be altered." Duffy also thought that the end, where the Ballarat affair was described, should come out.

Marcus Clarke's reception of this criticism was most warm and humble. He wrote: "I will act upon your advice and cut off the beginning and end." He not only did this, but introduced the different motive for Dawes's silence and made other changes. In 1874, an edition was published in Melbourne. Next year, practically the same book, with the advantage of some slight polishing, was issued in London and this is the short version which has run to a multitude of reprintings since.

So far, so usual. Many a good serial has been modified and re-treated for book-publication. The strange aftermath is that the long serial version has not been allowed to die, and at present seems likely to establish itself as the version which will be read by Australians in the future.

The *Australian Journal* re-serialized the original *His Natural Life,* together with illustrations, immediately on the death of Marcus Clarke in 1881. We are told that, on this occasion, the story "benefited the circulation to a very material extent." As mentioned, the magazine printed the original story a third time five years later. (Meanwhile, an English short version in 1885 had coined the more resounding title, *For The Term of His Natural Life.*) The first book appearance of the tale as Clarke originally set it down did not occur until 1929, in Sydney, but three years ago, editions at three different prices, issued by New Century Press, used the full text except for a few thousand words of intermittent cuts designed to "modernise" the reading.

What is to be the opinion of posterity on the differing merits of these versions? Henry Lawson said, after coming on one of *The Australian Journal* re-serializations: "We read *For the Term of His Natural Life* as Marcus Clarke wrote it. The introduction was, I think, equal to Dickens in style. The sight of it in book form, with its mutilated chapters and melodramatic 'prologue,' exasperates me even now." Contrast this with "Banjo" Paterson's view: "The early chapters . . . were a grotesquely close imitation of Dickens and were therefore struck out when the book was published in England." (A mis-interpretation, that "therefore.") "The prologue, crude in workmanship and utterly regardless of probability, yet accords better with the general bold character of the work than did the original chapters."

My own opinion (for what it is worth) is that Clarke was well-advised to cut *His Natural Life,* but that he had absolutely no business to make such a hack job of it. Time and time again, reading the short book, one comes with a shock on references which seem to depend for understanding on earlier references not included. One is driven to look vainly back over foregoing pages for explanation. An example is the blood relationship of Frere and Dawes, suddenly mentioned as though one should know of it all along. Such shocks, not experienced in the serial version, cause irritation and a certain lessening of confidence in the author, who does not quite seem to be playing the game. The prologue is as tawdry a piece of blood and thunder as ever came out of the Victorian era, but it does have the effect of plunging the reader straight into the story's proper business, which is the voyage to Van Diemen's Land and the adventures of Dawes, John Rex, Captain Frere, Gabbett, Sylvia and others under the convict system. In the long book, the preliminary web of ironic circumstance woven to explain Dawes's transportation is unduly complicated, even though the style is "equal to" and very reminiscent of Dickens.

The short version's ending is superior, in my opinion, to that of the long. One is hardly prepared to accept another escape from death by Dawes. The fanciful narrative of Eureka conflicts too grossly with well-authenticated fact, while the hocus-pocus of the jewel alchemy revealed in the last pages is utterly weak and absurd compared with the emotional impact caused by ending the story tersely and logically, with the death of Dawes and Sylvia in each other's arms.

But, taken in either version, *His Natural Life* remains a great novel. Read to-day, it is as compelling, as richly, deeply absorbing as seventy years ago. True that it is soaked in that specifically Victorian fluid, melodramatic emotion earnest and unashamed. True that it reflects much of the flashiness of its author, lacks a truly sensitive, distinguished grain, takes sadistic delight in cruelty, waxes rhetorical and journalesy. True that the author makes the cardinal error of never letting you see into the mind of his hero, and thus denies him the reader's true sympathy based on self-identification. But the book has a plentitude of invention, a story to tell. John Rex's escape by way of the blowhole at Eaglehawk Neck is a classic example of graphic narrative. Other parts, particularly the treatment of Rev. North, show uncannily modern penetration into psychology. It is almost unbelievable that the picture of Rev. North could have been drawn by a man of 24. For its unremitting exposure of the brutalities of "the system," *His Natural Life* groups Marcus Clarke with Dickens and Dostoievsky among the nineteenth century sociological novelists who will be remembered. (pp. 102-04)

> Leslie Rees, " 'His Natural Life'—The Long and Short of It," in The Australian Quarterly, *Vol. XIV, No. 2, June, 1942, pp. 99-104.*

VANCE PALMER   (essay date 1946)

[*In the following excerpt, Palmer reviews prominent critical attitudes toward Clarke's works and attempts to determine the value of Clarke's achievement. His comments were originally published in the periodical* Meanjin *in March 1946.*]

The uncertain nature of Clarke's gifts has always troubled his critics. Was the power he showed in *For the Term of His Natural Life* an organic part of him, or was it communicated to him by the dark realities of the records? What was the relation between his intelligence and his creative impulse? And how could a man with that clear, sceptical mind be so uncritical of what he wrote as to send a story like **"Pretty Dick"** ("they always felt they had their Sunday clothes on in his presence") to the author he most admired, Oliver Wendell Holmes?

Sentiment here, irony there! It was not as if Clarke were one of those unlucky fellows who have been baffled and frustrated through sheer inability to hit on a theme that would compel their concentration, draw out their full talent, and impose an integrity upon them. He was extremely young (only twenty-five) when his great book was written. And its reception was of a kind to stimulate any writer and set him fruitfully to work.

"To me, I must confess," wrote the Earl of Rosebery, "it is the most terrible of all novels, more terrible than *Oliver Twist* or Victor Hugo's most startling effects, for the simple reason that it is more real."

Though Clarke could not have read these words they are typical of many printed in prominent journals, at home and overseas, when the book appeared. Charles Reade never wrote so powerful a romance, said George Augustus Sala, the great journalistic mogul of the day. Other critics prophesied that Clarke had it in him to become the most distinguished novelist of his time.

Yet, in the ten years that remained to him, he did not make an effort to put forth his full strength again. It was not the necessity to earn a living that inhibited him; he doesn't seem to have felt any inner pressure. By exercising the less creative part of his mind he could dazzle his friends of the Cave of

Adullam. He was mature, sophisticated, a man of the world yet at home in Bohemia. He could command a style that made the essays of other men look like papers written for literary clubs in the suburbs. To a man with no live coal inside him this would be enough: and, apparently, Clarke was free from such an uncomfortable source of heat.

Without his masterpiece, Clarke's case would be simple. There are always plenty of writers in every period who have skill with words and a gift of analysis, yet no power to construct anything of their own. And, soon after Clarke died, there was a tendency to dispose of the problem he presented by writing down *For the Term of His Natural Life.* It was suggested that there was something spurious about it; that it was a pastiche concocted with one eye on Balzac and the other on material very much more "prepared" than the ordinary raw substance of life.

Francis Adams, who came here in the middle 'eighties, found that a reaction had set in against Clarke. He was not considering Thomas Bent's absurd attack upon him in the House, nor the remark of the prominent editor (it was probably David Syme): "We have half-a-dozen men on the paper who can write stories as well as Clarke could." Rather was he thinking of the younger generation, of whom he said that nothing struck him more in his stay here than the keenness of their instinct, not only in things social and political, but (strangely) in things literary. This shrewd instinct of theirs, nourished on stark little *Bulletin* sketches, made them suspect that Clarke's writing was all surface texture. An admirer of Clarke, Adams was eager to rebuild his reputation. Clarke, he affirmed, was the author of the only real prose yet written in Australia.

"His essay on *The Future Australian Race* is as utterly alone in the domain of Australian social criticism as his essay on "**Abel Jansen Tasman**" is in the domain of prose literature. It is the only thing written about the Australian civilization that can be said to count at all."

Fellow-feeling had perhaps a little to do with Adams' judgement. Cultured, cut off from his English roots, at once attracted and repelled by the country he had come to, he had much in common with Clarke. They both wrote a brilliant prose; they loved broad and sweeping generalizations and were weak in detail. And the novels of Francis Adams, like those of Clarke, had the hard glitter of intelligence in them but rarely beat with a human pulse.

Lacking the ultimate creative quality himself, Adams could throw no real light on Clarke's uncertain possession of it. His account of the writing of *For the Term of His Natural Life* belongs to a romantic legend. Here was the perverse and brooding genius, conscious of his weakness and his power, fearful that his great gifts were being frittered away, determined to achieve something before night fell.

"It was a writer of this complex constitution who, feeling the ground slipping from under his feet, made one desperate effort to concentrate himself in a masterpiece . . . "

But why should Clarke feel the ground slipping so hopelessly from under his feet at twenty-five? And is there proof that he went to Port Arthur with any intent than to earn money for a holiday?

The truth seems to be where A. G. Stephens found it [see excerpt dated 1941]. Clarke was essentially a professional writer, like his English contemporaries and forerunners. He had not much original impulse, but he had a keen intelligence and a

sharp sense of craft. When he was dealing with fresh matter, as in [*Holiday Peak, and Other Tales*], his "literary attitude" gave his work a brittle falsity, but he was fortunate, when young, to come upon a subject that might have been handled by Hugo or one of his favourite novelists.

"Given the ore he could refine it," says Stephens, "given the situation, the scene, the men, he could bring all the contours and contrasts into prominence. His style is an admirable journalist's style, but not always good from the point-of-view of literature."

Is this underestimating Clarke's achievement? Perhaps; a little. But it largely depends upon how you value the element of craft in the novel, the ability to work well according to a traditional pattern. Latterly we have come to place more emphasis on poetic vision, the power to pour imagination over a thing and make it show a new face. Clarke had very little of this; though warm of heart in the daily affairs of life, his imagination was always cold; he was the professional, moved by nothing but his own sense of skill. If you want to see the difference between the two kinds of force in action you should re-read Price Warung's story of the Ring in *Tales of the Old Regime.* Price Warung was a much inferior workman to Clarke; he had neither his alert mind nor his skill with words, but dealing with the same material as Clarke he occasionally makes the heart beat faster by twitching away the period backcloth and showing his human figures against a background of eternity. (pp. 167-69)

> Vance Palmer, "Marcus Clarke and His Critics,"
> in Twentieth Century Australian Literary Criticism,
> edited by Clement Semmler, Oxford University Press,
> Melbourne, 1967, pp. 167-69.

BRIAN ELLIOTT (essay date 1958)

[*Elliott is an Australian literary critic, biographer, and novelist. His* Marcus Clarke, *from which the following excerpt was drawn, is the major critical and biographical study of the author. Elliott here explores Clarke's purpose in writing* His Natural Life *and compares the work with* The Broad Arrow, *an earlier Australian novel of convict transportation.*]

[Clarke's] motive in planning a novel on [the theme of convict transportation] was essentially neither descriptive nor expository. As it first took shape in his mind the story was broadly historical, but it emerged finally as a psychological romance. All that he claimed for the book historically was that he had endeavoured "to set forth the working and results of an English system of transportation carefully considered and carried out under official supervision; and to illustrate it in the manner best calculated, as I think, to attract general attention to the inexpediency of again allowing offenders against the law to be herded together in places remote from the wholesome influence of public opinion, and to be submitted to a discipline which must necessarily depend for its just administration upon the personal character and temper of their gaolers" To argue the inexpediency of doing again what had been firmly and finally repudiated was not to serve a very urgent purpose; the truth is that his preface to the revised version of *His Natural Life,* in which this statement occurs, was an afterthought, and amounted only to a pious rationalization. He had no intention originally of writing a pamphlet against the system. He had no special sympathy for convicts as a class. He was merely interested in writing a novel and saw that this subject afforded excellent scope for his talents.

"The convict of fiction," declares the Preface, "has been hitherto shown only at the beginning or at the end of his career. . . . Charles Reade has drawn the interior of a house of correction in England, and Victor Hugo has shown how a French convict fares after the fulfilment of his sentence. But no writer—as far as I am aware—has attempted to depict the dismal condition of a felon during his term of transportation." From the first Clarke had decided to centre his story upon a single convict hero, conceived upon the grand scale, in whose soul all that was terrible in the system was to find dramatic expression. He was primarily interested not in the discipline of prisons nor in the private mentality of a criminal, but in the survival against odds of a tortured human spirit. It was not merely in deference to polite Victorian convention that he made Rufus Dawes innocent of the crime for which he was transported, but rather because it was as a suffering man and not specifically as an offender against society that he wished to portray him.

In the character of his hero therefore Clarke exploited the popular legend of concentrated individual suffering, and in the end made a kind of convict Lear of Dawes. As in Lear are united all the agonies of helpless age, so in Dawes were symbolized the helplessness and frustration of the spirit crushed by the processes of a cruel system. But he was not quite correct in his claim that no novelist before him had attempted to depict the dismal condition of a felon during his term of transportation. He can surely not have been ignorant of at least one Australian predecessor: Caroline Leakey, whose novel *The Broad Arrow* (1859) had been actively concerned to do just that. (pp. 145-46)

Too much should not be made of the parallels between *The Broad Arrow* and *His Natural Life*. In outline the final version of *His Natural Life* bears a general resemblance to *The Broad Arrow*. But the correspondences are superficial. Maida Gwynnham is represented as the guileless dupe of her lover, to shield whom she suffers. She is transported to Tasmania, is formally assigned out as a servant in a decent household and appears about to recover the self-esteem she had lost when she is innocently involved in a further criminal situation, and her explanation is discredited. She is severely punished, becomes ill, and eventually dies in the prison hospital just too late to meet the eyes of her repentant seducer, who has come to Tasmania to be with her and to atone for his sin. For a considerable number of pages the story is occupied with descriptions of a journey by ship to the secondary penal settlement at Port Arthur and of life at the settlement itself.

On the surface, this is very like the scheme of *His Natural Life:* Richard Devine, alias Rufus Dawes, is transported for a crime he has not committed and conceals his innocence for honourable reasons. He is then involved in a series of degenerative situations—which Clarke relates in much greater detail than Caroline Leakey—and thus sinks deeper and deeper into degradation, until he dies, having become in most respects the mere outward shell of the man Richard Devine should have been. Maida Gwynnham dies pathetically and nobly, Dawes is permitted a heroic death by drowning, and accorded a highly improbably and romantic reunion in death with the woman whom he has loved with dogged devotion all through his sordid and loveless career. But these deaths are really only devices to end the novels. There is a vital difference in the two writers' aims. Caroline Leakey made a stoic heroine of Maida Gwynnham; in spite of her lapse she retains a proud spirit, a spiritual virginity to the end. Like Clarissa Harlowe, she dies in the grand manner, literally of tuberculosis but spiritually of sheer

pride and injured innocence; her death is a purification. Dawes in his lifetime suffers death in the soul: and only his one inextinguishable spark of humanity, his love of Sylvia Vickers, prevents him from descending to the inhuman levels which some other characters in the book occupy—the cannibal beast, Gabbett, the diabolical and heartless official bully, Frere.

The character of Dawes is a psychological study but not an essay in psychological realism. Some part of *The Broad Arrow* is designed to give factual information about the system, although by 1859 transportation to Tasmania had been discontinued. The descriptive impulse had already begun to give place to the historical. It is difficult to discover any part of *His Natural Life* which is designed merely to be illustrative: Clarke wrote it neither as a descriptive nor an historical story. It differed significantly in this respect from *The Broad Arrow* and from such a story, for example, as *Uncle Tom's Cabin*. Ironically, however, its effect was potent in that way. In the later years of the century popular recollection of the convict days had very largely faded and *His Natural Life* was the most tangible evidence of it available. What was known of the system was disliked, but the novel presented a picture which, though sensationally distorted, was firmly documented, and in addition had the appeal of a heroic framework.

His Natural Life also introduced to Australian fiction a new historical pattern which Clarke hardly intended. Among recent historical novels one formula is constantly repeated. It is that of the fine young Englishman who battles with the bush and in the end qualifies as an Australian pioneer, but at the cost of all his conscious English inheritance. He is a kind of phoenix-figure from whose ashes rises the archetypal Australian character. There is no personal triumph in his subjection of the bush; his triumph is not his own but the country's. In his own person the country destroys him utterly; it not merely wears him out physically but it coarsens his soul. But from his ruin springs a generation which is no longer heroic, but humane. The implication is that false values, artificial culture, unreal distinctions of rank and class have been purged away, leaving the basic British man; the Australian individual who survives is a simple unit in a just society. This romantic ingenuous view of history belongs to a phase which is already passing, but it was sympathetically entertained for many years. The exaggerated legend of convict suffering and official oppression was invented to counter the embarrassment which many felt at the penal origin of Australian settlement. Rufus Dawes was no gentleman pioneer, although Tom Crosbie in the unrevised form of the novel might in some measure be considered one—not of the land, but in the world of business and affairs. In Dawes as a convict Clarke provided later fiction with a striking pattern of the ever-varied, accumulative, and killing frustration which the pioneers encountered and which became for the novelists the real test of the spirit's vitality. The survival of the spirit through every onslaught of adversity is a constant theme of Australian romanticism. Therefore in transferring the formula from Clarke to the historical novel the writers have not shifted ground very far. When they wrote, *His Natural Life* had been for several generations part of the background of the general Australian imagination.

After a period of fifty years when its prestige was never seriously challenged, it is understandable that popular taste should at present be disposed to regard *His Natural Life* with a certain reserve. Since the vigorous renaissance of creative energy in Australia from the late twenties or early thirties, Colonial writing has been in eclipse, and *His Natural Life* has suffered the logical consequence of this healthy expansion of the native point of view. The Colonial perspective is not yet distant enough to become attractive in itself. But it is not right to condemn *His Natural Life* as an historical novel when it is clear that history, as such, was not Clarke's object.

The struggle of Rufus Dawes is a struggle with life, not primarily with a local or historical environment. Clarke would not have cared to write mere embroidered history. For him a novel was first of all a work of imagination, and while it was necessary that the data should be true, to have made invention the servant of historical fact would have seemed to him the abrogation of the writer's freedom. (pp. 147-50)

> Brian Elliott, in his *Marcus Clarke, Oxford at the Clarendon Press, 1958, 281 p.*

H. M. GREEN (essay date 1961)

[*In the following excerpt, Green analyzes the journalistic and theatrical characteristics of* His Natural Life *and evaluates Clarke's literary achievement.*]

Marcus Clarke was one of the most brilliant journalists that Australia has produced, or helped to produce. He was a journalist essentially: after reading his books, and without even knowing that he had ever written an article for a newspaper, the editor of the London *Daily Telegraph* asked him to write some leading articles and suggested that he should join its staff in London: Clarke perferred to remain in Australia, but became the paper's Australian correspondent; and just before his death it had been proposed that he should travel through the Australian colonies and the South Sea Islands as special correspondent of the London *Daily Telegraph* and the *Sydney Morning Herald*. He was so quick and sensitive that he could take something of the colour of every phase of life he touched, but usually he intensified it, making it more striking if less real; and when he achieved excellence he could not maintain it for long; he is far better in short passages than in anything as a whole. Also, even at his best his taste is not quite sure: he loved drama, and he could be exceedingly dramatic, but too often it turned into melodrama under his hands; he loved pathos, and he could be exceedingly pathetic, but too often it slopped over into sentimentality; he would sacrifice much to produce a striking effect, and he produced some effects that were very striking, but sometimes his sacrifice included the probabilities. All these characteristics appear in *For the Term of His Natural Life*. Clarke studied the records of "the System" [of convict transportation from England] with great care, and nothing he described was too cruel or too brutal to have happened under it; indeed some of the most terrible things in the book had actually occurred: but it is more than unlikely that so many horrors, so much injustice and misfortune should have grouped themselves together in the story of any one man's life. There is a whole series of improbabilities that become more and more manifest as one reads. The events that bring about the transportation of Devine, or Dawes; the planning by Sarah Purfoy of the mutiny on the convict ship, when her lover might have been freed so much more surely and safely by assignment to her in the colony; the convenience of Mrs. Vickers's death and Sylvia's loss of memory so that Frere and not Dawes might appear as the hero of the marooning episode at Hell's Gates; the likeness between Devine and his half-brother Rex, which is not noticed on board the ship, and yet is sufficient to ensure Rex's easy acceptance as Devine even by Devine's own mother: the cumulative effect of such things as these casts an atmosphere of unreality over the whole book. Besides, even if we could accept the premises on which the story is founded, we cannot accept the characters and emotions as they are handled: individually, many of them are credible enough, but again it is impossible to accept them in the mass: Frere is at times too inhuman; Sylvia, who was a child of strong character, is little more than a romantic puppet when she grows to womanhood and marries Frere; Meekin is a caricature; the pathos of the episode between Sylvia and the two little convict boys who afterwards kill themselves is overdone. No chance is missed of adding to the almost unrelieved misery of the story, and especially the miseries of Dawes: Clarke does his utmost to squeeze the last drop of emotion out of the reader; but he defeats his own end, for after a while from pitying we cease to believe, and may even become bored; and the language of the story is often theatrical, apart from what it has to convey. In fact there are faults enough to damn most novels. Yet this novel contrives to rise triumphant above its faults. It accumulates force like a great wave. The story proceeds from its melodramatic opening to its sentimental conclusion with a deliberate relentless motion that one feels nothing can check; and if the gloomy and brutal world within which it moves is not quite a human world, it is filled with life and force. Both action and characterization are, in spite of exaggerations, extraordinarily vivid. Setting aside Dawes himself, his parents, Sylvia as a grown woman, the two little convict boys, Meekin, and perhaps even North, every person in the book, even the incidental sailors, convicts and officials, is not only sharply individualized, so far as he goes, but warmly alive, though their life is not quite like ours. Among the minor characters, Blunt, the old sea-captain, is particularly good, and it is worth noting how the vain, extravagant, and shrewish Mrs. Vickers can behave with courage in emergency, and take a dying sailor's head upon her bosom. But the most vivid of all the characters are Frere and Sarah Purfoy, and the most vivid of the actions are those with which Frere and Sarah are closely concerned: Sarah is aglow with colour and vitality, attracting those rough men as a magnet attracts iron filings; Frere is a magnificent barbarian, with brains enough for his purposes, a dominant personality, and a courage and determination that takes hold of the reader almost in spite of himself. Sarah and Frere, Sarah and Blunt, Sarah and the soldier Miles: some of the scenes in which these people figure conduct themselves before the eyes as on a stage in a play by a dramatist of power. For there was one thing Clarke could do supremely well: he could make character in action come alive; men and women doing things at a dramatic crisis. The moving scene unrolls swiftly before us, the actors showing, as though they were transparent, what they are by what they say and I do; I said "the actors," and there is this about such scenes of Clarke's: extraordinarily lifelike, they are not quite like life; the effect produced is more like that of excellent acting, of life at one remove. In the following passage for example; it is magnificently conceived, and, but for the overloading of the style and the general atmosphere of the theatre, magnificently carried out; it is introduced to illuminate an aspect of the character of Frere:

> One day a man named Kavanagh, a captured absconder, who had openly sworn in the dock the death of the magistrate, walked quickly up to him as he was passing through the yard, and snatched a pistol from his belt. The yard caught its breath, and the attendant warder, hearing the click of the lock, instinctively turned his head away, so that he might not be blinded by the flash. But Kavanagh did not fire. At the instant when his hand was on the pistol, he looked up and met the magnetic glance of Frere's

imperious eyes. An effort, and the spell would have been broken. A twitch of the finger, and his enemy would have fallen dead. There was an instant when that twitch of the finger could have been given, but Kavanagh let that instant pass. The dauntless eye fascinated him. He played with the pistol nervously, while all remained stupefied. Frere stood still, without withdrawing his hands from the pockets into which they were plunged.

"That's a fine pistol, Jack," he said at last.

Kavanagh, down whose white face the sweat was pouring, burst into a hideous laugh of relieved terror, and thrust the weapon, cocked as it was, back again into the magistrate's belt.

Frere slowly drew one hand, took the cocked pistol and levelled it at his recent assailant. "That's the best chance *you'll* ever get, Jack," said he.

Kavanagh fell on his knees. "For God's sake, Captain Frere!"

Frere looked down on the trembling wretch, and then uncocked the pistol, with a laugh of ferocious contempt. "Get up, you dog," he said. "It takes a better man than you to beat me. Bring him up in the morning, Hawkins, and we'll give him five-and-twenty."

As he went out—so great is the admiration for Power—the poor devils in the yard cheered him.

And Gabbett's struggle on the ship during the mutiny, first with Frere and then with the sailors; here is the second part of it:

Shaking his assailants to the deck as easily as a wild boar shakes off the dogs which clamber upon his bristly sides, the convict sprang to his feet, and whirling the snatched-up cutlass round his head, kept the circle at bay. Four times did the soldiers round the hatchway raise their muskets, and four times did the fear of wounding the men who had flung themselves upon the enraged giant compel them to restrain their fire. Gabbett, his stubbly hair on end, his bloodshot eyes glaring with fury, his great hand opening and shutting in air, as though it gasped for something to seize, turned himself about from side to side—now here, now there, bellowing like a wounded bull. His coarse shirt, rent from shoulder to flank, exposed the play of his huge muscles. He was bleeding from a cut on the forehead, and the blood, trickling down his face, mingled with the foam on his lips, and dropped sluggishly on his hairy breast. Each time that a man came within reach of the swinging cutlass, the ruffian's form dilated with a fresh access of passion. . . . At one moment bunched with clinging adversaries—his arms, legs, and shoulders a hanging mass of human bodies—at the next, free, desperate, alone in the midst of his foes, his hideous countenance contorted with hate and rage, the giant seemed less a man than a demon, or one of those monstrous and savage apes which haunt the solitudes of the African forests. Spurning the mob who had rushed in at him, he strode towards his risen adversary, and aimed at him one final blow that should put an end to his tyranny for ever.

(pp. 218-21)

The style of *His Natural Life* is in keeping with the rest of it. It is a vigorous, packed and glittering style: impressive, if rather obviously intended to impress; dramatic, with a tendency to become theatrical. It has been suggested that Clarke owed a debt to Balzac, but he owed a much more obvious debt to

Dickens and Victor Hugo, a debt which is by no means confined to style; and he may well have owed something to Charles Reade; by way of contrast with the passages just quoted here is a shorter passage in which there is no movement:

In the breathless stillness of a tropical afternoon, when the air was hot and heavy, and the sky brazen and cloudless, the shadow of the *Malabar* lay solitary on the surface of the glittering sea.

Effective as is this passage, it is perhaps a little too evident that each word has been weighed with great care; there is lacking the final touch of art that would conceal the art itself, making it seem as though the words had flowed spontaneously from the pen. The same sort of thing, careful balance of phrases, careful antitheses, effective but obviously painstaking general arrangement, is equally evident in the passage near the beginning of the book which describes the stowing of the convicts in the 'tweendecks of the *Malabar*. Clarke's feeling for the effective, the dramatic, the theatrical comes out too in his liking for a "curtain," a short final paragraph to nail down a climax: at the end of Gabbett's struggle with the sailors comes this:

Authority was almost instantaneously triumphant on the upper and lower decks. The mutiny was over;

and after the description of the figure of the lonely convict standing on the barren cliff at Hell's Gates:

This solitary man was Rufus Dawes.

These are outstanding examples, but the ends of many chapters are nailed down in some such fashion. In Australian fiction *His Natural Life* will always hold a high place, though it is no longer possible to speak of it as "the great Australian novel," even assuming that such a thing can exist. And in the literature of "the System" it is not likely that any novel will surpass it; it is worthy indeed of a wider range of comparison than Australia can yet afford. But when we compare it with *Les Misérables* for instance or *Wuthering Heights,* though both of these share some of its defects, it takes a lower place. Clarke had not Hugo's genius, and he lacked the utter sincerity, the complete obliviousness of everything beyond the immediate object, that marks Emily Brontë: we feel that she thought of nothing but to make her book as good as she could make it; that it did not enter into her mind to work up effects for her readers, that indeed she did not think of her readers at all. We cannot feel like this about Clarke's book: there, we are too often conscious that its writer is glancing sideways at the gallery, and that sometimes he either shared its tastes or allowed them to be substituted for his own. And though Hugo also had an eye to the gallery and sometimes shared its tastes, the immense personality that informs and raises the claptrap of which he is sometimes guilty carries through what Clarke was not always abel to carry through. *His Natural Life* is in its kind a masterpiece, but it is by no means among the greatest in its kind. (pp. 221-22)

In Marcus Clarke journalism and literature were at war, and the result was complicated by the circumstances in which he found himself. In so young and undeveloped a country as Australia it was impossible that the most characteristic aspects of his talent should find full expression; yet it is a question whether without the stimulus afforded by migration and entirely new surroundings he would have made any mark at all outside the journalistic world. Journalism claimed him in Australia as it would have claimed him anywhere; it absorbed more and more of his forces, so that his one serious literary achievement represents an excursion out of the world in which he lived his ordinary writing life. It would seem that the best that might have been hoped from Clarke was not actually anywhere realizable, so that we may be glad that he used the single opportunity, which was afforded by journalism, of breaking as free from it as he could ever in any case have broken free; and we may be grateful for a literary achievement which is real and definite, even if it represents only one aspect and that not the most characteristic of a diverse and brilliant talent. (pp. 224-25)

H. M. Green, "Fiction: Clarke and Boldrewood," in his A History of Australian Literature, Pure and Applied, 1789-1923, Vol. I, *Angus and Robertson, 1961, pp. 215-35.*

BILL WANNAN (essay date 1963)

[*In the following excerpt, Wannan appraises* His Natural Life.]

The high regard in which Clarke's great novel was once held has . . . been depreciated somewhat in more recent years. Brian Elliott has put the matter succinctly [see excerpt dated 1958]: "After a period of fifty years when its prestige was never seriously challenged, it is understandable that popular taste should at present be disposed to regard *His Natural Life* with a certain reserve. Since the vigorous renaissance of creative energy in Australia from the late twenties or early thirties, Colonial writing has been in eclipse, and *His Natural Life* has suffered the logical consequence of this healthy expansion of the native point of view."

The critical reader in our time is somewhat dismayed by the absurdities of the plot; the melodramatic coincidences; the depressing atmosphere, at times, of a musty mid-Victorian charade. The book's imitations and echoes of Dickens, Dumas, Balzac, Hugo, Thackeray and Defoe, with little of the tremendous zest and creative power of the originals, leave one disappointed and sometimes embarrassed. The Reverend Mr. Meekin, for example, is a Dickensian character without any of the depth, the understanding, the ironic humour of Dickens.

Sylvia is another character who rarely comes fully to life. There is some justice in Miles Franklin's reference to Sylvia as "bearing resemblance to little Eva" [see Additional Bibliography].

Clarke attempted too much in this novel. His mind was seething with the stories he had culled from old books and files in the Public Library—the stories that he wrote down in the series "Old Tales Retold." He included a number of these separate chronicles, in a somewhat altered form, of course, within the framework of his book: and the result is that too many raisins have got into the pudding. The Tichborne case; the cannibalism of Alexander Pearce and his convict companions; the mutiny on the *Frederick* brig; the escape of the prisoners aboard the *Cyprus* brig; the tragic mutiny of convicts under the leadership of William Westwood (alias "Jacky-Jacky") on Norfolk Island; the wreck of the convict ship *George the Third;* the success-story of Mary Reiby in Sydney: all such episodes taken directly from history may have helped to fill out the instalments of the novel, considered as serial fiction, but they clutter up the central narrative so decisively that the work loses in artistry far more than it gains in bulk and variety.

And yet, despite the over-burden of plot and sub-plot; the clichés of Victorian England; the frequent failure of the characterization; the melodrama and the occasional mawkishness—despite these and other faults, *His Natural Life* has a core of greatness that is apparent to all who take up the book. There are few readers who do not become passionately involved in the fate of poor Rufus Dawes. In Maurice Frere's relentless determination to destroy him, there are the elements of a tragedy as powerful and as real as that of *Moby Dick.* Captain Ahab and Captain Frere, so different in their characters and purposes, are yet cast in the same mould.

In that strange figure, the Reverend James North, Clarke has created one character who is excitingly alive, and modern. He is a type of the priest so compellingly portrayed in Graham Greene's *The Power and the Glory.* James North is a fully realized character—one of the most poignantly tragic figures in all English fiction. In his creation, Clarke has reached into the most profound psychological deeps. Guilt-ridden, contradictory, compassionate, whisky-sodden, heroic North bears testimony to Marcus Clarke's genius as a writer—a genius that he dissipated elsewhere in so much that was trivial. It is not easy to accept the fact that the mind which created such a complex and subtle character as North, occupied itself with the Gothic absurdities of **"The Mind-Reader's Curse"** and with the trivialities of *Chidiock Tichbourne.*

By comparison with the Reverend North, Rufus Dawes is an almost shadowy figure. In his delineation he lacks the clergyman's psychological complexity. But as we become immersed in Dawes's story we grow to accept him as a symbol of all humanity that is beset by the forces of evil; nor is he so vaguely sketched that we cannot identify ourselves with his struggle to retain the last vestiges of human dignity. We are genuinely touched by his tears, for they represent his—and our—affirmation of humanity. We honour him as, twisted in agony from the remorseless floggings imposed by Frere, he refuses to capitulate to the enemy by becoming a convict constable. Urged to do so by the Reverend North, he cries out with scorn: "And betray my mates? I'm not one of that sort."

In a world that has known the nightmare evil of Hitler and all his works, *His Natural Life* must remain as a thoroughly relevant commentary on the triumph of the human spirit in the face of almost overwhelming terror and brutality. (pp. xvi-xviii)

Bill Wannan, in an introduction to A Marcus Clarke Reader, *edited by Bill Wannan, 1963. Reprint by Angus & Robertson Ltd., 1964, pp. vii-xxiv.*

L. T. HERGENHAN (essay date 1965)

[*Hergenhan links the pattern of Christian redemptive symbolism in* His Natural Life *to characterization and thematic structure in the novel. For additional commentary by Hergenhan, see excerpt dated 1984.*]

R. G. Howarth [see Additional Bibliography] has suggested that *His Natural Life* is more than a novel of social protest, that it becomes 'a tragedy of a human soul; but beyond that, Rufus Dawes is the figure of martyred humanity—it might be of Christ himself in mortal form, crucified, tortured, abandoned and finally released from the horror of "life".' There is some truth in this view though the Christian symbolism and the treatment of Dawes are more complex than it suggests. In Books II and III Dawes faces the 'desert' and a scourging, and there is a hinted parallel with the life of Christ which is to be explicitly developed later. But Dawes is not simply a Christ-figure, he is both like and unlike the Redeemer, and once again man's duality is stressed. Dawes as man is made partly in God's likeness, and this is made apparent in the goodness of which he is capable in a world of evil. On the other hand

Dawes is partaker of man's fallen nature and so is capable of denying God's image in himself. Thus during his scourging, which represents a kind of crucifixion in its extreme of suffering, his lonely spirit, cut off from any form of succour, is crushed at last, but unlike Christ, who suffers the same temptation, he succumbs to despair. Christ had also conquered in the 'desert'. The moral duality underlying this symbolism is also to be found in the way it is applied to North, as we shall see later; for Dawes is not the only Christ-figure in the novel.

Critics of *His Natural Life* have stressed the importance of Dawes' being an *innocent* sufferer. But he does not retain his innocence and it is just as important to recognize his spiritual corruption. His flogging at Port Arthur marks not only the peak of his physical sufferings but also a moral surrender that is without parallel in his earlier afflictions:

> The self-reliance and force of will which had hitherto sustained him through his self-imposed trial had failed him—he felt—at the moment when he needed it most; and the man who had with unflinched front faced the gallows, the desert and the sea, confessed his debased humanity beneath the physical torture of the lash. He had been flogged before, and he had wept in secret at his degradation, but he now for the first time comprehended how terrible that degradation might be made, for he realized how the agony of the wretched body can force the soul to quit its last poor refuge of assumed indifference, and *confess itself conquered.*

Dawes thus becomes dehumanized, in the sense of losing essential human values, in a similar way to the other debased wretches who throng the novel and are not restricted to the convict elements. Dawes' forced surrender, the collapse of his mind under physical suffering beyond endurance, a form of violation more common in twentieth century than in nineteenth century literature, would seem to refute the idea of the inviolability of the human will. But Clarke is true to his time in assuming that moral responsibility has not been abrogated—Dawes is somehow to blame for his lapse, he has 'sinned'. The moving case of Kirkland, the innocent who is driven out of his mind and forced into suicide-attempts by the unnamed form of defilement he endures during an enforced night with the worst convicts, raises the same problem of the limits of human responsibility, but here Clarke is non-committal, suggesting, if anything, that Kirkland is to be pitied as a victim rather than harshly judged.

In his fall Dawes succumbs to the 'debased humanity' which lurks in everyone (Kirkland has encouraged Dawes to apply the cat by insinuating that he is 'no more than another man'). Dawes' corruption by despair—a deadlier menace than cruelty in Clarke's nightmarish world—is important to the novel as a whole, because it provides the main indictment of the penal system in particular, and of man's inhumanity in general. It shows that not only does the system preclude reform and encourage further degeneration, but that it can corrupt the most worthy, those most capable of resisting—and *corruptio optimum pessima.*

Dawes' moral collapse is important because it enables Clarke to continue the development of his themes. As has often been remarked Dawes passes from one 'hell' to another, and though he undergoes progressive degradation there is some attendant monotony. But the novel does develop. Book IV does more than add to the accumulation of horrors of the system by exposing conditions at Norfolk Island; more importantly it enlarges the moral references by showing how a soul which has reached the depths of degradation can be regenerated. In other words the emphasis of this Book is on redemption, and this was underlined in the revised version by the retitling of what became the penultimate chapter 'The Last of Norfolk Island' as 'The Redemption.'

The role of the Rev Mr North as would-be redeemer is of more interest than has been allowed; it offsets weaknesses in his presentation and explains the concentration on his diary entries. North is first introduced towards the end of Book III when Dawes has given in to despair. North, the dipsomaniac priest, has Dostoievskian qualifications for his role as 'saviour':

> He who would touch the hearts of men must have had his own heart seared. The missionaries of mankind have ever been great sinners before they earned the divine right to heal and bless. Their weakness was made their strength, and out of their own agony of repentance came the knowledge which made them masters and saviours of their kind. It was the agony of the Garden and the Cross that gave to the world's Preacher His Kingdom in the hearts of men. The crown of divinity is a crown of thorns.

Dawes responds to North's deeply felt sympathy, and to 'a glimpse of a misery more profound than his own'; but when the drunken North fails to visit him in hospital he sinks again into 'sullenness and despair' in reaction against the false priest, Meekin, who is fatally cut off from moral reality by his engrossing self-concern. Clarke's conception of North may have been partly the outcome of a reaction against Charles Reade's ideal portrait of the reforming clergyman, the saintly Mr Eden, in *It Is Never Too Late To Mend,* a work whose influence Clarke acknowledged. It is a mark of the harsh pessimism of *His Natural Life* that North not only ultimately fails as a priest and a man but becomes in part a demoniac figure, and is succeeded at Norfolk Island by 'the saintly Meekin'. When next we meet Dawes at Norfolk Island he has been 'brutalized' not only by the cruel system but by his own 'sin'. He reminds North of 'How habitual sin and misery suffice to brutalize the face divine!' There is here a possible word-play on Dawes' real surname 'Devine', with the suggestion that he has destroyed God's likeness in himself.

North assumes much more prominence in the abridged novel than in the original version, although his role remains substantially unchanged. In fact he becomes one of the chief characters. Besides providing the interest of a new character North helps to widen the concerns of the novel. He enlarges the moral reference by taking it *explicitly* beyond the convict system (hitherto the novel has implicitly transcended the system because Clarke penetrates to the enduring human nature behind it). North struggles against inner unworthiness not external persecution, yet his soul and mind are at stake and his self-torment is comparable to the suffering of the convicts. Like those who are degraded by the system, whether victims or masters of it, North 'loses his humanity', and is assailed by 'bestial' desires. Tormented by self-loathing, despair and 'monstrous imaginings' he loses faith in God and in life itself, facing a spiritual death like that endured by Dawes. In fact the moral counterpointing of Dawes and North provides the main interest and force of the final Book. Like Dawes, North is inspired by the goodness of Sylvia, but what begins as an exhortation to virtue ends as an ugly occasion of temptation. Drunkenness and lost of religious faith add to North's afflictions, with which he is rather over-loaded.

North wavers in his battle against his desires, and in him is presented a microcosm of what Clarke described as 'the terrible

Duality which is Man'. North has gone to Norfolk Island hoping to find there his 'purgation', and he sees his chance in the redemption of 'the notorious Dawes': 'Between these two—the priest and the sinner—was a sort of sympathetic hand'. When North speaks to Dawes of 'hope of release, of repentance, of redemption', Dawes sneeringly replies:

> 'Who's to redeem me?' he said, expressing his thoughts in phraseology that to ordinary folks might seem blasphemous. 'It would take a Christ to die again to save such as I.'

Later Clarke writes:

> 'It seemed to the fancy of the priest—a fancy distempered, perhaps by excess, or superhumanly exalted by mental agony—that this convict, over whom he had wept, was given to him as a hostage for his own salvation. 'I must save him or perish', he said. 'I must save him though I redeem him with my own blood.'

Later on the suggested parallels to Christ's role as redemptive saviour are not modified as in the above passages, and are apparently endorsed by the author.

Dawes refuses to give way again to despair under the renewed persecution of Frere, because he 'clung to North as the saviour of his agonized soul'. Under North's influence Dawes is regenerated though it is a weakness in the novel that this process is more talked about than demonstrated. Dawes has a premonition that 'the strange wild man of God' has 'become a man of evil', and this proves true. North, by this time verging on madness, loses the battle with himself, and his 'diseased imagination suggests that he should destroy his own fame in the eyes of the man whom he had taught to love him', then desert him and go away with Sylvia. His transformation from the divine to the demoniac is thus vividly exemplified, and the roles of Dawes and North become reversed.

Dawes reproaches North and forbids him to destroy his own soul and Sylvia's. North is confounded 'at this sudden reversal of their position towards each other'. Dawes now claims a divine mission: 'That God who sent you to save me from despair, give me strength to save you in my turn'.

In answer to North's plea of his love for Sylvia, Dawes tells him the cause of his own misfortunes to show him what true love means. This cause was different in the revised version. Instead of enduring transportation to hide his father-in-law's disgrace from a wife he does not really love, Dawes suffers to hide the guilt of an adulterous mother. The motive is not made convincing in either case, but in the second it is made to relate more closely to the moral scheme of the novel. This is brought out in an additional paragraph that was prefixed to the re-titled chapter 'The Redemption' in the revised version:

> That is my story. Let it plead with you to turn from your purpose, and to save her. The punishment of sin falls not upon the sinner only. A deed once done lives in consequence for ever, and this tragedy of shame and crime is but the outcome of a selfish sin like yours. [i.e. the sort of indulgence North is contemplating]

Dawes' unselfish love of both his mother and Sylvia stands in contrast not only to North's unworthy passion but to the brutish Frere's loveless attachment to Sylvia, which reaches its repulsive culmination in this final Book.

North has yet more frightful revelations to make to Dawes: he admits to robbing the murdered Lord Bellasis and not testifying to Dawes' innocence at the trial. This agonized confession would seem to presage forgiveness and redemption, but the fate of North from this point on is rather confused. Painfully aware of his own baseness as a 'despised outcast' (whereas Dawes is 'a hero—a martyr') he rushes to his cottage instead of to the ship, aware of nothing but his own anguish. He does not notice the absence of the gaoler for 'he was not in a condition to notice anything'. He feels he must now 'fulfil the doom he might once have averted' (presumably suicide), and at that moment glimpses Dawes who has taken the opportunity to escape, rowing to the ship disguised in North's cloak:

> He remembered how he had said, 'I will redeem him with my own blood!' Was it possible that a just heaven had decided to allow the man whom a coward had condemned, to escape, and to punish the coward who remained?

(We are reminded by this that North's role has already been mixed; previously at Port Arthur he has failed to act as redeemer and has instead contributed to Dawes' corruption by his weakness. This reversal of roles thus occurs a second time at Norfolk Island though here the result is different). North acquiesces in Dawes' escape instead of initiating it, though he presumably has no option. He then commits suicide, believing he is a mere 'corrupt shell'. It is ironic that this should be the fate of the 'free' man of God, not of the victim of the system. From this evidence it seems clear that the final phase of Dawes' redemption, and his release from the system, was the work of Providence in which North had to acquiesce. North, by his despair and gratuitous suicide (so far as Dawes' escape is concerned), is truly a lost soul, his self-murder representing a moral horror less sensational than Gabbett's murderous cannibalism, yet testifying along with it to man's 'debased humanity'—his destructive propensity for evil. The would-be redeemer thus fails to save his own soul.

Brian Elliott sees North as 'another Sidney Carton' [see excerpt dated 1958] and it would seem that Clarke wanted the reader to view him in an even grander, if similar, light; yet the evidence of both versions of the novel points in an opposite direction: North falters when he is on the threshold of winning his own and Dawes' salvation. (The comparison with Sidney Carton suggests that Clarke is working on a more complex level of character and theme if not of plot.) It would seem that Clarke wanted simultaneously to ennoble North and to damn him, and that he tries to have it both ways with some resultant confusion. This same ambivalence or uncertainty, perhaps signifying a mind divided against itself, is played out through the counterpointing of Dawes and North and through the unexpected but dramatic exchanging of their roles. It is certainly true that in spite of its ineffectually hopeful strain *His Natural Life* appeals to the reader as an oppressively dark novel springing from, and conveying, a harshly pessimistic view of man. It is Clarke's strength that he becomes in his own words 'poet of our desolation' (preface to Gordon's poems), and his grasp of desolation, with its striking emotional resonance as well as its insight, must have been rooted in some bitter part of his experience.

To return to the fate of Dawes following North's suicide; Dawes, acting consistently in his exchanged role and now redeemer in his turn, saves Sylvia from spiritual, if not physical, death, and so achieves his apotheosis:

> Then a pair of dark eyes beaming ineffable love and pity were bent upon her. . . .

She only considered in her awakening the story of his wrongs, remembered only his marvellous fortitude and love, knew only, in the last instant of her pure, ill-fated life, that as he had saved her once from starvation and death, so had he come to save her from sin and despair.

Though we may have reservations about Clarke's success in embodying his affirming theme, especially at this point, the ending of the novel will seem less arbitrary and melodramatic if it is seen as being carefully prepared for on a thematic level, as being part of a design at least admirable in intention.

Another strand of interest in Book IV of *His Natural Life* which has not been mentioned, but which is relevant to Dawes' redemption, is the story of John Rex's escape, his masquerade in England as Richard Devine, and his eventual detection and escape. In the original version this story was mainly dispersed through the additional lengthy Book. Clarke did not change its substance, but he drastically abridged it, and Rex's inglorious 'escape' from England now forms its conclusion. At first sight it would appear to have little relevance to the regeneration of Dawes and its attendant problems, but it does contribute to the moral scheme of Book IV (especially in the revised version), though its main function may be still to provide added plot-interest.

When Rex gains his freedom and goes to London to become a rich man he is progressively dehumanized, and this is seen not as the result of his convict experiences but of his innate moral brutishness. (The novel also suggests by the way that Gabbett's bestiality is natural to the man and not the product of the system under which it reaches a grisly flowering.) Like North and Dawes, Rex, though morally obtuse, has had his moment of choice in which it has been open to him to reform his life. When he is trapped alone in the caverns of the Blow-hole, his guilty imagination calls up visions 'of death and horror'; these are vividly evoked and are a kind of equivalent of his corrupt life:

> The naturalist, the explorer, or the ship-wrecked seaman would have found nothing frightful in this exhibition of the harmless life of the Australian ocean. But the convict's guilty conscience, long suppressed and derided, asserted itself in this hour when it was alone with Nature and Night. The bitter intellectual power which had so long supported him succumbed beneath imagination—the unconscious religion of the soul. If ever he was nigh repentance it was then. Phantoms of his past crimes gibbered at him, and covering his face with his hands he fell shuddering upon his knees.

Unlike the more sensitive North, Rex is not long tormented by such fantasies; but if he escapes his conscience and the law he does not avoid his retribution.

The Blow-hole incident, with its suggestions of the infernal and nightmarish nature of the place and its 'terror of solitude' suggests Rex's brief descent into the dark world of his own mind; but to insist on this might be to give the episode more significance than it can bear.

When Rex returns to London, 'the impulse of poverty and scheming having been removed, the natural brutality of his nature showed itself freely'. At the height of one of his most outrageous debauches he is an 'animal, torn, bloody and blasphemous'. It is appropriate that Rex, who cannot possibly become a Richard Devine [Dawes] in any sense, should be revealed as an imposter, and it is appropriate that his retribution

is not a return to convictism but a paralytic stroke which physically reduces him to the animal level on which he has always moved morally:

> The infernal genius of Sarah Purfoy had saved him at last—but saved him only that she might nurse him till he died—died ignorant even of her tenderness, a mere animal, lacking the intellect he had in his selfish wickedness abused.

So Rex, the 'King' of knaves, escapes from physical death at Eaglehawk Neck only to endure a living death. Like Dawes and North he has had a woman's devotion to regenerate him, but he uses it and religion (admittedly in the weak form of Meekin's ministrations) for his own ends. The repudiation of her love leads directly to his unmasking. The contrast between the retribution that overtook Rex, and the ends of North and Dawes, was heightened in revision by the bringing forward and condensing of the 'discovery' of Rex which allowed for a dramatic juxtaposition.

In the first three Books of *His Natural Life* Clarke spreads his net wide to include a variety of incident and character while retaining Dawes as central figure, but in the final Book the attention is narrowed to three individuals, Dawes, North and Rex. A desire to emphasize and extend this thematic relationship may help to explain, and partly to justify, what appears to be the most crude instance of Clarke's straining of coincidence, namely his involving the above three characters in the crime from which the whole action of the novel springs, the murder and robbery of Lord Bellasis. If seen in relation to the development of the novel, it is likely that Clarke is not using this melodramatic device merely for its own sake. Through it the three different natures are involved with evil at various levels of guilt and innocence, and their consequent fates are carefully weighed against one another so as to provide a paradigm of man's destiny.

Of course, to find a thematic coherence, or to draw attention to underlying conceptions in a novel is not to demonstrate that they are effectively embodied; and in the case of *His Natural Life* as we have already glimpsed, Clarke falls short of full realization of his aim of infusing an 'ideal' element. But the attempt takes an interesting form, and is flawed rather than downright unsuccessful. At the very least the working out of his themes in the final Book testifies to a careful regard for design at a deeper level than plot, which marks the whole novel and with which it is rarely credited.

Clarke shows restraint in handling his Christian symbolism, and it gains some power from the deep feeling that lies behind it but does not always achieve adequate expression. The flaws are obvious. The ending of the novel is conventionally strained and rhetorical, and there are some false notes of melodrama and sentimentality in the presentation of the introspective North. But the agony of this self-divided figure, with his destructive tensions and contradictions, is conveyed with some force, and he is effectively balanced against Dawes.

Clarke does not unduly distort North's character or rob it of its humanity by giving it its wider meaning. As would-be redeemer he is fulfilling the orthodox role as Christ's representative. Admittedly North's aspiration moves on an heroic level but this is offset by his human weaknesses; and moreover the underlying morality is not merely a conventional gesture. The notion that only priests who have themselves suffered the agonies of sin and repentance can conquer men's hearts is less orthodox; it may owe something to Dostoievsky and to Hawthorne's version of the 'Fortunate Fall'. And in Clarke's hands it is no mere romantic formula but is evidently animated by deep conviction in spite of some weaknesses of presentation. Similarly, Dawes in his regenerated goodness is Christ-like because he has been proved in the furnace of suffering (though not without the intervention of God's grace through the person of North). Clarke's 'myths', then, though they have about them something of the adulterating ideal that has not been refined away by conversion into deeply felt experience, are far from being divorced from experience and hence lacking in human meaning in the manner of inferior idealizations.

The kind of synthesis or rationalizaton Clarke attempted was a conventional ingredient in the Victorian novel of social protest which not only revealed festering social ills but also indicated a way of remedying them. However, Clarke offers no easy solutions like many of his contemporaries; and he links his social ills with what is enduring in human nature. Moreover, the affirmatory strain, even in the work of such novelists as Dickens, Charles Kingsley and Charles Reade, is often more crude and 'undigested' than in *His Natural Life*. If Clarke failed to realize his views of good and evil with equal success, and to merge them in a single powerful vision, he failed in a supreme task. (pp. 38-49)

> L. T. Hergenhan, "The Redemptive Theme in 'His Natural Life'," in Australian Literary Studies, Vol. 2, No. 1, June, 1965, pp. 32-49.

HAROLD J. BOEHM   (essay date 1972)

[In the following essay, Boehm demonstrates how Clarke uses complex patterns of internal and external conflict and animal and prison imagery to reveal theme in His Natural Life.]

The cumulative power of Marcus Clarke's novel on the convict system, *His Natural Life,* has been acknowledged by every major critic who has written on the work, in spite of certain reservations about the melodrama and overwriting in sections of the novel. Nevertheless, relatively little has been done on the source of the narrative, from which much, though not the ultimately significant portion, of the impact of the novel springs. That Clarke borrowed heavily from various sources for the events and characterizations of *His Natural Life* is evident from the sources listed in the appendix of the novel; however, a careful look at them and an attentive re-reading of the book reveal a skill and artistry in the novel which are not explained by the quality of the original material. Clarke obviously discovered a theme in his readings, but it was a theme obscured by the variety of the materials; therefore, in the revised (novel) version of the story, he carefully structured the materials he had come across around a central conflict, added a pervasive network of appropriate imagery, and thus aimed every detail in the book at one coherent (though complex) thematic statement. It is from this process of patterning that the most telling effect of the novel springs.

The resulting structure (using structure as a term which includes all the elements—particularly, here, conflict, imagery, and theme—which make up a work of fiction) can best be seen as an interlocking pattern of various forms of disintegration, counterpointed by or coupled with a weaker, though still significant, line of regeneration and accretion. The positive side of the novel, the weaker rising line of affirmation, has been dealt with by L. T. Hergenhan in his article "The Redemptive Theme in *His Natural Life*" [see excerpt dated 1965]. But even he admits the "source of the novel's main power" is Clarke's

"realization of evil and suffering."... The images of waste and destruction used to describe Van Diemen's Land ("a biscuit at which rats have been nibbling," "melted lead" upset by a careless giant and "spilt" into the ocean) could be taken as types for the action or movement of the novel: it is a book about wasted, destroying, or self-destroying lives; the nibbling process is insidious and pervasive. But in order to see the pattern emerging, each of the major elements—conflict, imagery and theme—must be examined in turn.

There are two broad types of conflict in the story, external and internal. All the characters in *His Natural Life* are to some degree pitted against the world in which they live; more apparently, character struggles against character in the oppositions both inside and outside the world of the felon; and finally, most of the major figures find themselves torn by a bitter, and, in at least James North's case, self-destructive internal conflict. Initially at least, the general conflict, both external and internal, is between good and evil. In the simplicity of its oppositions, then, the book follows one of the conventions of melodrama. That convention, however, is given a twist: in *His Natural Life,* evil, almost without exception, triumphs over good. The price that is paid by the victor is moral disintegration.

The effects of the world in which all the characters make their way may be inferred from the arguments that follow; my analysis will be confined to external and internal conflicts involving the characters themselves. The central external conflict, that between Rufus Dawes and Maurice Frere, contains the most readily apparent embodiment of the pattern mentioned previously. It can best be pictured as a simple diagram: on the one hand we have the rise of the fortunes of Maurice Frere, much of which is dependent on his initial ruthless exploitation of Dawes's skill and courage; on the other, the decline of those of Rufus Dawes. Everything Dawes, the good man, loses, Frere gains. Dawes loses the respect of the honest elements of society; Frere, by means of increasingly cruel practices, wins their respect, but not their affection. Dawes loses the love of Sylvia Vickers; Frere, though he uses cowardly means, gains it, only to slowly destroy what he has unjustly attained. Dawes sinks lower and lower into the hell of convictism; with ruthless and cruel efficiency, Frere rises higher and higher in its authoritarian superstructure. Dawes loses his fortune; John Rex usurps it. Finally, Dawes loses his life; Frere remains alive, in the barren world he has created, to torment prisoners on Norfolk Island.

Similarly, in the external conflict between Frere and North, it is the humane North who loses his battles to better the lot of the prisoners; in the Kirkland incident it is Frere who finally undermines North's attempts to bring Burgess, the commandant of Port Arthur, to account for his cruelty. On Norfolk Island their relations further deteriorate, until North finds that "for a prisoner to be seen talking to the clergyman was sufficient to ensure for him a series of tyrannies." Finally, his inner conflict and Frere's persecution of him and the prisoners he attempts to serve, drive him to decide to leave Norfolk Island and abandon his attempts.

In John Rex's conflict with whatever justice lies with the government side, it is Rex who finally circumvents the law and evades punishment. For his ruthless use of Sarah Purfoy and Lady Devine he suffers the same moral disintegration Frere undergoes, but his final punishment is not inflicted by the system he circumvents. Likewise, Sarah Purfoy, and through Sarah's influence, Captain Blunt, follow a life of evil and prosper. Sarah is obviously the mistress of a house of prostitution, the *George the Fourth,* in Hobart Town; judging from the description of the "handsomely furnished" house, she has profited in the trade. Later she uses the stolen money kept for Rex and herself in London to build a sizeable fortune in New South Wales. Blunt does her errands, including picking up the fugitive Rex, for her, and evidently is rewarded both by her and by Frere, who procures command of the *Lady Franklin* for him. The good characters, on the other hand, are either killed, as is the "faithful watch-dog" Bates, or to some extent compromised. Thus evil, at least externally, wins over good.

For every external conflict involving a major character, there is likewise an internal conflict between the two opposing forces, good and evil. All the major characters—including Sylvia—and, with (perhaps) the exception of Sarah Purfoy, all the significant minor characters, go through this process of gradual dissolution or destruction. Frere grows progressively more brutal; Dawes is more and more affected by his degrading surroundings; North and Rex progressively lose their powers of restraint; even Sylvia becomes, because of her marriage to Frere, less and less of a woman, and finally a runaway; Gabbett sinks from bestiality to complete degradation and finally into madness. The whole world depicted in *His Natural Life,* degree by degree, loses its morally restorative characters and powers.

Internal conflict might reasonably be expected to be weakest in Frere: there is, however, a significant attempt by Clarke to present a weak, but nonetheless real, "good" (or at least more human) side to his character, which is gradually destroyed by his own actions. The reader is told Frere's five years as commandant at Maria Island "had increased that brutality of thought" which is his most salient characteristic; yet, when the half-starved, half-mad convict Dawes suddenly appears at the outcasts' fire (and they have very scanty provisions to begin with) the idea of killing Dawes while he sleeps occurs to Frere, "but, to do him justice, the thought no sooner shaped itself than he crushed it out." He later commits a great wrong against Dawes, but there is evidence he suffers some remorse for what he has done: before she marries Frere, Sylvia constantly, though unconsciously, torments him by stating half playfully "if you hadn't saved my life, you know, I shouldn't love you a bit." Finally Frere, hearing a convict servant whistling as he works in the garden, states uncharacteristically, "They're not so badly off," and half confesses his unworthiness to Sylvia. Later he is driven to ask her directly if she would have loved him had he not saved her, as she supposes he has; her answer is again qualified, and Clarke states: "If there had been for a moment any sentiment of remorse in his selfish heart, the hesitation of her answer went far to dispell it." Finally even this suggestion of remorse is crushed out, when after their marriage Frere brags to North about his "rescue" of Sylvia: "That was how we fell in love," said he [Frere], tossing off his wine complacently." And on Norfolk Island he reaches the nadir of callousness when he taunts Dawes with the remark: "Have you made any more boats?"

Dawes also undergoes an internal conflict, because of the brutalizing forces acting on him. He is forced into making a number of choices; and at first they are rather simple, between good and evil. He wavers when he throws himself into the ocean from Grummet rock; but he chooses for the good when he decides not to take the coracle he has built and leave Mrs Vickers, Sylvia, and Frere to starve. His betrayal by Frere causes him to take a downward course, but he retains faith in the memory of Sylvia. When that is destroyed by Sylvia's inability to recognize him, he takes another turn for the worse.

HIS NATURAL LIFE

BY

MARCUS CLARKE

Author of OLD TALES OF A YOUNG COUNTRY, HOLIDAY PEAK, &c.

MELBOURNE: GEORGE ROBERTSON
33 AND 35 LITTLE COLLINS STREET WEST
1874

The title page of the first edition of His Natural Life.

He later consents to flog Kirkland—a deed considered worse than all others by the convicts—but stops after fifty-six lashes and refuses to go on, though he is himself flogged for it. This flogging and the substitution of Meekin for North in the chaplaincy at Port Arthur causes Dawes to despair further, and on Norfolk Island he becomes the leader of the "Ring," which has "strangled in their hammocks" two convict informers. Frere finally breaks the man partially. Despite the enormous pressure of the forces working towards his brutalization, Dawes is able occasionally to reverse the process and briefly regain part of his rightful nature; though, significantly, his final symbolic and actual freedom occurs only moments before his death.

Like Frere, Rex seems at first to have some good qualities: Bates says: "John Rex, you were never made to be a convict, man!" Rex is later described as a "reader of hearts"; thus it is apparent he has some sensitivity, though it may be used for a bad end. Again like Frere, Rex only occasionally gives way to moral considerations; still, there are two significant occasions when he wavers in his villainy. The first is the night he spends in the Devil's Blowhole, in which the gibbering forms of his past press in on him; "if ever he was nigh repentance it was then." But in daylight the pangs of remorse are snuffed out. The second occasion is during his deception of Lady Devine: he once feels "inclined to confess all, and leave his case in the hands of the folk he had injured"; and later Sarah urges a similar course of action. But he suppresses both. And he too destroys himself.

The clearest and strongest internal conflict is in the Rev. James North. His tortured downward movement is set out in graphic detail. But once again, evil triumphs over good; North succumbs to his dishonest desires and literally destroys himself. It is this conflict, however, which is most removed from the simple opposition of good and evil—North's decision to take Sylvia from her husband, considering the circumstances, is not an entirely blameworthy one. Good and evil become almost hopelessly mixed here, and the last chapter is unsatisfactory because Clarke seems forced to reduce the complex moral dilemma that North undergoes to a simple good/evil opposition.

Sylvia also experiences internal conflict, though hers is not examined in the detail North's is. She too succumbs to her desires and chooses what Clarke, in spite of his sympathy, obviously feels is the wrong course, in deciding to run off with North. This act of "despair," however, is only the end of a long chain of forced abandonment of her best womanly qualities. Her disintegration, like Dawes's, is mainly against her will; overwhelming circumstances force her to suppress or give up the best qualities she possesses.

It is apparent, then, that the simple diagram of the pattern of *His Natural Life* mentioned earlier must be modified in order to express the complexity of the last two books of the novel. Rex, the convict, like Frere the commandant, rises in the physical world but declines morally; he also experiences the love of a woman, Sarah Purfoy, but it does not keep him from betraying her though she has devoted her life to making him a free man. Like the convict Dawes, he also makes a series of choices which leads to the final one between good and evil; unlike Dawes, Rex consistently chooses the evil alternative: in his rejection of Sarah's faithfulness, his resistance to the impulse to confess to Lady Devine the identity and whereabouts of her real son, and his misuse of the Devine fortune. Finally, his outward state matches his inward corruption, and he becomes a mere animal.

On the other hand, North wages a constant war with himself. His decline is a tortured, self-aware sliding into what almost becomes a compulsion. But, in spite of the compulsive drinking, Clarke ensures that North makes a number of other choices for which he can be held responsible. North knew Dawes was innocent in England, but out of fear of exposure did not reveal Dawes's true role in the murder of Lord Bellasis. This is not to deny that North has impulses for the good: he genuinely tries to save Kirkland from the triangles, and later presses the injustice of the case in order to ameliorate the condition of the other prisoners. His affection for Dawes is also genuine, though ultimately it is compromised by his decision to run off with Sylvia, thus to his mind at least destroying all the good he has accomplished.

Thus North's spiritual decline counterpoints Dawes's tortured spiritual regeneration. Though Rex is on the other side of the bars, he mirrors Frere's simultaneous rise and decline on the two levels mentioned. Meekin, wherever he appears in the novel (and we are reminded in Book Four that he will soon take North's place on Norfolk Island), remains always the same. He learns nothing from the suffering taking place around him. He neither declines nor rises on either a spiritual or material plane; he simply moves, morally obtuse and complacent as he was at the beginning, from place to place. He is at Hobart Town, Port Arthur, and later will be at Norfolk Island; his baseness is constant, and from it we can better judge the decline or rise of the other characters.

The imagery which ties the book together follows the same pattern as the conflict, from the crude to the complex. . . . [There] are three major sets of images in the novel: animal imagery, prison imagery, and images of "value" which surround Sylvia and her relationship with Dawes. The omnipresent animal imagery has been quite competently examined by Dr. L. T. Hergenhan, but it is so integral to the novel that, even at the risk of repetition, at least a brief examination seems to be necessary.

The animal imagery used is both general and particularized in its application. All the major characters except Sylvia are described in animal terms; the convicts are consistently described as "wild beasts" of one sort or another, both by the characters in the novel and by Clarke himself; finally even the minor characters and inanimate objects are presented in animal terms. Bates, the pilot at Macquarie Harbour, is "like a faithful watchdog"; Sarah has a "tigerish look" and leaps out of the ship's cabin "like a panther"; Sarah and John Rex are two "birds of prey" who victimize "lambs" and "pigeons" in London; the convict ship *Malabar* itself becomes a "huge sea monster"; the gaol at Port Arthur responds like "a tame animal" to the hands of Frere and Burgess when they show Sylvia around; the boat the convicts escape in from Eaglehawk Neck is like "a six-legged insect"; and so on. Clarke describes a world of predators and the preyed upon: there are no other classifications which can exist for long.

There is, however, a clear differentiation in the use of animal imagery connected with each character. At the lowest level, Matthew Gabbett the cannibal is compared to a "wild boar," a "wounded bull," and is "less a man than a demon, or one of those monstrous and savage apes" of Africa. Later, in a key passage, Clarke says of Gabbett:

> . . . looking at the animal, as he crouched, with one foot curled round the other, and one hairy arm pendant between his knees, he was so horribly unhuman, that one shuddered to think that tender women and fair children must, of necessity, confess to fellowship of kind with such a monster.

The important point here is not so much that Gabbett is an unhuman monster, but that he shares a common nature with all men and that he is therefore not so much an aberration as an exaggeration. Gabbett's utter debasement is, of course, demonstrated in the premeditated cannibalism practised in the Port Arthur escape.

Maurice Frere is only a step above Gabbett, though his viciousness is mitigated by some good feelings, such as his early love for Sylvia. Frere is compared to a "bulldog," called a "smoking animal," often slips into his "native coarseness," is "impatiently brutal," and his marriage, according to Clarke, is a "marriage of the Minotaur."

> When the animal and spiritual natures cross each other, the nobler triumphs in fact if not in appearance. Maurice Frere, though his wife obeyed him, knew that he was inferior to her, and was afraid of the statue he had created.

His treatment of convicts reflects the brutality of his nature: he calls them "dogs" and "brutes," and treats them as such. All the better parts of his nature are slowly destroyed by his growing brutality until he becomes what he considers the convicts to be.

John Rex goes through a similar process of disintegration. He is the counterpart of Frere on the other side of the law. As long as he is constrained by circumstances he plays the part of the gentleman, but when he is safe in his role of Richard Devine he "suffered his true nature to appear. He was violent to the servants, cruel to dogs and horses, often wantonly coarse in speech, and brutally regardless of the feelings of others." When drunk he becomes an "animal, torn, bloody and blasphemous." The "natural brutality of his nature showed itself freely." Like Frere, he frequently admits to being a "brute." Finally, when he is discovered and has a stroke, he is "like a beast in the shambles that has received a mortal stroke," and Sarah takes him away to "nurse him till he died—died ignorant even of her tenderness, a mere animal, lacking the intellect he had in his selfish wickedness abused."

James North is also described in animal terms at times, though these are usually self-descriptions recorded in his diary. In his attempt to keep himself from drinking the night before Kirkland's punishment:

> . . . he told himself that another's life depended on his exertions, that to give way to his fatal passion was unworthy of an educated man and a reasoning being, that it was degrading, disgusting, and bestial.

When he fails, he tells Dawes he is "a besotted beast." Later he says of his craving "a hideous wild beast seems to stir within me, a monster, whose cravings cannot be satisfied," which "can only be drowned in stupefying brandy." "I feel all the animal within me stirring." "By day I feel myself a wolf in sheep's clothing . . . At night I become a satyr . . . I lose my humanity. I am a beast." North struggles heroically against his obsession, but ultimately fails.

Dawes too becomes an animal in the penal institutions, but his is a descent into brutality imposed from without. All the others to some degree choose to become brutes; Dawes is forced into it.

Opposed to this imagery of degradation is the set of images connected with Sylvia and with Dawes's relations to her. As a child, she is not of the beast-like world around her: she is a "fairy," an "elfin creature"; to Dawes the "sudden apparition of this golden haired girl" after his misery at Macquarie Harbour is providential: she becomes "his good angel, his protectress, his glimpse of heaven"; later, after Frere has usurped Dawes's rightful place, she becomes Maurice's "good angel"; when Sylvia doesn't recognize Dawes in court his "dream child" is destroyed, and "the beauty had gone from earth, the brightness from heaven." The world which Clarke depicts cannot allow such goodness and beauty to exist for long and on Norfolk Island, after several years of marriage to Frere, she becomes a "nervous invalid," a "statue," "artificial ice."

There are false hopes of happiness for Dawes and Sylvia before their final union in death. When Dawes learns from Frere that he is a rich man, and his success in building the coracle gives him some hope of a pardon so that he may claim it, he fixes his eyes "upon the sea, weltering golden in the sunset." But his hopes are dashed. Similarly, Sylvia believes Frere has actually rescued her and after her marriage to him the bride and bridegroom depart "through the golden afternoon"; but her dreams are also destroyed. The images are repeated in the scene in which Sylvia rescues Dawes from the "stretcher":

> Rufus Dawes, awakening from his stupor, saw, in the midst of a *sunbeam* which penetrated a window in the corridor, the woman who had come to save

> his body supported by the priest who had come to save his soul . . . (my italics.)

North takes Sylvia out of the prison, and it is at this moment that he decides to run off with her:

> The convict's arms fell, and an undefinable presentiment of evil chilled him as he beheld the priest— emotion pallid in his cheeks—slowly draw the fair young creature from out the sunlight into the grim shadow of the heavy archway. For an instant the gloom swallowed them, and it seemed to Dawes that the strange wild man of God had in that instant become a man of Evil—blighting the brightness and the beauty of the innocence that clung to him. For an instant—and then they passed out of the prison archway into the free air of heaven—and the sunlight glowed golden on their faces.

But the golden sunlight is an illusion; no happiness lies ahead for Sylvia with the debased priest. Dawes escapes from the island, and Syliva realizes in the midst of the fatal storm, "that as he had saved her once from starvation and death, so had he come again to save her from sin and from despair." After the storm, the bodies of Sylvia and Dawes, clasped together, "golden in the rays of the new risen morning," drift out to sea. The success of this last image is the result of the careful preparation in earlier chapters.

One final set of images remains to be examined: the prison images used in the novel. In their metaphorical significance, these images concern mainly Rex, North, Frere and Dawes— the reality of gaols, of course, permeates the work. John Rex, though he is free while Dawes is confined, finds that freedom is not a purely physical condition:

> After he was landed in Sydney, by the vessel which Sarah Purfoy had sent to save him, he found himself a slave to a bondage scarcely less galling than that from which he had escaped—the bondage of enforced companionship with an unloved woman.

Rex chafes at this confinement and "ceaselessly sought means of escape from this second prison house." "Twice he tried to escape from his thraldom, and was twice brought back." He finally succeeds in escaping her "thraldom," goes to England and impersonates Richard Devine, and "for five or six months he thought himself in Paradise." Then he began to find his life insufferably weary." Later Sarah finds him. "It was hard, in the very high tide and flush of assured success, to be thus plucked back into the old bondage." Finally, when Rex has his stroke, he is bound forever to Sarah.

James North's imprisonment is more subtle, but none the less binding. He says of his propensity for drink: "I have striven with my familiar sin, and have not always been worsted. Melancholy reflection. 'Not always!' '*But yet*' is as a gaoler to bring forth some monstrous malefactor." On the next page he quotes four lines of poetry which he feels express his predicament:

> What art thou, thou tremendous power
> Who dost inhabit us without our leave,
> And art, within ourselves, another self,
> A master self that loves to domineer?

"Circumstances," he says, "have made you what you are, and will shape your destiny for you without your interference." He adds that the maxim "man is a slave of circumstances" is "a doctrine which I am inclined to believe, though unwilling to confess." Finally, when he asks Sylvia to run away with him, he finds she is already scheduled to leave on the same ship which will take him from the island; his reaction is predictable: ''It was not of my seeking. Fate has willed it. We go together!'' But he cannot deceive himself long: ''. . . he had succumbed to his passion, and to win the love for which he yearned had voluntarily abandoned truth and honour; but standing thus alone with his sin, he despised and hated himself.'' It is the mark of North's failure to free himself from his demon that he finally kills himself.

Frere's loss of freedom is yet more subtle. He gradually rejects all the good around him until he is left with the one thing he has chosen—the prison. He talks only about the convicts and convict discipline; his ''love for [Sylvia] had burnt itself out . . . his apparent affection had been born of sensuality, and had perished in the fires it had itself kindled.'' He so ruins his home life that he invites North to dine with them: ''. . . though he disliked the clergyman, yet [he] was glad of anybody who would help him to pass a cheerful evening.'' They are finally reduced to petty bickering about Sylvia's refusal to sew on buttons for Frere. Maurice can be happy nowhere but in the scenes of misery he has himself created.

Dawes, on the other hand, though his body is in chains, is constantly striving to free his soul. For most of his imprisonment the struggle is simply to preserve his constantly threatened integrity. And, though he falters at times, Dawes is able briefly to free his body, and finally liberate his soul. As Sylvia and he wait for the end on the doomed *Lady Franklin,* ''they felt as beings whose bodies had already perished, and as they clasped hands their *freed* souls, recognizing each the loveliness of the other, rushed tremblingly together'' (my italics).

As is evident from the conflict and imagery of **His Natural Life,** Clarke began the book as a rather simple tale about the convict system. But, as he grew more and more interested in his characters and their fates, especially the tormented James North, he realized that not just Rufus Dawes but all men wear the yellow jacket. Convicts and ''free'' men alike must work out their own destiny, and if they are ever to be truly free they must shed the yellow jacket of their own making. Fate is, thus, partly of our own devising:

> . . . a thousand memories, each bearing in its breast the corpse of some dead deed whose influence haunts us yet, are driven like feathers before the blast, as unsubstantial and as unregarded. The mists which shroud our self-knowledge become transparent, and we are smitten with sudden lightning-like comprehension of our own misused power over our fate.

The specific theme of the work deals with the effect of the convict system on the human soul; but the general theme concerns the struggle of the individual to affirm the good in a world filled with evil.

The specific theme is stated early in the book in a chapter entitled ''The Barracoon'' (called ''How Society Made Its Criminals Forty Years Ago'' in the serial version). Clarke is describing the hold of a convict ship in which hardened criminals and first offenders are placed side by side:

> Each new-comer was one more recruit to the ranks of ruffianism, and not a man penned in that reeking den of infamy but became a sworn hater of law, order, and ''free-men.'' What he might have been before mattered not. He was now a prisoner, and—thrust into a suffocating barracoon, herded with the foulest of mankind, with all imaginable depths of blasphemy and indecency sounded hourly in his sight and hearing—he lost his self-respect, and became what his jailers took him to be—a wild beast to be locked under bolts and bars, lest he should break out and tear them.

The use of the words ''penned,'' ''den,'' ''herded,'' and ''wild beast,'' combined with the earlier description of the exercise pen on deck as a kind of ''cattle-pen'' and numerous references to ''wild beasts'' when the convicts are being discussed, makes obvious the major role animal imagery plays in the theme of the novel. Here the theme is as simple as it seems—treat a man like an animal and he will become one. It is not until later in the novel that Clarke develops the complexities of his subject matter.

On the other hand, the effect of this transformation is not so simple: instead of the convict hating the law or the social system which put him into the situation in which he exists as a brute, his hatred becomes general. Dawes, after going through six years of punishment, is cast up by chance with the abandoned party at Macquarie Harbour; Frere, intimidated by his savage appearance, asks the ''wretch'': ''. . . why should you wish to be revenged on *me*?'' Dawes replies: ''If I am a wretch, who made me one?. . . I was born free—as free as you are. Why should I be sent to herd with beasts?'' Frere defends himself on the grounds that he did not make the laws, and asks: ''. . . why do you attack me?'' Dawes replies: ''Because you are what I *was*. You are FREE!. . . You can love, you can work, you can think. I can only *hate!*''

The writing is melodramatic, but the point is clear. The process is not irreversible, though: as Sylvia and Mrs Vickers become more and more dependent on him, Dawes himself begins to change:

> Rufus Dawes was no longer the brutalized wretch who had plunged into the dark waters of the bay to escape a life he loathed, and had alternately cursed and wept in the solitudes of the forests. He was an active member of society—a society of four—and he began to regain an air of independence and authority.

As soon as the task is complete, however, and the four have the means to escape to civilization, the environment changes again:

> As long as escape was impracticable, he had been useful, and even powerful. Now he had pointed out the way of escape, he had sunk into the beast of burden once again. In the desert he was ''Mr'' Dawes, the saviour; in civilized life he would become once more Rufus Dawes, the ruffian, the prisoner, the absconder.

Dawes, of course, is thrown back into his life of misery when Mrs Vickers dies, Sylvia loses her memory after suffering a fever, and Frere lies about Dawes's role in the escape. But the memory of his brief enjoyment of the privileges of humanity sustains him until he escapes and Sylvia, not remembering this true role in the affair, has him recaptured. It is in the subsequent flogging of Kirkland and Dawes's endurance of the lash that Dawes finally breaks, though it is only a temporary lapse. Again, the breakdown is expressed in animal imagery: Dawes, after enduring a hundred and twenty lashes:

> . . . shrieked imprecation upon Burgess, Troke, and North. He cursed all soldiers for tyrants, all parsons for hypocrites. He blasphemed his God and his Saviour. With a frightful outpouring of obscenity and blasphemy, he called on the earth to gape and swallow his persecutors, for heaven to open and rain fire upon them, for hell to yawn and engulf them quick. It was as though each blow of the cat forced out of

him a fresh burst of beast-like rage. He seemed to have abandoned his humanity.

At Port Arthur, then, as at Macquarie Harbour, the effect of treating a man like a brute is to rob him of his ability to discriminate, to make his hatred general instead of particular, and to inspire in him a desire for revenge, not only on his persecutors, but on all men and on the God who allows such evil to flourish.

Seven years later the effects of being surrounded by men made into animals by the gaols and those whose nature was brutalized from youth, and the lack of anything to believe in or to hope for, show themselves in Dawes. The Rev. James North writes in his diary:

> He was much changed from the man I remember. Seven years ago he was a stalwart, upright, handsome man. He has become a beetle-browed, sullen, slouching ruffian. His hair is grey, though he cannot be more than forty years of age, and his frame has lost that just proportion of parts which once made him almost graceful. His face has also grown like other convict faces—how hideously alike they all are!— and, save for his black eyes and a peculiar trick he had of compressing his lips, I should not have recognized him.

Dawes, and therefore all convicts, have no choice but to draw examples from the dehumanized convicts around them, or from the often brutal or callous warders who watch over them. For Clarke then, one of the most harmful effects of prison life is the separation of the individual from good society.

From this point on Dawes remains the brutalized wretch he is when North sees him on Norfolk Island until Sylvia rescues him from the "stretcher." This act again gives Dawes something to hope for, and is in part responsible for his ability to withstand North's self-revelation of crime and hypocrisy. The animal imagery associated with Dawes then is primarily imposed from without: he is made into a wretch and a brute; these are not his natural characteristics.

The specific theme involving the effect of the convict system on the human soul is epitomized in Rufus Dawes, though it is also exhibited in such scenes as Kirkland's flogging. But it is in the characters of John Rex (after his escape from Port Arthur), Maurice Frere in the fourth book, and particularly the Rev. James North that Clarke realizes the more pervasive and more insidious interior gaol; it is this theme which makes the novel universal in its application. What was intended to be an occasional piece on the even then defunct convict system was gradually transformed in Clarke's imagination to a statement about man's capacity for evil; and ultimately it became a searching examination of the meaning of freedom. The threads Clarke found in the old almanacs, journals, and convict indents weaved themselves into a pattern in the light of his gifted imagination. The imagery, and in part the theme, were suggested by the sources themselves, but the structure is Clarke's; and the vision of the yellow jacket which every man in his secret heart wears was born of the bitterness of life, and embodied in the bitterness of the transportation system. This is Clarke's achievement. (pp. 57-70)

> *Harold J. Boehm, "The Pattern of 'His Natural Life':*
> *Conflict, Imagery, and Theme as Elements of Struc-*
> *ture," in* Journal of Commonwealth Literature, *Vol.*
> *VII, No. 1, June, 1972, pp. 57-71.*

MICHAEL WILDING   (essay date 1976)

[*In the following excerpt, Wilding attempts to demonstrate that Clarke's short stories anticipated those of Henry Lawson, who is often credited with establishing the outback as a setting in Australian fiction.*]

The Lawson tradition of the Australian short story, that you take your material from the bush, the outback, up-country, had already been established by Clarke. The short story was seen as the appropriate form for those materials. With Clarke, however, the tradition was not a reductive one: to write about the country you turned to the short story, certainly; but to write a short story, you did not have to turn to the country. He also wrote urban melodramas, historical fantasies, speculative gothic stories, and naturalistic stories that were not set in the country; and these different settings and types were an important part of his short story output.

Yet when Clarke came to collect his first volume of stories, *Holiday Peak,* he gathered together stories that were all, despite their very great variety in manner, set in the Australian up-country. A tradition was established.

Holiday Peak is a collection designed to show the range of Clarke's writing. The up-country setting provides an overall unity; but formally the pieces include fantasies (the title story, for instance), naturalistic stories, and sketches. He even includes one piece that was originally written as a "Peripatetic Philosopher" column, **"Arcades Ambo"**. An Addisonian essay, it portrays the changing nature and conditions of the squatters, contrasting a description of the old style squatter Robin Ruff with the new style young gentleman squatter leading an elegant, wealthy life, Dudley Smooth. The Latin title, the names denoting the types of the characters, indicate the English essay genre to which the piece belongs. And we are presented with the two antithetical types. Ruff "is six feet high, his hands are knotted and brown—mottled with sun and hardened with labour. His shoulders are broad, his head well set up, his eyes confident." Whereas Dudley Smooth "was of a very different stamp. Mr. Smooth was a very young gentleman. His hands were brown but well-kept, and his whiskers were of a fine yellow floss-silk order, like the down on a duckling. He had but lately come down from his station, but was arrayed in the most fashionable of fashionable garments". Yet these eighteenth century antitheses are seen, even as they are formulated, as belonging to the past. In this new world there are no static, permanent structures; the antitheses now are a dynamic dialectic from which a new force is emerging. Smooth

> has not arrived at the glory of his next neighbour, the Hon. Tom Holles, younger son of the Marquis of Portman-square, who was educated at Oxford and Cirencester, and has taken up squatting on scientific principles. The Hon. Tom washes his sheep in an American dip at the rate of 200 a minute, drafts cattle in lavender gloves, has nearly perfected a shearing machine, quotes Aeschylus to his overseer, prohibits all swearing, except on Sundays, and has named his bullocks after the most distinguished of the early Christians. The Hon. Tom belongs to a later phase of development, and Dudley is far behind *him* in civilisation, but he stands out in alarming contrast to poor honest, simple-minded Robin Ruff.

The Peripatetic Philosopher's facetious note catches that eighteenth century contempt for enthusiasm, for faddish belief in progress; but at the same time the realities of scientific advances, of the technologies of that older New World of the

United States have begun to intrude. The *Australasian* readers may have laughed at the Hon. Tom and admired the traditional antitheses of the Ruffs and the Smooths. But Clarke knew the Hon. Toms were on their way. And he had to look for a new literary tone to accommodate them.

There are two pieces in **Holiday Peak** that are sketches of a very different nature—far less formally stylized, essayistic pieces. These are "**An Up-Country Township**" and "**Grumbler's Gully**"; and they have a direct, naturalistic manner, a contemporary, immediate, documentary note. "**An Up-Country Township**" is a description of Bullocktown: Clarke used Bullocktown and its environs as the setting for practically all his up-country stories. Hamilton Mackinnon records that "'**Bullocktown**' is well known to be Glenorchy, the post-town of the Swinton Station, and all the characters in it are recognisable as life portraits presented with that peculiar glamor which his genius cast over all his literary work." The Bullocktown setting provides something of a Balzacian unity for these separate yet interrelating stories; we finally assemble a topography and sociology of a representative Australian country area; though the enforced unification of setting creates some tensions when naturalistic stories and sketches, melodramas, and utter fantasies are yoked together.

"**An Up-Country Township**" itself, however, is in a strictly naturalistic mode—and that distinctively low-keyed, wry, dry, ironic, Australian naturalism.

> Bullocktown is situated, like all up-country townships, on the banks of something that is a flood in winter and a mud-hole in summer. For general purposes the inhabitants of the city called the something a river, and those intelligent land surveyors that mark "agricultural areas" on the tops of lofty mountains, had given the river a very grand name indeed.
>
> The Pollywog Creek, or as it was marked on the maps, the Great Glimmera, took its rise somewhere about Bowlby's Gap, and after constructing a natural sheepwash for Bowlby, terminated in a swamp, which was courteously termed Lake Landowne. No man had ever seen Lake Landowne, but once, and that was during a flood, but Lake Landowne the place was called, and Lake Landowne it remained; reeds, tussocks, and brindled bullocks' backs to the contrary notwithstanding.

In "**Arcades Ambo**" Clarke was using the urbane essayist's tone, looking at characters out there, observing them with a knowing, worldly, distant attitude; sympathetically, certainly, but not with the sympathy of the participant in that world; the essayist is an urban man of letters with a good classical education. But in "**An Up-Country Township**" there is a marked difference; here the writer is expressing an identity of stance with the inhabitants of Bullocktown—laughing wryly at the city-based surveyors who know nothing of the actualities of the country they map. The Great Glimmera is known to the Bullocktonians as the Pollywog Creek, and it is as the Pollywog Creek that it is introduced, the distant, formal, official name added as a subordinate, secondary piece of information. Interestingly, what starts out as if it is a third person narration, evolves into a first person account—stressing even further the identity of the narrator's stance with the Bullocktonians. Here is somebody writing about the country with the values and assumptions of those living in the country: not as an urban, literary, pastoralizing intellectual. This is the sort of stance we so admire in Lawson's best writing. Clarke, however, differs in a major tonal aspect from Lawson here. Though Clarke is

writing from the stance of the country inhabitant, he is not writing as a country worker. Lawson made that further move in vocabulary, rhythm, and tone. Clarke is still writing as the well educated countryman who can recognize a classical allusion. But importantly he does let the country worker speak, and he frequently puts his narratorial support behind the quoted speech of those workers; though making it clear that while he is used to mixing with people who talk in this colourful and lively way, and democratically happy to mix with them, he himself does not speak in this way. He will quote Wallaby Dick, but not imitate or simulate that manner for himself.

> There was a church in Bullocktown, and there were also three public-houses. It is not for me to make unpleasant comments, but I know for a fact that the minister vowed that the place wasn't worth buggy-hire, and that the publicans were making fortunes. Perhaps this was owing to the unsettled state of the district—in up-country townships most evils (including floods) are said to arise from this cause—and could in time have been remedied. I am afraid that religion, as an art, was not cultivated much in Bullocktown. The seed sown there was a little mixed in character. One week you had a Primitive Methodist, and the next a Hardshell Baptist, and the next an Irvingite or a Southcottian. To do the inhabitants justice, they endeavoured very hard to learn the ins and outs of the business, but I do not believe that they ever succeeded. As Wallaby Dick observed one day, "When you run a lot of paddocked sheep into a race, what's the good o' sticking half-a-dozen fellers at the gate? The poor beggars don't know which way to run."

Drinking is a recurrent theme of the Bullocktown stories. Most of the sketch of "**An Up-Country Township**" revolves round the description of the three public houses there. Similarly, "**Grumbler's Gully**" describes a mining township twelve miles from Bullocktown, and consists mainly of a description of its hotels. And though Clarke departs from them in order to describe the main street, the gossip, the cemetery, and the religious sects, it is to the hotels he returns at the end of his piece. And what began as a genial, comic sketch of a mining township develops a suddenly bitter note. He describes the life of Daw, the editor of the local newspaper.

> Daw writes about four columns a day, and is paid £250 a year. His friends say he ought to be in Melbourne, but he is afraid to give up a certainty, so he stays, editing his paper and narrowing his mind, yearning for some intellectual intercourse with his fellow creatures. To those who have not lived in a mining township the utter dullness of Daw's life is incomprehensible. There is a complete lack of anything like cultivated mental companionship, and the three or four intellects who are above the dead level do their best to reduce their exuberant acuteness by excess of whisky-and-water. The club, the reading-room, the parliament, the audience that testifies approval and appreciation are all found in one place— the public-house bar. To obtain a criticism or a suggestion one is compelled to drink a nobbler of brandy.

In most of the Bullocktown stories Clarke finds the hotels and public houses places of amusement, and the drinking part of the geniality of social interchange. In "**Grumbler's Gully**" it is a torment. "To sum up the jollity of Grumbler's Gully in two words—'What's yours?'"

This powerful sketch was the only one of Clark's stories that also achieve publication outside Australia, appearing in *All the*

Year Round, the journal edited by Charles Dickens, as **"An Australian Mining Township".** Its bitter note gives an authenticity: this is not a glorification of outback life, but an insider's view of the destructive restraints and limitations that that sort of life produced. (pp. 74-8)

Holiday Peak derived its unity as a collection from the up-country setting of its stories. *Four Stories High* derives its unity from the clubman's *Canterbury Tales* device of the four characters each telling a story. The stories told involve events and characters and references ranging through England, France, Asia, and Australia, through city and country, through tribal societies and cosmopolitan sophistication. There is none of the exploration of a milieu, of **"Bullocktown"**, that there is in *Holiday Peak.* But there is an exploration of a mood, of a sense of loss, of despair, of exile.

The naturalistic sketches and the formula magazine melodramas are well represented in these two volumes of stories—though there are other examples of his work in those genres that he never collected. But the third major group of his short stories, the speculative and metaphysical fantasies, were only collected into volume form after his death. This genre of story has come back into fashion now with the North American and European discovery of the work of Jorge Luis Borges and other Latin American writers. Borges, of course, acknowledges his admiration for the work of such turn of the century English writers as Stevenson and Chesterton, who were writing in this English fantasy tradition. It was a major strand of the short story in English—but its lack of distinctively "Australian" materials has prevented its recognition as a component of an Australian fictional tradition.

Clarke's *The Mystery of Major Molineux and Human Repetends* is a posthumous volume collecting two of his stories in this area. One of them, **"Human Repetends"**, first published in *The Australasian,* 14 September 1872, looked back to his life in England and the circumstances surrounding his coming to Australia. . . . The narrator, Hugh Pontifex emigrates to Australia and ends up writing for *The Argus.* But the interest of the story lies not so much in these autobiographical motifs, as in the theme of what De Quincey called "unutterable and self-repeating infinities". The story belongs to a formula that has emigrated from English writing but that is alive and well and living in Argentina: Jorge Luis Borges's "Theme of the Traitor and Hero" is one recent version of it—appropriately, unending versions of it crop up in different centuries in different continents. "There are in decimal arithmetic repeated 'coincidences' called *repetends.* Continue the generation of numbers through all time, and you have these repetends for ever recurring."

Pontifex has to sell all his belongings; but he retains a fifteenth century engraving signed Finiguerra of an unknown, beautiful woman with whose image he is infatuated. One day he sees her in Melbourne. He spends the next three days looking for her after that brief glimpse—only to discover she was murdered by drowning in the Yarra the night he saw her. At the inquest of the girl, whose name was Jenny Gay, he meets Warrend who also has a copy of the engraving, and who knows the story attached to it.

> Jehanne La Gaillarde was a woman whose romantic amours had electrified the Paris of Louis XI. She was murdered by being thrown into the Seine. "All attempts to discover the murderer were vain, but, at length, a young man named Hugues Grandprête, who, though he had never seen the celebrated beauty, had

fallen in love with her picture, persuaded himself that the murderer was none other than Sieur De la Forêt . . . followed De la Forêt to Padua, and killed him."

Pontifex remembers that the man he saw Jenny Gay with was called Forrester. All the names fit: Sieur De la Foret/Forrester; Grandprete/Pontifex; Finiguerra/Warrender; Jehanne la Gaillarde/Jenny Gay. The whole pattern is repeating itself, inexorably. The narrator waits to fulfil his unwilling part in the inevitable design. "I live here in Melbourne at the seat of his crime because it seems the least likely place again to behold him. . . . But I *shall* meet him one day, and then my doom will be upon me, and I shall kill him as I killed him in Padua 400 years ago!''

"The Mystery of Major Molineux", one of the last things Clarke wrote, is a fine piece of Tasmanian Gothic. It has a Major who never appears on Thursdays, his toothless, glassy-eyed housekeeper Mary Pennithorne, and his surly, animal-like ex-convict manservant, Bagally. They inhabit the "Wuthering Heights" style forbidding house, Castle Stuart, where visitors are accommodated only grudgingly and where a ghostly face appears at a window on a storm-wracked night. Amongst all this broods the hint of some sexual evil. There is the grave of the transported forger Arthur Savary who suicided, it seems, when he discovered his wife was having an affair with the Major's brother-in-law; there was the mysterious death of beautiful young Agnes Tremayne after she discovered what happened to the Major on Thursdays; and then there is beautiful young Beatrice Rochford, recovering from concussion after a horse fall, found dead with an expression of extreme horror on her face after a brief visit from the Major—who promptly commits suicide. We never know what the horror is, what form the possession by devils that the Major says he suffers, takes. The narrator, who is in love with Beatrice, though she is young enough to be his daughter, spends a Thursday night of horror with the Major, but never reveals what happens. This unexplained mystery creates the suggestive suspense, but finally the story is unsatisfactory just because too much is missing when so much of the rest of the story is circumstantially detailed. (pp. 92-4)

> *Michael Wilding, "The Short Stories of Marcus Clarke," in* Bards, Bohemians, and Bookmen: Essays in Australian Literature, *edited by Leon Cantrell, University of Queensland Press, 1976, pp. 72-97.*

JOHN COLMER   (essay date 1983)

[*In the following excerpt, Colmer discusses narrative structure in* His Natural Life *in terms of Clarke's attitude toward colonialism as a political system.*]

There are good reasons for [the continuing popularity and success of *For the Term of His Natural Life*]. To begin with it is a rattling good story, even if the plot creaks in places. Then, it opens the reader's eyes to an important phase in Australia's history that many would prefer to forget, but which nevertheless exercises a curious fascination for everyone in the world. It is a brilliant piece of historical documentation, an inspired piece of creative journalism, based on Clarke's investigation of convict records in Melbourne and his research as a journalist on holiday in Tasmania a few years after the last convict had been transported to Australia. It is also a challenging book about justice and injustice in a closed system, about the extent to which punishers and punished are victims of the penal system and therefore by implication about the extent to which we are all prisoners of established systems. Finally, it is a novel about the powers of human endurance and the redemptive power of love. Both in form and substance it fits Henry James's description of the typical mid nineteenth-century novel; it is a 'huge baggy monster'. (p. 133)

If we stand back from this huge baggy monster and examine its structure, something interesting emerges that is worth following up because it may lead to a clearer understanding of the novel's imaginative effect and of certain internal contradictions. I think we can detect two large-scale deep structures and they are in some sense contradictory.

The first structure involves the repeated ironic reversals of intention or expectation. Almost every action in the novel produces the opposite effect to the one expected. Two examples at this stage of the argument must suffice. Rufus Dawes's well-intentioned desire to warn the captain and crew of the mutiny planned on the convict ship *Malabar* leads to his being punished as the ringleader of the mutineers. Another example is the way in which Rufus Dawes's enterprise and benevolence in helping Maurice Frere, Mrs Vickers, and Sylvia to escape from Hell's Gates leads to further severe punishment. Such reversals are not simply typical products of the penal system, since the structure of ironic reversal extends well beyond the confines of the various penal settlements to the action in England that precipitates Richard Devine's transportation as Rufus Dawes. His attempt to save his mother's honour leads to his transportation. There is the additional irony that his quixotic action was carried out in ignorance of the fact that her secret was safe and the deceived husband had died before carrying out his plan to disinherit his 'son' Richard/Rufus in favour of his nephew, Maurice Frere.

This pattern of ironic reversal of expectation can be seen as an expression of Marcus Clarke's world-view. Its genesis was both personal and public. In England all his youthful expectations were frustrated and reversed when the large inheritance of £70,000 he expected from his father turned out to be non-existent. As a result, he left England to seek fame and fortune in the antipodes, but found it necessary to plunge desperately into the competitive life of Melbourne journalism in order to survive. Alcohol, to which he turned as an escape from hackwork and penury, provided a guilty bondage, as it is for the strongly-drawn fictional character, the Reverend James North. In both these crucial phases of Clarke's personal life, migration and alcoholism, the deep structure was an ironic reversal of expectation. A similar structure is apparent in certain large-scale events. For many nineteenth-century British migrants, the search for a new Eden in Australia led to a hell of frustration and disappointment, and the unfulfilled Edenic quest is one of the dominant themes in Australian literature. Looked at from one point of view it can be seen that colonialism as a political system produced the opposite effects to those that its champions proclaimed: it produced dependence, not freedom; economic exploitation, not plenty for all; imprisonment within an arbitrary and alien system, not liberty and freedom to create a new model society.

The other deep structure that can be detected in the novel is a pattern of redemptive sacrifice and suffering. In fact, this surfaces as a major theme and has been the subject of a special study [see excerpt by L. T. Hergenhan dated 1965]. Against all the odds of probability and in contradiction with the tragic transformations of good actions into evil consequence that permeate the novel, the redemptive structure reveals a process of defeat turning into triumph through sacrifice and love, a love

that is symbolized in the somewhat sentimental but traditional symbol of the rose that Dawes treasures because it is associated with the angelic Sylvia. This Christian structure, calculated to appeal to the orthodox piety of nineteenth-century readers in Australia and Britain, is part and parcel of Victorian melodrama. But the conventional pattern of religious values is undercut in a variety of ways. The two public embodiments of the Christian system, Meekin and North, are frauds and shams. Meekin is a platitudinous society-man with no feeling for the convicts' sufferings; he thinks that Port Arthur is a paradise and is delighted with the convict system because it is so complete. North is wracked by his own guilty alcoholism and loss of faith. There is a further irony in the fact that when Dawes discovers his religious need after being brutally flogged, and calls for a chaplain, it is the superficial Meekin who comes, not the sympathetic, guilt-stricken North. Then the villainous John Rex's manipulation of others by means of empty confession and false piety exposes Christian values in an ironic light. And Sarah Purfoy's criminal attempt to reinstate John Rex in society as the returned, Tichbourne-type, heir serves as an obvious parody of the redemption theme worked out through the relations between Dawes and Sylvia. At the end of the chapter 'Fifteen Hours', Clarke specifically comments that 'the infernal genius' of Sarah Purfoy had 'saved' her lover at last.

Previous accounts of this colonial classic have employed more conventional ways of analysing the structure or design of the novel, paying attention to its formal division into four books or else comparing the serial and the book version. Valuable as such approaches have been in drawing attention to Clarke's artistry, they have not been able to illuminate the novelist's world-view or its relation to a particular phase of British colonialism. By looking more closely at the deep structures it is possible to expose important internal contradictions that are not peculiar to this one work or to this author but are characteristic of colonial and imperialist structures of society and much related literature, as may be seen in the structure of promise and withdrawal in E. M. Forster's *A Passage to India*. In seeking to place the author and his work in an appropriate cultural and political context in this fashion, I am making a similar assumption to that made by Chomsky in linguistics, Lévi-Strauss in anthropology, and Lucien Goldmann in genetic structuralism: that is, I am assuming that our major concern is not with the accidental materials of human experience but with the structure of human experience as this reveals itself in language, social rituals, literary structures and signs. As Goldmann frequently insists, genetic structuralism rests on the belief that common mental categories underlie both literary structures and social forms, or at least that there is a homologous relation between the two.

A novelist can create a closed society to serve as a model or a metaphor for society as a whole, as Huxley does in *Brave New World*, as Orwell does in *Animal Farm*, and, closer in some ways to Marcus Clarke, as Solzhenitsyn does in *The First Circle*, which is also a prison novel. The prison system, as Foucault suggests, can be seen as a model of the way society is based on the exercise of power, on the imposition of restrictive laws. In *For the Term of His Natural Life*, the various closed societies, on the prison ship *Malabar* and at the penal settlements at Macquarie Harbour, Port Arthur, and Norfolk Island, may be seen as models or metaphors for the system on which colonial society as a whole is based. Interestingly enough, at Norfolk Island the roles of the oppressors and the oppressed are reversed. As the result of the creation of the notorious

'Ring' by the prisoners, the officials live under a tyranny of fear, an ironic variation on the situation at Macquarie Harbour.

In contrast to these closed repressive societies we are presented with two other models: one is the model represented by the bestial prisoner Gabbett's regression to savagery and cannibalism; the other is the emergence of a natural order in the isolated community at Hell's Gates, consisting of Mrs Vickers, Frere, Grimes, and Sylvia, into which the runaway convict Dawes bursts like an apparition, stretching out his hands and hoarsely articulating the single word, 'Food'. Without the colonial apparatus of power to support him, Frere now drops into the background and Dawes becomes a mixture of Robinson Crusoe and Admirable Crichton. Incidentally, the Crusoe myth of individual resourcefulness and economic self-sufficiency is foreshadowed by the references to Defoe's novel in the accounts of Sylvia's reading. It is Dawes who builds the shelter; it is Dawes who has the imagination to construct the coracle. What this part of the novel seems to say is that if the unnatural controls are removed, if the machinery of colonial power is no longer operative, goodness and intelligence triumph over selfishness and stupidity. Indeed, the point has already been made in the preceding section when John Rex and the mutineers ridicule Frere's bullying tactics. Clarke comments that Frere's 'authority—born of circumstance, and supported by adventitious aid—had left him'. A little later the point is made that 'Maurice Frere's authority of gentility soon succumbed to Rufus Dawes's authority of knowledge'. But it is the authority not only of intelligence and knowledge but of good that Dawes demonstrates. This idea is raised to symbolic status when the child Sylvia writes on the sand the words 'GOOD MR DAWES', a successful piece of symbolic heightening in a predominantly realistic documentary novel.

The formal structure of the novel consists first of an 'Author's Preface' and a brief, tightly packed 'Prologue' to which many readers will find themselves returning to check what happened at the murder of Lord Bellasis, the father of both Dawes and John Rex, although in fact the full details are not revealed until towards the end of the novel. There follows the main narrative divided into four books; 'Book One, The Sea—1827'; 'Book Two, Macquarie Harbour—1833'; 'Book Three, Port Arthur—1838'; 'Book Four, Norfolk Island—1846'. Then comes the brief 'Epilogue' recording the death of the hero and heroine in the tempest: 'The arms of the man were clasped round the body of the woman, and her head lay on his breast.' This is followed by an 'Appendix' in which Clarke gives details of some of his historical sources, a device to enhance the historical authenticity of his sensational and melodramatic story. As in much recent American and Australian fiction (Frank Hardy's, for instance), the distinction between history and fiction is deliberately broken down. Moreover, in Clarke's novel there is an implicit contrast between the novelist's true history and the false comforting myths enshrined in Sylvia's schoolbook History of England, a book whose only use is to fuel the fire that attracts the brig to the rescue of the party in the frail coracle.

The titles of the four books indicate that the action covers a twenty-year period. In the course of this we witness the transformation of the youthful Richard Devine into the grey-haired convict on Norfolk Island. Clarke's manuscript journal shows how carefully he worked out the age of his characters at various moments in the plot. The titles also point to changes of scene involving sea voyages all of which are important elements in the narrative, since without such major changes this classic study of passive suffering and heroic endurance in a colonial convict-society would have been intolerably static. Each of the four books has a set-piece of exciting and sensational action: mutiny, shipwreck, flogging, and melodramatic escape. The titles, 'Prologue', and 'Epilogue', together with the strongly dramatic scenes, suggest that the general effect is of a play with four acts and a multiplicity of scenes. Four features of the dramatic design deserve notice. The reappearance of the same group of colonial administrators in a social setting of polite chitchat around the figure of Major Vickers in each of the books acts as an ironic contrast to the savagery of the convict gang, as may be seen most clearly in Book Two, Chapter 3, 'A Social Evening', where Lieutenant Frere, newly arrived at Macquarie Harbour, drops his callous remarks about the convicts over the tea cups and prescribes severe flogging as the certain remedy for all problems. 'Why don't you flog 'em?', says Frere, lighting his pipe in the gloom. 'By George, sir, I cut the hides off my fellows if they show any nonsense'. Secondly, the dramatic tensions built up in the first two books erupt into a whole series of violent events in the following books; such as Dawes's abortive escape, the young boy Kirkland's flogging, the suicide of the little boys, Rex's flight, and the hideous fate of the men lost in the bush. Thirdly, the deliberate juxtaposition of scenes of physical and mental suffering, as in the contrasting scenes of Dawes's dumb physical suffering and North's eloquent mental self-flagellation, powerfully enforces the sense of constricting and inescapable influences at work in this closed society. Fourthly, the symbolism of the sea permeates all four books, thus creating a dramatic unity within the novel as a whole. It is the sea that finally unites Dawes and Sylvia in a redemptive death.

> At day-dawn on the morning after the storm, the rays of the rising sun fell upon an object which floated on the surface of the water not far from where the schooner had foundered.
>
> This object was a portion of the mainmast head of the *Lady Franklin*, and entangled in the rigging were two corpses—a man and a woman. The arms of the man were clasped around the body of the woman, and her head lay on his breast.
>
> The Prison Island appeared but as a long, low line on the distant horizon. The tempest was over. As the sun rose higher the air grew balmy, the ocean placid; and, golden in the rays of the new risen morning, the wreck and its burden drifted out to sea.

Naturally enough in a novel originally written for serial publication, there are many sensational sections that serve little purpose in the overall dramatic design; but it is undeniably true that in revising the novel for book publication Clarke tightened up and improved the design enormously, especially as it related to Sylvia in the last book. The huge baggy monster does in fact possess order, shape, and expressive pattern.

In looking at the parts, it is a mistake to dismiss the 'Author's Preface' and 'Appendix' as irrelevant to an understanding of the novel. The 'Preface' makes it clear that Clarke recognizes that his novel belongs to a fairly new genre, that is, novels about crime and punishment, such as Charles Reade's *It's Never Too Late to Mend* and Victor Hugo's *Les Misérables*. But, rightly, he claims that he is the first novelist to write about transportation. The second thing to notice is that although the system of transportation had come to an end when Clarke wrote, he draws attention to the continued danger of such a system elsewhere. I think it is clear that his main intention in writing the novel was not to bring about reform, but rather to exploit a growing concern with crime and to satisfy the popular interest in Australia's early history. But it was also to explore a pattern of experience which was of vital concern to him personally and to all involved in the promise and disillusionment of colonialism. As in so many great novels, there is a creative interaction of communal and personal preoccupations. As Goldmann argues, literary structure may be seen as the joint product of the creative mind and the community.

When Clarke wrote, the population of Australia was small, and novelists therefore wrote as much for British as for Australian readers. This accounts partly for the abundance of explanatory details, geographic and historic. However, in 1870, he is writing about the Australia of forty years ago, and so even his Australian readers would need abundant historical information. Scholars have investigated his use of the convict records he consulted on his brief visit to Tasmania. As readers our concern is with how well this material is deployed. Naturally enough, long informative passages loom larger in the first part of the book, although there is certainly a rather long and intrusive account of Norfolk Island in Book Four, at the beginning of Chapter 3; but, in fact, this description of Norfolk Island skilfully leads up to our first surprising view of Rufus Dawes, now the leader of the notorious Ring. One very obtrusive piece of documentary writing is the account of prison quarters on the convict ship *Malabar:* here the action halts, the novelist retires while the journalist takes over.

A quite different use of documentary material is Clarke's careful creation of scenes to bring home to the reader certain aspects of the penal system: the barbarity of the floggings, the callous detachment of the prison officials, the dehumanizing effect of the whole system on everyone involved. Apart from using intensively dramatic but in fact fairly restrained flogging scenes, Clarke uses two quite different kinds of dialogue to reveal the effects of the dehumanizing process: the impersonal dialogue of the officials and the bestial utterances of the prisoners. For example, at the end of the chapter (Book Two, Chapter 3), when he hears of Gabbett's return, Frere says casually and callously 'Gad, he's had a narrow squeak for it, I'll be bound. I should like to see him'. Frere's words suggest that he regards Gabbett as a kind of performing animal who is to be displayed for his amusement. In the following chapter Clarke presents the reader with the sinister, brutal dialogue between the returned cannibal giant, Gabbett, and his interrogators. It is set off by the ironic sentence: 'The intelligent Troke, considerately alive to the wishes of his superior officers, dragged the mass into a sitting posture, and woke it'. Here the noun 'mass' and the impersonal 'it', instead of the personal pronoun 'him', signal to the reader that Gabbett has been reduced from a person to a thing. This reduction, as both the German philosopher Kant and the English Romantic poet Coleridge stated, is the basis of all tyranny. According to Coleridge it is a 'sacred principle' that 'a person can never become a thing nor be treated as such without wrong'.

The dialogue then dramatizes the respective attitudes of Vickers, the Commandant (a man who does everything according to the rule book), Frere, the warder Troke, and the prisoner Gabbett:

> 'Well, Gabbett', says Vickers, 'you've come back again, you see. When will you learn sense, eh? Where are your mates?'
>
> The giant did not reply.
>
> 'Do you hear me? Where are your mates?'
>
> 'Where are your mates?' repeated Troke.

'Dead', says Gabbett.

'All three of them?'

'Ay.'

'And how did you get back?'

Gabbett, in eloquent silence, held out a bleeding foot.

'We found him on the point, sir', said Troke, jauntily explaining, 'and brought him across in the boat. He had a basin of gruel, but he didn't seem hungry'.

'Are you hungry?'

'Yes.'

'Why don't you eat your gruel?'

Gabbett curled his great lips.

'I have eaten it. Ain't yer got nuffin better nor that to flog a man on? Ugh! ye'r a mean lot! Wot's it to be this time, Major? Fifty?'

And laughing, he rolled down again on the logs.

'A nice specimen!' said Vickers, with a hopeless smile. 'What *can* one do with such a fellow?'

'I'd flog his soul out of his body', said Frere, 'if he spoke to *me* like that!'

Troke and the others, hearing the statement, conceived an instant respect for the new comer. He looked as if he would keep his word.

This compact piece of dialogue epitomizes the futility of the penal system and the dehumanizing effect on all. It also, of course, through the enquiry into where Gabbett's mates are and the reference to the fact that he did not seem hungry, alerts us in the most sinister manner to the theme of survival through cannibalism. In the novel the reader is made to feel that the convict system in colonial society is a kind of cannibalism.

If the penal system is as comprehensive in its dehumanizing effects as Clarke suggests it is, how, we might ask ourselves, can anyone rise above it? If the constricting and repressive environment has such a determining effect, who can escape its influence? Specifically, how can Sylvia, whose whole education and experience have been within the closed societies of the penal settlements, remain largely untouched? How can she act as a symbol of good and agent of redemption? Specifically, how can Dawes, whose progressive deterioration we observe until he becomes the leader of the Ring on Norfolk Island, be an active participator in the redemptive pattern that affects Sylvia, North, and himself at the end of the novel?

One answer would be that love and suffering can triumph over environmental influence. According to this view, there is an indestructible disposition for good in man which may be driven underground but will eventually surface. Sylvia is an interesting case here. Her loss of memory of what happened at Hell's Gates enables Frere to claim that he was her saviour, not Dawes, that he made the coracle, not Dawes, and that Dawes intended to murder them. This is something more than a convenient bit of artificial plotting. The series of scenes that show Sylvia struggling to recover a lost memory of a good action enacts the whole process by which something good which is driven underground may surface at a later date. And in the following passage the struggle to remember is linked with the recurrent flower-imagery, which symbolizes the indestructible power of love: 'what was the link between her and the murderous villain? How came it that she felt at times so strange a sympathy for his fate, and that he—who had attempted her life—cherished so tender a remembrance of her as to beg a flower which her hand had touched?'

In spite of this, however, the sudden emergence of good at the end of the novel is not entirely convincing. Several reasons may be given. Of these, two deserve special attention. Firstly, we know too little of what goes on inside the minds of Dawes and Sylvia. They have no inner lives to speak of. This is immediately apparent when we compare them with Mr North, whose confessional journal dramatizes his intense inner conflict, his struggle to resist temptation and to do good. The second reason for the not wholly successful rounding off of the redemptive theme is that there is a significant silence, a gap, a rupture in the narrative. This occurs at the end of Book Four, Chapter 14, 'Getting Ready for the Sea', when Dawes, after saying to North 'You shall not destroy your own soul and hers! You love her! So do I! and my love is mightier than yours, for it shall save her', then promises to tell him his story: 'I will tell you the secret of my life, the reason I am here. Come closer'. This is followed by six dots and no story.

Now, it may be argued that Clarke showed great artistic tact in not repeating what the reader already knows. But it may be equally well argued that this silence, this gap, this rupture in the narrative is highly expressive in a way the author did not intend. It is the gap the author cannot fill between the two contradictory deep structures I described at the beginning of this essay: the pessimistic, deterministic, fatalistic structure, based on personal life and colonial experience, and its opposite, the optimistic structure of Christian redemption, based on the ideas of innate goodness, confession and repentance, and the exercise of free will. The actual confession that leads North to abandon his guilty love for Sylvia and that lands Dawes into Sylvia's arms has to be taken on trust. In the same way the quality of the love that each has for the other has largely to be taken on trust, since they rarely meet and Dawes is an inarticulate worshipper of a goddess. As a further complication the goddess has lost the all important segment of her past that would open her eyes and soften her heart. However, the sense of artifice is counteracted by the subtlety of all those passages that refer to Sylvia's response to a voice out of the past that she cannot place.

Clarke's method of representing the relationship between Dawes and Sylvia is symbolic, not naturalistic or deeply psychological, although the handling of Sylvia's suppressed memory is a subtle anticipation of later psycho-analytic fiction. Sylvia is consistently associated with the sun, with light, the rose of love, and flowers. And Dawes worships her through such treasured fetishes as the blue scrap of her dress and the flowers from her garden. The most dramatic presentation of the conflicting emotions involved is the scene when Sylvia visits the prison and demands that Dawes should be released from torture (Book Four, Chapter 13). Dawes awakens to see her 'in the midst of a sunbeam', only to experience an undefinable sense of evil as the priest, North, draws her away; he 'slowly draw[s] the fair young creature from out the sunlight into the grim shadow of the heavy archway'. It remains an open critical question whether such a highly symbolic mode can be successfully fused with a realistic documentary manner of narration. Disraeli succeeds in fusing them in his novel *Sybil*. Clarke is perhaps less successful in *For the Term of His Natural Life*: we often resist the symbolic heightening of action as obtrusive, dishonest, and sentimental.

Like *Great Expectations*, Clarke's novel had two endings. In the serial, Dawes survived. And Clarke was most reluctant to polish off his dearly loved, much suffering, ennobled victim, presumably because he had split his own psyche between the dumb noble suffering Dawes and the guilt-stricken alcoholic priest North. But as the result of taking others' advice, Clarke kills Dawes, yet grants him his happiness and union with Sylvia in death. In the split, one part of the author's psyche murders itself, the other achieves a joyful union with the ideal woman as he expires.

There is a comparable split in the presentation of woman in this novel. This is somewhat similar to the split in the American novel between fair goddess and dark temptress analysed by Leslie Fiedler in *Love and Death in the American Novel*, or the division in Australian society analysed by Anne Summers in *Damned Whores and God's Police*. Except during her pert childhood, Sylvia is passively good; what vitality she possesses is drained from her and 'absorbed' by Maurice Frere who thrives on this piece of male cannibalism, as North notes in his diary entry for 22 March. It is the wicked *femme fatale* Sarah Purfoy who possesses all the intelligence, sexual vitality, and will. Modern feminist criticism might have some pretty harsh things to say about this novel.

So, too, will readers intolerant of coincidence and sensational plotting in a novel. As Barry Argyle points out in *An Introduction to the Australian Novel*, the whole plot mechanism is an old one: 'the disinherited love child (Richard Devine); his punishment for a crime he did not commit; the resemblance between the hero [Richard] and the villain]John Rex]; and the use of coincidence to keep it all going'. Even the Reverend James North, a late comer in the story who adds great psychological depth to the exploration of guilt and remorse, was connected with the murdered nobleman Lord Bellasis. The connexion was through gambling debts; and if he had spoken out, Richard Devine, who becomes the convict Rufus Dawes, would never have been falsely accused.

Coincidences abound, but out of this intricate web of coincidence and deliberate doubling and parallelism, Clarke seems to express something profound though not easily defined about man's ambivalent nature: about guilt, self-hatred, and self-destruction. We need to notice that John Rex, who poses as the returned heir, and the Reverend James North, who resolves to redeem the broken Dawes, are both closely connected with Dawes in his early life and both destroy themselves. The case of North is the more interesting. His attempt to redeem Dawes involves an attempt to gain his own redemption. But when this is nearly in sight North suddenly surrenders to self-hatred and tries to destroy Dawes's new found faith. North then carries his self-destructiveness to its logical end, suicide. His ambivalent attitude to Dawes reflects his own ambivalence. In a remarkable passage of self-analysis North diagnoses the relationship between personal injury and hatred. 'If a man had injured me, the fact of his living at all would be sufficient grounds for me to hate him; if I had injured *him*, I should hate him still more'. He then goes on to quote Tacitus, who says that 'the hatred of those most nearly related is inveterate'. The phrase 'those most nearly related' can be applied to Dawes and North, as well as to North's divided nature, since he robbed the corpse of Lord Bellasis and could have saved Dawes from transportation and therefore prevented all his suffering if he had confessed.

It is a pity that this kind of acute psychological insight into guilt and self-hatred is not accompanied by an equally deep insight into the nature of love in relation to Dawes and Sylvia. The strength of the novel lies in its tribute to man's capacity to endure: this makes it a very Australian work. It also lies in its profound image of colonial society and of the alienated individual. Silent suffering proves a more successful theme than dumb adoration, which is the essence of Dawes's love for Sylvia. And so one is forced to the conclusion that *For the Term of His Natural Life* is a flawed masterpiece. Although it raises suffering to a heroic level and presents a powerful critique of colonial societies based on power and arbitrary rule, its vision of the redemptive power of love is sentimental and unconvincing, a typical product of the alcoholic's maudlin belief in the saving power of a good woman. (pp. 134-44)

> John Colmer, '' 'For the Term of His Natural Life':
> A Colonial Classic Revisited,'' in The Yearbook of
> English Studies, Vol. 13, 1983, pp. 133-44.

LAURIE HERGENHAN (essay date 1984)

[*In the following excerpt, Hergenhan relates aspects of Clarke's colonial experience to theme and purpose in* His Natural Life. *For additional commentary by Hergenhan, see excerpt dated 1965.*]

Since the 1950s, a number of reappraisals of *His Natural Life* have shown that it is a complex novel open to various interpretations. I shall concentrate on qualities which have received less attention: on the novel as embodying aspects of social and spiritual dispossession, which were problems of the Victorian England of Clarke's own day and which also provide an ''objective correlative'' for Clarke's own personal experiences as enforced immigrant. The novel has not been considered in any detail as a projection of Clarke's own experience. Although this involves speculation, it is a legitimate enquiry. Clarke's sense of exile would have sharpened his sense of the shortcomings of the upper-class society from which he was displaced, particularly of the social power which he had experienced in his loss of a promised position among the privileged classes. This conjunction of personal and larger social concerns is apparent in the novel's underlying recognition that the prison is not a world apart but a revealing expression of social power. . . . Clarke's novel is about colonial failure, but about a social rather than an individual failure.

In his ''Author's Preface'' to the novel, Clarke claimed as his aim, and as justification of the novel's violence, the social purpose of helping to prevent such atrocities ever happening again. From a twentieth-century viewpoint this has been seen as flogging a dead horse but, while Clarke was writing long after the convict system had been abolished, crime and punishment was still one of the most debated topics in Europe and Australia. Two articles concerned with it were published in the late 1860s in the *Colonial Monthly* when it was under Clarke's editorship. Apropos of a recent parliamentary report in Victoria, one of these articles dealt with a contemporary ''model prison'' at Mettray in France. This ''open'' prison for juvenile offenders, called a ''*colonie*'' was recommended as a ''Mecca'' of penal reformers and as a place to visit by ''our [Australian] colonists'' when in Europe. The choice of the name ''*colonie*'' inevitably sets up parallels with imperialist subjugation. (Mettray is one of the main prisons featured in Jean Genet's autobiographical *Miracle of the Rose* where it confirms him and others as subverters of society.) The Mettray article quoted with approval the observation that it is ''a wonderful prison, where there is no key but the *clef des champs* and where children remained captive because their masters have discovered the key to their hearts''. Foucault, writing over a hundred years later, pointed out that one of the main changes in pun-

ishment from the eighteenth century was to replace bodily punishment by punishment that ''acts in depth upon the heart, the thoughts, the will, the inclinations'', in other words, upon the ''soul'', which is an ''historical reality''. In *His Natural Life*, punishment is seen in this way, as conquering souls, not simply as subjugating bodies, as the ''key to hearts'' in the sense of locking them up or raping them.

Such overlooked contemporary relevance may help to account for the fact that critics have found a discrepancy between Clarke's stated reasons for writing *His Natural Life* and its passionate feeling. But, more importantly, there is some evidence from Clarke's life and journalism that his imaginative identification with the convicts derived from the painful dislocations of his colonial experience. It may be that [James Tucker, author of *Ralph Rashleigh*] and Clarke wrote the only convict novels drawing directly on the painful experiences of colonial exile but giving them a transferred embodiment, the one fantasizing a re-entry into the lost society, the other expressing the hopelessness of such a dream. (pp. 48-9)

Clarke remained in two minds about life in colonial Australia. He initially recoiled from the radicalism and vulgarity but appreciated the ''amount of humbug forced out of one by the force-pump of society here''. Humbug and pretension were targets of his lively journalism. His inherited conservatism of class privilege was modified, if never eradicated, by some appreciation of the ''radicalism'' he initially despised. Both tendencies are embodied in a gentleman hero, Rufus Dawes. Clarke, initially feeling ''a literary Ishmael'', became a talented, productive journalist and man of letters in post-goldrush Melbourne, and an entertaining *bon vivant*. But his personal life became increasingly afflicted by a self-destructiveness, expressing itself in the instability of recurrent bankruptcy, of drinking, and in the failure of his family life. Around him he saw a number of talented writers and journalists who ended up in the gutter. It is probably no accident that the linked struggles of Rufus Dawes and North in *His Natural Life*, at their deepest levels, is to maintain a sense of their human worth, of identity and relatedness to mankind against the stresses of outward circumstances and inner weakness. It would seem that Clarke, in spite of some success in colonial ''adaptation'' hoped to return to England but had to turn down an offer, apropos of the success of his novel, to join the London *Daily Telegraph*.

When Clarke visited Port Arthur as a journalist in 1869, he found there haunting human remnants of the abandoned convict system—''the smell of it remained—remains''. With ''no maudlin sympathy'' for convicts, he yet recognized ''how thin is the planking of 'favourable circumstances' which is between the best of us and such a fate''. This was no pious reflection, as both his life in Melbourne and the feeling of *His Natural Life* showed.

His journalism drew on such experiences and observation, and in it the images and the feelings of *His Natural Life* found foreshadowing expression. The most relevant journalistic pieces are the **''Lower Bohemia''** series of articles on the outcast poor of Melbourne, *Old Tales of a Young Country*, a collection of historical tales and a byproduct of Clarke's research for his novel; and his famous preface to Adam Lindsay Gordon's poems.

The world of Melbourne's destitute aroused the fellow-feeling that Port Arthur reinforced in Clarke a year later. But in the Melbourne sketches he also gained a vision, and with it a cluster of images, which was to enlarge the fate of the city outcasts and those in *His Natural Life*. These images revolve around

Robinson Crusoe and the "modern civilization"-wilderness opposition, seen in terms of sea and desert, the city and wild nature, Ishmaelites and wild beasts, civilized man and savages. This conception, (perhaps an expression of Clarke's lost metropolis-antipodes dilemma), embracing European (and American) society, also had its roots in formulations of the role of the Australian colonial in early works of history and literature. *Robinson Crusoe* was both a work admired by Clarke as a "superb romance of reality", and the source of a common colonial image: the resourceful, independent Englishman subduing wild nature, and "wild" man to his own purposes of survival and self-assertion. In such tales the hero either went home to England like Robinson Crusoe (and Rufus Dawes in the unrevised, serial version of *His Natural Life*), or laid claim to the new land. This latter imperial spirit is exemplified in a passage from one of the popular early guide books for intending settlers:

> I vanquished this wilderness, and made the chaos pregnant with order and civilization, "alone I did it!" I feel myself a man with a reasonable soul and a contriving intellect; I am no longer a small screw in a complicated machine; my whole powers are put forth, and every faculty put to its providential use.

In "**Lower Bohemia**" the city struggle of self-help, or of every man for himself, is "more desperate than Crusoe's because in modern civilization there is "no ship from which to draw stores and ammunition". This bankruptcy is spiritual as well as referring to the destitute poor. Clarke explicitly draws on the American frontier and its novelists (such as Cooper) as well as on *Crusoe*, and also implicitly on images of the city in nineteenth-century novelists, such as Dickens and Balzac, the two he had placed highest. American history and literature were a greater influence on Clarke than has been realized. The city was not, however, the setting in which he most intensely expressed his vision of the savagery of society. He transposed it instead into the natural wilderness of Van Diemen's Land, an antipodean form of wilderness—or a "moral Ultima Thule" as he and Tucker both called convict Australia. In this setting, with prisons as "natural" outposts, Clarke questioned concepts of civilization and what was "natural" for it, thereby also crticizing his "disowning" motherland. But the two deserts: the "locked doors" of the city; and the "indifference of nature worse than her wrath", find expression in *His Natural Life* in despair and in the closed hearts and minds of those who acquiesce to the system. In the Melbourne sketches it is the outcasts, in *His Natural Life* the brutalized convicts, who replace the Comanches, the prison officers who replace the police as authority figures. The combination of physical wilderness and prison society gives the novel much of its power.

Also contributing to Clarke's vision in "**Lower Bohemia**" and his novel was the threat of the survival of the fittest version of Darwinism to nineteenth-century society's view of itself. The Romantic idea of nature as a source of consolation and inspiration was giving way to the view of predatory nature as an analogue of society. The alien colonial landscape offered a ready vehicle for this threat. In "**Lower Bohemia**", drawing on both *Crusoe* and his contemporary Melbourne, Clarke found one of the master symbols of *His Natural Life*—cannibalism. It came in the form of the half-crazy hangman who had ended up as one of the derelicts on the Yarra bank, plagued by the criminal class that society employs him to persecute:

> His reason for living in the stone-heaps is that if criminal Bohemia knew that he had a settled abode, they would annoy and maltreat him. It struck me as

a curious comment upon capital punishment, that the executor of justice should be forced to live like a dog by reason of his office. . . . I was in the midst of the Crusoe's desert island of modern civilization, and I had suddenly come upon that Footprint,—instinct with a terrible significance—which was alone wanting to make the parallel complete.

The kind of significance Clarke found in the Melbourne "underworld" is found also in *Old Tales* which, along with *His Natural Life,* was commenced six months later, after the intervening trip to Port Arthur. The title echoes that of Hawthorne's *Twice-Told Tales,* and it has been suggested that Clarke was doing for Australia what Hawthorne had done for America: aiming "consciously to create a history, to draw attention to the romantic past, the archetypal characters and situations". As Michael Wilding adds, there is, however, nothing of Hawthorne's "pale tint of flowers that blossomed in too retired a shade", but rather passionate and violent adventure. The tales deal with "exile and brutality", but equally dominant are the basic motifs of freedom and imprisonment, rebellion and suppression. These are played out through both convict and early settler situations: through escape and recapture, reimprisonment or death, and through the re-emergence of the Crusoe theme in those convicts or "free" men who perform feats of survival as shipwrecked sailors, explorers, escapees or bushrangers.

While *Old Tales* as a whole is more positive than "**Lower Bohemia**" in its celebrating of the human spirit of adventure and resilience, these are offset by their suppression and defeat. Clarke concludes "**The Last of Macquarie Harbour**": "Despite their treachery, their romantic story makes one hope they got their longed for liberty at last." The alternatives of liberty, rebellion and oppression are also embodied in *His Natural Life*. In the serial version, Dawes eventually returns to England via the goldfields and adventures in Victoria; in the revised version, in keeping with the original epigraph, death is the only escape, as for many unfortunates of *Old Tales* and of the Melbourne outcasts.

Another journalistic expression, drawing on colonial experience, of concerns of the novel is found in Clarke's preface to Gordon's poems. This appeared shortly after the revised novel. Such phrases as "the desolation", the "sullen despair", the "funereal, secret, stern" Australian forests, suggest feelings which are familiar from Clarke's writings and life and which are in search of a correlative. Clarke was helping to pioneer a literary sensibility suitable to the environment and it is interesting that once again he turns to American models, deriving the "keynote" of "weird melancholy" from Hoffman, Hawthorne and Poe. Poe's atmosphere, suggestive of disturbed psyches, does have relevance to colonial disorientation in Australia, though of course in Clarke it could degenerate into atmospherics. Hawthorne's guilt and gloom were underpinned by a more tangible psychological reality. His "weird power of [moral] horror" made *The Scarlet Letter* and its evocation of America's Puritan past a frightening book for Clarke. The influences of Poe and Hawthorne are incorporated into *His Natural Life* along with many others, European and local. The novel depends on literary models as well as on the documentary source of the convict records. For instance, the Reverend North owes something to Hawthorne's Mr Dimmesdale.

At the end of the Gordon preface, Clarke attempts to introduce a reconciling note by glancing at a time when Australians will become attached to their physical environment to the point of loving even its different, unlovely aspects:

The phantasmagoria of that wild dream-land termed the Bush interprets itself, and the Poet of our desolation *begins* to comprehend why free Esau loved his heritage of desert sand better than all the bountiful richness of Egypt (my italics).

This passage has the force of longing rather than of conviction in its expression of the freedom to be won by exile. More convincing are some preceding images of recoil, "the shrinking into insignificance [of] the trim civilization which bred [the colonial]" before the challenges of the old/new continent—challenges not simply of landscape, as *His Natural Life* demonstrated. In it, Clarke found his role "as poet of our desolation" in celebrating a tragic sense of loss rather than reconciliation.

Linked with the experience of colonial exile as a source of *His Natural Life* is its informing sense that systems of punishment are a symptom of the society they serve. The system Clarke dealt with reflected changes in European society in the eighteenth and early nineteenth centuries. With the decline of princes as sovereign powers, punishment by torture as a public spectacle decreased and was replaced by imprisonment. At the same time the judicial process became separated from its administrative arm so that those who carried out the punishment became more autonomous and the judiciary no longer took the public responsibility for the violence bound up with punishment. All the arbitrariness of judges and princes under the old system was "gradually reconstituted on the side of the power that administers and supervises the punishment. It is the sovereignty of knowledge possessed by the warder . . . let us call it the Declaration of Carcereal Independence. . . . The sign of this autonomy is very apparent in the 'useless' acts of violence perpetrated by warders or the despotism of an administration that has all the privileges of a closed community. Its roots lie elsewhere"—in society's need for "the prison's positive technical role" in transforming individuals. The "margin by which the prison exceeds detention is filled . . . by techniques of a disciplinary type. And this disciplinary addition to the judicial is what, in short, is called the penitentiary." This typifying social process, with its "roots" and the key place of the "natural penitentiary", is embodied in *His Natural Life* even if it lacks the formulations (and hindsight) of a Foucault.

The focusing on "civilization" and on what is "natural" for it is constantly used to deepen the novel. An early passage from the chapter on conditions on the convict ship shows Clarke concerned with the social significance behind the physical squalor and brutality he portrays so vividly:

> Society was the common foe, and magistrates, jailers, and parsons, were the natural prey of all noteworthy mankind. Only fools were honest, only cowards kissed the rod, and failed to meditate revenge on that world of respectability which had wronged them. Each newcomer was one more recruit to the ranks of ruffianism, and not a man penned in that reeking den of infamy but became a sworn hater of law, order, and "free-men" . . . he lost his self-respect, and became what his jailers took him to be—a wild beast to be locked under bolts and bars, lest he should break out and tear them.

This "natural" class conflict (appearing previously in **"Lower Bohemia"** in the same imagery) shows the transformation society enforces through its authority figures of magistrates, jailers and parsons. The transformation aggravates and yet controls the divisiveness, the "war", which is blamed on the lower and criminal classes. The creation of wild beasts legitimizes

the exercise of total power by jailers who in *His Natural Life* are far removed indeed from the sentencing magistrates. The convict system is based on self-interest and revenge and in turn it breeds them; the jailers are inevitably brutalized by their treatment of convicts. Foucault comments: "A whole series of illegalities . . . [arose from] struggles in which those struggling knew that they were confronting both the law and the class that had imposed it." In *His Natural Life* the class system, as well as precipitating the action (albeit melodramatically) of the revised version, is shown at many points to sustain the convict system. It was maintained by so few over so many that it has subsequently been wondered why convicts did not collectively rebel instead of in isolated groups (as in the Macquarie Harbour mutiny in the novel). One episode suggests part of the answer. A convict's nerve fails and he is unable to pull the trigger when he steals Frere's gun and turns it on the tyrant. Frere triumphs in "ferocious contempt" and is cheered by the convict gang, "so great is the admiration for Power" among the repressed.

Another scene which again shows awareness of issues of social dispossession occurs when Dawes as escapee vainly appeals to Sylvia in her Hobart garden. This scene, an unconscious betrayal (Sylvia has suffered loss of memory) preceding Dawes' calvary, is carefully prepared for. Under the branches of "the English trees (planted long ago)", sitting with her "face to the bay and her back to the house", Sylvia has just finished reading the narrative of John Rex (Dawes' half-brother) about his seizure of the ship, the *Osprey*, at Macquarie Harbour, the subsequent voyage round the world, then his recapture and return to Van Diemen's Land. (This narrative forms the basis of two of the *Old Tales of a Young Country*.) Sylvia feels that if the narrative were related "truly", she would understand "something strange and terrible" which has been hidden from her, as though "she had held ajar the door of some dark room into which she longed and yet feared to enter". Through this gradual awakening, Clarke makes symbolic use of a device found in other convict fiction, and in Dickens: the attempt to come to terms with a dark past, as a means of discovering the truth about society as well as self. Sylvia has been disturbed by the puzzling discrepancy between the human affirmation of this "wonderful relation" of Rex's travels (another version of *Crusoe*) and its "vague horror". Authority and received opinion have their ready explanation.

> Was the opinion of Maurice Frere the correct one after all, and were these convict monsters gifted with unnatural powers of endurance, only to be subdued and tamed by unnatural and inhuman punishments of lash and chain?

Here the irony of the novel's title is momentarily spelt out. Sylvia half senses the truth: in a moment of vision she pictures the convict island, and indeed all society, as built on repression and "blood", but her social education converts this into a threat only from "below", the "smouldering volcano of revolt and murder" that must never be allowed to explode. Only through marriage with Frere and knowledge of the convicts does she come to realize that authority or power itself can be evil and to experience in herself some liability to corruption in her "struggle for liberty".

> Her fancies growing amid the fast gathering gloom, she shuddered as she guessed to what extremities of evil might such men proceed did an opportunity ever come to them to retaliate upon their gaolers. . . . What if the whole island was but one smouldering volcano of revolt and murder—the whole convict population but one incarnated conspiracy, engendered and bound

together by the hideous Freemasonry of crime and suffering! . . .

> Oh, how strangely must the world have been civilized, that this most lovely corner of it must needs be set apart as a place of banishment for the monsters that civilization had brought forth and bred! She cast her eyes around, and all beauty seemed blotted out from the scene before her. The graceful foliage melting into indistinctness in the gathering twilight, appeared to her horrible and treacherous. The river seemed to flow sluggishly, as though thickened with blood and tears. . . . Oppressed by a terror of loneliness, she hastily caught up the manuscript, and turned to seek the house, when as if summoned from the earth by the power of her own fears, a ragged figure barred her passage.
>
> To the excited girl this apparition seemed the embodiment of the unknown evil she had dreaded.

In developing these intimations of social evil, Sylvia is to learn how "civilization had brought forth and bred" its monsters. Despite melodramatic touches, the scene is finely conceived in its suggestion of larger meanings, and also in its contribution to the novel's structure: it echoes and it foreshadows. Reminiscent of Hawthorne, it looks forward to Conrad's revelations of the treacherous divisions between civilizaton's surfaces and depths through the use of colonial/antipodean wilderness, masters and slaves. There is a parallel, too, to Patrick White's *A Fringe of Leaves* in which Ellen Roxburgh, in the haven of the obscene peace and plenty of the commandant's garden at Moreton Bay, is tortured by screams of convicts beyond.

Sylvia feels a "terror of loneliness" as the solidity of the trusted world melts into nightmare. This suggests the existential aloneness of nineteenth-century man, sharpened by colonialism, a further development of Crusoe's situation, which is one of the novel's main themes. It is a vision of man without religious or social faith whose identity is challenged more by the indifference than the cruelty of the natural world. The cumulative sense of man adrift, insignificant and alone, is strikingly embodied in the scene in which the boats from the lighted convict ship, the *Malabar*, row out into the dark towards the blazing *Hydaspes*. The scene figuratively enacts the trauma of leaving the homeland and civilization itself, and both are shown, in a sudden change of perspective, to be insubstantial:

> On board the prison ship, surrounded with all the memories if not the comforts of the shore they had quitted, they had not realized how far they were from that civilization which had given them birth. . . . That defiance of nature which is born of contact with humanity, had hitherto sustained them. . . . But now— with one ship growing smaller behind them, and the other, containing they knew not what horror of human agony and human helplessness, lying a burning wreck in the black distance ahead of them—they began to feel their own littleness. . . . *Then* the black hull rising above them, had seemed a tower of strength, built to defy the utmost violence of wind and wave; *now* it was but a slip of wood floating—on an unknown depth of black, fathomless water.

Men, alone or in groups, wandering vainly through an empty "desert" landscape, is a recurrent motif of *His Natural Life* in an early foreshadowing of Nolan and other modern Australian painters. Clarke was the first Australian novelist to make a thoroughgoing symbolic use of landscape and it suited his purposes of widening his themes to aim at generalized more than particular effects.

But Clarke does not fail to link the natural wilderness with civilization, just as the theme of isolated man in nature is linked with brutalization in society, his "losing [of] his humanity". The most memorable wilderness episode is the cannibal one, a parody of Psalm 23 in which Gabbett leads his flock not by green pastures but through a desert landscape, carefully described some chapters before as "delightfully barren", without "a scrap for a human being to make a meal on [though] the West Coast is worse". The episode ends succinctly: "At Hobart Town he [Gabbett] was recognized as the only survivor of the nine desperadoes who had escaped from Colonel Arthur's Natural Penitentiary."

The "worst" west coast of Macquarie Harbour, to which Dawes is initially consigned, is used both as a foreshadowing phase and for contributing individually to the novel. At this "very extreme of civilization", with its "perpetual warfare with the wind and the waves", Dawes is subjected to "the power of the wilderness". Here, Clarke not only develops the extreme brutalities of the system but also draws attention to what they deny in man.

Dawes' rescue of the marooned party is used as a Crusoe idyll (with Crusoe explicitly recalled) and a social fable, as well as being a "wonderful" tale, a prefiguring of the human feat of the extraordinary *Osprey* narrative of escape which Sylvia is to read about later. Clarke adapts the Crusoe symbolism outlined by Jack Lindsay:

> If we see Defoe as merely inventing astutely a picture of the isolated bourgeois man, we miss the whole dynamic, which is pastoral and concerned to show man in brotherly union with nature. Defoe . . . sees the dialectics of struggle, of desire for brotherhood and terror of human contact, which takes the utopian dream of a happy life in harmony with nature and fuses it with contemporary bourgeois reality.

In Clarke, for dispossessed convicts there is no union with nature, or within society, except as a temporary expedient.

In the Macquarie Harbour episode, where the convict Dawes displaces Captain Frere as the leader and "saviour" of the marooned party, "a society of four" forms a social fable. In essence it shows that power and authority, which in society are based on arbitrary class distinctions, are replaced in "natural" surroundings by individual ability, or the "natural" but unrewarded feats celebrated in *Old Tales*. There is also a testing of the Rousseauistic ideas of natural or savage man as basically good. This involves a testing of selfish individualism against communality.

In this fable, Clarke copies the Crusoe situation in terms of plot but debunks its myth by exploding the idea of European man's union with nature and his self-sufficiency (an eighteenth-century idea with links with Victorian self-help). Clarke's episode parallels similar ones in *A Fringe of Leaves,* but the Crusoe parts of *Ralph Rashleigh* and *Timeless Land* are contrastingly romanticized, asserting the triumph of man's natural ingenuity and goodness in a "natural" environment. Clarke also debunks Rousseau doctrine because the assertion of "natural" man is shown in *His Natural Life* as not possible inside society, to which the party is forced to "escape" from inhospitable nature. The terms of Dawes' re-entry into "free" society are shown to be repugnant because of its conventions and rigidity. "He had performed a prodigy of skill and daring" and yet he would at most attain the freedom of a servant. "What more could a convict expect?" The resulting bitterness of Dawes may mirror Clarke's own feelings that even if he "proved" himself in colonial society he could only re-enter English society as a second- or third-rate member. Dawes' temptation (and Clarke's?) is to follow society's individualistic values and save himself at the expense of his fellows, returning into society disguised (as Rex does). Dawes cannot resist the appeal of love (through Sylvia) but the price is self-sacrifice, an echo of his motive for his original voluntary surrender of his place in society, to conceal his mother's shame.

His Natural Life questions whether there are any alternatives to self-sacrifice or sacrifice of others. A limitation is that in its attempt at synthesis it insufficiently questions the self-sustaining, hypocritical ethos of self-sacrifice and can use it as a tired convention. It is from the possibilities of love, and the conflicts and denials involved with it, that the novel tries to weave some reconciliation. Although some opposition is set up between determinism and man's "misused power over fate", it is in the constraints on this power that the tragic weight of the novel lies. An ironic criticism of the Victorian notion of self-help is involved.

Clarke widens the scope of *His Natural Life* by extending important roles to those helping indirectly to maintain the system, such as the clergy, and those who, like Sylvia and Sarah Purfoy, might appear to be outside it or to have escaped what it stands for. As in the convict novels of Penton and White, marriage is used as an analogue of the convict situation, bringing out the arbitrary moral laws by which society keeps its free members in subjection. Sylvia comes alive in her role as wife and so her sentimental role as Dawes' "good angel" is offset. She marries Frere out of deluded gratitude, believing that he is her "saviour". Victorian taboos prevented Clarke from exploring the marriage but it is outlined with the psychological perception that can be one of the novel's strengths. Clarke explicitly states (through North) that he is not able to follow Balzac's example to "set forth in bare English the story of this marriage of the Minotaur". Frere marries Sylvia as an extension of his sexual power over her inexperience. This in turn provokes her resistance which, ironically gives her some power over him. Her frigidity both frustrates and attracts him.

Through Sylvia's recoil from Frere, Clarke comments on the slim possibilities of escape from the institution of marriage and at the same time expresses the disappointment of his own domestic life. The novel looks unsentimentally at the consequences of adultery in Victorian times through the attraction of Sylvia and North for one another. Even if one opposes convention and law in regarding "marriage without love as the coarsest of adulteries", which morally frees a partner, difficulties arise as to whether she (or he) is willing to risk the public disapproval and "legal offence", whether she can cope with the psychological upheaval, and whether the new love will last. These difficulties, compounded by women's economic dependence, parallel the seeming impossibility of Dawes' "escape" from convictism back into society (and of Clarke's return to England).

What is shown to be "wrong" with the adulterous plans of Sylvia and North is not the challenge to social forms, or selfishness (the novel's ostensible reason), but the underlying one that they are driven to it by despair, socially enforced in Sylvia, self-inflicted in North. Accordingly, when Dawes intervenes at the end to "save" Sylvia this is not simply a reliance on melodrama, the heroine's purity defended from the villain. Neither Sylvia nor North is restricted to such stereotyped roles. Dawes saves Sylvia from despairing in a sudden release from his own despair. The fact that such mutual release can result

Clarke at around twenty years of age.

only in death, and no other liberation, embodies Clarke's tragic view of the possible extremes of society's power. The ending, with Dawes and Sylvia perishing in a cyclone, though it is reached by creaky and confusing twists of plot, is figuratively appropriate and grows out of the novel as a whole, including its revolving of the possibilities of "escape". Through the situation of impending death, Clarke uses telescoping effects of effective melodrama in what is a moving adaptation of the novelistic "recognition" scenes. Sylvia's "shock of recovered memory" is used to figure a moment of moral awakening, as past and present are reconciled. In an intuitive leap she understands Dawes' life of imposed suffering and what it has suppressed. He "understood in his turn the story of the young girl's life, and knew how she had been sacrificed". When Dawes "saves" Sylvia for this second time it is with an affirmation, not a sacrifice, of self and through the communion of their shared recognition. Though in the final scenes Clarke was obviously toying with the hackneyed idea of heroic self-sacrifice as a means of ending the novel, this does not enter into the final scene. North's role as redeemer and a Sidney Carton becomes confused but he remains memorable as a portrait of self-brutalization, which shocked some contemporary reviewers.

The conclusion echoes the immediately preceding scene in which Dawes tells North "the secret of his life" and the underlying motive of self-sacrifice which precipitated the novel's action (in the revised version):

> "Love!" cried Rufus Dawes, his pale face radiant. "Love! Oh, it is you who do not know it. Love is the sacrifice of self, the death of all desire that is not for another's good. Love is Godlike! *You* love?—no,

no, your love is selfishness, and will end in shame!
Listen, I will tell you the history of such a love as
yours".

The notion of the voluntary "sacrifice of self" is the conventional, false Victorian conception touched on earlier and belied by the ending and other aspects of the novel. It involves a renunciation of freedom, whose hurt is denied and cloaked by resignation and idealism. It may well be that Clarke's own enforced renunciation of the "mother" country is echoed in this scene and in the first chapter. In the latter, the anger necessarily involved is directed against the putative, cruel father who, in what has been described as a transferred Oedipal act, is killed by Dawes' half-brother Rex. The main force of the novel lies in the presentation of the sacrificing of people in the name of society and in support of its power. Where self-sacrifice does enter in, as at Macquarie Harbour and in Sylvia's marriage, it is convincing not when it is used as a convention but when it is seen as a socially enforced frustration of the self and of what it can contribute to others.

The strengths of *His Natural Life* as a whole are brought out if one compares the revised ending with the preferred one of the reader who advised Bentley for the London (1875) edition, Geraldine Jewsbury. While praising the novel's power, she thought a happy ending was called for. Since the whole point of the story was for her to "show what transportation used to be—and what Norfolk Island was", some "vista of life and comfort" should "soften off" the end. Accordingly, she recommended, that, although "all *personal* hope and happiness is and must be at an end" for Dawes after his convict experiences, these must be used by devoting himself to the abolition of the Norfolk Island jail and aiding "poor wretches" at large.

While the glibness of these suggestions should not lead us to overrate Clarke's conclusion, they help to suggest its clear superiority and also that the novel's whole conception of convicts and society is much more far-reaching and probing than Jewsbury's preconceptions allowed her to glimpse. As Clarke did to some extent, she chose self-sacrifice as a reconciling motif, but in her formulation it is to be used as appeasement, to confirm the essential rightness of society. On the other hand, Clarke uses the motif in his attempts to reconcile his vision of men as predators with that of men as potential brothers so as to achieve the darkness of tragedy rather than of despair. For there is a genuine impulse in the novel to grant the need for love and communality, even if society can be inimical to them and if human nature makes them precarious. It is not too fanciful to see this, and the novel as a whole, as incorporating Clarke's own struggle to come to terms with the loss and trials of colonial dispossession. (pp. 49-61)

> *Laurie Hergenhan, " 'Poet of Our Desolation': Marcus Clarke's 'His Natural Life',' in his* Unnatural Lives: Studies in Australian Fiction, *University of Queensland Press, 1984, pp. 47-61.*

ADDITIONAL BIBLIOGRAPHY

Allen, L. H. Introduction to *For the Term of His Natural Life*, by Marcus Clarke, pp. v-xix. The World's Classics. London: Oxford University Press, Geoffrey Cumberlege, 1952.
> A biographical and critical sketch.

Barnes, John. "Australian Fiction to 1920." In *The Literature of Australia*, rev. ed., edited by Geoffrey Dutton, pp. 149-95. Harmondsworth, Middlesex, England: Penguin Books, 1976.
> A largely negative critique of *His Natural Life* that focuses on its melodramatic and theatrical characteristics.

Boehm, Harold J. "*His Natural Life* and Its Sources." *Australian Literary Studies* 5, No. 1 (May 1971): 42-64.
> Explores Clarke's use of historical materials in *His Natural Life*.

Burrows, J. F. "*His Natural Life* and the Capacities of Melodrama." *Southerly* 34, No. 3 (September 1974): 280-301.
> Examines the concept of melodrama and discusses the effectiveness of melodramatic elements in *His Natural Life*.

Edwards, P. D. "Charles Reade, Wilkie Collins, and Marcus Clarke." *Australian Literary Studies* 11, No. 3 (May 1984): 400-04.
> Labels Clarke's *His Natural Life* a "sensation novel" and reproduces letters written to Clarke by two prominent sensation novelists of the Victorian era, Charles Reade and Wilkie Collins.

Franklin, Miles. "First Novel by a Native-Born: *Gertrude the Emigrant*. First Four Novels of Adequate Tonnage." In her *Laughter, Not for a Cage: Notes on Australian Writing, with Biographical Emphasis on the Struggles, Function, and Achievements of the Novel in Three Half-Centuries*, pp. 28-68. Sydney: Angus and Robertson, 1956.
> Contains biographical and critical material on Clarke and *His Natural Life* as well as a plot summary of the novel.

Hergenhan, Laurie T. "The Corruption of Rufus Dawes." *Southerly* 29, No. 3 (1969): 211-21.
> Traces the progressive degradation of Rufus Dawes during his brutal exposure to the "System" of convict transportation in *His Natural Life*.

———. "Marcus Clarke and the Australian Landscape." *Quadrant* 13, No. 4 (July-August 1969): 31-41.
> Discusses Clarke's description of the Australian bush in his preface to Adam Lindsay Gordon's collection of poetry *Sea Spray and Smoke Drift*.

———. "The Contemporary Reception of *His Natural Life*." *Southerly* 31, No. 1 (1971): 50-63.
> A survey of contemporary British and Australian reviews of *His Natural Life*.

Howarth, R. G. "Marcus Clarke's *For the Term of His Natural Life*." *Southerly* 15, No. 4 (1954): 268-76.
> An introductory essay on *His Natural Life*.

Irvin, Eric. "Marcus Clarke and the Theatre." *Australian Literary Studies* 7, No. 1 (May 1975): 3-14.
> Discusses the production history of Clarke's theatrical works and attempts to determine why Clarke failed as a dramatist.

McDonald, Avis G. "Rufus Dawes and Changing Narrative Perspectives in *His Natural Life*." *Australian Literary Studies* 12, No. 3 (May 1986): 347-58.
> An analysis of narrative technique in *His Natural Life*. McDonald contends that Clarke's use of a flexible point of view reconciles realistic and idealistic elements in the depiction of Rufus Dawes's character.

McLaren, Ian F. *Marcus Clarke: An Annotated Bibliography*. Melbourne: Library Council of Victoria, 1982, 393 p.
> A comprehensive bibliography of writings by and about Clarke.

Murdoch, Walter. "Marcus Clarke." In his *Loose Leaves*, pp. 50-5. Melbourne: George Robertson and Co., 1910.
> An overview of Clarke's major works.

Nesbitt, Bruce. "Marcus Clarke, 'Damned Scamp'." *Australian Literary Studies* 5, No. 1 (May 1971): 93-8.
> Investigates Clarke's sources for *His Natural Life* and questions whether Clarke relied on James Erskine Calder, an Australian surveyor also interested in the history of convict transportation.

O'Leary, P. I. "Studies in Australian Literature: Henry Kingsley and Marcus Clarke." In his *Bard in Bondage: Essays of P. I. O'Leary,* edited by Joseph O'Dwyer, pp. 33-7. Melbourne: Hawthorn Press, 1954.

   A brief biographical and critical study of Clarke.

Pollard, Arthur. "Three Ways of Treating Convicts: An Examination of Three Australian Novels." In *Australian and New Zealand Studies: Papers Presented at a Colloquium at the British Library, 7-9 February 1984,* edited by Patricia McLaren-Turner, pp. 59-65. British Library Occasional Papers, no. 4. London: British Library, 1985.

   Compares three fictional portrayals of convicts in the early Australian penal system: Clarke's *His Natural Life,* William Gosse Hay's *The Escape of the Notorious Sir William Heans,* and Thomas Keneally's *Bring Larks and Heroes.*

Poole, Joan E. "Marcus Clarke: 'Christianity Is Dead'." *Australian Literary Studies* 6, No. 2 (October 1973): 128-42.

   Relates Clarke's negative view of organized Christianity as outlined in his essay *Civilization without Delusion* to the religious theme in *His Natural Life.*

Tinkler, John F. "Marcus Clarke's *Old Tales of a Young Country.*" *Southerly* 33, No. 4 (December 1973): 394-408.

   Compares Clarke's first edition of *Old Tales of a Young Country* with later, edited versions, arguing that the original possesses a unity of theme, tone, and image that makes it more than just a random selection of journalistic writings.

————. "Canadian Cultural Norms and Australian Social Rules: Susanna Moodie's *Roughing It in the Bush* and Marcus Clarke's *His Natural Life.*" *Canadian Literature* 94 (Autumn 1982): 10-22.

   Examines how British culture and society were assimilated in colonial Australia and Canada through a discussion of Clarke's *His Natural Life* and Moodie's *Roughing It in the Bush.*

Wilding, Michael. "Marcus Clarke in the Colonial City." *Southerly* 33, No. 4 (December 1973): 441-50.

   A review of *A Colonial City: High and Low Life—Selected Journalism of Marcus Clarke.* Wilding focuses on Clarke's versatility as a journalist.

————. "Marcus Clarke's *Chidiock Tichbourne.*" *Australian Literary Studies* 6, No. 4 (October 1974): 381-93.

   Considers the sources for Clarke's novel *Chidiock Tichbourne* and discusses its themes of emigration, expatriation, and homosexuality.

————. Introduction to *Marcus Clarke,* by Marcus Clarke, edited by Michael Wilding, pp. ix-xxx. Portable Australian Authors, edited by L. T. Hergenhan. St. Lucia, Queensland: University of Queensland Press, 1976.

   A biographical and critical essay.

————. *Marcus Clarke.* Melbourne: Oxford University Press, 1977, 52 p.

   A study of Clarke's life and work.

Gustave Flaubert

1821-1880

French novelist and short story writer.

The following entry presents criticism of Flaubert's novel *L'éducation sentimentale: Histoire d'un jeune homme* (1869; translated as *Sentimental Education: A Young Man's History*, 1898). For additional information on Flaubert's career and *Sentimental Education*, see *NCLC*, Vols. 2 and 10.

Sentimental Education is considered Flaubert's most sustained and successful effort to portray contemporary bourgeois society. In this novel the author sketches the manners and mores of his generation, describing the circumstances behind the February Revolution of 1848 and the reaction that followed it. Although not as well known or as widely read as *Madame Bovary*, Flaubert's most famous work, *Sentimental Education* is consistently regarded as one of his greatest achievements both for its commentary on French life in the nineteenth century and for what it reveals, through its autobiographical content, about one of the greatest writers of France.

Flaubert was born in Rouen, where his father was chief surgeon and clinical professor at the city hospital, the Hôtel Dieu, and his mother was a well-known woman from a provincial bourgeois family. Flaubert lived with his parents, brother Achille, and sister Caroline in an apartment at the hospital. As a youth he attended the Collège Royal de Rouen, traveled with his family throughout France, and spent summer vacations at Trouville. It was in Trouville that he first met Maria-Elisa Schlésinger, a married woman for whom he harbored a lifelong infatuation and who deeply influenced the character and direction of *Sentimental Education*. Although Flaubert was interested in literature and began to write at an early age, upon receiving his baccalaureate he honored his parents' wishes and reluctantly began law school in Paris. In 1844 his studies were disrupted when he experienced the first attack of what is now believed to have been epilepsy. As a result, he abandoned his plans for a law career and devoted himself to writing. Both his father and sister died in 1846, and the author, his mother, and his infant niece moved to the family home at Croisset, near Rouen. Except for several trips abroad and to Paris, including one to the city in 1848 to observe the February Revolution "from the point of view of art," Flaubert remained at Croisset until his death.

The third of Flaubert's five major novels, *Sentimental Education* was written between 1863 and 1869. Yet the idea for the work had been formed years before while Flaubert was composing three autobiograhical studies, which remained in manuscript throughout his life: *Mémoires d'un fou, Novembre,* and a first version of *Sentimental Education* (commonly known as the version of 1845). As early as 1838 Flaubert had begun *Mémoires d'un fou*, a reflective essay in which he recounted the agonies and frustrations of his love for Schlésinger. Shortly after, in 1841 and 1842, he composed *Novembre*, a tale of a man who, recognizing that he was not made for this world and could never adapt himself to it, "died, but slowly, little by little, by the force of thought alone, without any organ being ill, as one dies of sadness." Then, in 1845, he completed the first version of *Sentimental Education*, which he had begun in

1843 in Paris. This work, which contrasts the respective rewards of love and art, is based on the author's unfulfilled love for Schlésinger and strongly prefigures the 1869 version of *Sentimental Education*. In the original work the main character, Jules, who like Flaubert has been disappointed in love, resolves to become "a great and grave artist." For over a decade Flaubert struggled to realize Jules's dream for himself, publishing his first major novel, *Madame Bovary*, in 1857. Two years later, well into the writing of the historical novel *Salammbô*, he wrote to Ernest Feydeau: "The deeper I plunge into antiquity, the more I feel the need to do something modern, and inside my head I'm cooking up a whole crew of characters." Commentators agree that this "crew of characters" ultimately became the cast of *Sentimental Education*.

The novel begins in 1840, during the July Monarchy of King Louis Philippe. Like Flaubert at the time, the hero of the novel, Frédéric Moreau, is an unenthusiastic law student in Paris. For years he has been in love with Madame Arnoux (believed to have been modeled on Schlésinger), a married woman he met by chance when he was eighteen. Frédéric becomes a close friend of Madame Arnoux and her philandering husband, but he does not declare his love for her. Back home at Nogent-sur-Seine after finishing his studies, Frédéric begins work in a law office, only to return to Paris when he inherits money from his uncle. Here again Frédéric's experiences are similar to those of Flaubert, who was relieved of the need to work by an inheritance at about the same age. Frédéric renews his visits with the Arnoux, and Madame introduces him to a courtesan, Rosanette. Frédéric courts both women, but neither accepts his advances. In distress, he considers marrying a childhood acquaintance, however, Madame Arnoux, now extremely jealous, deepens their relationship while insisting that it remain platonic. This makes Frédéric all the more determined: he rents an apartment and attempts to lure her there by deception, but her son's illness forestalls the plan. As the February Revolution of 1848 rages in the streets, the angered Frédéric turns to Rosanette, with whom he then lives for a time. Soon he admits to himself that he will never consummate his love for Madame Arnoux. He takes a second lover, the rich and aristocratic Madame Dambreuse, and upon the death of her husband the two plan to marry. But on 2 December 1851, the day of Louis Napoleon's coup d'état, Frédéric learns that the Arnoux are bankrupt and that they have left Paris. Immediately, in apparent loyalty to the woman he desires most, he leaves his two lovers but does not go to Madame Arnoux. Nearly sixteen years pass before she visits him in March 1867. The two recall past times and walk in the streets of Paris. She cuts off a lock of her hair, now white, gives it to Frédéric, and says good-bye. As the novel concludes, Frédéric and his friend Deslauriers sit together and remember the dreams and companions of their youth.

As he explained in a letter to his friend Mademoiselle Leroyer de Chantepie in 1864, Flaubert set out in *Sentimental Education* to write "the moral history of the men of my generation—or, more accurately, the history of their feelings. It's a book about love, about passion; but passion such as can exist nowadays—that is to say, inactive." Flaubert was tormented by doubts about the project. While he intended to sketch bourgeois characters, he scorned the bourgeoisie and feared his readers would too. He also doubted his ability to depict the characters effectively. To Alfred Maury he wrote in 1866: "I fear [*Sentimental Education*] may prove to be a mediocre work, because the conception is faulty. I want to depict a psychological state—an authentic one, in my opinion—which has not yet been described. But the ambience in which my characters live and move is so crowded and teeming that time after time they barely manage to avoid disappearing into it." Here Flaubert expresses a concern that occupied him throughout his career and that was particularly pressing with *Sentimental Education*: his desire for total accuracy in descriptions of events, settings, and motivations, but never at the expense of the narrative itself. This is why, as numerous letters and working notes testify, Flaubert labored meticulously on the novel, painstakingly gathering information on Parisian social life, human behavior and psychology, and other more mundane subjects—a task he had begun in 1848 when he visited Paris, and possibly well before. This is also why he endeavored to make his characters, even the minor ones, representative of types he had personally observed: Dussardier, the hater of oppression; Sénécal, the dogmatic socialist; Hussonnet, the bohemian; Monsieur Dambreuse, the capitalist; Deslauriers, the man of good sense, who also functions as Frédéric's and, according to most critics, Flaubert's alter ego. In this way the novelist becomes historian and the scholar shows himself to be an artist, for as commentators agree, while history expands and elucidates Flaubert's plot, fiction supplies the background for political events.

Flaubert's many misgivings about *Sentimental Education* were realized immediately after the work's publication. Critics derided the book: they accused him, as they had with the oth-

erwise generally lauded *Madame Bovary*, of baseness and vulgarity; questioned his morality; attacked the novel's descriptive passages as tedious and redundant; deplored the absence of a strong hero; labeled the narrative awkward and disjointed; resented Flaubert's exposure of illusions held dear about the political events of 1848; and even claimed that Flaubert had lost forever what literary skills he may have once possessed. The reviews were so negative, in fact, that Flaubert suspected he was the victim of a plot to defame him. Yet modern scholars generally agree that the explanation is much simpler: most readers were not ready for what appeared to them to be a novel in which subject, plot, and character were merely background features, and few could easily bear its despairing tone and bleak atmosphere. However, some lesser-known critics saw genius. Paul de Leoni, for example, said in *Le pays*: "The book is serious, vigorous, gripping, and belongs to the family of *Madame Bovary*." Almost alone among eminent reviewers, George Sand praised the novel's structure and declared *Sentimental Education* to be "all the work of a master." But by the end of the century, probably owing, commentators believe, to the appearance in the meantime of many "non-fictional novels" (the term comes from Théodore de Banville, who used it in a positive valuation of *Sentimental Education* published after Flaubert's death), the work was favorably reviewed by such luminaries as Émile Zola and Henry James. Moreover, a number of disciples, including Guy de Maupassant and Joris Karl Huysmans, wrote their own *"éducations sentimentales,"* stories of lives that came to nothing. In the twentieth century, *Sentimental Education* is generally ranked second only to *Madame Bovary* among Flaubert's works, although a few commentators consider it the author's greatest achievement. Critics have explored the work from many angles, focusing especially on autobiographical elements, characterization, historicity, method of composition, structure, chronology, and point of view. Some have sought to isolate a high moral purpose in the narrative and to counter claims that certain sections, most notably the brothel episode at the end, are not integral and are there simply for shock value. Outside the realm of pure literature, historians have looked to *Sentimental Education* as a record of daily life in France during and immediately after the July Monarchy, and several philological studies have been made of the work. Today, *Sentimental Education* is recognized as a masterwork by a master artist, "one of the great novels of its age," according to Maurice Nadeau, "and one whose youth never fades."

GUSTAVE FLAUBERT   (letter date 1864)

[*In the following letter to Mademoiselle Leroyer de Chantepie, a minor woman of letters with whom Flaubert corresponded often, Flaubert expresses his concerns about the early progress of* Sentimental Education.]

No, chère Demoiselle, I have not forgotten you. I think of you often, of your mind, which is so distinguished, and of your sufferings, which seem to me utterly without remedy.

Our existences are perhaps not as different as they appear to be on the surface and as you imagine them to be. Between the two of us there exists something amounting to a bit more than mere literary sympathy, I believe. My days are spent in solitude, somber and arduous. It is thanks to work that I am able to stifle the melancholy I was born with. But often the old dregs resurface, the old dregs that no one knows of, the deep, secret wound.

Here I am, harnessed now and for the past month to a novel about modern life, which will be laid in Paris. I want to write the moral history of the men of my generation—or, more accurately, the history of their *feelings*. It's a book about love, about passion; but passion such as can exist nowadays—that is to say, inactive. The subject as I have conceived it is, I believe, profoundly true, but for that very reason probably not very entertaining. Facts, drama, are a bit lacking; and then the action is spread over a too extended period. In short, I'm having a good deal of trouble and am full of anxieties. I shall remain here in the country for part of the winter, in order to push ahead a little with this long task. (pp. 79-80)

> *Gustave Flaubert, in a letter to Mademoiselle Leroyer de Chantepie on October 6, 1864, in his* The Letters of Gustave Flaubert: 1857-1880, *edited and translated by Francis Steegmuller, Cambridge, Mass.: The Belknap Press, 1982, pp. 79-80.*

GUSTAVE FLAUBERT (letter date 1864)

[*In the following letter to his close friend Madame Roger des Genettes, Flaubert recounts his fear that* Sentimental Education *will be an artistic failure.*]

Just now I am in complete solitude. A fog has been gathering, deepening the silence and seeming to shroud me in a great whitish tomb. I hear no sound except the crackling of my fire and the ticking of my clock. I work by lamplight ten hours out of the twenty-four, and time passes. But I waste so much of it! What a dreamer I am, in spite of myself! I'm beginning to be a little less discouraged. When you next see me, I'll have done almost three chapters—three, not more. But I thought I'd die of disgust during the first. One's faith in oneself is worn down with the years, the flame dies, strength declines. I have a fundamental reason for being depressed—the conviction that I'm writing something useless; I mean contrary to the goal of Art, which is exaltation, of one kind or another. But with the scientific requirements of today, and a bourgeois subject, that goal seems to me altogether impossible. Beauty is not compatible with modern life. So this is the last time I'll deal with it: I've had enough.

> *Gustave Flaubert, in a letter to Madame Roger des Genettes in December , 1864, in his* The Letters of Gustave Flaubert: 1857-1880, *edited and translated by Francis Steegmuller, Cambridge, Mass.: The Belknap Press, 1982, p. 80.*

GUSTAVE FLAUBERT (letter date 1866)

[*In the following letter to Alfred Maury, a professor at the Collège de France who wrote extensively on psychology and religion, Flaubert describes the artistic and conceptual problems he has encountered in writing* Sentimental Education.]

You are too kind, my dear friend. I do not share your hopes concerning the novel I'm now writing. On the contrary, I fear it may prove to be a mediocre work, because the conception is faulty. I want to depict a psychological state—an authentic one, in my opinion—which has not yet been described. But the ambience in which my characters live and move is so crowded and teeming that time after time they barely manage to avoid disappearing into it. Thus I am forced to relegate to a middle ground precisely those things that are the most in-

teresting. I skim over many subjects that one would like to see treated more deeply. My purpose is complex—a bad aesthetic method: in short, I think I have never undertaken anything more difficult. We must trust in God, after all! (pp. 81-2)

> *Gustave Flaubert, in a letter to Alfred Maury on August 20, 1866, in his* The Letters of Gustave Flaubert: 1857-1880, *edited and translated by Francis Steegmuller, Cambridge, Mass.: The Belknap Press, 1982, pp. 81-2.*

GUSTAVE FLAUBERT (letter date 1868)

[*Flaubert discloses to George Sand, a highly prolific French novelist and woman of letters, his apprehension that both "patriots" and "reactionaries"—by "patriots" Flaubert means those defeated in June 1848, by "reactionaries" the triumphant bourgeois—will respond harshly to* Sentimental Education. *For Sand's response, see excerpt below dated 31 July 1868.*]

I've been slaving away madly for the past six weeks. The patriots won't forgive me this book, nor the reactionaries either! So much the worse: I write things as I feel them—that is, as I believe they exist. Is this foolish of me? But it seems that our unhappy condition is attributable exclusively to people of our own kind? All the Christianity I find in Socialism appalls me! Here, for example, are two little notes now lying on my table:

"This system [Louis Blanc's own] is not a system of disorder. For it has its source in the Gospels. And from this divine source *there cannot flow* hatred, warfare, total conflict of interests. For the doctrine formulated from the Gospels is a doctrine of peace, union, and love." (L. Blanc)

"I even make bold to assert that with the disappearance of respect for Sunday, the last spark of poetic fire has been extinguished in the souls of our rhymesters. As the saying has it: 'Without religion, no poetry.'" (Proudhon)

Apropos of the latter, I beg of you, chère maître, to read, at the end of his book on the celebration of Sunday, a love story entitled, I think, *Marie et Maxime*. One must know this to have an idea of the Style of our Thinkers. It should be placed with the excursion to Brittany in *Ça et là*, by the great Veuillot. This doesn't prevent some of our friends from admiring these two gentlemen. Whereas they deride Voltaire.

In my old age I intend to write criticism: it will relieve me. For I often choke on suppressed opinions. No one understands better than I Boileau's outbursts against bad taste: "The stupidities I hear uttered at the Academy are hastening my end." There was a man for you! (p. 116)

> *Gustave Flaubert, in a letter to George Sand on July 5, 1868, in his* The Letters of Gustave Flaubert: 1857-1880, *edited and translated by Francis Steegmuller, Cambridge, Mass.: The Belknap Press, 1982, pp. 116-17.*

GEORGE SAND (letter date 1868)

[*Sand was one of France's most celebrated and controversial writers. Writing effortlessly, yet maintaining an impressive richness of style and unity of construction, she produced nearly sixty novels, a lengthy autobiography, numerous essays, and approximately 20,000 letters during her lifetime. Flaubert met Sand shortly after she published a highly favorable review of* Madame Bovary *in 1857, and the two became close friends and corre-*

spondents. Here, Sand responds to Flaubert's letter dated 5 July 1868 (see excerpt above).]

You disturb me when you say that in your book you'll blame the patriots for all that went wrong [in 1848]. Is that really true? They—the vanquished! Surely it's enough to be defeated through your own fault, without having your nose rubbed in all your stupidities. Have pity! There were so many splendid souls even so. The Christian aspect was a fad. I confess that Christianity has always been seductive. When you see only its gentle side, it wins your heart. But you have to think of all the harm it has done. I'm not surprised that a generous heart like L. Blanc should have dreamed of seeing it purified and restored to its ideal. I too had that illusion, but as soon as you take a step back into the past you see that it cannot be revived, and I am sure that today L. Blanc is smiling at his dream. One must think of that, too. One must tell oneself that all who had some intelligence have come a very long way in the past twenty years, and that it would not be generous to reproach them for what they themselves probably regret. As for Proudhon, I never thought him sincere. He was an orator—of genius, so it is said. I don't understand him. He is a kind of perpetual antithesis, insoluble. I think of him as one of those sophists old Socrates made fun of.

I trust you to be *generous*. With a word more or a word less, with the hand wielding its strength gently, one can flick the whip without causing a wound. You are so good—you cannot be cruel.

> *George Sand, in a letter to Gustave Flaubert on July 31, 1868, in* The Letters of Gustave Flaubert: 1857-1880, *edited and translated by Francis Steegmuller, Cambridge, Mass.: The Belknap Press, 1982, p. 117.*

GUSTAVE FLAUBERT   (letter date 1868)

[*Flaubert addresses Sand's concern, expressed in a letter of 31 July 1868 (see excerpt above), that in* Sentimental Education *he will hold the patriots responsible for their own defeat in 1848.*]

I expressed myself badly if I told you that my book will "blame the patriots for all that went wrong." I don't recognize my right to blame anyone. I don't even believe that the novelist should express his opinion on matters of this world. He can communicate it, but I don't like him to state it. (Such is part of my poetics.) Thus I confine myself to describing things as they appear to me, to expressing what seems to me to be true. Hang the consequences. Rich or poor, winners or losers—I take no account of all that. I want to have neither hate, nor pity, nor anger. As for sympathy, that's different. One can never have enough of it. The reactionaries, by the way, will be treated even less gently than the others. For they seem to me more criminal . . .

Now let me say that since I have absolute confidence in the greatness of your spirit, I will read my third part to you when it's done, and if there is something in my work that seems cruel to you I'll remove it. But I'm convinced in advance that you'll make no objection. As for allusions to individuals, there isn't a trace. (pp. 117-18)

> *Gustave Flaubert, in a letter to George Sand on August 10, 1868, in his* The Letters of Gustave Flaubert: 1857-1880, *edited and translated by Francis Steegmuller, Cambridge, Mass.: The Belknap Press, 1982, pp. 117-18.*

GUSTAVE FLAUBERT   (letter date 1868)

[*In the following excerpt from a letter to his businessman friend Jules Duplan, Flaubert seeks information about certain technical and historical matters he intends to treat in* Sentimental Education.]

Here's the thing.

I tell—or rather, a cocotte in my book tells about her childhood. She was the daughter of workers in Lyons. I need details about the homes of such people.

1. A few lines about the living quarters of Lyons workers.

2. The "canuts" (as I think the silk weavers are called) work in very low-ceilinged rooms, don't they?

3. In their own homes?

4. Their children work too?

I find the following in my notes: the weaver working at a Jacquard loom is continually struck in the stomach by the shaft of the roller on which the cloth is being wound as it is completed.

5. Is it the roller itself that strikes him? Clarify, please.

In short, I want to write a four-line description of a working-class domestic scene, to contrast it with another interior that comes later—the luxurious establishment in which our heroine is deflowered. Her tambourine is punctured by a Saint-Florent. Unfortunately I have no room to expatiate on these people. If you know one of your compatriots whom you want to "stigmatize," send me his photograph. But all this is unimportant: what I need is my picture of "canuts" doing their work amidst their household paraphernalia.

It would be kind of you to send me this information right away. I need it.

> *Gustave Flaubert, in a letter to Jules Duplan in August or September, 1868, in his* The Letters of Gustave Flaubert: 1857-1880, *edited and translated by Francis Steegmuller, Cambridge, Mass.: The Belknap Press, 1982, p. 118.*

GUSTAVE FLAUBERT   (letter date 1868)

[*Flaubert informs Sand of the progress he has been making on* Sentimental Education. *For additional commentary by Flaubert on the Fontainebleau passage, see excerpt below dated 16 September 1868.*]

I'm working furiously. I've written a description of the forest of Fontainebleau that made me want to hang myself from one of its trees. I had interrupted myself for three weeks, and had great trouble getting back into my stride. I'm like a camel—you can't stop him when he's on the go, nor make him start when he's resting. I still have a year's work ahead. After that, no more bourgeois, definitely. Too difficult, and too ugly. It's time for me to do something good that I'll enjoy.

> *Gustave Flaubert, in an extract from a letter to George Sand on September 9, 1868, in his* The Letters of Gustave Flaubert: 1857-1880, *edited and translated by Francis Steegmuller, Cambridge, Mass.: The Belknap Press, 1982, p. 119.*

GUSTAVE FLAUBERT   (letter date 1868)

[*Flaubert recounts to Duplan the gathering of information for the Fontainebleau episode in* Sentimental Education.]

Look what's happened. After making the trip to Fontainebleau and back by train, I was struck by a doubt: and now I'm sure, alas! that in 1848 there was no railroad between Paris and Fontainebleau. This means I have to scrap two passages and begin afresh. I see in *Paris-Guide* that the line to Lyons began only in 1849. You can't imagine what a nuisance this is for me. So—I need to know: 1. how, in June 1848, one went from Paris to Fontainebleau; 2. perhaps *part* of the line was already in use? 3. what coaches did one take? 4. and what was their terminus in Paris? Here is the situation: Frédéric is at Fontainebleau with Rosanette; he hears that Dussardier has been wounded (this is June 25), and he leaves for Paris with Rosanette, who doesn't want to be left behind. But on the way she loses her courage and comes no farther. He arrives in Paris alone. Because of the Saint-Antoine barricades he has to make a long detour before reaching Dussardier, who lives at the far end of the faubourg Poissonnière.

Can you recall what the ambulances looked like? If you remember any details of the nights in Paris that week, send them to me.

My hero wanders through the streets the last night, June 25-26 (everything ended on the 26th).

Now you see the situation as clearly as I. Be a good chap: try to find me definite information.

My bugger of a novel is draining the very marrow of my bones. I'm dog-tired, and beginning to be depressed.

In 1848 the line between Corbeil and Paris was open. Remains to know how one got from Fontainebleau to Corbeil . . .

> *Gustave Flaubert, in a letter to Jules Duplan on September 16, 1868, in his* The Letters of Gustave Flaubert: 1857-1880, *edited and translated by Francis Steegmuller, Cambridge, Mass.: The Belknap Press, 1982, p. 119.*

GUSTAVE FLAUBERT   (letter date 1869)

[*In the following excerpt from a letter to Duplan dated "Sunday morning, May 6, 1869. 4 minutes before 5," Flaubert describes the profound relief he feels in having just completed* Sentimental Education.]

Fini! mon vieux! Yes, my book is finished! This calls for your stopping work and coming to embrace me.

I've been at my desk since 8 o'clock yesterday morning. My head is bursting. No matter—there's a tremendous weight off my stomach!

> *Gustave Flaubert, in a letter to Jules Duplan on May 6, 1869, in his* The Letters of Gustave Flaubert: 1857-1880, *edited and translated by Francis Steegmuller, Cambridge, Mass.: The Belknap Press, 1982, p. 129.*

EDMOND DE GONCOURT AND JULES DE GONCOURT   (journal date 1869)

[*The Goncourt brothers were literary innovators who are noted for their diverse contributions to the world of letters. In their best-known work,* Journal des Goncourts, *a diary that contains a detailed record of Parisian literary life, the brothers proved themselves adept historians of their age. In the following passage from the* Journal, *they describe their reaction to Flaubert upon his completion of* Sentimental Education.]

Flaubert's book, his Parisian novel, is finished. We see the manuscript on his green baize table, in a box made especially for it and bearing the title to which he stubbornly clings: **L'Education Sentimentale,** with the subtitle *L'Histoire d'un Jeune Homme.*

He is about to send it to the copyist, for ever since he began to write he has kept for himself as a sort of religion the immortal monument of his manuscript. This fellow makes a somewhat ridiculous ceremony of even the slightest things connected with his painful creation. Decidedly, in our friend we do not know which is more gross, his vanity or his pride!

> *Edmond de Goncourt and Jules de Goncourt, in a journal entry on May 23, 1869, in* Paris and the Arts, 1851-1896: From the Goncourt Journal, *edited and translated by George J. Becker and Edith Philips, Cornell University Press, 1971, p. 114.*

GEORGE SAND   (letter date 1869)

[*Sand tells Flaubert that she believes* Sentimental Education *is "all the work of a master."*]

I wanted to reread your book, and my daughter-in-law has read it too, and several of my young friends, all of them sincere and spontaneous, and not at all stupid. We are all of the same opinion, that it is a splendid book, with the strength of the best of Balzac and more real—that is, more faithful to the truth from beginning to end. It takes the great art, the exquisite form, and the austerity of your work to make us willing to forgo the flowers of fantasy. Nevertheless you do fill your painting with poetry, whether or not your characters are aware of it. Rosanette at Fountainebleau doesn't know what plants she's treading on, but she is poetic all the same. It is all the work of a master—so live as calmly as you can in order to last long and produce much.

I have seen two scraps of articles that don't seem to begrudge you your success, but I know little of what goes on except that the papers seem given over to politics. Keep me informed. If they didn't do you justice, I'd be angry and say what I think. That's my right.

> *George Sand, in a letter to Gustave Flaubert on November 30, 1869, in* The Letters of Gustave Flaubert: 1857-1880, *edited and translated by Francis Steegmuller, Cambridge, Mass.: The Belknap Press, 1982, p. 135.*

GUSTAVE FLAUBERT   (letter date 1869)

[*In the following excerpt from a letter to Sand, Flaubert ponders the early critical reception afforded* Sentimental Education.]

Your old troubadour is being greatly berated in the press. Read last Monday's *Constitutionnel* and this morning's *Gaulois*—they mince no words. They treat me like a cretin and a scoundrel. Barbey d'Aurevilly's piece in the *Constitutionnel* is a model of this genre, and the one by our friend Sarcey, though less violent, is no less uncomplimentary. These gentlemen protest in the name of morality and the ideal! I have also been flayed in the *Figaro* and in *Paris*, by Cesena and Duranty.

I don't care in the least, but it does surprise me that there should be so much hatred and dishonesty.

The *Tribune*, the *Pays*, and the *Opinion Nationale*, on the other hand, have praised me to the skies.

As for my friends—people who received copies adorned with my signature—they are afraid of compromising themselves, and speak to me about everything except the book. Instances of courage are rare. Nevertheless, the book is selling very well despite the political situation, and Lévy seems satisfied.

I know that the Rouen bourgeois are furious with me because of old Roque and the cellar of the Tuileries. Their opinion is that the ''publication of such books should be forbidden'' (I quote verbatim), that I favor the Reds, that I am guilty of fanning revolutionary passions, etc. etc. (pp. 135-36)

All the papers adduce as proof of my baseness the episode of la Turque—which they garble, of course; and Sarcey compares me to the marquis de Sade, whom he admits he hasn't read!

None of this destroys my composure. But I keep asking myself: Why publish? (p. 136)

> *Gustave Flaubert, in a letter to George Sand on December 3, 1869, in his* The Letters of Gustave Flaubert: 1857-1880, *edited and translated by Francis Steegmuller, Cambridge, Mass.: The Belknap Press, 1982, pp. 135-36.*

GUSTAVE FLAUBERT　(letter date 1869)

[*Distressed by the unfavorable reception given* Sentimental Education *during its first few weeks of publication, Flaubert implores Sand to publish a review of the work. Sand quickly acceded to the request, publishing one two weeks later in* La liberté.]

The way they're all jumping on your old troubadour is unheard of. People who have received a copy of my novel from me are afraid to talk to me about it, for fear of compromising themselves or out of pity for me. The most indulgent are of the opinion that what I have written is merely a series of scenes, and that composition and pattern are completely lacking. Saint-Victor, who extols the books of Arsène Houssaye, won't write about mine, finding it too bad. Voilà. [Théophile Gautier] is away, and no one (absolutely no one) is coming to my defense.

Therefore (you can guess what's coming), if you would care to take on that role you'd oblige me. If it embarrasses you, do nothing. No mere indulgence between us two. (p. 136)

> *Gustave Flaubert, in a letter to George Sand on December 7, 1869, in his* The Letters of Gustave Flaubert: 1857-1880, *edited and translated by Francis Steegmuller, Cambridge, Mass.: The Belknap Press, 1982, pp. 136-37.*

GEORGE SAND　(letter date 1869)

[*Sand reassures Flaubert of the excellence of* Sentimental Education *and summarizes her review of it.*]

You seem surprised by the ill will. You are too naif. You don't know how original your book is. You don't realize how it *must* vex people by its very strength. You think you write things that will go as smoothly as a letter in the mail. That's what you *think!*

In my article I emphasize the *structure* of your book. That is what people understand the least, and it's the book's strongest feature. I have tried to make simple readers understand how they should read it, for it's the simple readers who make a book a success. Clever, malicious folk don't want others to

succeed. I haven't concerned myself with them—it would do them too much honor. (pp. 137-38)

> *George Sand, in a letter to Gustave Flaubert on December 10-11, 1869, in* The Letters of Gustave Flaubert: 1857-1880, *edited and translated by Francis Steegmuller, Cambridge, Mass.: The Belknap Press, 1982, pp. 137-38.*

GEORGE SAND　(letter date 1870)

[*Sand attempts to account for continuing critical attacks on* Sentimental Education *and relates words of praise offered about the book.*]

Your book is still being attacked. That doesn't keep it from being a beautiful and good book. Justice will be done later; justice is always done. It hasn't come at the proper time, apparently; or, rather, the time is *too* right. It confirms the present confused state of people's minds all too strongly. It rubs the raw wound. People recognize themselves too clearly in it.

Everyone adores you here, and our consciences are too clear for us to be offended by the truth: we speak of you every day. Yesterday Lina was telling me that she greatly admired everything you do, but that she preferred *Salammbô* to your depictions of modern life. If you had been concealed somewhere nearby, this is what you would have heard coming from her, from me, and from the others:

He is taller, larger, than the average person. His mind is like him, out-size. In this he has at least as much of Victor Hugo as of Balzac, but he has the taste and discernment that Hugo lacks, and he is an artist, which Balzac was not.—Does that mean he is greater than both of them?—*Chi lo sa?* He hasn't yet spoken with his full voice. The immense capacity of his brain confounds him. He doesn't know whether to be a poet or a realist, and since he's both, that troubles him.—He must learn to cope with his own great radiations. He sees everything, and wants to grapple with everything at once.—In that he is unlike the public, which wants to take its nourishment in small mouthfuls, and chokes on anything big. Nevertheless the public will make its way to him, when it understands him.—It will even reach him quite soon if the author will deign to *want* to be understood.—For that, he will perhaps have to make some concessions to the laziness of its intelligence.—But we must think carefully before daring to offer him that advice.

Such is the résumé of what we have all been saying. It isn't without value to know the opinions of good people and young people. The youngest say that *L'Education sentimentale* made them sad. They didn't recognize themselves in it, they who haven't yet lived. But they have illusions, and they say: Why does this man, so good, so lovable, so gay, so simple, so sympathetic, want to discourage us from living? It isn't properly thought out, what they say, but since it's instinctive, it should perhaps be taken into account. (pp. 140-41)

> *George Sand, in a letter to Gustave Flaubert on January 9, 1870, in* The Letters of Gustave Flaubert: 1857-1880, *edited and translated by Francis Steegmuller, Cambridge, Mass.: The Belknap Press, 1982, pp. 140-41.*

W. P. MORRAS　(essay date 1870)

[*Morras discusses Flaubert's realism in* Sentimental Education. *For additional commentary by Morras on the novel, see NCLC, Vol. 2.*]

One of Rembrandt's pictures represents an anatomical demonstrator, who has just cut open the trunk of a corpse and exhibits its entrails to a class of young but grave-looking men. The spectator feels himself at once attracted and repelled by the picture. After he has long contemplated it he averts his gaze and draws a breath of relief.

Such is the impression produced on reading and laying down Gustave Flaubert's last novel. We question whether a work like *L'Education Sentimentale* has ever been written out of France. Many readers will probably add, "No, Heaven forbid!" But it is exactly because we need not apprehend that American authors will go too far in realistic delineations that it is safe to explain what invests books like Flaubert's with their peculiar value and painful fascination. It is of no consequence that this value and fascination are those of an anatomical lesson. Anatomy belongs to art: no artist has been the worse for a visit to the dissecting-room. Something may therefore be even learnt from an author who prepares the soul like a corpse, exposes and strips it with ruthless hand, dissects it with the sharp knife, and subjects its most delicate tissues to the microscope. The anatomist cannot teach us to create living beings, but we may learn from him all about the bones, muscles and nerves, without which nothing human can exist. This of itself repays the trouble. (p. 439)

[Flaubert] has just published his third work, *L'Education Sentimentale,* which relates the story of a young man named Frédéric Moreau. The hero is already nineteen years old when we make his acquaintance. Of his infancy and boyhood nothing more is said than that he lost his father early; that he was reared at Nogent, a small provincial town, by his mother; and that he received his schooling at the Lyceum of Sens. The mother is not described as sentimental. Not to prejudice the future career of her son, for whom she entertains ambitious views, she "did not like to hear the government censured in her presence." Nor are any sentimental influences to be traced back to the Lyceum. But Frédéric had early intoxicated himself with the poets of love and the passions, and considered his life already a failure at eighteen. "I could have achieved something with a woman that loved me. . . . Why do you laugh? Love is the food, and, as it were, the atmosphere of genius. Extraordinary emotions of the mind produce great results. But I refrain from seeking her whom I miss. Were I to discover her now, she would spurn me. I belong to the disinherited, and shall descend to the grave with a treasure either of glass or diamonds—I know not which." The story of this unhappy genius hinges chiefly on his love-affairs, and it is they that educate him. Represented at the outset of his life as an inquisitively-sensual and clumsily-bashful youth, we leave him a worn-out, satiated man in the fifties. The closing chapter of the novel relates a conversation between Frédéric and Deslauriers, a former schoolmate. If the main object of Frédéric's life was love, that of Deslauriers was power and distinction. Surveying the past with the eyes of altered men, both discover that their lives have been failures. Here are the reasons why:

"Perhaps for not having kept in the straight line?" said Frédéric.

"That may apply in your case," answered his friend. "I, on the contrary, have sinned by an excess of straightness, and paid no attention to thousands of subordinate things which are mightier than all. I had too much logic—you had too much feeling."

Feeling? Let us substitute the word sentiment for it. We can here learn the difference between these two. In one of those rare passages in which the author expresses his own opinions in two words, he calls his hero "the man of all weaknesses." In Frédéric the feeling is decidedly weak. Sensibility is the exact opposite of strength of feeling. Frédéric is a proof that excess of feeling destroys all force of character. His sensibility does not arise from any delicacy of mind, but from a nervous excitability: he is not soft-hearted, but weak-hearted. He succumbs to every impression, yet none retains a hold on him; he entertains an exalted opinion of his own excellence, but is capable of any meanness; he can even be magnanimous when a momentary nervous excitement carries him away. In a troubled period, amidst a disaffected society, which feels the ground tremble under its feet and finds no God in the heavens above; which sentimentalizes with the skeptical poets and looks to optimistic world regenerators for the reign of Proletarianism and the emancipation of the flesh; which discovers daily new rights, but scouts old duties; which dreams of an unlimited capacity for enjoyment, while it is incapable of any; which, disgusted with reality, flies to romance, and expects from it a solution of the great problems that oppress the Present,—such a period and such a society must give birth not only to many real men bearing a near resemblance to Frédéric Moreau, but to that ideal type—that compound of naïve egotism and affected martyrdom.

The hero of Flaubert's novel occupies therefore the same relation to the favorite characters of French romanticism as Don Quixote does to the heroes of knightly poetry. With historical gravity and circumstantial accuracy, as though it involved the most vital affairs, Flaubert relates Frédéric's various amours. Frédéric, it is true, calls the love with which he is inspired by Madame Arnoux, the virtuous wife and mother whom he fails to corrupt, his principal love, "his *grande passion.*" But this great love does not prevent him from living with Rosanette, the lorette, from promising marriage to the alluring Louise, his neighbor, from becoming first the lover and then the betrothed of Madame Dambreuse, the heartless fine lady. And all these love-affairs are simultaneous. That we may not suppose the author to feel something like an idealizing weakness for any one among his female characters, he takes special care to inform us that even the most virtuous of them are frail. Louise, the girl betrayed by Frédéric, marries his friend Deslauriers, and subsequently runs away with an actor. Madame Arnoux, with whose modesty and virtue we deeply sympathize, must at last, when a woman with white hairs, pay her former tempter an equivocal visit, from which she comes out pure only because Frédéric, "as much from prudence as from a reluctance to lower his ideal," prefers to turn on his heel and to roll up a cigarette.

The scene of the story is laid in Paris and in Frédéric's native town: the period extends from the year 1840 to 1868. We are not for a moment disconnected with the public events of the time, with the social and political life of France and her capital. Love-adventures in Paris have not exactly the character of idyls, in which two souls entirely forget the outside world. The women whom Frédéric loves are wives, lorettes and daughters. The realist cannot ignore their husbands, fathers, lovers and friends. These men sustain other relations—of love, business, friendship—into which we are also initiated. Thus the number of those whose nearer or remoter acquaintance we make becomes almost endless. All classes of society, which know each other and are thrown into close contact in Paris, are introduced to our notice: the whole nation acts the part of a chorus. All that takes place during the period is grouped together in the frame. When the realist therefore tells us love-stories dating from the year 1840 to 1868, we hear also of the Guizot ministry, the radical opposition, the Protectionists, the Socialists, the February revolution, Lamartine, Ledru-Rollin, Cavaignac, the July battles, the 2d of December, etc. Whatever comes within the scope of Frédéric Moreau's horizon is mentioned, and, if possible, described. And this is always done with the same unvarying, indifferent impartiality. The author takes the part of the virtuous woman against the dissolute girl as little as he takes that of the Revolution against Order, or that of Order against the Revolution. He observes, he describes both—keenly, but unsympathetically. He belongs to no party: no catchword attracts him, no enthusiasm blinds him. He knows the men of order and law, the supporters of the *status quo,* the expectant flatterers of power; the banker who only lives for his millions; the dandified viscount of the Faubourg St. Germain; the aspiring public prosecutor: there are egotists, hypocrites, cowards, intriguers and roués. On the other side, the description of the men of Liberty is neither better nor worse. Deslauriers, the democrat, who wants to rise at all hazards, becomes a delegate of the Republic, then a prefect of the Empire, and is finally disgraced on the ground of his over-zealous Imperialism. For this reason he laments his "straightness." Senecal, the Socialist, finds himself in 1848 deceived in his hopes of the Proletarians, and hunts down the republicans in the capacity of police agent on the 2d of December. Another, Citizen Regimbart, spends his life in the cafés and waits for the return of 1793: his wife has to work to pay for his absinthe. Arnoux, the irrepressible publisher of *"L'Art Industriale,"* Mecænas of the fine arts, speculator in houses, manufacturer of porcelain, fights on the 24th of February at the barricades, and tries afterward to escape financial ruin by dealing in the pictures of saints and in consecrated tapers. The only honest republican—nay, the only honest man in the novel—is the clerk called [Dussardier], a young fellow of genuine enthusiasm, disinterested, brave, honorable, but of limited mental capacities; he alone comes to a tragic end. The accuracy with which all these characters are sketched is truly admirable. A glistening chandelier, an elm swayed in the breeze, a cynical journalist,—all are objects entitled to the same faithful description from the realist, and all possess for him the same small human interest. The realist also devotes the same pains to a description of a masked ball at the house of a lorette, a race at the Champ de Mars, or the funeral of the millionaire Dambreuse, as to the description of the plundering of the Tuileries or a session of the "Club de l'Intelligence."

But this is exactly the rock on which the realist is wrecked. What does it mean when we say that the poet shall hold the mirror up to Nature? What mirror is capable of reproducing Nature? And what Nature is capable of being so reproduced?

Reality is endless in time and space: manifestation follows manifestation, and how can such a picture be framed? The task would be a hopeless one, even if the mirror which is to reflect Nature were an inanimate body, like a surface of glass or metal, on which things leave their impression as they pass. In their unlimitability, in their chaotic confusion, in their unsteady flight, how could they leave behind them a distinct picture? Things paint themselves not on an inanimate surface, but in the living spirit of the poet; and this living spirit, after it has passively received the impressions, forms them actively into a durable picture. It forms and arranges them into a picture, not by trying to portray all objects, but by retaining among them the essential, the important, the enduring, the necessary: in one word, it gives the law instead of the accident, the truth instead of the reality, but—for it is the poet and not the phi-

losopher—the law in the form of the accident, the truth in the garb of the reality.

In vain, therefore, the poet wants to persuade us that he only feels, not creates—only gives back Nature without any additions from himself. By giving back Nature he creates—he creates with greater or less consciousness: naïvely or reflectively he lets his own *I* appear or hides it, and is subjective or objective; but it is always he who gives shape to the material furnished by the outer world, and it is he who always does this in drawing an ideal picture of the real world. Hence, it were false to represent the difference between the realistic and the idealistic schools as though the former gave us the real and the latter the ideal. Both elements necessarily enter into poetic composition, and these definitions apply only to the differences of the relations between the one and the other. Every poet is at one and the same time an idealist and a realist, but it is a great poet alone who can be as much the one as the other. Only the poet in whom idealism and realism perfectly balance each other is true: untrue is not merely he who, instead of reflecting Nature, describes his own conceptions of her, but also he who gives the things themselves without their essence. (pp. 441-43)

In fact, the realist deceives only himself with his objectivity. He fancies himself without party, yet takes the part of sensuality against the spirit, of chance against law, of destiny against freedom. He manifests no sympathy for his creations: he suffers Madame Bovary, Salammbo, and Frédéric Moreau to become the unresisting prey of circumstances and their nerves; but it is not mere chance that makes his characters such suffering, receptive beings, utterly incapable of self-help: it proves his own inability to create different ones. He is himself a poetical Frédéric Moreau of exceedingly delicate sensuality, but a man who cannot rise above the reproduction of this sensuality. If he were to persuade us successfully that there are no characters but such as he paints in the real world, he would still leave unsolved the riddle why quite different beings haunt our imagination—beings who seem to us all the more interesting on account of their activity, power and independence. He wants to give us the full reality, while we feel it to be only half the truth—that his world is merely a world of a lower degree, and that only the weakness of his vision keeps him from seeing a higher world. Thus this realism, destitute of the ideal, is subjectively contracted, and therefore as untrue as the idealism which rejects reality. This one caricatures Nature, that one cripples her. The one invents misconceptions which are untenable—the other dissects corpses, thinking thus to learn the secret of life. (pp. 445-46)

W. P. Morras, "Gustave Flaubert, the Realist," in Lippincott's Magazine of Literature, Science and Education, *Vol. VI, No. 22, October, 1870, pp. 439-46.*

ÉMILE FAGUET (essay date 1899)

[*Faguet, a French literary historian and critic, was influential during the late nineteenth and early twentieth centuries. His critical writings are recognized for their emphasis on the work itself and their understanding of the history and evolution of French poetry. Faguet's study* Flaubert, *from which the following excerpt is drawn, was first published in 1899 in French. Faguet discusses Flaubert's apparent motives in writing* Sentimental Education, *especially as they are reflected in Madame Arnoux and Frédéric Moreau, and judges the success of the work as realist fiction. For additional commentary by Faguet on* Sentimental Education, *see NCLC, Vol. 2.*]

Flaubert, when he conceived *L'Éducation Sentimentale,* seems to have had three designs in view, which, let us own it at once, was perhaps too many: Firstly, to write a contrast to **Madame Bovary** by painting a *pure* woman of the *bourgeois* world, very much in love, but an absolutely good woman; secondly, to write a fellow book to **Madame Bovary** by painting a man who, as a man, is somewhat similar to Mme. Bovary as a woman; thirdly, to give a description of Paris and of some French society between 1840 and 1852.

It may be said that he succeeded admirably in his first object and fairly well in his second and in his third, that the general result is uncertain, and that the effect of the whole is not very happy.

Mme. Arnoux is his *pure* woman. I think it is because of her that he believed . . . that he had written a book which was half realistic and half idealistic. It is a mistake. A good and pure woman, Mme. Arnoux remains, however, well within the bounds of true Realism; she is admirably real. Only it is probable that Flaubert, either from his own idea or under the influence of his time, gave the name of Realism solely to the description of immoralities, and therein lies the error. Realism is a picture of average human lives. Mme. Arnoux is well within the average, and one of the beauties of the work is the mastery with which Flaubert has constantly and firmly held her within that average.

Mme. Arnoux is a healthy, well-bred girl of the provincial middle-class. She has excellent physical health, which is not a detail but an essential point; she has been brought up at home, simply, gently and correctly, until her marriage. She has no imagination. She never reads. After these two statements, it is useless to add that dreaming is unknown to her and that she has never lived beyond her horizon. Sensibility, which does not depend on imagination, and to which imagination merely gives a special form, is very strong within her. She is born to love a good, even a mediocre husband, her children and her grand-children. She marries a man of the kind that the middle-class in France calls a 'good fellow'; a flighty, vulgar, boasting man, without any moral sense; a man who gambles in business and runs after women; a man willing to oblige, dishonest, generous and familiar with every one; a dispenser of cigars, jokes, protestations and friendly digs in the ribs. She loves him; she loves him to the end, not only enough to put up with him but to pity him, which is touchingly stupid.

The possible lover appears. He is not *repulsed*. Mme. Arnoux is so virtuous, not so much from a sense of duty as from the very essence of her nature, that she is not one of those who need to repulse. She simply loves him who has pleased her with an almost tranquil certainty that she will never give herself to him. She loves him with pain and with delight. She rests on him her weary eyes, weary with tears and with the sights that they see. He is the brother she has never had and whom her sad life lacks. If she had read anything she would say to him: 'Thou alone art my brother, my father, my mother, all the pure affections which are necessary to a loving soul.' A beautiful trait, and a very simple one, though it would not have occurred to an ordinary writer, is that she is so pure that she makes him pure also, at least whilst he is with her. (pp. 134-37)

There is not a touch that might give Mme. Arnoux an air of romance, of 'lyrical' romance as Flaubert called it. Mme. Arnoux is not eloquent; she is not witty; she takes no attitude; she never speaks of her duty, hardly ever of her love. She is a good little *bourgeoise* from head to foot. She is simplicity itself. We all have met her, have passed her in the street, and have probably thought her insignificant. Only, hers is a straightforward nature, with a calm imagination, much self-respect, but no self-admiration, and a deeply loving heart; the whole, simply drawn character is charming and almost heroic. In order to measure the difference both in conception and in the process of description, think of the pure woman in *Le Lys dans la Vallée,* Mme. de Mortsauf, and see how Balzac's romanticism and bad taste have spoilt a fine portrait. Never was Flaubert's sense of truth more lively or his taste more perfect than in his picture of Mme. Arnoux.

Frédéric Moreau is the type of the little *bourgeois,* fairly gifted, fairly intelligent, with some natural distinction, a good education, and an absolute lack of strength of character. He is 'a man of every weakness,' as Flaubert tells us, perhaps somewhat late in the novel. He is the man who 'promises himself every night that he will be bold,' and who promises himself every morning that he will be somebody. He is endowed with a marvellous incapacity for action. . . . [He] is a passive being, dependent on his friends, his mistresses, his acquaintances, circumstances, on everything in fact except on himself. It is wonderful to see him a philosopher under the influence of one friend, a journalist at another's bidding, and a politician under the impulse of the events of 1848; he lends to one man, promises money to another, gives to one the sum he had put in reserve for another, and only at the age of fifty discovers that his life has been but a zig-zag, and that his real and imperious vocation was to do nothing at all.

Such a man would be in love all his life long, without violence, but with a sort of natural obstinacy. Laziness always having the effect of making a man live by his feelings alone, a lazy man can hardly be anything else than a lover or a dilettante. The most distinguished members of that human family become dilettanti, the others are perpetual lovers. Frédéric is something of a dilettante, and is eternally in love, simply because he seeks easy sensations, and also yearns to be ruled. It is in this that Frédéric resembles Mme. Bovary. He has the same fundamental indolence and the same constitutional dreaminess, the same untidiness in his habits and the same easy generosity, the same romanticism (more superficial in Frédéric) and the same vision of distant travels and of the picturesque East, also the same sensual ardour and the same incapacity to think of anything for long except love.

> He kept up his literary plans through a sort of point of honour with himself. He wished to write a History of Æsthetics, the *result of his conversations with Pellerin,* then to dramatise the French Revolution and to compose a big play *under the indirect influence of Deslauriers and of Hussonnet.* In the midst of his work the face of one or of the other [of his mistresses] would pass before him; he struggled against the yearning to go to her, and presently gave way to it.
>
> (pp. 140-43)

One essential trait is an admirable piece of observation, rendered with astonishing technique. Frédéric's only strength lies in his imagination, as is the case with all weak beings. Therefore 'crystallisation,' to employ Stendhal's word—meaning the effect of imagination upon love and the tenfold development of love through the collaboration of creative imagination—is extraordinarily powerful in Frédéric's case. In a being who is helpless in action, imagination takes the place and does the work of other faculties, moulding matter, travelling to the ends of the world, building palaces, planting parks, opening avenues and creating the universe which Desire demands. If it is applied to love, having been set in motion, whipped and spurred by love, it surrounds the loved object with draperies of its own weaving and embroidering; it builds, paints, sculpts and decorates a museum or a temple. It plunges both hands into Nature's bosom and brings every treasure to the loved one. Such are the splendid jewels which imagination throws over and around the loved object. That is 'crystallisation.' And see Frédéric at work in the process:

> The contemplation of this woman enervated him like the use of too strong a perfume. It reached the depths of his temperament, and became almost a *genral manner of feeling*. Prostitutes whom he met in the gaslight, singers uttering their trills, circus riders galloping by on their horses, middle-class ladies in the streets, *grisettes* looking out of their windows, each and every woman reminded him of that particular woman either through some likeness or through some violent contrast. He looked into the shop-windows at shawls, laces or jewels, imagining them draped round her, ornamenting her bodice or sparkling in her dark hair. The flowers in florists' stalls blossomed that she might choose them in passing; small satin slippers trimmed with swansdown in a shoemaker's shop seemed to be waiting for her foot; every street led to her house, cabs waited on the rank to take him there quicker. Paris was centred in her person, and the great city with all its voices sounded like an immense concert around her.

It is a development, though Flaubert was unaware of it, of the Abbé Cotin's celebrated line—

Tout m'en fait souvenir et rien ne lui ressemble.

[Everything brings her to my mind and nothing resembles her.]

And it is Stendhal's 'crystallisation' in all its precision. But note that it is the crystallisation of an imaginative man who is not a poet. A poet would himself create the dazzling crystals which cling as from their own accord to the delicate stem of his love. Each mica that Frédéric every moment adds to his is borrowed from reality, for he has enough imagination to bring the whole world to his mistress, but not enough to create a universe around her. It is but a half-imaginative crystallisation.

Frédéric is loved, moreover, as such men always are. Women are attracted by strong men, but they succumb to weak ones. They are not afraid of them. They love them as they love supple silky garments and soft furs. Frédéric is loved by a lady of the middle-class, by the wife of a great financier, by a courtesan and by a precocious and fanciful girl. He loves them all: the first one respectfully, the second through vanity, the third through sensuous greed, and the fourth from curiosity, in each case with a timidity which delights and enchants them. He finds himself extraordinarily encumbered with them all, and unable to decide between them, indecision being a fundamental part of his nature. They all end by escaping him, some after having been his, others after having been desired and desirous, and he finds himself towards the end of his life alone with himself, looking back upon a life which has been an absolute failure and which has never been happy. Such is Frédéric's *sentimental education,* or rather, for the title is none other than an improper expression, the series of sentimental experiences through which Frédéric learns that life is a great deceiver, and especially that he himself is a fool.

On the whole, Frédéric might be the son of Bovary and of Mme. Bovary. He has the flabbiness, passiveness, timidity and indecision of the one; and from the other he has inherited some

intelligence, some imagination, romantic tastes, a very feeble moral sense, improvidence, carelessness and an exacting sensuality. That middle-class young man is the epitome of his race. His end seems a little less sad than that of his spiritual parents, but it is not so in reality. It is *nothingness,* far more so than that of Bovary and Emma. Bovary dies of a complex grief in which the despair of love holds a great share, and which is still noble to a certain extent. Emma dies in order not to go down to the very bottom of the degradation into which she has fallen, and there is still some nobility about that. Emma and Bovary have some spring left in them. When a spring breaks, it is a proof that such a thing existed. Frédéric does not break, he glides and disappears into nothingness. His old age is purely vegetative. His end will be that of a poor little *bourgeois* of the provinces, events in whose life consist in drawing his little income on one day, on another day having his hair cut or buying a new coat. Even the memory of Mme. Arnoux disappears from his mind or becomes unwelcome; thus in his last conversation with Deslauriers he counts as his only pleasant recollection that of the first awakening of his senses, long before his first meeting with Mme. Arnoux, and suggests that the memory of his whole life is rather painful than otherwise. Men like Frédéric carry within themselves the means of finding nothingness before death. (pp. 144-48)

Finally, one of the author's intentions was to show us a picture of Paris and also of French society in 1840-55. He has not succeeded very well. I must confess that if you question most of his contemporaries on that point they answer, 'It is quite correct;' I myself have observed among survivors of that time some of the intellectual habits which he derides in *L'Éducation Sentimentale.*... His 1848 is exact but incomplete.... We feel as if we were reading a pamphlet when we had wished to read some history, and when it would have been natural to give us a few pages of history whilst keeping to the tone of the novel.... A great pictorial novel like *L'Éducation Sentimentale* should in well-chosen places have presented to us a true picture of the opinions of the middle-class in 1840-48; and to be true it should have contained some naïve generosity, some empty lyrism, sincere and candid ignorance, some ridicule, a little that was grotesque and a little that was odious. And Flaubert has only given us—perhaps only seen—a very small portion of that picture. And, having thus expressed what I believe to be a necessary criticism, let me be allowed to give my personal impression as an ordinary reader, and to confess that the historical part of *L'Éducation Sentimentale* amuses me enormously, and that, frankly speaking, I prefer it to the whole of the rest of the book. But my opinion as a critic must stand.

With all its merits mixed with faults of a slight nature, *L'Éducation Sentimentale* is not an interesting book, and it never has conquered the public. Flaubert himself said of it: 'I made a mistake.' What is the cause of that? Scherer said: 'It is because it is badly composed.' On the whole I am inclined to agree with him. I own that incidents do not command one another, do not *necessitate* one another; that many of them seem stuck in with no particular reason why they should be here instead of there; and that the book gives the impression of being made up of pieces put together with skill but with an obvious skill. It is so, no doubt, and the proof of it is that the interest *does not grow*. That is a sure sign; the interest is kept up but it does not grow. In every book which is not only cleverly constructed but *organised*, in every book which is an organism, in which the *dénouement* is so absolutely the consequence of every incident that it is its final cause, and that the book is as it were engendered by its conclusion—in every such book, I say, the interest is not only kept up but growing and increasing all the time, and that is not the case with *L'Éducation Sentimentale*. I acknowledge all that, but, however, I do not think it can be said, properly speaking, that *L'Éducation* lacks in composition.

The general composition, at least, is quite good. The author follows his principal character, step by step, in his progress towards annihilation; he hardly ever drops this thread, and that is the general composition of the work. It is the history of an illusion and a disappointment, or rather of all illusions ending in general disappointment. The plan consists in showing the illusions of youth dropping one by one, and being reduced to one, the illusion of love; this last, more persistent than the others, falls away in its turn, and the individual, because he was made up of delusions, is finally reduced to pure nothingness. And if you remember the book in its complete sequence you will find that the plan is very thoroughly followed. No, the composition of *L'Éducation Sentimentale* is somewhat loose, but it exists, and though not quite careful enough, it is fairly clever.

The true reason of the undeniable boredom with which this novel inspires us is that the principal person is himself a bore, the author having made a hero of the greatest bore he ever created. Frédéric is the central person, the one *whom we never leave*. Now he is not merely disagreeable, for that would be nothing, but he bores us, he sends us to sleep. He is insignificant in himself, it is part of his character to be so. As soon as we know him, we know of our certain knowledge that he will never do anything in the least interesting, that it is impossible to him to do so, that fate intends him to be nothing or next to nothing in every circumstance of his life. Now it is to him that we are tied, so to speak, him from whom we cannot get away during six hundred pages. Nothing is to be done, and the greatest talent could not prevail against such an impression. We find ourselves seized by an immense boredom, made up of itself first and then of the expectation of that which awaits us with such a travelling companion.

Do not let us say 'it should have been . . .' Do not let us suggest Mme. Arnoux as a principal person, or Deslauriers, or Arnoux. The novel being conceived as it was, Frédéric had necessarily to be the centre of it. The novel is fundamentally a study of a disease of the will in the middle-classes in France; and that being so, Frédéric had to be the centre of it. But then that constituted a fundamental fault in the book, dooming it to be dull. It always will be dull.

The general spirit and intention of the book are less clear than in *Madame Bovary*. Those who hold as essential that there should be no ideas, not even mere suggestions of ideas, in a novel, but only a picture, and who would say '*Pingitur ad pingendum*,' must be absolutely satisfied with *L'Éducation*. Those who, while hating a 'thesis,' and the obvious intervention of the author into his work with the intention of pleading a cause, yet do not at all dislike that a novel should inspire and suggest a general idea, are less satisfied with *L'Éducation* than with *Bovary*. Seen from this point of view, *L'Éducation* is merely a series of accusations. The general idea which emerges from it is something like this: 'Men of the middle-class, when they are not scoundrels, are fools, and those who are fools are also devoid of moral sense. It is the same for the women, save a few exceptions, of whom I have found a very agreeable one.' Here we have the accusations.

As a matter of fact, all Flaubert's realistic works are of this kind; but sometimes, as in *Bovary*, he goes further than his

accusations, and whilst making them, very bitterly too, he also inspires an idea which may be a leading idea, which may be salutary and which at any rate is an idea. *L'Éducation* may be considered as relatively more moral than *Bovary*, but *Bovary* seems to me more intellectual.

There is one more remark that I should blame myself for not making. It is characteristic of good books that the more we read them the more excellent we find them. I need not say that such is the case with *Madame Bovary*. But I must add that, in a less degree, such is also the case with *L'Éducation Sentimentale*, which is a proof that this is not really a poor book. I never read *L'Éducation* over without thinking it a little better; I have nearly reached the point when it hardly bores me any more. That comes of the fact that the beings created by Flaubert, even when they are not sufficiently alive, are always full, always have a great many thoughts in them, thoughts more or less connected, more or less animated, but numerous. They will bear examination, they will bear meditation, they will even bear that we should see in them what is not there; but that itself is only possible with creations that are already solid, and in literature we can only add to what is already full. I wished to make this observation because it might lead people to read *L'Éducation Sentimentale* once again, and it has that fault that it does not tempt one to read it over again. It is like those persons who improve on acquaintance, but who do not inspire a desire to become acquainted with them. I am not speaking for the fanatical admirers of *L'Éducation*—for there are some,— I speak for the others who are many. I should like them to say to themselves in Sévère's words, 'And perhaps one day I may know her better,' and I must say that this is the beginning of appreciating it more. On the whole, if Flaubert had not written *Madame Bovary* he would still have written his masterpiece. Every author must have one. And I do not think it would have been *Salammbô*. I think it would have been *L'Éducation Sentimentale*. (pp. 151-58)

> *Émile Faguet, in his* Flaubert, *translated by Mrs. R. L. Devonshire, Houghton Mifflin Company, 1914, 238 p.*

HENRY JAMES   (essay date 1902)

> [*James was an American-born English novelist, short story writer, critic, and essayist of the late nineteenth and early twentieth centuries. He is regarded as one of the greatest novelists of the English language and is also admired as a lucid and insightful critic. As a young man he travelled extensively throughout Great Britain and Europe and benefited from the friendship and influence of many of the leading figures of nineteenth-century art and literature: in England, he met John Ruskin, Dante Gabriel Rossetti, William Morris, and Leslie Stephen; in France, where he lived for several years, he was part of the literary circle that included Flaubert, Émile Zola, Edmond de Goncourt, Guy de Maupassant, and Ivan Turgenev. Thus, his criticism is informed by his sensibility to European culture, particularly English and French literature of the late nineteenth century. In the following excerpt from an essay originally published in 1902, James offers his reaction to Flaubert's portrayal of Frédéric Moreau and Madame Arnoux. For additional commentary by James on* Sentimental Education, *see NCLC, Vol. 2.*]

Why did Flaubert choose, as special conduits of the life he proposed to depict, such inferior and in the case of Frédéric such abject human specimens? I insist only in respect to the latter, the perfection of Madame Bovary scarce leaving one much warrant for wishing anything other. Even here, however, the general scale and size of Emma, who is small even of her sort, should be a warning to hyperbole. If I say that in the matter of Frédéric at all events the answer is inevitably detrimental I mean that it weighs heavily on our author's general credit. He wished in each case to make a picture of experience—middling experience, it is true—and of the world close to him; but if he imagined nothing better for his purpose than such a heroine and such a hero, both such limited reflectors and registers, we are forced to believe it to have been by a defect of his mind. And that sign of weakness remains even if it be objected that the images in question were addressed to his purpose better than others would have been: the purpose itself then shows as inferior. *L'Éducation Sentimentale* is a strange, an indescribable work, about which there would be many more things to say than I have space for, and all of them of the deepest interest. It is moreover, to simplify my statement, very much less satisfying a thing, less pleasing whether in its unity or its variety, than its specific predecessor. But take it as we will, for a success or a failure—M. Faguet indeed ranks it, by the measure of its quantity of intention, a failure [see excerpt dated 1899], and I on the whole agree with him—the personage offered us as bearing the weight of the drama, and in whom we are invited to that extent to interest ourselves, leaves us mainly wondering what our entertainer could have been thinking of. He takes Frédéric Moreau on the threshold of life and conducts him to the extreme of maturity without apparently suspecting for a moment either our wonder or our protest—"Why, why *him?*" Frédéric is positively too poor for his part, too scant for his charge; and we feel with a kind of embarrassment, certainly with a kind of compassion, that it is somehow the business of a protagonist to prevent in his designer an excessive waste of faith. (pp. 81-3)

We meet Frédéric first, we remain with him long, as a *moyen,* a provincial bourgeois of the mid-century, educated and not without fortune, thereby with freedom, in whom the life of his day reflects itself. Yet the life of his day, on Flaubert's showing, hangs together with the poverty of Frédéric's own inward or for that matter outward life; so that, the whole thing being, for scale, intention and extension, a sort of epic of the usual (with the Revolution of 1848 introduced indeed as an episode,) it affects us as an epic without air, without wings to lift it; reminds us in fact more than anything else of a huge balloon, all of silk pieces strongly sewn together and patiently blown up, but that absolutely refuses to leave the ground. The discrimination I here make as against our author is, however, the only one inevitable in a series of remarks so brief. What it really represents—and nothing could be more curious—is that Frédéric enjoys his position not only without the aid of a single "sympathetic" character of consequence, but even without the aid of one with whom we can directly communicate. Can we communicate with the central personage? or would we really if we could? A hundred times no, and if he himself can communicate with the people shown us as surrounding him this only proves him of their kind. Flaubert on his "real" side was in truth an ironic painter, and ironic to a tune that makes his final accepted state, his present literary dignity and "classic" peace, superficially anomalous. . . . I find myself feeling . . . in presence of *L'Éducation* how much more interesting a writer may be on occasion by the given failure than by the given success. Successes pure and simple disconnect and dismiss him; failures—though I admit they must be a bit qualified—keep him in touch and in relation. Thus it is that as the work of a "grand écrivain" *L'Éducation,* large, laboured, immensely "written," with beautiful passages and a general emptiness, with a kind of leak in its stored sadness, moreover, by which its moral dignity escapes—thus it is that Flaubert's ill-

starred novel is a curiosity for a literary museum. Thus it is also that it suggests a hundred reflections, and suggests perhaps most of them directly to the intending labourer in the same field. If in short . . . Flaubert is the novelist's novelist, this performance does more than any other toward making him so.

I have to add in the same connection that I had not lost sight of Madame Arnoux, the main ornament of *L'Éducation,* in pronouncing just above on its deficiency in the sympathetic. Madame Arnoux is exactly the author's one marked attempt, here or elsewhere, to represent beauty otherwise than for the senses, beauty of character and life; and what becomes of the attempt is a matter highly significant. M. Faguet praises with justice his conception of the figure and of the relation, the relation that never bears fruit, that keeps Frédéric adoring her, through hindrance and change, from the beginning of life to the end; that keeps her, by the same constraint, forever immaculately "good," from youth to age, though deeply moved and cruelly tempted and sorely tried. Her contacts with her adorer are not even frequent, in proportion to the field of time; her conditions of fortune, of association and occupation are almost sordid, and we see them with the march of the drama, such as it is, become more and more so; besides which—I again remember that M. Faguet excellently notes it—nothing in the nature of "parts" is attributed to her; not only is she not presented as clever, she is scarce invested with a character at all. Almost nothing that she says is repeated, almost nothing that she does is shown. She is an image none the less beautiful and vague, an image of passion cherished and abjured, renouncing all sustenance and yet persisting in life. Only she has for real distinction the extreme drawback that she is offered us quite preponderantly through Frédéric's vision of her, that we see her practically in no other light. Now Flaubert unfortunately has not been able not so to discredit Frédéric's vision in general, his vision of everyone and everything, and in particular of his own life, that it makes a medium good enough to convey adequately a noble impression. Madame Arnoux is of course ever so much the best thing in his life—which is saying little; but his life is made up of such queer material that we find ourselves displeased at her being "in" it on whatever terms; all the more that she seems scarcely to affect, improve or determine it. Her creator in short never had a more awkward idea than this attempt to give us the benefit of such a conception in such a way; and . . . I may as well speak of it at once as a mistake that gravely counts against him. It is but one of three, no doubt, in all his work; but I shall not, I trust, pass for extravagant if I call it the most indicative. What makes it so is its being the least superficial; the two others are, so to speak, intellectual, while this is somehow moral. It was a mistake, as I have already hinted, to propose to register in so mean a consciousness as that of such a hero so large and so mixed a quantity of life as *L'Éducation* clearly intends; and it was a mistake of the tragic sort that is a theme mainly for silence to have embarked on *Bouvard et Pécuchet* at all, not to have given it up sooner than be given up by it. But these were at the worst not wholly compromising blunders. What *was* compromising— and the great point is that it remained so, that nothing has an equal weight against it—is the unconsciousness of error in respect to the opportunity that would have counted as his finest. We feel not so much that Flaubert misses it, for that we could bear; but that he doesn't *know* he misses it is what stamps the blunder. We do not pretend to say how he might have shown us Madame Arnoux better—that was his own affair. What is ours is that he really thought he was showing her as well as he could, or as she might be shown; at which we veil our face. For once that he had a conception quite apart, apart I mean from the array of his other conceptions and more delicate than any, he "went," as we say, and spoiled it. Let me add in all tenderness, and to make up for possibly too much insistence, that it is the only stain on his shield; let me even confess that I should not wonder if, when all is said, it is a blemish no one has ever noticed. (pp. 84-8)

> *Henry James, "Gustave Flaubert," in his* Notes on Novelists, with Some Other Notes, *Charles Scribner's Sons, 1914, pp. 65-108.*

GEORG LUKÁCS   (essay date 1916)

[*Lukács, a Hungarian literary critic and philosopher, is acknowledged as a leading proponent of Marxist thought. His development of Marxist ideology was part of a broader system of thought in which he sought to further the values of rationalism (peace and progress), humanism (socialist politics), and traditionalism (Realist literature) over the countervalues of irrationalism (war), totalitarianism (reactionary politics), and modernism (post-Realist literature). In such major works as* Studies in European Realism *and* The Historical Novel, *Lukács explicated his belief that "unless art can be made creatively consonant with history and human needs, it will always offer a counterworld of escape and marvelous waste." In the following excerpt from a work first published in 1916 in* Zeitschrift für Aesthetik und Allgemeine Kunstwissenschaft, *he enumerates the qualities in* Sentimental Education *that make it a novel of disillusionment.*]

In the Romanticism of disillusionment, time is the corrupting principle: poetry, the essential, must die, and time is ultimately responsible for its passing. That is why in such novels all value is on the side of the defeated protagonist, who, because he is dying, is endowed with the beauty of wounded youth, while coarseness, harshness, the absence of an idea, belong entirely to time. Only as a post-facto correction of this one-sided lyrical opposition to the victorious power does self-irony turn against the dying essence by endowing it, negatively, with the attributes of youth; the ideal is said to be constitutive only for the soul in a state of immaturity. The overall design of the novel is bound to be deformed if positive and negative values are so distinctly divided between the two sides of the struggle. A form cannot really deny a life principle unless it is capable of excluding it *a priori* from its realm; as soon as it has to admit that principle, it must admit it as positive; and so this principle, not only as an opposing force but in its own right, becomes a precondition of the realisation of value.

Time is the fullness of life, although the fullness of time is the self-abolition of life and, with it, of time itself. The positive thing, the affirmation which the very form of the novel expresses no matter how inconsolably sad its content may be, is not only that distant meaning which dawns with a mild radiance on the far side of the search and the failure to find, but also the fullness of life which is revealed precisely through the manifold failures of the struggle and search. The novel is the form of mature virility: its song of comfort rings out of the dawning recognition that traces of lost meaning are to be found everywhere; that the enemy comes from the same lost home as the knight and defender of the essence; that life had to lose its immanence of meaning so that it might be equally present everywhere.

Thus it is that time becomes the carrier of the sublime epic poetry of the novel: it has become inexorably existent, and no one can any longer swim against the unmistakable direction of its current nor regulate its unforeseeable course with the dams of *a priori* concepts. Yet a feeling of resignation persists: all

this had to come from somewhere, must be going somewhere; even if the direction betrays no meaning, it is a direction none the less. From this feeling of resignation mixed with courage there spring experiences of time which are authentically epic because they give rise to action and stem from action: the experiences of hope and memory; experiences of time which are victories over time: a synoptic vision of time as solidified unity *ante rem* and its synoptic comprehension *post rem. In re,* there can be no simple, happy experience of this form or of the times which have produced it. Experiences of this kind can only be subjective and reflexive; nevertheless there is always in them the form-giving sense of *comprehending a meaning*; they are experiences in which we come as near as we can, in a world forsaken by God, to the essence of things.

Such an experience of time is the basis of Flaubert's *L'Education sentimentale,* and the absence of such an experience, a one-sidedly negative view of time, is what has ultimately been responsible for the failure of the other major novels of disillusionment. Of all great works of this type, *L'Education sentimentale* appears to be the least composed; no attempt is made here to counteract the disintegration of outside reality into heterogeneous, brittle and fragmentary parts by some process of unification or to replace absent connections or valencies of meaning by lyrical mood-imagery: the separate fragments of reality lie before us in all their hardness, brokenness and isolation. The central figure is not made significant by means of limiting the number of characters, by the rigorous convergence of the composition upon the centre, or by any emphasis upon the central character's outstanding personality: the hero's inner life is as fragmentary as the outside world, his interiority possesses no lyrical power of scorn or pathos that might set it against the pettiness of reality. Yet this novel, of all novels of the nineteenth century, is one of the most typical of the problematic of the novel form; in the unmitigated desolation of its mater it is the only novel that attains true epic objectivity and, through it, the positiveness and affirmative energy of an accomplished form.

This victory is rendered possible by time. The unrestricted, uninterrupted flow of time is the unifying principle of the homogeneity that rubs the sharp edges off each heterogeneous fragment and establishes a relationship—albeit an irrational and inexpressible one—between them. Time brings order into the chaos of men's lives and gives it the semblance of a spontaneously flowering, organic entity; characters having no apparent meaning appear, establish relations with one another, break them off, disappear again without any meaning having been revealed. But the characters are not simply dropped into that meaningless becoming and dissolving which preceded man and will outlast him. Beyond events, beyond psychology, time gives them the essential quality of their existence: however accidental the appearance of a character may be in pragmatic and psychological terms it emerges from an existent, experienced continuity, and the atmosphere of thus being borne upon the unique and unrepeatable stream of life cancels out the accidental nature of their experiences and the isolated nature of the events recounted. (pp. 122-25)

> *Georg Lukács, "The Romanticism of Disillusionment," in his* The Theory of the Novel: A Historico-Philosophical Essay on the Forms of Great Epic Literature, *translated by Anna Bostock, The M.I.T. Press, 1971, pp. 112-31.*

ALBERT THIBAUDET   (essay date 1936)

[*Thibaudet was an early twentieth-century French literary critic and follower of the French philosopher Henri Bergson. His work is considered versatile, well-informed, and original, and scholars cite his unfinished* Histoire de la littérature française de 1789 à nos jours, *first published in 1936, as his major critical treatise. In this work, Thibaudet classified authors by the generations of 1789, 1820, 1850, 1885, and 1914-18, rather than by literary movements. Here, in an excerpt from his discussion of the generation of 1850, he argues that* Sentimental Education *is Flaubert's masterpiece.*]

Flaubert's third novel, *L'Education sentimentale,* was a complete failure with the public and the critics of the last months of the Empire. Even as late as 1935, university criticism as a whole spoke of it almost unanimously as Flaubert's mistake, the paradox of realism, a picture of wasted lives in a wasted work. Novelists, on the other hand, held it in great regard; its influence on naturalism was profound; today a whole section of literary opinion views it as Flaubert's masterpiece, ranking it above *Madame Bovary.* Roughly, this latter view is the correct one.

It was the book that, even more than *Madame Bovary,* required the genius of realism. The principle is that of Henri Murger and Champfluery: take as the subject the author and his friends; thus, with Courbet, *L'Atelier du peintre* came after that *Enterrement d'Ornans* that is *Madame Bovary* (let us risk the grimace that Flaubert would make at this comparison). But what transformations, what stylizations! First of all, if Flaubert used in Frédéric Moreau his own life, his personal experience, his love for Mme. Schlesinger, he was careful not to make his hero a writer like himself; he took him away from literary mechanisms to offer him to pure, ordinary, average human experience, to the ''just like the rest of us'' on which every visionary, however great, always falls back in the end. Second, from the group of the painter's studio (all the characters in *L'Education,* Maxime du Camp said, really existed), the painter creates the group of the painter's generation, which was twenty to thirty years old in 1848, a generation in bankruptcy, it thought, in the Revolution and the *coup d'état.* Flaubert's great novel thus became a document in the manner of Balzac. Finally, the character of Marie Arnoux, in whom Flaubert immortalized the only prolonged passion of his life, is very rightly considered one of the purest and most perfect portraits of women in fiction. But around her, around Frédéric, there are at least a dozen characters portrayed with unmatched technique, sureness, and success.

Thus *L'Atelier du peintre* deserved to become the painter's school, the school of the most important area of the novel between 1879 and 1900. Undoubtedly the author of *L'Education* himself owed something to the Goncourts, who, beginning in 1860, had stylized the realistic novel. But the Goncourts had everything that was necessary to make their school dangerous, Flaubert everything that was necessary to make his beneficial. The style itself moved down a step toward simplicity and reality. He virtually abandoned that music, those oratorical cadences, that contributed to the aging of *Madame Bovary* and *Salammbô.* He achieved a perfect balance between a rigid style and a flowing style.

Indeed, the lack of success of *L'Education* added to its worth and its influence. There was a school of the conformist novel, and a very distinguished school it was, that of Octave Feuillet and *La Revue des deux mondes,* which flattered the reader and especially the woman reader, which aimed for the consensus of writer and public, of novelist and subscriber. But art progresses only through disharmonies. The last page of *L'Education,* which evoked outcries for thirty years, inflicts a healthy discomfort on the reader, sustains the atmosphere of the novel

in a nonconformism. And what it says is true: desires are often what is best in a whole life. Through his *Correspondances* we know Flaubert well enough to understand that this was his own case, and it is as good as any other. (pp. 302-03)

> Albert Thibaudet, ''Flaubert,'' in his French Literature from 1795 to Our Era, *translated by Charles Lam Markmann, Funk & Wagnalls, 1968, pp. 298-305.*

ANTHONY GOLDSMITH   (essay date 1941)

[*Goldsmith discusses* Sentimental Education's *combination of romanticism and realism, suggests why the work was given a hostile reception upon publication, and comments on its closeness to the drama.*]

As a young man Flaubert had shared to the full the frenzied idealism of his contemporaries. At the age of twenty-five he had produced a first and highly romanticized version of *L'Éducation sentimentale.* But in the twenty years that separate this early unpublished effort from the present volume his intellect had rebelled against the romantic school; he had grown to hate their self-dramatization, their contempt for the humble truth, and the distorted view of life which they imposed on their devotees. In *Salammbô* he had for the time being satisfied his taste for the gorgeous setting, the exotic background. Now he was determined to write a realistic novel about his own generation, to place the passions of his youth in final perspective, and to purge himself, through observation and irony, of the pernicious influences that had once obsessed him. Such was his aim in *L'Éducation sentimentale*; but the design was not completely carried out. Flaubert's emotions were too strong for his intellect; the strain of romanticism in his temperament was ineradicable; and, although the greater part of the book is written in a spirit of detached and sardonic realism, the central subject, the love-story of Frederic Moreau and Mme Arnoux, is pure romance. It is treated throughout, not with the cold objectivity which Flaubert intended, but with a strangely lyrical tenderness.

The explanation of this inconsistency is to be found in Flaubert's private life. Marie Arnoux is clearly identifiable as Elisa Schlésinger, from whom Flaubert had conceived an adolescent passion, when he first met her, in 1837, on the beach at Trouville. . . . [The] charm of Elisa was largely dependent on her inaccessibility. She represented for him the joys which he felt had always eluded him, and his attitude is well expressed in his last letter to her, written in 1872, three years after the publication of *L'Éducation sentimentale.* 'The future,' he wrote, 'has no more dreams for me. But the old days come before me, as if bathed in a golden mist, and from that luminous background, whence beloved phantoms stretch out their arms to me, the face that shines out most brightly is yours. Oh, unhappy Trouville!'

This idealization persists in *L'Éducation sentimentale.* Mme Arnoux occupies a position of unique privilege among Flaubert's characters. She alone is spared that deep and devastating analysis to which he was accustomed to subject his creations. Among so many profoundly observed types, she remains a shadowy figure—aloof, mysterious, impenetrable. It is as if Flaubert, obscurely aware of the real deficiencies of his ideal, and fearing to destroy his fragile day-dream, shrank from applying the dissector's knife to his heroine. Sometimes the veil is nearly lifted. '*Quelle bourgeoise!*' exclaims Frederic, in an interlude of clear-headedness; but a moment later he is back in the clouds again. Thus the main theme of the book, so far from being the detached, impersonal narrative planned by the author, becomes a monument, constructed with tenderness and pity, to Flaubert's own frustrated adolescence.

Artistically, this contradiction is of immense advantage. A purely ironic approach to the subject might have justified the charge of coldness and lack of heart so often brought against *L'Éducation sentimentale*. As it is, Frederic's unswerving devotion achieves a certain nobility, and Flaubert's exquisitely poetic treatment of the whole theme perfectly balances the surrounding realism.

When *L'Éducation sentimentale* was first published, in November 1869, it was received with the utmost disfavour. Many critics preferred to pass it over in silence, rather than offend the author of **Madame Bovary** and **Salammbô**. Those who expressed their views were nearly all censorious to the point of malevolence, and the public was not inclined to disagree with them. This almost universal hostility, although it amazed Flaubert, was not really surprising. For the whole tone and atmosphere of the novel is opposed to the spirit of the nineteenth-century. Flaubert did not share the inflated optimism or the faith in material values that were characteristic of his era, nor did he conceal his distaste for the bourgeoisie, great and small, who then dominated France. Flaubert's social scepticism was perhaps pardonable in **Madame Bovary,** for the exposure of corruption and hypocrisy in a provincial village might be interpreted as an implied compliment to the capital; but in *L'Éducation sentimentale* the society of Paris itself is made a target for satire—a satire which is all the more penetrating because it is based on meticulous observation and expressed with all the tremendous force of the author's mature style. Flaubert's description of M. Dambreuse, the banker, as a person who 'would have paid for the privilege of selling himself,' with his associates 'who would have sold France, or the whole human race, to safe-guard their fortune, to spare themselves a moment's uneasiness or embarrassment, or else out of sheer servility, through their instinctive reverence for brute strength,' was scarcely calculated to secure him the patronage of the wealthy. Moreover, the generation that grew up in the stable, confident decades following the Franco-Prussian War, was satisfied with its surroundings, and had little sympathy with the rebellious Radicalism and the thwarted ideals of Flaubert's young romantics. 'The reaction after '48,' wrote Flaubert, 'dug a gulf between one France and the other'; to the young people of the seventies Flaubert and his contemporaries seemed *de vrais fossiles*.

And it was not only the content, but the form of the book that puzzled and irritated the contemporary reader. Accustomed to the melodrama of Hugo and Dumas, he found Flaubert's unemphatic narrative dull, discursive, and episodic—a chronicle, not a novel. George Sand was almost the only critic who perceived the subtle dramatic structure which knits together the apparently inconsequent incidents of the book. 'The story of the novel,' she wrote, 'as complex as life itself, is bound together and interwoven with remarkable artistic skill. Each character emerges on the surface, but each does so in his turn. . . . They cross the stage swiftly, yet always marking a further step along the path they follow, as they let fall a vigorous summary, a brief dialogue, sometimes a single phrase, a word, which crystallizes, with a simplicity terrible in its strength, the particular obsession of their brain.' George Sand, in using the language of the theatre, seems to have realized how close *L'Éducation sentimentale* is to drama—not, indeed, to the styl-

ized rhetorical tradition of the French stage, but to the modern realistic drama of character, already evolved by Turgenev and soon to be further developed by Tchekov. The writers of this school do not go beyond everyday life for their subject-matter; they avoid stilted plots; they do not moralize. Their main preoccupation is with human psychology; and their seemingly casual and naturalistic dialogue is really selected with extreme care in order to illuminate the characters and their relationship with one another. Once the absolute reality of the characters has been established, the small incidents of their lives become as absorbing as the most sensational melodrama. The broad effects of classical tragedy cannot be achieved by these means; but to a great artist they offer wide scope for delicate pathos and subtle emotional nuance. This was the method used by Turgenev in his exquisite play *A Month in the Country*; and it is exactly the method employed by Flaubert in *L'Éducation sentimentale*. A technical device accentuates the dramatic aspect of the book. In order to bring out the intense and typically romantic egotism of his hero, Flaubert presents nearly the whole story through the eyes of Frederic. The other characters are not depicted, as in most novels, through their thoughts; they are exhibited objectively, from the outside. Arnoux, Rosanette, Louise, and the rest are brilliant feats of characterization, yet scarcely ever do we know what they are thinking; the whole impression is achieved, as in a first-class play, by the subtle selection of dialogue and action. It is worth noticing, too, that Flaubert divides his work into three parts, like the acts of a play, and closes each with a magnificent 'curtain,' reserving, like a skilful playwright, his most telling effect for the end of the second part.

L'Éducation sentimentale is a book about failures. All the characters are frustrated; Frederic is as far from achieving his ideal as Arnoux is from discovering the copper-red of the Chinese potters. Worldly success provides no exemption from the general doom, and M. Dambreuse, the millionaire, is perhaps the saddest failure of all. Nor are these people allowed the consolation of a grand tragic finale, a theatrical funeral pyre. Their exit in the last chapter is abrupt, almost undignified. And, to darken the picture still further, Flaubert attributes their failure neither to the age they lived in, nor to their own weaknesses, but to the futility of life itself, thwarting all endeavour, and, in the last resort, making true happiness unattainable.

Yet, in spite of its pessimism, *L'Éducation sentimentale* is not a gloomy book. Flaubert is a great enough artist to make a success of his chronicle of failure. Life may be futile, but *L'Éducation sentimentale* is not. It brings the reader into contact with all that was best in Flaubert's artistic personality—his wit, his profound wisdom, his immense vitality. And the reader leaves the encounter, not depressed, but inspired. (pp. x-xiv)

Anthony Goldsmith, in an introduction to Sentimental Education *by Gustave Flaubert, translated by Anthony Goldsmith, J. M. Dent & Sons Ltd., 1941, pp. ix-xiv.*

LOUISE BOGAN   (essay date 1942)

[*Bogan was a distinguished American poet whose work is noted for its subtlety and restraint. She served for many years as the poetry critic at the* New Yorker *and is the author of* Achievement in American Poetry: 1900-1950, *a respected volume of criticism. In the following excerpt, she describes the importance of money, authority, and self-interest in* Sentimental Education, *adding commentary on the current relevance of the work.*]

The most important novel to be published in English in 1941 was the first intelligent translation into English of Flaubert's *L'Education sentimentale*. This novel, first published in 1869, was written after *Salâmmbo* and just before the final version of *La tentation de Saint Antoine*. It is now generally acknowledged to be Flaubert's masterpiece. A profound and sardonic comment on Flaubert's own generation and the France of his youth, it is in every way pertinent to the human and social dilemmas of our own day.

The novel was viciously attacked by the critics and neglected by the general public, at is appearance. Only a few friends—Banville, the Goncourts, George Sand—understood Flaubert's intentions or appreciated his success in putting them through. Sand realized that Flaubert's readers were still too close to the events described, and too involved in the Second Empire point of view, to wish to appreciate the book's ruthless analysis of social change and human motives. They recognized themselves too easily. And Sand complained that Flaubert gave no overt clue to where his sympathies lay. She wanted "an expression of blame . . . to condemn the evil. People do not understand that you wanted precisely to depict a deplorable state of society which encourages bad instincts." Flaubert had run into this sort of obtuseness in the French public and government before this. It had brought about the suit against the morals of *Madame Bovary*. He was incapable of agreeing with Sand's rather sentimental moralistic demands. His idea of the relation between the individual and society was far more complicated than hers. Society warped the individual, but was it not individuals who had created, and blown up to enormous proportions, the governments which symbolized this hampering agency? Perhaps the basic evil lay deeper, in the constitution of the human heart.

Flaubert was depressed by the book's failure. He wrote in 1874 to Turgenev that he was still astonished that this work had never been understood. He finally decided that the book lacked "the *falseness* of perspective." "Every work of art," he said, "ought to have a point, a summit, make a pyramid . . . or better, the light should strike some point of the sphere. Now, there is nothing of that sort in life. But Art is not nature!" Here Flaubert partially understands that in this novel he has created a new genre. Critics, including Henry James, have misunderstood the book's conclusions because they were in no way dealing, here, with another *Madame Bovary*: not with "realism" or "romance," but with satire of a high but hidden order.

There is no doubt that *Sentimental Education* is a difficult book to get the hang of, at a first reading. The reader must have a fair working knowledge of reaction and revolution in nineteenth-century France. To use a figure of Lowes Dickinson's, France was, throughout the century, politically in a state as though tracked by the Furies. It was a century of nervous unrest and of new and untried theory. And all theories, once applied, backfired in the most appalling way. The revolt against the Orleans line brought in the July monarchy (1830) and Louis Philippe's dead-weight bourgeois rule. Universal suffrage, granted after 1848 and thought to be the instrument to establish the kingdom of God on earth, resulted only in Louis Bonaparte, and after three years of the Second Republic, the Second Empire. Paris fought for freedom; the provinces, fighting for the still unlaid ghosts of the old regime and Napoleon, finally voted away the newly granted franchise itself. Added to the political melee was the social one. The Industrial Revolution struck France in the '30's, in the factories of Lyons. All political parties were thrown into the rise of money, and the new concept of the right to work. The resulting confusion was severe. It is precisely this confusion, and its results, mirrored in the characters of the men and women who were at once its creators and its victims, that Flaubert here describes.

The book, written under the Second Empire, covers the period from 1840 to Louis Napoleon's coup d'état of December, 1851—save for the last two chapters, which form a code to the whole. The action, excepting a few short passages, is seen through the eyes of Frédéric Moreau, of the provincial landed middle class, newly come to Paris, as the book begins, to pass his law examinations. A new spirit is in the air. The tradition of romanticism, and of the bohemian painter, writer, and poet, is almost completely threadbare. The period of the career based on money deals of one sort or another (*"Enrichissez-vous"* was said to be the counsel of Louis Philippe to his subjects) had begun. Art and industry, art and journalism, stood opposed, in spite of naive efforts to reconcile their purposes. (*Industrial Art* is the name of the magazine run by Arnoux, the husband of the woman Frédéric comes to adore; the paper of the unprincipled Hussonet begins under the name of *Art* and ends up entitled *The Man About Town*.) Stock-jobbing, loans, investments, and mortgages were the preoccupation of deputies and ministers. Borrowing a little money and making more, getting in with "influential" people, occupied the minds of law students, writers, painters, and hangers-on. The movement of opportunism elaborates and expands into a mounting frenzy. Notes fall due; debts pile up; the fate of men and women depends on the worth or worthlessness of shares. Bankruptcies, auctions, bailiffs finish the hopes of guilty and innocent alike. Underneath runs the theme of personal treachery. Friends betray one another; old men revenge themselves in their wills; women take it out on rivals by holding over them old debts and promissory notes.

The revolts of Republicans and the new Socialists against bourgeois rule form the book's secondary theme. The theorists make plans and hold to rigid formulas. Spontaneous outbreaks of the people link up with the planned action of the revolutionaries. Barricades go up; arms are requisitioned from the citizens. The crow swarms into the Tuileries; grand pianos and clocks are flung out of windows. One of the book's great set-pieces describes the Paris street fighting in 1848. And the book closes with Paris again under arms: the dragons, aided by the police, galloping against the citizens under the gaslight with sabers drawn—and the Second Empire has begun.

Sénécal, the democratic dogmatist who develops by degrees into a tyrant and member of the police, is the character which has astonished modern readers by its deadly accuracy and contemporary pertinence. "Where are the labor poets?" Sénécal asks, when shown a library. He wants, in literature, content and not form. He thinks *tableaux vivants* corrupting for the daughters of the proletariat. As a factory overseer, he extracts fines ruthlessly. "Democracy," he remarks, "does not mean license for the individual. It means a common level under the law, the division of labor—order!" "You've left out humanity," Frédéric answers. It is Senecal who kills Dussardier, "the good fellow," the honest believer in Socialist virtue "who attributed all the evil on earth to authority."

And Flaubert traces down "an insane desire for authority, of whatever kind if only it be authority," in all these people who have lost so many natural links to life. "France, feeling herself without a master [after '48] began to cry out in terror, like a blind man without a stick, or a child that has lost its nurse." And the reader continues to recognize these characters. There is something startlingly familiar in Housonet, the journalist who prints gossip and slander as news, who "extols the fifth-rate and disparages the first-class minds." Arnoux, the intermediate type between bohemian and business man, infected with the failings of both—"his mind was not elevated enough to attain to art nor ordinary enough to think solely of profit, so that he was ruining himself without satisfying anyone"— is closely akin to Frédéric, who feels the resemblance. Arnoux is a gourmet and gives little dinners "with ten kinds of mustard." Deslauriers, Frédéric's friend, in the words of the Goncourts, is "with his fond envy, his intermittences of perfidy and friendship, his solicitor's temperament, a perfectly drawn type of the most widespread kind of scurvy humanity.' Mlle Vatnaz, the emancipated woman, venomous, the dupe of her passions, a literary hack and go-between with a business head, is still not a complete grotesque.

Then there is the gallery of "conservative humbugs," male and female, whom Flaubert does not spare. "Bigotry of the rich rivaled the frenzy of the starving. . . . Property began to be confused with God, and attacks on it . . . almost resembled cannibalism." But Flaubert was out to show up "the bourgeois in blouses as well as the bourgeois in coats." He examines with the same detachment social theorists, the hysterics, terrorist, and fakes on the fringes of the Socialist movement, and the conservative money and power jugglers and their "distinguished" circle, ready to grease the palm of any government that came into power. The stupidity of the workers' meeting and the complicated spite of the dinner party are both analyzed. Flaubert wished to clear the reader's mind of all "accepted ideas" concerning the supposed nobility of either group. Suddenly, at the end of the book, we look back and see how each category has received its touch of clearsightedness: these liberals who are at bottom neurotic reactionaries; these members of a new middle class who not only "have no interest in the things of the mind," who do not act according to motives of patience, pity, duty, love, or generosity, but *actually do not know that such qualities exist.* And has Flaubert spared from his satiric justice of treatment the supposed prototype of a lifelong love of his, Mme Arnoux? She has been thought to stand in the book as an unclouded exponent of womanly sweetness and virtue. Is she not, rather, a sort of Madame Bovary in reverse—a woman who rejects passion because she pietistically fears God's punishment, whose virtue brings her to the pass of offering herself, in age, to a man who suddenly sees the true incestuous nature of his devotion to her?

The profound psychological truth of the book's two final chapters is unequaled in modern literature. For in these two scenes Flaubert's uncanny knowledge of the pathology of modern life becomes startlingly evident. The nostalgic reminiescence of Frédéric and Deslauriers, casting back to their youthful frightened visit to the prostitute's house, reveals the continuing infantilism of these two grown-up children who have never been able to lift themselves over the threshold of maturity, who cannot learn, who can only, in spite of some native decency and generosity, repeat, and flee life's consequences. The modern split between emotion and reason stands revealed. Flaubert elsewhere remarks: "You do not possess Christianity any more. What do you possess? Railroads, factories, chemists, mathematicians. Yes, the body fares better, the flesh does not suffer so much, but the heart continues to bleed. Material questions are resolved. Are the others? . . . And as you have not filled that eternal yawning gulf which every man carries in himself, I mock at your efforts, and laugh at your miserable sciences which are not worth a straw." *Sentimental Education* is a hand-

book to the present because the gulf of which Flaubert speaks, after seventy years, has not been filled but only widened and deepened. The thirst for some saving authority has grown stronger, the childish bigotries more complete. Let us examine our theorists, Flaubert says, and throw out their false premises. Let us enlarge the provable human data. Have these nervous insurrections accomplished anything; are we following the "advanced notions" of a parcel of "buffoons"? Should "the government of a country be a section of the Institute, and the last section of all"?

Some partial answers lie in this novel, panoramic and profound, written in the "ivory tower" of Croisset and published one year before the inauspicious events of 1870 which ushered in the Third Republic. (pp. 301-02)

> *Louise Bogan, " 'Sentimental Education' Today," in* The Nation, *New York, Vol. 155, No. 14, October 3, 1942, pp. 301-02.*

EDMUND WILSON   (essay date 1948)

[*Wilson is generally considered twentieth-century America's foremost man of letters. A prolific reviewer, creative writer, and social and literary critic endowed with formidable intellectual powers, he exercised his greatest literary influence as the author of* Axel's Castle, *a seminal study of literary symbolism, and as the author of widely read reviews and essays in which he introduced the best works of modern literature to the reading public. In the following excerpt, Wilson studies* Sentimental Education *as a sociocultural testament, chiefly one involving socialist theories and bourgeois politics. For additional commentary by Wilson on* Sentimental Education, *see NCLC, Vol. 2.*]

[It is] in *L'Education sentimentale* that Flaubert's account of society comes closest to socialist theory. Indeed, his presentation here of the Revolution of 1848 parallels in so striking a manner Marx's analysis of the same events in *The Eighteenth Brumaire of Louis Napoleon* that it is worth while to focus together the diverse figures of Flaubert and Marx in order to recognize how two of the most searching minds of the century, pursuing courses so apparently divergent, arrived at almost identical interpretations of the happenings of their own time.

When we do this, we become aware that Marx and Flaubert started from very similar assumptions and that they were actuated by moral aims almost equally uncompromising. Both implacably hated the bourgeois, and both were resolved at any cost of worldly success to keep outside the bourgeois system. And Karl Marx, like Flaubert, shared to some degree the romantic bias in favor of the past. The author of *Das Kapital* can hardly, of course, be said to have had a very high opinion of any period of human history; but in comparison with the capitalist nineteenth century, he did betray a certain tenderness for Greece and Rome and the Middle Ages. He pointed out that the slavery of the ancient world had at least purchased the 'full development' of the masters, and that a certain Antipater of Thessalonica had joyfully acclaimed the invention of the water wheel for grinding corn because it would set free the female slaves who had formerly had to do this work, whereas the bourgeois economists had seen in machinery only a means for making the workers work faster and longer in order 'to transform a few vulgar and half-educated upstarts into "eminent cotton spinners," "extensive sausage makers" and "influential blacking dealers."' And he had also a soft spot for the feudal system before the nobility had revolted against the Crown and while the rights of all classes, high and low, were still guaranteed by the king. Furthermore, the feudal lords, he insisted, had spent their money lavishly when they had it, whereas it was of the essence of capitalism that the capitalist saved his money and invested it, only to save and reinvest the profits.

Karl Marx's judgment on his age was the *Communist Manifesto*. Let us examine the implications of Flaubert's political novel. The hero of *L'Education sentimentale*, Frédéric Moreau, is a sensitive and intelligent young man equipped with a moderate income; but he has no stability of purpose and is capable of no emotional integrity. He becomes aimlessly, will-lessly, involved in love affairs with different types of women and he is unable to make anything out of any of them: they simply get in each other's way till in the end he is left with nothing. Frédéric is most in love from the very beginning of the story with the virtuous oval-faced wife of a sort of glorified drummer, who is engaged in more or less shady business enterprises; but, what with his timidity and her virtue, he never gets anywhere with her—even though she loves him in return—and leaves her in the hands of the drummer. Flaubert makes it plain to us, however, that Frédéric and the vulgar husband at bottom represent the same thing: Frédéric is only the more refined as well as the more incompetent side of the middle-class mediocrity of which the dubious promoter represents the more flashy and active aspect. And so in the case of the other characters, the journalists and the artists, the members of the various political factions, the remnants of the old nobility, Frédéric finds the same shoddiness and lack of principle which are gradually revealed in himself—the same qualities which render so odious to him the banker M. Dambreuse, the type of the rich and powerful class. M. Dambreuse is always ready to trim his sails to any political party, monarchist or republican, which seems to have a chance of success. 'Most of the men who were there,' Flaubert writes of the guests at the Dambreuse house, 'had served at least four governments; and they would have sold France or the human race in order to guarantee their fortune, to spare themselves an anxiety or a difficulty, or even from simple baseness, instinctive adoration of force.' 'Je me moque des affaires!' cries Frédéric when the guests at M. Dambreuse's are complaining that criticism of the government hurts business; but he cannot give up going to the house, because he always hopes to profit by Dambreuse's investments and influence.

The only really sympathetic characters in *L'Education sentimentale* are again the representatives of the people. Rosanette, Frédéric's mistress, is the daughter of poor workers in the silk mills, who sold her at fifteen as mistress to an old bourgeois. Her liaison with Frédéric is a symbol of the disastrously unenduring union between the proletariat and the bourgeoisie, of which Karl Marx had written in *The Eighteenth Brumaire*. After the suppression of the workers' insurrection during the June days of '48, Rosanette gives birth to a weakly child, which dies at the same time that Frédéric is already arranging a love affair with the dull wife of the banker. Frédéric believes that Mme Dambreuse will be able to advance his interests. And bourgeois socialism gets a very Marxist treatment—save in one respect, which we shall note in a moment—in the character of Sénécal, who is eternally making himself unpleasant about communism and the welfare of the masses, for which he is ready to fight to the last barricade. When, later, Sénécal gets a job as foreman in a pottery factory, he at once becomes a harsh little tyrant; and as soon as it begins to appear, after the putting-down of the June riots, that the reaction is sure to triumph, he decides, like certain radicals turned fascists, that the strong centralization of the government is already a kind of communism and that authority is in itself a great thing.

You have, on the other hand, the clerk Dussardier, a strapping and obtuse fellow, who is one of the few honest characters in the book. When we first see him, he has just knocked down a policeman in a political brawl on the street. Later, when the National Guard, of which Dussardier is a member, turns against the proletariat in the interests of law and order, Dussardier fells one of the insurgents from the top of a barricade and gets at the same time a bullet in the leg, thereby becoming a great hero of the bourgeois. But the poor fellow himself is unhappy. The boy that he had knocked down had wrapped the tricolor around him and shouted to the National Guard: 'Are you going to fire on your brothers?' Dussardier is not at all sure that he ought not to have been on the other side. His last appearance is at the climax of the story, constitutes, indeed, the climax: he turns up in a proletarian street riot, which the cavalry and the police are putting down. Dussardier refuses to move, crying 'Vive la République!'; and Frédéric comes along just in time to see one of the policemen kill him. Then he recognizes this policeman: it is the socialist, Sénécal.

L'Education sentimentale, unpopular when it first appeared, is likely, if we read it in youth, to prove baffling and even repellent. The title may have given the impression that we are going to get a love story, but the love affairs turn out invariably to be tepid or incomplete, and one finds oneself depressed or annoyed. Is it a satire? The characters are too close to life, and a little too well rounded, for satire. Yet they are not quite vitalized enough, not quite responsive enough, to seem the people of a straight novel. But we find that it sticks in our crop. If it is true, as Bernard Shaw has said, that *Das Kapital* makes us see the nineteenth century 'as if it were a cloud passing down the wind, changing its shape and fading as it goes,' so that we are afterwards never able to forget that 'capitalism, with its wage slavery, is only a passing phase of social development, following primitive communism, chattel slavery and feudal serfdom into the past'—so Flaubert's novel plants deep in our mind an idea which we never quite get rid of: the suspicion that our middle-class society of manufacturers, businessmen and bankers, of people who live on or deal in investments, so far from being redeemed by its culture, has ended by cheapening and invalidating all the departments of culture, political, scientific, artistic and religious, as well as corrupting and weakening the ordinary human relations: love, friendship and loyalty to cause—till the whole civilization seems to dwindle.

But fully to appreciate the book, one must have had time to see something of life and to have acquired a certain interest in social and political dramas as distinct from personal ones. If one rereads it in middle age, one finds that the author's tone no longer seems quite so acrid, that one is listening to a muted symphony of which the varied instrumentation and the pattern, the marked rhythms and the melancholy sonorities, had been hardly perceptible before. There are no hero, no villain, to arouse us, no clowns to entertain us, no scenes to wring our hearts. Yet the effect is deeply moving. It is the tragedy of nobody in particular, but of the poor human race itself reduced to such ineptitude, such cowardice, such commonness, such weak irresolution—arriving, with so many fine notions in its head, so many noble words on its lips, at a failure which is all the more miserable because those who have failed in their roles have even forgotten what roles they were cast for. We come to understand the statement of Mr. Ford Madox Ford that he has found it is not too much to read the book fourteen times. Though *L'Education sentimentale* is less attractive on the surface and less exciting as a story than *Madame Bovary,* it is certainly the book of Flaubert's which is most ambitiously planned and into which he has tried to put most. And once we have got the clue to the immense and complex drama which unrolls itself behind the half-screen of the detached and monotonous style, we find it as absorbing and satisfying as a great play or a great piece of music.

The one conspicuous respect in which Flaubert's point of view on the events of 1848 *diverges* from that of Marx has been thrown into special relief by the events of our own time. For Marx, the evolution of the socialist into a proletarian-persecuting policeman would have been blamed on the bourgeois in Sénécal; for Flaubert, it is a development of socialism implicit in socialist beginnings. He distrusted, as I have shown above, the authoritarian aims of the socialists. It is Flaubert's conception that Sénécal, given his bourgeois hypocrisy, is still carrying out a socialist principle—or rather, that his behavior as a policeman and his yearnings toward socialist control are both derived from his impulse toward despotism.

We may not be prepared to conclude that the evolution of Sénécal represents the whole destiny of socialism, but we must recognize that Flaubert had here brought to attention a danger of which Marx was not aware. We have had the opportunity to see how even a socialism which has come to power as the result of a proletarian revolution can breed a political police of almost unprecedented ruthlessness—how the example of Marx himself, with his emphasis on dictatorial control rather than on democratic processes, has contributed to produce this disaster. Flaubert, who believed that the artist should rid himself of social convictions, has gauged the tendencies of a political doctrine as the greatest of doctrinaires could not; and here the attitude he proposed has been justified. (pp. 78-83)

> Edmund Wilson, "The Politics of Flaubert," in his The Triple Thinkers: Twelve Essays on Literary Subjects, *revised edition, Oxford University Press, 1948, pp. 72-87.*

MARTIN TURNELL   (essay date 1950)

[*Turnell isolates elements in* Sentimental Education *that contribute to what he terms its "curious dullness"—its overall failure to achieve greatness—praising, however, a few features of the novel as effective and successful.*]

French critics used to be fond of debating the comparative merits of *Madame Bovary* and *L'Éducation sentimentale*. The later book is undoubtedly far more ambitious. The eminent novelist turns his back on the loves of a country doctor's wife and attempts a full-length study of high society as seen through the eyes of a rich young man. It can hardly be maintained that the result is a success or that as a work of art it is comparable to *Madame Bovary*. For the larger canvas does not suit Flaubert. Instead of providing him with greater scope, it throws into relief the limitations of his sensibility which is reduced to a pathetic trickle winding through the endless wastes of words. Love, politics, art—all wither beneath his touch and are submerged in a common futility. Pellerin, the bad painter, is a successful minor character, but as social criticism the book is a failure. 'Oh, how tired I am', he wrote in a tell-tale sentence in a letter to George Sand, 'of the ignoble worker, the inept bourgeois, the stupid peasant and the odious ecclesiastic.' The truth is that in spite of his honesty, Flaubert did not possess either the penetration or the temper which go to the making of the great social critic. His irony is almost always too heavy, too obvious. There is an undercurrent of *rancœur*, an exas-

peration with stupidity which is continually breaking out in crude denunciation.

We must not be misled by Flaubert's sub-titles. Whether he calls a book 'Moeurs de Province' or 'L'Histoire d'un Jeune Homme', his basic interests are the same, and the resemblances between the two books are in general more striking than their differences. Frédéric's love story does, however, introduce some interesting variations and since the claim is implicit in the book, *L'Éducation sentimentale* must be considered as a social document as well as a study of personal relationships.

In *L'Éducation sentimentale* Flaubert drew directly on his personal experience. Frédéric Moreau is a portrait of the artist and his devotion to Mme Arnoux is founded on Flaubert's own devotion to Élisa Schlésinger. We may suspect that Flaubert adopted this course partly to avoid the conflict which we find in *Madame Bovary* and partly to give his personal experience a wider context and more representative significance. It could be argued that in *Madame Bovary* he was exposing what is in essence an immature state of mind, but no such excuse can be made for the failure of *L'Éducation sentimentale*. The book, indeed, belies its title. There is no 'education' and no development. Frédéric is eighteen at the beginning of the book and forty-five at the end of it; but except that he is worn out by his frivolous life, the Frédéric whom we take leave of after nearly six hundred pages is fundamentally the same as the Frédéric whom we meet on page one. For there seems to be little doubt that Flaubert was more at home with the 'literary' emotions of parts of *Madame Bovary,* and his attempt to write a novel about his own experience explains the psychological barrenness of *L'Éducation sentimentale.*

The one positive force in Frédéric's life appears to be his love of Mme Arnoux, but on closer inspection it turns out to have a different significance:

> Et ils s'imaginaient une vie exclusivement amoureuse, assez féconde pour remplir les plus vastes solitudes, excédant toutes les joies, défiant toutes les misères, où les heures auraient disparu dans un continuel épanchement d'eux-mêmes, et qui auraient fait quelque chose de resplendissant et d'élevé comme la palpitation des étoiles.
>
> [And they imagined a life that would be all love, and yet rich enough to fill the widest deserts; surpassing all joys, defying all sorrows, they would open their hearts to each other for hours on end. It was a life which might have become something splendid and sublime, like the twinkling of the stars.]

We recognize this as the familiar language of the romantic lover, the familiar hunt for an impossible love 'excédant toutes les joies' and producing 'un continuel épanchement d'eux-mêmes . . . comme la palpitation des étoiles'. But in this book the critical attitude which informed *Madame Bovary* is largely absent. Flaubert takes romantic love seriously and there is no trace of irony in his treatment of it. It is, perhaps, the greatest weakness of the novel that it reproduces so closely the history of Flaubert's connection with Élisa Schlésinger and that no attempt is made to transform the material into something more impressive. Mme Arnoux marks the stage at which the emotional development of both Frédéric and his creator was arrested. In the novel as in life the love affair is never consummated not because of moral scruples or because the woman would not have 'yielded' had she been pressed, but because romantic love must of its nature be unhappy and its object inaccessible. We may suspect that at bottom the high-minded devotion is a defence-mechanism, a prolonged adolescence which provides a refuge from the responsibilities of adult life.

I have spoken of the similarities between the two novels. It is interesting to compare Frédéric's *déception* when he meets Mme Arnoux again after an absence in the country with Emma's in the presence of Léon:

> Frédéric s'était attendu à des spasmes de joie; mais les passions s'étiolent quand on les dépayse, et, ne retrouvant plus Mme Arnoux dans le milieu où il l'avait connue, elle lui semblait avoir perdu quelque chose, porter, confusément comme une dégradation, enfin n'être plus la même. Le calme de son coeur le stupéfiait.

> [Frederic had been anticipating paroxysms of joy; but passionate feelings seldom survive a change of atmosphere, and, meeting Mme Arnoux again in an unfamiliar setting, he felt that her stature was somehow diminished, that she had suffered an indefinable deterioration—in short, that she had changed. His own calmness astounded him.]

Frédéric's 'spasmes de joie' resemble Emma's 'félicité profonde', and 'le calme de son coeur' expresses an emptiness which hardly differs from 'elle s'avouait ne rien sentir d'extraordinaire'. There is, however, one important difference. Frédéric's 'calm' is final; it is not followed by the *long frisson* or at any rate not until the discovery of Rosanette.

Flaubert tried to make Frédéric's story more interesting by giving him a greater variety of mistresses. Lousie, Mme Arnoux, Rosanette and Mme Dambreuse stand for Innocence, the Romantic Idol, Nature and Civilization. Mme Arnoux is not the only one who is a portrait from life. We cannot identify the charming though shadowy Louise who may have been a pure invention; but Rosanette—the only one of the four whose vitality is genuine and who really comes to life—like Marie in *Novembre* is to some extent a portrait of Eulalie Foucaud de Lenglade. Although Flaubert had Maxime Du Camp and Mme Delessert in mind when he wrote the parts about Mme Dambreuse, she certainly plays the same role in Frédéric's life as Louise Colet did in Flaubert's. She is the woman who for a moment satisfies Frédéric sexually and to some extent emotionally or possibly socially. When she persists in buying a small box at the sale which follows the Arnoux bankruptcy, Frédéric seizes his opportunity. She is just as brutally *éconduite* as Louise Colet when she forced her way into Croisset. (pp. 280-83)

One of the worst faults of *L'Éducation sentimentale* is its diffuseness. There are pages when words revolve like pieces in a kaleidoscope without forming any pattern. Then, suddenly, each of the pieces falls into place and the pattern is there:

> Frédéric l'observait. Le peau mate de son visage paraissait tendue, et d'une fraîcheur sans éclat, comme celle d'un fruit conservé.

> [Frederic watched her. Her lustreless skin seemed to be stretched over her face; it had freshness but no bloom, like a preserved fruit.]

The homely image is a shrewd comment not only on Mme Dambreuse, but on the society which produced her. This time every word is 'right'. The *tendue* makes us feel the strain under which all these people were living. The 'fraîcheur sans éclat', reinforcing the implications of 'la peau mate', suggests the curious artificiality of their lives, lives without genuine vitality depending on cosmetics and patent medicines; and though they possessed undeniable virtues, they were the virtues of 'un fruit conservé'.

This sentence acquires a symbolical value and in the manner of the novelists who followed him, Flaubert refers back to it later in the book, playing on its latent implications:

> Outre sa visite du soir, il lui en faisait quelquefois une autre vers la fin du jour; et il avait une gradation de joies à passer successivement par la grande porte, par la cour, par l'antichambre, par les deux salons; enfin, il arrivait dans son boudoir, discret comme un tombeau, tiède comme une alcôve, où l'on se heurtait aux capitons des meubles parmi toute sorte d'objets. . . .

> [Apart from his evening visit, he often paid her another in the late afternoon; and he experienced an ascending scale of pleasures as he passed in succession through the front door, the hall and the two drawing-rooms. At length he reached her boudoir, which was as quiet as a tomb, and warm as an alcove. One stumbled against padded furniture among a whole medley of objects. . . .]

The *tombeau*—a word that Flaubert sometimes used too melodramatically—gives the right sense of atmosphere here and the 'tiède comme une alcôve' the feeling of warm, stuffy, airless life. It is caught up a few pages later when we read:

> Il semblait à Frédéric, en descendant l'escalier, qu'il était devenu un autre homme, que la température embaumante des serres chaudes l'entourait, qu'il entrait définitivement dans le monde supérieur des adultères patriciens et des hautes intrigues.

> [As Frederic went down the staircase, he felt that he had become a different man, that the heavily perfumed air of conservatories surrounded him, that he had finally made his way into the higher world of patrician liaisons and aristocratic intrigues.]

The 'serres chaudes' refers back to 'tiède comme une alcôve' and the 'fruit conservé'. The different *gradations* described in the middle passage enable the author to get underneath the skin of his hero, making us feel his snobbish satisfaction as he disposes, one after another, of the different 'obstacles' which separate him from his lady's couch. But the boudoir—the goal for which he is making—is ironically also a *tombeau* because Frédéric's love contains the seeds of its own dissolution. 'En descendant l'escalier' in the last passage is also ironical. It is the moral *descent* which appears to lead *up* to the 'adultères patriciens' and the 'hautes intrigues'.

In another place we are told of Frédéric's departure from one of his meetings with Mme Dambreuse:

> Il huma dans la rue une large bouffée d'air; et, par besoin d'un milieu moins artificiel, Frédéric se ressouvint qu'il devait une visite à la Maréchale.

> [All the same, he drew in a large mouthful of air in the street; and feeling the need for a less artificial environment, he remembered that he owed a visit to Rosanette.]

The tug-of-war between Mme Dambreuse and Rosanette symbolizes the conflict between a dying society and what is real and vital in Frédéric's own make-up.

These passages recall an interesting comment on Rosanette's *cabinet de toilette*:

> On voyait, tout de suite, que c'était l'endroit de la maison le plus hauté, et comme son vrai centre moral.

[It was obvious at once that this was the most important room, the focal point, as it were, of the house.]

This sentence seems at first to place the *poule de luxe* with the same finality as Mme Dambreuse; but this time Flaubert is not completely successful. He should have begun, one feels, with a brief description of the *cabinet de toilette* and this sentence should have been the climax of a passage in which every object had its place. Instead, the process is reversed. It is the opening sentence and is followed by.

> Une perse à grands feuillages tapissait les murs, les fauteuils et un vaste divan élastique; sur une table de marbre blanc s'espaçaient deux larges cuvettes en faïence bleue; des planches de cristal formant étagère au-dessus étaient encombrées par des fioles, des brosses, des peignes, des bâtons de cosmétique, des boîtes à poudre; le feu se mirait dans une haute psyché; un drap pendait en dehors d'une baignoire, et des senteurs de pâte d'amandes et de benjoin s'exhalaient.

> [The walls, the armchairs, and the enormous spring divan were covered in chintz, with a bold pattern of leaves; on a white marble table stood two large basins in blue faience; the glass shelves above were loaded with bottles, brushes and combs, sticks of make-up, and powder boxes; a tall cheval glass reflected the fire; a cloth hung over the edge of a bath, and the scents of almond paste and benzoin filled the air.]

Flaubert was attempting something not unlike Swift's finale in the description of his mistress's boudoir, but he fails because he adopts the wrong method. His description not only robs individual objects of their significance, it destroys the effect which he has already created in the admirable opening sentence.

The preoccupation of the nineteenth-century novelists with the physical appearance of the external world, their obsession with the impact of material reality on their sensibility is a curious phenomenon. The great French writers of the past had displayed a singular lack of interest in the external world and in 'Nature'; their whole attention was focused on the drama going on inside the mind. Feelings were determined by the clash of personalities, never by the sense of being hemmed in by unending rows of houses. We have little idea what their characters looked like, what sort of clothes they wore or what sort of houses they lived in. Descriptions of their persons were for the most part purely formal; clothes and nature were only interesting in so far as they illuminated the inner drama. Thus we have Phèdre's:

> Que ces vains ornements, que ces voiles me pèsent!

and Antiochus':

> Dans l'Orient désert quel devint mon ennui.

The interest in nature which emerged during the eighteenth century was a reaction against the excessively civilized order of the seventeenth century. It is not surprising that this feeling should have developed into nature-worship or that nature should later have been regarded as a sanctuary, a refuge from the horrors of industrial civilization. It has not, perhaps, been sufficiently remarked that the converse is also true. Nineteenth-century materialism—the preoccupation with buildings, money and clothes—was a desperate attempt to find something solid and enduring, something which one could touch and feel, in a world of dissolving values. In Baudelaire it produced great poetry of a new kind and even Balzac's interest in the physical is a sign of vitality. Flaubert's preoccupation was of a different order. 'Pour qu'une chose soit intéressante,' he remarked in a letter to Alfred Le Poittevin, 'il suffit de la regarder longtemps.'

L'Éducation sentimentale is in the main an illustration of the falsity of this disastrous maxim:

> La plaine, bouleversée, semblait de vagues ruines. L'enceinte des fortifications y faisait un renflement horizontal; et, sur les trottoirs en terre qui bordaient la route, de petits arbres sans branches étaient défendus par des lattes hérissées de clous. Des établissements de produits chimiques alternaient avec des chantiers de marchands de bois. . . .

> [The straggling houses on the plain looked vaguely like a ruined city. Beyond rose the level ridge of the fortifications; on the muddy footpaths fringing the road stood small, branchless trees, protected by wooden frames studded with nails. Chemical factories alternated with timber merchants' sheds. . . .]

This extract—there is a great deal more of it—is taken from an account of one of Frédéric's journeys to Paris; but Flaubert uses precisely the same method in other contexts. The first thing that strikes us is the writer's complete lack of interest in what he is describing. The next is the manner in which the objects are set down, one after another, like a catalogue. 'La pleine, bouleversée, semblait de vagues ruines' is a good description of the process. For the whole scene disintegrates into 'vagues ruines', into a mass of inanimate objects which are without any relation to one another or to the observer. Instead of words becoming things as they must do in good prose, things become words and the words fall on the page like lumps of lead, meaninglessly. Flaubert's Paris is simply a confused mass of bricks and mortar. It is not comparable to Baudelaire's Paris or to Joyce's Dublin or Conrad's London in *The Secret Agent*.

Flaubert himself seems to have been aware that there was something wrong and in other places he is obviously at pains to cover the gaps:

> Mais le soleil se couchait, et le vent froid soulevait des tourbillons de poussière. Les cochers baissaient le menton dans leurs cravates, les roues se mettaient à tourner plus vite, le macadam grinçait; et tous les équipages descendaient au grand trot la longue avenue, en se frôlant, se dépassant, s'écartant les uns des autres, puis, sur la place de la Concorde se dispersaient. Derrière les Tuileries, le ciel prenait la teinte des ardoises. Les arbres du jardin formaient deux masses énormes, violacées par le sommet. Les becs de gaz s'allumaient, et la Seine, verdâtre dans toute son étendue, se déchirait en moires d'argent contre les piles des ponts.

> [But the sun was now setting, and a cold wind stirred up eddies of dust. The coachmen thrust their chins down into their neckcloths, the wheels turned faster, the asphalt grated; and all the carriages swept down the long avenue at a brisk trot, jostling, swerving, overtaking; then, at the Place de la Concorde they scattered. The sky behind the Tuileries took on the hue of its slate roof. The trees in the gardens became two solid masses, tinged with purple at the top. The lamps were lit; and the pale green expanse of the Seine broke into shot silver against the piles of the bridges.]

This passage has the same faults as the previous one, but Flaubert's subterfuges are not without interest. His use of three verbs together all expressing movement—'se frôlant, se dépassant, s'écartant'—was a favourite trick and it is employed here to give the monotonous prose a specious life. This also applies to the colours. Flaubert had little eye for colour. It is a sign of his lack of sensibility that he nearly always chose the

A portrait by Thomas Couture of George Sand, Flaubert's frequent correspondent while he was writing Sentimental Education.

dull, commonplace colours like *violacées* and *verdâtre*. The last sentence like so many in Flaubert reminds one uncomfortably of a crude coloured lithograph.

The late Jean Prévost has spoken of Flaubert's style 'qui rend tout immobile', and in reading him we constantly have the impression that the tempo of life is being deliberately slowed down, that a strange immobility is stealing over human feelings which stiffen and die, crushed beneath the impact of their surroundings. Turn, for example, to the account of Frédéric's and Rosanette's visit to Fontainebleau:

> Les résidences royales ont en elles une mélancolie particulière, qui tient sans doute à leurs dimensions trop considérables pour le petit nombre de leurs hôtes, au silence qu'on est surpris d'y trouver après tant de fanfares, à leur luxe immobile prouvant par sa vieillesse la fugacité des dynasties, l'éternelle misère de tout;—et cette èxhalaison des siècles, engourdissante et funèbre comme un parfum de momie, se fait sentir même aux têtes naïves. Rosanette bâillait démesurément. Ils s'en retournèrent à l'hôtel.

> [There is a peculiar melancholy about royal residences, which is probably due to their inordinate size, compared with the number of their inhabitants, or to their silence, which is somehow surprising after the trumpets that have sounded there, or it may be because of their fixed and motionless splendour, which proves by its antiquity the transience of dynasties, the inevitable decay of all things; and this emanation of the centuries, numbing and deathly as the smell of a mummy, affects even the shallowest mind. Rosanette was yawning vastly. They went back to their hotel.]

Flaubert's starting point is the 'mélancolie particulière' which the visitors experience when confronted by historic monu-

ments. It is connected at once with their physical proportions, with the 'dimensions trop considérables pour le petit nombre de leurs hôtes', with the silence and the 'luxe immobile'. Size is linked with age and the 'mélancolie particulière' transformed into 'l'éternelle misère de tout'. The repetition and the use of the heavy Latinized vocabulary give the prose its soporific quality; we feel the 'exhalaison des siècles' enveloping the visitors and overpowering them. The whole experience peters out in a sense of vacancy, in 'Rosanette bâillait démesurément'. The reader himself feels tempted to yawn as Frédéric and Rosanette suddenly turn for home, their minds a blank.

This no doubt is a description of a particular incident, but the method is characteristic and it enables us to understand the curious dullness of *L'Éducation sentimentale.* Flaubert's obsession with bricks and mortar, with distance, size and shape, turns his characters into ridiculous dwarf-like creatures who move convulsively through this dead silent world like the figures in an animated cartoon.

It is, indeed, of a film that the book continually reminds me— a film of inordinate length which in spite of good 'shots' and even good 'sequences' has almost every fault that a film can have. There are times when the picture is out of focus, when the sound-track degenerates into an incoherent mutter or fails altogether, or when the camera goes tracking interminably over the roofs and façades of buildings, nosing in and out of doors and windows and prying into backyards without the mind being able to grasp the significance of what is being shown. At other times it dwindles into a jerky, meaningless flicker. Then, suddenly, a scene is thrown into sharp relief, some object assumes, for a moment, immense significance, only to be swallowed up again in the endless meandering. (pp. 284-91)

The whole of *L'Éducation sentimentale* is in a sense an account of a journey through life, but a journey in which the traveller is a spectator rather than an actor, in which life is *seen* from the deck of a ship or the inside of a coach instead of being *lived,* emphasizing the paucity of Frédéric's contacts with life and not the richness of his experience. . . . (p. 292)

[The account of Frédéric's journey to Nogent], in which 'Life' is significantly symbolized by 'young love among the orange groves', illustrates the dream-like quality of Frédéric's journey. For *le rêve* plays the same part in his psychology as it does in Emma's. There is a continual movement away from comfortless actuality towards the 'oranges groves' and the 'pays à noms sonores' of the dream-world. There are moments when the dream changes into an hallucination or a nightmare, as it does in the accounts of parties in both books. Actuality disintegrates to reveal the hideous and terrifying shapes of the nightmare:

> Presque toutes portaient un bouquet de violettes à la main. Le ton mat de leurs gants faisaient ressortir la blancheur humaine de leurs bras; des effilés, des herbes, leur pendaient sur les épaules, et on croyait quelquefois, à certains frissonnements, que la robe allait tomber. Mais la décence des figures tempérait la provocation du costume; plusieurs même avaient une placidité presque bestiale, et ce rassemblement de femmes demi-nues faisait songer à un intérieur de harem. . . .

> [Almost everyone carried a bunch of violets. The dead colour of their gloves intensified the natural whiteness of their arms; ribbons and pearls hung down their shoulders; sometimes, when one shivered, her dress seemed about to fall. But the daring of their costumes was counterbalanced by the respectability

of their faces; some wore an expression of almost animal complacency, and this assemblage of half-naked women made him think of the inside of a harem. . . .]

This illustrates very well the alternation of nightmare and reality. The procession of women with their violets suggests some strange rite which is emphasized by 'le ton mat de leurs gants', then relieved by the 'blancheur *humaine* de leurs bras'. The feeling that their clothing may suddenly fall off takes us back to the world of the nightmare where one's trousers are always falling down. We come back again to reality in 'la décence des figures' only to switch to the nightmare with its fearful shapes in 'une placidité presque bestiale' and the 'intérieur de harem'.

The best illustration of all, however, is the account of the fancy dress ball at the Maréchale's:

> Alors, toutes les femmes, assises autour du salon sur des banquettes, se levèrent à la file, prestement; et leurs jupes, leurs écharpes, leurs coiffures se mirent à tourner.
>
> Elles tournaient si près de lui, que Frédéric distinguait les gouttelettes de leur front;—et ce mouvement giratoire de plus en plus vif et régulier, vertigineux, communiquant à sa pensée une sorte d'ivresse, y faisait surgir d'autres images, tandis que toutes passaient dans le même éblouissement, et chacune avec une excitation particulière selon le genre de sa beauté. La Polonaise, qui s'abandonnait d'une façon langoureuse, lui inspirait l'envie de la tenir contre son cœur, en filant tous les deux dans un traîneau sur une plaine couverte de neige. Des horizons de volupté tranquille, au bord d'un lac, dans un chalet, se déroulaient sous les pas de la Suissesse, qui valsait le torse droit et les paupières baissées. Puis, tout à coup, la Bacchante, penchant en arrière sa tête brune, le faisait rêver à des caresses dévoratrices, dans des bois de lauriers-roses, par un temps d'orage, au bruit confus des tambourins. . . . Mais la Débardeuse, dont les orteils effleuraient à peine le parquet, semblait recéler dans la souplesse de ses membres et le sérieux de son visage tous les raffinements de l'amour moderne, qui a la justesse d'une science et la mobilité d'un oiseau. Rosanette tournait, le poing sur la hanche; sa perruque à marteau, sautillant sur son collet, envoyait de la poudre d'iris autour d'elle; et, à chaque tour, du bout de ses éperons d'or, elle manquait d'attraper Frédéric.

[Then all the women, who had been sitting on sofas round the room, got up quickly in a line; and their skirts, their scarves, their head-dresses began to revolve.

They came so close to Frederic that he could even see the drops of sweat on their foreheads; and this dizzy, spinning movement, growing ever faster and more rhythmic, aroused a kind of intoxication in his mind, filling it with strange thoughts, while the women swept by him in a single, dazzling whirl; and each, with her special beauty, excited a different desire. The Polish girl's languorous surrender to the dance made him long to hold her to his heart, while they travelled together in a sleigh over a snow-covered plain. The Swiss girl, waltzing with her body upright and her eyelids lowered, opened to him vistas of quiet joy in a chalet beside a lake. Then suddenly the Bacchante, bending her dark head backwards, made him dream of ravenous kisses among groves of oleander, in thundery weather, to the murmur of tabors. . . . But the *débardeuse*, whose light toes scarcely skimmed the floor, seemed, with her supple limbs and serious face, to suggest all the refinements of modern love, which combines the precision of a science with the restlessness of a bird. Rosanette was dancing with her hand on her hip; her wig bobbed up and down on her collar, scattering powder all around her; at every twirl she almost caught Frederic with her golden spurs.]

The ritual element is introduced by the dancers all filing into the ballroom. The connection between the 'mouvement giratoire de plus en plus vif et régulier, vertigineux' and the movement of the journeys is evident. Frédéric, as usual, is a spectator—naturally he does not dance—but this time it is life which revolves about him. Its shapes suddenly draw near to him, beckoning to him, then move away tantalizingly. The movement of the dance merges into the imagined movement of the sledge gliding over the snows, changes to the calm of a Swiss lake, then to the 'bois de lauriers-roses' and ends with the refinements of 'modern love'. Rosanette, who is described later among the débris of the party as 'fraîche comme au sortir d'un bain . . . les joues roses, les yeux brillants', is a symbol of the Natural Woman, and the way in which the ends of her gold spurs keep just missing Frédéric stands for his intermittent contacts with reality.

I have dwelt at some length on passages which are not always in themselves of great intrinsic value because of the light that they throw on Flaubert's sensibility. Certain conclusions emerge from the analysis of these different passages. Flaubert had no gift for *direct* description. His descriptive prose is almost invariably dull and lifeless. His sensibility lacks freshness and he has no power of making us see material things in a new way or of selecting what is significant in the scene before him. His originality appears rather in sudden glimpses into the *moral* significance of a person or a place such as we find in the comment on Rosanette's *cabinet de toilette*, in the critical appraisal of a section of society that we find in the account of la Vaubyessard or in the passages in which he reshapes feelings which are largely derived from his own reading as he does in Emma's 'daydream'. I think that we must go on to say that his sensibility was not simply limited and intermittent, but was undoubtedly defective. It was a sensibility which only touched life at comparatively few points, and we have seen from his descriptions of urban life that there was a wide variety of situations in which it failed to register at all.

The implications of this criticism are far-reaching. Mme Dambreuse is practically the only character who has any roots in the society which Flaubert is studying and she is the only point at which there exists a tenuous relationship between Frédéric and this society. For one of the main weaknesses of the book is the gap between the account of Frédéric's *amours* and the account of society. The social life, the political meetings and the revolutions which Flaubert described so laboriously are no more than a drab and uninteresting background for what is after all a series of not very exciting liaisons.

These conclusions seem to me to be confirmed by the famous opening of Part III, chapter 6:

> Il voyagea.
>
> Il connut la mélancolie des paquebots, les froids réveils sous la tente, l'étourdissement des paysages et des ruines, l'amertume des sympathies interrompues.
>
> Il revint.

Il fréquenta le monde, et il eut d'autres amours encore. Mais le souvenir continuel du premier les lui
rendait insipides; et puis la véhémence du désir, la
fleur même de la sensation était perdue. Ses ambitions d'esprit avaient également diminué. Des années
passèrent; et il supportait le désœuvrement de son
intelligence et l'inertie de son cœur.

[He travelled.

He knew the melancholy of the steamboat; the cold
awakening in the tent; the tedium of scenery and
ruins; the bitterness of interrupted friendship.

He came back.

He went into society. He had other loves still. But
the ever-present memory of the first destroyed their
savour; and, besides, the violence of desire, the flower
of sensation itself, had withered. His intellectual ambitions had also dwindled. Years passed; and he endured the idleness of his mind and the stagnation of
his heart.]

This is undoubtedly one of the most accomplished pieces of
prose in the whole of Flaubert's work and in its way it is a
complete success. For . . . it is an artistic whole. The feeling
are completely dissolved into the images. There is no impression either that feelings are being released for which no adequate words can be found or that words are being used to
conceal a failure of sensibility. The short, sharp sentence: 'Il
voyagea' marks a break with the old life, the life which had
ended with the violent death of Dussardier during the riots,
and concentrates the attention on the 'remedy'. The 'blanks',
which Proust rather perversely described as the most beautiful
thing in the book, prolong the effect of the words, suggest long
periods of time passing, vast distances traversed. The weariness
and boredom of life on a liner lead to the cold and loneliness
of camping expeditions in the desert. For Frédéric becomes
the Romantic Traveller seeking escape from urban civilization;
but, as we should expect of a hero whom his creator described
in a moment of exasperation as 'l'homme de toutes les faib-
lesses', the famous sights—fresh landscapes, historic ruins—
only produce a vague *étourdissement* in the blasé traveller.
They are death-symbols which replace the life-symbols of Frédéric's earlier journeys. The attempt to escape from his own
isolation, to integrate himself into society dissolves into l'a-
mertumes des sympathies interrompues'.

'Il revint' has the same emphasis as the opening sentence. It
marks the failure to rebuild and the sudden return. The next
sentence describes the resumption of the empty, frivolous life
which had driven him away. The third explains the fundamental
immaturity of his outlook and his love for Mme Arnoux is seen
for what it is—an adolescent admiration which has prevented
development and adaptation. The remarkable phrase, 'et puis
la véhémence du désir, la fleur même de la sensation était
perdue', shows Flaubert—always more successful when describing disintegration and collapse—at his best. The sensation
is presented with startling clarity, linking spiritual and physical
destruction. The final sentence welds the two into a whole: 'le
désœuvrement de son intelligence et l'inertie de son cœur.'

The passage has the internal coherence and economy of a
seventeenth-century *tirade*, moving with mathematical precision from one feeling to another, from the mood of boredom
and loneliness to the mood of complete vacuity. The friction
between one set of feelings and another ends by destroying all
feeling. It was because Flaubert excelled in descriptions of
inertie that the second part of the passage is still more im-

pressive than the first. His 'Symbolist' technique was never
used with better effect. A whole life is crowded into these few
sentences. It is an admirable example of Flaubert's art certainly, but it knocks the rest of the book sideways, standing
out with a sombre splendour against a drab and colourless
background.

> It is the tragedy of nobody in particular [Mr. Edmund
> Wilson wrote of *L'Éducation sentimentale* (see ex-
> cerpt dated 1948)] but of the poor human race itself
> reduced to such ineptitude, such cowardice, such weak
> irresolution—arriving, with so many fine notions in
> its head, so many noble words on its lips, at a failure
> which is all the more memorable because those who
> have failed are hardly conscious of having done so.

Flaubert would have been highly gratified by these kind words;
but though they may very well describe his intention, they
seem to me to underline the immense gap between intention
and execution. For his characters simply will not bear the social
significance that he tries to attach to them. The doubts that one
felt about *Madame Bovary* become certainties. *L'Éducation
sentimentale* seems to me to be profoundly lacking in the famous French maturity, in that wisdom which is so abundantly
present in *Adolphe* and gives it its peculiar place among modern
novels. All Flaubert's characters—the principals as well as the
minor characters—are *ratés*. They are doomed to failure from
the start, but no one is less able than their creator to explain
how or why this is so.

While I do not feel able to share Mr. Wilson's high opinion
of the book, I do not think that it can be dismissed as a worthless
failure, as a mere example of the *platitude bourgeoise*, as some
critics would have us believe. It is a work of importance in its
way and for many of Flaubert's admirers it remains his masterpiece. For these readers it is a great book because it seems
to them to express better than any other the contemporary
'mess', the widespread disillusionment which has followed the
collpase of traditional beliefs. The book does, to be sure, leave
us with a sense of waste, a slow corrosion spreading over all
feeling; but we also have the impression that the situation is
an artificial one which depends on an incomplete analysis of
the *données* and that the true explanation is to be found in the
aberrations of the author's own personality, in the cultivation
of a highly refined sentimentality which is concealed behind a
certain bluntness, a certain matter-of-factness in the writing.

French critics may have valid reasons for their preference, but
I find something sad in the excessive admiration for the book
in Anglo-Saxon countries, and the readiness to accept its author
as the interpreter of the modern world to itself seems to be the
sign of a fundamental lack of self-confidence. There is no doubt
that Anglo-Saxon readers are altogether too inclined to identify
themselves uncritically with Flaubert's characters, to admire
them because they are *ratés*, to see in them the reflection of
their own personal failures. (pp. 292-98)

> Martin Turnell, ''Flaubert,'' in his The Novel in
> France: Mme de la Fayette, Laclos, Constant, Sten-
> dhal, Balzac, Flaubert, Proust, *Hamish Hamilton,
> 1950, pp. 247-311.*

STRATTON BUCK   (essay date 1952)

[*Buck studies the sequence of time in* Sentimental Education,
linking the chronology and structure of the novel.]

In his excellent edition of the *Education sentimentale*, M. René
Dumesnil has established for the novel a chronological plan

showing in detail in which month and year each of the incidents and events of the story is supposed to have taken place. This analysis is valuable to students of the novel. It reveals, perhaps as nothing else can, the scrupulous care which Flaubert exercised in his effort to make his historical background absolutely accurate, and opens the way for interesting reflections, not only on his realism, but also on his method and purposes in blending history and fiction.

Unfortunately, M. Dumesnil's *plan* fails (doubtless because his purpose was to provide an outline for reference rather than to study the chronological structure of the novel) to call attention to certain peculiarities and discrepancies in the passage of time in the story. It seems important to me that these be observed, for they bring out interesting facts about the organization of the **Education sentimentale,** and suggest speculation on certain aspects of Flaubert's genius.

The peculiarities to which I refer are found almost entirely in what I shall call the transitional passages of the novel, for, contrary to appearances, the **Education sentimentale** is not a continuous narrative covering the years 1840 to 1851, but rather a story in three episodes. Because it does not give a satisfactory account of the passage of time in the transitional passages, M. Dumesnil's *plan* obscures this fact. These transitions occur at the end of Part I of the novel, and in chapter iii of Part III. An examination of the text will reveal that these chapters devote only a few pages to the passage of many months, and that in them the exigencies of the ordinary calendar are not observed.

This cavalier treatment of time is the more peculiar when one considers the regularity with which the weeks, seasons, and years pass in the rest of the novel. In the greater part of the work, as M. Dumesnil's *plan* shows so clearly, it is possible to follow Frédéric and his acquaintances month by month through the decade in which Flaubert cast their story. Not only is the calendar accounted for fully, but each of the hundreds of allusions to contemporary events is made at the proper moment, and we know that the several characters are living in real, historical time. In this way, the novel goes forward quite normally from its beginning in September, 1840, to the moment when Frédéric completes his law course and celebrates the event by a picnic with his friends.

The passage of time within the story indicates plainly that we are now in September, 1843, and Dumesnil, in his *plan*, dates the gathering accordingly. He fails to observe the apparent discrepancy which occurs when "Regimbard accusait la Camarilla de perdre des millions en Algérie." This is an allusion to the debates which accompanied the signing of a treaty with Morocco, debates which excited the French in August and September, not of 1843, but of 1844. We must now conclude either that Flaubert has been guilty of one of his very rare anachronisms, or that he has deliberately skipped a year in the time plan of the story. The pages which follow force us to accept the second assumption.

A few days after the picnic, Frédéric goes home to Nogent, where his mother informs him that his fortune is far smaller than he had anticipated. He remains in Nogent until, on December 12, 1845, he receives the news that he has inherited his uncle's wealth. This residence in Nogent is the subject matter of the transitional chapter vi of Part I. It allows, quite clearly, for a time lapse of only fifteen months. While the succession of Frédéric's monotonous occupations is kept deliberately vague, the author observes the passage of the seasons. "Les six premiers mois, surtout, furent abominables." This

carries us from September to March, when "sa mère l'appela. C'était pour le consulter à propos d'une plantation dans le jardin." Spring gives way to summer, and Frédéric refuses an invitation of M. Roque because "il n'avait pas un costume d'été convenable." Then, December 12, 1845, the great news comes. But the hero has spent only fifteen months at home, and consequently could not have left Paris until September, 1844.

M. Dumesnil's *plan,* allowing for no such vagary, has Frédéric spend all of 1844 in Nogent. I believe, however, that the text of the novel bears out my contention. Flaubert does not acknowledge the existence of the year preceding September, 1844. The succession of months is observed, but we move from August, 1843, to September, 1844.

In the following chapter (Part II, chapter i), the calendar year, 1846, is disposed of by the same sort of artistic sleight of hand. Having learned of his inheritance, Frédéric returns to Paris, where he arrives on the morning of December 15. He renews quickly his relations with the Arnoux, meets Rosanette, establishes his residence on the Rue de Rumfort, and invites his old Latin Quarter friends to a house warming. This gathering takes place in January of what should be 1846, but the conversation touches on the Spanish marriages, the frauds at Rochefort, the reorganization of the St. Denis chapter, and the murders at Buzançais. None of these events had occurred at the beginning of 1846; all of them were live topics of conversation in January of the following year. There can be no question of anachronisms, for from this point the action of the novel moves normally through the years 1847 and 1848. For the second time, Flaubert has eliminated a year from the story by the simple expedient of moving forward as if no such year had existed.

Thus the first episode of the novel, relating Frédéric's student days in Paris, ends in August, 1843; the second episode, telling of his various adventures before and during the February revolution, does not begin until January, 1847. The transitional chapter vi of Part I, however, accounts for only fifteen months. The other two years elapsing are simply not considered by the novelist. One is eliminated just before the transitional chapter begins; the other is dismissed just after it ends. There is no apparent break in the continuity of the narrative. Each time, the leap of exactly twelve months is accomplished so neatly that it has escaped the notice of a student as familiar with the novel as is M. Dumesnil.

In the second episode, the orthodox calendar recovers its power, and it is possible to follow the plot month by month, and sometimes week by week, until July, 1848. This brings us to part III, chapter iii.

This twenty-three page chapter marks a second transition and relates events extending from August, 1848, until May, 1850. It opens with a very brief description of Frédéric's life with Rosanette in the summer of 1848, then moves rapidly to January, 1849, when the hero calls on Mme Arnoux and is interrupted by his mistress. The incident can be dated by the allusion to the *proposition Rateau.* Furious, Frédéric returns home with Rosanette, who, to check his violence, informs him that she is pregnant. The anger of the protagonist is quelled by this news, but "dès lors, toutes les défectuosités de la Maréchale lui apparurent. . . . Le tête à tête devenait triste. Ce fut un soulagement pour lui, quand les soirées de Mme Dambreuse recommencèrent." We are still in January, 1849, and not, as Dumesnil's *plan* would have it, 1850. Frédéric goes to la Vatnaz to settle Rosanette's obligation, not the following autumn or winter, but "le lendemain" of the visit to Mme Arnoux.

The return to the Dambreuse receptions marks the beginning of a rapid telescoping of the events of the next sixteen months. In five pages, the author describes the situation in the capitalist's household from the time of Martinon's proposal of marriage to Cécile until their wedding in May, not June, 1850. It is at this point that Mme Dambreuse yields to Frédéric's suit, that Deslauriers, much chastened, returns to Paris, and that the third episode of the novel may be said to begin. There has been no break in the continuity of the narrative, but almost imperceptibly the action of the novel has moved forward sixteen months. It is difficult for the reader to realize that so much time has elapsed.

Indeed, the usually rapid passage of time in these pages appears to have led the author himself into a ridiculous bit of confusion. Rosanette, who announces her pregnancy in January, 1849, is not delivered until February, 1851, or twenty-five months later. The most probable explanation of this blunder lies in a hypothetical revision of the pages we have been discussing. The passage concludes, as we have seen, in May, 1850. Had the pregnancy been declared at this point, the term would have been quite normal. My supposition is that, in an earlier redaction, Flaubert had *la Maréchale* reveal her condition close to the end of the chapter, after the description of the Dambreuse salon and household. In rewriting and reorganizing, he changed later the position of the incident, forgetting that in these pages a change of only a few paragraphs could involve a difference in time of sixteen months. Thus, the not very patient Rosanette is forced to endure a pregnancy of Gargantuan duration. In any case, the second transition is accomplished only with considerable confusion.

The concluding episode, beginning with Cécile's marriage to Martinon and Mme Dambreuse's surrender to Frédéric, continues normally from May, 1850 to the *coup d'état* of December, 1851.

The *Education sentimentale* is, then, a story in three episodes: the first of these extends from December, 1840 to August, 1843; the second begins in January, 1847, and ends in July, 1848; the third and last relates events occurring between May, 1850, and December, 1851. Within these episodes, the action of the novel is clearly and soundly established in historical time. It is possible to follow the passage of years and months; the hundreds of allusions to political and social events appear in their proper chronological places.

This scrupulous accuracy in the main body of the novel stands in strange contrast to the peculiar handling of time in the connecting or transitional chapters. In passing from 1843 to 1847, two full years are eliminated from consideration by what appears to be a conscious act of prestidigitation on the part of Flaubert. Thus Frédéric's stay at Nogent is reduced from thirty-nine to fifteen months. The transition from 1848 to 1850 is condensed into twenty-three pages, with the resultant absurdity of Rosanette's twenty-five month pregnancy, an absurdity of which, one trusts, Flaubert was unaware. (pp. 86-92)

Stratton Buck, *"The Chronology of the 'Education Sentimentale',"* in Modern Language Notes, *Vol. LXVII, No. 2, February, 1952, pp. 86-92.*

ANTHONY THORLBY (essay date 1956)

[*In this discussion of Flaubert's development as a writer, Thorlby compares the first and second versions of* Sentimental Education, *focusing especially on the artistry of the later work.*]

Flaubert's earliest works amount to a series of fragmentary confessions in imitation romantic style with such characteristic titles as *Agonies, Les Mémoires d'un fou,* and *Novembre: Fragments de style quelconque.* Like the less successful juvenilia of other writers, their interest is more documentary than literary; they offer, apart from some biographical information, an interesting insight into the development of Flaubert's art. They are emotionally pretentious in their bid for intense imaginative experience, but at the same time self-conscious and genuinely doubtful about the value of all this inwardness. Flaubert realized that there was something of a pose in his cultivation of romantic feeling and played with the idea of whether he really meant it. How could he set himself up as a poet, when, 'speaking of the soul, he began to laugh'? That tormenting question as to the value of it all, which was to inspire his life-long search for an unquestionable form of artistic accomplishment, is the constant theme of his earliest writing. 'What is the good of learning the truth when it is bitter?' The question is merely elaborated in a variety of impassioned contrasts between all the exotic and erotic dreams of romantic adolescence and the bitter truth of misery and decay; but always with the doubt that an impassioned response is vain, because the 'human heart is lost in an enormous solitude', and the passions are but 'travellers in the desert'. (pp. 20-1)

Flaubert grew suspicious of the whole life of feeling and the conventional realms of romantic experience. For it seemed to him that such sentimental self-indulgence prevented him from earning any real experience of life. He has imagined love, beauty, glory, religion, but all these things have remained unrealized, and he is left with nothing except a wasted existence and the sense that he has been cheated of something, that he has exhausted the potentialities of life without ever *really* feeling anything.

Devoured by limitless passions . . . , tempted by all the voluptuous pleasures of thought and desiring all the poetries, all the harmonies . . . I feel annihilated in an abyss of misery . . . I saw no longer anything, I felt nothing . . . I imagined that I had within me a supreme incarnation . . . and that these torments were the life of the god I bore in my entrails. To this magnificent god I sacrificed every hour of my youth; I made of myself a temple to contain a divinity, and the temple remained empty . . . I had no use for real life, and it used me up, consumed me.

Flaubert's emotional overstraining to find even in this experience some real significance was self-defeating. The romantic yearning of the spirit was likely to end simply in a suicidal exhaustion of passion—the fate of Emma Bovary. Everywhere Flaubert perceived the compulsion of some feeling, "freedom, belief, God, virtue', the illusions created by the soul to obscure the ultimate nothingness. When he wanted to leave the spectacle of his own miseries, all he could find was 'the same comedy perpetually repeated with the same actors'.

The fatality which had oppressed me since my youth, now extended itself over the whole world; I watched it operate in all the actions of men as universally as the sun shines on the surface of the earth. It became for me a ghastly divinity which I adored as an Indian does the advancing Colossus that passes over his prostrate body.

Flaubert's realism represents an attempt to express the illusions of feeling without making himself or his work the victim of illusion. It might not be possible to deal with the world in terms of feeling, but realistic fiction offered a way of treating feeling from the point of view of the world. . . . His conception of what the world and reality were was originally determined by the predicament of romantic feeling. Reality was misery, vice, illusion, folly—the predicament of feeling, in fact, looked at from the other side. Reality became interesting at just those points where the vain passions and thoughts of men were sacrificed to it.

There is already in Flaubert's *Novembre* a desire to analyse this reality dispassionately. The scene in which the hero is initiated into the sentimental facts of life as he lies in bed with a prostitute who tells him her story makes a crude mixture of romantic and realistic styles. There is at once the romantic sentiment for a woman who has lived for love, and a realistic sense of the frustration and hopelessness of the situation. The ideal of feeling which she symbolizes is matched against the cynical egoism of men and the commercial foolishness of women. The end of the book describes the hero in the third person, and this break in the narrative form from the first person marks an interesting development in Flaubert's literary career. For the immediate result is an almost complete loss of stature in the hero; when the lyrical passion and integrity of his feelings are taken away, he appears as an aimless young man futilely wasting away his life. Flaubert had found a way of ending his narrative, but not of resolving the problem of feeling.

The first *L'Education sentimentale* (1845) was, as the title suggests, to give fuller treatment to this problem, and it was also Flaubert's first full-length novel. The story is of a young man called Henry who comes to Paris full of extravagant expectations and engages in an adulterous love affair; he leaves behind him in his provincial home-town a friend called Jules, who reminds him of their youthful dreams. What Henry's education teaches him is that reality does not correspond to expectation; what Jules' education teaches him is the unreality of the imaginative life. Again the narrative peters out, with the two friends meeting again in a state of aimless disillusion. Flaubert's new contribution to the problem lies in his understanding of the term 'sentimental'.

Sentimentality has meant many different things in the history of literature. For Flaubert it characterizes the quality of romantic emotion: that is, it is not so much direct or 'real', as associative—less a passion than an aspiration. Thus Henry's feelings for his mistress, his actions, his surroundings are stimulated as much by his associations with the words adultery, adventure and Paris as by the things themselves. And Flaubert notes the same tendency in Jules:

> What made one sorry for him was that he did not know how to distinguish between what is and what should be; he was always suffering from the lack of something, he was perpetually expecting something indefinable which never arrived.

This might be considered a very ordinary state of affairs, but Flaubert's conception of it is distinctive. The very idea of a 'sentimental education' is based on an assumption that every interest, activity and accomplishment is essentially sentimental; if not actually inspired by love, it follows the same pattern of feeling and its value is emotional. Flaubert's realism aimed at analysing this romantic psychology and thus dispelling the illusions of feeling as unreal. His analysis of character is dominated by his concept of the role played by sentimental ideas. The whole spiritual energy of man seemed to him to be devoted to the vain pursuit of love, beauty and happiness. Man develops a 'sentimental' attachment for certain people, things and places, which appear to promise that indefinable something that he

desires. The attachment is sentimental because the feeling and the reality do not correspond to one another, as time invariably shows. But until time has taught its lesson, both heart and mind are at the mercy of their illusions which sentimentalize the world.

The artistic difficulty lay in the fact that, so long as Flaubert tried to realize his idea with the help of a hero, he had to go along with his hero's illusions until he had learnt his lesson. Thus while Flaubert is tracing all the stages of Henry's romantic experiences, he writes sentimentally—to the full extent of his hero's feeling. Further, when the romantic feeling has burnt itself out, there is nothing left, and the hero ceases to have the emotional integrity or interest of a hero. And at this point reality itself becomes uninteresting, because it lacks the association with sentiment. Henry himself is made to realize this dilemma towards the close of the novel. Thoroughly disillusioned, his love exhausted, he is faced with an impossible alternative: not to take it seriously, which is to accept existence at the unpoetic evaluation of the bourgeois mentality he spurns, or, to recognize the eternal nothingness of life's illusions, which leaves him nothing to live for. Henry seems to get over it and becomes a non-entity; Jules evidently chose the second possibility, as Flaubert explains at the moment when his second hero thinks he is in love:

> Was he in love? He doubted it himself later when he had lived for so long an ideal life of the imagination, in the midst of celestial loves and impossible feelings, and came to deny beauty because he had loved it too much and to laugh at all the passions because of the force with which he had studied them. But at this time he was still serious about life with all its illusions, and had not tried to measure his love against the scale of the infinite: a sinister mania which disgusts us with the greatest things and makes us old too early.

So Henry stops believing in love, and Jules stops believing in life; the two terms are wrenched apart and the novel ends. It ends with a kind of survey of material for its possible continuance, but the sentimental liason between reality and feeling has been broken, and there is no artistic incentive left to sustain the fiction. Flaubert had not yet discovered how to detach himself from the sentimental disintegration of his hero and integrate his material on a 'purely' artistic basis.

The final version of the second *L'Education sentimentale,* though it bears little external similarity to the first, illustrates by contrast Flaubert's achievement of artistic detachment. Only the difficulty involved in the convention of a romantic hero survived and caused Flaubert some uneasiness lest the novel fail by the failure of his new pupil, Frédéric Moreau. Flaubert interpreted the central weakness of the first version as a lack of causality in the lives of his heroes. The book had been, he said, 'an attempt to fuse the two sides of my nature', by which he meant the lyrical and the realistic. The question of causality was inevitably a major issue, because each side established a different claim on it. Feeling claimed a heroic determination, while reality exposed a causal helplessness. Flaubert now went to such lengths to stress the objective concomitants to Frédéric's most indeterminate feelings, that he fell into the reverse error from his earlier lyrical extravagance; he characterized the error by saying that 'the background devours the foreground'

Frédéric Moreau and his friends are in danger of becoming mere historical representatives of the various elements which make up the period 1840-1848; their reactions may be satisfactorily explained in terms of the political, artistic or commercial interests of the time. But the action of the novel as a whole betrays the strain of two unreconciled tendencies: Flaubert's desire to integrate his material 'purely objctively', and his concessions to the subjective integrity of his characters. George Sand located the weakness of the novel in 'the absence of any interaction between the characters'. This criticism cannot be taken quite literally; there is both action and interaction, but the two things do not fit together properly. The main theme of the action, which centres around Frédéric's love for Mme. Arnoux, is never fully realized. This is partly because it is an essentially unrealisable passion; when Frédéric first sees her, his 'desire for physical possession disappeared before a profounder longing, in an afflicting curiosity which knew no bounds'. From the start it is a sentimental experience. But the action remains unrealized also on artistic grounds for Flaubert wishes to expose this experience as it is in reality. And here he sees it as a complex of interactions between things and people and events, which inevitably end in disillusion, not because Frédéric 'fails', but because this is how reality is: indifferent to human illusions of feeling. Flaubert has denied his hero the power of effective motivation, but it is not clear whether this is a flaw of character, a weakness in characterisation, or a genuine insight into the really impersonal movement of things. The indeed ambiguous nature of reality is not rendered with complete aesthetic clarity, but interferes with the artistic effectiveness of the novel. There is a suggestion throughout of two planes that never meet, which gives to Frédéric and his friends an appearance of weak incompetence always below the level of their fate.

The artistic integration of the novel is based on a perpetual contrast between feeling and reality. The opening chapters build up a subtle complex of sentiment between the poles of Frédéric's ambition and his mother's expectation, Deslaurier's enthusiasitic plans and Frédéric's love-sick idleness, Mme. Arnoux's perfection and her husband's brash flirtatiousness, Frédéric's idealistic notion of the Parisian *monde* and the tough mentality of bourgeois self-advancement, between all the dreams of love and hope and the cynical practices of commerce in the world. The constant pole of feeling is symbolized in Mme. Arnoux; Frédéric 'was in love with everything connected with Mme. Arnoux, her furniture, her servants, her house, her street'—indeed with Paris itself. Everything in Frédéric's life, from his interest in art to his interest in politics, from his affair with Rosanette to his forsaking of the wealthy widow Dambreuse at the auction of the Arnoux property 'for the sake of Mme. Arnoux', is characterized as a sentimental experience. Frédéric's sentimental response supplies the artistic interest for Flaubert's realistic picture of Parisian society.

Proust likened the style of *L'Education sentimentale* to 'the monotonous, perpetual movement of a moving staircase'. Things, he observed, have as much life as men, and what would conventionally have been action turns into a uniform aesthetic impression. Frédéric's feelings are merely associated with the larger movement of things of which he is a part; at no time is the 'action' associated directly with his point of view and in several scenes he might just as well not be there at all. The end is reached because time runs out on him: a fact which Mme. Arnoux acknowledges when she leaves Frédéric for the last time with a lock of her white hair—'and that was all'.

In concluding the novel Flaubert betrayed the uneasy compromise he had been making all along between his stylistic detachment and his obligations to his hero. He had to wind up the themes he had introduced into his hero's life, and from Frédéric's point of view; at the same time he had to maintain towards the expiry of Frédéric's feelings the stylistic attitude of pure indifference proper to realism. Flaubert resolved this dilemma by administering a series of sentimental shocks to which Frédéric has no further power of response. It is doubtful whether the scenes which dispose of M. Roque and his daughter, Dussardier and Sénécal, Rosanette, Mme. Dambreuse and Mme. Arnoux, and last of all the two friends, Deslauriers and Frédéric, are examples of pure realism or overstrained sentiment. The closing chapter which dispassionately represents Frédéric and Deslauriers talking over old times like men of the world, and leaves them recalling as 'the best time we ever had' how they were once humiliatingly laughed out of a brothel, makes a last, too obvious, contrast with their 'dreams of love' and their 'dreams of power'. This kind of contrast lies at the core of Flaubert's artistic conceptions, but it is always in danger of falling into bathos.

Critics of Flaubert have suggested that there is a biographical explanation of why he made some concession to feeling in *L'Education sentimentale.* Mme. Arnoux, who alone is spared realistic analysis and keeps Frédéric in the role of a romantic hero where she is concerned, has been identified with Mme. Schlésinger for whom Flaubert once conceived a youthful passion. He always looked back on 'the old days', as he later wrote to her, 'as though they were bathed in a golden mist'; and he believed, as Frédéric might have done, that 'what little of value still remains to me, comes from that time'. The explanation seems likely, and would perhaps account for the lengths to which Flaubert went to submerge this feeling in the drift of a historical narrative. Certainly the novel lacks the power of *Madame Bovary,* where the sentimental action merges exactly with the objective analysis of events. (pp. 22-8)

> *Anthony Thorlby, in his* Gustave Flaubert and the Art of Realism, *1956. Reprint by Yale University Press, 1957, 63 p.*

RAYMOND GIRAUD　(essay date 1957)

[*Giraud examines the relationship between money, social class, and romantic attachment in* Sentimental Education. *For additional commentary by Giraud on the novel, see* NCLC, *Vol. 2.*]

Frédéric comes of a modestly well-to-do provincial *rentier* family, is of vaguely aristocratic origin on his mother's side and has expectations of a comfortable inheritance from a rich uncle who has made his money in business. Frédéric and his mother are ashamed of the rich uncle because of his debasing commercial activities; nevertheless, they feel no qualms about looking forward to his death and the inheritance of a fortune that will enable Frédéric to pursue a socially esteemed career like diplomacy. When, very early in the novel, Uncle Barthelémy does die and surprise the Moreaus by willing all his money to Frédéric, there are no tears wasted on him. The Moreaus are unreservedly overjoyed; their ship has finally come in. (p. 162)

There are curious associations in Frédéric's mind between money and his misty love for Marie Arnoux. His half-hearted and inactive courtship of this married woman must be accompanied by signs of a comfortable bourgeois way of life. Like the hero of *Novembre,* he is ashamed of a social and economic position inferior to that of the husband of the woman he loves. His first reaction to unexpected wealth is the joyful thought of how it will affect his relations with Mme Arnoux. The course of Frédéric's sentimental evolution can, in fact, be traced by reference to some crucial moments of his financial history.

The first crisis arrives when Mme Moreau informs her son that as a result of various misfortunes he will inherit an income of only 2,300 francs a year. Although, at the time, many workingmen were obliged to support a family on less than 1,000 francs, Frédéric is crushed by the news. (''Ruined, stripped, lost!'') He curses his fate and savagely wishes to relieve his feeling by beating someone up.

Frédéric's first concern in connection with this revelation of poverty is for his relations with Mme Arnoux. He feels his friendship with the Arnoux is based on his insinuations of great expectations, that Mme Arnoux will despise him as a liar and a fraud. Poor, he can never see her again. ''He could not always live up on the fifth floor, with the door-keeper for his servant, and come calling on her wearing his old black gloves worn blue at the finger tips, a greasy hat, the same frock coat for a year! No! No! Never!''

His despair gives rise to fresh dreams. Frédéric reminds himself that others have been and are as poor as he. He loathes himself for attaching so much importance to money. Without it, he will have all the more reason to accomplish great things. And he already sees himself feverishly at work in a garret, while Mme Arnoux, far from scorning and abandoning him, will be moved to new tenderness by his trials, and admire his energy and courage. This is silly romantic dreaming; Frédéric will never be able to work, and Flaubert despises him for it. What is significant in this action is that one of Frédéric's ideals is unrealizable without wealth, and that another, that of the self-pitying, martyred romantic hero, is awakened by his destitution. Frédéric would never be happy if he were poor. But he has read enough and knows enough about the structure of contemporary society to feel guilty toward those less fortunate than he and to have the feeling, if not the conviction, that money is despicable, is a corrupting influence and is not necessarily related to merit. His relations with Deslauriers, for example, who is poorer—and bitterer—than he, are marked by his feelings of guilt about his social successes and more comfortable situation.

It is again of Mme Arnoux that the hero of the *Education* first thinks when he hears a few months later that he will inherit his uncle's fortune. His immediate reaction to the news takes the form of a dream of the imagined future. ''An income of twenty-seven thousand francs! He was convulsed in a frenzy of joy at the idea of seeing Mme Arnoux once again. With the clarity of a hallucination, he saw himself at her side in her apartment, bringing her some gift wrapped in tissue paper, while before the door stood his tilbury—no! rather a coupé! a black coupé with a manservant in brown livery. He could hear his horse pawing the ground and the clinking of its curb-chain mingling with the murmur of their kisses.''

At this early stage of Frédéric's youth, wealth symbolizes a way of life, that of the elegant, idling dandy, the same sort of life to which Lucien de Rubempré aspired in the second part of *Les Illusions perdues*. There is the added complication that this way of life is important to Frédéric mainly as a requirement for his continued courtship of Mme Arnoux. Frédéric does not seek actively to enrich himself; his material well-being is important to him primarily for sentimental reasons.

Money is also an important factor in Frédéric's relations with Louise Roque and Mme Dambreuse, two women whom he courts but does not love. In both of these affairs, his interest is more selfish and his sentiment is less ethereal. Nevertheless, neither of these relationships is totally exempt of elements that were already present in Flaubert's youthful writings.

Frédéric courts Louise Roque for one reasons: He has lost 60,000 francs on the stock market and has thought of recouping his losses by making a good marriage. Deslauriers reminds him that Louise is available, whereupon Frédéric sets out immediately for Nogent-sur-Seine. There he discovers that both his mother and Louise's father favor the marriage and that the girl is ardently in love with him. Once more, however, it is clear that Frédéric is not uniquely concerned with material gain. He hesitates to reply definitely to Louise's own proposal of marriage and is disturbed and embarrassed by the violence of her passion. Other factors complicate the situation: Frédéric is once more welcome at the Dambreuses; Rosanette seems ready to become his mistress; and he is nostalgic for Paris. Feeling that he is being given no time to come to a decision which presumably he had made before his arrival, Frédéric leaves everything in the air and returns to Paris.

Once back, with a safe distance between himself and the field of action, he is able to deal with the matter in a way that can have no consequences: He dreams about it. ''The idea of getting married no longer seemed exorbitant to him. They would travel, they would go to Italy and to the Orient! And he pictured her standing on a little knoll, viewing the countryside, or clinging to his arm in a Florentine gallery. . . . Once outside her surroundings, in a little time she would make a charming consort. Besides, he was tempted by M. Roque's fortune. Nevertheless, such a consideration repelled him as a weakness, a degradation.''

This action has an element of baseness in it. Frédéric's approach to Louise because of her money is relieved and tempered by his embarrassment, his consciousness of the ignobility of what he has started to do and his inability to carry out his first intentions; but mingled with this combination of weakness and virtue are Frédéric's snobbish feelings about Louise's social origin and her rusticity, her total lack of the maturity of Mme Arnoux, the verve of Rosanette and the sophisticated worldliness of Mme Dambreuse. Thus his rejection of Louise is only partly motivated by virtue; it is also connected with his snobbishness, vanity and indecisiveness.

Mme Dambreuse is quite a different woman, as well as a different social type, from all the others whom Frédéric courts. He had admired her for years before she became his mistress. It was chiefly her social grace, all that she represented of a world above his own, that attracted him to her. This is still the only charm she exerts over him when he becomes her lover and then husband.

> It seemed to Frédéric, as he descended the staircase, that he had become another man, that he was being steeped in the perfumed warmth of a hothouse and was definitely entering the higher society of patrician adultery and lofty intrigue.

> His joy at possessing a rich woman was spoiled by no contrast. The sentiment harmonized with the setting.

This is evidently an echo of Flaubert's earlier lyric dreams of adultery in *Novembre*. Here, of course, he ironizes the sentiment and does not associate himself personally with Frédéric's juvenile vanity and social *arrivisme*. It is at this moment of the action, it would seem, that Flaubert withdraws most of what little sympathy he had retained for his hero.

Frédéric is at first charmed by the novelty of his mistress' social graces. He admires her coolness and aplomb when they are together in company. He contemplates with delight the elegance of her attire and is impressed by the expensive and tasteful gifts she sends him. But these spurs to his senses are soon blunted and ineffective. It becomes particularly disillusioning to see Mme Dambreuse in dresses that display her meager endowments. Frédéric is compelled to counterfeit passion by imagining in their place the fuller charms of Rosanette or Mme Arnoux.

To be excited by the idea of possessing a rich lady of fashion may be an adolescent emotion, yet it is not necessarily a base one. The disillusionment of Frédéric's senses, however, is accompanied by what Flaubert calls a sentimental atrophy. "This atrophy of the feelings left his head entirely free, and more than ever he thought ambitiously of a high position in society. Since he had his foot on such a stepping stone, the least he could do was to make use of it." Frédéric's subsequent marriage is a calculated act, devoid of sentiment. That Dambreuse had left his widow no money is Frédéric's ironically just punishment. Had he married Louise, whose attractions were not entirely limited to her fortune, Frédéric might have fared a bit better, even if she too had been impoverished.

An incident in which Maxime du Camp played a major role is said to have inspired this part of the action of the novel. This is not difficult to believe. Here alone, out of all Frédéric's sentimental adventures, is the pursuit of money and of social position unrestrained by the hero's feelings of disgust, guilt or contempt for his own behavior and untempered by the admixture of other motives and considerations that might evoke some sympathy from the reader. (pp. 163-68)

In short, Frédéric's capacity to love sincerely has been corrupted by the material values of bourgeois society. His potential nobility, his dreams of beauty, are relics of childhood, attenuated or transformed into indecision, the inability to work and a welter of out-of-date juvenile illusions. Frédéric has neither revolted against society nor been integrated into it in a solid and productive way.

Flaubert himself admired a certain kind of bourgeois competence. In the character of Dr. Larivière, who attended Emma Bovary at her deathbed, he raised a memorial to his father, a competent, respected physician, dedicated to the highest ideals of his profession. Some of the virtues of this man were transmitted to his bourgeois-hating son. Flaubert too was dedicated to his work and practiced it with the laboriousness and conscientiousness that distinguished his father's exercise of the profession of medicine. Mme Commanville relates that when she was a little girl, she thought vaguely that the words "Madame Bovary" were a synonym of work. He won the battle that raged within himself, conquering what he considered his juvenile impulses and subjecting himself to a rigid and painful discipline. In Frédéric he paints a man whose will and desires were weaker and who retained only the illusions of his youth. (pp. 168-69)

> Raymond Giraud, "Gustavus Flaubertus Bourgeoisophobus," in his The Unheroic Hero in the Novels of Stendhal, Balzac, and Flaubert, *Rutgers University Press, 1957, pp. 132-84.*

BEN F. STOLTZFUS (essay date 1957)

[*Stoltzfus argues that Frédéric Moreau's love for Madame Arnoux, which Flaubert presents in tandem with other evidence of the protagonist's weakness of character, signals a neurosis involving compulsion and self-destruction.*]

The story of Frédéric Moreau [in *L'education sentimentale*] is a detailed account of the events and circumstances which, with cyclical banality, grind his life into a meaningless void. It is the story of a man whose neurotic love for a woman determines the pattern of his whole existence. It is, as Thierry Maulnier says: "l'applatissement progressif d'une âme par la vie . . . un roman du vide, de l'échec, du néant de l'existence." Moreau's mental decomposition (not to mention the lives of the other characters) begins with Flaubert's significant statement: "C'était lé premier de ses rêves qui s'écroulait," and progresses relentlessly for four hundred pages until he confronts Moreau with the old age of Mme. Arnoux (the final disenchantment). If the novel seems to lack a unity of plot, it does, on the other hand, have an interior unity, that of human motivation, which is the struggle of a neurotic personality to solve an impossible problem. Deslauriers, Moreau's friend, attributes his failure in life to *trop de sentiment.* "Vous êtes mon occupation exclusive,. . . le but, le centre de mon existence." These are the words of Moreau to Mme. Arnoux. She is, indeed, the center of his life, and he is helplessly caught in a blind, self-destructive effort: "si jamais je la trouve, elle me repoussera. Je suis la race des déshérités." This is the essential tragedy of the novel. Moreau feels that he will be rejected, yet in spite of himself, he acts and chooses only through the vision of an obsessive love. As though in a classical tragedy, he acts out his premonitions and affirms the weakness of his character. His character is his fate and the tragedy is within himself. In fact, lost hopes and ambitions litter the pages of the book. And a lack of identity as a person is perhaps his most significant personality trait. If in the existentialist sense we define ourselves by choice and action, Moreau lives in the empty world of his undefined self. An inner conflict breeds his irresistible attachment to Mme. Arnoux. It is not enough however, to say that he acts through too much sentiment. Perhaps we can shed some light on his problem by searching for the answers to the three following questions. (1) Why was his love for Mme. Arnoux so dominant as to exclude practical contact with reality? (2) Why, when the occasion did present itself, was he incapable of fulfilling his major desire, that of possessing her? (3) Why was he blindly obedient to her wishes?

Flaubert hints at an answer both at the beginning and at the end of the book. In the beginning, Moreau has just seen Marie Arnoux on the boat and he is walking on the road, alone: "Il cria très haut 'Marie!' Sa voix sé perdit dans l'air. Une large couleur de pourpre enflammait le ciel à l'occident. . . . Un chien se mit à aboyer dans une ferme, au loin. Il frissonna, pris d'une inquiétude sans cause." Leaving aside the romantic element of the dog barking, let us visualize Moreau calling "Marie!" at the top of his voice. He has seen her only once, yet she is "le point lumineux où l'ensemble des choses convergeait." It is not enough merely to say that this was "love at first sight." This seems to have for him a profound emotional significance. The name, "Marie," the flaming sky, his anxiety, all are premonitions, the prelude to the drama of his life, which, as we read on, unfolds with relentless determinism. What is this "inquiétude"? Just prior to the cry of longing, or suffering, or anxiety, or perhaps all three, Moreau had been riding "bercé par le mouvement de la voiture, les paupières à demi closes, le regard dans les nuages, il s'abandonnait à une joie rêveuse et infinie." He is daydreaming and free-associating and perhaps bringing to consciousness repressed material from his subconscious. His compulsion to cry out seems to indicate this. The resultant anxiety tells us that perhaps all is not well, that, as Carl Jung says, repressed desires fester in our flesh (*Modern Man in Search of a Soul*), that they affect our behavior in unpredictable ways, with a notorious disregard for will-power (this being Moreau's weakness). What is the nature of these repressed desires? Freudians speak of the child's sexual attachment to the mother, his rivalry with the father for the mother's affections, and the repression of guilt because of the incest taboo. Flaubert suggests an analogous reason for Moreau's behavior. Mme. Arnoux has come to see him for the last time and he suspects that she has decided to offer herself to him. Yet, in spite of his desire, "il sentait quelque chose d'inexprimable, une répulsion, et comme l'effroi d'un inceste." Significant also is the fact that whenever we meet Mme. Arnoux she is with her children. Descriptions of her house, her room, her garden, her visits, always include their presence. Henry James objects to her as a character on the grounds that she does not realy live. But is that really so? Are we not seeing her exclusively through Moreau's love-sick eyes? And we see her therefore, as an obsession, a mother image, a symbol of purity, honor, virtue, and devotion to family. Moreau cannot bring himself to violate this ideal though the occasion presents itself many times (the dramatic episode of the sick child with the membranous croup being only an exception to the general rule, and Moreau, by renting a room in a cheap hotel, only temporarily degrades this "purity").

Moreau's weakness of character is but an elaboration of this central theme, his obsessive love for Mme. Arnoux. His weakness, however, is essentially a manifestation of his divided self. He lives in her shadow. Her choices are his choices, her whims are his laws, her troubles are his cue for resolute action. She was for him "une manière générale de sentir." His altruism stems merely from his incapacity to live without seeing her. He decides to get a *Conseil d'Etat* job because Mme. Arnoux thinks it would be good for him. He neglects an important business rendezvous with M. Dambreuse in order to go to the country to see her. He sleeps with Rosanetta to avenge his hurt pride: "ça me vengera!" He defends Mme. Arnoux's reputation in a duel, and he was finally "plein de désirs contradictoires et ne sachant même plus ce qu'il voulait. . . ."

We might ask if this is the behavior of a well-adjusted personality. A psychologist would in all probability say no. Moreau's actions are compulsive, and in the long run self-destructive. He is not choosing for himself, but for his shadow, represented by his neurotic love for Mme. Arnoux. His choices, therefore, are negative and self-damaging; they do not resolve the conflict, they merely perpetuate it and thus increase his sense of futility. The tragic aspect of Moreau's life is that he tries alternate solutions only to fail miserably. Flaubert offers him all possible choices. The physical love of Rosanette, the social position of Mme. Dambreuse, the complete love of Louise Roque. Ultimately he rejects all of them. Yet Mme. Arnoux is unattainable and he knows it. That is why Moreau feels the ennui, the "néant de son existence," as Maulnier calls it. He has arrived at an impasse. With Mme. Arnoux gone "il éprouvait une tristesse démesurée, une envie de mourir." This is the reason for his inevitable return to her. He needs her as a child needs its mother and he also needs the love she can offer him as a man. Yet caught in the ambivalence of his attitudes he is unable to reconcile his vision of her as a mother image and as a potential mistress. Caught in the web of his own neurotic personality he functions in an undifferentiated world in which the facts of external "reality" cede to the force of his inner compulsions. We are confronted therefore, at the end of the book, with a total nihilism. Moreau rejects all that he ever wanted, and Mme. Arnoux, in a symbolic gesture, cuts her hair and leaves the faded strands of her sex on his bed.

This moment in his life, which was to have been the most sublime, is empty, meaningless, and her gesture, like a Joycian epiphany, casts sudden insight into the useless cycle of Moreau's existence. (pp. 509-11)

Ben F. Stoltzfus, "The Neurotic Love of Frédéric Moreau," in The French Review, *Vol. XXXI, No. 2, December-January, 1957-58, pp. 509-11.*

HARRY LEVIN (essay date 1963)

[*Levin is an American educator and critic whose works reveal his wide range of interests and expertise. He has long been an influential advocate of comparative literature studies, and he has written seminal works on the literature of several nations, including* James Joyce: A Critical Introduction; The Power of Blackness: Hawthorne, Poe, Melville; *and* The Gates of Horn: A Study of Five French Realists. *In the latter work, from which the following excerpt is drawn, Levin discusses Flaubert as a realist who attempts to uncover and depict the sentimentality and illusion of his age. Here, he probes autobiographical elements in* Sentimental Education *and briefly considers its characters, setting, artistry, and point of view.*]

Though the full and final *Education sentimentale*, from its flashback of boyhood to its epilogue in middle age, covers thirty-five years, the story itself falls within the crucial decade, 1840-1851, and the central section is closely synchronized with the happenings of 1848. Those dates perforce had broadened Flaubert's subject, assigning to politics a share of the attention that had hitherto been concentrated on love. But the novel parallels his youthful confessions by starting from the grand Platonic passion of Flaubert's lifetime. Though the cherished heroine, Madame Arnoux, "looked like the women in romantic books," she was tenderly drawn from life—or rather, from memory. Her husband, Jacques Arnoux, the proprietor of *L'Art industriel*, seems to have been modelled upon the music publisher Maurice Schlésinger, of whom Wagner has left us a much less amiable portrait. Madame Schlésinger's biography, it would seem, was actually more eventful than Flaubert's delicate version of it would suggest. Indeed, because of an imprudent first marriage, about which he cannot have known, she was not yet married to the father of her child when the three made such a binding impression upon young Flaubert. Life, in this instance more romantic than literature, was tamed and muted by it. His devotion, like his hero's, was kept alive by the necessity of worshipping from afar, where fulfillment would undoubtedly have broken the spell. Frédéric Moreau's revulsion from Marie Arnoux, many years later, is "like the dread of incest." Their reunion, based again on actuality, is a last farewell. Leaving him a lock of her white hair, she kisses him on the forehead "like a mother."

Except for this encircling situation, *L'Education sentimentale* is not an autobiography. Frédéric ceases to be identifiable with Flaubert from the day he passes his law examinations. When he courts the wordly Madame Dambreuse, he seems to be retracing the slippery footsteps of Maxime Du Camp, with whom Flaubert had witnessed the Paris insurrection. Du Camp himself had written *Mémoires d'un suicidé* and *Les Forces perdues*, two weak novels about weak young men, contemporaries of his and Flaubert's and Frédéric's. Flaubert's book was characteristically strong, but it was concerned with the same groping protagonist, the composite post-romantic, the generic veteran of 'forty-eight. "I want to write the moral history—sentimental would be truer—of the men of my generation," he had explained, hesitating significantly over the adjective [see excerpt dated 6 October 1864]. The title might apply to all of his novels, Proust would point out, and not least to **Madame Bovary**. For, in substituting *sentiments* for *moeurs*, the novel shifts from an objective to a subjective approach; and if sentiments may be defined as untested emotions and illusory ideas, then Flaubert proposed to apply the test of reality. "What does that mean, reality?" asks his painter, Pellerin. "Some see black, others see blue, most people see stupidly." Few of them are cold-blooded enough to be clear-sighted; their vision is colored by lovers' reveries or politicians' slogans. The sentimentalist, the man who lives by illusions, has been let down more gently in English fiction than in French. In sounding the hollowness of sentimentality, Flaubert was performing the habitual task of the realist. But instead of pointing his attack at a single illusion, as Brandes acutely remarked [see *NCLC*, Vol. 2], he simultaneously tackled all the contradictions and disappointments of an illusion-ridden age.

Was there anything left that was not illusion, any manifestation of Schopenhauer's countervailing force, the will? Not in that tired liberal, "that man with very weakness," that hero foredoomed to failure, Frédéric Moreau. Henry James's description of him as an abject and inferior human specimen, "positively too poor for his part" [see excerpt dated 1902], bounces back when Edmund Wilson describes him as "a perfect Henry James character." Yet the part calls for indecision and ineffectuality because Frédéric's position is a false one. Because of his emotional involvement with Marie Arnoux, he responds half-heartedly to every other stimulus. Pampered by a private income— and, when he has run through that, a second inheritance—he dabbles as a dilettante among the serious pursuits of other men. Having grown up under the tutelage of Werther and René, having dreamed—like Lucien de Rubempré—of becoming "the Walter Scott of France," Frédéric has been speeded to Paris by the advice of his brash friend Deslauriers, to emulate the heroes of the *Comédie humaine*. Alas, he shows neither the ambition of Rastignac nor, for that matter, the sensibility of Julien Sorel. The young man of the 'thirties, the Amaury of Sainte-Beuve's *Volupté*, had erred with conviction and sinned with enthusiasm. No source of comparison is more revealing than the scene in which Balzac's hero, standing upon the heights of Père-Lachaise between a funeral and a dinner engagement, flings his dramatic challenge to the city. Bearing this in mind, consider the passage where Frédéric walks home from his first dinner with Madame Arnoux, and Flaubert rounds off his sensitive impressions with an irony which is almost a repudiation:

> The gas-lamps gleamed in two straight lines indefinitely, and long red flames wavered in the profundity of the water. It was the color of slate, while the sky, which was clearer, seemed to be upheld by large masses of shadow which arose on both sides of the river. Some buildings, which were hardly noticeable, augmented the darkness. A luminous haze floated over the roofs beyond; all the noises mingled in one monotonous hum; a light breeze stirred.
>
> He had stopped in the middle of the Pont-Neuf. Bareheaded, chest expanded, he breathed in the air. All the while he felt as if something unquenchable were welling up from the depths of his being, a flow of tenderness which left him weak, like the movement of the waves before his eyes. Slowly the clock of a church struck one, like a voice calling to him.
>
> Then he was seized by one of those shudders of the soul in which you seem to be transported to a higher world. An extraordinary power, whose purpose he did not know, had come to him. He seriously asked

himself whether to be a great painter or a great poet; and he decided in favor of painting, for the requirements of that profession would bring him close to Madame Arnoux. So he had found his vocation! The aim of his existence was now clear, and the future infallible.

Painting is an anticlimax, as law and literature have been, and as business and politics will turn out to be. Yet if Frédéric does not climb so high as Rastignac, at least he does not sink so low as Rubempré, and his dearly bought failures retain a muddling idealism which would be absent from the cheap success of *Bel-Ami*. Maupassant's ladies' man will complete the demoralization of the hero, after the Second Empire has dissipated the Napoleonic ideal. For Frédéric the boudoir proves more hazardous than the barricade. While the Reform Banquets are kindling a revolution, he is arranging a rendezvous with Madame Arnoux. She fails to come at the last moment, and he "reforms" on the rebound by spending the night with Arnoux's mistress, Rosanette. Next day that pathetic little tart declares herself for the Republic "as Monsieur the Archbishop of Paris had already done," continues Flaubert, "and as would do, with a marvellous quickness of zeal, the magistracy, the council of state, the Institute, the marshals of France . . . all the Bonapartists, all the legitimists, and a considerable number of Orleanists." But, having preferred the matronly Madame Arnoux to his girlish fiancée Louise Roque, Frédéric now neglects Rosanette for the wife of the aristocratic capitalist Dambreuse. It is a far cry from the bohemianism of the studios to the business transacted in her salon. "The majority of the men there had served at least four governments; and they would have sold France or the human race to guarantee their fortunes, to save themselves trouble or embarrassment, or even out of simple meanness or instinctive adoration of power."

As for the people, when Frédéric has the leisure to watch them fighting in the streets, looting the Tuileries, or sprawling on the throne itself, he agrees that "heroes smell bad." The uprising of February gives way to the suppressions of June as the middle class, dressed in the uniform of the National Guard, steps in. The crusty Père Roque, after shooting a youth who has begged for bread, rushes home to lunch, and goes to bed crying: "Oh, these revolutions!. . . I am too sensitive!" Yet if power corrupts, for Flaubert, enslavement ennobles, conferring tragic dignity upon one character in his gallery of radicals. This is Dussardier, the man of good will who became a revolutionist because he happened to be walking down the Rue Transnonain when the bloody reprisals occurred which made that street a synonym for counter-revolution. His love of simple justice and hatred of the police are juxtaposed to the rigid theories and utopian authorities of Sénécal, who combines "the reason of a geometrician with the faith of an inquisitor." These gifts equip the latter to rationalize the dialectic of those events which convert him into a factory-manager and then a police-agent. The climax arrives with the *coup d'état* of 1851, when Dussardier's last outcry of "Vive la République!" is cut off by Sénécal's pistol-shot—a denouement which subsequent events have converted into a parable. Frédéric, a witness to this episode, has just witnessed another revelation: the marriage of the opportunistic Deslauriers, a prefect under the incoming regime, to the heiress Louise. Again, as when Frédéric missed both Madame Arnoux and the insurrection, private and public frustrations have converged.

Repeatedly and decisively he has missed the boat. Everything has conspired, as it were, to fail him. A feeble duel has been stopped at the first scratch. Rash speculations and friendly loans have cost him his second fortune. His political candidacy has gone by default. After a fraudulent bankruptcy and a disastrous trial, the Arnoux *ménage* has fled to the provinces. The auction of their effects, so hallowed by his sentiments, is the final disintegration. Every blow of the auctioneer's hammer knocks down an illusion. What, after all, has Frédéric Moreau learned in the school of experience? Not the esthete's "secret of success in life," nor the mellow wisdom that ultimately rewarded the conscientious endeavors of Wilhelm Meister. Though Goethe laid down the pedagogical formula, Flaubert's conclusions have more in common with the self-deprecating ironies of that pedagogue *manqué*, that assistant professor of failure, Henry Adams. For both, the educational process is less a matter of learning than of unlearning, the result of which is negative— even, for Frédéric, nihilistic. Yet for the reader, Flaubert told Du Camp, his book taught history-lessons which, had there been time to meditate upon them, might have prevented France from returning to the barricades in 1870. Was it to be taken as Flaubert's critique of revolution, even as Stendhal's writing had been a critique of reaction? Why then should it evoke such admiration from the syndicalist author of *Réflexions sur la violence*, Georges Sorel? Its pros and contras, its manifestoes and credos, operate to neutralize each other. Rulers and reformers, proletarians and police appear and vanish in turn, like the visions that bedevil Saint Antoine. Instead of Sancho Panza's two eternal parties, the Haves and the Have-Nots, Deslauriers adds the historic dimension by distinguishing three, all of them impelled by the very same motive: "those who have, those who no longer have, and those who try to have."

Flaubert stands aside from all of them. He indicates his own role when he testifies in a letter, "I have been present as a spectator at nearly all the riots of my time." Bored and passive as Frédéric himself, he had marched with the National Guard. Living through the official lies of the Second Empire, he became retrospectively interested in the missed opportunities of the Second Republic. The abyss across which he viewed them interposed a coldness in the most heated debates, a dryness in the most exciting conspiracies. Though *L'Education sentimentale* is subtitled *Histoire d'un jeune homme*, its outlook is replete with weariness and apathy. "Ouf! I have finished my mournful work," he wrote to Du Camp. "Our entire youth has just passed before me. I am broken up over it." In the book, after Frédéric's anticlimactic reunion with Madame Arnoux, he has another with his unfaithful friend Deslauriers, who—always too clever for his own good—is also pretty much the worse for wear. Reverting together nostalgically to anecdotes of their shared adolescence, they recall an occasion when Frédéric's trepidations kept them from entering a local brothel. Now Deslauriers echoes his agreement with Frédéric: "We were better off then!" Thus the last word expresses our perennial yearning for innocence, our universal revulsion from guilty knowledge. It rounds out the book by protesting against wasted years, frustrated loves, corrupted hopes. It throws light on Flaubert's arrested emotional development, his lifelong desire to be sheltered from the contingencies of adult existence, his single-minded concentration on what ordinary men regard as a casual pastime. It suggests explanations for the reduplicating patterns of friendship that run through his work, for the maternal images in which his most impressive heroines are shaped.

Immediately after her husband dies, Madame Dambreuse proposes to Frédéric, who entertains her proposal for mercenary reasons. The sterility of this connection is symbolized when, discovering that the money is bequeathed elsewhere, she sits beside the emptied strong-boxes like "a mother in mourning before an empty cradle." It was a sick child, claiming a mother's attention and incidentally recovering, who thwarted Frédéric's assignation with Madame Arnoux. It is more than coincidental that the token of his relations with Rosanette should be an illegitimate child who dies in infancy. A pitiful and hideous pastel of the dead infant, "a veritable *nature morte*," is sketched by Pellerin—and by Flaubert as well. His notes show that he had prepared himself with particular thoroughness on the pathology of children's diseases. Nothing could more strongly emphasize this Flaubertian trait than the manner in which Octave Feuillet, whose *jeune homme pauvre* is so debonair a contemporary of Frédéric, glides over the scientific details of a similar case: "We shall not dwell upon this scene of poignant cruelty. . . ." The Flaubert that loved animalities was not less strongly attached to such situations by their latent tenderness. In his own childhood he had cultivated a precociously morbid streak; in later life he preserved an ever-youthful sense of wonder. Hence the underlying contradiction of Flaubert's personality reasserts itself in *L'Education sentimentale*, where the dispirited banalities that his theme presents are redeemed by a poet's freshness of perception. When Remy de Gourmont was moved to call it "our *Odyssey*, and the most beautiful poem in French," he was not simply indulging in mock-heroic overstatement. For Flaubert's Dublin disciple, James Joyce, would demonstrate anew how the wanderings of a latter-day Odysseus could be charted against the divagations and distractions of the city.

After the pallid human figures, spectators rather than actors, have been relegated to the sidelines, it is Paris that occupies the foreground of *L'Education sentimentale*—not the flamboyantly romantic metropolis of Balzac, but a more subdued, more subtle, more poetic vista. The narration detaches itself sharply from the characters, while lingering suggestively over the setting. The description is all but untranslatable: words move, lights "balance," shades "descend." Intermittent rain, the rain that beats through the cadences of Verlaine and Rimbaud, dampens the greying soul of Flaubert's protagonist. Through Frédéric we apprehend the sight and smell of gaslight, the rumbling of the omnibuses, the sensation of wet pavements, and—whenever he goes to the country—"a nostalgia for the boulevards." The pace and direction of the novel are set by his dilatory walks through the streets, and accelerated by the march of history to the abortive climax of street-fighting. To render "the great city with all its noises," rustling around his heroine "like an orchestra," Flaubert has utilized every artistic medium. Step back and squint: the ugliest negations of his subject assume a positive beauty of composition; the most embittered controversies dissolve into a mood of esthetic contemplation. The term "impressionism" would not be current until 1874, when Monet exhibited his *Impression: soleil leyant;* but members of that school were gathering at Batignolles when Flaubert published his book, and of them it constantly reminds us: of Pissarro, when Frédéric strolls down the boulevard; of Manet, when he joins his friends at a café; of Monet, when he glimpses reflections in the river; of Degas, when he takes Rosanette to the races; of Renoir, when he kneels at the feet of Madame Arnoux. (pp. 223-31)

> *Harry Levin, "Flaubert," in his* The Gates of Horn: A Study of Five French Realists, *Oxford University Press, 1963, pp. 214-304.*

VICTOR BROMBERT (essay date 1966)

[Brombert explores the importance of the prostitution theme in Sentimental Education, *commenting particularly on the brothel*

scene. For additional commentary by Brombert on Sentimental Education, *see NCLC, Vol. 2.]*

Ten years after the publication of *L'Éducation sentimentale,* Flaubert was still pained by the critics' hostile reaction. To his friend Turgenev, he wrote in 1879: "Without being a monster of pride, I consider that this book has been unfairly judged, especially the end. On this score I feel bitter toward the public." Few endings of novels have indeed baffled, even outraged more readers. The hero's flat assertion that an adolescent excursion to a brothel has been the most precious experience of a lifetime confirmed suspicions that Flaubert was an incurable cynic. It was bad enough that the "hero," Frédéric Moreau, after a life distinguished by failure, returns to the somnolence of a provincial existence, a death-in-life which corresponds to a total abdication and to a permanent vocation for nothing. But did the author have to bring Frédéric and Deslauriers together in this scene, pointing up the weakness and bad faith inherent in their reconciliation? Did he have to indulge in an inventory of decay? And does the exalted expedition to the provincial bawdyhouse not cheapen whatever might have been salvaged (the very memory of Mme Arnoux!) by stressing venal love and by linking almost perversely the prurient excitement of early adolescence with the impotence of precocious senility?

Yet Flaubert felt surer of the validity of this scene than of almost any other scene in the novel. Endings were for him a matter of utmost concern even when, as in *Madame Bovary* or *L'Éducation sentimentale,* they may at first appear like an unfunctional appendix. But the anticlimactic last three chapters in *Madame Bovary* are far from gratuitous. In *L'Éducation sentimentale,* the ending is even more intimately bound up with the very structure and meaning of the book. Paradoxically, it almost engenders the very beginning. It is an epilogue, no doubt: but this epilogue echoes and parallels one of the earliest passages in the book. I refer to the second chapter, which is partly a flashback to Frédéric's and Deslauriers' childhood, and partly an early conversation between the two friends as they look forward to the future, but already have a past to talk about. Thus the book can be said to begin and to close with a conversation between Frédéric and Deslauriers in which projects or reminiscences take priority over action. The immediate effect of this extension in time (the prologue carries us back to 1833, the epilogue forward to the winter of 1868) is a feeling of temporal circularity and erosion. All the dreams have come to nought. And already during the first conversation, the light the two friends can see shining from the small window of the *maison basse,* the house of ill repute, seems like a shimmering symbol of unattainable desire. "I am of the race of the disinherited," says Frédéric, convinced before the event that no worthwhile woman will ever love him. In the meantime, they do not have enough money to respond to the blinking light. But they do remember a common adventure of some years back, the same adventure that, twenty-seven years later, they will tell each other, agreeing that it had been the best moment of their lives. "C'est là ce que nous avons eu de meilleur."

If, however, we look at this last scene more closely, we must notice that the bordello motif is not exploited for its sheer anecdotal value, nor even primarily to allow for the devastating final comment. The episode, as remembered by the two friends—though it occurred some time before the events of the novel itself—does in fact sum up, in miniature fashion, a whole pattern of events and meanings. What happened is banal enough: on a late Sunday afternoon, the two boys plucked some flowers, gathered them into bouquets and proceeded furtively to the house of "La Turque."

Frédéric presented his bouquet, like a boyfriend to his fiancée. But the heat of the day, the fear of the unknown, a kind of remorse, and even the excitement of seeing at a glance so many women at his disposal, affected him so much that he grew very pale and could neither move nor speak. They all laughed, amused at his embarrassment. Thinking that he was being made fun of, he ran away; and since he had the money, Deslauriers was forced to follow him.

Several aspects of this passage deserve analysis. To begin with, the author provides here a subtly nuanced sketch of Frédéric's character. The naïve gesture of appearing with flowers at a brothel points up a latent and ineffectual idealism. The comparison with the boyfriend and his fiancée is touching enough, but suggests a tendency to see reality through a deforming imagination. The heat which paralyzes him reminds us of many other states of dreamy indolence in Frédéric's life. The vague sense of guilt, which, one must assume, is here related to a mother-image, is elsewhere associated with the pure and "maternal" image of Marie Arnoux. The multiplicity of women making the choice impossible corresponds not only to the constant and inconclusive wavering, within the novel, from one woman to another, but to Frédéric's basic inability to focus on anything and impose a single direction on his life. The immobility, the speechlessness and the ultimate flight underline a chronic timidity, the fear of judgment and humiliation. Thus he also tears up his first letter to Mme Arnoux: ". . . he did nothing, attempted nothing—paralyzed by the fear of failure." And the flight itself corresponds, of course, to a flight from the realities of the capital and a return to the sheltered life of the province.

But there is more to this passage. The naïve arrival in the whorehouse, the flustered departure, the very *fiasco* of the expedition symbolize the poetic illusion that clings tenaciously to unfulfilled love. It symbolizes the orgyless orgy, the love-dream remaining pure because it was unrealized. After all, Frédéric leaves "La Turque" chaste! The debauches have been of the imagination: mere velleities. So that the final comment ("C'est là ce que nous avons eu de meilleur"), far from being exclusively a cynical remark, or a symptom of arrested development, must also be interpreted as a lasting nostalgia for innocence. This preference for the past conceals another form of idealism. Memory illumines. And although both friends seem to have lost everything, this final dialogue between the man who sought Love and the man who sought Power reveals that it is the search for Love (no matter how clumsy and frustrating) which retrospectively bestows the only meaning. The episode thus combines, in the most ambiguous manner, touching illusion and adult disillusionment, flights of fancy and retreat into the self, attraction to the multiform manifestations of life and paralysis caused by the very proliferation of forms and possibilities, eternally youthful memories and the pathos of aging. In other words, it is a retrospective prolepsis of the very essence of the novel. Even the relationship of Frédéric and his friend is prefigured in the terse remark that since the one had the money, the other was obliged to follow him!

The bordello motif, or in a more general sense the image of the Prostitute and the theme of Prostitution, is at the core of *L'Éducation sentimentale.* Frédéric's erotic sensibility and erotic dreams as a boy crystallize around visions of satin-covered boudoirs where he and his friend will experience "fulgurant orgies with illustrious courtesans." Such exotic passions are inevitably linked to dreams of success. He and Deslauriers spend so many hours constructing and peopling their harems that they are as exhausted as though they had indulged in real debauches. Later, when Frédéric actually penetrates into the world of Parisian women, he is almost overcome by the luxurious *odor di femmina.* There is, to be sure, a certain literary tradition behind this particular mystique of the senses. Romanticism had cast the eternal hetaera, whether simple *fille de joie* or high-class courtesan, in the role of initiator into the deep mysteries of life. Even social, artistic and political success—in nineteenth-century literature—is often related to one form or another of prostitution. Such literary expressions no doubt correspond to certain social and psychological patterns: the bourgeois adolescent looked at the prostitute with mixed feelings of admiration, contempt, desire to redeem and even a yearning for profanation. There is for instance a curious letter from Alfred Le Poittevin to Flaubert which tells of the young man's desire to desecrate in the company of a whore places where he has been "young and credulous." As for Flaubert himself, it is clear that he is haunted by the image of the prostitute, whom he associates, in an almost Baudelairean manner, with equally complex monastic and ascetic urges.

In the novel, the bordello motif and the theme of prostitution assume in part a satiric function. The world of the *lorettes* into which Frédéric is ironically introduced by Mme Arnoux's husband, appears to him at first in the guise of a masked ball, where the most tempting display of flesh, costumes and poses inevitably brings to mind the variegated offerings of an elegant house of prostitution providing "specialties" for every whim. Frédéric is so dazzled that, during the first moments, he can distinguish only silk, velvet and naked shoulders. Then, gradually, he takes stock of the contents of this Parisian seraglio: the languorous Polish beauty, the placid and falsely modest Swiss siren, the provocative Fishwife, the Primitive with peacock feathers, the avid Bacchante, the carnival Workwoman— all the "refinements of modern love" dance before him, and the beads of perspiration on their foreheads further suggest a hothouse atmosphere. This scene, ending in a collective hangover the following morning, recalls the famous Taillefer orgy in Balzac's *La Peau de chagrin:* the same display of available carnality, the same specter of disease and death, the same garish coupling of the lascivious and the macabre. Only Flaubert is not concerned with sheer pyrotechnics. He is not out to rival Petronius' description of decadence in the *Satyricon.* His aim is neither sensational nor allegorical. He works and weaves his images patiently and deliberately into the general pattern of the novel. But there are some immediate effects, and the most noteworthy is a vertiginous proliferation of forms and gestures which ultimately transforms human beings into mechanized objects. In her drunken stupor, one of the women imitates "the oscillation of a launch."

The easy-virtued world of Rosanette is not the only one to be described in terms of lupanar images. Frédéric's suggestive vision imposes these very same images onto the assembly of elegant feminine guests in the salon of Mme Dambreuse. The upper-class ladies all sit in a row, "offering" their bosoms to the eye; the rustling of their gowns suggests that dresses are about to slip down. The lack of expression on their faces is in perverse contrast to their "provocative garments." The animal-like placidity of these ladies in décolleté evokes the "interior of a harem." Flaubert's intention becomes quite explicit, for he adds: "A more vulgar comparison came to the young man's mind." Here too, the salon provides a sampling of physical and regional types to satisfy every possible taste: English beauties with keepsake profiles, Italians with ardent eyes, three Norman sisters "fresh as apple trees in April"—an alluring

and appetizing display of sophisticated impudicity. The total effect is once again dehumanization: the crescendo of feminine chatter sounds like the cackle of birds.

Even public locales (cafés, restaurants, *bals publics*) are seen as places of prostitution, for instance the Alhambra, where, according to Deslauriers, one can easily get to know "women." The exotic name corresponds to fake exotic architecture, or rather to jarring elements of architecture: Moorish galleries, the restaurant side in the form of a Gothic cloister, Venetian lanterns, a Chinese roofing over the orchestra, neoclassical painted cupids. This shocking combination is not merely a sign of vulgarity. It represents the particular attempt at facile poetry, or rather at facile estrangement, which is the special function of all purveyors of bought pleasures. In this light, the bordello becomes the convenient metaphor for any catering to the thirst for illusion. The Alhambra provides sensual pleasures for the public. The reader witnesses a collective debauchery: the last firecracker of the evening provokes an orgastic sigh. But in reality, nothing really happens. The policemen who wake up Frédéric on the boulevard bench where he has fallen asleep, and who are convinced that he has "fait la noce," are as wrong as his own mother concerning his visit to "La Turque." For Frédéric, it has been an innocent orgy, combining in characteristic fashion exposure to depravity with an exacerbated yearning for ideal love. Frédéric's only activity right after the Alhambra is to stare at Mme Arnoux's window.

This aspect of the metaphorical unity of *L'Éducation sentimentale* is further strengthened by the presence of key characters who, in one form or another, are for sale. The most important of these is Rosanette Bron, "La Maréchale." That Rosanette is a kept woman, and most often kept by several men at the same time, is of course no secret. Her true calling is perhaps never more graphically suggested than by her portrait, commissioned by M. Arnoux, eventually purchased by Frédéric, but which in the meantime stands exposed in the window of a gallery with the following words written in black letters underneath: "Mme Rose-Annette Bron, appartenant à M. Frédéric Moreau, de Nogent." True to her vocation, she specializes, one might say, in sexual provocation. Innumerable passages in the novel stress this talent. Her laughter has a whiplike effect on Frédéric's nerves. At times, she assumes the poses of a "provocative slave." Most often, her sex appeal is less indolent: her way of pulling up her stockings, her movements, her very chignon are "like a challenge." When she eats, and the redness of the fruit mixes with the purple of her lips, the insolence of her look fills Frédéric with mad desires. As for her innumerable caprices, her disconnected cravings, they correspond to the usual versatility associated with the prostitution metaphor; only here the multiplicity of forms and possibilities is internalized. The capricious, unpredictable nature of Rosanette also corresponds to her treachery—and in a broader sense, to the theme of treason so important in this novel. Hers is partially an irresponsible type of cruelty best exemplified by her coldly abandoning Frédéric at the Café Anglais after accepting from de Cisy a bracelet with three opals.

A far more cold-blooded selfishness is the main feature of the "grande dame," the regal prostitute Mme Dambreuse. Frédéric finds that she has something "languorous" and "dry." Her sterile cupidity appears in full light when, after the death of her husband, and in the presence of her lover, she stares, disconsolate, into the empty strong box! As for the perfidious Vatnaz, the eternal procuress, she provokes only disgust. The mere touch of her "thin, soft hand" sends shivers down Frédéric's spine. The world of Paris thus insistently proposes to Frédéric images of prostitution: *lorettes* at the hippodrome; streetwalkers under the gaslight; scenes of slave markets with lewd sultans and cheap puns in boulevard plays. At the horse races, he glimpses an obscenely made-up queen of the burlesque theater known as the "Louis XI of prostitution." Everywhere he turns, it would seem that, as in Baudelaire's *Tableaux parisiens*, "La Prostitution s'allume dans les rues."

But actual prostitution is of course not the only form of prostitution. There are less literal manifestations, all pointing to some manner of depravity. For the bordello motif is closely bound up with Frédéric's apprenticeship of life. His "education" in Paris—the subject as well as the title of the novel place it squarely in the tradition of the *Bildungsroman*—is to begin with the discovery of one type or another of pandering, cheapening or desecration. One could almost take one by one every character and every activity. The very name of Arnoux's hybrid establishment, *L'Art industriel,* is like a profanation of art. And his career sadly illustrates this profanation: an amateur painter, he is in turn director of an art magazine, an art dealer, the owner of a pottery factory manufacturing "artistic" soup plates and mythological decorations for bathrooms. With every chapter he takes a step down. After designing letters for signboards and wine labels, and going bankrupt through shady deals, he has the idea of a *café chantant* and of a military hat-making business, and he finally winds up dealing in beads and cheap "religious art." The very word "décadence" aptly sums up his career. There is the same brutal deflation in the life of Pellerin, the painter who wanted to rival Veronese, then places his art in the service of politics, and ends up being a professional photographer. The actor Delmar, a coarse histrion, similarly illustrates the prostitution of art: he sells out his vulgar talent to political parties, and gives public recitals of humanitarian poetry on . . . prostitution. This propensity for selling out is most strikingly symbolized by the epitaph-like résumé of the life of the financier Dambreuse, who "had acclaimed Napoleon, the Cossacks, Louis XVIII, 1830, the working-man, every régime, adoring Power with such intensity that he would have paid in order to have the opportunity of selling himself."

As for Frédéric himself, much could be said. In a letter to Amélie Bosquet, written some ten years before the publication of *L'Éducation sentimentale,* Flaubert makes this revealing confession: "One has spoken endlessly about the prostitution of women, but not a word has been said about that of men. I have known the tortures of prostitutes, and any man who has loved for a long time and who desired no longer to love has experienced them." Unquestionably Frédéric's ambiguous situation vis-à-vis the Arnoux household, combining the duplicity of an adulterer, the frustrations of an unsuccessful suitor and the embarrassment of being Arnoux's rival not only with his wife, but with his mistress, exposes him to complex compromises and turpitudes. His dilettantish vacillations and reliance on others are almost those of a "kept" person. Frédéric is not only weak (Flabuert often depicts strong women and weak, virginal men), but passive and "feminine." He holds, for his friend Deslauriers, "un charme presque féminin." The projected marriage to Mme Dambreuse, for money and social prestige, shows us Frédéric morally at his most depraved.

Finally, the prostitution motif provides a link between individual and collective attitudes. Society itself, as represented by various groups, corporations or institutions, is the great whore who always embraces the winner. Like Rosanette, who after despising the revolutionaries now declares herself in favor of the Republic, so do all the representative authorities—"as his lordship the Archbishop had already done, and as the magistracy, the Conseil d'Etat, the Institut, the marshals of France, Changarnier, M. de Falloux, all the Bonapartists, all the Legitimists, and a considerable number of Orleanists were about to do with a swiftness displaying marvelous zeal." Politics in particular, which held a somewhat perverse fascination for the apolitical Flaubert, is viewed as a slattern. During the obscenely violent and profanatory sack of the Tuileries palace, a slut is seen, on a heap of garments, assuming the motionless, allegorical pose of the Statue of Liberty.

The bitterness of an image such as this stresses the coarseness and the fickleness of political allegiances. But it is part of a more general theme of betrayed ideals. *L'Éducation sentimentale* is a novel of bankruptcy and of pathological erosion. Certain chapters accumulate one form of betrayal on top of another, until the feeling is that of an immense desertion. Friendship, ambition, politics, love—nothing seems immune from this chronic deterioration and devaluation. The most brutal manifestation of this aspect of the novel is the double betrayal of the political turncoat Sénécal, the former Socialist now turned police agent, who during the coup d'état of 1851 coldbloodedly kills the sentimental revolutionary Dussardier. This stunning act, which leaves Frédéric agape, is like an allegory of treason destroying idealism.

And it is no gratuitous coincidence that makes Frédéric the witness to this despicable deed. The images of prostitution and degradation exist primarily in relation to Frédéric's personal vision, to his longings, his sadness, his disappointments and his defeats. The bordello motif may permeate the novel as a whole and may have a universal significance within its context. It represents ersatz on all levels, transmuting almost every gesture into parody: the duel with de Cisy is no real duel; the props Pellerin uses for his "Venetian" portrait are fake props; all creative efforts are derivative. But it is in relation to Frédéric's "sentimental education" that all this counterfeit acquires dramatic meaning. No matter how obviously depraved the objective world may be, it is his sentimental life which, subjectively, is most affected by the principle of degrading vicariousness. Thus Frédéric bounces from one woman to another, permanently oscillating between contradictory desires and contradictory experiences, always driven to seek a poor substitute for the *authentic* experience he dreams of, and which, in the process, he steadily defiles. One desire awakens a contradictory desire, suggesting a repetitive discontinuity. "The frequentation of the two women provided, as it were, two strains of music in his life, the one playful, passionate, amusing: and the other almost religious. . . ." And there are not two women in his life, but four—if one includes the young girl, Louise Roque. This oscillation at times obliges Flaubert to resort to devices which appear extraneous: chance encounters, unexpected letters, coincidences which further underline the passivity of the hero and his easy surrender to the easiest path. Almost symbolically, at one point, the "strumpet" Rosanette (Flaubert actually uses the word "catin") interrupts a love scene in progress, thus making the ideal "irrevocably impossible."

What is worse, Frédéric *uses* the image of one woman in his relationship with another. It is bad enough that he has learned to make one sentiment serve multiple purposes: in his courtship of Mme Dambreuse, he "makes use of his old passion" for Mme Arnoux; he repeats to Mme Dambreuse the very oath he just uttered to Rosanette, sends them both identical bouquets and writes them love letters simultaneously. Even more sadly, he has to rely on substitute images to stimulate himself sexually. "He found it necessary to evoke the image of Rosanette or of Mme Arnoux." (Thus Flaubert himself once told the Goncourts that "all women he ever possessed were no more than the mattress for another woman he dreamed of.") In the novel, this sexual substitution takes place quite literally when Frédéric, desperate because Mme Arnoux failed to show up at their rendezvous, makes love to Rosanette on the very bed he had so devoutly prepared for Mme Arnoux.

Such a pattern of substitution and profanation—underlined by the permanent prostitution motif—leads to contradictory results. On the one hand, we witness a strange paralysis, reminiscent of the scene in the brothel when Frédéric could not make his "choice." Life is a planned orgy which never quite amounts to one. As boys, Frédéric and Deslauriers had such extravagant dreams that they were "sad as after a great debauch." Frédéeric feels destined to accept defeat before even attempting a victory. He has a keen sense of loss before even having possessed. His imagination builds and furnishes Moorish palaces (always the exotic yearning!); he sees himself lounging on cashmere divans listening to the murmur of fountains—and these sensuous dreams become so precise "that they saddened him as though he had lost them." Make-believe and mental aphrodisiacs turn out to be manifestations of impotence.

The other result appears as a complete contrast to this atony: a vertiginous proliferation. But this proliferation, much like the dizzying display of women at "La Turque," only leads to another form of futility. Innumerable examples in *L'Éducation sentimentale* illustrate this coupling of diversity with sterility: the different esthetic "theories," the contradictory literary projects, the cacophony of political ideas, the jarring clash of opinions and inept clichés. Polymorphism, in the Flaubertian context, is nearly always a sure sign of an almost hypnotic attraction to nothingness, a suicidal yearning for annihilation. "Exhausted, filled with contradictory desires, no longer even conscious of what he wanted, he felt an extraordinary sadness, the desire to die."

It is significant that this allurement to nothingness, so explicitly stated, should be experienced by Frédéric while in the company of a high-class prostitute. For somehow, in Flaubert's own imagination, prostitution and an almost ascetic staring into the emptiness of existence are closely related. To Louise Colet he writes that the sight of streetwalkers and of monks "tickles" his soul in its deepest recesses, that prostitution evokes simultaneously "lewdness, bitterness, the nothingness of human relations. . . ." The theme of sterility and even abortion in *L'Éducation sentimentale* is illumined by a comment such as this. Flaubert's admiration for the marquis de Sade, which he shares with Baudelaire, makes him suspect Nature and explains in part why he views the Prostitute both as an antiphysis and the very incarnation of sterility. With bitter irony, Flaubert describes the "maison de santé et d'accouchement" where Rosanette gives birth to a sickly offspring in terms that are most equivocal: the chambermaid looks like a "soubrette," the director of the establishment is called "Madame," the establishment itself (with its closed shutters and continuous sounds of piano playing) is called a "maison discrète"—leaving little doubt as to the analogy the author had in mind. Originally, Flaubert had even planned to have the "Madame" explain to Frédéric how to dispose of the newborn baby! And when the sickly child soon after dies, Rosanette's grief coincides with the grief of Mme Dambreuse as she realizes that her husband has left all his wealth to someone else. "A mother grieving beside an empty cradle was not more pitiful than Mme Dambreuse at the sight of the open strong-boxes." The theme of sterility could not possibly be pushed much further.

Profanation, betrayal, sterility . . . and yet. And yet the reader is never permitted to forget the ideally pure figure of Mme Arnoux. Frédéric may use other women, and forget himself with them; they are nothing but substitutes for an ideal. One might even say, paradoxically, that profanation is here in the service of purity. Ever since *Mémoires d'un fou,* written at the age of seventeen, Flaubert was haunted by the contrasts between idealized woman *(le ciel)* and cheap love *(la boue).* The narrator of *Mémoires d'un fou,* still writing under the recent impact of his meeting with Mme Schlésinger, the model for Mme Arnoux, feels guilt and shame because he has lost his virginity with a promiscuous creature, "as though my love for Maria were a religion that I had profaned." In *Novembre,* written at the age of twenty, he attempted to synthesize in one figure the dual visage of woman. *L'Éducation sentimentale* again insists on a polarity. It is clear that the very concept of immaculate beauty required, in Flaubert's imagination, the drama of inaccessibility, as well as the antithesis of corruption.

This persistent idealism, strengthened by profanation as though made holier by it, is implicit in the bordello exploit, the subject of the last scene of the book. Just as the narrator of *Mémoires d'un fou* was haunted by the loss of virginity, so here Frédéric is filled with nostalgia for a lost innocence. For the memory is altogether a chaste one, and even on the level of sheer venery, the incident is marked by a sort of poetry of unrealized love. The memory, however, coming as it does at the end of the book (and especially after the ultimate, deeply moving encounter with Mme Arnoux), acquires an additional aura. And it is significant that Frédéric says not a word of this unforgettable last meeting to Deslauriers. For this is a private realm, a regal chamber open to no one. All throughout the novel it is Mme Arnoux's image that shines forth from behind the Parisian fog, keeping alive an "invincible hope." The very name Marie (the same name as in *Mémoires d'un fou* and in *Novembre*) suggests purity. And in the service of this "image," despite all his weaknesses and abdications, Frédéric acquires nobility. For the sake of this "image," he has in the long run given up everything. (pp. 125-40)

> *Victor Brombert, in his* The Novels of Flaubert: A Study of Themes and Techniques, *Princeton University Press, 1966, 301 p.*

BENJAMIN F. BART (essay date 1967)

[*In the first part of the following excerpt, Bart considers the role of the Revolution of 1848 in* Sentimental Education. *In the second part, he examines the work's aesthetic and stylistic devices.*]

From the very start, Flaubert's *Education* was to be far more than *Sentimental:* that was part of why he found this title inadequate. The book dealt with the art and the finance of his period, its upper social levels and the demimonde, its commerce and its industry, quite as much as with its love life. But for him the principal event of his generation had been the Revolution of 1848 and, almost from the outset, it was to occupy a central position in the novel.

"With Louis-Philippe's abdication something disappeared which will never return," Flaubert had written to Bouilhet from the Near East in 1850. Hence like *Salammbô, A Sentimental Ed-*

ucation has two main focuses, the personal lives of its principal characters and the major political events which put an end to a whole world Flaubert had known. Fiction and history fuse throughout the long episode of the Revolution—nearly seventy-five pages—which opens Part Three. It was a *tour de force* which caused Flaubert much anguish as he struggled to insert his characters and their necessary actions into the fixed data of the events which actually transpired. The background threatened constantly to overwhelm them, as it had so dangerously in *Salammbô*. This was, he fully realized, the grave risk of the historical novel as he conceived it; and the difficulty was compounded in his situation, since his characters, this time, were so much less interesting than the real people whose deeds he had to mention. Moreover, there was the delicate problem of what to choose among the vast body of data available to him.

Despite all his difficulties and the dangers he foresaw, Flaubert was on the whole successful. His novel has remarkable historical accuracy and one does follow the progress of the Revolution. On the other hand the reader is not forced to keep track of history in order to follow the lives of the protagonists. Perhaps the only failure of technique is that the modern reader—for whom these events are long past—has real need for the copious explanatory footnotes which accompany most editions today.

This section of the novel is a chronicle of 1848. Flaubert had long been convinced that he had great gifts for political intrigue; *A Sentimental Education* was to be his occasion to demonstrate his political insight. Unfortunately, as with *Madame Bovary*, the demonstration had to be in reverse, shown only ironically through the catastrophic errors of all involved. Deslauriers incarnates the revolutionary for personal gain; Sénécal's ferocious desire for power and for justice is coupled with a fanatic desire for order which leads to his becoming a police agent; their friend Dussardier is the idealist seeking to protect and elevate the weak and the downtrodden. And it is in the ironic nature of Flaubert's view of the world that Dussardier should finally be shot by Sénécal.

Some of the events of 1848-52 Flaubert had witnessed personally. He and Du Camp had attended one of the Reform Banquets which preceded the outbreak of the Revolution. Flaubert and Bouilhet had gone into Paris on the following February 23 to study the actual fighting. They considerably misunderstood what was happening: although they did notice the firing, they went off with Du Camp to listen to Bouilhet recite some of his poetry. Frédéric's conduct stemmed from that of Flaubert and his friends. And when, on the twenty-fourth, Frédéric walked about Paris and witnessed various events, he was retracing the steps Flaubert and Du Camp took and which Du Camp had in part related already in a volume of his. Flaubert may even have used Du Camp's notes; he certainly took none himself. Again, by pleasant good luck, he was in the capital at the time of Louis-Napoléon's *coup d'état,* which Frédéric missed in order to go to Nogent, where he hoped to marry Louise.

A Sentimental Education involves a great deal more than the mere external events of the Revolution of 1848, for Flaubert proposed to treat of the major attitudes and theories of the Utopian Socialists. He even put off beginning his novel for some months while he read their publications. Finally a worried Bouilhet became almost sharp in his admonitions to start writing. Flaubert did at last, but he returned once more for long

months in 1866-67, reading widely and asking older friends like Sainte-Beuve and George Sand for further suggestions.

In the novel, as the long pent-up rage of the mob burst loose, Frédéric moved from one part of the city to another to watch the rioting. At first all seemed to be play acting. But as the fighting grew more bloody, even the peaceful Frédéric "felt his Galic blood surging" under the magnetism of the excited crowds. He trembled all over and was seized with an immense love, a sort of supreme and universal tenderness, as if the heart of all humanity were beating within his breast. These high hopes, which so many of his generation entertained, were what had made the outcome of the Revolution so bitter a farce to a Flaubert, a Baudelaire, a Hugo, a Leconte de Lisle, and countless thousands of others.

The Socialists were the particular bête noire of Flaubert. Already in the Levant he had declared them monstrous in their stupidity. Now as he read and reread them in the 1860's, he was appalled. They all shared a common hatred for liberty, for the Revolution of 1789, for any sort of sound philosophy. Essentially medieval in outlook, they turned toward the past, not the future as they claimed. Their debt to religion was crippling; they had pillaged de Maistre and Lamennais. What despots they were! Flaubert's righteous indignation grew as he read. All of them, he came to state, based their belief ultimately on biblical revelation and sought to have man expiate some sort of original sin.

Deslauriers expressed much of Flaubert's thinking, attacking Saint-Simon and the other Socialists as a band of jokers who wished to redo Catholicism under a new guise. Sénécal illustrated the nature of the problem. Defending the position of the Revolution, he demanded the application of the principles of the Gospels, to which he added garbled elements from Rousseau and the nineteenth-century thinkers. He envisaged a virtuous democracy which would be a cross between a small farm and a factory, "a sort of American Sparta in which the individual would exist only for society."

As the Revolution faded into dissension and chaos, Deslauriers was again charged with expressing Flaubert's views. He complained that the hopelessly inept masses, prostrating themselves before one god after another, could always be bought by anyone who promised to feed them. Frédéric, too, castigated the revolutionaries as petty bourgeois and fools who had defrauded the workers of almost everything. Progress could be accomplished only by an aristocracy, perhaps only by a single powerful man.

The reactionaries, however, fared no better. Flaubert pointed out that they lacked the indispensable man to guide them to true conservatism; Thiers, their nominal leader, was as inept as the Socialists. The party was doubly damned: since salvation lay only through them, their failures made them criminal. Still worse, when they regained power, their cruelties and brutalities equaled those of the Socialists. The common sense of the nation seemed upset and, added Flaubert, there were men who remained idiots forever after. The divine right of kings and the sovereignty of the people were two equally absurd notions. For too long metaphysics had reigned in political thought, and all of society was rotted. It was time to treat political theory scientifically, as it was for esthetic theory. Otherwise chaos would always reign, changing only in the particular forms of idiocy worshiped at the moment. Thus patriots, Socialists, and reactionaries among Flaubert's readers could each find his own dish and put the book down with distaste or with fury at its author. Only time could heal these perspectives, and there has not yet been that much time. (pp. 521-24)

• • • • •

Camus has observed that the French novel has always sought to unite the fatalism of man's conditioned destiny with the notion of art, which is man's supreme manifestation of his liberty. It has been a sort of ideal terrain upon which the forces of destiny could struggle with the power of man's free will, giving him an opportunity for revenge and a chance to surmount his difficult fate by imposing a form upon it. It remains to determine to what extent Flaubert succeeded in imposing a form upon his material in *A Sentimental Education.*

Nature is beautiful only to those who know how to look at her, proof to Flaubert that everything is subjective. But equally he felt his novel was written in terms of certain scientific exigencies over which he had no control. In fact, any novel must be scientific, that is, it must remain within the limits of general probabilities. In addition, his particular novel was attempting to combine the epic and the satiric in an historical framework. It was to be a kind of "epic of mediocrity," as Gide later termed it, a satire of his generation. It was also to record, still within the novel form, the moral, political, and emotional history of his generation. Lastly, *A Sentimental Education* was to have the essential quality of all art for Flaubert: it must produce a vague exaltation in the reader through his participating in the lives of the characters.

It cannot be seriously maintained that *A Sentimental Education* is the entirely successful resolution of the wager involved in seeking to unite all these themes and subjects. Rigorous scientific demands, a bourgeois subject, fixed historical data, mediocre personalities, and an effort to produce in the reader a vague exaltation: no wonder Flaubert staggered under the burden, which a lesser man would not have undertaken. As he neared the end, even he declared that the attempt had been foredoomed.

Flaubert used to say of his novel that the trouble was it did not form a pyramid. This was apparent even in the initial planning, which is one reason why he put off starting for so very long. Many years after it was completed, he still affirmed that the *Education* lacked that falseness of perspective which is essential to art. It offered no progression of effect, and hence the reader had the same impression at the end that he had at the beginning. Somehow Flaubert had been so preoccupied with adhering to reality that he had failed to choose adequately within what it offered him. No one, he felt, had pushed probity further than he had; but since art and reality were separate domains, he had failed.

Flaubert also feared, even when far along in the writing, that his book suffered for lack of a main scene. To him it seemed to have no set pieces, not even any metaphors, because any embroidering that he might have done would have rent the basic fabric. He was worried—but he need not have been. The work abounds in major scenes, the initial one on the boat, the dinners and balls, various episodes in the Revolution of 1848, the whole stay of Frédéric and Rosanette in the Forest of Fontainebleau, and countless others. And of course it closes with the great scenes of the final visit of Madame Arnoux and the conversation between Frédéric and Deslauriers.

Flaubert intended *A Sentimental Education* to be impersonal, impartial, impassive, and objective. In fact, however, he was constantly and obviously present in his novel. Taine wrote him that he kept discovering the author's private feelings everywhere; he doubted, though, that readers who did not know him could do so. Maupassant, writing a little later and hence with more experience of what readers did discover, could be more perceptive. Speaking of Flaubert's manifest exasperation over human stupidity, he conceded that Flaubert's works did have a bitter savor which came from his constant discovery of mediocrity, banality, and stupidity everywhere. Flaubert, Maupassant pointed out, noted it in *A Sentimental Education* in almost every paragraph, by a word, by the slanting of a phrase, or by the general tone. Hence, Maupassant felt, the distaste which a number of readers experienced in reading the work.

Speaking of Thiers, whom he hated, Flaubert once asked how he could legitimately express his adverse opinion without appearing to be an imbecile later on. He decided, as before, that the best procedure was to content himself with depiction: dissection was a vengeance. And yet he promised his friends he would give the political leader his due, and he did by having one character declare Thiers's writing as beautiful as his thoughts were profound. Since probably not even Thiers thought his prose remarkable, the intent was clear. George Sand was worried and begged him to be generous. He promised to show her the manuscript and remove anything ill tempered or nasty; he did read it to her, but to no avail. She would have had to ask for a complete rewriting, and then it would have been another book.

Many of the devices Flaubert employed to express his own opinions he had elaborated earlier for *Madame Bovary*. The "poor" little face of Madame Arnoux's sick child joins the "poor" *Maréchale* in revealing Flaubert's sympathy, as had the "poor" hands of the dying Emma. Deslauriers not unreasonably phrased Flaubert's views on political theory; the artist Pellerin felt his nostalgia for bygone ages. Madame Arnoux observed correctly that her husband had been the only honest man at a dinner party. But in *A Sentimental Education*—as opposed to his earlier novels—Flaubert seems for the first time curiously unaware that such statements must be made by characters whom the reader can trust. When Pellerin expresses Flaubert's own doctrines on esthetics, the reader becomes uneasy. Is this bumbling charlatan to be believed when he asserts that so-called realism is silly and when he insists upon grandeur and impersonal exaltation as the aims of art? Or that these must be based upon ideas, of which he has almost none? He speaks for Flaubert and not for himself, but this the reader cannot know.

Ironic juxtaposition had been immensely effective in *Madame Bovary*, as in the Agricultural Fair. Here, too, Flaubert used the device as a means to avoid having to intervene himself; he could limit his role to arranging the sequences. When a desperate Frédéric returned from Fontainebleau to Paris during the Revolution, he hurried down to the Seine; at a window an old man was weeping over what had happened. The river, however, flowed as peacefully as before, the sky was clear and blue, and in the Tuileries Gardens the birds were singing.

More complex and richer in ambiguity are the oppositions between Frédéric and Rosanette at Fontainebleau. Royal residences, Flaubert explained, have a particular melancholy about them when, in their old age, their emptiness suggests the flight of time and the impermanence of man. This direct intervention by the author described the setting and, presumably, a reaction of Frédéric's. Now, using ironic juxtaposition, Flaubert had only to add that Rosanette was overcome with huge yawns.

At times, apparently unaware that he was intervening, Flaubert would state that "Madame Arnoux did not see that . . ." or "Frédéric told everyone, and believed himself, that . . ." Such devices can add richness when it is not entirely clear whether it is Flaubert or a character who is making the observation. During the visits Frédéric and Rosanette made to their child at the wet nurse's, "the two women would chatter on for hours, uttering unbearable stupidities."

Aphorisms and general observations, a long tradition in French literature, had already had their place in *Madame Bovary*. Although they were less common in *Salammbô*, they are constant here: "There are men whose only mission in life is to serve as intermediaries for others; one crosses them like a bridge and goes on." There can be no doubt who makes the assertions, and a large proportion of them are contemptuous. Hence, perhaps without being consciously aware of it, the reader elaborates an unpleasant picture of Flaubert: "Certain men delight in making their friends do disagreeable tasks." Or there are fuller statements, for instance the disillusioned and cynical assertion that "women's hearts are like those pieces of furniture with secret drawers; with vast effort and many broken nails, one gets them open to find only a dried flower, bits of dust, or nothing at all!" Maupassant was right: the reader does learn Flaubert's bitter view of humanity. And he will not necessarily concur or even—if he senses himself attacked—be willing to allow it.

Such aphorisms proved insufficient to carry the burden of Flaubert's scorn for his fellow man. For conservatives who were shocked by the audacity of certain Socialist theories in 1848, he observed that these ideas had all the novelty of Mother Goose and had been amply debated for forty years. He went on to affirm that they frightened the bourgeois as much as a rain of meteors would have; and he capped his insults with the observation that these ideas aroused indignation by virtue of the law that any idea, merely because it is one, always provokes hatred in such people. Later, he went on, such concepts would draw praise in proportion to the amount of this execration. He also stated that the corollary of this law was that any idea, however mediocre, is always superior to its detractors.

Flaubert did not leave the liberals in peace, either. He informed them that in 1848 France no longer felt a master over her and so began to whimper with fright like a blindman who cannot find his stick or a muling child who has lost his nurse. Now all groups had grounds for complaint, precisely as he wished, to match his all-encompassing hatreds. He continued to maintain his familiar esthetic canons as before, but he was now confusing an impartiality in which no one is blamed with one which deals out blows to all sides equally.

Flaubert's intrusions of this sort have succeeded in annoying a very considerable number of readers, and their antipathy may exceed their pleasure; nevertheless the novel can charm and always has delighted many others, for Flaubert made advances in style here which are not to be found in his earlier works. Thus, a strange, ambiguous form of intervention becomes prominent now. The technique sets the page apart not only from the reader but, oddly enough, from the author as well, for Flaubert offers suggestions which were "perhaps" the true explanation or situation: Frédéric's writing of others is "perhaps the only way not to suffer." Sénécal, taking leave of Frédéric after a long talk, made a confession which—Flaubert adds in parentheses—"was the aim of his visit perhaps." Reader joins author in speculation about what these creations of his were doing. No one, apparently, really knows, and the rich ambiguity of life is respected. The contemporary novelist, Alain Robbe-Grillet, has objected to earlier fiction on the ground that meaning in the world can never be more than partial, provisional, or even contradictory. How then, he asks, can the work of art claim to illustrate any a priori meaning whatsoever? If reality has a meaning, he insists, the contemporary artist does not know it. Flaubert's "perhaps" leaves his position safe.

Another device which has a strange effect upon the reader appears in descriptions where Flaubert wished one to sense the look of certain places: Fontainebleau, the site of the porcelain factory, the countryside about Nogent, and others. Unlike Yonville, these sites are real; and unlike Carthage, they were still in existence and familiar to many of his readers. Moreover, Flaubert had visited them and seen for himself what was there. He seems to have become intrigued with the possibility of suggesting the physical presence of the reader at the site. Hence, everything which is permanent, there at the time of the novel and still there at the time of the writing, he described in the present tense, reserving past tenses for what was only temporarily present or occurred only at the specific moment his characters were there. When Frédéric went out to see Madame Arnoux at her husband's factory outside Paris, all these tenses came into play:

> A great flat boat was going downstream with the current . . . a woman passed . . . He found himself on an island, where one sees on the right ruins of an abbey. A mill was turning, damming up the entire width of the other branch of the Oise River, which the factory overhangs. The size of this building greatly astonished Frédéric.

Free indirect discourse, already common in *Madame Bovary*, appears in even more nuanced situations, as when Frédéric, upon his return from the Dambreuse ball, summed up his evening while he prepared for sleep. Using free indirect discourse, including even a parenthetical thought, Flaubert phrased Frédéric's musing: "First of all, his evening dress (he had observed

Maria-Elisa Schlésinger, the probable model for Madame Arnoux in Sentimental Education, *and her infant son.*

himself in the mirror several times), from the cut of his coat to the bow of his slipper, left nothing to be desired.'' From this Flaubert slipped easily to direct questions and then back again to indirect, before finally becoming the traditional omniscient author stating what happened next. He is reporting Frédéric's speculations on Madame Dambreuse: ''It would be tremendous to have a mistress like her! Why not, after all? He was surely as good as the next man! Perhaps she was not so difficult to get! Next Martinon came to mind; and, as he fell asleep, he was smiling in pity over the poor man.''

As with his earlier novels, Flaubert gave constant, scrupulous attention to the details. The adjective ''monotonous'' recurs with just enough frequency and in sufficiently startling places to set the tone: the grass as Frédéric approaches the Arnoux factory is of a monotonous green; the men's ties at an evening party have a monotonous whiteness. Images foreshadow the synesthesia so popular with a later generation: ''the silence, which was profound and absolute, a black silence.'' Occasionally, however, in *A Sentimental Education* the care and attention can become obvious and preciosity enters, an ill-assorted partner for the almost frozen majesty of so much of Flaubert's writing. There is a kind of self-conscious pirouette to a sentence describing Madame Dambreuse: ''She wore a mauve gown trimmed with lace, the ringlets of her coiffure more abundant than usual, and not a single jewel.''

Concision is effective in such sentences; it can become a defect. In a formidable sentence Flaubert described three sorts of women present at the Alhambra seeking three sorts of men and wearing gowns of three different colors: ''Lorettes, shopgirls, and prostitutes had come there, hoping to find a man of wealth, a lover, a gold piece, or simply for the pleasure of dancing; and their gowns with tunics of water green, cerise-blue, or purple, passed and moved about among the ebony trees and the lilacs.'' There is, of course, a certain pleasure in piecing it all together—it does work out—but the novel has been interrupted while the author performed a *tour de force*. And surely he cannot be thought of as absent from the page.

Transitions from one paragraph to the next continued to demand Flaubert's attention. The sentence stating that France wept in terror at no longer feeling a master is the final one in its paragraph. The next paragraph, switching subject completely, does so by an ingenious recall: ''Of all Frenchmen, the one who trembled most was Monsieur Dambreuse.'' On occasion, however, a kind of stiff self-consciousness makes the reader aware of the technique, and what should be an imperceptible transition becomes an interruption. For really no inherent reason one paragraph ends with the statement that Frédéric became as punctual as Regimbart. The remark serves only to validate the opening sentence of the following paragraph: ''Every day Regimbart . . .'' But the reader's mind was too far from Regimbart when he entered as a point of reference for the device to be anything but distracting. So many transitions are so well motivated that it is a surprise to meet fortuitous ones, like the occasion on which Frédéric, walking aimlessly, looks up to see the sign in front of Arnoux's and so enters to pursue the acquaintance begun on the boat. Life, Flaubert would have responded, is like that, equally fortuitous, ephemeral, and trivial.

Flaubert's views on form occasionally raised serious difficulties. Less and less did they include observance of the simple requirements of grammatical structure or elementary composition: the demands of harmonious sound or flow could at any time supersede more pedantic rules for correct French. Du Camp, who was certainly being pedantic, found some 251 allegedly incorrect phrasings in the manuscript of *A Sentimental Education* when Flaubert submitted it to him. While many of these are no more than trivia, still readers will join him in his objection—which Flaubert declined to recognize—to the statement that one o'clock struck slowly. And, as Du Camp's mistress pointed out, there are innumerable pronoun references in the novel which—though actually correct—are so confusing that one has to read the passages several times to understand them.

Flaubert's interest and concern for style were elsewhere, in his concept of it as a special way of perceiving. The problem was as fundamental a matter as how one looked at simple physical objects, for that seeing would then condition the mode of description, making demands which far transcended mere antecedents for pronouns. After *la Maréchale* had described to Frédéric how her mother had arranged the sale of Rosanette's virginity, Flaubert let the unperturbed indifference of nature make the ironic comment he needed; but to do so he had to see all nature about them actively pursuing its own course. The leaves rustled; in a clump of grasses, a large foxglove swayed; the light flowed like a wave over the turf; and the silence was cut at rapid intervals by the grazing of a cow which had moved out of sight.

Light Flaubert frequently called upon to move or play about his characters in this fashion. The porcelain globes of a lamp poured out a light which undulated like white *moiré* satin against the walls. Or a lamp cast a luminous circle on the ceiling, whitening it, while in the corners shadows spread like black veils super-imposed one upon another. A white light falling on Rosanette from the candelabra infused her skin with mother-of-pearl tones, put pink on her eyelids, and made her eyeballs shine. Light was to Flaubert the agent creating what it falls upon, as it had been in Greece.

Perhaps the greatest single example is the description of the afternoon sunlight as Rosanette and Frédéric returned from the races in their carriage and drove down the Champs Elysées. They looked out on the rising vapor, through which the sunlight shone. ''Passing under the Arc de Triomphe, it spread out a reddish glow at a man's height, which made the wheel hubs, the door handles, the ends of the shafts, and the rings on the seats sparkle.'' Now, changing to a new subject—but the reader realizes this only slowly—Flaubert described the individual trees and people as forming a great wholes. ''And, on both sides of the broad avenue, like a river in which the manes, the clothes, and the heads of people were undulating, the trees, shining from the rain, rose like two green walls.'' The description closes on a return to the sky and its feel and color, essentially a return to light: ''The blue of the sky, above, reappearing here and there, had the softnesses of satin.''

The effect of this light is hallucinatory, and hallucinations in *A Sentimental Education* run the gamut from such odd modes of perception to nightmares, as when Frédéric fell asleep after the ball at Rosanette's, through hypnagogic dreams as characters doze, to artistic and finally quasi-epileptic hallucinations. Sometimes no more than a character's effort at recall was involved. Frédéric, in the carriage on the way to Nogent, remembered his first meeting with Madame Arnoux so vividly that he became aware of objects he had not consciously noiced when he was with her. At other times, it was still only his lively imagination at work: calling on Madame Arnoux, he saw the alcove containing her bed and came to imagine her head on the pillow so clearly that he had trouble in not seizing the real woman before him.

In Frédéric hallucination could become almost a deliberate creation. Resting beside Arnoux while sharing his guard duty, he noticed that his companion had fallen asleep with his gun so placed that if it were accidentally discharged, it would kill him . . . and free his wife. Like Saint Anthony meditating upon evil, Frédéric found he really wanted to commit the murder and became frightened: "In the madness of his dream, the rest of the world began to disappear and he was conscious of himself only through an intolerable tightness around his chest."

The dream about Arnoux was deliberately produced; or at least Frédéric was consciously collaborating in its production. Sometimes the hallucination passed beyond voluntary control. When he considered the idea that he was the father of Rosanette's child, he found it grotesque; but as his thoughts wandered on, it occurred to him that the mother might have been Madame Arnoux. "And his dream became so gripping that he had a sort of hallucination" and imagined the little child before him on the rug.

Madame Arnoux several times triggered these experiences in Frédéric, as Elisa had with Flaubert in the early days, when he would imagine she was behind him. After Frédéric's inheritance allowed him to return to Paris and thus see her again, "with the clarity of a hallucination, he saw himself beside her. . . . At the door his tilbury—no, a coupé rather—would be standing." He could hear the noises made by the horse. He would receive her and her husband in his house, which he furnished in his imagination. This life would last indefinitely, he felt, just as Charles Bovary had about his dreams for little Berthe. The stream of consciousness was being foreshadowed when Frédéric imagined a tilbury and then corrected himself; sounds, too, made the dream richer, though it lacked odors or tastes. It ended by approaching the epileptic seizures Flaubert knew: "These images were appearing so tumultuously that he felt his head beginning to turn."

The image of "moving with the extraordinary ease one feels in a dream" recurs, too, on one of several walks during which Frédéric slipped into a dream state. After an unfruitful visit to Madame Arnoux, he moved at random, seeing nothing, striking his foot against stones, and losing his way. He was brought back to himself only by a sound, as was Emma Bovary outside the convent, in this case the noise of the worker's shoes as they left the factory. Earlier, after his first dinner at the Arnoux home, he walked the streets of Paris, equally unconscious of where he was, of space itself, in fact. He went on aimlessly, lost, drawn forward by an invisible force. This time he was revived by feeling the damp air about him: he had returned to consciousness along the quays of the Seine.

Other characters, too, lost their sense of time while walking; but it was reserved to Frédéric to have the onset of an epileptic attack. Seeking desperately for a friend once, he was trying with all his forces to recall the cafes the man used to frequent: "all the names . . . spurted forth from his memory at the same instant, like the thousand elements of a piece of fireworks." Flaubert and Emma Bovary had both experienced this before Frédéric: it was the greatest anguish any of them knew. (pp. 526-36)

Benjamin F. Bart, in his Flaubert, *Syracuse University Press, 1967, 791 p.*

MAURICE NADEAU (essay date 1969)

*[The following excerpt is drawn from a work originally published in French in 1969. In his appreciative interpretation of Senti-*mental Education, *Nadeau discusses Flaubert's depiction of characters and their historical milieu, also describing some of the structural and thematic problems Flaubert faced in laying out the narrative. In the last section of the essay, Nadeau refers to several of the letters excerpted at the beginning of this entry.]*

Some books arouse admiration and respect. Others one merely likes and keeps reading over again, building up a sort of secret relationship with them, though they are not necessarily masterpieces. Some excite an initial enthusiasm, but seem strangely faded ten or fifteen years later. It is only rarely that one likes and is impressed by a book to begin with, and then with every reading finds it more and more rich and moving and profound. *L'Education sentimentale* is like that—one of the great novels of its age, and one whose youth never fades.

The beauty here is less systematic than that of **Madame Bovary** with its purity of line; less stiff and showy than that of **Salammbô**. Instead of leaping to the eye, the beauty of *L'Education sentimentale* hides behind what is said or, more often, suggested; it has to be found out.

Flaubert the painter is still there, laying on touch after touch to create a general color. Here it is the greyness of life in all its shades: blue for the voyage up the Seine aboard the *Ville-de-Montereau;* red for the revolution of 1848; ashen for the final scenes. Yet the neutral tone into which both private lives and great public events all fade never calls attention to itself. What one does perceive is a kind of music, already familiar to those who have read **Mémoires d'un Fou, Novembre,** and the first **Education**. It forms part of a great symphony in a minor key, crossing the threshold of skin and nerve to penetrate right to the marrow of our bones. It is more heartrending than the plaints of earlier days, because the cry of despair is now serene.

A Novel of Failure

Flaubert used to talk of the *"grotesque triste* (dreary grotesqueness)" of life, as if to exorcize and avenge himself on it rather than succumb to it. But now he speaks of the futility and hopelessness of any attempt to escape: every life is a failure in the long run for everyone in turn, the world rushes only downhill. There is no happiness except in the past, walled up in the memory and impossible to live over again. And a good thing too. "We'd have loved each other so well," say a couple who have never been able to belong to one another, and that could be the summing-up. But Flaubert insisted on making it fiercer still, and what survives of the ruined lives of Frédéric and his false friend Deslauriers, that "best thing" they have in common, is their farcical visit to the establishment of "La Turque."

Like the first **Education**, like **Madame Bovary**, like **Salammbô**, this is a novel of failure. The history of Frédéric Moreau belies both its title and its sub-title, *Histoire d'un jeune homme*. When his "education" is over, the "young man" from Nogent is neither stronger nor wiser nor more hardened than he was before, and when he leaves Paris he is thirty. He uses the next fifteen years to so little purpose they can be dealt with in ten lines. It is as if Frédéric were only waiting for the final confrontation with the great unfulfilled love of his youth to realize fully his own failure. Then, going over old times with Deslauriers, he accepts it. Once he was full of ambition and longed for fame, wealth, and love, but he was reduced to the common level by life, circumstance, and his own weakness. Now, in the "idleness of his mind and inertia of his heart," all that remains is for him to live and die a *petit-bourgeois*, existing on unearned income. This is how great designs and ranging thoughts may end. At one time Flaubert thought of calling the book *Les Fruits secs* (literally dried or withered fruit, a figurative equivalent of "duds," "failures").

The Son of Madame Bovary

But, it has long been objected, Frédéric Moreau never really had any great design, was never really borne along by a splendid ideal. What fate had he then a right to, this "mediocrity" whom even Flaubert himself describes as a "man with every weakness"? He only wants what young boureois usually expect and consider their due, without their having to make any effort or show any perseverance. Frédéric left things to circumstance, and the fact that circumstance was unfavorable was enough to make him give up.

Why then does he win our sympathy? Why have so many young men recognized themselves in him? In the first place, he is not so mediocre as all that, either in his desires or in his intentions. He is not out for money—he has, or will have, sufficient—or honors, or for the power attached to high office and such careers, political and other, as dictate public opinion. It is as if as soon as he entered on life he saw the emptiness of what most men strive for. All he wants is to be recognized for what he is, to emerge from the anonymity of the crowd, and to live for himself, freely and independently. It is for this reason he is drawn by the glitter of Paris, rather than in order to read law and become a judge or a barrister. As he dreams of his future in his room at Nogent, or on the boat going back there, or in the country with Deslauriers, he never sees himself as exercising any profession, but following some occupation that lies outside common or garden society. He "thought of an outline for a play, subjects for paintings, future passions"— "he aspired to be one day the Walter Scott of France"— "above all else he valued passion; Werther, René, Franck, Lara, Lélia and others less distinguished aroused almost equal enthusiasm in him." He feels himself to be, and wants to be, an artist, though whether a musician, a writer, or a painter he does not know—he is attracted by every art in turn, sometimes several simultaneously. But the main thing for him is to experience a *grande passion*. "Love," he tells Deslauriers, "is the food, the atmosphere of genius. Unusual emotions produce sublime works . . ." Brought up on Byron, Chateaubriand, Victor Hugo and George Sand, he moves naturally among the great clichés of Romanticism. If he is the son of Madame Bovary, he is a son who has been educated into a "Parisian"; he is a cut or two above his mother.

"The Men of My Generation"

From the very first pages of the book we know he will fail all along the line, that he will not realize any of his ambitions, and that he will not have the strength or courage for the "grand passion" he aspires to. The symphony's main theme is stated in the opening bars, where the whole story is, as it were, already relegated to the past. "*J'aurais fait quelque chose avec une femme qui m'eût aimé* (I would have achieved something with a woman who loved me)." Deslauriers, who sees the funny side of this precocious world-weariness, laughs, and Frédéric recovers and adopts the only tense suitable for one of his age: the future. But he still comes to the same negative conclusions.

> *Quant à chercher celle qu'il me faudrait, j'y renonce!*
> *D'ailleurs, si jamais je la trouve, elle me repoussera.*
> *Je suis de la race des déshérités, et je m'éteindrai*
> *avec un trésor qui était de strass ou de diamant, je*
> *n'en sais rien.* (As to looking for the right woman,
> I shall not try! Anyhow, if ever I do find her she'll

reject me. I am one of the outcasts of fortune, and when I die I shan't know whether the treasure I clasped was paste or diamonds.)

Once again the past encroaches on the future, and while Frédéric succumbs anew to Romanticism to the extent of affecting superiority to his own fate, at the same time he entrenches himself in renunciation, rejection, skepticism. It is not that he is exceptionally lucid about himself. He is too young; that will come later.

At present it is his dreams which see clearly for him and which already come up against reality. The time for grand passions is over. It is 1840, the age of *le roi bourgeois*, the Citizen King.

The practical-minded Deslauriers brings him rudely back to earth: since he has a black coat and white gloves, he ought to take up with M. and Mme Dambreuse. "Think of it, he's got millions! Set yourself out to please him, and his wife as well. Become her lover!" Frédéric is indignant: that is not the kind of success he is after. His friend tells him to remember Rastignac in *La Comedie humaine*. But that is just what he does not want to be. Nevertheless, he does waver slightly and agree that his "despair is foolish." Forgetting Mme Arnoux, or including her in the prediction which had been made about the other, he could not help smiling." The novel has only just begun and Frédéric is already compromising mentally. He is not a "mediocrity," but he is impulsive and weak. He literally does not know what he wants. So he leaves it to circumstance, and hopes circumstance will prove favorable.

If he were the novel's only interest one might accuse the author of having made things too easy for himself. But Deslauriers is there as a corrective. He is a strong, ambitious character who means to "arrive" and has no scruples to stand in his way. He later tries to supplant Frédéric with Mme Arnoux, to get into the good graces of the Dambreuses, to influence opinion through a newspaper, and to play a part in politics. He does in fact hold office for a while under the provisional government, and makes a "good match," thereby doing Frédéric out of this last chance. But his is a poor success. He is of such vulgar stuff, so steeped in greed and envy, that he overdoes it every time, and transforms into immediate or ultimate defeat all the possibilities of victory purchased by effort and ever-increasing degradation. His wife "runs away with a singer," and he too will die empty-handed.

Others—Hussonet, Cisy, Martinon—are different from both Frédéric and Deslauriers. They find their own level in society, as blackmailers, climbers, dowry-hunters. As lacking in character as Frédéric, they are also without the scruples and delicacy of mind and feeling which at least keep him from being abject. But abjection is too large a word for these air-balloons, these corks on the water. They are no more than foam on the wave which carries Frédéric along, and which he lets toss him from one situation to another, from Rosanette to Mme Arnoux, and from Mme Arnoux to Mme Dambreuse.

The only ones who see farther than their own interests and have some conviction or ideal belong to the "lower classes": Dussardier, a shop assistant whose magnanimity makes up for the simplicity of his ideas; Sénécal, the "mathematics tutor" who is spoken of as "a future Saint-Just." They are both republicans and socialists, Dussardier out of hatred for injustice and warmth of feeling, Sénécal out of cool rationalism. But alas, Dussardier, who believes in the fine words of Lamartine, fires on one of his class brothers in June 1848, considers himself half responsible for this betrayal, and by way of absolution gets himself killed by a policeman during Louis-Napoleon's *coup d'état.* Fate has arranged things well: in the policeman, Frédéric, "staring open-mouthed, recognized Sénécal." The wheel has come full circle, and if Flaubert's only purpose has been to write, as he said, "the moral history of his generation," [see excerpt dated 6 October 1864], these parallel destinies all ending in moral, intellectual, or political bankruptcy would be enough to show us why the Prince-President later became Emperor of the French.

A Vast Miscarriage

But *L'Education sentimentale* is something very different from a moral history; its essence is to be found elsewhere. And yet Frédéric's unfulfilled passion for Marie Arnoux, the impossibility of its living and growing though everything shows it is requited; the faint-heartedness on one side and excessive reserve on the other which gave rise to so many "*intermittences,*" as Proust called them, so many eclipses, so much compromise, frustration and suffering; this unhealthy blighting of what should have flowered—all this would be less comprehensible if it did not take place against the background of an even vaster miscarriage. The generation of 1820, their ears still ringing with the loud exhortations of Romanticism, were reduced to inaction, confronted with a mean and cramping reality. Unable to live their dreams, they settled for dreaming their lives. Frédéric is the incarnation of this generation, and his behavior is typical, almost symbolic. He does not take part in the "February Days," he is merely "present." He enjoys the barricades, the riots, the sight of the people in arms, as a spectacle; the looting of the Tuileries he finds in bad taste. He is so afraid of being duped he will not believe in any change, and declares people will always be the same. When the provisional government massacres the proletarians in June he is at Fontainebleau with Rosanette. After the *coup d'état* he lets it be understood that that was not what he wanted. Most of his young bourgeois friends had thought and acted the same way.

L'Education sentimentale would not possess the virtually inexhaustible richness it has without this political and social backcloth, this tapestry into which the story of Frédéric and Mme Arnoux is woven, this turmoil of events which reveals people as they are deep down—rich men, business men, republicans, artists, and even women of easy virtue. History confirms the accuracy and perfect objectivity of the picture, but that scarcely matters: Flaubert was not aiming at historical reconstruction. The truth he aimed at and attained was larger, more general, more typical. Dambreuse is our contemporary, and so is the sinister Père Roque, and you may pass Sénécal still in the Paris streets today, with his stubble haircut and his pseudo-priestly or professional air. More than one generation since 1820 has had its Days of February and June; more than one has been made up of disappointed dreamers and thwarted climbers. Many an adolescent, reading the *Education,* has learned to make his own self-examination. The truth as brought up to date by Flaubert is valid for all "lost" or "sacrificed" generations, and for all "angry young men." (pp. 175-81)

Flaubert's Problems

It took Flaubert five years to write *L'Education sentimentale,* from 1864 to 1869. The work was long and hard. Though he complained less than before about "the throes of style," he experienced, as he had over *Madame Bovary,* moments of suffering, periods of discouragement, attacks of distaste at being tied to a "bourgeois subject." "It's about time I amused myself

at last," he wrote to George Sand. He meant he would like to treat a more congenial subject, one which would require less research of all kinds, less hunting after details apparently unimportant but which for him had to be absolutely accurate. He had already expressed such a wish to Louise Colet. As the years went by bringing the death of friends, especially that of Bouilhet in 1869, and accentuating the fact that he was old before his time, he entrenched himself more firmly every day in pessimism, and, despite his social life in Paris, in solitude. He did not know the worst was yet to come.

His first concern in writing "the moral history of the men of [his] generation" was to create a truthful work, *i.e.* one that was impartial and objective and did not betray his own sympathies and preferences. This concern derived from his theories about a "scientific and impersonal" art, and a novel which "should . . . remain within the limits of general plausibility." He wrote to George Sand: "Rich or poor, victors or vanquished, I don't accept any of all that"—meaning the exalting of the one and debasing of the other. "I don't want to have love or hate or pity or anger"; he hoped to "bring Justice into Art." Then, he went on, "the impartiality of description would have the majesty of law—and the precision of science."

He had to ask himself whether this concern was compatible with his wider aim of creating a work of art, and with the need to give form to what can only be called the author's opinion on "the things of this world."

On the theoretical plane he met with no answer to the first question. He believed what he was in the process of creating was "something useless, by which I mean contrary to the aim of Art, which is vague exaltation. But with the present scientific demands [*i.e.* his own] and a bourgeois subject, that seems to me fundamentally impossible. Beauty is not compatible with modern life. . ."

This was one of the bees in Flaubert's bonnet. But there is more than one kind of artistic beauty, and while *L'Education* does not observe the canons of classical art or of those of the novel as generally written in Flaubert's day, it is this very fact which lends it its eternal freshness and has made it a universal influence on the modern novel.

As to the "form" to be adopted "to express one's opinion now and then on the things of this world without running the risk of seeming an idiot later," one can only agree with Flaubert that it is "a tough question, *un rude problème.*" But to this question he did find an answer. Regarding the things of this world, "It seems to me the best is simply to paint them." Simply? What he did was paint them in his own way, with their good side and their bad, their causes and their effects, with a scalpel for instrument. "Dissection is revenge," or in other words the expression of opinion is revenge, because for a pessimist to dissect men is enough to show they are bad and that life drags us towards the void. *L'Education,* like *Madame Bovary,* was to be a work of criticism, even of social criticism. When Flaubert wrote to George Sand, "I confine myself to showing things as they appear to me, to expressing what seems to me the truth," he added at once, "Damn the consequences!" showing how few illusions he had about what the reactions would be.

It was not the vanquished who were likely to be angry. They are dreamers rather than men of action, and Flaubert was irresistibly attracted to dreamers, and satisfied merely with showing their ludicrous side. But what would be the response to the picture of the frightened and cynical bourgeois at the Dambreuses', the shot fired by Père Roque at the prisoner in the Tuileries, and the murder of Dussardier by Sénécal? He had only had to show the characters as they were and describe the situations in detail to reveal the fundamental significance of the events. The impartiality and objectivity of the description add to its force and make it inexorable. Flaubert's powerful searchlight on events makes even those who, like Frédéric, are apathetic about them, appear different and in this respect less sympathetic.

Heroic Self-restraint

Another difficulty was how to insert individual stories into a picture of an age, with its great events dictated by history. First of all there was the love of Frédéric for Mme Arnoux, which with all its vicissitudes and consequences had to run right through the book and make its presence constantly felt. Then there were the adventures of dozens of other characters, which as in real life did not always fall into convenient groupings and were not sufficiently interesting to hold the limelight. Nevertheless the reader had to feel the presence of Hussonet, Cisy, Martinon, and many other minor figures. And how was Flaubert to confine himself to painting a back-cloth when public events erupted on to the front of the stage and monopolized attention? The author also had to be careful to preserve the over-all greyness of tone he was aiming at.

All these problems Flaubert put to himself and to his correspondents. "Will character-descriptions interest you?" "Historical characters are more interesting than fictional ones, especially when the latter have moderate passions; one is less interested in Frédéric than in Lamartine." "I am afraid lest the backgrounds eclipse the foregrounds." And so on. He solved these difficulties by returning to them again and again, making changes like a painter muting his colors and transferring them from places where they catch the eye too much. He had to weave within the framework of his main tapestry without allowing himself any "embroidery" that might unbalance it. "No big scene, no purple passages, no metaphors even." He deliberately held back his abilities as a writer and the resources of his temperament, the whole skill of which a novelist is generally so proud, and by this heroic self-restraint he achieved the perfect work of art which is the *Education,* that long flow of dream, love, and nostalgia, the closest possible image of time which passeth and returneth not. (pp. 186-89)

> *Maurice Nadeau, in his* The Greatness of Flaubert, *translated by Barbara Bray, The Library Press, 1972, 307 p.*

R. J. SHERRINGTON   (essay date 1970)

[*Sherrington investigates point of view in* Sentimental Education.]

[By] far the greatest part of *l'Education* is presented from Frédédric's point of view. For Flaubert, this has the advantage that several problems of unity in tone and structure are largely solved from the beginning, in spite of the complexity of the material he has to present. In choosing this solution, he would appear to have benefited from the experience gained in his two earlier works. To put the matter in its broadest terms, it can be said that *Bovary* is primarily the story of an individual, while *Salammbô* is the story of a society in crisis. *L'Education* tries to be more broadly-based than either, a combination of both, with neither aspect significantly more important than the other. Flaubert had used the technique of individual points of view with some success in his first novel, and added to it the method of combined point of view in his second. In *l'Education,* he was faced with the double problem of a more complex structure and a desire to tighten his method of presentation. This involved a certain modification of his earlier techniques.

His first important decision was to make individuals, rather than the society from which they had sprung, the centre of his new novel. In this he was greatly helped by the fact that the society with which he was dealing required less objectification than Carthage. In addition the crisis was internal, so that he had one and not two social structures to present. Thus he could more easily use a single witness to observe all aspects. His early plans show, moreover, that he had given considerable thought to selecting as his witness a central character whose social situation would permit him to observe a wide variety of social levels.

Having selected Frédéric as his witness, Flaubert had to consider ways of ensuring that his character represented typical aspects of the time and place: apart from his general theory of universality, he is concerned with 'l'histoire morale des hommes de ma génération' [see excerpt dated 6 October 1864]. This involved presenting the reader with the idea, scarcely imagined by the majority of literate people in the complacent Second Empire, that his generation had totally failed to meet the challenge of modern life (compare his lamentations about the defeat of France in 1870); it also involved offering an explanation of this failure. Impersonality enters the picture, for Flaubert felt he could not stand up and wave his arms in fury as a Victor Hugo, or even a Balzac, did. He must *show* his hero failing, and through him show everyone else failing as well—as in a Shakespearian tragedy, the stage must finally be strewn with bodies, at least morally. In *Bovary,* he had shown Emma's failure by two main methods: by contrasting her point of view with that of others, and by contrasting her point of view at one time with that at other times. He has now realized that it is not necessary to use both these methods. It is possible to achieve substantially the same result with very little intervention of other points of view. The development is based on the assumption that most people damn themselves simply by being themselves. They usually have such monumental egotism that they seldom see the rest of the world except emotionally, in relationship to themselves ('voir les choses comme elles sont'?), and at the same time have thought so little about moral and other problems that they are convinced all the answers are simple and straightforward ('ne pas conclure'?). Since the concluding is based on observation and experience, it follows that it is continually varying with emotional responses to these experiences. It also follows that *all* conclusions are logically false, even though there may be a 50-50 chance of their being true in fact. Flaubert's method is to avoid deciding which ones are true (he has sufficient humility to believe he is incapable of this), and to restrict himself to demonstrating that all are logically false. Frédéric's emotional responses inevitably result in conclusions which show nothing but inconsistency and contradictions. This is achieved without the assistance of contrasting points of view.

The chief danger of the method, especially in such a long and complicated book, is that the reader will not make the comparisons which are an essential part of it. This was already a danger in *Bovary,* but it is much greater here. If the comparisons are not made, a 'Frédéric Moreau, c'est moi' equation will be unavoidable, and indeed several critics accept this equation. But one of the outstanding traits of Flaubert's character, as revealed in his correspondence, is his constant self-examination;

and this is what Frédéric lacks most of all. There is no point in demonstrating that this or this theory or experience were common to Frédéric and Flaubert: such correspondences do not turn a novel into an autobiography. At best we could say that the novel *might* have been Flaubert's story, if he did not possess the critical faculties and single-mindedness so noticeably absent from Frédéric's character; but this is like saying a negro could pass for a European if it were not for the colour of his skin, and in any case it would mean that the novel could never have been written. Nor is the fact that Flaubert apparently identifies himself with Frédéric for most of the the book particularly relevant. What Flaubert is trying to say about Frédéric is to be found not in the content of any particular scene (which is all Frédéric himself can see), but in the inconsistencies between scenes (which Frédéric is incapable of seeing). That is, Flaubert relies very heavily on the structure of the book to communicate his thoughts, so that within any given scene his apparent identification with the hero, while having several practical advantages . . . , does not seriously affect his message—except for the unwary. Flaubert does not have to condemn Frédéric's behaviour, for it condemns itself. Beneath the apparently guileless factual record of Frédéric's experience there is a pattern of half-truths and delusions which can satisfy only a person like Frédéric. It is because he is satisfied with them that his whole life is consumed in running round in circles, with the result that at the end of the novel he is not more 'educated' then he was at the beginning. And all this is achieved impersonally, for it comes through even though he has been allowed to argue his own case. The author almost never intervenes to let the reader know directly how false Frédéric's life has been. (pp. 327-30)

[If] this is the case for the novel as a whole, there is no reason why it should not be so in the Mme Arnoux part of the story. Already in the early plans for the novel there was considerable evidence suggesting that the Schlésinger episode was neither the starting-point or the main inspiration for this novel; and in the novel itself there are several reasons for arguing that Frédéric deluded himself about Mme Arnoux as much as about anything else. Idealization there undoubtedly is, but the idealization is self-centred and intermittent—as false as any of his other attitudes. And it is Frédéric's idealization, not Flaubert's. The affair should be seen in perspective, as one aspect of a many-faceted book, and as an illustration of one side of Frédéric's character, revealing its true value only in comparison with other sides.

Changes in the point of view, then, do not have the same importance in *l'Education* as in either *Bovary* or *Salammbô*, but the communication of Frédéric's *Bovarysme* is perfectly adequate without them. The other task Flaubert had set himself was to show the *Bovarysme* of a whole nation. This is also achieved largely by using the same witness to register the actions and speech of others, and leaving the reader to effect the usual comparisons. Using the same witness preserves the external or mechanical unity of the work, while a deeper unity is achieved by making sure that nearly all the minor characters have at least some traits in common with one or more of the others, even of their enemies, and that all change their social or political position at least once, so that one can never be sure who will be on whose side at any given moment. The result is an immensely involved ever-changing series of cross-relationships—Flaubert no doubt working on the assumption that something of this nature must have happened, or the royalists, the republicans, and the bonapartists could not possibly have been successively victorious in such a short period. The

majority of Frenchmen, he argues, could not correctly be classified as any of these things, but as opportunists. These inter-relationships, and the comparisons they invite, increase the unity not only in the sense that the removal of one of the characters would leave a gaping hole in the structure, which could be patched only by modifying many of the remaining actions, attitudes and scenes. They also provide a seemingly infinite variety of ironic contrasts behind which Flaubert can hide his personal attitudes, and each character exhibits attitudes having sufficient points of contact with Frédéric's for us to conclude that the weaknesses in his character which are responsible for his downfall (or, more precisely, his lack of progress) are the same as those which caused the social troubles in the French nation. The technique adopted therefore ensures several of what for Flaubert were the cardinal virtues of a work of art: unity, universality, irony, impersonality.

The technique of a double or combined point of view, relatively important in *Salammbô*, is hardly to be found in *l'Education;* although it is not uncommon to have several people witnessing a scene at once, this does not seem to have the effect of increasing the objectivity of presentation. This is no doubt partly because the concept of 'crowd' as a powerful monster with many bodies but only one tiny mind, is not so important to this novel, which is more concerned with the failure of individuals. Instead, Frédéric himself is credited with varying degrees of perspicacity, depending on what he is looking at and how nearly it concerns him. He is most unreliable in his judgements of people, and especially of women; a little more reliable when it comes to viewing material surroundings, which generally inspire fewer debilitating emotions; and most reliable when he is called upon to witness a street rising. In the last case he is completely uninvolved emotionally, and Flaubert is free to make him wander through the streets, viewing the most interesting events, wherever they may occur. His eyes are used to give a comprehensive view of the Revolution, such as Dussardier, for example, would be quite incapable of giving—he is too busy fighting. Because of his character, Freédéric can replace the narrator in these scenes, so that the apparent unity of viewpoint can be continued.

The methods so far summarized account for over 80 per cent of the total length of the book. The remainder is presented by direct speech, by the omniscient narrator, or from the point of view of various secondary characters. Generalized commentary by the author is rare, except that he does display his cynicism and disgust with the French nation in a few pages. Flaubert may have felt that his customary impassiveness was impossible here—since Frédéric has shown no real interest in the political events, and since in any case the whole book has so thoroughly demonstrated the unreliability and shallowness of both him and all the other characters, the reader could not be expected to recognize an author's mouthpiece if one suddenly appeared at this stage. Yet most of the authorial comments confirm, rather than add to, what an attentive reader would already have inferred from the development of the action, so these comments are rather difficult to explain. The other intrusions by the narrator or secondary characters are usually in the interests of efficiency, of a comic effect, or of irony. They are minor, but do show that even now Flaubert is not tied to any one means of presentation. He will always choose that which is most suited to his needs, provided that it does not clash with his basic artistic tenets.

Thus the point of view technique developed in *Bovary*, and used again with variations in *Salammbô*, has now become even more important to Flaubert: it is used more often, in a more thoroughgoing fashion. It is also used more subtly (which is partly a side-effect of its being more nearly restricted to a single character): indeed, even some critics who have recognized its presence in *Bovary* have lamented its absence in *l'Education.* I have tried to show that it is indeed present, and that postulating its presence allows of an interpretation which differs from that which is most commonly accepted. It also permits the dismissal of one of the great 'problems' of the novel, the question of how Flaubert can talk so much about impersonality and yet apparently ignore his own principles in one of his two greatest works; and then the dismissal, too, of some of the uneasy compromises which have been offered to explain away this problem. If one tests the hypothesis by detailed examination of the text, it is found that it can be applied with considerable consistency. It is not difficult to advance theoretical reasons for accepting that such a technique would be attractive to Flaubert, because it allows him to put into practice most of his prized artistic dogma. And the application of it represents the culmination of efforts dating from at least the writing of *Novembre,* some twenty-seven years earlier, to express, in a manner consistent with these dogma, what Flaubert regarded as a fundamental psychological fact. (pp. 330-33)

R. J. Sherrington, in his Three Novels by Flaubert: A Study of Techniques, *Oxford at the Clarendon Press, 1970, 363 p.*

MARCIA K. MILLER (essay date 1971)

[*Miller examines the narrative structure of* Sentimental Education, *delineating parallels and correspondences between events in Frédéric Moreau's life and events in French history.*]

Although his masterpiece was misunderstood and neglected for years after its publication in 1869, it has been granted for some time now that in *L'Éducation sentimentale* Flaubert presents a brilliant picture of his hero Frédéric Moreau and of life in France (in Paris particularly) between the years 1840 and 1851. Still, the novel has seemed something less than a well-unified whole. It follows a traditional chronological line of narration, and yet, read this way, appears confusingly episodic. The many characters are introduced in abrupt fashion and pop in and out of the novel with disconcerting rapidity; events large and small occur in bewildering, seemingly unconnected succession. Flaubert himself explained this by saying that he was dealing with life, not art. In spite of this disclaimer, however, a close study of the novel shows that it does not imitate the formlessness of life, but is a carefully wrought structure. A number of critics have shown various patterns, particularly thematic motifs or symbols, that give structure to the novel. I should like to discuss one element of structure that is perhaps so obvious as to have escaped notice.

Perhaps the first important thing to grasp in reading *L'Éducation sentimentale* is that it is always two stories at once, each equally important: the story of Frédéric Moreau, and the story of France. They run parallel throughout, supporting and illuminating each other. This may seem to be a distinction without a difference, in relation to the idea that *L'Éducation sentimentale,* like most historical novels, presents a character and his times in a single matrix. But this is not so. Flaubert keeps his two stories distinctly separate in spite of the common ground they share and makes special use of a structural interplay between them as the book proceeds.

Let us see very briefly how this works out. The first two chapters are a sort of prologue to the novel. In them Frédéric, who is eighteen and has just taken his Bachelor's degree, goes home to visit his mother in the provinces. On the steamer which takes him from Paris he meets and falls deeply in love with the Parisian, Madame Arnoux. At his mother's house, he visits the friend of his boyhood, Deslauriers; the two have long dreamt of going to Paris to begin life together. Frédéric can think only of Paris. Throughout the novel he is opposed to his mother's plans for a prudent and successful life—to take a sound, dull position, marry the neighboring heiress Louise, voice no criticism of the government which could give him patronage. When, in ch. 3, he returns to Paris, he is on his own for the first time, embarking on a new life away from his provincial home and his mother, and preparing to make a great name (should it be as a lawyer or a poet?) that will win him fame and the attention of Madame Arnoux. He is intoxicated with the prospect of his freedom, indeed his life is to be an experiment in freedom. In the course of the novel he travels a number of times between Paris and the provinces. These journeys represent the two poles of his life and signify opposite goals and values—Paris, the unknown, the glamorous, the sophisticated, the exciting; the provinces, the familiar, the stale, the safe.

The journeying between the two poles is most effectively symbolized by the steamer journey in ch. 1. And here we see a first important correspondence between the two stories of Frédéric and of France. Just as Paris and the provinces are the twin poles of Frédéric's life, so they are the twin poles of the life of France and its political history during this period leading up to and following the revolution of 1848. That revolution belonged only to Paris and a few large cities with an urban proletariat, and it was to be negated largely because of the opposition of the provinces. The struggle between Paris and the provinces is crucial both for Frédéric and for France; hence again the importance of the opening journey.

In Pt. 1, which takes up two-thirds of the novel and is located largely in Paris, Frédéric's most important experiences center around his love for Madame Arnoux. He is undergoing the education referred to in the title, an education in sentiment, in emotions, an education of the heart involving him in new attitudes and activities. In turn France, in Pt. 1, is engaged in an experiment in a new freedom. Especially through a group of Parisians among whom Frédéric makes a number of friends, she is working towards the revolution that will come in 1848, after suffering the disappointments and disillusionment ensuing from the revolution of 1830. These Parisians are thus also undergoing an education in sentiment, the sentiment of a revived liberty, equality, fraternity. They see all wealth and power concentrated in the hands of the wealthy manufacturing and business class, with a proletariat that does not get its rightful share. But beyond this, they have no clear ideas of what they wish the revolution to accomplish for the country, any more than Frédéric has any clear idea of how he wishes to make his love for Madame Arnoux a part of his life. Here is another important correspondence between the two stories. Both Frédéric and the revolutionaries live largely on dreams and noble visions. We see the process of a sentimental education, alike in love and in revolutionary politics, since in both cases the sentiment is an idealistic aspiration of heart and spirit.

With Frédéric it is the almost religious yearning for a beautiful and virtuous woman; with many Parisians it is the yearning for a new freedom and justice. Among the Parisians, for example, there is the fiercely puritanical and dogmatic socialist

Sénécal, who, like an Old Testament prophet, demands the overthrow of a rich, corrupt, materialistic Establishment and a new life of simplicity and righteousness; there is the good, naive, stupid, young blue-blouse, Dussardier, who confidently looks toward a day when men of all classes will love each other like brothers. Both of these men, like Frédéric, pursue a vision; but they are not clear-sighted or hard-headed in seeing people or events around them. It is true, of course, that neither Frédéric, dreaming of Madame Arnoux, nor most of his compatriots, dreaming of freedom, seem pure in their idealism. When Frédéric is not worshipping at the shrine of Madame Arnoux, he is pursuing Rosanette, a small-time courtesan. Sénécal and Dussardier are the only two whose enthusiasm and work for the revolution is untainted by personal interest. All the others support the revolution for what it will bring them. Deslauriers, wanting power over men's minds, hopes it will make him the editor of a powerful journal; Pellerin, the third-rate painter who forges old masters, wants a government that will recognize and subsidize him as a great artist; the effete young aristocrat Cisy simply enjoys the fearful excitement of having radical friends. But all are affected nonetheless by the dreams and sentiments of the times, which are indeed the strongest force in their lives.

A third and most important correspondence between the stories comes at the end of Pt. I, the only break in the novel. Here Flaubert gives us the great climax of both stories, and they occur simultaneously, in a way that is surely meant to point up the parallelism of the two main strands of the book. For Frédéric, who seems finally to have realized his romantic dream by arranging an assignation with Madame Arnoux, the climax is her failing to appear, and Frédéric's bitterly vengeful invitation to Rosanette to take her place. For France the climax is at that same moment the outbreak of the February revolution of 1848. In the last lines of Pt. I Frédéric and Rosanette, making their way through the crowds of gathering revolutionaries to the house Frédéric has rented, hear a noise like the rending of a great piece of silk. It is the soldiers firing on the people protesting the official ban on the reformers' banquet. Symbolically a terrible ripping apart of the characters' lives has begun. The fruits of a sentimental education are about to be seen.

This double climax is employed by Flaubert in quite traditional but effective ways. It could neatly illustrate the old graphs showing a plot line rising to a peak two-thirds of the way through the story and then going downhill; it is intensely dramatic; and it does indeed represent a turning point after which events inexorably go in a different direction. As I have said, the fruits of a sentimental education appear in Pt. II, the last third of the book, which shows the lives of both Frédéric and France in hectic disarray. Frédéric, whose life has always been characterized by a certain amount of fecklessness and undirection, now exhibits these traits much more strongly. He makes an impulsive attempt to enter political life, suffers a single small humiliation, and retreats into a long rambling trip with Rosanette through the historical chateau country in an attempt to lose himself in the past. Returning to Paris, he maintains a half-hearted liaison with Rosanette, fathers an unwanted son who dies, and begins to court Madame Dambreuse for her high social position and wealth. His experiment in freedom ends in spiritual vacuity. Similarly, France enters a period of chaotic undirection. The February revolution begins with a disorganized mob in carnival mood sacking the Tuileries, and Flaubert includes the ominous detail of a prostitute who swathes herself in plundered robes and poses as a statue of liberty. As Victor

Brombert has pointed out [see excerpt dated 1966], the theme of prostitution is heavily stressed throughout the novel. We see this in the two stories. Frédéric has sold out his love for Madame Arnoux, bargaining for that of Rosanette. All parties in France after the revolution sell out for their own selfish advantages. It is said of M. Dambreuse, who represents the Establishment, that he acclaimed every regime in his lifetime no matter what its political principles, loving power so dearly that he would have paid to sell even himself (his funeral takes place appropriately in a church painted with scenes from the life of Mary Magdalene). Deslauriers reports bitterly that the workingmen in the trades unions are as bad as the manufacturers, that any one of them would sell his country for fifty centimes to get a tariff of three francs on the product of his work.

The lack of unified direction is graphically shown by the way the revolutionaries split into factions which engage in paralyzing and trivial quarrels among themselves. There is the memorable scene of the meeting of the political "Club of Intellect" (of which Sénécal is president), where there is: roaring applause for some young men who burned copies of the *Assemblée Nationale* in front of the Pantheon; a fight over which "workmen's hymn" to sing; a debate over the idea that European democracy should adopt a single language such as Latin; an unending speech on taxes; an attempt by a farmer to read a paper entitled "Manures"; an exhortation to inaugurate the Kingdom of God after the principles of the founder of Socialism, Jesus Christ; Pellerin's speech on art and his ejection from the meeting; and Frédéric's attempt to speak and his ejection by Sénécal as the crowd is harangued in incomprehensible Spanish by a revolutionary from Barcelona.

In Pt. II the hostility between Paris and the provinces is again seen. When the national workshops to assist the starving proletariat fail and the government plans to send these people to the country to farm, they prepare to riot against what is to them an unacceptably degrading mode of life. The National Assembly, chosen by universal suffrage in the spring of 1848—and here the provinces made their power felt—is extremely conservative and becomes increasingly repressive. The Socialists, representing the urban revolutionaries, rebel in June and are savagely crushed by the new government that was supposed to usher in an age of liberty and justice. Pere Roque as a patriotic supporter of the new government (he is, significantly, a neighbor of Frédéric's mother in the provinces) volunteers as a sentry at the prison into which the Socialists are crammed in frightful filth and deprivation, and takes pleasure in shooting any who appear at the vent-hole and ask for bread.

Throughout Pt. II the stories of Frédéric and France run parallel. Both are on a down-hill course of moral debasement. Both exhibit new and degrading ugliness, foreshadowed in Pt. I but seemingly unlikely then. Frédéric calculatingly schemes and works to make himself the lover and lackey of the cold, selfish, tyrannical Madame Dambreuse in order to win an important place in the wealthy aristocratic world. At the same time he goes through the motions of planning to marry Louise, and indulges in every sort of mean duplicity. The parallel between Frédéric and France is again made clear. As he becomes the servant of Madame Dambreuse, so France becomes again the servant of a crassly selfish, materialistic bourgeoisie while going through the motions of being a democratic republic. This parallel is heavily underlined by the way in which Flaubert shows how impossible it is eventually for either France or Frédéric to make any kind of new life, even a new beginning. As at the end of Pt. I, he does this with a deft double climax occurring at the end of the novel proper, before the last two chapters of epilogue. This climax is presented in only a few paragraphs, through two events that follow each other like gunshots. Frédéric, after breaking with Madame Dambreuse on a final noble impulse inspired by his love for Madame Arnoux, decides to start afresh by returning to the provinces and marrying Louise. He arrives in the village just in time to see her coming out of the church as the bride of Deslauriers. Upon this, the crash of his personal hopes, he hurries back to Paris and witnesses a similar crash of the hopes of the Republic. Crowds are out, barricades are up, the libertarians are making a last stand against Louis Napoleon's *coup d'état* of 1851. The police charge, and Sénécal, now an officer because he always prized authority over freedom, shoots his old friend Dussardier who is still fighting for the lost dream. And so both Frédéric and revolutionary France lose everything they once dreamed of possessing or accomplishing. Moreover, both are betrayed by their one-time friends.

The last two chapters, the epilogue, take place in 1867. They seem to belong only to Frédéric and round off two events that took place in the first two chapters of prolouge: his meeting and falling in love with Madame Arnoux on the steamer taking him to his mother's house (in ch. I), and his discussion with Deslauriers of a youthful escapade (in ch. 2). But in view of the parallels between the two stories they can certainly be taken as a comment on France as well. In the penultimate chapter Madame Arnoux, whom Frédéric has not seen for many years, comes unexpectedly to visit him, and afterwards he believes she came to offer herself to him. Might this not suggest, for the other story, the capitulation of France to Napoleon III?

In the final chapter Frédéric and Deslauriers reminisce about their youth, deciding that the best time of their life was their daring experiment in freedom when they visited the village brothel; here again we are reminded of the prostitution image which Flaubert uses so often in the political part of the novel. This visit was the one experiment in freedom that did not fail, simply because it never materialized, Frédéric taking fright and both boys running from the house as soon as they entered. Otherwise—and here we have an important concluding parallel between the two stories—the great experiment in freedom for Frédéric and for France, their education in sentiment, in idealistic aspirations of love and politics, ends in depressing failure. Everything has come full circle; the life of Frédéric and France is seen at the end as at the beginning. Frédéric is once again back in the provinces, leading a quiet, dull life and sharing the friendship of his boyhood companion Deslauriers. France is again ruled by the same powers that were dominant at the start of the novel, typified by M. Dambreuse, the ruthless banker and businessman who at first believed himself ruined by the revolution but who soon found himself and became president of the National Assembly elected in 1848. (After his death he is buried beside Benjamin Constant, the president of the Council of State after the failed revolution of 1830.) To emphasize the inutility of a sentimental education, Flaubert contrasts the failure of Frédéric and his revolutionary friends with the success of characters like M. Dambreuse and Martinon. These were usefully educated because they eschewed sentiment for hard business facts; they followed the head rather than the heart, and learned and prospered.

What then is Flaubert saying to us? We are at first likely to read the novel as a fiercely sardonic indictment of a sentimental education (whether in love or politics) as hopelessly weak and foolish, of idealistic aspirations as immature and silly fantasies,

of a romantic view of life as utterly unrealistic and escapist. We see a cynical stamp of approval set on those who live only with an eye on the main chance. All this is there, to be sure. But it is not the whole truth. For unheroic though Frédéric is, self-indulgent and vacillating, he is also amiable, kind, and generous; surely he is not worse than M. Dambreuse of unrelenting strength and purpose. The political idealist Dussardier is incredibly naive and trusting, a born martyr in every matter large and small, yet with his sweetness he moves us in a way that none of the other revolutionaries do. Flaubert's later proposed title for the novel *Les Fruits Secs* expresses the theme of disillusionment and sterility in *all* life, echoing the resignedly melancholy proverb, "Plus ça change. . . ." To the young reader this is profoundly depressing, but perhaps to the older reader not so much so. Though the ideals and aspirations of the heart must fail to be realized, there is yet no satisfactory alternative. They represent as real and necessary a part of life as anything else. To echo another proverb, take your choice, says Flaubert, and pay for it. So he gives us the two stories, that of Frédéric and of France.

Because of the marked and deliberate parallelism of the two strands of the novel, it is tempting to see countless detailed similarities between them. This can be done with profit up to a point, but it should not be carried to extremes. Certainly Frédéric is not a symbol of France or even of his generation—he is always himself—nor are the events of his life simply an allegory of the nation's history during these years. But an awareness of the parallelism is valuable in providing an understanding of the underlying unity of structure of the novel. It brings the sometimes confusing impressions of people and events into order. It causes the seemingly random succession of episodes to fall logically into place. And it greatly strengthens and enriches an appreciation of the theme of sentimental education. (pp. 130-136)

> *Marcia K. Miller, "A Note on Structure and Theme in 'L'education sentimentale',"* in Studies in Romanticism, *Vol. 10, No. 1, Winter, 1971, pp. 130-36.*

RENEE WINEGARTEN   (essay date 1974)

[*Winegarten examines Flaubert's views concerning revolutionary tradition and culture.*]

[Flaubert presents an] extreme example of literary as opposed to political commitment. It was as the dedicated exponent of literary commitment that he launched in his masterpiece, *L'Éducation sentimentale,* a devastating critique of the revolutionary myth, dogma, and tradition. That critique has never been equaled, let alone surpassed. The title, *Sentimental Education,* to which Flaubert was so attached that he used it twice and ignored Turgenev's advice to change it, gives only a partial idea of what the book is about. When the novel first appeared, it went largely unappreciated, and perhaps its full implications have only become apparent in our own day.

By the revolutionary tradition is meant the whole mystique of revolution as handed down from the French Revolution of 1789: the intoxication of the crowd storming the Bastille, the spontaneous heroism of the barricades, the self-denying courage of the victorious volunteers of 1792, the "Roman" patriotic ideals of the government of 1793, the stirring revolutionary phraseology and rhetoric, the exciting revolutionary festivals with their processions and the planting of trees of liberty, the whole atmosphere of living outside ordinary time in a supreme moment when everything suddenly becomes possible, the feeling of playing a vital part in a heightened drama. There existed a tradition of violent action. Boys brought up on the legendary deeds performed on the barricades looked forward to the day when they too could show their mettle like the youth in Delacroix's picture. Some would give their lives with exemplary valor for this new chivalry, this dream of revolutionary heroism. (pp. 170-71)

When Flaubert in his novel undertook to question this revolutionary mystique as revealed in the revolution of 1848, he was attempting to analyze the psychology of revolutions in general. As a novelist, his prime concern was with "the eternal element," the portrayal of general human principles through particular instances. One of these principles, Flaubert had perceived, was revolutionary imitation, the way the men of 1789 modeled themselves on their conception of republican Rome or austere Sparta, while those of 1848 modeled themselves on their conception of 1789 or 1793. What did it matter if the men of 1793 did not really understand Sparta, when the very act of imitation was the important thing? Concepts produce facts, or so thought Jules, the devoted novelist and Flaubert's other self, in the first version of *L'Éducation sentimentale* (begun in 1843 at twenty-one, completed in 1845, and unpublished in the author's lifetime), as he commented on revolutionary imitation years before Marx did so in *The Eighteenth Brumaire of Louis Bonaparte*. Of course Marx, unlike Flaubert, thought his bourgeois phase of revolutionary imitation would eventually be overcome by the proletariat. So far, it is not the German philosopher who has been proved correct.

Flaubert, who was scarcely kinder to the bourgeoisie than Marx, did not expect the proletariat of the future to behave otherwise than in accordance with general human laws. The novelist was sufficiently swayed by the positivism of his age as well as by its respect for science to feel that what was needed was scientific inquiry in place of dogma. Instead of credulous affirmation and belief, there should be Voltairean doubt, questioning, and discussion. "The Revolution must cease to be a dogma and must be restored to the realm of Science, like the rest of human affairs," he would tell George Sand during the Commune in 1871. "If people had been more knowledgeable, they would not have believed that a mystic formula can create armies and that the word 'Republic' is enough to conquer a million well-disciplined men." They would have known that the victory of the volunteers in 1792 was not all it was cracked up to be. "But no, always the same old refrain, the same old humbug!" Instead of invoking God and the saints, people now swore by the Republic and 1792; they foolishly wanted to recreate a legendary heroic situation although circumstances had completely changed, "but what does that matter, it's tradition."

His friends, those sharp-tongued gossips the brothers Edmond and Jules de Goncourt, in their journal also criticized the revolutionary myth. After reading pamphlets published during the French Revolution for a play they were writing, they decided that were it not for its bloodshed, the revolution and its great men would be regarded as merely stupid. "And what hypocrisy, what lies, this Revolution was made up of! The mottoes, the walls, the speeches, the stories—everything was then a lie. *The Humbug of the Revolution:* there is a book to be written! . . . Is there one fact about the Revolution that patriotism and party passions and journalism have not turned into legend? . . . And out of all the gulls and simpletons in society and in the streets who have their catechism of the Bastille by heart, how many know the number of prisoners that these horrible and devouring dungeons actually released to the light of day?

Three, wasn't it? or was it four?" While there is some truth in this sour view, it does overlook the fact that the Bastille was the symbol of a hated tyranny.

Flaubert had no more intention of being duped than had the Goncourt brothers. Still, unattractive as the modern age of revolutions in which he knew he was living might be, it was nonetheless fascinating to Flaubert the artist. At least, so he had felt when younger, and he had enough of the romantic in him to find storm more interesting than calm. His Jules wondered whether an artist did not enjoy more freedom in a period when there had been "a revolution to change the world and a hero to conquer it," when monarchies crumbled and peoples were born, than in an era of stability. He could not but feel that this was a difficult yet fruitful subject for art. It all came down to art.

Of all the great nineteenth-century novelists, Flaubert stands as the most complete and confident representative of European literary culture for its own sake. (Not until shattered by the Franco-Prussian War did he voice grave doubts about the value and importance of literature). That confidence in literature is doubtless one reason why later writers, from Proust to Sartre, have been so preoccupied with the challenge he presents. True, when Flaubert speaks of taking ten hours to produce three unsatisfactory lines, and of the labor pangs of style, allowance has to be made for exaggeration (Edmond de Goncourt remarked, in a note, on Flaubert's penchant for magnifying things). Moreover, Flaubert wrote to friends describing his creative struggles when he was tired after many hours of toil in pursuit of the right word. Nevertheless, in modern eyes, he appears the literary saint incarnate. He quite deliberately stressed the opposition of art and life. Literature became for this son of a Rouen surgeon a means of evading a confined, shabby bourgeois reality that was permanently repugnant to his limitless imagination; it offered also the agreeable possibility of commanding and castigating the world he rejected.

His pessimism was temperamental. He was only thirteen when he spoke of life as a grotesque joke. The nervous attacks he suffered as a young man have been qualified as psychosomatic, an attempt to elude any other career than the literary one he desired to pursue. The isolated style of life the novelist would adopt (but for his travels and his emergence for Magny dinners and attendance in Princess Mathilde's salon during the years of fame) is foreshadowed in that of the writer Jules in the first version of *L'Éducation sentimentale*. Jules withdraws from the world into obscurity, into a manner of life called at once "sterile" and "rich," in contrast with Henry who frequents political salons and progresses from republicanism and socialism to support of the regime. Not that Jules was spared misgivings: "Occasionally he still experienced the temptation to live and act," but irony prevented him from accomplishing any action, and analysis undermined feeling. Besides, Jules could perceive the "nothingness" of all human endeavor which made action vain.

Of feminine temperament (a hysterical old woman, his doctor called him) if not of homosexual inclination, Flaubert dreamed a lifelong impossible love for Madame Schlésinger, whom he first glimpsed when he was fourteen at Trouville. He found the muse gave less trouble than ties with any demanding flesh-and-blood female. During his liaison with the authoress Louise Colet, it has been estimated that he met her only six times in two years, and then was careful to arrange their rendezvous when he was not likely to be in the middle of writing a chapter. Years later he told George Sand that he had been afraid of life.

The writings of the Marquis de Sade haunted his imagination and encouraged him to dream of "limitless mastery and magnificent power." One could have the illusion of attaining power through the word, the literary imagination seeming godlike in its capacity to embrace all things. Unlike the literary activities, Flaubert appeared content with power in the imaginative world (where, as in *Salammbô,* for instance, he could pile on the pagan atrocities to his heart's content).

He possessed the anarchist inclinations so common to the literary temperament, veering between thoughts of self-destruction and world destruction. In his notebook, written in 1840-1841, when he was between the ages of eighteen and nineteen, he envisaged the political future as an era of barbarism: "I wouldn't mind a bit seeing all civilization crumble like a mason's scaffolding before the building was finished—too bad! . . . I'd enjoy being at the gates of Paris with five hundred thousand barbarians, and burning the whole city. What flames! What a ruin of ruins!" (The imaginings of his Nero complex would become reality sooner than he knew, with the siege of Paris by the Prussians, their occupation of his home in Normandy, and the destruction wrought during the Commune—disasters he conceived as the end of his world.)

It was quite early, then, that Flaubert took to expressing disdain and disgust with life. Life was meaningless. The attempt to attain a true and complete assessment in any field of endeavor was impossible. The novelist Jules, hearing historians express contradictory views on the French Revolution, on Robespierre (a blood-thirsty tiger or the gentlest of legislators), on the Mountain (a sacred host or a den of brigands), gave up talking about history. The history of the world is a farce, the young Flaubert had written in his notebook, adding, "Too bad that conservatives should be so despicable and republicans so stupid." Partisanship is absurd. Opposing views and parties cancel each other out: they are roughly equivalent.

This attitude is not very different from the total impression conveyed by *L'Éducation sentimentale* (begun in 1864 when Flaubert was forty-three and completed in 1869). The feeling of disillusionment it exudes was therefore neither the result of his personal experiences during the revolution of 1848 nor the consequence of his meticulous documentation for that novel. These merely confirmed his opinion. In Rouen, Flaubert had attended one of the reform banquets that preceded the February Revolution and sat with frigid disgust amid the patriotic enthusiasm. With his intimate friend, the poet Louis Bouilhet, he visited Paris to find out what was going on "from the artistic point of view." He saw the fighting in the streets and the sack of the Tuileries, and returned to Normandy the day after the proclamation of the Second Republic. What particularly pleased him about the revolution was the downfall of the bourgeois supporters of Louis-Philippe. Would the new government and social conditions be favorable to art? Could the new men possibly be more stupid than their predecessors?

In Rouen he briefly joined the National Guard and paraded when a tree of liberty was planted. A further visit to Paris before the June days elicited the opinion that all parties were equally inept and that it was enough to make a decent person vomit. And he was in Paris during the coup d'état of December 1851, saw people killed before his eyes, and was almost killed himself.

By the time Flaubert came to write his novel, which covers the period from 1840 to 1851 and beyond, he realized that while these experiences contributed a skeleton framework, they were insufficient. Not only did he read or reread the socialist thinkers and study the newspapers of the period, but he consulted his friends, including George Sand, who put him in touch with Barbès, the only revolutionary for whom Flaubert expressed esteem. (Barbès risked his life for liberty in the streets while I was phrase-making in my study, wrote the author of *Madame Bovary,* voicing a contrast that later writers were to find more oppressive.) Other correspondents were asked about methods of transport in 1848 and about the posts of the National Guard. His care was such that the book has been judged historically accurate in all but a few minute particulars.

The much-vaunted impartiality of Flaubert is another matter. He prided himself on impersonality: the novelist has no right to express his opinion on anything whatever, he told George Sand. Has God ever expressed his opinion? Great art should be scientific and impersonal. It should be as majestically just and impartial as science. This was an exhortation to a godlike indifference he wished to, but could not, feel. He often spoke of his ivory tower, but he remained passionately interested in what was going on outside. It was this which kept his anger on the boil.

He was permanently infuriated by baseness, pettiness, and folly. Indignant at eighteen, he savored his indignation and went on being angry all through life. This impotent rage fell indiscriminately upon all. What remained constant, in his view, was "a depth of stupidity in humanity which is as eternal as humanity itself." He did not entirely exempt himself from that censure, and the fury of self-laceration is one of the sources of the novel's power.

To Frédéric Moreau, the passive, ineffectual, flaccid protagonist of *L'Éducation sentimentale,* with his hopeless love for Madame Arnoux, Flaubert gave the ideal love he himself cherished for Madame Schlésinger; but the novelist savaged his antihero, through whom he portrayed his own shortcomings without the compensating factor of his genius. Frédéric has only the vast dreams of artistic fame, the ambitious plans for writing a series of plays on the French Revolution; he is far too weak willed to accomplish anything. He belongs to the generation of Flaubert's provincial school friends, molded by romantic revolt, dreaming of dramatic love affairs or conspiratorial glory; one of them penned an apology for Robespierre, while two others committed suicide. Instead of fulfilling the high hopes entertained of him, Frédéric fritters time away and becomes involved with women he does not really love: the plebeian courtesan Rosanette and the frigid, wealthy bourgeoise, Madame Dambreuse.

At first the sensitive Frédéric's friendship with the coarse-grained Deslauriers seems inexplicable. Despite the harm the latter occasionally does Frédéric, their union is indissoluble. They are in fact two faces of the same bourgeois phenomenon. In their old age, they both look back to a boyhood escapade, when they took some flowers to a local prostitute and fled, as the best moment of their lives. This is Flaubert's final comment on the ineffectualness of his generation, and on the bourgeois society he loathed, though he was inescapably a part of it.

Besides aiming to undermine bourgeois values and leave the bourgeoisie "stupefied," Flaubert sought to expose the nature of revolutionary attitudes and sympathies. This is how it was then, and how it always will be, he proposes. When the February Revolution erupts, Frédéric, enjoys himself hugely, probably as Flaubert himself had done roaming the streets with Louis Bouilhet and Maxime du Camp. At the barricades, Frédéric was fascinated. The wounded and dead did not look real. He felt he was watching a play. Then he was gripped by the magnetism of the enthusiastic crowds. He sniffed ''voluptuously'' the stormy air that reeked of powder. However, like his creator, Frédéric did nothing. The idea of standing for election appealed to him. He thought of the great men of the Convention, of the new dawn, how he should throw himself into the revolutionary movement and even hasten its progress; and besides he was attracted by the deputy's uniform, which he understood would be a waistcoat with lapels and a tricolor sash.

As for the republican lawyer Deslauriers, he had dreamed beforehand of the coming cataclysm, of how he would shatter the foolish tranquility of the bourgeois who were unaware that a new 1789 was on the way. ''Oh! how much more splendid it was when Camille Desmoulins . . . urged the people onwards to the Bastille! They lived in those days, they could make their mark, prove their mettle! Mere lawyers gave orders to generals. . . .'' Something of Flaubert's destructive urge, his satisfaction at the overthrow of the complacent ruling bourgeoisie, has passed into Deslauriers. But Deslauriers reveals, too, an ambitious envy, an impatience for an upheaval through which he could climb to a position of importance—feelings that Flaubert regarded as forming a considerable part of revolutionary psychology.

It was to the vulgar Deslauriers, however, that Flaubert gave his own views on Socialism. Deslauriers says of Saint-Simon ''and his church'' and of Fourier that they are ''a lot of humbugs who would like to give us Catholicism all over again.'' For Deslauriers, ''modern reformers (I can prove it) all believe in Revelation.'' This was the conclusion that Flaubert had reached as a result of reading Saint-Simon, Fourier, Leroux, and Proudhon for the novel. All these pedantic and despotic utopian socialist reformers, thought Flaubert, not only derived from religious revelation but were united by hatred of freedom and philosophical inquiry. Their outlook was medieval, dogmatic, Jesuitical, ''Catholic'' in a word. They had taken the wrong turn in following the path of Rousseau, sentimental father of envious and tyrannical democracy, instead of the major highway of Voltaire with his emphasis on justice and law. ''I believe our ills partly derive from Republican neo-Catholicism,'' wrote Flaubert to the historian of the French Revolution, Michelet. This was one of the novelist's favorite themes in his letters.

The true revolutionary of *L'Éducation sentimentale,* the future Saint-Just according to Deslauriers, is the mathematics teacher Sénécal, and it is plain from the first moment that the author detests him as much as Frédéric does. Disinterested the austere Sénécal may seem to be, but he is described as pedantic and clerical in appearance, with something hard and cold about his gaze. His view that art should serve an educational purpose would have been enough to give the game away. After work, Sénécal annotated Rousseau's *Social Contract* and out of his reading of Mably, Morelly, Fourier, Saint-Simon, Comte, Cabet he had evolved ''a sort of American Sparta where the individual would exist solely in order to serve the State, which was more omnipotent, absolute, infallible and divine than the Dalai Lama or Nebuchadnezzar.'' (In Flaubert's eyes, the state was ''hateful''.) Sénécal employed ''the good faith of an inquisitor'' to demolish everything opposed to his view. And — an outlook particularly offensive to artists—he hated any sign of preeminence.

As foreman in the pottery factory of the thoughtless and shady Arnoux, he proves a petty tyrant to the girls who work there. Frédéric finds Sénécal's behavior cruelly harsh, but Madame Arnoux observes that there is such a thing as necessary severity. It is a revealing moment. At a first reading, one tends to see Madame Arnoux through Frédéric's eyes, in a soft, beautifying haze. On closer scrutiny, she appears an ordinary bourgeoise (as indeed she qualifies herself), with the ideas and ideals of her class.

All the same, when Sénécal is arrested for complicity in a terrorist plot, Frédéric, despite his dislike for the pedagogue, feels an all-too-human sympathy for the terrorist, ''that admiration inspired by any man who sacrifices himself for an idea.'' More enthusiastic toward Sénécal is Dussardier, with whom he is contrasted. Dussardier—the trusting, idealistic, simple man of the people—sees in Sénécal the victim of authority to be helped whether guilty or not, and regardless of whether his intended act was odious. When only fifteen, Dussardier had witnessed in the Rue Transnonain the 1834 massacre of defenseless workers and their families immortalized by Daumier's lithograph, and since then he had hated government as the embodiment of injustice and evil. (This attitude Flaubert calls naïve, but it has something in common with his own.)

Unlike Frédéric, Dussardier fought on the February barricades, and believed implicitly in all the revolutionary ideals. He thought that with the proclamation of the Second Republic there would be universal happiness and the whole world would be free. Recruited into the National Guard, he kills a youth on the barricades; thenceforward his conscience troubles him, for the boy had draped himself in the tricolor and cried, ''Are you going to fire on your brothers?'' So shaken is he by the betrayal of his ideals, and so disillusioned by the workers (whom he finds no better than the bourgeoisie) that he wishes to get himself killed. He is last seen shouting ''Long live the Republic!'', cut down by a policeman whom Frédéric recognizes as Sénécal.

This astonishing climax is one of the best sign-posted in all fiction: it has the satisfaction of surprise joined with the fulfillment of the reader's suspicions. The transformation of Sénécal into the instrument of tyranny follows implacably from the deepening authoritarian nature of his views: ''The end justifies the means. Dictatorship is sometimes necessary. Provided the tyrant does good—long live tyranny!'' From the first, Flaubert makes it plain that Sénécal stands for tyranny under another name; ultimately there is no difference between his form of tyranny and that of the reactionaries. Both work to the same end. A decent, honest, simpleminded fellow like Dussardier, the only worthy character in the book, suffers for all the dupes and victims.

Besides its powerful strain of tragic irony, the novel presents a sustained satire on revolutionary conduct and attitudes. Here are the bands of students in revolt. Newly arrived in Paris, Frédéric asks the reason for the disorders in the university quarter and is told, ''I don't know . . . and neither do they! It's their fashion of the moment!'' Here are the ritual cries, slogans, and rhetoric. The revolutionary myth of the sovereign people is mocked when the sack of the Tuileries culminates in a prostitute's adopting the stance of a statue of Liberty.

Flaubert ridicules, too, the sense of unlimited possibility awakened by revolution, long before the slogan ''Be realistic, ask for the impossible'' was written on the walls of the Sorbonne in 1968. For Mademoiselle Vatnaz, the emancipation of the proletariat cannot be accomplished without the emancipation of woman, and she puts forward an extensive program summed up as "everything for women." Indeed, if rights for women are not granted, they should be seized forcibly by a female army. The artists demand an arts forum or exchange where masterpieces would be produced by pooling talent.

As for the students, their cry is simple enough:

> "No more academies! No more Institute!"
>
> . . . "No more matriculation!"
>
> "Down with university degrees!"
>
> "Let's keep them," said Sénécal, "but let them be conferred by universal suffrage, by the People, the sole true judge!"

These students form part of the audience of the ironically named Club of Intelligence. Frédéric hopes to obtain its support for his candidacy, but he is shouted down in favor of a Spaniard whom nobody can understand, in one of the most savagely comic scenes in the novel. Everyone was imitating a model. Some were copying Saint-Just, others Danton or Marat, while Sénécal "was trying to be like Blanqui, who imitated Robespierre." The words, gestures, images of the French Revolution are all there, but the great passions are lacking. Along with Heine and Herzen, Flaubert perceived that there existed a revolutionary conservatism.

However, if Flaubert is not kind to the revolutionaries, he does not spare the reactionaries either. In a few telling paragraphs he evokes the imprisonment of Sénécal below the Orangerie terrace, where hundreds of men, sick, dying, and dead, lie in their own excrement. From time to time, bayonets are thrust haphazardly through the railings into the mass. When a prisoner begs for bread, Monsieur Roque fires; then returns home to be coddled by his daughter: "Oh! these revolutions!. . .," he moans. "I'm too sensitive!" The bourgeoisie are frightened, cowardly, cynical, vicious, and vengeful. Their leading representative, the banker Dambreuse, is acidly characterized as one who changed his coat so often and loved power so much that "he would have paid to sell himself." Flaubert told George Sand that the reactionaries in the novel seemed to him more "criminal" than the rest [see letter dated 10 August 1868].

He came to hate the bourgeoisie less as a class than as a mentality—a mentality shared by the workers as much as by the property owners, for "the bourgeoisie now is all of humanity, including the people." Upon this humanity he wished to "vomit" his disgust. He detested the masses, who seemed to him irredeemably stupid; the herd; equality; democracy; universal suffrage (as silly as divine right, though a little less hateful). He would say of the Communards that he did not hate them because he did not hate "mad dogs." But he thought these "bloody imbeciles" should have been forced to clear the ruins of Paris with chains round their necks, like common convicts. However, because of romantic sentimentality, "people feel compassion for mad dogs, instead of for those they have bitten."

Ideally, what Flaubert would have liked was government by the mandarins, an aristocracy of men of letters and men of science, the sole true representatives and torchbearers of humanity. Only then, he felt, would it be possible to avoid the crimes committed as a result of pursuing ideals in politics.

It is not difficult to see what is missing from this choleric indictment uttered by one who loftily declined to participate in the shaping of events, and who knew little and cared less about the day-to-day workings of politics or the deeper economic causes of unrest. The equally pessimistic but liberal Russian novelist Turgenev, to whom he was devoted, revealed a more sympathetic understanding of the forces of conservatism and change.

Flaubert was like a man sawing away at the branch he was perched on. The supreme bourgeois-hating bourgeois artist, the epitome of nineteenth-century bourgeois literary culture in its withdrawal from, and distaste for, modern life, the critic of the revolutionary tradition—Flaubert worked to undermine the basis and values of that culture as surely as did any revolutionary. He was one of a long line of nineteenth-century bourgeois writers who helped to make the word "bourgeois" a term of opprobrium, and whose antibourgeois strictures would eventually decline into the destructive commonplaces of revolutionary and counterrevolutionary alike. (pp. 171-82)

> *Renee Winegarten, "Literary Commitment versus Revolutionary Tradition: Flaubert," in her* Writers and Revolution: The Fatal Lure of Action, *New Viewpoints, 1974, pp. 169-82.*

D. A. WILLIAMS (essay date 1978)

[*Williams explores Flaubert's apparently ambivalent attitude toward literary realism in* Sentimental Education, *focusing chiefly on his depiction of love, masculinity, and male sexuality.*]

Flaubert's reputation as a Realist was secured, much to his dismay, by the publication of his first novel, **Madame Bovary,** in 1857. But it is his second novel dealing with modern life, **Sentimental Education,** published in 1869, which on several scores constitutes his greatest achievement as a Realist. The central character of this second work is less unusual, less outstanding than Emma Bovary who, as Baudelaire pointed out, is in some ways an awe-inspiring figure, endowed with an energy, passion, and intensity of aspiration which lift her above the ruck of common humanity. Secondly, the references to contemporary social reality in **Sentimental Education** are far more copious than in **Madame Bovary.** Thirdly, Flaubert's aim in **Sentimental Education** is to show the mixed fortunes of a whole generation as well as the psychological development of Frédéric Moreau, whilst in **Madame Bovary** the emphasis is firmly on the destiny of a single individual. Lastly, whilst [according to Henry James] **Madame Bovary** 'confers on its sufficiently vulgar elements of exhibition a final unsurpassable form', **Sentimental Education** is characterized by a narrative mode and structure which are less conspicuous, less obviously designed to compensate for the novel's equally 'vulgar elements of exhibition'.

All these features of Flaubert's second novel dealing with modern life constitute an intensification of the Realism of **Madame Bovary**—an intensification which extends the form near to breaking point and leaves many readers dissatisfied. In trying to avoid the novel's customary distortion of reality, Flaubert flouts traditional expectations. His choice of a mediocre central character, his studied evocation of an uneventful existence, his presentation of an unusually detailed historical background, his deference to Frédéric's confused awareness, his opting for an extended and curiously unmemorable plot and a deeply concealed structure are all part of Flaubert's deepening commitment to the 'profoundly true' rather than to the entertaining or aesthetically pleasing.

The choice of main character in *Sentimental Education* has often perplexed critics. Flaubert was not obliged to choose 'such an abject human specimen' [see excerpt by Henry James dated 1902]; what then is the purpose of selecting so dull and nondescript a character, or as P. Cortland puts it, 'a faceless man in the crowd'? Even Flaubert had his doubts: 'Do such flabby characters offer any interest', he wonders. The issue is clearly of central importance as Gide realized when he wrote: '*Sentimental Education* raises an enthralling problem; is the least exceptional character the most representative?' The danger of having so disconcertingly null, so uninspiringly mediocre a character is that he will fail to command the reader's attention; but the reward, the possible gain if the Realist wager is accepted, is that such a character, since he so clearly lies closer to the median line of unexceptional averageness than more heroic characters, will be more likely to reflect the pattern and dramatize the problems of the 'average' reader. In such a character's very insignificance lies his significance.

Flaubert once clearly defined the lack of positive qualities in Frédéric Moreau, by amending the sub-title of the novel to *Histoire d'un jeune hommet,* using the diminutive form to pinpoint his hero's rather spineless, apathetic personality and foppish, ineffectual ways. The actual sub-title—*Histoire d'un jeune homme, Story of a Young Man*—avoids prejudging the issue, however, leaving the reader to form his own general conclusions about the inadequacy of Frédéric from the apparently neutral account of his life. The principal characteristic of Frédéric—as revealed by his various actions and utterances—is a relentless passivity, more generally associated with the heroine of a traditional novel. Frédéric spends most of his life suspended in a state of expectation. In the opening chapter, we are told that 'he considered that the happiness which his nobility of soul deserved was slow in coming'. Happiness for Frédéric is not a goal which is actively pursued but a reward which he passively waits to be accorded. Likewise, worldly success. On inheriting a large fortune, he announces his ambition of becoming a minister but makes it clear that he is prepared to do nothing to achieve this ambition. From the outset, Frédéric renounces all effort in the sphere of love, too ('As for looking for the woman of my dreams, I've no intention of doing that'). He expects women to offer themselves to him and excludes a more forceful approach to the opposite sex. His typical posture is supine—even in his daydreaming, he sees himself 'reclining on cashmere divans'. The opening scene in which he is seen on the old paddle-steamer richly anticipates his whole life. Throughout the novel Frédéric seems to drift aimlessly through life, to be borne along by the tide of circumstance. He will repeatedly be shown poised motionless in a moving world, surrounded on all sides by the prosaic, bustling activity of the crowd, a born spectator forever reluctant to participate but drawn into dubious complicity with the dallying of Arnoux who does what he does not dare to do, and all the time cherishing the illusion that his attachment to the idealized 'vision' of the perfect woman sets him apart from a humanity engaged in more mundane pursuits.

The sinuous course of the river prefigures Frédéric's failure to 'steer a straight course', the way in which he repeatedly takes the line of least resistance, passively succumbing to his own whims and desires rather than pursuing a social, political, or artistic objective. The words which recur in connection with his behaviour are 'lâche' and 'lâcheté'; they are usually translated by 'cowardly' and 'cowardice' but the French carries suggestions of flabbiness, pusillanimity, lack of energy and moral vigour. 'Cowardice' seems both to descend on Frédéric

from outside ('An immense cowardice overcame Madame Arnoux's admirer') yet also to form the liquid substance of which his flabby being is composed ('All his virtuous wrath sank in a sea of cowardice'). When G. Sand attributed the novel's poor reception to 'the lack of control that the characters have over themselves', she was probably thinking principally of Frédéric.

Such lack of willpower and spinelessness cannot be put down simply to the callowness of youth. Even towards the end of the novel, when he is more 'mature', Frédéric continues to give way to his own worst desires; his involvement in politics is interpreted as a sure sign of weakness and, despite the fact that he has now 'won' two women, he is dominated by both of them, meekly carrying Madame Dambreuse's missal when he accompanies her to church and becoming Rosanette's 'chattel'. Frédéric sometimes judges himself harshly, of course, but the reader is likely to accept his view that it is an act of cowardice to let Rosanette drag him away from Madame Arnoux just after he has sworn he loves her as much as ever. Frédéric's flabbiness emerges clearly from the contrast with other characters. All four women with whom he is involved are more forceful than he is. At the end of the novel, it is Madame Arnoux who seeks to consummate their love; Rosanette is forthright in the offers she makes and in Part III makes a determined attempt to give their relationship permanence; Madame Dambreuse precipitates the break by forcing Frédéric's hand at the auction; Louise Roque braves the Paris streets at night, having earlier accused Frédéric of not having the courage to take her away from Nogent. The other male characters are almost all actively committed to an enterprise of one kind or another; Arnoux to a variety of hair-brained artistic and financial ventures, Deslauriers to launching a political journal, Dambreuse to the consolidation of his fortune, Sénécal to Socialism, Dussardier to the ideal Republic, Pellerin to Art, Martinon to the advancement of his own career. Frédéric, on the other hand, is not committed to anything; a Jack-of-all-trades, he shows no clear purpose or consistent effort; he abandons his novel, ignores socially advantageous openings, makes little effort to win votes as a political candidate, betrays each of the women he loves.

Frédéric's lack of direction also contrasts with the more purposeful careers of the young men depicted by Balzac. Although he admired his work and recognized his achievement, Flaubert set out to dedramatize the earlier novelist's presentation of the young man's attempts at making his fortune. Frédéric lacks the boldness and driving ambition of an Eugène de Rastignac or a Lucien de Rubempré; despite the fact that fortune smiles on him in the shape of a substantial inheritance and openings in the fashionable world, Frédéric is, on the whole, indifferent to success and follows an idle and meandering course, unlike Lucien whose character 'urged him to choose the shorter . . . route'. Frédéric does have his frantic moments but these are when he is in pursuit of Madame Arnoux or rushing to see a wounded friend, neither of which advances his social career. The constant implication of *Sentimental Education* is that Balzac's portrayal of the young man's entry into society puts too much emphasis on social ambition which typically, in Flaubert's view, assumes less importance than emotional or sexual matters. (pp. 78-82)

One of the most obvious challenges to Balzacian mythology comes in the sphere of sexual relations. The young man in Balzac is led to believe that the key to social advancement lies in the exploitation of women who are to be regarded as post-horses, to be abandoned as soon as they have outlived their social or financial usefulness. Compared to Rastignac who, as Balzac puts it, soon gets the bit between his horse's teeth, Frédéric is slow to develop 'equestrian' skills. Flaubert, in fact, reverses the pattern, showing in a symbolic dream Rosanette astride Frédéric (who is teamed up with Arnoux) and 'tearing his belly open with her golden spurs'. The only woman likely to benefit Frédéric socially is Madame Dambreuse who represents [according to Alison Fairlie (see Additional Bibliography)] the necessary challenge to the post-Balzacian hero'. It is significant, however, that Frédéric for a long time lacks any interest in her despite Deslauriers's injunction that he should set about seducing her and, although at the end he is tempted by her fortune, he makes an un-Balzacian sacrifice when he refuses to enter the symbolic Dambreuse carriage.

Lurking in the background in Balzac's novels about young men trying to make their way in society is the criminal, even Mephistophelean figure of Vautrin, aiding and abetting the social ambition of his protégés. Such a figure is conspicuous by his absence in *Sentimental Education.* This means that Frédéric compromises himself in small-scale acts of treachery (as when he writes notes, at Arnoux's request, putting off guests from attending a big banquet launched by a rival), whereas Eugène and Lucien, through their association with Vautrin, compromise themselves irredeemably. Whilst Lucien is forced to accept as a last stigmata of Parisian life the money Bérénice has earned by prostituting herself, Frédéric commits the paltry crime of taking the savings of the impecunious Dussardier. Flaubert nowhere presents the development of Frédéric in terms of a struggle for his soul between the forces of good and evil; there is no suggestion of some larger cosmic drama which would heighten the significance of the events recorded.

Flaubert is also reluctant to present the young man's career in terms of a conflict between the individual and society, with the latter seen as a quasi-mythical entity against which the young man pits his strength. The reference to 'that vague, glittering, indefinable thing called *society*' casts doubt on the validity of thinking of society in generalized terms and Flaubert substitutes for such a monolithic entity a series of unrelated worlds with sectional interests which never unite to expel the young man from the metropolis. Society is not described as a machine in which one runs the risk of being ground to pieces or as an ocean of mud in which it is impossible not to be besmirched. If the lives of both Frédéric and Lucien follow a downward course, it is for very different reasons. Lucien fails because he has been unable to withstand the pressures of a commercialized world. His downfall is the inevitable consequence of his immersion in a degraded world. Frédéric fails, on the other hand, by virtue of the unfolding of an inner logic; he contains within himself the seeds of his own destruction in the form of totally unreal expectations which makes his final state, 'lost among the ruins of his hopes', a foregone conclusion.

Lastly, the attitude to the whole question of the education of the young man differs. Balzac regards the shedding of youthful illusions as potentially beneficial ('His education was beginning to bear fruit' is the comment in *Old Goriot* when Eugène begins to adapt to the harsh realities of Parisian life). Flaubert, in contrast, associates the loss of illusions not with the achieving of some kind of maturity but with impoverishment and emotional desiccation. One title Flaubert considered for the novel, *Les Fruits secs* ('Withered Fruit') points to the slow organic movement towards sterility which characterizes Frédéric's development. Instead of a pattern of growth and maturation, Flaubert describes a gradual running down of emotional energy, an 'atrophy of the heart', culminating in a state of complete mental and emotional inertia: 'he endured the idleness of his mind and the inertia of his heart'.

Flaubert is, of course, not challenging Balzac simply for the sake of it. Many of his rectifications of the Balzacian prototype are a function of his desire to 'represent a psychological state, true, in my estimation, but not yet depicted.' If, in comparison with some of Balzac's heroes, Frédéric seems lacking in energy, it is largely because Flaubert is concerned with 'passion of the kind that can survive nowadays, that is to say, inactive.' Uncomplicated, resplendent passion such as that felt by Mâtho in his previous novel, *Salammbô,* makes for colourful effects but Flaubert feels obliged to forfeit such effects, declaring: 'I see simplicity nowhere in the modern world.' Flaubert is determined to get to grips with the underlying psychological problems of modern man even if this means that his novel, judged by traditional criteria, runs the risk of being considered unsatisfactory.

In conversation with the Goncourt brothers, Flaubert once declared that man is more in need of a 'nervous emission' than a 'seminal emission' and throughout his work he implies that emotional longing takes precedence over physical desire. Flaubert does not, however, set up a false dichotomy between soul and senses, like Balzac in *The Lily in the Valley* or Sainte-Beuve in *Volupté,* for he believes that the 'genital organs are at the root of all passion' and that it is impossible to dissociate sexual and mystical impulses. Flaubert may have declared, at the time of writing *Sentimental Education,* that 'woman, for all men, is the ogive arch reaching up to the infinite' but he was convinced that, although what he called the 'religious adoration of woman', endemic in the modern age, was characterized by the repression of a sexual response, it was, in fact, fueled by sexual energy.

It is these 'generalities' of male sexuality, based more perhaps than he would admit upon his own personal experience, which Flaubert uses in *Sentimental Education* in order to construct his model of a complex form of sexual abstinence. In the opening chapter Frédéric is shown falling involuntarily into a worshipping posture and establishing a pattern that will persist throughout the book. Although he knows nothing about Madame Arnoux at this stage, he bows 'automatically' when she passes and 'with an almost religious impulse of the heart' makes a lavish gift to the harp player. A precondition and a consequence of this worshipping attitude is the suspension of sexual desire: 'the desire for physical possession gave way to a profounder yearning, a poignant curiosity which knew no bounds.' Subsequently, Frédéric insists on regarding Madame Arnoux as a saintly figure, despite the fact that she seems perfectly ordinary to every one else, and this is constantly shown to inhibit a sexual response since to think of her in sexual terms is to profane her image: 'He was restrained by a sort of religious awe. That dress of hers, merging into the shadows, struck him as enormous, infinite, impossible to lift; and precisely because of that his desire increased'. An obscure compulsion, compounded of sexual and mystical elements, drives Frédéric to raise Madame Arnoux 'to a position outside the human condition'. In a strangely paradoxical manner, the object of desire is pushed further and further away; a harassed middle-class woman of unexceptional appearance is transformed by Frédéric's reverential gaze into an awesome, saintly figure whose inaccessibility guarantees both the strength and the frustration of his desire.

Although both Frédéric and Madame Arnoux, after prolonged acquaintance, seek to put their relationship on a different footing, they are unable to shake off the idealized images they have built up. Even when he believes Madame Arnoux is about to yield, Frédéric is shown incongruously preparing the apartment in the rue Tronchet 'more reverently than somebody decking out an altar of repose'. If Madame Arnoux were to have attended the rendezvous, it would have been psychologically impossible for Frédéric to consummate his passion. This is made clear at the end of the novel when he rejects the offer Madame Arnoux makes of herself. All external obstacles have now been removed to reveal an underlying resistance to sexual contact in Frédéric, a resistance which is in part explained by the apotheosis of Madame Arnoux as a mother-figure.

'Religious adoration of woman' is shown both to shape and distort Frédéric's whole life. It makes for continuity—the 'golden thread' running through his otherwise base existence—but also has disruptive and damaging side-effects. On the one hand, the image of Madame Arnoux is the lodestar of his mental universe, the unmoving obsessional centre around which his world is made to revolve. In the first chapter she dominates an expanding world ('His world had suddenly become larger. She was the point of light on which all things converged') and throughout Part I remains the focal point of his metropolitan world: 'Paris depended on her person, and the great city, with all its voices, thundered like an immense orchestra around her'. All that is contiguous with the commanding centre is invested with significance; since the centre itself is taboo and Frédéric can rarely bring himself to look her in the eye, his attention digresses metonymically to her immediate surroundings, possessions, casual utterances, with the result that all the Realist detail becomes charged for him with quasi-mystical significance (cf. 'He looked at her work-basket with eyes full of wonder, as if it were something out of the ordinary'). One thing his passion does achieve—the rehabilitation of the commonplace.

In Part II a more complex organization comes into existence as Frédéric sets the sacred object of religious adoration in rigid opposition to the profane object of sexual desire, Rosanette. Madame Arnoux's image is enhanced and strengthened by the repeated contrast Frédéric makes with Rosanette, and, inasmuch as he believes he has found in her a focus for carnal desire, his response to Madame Arnoux is 'purified'. The beneficial effect of Frédéric's thralldom to the idealized image of the Madonna is perhaps most clearly illustrated in Part III for, once Madame Arnoux has been removed from his life, he undergoes a rapid moral deterioration. Frédéric, it becomes clear, has preserved a kind of integrity and a relative 'decency' by worshipping at Madame Arnoux's shrine.

But Frédéric's obsession also has undeniably deleterious effects. His basic passivity is compounded, if not explained, by his adoration of an idealized image, an adoration which is felt to be a kind of imprisonment: 'Incapable of action, cursing God, and accusing himself of cowardice, he turned restlessly about in his desire, like a prisoner in his dungeon'. Secondly, it puts everything else into the shade, impoverishing his relationships with others, undermining his friendship with Deslauriers and leading him to under-value Rosanette and attempt to restrict narrowly his response to her ('if, in Rosanette's company, his heart happened to be stirred he promptly remembered his great love'). Thirdly, it eclipses all his social and intellectual ambitions. Frédéric stakes everything on his relationship with Madame Arnoux with the result that other sides of his life suffer from neglect.

This would be less of a tragedy if Madame Arnoux's image survived untarnished but in fact it is repeatedly degraded and profaned. On several occasions Frédéric interprets his involvement with Rosanette as a form of treachery (cf. the scene at the races). Although he attempts a rigid compartmentalization of his responses to the two women, the pure woman is contaminated by the impure one. Sacred objects such as the casket are exposed to 'sacrilege' when moved into the orbit of the impure woman and it seems that an 'atrocity' is committed when Madame Arnoux's precious 'relics' are auctioned. But the urge to defile is also deeply rooted in Frédéric himself; when Madame Arnoux fails to turn up at the rendezvous, he substitutes Rosanette for her 'in order to degrade Madame Arnoux more completely in his mind'. The closest Frédéric ever gets to the ideal is when profaning it but, ironically, this also means that it is destroyed. *Sentimental Education* gradually reveals the way in which sacred and profane love are interdependent. A rigid opposition between the two is set up in Frédéric's conscious mind but there is a strong suggestion that at an unconscious level they are complementary rather than antithetical. At the source of Frédéric's erotic life is the brothel episode, though it is not described in full until the very end of the book. The reason why the episode is regarded as 'the happiest time we ever had' is that the two adolescents were able to combine two attitudes which later become mutually exclusive—on the one hand, the 'poetic', reverential attitude to woman implicit in the offer of 'big nosegays', on the other the practical realization that money is required to purchase her favours. The subsequent polarization of Frédéric's response to the opposite sex causes considerable psychological damage. Love and desire become mutually exclusive and he reacts to Madame Arnoux and Rosanette in a hopelessly partial manner. The psychological need to complete the incomplete and restore the ideal unity experienced in the brothel now gives rise to the painful drama of profanation; if Frédéric is to add the missing element, inevitably he will detract from her idealized image. *Sentimental Education* offers a sustained and perceptive study of the complex and problematic nature of male sexuality.

Flaubert's exploration of the religious adoration of woman is not conducted in a vacuum. Frédéric's reactions are not analysed in isolation; Flaubert is typically Realist in his assumption that 'human life is most truthfully presented in terms of the individual's milieu, of the particularity of social situation and historical circumstance.' 'Generalities' relating to male sexuality are illustrated in the context of a life which itself provides an excellent illustration of what Auerbach considers indispensable to Realism—'the embedding of random persons and events in the general course of contemporary history, the fluid historical background.' (pp. 82-8)

> *D. A. Williams, "G. Flaubert: 'Sentimental Education' (1869)," in* The Monster in the Mirror: Studies in Nineteenth-Century Realism, *edited by D. A. Williams, Oxford University Press, Oxford, 1978, pp. 75-101.*

JEFFERSON HUMPHRIES (essay date 1987)

[*Humphries examines* Sentimental Education's *structure as it mirrors major themes, focusing on the novel's "endless beginnings."*]

L'Education sentimentale begins with a love never to be requited, and ends with a recollection of unrequited lust. The opening of the novel looks forward to a 'sentimental' obsession with a woman who, 'pledged to another,' cannot, though she might like to, accede to it physically. From first scene to last, this is a story about incompletion, the stubborn incongruence of lust and love, and the impossibility of bringing either to term independently of the other. Desire, whether physical or emotional, or both, always fails to reach its object. Because this fictionalized desire cannot requite itself, complete its own circuit, neither can the novel be *read, finished;* the reader's striving (and for that matter, the writer's) is as frustrated as the protagonist, Frédéric Moreau's, each an allegorized, specular image of the other. There is no closure here, either in the story, or in the (story of the) reading of it. The question of which implies the other is as vertiginously unanswerable—and finally banal—as that posed by the proverbial chicken and egg. Frédéric's problem is ours, as readers. What exactly, literarily and psychologically is that problem?

The ending of the book looks back to a moment in Frédéric's adolescence when he very nearly divested himself of his virginity. He might easily have, had he not lacked the requisite nerve. On the one hand, we are thrust toward emotional frustration, while on the other we fall backwards onto sexual frustration. What of the middle? Where is it? What is there between these two specular extremes? Some sort of a morphological middle, of course, which works away from love, a predominately emotional desire, through a series of female metonymies of it—Madame Dambreuse, Rosanette, both of whom are surrogates, insufficient compensations for the primary object, who is Madame Arnoux—toward the seedy realization that Frédéric's greatest hour came before the beginning of the story we have read when, dropping a bouquet of furtively picked flowers, he broke and ran from a house of ill repute where he had hoped to pilfer his first taste of the fruits of desire. His friend Deslauriers had no choice but to abandon the project also, as Frédéric had the money to pay for it. There, allegorized, is much of the novel's plot; the ambitions of Deslauriers follow closely and covetously behind Frédéric's, preferring power, however, to love, as Deslauriers says, but not so much that he does not attempt to seduce each of Frédéric's loves, succeeding, he admits near the end of the book, only with Rosanette. He finally mimicks Frédéric's mannerisms, usurps his place of honor in his hometown, and marries Louise Roque who had destined herself for Frédéric. Deslauriers follows alongside, finally in Frédéric's footsteps, only to find that Frédéric has no shoes to fill. Where do the two main characters go from such a discovery?

> They resumed their lives.
>
> They had both failed in their lives, the one who had dreamt of love and the one who had dreamt of power. What was the reason for it?
>
> —Perhaps it's for lack of a straight line, said Frédéric.
>
> (pp. 531-32)

Indeed, that describes the difference between this and the standard Victorian formula for a narrative. It ends with no marriage, no children, no comfortable death in the bosom of a comfortable bourgeois family. We have come full circle, from a beginning, to before it, backwards, and regressed from the idealism of a first love, to the awkward scandalousness of a first lust. We have reached no terminus, no conclusion, but only exhausted the characters' possibilities of fulfillment, and we and Flaubert abandon them to live out their lives beyond the pages of the novel. This ending is much like that of ***Bouvard et Pécuchet,*** which is equally inconclusive, a verbal shrug which puts the characters back where they were as the story began,

no better off, and considerably the worse for wear: "They began," concludes the unfinished manuscript ("Ils s'y mettent").

L'Education sentimentale begins with a look at Paris through fog. Any reader, especially one familiar with Proust, takes this as a nostalgic look back. The novel will be written from a backward perspective, analeptically. But no. Frédéric has never been to Paris. This is Flaubert, not Proust. Flaubert's novels typically *seem* to look forward from the beginning. "Frédéric thought of the bedroom he would occupy there, of the outline of a play, of subjects of paintings, of future passions" ("Frédéric pensait à la chambre qu'il occuperait là-bas, au plan d'un drame, à des sujets de tableaux, à des passions futures"). The only play written in the course of the novel is by Hussonet and it is never produced. Frédéric never learns to paint competently. There are two notable paintings commissioned by him in the story, however, both by Pellerin. One is of Rosanette. Frédéric denies that he commissioned it for himself and only reluctantly accepts it. At the end of the novel, when Madame Arnoux thinks she recognizes its subject, Frédéric says she could not possibly, as it dates from the Renaissance. The other painting is of the dead son of Rosanette and Frédéric. It is described as an unmitigated atrocity. "He found," the novel's opening passage goes on bovaresquely, "that the happiness called for by the excellence of his soul was late in coming" ("que le bonheur mérité par l'excellence de son âme tardait à venir"). At the end of the novel, he finds that his *bonheur* still has not arrived and no longer expects it to. This narrative begins with expectation, with looking forward; it ends with the revelation that there was never anything to look forward to. There is no middle or end to it. The novel is a repeatedly frustrated beginning, a looking forward to something which never comes, and it ends only when its primary characters stop looking forward, stop 'beginning.'

One event which might be construed as an "ending" of sorts and an opportunity to look back on the beginning, on Frédéric's early years in Paris and the long infatuation with Madame Arnoux, is the public auction of the Arnoux's household belongings. Frédéric is about to embark on a respectable 'middle' to the story by marrying Madame Dambreuse. That event in itself might have imposed a closure at least on all the frustrated starts that came before it. But Frédéric is not wafted by this event, by the auction, into a wise and knowing resignation. He is sickened and repulsed by it. It would force him to see Madame Arnoux in the perspective of a dead woman, part of a past to which Frédéric no longer belongs. Frédéric turns away from the scene because he cannot bear to look back in such a way. If he had been able to stomach the experience, looking back and looking ahead (to a married life with Madame Dambreuse) might have been fused to give us a 'straight line' to the end of the novel. Madame Dambreuse wants to buy a trinket, an antique box that partakes of Frédéric earliest memories of the Arnoux household. It is emblematic of a first blissful vision of the Arnoux *foyer,* and of the impossibility of penetrating it to reach Madame Arnoux, also emblematic of Monsieur Arnoux's infidelity, his liaison with Rosanette, to whom he subsequently gave the box. The box has belonged to two other women Frédéric has loved, passing from one to the other through the hands of Arnoux. Now it is about to pass into the possession of a third, whom Frédéric is pledged to marry. In her, the milieu of marriage might supplant the gruesomely botched beginning with Rosanette, which culminated with the death of their son, and the eternally incomplete yearning for Madame Arnoux—to become what? Nothing but a new beginning marked and fueled libidinally by a metonymic association with the old ones. Frédéric refuses what he was willing to accept with Rosanette. He will not marry Madame Dambreuse if she buys the box, and so becomes tied to the long frustration emblemized by it. He accepted this in Rosanette, and knows where it led: to a dreadful portrait of a dead child. He will marry only if marriage promises to break his string of false starts and the years of obsession with Madame Arnoux. He yearns to find in Madame Dambreuse a middle and an end, children and finally death in old age. But Madame Dambreuse wishes to be loved by Frédéric as he loves Madame Arnoux. She wishes to replace Madame Arnoux who cannot be replaced, for she is the perpetually postponed middle and the always prolonged start, and it is true that Frédéric loves her as he will never love anyone else. Madame Dambreuse still wants to wear at least part of the Arnoux mantle. Frédéric knows by this that she can offer him no rupture, but only continuation. So he breaks the engagement. What does this leave him with, but his love of beginnings, and Madame Arnoux? Rosanette might have been a middle, but turned out only to be the beginning of one; he became interested in her only because she was the mistress of the husband of Madame Arnoux. Madame Dambreuse might have been middle or end or both, but she chose not to be, or did not know how to choose otherwise.

Another occasion for a 'middle' to insert itself is Frédéric's return to Nogent after completing his law degree. He finds, much to his dismay, that the fortune he thought to have inherited from his father does not exist. There is nothing to look forward to, nothing to fuel grand hopes and ambitions. Frédéric finds himself "ruined, stripped, lost" ("ruiné, dépouillé, perdu"). Either he abandons all his former aspirations and sets about supporting himself with a provincial law practice and eventually marrying the daughter of Monsieur Roque or even someone without her wealth. Or, he may wallow in despair, preferring to do nothing rather than sacrifice his grand projects. He chooses, of course, to wallow in despair. Or rather, to wallow in a hope which very much resembles despair.

> And her, Mme Arnoux, how to see her again now?
>
> That, moreover, was completely impossible, with only three thousand francs income. He could no longer live on the fifth floor, have the porter for a servant, and introduce himself with poor black gloves bluish at the end, a greasy hat, the same year-old overcoat. No, no, never! Yet existence was intolerable without her. Many people lived well who had no fortune. Deslauriers among others;—and he found himself cowardly to attach such importance to mediocre things. Perhaps poverty would multiply his faculties a hundredfold. He felt exalted, thinking of the great men who worked in attic rooms. A soul such as Mme Arnoux's ought to be moved by the spectacle, and she would soften towards him.

Because of his overpowering love for Madame Arnoux, Frédéric refuses to alter his plans in any way. If he cannot live so as to impress her and be close to her, he will not live at all, but simply subsist, passively. The love of Madame Arnoux, the hopes, the looking forward, are all bound up with the locale of Paris, which from the first page of the novel has represented all those things to which Frédéric aspires. To look at Paris is to look forward.

> Thus, this catastrophe was a blessing after all; like those shiftings of the earth which uncover treasures, it had revealed to him the secret opulences of his nature. But there was only one place in the world where they could be made worth something: Paris! For, in his ideas, art, knowledge and love (these three

faces of God, as Pellerin would have said), belonged only to the capital.

At first he resolves to return to Paris and Madame Arnoux despite his poverty. He thinks of writing a letter to the Arnoux, to break the news of his bad fortune, but the comforts of home, the pleading of his mother, the hopelessness of the situation persuade him not to go to Paris. He does not write any letter, and resolves to forget Madame Arnoux. But he cannot. He cannot stir himself to impress a prospective employer, because he cannot bring himself to forget Paris and his old love. Frédéric's *hamartia* is that he cannot conceive himself in the present, or even as having a distinct past, as constrained by circumstances of past and present which will allow of futures unlike the one to which he aspires. What can be done, the futures that could be his, don't interest him. Instead, he passively indulges in a 'nostalgia' for an impossible future.

> Yet, he missed even the smell of gas and the noise of the omnibus. He dreamed of all the words she had spoken to him, of the pitch of her voice, the light of her eyes,—and, thinking himself a dead man, he did nothing any more, absolutely.

That future does not become any more possible when he inherits his uncle's fortune. Madame Arnoux is still married, still possessed of an inflexible sense of duty to husband and children, and, more importantly, Paris still represents a distantly projected future to Frédéric, not a present comprising opportunities, a straight line which would lead through a middle to an end. The end is cut off from the beginning because Frédéric does not know how to navigate the middle distance. He does not want to discover how to navigate it unless it can lead him to Madame Arnoux. He will not admit a middle which will not lead him to the end he desires. He is about to bore himself to a premature end when his life is suddenly infused with the fortune of his uncle. The visions that occur to him on receipt of the letter announcing the inheritance reveal a great deal about Frédéric's designs on Madame Arnoux: "this [their meetings] would be renewed everyday, indefinitely," ("cela se renouvellerait tous les jours, indéfiniment"). Frédéric wants nothing more, expects nothing more, than to call resplendently on Madame Arnoux every day for the rest of his life, a chaste courtship. "He would receive them at home, in his house" ("Il les recevrait chez lui, dans sa maison"). He will receive *them*—husband and wife. He announces, with honesty of which he seems himself unaware, his intentions to his mother with jarring clarity:

> Hardly did he hold this happiness in his hands when someone wanted to take it away. He made a formal announcement of his resolve to reside in Paris.
>
> —To do what there?
>
> —Nothing.

Frédéric finds it impossible to do anything because the present is not real to him, nor the past except as it feeds his hopes for an ephemeral future:

> Like an architect drawing up the plan of a palace, he arranged, in advance, his life. He filled it with delicacies and splendors; it rose up to the heavens; a prodigality of things appeared in it; and this contemplation was so profound that exterior objects had disappeared.

This way of experiencing the world makes it impossible for Frédéric to realize any kind of union. His elaborately plotted and long hoped-for seduction of Madame Arnoux fails to come off because of her son's illness, which reaffirms her strong sense of bourgeois morality. This, however, a circumstance beyond the control of Frédéric but well within that of Flaubert, points to the coincidence of Frédéric's inability to 'live' a beginning through a middle to an end, and Flaubert's inability, in this novel, to write one. Both of which coincide with our frustrated desire to read through to an end. This sense of frustration which, more than anything else, is what the book is about, may be a large part of the reason why Victorian critics so hated it. Frédéric, of course, doesn't really care that Madame Arnoux fails to meet him as she promised to do. The event only reinforces his love for her, which has become more and more synonymous with his frustration. When she explains to him the reason why she had not been able to meet him, he replies "Thank you! Thank you! I doubt no more! I love you as always" ("Merci! Merci! je ne doute plus! Je vous aime comme toujours"). They indulge themselves in the following ludicrous exchange, almost parodic of so much earlier Romantic literature such as Balzac's *Duchesse de Langeais* and Constant's *Adolphe:*

—Poor boy!

—My life is so sad!

—And mine!

Everyone is unhappy with things as they are; things as they are can be altered by no more than a change of mind. But neither Frédéric nor Madame Arnoux is desirous of making that change of mind. Why not? Because it would necessitate inventing a real middle and passing into a real future, which could not resemble the Shangri-la that both Frédéric and Madame Arnoux seem to realize exists nowhere but in their hopes, in looking forward, in projection. And of course we have to wonder if Flaubert's unwillingness to have either character change his or her mind does not stem from a similar knowledge, a similar feeling about 'futures.'

Through much more of this novel, the reader anxiously waits for Frédéric to disburden himself of his virginity. He finally does, but with Rosanette, whom he does not love, and this means that Frédéric has not really (metaphorically) lost his virginity at all, after sleeping with Rosanette. He could only lose it by sleeping with Madame Arnoux. He cannot mix sex and love. To join sex with love would mean joining present and future, and Frédéric refuses this. So it is not surprising that we should find the following sentiment expressed in a scene in which Frédéric and Rosanette are as close as they will ever be, and Frédéric is as near to joining sex and love, beginning and end, as he will ever be:

> In the midst of the most intimate secrets, there are always restrictions, of false modesty, delicacy, pity. One discovers in the other *or in oneself* precipices or quagmires which prevent pursuit; one feels, moreover, that one would not be understood; it is difficult to express exactly whatever; and complete unions are rare [emphasis mine].

It is impossible not to wonder what Flaubert may have invested of himself in such a statement, particularly since this book has an undeniably autobiographical character. René Dumesnil writes of a typical passage that

> It's enough to replace the name of Frédéric Moreau by that of Gustave Flaubert, that of Marie Arnoux by Elisa Schlésinger, of Deslauriers by Alfred Le Poittevin, to read *Schlésinger Music Publications* instead of *Industrial Arts*, to find in this page, not the

fragment of a novel, but a confession, an autobiographical story.

There are then two senses in which this is a historical novel. In the one sense, it is as rigorously 'about' the history of France in the mid-nineteenth century as any novel of the period. It succeeds in being absolutely verisimilar by so successfully mixing the fictive story of Frédéric and Madame Arnoux with the 'true' one of Paris in the nineteenth century that we cannot separate one from the other. On the other hand, it confuses Frédéric the character with Flaubert the writer to such an extent that it is very difficult to tell them apart either. In both senses of 'history,' Dumesnil contends that the novel is much more 'observed' than invented.

Yet the two kinds of history are quite distinct one from the other. The historical backdrop of nineteenth century Paris gives the novel its middle. It does not (cannot) depend on Frédéric for a middle. Nor, in a sense, does it depend on Flaubert for one. The middle is there, it is 'true,' so that it does not have to be 'invented.' All that Flaubert need do is 'describe,' 're-produce,' dramatize and vivify 'actual' events. This gives the novel a sense of duration and progression. It does not, however, give it an ending. The history of France begins before the novel does and ends beyond anyone's view, Flaubert's or the reader's. Insofar as it partakes of the 'historical,' then, this novel is nothing but middle.

But this still leaves it without any distinct terminus. The autobiographical dimension does not provide one, but it may explain why there cannot be one. This novel constitutes, for Flaubert, a look back which is nostalgic not for the past but for the future, a future which will never be, a look back which is a look ahead at an enduring loss—a loss which precedes possession and precludes it. Elisa Schlésinger and Marie Arnoux are lost from the first moment they are perceived. The loss is always getting under way, always preceding possession and following after it; yet possession never is realized. The 'nostalgic look forward' at Paris, that paradox with which the story begins, emblemizes this problem. From such a perspective, from the author's vantage point, and from Frédéric's, the novel is a 'work of mourning' in the Freudian sense but one premised on a loss which precedes and precludes possession. Following the loss of a loved object, real or imagined, the ego must work through all its memories of and associations with the lost object in order to withdraw its libidinal investment. The work of mourning is complete when the sense of loss, which is synonymous with love for the lost object, is worked out, when the libidinal investment is exhausted. Then the ego can embark on new attachments. But the work of mourning is preliminary to a reconciliation with the present, with 'reality,' and to a 'middle,' and an end (see Freud, "Mourning and Melancolia," in *General Psychological Theory*), whereas Flaubert seems not to be interested in transcribing what follows the work of mourning, or in whatever 'possession' might precede it, but only in the work itself. When the last drop of libido is finally withdrawn from Marie Arnoux, and Frédéric turns from love back to lust, Flaubert has also exhausted (for the moment) his emotional investment in the novel, in the act of writing, and we, as his readers, have exhausted our interest in the novel as well. Flaubert's work of mourning, and Frédéric's, have coincided with ours, so that there is some sense of relief, and release, at the close of the novel. The larger 'historical' milieu takes over, provides an apparent exit—a middle—through which we, readers, Flaubert, writer, and Frédéric, may *seem* to leave the novel, the work of mourning, and to begin to work toward an ending, begin to 'live,' reconciled to 'reality,' to

The Flaubert residence at Croisset, where most of Sentimental Education *was written.*

'real' events, circumstances which admit of certain possible middles and certain possible endings, and not others.

This is why, it seems to me, the novel 'works' so ambiguously and yet so well, why it satisfies reader, writer, and Frédéric, without really inventing anything but a beginning. Dumesnil is right in saying that most of the novel is 'observed'—the middle against which the beginning, the work of mourning, is 'worked through,' and which gives us some place to be when the story is over, is nothing but 'observation,' recapitulation. But on the autobiographical level, he is quite wrong. This work of mourning is not observation or even simply recollection, as in Freudian psychology it ought to be. It is a nostalgia for the future, a looking back to a point that precedes the novel and follows after it. This nostalgia is a sense of longing for middle and end, that is, for writing and reading to be over so that 'life' may be reconciled to 'history,' the great ongoing middle, and proceed. But aren't history, contemporaneity, life, just more postponements, *pis-allers,* recommencements? Why should Gustave Flaubert's life, or ours, be any different from Frédéric's? How often does anyone get exactly what he expects, much less wants? Aren't we as 'fictive,' rhetorical, in our own more subtle fashion, as Frédéric, our 'lines' just as crooked and truncated as his? Aren't we just as nostalgic for impalpable futures, perfect shapes, endings? Whether we are the chicken and Frédéric the egg—whether reading or writing, life or art, is more important, which comes first—like whether Frédéric actually loved Marie Arnoux or some idealized image he had projected onto her, these are an idiot's questions. Any novel, any work of art or any object of desire, as Proust put it, is an optic, a speculum in which the reader/lover casts an image. Who is to say that the 'reality' is more important than, or

different from the image when it is only by the image that we know the 'reality,' only by interpretive 'fictions' that we know 'history'? The novel, by dissolving the conventional distinction made among history, autobiography, and fiction, pouring each into the others, poses this problem. So that Frédéric's strange forward-looking nostalgia and this novel balefully and fearfully suggest the impossibility of ever satisfying the desire which has called them into being (the desire to *know,* carnally and intellectually, as if there were any real difference), and called us to reading. Could it be, Flaubert seems to wonder, that all we ever really know, is what we lack? (pp. 532-41)

Jefferson Humphries, ''Flaubert's 'L'education sentimentale' and the Problem of Reading 'History': Endless Beginnings,'' in Southwest Review, *Vol. 72, No. 4, Autumn, 1987, pp. 531-41.*

ADDITIONAL BIBLIOGRAPHY

Aynesworth, Donald. ''The Poetry of Violence in *L'education sentimentale.''* *Nineteenth-Century French Studies* 11, Nos. 3-4 (Spring-Summer 1983): 285-301.
    Probes Flaubert's use of violence in *Sentimental Education.*

Baldick, Robert. Introduction to *Sentimental Education,* by Gustave Flaubert, translated by Robert Baldick, pp. 7-13. Harmondsworth, Middlesex, England: Penguin Books, 1964.
    A concise survey of major issues in *Sentimental Education* criticism.

Bourget, Paul. ''A Lecture at Oxford: Gustave Flaubert.'' *The Fortnightly Review* LXII, No. CCCLXVII (1 July 1897): 152-64.

Contains scattered brief references to *Sentimental Education,* chiefly treating the novel as a reflection of what Bourget terms Flaubert's theory of "Art for Art's sake."

Buck, Stratton. "Testament of Youth." In his *Gustave Flaubert,* pp. 124-42. Twayne's World Authors Series, no. 3. New York: Twayne Publishers, 1966.

A close study of *Sentimental Education,* emphasizing its structure, major themes, and setting.

Carlut, Charles; Dubé, Pierre H.; and Dugan, J. Raymond. *A Concordance to Flaubert's "L'Education sentimentale."* 2 vols. Garland Reference Library of the Humanities, vol. 125. New York: Garland Publishing, 1978

A key-word-in-context concordance to the 1869 text of *Sentimental Education.*

Cortland, Peter. *The Sentimental Adventure: An Examination of Flaubert's "Education sentimentale."* Studies in French Literature, no. 15. The Hague: Mouton & Co., 1967, 203 p.

Maintains that the universality of human failure is the dominant theme of *Sentimental Education.*

———. "*Sentimental Education.*" In his *A Reader's Guide to Flaubert: An Analysis of the Texts and Discussion of Current Criticism,* pp. 83-126. New York: Helios Books, 1968.

A broad reading of *Sentimental Education* examining its realism and sentimentalism.

Culler, Jonathan. "The Perfect Crime: The Novel, Description and Meaning." In his *Flaubert: The Uses of Uncertainty,* pp. 91-108. Ithaca: Cornell University Press, 1974.

Briefly compares Flaubert's prose style in *Sentimental Education* with the writing of Honoré de Balzac.

Danahy, Michael E. "The Esthetics of Documentation: The Case of *L'éducation sentimentale.*" *Romance Notes* XIV, No. 1 (Autumn 1972): 61-5

Explores the aesthetic implications of Flaubert's use of historical details in *Sentimental Education.*

———. "Narrative Timing and the Structures of *L'éducation sentimentale.*" *The Romanic Review* LXVI, No. 1 (January 1975): 32-46.

Analyzes the function and meaning of narrative timing in *Sentimental Education.*

———. "Chronoscapes in *L'éducation sentimentale.*" *Australian Journal of French Studies* XV, No. 5 (September-December 1978): 263-65.

Investigates the function and meaning of landscapes in *Sentimental Education.*

———. "A Critique of Recent Spatial Approaches to Flaubert and Related Theory of Fiction." *Nineteenth-Century French Studies* X, Nos. 3-4 (Spring-Summer 1982): 301-16.

Reviews criticism of spatial design in *Sentimental Education.*

Denommé, Robert T. "The Theme of Disintegration in Flaubert's *Education sentimentale.*" *Kentucky Romance Quarterly* XX, No. 2 (1973): 163-71.

Maintains that Flaubert imposed little structural unity on *Sentimental Education* in order to complement the seemingly disconnected wanderings of the protagonist.

———. "Flaubert's Portrayal of Mood and Temperament in *L'education sentimentale.*" *Nineteenth-Century French Studies* VII, Nos. 1-2 (Fall-Winter 1978-79): 59-75.

Approaches *Sentimental Education* as a mirror of Flaubert's views concerning psychology and the emotions.

Fairlie, Alison. "Some Patterns of Suggestion in *L'education sentimentale.*" *Australian Journal of French Studies* VI, Nos. 2-3 (May-December 1969): 266-93.

Contends that Flaubert intended *Sentimental Education* to stimulate the reader "to be himself the artist in strenuously interpreting patterns of evocative and deliberately ambiguous detail."

Furst, Norbert. "The Structure of *L'education sentimentale* and *Der grüne Heinrich.*" *PMLA* LVI, No. 1 (March 1941): 249-60.

Observes similarities between the 1869 version of *Sentimental Education* and the 1880 text of Gottfried Keller's *Der Grüne Heinrich.*

Gans, Eric. "*Education sentimentale*: The Hero as Storyteller." *MLN* 89, No. 4 (May 1974): 614-25.

Considers the meaning of the brothel scene in *Sentimental Education.*

Gerhardi, Gerhard C. "Romantic Love and the Prostitution of Politics: On the Structural Unity in *L'education sentimentale.*" *Studies in the Novel* IV, No. 3 (Fall 1972): 402-15.

A close study of the narrative structure of *Sentimental Education.*

Goodman, Paul. "Novelistic Plots." In his *The Structure of Literature,* pp. 127-83. Chicago: University of Chicago Press, 1962.

Examines *Sentimental Education* as a "remarkably pure" example of a sentimental novel in which "'nothing happens'."

Green, Anne. "Flaubert, Bouilhet and the Illegitimate Daughter: A Source for *L'education sentimentale.*" *French Studies* XL, No. 3 (July 1986): 304-10.

Cites Louis Bouilhet's 1858 drama *Hélène Peyron* as the source of the Cécile Dambreuse story in *Sentimental Education.*

Grover, P. R. "Two Modes of Possessing—Conquest and Appreciation: *The Princess Casamassima* and *L'éducation sentimentale.*" *The Modern Language Review* 66, No. 4 (October 1971): 760-71.

Notes similarities between *Sentimental Education* and Henry James's 1886 novel *The Princess Casamassima.*

Haig, Stirling. "Madame Arnoux's *Coffret*: A Monumental Case." *Romanic Review* LXXV, No. 4 (November 1984): 469-82.

Probes the semantic potential of Madame Arnoux's casket.

Hearn, Lafcadio. "The Friends of Flaubert." In his *Essays in European and Oriental Literature,* edited by Albert Mordell, pp. 65-73. New York: Dodd, Mead and Co., 1923.

A reprint of an 1884 review in which Hearn describes *Sentimental Education* as "now almost unreadable—the only one of [Flaubert's] novels which may justly be considered a literary failure."

Jackson, Ernest. "*L'education sentimentale* and *Bouvard et Pécuchet.*" In his *The Critical Reception of Gustave Flaubert in the United States, 1860-1960,* pp. 90-105. Studies in French Literature, no. IX. The Hague: Mouton & Co., 1966.

Evaluates selected American criticism of *Sentimental Education.*

James, Henry. "Gustave Flaubert." *Macmillan's Magazine* LXVII, No. 401 (March 1893): 332-43.

A general appraisal of Flaubert's life and works in which the critic describes *Sentimental Education* as "cold as death."

Knight, Diana. *Flaubert's Characters: The Language of Illusion.* Cambridge: Cambridge University Press, 1985, 125 p.

Contains scattered references to characterization in *Sentimental Education.*

Moon, H. Kay. "Description: Flaubert's 'External World' in *L'education sentimentale.*" *The French Review* XXXIX, No. 4 (February 1966): 501-12.

Maintains that Flaubert used physical description in *Sentimental Education* to enhance moods and help define characters.

Raitt, A. W. "The Art of Decharacterization in *L'éducation sentimentale.*" In *Critical Essays on Gustave Flaubert,* edited by Laurence M. Porter, pp. 130-39. Critical Essays on World Literature, edited by Robert Lecker. Boston: G. K. Hall & Co., 1986.

Contends that, contrary to his practice in *Madame Bovary,* Flaubert deliberately deprived the characters in *Sentimental Education* of any clearly defined identities.

Sartre, Jean-Paul. *The Family Idiot: Gustave Flaubert, 1821-1857.* Translated by Carol Cosman. Chicago: University of Chicago Press, 1981-87.

Part one and book one, part two, of *L'idiot de la famille: Gustave Flaubert de 1821 à 1857* (1971), Sartre's multipart biography of

Flaubert. The work contains scattered brief references to *Sentimental Education,* chiefly concerning psychosexual aspects of the novel.

Sonnenfeld, Albert. "Flaubert's *L'education sentimentale:* A Century of Relevance." *Laurels* 53, No. 1 (Spring 1982): 45-56.
> Praises the present day "relevance" of *Sentimental Education,* noting parallels between contemporary politics and the political situations depicted in the novel.

Spencer, Philip. "The Testament of Failure" and "The Reckoning." In his *Flaubert: A Biography,* pp. 164-83, pp. 184-95. New York: Grove Press, 1953.
> Surveys the events in Flaubert's life that led to the writing of *Sentimental Education.*

Starkie, Enid. *"L'éducation sentimentale."* In her *Flaubert the Master: A Critical and Biographical Study (1856-1880),* pp. 140-78. New York: Atheneum, 1971.
> A psychological interpretation of *Sentimental Education,* emphasizing autobiographical elements in the work.

Thiher, Roberta Joyce. "Dehumanization through Style." *Romance Notes* X, No. 2 (Spring 1969): 265-67.
> Argues that Flaubert created a "mechanized, depersonalized atmosphere" in *Sentimental Education.*

Ullmann, Stephen. "Word-Order as a Device of Style: Flaubert, *L'education sentimentale."* In his *Style in the French Novel,* pp. 161-67. New York: Barnes & Noble, 1964.
> A rigorous investigation of syntax in *Sentimental Education.*

Williams, D. A. "Sacred and Profane in *L'éducation sentimentale."* *The Modern Language Review* 73, pt. 4 (October 1978): 786-98.
> Examines the opposition between Madame Arnoux, an object of religious adoration, and Rosanette, a profane object of sexual desire, in *Sentimental Education.*

Washington Irving

1783-1859

(Also wrote under the pseudonyms of Geoffrey Crayon, Diedrich Knickerbocker, Jonathan Oldstyle, and Launcelot Langstaff) American short story writer, essayist, historian, biographer, and editor.

The following entry presents criticism of Irving's prose collection *The Sketch Book of Geoffrey Crayon, Gent.* (1819-20). For additional information on Irving's career and *The Sketch Book,* see *NCLC,* Vol. 2.

The Sketch Book of Geoffrey Crayon, Gent. is considered a landmark work in American fiction. The book not only introduced the modern short story form in the United States, but was also the first work by an American author to gain recognition abroad. Noted chiefly today for the stories "Rip Van Winkle" and "The Legend of Sleepy Hollow," the collection was widely popular in its time in both England and the United States, and it remains Irving's best known and most critically acclaimed achievement. Purportedly the work of Geoffrey Crayon, Gent., a genteel, good-natured American wandering through Britain on his first trip abroad, *The Sketch Book* consists largely of his travel impressions. These sketches of English life are picturesque, elegant, and lightly humorous in the tradition of the eighteenth-century essayists Richard Addison and Oliver Goldsmith, Irving's literary models. The pieces from the book that have endured, however, are those in which Irving abandoned the Crayon persona and wove elements of legend, folklore, and drama into narratives of the New World. "Rip Van Winkle," the story of a lackadaisical Dutch-American who slumbers for twenty years, and "The Legend of Sleepy Hollow," which recounts Ichabod Crane's meeting with a headless horseman, have long been considered classics. Critics generally agree that these were the models for the modern American short story and that both tales introduced imagery and archetypes that enriched the national literature. Authors as varied as Herman Melville and T. S. Eliot wrote poems inspired by "Rip Van Winkle," and critics note that characters based upon Rip, Dame Van Winkle, and Ichabod abound in American fiction.

Irving was thirty-five years old and living in England when he wrote *The Sketch Book.* The Liverpool branch of his family's import-export firm, where he had been working the past three years, had gone bankrupt, and after years of wavering indecisively between a legal, editorial, and mercantile career, he decided to make writing his livelihood. He already enjoyed a minor literary reputation in the United States for two satirical and humorous works that had appeared a decade previously. The first, published in 1807-08, was entitled *Salmagundi; or, The Whim-Whams and Opinions of Launcelot Langstaff, Esq., and Others.* Written in collaboration with Irving's brother William and their friend James Kirke Paulding, *Salmagundi* contained essays and poems poking fun at the political, social, and cultural life of Irving's native New York City. It proved highly popular, and in 1809 Irving enjoyed a second success with the single-handed effort, *A History of New York, from the Beginning of the World to the End of the Dutch Dynasty.* Narrated by the fictional Diedrich Knickerbocker, a fusty, colorful Dutch-American, *A History of New York* provided a com-

ical, deliberately inaccurate account of New York's past. The favorable reception of this work was shadowed, however, by the death of Irving's fiancée, Matilda Hoffmann, and Irving floundered for the next several years, choosing not to write again until 1818, when he found himself in England, jobless, with no prospects. He then began recording impressions, thoughts, and descriptions in a small notebook. These, polished and repolished in Irving's meticulous manner, became the pieces that make up *The Sketch Book.*

The Sketch Book comprises some thirty parts: about half English sketches, four general travel reminiscences, six literary essays, two descriptions of the American Indian, three essentially unclassifiable pieces, and three short stories: "Rip Van Winkle," "The Legend of Sleepy Hollow," and "The Spectre Bridegroom," a tale set in Germany that draws upon German legend. The book was published almost concurrently in the United States and England in order to prevent the literary piracy to which literary works were vulnerable before international copyright laws. The American edition was produced under the supervision of Irving's brothers in seven paperbound parts in 1819-20. In England the publisher John Murray, encouraged by Irving's friend Sir Walter Scott, brought out two clothbound volumes in 1820. The miscellaneous nature of *The Sketch Book* was an innovation that appealed to a broad range of readers; the work received a great deal of attention and sold briskly, and Irving found himself America's first international literary celebrity. The book's considerable profits allowed Irving to devote himself full-time to writing, and he became in addition the first American author to support himself solely by his literary work.

The Sketch Book was favorably received: reviewers in the United States generally were delighted with the work of their native son, and even English critics, normally hostile to American authors, accorded the book favorable—if somewhat condescending—notice. Among the pieces singled out for praise in the early reviews were "The Author's Account of Himself," Geoffrey Crayon's charming self-introduction; such descriptive sketches as "Stratford-upon-Avon" and "Westminster Abbey"; and, most frequently, the three short stories, particularly "Rip Van Winkle." Critics found Irving's style pleasingly elegant and humorous, although some, including the American Richard Henry Dana, complained that there was a lack of intellectual content beneath the decorative surface. Dana also observed that in adopting the authorial persona of Geoffrey Crayon—with his prose style modeled after the eighteenth-century essayists—Irving lost the robustness, high color, and comic vigor of his previous incarnations as Launcelot Langstaff and Diedrich Knickerbocker.

The Sketch Book was a perennial favorite of American readers during the nineteenth century, and Irving was lionized throughout his long life by literati and the public alike. Many critics, however, voiced skepticism about the originality and artistic stature of this elegant "Father of American literature," as Irving was commonly called. Ralph Waldo Emerson termed him "only a word-catcher," and Edgar Allan Poe, whose own masterful short stories built upon Irving's example in *The Sketch Book*, wrote in 1838: "Irving is much overrated, and a nice distinction might be drawn between his just and his surreptitious and adventitious reputation—between what is due to the pioneer solely, and what to the writer." In this statement, Poe accurately predicted the critical response to Irving after the turn of the century. Judging *The Sketch Book* as a stylistic rather than an artistic achievement, such commentators as Fred Lewis Pattee focused on the work's pioneering contribution to the development of the short story form, as well as on Irving's key place in establishing the profession of letters in the United States. Indeed, from the turn of the century until the burgeoning of American literary scholarship in the 1950s, Irving and *The Sketch Book* were more often treated as subjects for literary histories than as subjects for literary evaluations.

Beginning in the 1950s, however, critics turned to *The Sketch Book*'s famous tales to explore in depth many notable artistic and thematic innovations, including the use of folklore, myth, and fable; the expression of the tenuousness of time and reality; landscape as a reflection of theme and mood; and the tension between imagination and creativity versus materialism and productivity in nineteenth-century America. In the latter category, many critics read Rip's long sleep as a rejection of the capitalistic values of his society—ferociously personified by the shrewish Dame Van Winkle—and an embracing of the world of the imagination. Some critics offer biographical readings of "Rip Van Winkle," regarding it as Irving's rationalization of his own somewhat lackadaisical attitude toward work and his career. Critics view Ichabod Crane, too, as a symbol of the outcast artist-intellectual in American society, although he has been considered, conversely, as a caricature of the acquisitive, scheming Yankee Puritan, a type that Irving lampooned regularly in his earlier satirical works.

While most of *The Sketch Book* is regarded today as little more than pretty, derivative prose, the work is acknowledged as significant to American literary and publishing history. Critics agree that in "Rip Van Winkle" and "The Legend of Sleepy Hollow," Irving set an artistic standard that he himself never surpassed, even in the course of a long and productive literary career. In their continuing attention to these two stories, critics affirm that while *The Sketch Book* may belong properly to literary history, "Rip Van Winkle" and "The Legend of Sleepy Hollow" belong to literary art.

(See also *Dictionary of Literary Biography*, Vol. 3: *Antebellum Writers in New York and the South;* Vol. 11: *American Humorists, 1800-1950;* and Vol. 59: *American Literary Critics and Scholars, 1800-1850.*)

THE EDINBURGH MONTHLY REVIEW   (essay date 1820)

[*In the following excerpt, the reviewer praises Irving's style and humor in* The Sketch Book *while faulting the "coarseness and vulgarity" of some of the portraits.*]

Early as we thought to be in paying our respects to Mr. Crayon, we find that his fame has got a-head of us. The first volume of his spirited sketches [in *The Sketch Book*] has had the good fortune already to witness a second edition.... Giving full credit to ... their [American] origin, we cannot forbear expressing our satisfaction at the decided and well-deserved success of [Mr. Washington Irving's] labours. We consider it both as an evidence of the liberality of our countrymen, and an encouragement to hope for a better understanding between them and their transatlantic neighbours, than has for some time past existed. In saying this, we have no hesitation to admit that the praise of the advance towards good-fellowship is due to the author; and we shall be content to claim for ourselves the negative merit of being neither insensible to the excellencies of temper and talent which have prompted and enabled him to attempt it, nor ungrateful for the benefits which are likely to result from its accomplishment. (pp. 303-04)

[Mr. Crayon] is altogether a most agreeable writer—full of fancy and warm thought—alive in every sense, and at every nerve, to the beauties of nature—just to the fair demands, and liberal to the failings of his species; but by no means void of that spirit which makes a man what Dr. Johnson called a "good hater;" and far less a victim to that spurious sentimentality which can find an apology for every vice. He is a lover of the antique in national history, by the way, no ordinary excellence in an American; he is fond of our literature, our customs, our tastes, and our oddities—fond of them, we mean, in a degree, and with a sincerity, which may be allowed fairly to bespeak him to be part and portion of the English commonwealth. His sketches, moreover, put us in mind of some of the best papers in the *Tatler* and *Spectator*, but it is to convince us that in several respects he excels them;—then, again, to a descriptive power, a richness of humour, and a familiarity with the marvellous and the preternatural, which render the writings of the author of *Waverley* so graphic and so impressive, he joins a tenderness of soul that might lead him into feminine weakness, if the wings of his imagination did not bear him rapidly over the objects that would seduce him;—and, finally, he has a copiousness and a fluency of expression, which make him quite at home on any subject that happens to engage his attention.

The sketches are on various topics, no otherwise connected than as they are the product of the same kindly heart, and the same vivid genius. They are sometimes pathetic, sometimes simply narrative; a few of them have rather a didactic appearance; but perhaps the most predominant feature of the book is that sort of humour which delineates character with a view to harmless merriment, rather than the excitation of the satirical feelings. After such commendation, we may be allowed a word or two in reprehension of a fault; and we deliver them now, that we may neither interrupt the course of our selections, nor destroy any agreeable impression which these may produce on the minds of our readers. Mr. Crayon seems to us defective in taste, and in consequence to degenerate at times into common-place vulgarities, which are generally at variance with the aspirings and the capabilities of his mind. We speak not of any peculiar expressions of an offensive nature,—nor do we censure his choice of familiar objects for his pencil. Our allusion is to certain hackneyed, and consequently gross caricatures, which could have been looked for only in the portfolio of a venal libeller, or the window of a dealer in low prints. For example: "A snuffling well-fed vicar, who is a privileged guest at all the tables of the neighbourhood, and who had been the keenest fox-hunter in the country, until age and good living had disabled him from doing any thing more than ride to see the hounds throw off, and make one at the hunting dinner." Such is the viciously low picture of a Church of England clergyman! In the same style, and in the same piece, entitled "**The Country Church**," we have the trite contrast between the modestly dignified deportment and easy manners of the family of a nobleman of high rank, and the vain-gloriousness and airs of that of a wealthy citizen, with his consort "a fine, fleshy, comfortable dame." Besides their coarseness and vulgarity, there is a degree of invidiousness in such portraits, to which a man of high spirit would disdain to afford a tenement in his breast. We dislike them the more, because, as they cannot have been drawn for any individuals, they must be conceived to be either copied from the worst authorities, or to be intended for likenesses of genera and species. Either supposition is disadvantageous to the painter. (pp. 304-306)

The first paper, "**The Author's Account of Himself**," tells us of his predilection for travelling in general, and his special desire to visit Europe. The reasons for this preference are shortly, but finely stated. (p. 306)

Alas! there are many, who, if we may judge from their writings, take a pleasure in fomenting those discords [between America and England] which have already proved so injurious; nor can it be denied, that several of our own countrymen have laboured very inconsiderately in this cruel work. Such is the opinion of our author, who expresses himself on the subject with a tenderness, and, at the same time, a force of thought, which ought to give the highest efficacy to his well-timed rebuke. See what he says in his sketch, entitled "**English Writers on America**." (pp. 306-07)

Among the pieces of a pathetic cast, but which are also narrative, in so far as they are stories, we may mention "**The Wife**," "**The Broken Heart**," "**The Widow and Her Son**," and "**The Pride of the Village**," as very good of their kind, though no way remarkable for invention, the incidents being of pretty common occurrence in works of fiction. Somewhat allied to them, but possessed, also, either of a spice of humour, or of a large admixture of something approaching to epic machinery, are, "**Rip Van Winkle**," "**The Spectre Bridegroom**," and "**The Legend of Sleepy Hollow**." The sketches in which

humour predominates, are chiefly "**The Boar's Head Tavern, Eastcheap**," "**Little Britain**," "**The Angler**," and those relating to Christmas. But though we have thus classified these sketches, for distinction's sake, the reader will easily imagine, from the slightest allusion to them, that the various qualities on which the arrangement is founded, are frequently mixed up, so as to give a very composite appearance to every individual production. (p. 315)

"**Little Britain**," is one of the liveliest [sketches] in the book, though not finished off with most care. Mr. Crayon says it was put into his hands by an odd-looking gentleman in a small brown wig and snuff-coloured coat, with whom he happened to become acquainted in one of his perambulations through the metropolis; and that the same individual is engaged in a full and particular account of the very interesting region in which he resides. We think it decidedly in his own rich and highly coloured style. Of the locality of the cluster of narrow streets and courts denominated Little Britain, in the center of London, there are few of our readers, we take for granted, who need to be informed. (p. 329)

We shall conclude our survey of these sketches with noticing one of them, of which we have not hitherto made mention. It is entitled "**Stratford-on-Avon**," and is of course full of allusions to the "master-poet," from whom the place so called has derived its fame. Few persons have gone there on a poetical pilgrimage, possessed of more poetical feelings than seem to be enjoyed by Mr. Crayon, or more capable of expressing what those feelings are. Little of novelty, however, at least as to description, could be expected from him or any one else—the ceaseless inquiries of multitudes of votaries leaving scarcely a ray of hope for the most diligent of their successors. But there is an air of originality, as well as great beauty, in what he says on the most frequently treated topics. (p. 332)

A review of "The Sketch Book," in The Edinburgh Monthly Review, *Vol. IV, No. XXI, September, 1820, pp. 303-34.*

THE MONTHLY REVIEW, LONDON   (essay date 1820)

[*In the following review of* The Sketch Book, *the anonymous author approves Irving's elegant prose style and attitude toward the British, but faults his tendency to overwrite.*]

No: these are not *crayon* sketches; they have not the careless freedom, the broken outline, the random roughnesses of the crayon. On the contrary, it is evident that the camel-hair pencil has lent them its softness; they are smooth and polished, and have all the tint and finish of water-coloured drawings. Without aspiring to the higher merit of strength and originality in design, they are intitled to the praise of elegance in execution.

We understand that the real name of the author is Washington Irving; and that he is an American gentleman who, after having visited various parts of his own country, and indulged his taste for the sublime and beautiful in natural scenery among his own stupendous mountains, lakes, and rivers, became anxious to visit Europe, and see men and manners in more variety and more advanced refinement. Great Britain might well be the object of peculiar attraction; where literature, science, and philosophy spread their immeasurable and blooming branches from one end of the kingdom to the other; inviting by their fragrance, and collecting under their shadow in the north and the east, in the south and the west, societies of men who emulate each other in moral and intellectual attainments.

It is matter of regret with us that the author, who modestly expresses his consciousness that much of the contents of his papers can be interesting only to American readers, has any cause to say that 'he is aware of the austerity with which the writings of his countrymen have hitherto been treated by British critics;' mildly adding that he solicits for his own production that courtesy and candour which a stranger has some right to claim, who presents himself at the threshold of a hospitable nation. (pp. 198-99)

Among the miscellaneous matter which composes these volumes, one article is headed **"John Bull."** In looking at the picture of himself, no man perhaps can form an accurate judgment of the resemblance: but the drawing in this case is spirited, the colouring good, and the portrait altogether so pleasing, that, notwithstanding certain excentricites of feature, we are rather flattered with the hope of its being a likeness. . . . Ample credit is given to the good qualities of John Bull, and the most indulgent allowance is made for such as are questionable. (p. 202)

Mr. Irving has studied the manners of the English in their rural occupations and festivities, as well as in the busier and more varied engagements which develope the national character in our metropolis and other large cities. His sketches intitled **"Rural Life in England"**; **"The Country Church"**; **"The Stage Coach"**; **"Christmas Day"**; **"The Christmas Dinner,"** &c.; and some others, not forgetting **"Little Britain"**; are touched with great spirit and vivacity. (p. 204)

[Mr. Irving] is probably a young man, and in that case his enthusiasm should excite our envy rather than our censure; otherwise, we should say that he is a little too romantic, and that he festoons his descriptions somewhat gaudily with epithets and apostrophes. (p. 207)

A review of "The Sketch Book," in The Monthly Review, *London, Vol. XCIII, October, 1820, pp. 198-207.*

THE QUARTERLY REVIEW   (essay date 1821)

[*After reflecting on the inferiority of American literature, the anonymous British reviewer praises* The Sketch Book's *style and subject matter. The critic also makes a judgment affirmed unanimously by later critics: that "Rip Van Winkle," "The Legend of Sleepy Hollow," and "The Spectre Bridegroom" are Irving's outstanding efforts in the book.*]

This [*The Sketch Book*] is one of the best samples which we have yet seen of American literature; for though it is, as indeed it professes to be, of a light and unpretending character, it is good of its kind; full of imagination, and embellished with a delicacy of feeling, and a refinement of taste, that do not often belong to our trans-Atlantic descendants.

The age of fine writing will always come late in the annals of a nation; and there is nothing in the history of the rise or progress of America to make her an exception to the general rule. The genius of her people, as might be expected from their origin and their pursuits, is rather directed to what is useful and mechanical; and indeed while they have still so much uncultivated land, we can scarcely expect that any great encouragement should be given to the cultivation of mind. Accordingly, we find that, while she would gladly rival our broadcloths and our cutlery, she is content to import our poetry, our romance, our philosophy and our criticism. (pp. 50-1)

[The story of Irving's **"Voyage to England"**] is very beautifully told; and it is a decisive proof of the talent and taste of the author, that he has been able to confer an air of novelty on so hacknied a subject:—but natural feelings expressed in the language of nature and good sense must always be contemplated with interest and pleasure. He lands at Liverpool, and, in the first fervour of a traveller's enthusiasm, (breaking loose after the confinement of a tedious voyage,) indites a long chapter upon Mr. Roscoe! The name of Roscoe will always maintain a certain place in the calendar of literature; but is it not a little hyperbolical to talk of him 'as one of those men whose voices have gone forth to the ends of the earth,'—'who pass before our imaginations like superior beings radiant with the emanations of their own genius, and surrounded with a halo of literary glory.'? We know not how it may be at the 'ends of the earth;' but we suspect that there are a great many worthy people on this side of 'the Land's End' who never heard of the historian of Leo and the Medici; and who are only acquainted with Mr. Roscoe as the weakest of all political writers and speakers, and the unsuccessful candidate for Liverpool.

The next chapter, entitled **"The Wife,"** is pretty; but we doubt whether it is natural, and are sure it is not English nature. There is an affectation in the sentiment, and an artificial smartness in the getting up of the incidents, which would almost lead us to suppose it was a translation from the French. We like **"Rip Van Winkle"** much better; in this there is a spirit, and an originality that occasionally remind us of the great Northern Enchanter.

"Van Winkle" is followed by a long chapter, which has for its title **"English Writers on America,"** written for the most part in a spirit of good sense and moderation which could scarcely be expected from an American,—even when intended for publication on this side of the water. There are some traits of national obliquity; but there is much that is praiseworthy and excellent; and we think the perusal of it may be of great service on both sides of the Atlantic. (pp. 52-3)

The last, and perhaps the best, chapter in the first volume is **"The Spectre Bridegroom"** a romantic tale, which the author, in a pleasant introduction, represents as the narration of an old Swiss traveller at the fireside of an Inn Kitchen in the Low Countries. Our author, we think, succeeds best in his narrative pieces, which are written in a style at once playful and picturesque, and we should be glad to see a whole series of "Tales of the Inn Kitchen" executed in the same lively manner. (p. 58)

"Little Britain" is tiresome enough, and we could willingly have dispensed with **"Philip of Pokanoket"**; but—*quot homines tot sententiæ:* there may be persons in the world who will prefer these, with the articles **"The Art of Book-Making"** and **"The Mutability of Literature"** in the first volume, to any other parts of his work, and therefore we acknowledge the force of Mr. Crayon's reasons for serving up a variety of dishes to please a variety of tastes.

He is generally very happy in what is called *sentimental* description—in that lively transmission of sensations and impressions which not only places before the eyes of the reader an animated picture of the scene described, but imparts at the same time the *feelings* which it is calculated to inspire. (pp. 58-9)

"John Bull" is a clever allegory, and if we do not acknowledge it to be a faithful portrait, we must at least allow that it is a spirited caricature, abounding in lively and laughable strokes of satire. But an allegory cannot be continued through a long chapter without becoming tedious; and we pass on to **"The Legend of Sleepy Hollow."** The scene of this pleasant tale is laid in the neighbourhood of a village situated on the banks of the Hudson, where, it seems, there is a little valley, or rather 'lap of land,' among high hills which has long been known by the name of Sleepy Hollow. The air of this sequestered glen has a kind of magical influence, disposing the mind to dream dreams and see apparitions, and accordingly the superstition of the inhabitants has peopled it with a fearful race of imps and hobgoblins. The head—we beg pardon—the ringleader of the apparitions, however, is a Hessian trooper, whose head has been carried away by a cannon-ball during the revolutionary war; and the belief of the neighbourhood is, that (the body of the trooper being buried in the churchyard) the ghost rides forth to the scene of battle in nightly quest of his head, and that the speed with which he is often seen to rush along the Hollow in his way back is owing to his being 'belated,' and in a hurry to reach the churchyard before daybreak. (p. 59)

["**The Legend of Sleepy Hollow**"] with "**Rip Van Winkle**" and the "**Spectre Bridegroom**," will, we think, be more read and admired than any other parts of the book. There is in the author's sketches of this kind a force and facility of touch, that bespeak the hand of a master. His style is in general remarkable for sprightliness and elegance;—though where he has not the care and conduct of a story to keep his pen within bounds, he is too apt to fall into a habit of stringing pretty sentences together in an artificial style of composition, in which the constant attempt to be sweet is carried almost to cloying; apparently, not aware that

> ————the sweetest honey
> Is loathsome in its own deliciousness.

And, when in this mood, there is so sempiternal a sameness of sentiment and expression, that as soon as we have read the first opening words, we seem to know exactly how the period will end. We had marked down a few phrases as Americanisms, but upon referring to our dictionary, we find many of them might be defended by authority, though there are certainly some words, such as 'deviltry,' 'bedroofed,' 'umbratile,' and others of the same school, that have rather an outlandish air. (p. 66)

The author before us is the best writer of English, in our estimation of that term, that America has produced since the era of her independence. He seems to have studied our language—where alone it can be studied in all its strength and perfection—in the writings of our old sterling authors; in working these precious mines of literature, he has refined for himself the ore which there so richly abounds. His work, too, is exclusively English, and is not indebted for any of its charms to the common aid of classical allusion or quotation;—of which we do not recollect a single instance in either of his volumes. We take leave of him with the highest respect for his talents, and a warm feeling of regard for those amiable and benevolent qualities of heart and mind which beam through every page of his book. (p. 67)

A review of "The Sketch Book," in The Quarterly Review, *Vol. XXV, No. XLIX, April, 1821, pp. 50-67.*

[WILLIAM HICKLING PRESCOTT]   (essay date 1822)

[*Prescott, an American author and historian who specialized in the study of Spain, is best known for his* A History of the Conquest of Mexico. *In the following excerpt from his review of two books styled after* The Sketch Book, *Prescott discusses the influence of Irving's work on American essayists and on the reading tastes of the American public.*]

The style hitherto predominating in the compositions of men of education in our own country, has been for the most part that plain, unvarnished style, better fitted to give information than delight; well suited to an intelligible disclosure of facts, but foreign to all the ambitious purposes of fine writing. Still we have had examples of this in more than one name, that will be remembered with gratitude by posterity. Franklin, Dennie, Ames, and Buckminster, to mention no others, have left us evidence of the distinctive physiognomy of their minds, no less in the peculiar merits of their style, than of their sentiments; and many more, were it not invidious, might be enumerated, who, in the present increasing appetite for letters, are cultivating with success the most refined beauties of English composition. *The Sketch Book,* however, is the only one pertinent to our purpose, as developing a new form, and constituting the last link in the series of periodical essay writing. (pp. 331-32)

That species of periodical essay writing, which had continued in Great Britain, with little intermission, from the first appearance of the *Tatler,* disappeared under this extreme popularity of reviews and magazines. It has, however, arisen within a few years in our own country, with new and very different attractions. *The Sketch Book* certainly forms an epoch in the history of this kind of literature; for although of the same generic character with the British essayists, it has many important specific peculiarities. The former were written . . . with a direct moral tendency, to expose and to reform the ignorance and the follies of the age. *The Sketch Book,* on the other hand, has no direct moral purpose, but is founded on sentiment and deep feeling. In its comic scenes (which by the bye we think its best) we have the broad caricature of a truly original humor, but not a faithful delineation of the state of society in any age or place. Neither do the beautiful pictures of English life hold out any direct moral aim, but are distinguished by the same rich coloring of sentiment that pervades, and, in fact, gives a character to the whole work. In one word, as the principal object of the British essayists was to instruct, so they have for the most part given a picture of common life, in simple language; while the principal object of *The Sketch Book,* being to delight, scenes only of exquisite emotion are selected, and painted in the most exquisite, but artificial language.

We confess, that we are somewhat apprehensive of the influence of a work, uniting such uncommon richness of thought and expression, upon our general taste, and doubt it may give younger readers, at least, a disrelish for the more simple and less stimulating compositions of Goldsmith and of Addison. Of one thing we are positive, that it is the very worst model in the world for the imitation of writers, especially of young writers, who, wanting genuine sensibility, will only expose the beggarly condition of their thoughts the more, by arraying them in this gorgeous apparel. (p. 333)

[William Hickling Prescott], "Essay Writing," in The North American Review, *n.s. Vol. 14, No. XXXV, April, 1822, pp. 319-50.*

GEOFFREY CRAYON [PSEUDONYM OF WASHINGTON IRVING] (essay date 1822)

[*In the following footnote from his book* Bracebridge Hall, *published in 1822, Irving responds to charges that he "plagiarized" German folklore in "Rip Van Winkle."*]

I find that the tale of "**Rip Van Winkle,**" given in the *Sketch Book,* has been discovered by divers writers in magazines, to have been founded on a little German tradition, and the matter has been revealed to the world as if it were a foul instance of plagiarism marvellously brought to light. In a note which follows that tale I had alluded to the superstition on which it was founded, and I thought a mere allusion was sufficient, as the tradition was so notorious as to be inserted in almost every collection of German legends. I had seen it myself in three. I could hardly have hoped, therefore, in the present age, when every source of ghost and goblin story is ransacked, that the origin of the tale would escape discovery. In fact, I had considered popular traditions of the kind as fair foundations for authors of fiction to build upon, and had made use of the one in question accordingly. I am not disposed to contest the matter, however, and indeed consider myself so completely overpaid by the public for my trivial performances, that I am content to submit to any deduction which, in their afterthoughts, they may think proper to make. (p. 247)

> *Geoffrey Crayon [pseudonym of Washington Irving], "The Historian," in his* Bracebridge Hall; or, The Humourists, *edited by Herbert F. Smith, Twayne Publishers, 1977, pp. 246-47.*

[EVERT DUYCKINCK?]   (essay date 1845)

[*Duyckinck was an American editor, critic, and literary historian who coauthored with his brother, George Duyckinck, the* Cyclopaedia of American Literature. *This anthology and critical survey was influential in establishing the validity of American literature and promoting its study. Duyckinck lived and worked in New York City and was a friend of many noted American authors, including Irving. In the following review of* The Works of Washington Irving, *signed "E. D." and believed to be by Duyckinck, he discusses Irving's significance as an innovator in American literature and offers a brief appreciation of* The Sketch Book.]

To Washington Irving must be conceded the high honor of having originated what our friend Judge Meek forcibly terms "Americanism in Literature." He was among the first, if not the very first, of our native writers, to spurn the literary dictation of the British critics; and, in *Salmagundi,* (in which Mr. Paulding was his coadjutor,) the declaration of our literary independence was first boldly proclaimed. . . . (p. 71)

[*The Sketch Book* is a] faithful transcript of the first impressions of an educated and intelligent American traveller, visiting for the first time the land of his ancestors, invested with all the eloquence which true feeling and genius, when combined, must produce,—it at once took captive the hearts and judgments of the sensible portion of both the English and American public, and compelled even the British critics to admit, that an American had actually written a good and sensible book. Its earnestness and sincerity are its chief characteristics. He evidently conveyed the impressions produced upon his mind, without "extenuating or setting down aught in malice." It is the most candid and impartial record of travel we recollect ever to have met with. . . . (pp. 88-9)

In *The Sketch Book,* Mr. Irving did not attempt, like most tourists, to give a guide-book of routes and distances, the population of the different cities, or the number and size of the various public buildings,—but simply to record the general impressions produced upon his mind, by the scenes through which he passed, and the recollections which they awakened; interspersed with graphic sketches of national and individual character. (p. 89)

[Mr. Irving] is what our Gallic neighbours would term a capital Raconteur; there seldom being any superfluous flourishes about his style, which runs smoothly and placidly to its destined point. But his great forte undoubtedly is in his humor, which, chameleon-like, seems to take the hue of that to which it is nearest. Thus, the humor of Diedrich Knickerbocker is as widely different from the sportive fancies of Geoffrey Crayon, as delftware is from porcelain; yet both are part and parcel of the same peculiar temperament. Our author, in his different writings, sometimes startles us by the apparent incongruity of his sentiments, and almost persuades us, as Mrs. Malaprop says of Cerberus, that "he is two gentlemen at once." Yet this is one of the rare but high privileges of genius, to enter into and identify itself with feelings and sensations, apparently the most adverse and repugnant; and thus the broad, coarse humor of Knickerbocker, is not incompatible with the refined and pensive musings of Geoffrey Crayon over the tomb of Shakspeare, or in his wanderings by the haunted windings of the Avon.

The humor of Mr. Irving is peculiar to him, and . . . akin to that of Goldsmith in some of its phases; while, in others, it bears some affinity to that of Swift, the mighty master of sarcastic pleasantry,—with this difference, however, that no poison lurks beneath his honey, and that his satire is not directed by the malignant spirit, which stung and tortured into convulsive merriment the mighty but erring genius to whom we have compared him. (pp. 91-2)

> [*Evert Duyckinck?*], *"Writings of Washington Irving," in* The Southern Quarterly Review, *Vol. VIII, No. XV, July, 1845, pp. 69-93.*

HENRY WADSWORTH LONGFELLOW   (essay date 1859)

[*Longfellow was the most popular American poet of the nineteenth century. Widely acclaimed in his day for such works as* The Song of Hiawatha *and* The Courtship of Miles Standish, and Other Poems, *Longfellow and his poetry have since his death suffered a serious decline in critical and popular interest. The following excerpt is from a memorial tribute to Irving and* The Sketch Book *delivered at a meeting of the Massachusetts Historical Society soon after his death.*]

Every reader has his first book: I mean to say, one book, among all others, which, in early youth, first fascinates his imagination, and at once excites and satisfies the desires of his mind. To me, this first book was *The Sketch-Book* of Washington Irving. I was a schoolboy when it was published, and read each succeeding number with ever-increasing wonder and delight,—spell-bound by its pleasant humor, its melancholy tenderness, its atmosphere of revery; nay, even by its gray-brown covers, the shaded letters of the titles, and the fair, clear type,—which seemed an outward symbol of the style.

How many delightful books the same author has given us, written before and since,—volumes of history and of fiction, most of which illustrate his native land, and some of which illuminate it, and make the Hudson, I will not say as classic, but as romantic, as the Rhine! Yet still the charm of *The Sketch-Book* remains unbroken; the old fascination still lingers about it; and, whenever I open its pages, I open also that mysterious door which leads back into the haunted chambers of youth.

Many years afterward, I had the pleasure of meeting Mr. Irving in Spain; and found the author, whom I had loved, repeated in the man,—the same playful humor, the same touches of sentiment, the same poetic atmosphere, and, what I admired still more, the entire absence of all literary jealousy, of all that mean avarice of fame, which counts what is given to another as so much taken from one's self. . . . (pp. 393-94)

One summer morning, passing his house at the early hour of six, I saw his study-window already wide open. On my mentioning it to him afterwards, he said, "Yes: I am always at my work as early as six." Since then, I have often remembered that sunny morning and that open window, so suggestive of his sunny temperament and his open heart, and equally so of his patient and persistent toil. . . . (p. 394)

> *Henry Wadsworth Longfellow, "Remarks of Mr. Longfellow," in* Proceedings of the Massachusetts Historical Society, *December, 1859, pp. 393-95.*

SCRIBNER'S MONTHLY   (essay date 1876)

[*In the following excerpt from a negative assessment of Irving, the critic contends that Irving failed to introduce new themes or techniques to American literature. The critic further suggests that in "Rip Van Winkle" and other writings, Irving was more concerned with superficial style than substance.*]

[Exactly] what are the results of Irving's American associations? How far do they extend? To me it seems that the conquest over something hitherto unsubjected to literature, and the substantial gain to America of handiwork containing the germ of a new order of thought or feeling, is in Irving's books almost nil. What is his view point? Almost entirely that which leads to a search for the mere picturesque. The lightness and vagueness of theme with which he is content is very manifest in *Wolfert's Roost*, in the *Tales of a Traveler,* and the introduced narrative of *Bracebridge Hall*; and at times the minute atom of real emotion or definite incident at the bottom of these, is almost stifled by his insatiable desire of words. But the most remarkable example is his treatment of the Rip Van Winkle legend [in **"Rip Van Winkle"**]. There is hardly a suspicion here of the real depth of pathos which has since been revealed to us in the same story on the stage. As elsewhere, Irving shows in his sketch of this tradition an excellent sense of what constitutes elegant entertainment; his perception of the gentlemanly in literature is admirable; he contrives good conventional contrasts, and rounds in the whole with a sonorous and well-derived style. It is the most completely "polite" writing. But the absence is as complete of anything like profound insight, deep imaginative sympathy, or genuinely dramatic rendering of character and circumstance. As for any new distillation of truth from his New World subjects, we must forego that entirely. All this finds parallel, too, in his style, which the systematic and loyal puffing of half a century has not been able to make into anything else than a patent-leather Addisonian one. For simple surface execution, it may be agreed, he has been equaled by few in his time; and *Bracebridge Hall* is a most remarkable revival of an obsolete and very acceptable style; but from this sort of imitation the same unconscious insincerity is as inseparable as it is from the recent French reproductions of Japanese porcelains. They are even better, one may say, than the originals, and yet the more refined and enduring value of the first product is entirely absent from the imitations. Thackeray's *Henry Esmond* is the only English fiction of this century, I suppose, which in point of antiquated style comes upon the same ground with *Bracebridge Hall*; but there, instead of being an anachronism, the style is a part of the dramatic unity, and again it is penetrated at every point and nobly uplifted by the atmosphere of powerful human passions. Thus, Irving's superficial treatment of theme and acquired style operate against the originality of his few American fictions. (pp. 800-01)

This brings us to his humor. . . . There is a smack of college wit about it, especially in the excess to which he carries pretended derivations of local and personal names. There is always in Irving's writing the mild, sweet radiance of a graceful, uncontaminated spirit which comes forth here and there in a sort of subdued and gentle smile; and this is something to be prized. But his humor never develops into the full, rich laugh that belongs to Scott and Dickens. It is always a smile, as his drawing is sketching. There is something full of meaning in that oddly logical title of his most popular work, *The "Sketch" Book*. He was, in strict analysis, an amateur. But it will not do to play the amateur, when one is laying the foundation of a national literature. (p. 801)

> *"Poe, Irving, Hawthorne," in* Scribner's Monthly, *Vol. XI, No. 6, April, 1876, pp. 799-808.*

EDWIN W. BOWEN   (essay date 1906)

[*Bowen offers a brief appreciation of* The Sketch Book, *citing "The Wife," "Rip Van Winkle," and "The Legend of Sleepy Hollow" as the book's best stories. The critic also suggests that Irving's achievement lies in his prose style rather than in intellectual depth.*]

At thirty-six Irving settled down to literary work in London, and the first product of his labors was the famous *The Sketch-Book*. Though resident in the British metropolis, his heart was in America,—on the historic and picturesque Hudson along whose banks, in his earlier years, he had so often roamed and hunted game, in quest of health. . . . *The Sketch-Book* is distinctively American, racy and smacks of the soil. The old legends of the Hudson are here clothed with life and beauty and are now recognized almost as a part of our national history. Irving gave these local traditions of our American Rhine celebrity and currency, and they have now become as familiar as household words.

The treatment of *The Sketch-Book* is somewhat unequal. Some of the sketches are naturally better than others. A popular vote would probably put **"The Wife," "Rip Van Winkle"** and **"The Legend of Sleepy Hollow"** easily first, and this verdict would be confirmed by critical judgment. While all are good, these three sketches are felt to be the finest. Their tender pathos, imaginative humor, simplicity and grace have already endeared these three to the hearts of thousands of readers who have lingered, almost spellbound, over their pages; and their charm and beauty will, no doubt, commend them to generations of readers yet unborn. Of this trio **"Rip Van Winkle,"** in the popular estimate (perhaps also in the estimate of the critics), is entitled to first place. This, even more than the others, Irving seems to have suffused with the soft hues of his romantic fancy and to have invested with unusual glamour and pathos. (pp. 174-75)

Irving scored a signal success in *The Sketch-Book*. The volume met with a reception, on both sides of the Atlantic, which far exceeded the author's most sanguine expectations. Irving himself had some misgivings about the publication of the book. Speaking, in a letter to a friend, of the cordial reception given it, he wrote in 1819:

> The manner in which the book has been received, and the eulogiums that have been passed upon it in the American papers and periodical works, have completely overwhelmed me. They go far, *far* beyond my most sanguine expectations, and indeed are expressed with such peculiar warmth and kindness

as to affect me in the tenderest manner. The receipt of your letter, and the reading of some of the criticisms this morning, have rendered me nervous for the whole day. I feel almost appalled by such success, and fearful that it cannot be real, or that it is not fully merited, or that I shall not act up to the expectations that may be formed. We are whimsically constituted beings. I had got out of conceit of all that I had written, and considered it very questionable stuff; and now that it is so extravagantly bepraised, I begin to feel afraid that I shall not do as well again. . . . I hope you will not attribute all this sensibility to the kind reception I have met to an author's vanity. I am sure it proceeds from very different sources. Vanity could not bring the tears to my eyes as they have been brought by the kindness of my countrymen. I have felt cast down, blighted, and broken-spirited, and these sudden rays of sunshine agitate me more than they revive me. I hope—I hope I may yet do something more worthy of the appreciation lavished on me.

(pp. 175-76)

Irving richly deserves the distinction usually accorded him of being the first American author to win for himself a conspicuous and unfading name in the department of letters. . . . This honor has been achieved not by our author's intellectual force and acumen, nor by his creative imagination and incisive literary touch, but by the free play of his romantic fancy, his pervading sentiment, his unfailing, delightful humor and his charming style. Herein lies the secret of his success. (p. 181)

Irving appeals to the sensibilities rather than to the intellect, to the heart rather than to the head. His register, to use a musical term, is not great; his range is not wide. There are notes he never sounded, depths and heights he never reached. The tragedy of life, the profoundest problems of human existence, the realm of philosophical speculation—these were to Irving an unexplored country which his creative mind never entered. The subtle analysis of Poe and the perplexing social problems and deep mysteries of Hawthorne had for Irving no special interest or attraction. He did not make his works a medium for communicating to the world mere metaphysical exercises of marvelous originality, or great moral truths. Such studies awaken in us the spirit of inquiry and speculation, disturb our peace of mind and tend to unsettle our convictions. Irving's works, on the other hand, induce to repose and quiet musing; they do not agitate or ruffle our spirits. They reflect their author's own quiet and reposeful nature, as that nature is enlivened by a delightful vein of humor and sentiment. For this reason Irving is not especially stimulating or suggestive. He is the author to be read when one desires particularly amusement and unfeigned delight. (pp. 181-82)

Edwin W. Bowen, "Washington Irving's Place in American Literature," in The Sewanee Review, *Vol. XIV, No. 2, April, 1906, pp. 171-83.*

HENRY SEIDEL CANBY (essay date 1909)

[*Canby, an American scholar and author, was a founder and editor of the* Saturday Review of Literature. *Among his many books is* The Short Story in English, *excerpted here, which was long considered the standard college textbook on the genre. Canby asserts that Irving was significant to the development of the short story because he applied humor and eighteenth-century ideals of balance and restraint to essentially romantic subject matter.*]

There is no prose short story in [the early nineteenth century] which does not reveal inferiority, and often an abysmal inferiority, when tried by the touchstone of "**Rip Van Winkle,**" or "**The Legend of Sleepy Hollow.**" . . . Amidst all the welter of pathetico-mystico slush which filled the periodicals of these years, an obscure American suddenly elevates the popular kind of short story into masterpieces which belong to our permanent literature.

The critical problem is a nice one. First, just what did Irving accomplish when he wrote the best of his stories; next, how did he accomplish it; and, finally, what is the place of his achievement in the evolution we are tracing? The materials are in *The Sketch Book, Tales of a Traveller,* and *The Alhambra,* in which three works his most noteworthy contributions to the short story were contained. (pp. 218-19)

To begin with, just what was it that Irving did accomplish? There is a disposition, in contemporary criticism, to disparage the first American writer who became "classic." The tendency shows itself by implication, rather than in the open, and seems to result from the sudden rush to appreciate the modern short story. Irving certainly did not achieve the "short story," or short-story, or Short Story, as the modern product has been variously written down. Professor Baldwin has aptly suggested in this connection, that if "**Rip Van Winkle**" should be retold to-day it would be a very different narrative. The return of old Rip to his village would be the situation chosen for emphasis by the narrator; the Catskill episodes would sink to mere foothills of antecedent action; the confusion of the returned hunter would rise to the heights of climax. Indeed, it is true that the technique which has put so many hitherto unconsidered situations into literature, and the short-story form, was not in Irving's grasp, or, better, was unknown to him. Yet, since nothing could be more different in artistic purpose than these idyllic tales of the Hudson River Dutch and the stories of Poe, Harte, or Kipling, nothing is more useless than to compare their technique to the detriment of either. Intensity, emphasis, excerption of a single situation is the aim of the more modern story-tellers; breadth within limits, balance of parts, an easy telling of several related incidents, the accomplishment of the first American master of the tale. When successful, the simple, unemphatic, but well-balanced tale is no whit inferior to the highly artificial mechanism of "The Cask of Amontillado" or "They"—it is merely different. The simpler structure was less sure of success in a few pages; witness the many good plots spoiled in these early decades. But Irving mastered this simplicity and made it successful; restrained pathos, mystery, and sentiment with humor; balanced the fashionable introduction with the requisite weight of story; carried fluency and restraint to the end. He may be said to have discharged his debt to the rhetorician; and, though he did not achieve the modern short story, it is not impossible that his particular success, the proportioning of the simple tale, may belong to a more durable variety of art.

The second question, What made him so successful with the simple tale while his contemporaries were crowding the periodicals with failures? is not so easily answered. Perhaps humor was the talisman which saved Irving from contagion; that gentle, urbane humor which smiles from behind Ichabod Crane and Rip. It must have been a sense of humor that restrained him from the excesses of the average contributor. Supply a theme which, lending itself to sentiment, forbade the humorous, and he stopped just short of the common complaint of the annuals. "**The Pride of the Village**" in *The Sketch Book,* "**The**

Young Italian'' of *Tales of a Traveller,* are unhumorous—and on the brink. (pp. 219-20)

But there is another reason for the success of [Irving] in the exquisitely simple, perfectly balanced tale, a reason which regards the structure as much as the contents of the story. It must be set forth in order to relate his work to the development of the short story, as well as to complete the explanation of his triumph. This reason is to be found in the nature of the models upon which he formed his style.

The question, Where did Irving learn his art? may be answered, to the degree in which answer is possible, with ease and rapidity. The bent of his genius is in exact conformity with his age. He is a late romantic, he belongs to the generation after the Gothic romance, the generation of the historical romance, and the pathetic, ghastly, mysterious tale. His subjects are those of his times. But his method, his style, his view-point differ . . . from those of his contemporaries. This difference must certainly be ascribed in part to his well-known fondness for the literature of the early eighteenth century. No argument is needed to prove a general influence. The form of *The Sketch Book* is reminiscent of *The Spectator,* and *Bracebridge Hall* was evidently inspired by Sir Roger de Coverley; Irving's style is Addisonian; his humor an Augustan urbanity; he is inclined to study manners in a very eighteenth century fashion. If his interests stamp him romanticist, his manner as certainly marks him a student and often an imitator of the age of Pope, Steele, and Addison. But, to these obvious debts, I would add one more. The resemblance between the periodical narrative of the eighteenth century and these perfectly balanced tales of Irving has been noticed only as far as their characters, Will Wimble and Rip, the squire of Bracebridge Hall and Sir Roger, betray evidences of kinship. It goes much deeper. We will not presume to say that Irving learned his proportioning sense of humor from *The Spectator* or *The Tatler,* although doubtless he was not uninfluenced by the Queen Anne temperament. But it is notable and significant that one finds the balance, the restraint, the exact adaptation of means to end, precisely what the short stories of the romanticists lacked, precisely what Irving attained, in the periodical narratives of the early eighteenth century which were his early and revered reading. Put the question this way. How would a close student and admirer of the narratives of *The Spectator,* or *The Rambler,* treat a romantic story of pathetic love, a mysterious legend, or any example of the narratives most cherished in Irving's day? Would he be mawkish in the telling, extravagant, grossly improbable? Could he be, with such models! A theoretical application of an eighteenth century manner to the romantic tale of Miss Roberts in the annual before me, gives, to the assertion that he could not, a pragmatic value. Most certainly Irving was a romanticist, but, quite as certainly, he learned order, restraint, and symmetry from the masters of the short story in the eighteenth century.

This criticism, so far, may seem to be a narrow one. It has been based upon only two stories, the Dutch tales of *The Sketch Book.* But these are the best as well as the earliest of Irving's successful narratives. He never afterwards reached their level. He often fell far below it. (pp. 222-24)

> Henry Seidel Canby, ''The Early Nineteenth Century,'' in his The Short Story in English, *Henry Holt and Company, 1909, pp. 209-26.*

JOHN MACY (essay date 1913)

[*In an appreciation of ''Rip Van Winkle,'' Macy suggests that commentators have overemphasized Irving's reliance on eighteenth-*

century writers and that he is less than the ''immortal'' American author some have claimed him to be.]

Rip took his place at once among the favourite heroes of fantastic story. . . . [''**Rip Van Winkle**''] is so simple, so familiar, that in rereading it one may easily take it for granted and not be struck by its genius. To be convinced that it is a masterpiece one needs but to reflect how infrequently such a tender weanling is adopted as the child of time. A little thing that happens seldom is important.

The story of Rip is based on a German legend, and the origin accounts in some measure for the elementary directness of the tale, a virtue that sophisticated art cannot easily counterfeit, but can easily destroy. Irving has preserved the quality of a folk-tale, and at the same time he permits himself the privilege of winking at the reader over the head of [the fictitious narrator] Knickerbocker.

''**Rip Van Winkle**'' is not an accidental, solitary success. All the stories in *The Sketch Book,* notably ''**The Legend of Sleepy Hollow,**'' and other yarns comic and creepy in *Bracebridge Hall,* and *Tales of a Traveller,* are well told, with sprightly verve and grace. There are no afterthoughts or under-purposes. The attitude is that of a familiar raconteur who has no object in the world but to entertain his company, to puff his pipe in fireside ease and give the tale as 'twas given him. This style of narrative never hints that it is difficult to do and deceives one into overlooking its remarkable rare excellence.

Irving's avowed debt to Goldsmith and his fondness for tales of British squiredom warrant to some extent the view that he is an imitator of the English essayists and character-sketchers of the eighteenth century. He has been called a ''belated'' American Goldsmith. There has arisen in one quarter the curious notion (a theory running wild with a little fact in its mouth) that American literature is habitually a generation behind English literature. Even Holmes, a very modern man, is accounted for in terms of the ''eighteenth-century spirit.'' The truth seems to be that nineteenth-century thought everywhere is eclectic, and of its many voices each is germane to the times.

Any man, anywhere, writing at the opening of the last century is inevitably dependent on the eighteenth century. . . . Irving is no more filled with the eighteenth-century spirit than are many of his British contemporaries. Byron and Scott are his heroes no less than Goldsmith, and he makes pilgrimages to Newstead Abbey and Abbottsford. His attitude toward Johnson is that of the nineteenth-century romantic making a case for the gentle poetic Goldsmith against the kindly tyranny of the critical prosaic bear.

Irving is not, of course, akin to the spirit of revolt that now seems the most significant fact of the age of Wordsworth; he is a conventional man, with no very profound convictions, no intense theory of life. His philosophy is that of the amiable, gifted man of the world of all times and places; ''I have always had an opinion that much good might be done by keeping mankind in good humour with one another.'' Such a philosophy does not proceed from a nature that is torn by everlasting problems, but it is not referable to any special period of literary thought; it is as near to Scott as to Addison, it is as remote from Swift as from Shelley. (pp. 25-8)

Certain American books have sufficient depth and breadth to be called masterpieces; they stand self-contained and all but assured of immortality. . . . Other books, like Emerson's *Essays* and Whitman's poems, contain matter of loftiest quality yet in such brief form that the author's title to mastery lies in the collected work, rather than in any single unit of art. In neither of these ultimate classes can Irving be included. Though one would not wish to quarrel with whoever should call "**Rip Van Winkle**" a self-secure masterpiece, nevertheless Irving is, for all his bulky histories, essentially a sketcher, a miscellanist. His place is on one of the gentler lower slopes of literature in the company suggested by the sub-title of **Bracebridge Hall**— "The Humourists, A Medley." (pp. 32-3)

> *John Macy, "Irving," in his* The Spirit of American Literature, *Doubleday, Page & Company, 1913, pp. 18-34.*

THE NATION, NEW YORK   (essay date 1919)

[*In the following excerpt, the critic assesses the vitality of* The Sketch Book *one hundred years after its publication and remarks on Irving's central importance to the development of the short story form.*]

Many busy pens have written many centennial articles this year, and yet no one has paid the proper honors to that blithe centenarian who still survives with most of his faculties about him—Mr. Geoffrey Crayon. It was during 1819 that he gave nearly all the happiest strokes to his **The Sketch Book**; indeed, it was almost exactly a hundred years ago this week that he put into final form "**The Legend of Sleepy Hollow**," beyond which his art was never able to go though he wrote four hearty decades longer. Earlier in the year he had already enlivened and enriched the universe with "**Rip Van Winkle**," and between these two indisputable climaxes of his achievement had brought forth nearly the whole of the earliest volume of belles-lettres by an American to catch and hold an international audience. The vogue of **The Sketch Book** is perhaps not what it was during its first half century. Of how many books cannot such a thing be said? But it has never ceased to amuse, and it has long stood in the decisive position of that classic in English which youthful foreigners, from Switzerland to Japan and in most of the lands that lie between, are likely to study first in learning the English language. To have done for a hundred years what Addison with his *Spectator* did the hundred years before points to a vitality in Mr. Crayon which not a few of us may have overlooked. We have been taking him for granted, as a natural part of the landscape of letters, hardly conscious how much we should lack if he had never lived.

Let us admit, of course, that like some other gentlemen of the old school he has about him certain airs and graces that we smile at in 1919. He was the child, for instance, of a generation to whom tears must have been less salt and hot than we think tears now, else they could never have been endured in such multitudinous floods; witness his stories "**The Wife**" (all that fuss made over a wife who continues to love her husband though he has lost money!) and "**The Pride of the Village**." Mr. Crayon trifled, too, with village antiquities a good deal in the curious spirit of Sylvanus Urban, though in a mellower style than Mr. Urban often used. Consider such philanderings with "nature" as "**Rural Life in England**" and "**Rural Funerals**." In general it may be said that Mr. Crayon hankered for the past with a tender insistence upon the solidity of old beef and the flavor of old ale and the color of old customs. . . .

But Mr. Crayon must not be looked at as merely a man who poured all his forces into no matter how prosperous a stream. He stands sturdily at the source of the modern short story, which begins with "**Rip Van Winkle**." Before it, "The Vision

of Mirza" and *Moral Tales*; after it, an old art learning so many new tricks that it sometimes seems a new one. In place of allegories and apologues and sketches of character and manners we have for a century had stories of actual persons and specific situations, pointing morals a shade (or several shades) less obtrusively, and set down less in the service of satire or moralism than at the instigation of sheer delight in the variety and color of life. Yet of the thousands of such tales which have been written none has surpassed "**Rip Van Winkle**" and "**The Legend of Sleepy Hollow**" on their own ground. They have ripened not faded, sweetened not withered, with age. And while their lines have gone out through all the earth, so that Rip is everywhere the symbol of those fortunate souls who can hibernate their cares away, they belong to the soil as do no other American legends. Oddly enough, when he wrote these stories Mr. Crayon had never seen more of Rip's Catskill village than he could see from the deck of a Hudson River sloop; the story of the Headless Horseman was first told him in England, when he had been absent from his native state for a dozen years. Homesickness, which had forgotten irrelevant details, helped his imagination. Nor let it be unnoticed that Diedrich Knickerbocker appears as the narrator. Therein lies a large part of the secret. The urbane and smiling cosmopolite collaborated with the homebred, assiduous antiquary. When Geoffrey Crayon called Diedrich Knickerbocker into consultation, experience shook hands with knowledge, and breadth with depth; English made common cause with Dutch; conquering New York embraced a reconciled Nieuw Amsterdam.

> *"Geoffrey Crayon," in* The Nation, *New York, Vol. CIX, No. 2840, December 6, 1919, p. 710.*

EDWARD J. O'BRIEN   (essay date 1923)

[*O'Brien was an American poet and critic who edited numerous collections of short stories, including the annual* The Best Short Stories *(1914-1940), and wrote* The Advance of the American Short Story, *a study of the genre excerpted below. O'Brien names Irving as the central innovator in the American short story tradition. He also suggests that Irving made an implicit statement in his writings against materialism and that critics exaggerate his reliance on eighteenth-century authors.*]

The history of the American short story before Hawthorne and Poe is for the most part of mere academic interest. (p. 20)

The only writers to whom there is the slightest need of our paying any careful attention . . . are Washington Irving and William Austin. Irving presents us at once with a date and a point of departure. The date is 1819, when he published **The Sketch Book,** and the point of departure is "**Rip Van Winkle**," which for every sane and practical purpose is the beginning of our short story history. If we examine **The Sketch Book** attentively, we shall see that the short story begins by detaching itself from the essay. It is timidly experimental, but the steps of the process are tolerably clear. (pp. 21-2)

By temperament, the American who was a pioneer was impatient and restless. In general, as a writer he could not content himself with a literary form which demanded a long apprenticeship, much exhausting experimentation, and an uncertain public response. In like manner, as a reader, he would not concentrate willingly on a long piece of work, or respond to it with any great degree of sympathy, unless he was more or less vitally implicated in some immediate and pressing problem which it raised. (p. 25)

[The] short story from a pioneer's point of view has the merit of being brief and of condensing emotion into a moment as it flies. It satisfies his gregariousness without affronting his conscience. It requires no leisure to grasp its point. It requires less leisure on the author's part than the novel to express his feeling. Moreover, it solves his own unconscious conflicts with a greater economy of energy and with greater apparent clarity and force. Its chance of survival and development in a pioneer civilization was infinitely greater than that of the novel, and to this day the short story is our characteristic literary form. . . . (p. 26)

[We] may perceive in [Irving's] writings one significant fact, I think, which is usually ignored. He was in quiet revolt against the American life of his time. I do not mean that his life in Europe denationalized him. While living in Spain, his letters show, on the contrary, that he was homesick for America. I mean that he foresaw the coming suppression of spiritual by material values in his own country and sought to stem that tide. Those critics who are actively questioning our own contemporary values, and who are disposed to find fault with him, would have had his sympathetic esteem and coöperation. Strain is not always a sign of intensity, he might have pointed out to them, but with their general thesis he would have had no quarrel. To those who say that Irving had no explicit message, we may reply that he had an implicit ideal. (pp. 28-9)

Irving's two best stories are **"Rip Van Winkle"** and **"The Legend of Sleepy Hollow."** . . . Coming to these stories after reading the work of his American predecessors, we perceive at once that Irving owes nothing to the style of his fellow-countrymen. The influence, however, of Defoe, Goldsmith, Addison, and Steele are plain, though he has his eye fixed much more directly upon the object than Addison and Steele. He has Defoe's verisimilitude of manner and Goldsmith's verisimilitude of visual rendering. The influence of Defoe does not appear to have been stressed hitherto, although it is well-known that *Robinson Crusoe* was a favorite book of his boyhood.

He has the "sense and sensibility" of Goldsmith, and also his gift of gentle satire. George Saintsbury has remarked in his *Peace of the Augustans* that Goldsmith is inimitable, and has pointed out that Thackeray, who could write like Steele or like Horace Walpole, to take two very different contemporaries of Goldsmith, never attempted to imitate him. Well, Irving probably did not try to imitate him, but his sensitive and unconscious assimilation of Goldsmith's style, no doubt while reading *The Vicar of Wakefield* over and over again as a boy, accomplished the feat.

In later years, Irving was influenced by his friend Sir Walter Scott, but this influence is to be observed chiefly in the more deliberate direction of his interest toward the historic past, and for our purpose in this study it need not be further discussed, except to point out that it may have helped to determine the subject matter of the stories told in *The Alhambra.*

It has been the fashion of short story critics during the past few years to refer slightingly to **"Rip Van Winkle"** and **"The Legend of Sleepy Hollow,"** and to claim that their technique is crude. One critic, for example, whose study of the American short story has been unusually careful and valuable, Professor Baldwin, has pointed out that a writer who was relating the story of Rip Van Winkle to-day, "would begin with Rip's awakening, keep the action within one day by letting the previous twenty years transpire through Rip's own narrative at the new tavern, and culminate on the main disclosure." We might readily suppose that Euripides would have handled *Hamlet* in

a similar manner. Such speculations are not only useless, but actually harmful. It is a necessary, but frequently forgotten, platitude of criticism that we must measure a writer's achievement by what he sets out to do, and govern our appreciation accordingly. We must not judge Irving's technique to be inferior because it is different from that of Kipling, or because it is earlier. Each kind of writing has great merit. The one has ease, and the other intensity. It is, of course, arguable that the ideal short story should have both qualities, but the historical fact remains that intensity and ease have not yet been fused into a masterpiece by a short story writer in any language.

Furthermore, the point may be made that Irving's characteristic qualities of restraint and quiet balance have the merit of forestalling any reaction against his subject. There is an unfortunate tendency nowadays, which may perhaps be regarded as an excess of virtue, to value a short story in so far as it gives us a shock of surprise. As I have said before, it is the stories to which we can return again and again with a sense of refreshment and familiar recognition that survive the day for which they were written. By this test **"Rip Van Winkle"** and **"The Legend of Sleepy Hollow"** will outlast many changing literary fashions. (pp. 29-32)

> Edward J. O'Brien, "The Forerunners: Irving, Austin, and Others," in his The Advance of the American Short Story, *Dodd, Mead and Company, 1923, pp. 20-41.*

THE TIMES LITERARY SUPPLEMENT (essay date 1936)

[*In a derisive overview of Irving's literary career, the anonymous critic maintains that Irving's works lacked substance and that, while his style could be pleasing, it was obsolete, even in Irving's time.*]

"Authors, like coins, grow dear as they grow old," said Pope. Not all. Perhaps Irving was born too old. He was outdated from the start. The honours due to him are the honours due to one of the originators of imaginative literature in the United States. Yet a re-reading of his work brings curious questionings. How is it that a vital literature originated in anything so unoriginal as Irving's imitations of writers already outmoded? . . . Decaying customs and dead habits were his subjects, and a memory for the obsolete in writing formed his style. He was indeed a master of the obsolete in style and substance. His knowledge of the use of a disused technique and his acquaintance with discarded ideas are astonishing and almost deserve fame. His manner is drained of volition, and he seems void of responsibility. . . . Nearly everything that Irving acquired—style, subject, outlook—is secondhand and impoverished. His interests are homely; he takes us into his confidence though he has little to confide; pours into our ears a copious but thin flow of emotions. His mind runs on anecdotage and quotation. He interweaves his feelings with the landscape, utterly unabashed by their subjective quality and their insignificance. He could assimilate but not recreate. (p. 229)

The Sketch Book may be taken as the epitome of his work—and in a sense of his life. As fearless in declaring himself as in writing a platitude, he explained that he hoped in this work to escape "from the commonplace realities of the present and lose myself among the shadowy grandeurs of the past." He had travelled, he confessed, pencil in hand and had brought home a portfolio filled with sketches. They showed him making a momentous passage from the new world to the old, "musing for hours together on the tranquil bosom of a summer's sea," with "finny herds" roaming "its fathomless valleys"; admiring the "refreshing verdure" of English rural life; our churches, castles, parks and particularly the "moral feeling" that pervades them—with never a hint that the world had moved since Goldsmith's day, that industrialism was disturbing the "calm and settled security" that spoke to him so "deeply and touchingly."

All his descriptive epithets are counters, he never breaks into an original phrase; but he did have a gift for keeping a careful balance in the tone and rhythm of his sentences. That and his sentimentality was the secret of his popularity; as to-day they may explain why he has few to admire him. In Westminster Abbey he works up the right mood for "solemn contemplation" by intoning clichés in every device of cadence of which he was capable. But after Sir Thomas Browne's harmonies on mutability what a tinkle of words is this over "the congregated bones of the great men of past times who have filled history with their deeds and the earth with their renown." There is something to be said on the credit side. *The Sketch Book* does contain a story which may survive those "dilapidations of time" which Irving never ceased to lament. The plagiarism from a German source for "**Rip Van Winkle**" is a less important matter than some writers have pretended. Irving made the legend his own in the Catskill Mountains; and a re-reading brings again a childish thrill at the sight of the weird brotherhood of Dutchmen whose game of bowls sent the echoes rumbling through the ravine like peals of thunder. (p. 230)

"A Master of the Obsolete: Washington Irving in the Shadows," in The Times Literary Supplement, *No. 1781, March 21, 1936, pp. 229-30.*

FRANCIS V. LLOYD, JR. (essay date 1946)

[*Lloyd suggests that "Rip Van Winkle" is a satire on the narrowness of small-town thinking.*]

In answer to [the question] . . . as to whether there is a "theme" in Irving's "**Rip Van Winkle**" I think it would be fair to assume that the author of Knickerbocker's *A History of New York* . . . might be expected to "protest against the theory of the small town mind." At this most lively period (1809-1819) of Irving's thinking, satire and native humor were his predominant characteristics.

Specifically, consider two scenes. The one depicting the "club of the sages, philosophers, and other idle personages of the village" which met before the inn and listened to the news of a month's old newspaper read out by the local schoolmaster and watched the patriarch of the group express his opinions by smoke signals emitted from his pipe, is highly satirical of the Babbitts of those times. The other scene is Rip's return. The state of things in this scene of the village is symbolized for me by the sign on the inn which once portrayed "the ruby face of King George" but which now, after the substitution of a sword for a sceptre and the addition of a cocked hat to the head, was labeled George Washington. In other words, there was no basic change in the village despite the Revolution.

Whether all this can be dignified as a "theme" or not—and that word may well exaggerate the spirit of Irving—it would still appear to be satire of a way of life that Dreiser, Lewis and Wolfe tried later to expose in one form or another.

Francis V. Lloyd, Jr., "Irving's 'Rip Van Winkle'," in The Explicator, *Vol. IV, No. 4, February, 1946, Item #26.*

SARA PURYEAR RODES (essay date 1956)

[*In the following excerpt, Rodes describes Irving's effective use of folklore in "Rip Van Winkle" and "The Legend of Sleepy Hollow" and recounts the original folktales from which Irving drew his stories.*]

Washington Irving, who dearly loved the antique and the quaint, was one of the first [American writers] to recognize the romance in the tall tales and rough practical jokes of the frontier. Perhaps this was easier for him because his folk surroundings were Dutch while he himself was from a Scotch Presbyterian background, so the contrast helped him to be objective. Even as a youngster hunting along the shores of the Hudson, he saw the Dutch tales as fascinating scraps of literature; and as a man studying the folklore of Europe, he remembered the distinctive tales of his homeland. In 1817, a visit to Sir Walter Scott inspired Irving to help the local American countryside realize its romance and tradition as Scott had done in Scotland; and within the limits of his material and his ability, he quite succeeded. Of his seven tales and several sketches of the Hudson, only "**Rip Van Winkle**" and "**The Legend of Sleepy Hollow**" became classics; but all the tales have the aura of the Dutch Hudson and the true flavor of folklore about them, and all were appreciated by Irving's first American readers.

Irving uses three distinct elements in his tales—authentic setting and local characters, folk material, and fabrications from his own imagination. Sleepy Hollow with Brom Bones clattering up and down its stony roads was a reality. Village housewives, inns and hunting parties are those which Irving had actually known in his youth. He uses the folk material in a variety of forms. Local *sagen* and accounts of practical jokes are scattered freely through all the tales to add tone and richness while both local legends and long established folk tales are used as basis for three of the better stories—"**Rip Van Winkle**," "**The Legend of Sleepy Hollow**" and "**The Devil and Tom Walker**." However, Irving is thoroughly capable of creating pure fiction from his own imagination. He is especially good at elaborating and embroidering the skeleton of a local tradition so that it becomes an involved and romantic tale such as that of "**Dolph Heyliger**." (pp. 143-44)

Irving's two most well known American tales are also those in which he uses folklore most effectively. They vary widely. "**The Legend of Sleepy Hollow**" is a "mere whimsical band to connect descriptions of scenery, customs, manners, etc.," which also recounts folk traditions, *saga* and beliefs of various sorts in a loosely connected structure with just enough plot to hold the story together. "**Rip Van Winkle**" is the American version of an ancient folk tale in which Irving keeps very close to the folk version and with which he makes his greatest contribution to and use of American folklore. These two stories are the best of Irving's folklike tales. In them, one can see the real contribution which folklore can make to the art of literature.

"**The Legend of Sleepy Hollow**" has a wide variety of folk material. Folk attitudes, homey descriptions, local *sagen*, and ghosts lengthen the tale while the entire story is a practical joke, true to the ribald humor of American folklore. Localities have special prejudices. Irving uses two of the special Hudson Dutch folk notions in his satire of Ichabod Crane. The prosperous Dutch farmers had little use for education and even less for the clever New Englanders, so by satirizing Ichabod, Irving catches both attitudes. His descriptions of Sleepy Hollow and the people there were so realistic and homey that old timers of the lower Hudson River claimed to have known Brom Bones himself. In this loosely organized tale, Irving could take time for his characters to recount to one another several local *sagen,* similar to tales collected by other writers interested in the Hudson. These of Sleepy Hollow are based in historical fact and embroidered with native imagination instead of being old tales transplanted to the New World.

> Many dismal tales were told about the funeral trains and mourning cries and wailings heard and seen about the great tree where the unfortunate Major Andre was taken, and which stood in the neighborhood. Some mention was made also of the woman in white, that haunted the dark glen at Raven Rock, and was often heard to shriek on winter nights before a storm, having perished there in the snow.

The ghost of the Hessian trooper is of quite a different character from Irving's other ghosts. The mood of **"The Legend of Sleepy Hollow"** as a whole is more skeptical and less romantic than Irving's other tales; and this of course basically determines the interpretations of the ghost. In the story of **"Dolph Heyliger"** the ghost has a vital but friendly part to play in the action and is portrayed somewhat moderately. The ghost of **"Wolfert Webber"** is a more terrifying character, but his part also is realistic in relation to the plot, so his introduction and ghostly appearances must be kept within bounds but the ghost of Sleepy Hollow is not real; he is merely a huge practical joke. Therefore, Irving can go to extremes with this ghost. In other stories, the introduction of the ghost is carefully prepared for with many forewarnings; in **"The Legend of Sleepy Hollow,"** his preparation is much shorter and more intense. This ghost is more formidable and ghastly than Irving's other ghosts and, in proportion, less believable. The reader may be willing to suspend disbelief for a pirate in a distant doorway but recoils against a headless apparition riding the night roads beside him. For this reason, Irving makes the whole affair with the ghost move swiftly so as not to be asking too much of his readers. Although the story as a whole is slow and descriptive, the sections dealing with the Hessian move comparatively quickly. The mood of terror is developed almost entirely within Ichabod's ride from Katrina Van Tassel's home to the little bridge and everything the schoolmaster passes contributes to building up the terror. The tension corresponds to the pace of Ichabod's horse who is soon racing wildly and uncontrollably in the wrong direction. Immediately, the pumpkin head breaks and the joke is sprung.

This humorous use of the supernatural is more acceptable to the modern reader than the more serious interpretations of Irving's other tales. Irving uses his talent for comic satire as well as his talent for sympathetic description throughout the whole story and indirectly applies this satire to the belief in supernatural spirits as well as to Yankee schoolmasters. This light treatment of ghosts is not usual in the type of European folk tales which Irving admired but is thoroughly in harmony with the disrespectful American folk attitude toward the traditional ghost. By his use of humor and the practical joke, Irving brought **"The Legend of Sleepy Hollow"** much more closely in touch with the spirit of American folklore than are his other tales except **"Rip Van Winkle."**

In creating the American version of the story of Rip Van Winkle, Irving did his nation a real favor, for he brought into American folklore one of the oldest folk themes of western culture and made of it an excellent and pleasant tale. It is his best work. Although Irving's version is a conscious literary one, it is also a tightly woven folk tale which allows little except the actual folk tale material to enter into it. As a universal folk tale, the story was so well known that Irving was criticized immediately upon its publication for not acknowl-

edging a source. He answered that the tale was found so frequently in the European folk tradition that he had thought no acknowledgment was necessary. It may well be that Irving did not have one direct source for this tale. He was well acquainted with folk tales from many countries. In writing **"Rip Van Winkle,"** he may have fused his personal experiences in the Catskills with his reading to produce the tale; he may have been translating and Americanizing the German tale of Peter Klaus; or he may have been writing a polished version of a tale he had first heard from the Dutch settlers on the Hudson. It is impossible to denote one of these possibilities as the definite source for the tale, although one is inclined to think that Irving's reading in German folklore was inspiration for the actual writing of **"Rip Van Winkle."** No matter what the immediate source of the tale, Irving's production is the version in English of a folk tale known to many peoples. (pp. 147-49)

Two tales, widely separate in setting, are strikingly similar to Irving's version of **"Rip Van Winkle."** One is the tale of the Greek, Epimenides; the other is the German, Peter Klaus. The ancient Greeks told the story of Epimenides, who went to the mountains in search of stray sheep. At noon, he went into a cool cave to escape the heat of the sun. There, he fell asleep and slept for fifty-seven years. When he returned home, everything was changed. His house was gone and he could not recognize anyone in the village. He was a stranger among strangers until his youngest brother, now an old man, finally recognized him.

Two versions of the German tale of Peter Klaus, who visited the sleeping emperor Frederick Barbarossa, show striking similarities to the tale of Rip, one at the beginning of the story, another at the end. Peter Klaus was herding his goats on the mountain when he saw a young man who silently beckoned to him. He followed the young man into a deep dell surrounded by craggy precipices. There were twelve knights playing skittles, and these were also silent. Looking about, Peter saw a jug of wine. He drank and was at first filled with joy and life but soon fell asleep. When he awoke, he found himself in the fields again; but his goats and dog had disappeared. Trees and bushes were much taller than he remembered them. Returning to the village, he could not recognize the houses or people. He met a few acquaintances in the streets, but they were strangely old. Finally, after many questions, he discovered that he had been asleep for twenty years. Another version tells that Peter Klaus, the goatherd of Sittendorf, tended his goats in the Kypphauser Mountains. He began to notice that one of his goats came late to the enclosure every evening. He watched her carefully and discovered that she slipped through a crack in the mountain. He also went through the crack and found a cave in which the goat was eating oats that dropped from the roof. He heard the stamping and neighing of horses above him. A man appeared and silently motioned that Peter should follow him. They went up a flight of steps and out into a hollow surrounded on all sides by high rocks and overhung with bushes. Here twelve knights were silently playing nine-pins, and Peter was silently instructed to set them up. He was badly frightened but slowly took heart; and, looking around, he found a tankard from which he took a drink. The liquor was good; so he drank often to refresh himself as he ran back and forth with the nine-pins. Soon, the liquor put him to sleep. He awoke in the place where he usually counted his goats. He was surprised that the trees and bushes were taller than he remembered; and he could not find his goats. Returning to the village, he recognized the houses but not the people. Even their clothes were strange. When he asked about his goats, people merely stroked their chin. When he stroked his in return, he discovered that his beard was a foot longer than it had been when he fell asleep. He decided that the world was enchanted. His home was decayed, and a new goatherd and dog lived there. Soon a crowd gathered and began asking questions. Peter asked about his friends, but they were all dead. Then he saw a young woman with two children who looked like his wife. She told him that her father, Peter Klaus, had not been seen for twenty years. He told his name, was recognized by an old woman, and was welcomed by the people. Although the similarities between the tale of Peter Klaus and **"Rip Van Winkle"** are certainly striking, one cannot say that Irving was merely rewriting the German tale. The general theme is too universal for such a narrow interpretation.

Irving has actually enriched the basic folk tale by bringing together several folk themes although a casual reading does not show any great difference between the two tales of Rip and Peter Klaus. Irving has spun the folk themes of the long sleep, the shrewish wife, and the origin theme together into one tale so smoothly that they have become a real unity. He uses the shrewish wife theme, in the form of Rip's ill-tempered wife, as a motivation for the first part of the action. The long sleep theme, in the form of Rip's sleep on the mountainside, is, of course, the center of the story; but perhaps the most appealing idea in the story is the notion that the thunder of the Catskills is made by Hendrick Hudson and his crew playing at nine-pins. Irving may have heard of this idea from American folk tradition or imported it himself; but in either case it is an excellent piece of Americanization of a European folk theme. Henry Hudson is an excellent choice for an early New York Dutch folk hero; so that if Irving did originate or himself import this addition to his tale, he is greatly to be praised. His handling of the supernatural quality of this old adventuresome crew is also done with more skill than usual. He does not blatantly introduce ghosts but merely surrounds his strange figures with an air of mystery. He is careful never to identify them. His descriptions of the spirits fit well descriptions of ancient Dutch seamen and yet include many of the traditional attributes of dwarfs. In this tale, Irving truly succeeded in his portrayal of the supernatural, even to the satisfaction of the skeptical American reader. The story of Rip would never have become so popular if Irving had not succeeded in giving it a thoroughly American character even though he was writing a more European type folktale.

The story of **"Rip Van Winkle"** has become an integral part of American folklore. It was popular immediately upon publication and was widely read. Within a few years, several dramatic versions had been composed, the most successful of which was that of Joseph Jefferson. Jefferson played his version in Europe and America for years and was so famous in the role that many people who would never have read the story came to know of Rip's adventures. Rip soon became part of the folk consciousness of the Hudson. Since Irving did not specifically designate the village in which Rip lived, several of the Catskill towns hastened to claim him. Rip Van Winkle is not an American folk figure who owes his existence to the literary production of Washington Irving. With his Hudson River tales, Irving made a real contribution to the appreciation of American folklore. (pp. 150-52)

Sara Puryear Rodes, "Washington Irving's Use of Traditional Folklore," in Southern Folklore Quarterly, *Vol. XIX, No. 3, September, 1956, pp. 143-53.*

TERENCE MARTIN (essay date 1959)

[*In the following excerpt from a discussion of "Rip Van Winkle" and "The Legend of Sleepy Hollow," Martin demonstrates how Irving's stories reflect nineteenth-century American views on imagination and creativity.*]

Irving's America (as R.W.B. Lewis has reminded us in *The American Adam*) was a new nation which saw itself, fresh and innocent, as emancipated from history; concomitantly, this new nation desired to elicit confidence from within and without by assuming an immediate adulthood in the family of nations.... Because hope for the future entailed and fed on responsibility and stability in the present, a belief both in progress and practical conservatism sustained this anamalous self-image.

The conservative impulse of America generated by the desire for immediate adulthood quite naturally had its effect on the working of the creative imagination; the writer, as we know, worked in the context of a pervading mistrust of the imagination. Especially in the adverse criticism of fiction and the novel, which came from pulpits, commencement addresses, and at times from writers themselves, do we sense the suspicion of the imagination which the writer might at once confront and share. (pp. 137-38)

[There existed an] American version of the theory that poetry and art belong properly to primitive, that is, culturally childish, societies, a theory given much attention by the Anglo-European eighteenth century.... But a more specifically American use of the idea was the attempt to insist on personal adulthood by equating the imaginative and the childish. Childhood, says [The Reverend James Gray of the Philadelphia Academy for Young Ladies in 1810], is the time for imaginative indulgence; adulthood brings with it a demand for fact and doctrine. That he sees progression here is clear; the adult perforce grows away from "the region of fiction" to a higher and better reality. Likewise, a childish (primitive) society might legitimately take an interest in things imaginative; such a society, however, was precisely what America wanted not to be. And the proof and the price of cultural adulthood was the willing renunciation or at least containment of the imaginative order. Gray admits that he is as "liberal" on the matter as he can afford to be: he is concessive toward childhood, but he celebrates adulthood; he is concessive toward fancy, but he celebrates fact and doctrine; he is concessive toward the youthful mind as the region of fiction, but he celebrates the adult demand for "more substantial food." In the terms of Gray's argument, representative rather than original, only a culturally childish America could provide the proper nourishment for fiction.

Gray's consideration of fiction and responsibility explains more fully why America wished to assume an immediate adult status—there was simply no time for childhood.... Conservative, self-consciously adult, America had no place for ghosts and hobgoblins; as a new nation it did not feel that it could afford to indulge its imagination. The exigencies of the adult (better) world were all too apparent.

But if America did not want to be very young, neither of course did it want to be very old. As a nation which lacked a past, which was beginning history again in a better way, America had to shrug off as it were the implications of history; antiquity, mystery, evil—all products of the process of history—were not a substantial part of the American vision. From one point of view (shared by Emerson, Thoreau, Whitman, and others) this was a good thing: getting rid of the past meant living more fully in the promise of the present. From another point of view,

F.O.C. Darley's drawing of Ichabod Crane's school for an early edition of ''The Legend of Sleepy Hollow.''

however, the lack of a past had its lamentable side: the result was a cultural thinness and bleakness which left little for the writer to work with. (pp. 138-39)

For Hawthorne, romance and poetry implied an atmosphere of ruin. That he could not write romance easily about America is significant, measuring his hope in an America free from the consequences of historic process. Romance would not thus seem to belong by nature to America. But with the primitive condition and what it appeared to offer effectively and unequivocally ruled out by the desiderata of American society, a number of our early writers (Charles Brockden Brown, Irving, Poe, and Hawthorne among them) did attempt to create an art based at least implicitly on an aesthetic of age or shadow. They pretended shadow, ruin, decay as prerequisites of imaginative creation; at times they wrote as if America were very old. In view of the American self-image it was a massive pretense. But it produced a significant body of fiction which reflected the tension between what America wanted to be and what these writers had to pretend it to be.

The work of Washington Irving reflects significantly the quality of this tension between imaginative endeavor and cultural tendency. In *Bracebridge Hall* Irving tells us that he had experienced England with ''the delightful freshness of a child,'' but that he was ''a grown-up child.'' He admits in *The Sketch Book*

that the scenic splendor of America has failed to stimulate him imaginatively; in Europe are ''all the charms of storied and poetical association.'' America is filled with youthful promise, but Europe is rich ''in the accumulated treasures of age.'' He longs for a meditative antiquity, for the ''shadowy grandeurs of the past,'' in place of the ''commonplace realities of the present.'' Irving's most profoundly felt imaginative need was to escape from such ''commonplace realities,'' from—in Hawthorne's phrase—the American insistence on actualities. (pp. 140-41)

Although (and because) they are known to all, **''Rip Van Winkle''** and **''The Legend of Sleepy Hollow''** will repay a close analysis and reveal Irving's mode of literary creation in such a culture. Early in his tale of Rip, Irving speaks of the ''magical hues and shapes'' of the Kaatskill mountains; next he calls them ''fairy mountains.'' The terms ''magical'' and ''fairy,'' apparently incidental, adjectively subordinate, invite the reader away from the ''commonplace realities of the present'' to a region of greater imaginative latitude. In beginning his account of Rip's famous adventure, Irving constructs his scene so as literally to remove it from ''broad and simple daylight.'' Rip gazes into a wild and lonely mountain glen which is ''scarcely lighted by the reflected rays of the setting sun.'' Out of this shadowy glen, the American equivalent for the ''shadowy grandeurs'' of the past, Rip hears a voice calling his name and meets a "strange" figure in antique Dutch dress. In silence and wonder Rip helps the man carry a keg of liquor up a wild mountain: "there was something strange and incomprehensible about the unknown, that inspired awe and checked familiarity." The reader is now, with Rip, in a realm of the strange and unknown that inspires awe and checks familiarity. Only after such careful preparation, after guiding us away from the commonplace practicality of everyday life, does Irving introduce, in four brief paragraphs, the purely marvelous element of the story—the company playing ninepins. At the end of these paragraphs Rip falls into a sleep; when he awakens—on a "bright sunny morning," with the "birds hopping and twittering among the bushes"—we are back in the world of actuality. Rip returns to the village to find not only the people but "the very character of the people" changed.

Irving has taken Rip out of the context of everyday reality, but then has deliberately put him back in it. The tale, in its beginning and end, has historical location. And when Rip returns at the end of the tale he finds a metamorphosed community, no longer even the same country. The image of George Washington—the father of a new country—has replaced that of George III on the sign at the inn, and Rip has no way of orienting himself in terms of this new father image. Irving has had Rip sleep through the American Revolution, through what we might call the birth pangs of our country, and return to a "busy, bustling, disputatious," self-consciously adult United States of America. There his uncompetitive spirit, his predisposition to idleness, his inclination to imaginative indulgence are badly out of place; he is no more at home than he was with Dame Van Winkle, who prefigured the bustling, disputatious tone of this new world, though she at least knew him. Irving does not exact the full penalty from Rip; he allows him to settle in a corner of this world, but with a function extremely limited and marginal. Nonetheless, the tale dramatizes Rip's loss of identity, and, by inference, the loss of identity of the imaginative function. Rip's miraculous sleep has left him ignorant of the American Revolution—the magical, the marvelous, the imaginative, and the indolent have had no place in the founding of the new republic. And when these qualities return in the person of an antique but childlike man, there arises a sense of embarrassment overcome only when he is known to be harmless, one who will not interfere.

In **"The Legend of Sleepy Hollow"** Irving goes to even greater lengths in creating a never-never land to contain his tale: "a drowsy, dreamy influence" hangs over the land and pervades the atmosphere; the people have trances and visions and entertain marvelous beliefs. Haunted spots and "twilight superstitions" abound in the neighborhood. All of this of course prepares for the bold reference to the Headless Horseman. And, as if to urge a spirit of enchantment upon his readers, Irving states that even visitors to Sleepy Hollow become bewitched: inhaling the "witching influence" of the air, they begin to "grow imaginative, to dream dreams, and see apparitions." The quotation holds the key to Irving's method of literary creation: the wide-awake reader, dwelling in the "broad and simple daylight" of the actual world, is invited to enter Irving's sleepy region (Gray's "region of fiction"), to dream there under the bewitching influence of fictional apparitions.

Irving's introduction of Ichabod Crane defines a particular problem of the early American writer. "In this by-place of nature," he writes, "there abode, in a remote period of American history, that is to say, some thirty years since, a worthy wight of the name of Ichabod Crane." The archaic substantive *wight* serves to emphasize the incongruity of the introduction; only in the America of the time could a remote period of history be defined as thirty years. That Irving could speak ironically about the poverty of the past in America did not make it less a fact for him to deal with. Without a large, commonly shared, and hence more than personal past to work with and out of, the writer himself had to contain and be the measure of antiquity.

Ichabod Crane personifies the protagonist as comic figure. "His appetite for the marvelous, and his powers of digesting it, were . . . extraordinary; and both had been increased by his residence in this spellbound region. No tale was too gross or monstrous for his capacious swallow." Throughout the tale Irving plays on the idea of Ichabod's tremendous appetite and his "capacious swallow." But not only does this appetite pertain to the marvelous: Ichabod is a "huge feeder"; he contemplates with longing the largesse of the Van Tassel farm; the very prospect of winning the hand of Katrina comes to him in terms of a superabundance of food. In a manifold sense he yearns to swallow the world and thereby realize an oral heaven. By fitting the notion of gullibility into the dominant metaphor of Ichabod's oral preoccupation, Irving emphasizes the childlike quality of his protagonist. Ichabod can swallow and digest anything; therefore he is always and increasingly gullible. But growing up involves learning what not to swallow, in every sense of the word. Ichabod has failed utterly to learn this first lesson in the practical knowledge of survival precisely because of his extreme addiction to the imagination. Irving couples the oral stage and imaginative indulgence; both signify childhood. There is, moreover, a price to be paid for continuing in childhood. In our natural laughter at the story, we often forget that Ichabod goes down to defeat because he is overimaginative. For he loses all chance for the double prize of Katrina and the wealth of the Van Tassel farm when, terrified by his excessive imagination, he is literally run out of the region by Brom Bones impersonating the Headless Horseman. Brom Bones—the scoffer at superstition, who boasts that he has ridden a winning race against the Headless Horseman—triumphs, marries Katrina, and is the victor of the tale. It is a victory for common sense and hard-headed practicality over imaginative indulgence.

In each of these tales Irving has created his setting as a writer of romance; he overcomes the difficulty of creating imaginatively in the "broad and simple daylight" of his America by positing shadow, mystery, superstition. He writes, in short, as if his settings had antiquity, as if America had a past. Into each tale, however, he introduces a childlike protagonist, whom we may recognize as primitive if we allow for the fact that Irving would share the disbelief in contemporary primitivism and would create such a character out of that disbelief. Rip Van Winkle, with his "insuperable aversion to all kinds of profitable labor," delights in playing with children, and they in turn love him; he is a favorite among the village wives; not a dog in the neighborhood will bark at him. Ichabod Crane spends much time telling ghost stories with the old Dutch wives of Sleepy Hollow; he is the "playmate" of his larger students. In bringing each of these protagonists to a kind of defeat, Irving is echoing James Gray's pronouncement that America must be mature, must call for "substantial food." Rip and Ichabod lose out because they fail to see the necessity of demanding "fact and doctrine," which are at once the prerequisite for and the evidence of personal and cultural maturity. They are would-be heroes, but would-be heroes of the imagination, who cannot withstand or successfully come to terms with the terror that is the lot of such a hero, the terror implicit in Rip's loss of identity, explicit in Ichabod's flight. They defeat themselves.

It would appear that for Irving there is no place, or a very limited place, for the hero of the imagination in the culture of early America. A nation of Rips and Ichabods, Americans might reason, would soon be no nation at all.

Not even the settings can endure in these tales. It is as if Irving must admit that this is not a real past, that he will not persist in playing with the imagination. In **"Rip Van Winkle"** the village is transformed from "drowsy tranquility" to a bustling disputatiousness. There are no more shadows in Rip's world. In Sleepy Hollow, to be sure, the people remain unchanged. But we have been shown who is master there: it is Brom Bones (whose true name, Brom Van Brunt, also suggests the kind of strength Irving wants him to have), perhaps the first American bully, who can play upon fear and superstition to get what he wants. His apparent audacity in impersonating a ghost shows how fully in control Brom Bones is. For this impersonation is audacious only if we see it from the point of view of the villagers of Sleepy Hollow. To Brom Bones, to the only authentic American in the tale, it must literally be child's play. Irving has thus shown his American readers images of themselves in the changed village of **"Rip Van Winkle"** and in the character of Brom Bones. The manner of each tale suggests that Irving did not find these images entirely flattering, albeit necessary, and, indeed, readers have never found them attractive. Instinctively we sympathize with Rip and Ichabod; we laugh at them and in doing so at what there is of them in us; at the same time, we regret their failure. But what we regret is only what we had to give up to become what we are.

Irving's most characteristic fiction involves variations on the basic pattern of victory for the practical and defeat for the impractical and visionary. In **"The Spectre Bridegroom,"** Herman Von Starkenfaust's bold decision to impersonate a dead lover wins for him a beautiful wife. The "very manly" aunt in **"The Adventure of My Aunt"** exposes a robber by her refusal to be frightened when the eyes of a picture on the wall begin to move, while the unfortunate Young Italian of **"The Adventure of the Mysterious Stranger"** confesses that he has always been "a visionary, imaginary being." At the end of the Italian Banditti section of *Tales of a Traveller,* it is the Englishman, vexatious, hardheaded, insensitive, blind to chivalric courtesy, who saves the lovely Venetian Lady from the bandits whom he alone has scorned. **"Dolph Heyliger"** shows us how Dolph's daring to sleep in a haunted house ultimately leads him to wealth and a beautiful girl. For the grown-up person, for the practical and bold, the prize is wealth and beauty; for the childish, visionary, imaginary being, the price is the same wealth and beauty. Brom Bones, Herman Von Starkenfaust, and Dolph Heyliger are all recognizably related by a success that comes from their control of the imagination. The others, those duped by their imaginations, share the brotherhood of failure. (pp. 141-45)

> Terence Martin, "Rip, Ichabod, and the American Imagination," in American Literature, *Vol. XXXI, No. 2, May, 1959, pp. 137-49.*

ROBERT A. BONE (essay date 1963)

[*Bone, an American critic, is the author of the critical histories* The Negro Novel in America *and* Down Home: A History of Afro-American Short Fiction from Its Beginnings to the End of the Harlem Renaissance *. In the following excerpt, he reads "The Legend of Sleepy Hollow" as a parable representing the victory of materialism over the artistic life. His view of Ichabod Crane*

as a caricature of the defeated artist-intellectual was refuted by Martin Roth (see excerpt dated 1976).]

Increasingly [in the early nineteenth century] the American writer found himself in an atmosphere of trade and commerce profoundly hostile to his art. In self-defense he turned to the Romantic movement, at the heart of which lay a spirited defense of the imagination.

During the Romantic period, the concept of imagination was itself transformed. Closely associated with devotional practices in the past, it now became more or less secularized. . . . As the role of the artist became increasingly differentiated from that of the clergyman or philosopher, the stage was set for a new phase in the history of the American imagination. *Henceforth the pressure of commodities would be experienced as a threat to the artistic process as such.*

It is Washington Irving's distinction first to have explored this theme. His interest in folklore, myth and legend provides him, in his best work, with a means of confronting the prosaic temper of his time. The folk tale, with its elements of fable and of fantasy, is an ideal medium, and it is here that Irving's creative powers reach fulfillment. **"The Legend of Sleepy Hollow"** is at once his finest achievement and his most enduring contribution to our literary history. For in the mythic encounter of Ichabod Crane and the Headless Horseman, the crisis of the modern imagination is first revealed.

The story begins with an epigraph from "The Castle of Indolence," by the Scottish poet James Thomson:

> A pleasing land of drowsy head it was,
> Of dreams that wave before the half-shut eye;
> And of gay castles in the clouds that pass,
> For ever flushing round a summer sky.

These lines serve primarily to establish the drowsy atmosphere of Sleepy Hollow, but are not without thematic relevance. "Dreams," "castles in the clouds," are suggestive of the imaginative faculty which is Irving's real concern. Moreover, the poem deals at length with the economic foundations of the arts; that is, with the question of patronage. This is one of the central issues which Irving means to raise.

Thomson is a spiritual cousin of Ben Franklin, and the poem amounts to a Calvinist homily on work. It is an allegorical attack on the slothful propensities of the leisure classes, and a sturdy defense of the Protestant ethic. Thomson is a poet, however, and he cannot suppress certain misgivings about the benefits of industry and progress. In particular, he deplores the loss of patronage which attends the passing of a cultured aristocracy. A jarring note thus intrudes upon his celebration of the Protestant virtues. In the old order, indolence brought social stagnation, but afforded a leisurely pursuit of art. The rise of the middle class portends great material prosperity, but leaves the fate of the poetic imagination in doubt.

This is precisely the mood of **"The Legend of Sleepy Hollow."** Dimly, uneasily, Irving sees the precarious position of the artist in bourgeois society. He is therefore of two minds as he contemplates the demise of Dutch colonial America. Fundamentally he approves of movement, activity and progress. Yet the story is saturated with nostalgia for the sheltered, protected, *embosomed* world of Sleepy Hollow, where dreams and reveries, ghosts and apparitions, still nourish the "visionary propensity."

Tarry Town emerges as a symbol of the colonial past, in which we tarry for a moment before moving on. The atmosphere is simple, uncomplicated, pastoral. It is established by such adjectives as quiet, listless, drowsy, dreamy, and such nouns as murmur, lull, repose, tranquillity. Captivated by the mood he has created, the narrator recalls his first exploit in squirrel hunting:

> I had wandered into [a walnut grove] at noon time, when all nature is peculiarly quiet, and was startled by the roar of my own gun as it broke the Sabbath stillness around, and was prolonged and reverberated by the angry echoes.

It was a shot heard round the world. The disruptive roar of the gun heralds the introduction of the Hessain trooper, "whose head had been carried away by a cannon-ball, in some nameless battle during the Revolutionary War." To the quiet repose of the opening pages, Irving counterposes the furious speed of the galloping Hessian. He is seen "hurrying along in the gloom of the night, as if on the wings of the wind." He embodies the sudden violence of the Revolution, which brought the pastoral phase of the national life to an end. A new spirit is abroad in the land, the mercenary spirit of a Hessian soldier.

At this point it may be well to review the basic features of the plot, so as to establish a solid foundation for a symbolic interpretation. In essence, we have a romantic triangle. Ichabod Crane and Brom Bones are rivals for the hand of Katrina Van Tassel, the daughter of a prosperous Dutch farmer. Ichabod is defeated under comic circumstances, and as a result, his values are profoundly altered. Humiliation and defeat transform his life, but what is the inner meaning of these events?

As the three principals are introduced, certain details of characterization point to Irving's theme. To begin with, Ichabod's New England origins are heavily underscored:

> He was a native of Connecticut, a state which supplies the Union with pioneers for the mind as well as for the forest, and sends forth yearly its legions of frontier woodsmen and country schoolmasters.

His favorite book is Cotton Mather's *History of New England Witchcraft*. Great stress is laid upon his appetite, which is at once natural and supernatural, encompassing both the gustatory and the marvellous. In this he reflects the dilemma of his Puritan ancestors: the contest in his soul might be said to turn upon the question of which appetite will come uppermost.

The ascetic circumstances of his existence are suggested by the shabbiness of his schoolhouse and the itinerant character of his life. As he moves from home to home among his pupils' families, he carries "all his worldly effects tied up in a cotton handkerchief." His poverty, however, is not without its compensations. Because of his itinerant habits, he is welcomed as a bearer of news and gossip. He is esteemed by his neighbors as a man of letters, "for he had read several books quite through." He instructs the young people in psalmody, and his tales of the supernatural are a popular feature of village entertainment. Ichabod embodies, in short, the primitive impulse of a frontier society toward culture.

Since culture is viewed with suspicion in frontier communities, Ichabod is thought, "by all who understand nothing of the labor of headwork, to have a wonderfully easy time of it." Highly vulnerable to criticism, he is forced to justify his existence on utilitarian grounds:

> That all this might not be too onerous on the purses of his rustic patrons, who are apt to consider the costs of schooling a grievous burden, and schoolmasters

as mere drones, he had various ways of rendering himself both useful and agreeable.

There is something in the comic absurdity of Ichabod's situation which raises echoes of Cervantes. At one point, in fact, Ichabod rides forth "like a knight-errant in quest of adventures," astride a broken-down plough horse. In the light of these allusions, the character of Ichabod acquires a new dimension. Like Don Quixote, he is comic in appearance and behavior, but he must be taken seriously as a symbol of man's higher aspirations. Such a portrait requires a certain complexity of tone. For Ichabod is at once a comic and a tragic figure; he is, in Wallace Stevens' phrase, "A clown, perhaps, but an aspiring clown." In a portrait which is permeated with self-irony, Irving caricatures the position of the artist-intellectual in American life. Ichabod Crane is the first example in our literature of the comedian as the letter C.

Ichabod's antagonist is Brom Bones, "the hero of the country round." Brom's symbolic role is defined by a series of associations with the Headless Horseman. He is linked to the goblin rider by his skill in horsemanship and by the hurry-scurry of his midnight escapades. Like the Hessian, he scours the countryside with a squad of hard riders who dash about "like a troop of Don Cossacks." As the story reaches a climax, Brom becomes the literal incarnation of the Hessian trooper, for it is he, disguised as the Headless Horseman, who pursues Ichabod to his doom. Symbolically, Brom is the embodiment of the Hessian spirit, of mercenary values which threaten to engulf the imagination.

While Ichabod exists on the periphery of his culture, Brom occupies the very hub. Invisible spokes radiate from him to the entire male population of Sleepy Hollow. What is the "tough, wrong-headed, broad-skirted Dutch urchin who sulked and swelled and grew dogged and sullen beneath the birch" but a schoolboy version of Brom Bones? Brom's gang, whose behavior suggests the juvenile-delinquent phase of male development, harries the schoolmaster by smoking out his singing school and breaking into his schoolhouse after dark. (pp. 168-72)

Katrina is a pivotal figure; she provides the measure of Ichabod's social worth. The bestowal of her favors amounts to a kind of community sanction, for if Ichabod's society takes him seriously it must supply him with a wife. It is of course Brom Bones that she chooses; she has been flirting with the schoolmaster only to arouse the jealousy and ardor of his rival.

Irving's sketch of Katrina blends humorously with his description of her father's farm. She is "plump as a partridge; ripe and melting and rosy cheeked as one of her father's peaches." She wears "ornaments of pure yellow gold" whose colors call to mind the golden ears of Van Tassel corn, and "the yellow pumpkins . . . turning up their fair round bellies to the sun." As Ichabod surveys his future prospects, the metaphors proclaim his gustatory love:

> In his devouring mind's eye . . . the pigeons were snugly put to bed in a comfortable pie, and tucked in with a coverlet of crust; the geese were swimming in their own gravy; and the ducks pairing cosily in dishes, like snug married couples, with a decent competency of onion sauce.

Faced with such temptations, Ichabod is defeated from within. Consider the implications of his name. "Ichabod" is from the Hebrew; it means "inglorious," or literally, "without honor." Ichabod is a turncoat; in pursuit of material comfort, he betrays a spiritual tradition. Confronted with the opulence of the Van

Tassels, he succumbs to the sins of covetousness and idolatry. His imaginative faculty is perverted, deflected from its proper object:

> . . . his busy fancy already realized his hopes, and presented to him the blooming Katrina, with a whole family of children, mounted on the top of a wagon loaded with household trumpery, with pots and kettles dangling beneath; and he beheld himself bestriding a pacing mare, with a colt at her heels, setting out for Kentucky, Tennessee, or the Lord knows where.

Here is the New England imagination turned mercenary, placed in the service of the westering impulse. Brom Bones has only to bury the body.

Ichabod's encounter with the Headless Horseman is the dramatic climax of the story. The stage is set so carefully, however, that a closer look at the backdrop is in order. Dominating the landscape is an enormous tulip tree known in the neighborhood as Major André's tree. André was a young British officer, appointed by his superiors to consummate with Benedict Arnold negotiations for the betrayal of West Point. Captured by American militiamen after a midnight interview with Arnold, he was executed as a spy. In effect, he was a scapegoat, hanged for Arnold's crime. As a result, he occupies an ambiguous position in American history. This ambiguity seems to be the point so far as Irving is concerned:

> The common people regarded [Major André's tree] with a mixture of respect and superstition, partly out of sympathy for the fate of its ill-starred namesake. . . .

It is just this note of sympathy which Irving means to strike. Systematically he links "the unfortunate André" with "the unfortunate Ichabod," using the historical figure to control his tone. Let there be no mistake: Ichabod betrays the race of Cranes. The betrayal occurs at the quilting party, as he contemplates the possibility of becoming lord of the Van Tassel manor:

> Then, he thought, how soon he'd turn his back upon the old schoolhouse; snap his fingers in the face of Hans Van Ripper, and every other niggardly patron, and kick any itinerant pedagogue out of doors that should dare to call him comrade!

But Irving wishes to soften the effect of this betrayal by shifting the burden in large part from Ichabod to his society. The reader is to respond to Ichabod rather as an André than an Arnold: not entirely guiltless, but largely the victim of circumstance. Yet the veiled threat remains. Irving recalls, by his allusion to Arnold, a famous episode in which the nation's neglect and ingratitude was repaid by treason. Be niggardly with your patronage, he warns the Hans Van Rippers, and your artists will desert to the enemy camp.

At the very spot where Major André was captured, Ichabod is accosted by the Headless Horseman. The schoolmaster is an unskillful rider; he attempts an evasive maneuver, but to no avail. With a fizzle and a sputter, Gunpowder ignites from the spark of his rider's fear, and off they fly, with the apparition in hot pursuit. As they near the safety of the bridge, the goblin rider rises in his stirrups and hurls his head at Ichabod, tumbling him into the dust.

What is the meaning of this parable? Ichabod is overwhelmed by the new materialism, but at an awesome price to society. For in order to conquer, the Hessian must throw away his head. The next morning a shattered pumpkin is found in the vicinity of the bridge. The organ of intellect and imagination has become an edible. The forces of thought have yielded to the forces of digestion.

Defeated by the spirit of the age, Ichabod reconstructs his life along more worldly lines. As rumor has it,

> . . . he had changed his quarters to a distant part of the country; had kept school and studied law at the same time, had been admitted to the bar, turned politician, electioneered, written for the newspapers, and finally had been made a justice of the Ten Pound Court.

It is hardly necessary to recall the unfortunate Irving's legal career to sense the diminution of spirit which the author intends. "The Ten Pound Court" unmistakably conveys the pettiness and triviality of Ichabod's new occupation. The community suffers a loss, the nature of which is defined by Ichabod's curious estate. A book of psalm tunes, a broken pitch pipe, Cotton Mather's *History of Witchcraft,* a book of dreams and fortune-telling, and an abortive attempt at verse in honor of Katrina: these crude tokens of the imaginative life are left behind as the schoolmaster vanishes from Sleepy Hollow.

The postscript is an ironic defense of the literary imagination. The time is "the present," and it is clear that the descendants of Brom Bones are in the saddle. Folklore and legend, ghost stories and old wives' tales, have been superseded by an age of reason and common sense. Fiction itself has become suspect. Writing in a hostile climate, Irving supplies his fictional world with the trappings of historical research and objectivity. Hence the **"Postscript, Found in the Handwriting of Mr. Knickerbocker."**

This postscript recapitulates the theme; the dramatic situation alone has changed. The scene is "a Corportion meeting of the ancient city of Manhattoes, at which were present many of its sagest and most illustrious burghers." The role of Ichabod-Irving is played by a shabby narrator with a sadly humorous face, who is an entertaining storyteller, but is "strongly suspected of being poor." He has just told a tale called **"The Legend of Sleepy Hollow."** The role of Brom-Hessian is assumed by the sleepy aldermen who comprise his audience, and in particular by a literal-minded burgher who inquires as to the moral of the story, and what it goes to prove?

The narrator avoids a direct reply. The meaning of the story, Irving intimates, will not yield to purely logical methods. The art of fiction has nothing to do with "the ratiocination of the syllogism." The reader's imagination must supply the moral:

> The story-teller, who was just putting a glass of wine to his lips, as a refreshment after his toils, paused for a moment, looked at his inquirer with an air of infinite deference, and, lowering the glass slowly to the table, observed, that the story was intended most logically to prove:—
>
> That there is no situation in life but has its advantages and pleasures—provided we will but take a joke as we find it:
>
> That, therefore, he that runs races with goblin troopers is likely to have rough riding of it.
>
> Ergo, for a country schoolmaster to be refused the hand of a Dutch heiress, is a certain step to high preferment in the state.

(pp. 172-75)

Robert A. Bone, ''Irving's Headless Hessian: Prosperity and the Inner Life,'' in American Quarterly, Vol. XV, No. 2, Summer, 1963, pp. 167-75.

JOHN CLENDENNING (essay date 1964)

[*Clendenning discusses Irving as a satirist of the Gothic form, describing how he made innovative use of the Gothic mode in such stories as ''The Legend of Sleepy Hollow'' and ''The Spectre Bridegroom.''*]

Washington Irving was about half-way between modern fiction and the [gothic] cult of Mrs. Radcliffe. When he began producing his major works—*The Sketch Book, Bracebridge Hall,* and *Tales of a Traveller*—the popularity of gothic novels was falling apart, and a period of reaction, represented chiefly by Jane Austen's *Northanger Abbey* (1818), was under way. . . . [Instead] of continuing an exhausted tradition, Irving hoped to find some original use for gothic material. To be sure, he did not always succeed, but at his best he became a skillful parodist and a highly suggestive psychologist. (pp. 90-1)

[As] innovator of the so-called ''sportive'' gothic, Irving was a master. Although the term ''sportive'' is too vague, it is generally assumed to describe a tale which employs an abundance of ''machinery'' assembled in a light-hearted tone, as is characteristic of ''The Legend of Sleepy Hollow.'' So pervasive is this tone that the mystery and terror common to most gothic tales are permitted to flourish only in the ironic sense that melodrama is used to promote humor and satire. How Irving managed to employ the machinery without its usual tone is not easy to determine. Certainly his zestful narrator, whom he had used earlier in his Knickerbocker *A History of New York* and who was conspicuously missing in ''The Story of the Young Robber,'' provides the basic ingredient for the humorous tone. The structure of ''The Legend of Sleepy Hollow'' also guards against gothic terror, for though the headless Hessian dominates the last pages of the story, he is preceded by amusing details that never lose their influence on the narrative. Finally, the central characters themselves resist a melodramatic treatment. The original gothic hero . . . claimed only an ideal existence, whereas Ichabod Crane, the prototypic Yankee schoolmaster who wants only food, comfort, and a plump Dutch wife, brings to the story such a weight of actuality that a world of haunted forests seems, by contrast, absurd.

This local-color element is, on the simplest level, what Irving made the story's central interest: the Connecticut Yankee meets the New York Dutch. The same element, however, by itself so superficial, gives way to an exploration of the role of imagination and the artistic process. Ichabod, we are told, was ''an odd mixture of small shrewdness and simple credulity.'' Having the wit of a Yankee peddler, he is careful to win the affection and confidence of the village. But having also the superstitions of a Puritan, he trembles in fear. One quality enables him to deal with the world as he wishes; the other eventually causes him to leave town at midnight, fearful for his life, never to return. But the ''odd mixture'' is really two applications of the same thing; for what chiefly characterizes Ichabod's mind is his rich imagination, a mind which dreamingly arranges the pieces of his experience—sometimes giving vivid impressions of himself luxuriating in food, wealth, and women, and giving also clues for realizing them. Thus the New England pedagogue manages, until the end of the story to stay a few steps ahead of the intellectually lethargic Dutch. And when Ichabod is defeated, Brom Bones is not the real victor:

he merely stimulated the Yankee's self-destructive imagination. Thus the capacity that enables Ichabod to see the world as it may be—a ''sumptuous promise of luxurious winter fare''—is the same irresistible curse which makes ghosts and goblins as palpable as pigeon pies. The story can, then, be understood as an allegory of the artistic process itself, for the literary artist must imaginatively create legends for the world's sleepy hollows. But the limits on the imagination . . . demand that the artistically created world co-exist with actuality. Permit the imagination to be wholly separated from human experience—as gothic fiction constantly separates them—and the art is destroyed. . . . Thus, the gothic material in ''**The Legend of Sleepy Hollow**'' serves a vital function. Constantly juxtaposed with the actual world, it represents the extreme form in literary art of the imagination disassociated from life. Hence, if Irving has given us a ''sportive'' gothic, he has not done so uncritically.

But ''sportive'' gothicism is not parody, though Irving's critics have tended to confuse them. ''**The Legend of Sleepy Hollow**'' is only allegorically an attack on gothicism; parody reveals the excesses of a genre by imitating it. This distinction should be clear enough if we examine a genuine parody of gothic fiction, ''**The Spectre Bridegroom.**''

Unlike the other *The Sketch Book* tales, this story has the stereotypic setting of medieval Germany, complete with the satiric names, Baron Von Landshort, Herman Von Starkenfaust, and Katzenellenbogen. For his plot, Irving chose the impossibly obvious formula of the supernatural *expliqué*, popularized by Mrs. Radcliffe and imitated extensively in America: the hero pretends to be the ghost of the murdered bridegroom in order to win the affections of the heroine and the confidence of her family. The major element, however, which makes ''**The Spectre Bridegroom**'' a travesty is not the artificial structure, the grotesque setting, or the ridiculous names, but rather the minds of the characters. Irving presents a society which, craving the supernatural, is ideally prepared to find it. The daughter's literary fare consists exclusively in ''church legends'' and ''the chivalric wonders of the Heldenbuch.'' Her morbid imagination is clearly indicated by the agonized expressions of the saints she embroiders, who ''looked like so many souls in purgatory.'' Other members of the family seem equally drawn to gothic themes. The baron's greatness seems to consist chiefly in his ability to tell ghost stories. ''He was much given to the marvellous and a firm believer in all those supernatural tales with which every mountain and valley in Germany abounds.'' Indeed, young Starkenfaust got his idea of posing as a spectre from one of the baron's stories, and the family's commitment to the supernatural explanation was their own idea. Like Catherine Morland in *Northanger Abbey*, the Katzenellenbogens attempt to interpret their experience in terms of German legends. In fact, the poor relation who suggests the truth—that the spectre may be some evasive young cavalier—draws upon himself the ''indignation of the whole company.'' And when the hoax is finally revealed, one of the aunts is ''particularly mortified at having her marvellous story marred. . . .'' The most important facet of this parody, therefore, is Irving's interest in the psychology of gothicism. Turning the external gothic theme inward, he treated the supernatural world as an expression of an excessively morbid imagination.

If ''**The Spectre Bridegroom**'' is a delightful though serious parody of the gothic tale—particularly of the Radcliffian supernatural *expliqué*—Irving designed other stories to render it quite as ridiculous, but in an exactly opposite manner. Instead of resolving the supernatural in natural terms, his heroes sometimes—as in **"The Bold Dragoon,"** for example—disguise their very embarrassing natural activities under a gothic mask. . . . Irving has given us what we may, in fact, call the *inverted* gothic story—not unlike Chaucer's "Miller's Tale"—in which the lusty dragoon escapes recrimination for his midnight peccadillo with the landlord's daughter by throwing up an absurd haze of supernaturalism.

Although this form has failed to survive in modern fiction, it was one of Irving's favorites. In **"Dolph Heyliger,"** for instance, we have a similarly inverted gothic tale, in which the picaresque hero returns with his life's fortune and a ghost story to explain how he got it. Doubts of Dolph's honesty are never uttered, not of course because his character is spotless but because it is noted that he is "the ablest drawer of a long-bow in the whole province."

If we consider **"Rip Van Winkle"** in the context of **"Dolph Heyliger"** and **"The Bold Dragoon,"** it appears that this most famous of Irving's stories also employs the techniques of inverted gothicism. Like Dolph, Rip disappears, only to return later with a supernatural account of his absence. And like the dragoon's story, Rip's tale is "authenticated" in a fashion which is as irrational as the story itself; crucial testimony is given by Peter, "the most ancient inhabitant of the village, and well versed in all the wonderful events and traditions of the neighborhood." The gullible narrator, old Diedrich Knickerbocker, who relates the story without a flicker of doubt, believes Rip's account because (1) stranger stories have been told, (2) Rip was "venerable," "rational," and "consistent," and (3) the story had been recorded by an illiterate country justice. Indeed, the whole community refused even to consider what they should have suspected from the first: that Rip had finally become exasperated with his "termagant wife," took his dog and gun, and deserted. He was, long before his disappearance, a great teller of ghost stories and a notorious malingerer—exactly the sort of man who would ramble for twenty years, then return with a bit of gothic nonsense designed to amuse the town and avoid its scorn. The final paragraph of the story seems to point directly toward this conclusion. Old Knickerbocker admits that Rip had several versions of his account: "He was observed, at first, to vary on some points every time he told it. . . ." Only later did Rip settle down to the story as we have it related. Those few who doubt it suspect that Rip has lost his faculties. The others—men, women, children—have the story memorized. Some even literally believe that thunder is the sound of "Hendrick Hudson and his crew . . . at their game of nine-pins. . . ." We have, then, a society willingly trying to turn life into a gothic legend; as such, **"Rip Van Winkle"** is a brilliant satire on the gothic mind.

But what should we make of Rip? Only he escapes Irving's satire, for he unites both Starkenfaust and Ichabod: the poseur in one sense, the artist in another. Like Irving himself, and like countless writers in America, Rip's problem is that of a vocation. What is a creature of the imagination to do in a world whose values are represented by Dame Van Winkle? Art in such a world is, as Hawthorne complained in his sketch "The Custom-House," driven to become a mere escape. Thus, the youthful Rip spends his days "telling endless sleepy stories about nothing." Finally, "reduced almost to despair," he is driven to an actual escape: he rambles off, a sad counterpart to Odysseus, not to return for twenty years, a ragged old man, greeted by his dog with a snarl. Yet one quality in him has not been destroyed by age; his imagination is even richer than before, and he had "arrived at that happy age when a man can

be idle with impunity. . . ." Perhaps that was what brought him home, the hope that his world could finally accommodate him. It does: Rip becomes an honored village patriarch and chronicler. Unlike Ichabod, therefore, Rip is not defeated by his gothic imagination, because, for him, it was never dissociated from life. Even if the village skeptics are right, and they may be, in believing that old Van Winkle is edging toward senility, he is granted "an old man's frenzy," which Yeats hoped for and which he recognized in King Lear and William Blake. Imagination alone, whether inspired by frenzy or plain cunning, makes Rip's life significant. Thus, in **"Rip Van Winkle,"** Irving accomplished a judgment of the extremes of the gothic mind and a frail reconciliation between it and the role of the artist.

In most of these modifications of the gothic tradition, Irving's "psychology" played an important part. The too richly imaginative Ichabod Crane, with Puritan superstitions whirling in his brain, was able to manufacture his own midnight goblin, whether or not the external world of fact could give evidence of it. An imitation spectre bridegroom captured the credulity of nearly all the Katzenellenbogens, nourished as they were on the gothic thrills of German legend. (pp. 92-7)

I do not pretend that Irving was a great artist; he was not. But as a parodist, he mirthfully helped to destroy all that was crude in gothic fiction. More importantly, one cannot deny that he anticipated the advanced gothic fiction of Poe and Hawthorne. Then following admittedly in their wakes, we have French symbolism and Henry James—two fundamental forces behind twentieth-century fiction. We should not be surprised, therefore, to find traces of Irving's "sportive" gothic in the works of William Faulkner or his subjectified "machinery" in the midnight novels. (p. 98)

> *John Clendenning, "Irving and the Gothic Tradition," in* Bucknell Review, *Vol. XII, No. 2, May, 1964, pp. 90-8.*

GEORGE MONTEIRO (essay date 1968)

[*Monteiro discusses "The Pride of the Village," a story from* The Sketch Book *that he feels has been neglected. The critic seeks to demonstrate that the tale is more than the mere exercise in sentiment some would claim it to be.*]

The continuing high assessment of Irving's two most famous stories, **"Rip Van Winkle"** and **"The Legend of Sleepy Hollow,"** has unfortunately deflected critical attention from the other pieces which make up *The Sketch Book.* (p. 347)

I should like to consider **"The Pride of the Village"** as a neglected example of Irving's subtlety and conscious artistry. If there is pathos in this account of a young girl's death, I suggest that Irving earns a more subtle effect than he is normally given credit for. Without minimizing its element of sentimentality, I should like to turn to aspects of this particular tale which reveal it as something finer and more durable than a pallid exercise in sentiment.

It is not often noted that "Geoffrey Crayon, Gent.," the name given on the title page of *The Sketch Book,* identifies the protagonist of **"The Pride of the Village."** A sentimentalist haunting churchyards and following funerals, Crayon finds himself at dusk in a "rural and retired" English village. After an early dinner he takes a leisurely walk which ultimately brings him to the village churchyard where a funeral is taking place. He then returns to the inn where he learns that he has witnessed the funeral of a young girl who had been "the pupil of the village pastor, the favorite lamb of his little flock." He is told a melodramatic tale about a May day queen who had attracted the attention of a soldier temporarily quartered in the neighborhood. He had courted her in "that unthinking way in which young officers are too apt to trifle with rustic simplicity." Their love prospered until the young officer, misjudging her virtue, suggested impetuously that she follow him to the Continent when his regiment is ordered to move. For the first time recognizing the nature of his view of their relationship, she refused. Retreating into solitude, she became "fervent in her devotions at church," until the old people of the village came to view her as "something spiritual" rather than material. Her health failed precipitously, and just before her death she wrote in forgiveness to the young officer. He returned immediately, but too late. The tale concludes when the narrator reveals that at a later date he again visited the church, seeing there "the chaplet of flowers and the gloves, as on the day of the funeral."

The first thing to note is that Irving is less interested in the conventional elements of a love tragedy than he is in the phenomenon of the young girl's wasting away from life into death. Through the sentiment accruing to this basic plot Irving works this far-more-significant theme. The words for "the burial of the dead" quoted in the tale—"Earth to earth—ashes to ashes—dust to dust!"—refer explicitly to the passing of human vanity. At the moment of the young girl's death her father comforts himself "with the assurance that the dead are blessed which die in the Lord." But her mother thinks of something quite different from traditional consolation: she "only thought of her child as a flower of the field cut down and withered in the midst of its sweetness." Indeed, the mother is "like Rachel, 'mourning over her children, and would not be comforted.'" These conflicting views—the father's and the mother's—serve to prepare the reader for the narrator's perspective, one which plays havoc with any simple view we might have of his melancholy.

We are informed by the narrator that the father just before his daughter's death has been "reading a chapter in the Bible," which "spoke of the vanity of worldly things, and of the joys of heaven." It may be useful to recall the opening verse of Ecclesiastes, where the Preacher inveighs against the vanity of those who become inordinately attached to this world:

> Vanity of vanities, saith the Preacher, vanity of vanities; all is vanity.
>
> What profit hath a man of all his labour which he taketh under the sun?
>
> One generation passeth away, and another generation cometh: but the earth abideth for ever.
>
> The sun also ariseth, and the sun goeth down, and hasteth to his place where he arose. (1:2-5)

Irving's use of Ecclesiastes provides perspective for the sentiments, even the descriptions, which pervade **"The Pride of the Village."** For example, Crayon notes on the day of the funeral that "there was a broad tract of golden sky in the west from which the setting sun gleamed through the dripping leaves, and lit up all nature with a melancholy smile. It seemed," he decides, anticipating ironically the close of his tale, "like the parting hour of a good Christian, smiling on the sins and sorrows of the world, and giving, in the serenity of his decline, an assurance that he will rise again in glory." It is ironic that in Ecclesiastes such reassuring permanence, denied to man, is largely restricted to the earth and the sun.

There are other ways in which Irving plays off Ecclesiastes against a sense of earthly life and values. What keeps the young officer from an immediate, unfettered love are his vain earthly concerns: "the sordid distinctions of rank and fortune," the "old obstacles"—"His rank in life—the prejudices of titled connections—his dependence upon a proud and unyielding father." When the Preacher implores men to sever their attachments to worldly things, he offers dramatic figures of death, the ultimate casting off of "old obstacles": "the silver cord be loosed, or the golden bowl be broken." Irving's discussion of the girl's wasting away from life is put explicitly in the images of Ecclesiastes: "The silver cord that had bound her to existence was loosed, and there seemed to be no more pleasure under the sun."

Ecclesiastes insists that in days of light we evoke darkness, in youth we think of death, on earth we contemplate eternal judgment. Man does well to remember his unavoidable fate: "All go unto one place; all are of the dust, and all turn to dust again." But if this is one of the morals of Ecclesiastes, it is hardly Irving's. For **"The Pride of the Village,"** despite Irving's allusions to the Preacher's words, offers no such moral.

Dwelling upon Ecclesiastes, and with his mind on the wasteful death of the young girl, Crayon experiences conflicting sentiments. Obviously the title of the sketch refers to something beyond the fact that the maiden is the choice member of the community. For despite her own innocence, she serves as vessel for the communal vanity of the villagers. She is a locus for material values; innocence, youth, and beauty make her the "pride of the village," the "favorite of the flock," and, significantly, the object of their vanity. As their May queen she participated in the "faint observance of the once-popular rites," fostered now by the village pastor, who is described as "one of those simple Christians that think their mission fulfilled by promoting joy on earth and good will among mankind." But Crayon's attitude toward the pastor's simple pagan ceremony suggests that his sentiments differ markedly from the Preacher's. He is aware of the idea that because all earthly things are transitory "all is vanity," but he is unwilling to surrender what is mortal. If he too readily shares a portion of the Preacher's fatalistic vision of human experience, he is nevertheless reluctant to respond to the Preacher's final imprecation to cut loose from all vanity.

Crayon's final observation is relevant to our understanding of this conflict between worldly, that is to say, human values, and the spiritual redemption of those who transcend the things of this world. He concludes his account with a description of his return to the church where he had witnessed the girl's funeral:

> The church door was open, and I stepped in. There hung the chaplet of flowers and the gloves, as on the day of the funeral; *the flowers were withered, it is true, but care seemed to have been taken that no dust should soil their whiteness.* I have seen many monuments where art has exhausted its powers to awaken the sympathy of the spectator, but I have met with none that spoke more touchingly to my heart than this simple but delicate memento of departed innocence. (Italics added.)

Ecclesiastes warns that "the dust [shall] return to the earth as it was: and the spirit shall return unto God who gave it." Still, it would be simple enough to miss the "worldly" implication of Irving's sentences: the clear note that, in tacit challenge to the Preacher's warning that dust returns to dust, the flowers, if withered, have been so cared for that no ''dust'' soils them. And with the sounding of this note we discern that the scene itself has become a defiant monument of sentiment to the girl's touching death.

Let me conclude these remarks with a reasonable disclaimer. I cannot insist that this tale will appeal to every modern reader. Some of the simple sentiments, presented discursively, which so readily pleased its first readers are precisely what put off, at first encounter at least, many of today's readers. It may be granted that Irving's rather easy dependence upon certain sentimental conventions remains for us an aesthetic problem. Still, it is necessary to point out that ''The Pride of the Village'' is more complex both in purpose and effect than is customarily acknowledged. (pp. 348-50)

> *George Monteiro, ''Washington Irving: A Grace Note on 'The Pride of the Village',' in* Research Studies, *Vol. 36, No. 4, December, 1968, pp. 347-50.*

WILLIAM L. HEDGES (essay date 1969)

[*Hedges, an American scholar and author, has written and edited several works on American literature, including* Washington Irving: An American Study, 1802-1832 *(see Additional Bibliography). In a survey of* The Sketch Book *excerpted below, Hedges comments on the book's impact on American literature and discusses sentimentality and mock-sentimentality in Irving's work.*]

[The style of *The Sketch Book*] is a familiar style, still basically formal but not academic or complex, fond of homely English and American nouns and verbs. It is symmetrical without seeming to strain; it runs naturally to abundant metaphor. Neither pretentious nor overly rhetorical, the style suggests that Irving did not have to work hard at being literary—which is something that cannot be said of much American writing between 1776 and 1820. (p. 58)

For the English reader there was little in *The Sketch Book* that was new. Crayon hedges himself about with scraps of verse and prose culled from British authors, both famous and forgotten, which he uses for epigraphs or as illustrations in footnotes and text. In fact much of the work is *about* literature, **''The Boar's Head Tavern, Eastcheap,''** for instance, which Crayon calls a ''Shakespearian Research,'' or its companion piece, **''Stratford-on-Avon,''** or **''The Royal Poet,''** a sketch which resurrects a long verse narrative written by James I of Scotland during his imprisonment in Windsor Castle. In **''The Art of Book-Making''** Crayon falls asleep in the British Museum and has a nightmare about authors borrowing from works of obscure predecessors, a fantasy which is virtually continued in **''The Mutability of Literature''** as he commiserates with a little quarto volume in the library of Westminister Abbey on what the passage of time does to literary reputations. Furthermore, even when he is not talking about an author or talking to an old book, Crayon may remind the reader of earlier British literature. In **''Westminster Abbey,''** for instance, he suggests Goldsmith or Addison; on a trip to the country, he slightly resembles the Spectator visiting Sir Roger de Coverley. Indeed, his very sound has affinities with the language of Addison and Goldsmith. This is in part what it meant for Irving to be hailed as the first literate American—that he had mastered a familiar English prose style. (pp. 58-9)

On the whole it is vestiges of the English past that catch Crayon's eye rather than the English present, about which *The Sketch Book* has nothing to say that compares with the perceptiveness of, say, Hawthorne's *Our Old Home* or Emerson's

English Traits a generation later. Irving's fondness for old England may have disarmed criticism there and thus contributed to the success of his book. But for all the merits of **''Rip Van Winkle,''** **''The Legend of Sleepy Hollow,''** and two or three other individual pieces, the book would not be worth reading as a whole were it not for the fact that the curiosity about England, embodied in Geoffrey Crayon, reflects a particularly American emotional need.

''The Author's Account of Himself'' presents *The Sketch Book* as a portfolio of observations made by Crayon in the course of his travels abroad. But Irving did not quite trust his basic structural scheme. He must have sensed that to hold his audience he had to have occasionally a more pronounced dramatic interest than Crayon could provide alone. We read only a few sketches before encountering, without apology or explanation, a story about America, **''Rip Van Winkle,''** which, instead of being attributed to Crayon, is presented as ''A Posthumous Writing by Diedrich Knickerbocker.'' Three other narratives in the original edition of *The Sketch Book*—it was slightly expanded later—have little or nothing to do with Crayon's trip to England. Otherwise, however, the book adheres to the stated format. And as Crayon's personality emerges, a unity of interest and feeling develops which compensates for Irving's casualness about the structure, so much so that one finally wants to read **''Rip Van Winkle''** and **''The Legend of Sleepy Hollow,''** if not as stories told by Crayon instead of Knickerbocker, then at least as stories that have touched Crayon almost personally. (pp. 59-60)

Crayon obviously has not felt completely at home in what he calls ''the common-place realities of the present'' in the United States. To appreciate him, one has to imagine what it was like to grow up in a country relatively barren of native belles-lettres, of fine arts, or of a meaningfully formulated history, a country in which practical considerations were apt to undermine cultural aspiration, a country frequently sneered at by Europeans as intellectually backward. Crayon sneers back in observing the ''swelling magnitude of many English travellers'' to America, and in his essay **''English Writers on America''** he makes clear the resentment felt in his country against European criticism. He also makes fun (by pretending to accept it) of the pseudo-scientific view of Buffon and other Europeans that animal life deteriorates in America, man included. Crayon goes to England, he says, to see ''the gigantic race'' from which he has ''degenerated.'' But the exaggeration may mask a fear that there is some truth in the theory.

At any rate, through Crayon, Irving becomes the first of a series of major American writers to make an issue of the contrast between the drabness, the plainness, the ordinariness, the newness of America and life in Europe as he sees it, encrusted with ''the accumulated treasures of age.'' James Fenimore Cooper, Nathaniel Hawthorne, and Henry James were to speak explicitly of the hardship which the American writer labored under in a society destitute of the monuments and works of art, the traditional rituals and symbols, the long established institutions and customs that to those authors gave interest to the surface of life in Europe.

A sense of the barrenness of the American scene was increasingly after 1820 to help turn the attention of the native writers to history—a tendency encouraged by the example of Sir Walter Scott, with whom Irving discussed literary strategy while preparing *The Sketch Book*. Cooper, Hawthorne, William Gilmore Simms, John P. Kennedy and others, drawing on history for picturesque material, gradually developed a tradition of American romance and in the process often gave poetic or mythical, if not precisely historical, meanings to portions of the American past. Several of Irving's American stories also utilize the past, while in Crayon he almost literally depicts the American writer searching for values in culture and tradition.

Yet the quest for a meaningful past constantly verges on grave-yard rumination. Mutability is the most persistent note of *The Sketch Book*. Crayon cuts a ludicrous figure occasionally, as when he speaks of himself as eager to ''loiter about the ruined castle—to meditate on the falling tower'' and ''lose'' himself in the past. To look at vestiges of the past is sooner or later to be reminded of the process of decay. Interpreting the floral imagery of English funerals and burials, Crayon seems to sense how naturally and deeply rooted in a culture poetry and symbolism can be—a vital realization for an American. But in reaching it he reveals openly his own anxiety about death. Funeral rites and monuments to the dead only partly distract the living from awareness of the inevitability of decay and oblivion. (pp. 61-3)

In spite of his awareness of the danger of mawkishly indulging in pathos [Irving] sentimentalized parts of *The Sketch Book* beyond anything that modern taste can bear. Crayon gives disquisitions on broken hearts and maidens dying of disappointed love. His sketch **"The Widow and Her Son"** weeps for bereaved motherhood. The prospect of economic failure and the breaking up of homes and families repeatedly looms before Crayon, a negative manifestation, doubtless, of the same need which impels Irving to find houses and traditions in which Crayon can at least temporarily feel at home.

Curiously, however, certain pieces of fiction in *The Sketch Book* undercut the sentimentality, just as Crayon's fantastic confrontations with forgotten books mock his literary aspirations. Woman's devotion, the wife as guardian angel, home and marriage as refuge from the vicissitudes of the world— these are the daydreams of Geoffrey Crayon. His book includes, however, not only the extravagantly idealized bride of the sketch called **"The Wife"** but the termagant Dame Van Winkle as well. (pp. 63-4)

The other well-known American story, **"The Legend of Sleepy Hollow,"** makes fun of a bookish bachelor who dreams of a comfortable marriage and is unable to provide it for himself. A tale called **"The Spectre Bridegroom"** presents a young couple defying with great resourcefulness a stupid and destructive prejudice which family pride has maintained as an honorable tradition. *The Sketch Book* appears finally as the work of a somewhat self-mocking sentimentalist. (p. 64)

We associate sensibility, graveyard melancholy, and the vogue for ruins with the era of Gray, Goldsmith, and Sterne, but *The Sketch Book* in 1820 gave impetus in America to a wallowing in soft emotion that lasted at least another forty years. Following Geoffrey Crayon, the figure of the idle daydreaming bachelor became a literary commonplace. The emotional binge was sustained by a vast subliterature of gift-books, annual publications produced largely for female readers, though it is clear that the American male was also susceptible to sentimentality. There was a soft-heartedness next to the hard-headed matter-of-factness which in this period was subduing the American continent. The avidity for sentimentalism suggests a national need for relief from the grinding pursuit of success and fear of failure, from tensions and anxieties known not only to Irving but to such writers as Hawthorne, Poe, and Melville. The dread and longing that underlie the haunted characters of these writers are not very different from the emotions which generated the sentimentalism of American literature in this period.

Irving's rhetoric distorts and greatly oversimplifies the strains to which a competitive economy subjects marriage, but, less sentimentalized, his ideal image of **"The Wife"** is a central force in Hawthorne, the symbol of man's need for a love that will bring him out of himself and out of an isolation into which pride, ambition, or greed tends to thrust him. Home, sweet home, the humble hearth, the comfortable pipe, the wife, the child, the old oaken bucket, the cottage in the valley, the green grassplot sheltered from commercial traffic, the oasis in the desert, the green isle in a savage sea—these images express a longing which informs American literature both at its worst and at its best in the first half of the nineteenth century. But at its best that literature is also obsessed with the man who consumes his life in longing, who refuses or is unable to settle down, who leaves home, who wastes his maturity in a lonely futile quest or who simply withdraws from life, who somehow destroys his house, his estate, or his wife and in the process brings about his own destruction. And this grotesque composite personage is in part the legacy of Crayon, Rip Van Winkle, Ichabod Crane, and a handful of characters in subsequent stories by Washington Irving. (pp. 64-5)

> *William L. Hedges, "Washington Irving: 'The Sketch Book of Geoffrey Crayon, Gent.','' in* Landmarks of American Writing, *edited by Hennig Cohen, Basic Books, Inc., Publishers, 1969, pp. 56-65.*

MARTIN ROTH   (essay date 1976)

[*Roth refutes the contention of Robert A. Bone (see excerpt dated 1963) and other critics that Irving identifies Ichabod Crane with the artistic imagination. On the contrary, according to Roth, Crane represents the Yankee-Puritan and other negative types lampooned by Irving in his earlier works* Salmagundi *and* A History of New York.]

Like *A History of New York* and **"Rip Van Winkle,"** [**"The Legend of Sleepy Hollow"**] is a tale of a Yankee invasion, but in it the Yankee is temporarily defeated, and his defeat is due primarily to the Yankee-American inability to assign any value to the world of dreams and imaginings. There is a hint of this theme toward the end of **"Rip Van Winkle"**: the villagers who doubt the reality of Rip's tale and insist ''that Rip had been out of his head, and that this was one point on which he always remained flighty'' are the new Yankees who have conquered the sleepy community of Hudson, New York, and converted it into secular logocracy. They can only identify imaginative vision as madness (which, in a positive sense, it is). (p. 161)

It has been argued by several critics that Sleepy Hollow dramatizes the conflict between the active and the imaginative life, and that Ichabod, despite the ridiculous figure he is made to cut, is a Quixotic projection of the artist—deliberately ridiculous as an emblem of the slightly comic position of the artist in America. [In a footnote, the critic cites Robert A Bone.] If, after fifteen years of trying, Irving finally managed to paint his enemy in rich colors, this can hardly be taken as evidence of an awakened sympathy for the type. For Ichabod Crane is definitely the enemy. Crane is not only a Yankee of Franklin's stamp, he also possesses many of the qualities of his earlier Puritan ancestors. Both attitudes involve a manipulation of nature, one for the purpose of accumulating material wealth and the other for the purpose of arousing piety through terror.

Irving's comic feud with schoolmasters and natives of Connecticut can be seen as early as *The Corrector,* and it was sustained throughout his subsequent works. The treatment of neither in **"Sleepy Hollow"** suggests any grounds for sympathy. Ichabod also corresponds to several other negative types in Irving's work. He is, for example, the sophisticated foreigner who debauches the tastes of the simple country girls, the homegrown equivalent of the French *émigré* in **Salmagundi.**

Ichabod Crane simply cannot be identified with the artistic imagination; there is too much sound evidence against this association. We are told "in fact" that Ichabod was "an odd mixture of small shrewdness and simple credulity"; these qualities are not imaginative, but they do relate directly to the Yankee-Puritan coupling referred to above.

Three times in the tale, Ichabod is seen engaged in "artistic" pursuits: he would amuse the maidens on Sunday by "reciting . . . all the epitaphs on the tombstones," and a sheet of paper is found, "scribbled and blotted in several fruitless attempts to make a copy of verses in honor of the heiress of Van Tassel." The third instance plays with the terms of creativity:

> As the enraptured Ichabod *fancied* all this, and as he rolled his great green eyes over the fat meadow-lands, the rich fields of wheat, of rye, of buckwheat and Indian corn, and the orchards burthened with ruddy fruit . . . his *imagination* expanded with the idea, how they might be readily turned into cash, and the money invested (italics mine).

Icahbod Crane is a petty capitalist and speculator.

Arguments linking Crane and the imagination generally hinge on his capacity for swallowing tales of the marvelous. Old Dutch wives tell him "marvellous tales of ghosts and goblins, and haunted fields, and haunted brooks, and haunted bridges, and haunted houses, and particularly of the headless horseman, or galloping Hessian of the Hollow."

> He would delight them equally by his anecdotes of witchcraft, and of the direful omens and portentous sights and sounds in the air, which prevailed in the earlier times of Connecticut; and would frighten them wofully with speculations upon comets and shooting stars; and with the alarming fact that the world did absolutely turn round.

Ichabod's voracious appetite for the supernatural is both "gross" and "monstrous." It is associated with his insatiable physical hunger which, as we shall see, is essentially sterile, an absorption which does not nourish.

There is a sense in which Crane does "create," however; he works at night, transforming nature into a place of terror:

> What fearful shapes and shadows beset his path. . . . How often was he appalled by some shrub covered with snow, which, like a sheeted spectre, beset his very path! . . . and if, by chance, a huge blockhead of a beetle came winging his blundering flight against him, the poor varlet was ready to give up the ghost, with the idea that he was struck with a witch's token.

This is comparable to the world of Hawthorne's "Young Goodman Brown"; Crane is not imagining; he is projecting the terror of his isolation (the spiritual isolation of the mobile and manipulative Yankee) upon the neutral darkness of nature. By transforming nature into a place of terror he expresses his fear of the natural and his own body, just as the transformation of the abundance of the Van Tassel farm into the neutral sterility of money expresses a similar fear. And the images that are evoked by his "excited imagination" terrify him in turn: "His only resource on such occasions, either to drown thought, or drive away evil spirits, was to sing psalm tunes." True creativity in **"The Legend of Sleepy Hollow"** is represented by the Van Tassel farm and by Brom Bones.

Brom Bones, Ichabod's opponent, is Irving's final version of the traditional *buck* of *The Spectator.* He is a sympathetic character: "with all his overbearing roughness, there was a strong dash of waggish good-humor at bottom." Although Ichabod Crane is not an artist, a case could be made for Bones—an artist, moreover, whose productions suggest Irving's own. After all, Brom Bones creates the legend of Sleepy Hollow out of the rumors of the community; its plot is the defeat of a Yankee, and its form is a hoax. Bones is a parodist—he "had a scoundrel dog whom he taught to whine in the most ludicrous manner, and introduced as a rival of Ichabod's . . . in psalmody"—and a burlesque artist—he "broke into the schoolhouse at night . . . and turned everything topsy-turvy."

Although the conflict at the center of **"The Legend of Sleepy Hollow"** is comparable to that of *A History of New York,* Irving uses the symbolism of the earlier work in a contrapuntal way to express the conflict. It is Ichabod who is given the classical vision of Cockaigne—". . . he pictured to himself every roasting pig running about with a pudding in his belly, and an apple in his mouth"—but it is here contrasted unfavorably with the natural abundance of Sleepy Hollow and becomes simply a sign of Ichabod's avarice. Ichabod, like Pantagruel, is a huge gullet; not only does he eat enormous quantities of food, but he eats superstition as well, with a "capacious swallow." He is a "huge feeder," and Katrina Van Tassel is "plump as a partridge; ripe and melting and rosy cheeked as one of her father's peaches." But although he eats voraciously, he remains as lean and skeletal as ever. The eating of Crane is likened to the devastations of a plague: he is compared to the grasshopper; and "to see him striding along the profile of a hill on a windy day, with his clothes bagging and fluttering about him, one might have mistaken him for the genius of famine descending upon the earth."

Ichabod Crane is literally defeated and expelled from Paradise as a result of a prank played on him by Brom Bones. The essential cause of his defeat, however, is his fear of the powers of the imagination, his fear of art—common to both the Puritan and the Yankee. This is reinforced in the contrast between his aversion and Brom Bones's easy entrance into the very legend that sends Crane flying:

> [Brom Bones] made light of the galloping Hessian. . . . He affirmed that, on returning one night from the neighbouring village of Sing Sing, he had been overtaken by this midnight trooper; that he had offered to race with him for a bowl of punch, and should have won it too, for Daredevil beat the goblin horse all hollow.

The defeat of Ichabod Crane is the most glorious moment of Irving's career, artistically and, perhaps, psychologically as well; for it fuses into one image the various meanings that made up Irving's American period. Within the context of *A History of New York,* Ichabod is defeated by his own conquest: the pumpkin was the Yankee emblem in that work, and it signaled the Yankee conquest of Fort Goed Hoop, where it "was hoisted on the end of a pole, as a standard—liberty caps not having as yet come into fashion."

Ichabod Crane is also defeated by his historical conquest. Irving has finally succeeded in undoing for a moment the American revolution by identifying the Dutch protagonist of his tale with the two historical enemies of Yankee America, the Hessians and the British in the person of Major André. In the third place, the Yankee is defeated by that value to which he had devoted his existence, and that is mind to the exclusion of body. The Horseman throws his head at Ichabod as if to say that he does not much need it, that he is quite comfortable in his subsequent untroubled state. Finally, Ichabod is defeated by American art, Dutch art; for the legend is a creation of the Dutch community generally and Brom Bones particularly. (pp. 163-66)

> *Martin Roth, in his* Comedy and America: The Lost World of Washington Irving, *Kennikat Press, 1976, 205 p.*

MARY WEATHERSPOON BOWDEN (essay date 1981)

[*In an overview of* The Sketch Book, *Bowden delineates the darker themes of the volume, asserting that Irving's repetition of images and ideas unifies the various sketches into an artistic whole.*]

In 1820, when *The Sketch Book* first appeared in England, England, having conquered Napoleon, was a nation divided. The corn laws left many hungry; many, as Irving pointed out to Brevoort, were starving; recent inventions had put many out of work; a public gathering at Manchester had ended with the cavalry attacking and wounding up to four hundred people; habeas corpus had been suspended; sedition laws were rigidly enforced; local magistrates had the power to imprison anyone they thought had made a face at authority. Any movement by radicals, or even liberals, led to harsher repressive measures on the part of the government. *The Sketch Book,* chiefly through its images, reflects Irving's attitude toward such an England. To one coming to it straight from Knickerbocker's *A History of New York,* it is depressing, nothing but melancholy, sentimentality, death, and graves. (p. 57)

Common themes include those of imprisonment, shipwreck, sterility, financial loss, and the role of the storyteller. Interlaced throughout the entirety is the Jeffersonian ideal of the virtues of agrarianism. While Irving attributes moral feeling to the rural life, its temple is a plentifully stocked barn. Independence of thought is associated not with the nobility, nor with the peasantry, but with the substantial farmer. While, in some respects, *The Sketch Book* is a traveler's guide to England and the English character, it is also Irving's statement of determination to make a mark for himself in the English literary world. (pp. 57-8)

The prelude, ["A Voyage to England"] is dominated by images of blankness and death: "the vast space of waters, that separates the hemispheres is like a blank page in existence . . . from the moment you lose sight of the land you have left, all is vacancy." The voyage is a gulf, "rendering distance palpable and return precarious." The vacancy is corrected by the artist, who transforms clouds into "some fairy realms." But reality intrudes even upon the artist; a drifting mast gives no indication of the ship's hapless crew, the captain tells of running down a smaller ship at night and being unable to help any survivors. Thus Crayon's voyage is one of terror. . . . (p. 58)

The rest of the essays of the first part deal with financial failure and how to cope with it. The first, "Roscoe," describes the financial misfortunes of the Liverpool banker and biographer of the Medicis. Roscoe had failed, and his library had to be sold, and Crayon likens the scene of the sale to "pigmies rummaging the armoury of a giant, and contending for pos-session of weapons which they could not wield." Thus the fate of one of the giants Crayon had expected of England. While Roscoe survives his loss through philosophy, Leslie, the chief character of "The Wife," is able to cope with his ruin because of his wife's virtues. While "The Wife," when read by itself, is extremely sentimental, its sentimentality is somewhat palliated by its context.

It is in this context that Irving introduces "Rip Van Winkle," his third story of financial failure. The first failure resorted to philosophy; the second, to his wife; the third, significantly, to story telling. "Rip" is both Irving's acknowledgement of his New York readers and his promise to return to them. (pp. 58-9)

In "English Writers on America," Irving criticizes the works the English have written about the United States. Although Americans resent these attacks, they should not: "the tissue of misrepresentations attempted to be woven round us are like cobwebs, woven round the limbs of an infant giant. Our country continually outgrows them." Irving warns English writers that, through their words, England "is instilling anger and resentment into the bosom of a youthful nation, to grow with its growth and strengthen with its strength." While throughout the essay England is pictured as a pigmy in comparison to America, Crayon still values England as "the fountain head from whence the literature of the language flows."

Having condemned English writers on America, in his next essay, Crayon becomes an American writer on the English, declaring that "the stranger who would form a correct opinion of the English character must not confine his observations to the metropolis." It is only in the country that Irving finds Englishmen at their best. There Irving discovers a "regular gradation from the nobleman . . . down to the labouring peasantry; and while it has thus banded the extremes of society together, has infused in each intermediate rank a spirit of independence.". . . Irving ends the essay with a poem which closes with these lines:

> A world enjoy'd; that wants no witnesses
> But its own sharers, and approving heaven,
> That, like a flower deep hid in rocky cleft,
> Smiles, though 'tis looking only at the sky.

This seems pleasant. But the reader turns the page and comes upon this quotation: "I never heard / Of any true affection but 'twas nipt / With care, that, like the caterpiller, eats / The leaves of the spring's sweetest book, the rose." While this quotation from Middleton is an appropriate headnote to its essay, "The Broken Heart," the juxtaposition of the two poems is striking. "The Broken Heart," too often reprinted alone, seems to appeal nicely to the sentimental taste for young love, disappointment, and death. But in context, it also serves to illustrate the cankers even in rural England. (pp. 59-60)

The bleakest section of *The Sketch Book* is part 3, for it abounds with images of imprisonment, death, and the present sterility of England. In "The Royal Poet," Irving deals with James I of Scotland, but does not emphasize his kingship, his ability as a soldier or a ruler, but with his imprisonment, after a voyage, in a strange land, in England. In describing the blessings of the imagination when the body is confined, Irving returns to his Magi image of ["The Art of Book Making"]: "it can create a world for itself, and with a necromantic power, can conjure up glorious shapes and forms, and brilliant visions, to make solitude populous, and irradiate the gloom of the dungeon." (p. 62)

The fifth part of *The Sketch Book* is the only one still reprinted as a section, usually under the title, *Old Christmas*. The title is appropriate, since Irving continually emphasizes that the bounty and plenty described are more familiar to the past than the present. . . . He has chosen Christmas, because, then, "heart calleth unto heart, and we draw our pleasures from the deep wells of living kindness." It is "the season of regenerated feeling—the season for kindling not merely the fire of hospitality in the hall, but the genial flame of charity in the heart." Thus, as indicated in the previous section, Crayon's pilgrimage is now to the well of the heart, rather than to the fountainhead of literature. The month of May being unobtainable, he is seeking warmth.

But the images Irving uses at the close of this first essay, **"Christmas,"** remind us that Crayon is still alone:

> The scene of early love again rises green to memory beyond the sterile waste of years, and the idea of home, fraught with the fragrance of home dwelling joys, reanimates the drooping spirit—as the Arabian breeze will sometimes waft the freshness of the distant fields to the weary pilgrim of the desert.

The pilgrim, however, still has more desert to cross, as Crayon emphasizes in his next paragraph: "stranger and sojourner as I am in the land . . . yet I feel the influence of the season beaming into my soul from the happy looks of those around me. Surely happiness is reflective." Crayon can only enjoy this reflected happiness. (p. 67)

From the beginning blankness and threat of death of [**"A Voyage to England"**] and the succeeding images of entombment, frigidity, and sterility, from the beginning quotation that the traveler must "live where he can, not where he would," Irving moves steadily from frigidity to the warmth of the heart, from the sterility of books to the fairyland of children, from the grave to resurrection, from storms to a safe harbor, from living where he must to the rat's looking "for some other nest" [in **"Little Britain"**] and relocating. *The Sketch Book* is a unified chronicle of progress. It cannot be called a novel, but it is far more than a random collection of sketches. In it, Irving shows his artistry. (pp. 78-9)

Mary Weatherspoon Bowden, in her Washington Irving, *Twayne Publishers, 1981, 201 p.*

ADDITIONAL BIBLIOGRAPHY

Aderman, Ralph M., ed. *Washington Irving Reconsidered: A Symposium*. Hartford, Conn.: Transcendental Books, 1969, 66 p.
   Comprises twelve articles on various aspects of Irving's career. Pieces dealing with *The Sketch Book* include "The Spell of Nature in Irving's Famous Stories" by Herbert F. Smith and "Irving, Hawthorne, and the Image of the Wife" by William L. Hedges.

Bruner, Marjorie W. "'The Legend of Sleepy Hollow': A Mythological Parody." *College English* 25, No. 4 (January 1964): 274, 279-83.
   Presents "The Legend of Sleepy Hollow" as a parody of ancient Greek myths and rites of Greek fertility cults, comparing various characters with figures from Greek mythology.

Cairns, William B. "Irving." In his *British Criticisms of American Writings, 1815-1833: A Contribution to the Study of Anglo-American Literary Relationships*, pp. 58-111. University of Wisconsin Studies in Language and Literature, no. 14. Madison: University of Wisconsin, 1922.
   A detailed account of the British reception of Irving's works, including *The Sketch Book*, from 1815 to 1833. Cairns includes bibliographical citations for the magazines discussed and often provides generous excerpts of the criticism.

Coad, Oral Sumner. "The Gothic Element in American Literature before 1835." *The Journal of English and Germanic Philology* XXIV, No. 1 (January 1925): 72-93.
   A historical overview of Gothicism in American literature that includes a survey of Gothic elements in *The Sketch Book*.

Current-Garcia, Eugene. "Soundings and Alarums: The Beginnings of Short Fiction in America." *Midwest Quarterly* XVII, No. 4 (Summer 1976): 311-28.
   A survey of the short story in the United States that affirms *The Sketch Book* as the first accomplished example of the genre.

Eby, Cecil D., Jr. "Ichabod Crane in Yoknapatawpha." *Georgia Review* XVI, No. 4 (Winter 1962): 465-69.
   Suggests that William Faulkner's novel *The Hamlet* is a reworking of "The Legend of Sleepy Hollow."

Ellis, Amanda M. "What Does Irving Say?" *English Journal* XVII, No. 7 (September 1928): 576-78.
   Briefly describes how the details of "Rip Van Winkle" were distorted in its various dramatic and juvenile adaptations.

Ellmann, Richard. "Love in the Catskills." *New York Review of Books* XXIII, No. 1 (5 February 1976): 27-8.
   Reads "Rip Van Winkle" as a parable of Irving's life.

Fetterley, Judith. "Palpable Designs: Four American Short Stories." In her *The Resisting Reader: A Feminist Approach to American Fiction*, pp. 1-45. Bloomington: Indiana University Press, 1978.
   A feminist revaluation of American literature discussing "Rip Van Winkle" as typical of most American fiction in its implicit exclusion of females.

Hedges, William L. *Washington Irving: An American Study, 1802-1832*. The Grouchen College Series. Baltimore: Johns Hopkins Press, 1965, 274 p.
   A study of Irving's relevance to American literary history. The critic states that his intent is "to define [Irving's] major contributions as a writer and to work out in detail his relation to his intellectual environment." *The Sketch Book* is discussed extensively.

Heiman, Marcel. "'Rip Van Winkle': A Psychoanalytic Note on the Story and Its Author." *American Imago* 16, No. 1 (Spring 1959): 3-47.
   A psychoanalytic, biographical analysis of "Rip Van Winkle." Heiman postulates that Irving wrote the story as a means of resolving the conflicts in his own life.

Hellman, George S. *Washington Irving, Esquire: Ambassador at Large from the New World to the Old*. New York: Alfred A. Knopf, 1925, 355 p.
   A biography utilizing previously unavailable notebooks, letters, and journals by Irving.

Hoffman, Daniel. "Prefigurations: 'The Legend of Sleepy Hollow'." In his *Form and Fable in American Fiction*, pp. 83-96. 1961. Reprint. New York: Oxford University Press, 1970.
   Credits Irving as the first American author to use folklore and fable in fiction. Hoffman details the folkloric origins of "The Legend of Sleepy Hollow" and locates its place in the comic tradition of American literature.

Irving, Washington. *Notes while Preparing "Sketch Book" &c. 1817*. Edited by Stanley T. Williams. New Haven: Yale University Press, 1927, 97 p.
   Reprints, with an explanatory introduction, the contents of the notebook Irving kept while he was writing *The Sketch Book*.

Kann, David J. "'Rip Van Winkle': Wheels within Wheels." *American Imago* 36, No. 2 (Summer 1979): 178-96.
   Examines the various levels at which truth is revealed and concealed in "Rip Van Winkle."

Leary, Lewis. *Washington Irving*. University of Minnesota Pamphlets on American Writers, no. 25. Minneapolis: University of Minnesota Press, 1963, 48 p.

A biographical and critical overview.

Lee, Helen. "Clue Patterns in 'Rip Van Winkle'." *English Journal* 55, No. 2 (February 1966): 192-94, 200.

Details the intricate pattern of clues contained in the plot, setting, characters, and language of "Rip Van Winkle." These clues, according to the critic, foreshadow the action of the story.

Lynen, John F. "The Fiction in the Landscape: Irving and Cooper." In his *The Design of the Present: Essays on Time and Form in American Literature*, pp. 153-204. New Haven, Conn.: Yale University Press, 1969.

Examines Irving's treatment of myth, time, and natural landscape in "Rip Van Winkle," highlighting Irving's use of symbolism and his depiction of the tenuousness of time and reality.

McClary, Ben Harris, ed. *Washington Irving and the House of Murray: Geoffrey Crayon Charms the British, 1817-1856*. Knoxville: University of Tennessee Press, 1969, 242 p.

Reprints Irving's correspondence with his first British publisher, John Murray, with an introduction and running commentary by the editor. Irving's letters reveal much about the publication of *The Sketch Book* and the state of literary relations between the United States and Great Britain.

Myers, Andrew B., ed. *Washington Irving: A Tribute*. Tarrytown, N.Y.: Sleepy Hollow Restorations, 1972, 86 p.

Eight articles by various contributors supplying the biographical, historical, and literary background to Irving's career.

————., ed. *1860-1974: A Century of Commentary on the Works of Washington Irving*. Tarrytown, N.Y.: Sleepy Hollow Restorations, 1976, 504 p.

Comprises forty-five biographical and critical essays written between 1860 and 1974. The critics represented include William Cullen Bryant, Henry W. Longfellow, George W. Curtis, Fred Lewis Pattee, Edward Wagenknecht, and William L. Hedges.

Pochmann, Henry A. "Irving's German Sources in *The Sketch Book*." *Studies in Philology* XXVII, No. 3 (July 1930): 477-507.

Compares the texts of three short stories—"Rip Van Winkle," "The Legend of Sleepy Hollow," and "The Spectre Bridegroom"—with what Pochmann considers their German sources. The critic also discusses Irving's knowledge of German literature.

Springer, Haskell. *Washington Irving: A Reference Guide*. Boston: G. K. Hall & Co., 1976, 235 p.

Lists secondary materials on Irving published from 1807 to 1974.

Tuttleton, James W. "Washington Irving." In *Fifteen American Authors before 1900*, edited by Earl N. Harbert and Robert A. Rees, pp. 330-56. Madison: University of Wisconsin Press, 1984.

A bibliographical essay listing Irving bibliographies, manuscripts, letters, and criticism.

Warner, Charles Dudley; Bryant, William Cullen; and Putnam, George Palmer. *Studies of Irving*. New York: G. P. Putnam's Sons, 1880, 159 p.

Biographical-critical essays by Irving's fellow authors Warner and Bryant and by his publisher Putnam.

Williams, Stanley T. *The Life of Washington Irving*. 2 vols. New York: Oxford University Press, 1935.

The standard biography.

Young, Philip. "Fallen from Time: The Mythic Rip Van Winkle." *Kenyon Review* XXII, No. 4 (Autumn 1960): 547-73.

A thorough examination of the mythic sources of "Rip Van Winkle." Young attempts to demonstrate the psychological complexity behind the seemingly simple tale.

Imre Madách

1823-1864

Hungarian dramatist, poet, essayist, and short story writer.

Madách is remembered for his dramatic poem *Az ember tragédiája (The Tragedy of Man)*, which is considered one of the greatest works of Hungarian literature. A philosophical examination of the universal struggle between good and evil, *The Tragedy of Man* has often been compared with such Western literary masterpieces as Johann Wolfgang von Goethe's *Faust* and John Milton's *Paradise Lost*. While the difficulty of translating the drama has rendered it virtually unknown to English-speaking audiences, *The Tragedy of Man* has been widely performed and studied in Europe. Madách wrote several dramas in addition to *The Tragedy of Man;* however, these works have received little critical attention, with most scholars agreeing that they lack the range and artistic mastery of *The Tragedy of Man*.

Madách was born in Alsósztregova, Hungary (now Czechoslovakia), into a wealthy and aristocratic family. As a child, he received the finest available education, studying at home with a private tutor, an art teacher, and a dance instructor. Madách developed a strong interest in history and literature at an early age, especially admiring the tragedies of William Shakespeare and Johann Friedrich von Schiller. He attended secondary school for a brief time and then, in 1837, he entered the University of Pest, where he studied philosophy and law and also composed poetry. Around this time, Madách began to develop the heart problems that would plague him throughout his life. In 1840, after falling in love with Etelka Lónyay, the fourteen-year-old sister of a friend, he wrote *Lant-virágok*, a collection of love poems in her honor. Madách was devastated when the romance ended and left Pest for several months to recuperate emotionally as well as physically at a nearby spa. When he recovered, Madách resumed his law studies and, upon graduation, was appointed to the first of a series of public offices from which his poor health often forced him to resign.

Madách combined his duties as a public servant with his literary career. In the early 1840s, he composed several historical dramas, among them *Commodus* and *Nápolyi Endre*. Although rarely read today, these works are considered of interest by critics for their treatment of themes that recurred in his later works, most notably in *The Tragedy of Man*. These themes include the tumultuous character of relations between men and women, the doomed condition of humanity, and the melancholy nature of life. In the winter of 1844-45, Madách met Erzsebet Fráter, a volatile young woman he married shortly thereafter. When Hungary entered into war with Austria in 1848, Madách was barred from combat because of his poor health. A devout patriot, he was deeply troubled by his inability to participate in the fighting, and Hungary's defeat caused additional anguish: he lost his closest friend as well as his sister and her family in the war. In 1851, Madách took a political refugee into his home, for which he was subsequently arrested and imprisoned. During Madách's incarceration, his wife had several flagrant affairs, and when he returned from prison in 1854, the two divorced, an event that left him isolated and depressed. Nonetheless, he continued to write. In 1859, he finished the drama *A civilizátor,* a satiric account of Austrian

bureaucracy in Hungary patterned after the writings of Aristophanes. The following year, Madách completed *The Tragedy of Man* and was elected to the Hungarian Parliament in Pest. He acquired a reputation as an eloquent speaker, which helped bring his work to the attention of the local literary community. Madách showed *The Tragedy of Man* to János Arany, a highly respected poet. Initially, Arany was unimpressed with the drama, calling it a derivative version of *Faust*. Yet, when pressured by Madách's friends to reexamine *The Tragedy of Man*, Arany realized the strengths of the work. Arany offered to help edit the drama and in October 1861, *The Tragedy of Man* was read aloud at a meeting of the Kisfaludy Society, a prominent literary organization. The work met with resounding acclaim and was published shortly thereafter. Madách was unable to duplicate the success of *The Tragedy of Man*, however, and the later pieces he submitted to the Kisfaludy Society for publication were poorly received. Madách never completed his last work, *Tündérálom,* due to illness, and he died on 5 October 1864.

Critics agree that Madách's reputation rests on *The Tragedy of Man*. Structured as a dramatic poem consisting of eleven dream segments, the work tells the story of Adam, Eve, and Lucifer through numerous historical reincarnations. Commencing with the dawn of creation, the action moves from ancient Rome and ancient Greece to the French Revolution and ends sometime in the future. Madách's Adam, intended as a reflection of Madách himself, is meant to be Everyman, eternally down-trodden and struggling. Lucifer is Adam's tempter, sabotaging him at every opportunity. Eve, conversely, represents hope. At the drama's end, Adam has resigned himself to suicide when Eve saves him with the news that she is expecting a child. Though Madách never intended his drama for the stage, it was first performed in 1883 and continues to be widely staged throughout Europe.

The Tragedy of Man has inspired an enormous body of criticism in Hungarian, but it has been the subject of relatively little commentary in English. Part of the reason for this is the difficulty of translating the work effectively. Most critics contend that it is almost impossible for a translator to appropriately recreate the spirit and beauty of *The Tragedy of Man* while at the same time rendering it suitable for performance. In spite of this, critical interest in Madách's drama has slowly emerged in the English-speaking world in recent years. This commentary, which emphasizes the work's unique combination of philosophical depth and dramatic impact, offers hope for increased understanding and appreciation of *The Tragedy of Man*.

*PRINCIPAL WORKS

"Az anya gyermeke sírján" (poetry) 1839; published in
     periodical *Honmüvész*
Lant-virágok (poetry) 1840
Commodus (drama) 1841
Nápolyi Endre (drama) 1841
Csak tréfa (drama) 1843
A férfi és nö (drama) 1843
A civilizátor (drama) 1859
Az ember tragédiája (verse drama) 1860
     [*The Tragedy of Man*, 1908]
Mózes (verse drama) 1860
Tündérálom (unfinished verse drama) 1864
Összes müvei. 3 vols. (dramas and poetry) 1880
Összes levelei. 2 vols. (letters) 1942
Összes müvei. 2 vols. (dramas, poetry, short stories,
     letters, speeches, and essays) 1942

*Individual dramas are chronologized by date of composition rather than first performance.

IMRE MADÁCH (letter date 1862?)

[*In the following excerpt from a letter to János Erdélyi, a Hungarian critic, Madách defends the philosophic intent of* The Tragedy of Man. *The date of the letter's composition is unknown, but it is believed to have been written in 1862.*]

What is meant to be the fundamental idea of [*The Tragedy of Man*] is that once man has broken away from God and is beginning to act, relying on his own strength, the course of his action takes him, in succession, through the greatest and most sacred ideas of mankind to the very end. It is true that he fails everywhere and that what brings about his failure everywhere is a weakness that is hidden deep within human nature and that he cannot cast off (that, in my humble opinion, would be the tragic element). But, although he thinks in despair that all endeavors he has made so far have been a drain of energy,

his development has gone ahead continuously, the human race has progressed although the struggling individual did not recognize it, and the guiding hand of God's providence makes up for that human weakness which he himself cannot conquer. This is what the "Strive and trust" of the last scene refers to. (pp. 53-4)

> *Imre Madách, in an extract from a letter to János Erdélyi in 1862?* in Imre Madách *by Dieter P. Lotze, Twayne Publishers, 1981, pp. 53-4.*

GEORGE ALEXANDER KOHUT (essay date 1896)

[*Kohut points out the various influences on* The Tragedy of Man *while stressing Madách's originality.*]

To English readers, Madách is a total stranger. His name is scarcely ever found in any encyclopædia or biographical dictionary; and strangely enough, no attempt has been thus far made to give even a selection from this latter-day Milton of Hungary.

It is not here intended to explain the origin and inner development of [*The Tragedy of Man*], nor to draw elaborate parallels between its author and his predecessors in other lands. Such a comparative critical study would be interesting as showing the spiritual kinship between master minds, centuries distant from one another, whose sympathies are in direct touch with our own ideals and life problems.

Madách will plead his own cause effectively enough. To him, however, who in reading the *Tragedy of Man* involuntarily makes such comparisons, and might be led unjustly to question the author's originality, the graceful adage *Grosse Geister treffen sich* (Great minds meet) will serve as an answer. He should rather say, with true artistic estimate, that the shading in the one landscape of a higher life helps to set off the vivid and brilliant coloring in the other; so that the whole, viewed side by side, presents a series of wondrous harmonies. Madách imbibed, no doubt, from foreign sources. He was familiar with *Paradise Lost*, and with the now obsolete but once much-lauded epic, *La Semaine* (The Week), of Milton's French predecessor Du Bartas; Alfieri's tramelogedia, *Abele*, and Gesner's *Death of Abel*, as well as Byron's *Mystery of Cain*, may also have come to his notice; Goethe's *Faust* appears more than once, and may be recognized in any incognito. Yet we cannot say with certainty that any one of these masterpieces influenced his own work, any more than Milton inspired the great German bard. We might as justly tax him with drawing upon Hebrew tradition for the entire plot of his drama, beginning with the fourth scene; for strangely enough, Adam's experiences with his mentor and Nemesis, Lucifer, are foreshadowed in the very same manner in a quaint legend of the Jewish Rabbis, told nearly twenty centuries ago. The comparative study of literature will reveal other facts equally amazing. It is of course self-evident that the morbid pessimism which rings its vague alarms throughout the book is that of Ecclesiastes, whose *vanitas vanitatum* is the key to his doleful plaint.

> I applied my heart to seek and to search out by wisdom concerning all that is done under heaven: it is a sore travail that God hath given to the sons of men to be exercised therewith. I have seen all the works that are done under the sun; and behold, all is vanity and a striving after wind. . . . And I applied my heart to know wisdom, and to know madness and folly: I perceived that this also was a striving after wind. For

in much wisdom is much grief; and he that increaseth knowledge increaseth sorrow.

This is the leading theme, and Lessing's soulful simile of the ideal, the grand *morale:*—"If God held truth in his right hand," says he, "and in his left the mere striving after truth, bidding me choose between the two, I would reverently bow to his left and say, 'Give but the impulse; truth is for thee alone!'"

Thus, after traversing many lands the world over; after plunging into every pleasure and being steeped in every vice; after passions human and divine have had their sway over his spirit,—Adam concedes to Lucifer that the world of ideals is illusory, existing only in fancy, thriving but in our own souls, nourished by sentiment, and supersensitive to the touch of grosser things. And yet the echo which answers his sad pleadings, as he cries out disheartened—

> O sacred poetry, hast thou then
> Quite forsaken this prosy world of ours?

is a wholly unexpected one in the grand *finale.* It teaches the doctrine of eternal hope, as the great Hebrew pessimist Koheleth summed it up, when ony the Hellenic intellect reigned supreme and the Hellenic heart was cold:—

> I have decreed, O man—strive ye and trust!

The ideal conquers in the end, should life and love not fail. Poetry and sentiment transform even this valley of the shadow of death into a Paradise regained. It is a song of the ideals in which salvation lies; and the words of the Lord with which the poem closes are, "Struggle and trust." (pp. 9515-17)

> *George Alexander Kohut, "Emerich Madách (1823-1864)," in Library of the World's Best Literature: Ancient and Modern, edited by Charles Dudley Warner & others, 1896. Reprint by J. A. Hill, 1902, pp. 9515-30.*

EMIL REICH (essay date 1898)

[Reich interprets The Tragedy of Man *as "a philosophy of History."]*

[In **The Tragedy of Man**], there is revealed all the sombreness of profound melancholy, wailing over the bootless struggle of Man since the unlucky moment of his creation. . . . [The] Hungarians, as a nation, are strongly inclined to pathos; just as the English are to satire and the French to irony. In the youthful members of the Magyar nation that bent is at times so strong as to dominate all the other modes and faculties of the soul. Hence the astounding wealth of grave Largos in Hungarian music, and the melancholy and despondent tone in many a great work of Hungarian poetry. Few poems can compare in unaffected sadness. . . . Madách's **Tragedy of Man (Az ember tragédiája)** is, as it were, the funeral march of humanity. It would be utterly wrong to compare it to Goethe's *Faust.* Although there is a general similarity in the drift of the two works, yet the poem of the luckless and suffering county official of an obscure Hungarian province is essentialy different from the drama of the Jupiter of German literature. Madách's poem is, reduced to its skeleton, a philosophy of History. He takes us from the hour when Adam and Eve were innocently walking in the Garden of Eden, to the times of the Egyptian Pharaohs; then to the Athens of Miliades; to sinking Rome; to the adventurous period of the Crusaders; into the study of the astronomer Kepler in the seventeenth century; thence into the horrors of the French Revolution; into greed-eaten and commerce-ridden modern London; nay, into the ultra-socialist state of the future, in which there will be no family, no nation, and no individuality amongst the countless individuals; and where the ideas of the preceding ages, such as Religion, Art, Literature, will, by means of scientific formulae, be shown up in all their absurdity; still further, the poet shows the future of the earth, when ice will cover the whole of its surface, and Europeans and other human beings will be reduced to the state of a degraded brute dragging on the misery of existence in some cave. In all these scenes, Adam, Eve and the arch-fiend (Lucifer) are the chief and constantly recurring *personæ dramatis.* In fact, all these scenes are meant to be prophetic dreams of Adam, which Lucifer causes him to have in order to disgust him with humanity in advance, and so, by driving him to suicide, to discontinue humanity. In paradise, Adam learns and teaches the lesson of man's incapability of enduring bliss; in Egypt, Adam, as Pharaoh, experiences the bottomless wretchedness of tyranny, where "millions live for the sake of one;" in Athens he is made to shudder at the contemptible fickleness of man when part of a crowd; in sinking Rome he stands aghast at the corruptibility of mankind, and in the Crusades at their fanaticism; in the study of Kepler he comprehends the sickening vanity of all attempts at real knowledge, and in Paris he is shown the godless fury of a people fighting for the dream called Liberty. So in the end, Adam, despairing of his race, wants to commit suicide, when, in the critical moment, Eve tells him that she is going to be a mother by him; whereby his intention of discontinuing his race by suicide is baffled. Adam then prostrates himself before God, who encourages him to hope and trust, making him feel that man is part of an infinite and indestructible power, and will struggle not quite in vain. Like Goethe's *Faust,* the great poem of Madách was not meant for the stage; yet, ike *Faust,* it has proved of intense effect on the stage too. It is . . . a philosophic poem excelling rather in the beauty and loftiness of the thoughts conveyed or suggested than by power of characterization or dramatic vigour. In general literature we should like to compare it most to the *De rerum natura* of Lucretius. The powerful melancholy of the Roman is of a kind with the gloom of the Hungarian; and while the former dwells more on the material and religious aspect of man, and the latter on social phenomena in all their width and breadth, yet both sing the same tempestuous *nocturne* of Man's sufferings and shortcomings, illuminating the night of their despondency by stars of luminous thought. Madách died at too early an age to finish more than this one masterpiece. His other poems are inferior. (pp. 217-20)

> *Emil Reich, "Dramatic Literature—Szigligeti—Madách—Csiky—Great, but Hitherto Ignored Importance of the Hungarian Drama," in his Hungarian Literature: An Historical & Critical Survey, Jarrold & Sons, 1898, pp. 207-25.*

ALEXANDER HEVESI (essay date 1930)

[Hevesi compares The Tragedy of Man *with Johann Wolfgang von Goethe's* Faust, *highlighting the differences between the two works.]*

The **Tragedy of Man** is one of the most curious works in universal literature, a dramatic poem of the type of Goethe's *Faust* and Byron's *Cain.* It is a grand poem of humanity for humanity, of which the hero is Adam, the eternal man, and the heroine Eve, the eternal woman.

It is curious to observe that both Goethe and Madách deny the "genre" to which their works belong. Madách announces in the title that his poem is the *Tragedy of Man.* Goethe called *Faust* a tragedy. But it must at the outset be remarked that neither of them is a tragedy; for both are mystery plays.

It is undeniable that Faust and Adam undergo most tragical experiences, and like Hamlet and King Lear they too have to pass through many different tragical events, but the difference between tragedy and mystery does not lie in the tragical character of the happenings; it depends entirely on the point of view from which the poet regards his subject, namely, whether he looks at it with the eyes of heaven or of earth; to be more precise, whether the tragical struggle of Man begins and ends on earth or begins and ends in heaven.

The tragedy of Shakespeare's heroes has its origin and end on earth; their fate is not to be faced, it is woven into their story and character. But neither Faust nor Adam surrenders to his fate or character. What is happening with them, is really the struggle of God and Satan; the human struggle develops according to the plan of God as in the mysteries of the Middle Ages. The culminating moment of all tragedies is death or annihilation; the culminating moment of all mystery plays is always redemption. (pp. 392-93)

When the first German edition of the *Tragedy of Man* was published . . . some German critics spoke of it as an imitation of Goethe's *Faust,* and they did not take the trouble to study this work seriously enough to see how far it was second-hand or second-rate. The same thing happened long before with Byron's *Manfred* which was also considered as fashioned after *Faust.* As to the *Tragedy of Man,* this attitude was by no means surprising, because immediately after the first Hungarian edition critics were to be found who compared the two works, easily discovering all the details which Madách seemed to have taken out of Goethe's great poem. Prague as the disciple of Kepler, the great astronomer. The typical love-scene in Martha's garden, the pair of loving couples, after the fashion of Spanish classical comedies, is repeated in the Byzantine scene by the author of the *Tragedy of Man.* At the first meeting of Faust and Gretchen, she is coming from church, and so is Eve as the light-hearted girl in the London scene of the Hungarian poem. More than this, there are some sayings to be found in the work of Madách which, at the very first glance, show how profoundly he studied the German master. But, on the other hand, no carping scholar of Madách can deny that behind the transparent veil of all these resemblances between the two works yawns a gap of half a century, and thus the very centre, the problem, the life-elements, the system, the plan, and the technique of the *Tragedy of Man* differ entirely from *Faust.* The German masterwork is the most successful revival in the second half of the 18th century of a great theme of the Middle Ages, perhaps the only one which Shakespeare left to following generations. To this Goethe added his intense inner life and experience during the first three decades of the 19th century. On the other hand, the dramatic poem of Madách could not have come to life before the second half of the 19th century, and, as I shall point out, only in Hungary of that period. Madách did, indeed, learn very much from Goethe, but he is not at all a spiritual brother or nephew of him. *Faust* is the key-stone at the top of an epoch. The *Tragedy of Man* is a fresh start, the beginning of a quite different development; it is a hint of the future, lighting up new paths. Between the two works there is a whole world.

What is the very centre of *Faust*? Man, standing between the real and the ideal, between moral good and evil, or according to medieval ideas, between God and Satan. On the other hand, in the centre of Madách's work (in spite of its title which was chosen by chance), it is not man but something more, of which Goethe did not even think, something which could not have entered his mind, but which is also to be found as one of the fundamental ideas of two great modern dramatists, the German Hebbel and the Norwegian Ibsen (both of them were quite unknown to Madách); this new element is simply the couple, man and wife, as one. The problem of man and wife, intended and determined, conceived, and created one for the other, that is the tragical gist of the great dramas of Hebbel and of Ibsen and that is the real essence of Madách's poem, as it was the great crisis in his private life.

I venture to say that precisely by taking from the Bible this couple, the symbolic man and wife of all times and all ages, Madách has succeeded far better in setting and solving this problem than any other dramatist. Adam and Eve do not stand for one couple, thay stand for all men and all women. This is the first essential difference we come across when comparing the compositions of Goethe and Madách. In Goethe's poem woman is but an episode, as is Gretchen in the first part and Helena in the second. Gretchen is the love passion of man, his ideal of charm and beauty. Yet the couple, man and wife as bound up for ever, is not to be found in Goethe. The problem of woman is conceived out of the poet's personal experience. Faust is Goethe, the man standing by and for himself; woman is never on the same level as he is. Whether she is beneath him as a narrow reality or above him as a heavenly ideal, they are never really together. How far from that is the modern position of woman as found in the *Tragedy of Man.* Eve always falls or rises with Adam; whether beneath him or above him, she is bound up with him for eternity.

The dissimilarity between the two works will grow still greater if we consider the rôle of the Devil. Appearances were never more deceptive than in the case of Mephistopheles and Lucifer. Mephistopheles is simply the other side of Faust's soul, his earthly part, his opposite, in whom vulgar reality, lust, negation are incarnated. When facing God, this same Mephistopheles is but a poor devil of the middle ages who is quite happy that the Almighty enters into conversation with him.

Madách's Lucifer is entirely the reverse. Against God he is strong and resolute: the spirit of negation of all times, living from all eternity. In Paradise he is the serpent of the Bible. But on earth, throughout the scenes of Adam's dreams he lacks activity. Very often he is lost in long criticisms. This had always been observed and censured as a failure in the character of Lucifer, and indeed it cannot be denied. But, on the one hand, it was a consequence of Goethe's authority, and, on the other hand of his own, quite genuine imagination, and indeed part of the originality of the work. The *inactivity* of Lucifer through the historical dream-scenes has for its cause the fact that unconsciously, by the very lines of his own conception, Madách was compelled to replace the Devil by another earthly, dramatic factor which, as thus conceived, was wholly unknown at the time when Goethe wrote the second part of *Faust,* and that is the environment, the *milieu,* the antipodes of all great men. This opposite force, this counterpart is represented in a very dramatic way by Madách in the mass, the multitude, the mob.

So we have the man, the woman, and the mass as three earthly actors. The negation, embodied in the person of Lucifer when he is facing God, takes the shape of the mass against Adam, the great representative of mankind. Adam, the great Man, the exceptional personality is found in a continual struggle with the mass, with the common run of humanity which denounces him and degrades every noble idea, turning freedom into demagogy, living Christianity into barren theology, science into quackery and so on.

The scene in space, one of the grandest conceptions, is only to be regarded from this point of view. Man, with the utmost effort of his higher mind, wants to break away from his environment, but in vain; the Spirit of Earth recalls him to his own sphere. Man is unable to live beyond this sphere. He is to bear the struggle with that hostile force of the mass which always tends to overwhelm him, to break him down.

Woman—and this is an entirely genuine and original idea of the Hungarian poet—is placed between the man and the mass. She is elastic, and may always be formed and fashioned. The evil emanating from the mass, influences her more profoundly than it influences the great man. . . . But there is among others a turning point in the whole drama which definitely shows the fundamental dissimilarity of the two works. This is the moment when the woman outdoes the man and proves to be stronger than anything else. In Goethe's world-poem woman is but the man's love and dream, his sexual and æsthetic ideal. Gretchen, when she becomes a mother, strangles her baby. There are but few things in all world literature more poetical than the story of that girl-mother, but if we go to the bottom, this tragedy never rises above the *drame bourgeois*. To Madách motherhood appears as the great driving power of mankind. First it saves human society in the Phalanstery, when all masculine wisdom has proved a failure, and at the end of the drama it prevents Adam from suicide, and thus preserves mankind. It is here that Madách is at his best.

The *Tragedy of Man* is a peculiarly Hungarian piece of literature. Yet, as none of the historical scenes relates to Hungary (which is only once mentioned during the whole poem), the question arises, wherein the Hungarian origin of the poem is realised. The answer is very plain. The political problem which is the kernel of the work, is really the same national anguish and anxiety that are to be found at the bottom of so many Hungarian works of poetry. Madách's starting point had been the national struggle and agony of the fifties. As a young man, he wrote two national tragedies dealing with the problem of how the harmony of the people and its leader could be attained, how a people can become a nation and how a nation can exist. And there is one scene to be found in the *Tragedy of Man*, where this Hungarian undercurrent of the whole conception becomes very obvious. Miltiades, the pure and bold hero, stands at the block bending his neck to it when the first demagogue cries: "Let him be put to death! Long live our Fatherland!" There speaks the mock patriotism which—at that time—had spread throughout all Hungary. Thus the *Tragedy of Man*, the most universal drama of Hungarian literature, was fashioned from the fundamental political problems of Hungary. (pp. 397-401)

> *Alexander Hevesi, "Madách and 'The Tragedy of Man'," in* The Slavonic Review, *Vol. IX, No. 26, December, 1930, pp. 391-402.*

ERDMANN D. BEYNON (essay date 1931)

[*Beynon views* The Tragedy of Man *as a reflection of Madách's own religious struggle, relating scenes in the drama to events in Madách's life.*]

Madách Imre's masterpiece, *Az Ember Tragêdiája, The Tragedy of Man,* has proven for over fifty years one of the most successful dramas on the Hungarian stage. This strange poem, however, enjoys the distinction of being the only great philosophical work ever composed in the Hungarian language. Part of its popularity is doubtless due to the peculiar temperament of the Hungarian people. The chief reason underlying its success, however, is the fact that the Madách wrote from his heart and so appeals to our hearts, as one of his admirers remarked. This philosophical drama is more than philosophy or drama: it is the struggle of the author's soul out of the darkest night into which despairing man may be cast, back to the sunlight and a happy trust in God. Thus we find that the background for the drama is Madách's own life; and it was out of his own life's tragedy and the calamity which befell his nation that Madách came to feel the universal sorrow of mankind.

The marvel of his life and of his drama is that he could feel this common woe. Throughout his life fate seemed determined to prevent all contact between him and suffering humanity. He was born in an ancient feudal castle which had belonged to his family for centuries. Being his mother's pet child, he was shielded from the rough-and-tumble of school life and educated by private tutors. Owing to his wealth he was considered the social equal of the greatest lord in Hungary. During his declining years he was one of his country's most honored citizens. His drama brought him great fame in the literary world: at the same time his wealth and nobility made him a commanding figure in the Parliament to which he had been elected. Yet between the tranquillity of his youth and the serenity of his later years there lay in his life a period of such storm and stress as fairly well epitomized the struggle of mankind. During these years Madách fought a tremendous battle with despair and disillusionment and was victorious in the end.

The Framework of the Drama

Madách used the biblical stories of the Fall of Man and of the Trial of Job as the vehicle by which he sought to set forth his views of the world. Had his theology been more liberal, he would doubtless have chosen some other canvas on which to paint the experience of the race.

In Madách's treatment of the story of the Fall of Man, he reveals the cause of his own pessimism. He makes the desire for knowledge and for immortality only phases of a craving for independence. Why should man rely on God, when by disobedience he may assert his own independence and sovereign power? Yet through this proud defiance man loses not only his trust in God, but Eden also. The Adam of Madách's poem leaves Eden without regrets for lost happiness but with a stern, defiant resolve to struggle on and enjoy his newly found independence. As Adam struggled, so Madách himself also struggled—and failed. This failure caused his pessimism. So the problem of his life as of his drama was not to have God's ways explained to him but to find that peace which comes from a childlike trust in God. In Madách's maturer judgment the greatest loss which our first parents suffered was the loss of God's companionship and the utter loneliness which followed. "I look about me in the wide world and neither in heaven nor on earth is there one friend who might cheer or comfort us." At the same time when he wrote these words, he himself knew what that loss meant.

Madách came somehow to think of his own personal sorrow and disillusionment as typical of the misery of the entire human race. That there might be a continuity in his presentation, he represented the same man, Adam—the father of the race—as being reborn in every different age of the world's history. Though each rebirth brings Adam into entirely new and different surroundings, he seeks in every age to solve the one question, "Is Life Worth Living?"

Do Power and Glory Make Life Worth While?

In choosing those particular epochs of human history best fitted to represent the whole, Madách was influenced by the stages through which he himself had passed. While he was yet a County Clerk of Nógrád, his home shire, he had known what it was to strive for fame. That this aim might be more distinctly seen, he represented Adam, the universal man, as being reincarnated in Pharaoh, at that glorious period when the Fourth Egyptian Dynasty ruled the known world. With pride the Pharaoh surveys the toiling millions who build his pyramid to leave to posterity an undying memory to his glorious name. At the moment of his greatest triumph Lucifer appears with the sinister question, "Oh, Pharaoh, art thou happy?" The universal man, though sitting on the throne of Khufu, is forced to answer: "I am not. I feel a void unspeakable within me. Only let not the rabble guess my inward pain, for then they would cease to worship me."

Though hindered by the taskmasters, a wounded slave rushes in and dies at Pharaoh's feet with these bitter words upon his lips: "Why should slaves live? To carry stones for pyramids—to please the strong—and leave descendants for the yoke, and then—die: millions for the sake of one." The Pharaoh soon forgot the slave's words as he forced that very slave's beautiful wife to marry him. She called his attention to the wailing of the toiling multitudes. He replies: "Now for the first time have I noticed this unpleasant sound. Let us pay no more attention to it." Yet somehow he cannot escape from that cry of woe. The pain of the oppressed and enslaved millions finds a response in his own heart. Power and glory at the expense of others bring no happiness. We do not know whether Madách had any foundation for this episode in Egyptian history: but he had abundant foundation for it in the sudden awakening of the Hungarian aristocracy of his day to the woe and sorrow of the serfs.

Is the Patriot a Truly Happy Man?

Madách had not held his political office for any length of time before he became thrilled by that patriotic fervor which swept over Hungary before the Revolution of 1848. The serfs were to be emancipated and made the equals of the nobles in order that all together might struggle for a free democracy. Madách looked beneath the surface and saw the ingratitude of the emancipated throng. To illustrate this Madách chose as most typical of the rewards of patriotic sacrifice that episode in the Persian Wars in which Miliades, the hero of Marathon, was returning wounded and unvictorious from Paros. The Athenian masses had clamored for the general's death, but grew fearful as he returned with his army. So they slunk away after begging his pardon. Suspecting nothing, he dismissed his army. When the people realized that they had nothing more to fear, they renewed their plot and condemned the patriot to death.

Throughout this scene Madách ever shows himself the haughty aristocrat whose patrotism is dampened by the feeling that the common people are not worthy that a nobleman should suffer or die for them. This disillusionment led Madách to resign his political office in August, 1943, and to live henceforth, for a time at least, with no higher aim than the gratification of his senses.

The Life of Self-Indulgence

During the years which followed his abandonment of a political career Madách learned from experience the sweets of a life of dissipation—and its sorrows too. Though a Hungarian country squire had no opportunity for pleasure on a scale similar to that enjoyed by the gilded youth of decadent Rome, still Madách felt that there was something in common between a Roman banqueting hall of Catullus' day and the wild parties in which he himself had taken part. Adam, the universal man, is reincarnated in Sergiolus, a young and wealthy patrician. Madách pictured in boldest language the sinful pleasures of wild carousal. 'Gladiators fought and slew each other that the sight of blood might make the kisses of courtesans more sweet." Lewd songs in contempt of ancient Roman morals beguiled the young patricians as they lolled in the laps of their mistresses. This scene doubtless has many reminiscences of Madách's own life. (pp. 65-7)

The life of bodily indulgence had no comfort to offer in the hour of sorrow and death. Some think that the death of a dear friend called Madách back from this wild life. He realized that his craving for pleasure had defeated its own ends. "The despised slave, after his week of toil, enjoys an hour of pleasure. His satiated master craves for such pleasure in vain. Pleasure is a cool drink to the weary toiler, but death to those who plunge into its waves."

Does Christianity Fail to Satisfy?

As Madách turned in disgust from a life of sensual gratification, he felt that urge toward heroic action which has stirred the hearts of crusaders in all ages. He too would fight for the ideal of purity and noble manhood and for the cross of Christ. So Adam, the universal man, becomes Tancred, the flower of chivalry, the noblest knight of the First Crusade. Weary after their long journey he and his knights enter Constantinople, but no shelter is granted them there in the very capital of Christendom. The citizens flee from them, for they know only too well the rapacious cruelty of many who have masked themselves under the cross. Even some of Tancred's men pursue hapless maids across the city. Throughout this scene we find that Madách is using the story of the Crusaders merely to show a type of the evils prevalent in Christianity to-day. Yet his dissatisfaction was with the Christianity he knew. He never overcame his pessimism until he was able to look beyond the church to Christ himself.

Madách is guilty in this scene of a grave historical anachronism, for he makes the First Crusaders engage in the Arian Controversy which was fought six centuries before their time. He was seeking to point out the foolish strife among the different people who bear the name of Christ. . . . Under the figure of the Arian Controversy Madách sought to describe the struggles between Catholics and Protestants and every controversy in which through lack of love men have set at naught the Spirit of Christ. How modern this poem is when we see Modernists and Fundamentalists set in array against each other to-day! (p. 68)

[A] fault of the church as Madách knew it is the vow of chastity imposed upon a young and oftentimes unwilling girl at the behest of her parents. It led him to exclaim: "Oh, Holy Mother, thou embodiment of pure love, didst not thou turn in disgust from such an unholy promise which puts the stamp of sin upon thy virtues and makes the grace of heaven a curse?" Did Protestant ever condemn more strongly the vow of celibacy than has this Catholic whose work is still studied to-day in the Catholic schools of Hungary? Quite naturally we find the following foot-note in the Catholic School edition of this poem: "Madách has expressed in many places the power and worth of Christianity in its service of mankind. These criticisms are one-sided and were shown to Adam by the devil in an effort to discourage him." Yet one cannot read this canto without feeling that Madách's criticisms of the church he knew came right from his own heart. In his utter disillusionment he could find no solace in the church. Worldliness, controversy and persecution, the destruction of the most sacred things in the name of religion had left the church without the power to make life worth while.

The Calm Life of a Philosopher

Adam turns from the strife of crusading Christianity and seeks repose in the library of John Kepler, the renowned astronomer. Kepler's life at Prague as the favorite of the Emperor Rudolph seemed to Madách for a time to typify the happiest existence possible for man. His wife was the beautiful heiress, Barbara von Mühleck; he was able to spend practically his entire time in the study of astronomy and philosophy, while admiring disciples hung on his every word.

Madách himself had known something of that philosophic calm which it was Kepler's privilege to enjoy to the full. In the years which followed his own marriage to the wealthy Frater Erzsike, he had lived quietly on his country estate, enjoying the favor of his wife's uncle, the Lord Lieutenant of the County. His quiet life was wrecked by the catastrophe of the Hungarian Revolution of 1848. He himself was imprisoned; on his release he found that his wife had been disloyal to him. His calm life was forever ended; it became an apple of Sodom. In the poem Madách changes several incidents of Kepler's life to make them harmonize better with his own sad lot. The most crushing tragedy of all was the bitter realization that after all the years spent by him in the study of philosophy he still knew nothing at all. Madách's disillusionment is so great that he makes Kepler cry out: "All teaching is folly: all knowledge is mere guesswork." Indeed Madách came to believe that philosophy itself was dangerous; if perchance philosophic catch-words should begin to permeate the thinking of the masses. That is the meaning of the "vision within a vision" which Kepler sees, standing as Danton beside the guillotine in the early days of the French Revolution. The mobs are shouting "Liberty, Equality, Fraternity," and in the name of these philosophic concepts are dragging men and women to the executioner. In that gory tragedy Madách saw the failure of philosophy.

Modern Democracy

From the somewhat mediæval seclusion of his own country, Madách looked eagerly toward the democratic states of the West and believed for a time that in them true happiness would be found for man. Individual freedom and unhampered competition seemed the goal toward which the human race had striven. He placed his universal man, therefore, in that place where more than anywhere else in his day such a life might be experienced. From the Tower of London the reincarnated Adam descends, thrilled by the myriad voices of the metropolis. When from the street, however, he views the surging crowds at closer range, the process of disillusionment begins. True, all are free: everyone may do as he sees fit. Therefore, in practice the strong oppress the weak and rogues earn their living by cheating others. With an uncanny insight Madách presents the seamy side of city life: and his words apply as well to the American city of to-day as they did to the London of his day: "When self-interest rules both capital and labor and sets them in array against each other, what happiness re-

mains in store for man?" He contrasts the material and industrial success of this age with its spiritual failure.

At the close of this canto people of every class are represented as approaching the grave. The mask of insincerity falls off. Neither tricks nor cunning nor the strength to crush avail any longer. All alike feel a most bitter sense of failure in life. The rich manufacturer, for example, says: "I have amassed money, but my treasure has brought me no happiness." Those who have sought the pleasures of the day find in their last hour that pleasure has brought them only pain.

Madách held that the cause of all this failure is because self-interest has ruled in the lives of men. With a sure touch he points out the greatest weakness of modern democracy when he represents Lucifer as saying: "I have drawn out the master-screw which held together the entire machine. That master-screw was reverence for God. And I have neglected to replace it with something stronger."

The Rule of Science

Madách was convinced that the individual freedom and unlimited competition of democracy entailed too much wasted effort and could not be stable. Even in his day there were strivings after a greater efficiency than could be based on individual enterprise. He prophesied that the state of the future would be socialistic, in the sense that science would rule and that every individual would be compelled to follow not his own wishes, but the dictates of science. To some extent his prophecy has already been realized—partly in the Soviet Republic, with its attempt to make real those theories of which Madách had already heard, and partly in our modern factory system whereby individuals become mere cogs in the machine.

Madách's problem was to find out whether such a state of human society would make men happy. If science rules, then all individual ambitions and emotions must be checked. "In the factory the man who learns to make bolts makes bolts all day long." In the name of efficiency arabesques are abolished from the backs of chairs. "Such ornaments make them no more comfortable for the weary laborer to sit upon." Cheaper substitutes are found for the metals of the past. Sages spend their time seeking some substitute for the sun's declining warmth.

That science may rule, children are educated in institutions and taught only those things which they should know in order to become efficient members of such a state. A child's future occupation is assigned to it according to the shape of its head. Marriages are determined by professors of eugenics.

In this reign of efficiency human nature has no choice save to rebel. The mother fights to keep her child. Lovers defy the laws of eugenics. How could genius live in such a barren world as has banished patriotism, love of home, heroism and beauty— all in the interests of efficiency? To Madách it seems a dead world—dead to everything worth while. He saw that such a system can never endure nor satisfy the human soul. There is something in man's nature so great that "to make bolts all day long every day of his life means for him spiritual death."

The Degradation of Mankind

That the effects of materialism may be seen more clearly, Adam is transported to the land of the Eskimo, where materialism is seen in its naked reality. This scene was undoubtedly suggested to Madách because of the close relationship between the proud Magyar aristocracy of Hungary and the lowly Ostyaks and Voguls who live along the Ob and its tributaries in Siberia. What made the difference between the Magyars and these degraded savages who are the only people in the world closely related to the Hungarian by blood and language? Was it a mere difference in environment? True, the Magyars lived on the fertile plains of central Europe, while the other Ugrian tribes lived on wind-swept plains near the Arctic. Was it not rather a difference in ideals? The Magyars had suffered much, but they struggled on and upward. The Ostyaks and Voguls were content with the struggle for a livelihood. Thus they sank almost to the level of animals! Men who live without ideals will revert to this type, so Madách believed. To the degraded Eskimo nothing matters save the catching of seals. His sole prayer is that men may decrease and seals increase, that his stomach may be well filled.

Is There Any Escape?

After Adam has thus seen the whole of human history at its worst, he craves some way of escape. In his descendants he is doomed to struggle on forever and to fail always to gain happiness. Madách's soul can find no solace in the loss of all consciousness in Nirvana. "Without purpose ahead or obstacle to overcome, what avails a mere existence? Though a hundred times I fail to reach my goal, what matters that? The purpose still remains. To struggle for a purpose makes life worth while." Man may long for calm but his soul was made for struggle.

The realization of the impossibility of escape brings Adam to his knees even as it brought Madách himself. (pp. 69-72)

The Solution

Like the author of the Book of Job, Madách found the solution of life's problems not in having them explained to him, but in catching a vision of God. In the closing canto, the Lord is represented as addressing the awakened Adam thus: "Do not ask further for the secret which the hand of God hath mercifully hidden from thine eyes." Once Madách found God, he was content. The very keynote of the last canto is, "Trust in God." Madách's pessimism vanished as his new-found trust in God made right the other problems of his life. "What an imperial power is man's to have free choice 'twixt sin and virtue and yet to know that ever o'er him stands the shield of grace divine!" Man's life has been a failure only in so far as he has lived for himself or for unworthy aims. If he loses God's friendship, there is a void in his life which nothing else can fill. The tragedy of the world is because men have never fully abandoned themseves to God. Was Madách then a pessimist? Yes, but of the same type as Saint Paul, Saint Augustine, Kempis, Luther or Wesley, who saw life without God as absolutely bad, while life with God appeared the only worthwhile existence for a human being. The Tragedy of Man will be no more when men, to quote the last line of the poem, "struggle for the right and trust in God." (p. 72)

Erdmann D. Beynon, "The Conversion of a Hungarian Pessimist," in The Methodist Review, *Vol. CXIV, January, 1931, pp. 65-72.*

JOSEPH REMENYI (essay date 1950)

[*Remenyi discusses the reasons why he considers* The Tragedy of Man *one of the theatrical masterpieces of nineteenth-century Hungary.*]

The road Hungarian playwrights traveled from the 18th until the middle of the 19th Century was of necessity an arduous one, and Madách's achievement no mean one. What set him apart from his playwriting colleagues was the fact he was the first who could be classed as a philosophical dramatist comparable with western European playwrights who wrote in a similar vein. (pp. 7-8)

One cannot divorce Madách's work from his life. That he tried to further the culture of his nation, that he was politically active, that the means he used to achieve his civic goal were noble—all this shows him as a man of public spirited disposition, but does not tell us anything about the integration of his whole being through his dramatic art. What he was striving to do as a citizen is primarily significant because he is the author of a play in which philosophy and drama are welded together. Although the author of other plays, including comedies, and although he wrote essays and lyric poems, it is *Tragedy of Man* that justifies his literary reputation.

It is not an extravagant claim to say that—without seeking a facile ground for analogy—to discerning Hungarian critics and audiences Madách's name calls up immediately an image of a prominent author in the same sense that Byron's name awakens such an image in an Englishman, or Goethe's name in a German. Goethe's and Byron's influence is evident in *Tragedy of Man,* but without Madách's aping them. Some of this influence is hypothetical, as one senses the originality of a creator, and of a reflective individual who, while pondering over the subject of man's fate, turned to the medium of the drama in order to take an objective cognizance of his own fate. (p. 8)

The final reckoning with reality, which excites every real creator, characterizes the Hungarian author's work. Burdened with the question of good and evil, conscious of the lamentable conditions of his own existence, of his nation and of humanity as a whole, and endowed with a catholic taste, Madách wrote a play that is the cry of a soul tormented by loss of hope and inspired by a desperate yearning for hope, yet—despite its subjective undertone—it is a singular contribution to dramatic literature. . . . [His] dramatically presented striving for a focus in human destiny, without which a full understanding of the play would be impossible, was implicit in the personality of the author. His life, indeed, had a profound influence upon his writing. The knowledge of certain biographical facts is necessary for the interpretation of the psychological and ethical perspective of the play, which gives us a key to the virtues and defects of Madách's art, to his personal problems, to his perpetual unrest, to his need to find relief from tragic uncertainty. Touched and moved and terrified by the world about him and the world within himself, Madách proved that sincere creative work is a heroic attempt to obtain an adequate explanation for the purpose of life. This irrepressible romantic nostalgia for truth is a confession, a concern with the inward and external world into which the author wished to bring order out of chaos.

The mystery that shrouds every human life would have been intolerable for him had he not tried to establish a creative relationship between its darkness and its possible clarity. His play is a dramatic effort to seize the essence of things. The manner in which Adam, the central character of *Tragedy of Man,* struggles with destiny, his communion with everything that is significantly desirable or undesirable in human life, mirrors the author's fundamental emotional, moral and metaphysical problems. (pp. 9-10)

[Madách] was able to step outside of his own social class for a universal vista, which he could not have done without establishing a creative correlation between individual, national and human issues. As dying trees on a roadside may remind one of forests and wilderness in autumn, so Madách was reminded by his own hapless lot and by the tragedy of his nation of the plight of mankind. The play shows how he could shake off the shackles of Hungarian destiny. (p. 13)

Tragedy of Man reveals Madách as a "pessimistic idealist" or, perhaps, the adjective "tragic" would be more applicable to him. The question: "what is the objective of life?" is answered by pointing to struggle and faith as the principles of human dignity. . . . It took Madách a year to write the play, but it is reasonable to assume that before 1857 when, according to a letter written to Pál Szontágh, the idea appeared in his mind the first time, he was interested in the warring of the ideal with the real human's life. While the characters are in substance concepts, they are not sketchily drawn. As creative portraits, Adam, Eve, and Lucifer do not rank below similar characters in other philosophical dramas. In surveying the major and minor characters one feels that Adam's experience is a paraphrased autobiography of Madách's spiritual journey. The various individual, political and social references, if we are to understand their meaning, are dramatized projections of the affections, idiosyncrasies and hostilities that the author experienced in his private and public life. (p. 23)

The author did not look for a scapegoat for all the ills of mankind, but maintained that Adam—irrespective of whether he judges things clearly or is possessed by fog-shrouded uneasiness—represents a man who is expected to defend the cause of his individuality and the task of humanity against the destructive challenge of desolate and futile facts and events. Based on his personal experiences and on a vital interest in the ultimate, the problems Madách found worthy of attention and the issues that were at stake in human life on an objective plane are ingeniously interwoven in the 15 scenes. Adam thinks and feels with his whole self. His "Weltschmerz" forces him to take a stand on the issues of human fate, and to do this—while tempted by resignation and inertia—requires courage.

The intensity and tension of Madách's personality and life prevented him from being "an artist refined out of existence," as it has been said about certain *mal-du-siècle* creators; but it also prevented him from being primarily a creative writer esthetically, which made the counselling of János Arany, a master of the Hungarian language and of prosody, necessary. Arany retouched and improved Madách's style. It is, obviously, wrong to isolate form from content or to deny the importance of the coupling of technique with purpose. There has to be absolute unity in a tragedy, as in other artistic works. But regardless of Madách's inability to control his material with flawless artistry, and of the fact that sometimes one misses the perfectly attuned ear of the real poet, the general effect of the play is that of a magnificent and creatively realized experience. The consistent characterization of Adam is the unifying force that keeps the play together, and, in moulding the tempo of the plot, enabled the author to produce a work which fulfills the noblest human and literary anticipations of man.

Next to Adam the portrayal of Lucifer must be considered. . . . It would have been quite natural for Madách to moralize about Lucifer. Instead of succumbing to moralizing, however, he portrays Lucifer creatively as a fit opponent of the Lord, as one who never seems to be at his wit's end, even when the inscrutableness of the Lord regarding man urges Lucifer cynically to encourage Adam. In fact, when Adam, responding to the Lord, declares "he cannot forget the end," it seems that despite his willing submission to the Lord he is besieged by the negating spirit of Lucifer, by his illusion-shattering magic, although the influence is ineffective.

Through Lucifer one witnesses not only the assertion of the spirit of eternal negation trying to uproot Adam's belief in the purpose of life, but also, because of his incapacity to subdue Adam to his will, man's opportunity to be master of his destiny. (pp. 24-5)

Some critics object to Madách's "enforced optimism" at the climax of the play. They seem to overlook the author's "tragic idealism," that is to say, they respond only to his gloomy and morbid moods and neglect to observe that in practically each scene, without offering positive panaceas to humanity, Adam—torn by conflicting forces—suggests an affirmative position or a yearning for it. Is Adam's problem resolved in the final scene? It is fallacious to condemn Madách for failing to explain the "trust" advice of the Lord; there was no need for explaining it. Humility is an ingredient of man's totality, a recognition of one's limitations. Adam, in submitting to the Lord, admits his humility, and shows his awareness of the Lord's indefinable intent regarding man.

As in music, where tones are dependent on each other for meaning, so in *Tragedy of Man* ideas and ideals are dependent on each other for the purpose of accepting struggle and faith as the categorical imperative of man's microcosmic and macrocosmic destiny. Struggle, in fact, is faith in action. There is nothing irrelevant to the outcome of the plot. But as some people seem to hear the human voice only when it reaches them through a loudspeaker, there are those who seem to need a kind of symbolic loudspeaker for the understanding of the almost inaudible voice of the writer. While the plot in *Tragedy of Man* moves continually in a dramatic sense it also moves emotionally and ideologically towards the goal of a nonsentimental philosophy of fortitude. (p. 26)

Joseph Remenyi, "Imre Madách," in Bulletin: National Theatre Conference, *Vol. XII, No. III, November, 1950, pp. 6-26.*

CHARLES WOJATSEK (essay date 1961)

[*Wojatsek analyzes* The Tragedy of Man *in light of events in both Madách's life and Hungarian history at the time of the drama's composition.*]

[The] philosophical and moral ideas expressed in [*The Tragedy of Man*] contain eternal human values, and exercise a constant, timeless influence on its readers. Madách's expression of the truths of life, clothed in images of beauty and phantasy forms a philosophical system embracing the meaning of the moral, intellectual, and sentimental world, set forth in terms of a world drama. *The Tragedy of Man* has so universal a character that only its language reveals it as the work of a Hungarian poet, whereas with other Hungarian poets national literature and history are very closely connected ". . . patriotism can be the subject of poetry only among the Hungarians, where we fight for our existence." Western readers have seldom heard of Imre (James) Madách, the great poetic genius of the Magyar land, because Hungarian literature is little known abroad. Universal culture would lose much, however, if the literature of small nations were neglected. The study of Hungarian literature can show us its cultural propinquity to Western Europe, and the profound concern of Hungarian writers for significant contributions to the nation's and world literature.

Madách presents in fifteen scenes the fate of mankind through the historical ages, but his prophetic vision anticipates the unknown form of future society beyond the description of past and present events. In spite of the disillusionments of the two main characters, Adam and Eve, throughout the ages, their role is not desperate, nor is the conclusion pessimistic. The man represents the logical element, while the woman embodies the emotional life in this dramatic poem. Lucifer is not the demon of supernatural force but the personification of negation, that part of the human soul which opposes the Creator. He is the spirit of doubt, of proud reason and sophistry. Each personality lives his own life. Concerning the meaning of *The Tragedy of Man* Madách said: "The basic idea of my work seeks to establish that when man separates himself from God and acts on his own initiative, relying on his own strength he does so through the most sacred ideals of humanity. It is true that he fails in every direction and human fallibility is everywhere his destroyer, hidden in the innermost essence of human nature, from which he is not able to free himself (this would be in my view the tragic element), although he regards with despair the fact that his efforts were in vain, in spite of this he always proceeded, mankind made progress even if the struggling individual did not notice it, and human weakness which he was unable to overcome is replaced by the leading hand of divine providence, to which "struggle and have faith" in the last scene refers" [see excerpt dated 1862?]. These are the words of the poet about his own work. He explains with them briefly the significance of this dramatic poem, and he quotes the last sentence of *The Tragedy of Man* to prove the noble value of human life and efforts.

Who was Imre Madách, the poet, who donated *The Tragedy of Man* not only to Hungarian, but in a larger sense to world literature? In order to understand this dramatic poem we must know Madách's life and the main events in Hungary during his lifetime which may offer the key to the psychology of creation. The theme of *The Tragedy of Man* is concealed in the private life of the poet, in the political events of the time, but he outlines them in his other dramas too, such as the Roman scene in *Commodus;* in [*A férfi és nő*], the problem of Eve; in [*Mózes*], the relationship of a great man to the people. In distinction to the romantic Faust of the beginning of the century, *The Tragedy of Man* belongs to the social drama of the second half of the century. (pp. 210-11)

Madách made careful studies and preparation to become a dramatist. Besides Hungarian literature, he read Latin, Greek, French, Italian and German. He knew Shakespeare from German translations. Madách examined history, seeking answers on the mystery and striving of human life. He believed that life on this earth has meaning, and if this earthly life is imperfect, there has to be another world, where only the soul exists. Only by following ideals in life can we find spiritual and intellectual harmony. In hundreds of his other poems we retrace the ideas of his great dramatic poem, for he borrowed first of all from his own writings, thus clarifying and deepening his visions and reflexions and achieving an aesthetic expression of a system of philosophy.

The plot of his dramatic poem, *The Tragedy of Man,* the most significant work of Hungarian dramatic literature, opens in the heavens, where a choir of angels praises God as the possessor of power, knowledge and magnificence. In this harmony Lucifer stands alone as the spirit of disagreement and of materialism. In Paradise, beneath the tree of knowledge, Eve is tempted by Lucifer to pluck the forbidden fruit. The curious woman calms her conscience with her own logic, that sin is part of the Lord's plan. It is Eve's explanation to cover her fatal step, her disturbed emotions, it is Lucifer's diabolic plan

but not the fatalistic determination of the writer who does not believe in an inexorable enforced command of a superior power which controls the human will. After the expulsion from Paradise it is clear to Adam that he must face the hardships of life, and he accepts the challenge in the spirit of human reason. Adam petitions Lucifer for the promised knowledge—the foreseeing of his own future. Lucifer shows Adam in dreams, in visions, the road beset with violent strifes that mankind will have to pursue to the end.

The form of presentation is a dramatic poem which was not planned for the stage but is, rather, a philosophy of history in literary form. From the history of mankind the poet develops his own philosophical view of life, using selected visions. It is Madách's poetic talent to solve philosophical problems by artistic means. He tries to answer the deepest problems and follow the highest intellectual concepts through the main ideological movements of different epochs. According to A. Szerb, a Hungarian literary historian, Madách follows the sequence of a Hegelian philosophy of history: thesis, antithesis and synthesis. With the passage of the ages the fundamental idea in this drama also changes to egotism and collectivism. "Dreams have a great role in poetry. In the drama the dream calls up the avenging spirits of the past, in the epic it foreshadows the future world, and shows the way, giving encouragement to the hero. In *The Tragedy of Man* it fulfills the former function. The dream is a favorable invention which tolerates the loose and freakish connections of the imagination, and is appropriate for linking history with a projection of the future. The historical ages are depicted with realism, every scene is independent, and each is dramatically presented." Madách chose the ages wherein he could find the dominating ideas to serve his own goals with poetic license and with the eye of a philosopher. This dramatic poem is not a textbook of history. From the history selected by Lucifer—who guides Adam in his dream—we can see only those times which lead to crises. (pp. 213-14)

In ancient Egypt Adam, as Pharaoh, is not happy. He desires immortal glory, and has pyramids built by his slaves to commemorate his name forever.

> THE SLAVE: What does the serf live for? At the strong
> man's behest.
> He carries stones for the pyramid, and as soon
> as someone
> Can replace him under the yoke, he dies.
> Millions for one man.

The Pharaoh, inspired with love for Eve, the wife of a dead slave, elevates her to his throne. Now he understands the grievances of the oppressed. He discovers that his ambitions were only vanity; his body will remain merely a mummy. He then abandons everything—his throne, his love,—and looks for a new life of significance and endeavor. The subjugation of millions of people cannot be the goal of his future. Unrestricted ambition did not make Adam-Pharaoh happy, because it was Lucifer who directed the events.

> ADAM: Only the crowd must not suspect my anguish—
> If they should pity me, they would no longer
> worship me.

Adam clings to the concept of his divine rule, though he knows it is a falsehood.

The antithesis of this scene is the desire for a collective government, which would enable the ruler to work for the benefit of his fellow men. The transition is psychologically natural. We are in ancient Athens, in the homeland of a proud and free people, who fight for their freedom and believe it virtuous to die in the defence of their native land. Adam, as Miltiades the supreme commander, saves his city-state from the enemy: but, later, the ungrateful people, at the instigation of demagogues, condemn their hero-patriot. The presentation of the psychosis of the masses in Athens indicates the author's unique observation of human nature. (p. 215)

When Miltiades dismisses his troops, he stand alone, powerless against the debased feelings of the crowd. The common people are delighted at the downfall of the hero. Adam learns that the masses enslaved by misery and poverty become serfs in mind and spirit, and would follow any strong agitator. Miltiades asks himself if this is the reward of sacrifice for the common good. In his naïvete he believed that such people desired freedom. Disillusioned in his ideals, he condemns the populace. Pallas rescues Adam-Miltiades from execution and thus religion spoils Lucifer's triumph.

Following the Hegelian philosophy of history, we find the synthesis, or the answer to the first two stories in the life of decadent Rome, where there are no dominating individuals nor a strong common spirit, neither egotism nor altruism. The Romans no longer believe in those ideals which once helped found their empire. Adam becomes selfish and misanthropic. The pursuit of pleasure, cupidity, immoderateness, cruelty and voluptuous enjoyments characterized those times. Adam, as Sergiolus, drinks and lives an easy, thoughtless life, with women of loose morals. This mode of living does not satisfy him; he is disgusted by the orgies, and looks for new possibilities. He envisions the nobility of the soul, and the Apostle Peter tries to hint at the discovery of a new world. (p. 216)

After the scene of Rome, Madách does not continue to apply the three Hegelian principles, but henceforth develops the conflict of two other motives—the opposing ideas of individualism and collectivism.

Adam wants to see a better world where chivalry and gallantry are the leading ideals. Now the age of chivalry is examined from the philosophical point of view. The magnificent moral principles degenerate. This age excelled in the defense of the cross and of womanhood. Large masses of people were so spiritually moved that they were willing to fight and suffer for their faith. (pp. 216-17)

In the seventh scene Adam's misanthropy changes to philanthropy. As Tancred, he sees with sorrow, that the Christians in Constantinople, are divided among themselves, killing each other regardless of age and sex because of the letter "i". Tancred fails to understand the difference between the two teachings of "homousion" and "homoiusion," which has aroused such hate. Tancred, who became a crusader to defend sacred ideals, is forced to realize that humanity is not mature enough for Christianity. Weary, he no longer wants the responsibility of leadership. But Lucifer predicts that his spirit will not let him stay idle. The natural anti-picture of the leading Adam-Tancred is Kepler who desires only relaxation.

In the next vision it is made clear to Adam, as Astronomer Kepler at the royal court of Emperor Rudolf in Prague, that astrology is worthless. He himself does not believe in it, but his wife, Borbala, always wants money, so that he is compelled to continue that unscientific game to make a living. Adam starts to meditate grievously on that woman whom he once loved and would now like to divorce, but the authority of the church makes this impossible. Madách revealed his own feelings about women in this scene, Borbala being none other than

his own unfaithful wife who led a gay and reckless life even during her husband's imprisonment. He shows woman from every point of view: saint and sinner, nun and bawd, loving mother and voluptuous instrument. Adam wanted to live in a quiet age, but his vigour projects him into a dynamic future.

The next picture is a dream within the dream. The whole vision shown by Lucifer is a dream, and now Adam as Kepler dreams. When he awakes after dreaming he is again in Prague. This scene is the French Revolution. Adam as Danton in the midst of the Terror, falls in love with Eve, who is dragged to the scaffold: finally he too is executed. Man did not find happiness by overthrowing the existing social order and established faith, or by following the new materialistic teaching.

After this dream Madách takes us back to the court of Rudolf, where we are shown the destructive forces of marital infidelity, which made Madách himself unhappy, when his wife became alienated from him during his imprisonment by the government of Vienna for political reasons. Adam, as Kepler, confesses to his disciples that his science is false, and it is necessary to destroy all books which would hinder the development of the next generation. Adam yearns to go to a new world where the discontented human spirit may attain its eager desire for evolution. It is a diabolic thought that every human effort ends in failure to be replaced with a new evil. This is what Lucifer wants to prove.

After the quiet life of a scientist, Adam finds himself with Lucifer at a noisy market place in London where life is free and offers unlimited possibilities for advancement. People of different occupations and various views are passing in front of our eyes. We can observe the power of instinct on the people. Eve, coming from the church with her mother, represents the religious aspect of life. A gypsy woman predicts the future for Eve, and helps to bring her together with Adam. The mass psyche is demonstrated when the people of the streets succumb to their lower feelings at the sight of a laborer being taken to the scaffold for his revenge on a person who seduced his wife while he was in the hospital. Only in the London scene has Lucifer supernatural power, which changes the jewels on Eve's neck into snakes, and melts the money given to the gypsy woman into mercury. Everybody feels aversion to life as it is and wants to start anew. . . . (pp. 217-18)

Now we have arrived at the point where, with poetic genius, the vision of Madách introduces us to the future world, the Communist system of government which represents the total triumph of materialistic philosophy and the rule of force in public life. This social system could have been foreseen only by a poet of prophetic inspiration. We are in the phalansterian or collective society where every person is the equal comrade of every other and the sciences and knowledge watch over the state. Adam becomes profoundly absorbed in the study of the phalansterian system. In this scene the scientist shows Adam and Lucifer the past world, the values of which are forbidden to be taught. There is no romance anymore; even the nurse-maids instead of crooning, talk about higher equations and geometry to the babies. All individuality, all the arts are extinct; the forced laborers, the slaves, do their monotonous assigned task until the end of life; devoid of spirit, inspired by no goal and no ideal. We read about the scientific and technical development of the future society. The most inhuman scene comes when the numbered workers leave their working place, and their output is judged. Their provisions, clothing, further duties and punishments depend upon it. Individual success and personal achievements are unrecognized. In this system the children are taken from their parents, and are put in common boarding places. Adam falls in love with Eve, from whom her child is taken in spite of her frantic protest. Adam wishes to escape somewhere else from the inhuman society.

Adam yearns for higher regions far from earthly rubbish. He flies with Lucifer into space. Once he is separated from the earth, from his reminiscences, Adam is eager to return, having discovered that life is worthless without love and struggle. He is unable to escape from the earth: he wants to be happy there where he has lost so many battles. He hopes that a new ideal may emerge, which will be worth working for. After so many failures he believes, in spite of Lucifer's guidance, in the greatness and creativeness of the human spirit.

In the last dream of Adam, we find ourselves in the far north among the Eskimos. Their view of life seems narrow-minded to Adam. Lucifer wants to augment Adam's existing despair. Adam despises the life of the Eskimos—that coarse struggle for a dim existence, and he shudders with horror at the Eskimo woman, offered to him by her husband in conformity with their customs.

Adam would like only to live in the present, with no wish to foresee his destiny. He is no longer willing to oppose God's will. (pp. 219-20)

The author makes an attempt to answer the most mysterious problems of mankind, the endeavour and meaning of human life. Rational and striving man is accompanied during his life by woman as spouse, as ideal or unfaithful lover. In none of the ages has man found happiness. As Pharaoh, he did not find spiritual equilibrium in the thirst for power. When he saw the misery of that age, he wanted to rid himself of the immoral rule. In Athens, the hero who fought for the people is condemned by the masses from whom he can expect no gratitude. Decadent Rome is judged in the light of ethics. Mankind abandons Christianity because instead of living by the laws of love they wage wars. The scientist regards his own teaching as trickery. Free competition oppresses the weak, and in a controlled society man becomes a slave. (p. 221)

[*The Tragedy of Man*] has universal character, independent of time and place, and seeks an answer to the mystery of life. Every age has its values— this is Madách's social philosophy— which are honored by contemporaries, yet are always altering. The animating, the life-giving element of human happiness lies in the will's determined striving for progress. Lucifer, on the other hand, seeks to show that there is not a single achievement that can bring luck or satisfaction to human life. In this lies the dramatic and philosophic significance of the scenes. Lucifer's success is not permanent; Adam is never his captive. The action is played in front of our eyes, and the dream pictures are the basis for psychological unity. Adam fails in every age by following Lucifer's instruction, but he always has sufficient strength for a further display of force, which helps him in the end to overcome his previous pessimism. Man has free will, and is not the prisoner of Satan. Constant struggle and activity is a psychological necessity. Adam is enthusiastic about the progress of humanity. He does not work for his own interest. The question is whether the human race can go ahead or not. In Adam the problems of mankind, of the eternal man as well as those of an individual dramatic character, are united. (p. 222)

Undoubtedly *The Tragedy of Man* would be pessimistic if Adam could not see after so many failures and disappointments that human life is striving toward the attainment of its goal. We must trust in the victory of an ethical order, and exert our best

Madách seated in a chair.

abilities for the reign of the noblest ideas on this earth. The exalted view of life makes Madách's work immortal and part of the common treasure of the human intellect, in spite of the difficulty of access to it, imposed by the Hungarian language.

Adam is the representative of reason, who looks for the causes of effects, ponders the consequences, and controls his passions. Determined to give purpose to life, he searches for ideals. We have seen another Eve in the different scenes, not the continuation of the old character. She does not interfere with the fate of Adam, who has his own separate dreams. He remembers the previous life, but we see a new Eve in every dream-picture, because it is psychologically impossible that two people could have the same dreams. The real combat is between Adam and Eve, Lucifer being the attendant only, the spirit of doubt, the satan of cold logic. The author expresses his most intimate feelings in this work, his personal and national tragedy. Without his unfaithful wife, Elisabeth Fráter, we would not have had *The Tragedy of Man*. The scene of the French Revolution and the rule of brutal power refers to the ruthless oppression of Hungarian independence in 1849 by the Habsburg dynasty and the Russian Tsar. In the subconscience of the author there is always the renewed and defeated, unhappy and endless struggle for an independent and integral Hungary. According to Madách's philosophy of life the forces of nature regulate the universe and similarly the moral law which is inherent in our human soul, in our conscience, rules our deeds. Madách stands on the basis of moral philosophy, and accepts the moral law as obligatory for human actions. (pp. 222-23)

Charles Wojatsek, "The Philosophical and Ethical Concept of 'The Tragedy of Man'," in Études Slaves et Est-Europénes, *Vol. VI, Nos. 1-2, Spring-Summer, 1961, pp. 210-27.*

ISTVÁN SÖTÉR (essay date 1964)

[*Sötér seeks to demonstrate that* The Tragedy of Man *is a "great synthesis" of nineteenth-century Hungarian culture and history.*]

The Tragedy of Man is a dissembling, secretive, enigmatic work of Hungarian literature. The fruit of the critical decade following the suppression of the 1848 War of Independence, it was written in the months between February 1859 and March 1860. This period was marked by equally profound political and ideological crises. Almost ten years had gone by since the failure of the Hungarian revolution when Madách began to write *The Tragedy.* The nation had not yet recovered; on the contrary, under the stress of Austrian oppression its moral reserves began to be depleted.

The revolutionary generation had grown up in an enthusiastic belief in ideas, in an absolute confidence in progress, in the cultivation of virtues and activities for the common weal developed by the enlightenment and nourished, even filled with dreams, by the romanticism and liberalism of the first half of the century. The downfall of the 1848 movements in itself forcibly belied the confidence and the day-dreams of this generation. Grand and inspiring ideas were not realized at a single stroke but, in reality, were seen to turn into their own contradiction; their brilliance was sullied by blood and mud, and man, claimed by romanticism to be a demi-god, was proved to be a feeble, fallen hero by history. History and revolutions are shaped by the will and spirit of the masses, but their motion is like that of the sea: the tide is always followed by ebb. *The Tragedy of Man* was produced at such a low water mark of time. Its poet stood on a deserted shore, feeling hopelessly lonely.

To the bitter historical experience another equally disillusioning experience was added. The generation reared on idealism was faced by a new trend in philosophy, the mechanical materialism triumphant in Germany. Buchner, Moleschott and their associates declared themselves for a crude and extreme materialism (of which Marx and Engels openly disapproved), and this materialism, enraptured by the achievements of the revolution in the natural sciences, had summary, apparently final answers to the most intricate philosophical problems. The soul was an illusion, ideas no more than smoke, morality an invention, and, what was still worse, man, the slave of circumstances, with his fate determined by blind material forces, figures, statistics and natural conditions, could do nothing to alter his lot. The generation of 1848 lost its bearings not only because of political developments; its ideological foundations had also been crushed. It was impossible to disregard the triumphant achievements of the revolution in the natural sciences; and, at first glance, these achievements seemed to confirm the theses of the mechanical materialists.

Hence the historical and philosophical crisis looming in the background of *The Tragedy of Man.* In the eyes of the dramatist it was aggravated by his personal crisis, by the wreckage of his unhappy marriage; happy love was condemned to bitter destruction. Moreover, how many dead, how many victims in his own family: a brother, a sister with her husband and children, all had lost their lives amidst the terrible ordeals and vicissitudes of the War of Independence. *The Tragedy* presents the history of mankind in dramatic vignettes, from the Garden of Eden, the history of Egypt, Athens, and Rome, through the imagined future phalanstery, to the cooling of the earth; behind this series of pictures, however, one must inevitably sense the tension produced in Madách's mind by his ideological and personal crises. Without it the series of historical pictures constituting *The Tragedy* would wane into a mere scholastic spectacle, because this hidden tension released in the poet deep intellectual, moral forces and a desire to resolve the crises—a desire that imbues the work with a painful, concealed lyricism, a nostalgia for the lost Garden of Eden.

The Tragedy of Man consistently presents scenes of failure and downfall. It belongs to the most profoundly pessimistic works. However, its true meaning lies in the poet's refusal to accept this pessimism, for the more merciless historical facts become, the more desperately he seeks to refute them. Refutation grows almost arbitrary, even senseless, but this only serves to render the wish for refutation still more violent and urgent. The generation bred on idealism and romanticism had to recognize the bitter lessons of history, the annihilation of dreams, and the doubts assailing beliefs and ideas. This recognition made the former enthusiasts adopt a contrary attitude: they became unbelievers and sceptics. Yet no more at home in their new scepticism than in their old enthusiasm, they came to wonder whether they should not return to their former happy beliefs, to their unsuspecting daydreams, to their old hopes attached to action. The world around them had changed, and so had they. In looking for something beyond enthusiasm and doubt, they were endeavouring to find something new, some reassuring explanation, some acceptable encouragement and an attainable harmony. This was the dialectical process of thoughts and emotions that took place in the minds of the quondam romanticists and idealists who had lived through the revolution. The same dialectical process animates *The Tragedy of Man* and turns it into a drama.

One hero of *The Tragedy* is Adam, who always believes unconditionally and is therefore invariably doomed to defeat, as were Madách and his generation. The other principal hero, Lucifer, has faith in nothing and doubts everything, therefore his spirit remains barren. Lucifer differs from Adam only in so far as he regards the repeated downfall and failure of Adam as a fixed law of life and its conditions. After suppressed revolutions the two extreme, polarized attitudes are not infrequently encountered: unconditional belief, on the one hand, and absolute scepticism and disillusionment on the other. In the closing scene of *The Tragedy* the Lord pronounces the moral that mankind needs both views: an abstract creed leads to inertia, because it is immobile and mere conjecture, like a theory that cannot be put to practical test. Doubt and denial may become the motive power, the leaven of a new creed and new activities. All this may, of course, be applied in the reverse order. Human virtue is hampered by fallibility, but the latter is sometimes apt to bring rescue from the blind and destructive exaggerations of virtue. Man is often saved by his own character, or by Nature, from the abstract and speculative, hence negative and harmful, exaggerations of his own ideas.

This escape, this protection conferred by failure, this support offered by weakness, this realism opposed to abstraction, is embodied in Eve, the third figure of *The Tragedy.* From the blind alleys of over-zealous belief and crude denial we can escape only along the path opened by the often underestimated reserves of human nature. In his disappointment and despair Adam wants to commit suicide, but Eve's motherhood makes suicide senseless and impossible. The personality of Eve thus intervenes in the sterile debate of belief and denial, rendering it fertile. Eden was lost through the frailty of Eve; however, only Eve is capable of recreating something from what has been forfeited. Here lies Eve's absolute superiority over Adam and Lucifer, and this was Madách's final effort to refute history by factors lying outside history.

The dialectical process taking place in the minds of the generation that had lived through the revolution was thus revived in the dramatic dialectics of the three principal figures of *The Tragedy.* (pp. 56-9)

Of the fifteen scenes of *The Tragedy,* the first three and the last constitute the framework, with the three principal characters (Adam, Eve and Lucifer) appearing in a biblical background. The first scene, in "Heaven", opening with a debate between the Lord and Lucifer, is undoubtedly reminiscent of one of the prologues to Faust; superficial readers have therefore shown a tendency to regard the whole Tragedy as an imitation of Faust. As a matter of fact, *The Tragedy of Man* fundamentally differs from Goethe's great work in conception and characterization alike. In form it certainly belongs to the populous family of verse dramas which, evidently inspired by Faust, flourished in the romantic period of the 1830's and even earlier in the works of Byron, then Lamartine and de Vigny, Andersen and Mickiewicz. . . . (p. 62)

In the scenes constituting the framework of the drama, Lucifer steps on the stage as the personification of denial and doubt. Madách put into his mouth the ideas of mechanical materialism, so much so that in the London setting, the phalanstery and the Eskimo scenes, several ideas and passages of Ludwig Bücher's popular book on mechanical materialism entitled *Power and Substance* can be clearly discerned in the stage tirades. In the so-called historical sequences the dramatic nature of Lucifer's figure loses vigour; he appears only as the companion of Adam, volunteering malicious comment on the events, since the failures of history furnish sufficient confirmation to vindicate his attitude.

The simple action of *The Tragedy* consists of eleven dream pictures evoked by Lucifer to show Adam the whole fate and history of Humanity with the intention of making him turn away from God in despair. These historical scenes incorporate all the ideas that had thrilled the young and liberal Madách and his generation to enthusiasm, ideas that had failed one after the other, either in earlier centuries or in the poet's own lifetime. Belief, disenchantment, disgust and flight, then again a new creed: successive dramatic situations, with Adam in the centre, reborn in every age, as historical periods follow one another.

In Egypt Adam appears as a Pharaoh who burns for freedom as did the Hungarian liberals, giving his slaves their release as did the latter their serfs. In the Athens scene he steps forward as Miltiades, who recoils both from the fickleness of the crowds and from demagogy, as Madách may have recoiled from the passions and excesses of the 1848 revolution. Adam, disappointed, reappears in imperial Rome as Sergiolus; disillusionment here seeks forgetfulness in hedonism, as did the generation beset by the *mal du siècle,* to which Madách belonged. Idealism is unable to do without illusions for any length of time and Adam pins his new hopes to christianity, again to be disappointed at Byzantium as Tancred. It is here that Eve, made unattainable to him by the grimly austere religiosity of the age, conjures up the memory of Eden with irresistible force. Their conversation is one of the most lyrical parts of *The*

Tragedy, tersely summing up the emotions that animated Madách's earlier poems.

> Dost not thou fear to gaze into the night
> That like a mighty heart with love does beat,
> When we, we only, are forbidden to love?

The stakes at which heretics are burnt reflect a lurid light on the tragedy of love associated with historical tragedy, and these stakes still blaze in the next scene, Prague, where we see our disillusioned Adam as Kepler, at the court of the emperor Rudolf. In Rome disappointment had plunged him into a life of pleasure; here it leads him to the asceticism of science. However, the age has no need of science and yearns after superstition instead. The future is revealed to the embittered Kepler—a dream within a dream—with the promise of the French Revolution, and Adam appears as Danton. From here too Adam must flee, back to the dream picture of Prague; this is the only historical scene which Madách does not make his hero reject. (pp. 62-3)

From history *The Tragedy* now steps into the present of Madách. A bustling fair is seen outside the Tower of London, presented as a symbol of established capitalism. The heart that has known Eden cannot experience happiness here either, and the dance macabre episode round the grave closing the fair echoes some of Madách's most personal lyric poetry. Eve is the only one to pass unharmed over the grave, for the power of "Love, poetry and youth" is not vanquished by death. . . . Adam flies into space to get away from earth, the scene of his torments and disappointments, but he is called back by the Spirit of the Earth, to face fresh torture and disappointment. In the next-to-last scene he sees the cooled globe with its last, remaining inhabitants who live the indigent lives of Eskimos. This is followed by the final scene of attempted suicide, the revelation of Eve's motherhood, and the enigmatic encouraging oration of the Lord closing the depressing series of failure and disappointment by calling on Adam:

> O, Man, strive on, strive on, have faith; and trust!

After such a uniform sequence of defeats this encouragement sounds almost like mockery. There have been critics who maintained that this last line was added by Madách to the words of the Lord as an afterthought, quite arbitrarily. However, it closely follows from the fundamental idea of *The Tragedy* and is actually prepared by the series of failures. Madách was unable to accept either natural or historical determinism. In *The Tragedy* the three principal figures represent three attitudes. Belief, denial and fallibility each separately may exercise useful as well as harmful functions: all that draws Adam away from the abstract quality of his ideas at the same time saves and preserves him. Belief both lends him strength and becomes his greatest weakness. However, in "created" reality, represented by the Lord, the three attitudes coincide, completing, balancing and aiding one another. The beginning of *The Tragedy* was dominated by monotonous celestial harmonies; this harmony, disrupted by Lucifer and mankind, is restored in the last scene: belief is as necessary as doubt, but the peculiar, "independent view" of Nature (Eve), serving its own ends, is still more important. This interdependence implies a modest encouragement, a carefully concealed confidence, which, owing to its dim, latent nature, may be pronounced only in the last words of the Lord, as if he himself had been hesitating, but could finally not resist pouring into words that which he only permitted to be guessed at before. (pp. 64-5)

From the close of the 18th century, the period of enlightenment, Hungarian literature unfolded in several waves, and *The Trag-*

edy of Man may be conceived as the summit of one of these waves. As with the literatures of many other small peoples, the aim of Hungarian literature was to establish a national bourgeoisie. To become modern, to express the ideas pervading the educated world, as did the literatures of the literate peoples of Europe, to tell of mankind all that could be told only by a Europe with a conscious and refined civilization, such were also the objectives of Hungarian literature. (p. 65)

By the middle of the 19th century, before the 1848 Revolution, the demand for a national character and a modern bourgeois message became . . . [very] urgent. In this period literature exhibited a deeper desire to become national and popular than it had in earlier eras, together with the wish to appeal to humanity. A union of the nation and of mankind, a simultaneous treatment of these two elements, was the highest ambition of the poetry of this period. This ambitious effort was personified by the poetry of the two greatest Hungarian poets of the mid-century, Petöfi and Arany. Madách was their contemporary, and he profited from them as much as from their romantic predecessors, particularly Vörösmarty, who also endeavoured to be national while addressing himself to humanity. The starting point of *The Tragedy of Man* was the national crisis; but the horizon embraced by the work reaches out to the fate of mankind.

Madách's work is a great synthesis of the doubts, meditations and hopes of an epoch; it summarizes all the concepts and creeds that were alive in the writer's age. It also represents the achievements of over half a century's progress in Hungarian literature. The demand for a national character and the appeal to folk poetry sometimes resulted in isolation. To be national occasionally involved turning one's back on the wider world; indeed, there have been periods when Hungarian poetry and Hungarian culture showed a tendency to wrap themselves up in outworn jingoism. Such an isolation is fraught with deadly dangers: the smothering of forces, a sinking into indolence and self-satisfied, smug provincialism.

Madách cut through the isolating wall which a narrow populist and national cult might have raised around Hungarian poetry. He voiced the persevering and unselfish endeavours of Hungary's best writers in addressing himself to the whole of mankind. (pp. 65-6)

> *István Sötér, "Imre Madách's 'The Tragedy of Man',"*
> in The New Hungarian Quarterly, *Vol. V, No. 16,*
> *Winter, 1964, pp. 56-66.*

ESTHER H. LESÉR (essay date 1978)

[*Lesér discusses the influence of the Western intellectual tradition on* The Tragedy of Man, *comparing it with works by Johann Wolfgang von Goethe and Georg Wilhelm Friedrich Hegel.*]

For someone desiring an objective insight into the Hungarian mental climate, Imre Madách's *Az ember tragédiája* is an ideal choice. Its translation into various languages has proved its wide appeal, and Hungarian scholars have acclaimed it as one of the masterpieces of their country's literature. This work conveys the spirit of the Hungarian *Geist* admirably, while simultaneously it reflects Western European cultural trends. It typifies, to some extent, Western literature involving one nation's absolute rule over another with an independent cultural heritage of its own. Both intellectually and spiritually, Hungary has belonged to a Western world which seldom thought of it as a member of its cultural body. This study will attempt to show that Hungary has been part and parcel of Western culture for some time, by analyzing the connections linking Madách's *Az ember tragédiája*, Goethe's *Faust*, and Hegel's "Vorlesungen über die Philosophie der Weltgeschichte." (p. 43)

At first glance, the work resembles a Faustian tragedy. Elements of the God/Devil/Man perspective; the theme of human striving; Man's relation to Woman; Man's wandering through the universe; as well as God's positive intervention at the end, all seem to indicate that the work was structured on the model of Goethe's *Faust*. Indeed, Madách did not hesitate to adapt materials from other authors. The heavenly choruses; the jewel motif in the London scene; the secondary plot of Lucifer and Eve analogizing Mephistopheles' and Martha's scenes, are indeed all derived from Goethe's *Faust*.

Close examination reveals, however, that these similarities pertain mainly to setting and method of presentation rather than to substance. Madách's concept of the theme and expression of his messsage differed greatly from Goethe's. First, the *Weltbild*: in *Faust*, the three-dimensional God/Man/Devil trilogy closely resembles the central concept of a mystery play. God is obviously omnipotent and omniscient regarding His creations, incuding Man, and even Mephistopheles. But Mephistopheles is a higher creation than Man; he has wider insight than Faust; Mephistopheles is the catalyst who challenges Faust's free will. In Goethe's work, Faust's surviving capacity for love is of the greatest importance, whereas Mephistopheles has rejected love and is thus incapable of love, God's principal quality. (p. 45)

In *Az ember tragédiája*, after the introductory chorus of the angels, the scene between God and Lucifer reveals a basic difference between Goethe's and Madách's work; here Lucifer is . . . actually one of the components of God's nature itself; Lucifer's existence is the negative aspect of the Divine. God's responses to Lucifer are rather unconvincing arguments. He appears as an oppressive, absolute ruler rather than as an omnipotent Lord. Lucifer defines his own nature. . . . (p. 46)

Lucifer's negative, cynical character and his spirit of rebellion in many ways parallels Adam's—and/or Madách's—view of the world. . . . Since Lucifer represents negation and is part of an original element of the universe, his significance is quite different from that of Goethe's Mephistopheles. Madách's Lucifer represents a dialectic antithesis to God the ruler, having an equal chance to rule the synthesis of the outcome of existence.

The yearning of the two heroes also bears examination: Goethe's Faust is an elderly scholar who has learned all he could from books, yet who yearns to learn more. . . . No marvel may ever overshadow Faust's God-given capacity to strive; in each phrase, Faust's striving, however unconscious, encompasses the three dimensions of God's Universal Creation.

Since Faust was a human and an earthling, Goethe did not have to make his God face the embarrassment of being betrayed by man in Paradise, and so Faust never rebels against God directly. Madách's Adam, however, was full of ambition for knowledge and eternal life. His eagerness was so intense that Madách failed to invest Eve with her traditional role as temptress. Like a rebellious Prometheus, Adam grasps the apple, the first tool of independence, without intending to share it with anyone, not even Eve. He desires self-identity, and the right to live or die as he wishes; he never repents his sin against God; all he demands from Lucifer constantly is his rightful share of wisdom.

Here, the traditional God is crippled by the existence of Negation (Lucifer), and is consequently half disabled in all his manifestations. Actually, Adam's character stands closer to Negation (Lucifer) than to God, because of his desperation over his own limitation as a man. He is unable to give or to receive love before having achieved self-liberation. (pp. 46-8)

Adam's desperate struggle must be carried on, chaining him to an endless earthly existence because, limited by the hopelessness of his task, he stubbornly focuses upon the sole issues of self-liberation and identification. This passionate desperation has much in common with Lucifer's, except that Adam is not pure negation, as Lucifer is. Hope, even against all logical odds, remains a dialectically extant possibility for Adam. Goethe's *Faust* therefore offers a conclusion, a restful final message, whereas Adam's restless spirit is constantly present on earth, dramatically pursuing his yearning.

Madách's Eve does not parallel Adam's qualities. Representing the fluctuation of the human mob, she declines into subhumanity in scene 14 with the rest of mankind. (p. 48)

The formal presentations of *Faust* and *Az ember tragédiája* are similar; the protagonists wander in the universe with the "Siebenmeilenstiefeln" of the Romantics, and the reader is able to visualize the message of each actor by the various episodes. Goethe retains neither chronology nor historical authenticity in his scenes. He maintains the same limitless focus as does the whole God/Mephistopheles/Faust complex. The logical and historical chronology of the visions in *Az ember tragédiája* focuses upon its own hidden message, which is completely unrelated to and even unconcerned with the universal message of Goethe's *Faust*.

Madách's depression over personal and national problems, combined with his reading of Hegel, especially the "Vorlesungen über die Philosophie der Weltgeschichte," reinforced his ideal about the unification and liberation of a nation through a strong leader. But he did not accept Hegel's notion of the leader's loss of individuality by immersing it in the *Volksgeist*. A summary of these Hegelian concepts is germane here:

> Kant's Republic of Wills, the English concern with individual rights—all this betokens for Hegel the fragmentation that is the death of a culture. . . . Individualism is for Hegel a symptom of a nation's decline.

> The greatness of a nation begins with its unification as a nation—that is the only way it can acquire a *Volksgeist* with which to participate in the development of World-Spirit. Such a unification is possible only with a strong leader . . .

Madách's refusal to accept Hegel's formulations completely was expressed throughout his entire life and work. One Hegelian point he found most incompatible was the rejection of Kantian individualism. This is indicated very strongly in the phalanster scene of *Az ember tragédiája*. Whereas for Faust people gain importance in his last moments of life, Adam is intensely involved with people in all scenes, from four through fourteen, and he strongly expresses his disdain for the mob. Adam's feelings here echo Madách's own, since he and his friends felt paralyzed in their attempts to help their people owing to the lack of popular support. (pp. 48-9)

Some Hegelian concepts were nonetheless deeply rooted in Madách's mind; he preferred the qualities of the crowd to the virtues of the leader, in terms reminiscent of the Hegelian dialectic. This pattern gives meaning to scenes four through fourteen, as well as to his concept of the triangularity of the God/Lucifer/Adam relationship. . . . (p. 49)

Madách sees that "küzdés" (struggle), having the goal of "haladás" (progress), ultimately equals "szabadság" (liberty). . . . Whereas Goethe, the Westerner, permitted his Faust to consume his entire existence by traversing the three dimensions of the Universe, Madách, the Hungarian freedom fighter, knew that such an approach would be aimless before attaining the initial platforms of self-identification and self-liberation. Thus he dispatched his Adam on an aimless, paradoxical earthbound life-voyage, with only the words of a distant God to sustain him. . . .

After writing *Az ember tragédiája,* Madách became more hopeful. His last work, *Mózes,* showed a more conciliatory mood to Hegel's concept of the hero. . . .

Madách was a poet of ideas, but not a philosopher; a romantic with a powerful sense of realism; and a Western European intellectual continually striving for freedom. To grant him his identity as belonging to the West, means to understand in part the prototypical "Hungarian Tragedy." (p. 50)

> *Esther H. Lesér, "A Hungarian View of the World, Expressed in a Faustian Tragedy: Some Considerations upon Madách's 'The Tragedy of Man'," in* The Canadian-American Review of Hungarian Studies, *Vol. V, No. 2, Fall, 1978, pp. 43-51.*

DIETER P. LOTZE   (essay date 1981)

[*In the following excerpt from his full-length study of Madách's life and works, Lotze examines the author's minor writings, including his poetry, prose tales, and dramas. For additional commentary by Lotze, see excerpt dated 1983.*]

Without *Az ember tragédiája,* it is not likely that the lyricist Madách would have attracted much critical attention. As it stands, some of his poems are rightly regarded as important preliminary studies for his play, and others are valued for the insight they give into the writer's soul. As a record of his emotional reactions to events in his own life and in the life of the nation, they add up to a remarkable interior autobiography.

The love poems in *Lantvirágok,* inspired by Madách's feelings for Etelka Lónyay, reflected a romantic view of love and the tendency to go from personal experience to more general concepts. The romantic glorification of love as a universal force holding the world together is still quite clear in the "Vadrózsák" (Wild Roses) cycle, probaby written in 1845 and dedicated to [his wife]. The thought already expressed in his play *Commodus* is now stated most strikingly: "The sacred chain of love is the universe, / And in it, we, too, are a tiny particle." The lover becomes part of this eternal force. The initial period of marital bliss led to poems expressing the fulfillment of love and the quiet happiness of domestic life. . . . (p. 34)

Madách's commitment to the cause of liberty was unconditional. "Költő és szabadság" (The Poet and Freedom) speaks in epigrammatic conciseness about this engagement. He violently opposed the willingness of some of his compatriots to accept a compromise with Austria after the war. "Csak béke, béke" (Only Peace, Peace) castigates those who are already negotiating peace while the graves of the heroes fallen for freedom are still bare and wounds are still bleeding. His indignation over the faint-heartedness of those who do not realize that the "peace" they desire is death becomes a statement of general philosophy that will be expressed in very similar terms in *Az ember tragédiája:* "Life is struggle, rest is death; / Even if there is a thunderstorm in the summer sky, / What are you afraid of?" **"Síri dal"** (Grave Song) vows in Petőfi's spirit the continuation of the war of liberation as the fight against despotism. From the struggle for Magyar liberty will spring the fight for world freedom.

Much of Madách's patriotic poetry—as well as his love and nature poems—is Romantic in spirit. But some of the works inspired by the war, such as the miniatures of military life in the cycle **"Tábori képek"** (Camp Images), are unsentimental and do not idealize the real world. In some other examples the poet, in describing landscapes or scenes from everyday life, emerges as a lyrical Realist. **"Ősszel"** (In Autumn) offers an idyllic but factual description of a rural estate and its denizens in their normal activities. **"Alföldi utazás"** (Travelling in the Great Plains) contains some stanzas that skillfully sketch the landscape of the region. **"Egy nyíri temetőn"** (In a Cemetery in the Nyír District), probably written in 1845, starts with a strikingly modern depiction of the desolate scenery with its bleak sand, hill next to hill like a field of graves; a stagnant pond below; and above, dressed in white, lonely birches rising up.... But—as in several other poems—this tone is not sustained throughout: the powerful images of reality soon give way to abstract thoughts and philosophical generalizations.

One of Madách's most successful lyrical creations is **"Dalforrás"** (Fountain of Song) which shows the influence of Petőfi's "Dalaim" (My Songs) although the message is quite different. In his poetry—as in his dramatic works—Madách made no attempt to hide the inspirations that had come from others, probably because he was sure of his basic originality of thought and emotion. **"Dalforrás"** seems to reflect the short time in the poet's life when he had found peace with himself and the world. It blends the Romantic longing for harmony with nature, pantheistic ideas, and patriotic feelings in a unique way, and its use of language and form is skillful. The middle of each stanza has the refrain-like repetition of the phrase, "I do not even know how far my soul reaches" and the expression of the sensation of unity with "the sun's light," "dawn," "the quiet night," "the mist of the pale autumn," and "the clouds of tempest." Surprisingly, the conscious interruption of this evocation of harmony between man and nature through the introduction of the theme of love of country does not seem inappropriate.

Many of Madách's philosophical poems touch on ideas and themes that later find their ultimate expression in *Az ember tragédiája*. **"A nő teremtése"** (The Creation of Woman) presents Lucifer as the rebel, and **"Az első halott"** (The First Death) deals with man's early sinfulness and outlines the function of womanhood that the Lord later describes to Eve at the end of Madách's drama. A recurring theme in these poems is the loss of the original harmony, and man's isolation and alienation. In **"Ó-és újkor"** (Old and New Times) the poet follows the example of Kölcsey and Arany in contrasting the world of harmony and joy of classical Greece with later times that brought only pain and unrest to humanity. But usually there is no such clear reference to a specific idealized period in history. It is the loss of Paradise, the loss of the original unity with God and nature that is mourned in the longer of the two poems with the identical title **"Hit és tudás"** (Faith and Knowledge). (pp. 35-6)

Madách's poetry as a whole reflects a sensitive and thoughtful author, aware of the literary trends of his period but searching for his own mode of expression; a man occasionally savoring joy and contentment but often given to gloomy despair; a patriot never wavering in his commitment to the cause of national freedom but deeply grieved by the events of his times; an individualist with the tendency to generalize from his personal experience; a Romanticist looking at reality; a lyricist on his way to writing a dramatic masterpiece.

Critics seem to agree that Madách's five prose tales represent the least successful aspect of his literary production.... They are marred by complicated and sometimes unclear plots and melodramatic effects, by poorly developed and unbelievable characters, and by a graceless prose style. There is surprisingly little evidence of artistic growth between **"Duló Zebedeus kalandjai"** (Zebedee Duló's Adventures) of 1842 and **"A Kolozsiak"** (The Kolozsi Family) of 1864, and the contrast between his narrative prose and his eloquent speeches is particularly striking.

"Duló Zebedeus kalandjai" is the humorous account of the first-person narrator's misadventures during a visit to Pest in an attempt to find a wife. The influence of Károly Kisfaludy's comic short stories is evident. The one remarkable feature might be the satiric portrayal of the country gentleman which precedes by three years Petőfi's similar description in his famous poem "A magyar nemes" (The Hungarian Nobleman).... (p. 37)

"Az ecce homo" (The Ecce Homo) seems intended as an illustration of Rousseau's philosophy. Spiridion has grown up in the Javanese jungle and is taken to Europe to face the corruption of seventeenth-century society, dominated by the Church. The abundance of melodramatic elements makes the story almost a parody of popular Romantic tales. There are the evil monk, scheming to have various people murdered so that their possessions will fall to the Church; the terror of the Inquisition; the rescue of the condemned from the burning stake; insanity; escape from a convent; incest; the murder of mother and infant by a conspiring physician; and the union in death of two half brothers who had become mortal enemies. By using the past as the setting for this story, Madách may again have followed Kisfaludy who chose contemporary backgrounds only for his humorous tales.

"Krónika két pénzdarab sorsáról" (Chronicle of the Fate of Two Coins) is another Romantic story that is rich in improbable twists. But it reflects the social consciousness of young Madách. Aristocrats and rich people are depicted as the villains, and the poor appear as the victims of society and its unjust laws....

"Hétköznapi történet" (Everyday Story) challenges society's condemnation of the "fallen woman" and presents in Júlia the emancipated female who finds an understanding and honest man whose devoted and faithful wife she becomes. (p. 38)

"A Kolozsiak" is the story of a woman's elaborate plans to avenge her husband's murder, committed by her brother-in-law.... The story is set in the seventeenth century following Thököly's *kuruc* uprising, but Madách makes little effort to sketch out the rich historic background.

It is obvious that Madách's imagination and his strong emotional reactions to his world did not find the appropriate medium in the prose narrative. While Kisfaludy was able to write successful short stories and to excel as a dramatist, the playwright Madách remained a frustrated storyteller.

In evaluating Madách's first dramatic attempts, it should be remembered that he was between seventeen and nineteen years old when he wrote *Commodus* and *Nápolyi Endre* (Andrew of Naples). He knew little about the theater, and Hungarian drama did not have enough of a tradition to give him much guidance.

It seems only natural for a beginning playwright to turn to historical themes supplying ready-made plots and characters. The atmosphere of decadent Rome and the poisoning of Emperor Commodus by his mistress Marcia in 192 A.D. provided the material for the four acts of Madách's prose drama which he apparently intended to rewrite later in iambic verse. Elements of Romantic horror fiction abound: the abduction of an innocent young woman by a depraved and powerful man; the mother who becomes insane in her grief; one brother's self-sacrifice for his sibling and their exchange of clothing to facilitate a prison escape; and the depiction of Christians facing death in the arena. There are shortcomings in plot and character development; some of the dialogue is awkward; but Madách already demonstrates one skill that points forward to *Az ember tragédiája:* he manages to paint a convincing picture of an historical period. (pp. 38-9)

While *Commodus*—and the *Brutus* planned by Madách—and the theme of tyrannicide may have some indirect connection with Hungarian history, *Nápolyi Endre* is the first of several dramas to deal directly with events in the nation's past. In the five-act prose play Madách also introduces a theme that will occur again and again in his work: the relationship between the sexes. The story of the assassination of the Hungarian Anjou prince Endre in 1345, most likely arranged by his wife Queen Johanna of Naples, gave Madách the opportunity to portray the clash of two cultures and to use again some of the Romantic elements of *Commodus*. The figures of the monk Robert as one of the conspirators and of Cabanis, the assassin who kills his own daughter by mistake, are popular contemporary stereotypes. Madách's lack of dramaturgical experience and his weakness in presenting believable characters and effective dialogue are as obvious as are his problems in combining the factual account of Ignác Aurél Fessler's comprehensive work on Hungarian history with the internal logic flowing from the action of a stage play. In the second act the visit of Endre's mother from Hungary, to convince her son to leave the hostile surroundings, is an historic event; but after her mission fails, she simply drops out of the drama. Shortly before Endre's murder, Durazzo, one of the conspirators, has a completely unmotivated and unexplained change of heart. Yet even this immature work—influenced, as his other plays of the time, by Victor Hugo, Schiller, and Shakespeare—shows promise and is an important first step toward the achievement to come almost two decades later. (pp. 39-40)

Fourteenth-century history again provides the background for *Mária királynő* (Queen Mary) and *Csák végnapjai* (Csák's Last Days). The two plays of 1843 depict Magyar resistance to foreign-born rulers; both deal with the question of female succession to the throne of Hungary; both combine historic facts with poetic invention but suffer from the same inadequate fusion of these elements as did *Nápolyi Endre*. Romantic subplots interfere with the effective presentation of important events in the nation's history. Inconsistencies in plot development and characterization and uneven poetic language reveal the twenty-year-old amateur with little theater experience. (p. 40)

In *Férfi és nő* (Man and Woman), although written during the same period as these historical plays, Madách turned from his nation's past to Greek myth, and from Kisfaludy to Sophocles. In his fragmentary essay of 1842, "**Művészeti értekezés**" (Discourse on Art), he had tried to develop a dramatic theory based on his study of the works of the Greek playwright. Now he selected the theme of Heracles between Deianeira and Iola, featured in *The Trachinian Women*. But his emphasis is quite different. Sophocles had concentrated on Deianeira and written a drama on the psychology of jealousy. Madách, in accord with European literary tendencies of the time, made Heracles the center of action and drew the portrait of a Romantic titan. His hero is torn between human love that threatens to tie him to earth and divine aspirations that are part of his dual nature. The tragedy is not brought about by man's unfaithfulness and disregard for established morality; Madách rather concentrates on the great man who is not understood by women. Only in death, which he freely chooses, is Heracles united with Hebe, the goddess of youth. Madách, the young poet, seems to say that man can achieve greatness only without woman and her ties to the material world. The mature playwright will later show that only with woman can man reach his goal: Adam and Eve belong together and complement each other. Yet the tendency to translate personal experiences and beliefs into generalized concepts emerges even in this youthful drama. While Heracles does not yet represent humanity, Madách makes him the prototype of maleness as he sees it.

The relationship between the sexes is also a prominent theme in his two social dramas. Only the first act of *Jó név és erény* (Good Reputation and Virtue) was completed, but the author's outline introduces the heroine as a woman of lower social rank who marries an aristocrat in order to elevate her status, then has him killed by her lover, and finally becomes insane when her fading youth and beauty cause her companion's passions to cool. Perhaps Madách did not complete the work because he was aware of the immaturity it reflected, but it is interesting to see how motifs from *Commodus* and *Nápolyi Endre* were transplanted into the Hungarian society of the 1830s and how there is almost a premonition of the type of woman whom he would meet and marry a short time later.

Csak tréfa (Just a Joke) is more important, especially as an insight into the reactions of the young writer to the society he encountered at Balassagyarmat. The devastating view of corruption in the administration of justice, the political opportunism and dishonesty, and the approach to matrimony based on economic considerations rather than love reflect personal observations. It is the poet himself who speaks through his hero, the idealistic politician Zordy who is destroyed through the manipulations of a powerful and scheming woman. Characteristically, Madách's experiences in Nógrád County are transformed into a view of the world. Zordy's tragedy is the recurring theme of the misunderstood and betrayed visionary. Jolán is the female who is too weak to follow her heart and instead enters a marriage of convenience. But in the singer Bianka the prototype of the emancipated woman emerges for the first time in Madách's dramatic work. Unfortunately, the play is marred by too many weaknesses to make its social criticism effective, and the impact of what could have been a precursor of Ibsen's portrayal of societal corruption is further blunted by Madách's selection of verse instead of prose.

Form and intent blend well, however, in his last drama before *Az ember tragédiája*. He called *A civilizátor* "a comedy in the manner of Aristophanes," and it is indeed carefully modeled after the works of the great satirist. The political burlesque ridicules the despised Bach regime just as Aristophanes had exposed the vices and follies of his time to the laughter of the Athenians. Madách imitates the strophe and antistrophe of the Greek chorus; and where Aristophanes had used birds, frogs, and wasps to provide the comments in his plays, the Hungarian satire features a chorus of cockroaches. This choice is ingenious. Not only does this insect elicit an immediate emotional response, but the Hungarian word for it, *svábbogár,* literally translates as "Swabian bug," and the German settlers in Hungary were generally called "Swabians" regardless of their specific origin. (pp. 41-3)

While Madách's comedy with its sometimes forced humor is no literary masterpiece, it is significant as a successful evocation of the spirit of Aristophanes. And it is an important political statement by a man soon to be elected to represent his community in the national Diet. (pp. 43-4)

With *A civilizátor,* the poet turned to the political situation of his times. *Az ember tragédiája* combines a look at history with a discussion of man's relationship to God. It is as if Madách had made a conscious effort to bring all these elements together in the last play he was able to complete.

Two months after finishing *Az ember tragédiája* Madách began to write *Mózes.* (p. 44)

In light of the fact that *Mózes* was written at a time when Madách was directly involved in the political affairs of his country as a parliamentary delegate, it is quite likely that the parallels between Hungarian conditions and those of his biblical account are not accidental. It has often been pointed out that the Jewish people could represent the Hungarians, trying to free themselves from the oppressive Austrian reign as represented symbolically in Pharaoh's Egypt. Aaron is frequently seen as Deák's counterpart, and Moses himself is interpreted as Kossuth or Széchenyi, depending on the critic's point of view. Madách certainly intended to do more than give a lecture on Hungary's past and present in the guise of a biblical drama, but his strong commitment to the ideals of Petőfi and Kossuth and his devotion to the laws of 1848, as evidenced by his political speeches, make it very probable that he was addressing his own nation when he had Moses exhort the Jews not to abandon the laws of the Ark of the Covenant. (pp. 44-5)

Mózes shows . . . as does *Az ember tragédiája*—the great individual in conflict with the cowardly, uncomprehending, and hostile masses. What Moses tells Abiram seems to exemplify a callous contempt of the people, and the attitude of the towering historic figures whom Hegel saw as the movers of world history. . . . But . . . Madách's attitude was not this contempt for the people as such but a stand against what he saw as the large-scale demoralization of his compatriots which had its parallel in the faint-hearted views of the Israelites who longed for the fleshpots of Egypt and for their protected slave existence. Only liberty could bring an end to this demoralization. And Moses comes to identify with the people whose leader God had appointed him to be. . . .

Moses dies without entering the Promised Land. But a free nation will be established on the soil of the regained homeland. This optimistic ending is unambiguous and indicates the poet's new attitude. Although philosophically and artistically *Mózes* is anticlimactic after *Az ember tragédiája,* it constitutes a fitting conclusion of Madách's struggles.

Only fragments are left of the poet's last play [*Tündérálom*]. (p. 45)

After wrestling with profound questions of philosophy and in the wake of his active involvement in national politics, the poet seems to have felt a need to escape into the fairy world of Vörösmarty's *Csongor és Tünde.* The completed segment,

which contains some of his best lyrical verse, reads like a whimsical parody of the opening scene of *Az ember tragédiája,* with Ilona the Fairy Queen resting on her throne, a choir of fairies singing, and the four fairies of song, charm (significantly named Tünde), whim, and imagination addressing their queen. (p. 46)

Madách's notes show that he had planned to bring various mythological figures—Hercules, Samson, Achilles, Helen—into his play and, perhaps more important, that he wanted to incorporate some motifs of traditional folktales, such as the prince with a pig's face whose spell is broken by a teardrop, and the lost fairy crown that changes into a girl. Having dealt in his dramas with Hungarian and world history, with biblical myth and philosophical speculation, the playwright appears to turn toward the popular culture that had inspired Petőfi and Arany. (pp. 46-7)

> *Dieter P. Lotze, in his* Imre Madách, *Twayne Publishers, 1981, 173 p.*

DIETER P. LOTZE (essay date 1983)

[*Here, Lotze analyzes Madách's comedy* A civilizátor *as a satire on contemporary Hungarian politics, exploring also the influence of Aristophanes on the work. For additional commentary by Lotze, see excerpt dated 1981.*]

[A] perusal of Madách's correspondence and of his literary works reveals a very distinct tendency towards satire throughout his life and development as a writer. His first-person account of the **"Adventures of Zebedee Duló"** ("**Duló Zebedeus kalandjai**") of 1842 sketches a satirical portrait of the Hungarian country squire who likes his dogs because they—unlike people—do not attempt to rise above their social status. Duló does not read, as books are only for those who need to learn, and he is, after all, a Hungarian gentleman. . . . Unfortunately, Madách is unable to sustain the tone of the opening of his narrative, and the rest of the tale reads like a poor imitation of a short story by Károly Kisfaludy. The playwright's contributions to the *Nógrádi képcsarnok* (Nógrád Picture Gallery), the collection of satirical epigrams he coauthored with Szontágh and Ferenc Pulszky in 1844, further attests to his ability to use wit and sarcasm in portraying people. The satirical trend reaches its culmination in the 1859 comedy *A civilizátor* (The Civilizer). But it continues not only in Lucifer's attempts to ridicule everything Ádám sees as great and ideal, but also in Madách's parliamentary speeches, and it is still evident in the dramatic fragment *Tündérálom* (Fairy Dream). Here Amor complains about the changed conditions on Mount Olympus and among human beings. He is no longer taken seriously in the realm of the gods, and on earth commercialism reigns instead of true love. His arrows cannot pierce the shield and armor of real estate registers and contract forms, and he himself is being replaced by "newspaper advertisements, aunts, old hags, cosmetics and profiteers."

But the focus of this study will be on the drama whose very subtitle emphasizes its satirical intent: Madách called *A civilizátor* a "comedy in the manner of Aristophanes". He wrote his play at the end of a period of deep personal depression and as a response to the sad conditions of his country. The war of 1848-49, in which he could not participate actively for health reasons, had brought tragedy not only to the nation but also into his own life. His favorite sister Mari, her husband, and their son had been brutally murdered by Rumanian insurgents. His idealistic and patriotic brother Pál was another victim of the war. In his poetry, Madách expressed his grief over the loss of those dear to him and his deep concern over the fate of his country. The Austrian revenge after the failure of the Hungarian struggle for freedom had been brutal, and the "Bach Regime" of the 1850s, named after the Austrian Interior Secretary Alexander Bach, governed Hungary like a conquered colony and attempted to change the traditionally independent country into a province of the Hapsburg "Gesamtmonarchie", the total unified monarchy. A repressive bureaucracy, staffed by officials whom the Hungarians mockingly called "Bach hussars" because of their extravagant uniforms, was an important tool in this effort. The Hungarian response was widespread passive resistance and refusal to pay taxes.

The Bach period was to have a profound impact on Madách's personal life, too. In 1851, he gave shelter to a political refugee. Probably denounced by a neighbor, the poet was arrested by the Austrian authorities and imprisoned for almost a year. During this period and in the time after his release, his marriage to charming but selfish Erzsi Fráter deteriorated. After his divorce in 1854, he completely withdrew not only from public life, but also from his friends and even from his family. His writing helped restore gradually the psychological and emotional balance of the "Recluse of Alsó-Sztregova" *A civilizátor* and especially *Az ember tragédiája* mark his breaking out of his self-imposed intellectual and physical exile. Significantly, he reentered political life as well and was elected to the 1861 Diet in Pest. It is this background we should keep in mind when looking at his "Aristophanic comedy".

A synopsis of the one-act play should make Madách's intentions quite clear. Uncle István, the Hungarian farmer, and his servants, Janó the Slovak, Uros the Serbian, Mitrule the Rumanian, Carlo the Italian, Miska the Hungarian, and Mürzl the German maid, are ready to sit down for their evening meal when an odd-looking stranger appears. Sitting on top of an immense bundle of paper in a wheelbarrow drawn by two dogs, he identifies himself as "Stroom, the great civilizer", who has left "Great Germany", his homeland, to "carry to the East the blessings of the West". Stroom manages to incite the servants to desert their master. He gains the support of Uros, who has been banned from the main table for a minor act of insubordination, by his promise of replacing the "established custom" with a formal legal system. The other servants are won over by his pledge of a system of absolute equality where the different nationalities would no longer have to accept orders from a Hungarian. (pp. 204-06)

The servants take over István's house and are ordered to make an inventory of all the items there when the army of Stroom's assistants arrives: long lines of cockroaches, the "irresistible carriers of civilization". They function as the Aristophanic chorus throughout the play, and from their ranks Stroom will appoint his judges, policemen, administrators, and teachers. (p. 206)

Madách's immediate target is the Bach Regime and its excesses. But in a wider sense, his satire is directed against Austria's longstanding efforts to make Hungary an integral part of the Hapsburg Empire. While the author was very familiar with German culture and—as *Az ember tragédiája* shows—was influenced by it, "German" becomes in this play a symbol for that continued threat of political, cultural, and linguistic domination from the West. The choice of cockroaches to present the chorus of "Bach hussars" is ingenious. Not only do these insects elicit immediate emotional responses, but their Hungarian name, "svábbogár" (or "sváb"), actually means

"Swabian bug", and "Swabian" was traditionally used in Hungary as a generic term for all German-speaking settlers, regardless of their specific origin. Thus, when the chorus mourns in the end that "Swabia has fallen, the sacred bastion", it acknowledges that Hungary can no longer be considered a province of Austria, governed by a German-speaking bureaucratic elite.

In his description of the way in which Stroom secured the support of István's servants, Madách gives a satirical but essentially accurate portrayal of Hapsburg's policy to divide in order to conquer. The symbolic representation of the different nationalities in the microcosm of Uncle István's farm reflects 19th century Hungary and her various ethnic groups, many of whom were as disgruntled about Hungarian cultural dominance as were the Magyars about Austrian attempts to Germanize them. Vienna very skillfully used to her own advantage these nationalistic tendencies and this resentment by the different minorities. In part, the war of 1848-49 came about because of these problems. Thoughtful Hungarians realized that a continuation of past policies would result in further instabilities. Thus, while the satirist Madách paints a picture of initial harmony of the nationalities under benevolent paternalistic leadership of the Hungarian master, the politician Madách, a strong supporter of Baron József Eötvös, eloquently expressed his concern about the question of the nationalities when he served in the 1861 Diet.

On the other hand, just as István's servants eventually realize their common interest and their common enemy and fight together with their master against the "Great Civilizer" and his cockroaches, many members of ethnic minorities identified completely with the Hungarian cause in the struggle against Hapsburg. (pp. 208-10)

After 1849, the victorious Austrians claimed that the existence of a privileged class in Hungary had prevented the people from achieving freedom and had kept the country from progressing. One of the professed goals of the Bach Regime was to rectify this deplorable condition, and Stroom's removal of István from his position of relative power is the caricature of that process. Of course Stroom immediately establishes himself as the new master; similarly, Francis Joseph's Austria was not the least interested in introducing democratic freedoms into the territory she controlled. A system of customs and traditions was being replaced with formal laws and regulations; conflicts between individuals were not solved on the basis of common sense and longstanding practice, but according to specific paragraphs of specific laws. This is how Stroom proceeds in the "celebrated and complicated case of Uros" who, instead of merely having to eat by himself, is now additionally faced with corporal punishment and a heavy fine. Of course the new administration—in the country as well as on István's farm—creates a veritable flood of paper that threatens to drown the people. The "Great Civilizer" decrees that István's home will be converted into a government office in order to hold all those documents that the people cannot carry on their persons; the stable will have to do as shelter for those who used to live in the farmhouse. He also replaces St. Steven, István's patron saint, with Sophia, protectress of hemp growers. . . . (pp. 210-11)

The inefficiency of the bureaucratic system is demonstrated when the farmhands rush to rescue an ox that has just fallen into the mire. Stroom interferes because this is the task of the police force he has set up. He reminds his cockroaches to follow established procedure and to keep proper records. When they arrive a while later with the dead animal, he considers the damage minor since at least the report was drawn up according to regulations.

Of course the bureaucracy thus introduced and the new way of dispensing justice are expensive; so fees are charged for everything, and a general income tax is imposed. Stroom also tries to introduce a new device that will grind up the corn cobs, hitherto thrown into the garbage, as feed for the Hungarians, so that their wheat may be taken away as another form of taxation rather than being wasted for their white bread. In exchange for their traditional currency, he supplies worthless paper money. Certainly Madách was not alone in charging Austria with the economic exploitation of his homeland.

But the author's most stinging sarcasm is reserved for another target, already indicated in the title of his play. Stroom represents not only the attempt to dominate Hungary politically, to change her governmental structure, and to exploit her economically. Even more, he stands for the cultural arrogance so frequently encountered in German-speaking countries: everything (and everybody) beyond the Eastern linguistic borders is "barbaric" and in dire need of Western civilization. Thus, the Austrian effort to Germanize Hungary was not solely a matter of political expediency, but also had its roots in cultural imperialism.

Stroom complains about the inadequacy of the Hungarian language that does not even contain an all-important world like "must". So the Magyars have to learn the word, "muszáj", and the concept behind it from the superior German civilization. Obviously a family name like "Magyar", which he considers "parvenue", can no longer be tolerated, so he renames István "Máder". Once again, Madách's choice is a happy one. Not only is "Mader" a perfectly plausible Austrian name—Viennese-born Joseph von Mader . . . taught law in Prague and is considered the father of medieval numismatics—but, more important, the German word "Made" means "maggot", and Stroom thus symbolically transforms the free Hungarian farmer into a member of his crawling army of vermin. (pp. 211-12)

Throughout the play, Madách mocks the philosophy of Georg Wilhelm Friedrich Hegel, or, to state it more accurately, the inane and arrogant use of Hegelian ideas and slogans by Stroom. In his lectures on the philosophy of history, Hegel had described the history of the world in terms of the dialectic progress in the consciousness of freedom. He saw the fusion of oriental Christianity and Germanic culture as the last and highest stage in this development and came to view the Prussian monarchy of his times as the most highly developed and thus inherently freest political system. The "blessings of the West" which the "Civilizer" wants to share with the pagan, uncultured Hungarians spring from this "Germanic-Christian" spirit. (p. 213)

Stroom appears most ridiculous when he tries to impress the Hungarians with his own knowledge of Hegel's philosophy. His listeners either poke fun at him or show incomprehension and disinterest. (pp. 213-14)

[A] careful study of *The Tragedy of Man* will yield ample evidence for Madách's familiarity with at least Hegel's lectures on the philosophy of history, and for the impact of Hegel's concept of a dialectic pattern in history, although the playwright most certainly did not agree with the German thinker's assessment of his own period as the highest point of development. How could any Hungarian in the 1850s have held that view? But a close reading of *A civilizátor* reveals no wholesale rejection of Hegelian thought, but rather an attempt to ridicule

those who—like Stroom—employed some of his terminology and argumentation, not in order to foster dispassionate philosophical debate, but rather to achieve their own selfish and very materialistic goals.

To what extent was Madách justified in attaching the label "Aristophanic" to *A civilizátor*? . . . [We] can infer from Madách's correspondence that he knew at least some of the works of Aristophanes. (p. 215)

Certainly there is a general thematic correspondence between Madách's satirical drama and most of the plays of Aristophanes. Both playwrights employed the medium of the comedy to castigate what they considered deplorable in the political or cultural area. Thus, the attitude of the Hungarian writer in ridiculing the oppressive Bach Regime and the cultural arrogance of the German-speaking countries is akin to the Greek author's attacks on Cleon or on Socrates and the Sophists whom he held responsible for undermining traditional morality.

But while both dramatists wrote satirical political comedies, their purposes were quite different. Madách knew that his biting attack on Austria and her policies had no chance of being approved by the censor. He did not write for the stage and probably intended to share the play only with his closest friends, if with anybody. Aristophanes, on the other hand, created his comedies for public performances at the Athens festivals, and he consciously employed them as political weapons. Through his hardly disguised assaults on specific personalities, he tried to bring about changes in government, and through making martial attitudes an object of derision, he attempted to facilitate an end to the war his country was waging.

Given the satirical intentions of Madách's play, his choice of symbolic names—such as István Magyar—or of symbolic characters—the servants and their nationalities, or the "Great Civilizer" himself—is natural and need not have been inspired by Aristophanic comedies where these devices abound. But it is highly unlikely that Madách would have come up with his chorus of cockroaches, had Aristophanes not established the model in his animal choruses. The insects that take over István's house were certainly modeled after the birds, wasps, and frogs in the Greek satires. And in each case the animals have some attitudes or characteristics that are symbolic. Wasps—like the Athenian jurors they represent—swarm, buzz, and sting; birds—in contrast to human beings—can escape from their misery by flying away. Madách's cockroaches—like good policemen and informers—can penetrate into any crack and dig into any dirt. In addition, they eagerly consume whatever is edible. But, except perhaps for István's use of flyswatters as weapons, Madách fails to derive the same comic effect from the employment of animals that Aristophanes achieved. (pp. 216-17)

Certainly the formal structure of the choral passages, the division into strophe and antistrophe in *A civilizátor* can be traced to Greek drama in general, and most likely to Aristophanes in particular. But in contrast to most Aristophanic comedies, Madách's satire lacks the *parabasis*, the characteristic episode in which the chorus, alone on stage, addresses the audience directly and becomes the mouthpiece for the author's opinions. The only faint echo of his might be the moment when the cockroaches implore their master not to initiate neverending civil court proceedings. But perhaps Madách found it too difficult to have this particular chorus serve as his spokesmen, or, more likely, he was not completely aware of this specific dramatic technique.

Both authors present in their works a blend of sophistication and burlesque. Slapstick humor and bawdiness can be found in Madách's play as well as in all Aristophanic comedies. To some degree, lewdness and vulgarity serve a function in the Hungarian play. Stroom objects early in the drama to István's use of the words "pants" and "maiden", as they make him blush and lead to dirty thoughts. When the same Stroom later pursues Mürzl, comparing himself to an overcharged battery on whose positive pole a flame is burning and who would like to find a negative spot in her lap to discharge his energy, and when he eventually marvels that the Hungarians get so upset because of the female sexual organ under lock and key—Madách abbreviates the vernacular here—then he reveals himself as the hypocrite he truly is. Yet, very much in contrast to the obscenity in the works of Aristophanes that seems to serve a purpose and furthermore is related to the culture of the age, even in this case the crudeness in Madách's work appears somewhat artificial and unmotivated. (pp. 217-18)

It is characteristic that such examples of coarseness are restricted to Stroom. It is obvious that the playwright attempted to ascribe only positive characteristics to István. He is kind, generous, just, patient, thoughtful, witty, considerate, and brave, and at the end demonstrates his willingness to forgive. In view of the satirical and symbolic intention of the play and its cast, one should perhaps not complain about the lack of believability of such overly noble character. Yet, after reading *A civilizátor,* one almost longs for a little of that vindictiveness so typical of the works of Aristophanes.

The comedies by Madách and by Aristophanes are topical. But the most significant difference may be that the best plays by the Greek author continue to be read and enjoyed long after their topicality has gone. . . . Madách's play, on the other hand, becomes meaningless without the specific historical setting. *A civilizátor* offers little to hold the attention of anyone unfamiliar with the conditions in Hungary in the 1850s.

Perhaps the lacking ingredient that could have made Madách's drama truly a "comedy in the manner of Artistophanes" was a sense of humor. The playwright emerges as a brilliant satirist, using sarcasm and wit to ridicule and tear down. But there is no attempt and no ability to view matters from the detached vantage point of a humorist. But then, such stance could hardly be expected from someone with Madách's experiences. As it stands, *A civilizátor* is important as a historical document, and it is important as a statement by a man soon to be elected to parliament and soon to give life and voice to the greatest satirist of them all, Lucifer in **The Tragedy of Man.** (pp. 218-19)

> *Dieter P. Lotze, "Of Cockroaches and 'Civilizing' Hungary: Imre Madách as an Aristophanic Satirist," in Neohelicon, Vol. X, No. 1, (1983), pp. 203-19.*

ADDITIONAL BIBLIOGRAPHY

Czigány, Lóránt. "Post-Revolutionary Disillusionment." In his *The Oxford History of Hungarian Literature from the Earliest Times to the Present*, pp. 198-216. Oxford: Clarendon Press, 1984.
    Contains a biographical and critical section on Madách with a lengthy analysis of *The Tragedy of Man*.

Jones, D. Mervyn. "An Aristophanic Drama from 19th Century Hungary." In *Kōmōidotralēmata: Studia Aristophanea Viri Aristophanei, W. J. W. Koster in Honorem*, pp. 108-14. Amsterdam: A. M. Hakkert, 1967.
    Praises the satire in *A civilizátor*.

Lotze, Dieter P. "The 'Poèmes d'humanité' of Guernsey and Alsó-Sztregova: Victor Hugo's *La légende des siècles* and Imre Madách's *The Tragedy of Man*." *Neohelicon* V, No. 2 (1977): 71-81.
    A comparison of *The Tragedy of Man* with Hugo's drama.

————. "Madách's *Tragedy of Man* and the Tradition of the 'Poème d'humanité' in European Literature." *Neohelicon* VI, No. 1 (1978): 235-54.
    Places *The Tragedy of Man* within the context of both European and Hungarian literary history.

————. "Madách's *Tragedy of Man:* Lessing Echoes in 19th Century Hungary?" *Lessing Yearbook* XI (1979): 133-41.
    Traces the influence of the German author Gotthold Ephraim Lessing on Madách.

————. "Imre Madách is Alive and Well and Dying in West Germany: Peter Michael Hamel's Opera *Ein Menschenstraum.*" *Hungarian Studies Review* XI, No. 2 (Fall 1984): 3-14.
    Discusses an opera based on both *The Tragedy of Man* and Madách's life.

Mark, Thomas R. "Madách Revisited: Toward a New Translation of the *Tragedy of Man*." *Canadian-American Review of Hungarian Studies* IV, No. 2 (Fall 1977): 145-54.
    Examines the difficulties inherent in translating *The Tragedy of Man* into English.

Németh, Béla G. "Populist Literature (*c*. 1840-*c*. 1870): Imre Madách." In *A History of Hungarian Literature*, edited by Tibor Klaniczay, pp. 271-76. Budapest: Corvina, 1982.
    An overview of Madách's life and works that focuses on *The Tragedy of Man*.

Riedl, Frederick. "Teleki and Madách." In his *A History of Hungarian Literature*, pp. 248-65. New York: D. Appleton and Co., 1906.
    Places *The Tragedy of Man* in the history of Hungarian literature.

Róheim, Géza. "Psychology and History, or *The Tragedy of Man*." In his *Psychoanalysis and Anthropology: Culture, Personality and the Unconscious*, pp. 461-87. New York: International Universities Press, 1950.
    A Freudian reading of *The Tragedy of Man*. Róheim interprets the drama as a reflection of human evolution.

Tezla, Albert. "Part I: Authors from 1450 to 1945, Madách Imre." In his *Hungarian Authors: A Bibliographical Handbook*, pp. 370-77. Cambridge: Harvard University Press, Belknap Press, 1970.
    Biographical information along with a list of Madách's principal works and a bibliography of works about the author.

(Jean) Charles (Emmanuel) Nodier

1780-1844

French short story writer, novelist, poet, dramatist, travel writer, autobiographer, journalist, bibliographer, and lexicographer.

Nodier is chiefly remembered for his *contes fantastiques,* fantastic tales in which he expanded the boundaries of short fiction during the early French Romantic period. In his most representative short stories—*Smarra; ou, Les démons de la nuit, Trilby; ou, Le lutin d'Argail (Trilby, the Fairy of Argyle), La fée aux miettes,* and *L'histoire du roi de Bohême et de ses sept châteaux*—Nodier explored elements of the fantastic, the subconscious, and the occult to create complex, experimental pieces that were not always understood in his own time and that are often cited as forerunners of the works of the surrealists. Nodier was also the versatile and prolific author of numerous works of lexicography, bibliography, and criticism, and the founder of an important literary salon that directly influenced many French Romantic writers. Thus, today Nodier is recognized as an innovator who helped alter the course of French letters.

Nodier was born in Besançon to an unwed lawyer and his housekeeper, the two of whom eventually married in 1791. Educated privately by a tutor and at the École Centrale in Besançon, he studied, among other subjects, botany, entomology, classical literature, and Greek. Though he obtained a post as librarian at the École Centrale in 1798, he made frequent trips to Paris searching for other employment. There, in 1803, Nodier was arrested and briefly imprisoned for composing and circulating *La Napoléone,* an incendiary verse satire mocking Napoleon. Released and banned from Paris, he lived under police surveillance for the next several years at Besançon and at Dôle, where he married Désirée-Liberté Charve in 1808 and later started a family. Following his marriage, Nodier worked as a journalist and contributing editor for a number of French and foreign periodicals. It was not until 1818 that he published his first major fictional work, *Jean Sbogar,* a novel concerning a dashing Illyrian bandit. Immediately successful, *Jean Sbogar* was followed within a few years by several novels and two tales of the fantastic with which the author is closely associated, *Smarra* and *Trilby.*

Nodier's literary career was well under way when, in 1824, in recognition of his historical, critical, and linguistic scholarship, he was appointed curator of Paris's Bibliothèque de l'Arsenal, one of France's greatest libraries. In Paris, he founded a salon that attracted the elite in the arts for several years, inspiring a rising generation of writers whose number included Victor Hugo and Alfred de Vigny. Nodier continued writing prolifically, publishing, among other works, *L'histoire du roi de Bohême* in 1830 and *La fée aux miettes* the following year. In 1833 he was elected to the French Academy. Despite increasing ill health, he remained active in French letters—particularly in the fields of bibliography and lexicography—until his death in Paris in 1844.

Nodier's literary accomplishments were diverse, but his tales of the fantastic remain his major literary legacy. These stories, which were posthumously collected in *Contes fantastiques,* share a common concern with dualisms, including sanity and madness and reality and dream. Nodier's better-known nar-

ratives display his knowledge of the subconscious and are considered remarkable for their anticipation of modern psychological theory. For example, *La fée aux miettes* alternates entirely between dreams and actual events, while in *Smarra,* the structure is concentric, unfolding stories within stories and dreams within dreams. Commentators have traced throughout the latter work repetitive images, words, and sounds highly suggestive of the dreaming state, citing it as one of the earliest experiments in literary illustration of psychological principles. Nodier also employed the supernatural to blur the distinctions between truth and illusion: in *Trilby,* a young married woman trapped in a routine of dull domesticity dreams about a charming sprite, who is symbolic of the supernatural. *L'histoire du roi de Bohême,* while featuring Nodier's characteristic mélange of dream and reality as well as a heightened attention to wordplay and sounds, significantly departs from the author's other *contes fantastiques.* Loosely structured around a fictional king's visit to his seven castles, the story, according to some critics, is ultimately a pastiche reminiscent of the works of François Rabelais and Laurence Sterne in which Nodier imitates their characteristic ramblings, digressions, and mock-serious tone toward revered institutions.

While Nodier commanded a substantial popular following throughout the nineteenth century, critical recognition was tinged with skepticism until well into the twentieth. This was due largely to hesitation regarding the psychological foundation of much of his work. However, Nodier's interpretation of the workings of the subconscious, its manifestation in dreams, and its power over human behavior has now been well substantiated by modern psychological theory and is frequently the subject of critical commentary. Nodier's effective use of the fantastic and the occult, as well as his innovative style, have also contributed to ongoing interest in his better-known *contes fantastiques* and to the acknowledgment of his importance to French literary history. He is deemed a significant forerunner of the French surrealists, who wrote of the same disorienting borderlands of the imagination and claimed him as an influence. And as Hilda Nelson has observed, "Nodier can be considered, if not the inventor, at least the initiator of the *conte fantastique* in France."

PRINCIPAL WORKS

Les proscrits   (novel)   1802; also published as *Stella; ou, Les proscrits*, 1808
La Napoléone   (pamphlet)   1803
Les essais d'un jeune barde   (poetry)   1804
Jean Sbogar   (novel)   1818
Thérèse Aubert   (novel)   1819
Adèle   (novel)   1820
Lord Ruthwen; ou, Les vampires   (novel)   1820
Le vampire [with Pierre François Adrien Carmouche and Achille François Élénore de Jouffroy]   (drama)   1820
Smarra; ou, Les démons de la nuit   (short story)   1821
Trilby; ou, Le lutin d'Argail   (short story)   1822
   [*Trilby, the Fairy of Argyle*, 1895]
L'histoire du roi de Bohême et de ses sept châteaux   (short story)   1830
La fée aux miettes. Inès de las Sierras   (short stories)   1831
Mademoiselle de Marsan   (novel)   1832
Oeuvres complètes. 13 vols.   (short stories, novels, prose, poetry, and drama)   1832-41
Les quatre talismans   (novel)   1838
Franciscus Columna   (short story)   1844
Histoire du chien de Brisquet   (short story)   1844
   [*The Woodcutter's Dog*, 1922]
Trésors des fèves et fleurs des pois   (short story)   1844
   [*Bean Flower and Pea Blossom*, 1846]
Contes fantastiques. 2 vols.   (short stories and novels)   1957

GEORGE BRANDES   (essay date 1882)

[*Brandes, a Danish literary critic and biographer, was the principal leader of the intellectual movement that helped to bring an end to Scandinavian cultural isolation. He believed that literature reflects the spirit and problems of its time and that it must be understood within its social and aesthetic context. Brandes's major critical work,* Main Currents in Nineteenth Century Literature, *won him admiration for his ability to view literary movements within the broader context of all European literature. In the following excerpt from* Main Currents, *he emphasizes the imaginative quality of Nodier's later works. Brandes's remarks were first published in Danish in 1882.*]

From the year 1824 onwards Hugo, Dumas, Lamartine, Sainte-Beuve, De Musset, and De Vigny met almost every Sunday evening at the house of a friend who that year took up his residence in the outskirts of Paris, near the Arsenal, in a modest dwelling which went by the name of the Little Tuileries. Their host was a man who in point of age belonged to the previous generation (he was born in 1780), but who in his mental attitude had anticipated the nascent literature, which he consequently at once and without hesitation took under his protection. His name was Charles Nodier.

Nodier's life had been one of strange vicissitudes; he had been an *émigré* in the Jura, a newspaper editor in Illyria, and now he was a librarian in Paris. His most remarkable characteristic as an author is that he is always from ten to twenty years in advance of every literary movement. His novel *Jean Sbogar,* the story of a species of Illyrian Karl Moor, which he planned in Illyria in 1812 and published in 1818, although improbable and uninteresting as a tale, is remarkable from the fact that its author, long before the days of Proudhon and modern communism, has put some of the most striking truths and untruths of the communistic faith into the mouth of his hero. (p. 32)

Men had forgotten the existence of such a book as *Jean Sbogar,* when Napoleon's memoirs came out and informed them that he had had it with him at St. Helena, and had read it with interest. The little novel belongs to Nodier's transition period. It was written before he had developed his characteristic individuality. This he did about the time of the formation of the Romantic School proper. He stood then, so to speak, at the open door of literature, and bade that school welcome. His review of Victor Hugo's boyish romance, *Han d'Islande*, is a little masterpiece of criticism, sympathetic and acute. It was the beginning of the warm friendship between the two authors. The appreciation of Hugo is so marvellously correct that in reading it to-day one can hardly believe that its writer was unacquainted with all the master's later works. It required no small amount of cleverness to foresee them in *Han d'Islande*.

The stories which Nodier now began to write possess a charm and attraction unique in French literature. They are distinguished by a mimosa-like delicacy of feeling. They treat chiefly of the first stirring of passion in the hearts of youths and maidens; the fresh dew of the morning of life is upon them; they remind us of the woods in spring. It is a well-known fact that there is some difficulty in finding French books of any literary value which are fit for young girls' reading; but such tales as Nodier's *Thérèse Aubert,* or the collection of stories entitled *Souvenirs de Jeunesse,* meet both requirements. The only risk run would be the risk of imbuing the young readers with fanciful platonic ideas; for these tales are as sentimental as they are chaste; the love which they describe may be a friendship with little of the sexual element in it, nevertheless it completely engrosses the little human being. It owes its charm to the fact that as yet no experience has made these minds suspicious and that no false or true pride prevents these hearts from revealing their emotions. As all the tales are founded on reality, on memories of their author's youth, the terrors of the Revolution form the dark background of them all, and they all end with a parting or the death of the loved one.

A childlike delicacy of feeling is the fundamental characteristic of Nodier's character. To the end of his days he remained a big, unworldly child, with a girlish shrinking not only from the impure, but even from the grown-up standpoint.

Above this groundwork of naïve freshness of feeling there rises, as second story, a wildly exuberant imagination. Nodier possessed such a gift of extravagant invention that one can hardly help believing that he must have been subject to visions and hallucinations; he had the dangerous quality peculiar to a certain type of poetic temperament, that of scarcely being able to speak the truth. No one, not even he himself, ever knew for a certainty whether what he was relating was truth or fiction. Jest is the mean between the two. Nodier was considered one of the most entertaining of Frenchmen, and he was not the least offended when he was told by his friends that they did not believe a word of what he was telling them. (pp. 33-5)

La Fée aux Miettes seems to me the best of Nodier's fantastic tales. There is undoubtedly too much of it; it is not without an effort that one follows all the wild twists and turnings of a fantasy which occupies 120 quarto pages, even though much of it is both interesting and charming. A poor, harmless lunatic in the asylum of Glasgow tells the story of his life. This is the setting of the tale, but we forget it altogether in the marvellousness of the events related. All the chords of human life are touched, jarringly and wildly. It is as if life itself passed before one's eyes seen wrong side out, seen from the perfectly permissible standpoint of the dreamer or the delirious fever-patient. (p. 38)

At its maturity his imaginative faculty is more wanton and bold. No longer contented with producing shapeless, unordered material, he presents his material to us with a grotesque, loquacious, satirical explanation. No Frenchman comes so near having what Englishmen and Germans call humour as Nodier. At times he seems to be positively possessed by whimsicality. Then he not only turns the everyday world topsy-turvy in his stories, but plays with his own relation to the story, satirises contemporaries, makes a thousand innuendoes, philosophises over the illusions of life. He takes even the art of the printer into his service to heighten his fantastic effects; or, more correctly speaking, in order to prove the absolute power of his personality over his material, he leaves not a single thing, not even the purely mechanical means of communication, untouched by his mood. In his famous tale, *Le Roi de Bohème et ses sept Châteaux,* he exhausted the resources of the printing establishment. At his command the letters become so long that they stretch from top to bottom of the page; he commands again, and they dwindle into the tiniest of the tiny; he screams, and they stand up on end in terror; he becomes melancholy, and they hang their heads all along the lines; they are inseparably mixed up with illustrations; Latin and Gothic groups alternate, according to the mood of the moment; sometimes they stand on their heads, so that we have to turn the book upside down to read them; sometimes they follow the narrative so closely that a descent of the stairs is printed thus:

> Hereupon
>   our
>   hero
>   went
>   dejectedly
>   down
>   the
>   stairs.

It is interesting to trace in the account of Nodier's life written by his daughter, the foundations of fact upon which he built his fantastic tales. It rarely happens that, as in *Inès de Las Sierras,* something real (in this case an old castle which Nodier had visited in the course of a tour he made with his family in Spain in 1827) forms the groundwork. Sometimes, as for example in *Trilby,* the point of departure is a legend; and it is significant that this particular legend should have been told to

Nodier by Pichot, the French translator of Scott and Byron. The idea of *Smarra* Nodier got from hearing the old porter of his house in Paris, who was too ill to sleep anywhere except sitting in his chair, relate his nightmares and dreams. The model for the Fée aux Miettes was an old woman who served in his father's house when he was a child, and who treated his father, a man of sixty, as if he were a giddy youth. This old Denise maintained that before entering the Nodiers' household she had been in the service of a Monsieur d'Amboise, governor of Château-Thierry. When she held forth on this subject, she mixed up with her own experiences reminiscences of the most extraordinary events and most antiquated customs; and the family, out of curiosity, caused inquiry to be made about this remarkable governor. The archives of the town showed that only one of the name had ever existed, and that he had died in 1557. One can see how the story of the fairy evolved itself out of this curious incident. The very slightest element of fact— a landscape, a legend, a dream, a lie, a mere mote—was enough for Nodier.

The amiable, clever man, whose house was for a number of years the rendezvous of the men of letters who made their *début* about 1830, the place where all the talented young beginners repaired to seek encouragement and, if possible, permission to read a ballad or a little piece of prose before the select company which assembled there on Sunday afternoons, this man in his proper person represents the extreme of Romantic fantasticality in the literature of the period. The fantastic supernaturalism which was the main characteristic of German Romanticism, is only one of the poles of French Romanticism; or, to speak more correctly, it is merely one of its elements— in some of the most notable men of the school a weak and subordinate, in others an important element, but an element always present. In Victor Hugo's case it announces itself at once, in his *Ronde du Sabbat,* and makes itself forcibly felt in the great *Légende des Siècles,* though in this latter the legend is only naïve history; we have a glimpse of it even in the rationalistic Mérimée (half explained away in *La Vénus d'Ille,* more distinct in *La Vision de Charles XI.* and *Les âmes du purgatoire*); it reigns, half-seraphic, half-sanguinarily sensual, in Lamartine's *La chute d'un ange;* it pervades Quinet's pantheistically vague *Ahasvère;* it appears in George Sand's old age in the pretty fairy-tales she writes for her grandchildren; it occupies even the plastic Gautier in the many tales in which he allows himself to be influenced by Hoffmann; and, as Swedenborgian spiritism, it actually, in a romance like *Séraphitus-Séraphita,* completes Balzac's great *Comédie Humaine.* But in no other author has it the naïve originality and the poetic force which distinguish Nodier. (pp. 41-2)

George Brandes, "Charles Nodier," in his Main Currents in Nineteenth Century Literature: The Romantic School in France, Vol. V, *translated by Diana White and Mary Morison, The Macmillan Company, 1904, pp. 32-42.*

MAXIMILIAN J. RUDWIN   (essay date 1924)

[In this excerpt from his discussion of the fantastic elements in Nodier's writings, Rudwin details his use of legend, myth, and the supernatural, focusing especially on his representation of Satan.]

French Romanticism is indebted to its schoolmaster for its fantastic element. The group of young men who gathered around Charles Nodier . . . Sunday evenings in his salon at the Arsenal . . . to carry out under his leadership the literary revolution called Romanticism followed their host to his holding in the country of fantasy. This writer fathered the Fantastic in French fiction. Nodier was a fanatic *fantaisiste*. He was obsessed with the phantasmagoric world. Reality was to him, as to Hoffmann, but a pretext for the flight of his imagination. This cultivated and learned man of letters, this editor and librarian, this bibliographer and lexicographer, this grammarian and historian, this botanist and entomologist, this traveler and man of affairs lived in a world of dreams. Nodier had a very complex character. He was at once sceptical and superstitious, heretic and mystic, revolutionary and royalist. This investigator and innovator felt an affinity for the frantic and fantastic. He had an infatuation for the accidental and exceptional, for the fabulous and monstrous, for the mysterious and miraculous. Our writer was passionately fond of fairy-tales and ghost-stories, of Eastern legends and Western myths. As a boy he read fantastic stories with such relish that he was willing, as he tells us himself, to give ten years of his life for the Fantastic.

Nodier's first novel, *Le Peintre de Saltzbourg,* already showed its author's preoccupation with the supernatural and suprasensual. His introduction to Taylor's collection of prints, *les Voyages pittoresques et romantiques dans l'ancienne France,* expressed the enthusiasm for national antiquities to which Nodier gradually rose. This marked the beginning of our writer's patriotic piety for the historic past of his country. His patriotism found a very beautiful expression in his story, *La Neuvaine de la chandeleur.* Nodier may with right be considered the pioneer of French folk-lorists. He was an untiring collector of medieval legends and popular beliefs. Nodier may be credited, together with Chateaubriand, with the restoration of medievalism in modern arts and letters. his essay, *Du fantastic dans la littérature,* is an apotheosis of the Middle Ages, which he calls the Golden Age of the Fantastic.

In this essay, our writer sketches the progress of the Fantastic through the ages. According to his point of view, it is the fantastic element which has been at all times the highest inspiration of the poet. Nodier fully realizes the difficulty of restoring this element in the literature of a period which has long ago abandoned its belief in the Supernatural. As a necessary condition for the resurrection of the Fantastic in the literature of his sceptical contemporaries, he therefore demands a suspension of disbelief on the part of both the writer and the reader. In order to obtain the reader's momentary suspension of incredulity, the writer must tell his story in such a way as not to arouse any doubt as to his own belief in its truth.

Nodier was *naïf* enough to think that he could reawaken in modern times the medieval faith in the marvellous and miraculous. Nevertheless, this *merveilleux naïf* was a step further than Chateaubriand's *merveilleux chrétien* toward the resurrection of the Supernatural in modern arts and letters. In contrast to Chateaubriand, our writer fully understood that the Supernatural was not merely material for stylistic embellishment. The aim of the supernatural element in art was to call forth in the reader that sort of emotion which could not be imparted by the world of realities.

Nodier's fantasticism may be defined as *le merveilleux germanique et celtique*. It comprises the lives of the saints, medieval traditions, popular superstitions, Germanic myths and Celtic legends. It embraces all the inhabitants of the extra-human realm: angels and saints, demons and ghosts, dragons and dwarfs, fairies and elves, sylphs and salamanders, goblins and griffins, vampires and valkyrs. Nodier himself, with his kind heart, delighted mostly in elfland and fairyland. Our au-

thor loved especially to tell stories of benevolent spirits but his appeal to the popular belief in angels and saints could easily be extended to the malevolent spirits. This is just what has happened, and diabolism has become an integral part of Nodier's fantasticism. As a matter of fact, the temptations of the devils surpass in number the interventions of the saints. Diabolical legends will be found even in the works of Nodier himself. A few of his stories deal with apparitions, sorcerers and devils.

Nodier's *Tablettes romantiques* contain the legend of Mont Saint-Michel. This mountain on the Norman coast is the eternal monument to the victorious leader of the hosts of Heaven in the war against the rebel angel. In his *Légendes populaires de la France,* . . . our writer included the legend, "**Le Château de Robert le Diable.**" Now Robert the Devil, the son of a duke and duchess of Normandy, was born, according to the confession of his mother, in answer to prayers addressed to the Devil. In another version of the story, the devil himself was Robert's father. However, when Robert learned of his diabolical descent, he turned from his father to God. During his courageous defense of Rome against the besieging Saracens, an angel bestowed upon our penitent celestial weapons with which he was given power to rout his enemies. Richard sans Peur, about whom this book also contains a legend, was another son of Satan. He, too, joined the cause of the good God upon learning of his infernal origin.

Nodier was among the contributors to *le Tiroir du Diable* and *le Diable à Paris,* collections of *tableaux parisiennes*. Our writer is also credited with the story, *le Violon du Diable,* but its authorship is very doubtful. His *Infernaliana* is wholly a diabolical book, as the title well implies. It contains anecdotes, brief novels, novelettes and short stories on ghosts, specters, demons and vampires.

Nodier repeatedly occupied himself with vampirism. The belief that a departed spirit returns to earth to feed on the blood of the living is very current among the Slavonic peoples. The word "vampire" itself is of Russian origin. In 1820 Nodier published a novel, *Lord Ruthwen, ou les Vampires,* and a melodrama, *Le Vampire,* which is an adaptation of the novel.

Vampirism also forms the subject of *Smarra, ou les démons de la nuit,* published the following year, the most admired and the most characteristic of Nodier's stories. This tale of Thessalonian superstition, written in the manner of the sorceries and diableries of the *Golden Ass* of Apuleius, swarms with demons of all sorts. The night, according to the belief of the early Christian poets, is full of demons. Smarra, a ghoul, who drinks men's blood, is the familiar spirit of a witch, who delights in filching men's hearts. On their nocturnal revels, the evil spirit and his mistress are accompanied by a thousand demons of the night: "stunted women with a drunken look in their eyes; red and violet serpents with fire-spitting mouths; lizards, who, from out of a lake of mud and blood show faces similar to those of living human beings; heads recently detached from the trunk by the soldier's axe but fixing their eyes upon me and running away skipping on reptilian feet."

Nodier aimed at a reconciliation of Classicism with Romanticism in *Smarra,* as may be seen from the famous verse by Chénier, which our writer placed as a motto at the head of the story. He also wished to pour new wine in old bottles. But in this book a new influence is already making itself felt. Nodier has now fallen under the fatal fascination of Germany. In his essay, *Du fantastic en littérature,* our writer hails Germany as the last retreat of the fantastic element in modern times. "Germany," he asserts, "is richer in this form of creations than any other country in the world." It is in his opinion "the favorite domain of the Fantastic." Nodier is chiefly responsible for the advent of Germanism in French Romanticism. He acquired his admiration for Germany through his personal contact with Mme. de Staël. German folk-lore and legend appealed strongly to our writer's fantastic spirit. Fantastic supernaturalism was the main characteristic of Romanticism in Germany; and it is from this country that it was imported into France. But it did not long remain a foreign importation. We must always bear in mind that whatever was introduced in France from abroad during the Romantic period received the national imprint of that country.

Nodier was especially attracted to a kindred spirit among the Romantic writers of Germany, Ernst Theodor Amadeus Hoffmann.... Our writer was a fervent admirer of this genial German author whom he resembled in his expression of fantastic revery, psychologic mystery, and eery enchantment. Hoffmann, more than any other German author, had fervent followers and devoted disciples in France. His influence on French Romanticism far exceeded even that of Goethe. (pp. 8-12)

Goethe was next to Hoffmann the German writer who most deeply affected the writings of Nodier. It is beyond our scope to show in this paper the influence of *Werther* on *Le Peintre de Saltzbourg*. What concerns us in this connection is the effect produced by *Faust* on our writer. This poem, especially in its diabolical aspect, strongly influenced French imagination. Nodier also admired *Faust*, and prepared . . . , in collaboration with Antony Béraud, a prose adaptation of the poem for the stage. In his essay, **Des types en littérature,** he mentions Faust and Mephistopheles among the admirable characters in literature. (p. 13)

[Nodier's **L'amour et le grimoire**], originally called *Le Nouveau Faust et la Nouvelle Marguerite, ou Comment je me suis donné au Diable,* is a burlesque of Faust. In it, Nodier brings down Goethe's lofty poem to the level of a very ordinary bourgeois affair. It is a pseudo-supernatural story and belongs to what is generally called explained Supernaturalism. This type of the Supernatural was the main characteristic of the English Gothic Novel at the end of the eighteenth century.

Maxime, who tells the story in the first person, summons Satan and offers his soul to the Devil on condition that the latter bring to his room at midnight a certain Marguerite to whom the young man has taken a passing fancy. Satan, however, turns a deaf ear and refuses to submit to the back and call of a mere school-boy who has by chance gotten hold of a grimoire (book of conjurations). By a curious coincidence, the girl appears in his room without the aid of the Devil. A friend of our young man, who has succeeded in persuading Marguerite to elope with him, has sent her up to the room of her would-be seducer there to await in hiding the morning mail-coach. Maxime's anxiety not to betray a trusting friend shows that he is too good a man to sell his soul to Satan. (pp. 13-14)

[In **Le Combe de l'homme mort**], based on a sixteenth century legend of a bargain with Beelzebub, Goethe's influence is less significant. On the eve of All Saint's Day in the year fifteen hundred and sixty-one, the Devil seized a man riding along the road and bore him off thirty leagues to a narrow valley in the Jura mountains. This man had murdered an old hermit in order to obtain his wealth, after having won his confidence through hypocritical piety, and when trapped by the villagers

and threatened with death, he sold his soul to the Devil in exchange for a thirty years' respite. The contract was written in Satan's scrawl on a slip of paper stained with blood and marked with five big black finger nails like a royal seal.

The man was as eager for knowledge as for wealth. After having escaped punishment through the aid of the Devil, he studied at the Universities of Metz and Strasbourg, sat at the feet of the famous sorcerer Cornelius and obtained his doctorate in four faculties. His reputation as a scholar spread far and wide and he was called to fill a chair at the University of Heidelberg. Men and women came from the four corners of the continent to study under this professor. Satan himself, attracted by this scholar's reputation, enrolled as one of his students. Our professor soon was elected rector of the celebrated university. He possessed fame and fortune and never thought of his pact with the Devil. But Satan has a better memory than even the rector of the University of Heidelberg. At the expiration of the term, the Devil was at hand to claim fulfillment of the terms of the contract. As the rector rode along the highway, pleased with himself and the world, the Devil appeared, snatched him up and brought him to the spot of the murder. When the rector ascertained his whereabouts, he was assailed by unpleasant memories. An old woman, urged on by the Evil One, helped along the poor professor's memory by a full and detailed recital of the events which had occurred thirty years before and which gave the valley its name—the Valley of the Dead Man. As he finally rushed out, anxious to disappear in the dark of the night, the Devil followed him and wrung his neck.

The Devil cannot kill a man unless the latter has entered into a pact with him and has forsworn God, as may be inferred from the counsel given to Job by his well-meaning wife. The Devil has no interest in a man's body. If he kills a man, it is only to obtain his soul. "When the term [of a devil-pact] is over," Victor Hugo tells us in *Notre-Dame de Paris*, "the Devil destroys the body in taking the soul, just as a monkey cracks the shell to eat the nut."

The conception of Satan as a university student is reminiscent of Wilhelm Hauff's *Mémoirs des Satan*.

The Devil retains in this story some elements of his former avatar as a hearth spirit. He is described as small of stature, with thick locks of flaming red hair, which almost cover his face, a face pale and yellow like the wax of an old candle and furrowed by wrinkled lines, little red eyes, more sparkling than red-hot coals, a huge mouth with innumerable teeth as pointed as pins and as white as ivory, and with hands long and lean, so transparent that the flame, over which he warms them, shines through them as if they were of horn. The Devil is dressed in a doublet and breeches of scarlet red and wears on the top of his head a woolen cap of the same color. It is this conventional costume that our Devil has in common with Goethe's Mephistopheles. (pp. 14-15)

Maximilian J. Rudwin, "Nodier's Fantasticism," in
The Open Court, *Vol. XXXVIII, No. 1, January, 1924, pp. 8-15.*

PAUL ROSENFELD (essay date 1944)

[*In this excerpt from an essay commemorating the centenary of Nodier's death, Rosenfeld admires Nodier's literary innovations.*]

London newspapers sometime in 1819 reported that Napoleon at Longwood recently had spent a night reading and annotating a French novel. This was *Jean Sbogar,* the depiction in a romantic plot of the character of a sublime Illyrian bandit. . . . The author was Charles Nodier, subsequently famous as the link between French classicism and romanticism, who in the present year, the centenary of his death, must be the subject of commemorations wherever literature remains in honor and the love of French literature persists.

The truthfulness of the report about Napoleon and the novel was afterward impugned. The story was called a clever inspiration of the publisher's. Yet if indeed it was a lie, it was an artistic one. *Jean Sbogar* introduced readers of fiction to a new cause of action which might readily have interested the imperial *Realpolitiker,* the former ally of Babœuf. This new cause of action naturally was not a sublime motive for banditry, a passion for justice, say, leading to banditry. Noble banditti long since had become familiar figures in novels, dramas, narrative verse. Their line led back to Lope de Vega: Schiller merely had sensationally continued it in *The Brigands,* Byron more recently in *The Corsair,* Scott very lately in *Rob Roy.* All these figures rose from the timeless conflict between law and liberty; the more recent from the interior conflicts of individualism, from the division and resentments in middle-class youth in a feudal society, tragic in the sensitive individual requiring freedom for work toward his goals. . . . A picture of banditry—what it comes to is revolt—inspired by individualism, even the noblest kind, could . . . doubtfully have been of interest to Napoleon; nor was the cause of action introduced into fiction by *Jean Sbogar* individualistic.

It was social. In Venetian society of the opening nineteenth century, the fiction begins, there figured a handsome man of mystery. Actually he was the Illyrian brigand, Jean Sbogar, but the fact was unsuspected, and a young patrician, Antonia, fell in love with him. One day he dropped his notebook, which, most prophetically, was "bound in Russian leather." Peering into it, Antonia read this aphorism among others similarly colored: "The robbery of the rich by the poor . . . in the last analysis is nothing save a reparation, a just and reciprocal displacement of a piece of bread or money, returning from the hand of a robber into that of the robbed." Was Nodier's outlaw echoing Babœuf? We do not know. This however is plain: under romantic decorations Nodier here introduced to readers of fiction the idea of the social revolutionary in the epoch propelled by Napoleon; the source of his passion. Since the novelist endowed his brigand with chivalry, magnanimity, a sharp ethical sense, the introduction was ceremonious and serious. *Jean Sbogar* thus was the first socialist novel, by which name we signify a fiction honoring the social motive of revolt. In its wake streamed all the novels expressing popular sympathy, making for social justice—from those of the 1840's by Sue, Sand, Gogol, Dickens, through those by Balzac, Zola, Tolstoi, to grandiose records of the social struggle like *Pellé the Conqueror.* (p. 18)

[Nodier was] a creator in the Greek sense; consistenly the inventor of the new in point of material or method; continually "forming new individualities from out a mass of scattered elements." In 1803, almost at the beginning of his career, he had produced a new method of fiction, the journalary form of the novel. He used it to present the type of the psychological solitary: so also have Hugo, Turgenev, Chekhov, Rilke, Bernanos, and almost all of the novelists who have followed him in using it. After *Jean Sbogar,* in 1839, he revealed yet another important new material for fiction in his exquisite [*La neuvaine de la chandeleur*]. This is the stuff of the pastoral novel—

which is not to be confused with idyls like *The Vicar of Wakefield* or naturalistic and objective studies of peasants and provincial people. The content of the pastoral novel is the lyrical expression of the very peasant or provincial spirit. The country fictions of George Sand probably constitute the classic French representatives of the type; the characteristic fictions of the Swiss C. F. Ramuz and Jean Giono, and stories of Sherwood Anderson's like "I'm a Fool," its chief contemporary ones. Yet another of Nodier's volumes, the humorous and fantastic [*L'histoire du Roi de Bohême et de ses sept châteaux*], anticipated a modern mold of poetry's. The book features expressive contrasts and dispositions of typography creating a sort of supplemental poetry; on one of its pages an arrangement of words in lines evoking an image identical with the one formed by the words' meanings. Rabelais and George Herbert had made experiments of the sort: Nodier's, however, far surpass theirs in wit. The anticipated modern poetic mold of course is the typographic poem of Mallarmé, Guillaume Apollinaire, and E. E. Cummings—that encroachment of poetry on the domain of the sensuous arts.

There are still other instances of his invention of means and materials. Innovation in art, indeed, appeared to Nodier "the seal of genius": in particular, those "irresistible innovations which obediently conform to the progress of social intelligence" and "proceed like naive emanations from the practical inventions of civilization." "Such is the genius of societies," argued he, "that no fundamental change can occur in their antique organizations unless an analogous movement operate in their means of speech." And it is precisely this brilliant inventiveness of his and his steady defense of innovation that are responsible for the elevation of the tone in which we commemorate the one-hundredth anniversary of his death over the one in which his contemporaries commemorated the actual event. Not that Nodier's personality and work were not much remarked on, much admired and praised, when he died. Long before, his apartment in the Arsenal in Paris had become "the little Tuileries," where not the fashionable but the literary world foregathered. There the young romantic school had grown conscious of itself under his paternal eye. But his innovations amused his contemporaries a little more than they impressed them. Sainte-Beuve, in the course of his famous, affectionate portrait of Nodier, a trifle patronizingly called him a *littérateur.* A *littérateur* of course is "an author without a specialty—whose talent, works, literary life resemble an army containing all banners, everything, indeed, save general headquarters."

Now, we do not deny that Nodier was a "polygrapher." Besides novels, he composed, in almost passionate excitement, poetry, criticism, and history; and was a philologist to boot, a bibliographer, and a student of botany and of butterflies, "whose brilliant hues he would seem to have transferred to his style." Neither do we in the least deny that Nodier excelled in nothing. His style, which was modest, sensitive, and charming, did want power.

It merely is that, looking back over the past century, we can perceive the startling results of the new methods and materials which amused his contemporaries; and moreover possess general reasons for seeing in all such inventions "the seal of genius"—reasons still other than those with which Nodier himself supplied us. One is the feeling that ultimately it is in forming new phenomena that art meets the many spiritual demands of society. For each vibration of the spirit has an appropriate form, and there always are new vibrations. Another is the feeling that we encounter the human spirit more purely, profoundly, thrillingly in what is fire-new and unprecedented than in what is influenced, imitative, and traditional. "Ontogeny recapitulates phylogeny!" We even suspect that without innovation there might not exist the possibility of tradition. To put ourselves in the way of understanding past men, it seems we must ourselves perform deeds in some way paralleling theirs: one can, it seems, understand only what in some fashion one is capable of accomplishing. And the past certainly generated the new. Hence, facing the fertile Nodier, we feel nothing save admiration, and revere his memory. (pp. 18-19)

> Paul Rosenfeld, "Nodier After a Century," in The Nation, New York, Vol. 159, No. 1, July 1, 1944, pp. 18-19.

RICHARD SWITZER   (essay date 1955)

[*Switzer considers Nodier's role in French literary history, arguing that he was "a major influence guiding and foreshadowing the post-romantic poetic development."*]

From the very beginning of his career, in the eyes of literary history Charles Nodier was a misunderstood author. He has acquired the undeserved epithet of *précurseur attardé du romantisme* and is known principally for the *cénacle* over which he presided. Nodier continues to be classed as a second rate romantic instead of being placed in his rightful position as an important precursor of symbolism and a significant author in his own right.

During his lifetime, to be sure, Nodier was well known and highly appreciated, but his fame came rather from the less significant parts of his work. An almost incredible example of this lack of comprehension on the part of Nodier's audience is found in the fate of his story **"Les deux Aveugles de Chamouny"**. The story is a delightful parody of the Werther-type story as it had degenerated in France. Moreover, as a parody of the Sterne-type digression which had become so popular in France, Nodier wove this parody episode by episode into his monumental pastiche, *Le Roi de Bohême*. In spite of this double faced parody, in 1844, after the death of Nodier, a collective edition of his stories removed this tale from the *Roi de Bohême,* pieced together the episodes, and presented it as a straightforward tale. It was accepted as such and continued to be reprinted.

Another example of the lack of comprehension is afforded by a second work, **Smarra**. This is certainly one of Nodier's finest works, and is perhaps the most interesting. Nevertheless it was originally received merely as another vampire tale. In fact, Nodier's reputation suffered so that his election to the Académie was delayed for several years.

This lack of understanding is not especially surprising. Contemporaries can seldom detect the true value of an author. In this case the public could not look ahead to symbolism and see to what an extent it was foreshadowed in the works of Nodier. What is surprising is that posterity has not yet seen fit to give to Nodier the place in literary history which he deserves. (p. 224)

Nodier's writings are truly encyclopedic. On one hand he produced works of pure science, of philology, of criticism. On the other hand he brought forth *œuvres d'imagination* which embrace the poles of literary expression. His prose is bare, stark, classic in **Le Chien de Brisquet**. In **Thérèse Aubert** we have a typical *roman sentimental* of the period. A satirical pastiche is presented with the **Roi de Bohême**. **Trilby** and **La Fée aux miettes** belong to the realm of the marvellous and

Smarra to the fantastic. This rather arbitrary terminology of marvellous and fantastic is necessitated by the vast difference between light and gay works such as **Trilby**, and **Smarra** which is somber and anguished.

Nodier's importance as a precursor is evidenced both in form and in content. It would be impossible here to discuss even a small fraction of Nodier's works from these two points of view, although it would be a rewarding study. Let us confine ourselves then to only two works of primary importance, **Smarra** and **L'Histoire du roi de Bohême et de ses sept châteaux.**

Let us consider first the second work, which in many ways is the more superficial. It is a magnificent pastiche from beginning to end, satirizing Sterne, Rabelais, Goethe, Cervantes, Swift, and an almost endless list of authors, a list limited only by the ability of the reader to recognize the pastiche. Nodier was possessed of an incredible erudition. All of this has flowed into the **Roi de Bohême**, necessitating an almost equal erudition on the part of the reader if he is to follow the author. Thus a complete understanding of the text can be the fruit only of patient and careful study.

Certain elements of great interest are, however, immediately apparent. The name of the work comes from the story referred to but never told in *Tristram Shandy*. And in the true manner of Sterne, we learn very little about the King of Bohemia, but a great deal about Popocambou-le-brèchedent, 42,633rd autocrat of Timbuctoo. The book is crowded with all sorts of amusing digressions. . . . (p. 225)

It is the form of the **Roi de Bohême** which first strikes the reader. Nodier is obviously fascinated with the various possibilities of typographical arrangement on the page. Rabelais had used these devices to a certain extent, but Nodier carries the process much further. He uses varying sizes and designs of type; he arranges pages in triangles; he presents two-line chapters, isolated in the middle of a page; he inverts the text; he uses the words to illustrate the text. . . . There is a serious and deliberate attempt to give to the printed work a significance beyond its literal sense; the work takes on an intrinsic value. This of course immediately brings to mind the typographical experiments of later authors such as Apollinaire.

The **Roi de Bohême** is no less significant from the point of view of content. There are three main characters, Théodore, Don Pic de Fanferluchio, and Breloque. But they are actually merely three facets of the author's own being, as he carefully explains to us. Théodore represents the imagination, Don Pic the memory, and Breloque the judgment.

In the course of his tale, Nodier presents frequent long lists in the manner of Rabelais. There is an immediate temptation on the part of the reader to skip over them hurriedly. But again, this is a place where it is necessary to proceed slowly in order to analyze Nodier's intentions. To realize these intentions it is necessary to read the lists aloud. At one point Nodier introduces a nine page list of insects. . . . Nodier was a great naturalist. No doubt he knew each one of these creatures. But he is not giving us here a test of our knowledge of natural sciences. What he is giving us is a juxtaposition of exotic and fascinating sounds. If we search for the meaning of the words, their significance is lost. They exist solely for their sound. The lists are moreover constructed with great care: from time to time, as the ear wearies of the strange sounds, Nodier adds . . . [a ridiculous epithet which serves] to re-focus our attention on the words themselves after this momentary respite.

Here again Nodier is strikingly modern, anticipating the host of modern authors who have striven to find an intrinsic value in words themselves, aside from their meaning.

The *Roi de Bohême* is an extremely significant work. Even more significant is one of Nodier's earlier works, his *Smarra*. . . . However, the important elements of *Smarra* require a closer examination than do those of the *Roi de Bohême*, if one is to understand their nature and importance.

Smarra is, to a certain extent, the result of Nodier's post as editor of the *Télégraphe* in Laybach during the French occupation of Illyria. The title itself is Slavic, Nodier tells us, for nightmare. This is in short the subject of the work, the description of a nightmare. (pp. 226-27)

The story which Nodier relates is vague and confused, as suited to a dream. It is divided into five parts: the Prologue describes the sensations of falling asleep; the Récit begins the dream, in which Lucius, approaching Larisse, is thinking of the delights that await him there. In the Épisode, the shade of Polémon describes his life under the enchantress Méroé, especially the tortures inflicted upon him by the incubus Smarra. In the Épode, within the framework of the dream, Lucius falls asleep and dreams a dream within a dream. Finally the Épilogue presents the awakening of Lucius.

The basic idea of the dream was suggested by Apuleius's *Golden Ass*, but there is little further resemblance. The story itself, moreover, does not exist for itself, but rather exists as the framework for a series of lyrical passages designed to arouse violent emotions in the reader.

Again we may examine the work from the two points of view of form and content. The form is basically a loose narrative holding together a series of evocative passages. As an example of one of these passages, let us examine the description of the coming of sleep:

> Il y a un moment où l'esprit suspendu dans le vague de ses pensées . . . Paix! . . . La nuit est tout-à-fait sur la terre. Vous n'entendez plus retentir sur le pavé sonore les pas du citadin qui regagne sa maison, ou la sole armée des mules qui arrivent au gîte du soir. Le bruit du vent qui pleure ou siffle entre les ais mal joints de la croisée, voilà tout ce qui vous reste des impressions ordinaires de vos sens, et au bout de quelques instants, vous imaginez que ce murmure lui-même existe en vous. Il devient une voix de votre âme, l'écho d'une idée indéfinissable, mais fixe, qui se confond avec les premières perceptions du sommeil. Vous commencez cette vie nocturne qui se passe (ô prodige! . . .) dans des mondes toujours nouveaux, parmi d'innombrables créatures dont le grand Esprit a conçu la forme sans daigner l'accomplir, et qu'il s'est contenté de semer, volages et mystérieux fantômes, dans l'univers illimité des songes.

The very nature of this passage forces upon us the question: is this a prose poem? In Aloysius Bertrand's *Gaspard de la nuit* of 1842, we have already the completely developed prose poem form. It would not then be surprising to find the beginnings of this form in earlier authors. Certainly it cannot be denied that if what Nodier presents us are not *poèmes en prose*, they are at least very close to that form. The narrative purpose has given way almost entirely to the lyric function of the words and ideas.

As for content, Nodier is undeniably a precursor in the utilisation of the dream as subject matter. Previous authors had on occasion used the dream, but there had been no attempt at the delicate shadings which are to be found in *Smarra* nor at the rich evocative possibilities of the subject, which are so carefully developed in the passage which has just been quoted. No one had, as did Nodier, ventured into the limbo lying between waking and sleep illustrated here. Again we must be impressed by the modernity of Nodier in presenting a passage whose overtones, for us, are definitely Proustian. The *coucher* at Combray is immediately recalled. Moreover, the idea of the exterior phenomenon entering into the person is a theme which Proust was to develop in the episode of the "petite madeleine."

The world of *Smarra* is not only the world of dreams, but also the world of the fantastic. Certainly this element is not new to literature; it is rather in the way that Nodier handles his material that the innovation is to be found. Anne Radcliffe still dominated the field of the *roman noir*. Almost without exception the French authors followed her example: the reader is cheated by the author in a sense, since the novel presents a series of frightening and seemingly inexplicable events which in the end are explained away by coincidence and trickery. There were really no apparitions, no element of the supernatural. All was coincidence, imagination, or the machinations of evil scoundrels.

There was of course a tradition of the fantastic in literature, influenced greatly by Jacques Cazotte who, in his *Diable amoureux* of 1772, had produced a novel of diabolism, but treated in a light vein. Nodier on the other hand not only presents his fantastic in somber tones, but he appears convinced of the reality of what he describes. We no longer have a calculating author devising means of mystifying the reader. Nodier draws the substance of *Smarra* from his innermost emotions and convictions. (pp. 227-28)

In *Smarra* as a whole, we do not see the scene clearly; it is not precisely ordered and delineated. It is suggestion which plays the major rôle. . . . In the same way *Ulysses* presents on the surface a jumbled mass of confused speeches and ideas, but a close analysis shows the careful plan of the author. Apparently unmotivated transitions find their motivation in the subconscious, in the chance association of images. The technique of using sentences broken off in the midst of a thought, the constant interruptions and flights of fancy, are identical in the two works.

Smarra is then a work of poetic prose whose subject matter lies in the dream world and in the borderline between sleeping and waking. The author is further preoccupied with the fantastic and the diabolical. The work is couched however in vagueness, where is given simply the suggestion as a point of departure for the imagination of the reader. In the *Roi de Bohême* we have seen the typographical experiments, the symbolism, and the fascination with words representative not of a thought concept but as entities in themselves.

Charles Nodier must inevitably be recognized as a major influence guiding and foreshadowing the post-romantic poetic development. His direct influence is undeniable. In the case of Gérard de Nerval, for example, we can find paragraphs and poems which unmistakably are inspired by Nodier. The less direct influences are more difficult to trace, but none the less real and important.

But beyond this, . . . [Nodier] remains readable to the person of today. The author's outstanding ability as a stylist, and above all his almost unrivalled force of suggestion, combine to make of Nodier a writer who deserves recognition in his own right. (pp. 231-32)

Richard Switzer, ''Charles Nodier: A Re-Examination,'' in The French Review, Vol. XXVIII, No. 3, January, 1955, pp. 224-32.

GWENDOLYN BAYS (essay date 1964)

[*Bays is an American educator and the author of* The Orphic Vision: Seer Poets from Novalis to Rimbaud. *In the following excerpt from that work, she discusses several of the visionary characters in Nodier's works.*]

[Nodier became] a member of a group in Paris, the *Méditateurs,* who practiced the smoking of opium in their meetings held at Passy. Under this powerful stimulant, Nodier conceived the possibility of making artistic use of the dreams evoked by the drug. In the Preface to *Smarra, ou les Démons de la nuit* he describes the dream as the source of poetry, myths, and the marvelous, and says that among primitive peoples and in children there exists between the waking and sleeping state a communication which civilized man has lost: ''The world of sleep contains a gate to heaven or to hell, to the sublime dream or to the nightmare.'' In the prologue of *Smarra,* set in a Lombard village, the lover Lorenzo is delighted to find his mistress, Lysidis, from whom he has been separated for a year. As they celebrate their reunion, Lorenzo tells Lysidis about his terrors during their separation. Abruptly, the scene changes to Thessaly at twilight and the hero, whose name is Lucius, is riding on horseback when, at the point of exhaustion, he has an hallucination: he is surrounded by a group of specters among whom he recognizes his friend, Polémon, who had been killed when the two were on the battlefield. The appearance of Polémon is accompanied by a sort of Walpurgis night scene amid demons and sorceresses. At the sound of a harp all come to order, and Polémon tells Lucius how the sorceress, Méroë, had cast a spell over him and delivered him into the power of Smarra, demon of nightmare. At length, Lucius falls into the clutches of Smarra and sees himself accused of assassination, condemned to death on the guillotine, and his head roll from the scaffold. In spite of this, Lucius' consciousness remains clear enough to be aware of the punishment of Polémon, who was delivered to bacchantes and had his heart torn out by them. With this, the nightmare ends and we are back in Lombardy with Lorenzo, who dreamed he was Lucius, but who awakens to find himself in the arms of Lysidis.

In addition to *Smarra, Jean Sbogar, Le Vampire,* and *Infernaliana,* a collection of stories inspired by a translation of the *Fantasmagoriana,* a similar German work, belong to this same general category of frenetic literature born of the Revolution. About 1830, a marked change may be noted in the writings of Nodier, which Viatte attributes to the fact that he had an experience of illumination in 1828. Whether or not this is true, there was in the life of Nodier a crisis accompanied by acute mental anguish and depression, partly due to the marriage of his daughter, Marie. Although he was still haunted from time to time by nightmares, these became infrequent and less frenzied in his imagination and in his writings after 1830. At this time, he began to turn his creative talents toward more simple, primitive human beings, those who have often been labeled ''insane'' by society. Nodier said he felt special attraction to them because they remain, even when awake, in the borderland of sleep, being unable to return to a waking state: ''How do I know if this alleged infirmity may not be the symptom of a more energetic sensitivity, of a more complete organization, and if nature in exalting all the faculties did not render them fit for perceiving the unknown?'' Thus, Nodier peoples his later works with these ''innocents'' who, because they are pure in heart, possess innate wisdom and visionary powers. The first of such characters is Michel in *La Fée aux miettes,* a simple carpenter, inmate of an asylum in Glasgow, who turns out to have more common sense than the doctors in the institution. The second is Soeur Françoise, the ninety-two-year-old nun in *Hélène Gillet* who refuses to pray for a miracle of some sort to save from the guillotine the innocent Hélène because she ''knows'' in advance that something extraordinary will take place to save Hélène. Another of these dream-world inhabitants is the hero of *Jean-François les Bas-bleus,* who has become deranged as a result of an unfortunate love affair. On one occasion, after having seen traces of blood in the sky, he predicts the execution of Marie Antoinette; on another, he is seized with horror in the public square of Dijon, where he begins calling the names of members of his family who are at that very moment being guillotined in Paris.

The last two of Nodier's seers are the hero of *Baptiste Montauban* and Lydia in *Lydie ou la Résurrection.* The first of these, Baptiste, like Jean-François, has become deranged as a result of an unfortunate love affair. In Baptiste's unusual gentleness combined with great strength of character Nodier suggests the idea of the magic power of saintliness, a theme which Balzac develops two years later in the novel *Séraphita.* Baptiste has a supernatural power of communicating with nature, and like Saint Francis of Assisi his particular talent consists in his ability to tame birds. In the second story, Lydia, a young wife, has become deranged since the death of her husband, George, who was killed while saving a family from their burning home. One night, in her sleep, Lydia succeeds in communicating with her dead husband, who conducts her into the Beyond and explains about an intermediary state in which persons remain for a time after death. For a year Lydia lives in continual communication with the spirit world at night and at the end of this time, when she dies, the narrator is pleased that she has at last joined her husband.

Such is a brief indication of the evolution apparent in Nodier's literary subject matter—from the black magic and the nightmare of *Smarra* to the white magic of his innocent seers, Jean-François, Baptiste Montauban, and Lydia. A forerunner in his introduction of the visionary and the dream into French Romanticism, Nodier not only knew how to create the nebulous atmosphere of the dream but also how to people his world with ethereal creatures. His seers, who are of simple character, instinctive and unlearned, contrast sharply with Balzac's sophisticated and scholarly seers, Louis Lambert and Séraphita. ''Revelation,'' Nodier concludes, ''has not been given either to beings of a nature superior to man nor to men obstinate in the sin of knowledge. . . . It has been given to the simple in spirit and in heart, who believe because they feel and not because they know.'' (pp. 78-80)

Gwendolyn Bays, ''The Seer in French Romanticism,'' in her The Orphic Vision: Seer Poets from Novalis to Rimbaud, *University of Nebraska Press, 1964, pp. 68-125.*

ALBERT J. GEORGE (essay date 1964)

[*George assesses Nodier's overall contribution to the development of French short fiction, focusing on* Trilby *and* La fée aux miettes.]

Nodier, unlike any other previous writer, dedicated his talent primarily to the brief narrative, winning popularity and a durable reputation for himself as a *conteur* of note. Contemporary with Xavier de Maistre, Chateaubriand, and innumerable lady practitioners of the form, he moved more naturally than they within its confines. Much of his work followed the standard recipe, but when he found himself unable to fit his thoughts into the accepted modes of expression, he moved beyond the strictures of the past to become perhaps the first author of his age to recognize short fiction as a form independent and valid in itself, not a dehydrated version of the novel or an episode foreshortened by unimaginative composition. When he laid down his pen, new areas of subject matter had been opened up to the creative imagination of later French writers.

To be sure, Nodier was little clearer than his predecessors on the precise nature of the medium he was handling. The words *conte, nouvelle, historiette, anecdote,* and *roman* were carelessly attached to his stories without concern for sharp theoretical distinction. In the preface to *Trilby,* Nodier called his tale both a *conte* and a *nouvelle;* the same blithe indifference toward nomenclature occurs in the preface of *Les Quatre Talismans* and the dedication of *Inès de las Sierras.* Length and subject matter seem the principal factors of differentiation. *Paul ou la Ressemblance* was entitled an *historiette* or an "histoire véritable et fantastique" while *Les Fiancés* was tagged a *nouvelle.* He called *Piranèse* a *conte psychologique, M. Cazotte* a fragment of a novel, and *Le Génie Bonhomme* a *conte fantastique.*

As one might expect, little of Nodier's work departs radically from previous practice, His roots lay too deeply in the eighteenth century for that, and sorties into new territory were as infrequent with him as with any of his contemporaries. Most of his narratives, in fact, did not survive his death for understandable reasons: the bulk of them belonged in an already weary tradition. The plots are anodyne, simple structures on which Nodier draped moral dissertations. They are peopled with flat characters who live emotionally superficial lives, uninspiring as illuminations of human conduct or as insights into the values of another age. And, unfortunately, these stories constitute the major portion of Nodier's production, among them the *Souvenirs de jeunesse,* many of the *Contes de la veillée,* and most of the so-called *romans.*

All are genial tales told in the tradition of the undisciplined anecdote. Each follows a chronological development and recounts the adventures of an innocent young couple whose love will be frustrated almost at the moment of fulfillment by parental fear of mésalliance, or by an illness that consumes one of the main characters, leaving the other a choice between suicide and life as a religious. Thus the *Neuvaine de la chandeleur* tells of a young man's worshiping a dream girl who died the day after he found her. In a like vein, *Les Aveugles de Chamouny* concerns the thwarted love of the heiress Eulalie and orphaned Gervais, both blind.

Even more emotional are the *Souvenirs de jeunesse,* a collection of lachrymose accounts of ill-fated love taken purportedly from a manuscript which fell into Nodier's hands. The reader is led from Séraphine to Thérèse, Clémentine to Amélie, Lucrèce, and Jeannette, while the author minutely examines his ego. The book catalogues the unknown writer's tragic love life: Thérèse and her young husband succumbed as victims of revolutionary justice; Clémentine refused to marry for fear of a mésalliance; when she died, the author entered a monastery. Later he persuaded Protestant Amélie to change her religion and marry him but almost immediately she succumbed to an unknown illness.

At first glance these stories show little variance from the trite practices of the past. This kind of expanded, formless anecdote

had been the specialty of ladies like Mme Cottin. But a second look reveals a primitive kind of pattern. Each is constructed to permit Nodier to arrange the incidents in a succession of sentimental peaks that culminate in the final catastrophe of young love betrayed by death. The story wanders along a path predetermined by the author's need to manipulate episode for the production of increasingly stronger emotion.

The plots meander as mood dictates, some of them complex, with incidents strung bead-fashion, since Nodier had no use for cause-effect relationships. There is almost a complete lack of tension, for the suspense he sought was not of the kind that would induce tightness of plot. The insoluble predicament of characters trapped by a hostile life provided him with far more interesting material. Thus, the *Fée aux miettes* made a direct emotional appeal to the reader; the *Proscrits* was "l'effusion d'un coeur vivement ému, qui se répond dans le coeur des autres." *Thérèse Aubert* made even its author weep while he wrote of Adolphe, a wounded Vendéen hiding from Republican pursuers, who fell in love with his rescuer, Thérèse, only to watch her die slowly of smallpox.

Pathetic stories and naïve plots, to be sure, but many of them provided Nodier with a vehicle for more serious purposes. He was attempting to reverse literary history and return the brief narrative to what it once had been: a literature for the people. Since he considered his tales an arm of morality, he often used situation to provide ethical dilemmas on which he could comment. The preface of *Hélène Gillet* asserted that all *contes* had to convey a message, a dictum to which Nodier willingly conformed. In the *Peintre de Saltzbourg* or the "diary of the emotions of a suffering heart," Nodier concluded with a discourse on the evils of suicide. *Paul ou la Ressemblance* contained a sermon on overcoming disappointment and sorrow; *Mademoiselle de Marsan,* a tale of secret societies, furnished opportunity for a lecture on tyranny, republicanism, and clandestine organizations. In *Jean Sbogar,* the most popular of Nodier's works, Antonia found the diary of her beloved Lothario to consist of a series of gloomy meditations. Lothario-Nodier resented the use of money, was convinced that cities were the curse of civilization, that murder constituted a sin, and capital punishment a still greater one. He had reason for the last, for Jean was executed for banditry by the French and Antonia dropped dead from shock. So keen was Nodier's interest in moralizing that on occasion he passed from the usual enlarged anecdote to the apologue, or moral fable, to satisfy his compulsive didacticism.

Because these stories carried a meager ideological burden, the means of expression were not particularly inspired. Most of them followed the oral tradition recommended by Diderot, according to which the author claimed the right to interpose. Since Nodier aimed at pure exposition rather than revelation or illumination, there is little conversation. He constantly interjected himself between reader and story because he considered his function that of directing attention to the implications of each situation. Hence digression and comment became important and intrinsic to his manner of storytelling. The characters assumed simple allegorical meanings, but were never trusted to carry the whole burden of the writer's intent.

This passion for preaching made Nodier vulnerable to critical attacks on the realism of his fiction. Consequently, he generally fell back on the story-within-a-story and the first person singular for verisimilitude. To bolster the meager probability of his work, Nodier relied on such clichés as the lost manuscript, the journal left by the hero, or the account taken from an old hagiographer. He assumed that these devices would protect him from charges of fantasy since he was dealing with "real" life. Thus *Thérèse Aubert* purportedly came from a manuscript discovered in a prison; *Adèle* was based on the correspondence between two young men; the *Peintre de Saltzbourg* appeared in diary form; *Soeur Béatrix* was drawn from Bzovius, an old historian. One entire collection appeared as *Souvenirs de jeunesse,* another manuscript entrusted to him. Often Nodier digressed to reassure readers that nothing had been invented, as in *Mademoiselle de Marsan,* or to insist that his stories could be taken literally since the author's natural bent was for "le vrai."

Naïve pretensions, perhaps, as hostile critics sneered, but necessary from Nodier's point of view. As he admitted in a footnote to *Les Quatre Talismans,* the workers and peasants—the only class which understood the obligations of life—formed his audience. For these readers of scant education, he made his characters of modest station, generally from rural areas. He hoped to replace the literary fare usually available to them and to pitch his didacticism at a level they could reach. His characters were types, familiar to ordinary folk in personality, if not in the tenor of their more exciting lives.

This kind of story, although it forms the major portion of Nodier's work, gives an inexact measure of the man. His talent offered more than moral dissertations on the sad fate of young lovers, for his mind contained the vision of a universe larger than the painful stories of Paul, Hélène, or Adèle. These originated in his experience with life, but so would the fairy tales, a reaction to the same circumstances, which constituted his greater claim to literary recognition.

The relationship of these fairy stories to Nodier is more apparent than that of the weepy tales he authored. Even his beloved daughter recognized in the author of *La Fée aux miettes* and *Le Trésor des fèves* a child who had lost contact with reality and become hostile to the world around him. He himself admitted in the *Souvenirs de la Révolution* that his most pleasant memories dated from early youth. (pp. 29-34)

The fairy tale gave Nodier the perfect form for combining his urge to teach and his desire to move beyond the restrictions of reality. "Once upon a time there were fairies," he began the *Génie Bonhomme* and in a humorous introduction he presented Bonhomme, a djinn of modest pretensions who gave Saphir and Améthyste, the grandchildren of Tropbonne, the secret of freedom from boredom: useful labor. This story, like *Trésor des fèves et Fleur des pois,* represents a tradition old in French literature when Nodier wrote. Writers like Madame d'Aulnoy, Mlle Lhéritier, and Perrault had accepted from folk art the general outline and assumptions of this kind of tale and their literary posterity had found no reason to challenge the custom. With them the genre received the sanction of the sophisticated and made its way into literature as a conscious art form. Just before the Revolution, in 1785, the fairy tale had experienced a resurgence of popularity with the publication of the *Cabinet des fées,* a collection of practically all these narratives written in French. Then, during the Empire, the fairy tale flourished again, partly because of the censorship of contemporary materials, partly because of the general stagnation in art. At this time the fairy tale turned into something close to the love story, with unhappy endings and melancholy characters.

Nodier was well acquainted with his distinguished predecessors, but he chose to speak to the same audience toward which he had directed his other work. Consequently, he kept his plots

on an elementary level and continued the bad literary habit of digressing on any topic that caught his fancy. The exigencies of a tightly controlled art bothered him not at all; his audience reacted only to plot, caring little for niceties of structure or fine points of characterization.

Trilby provided just the kind of narrative he liked. Nodier recounted in an intimate, folksy manner the love of a sprite for the Scottish lass Jeannie, using many of the ingredients traditionally involved in the concoction of a fairy tale. The story begins with a bit of local color, a short disquisition of the prevalence of elves and sprites in Scotland. There is the usual sage, the centenarian monk Ronald, who summons Trilby thrice, and thrice reads the litany of the Virgin. The elf uses the hoary device of disguising himself as an old man, deceiving nobody but Jeannie, and his end is foreshadowed by the interpolation of a legend of how a monk overpowered a giant through prayer. The tale ends in a cemetery, at which point Nodier falls back on the genie-in-a-box idea and multiplies the emotional impact by having Trilby sealed away for a thousand years.

The plot, however, contains divergences from the old recipe. There is no villain, no wicked giant or nasty ogre, and a priest brings about Trilby's downfall. Trilby is mischievous but never malicious; he prefers the company of the poor and disdains the rich. Those he favors prosper and are never threatened by sudden reversals of fortune. And Trilby loves Jeannie with a mundane passion surprising in a fairy tale. The streak of sensualism that runs through Nodier's work has often been noted, but here it is almost painfully evident. At night Trilby dances through Jeannie's hair, whispering endearments, and she dreams of him in what Nodier blandly calls her "rêves innocemment voluptueux." But no such statement can keep the dullest reader from recognizing Trilby's meaning when he begs Jeannie to recall him because he loves her. The words are seductive, for here Nodier could not disguise the fact that his plot revolves around the sprite's attempt to steal Jeannie from her husband, even though Nodier insisted on the other-worldly quality of his affection.

Basically, the story departs little from Nodier's customary manner. *Trilby* is an intimate but wandering tale that winds from one strong emotion to another. The lovers never surmount the difficulties which the author hurls in their path; their predicament is resolved by death and the intimation that their reward will come in the hereafter. Jeannie's tomb lies conveniently near the tree and her headstone carries a message for the young at heart: "Mille ans ne sont qu'un moment sur la terre pour ceux qui ne doivent se quitter jamais."

It would be easy to carp at Nodier, to titter at his description of how the wind sobbed a requiem for Jeannie. Even though he never succeeded in controlling his plot, some of his descriptions, particularly those of the loch and its surrounding mountains, should earn him a measure of forgiveness. He believed that the fairy tale suited his talents, and when critics disagreed he paraphrased Luke 18:16: "Permettez aux petits de venir, car il n'y a point de danger pour eux à écouter mes récits, et vous me connoissez assez pour me croire."

In 1831, he returned to the fairy tale with *La Fée aux miettes,* his most ambitious project, and in some ways his most significant contribution. In terms of length, the *Fée* falls outside any consideration of brief prose fiction, but actually it differs from Nodier's shorter works only in that it was expanded to volume size by multiplying the number of obstacles set before the hero. The story seems, in fact, an attempt to marry the structure of the romance to the fairy tale plot. Nodier utilized the framework technique to capture the attention of his readers, beginning near the end of his tale by having young Michel, a carpenter, recount the saga of his star-crossed love for the fairy queen Belkiss in a lunatic asylum.

Nodier called the *Fée aux miettes* a "bluette de peu de valeur," but obviously he had poured a great deal of himself into it. Michel's story dispensed with even that small bit of logic on which the element of the fantastic is usually superimposed. Nodier ignored cause and effect; the story moves along in an atmosphere if unreality, with the plot resting entirely on coincidence and arbitrary movement. Fantastic event piles on fantastic event in a weird mixture of dream sequences, strange metamorphoses, and irrational situations to produce an almost surrealistic effect. Poor Michel falls into bloody and terrible nightmares which foreshadow tragic events in a manner customary in fairy tales, kaleidoscopes of horror that hint at evil. Similarly, when the boy is to be tried for the murder of a bailiff who suddenly revives, he appears before a jury composed of animals. In *La Fée aux miettes,* as in Kafka's *Der Prozess,* there is a complete lack of communication between Michel and the judge, and his lawyer offers a defense so absurd as to seem ludicrous. Nodier, in fact, was indicting the legal profession for inconsistency, pedantry, and lack of concern with justice.

The book represents an excursion into what Nodier had come to accept as the "real" world, beyond time, where death was not really death, nor misfortunes endless. Michel, the dreamer, learned to his sorrow that the world of human prejudice and pragmatism refused to understand him. Therefore, Nodier created a better universe for the type of simple young man he thought himself and for whom he acted as benevolent Providence. Only in this kind of fantasy, Nodier argued in the preface, could happiness really be found.

In *La Fée aux miettes,* as in *Trilby,* Nodier used the basic ingredients of the fairy tale, liberally spiced with criticism. Michel loved Belkiss in all his adolescent innocence, but soon the affair took a more adult turn as Nodier described the worldly aspect of their love. Belkiss, or the Queen of Sheba, was the traditional good fairy who tested the fidelity of the mortal she favored. Following custom, she placed him in jeopardy three times, borrowed money three times, then required him to accomplish the impossible to save their love. Yet the reader follows the boy's adventures with the comfortable assurance that all will end well to the tune of the mandrake's song.

Because Nodier was expanding the fairy tale, approximating the structure normally used for the romance, the central themes are almost buried. As in *Trilby,* he intended to involve the reader emotionally with Michel's plight by moving from crisis to crisis. Nodier had inherited this method from the eighteenth century and it would have constituted a revolution of the first magnitude for him suddenly to have rejected it. In all fairness, he can be understood only in these terms.

The *Fée aux miettes* is difficult to read not just because of the complexity of episode and the author's propensity for slipping from "realism" to a conventional fairyland and thence to nightmares of Freudian proportions, but also because of the extremely heavy overlay of didacticism. In this respect Nodier was following the major precept of seventeenth- and eighteenth-century prose fiction: to teach morality, either by lecture or by horrible example. Michel is a naïve country boy who successfully resists the world's temptations. Some classified

him as a fool, or an epileptic, a fact which enhanced his value in Nodier's eyes, since he thereby became a better medium for expressing the subjective experiences that form an essential part of the plot. Nodier felt a special affection for this kind of protagonist, in his mind more in tune with things spiritual. (pp. 35-8)

The loose structure of *La Fée aux miettes* permitted interpolations either in the form of direct explanation or long sermons by the fairy and the uncle. Michel receives a goodly share of advice on matters as disparate as personal conduct and the gathering of cockles. He leads the good life of simple tastes, shares his wealth with friends, and remains true to his word and his love. Even under great pressure he shuns temptation. . . .

The didacticism, however, stands alongside biting irony. Beyond the pastiches of Fénelon, Cyrano de Bergerac, and Perrault, in addition to the essays on natural history, are indications of the lessons Nodier had learned from the master satirist Laurence Sterne. Nodier teases the reader with apparently serious remarks, or gives such facetious headings to his chapters as: "Le dernier et plus court de la narration de Michel, qui est par conséquent le meilleur du livre." Like Sterne he breaks off the story to address the reader, comments on his characters, or tosses barbs at unbelievers. Nodier mocked the critics with Uncle Toby's refrain, or called attention to a conclusion "which explains nothing and can be dispensed with." He whimsically named his characters Folly Girlface, the other woman; Master Finewood, the builder; or Jap Muzzleburn, the canine bailiff of the Isle of Man.

No doubt he enjoyed this kind of humor, but he also used it to strike back at those who objected to his work as the maundering of an unsophisticated mind. (p. 40)

In the development of the forms of short prose fiction, Nodier's is a name to be reckoned with, historically, as one of the first to dedicate a major part of his literary life to the brief narrative. Much of his work, written under pressure, did not extend beyond tales of thwarted love, arranged as stories-within-stories. Generally these narratives were only long anecdotes of the woes of frustrated young folk, which he attempted to justify as "true" or "historical." Occasionally he flirted with the apologue, or resuscitated the pseudo-diary and epistolary forms so fashionable in the previous century. Most of all he preferred the fairy tale, in which he could arrange incident to satisfy his outraged sense of justice. In this way he solved the dilemma facing him as an artist: how to be in a hostile world, yet not of it. He ventured into make-believe, folk stories, or dreams, always giving free hand to an incurable didacticism. Thus he performed what he considered the function of art when he acted as moral guide to his readers, whom he considered lesser beings. To the public he presented a grandfatherly personality, hiding the private one that cringed from life.

In these instances Nodier added little to the technique of brief fiction. Structurally he followed eighteenth-century usage by building his plot in terms of emotional crises. He showed little sense of the capabilities of the form, no willingness to depart from ancient tradition. . . . Perhaps he was misled by the audience he aimed at, the little people in the villages, for whom he pioneered a literature far in advance of George Sand and Lamartine. For the unsophisticated and the newly literate he used highly sensitive characters in stories full of pathos to teach a code of behavior. Consequently, he had no need of a story line that culminated in a crisis reached by the constant interaction of personality and incident. Successful as he may have been in his time, this insistence on emotional content has dated this part of his work. The increase of literacy and the changes which industrialization brought to France left him an author with a decreasing public and stole the freshness from his work.

It would not be fair, however, to dismiss Nodier cavalierly as only of historical importance. Parts of his writing still sparkle: the descriptions of Trilby and Jeannie on the lake, the unexpected flashes of wit. A fine vein of irony runs through his tales, sometimes directed at his own art, as though he sensed its thinness, sometimes aimed at readers silly enough to take him seriously. With a measure of good will and some historical imagination, one can still read him with pleasure.

More importantly, however, Nodier indicated to later writers the treasures they could find by exploiting the world of the subconscious. In *Smarra* he moved away from the comfortable exterior world which had satisfied previous generations into the untracked, illogical, and frightening reaches of the human mind. In so doing, he departed from the fictional universe of causality, chronology, and incident. With *Smarra* he opened up new and unexplored lands, indicating, like Chateaubriand, the possibility of depicting inner conflicts, reaction rather than action, suggestion in preference to exposition. A writer could then step away from his reader and move into the minds of his characters. (pp. 45-6)

> *Albert J. George, "Transition," in his* Short Fiction in France: 1800-1850, *Syracuse University Press, 1964, pp. 17-52.*

LAURENCE M. PORTER   (essay date 1972)

[*Porter offers a psychoanalytic interpretation of dream imagery and human relationships in* Smarra, *premised on the Jungian theory that "the central thrust of dreams and fantasies is the quest for individuation, the reconciliation of the unconscious with the conscious parts of the personality." For additional criticism by Porter, see excerpt dated 1974.*]

The revolutionary turmoil of the late eighteenth century called into question all of Europe's social, political, and religious institutions. Society seemed unable to improve itself; reason seemed unable to explain the world. Writers began to seek the basis of a new order in the supernatural realm; and they tried to apprehend this order with the non-rational faculties. In prose fiction, the dream-narrative became one of their most common vehicles. Outside France, Novalis and Blake came before and overshadowed Nodier; in France, the later dream-narratives of Nerval, Lautréamont, and Flaubert (*La Tentation de Saint Antoine*) are much better known. *Smarra ou les démons de la nuit; songes romantiques,* Nodier's masterpiece, has never received more than cursory attention. But *Smarra* is not only the first French narrative to create an elaborate semblance of dream-structure; it also portrays the dynamics of the human psyche in a way that strikingly anticipates the theories of modern psychoanalysis. In France there is no more subtle or complex rendering of dream-experience until Nerval's *Aurélia.*

Smarra's setting leaps capriciously from modern Italy to Athens and Thessaly under the Roman Empire to the same places in Ancient Greece three centuries earlier. The adventures of three couples—Lorenzo and Lisidis, Lucius and Myrthé, Polémon and Méroé—are tenuously, confusingly intertwined. But Nodier's preface to the original edition claims that *Smarra's* haphazard array of places and episodes conceals a drama as coherent as the plot of a classical tragedy. . . . Nodier's comparison of his dream-narrative's structure to that of a four-act play

corresponds exactly to Jung's description of dream-plot, based on the analysis of thousands of dreams: "There are a great many 'average' dreams in which a definite structure can be perceived, not unlike that of a drama. . . . [Its four phases are] the EXPOSITION . . . DEVELOPMENT of the plot . . . CULMINATION or *peripeteia* . . . the *lysis,* the SOLUTION or RESULT produced by the dream-work."

Nodier himself provided the essential clues to the hidden unity of his fantastic tale. He called *Smarra* the faithful account of a nightmare. And he elsewhere defined the nightmare as a drama with a thousand actors, in which the dreamer himself plays all the roles. Applied to *Smarra,* Nodier's definition of the nightmare means that all six major human characters and the monster Smarra can be interpreted as fragments of the protagonist's total self, exteriorized through the psychic mechanism of projection. *Smarra* has at most two characters, *Me* and *It: It* is the feminine phantom feared, desired, and woven from the dreamer's imaginings. The women Lisidis, Myrthé, and Méroé embody aspects of the Jungian anima, the feminine part of every masculine psyche which is repressed from ego-consciousness into the unconscious. It re-emerges, according to Jung, in the forms of "everything that functions like a mother" in our fantasy life.

Lacking the terminology of modern psychoanalysis, Nodier nevertheless proved himself clearly aware of the existence of a personal unconscious, and of the wish-fulfilling function dreams may serve. . . . He wrote several substantial essays on the dream. And at the beginning of the dialogue fantasy *L'Histoire du Roi de Bohème et de ses sept châteaux,* Nodier directly equates the three main characters with three different aspects of his own psyche: Théodore is his imagination; Breloque, his reason; and Don Pic, his memory. In short, as Nodier himself describes his art, it anticipates the principles of psychoanalytic dream-interpretation. There are no "accidents": every detail points to the hidden affective center of the dream, and every shift in plot, subject, characters or setting is motivated by the dreamer's inner conflicts. (pp. 331-32)

To interpret Nodier's *Smarra,* I rely primarily on Jung, who developed the most sophisticated, illuminating theories of dream-analysis available today. My basic assumption is that the central thrust of dreams and fantasies is the quest for individuation, the reconciliation of the unconscious with the conscious parts of the personality. The dream is an involuntary creative process, arising from the interplay of compulsions and strivings for self-realization (Adelson).

The dreamer's identity crisis dramatized in *Smarra* is not successfully resolved with the establishment of a mature personality. The recurring motif of thwarted or disastrous attempts to enter a city (Larissa; Athens; Corinth) embodies Lorenzo's anxiety about undertaking a mature sexual and emotional relationship with a woman. Whether this attempt be made in the spirit of conquest (Corinth), submissiveness (Athens), or curiosity (Larissa), it would be symbolically consummated by a character's entering the city. But as the dream ends, Lucius and Polémon, beset by the Thessalonian witches, are prevented from triumphing in their siege of Corinth.

Freud claimed that "dreaming on the whole is a regression to the dreamer's earliest condition, a revival of his childhood, of the instinctual forces which dominated it and of the methods of expression which were then available to him" (cited by Adelson). Nodier appears to concur, for he co-ordinates his narrative's steady retreat into the historical past with the dreamer's psychic state. The dreamer's memories regress through earlier periods of his life towards a semblance of infancy. Lorenzo has just married, Lucius has just left school, and Polémon is associated with an imagery of helpless children during his nightmare at the heart of the story. Méroé, the name of Polémon's mistress, sounds very like "mère." As the Queen of the Witches who eventually devours Polémon's heart, Méroé plays the role of the Jungian Terrible Mother, the awesome, possessive, dominating figure who denies her children an independent identity. (p. 333)

Nodier constructed *Smarra* like a *monde gigone,* a world of nested boxes where a story-within-a-story becomes the narrative frame for another story within itself, and so forth indefinitely at the pleasure of the author. The five titled divisions of the story are arranged A-B-C-B-A, as it were, to form three levels of experience:

I) LORENZO with Lisidis in their marriage bed
PROLOGUE . . . EPILOGUE.
II) LUCIUS with Polémon in his pleasure palace
RECIT . . . EPODE.
III) POLEMON in the nightmare with Méroé
EPISODE

Each level illuminates a different area of Lorenzo's psychic life. Polémon's nightmare presents what seems to be the mother-child relationship seen retrospectively by the adult, and as it colors his relationships with all other women. Lucius' psychic state, throughout his vague search for pleasure without a specific object, corresponds to what Erik Erickson has characterized as adolescent identity diffusion. Lorenzo's need to adjust to the new commitment of marriage has generated emotional stress. This reactivates earlier psychic states in Lorenzo's life, the memories of which are preserved in the unconscious. The unresolved conflicts of these earlier states inspire Lorenzo with feelings of helplessness and terror. By dramatizing these conflicts in what the psyche presents as dreams within dreams, Lorenzo attempts to rob them of reality. The main, initial dream represents an attempt to replace that which is rejected in the inner ones. (p. 334)

The prologue begins in a house in Arona, beside the Lago Maggiore. Like Nodier's other major dream narratives, *Trilby* and *La Fée aux Miettes, Smarra* is set near water as if to suggest the proximity of the unconscious depths to the protagonist's state of waking consciousness. As Lorenzo goes to bed with Lisidis, his bride of a week, he hopes her presence will ward off the terrifying nightmares which have been afflicting him. He ascribes them to having read the first book of Apuleius with its story of vampirism, and he attempts to dissociate Lisidis from them. . . . He dares not consider that his relationship to Lisidis may be the origin of his nightmares, as well as of the erotic fantasies that have preoccupied him for the past year. His psychic needs have polarized the attributes of Lisidis as he consciously and unconsciously imagines them. Consciously, he idealizes both her and himself, perceiving in each of them only the desirable qualities of selfless, trusting, protective love for the other. His fear of domination and his aggressive desire to dominate are repressed by being projected into the characters of classical Roman literature. And then he invokes the idealized image of Lisidis which he loves, to protect him against the darker image of her which he refuses to acknowledge.

Near the end of the story, we learn that Lorenzo's week-old marriage to Lisidis has just had its first social test at a dance in the magnificent palace on the Isola Bella. The presence of other attractive women has activated Lorenzo's desires to re-

gain his independence, either by abandoning Lisidis or by completely dominating her. He would like to be free to have any woman, without responsibility, while keeping Lisidis as a preferred but submissive servant. These feelings generate the harem fantasies, attributed to Lucius, of a pleasure-palace and a favorite slave Myrthé. But, feeling similar yearnings for independence, Lisidis has danced too long with a rival. The rival has made Lorenzo fear being dominated or rejected by her. In his dream, the surrogates Lucius and Polémon effect a partial catharsis of Lorenzo's guilt and fear by being dominated and punished in his place. From this perspective, the male rival at the dance becomes the monster Smarra, the true husband of the mother-wife Méroé in the dream. As a witch, Méroé embodies those aspects of Lisidis which Lucius is reluctant to acknowledge consciously, as well as his projected fears of her anger and retribution for his thoughts of infidelity. When Lorenzo talks to Lisidis at the beginning of the story, she has fallen asleep. At the end, he falls asleep while she talks to him. There appears to be little communication between the human beings, who mainly interchange two exteriorized fantasy projections.

A sensitive passage then describes Lorenzo's approach to the dream. Characteristically for visionary Romantic literature, the protagonist's perceptions move from gathering darkness, to sound, to a new and different light. Vision, an objective response to the outer world and the awareness of the barriers which distinguish different roles and forms, yields to the perception of sound. Sound impressions are more resistant to measurement and categorization than visual ones; they are discernible, but without weight, form, or shape. Here the perceptions of sound descend the hierarchy of consciousness towards a purely instinctual state: the regular steps of a townsman give way to the tread of home-bound mules, and finally to the unmeasured moaning of the wind. (pp. 335-36)

The *Récit* begins. Lorenzo, now asleep, imagines himself to be Lucius, the protagonist of Apuleius' *Golden Ass.* On horseback he has left the philosophical schools at Athens (Minerva, wisdom, rationality) to explore the magical region of Thessaly. As Nodier's *Histoire du Roi de Bohème* makes plain, journeys stand for dreams, and the act of riding a horse represents love-making. Even the horse's name, Phlégon (Greek *Phlegein,* to burn), evokes sexual desire. With the intermediary of Lucius' erotic fantasy, in other words, Lorenzo re-enacts his confusing, exciting transition through adolescence to mature sexual experience. He travels alone at night, through dark woods and beneath a foggy sky; that is to say, in a state of uncertain identity where the self has yielded to its instincts and is borne along by them. And the sorceresses reputed to haunt the forest are the imagined women who will teach Lucius the art of love. Their magic frightens the protagonist because, as Lorenzo, he feels guilty and disloyal towards Lisidis; as Lucius, he fears the unknown; and the mature sexual response to women he feels as Polémon, remains confused with the child's forbidden attraction to his mother. Lucius represses his fear of the dark journey by attributing it to his horse, as he will later attribute it to his friend Polémon. Phlégon starts in terror and speaks to warn his master of menacing phantoms. Exteriorized, these fears then take shape for Lucius as the phantoms of crippled beggars and hideous old men—potential future selves mutilated by the experiences which Lucius approaches. They embrace him with terrifying glee. But then the city of Larissa, "si chère à la volupté," comes into view. Cries of pleasure and the songs of the Thessalonian girls dispel Lucius fears.

Like Lorenzo at the beginning, in whom thoughts move from remembered nightmares to delighted appreciation of Lisidis,

Lucius progresses from terror to *volupté*. Such a movement of thought is typical of dream-sequences which end with a wish-fulfilling act to which the dreamer cannot give whole-hearted, conscious moral consent. A preparatory dream or dreams is necessary to overcome the dreamer's initial resistance, by veiling the thing desired in a symbolic disguise, and by purging the dreamer's feelings of fear and disgust. Only then can his wish emerge in recognizable form.

As Lucius observes the city, accumulated images of transparency now show it opening before the eye of desire. Its marble columns and cupolas resemble legs and breasts. . . . His desire, however, has not yet distinguished an object; the singing procession of girls that approaches him remains as a vague swarm, . . . and surrounded by a cloud of perfume, music and flickering iridescent light. The description of the scene, moreover, reflects a strong effort at sublimation. Song itself, particularly in the literature of Romanticism, often presents sexual pleasure in symbolic and idealized disguise (cf. *Atala, Sylvie,* etc.). And here the song inspires thoughts of pure first love and of a mother's (equivocal) devotion for her child.

Then one figure emerges from the undifferentiated crowd. "Grande, immobile, debout," she is the "apparence imparfaite de la bien-aimée qui n'est plus." Lucius claims to have mourned her faithfully for seven years, as he tries to ward off the guilt he feels at the "reproche effrayant" of the apparition. Since he has just left school, it is difficult to imagine how he would have had the time to love and to remain faithful to a romantic memory for so long. The female phantom's distinctive height evokes a mother seen by her child: the guilt Lucius feels may derive in part from his having forgotten his own mother in his pursuit of adult independence. But the number seven suggests that the principal meaning of the apparition attaches to the Lorenzo-Lisidis relationship. At the end of **Smarra**, Lisidis mentions that the day of the dance was the eighth day of their marriage. The details of the apparition to Lucius attempt to diminish Lorenzo's guilt concerning his fantasies of infidelity, by attenuating his obligations to Lisidis and by exaggerating his fidelity. she has been transformed from a wife to a fiancée; she is now dead (an emphatic oneiric equivalent of "forgotten"); and besides, Lucius/Lorenzo has already been faithful to her for seven years (days) before he attempts to enter the pleasure city of Larissa. Nevertheless, Lucius' psychic discomfort becomes too strong. He dehumanizes the scene of himself among dancing girls to that of a boat among waves; these are soon replaced by an abyss filled with torrents of ghoulish dead; that is to say, the anger of the "dead fiancée" has expanded until it fills the world. He rescues himself by taking flight. . . . The world shrinks beneath Lucius in an affective distancing which reduces the "dead fiancée" to insignificance. And at last this world becomes no larger than the hexahedral toy which children spin along the pathways of the Céramique, a district of Athens.

So the phantasmic anima-figure which prevented Lucius from entering the city of mature sexual experience drives him back to childhood. He returns to the city where he went to school, and there what he first sees is a children's game. But Lucius' desires, fears, and the anima figure have followed him back to Athens. In attempting to regress to the condition of a child, Lucius finds himself encumbered with an adult body, self-concept, and need for self-definition. . . . Lucius' trip to Thessaly amounted to a moratorium, obviating the need to compete and choose an occupation. Lucius' harem fantasies likewise conceal a wish to postpone or evade psychosocial self-defi-

nition, since the slave-girls obey Lucius rather than challenging him. Even under these ideally relaxed conditions, however, there remains the serious problem of coping with heterosexual intimacy. . . . The threat of identity loss becomes all the greater when in Lucius' fantasies, his psychic regression draws forth the devouring aspect of the anima from its lair in the infantile depths of his psyche.

Nodier chooses to make the transition from Larissa to Athens by mentioning the paths around the Céramique, because the paths in that section of Athens were lined with tombs commemorating warriors who like Lucius' friend Polémon had died for their country. (This common Greek name comes from the word *polemos,* war: as a surrogate for Lucius and Lorenzo, Polémon is placed at the center of Lorenzo's psychic conflicts and bears the brunt of them.) Inside an open square in Athens, Lucius then perceives a procession of sorceresses' male victims, tormented by nightmares. Their bodies tremble gently like a jew's-harp, and they slowly tread in a circle like the mechanical figures on a clock. By comparing the victims to toys—to little, inanimate things—Lucius as narrator controls his own fears and distances himself from their purgative re-enactment by the victims. the victims' endless circular movement suggests the ego-consciousness in the grip of a superior force; the development of the ego has been blocked until it will come to terms with the unconscious. (pp. 336-39)

Lucius recognizes his dead friend Polémon in the procession. They had besieged Corinth together with the armies of the Achean League (244 B.C.). Polémon threw himself in front of Lucius to intercept a lance hurled at his friend, and he died of his resulting neck wound. Since both men will be decapitated later in the narrative, the location of Polémon's wound here foreshadows a dissociation of mind and body, brought about because the claims of the body, or instinctual self, are inadmissible by the head or reflective self. The lance is the anima's weapon, striking unexpectedly from afar. *Smarra's* major source, the first book of Apuleius' *Golden Ass,* corroborates this association of lance and anima, for in Apuleius it is a sorceress and not a soldier who inflicts the neck wound. This incident telling of Polémon's being struck down outside a city he is trying to enter reduplicates the appearance of the reproachful phantom that prevents Lucius from reaching his pleasure-palace in the city of Larissa. Corinth, like Larissa, was renowned for the delights of love, for its temple to Venus and its expensive courtesans. In his correspondence, Nodier cited the familiar proverb "non licet omnibus adire Corinthum." Not everyone may go to Corinth, because its pleasures cost too dear. The power of the anima, unacknowledged by ego-consciousness, debars the protagonists from a mature love relationship.

The scene darkens, suggesting an imminent change to another level of consciousness. Lucius invited Polémon to his pleasure-palace (now transported from Larissa to Athens). They will listen to the harp and voice of Lucius' favorite slave-girl, Myrthé, whose songs have the power to drive away evil spirits and nightmares. This girl is herself an archetypal anima-figure in its protective aspect. Her name comes from the Greek work for perfume (*muron*) and from the name of the myrtle, a plant consecrated to Venus and the token of happy lovers. The many verbal refrains in Lucius' praises of her song create a walled-in, sheltering world of reassurance. And the harp itself can represent a tension between the material instincts (the frame and strings) and spiritual aspirations (the vibrations), resolved in harmony and self-control (Chevalier). But Myrthé has potentially some attributes of the Terrible Mother. That her father is a smith associates her with the underworld: she exercises enchantments and rules over familiar spirits. The nightmares from which Lucius says he suffers associate him with Lorenzo and Polémon, and Myrthé protects Lucius as Lisidis tries to protect Lorenzo. But Lucius' nightmares are peculiar to his state of identity diffusion. They signify a sense of inadequacy and fear of exposure to others. He dreams of losing his teeth and nails (the battlements which protect the inner man—[Cirlot]; of course, this also suggests castration). He dreams of being exposed to the crowds on the street in a transparent tunic; he fears that others can read into his soul and that they will find him despicable.

Nodier uses insect imagery in his description of Lucius' palace, to prepare the transition to the nightmare sequences of Polémon's story. The dark-haired cohorts of the blond Myrthé have stolen honey from the bees; their names—Thélaïre and Théis—not only evoke famous courtesans, but also are the names of species of insects. The spirits of intoxication fill the air like fireflies. The monster Smarra later appears among a swarm of phantoms that hover like gnats. Like a mosquito, he pumps blood from Polémon's chest, and later he will lick it with a tongue that uncoils like a butterfly's. Nodier lived for a time with the naturalist Girod de Chantrans, and was co-author of a treatise on the function of antennae in insects when he was eighteen. He chooses the names and characteristics of insects to represent nightmare apparitions, because insects represent an objective reality which can be precisely described, and yet their appearance and customs are completely alien. The social insects display a more elaborate community organization than one finds anywhere outside human society, and the semblance of purposefulness which this organization creates is analogous to the inhuman purposefulness of evil spirits. At the same time, the implied author's choice of insects as vehicles for his fantasies has a defensive element: because insects are small (''unimportant'') the fantasies appear less menacing.

The love-making which would be the natural conclusion of Lucius' harem fantasy is replaced by Polémon's story. As a soldier, Polémon will embody the impetus of male sexuality in Lucius, and run the risks Lucius fears to face directly. Polémon relates his persecution by Méroé. We are supposedly in Athens, but he offhandedly situates his adventure in Larissa. So Larissa has come to Athens; that is, Lucius/Lorenzo's adult desires have pursued him despite his attempted regression to childhood. At the same time, however, Polémon's relationship to Méroé suggests a child's relationship to its mother. He adoringly follows her everywhere. His love feelings reveal a disturbing abdication of personal will.... And the death of Méroé's husband, making her available, disguises the dreamer's wish for the death of his father.

Wordlessly, one evening, Méroé lures Polémon into her palace. She rests her head on his arm, and they fall asleep in this position, after making love, as did Lisidis and Lorenzo. But when Polémon lies quite still, Méroé rises quietly to invoke her familiar spirits and to prepare a magic potion. She compounds it of the veil in which a remorseful lover hid his head after having killed a woman's husband to possess her, and of the tears of a hungry tigress who devoured one of her young. In the context of the imagery of children, mothers, and helplessness which pervades Polémon's account of his nightmare, the ingredients of Méroé's potion suggest the child's Œdipal fantasy of replacing his father, and his resulting guilt, together with the child's unconscious response to his mother's love, experienced both as tenderly protective (the tears) and as de-

structively possessive (the devouring). The strength of the spell which Méroé as anima-figure casts is suggested by the *rhombus* top she spins: the world reduced to a toy. The cosmic harmony symbolized by the *ouroboros* of Méroé's bracelet (a snake with its tail in its mouth) breaks when the creature comes alive and slithers away hissing. In Jungian terms, this manifests ''a symptom of anguish expressive of a reactivation of the destructive potentiality of the unconscious'' (Cirlot). All the protective aspects of the mother fail, yielding up the ''child'' Polémon to destruction. The moon appears, as bloody as the iron shield on which a dead warrior is borne home from battle. Within the palace, colonnades open out endlessly (in this passage the columns suggest the mother's legs seen by a small child).... Polémon's vision of numerous, undifferentiated children, separated from the protective mother, suggests that he suffers from such dissociation here.

Polémon cries out in horror. To punish him for spying on her secrets, Méroé releases the monster Smarra from beneath the turquoise in her ring. (This gem is associated with lead, with Saturn, and thus with the nether regions.) Smarra embodies the child's Œdipal hostility towards the rival father. Through the mechanism of projection, this hostility is unconsciously attributed to the father himself, and is consciously perceived as a generalized, unidentified source of terror. (pp. 339-42)

Smarra drains Polémon's blood like a vampire, in a self-inflicted punishment.... In the background Polémon sees hideous reptiles of self-contempt, stunted drunken women expressing his repulsion at his wish for incest with the mother-figure, and severed heads evoking the punishment of castration, but more generally signifying a mind dissociated from a body whose desires it can no longer endure to contemplate. Every night thereafter Polémon's dreams re-enact the dreaded, desired incest fantasy. (p. 342)

The guilt induced by Polémon's adult sexuality superimposed on an infantile attraction to the mother represents only an intermediate stage in his drama of regression. Méroé as Terrible Mother will literally engulf him in the womb and destroy his independent existence. (p. 343)

Polémon finishes his story and falls asleep, but Lucius now sees Polémon's phantoms himself.... Polémon is also an aspect of Lucius and Lorenzo, and this contagion proves the failure of the defensive strategy of transposition in the dreamwork. Lucius sees that Myrthé's face is veiled by her long hair—an estrangement which prepares her transformation into a raging Bacchante and follower of Méroé in the next scene. When Lucius then closes his eyes, his first impressions are regressive, recollections of his school days and his family. A murmur of hostile voices tediously repeats some verses from Æschylus and the last advice of his dying grandfather.... The room seems to become suffused with blood; its rows of candelabras turn into shining lances held by two rows of soldiers; and Lucius is led between them towards his execution.

Lucius learns that he stands accused of having murdered Polémon and Myrthé. In effect this means that they are lost to him as psychic defenses. Myrthé can no longer be used artificially to embody only the protective aspects of the anima, and Polémon can no longer serve as Lucius' scapegoat. Lucius must assume the burden of Polémon's incest fantasy. (pp. 343-44)

In the watching crowd, the elements of Lucius' psyche unite to condemn him. A dwarf or the repressed ''unworthy'' side of the personality appears and claims Lucius has become little, like himself. The parent-figures appear in both individual and social aspects to judge their child—there is a man who resembles Lucius' father, a veiled woman, an old soldier (in this scene Lucius is described as a soldier—like Polémon) and a "femme du peuple" (cf. the crowd at Michel's execution in *La Fée aux Miettes*). The dream-work prevents the awareness of incestuous feelings from confronting Lucius directly, however. He attributes these regressive, guilt-provoking fantasies, by implication, to the crowd. . . . A little girl sings of Lucius' crimes, and her blue dress and spangled hair suggest the stars and sky (the heavens speak to condemn Lucius), but her madness shows that Lucius feels partially detached from her accusations. Indeed, he sees Polémon and Myrthé still alive. His severed head clings with its teeth to the execution platform, until it grows wings and can fly.

He becomes a bat rather than a bird. Because the incest wish has not clearly emerged in the dream, Lucius/Lorenzo cannot understand and then surmount it. His psychic development has been arrested. . . . Nodier makes this explicit by stating that Lucius' head finds no shelter, and by comparing it to a butterfly newly emerged from its chrysalis to beat its wings vainly against the pane which separates it from the light. As his female slaves transformed into Meneads arrive with Méroé and Smarra, to tear out and devour sleeping Polémon's heart, horrible decrepit children bind Lucius (become whole again) to his bed. He is bound to his present condition, and his possibilities for future development (the children) are withered and stunted. . . . When Lucius manages to leap out of bed, he finds himself in a warrior's tent beneath the walls of Corinth. Polémon, lying near him, is dead.

Lucius/Lorenzo slowly emerges from the dream in the epilogue. Talking in his sleep, he confuses his palace with his

A caricature of the author as a bibliophile.

Italian bedroom, and Lisidis' voice with the voices of phantoms. He accuses her of having abandoned Polémon to the witches: that is, of having withdrawn the maternal, protective aspect of her personality from the dependent child in himself. He calls on her to save him from Théis, Myrthé, and Thélaïre: that is, to reassure him that the compliant, subservient aspect of herself is her entire self, and that his fears of her aggressive domination are an illusion. These two demands, for protection and for submission from Lisidis, are mutually contradictory, although both call upon her to be entirely devoted to him. Lucius/Lorenzo cannot enter the city of maturity, because, embodying his dependent childish tendencies, Polémon has not yet been integrated with the rest of his personality. So long as this state lasts, his need for protection will activate his fear of being dominated by the other, and his desire for submission, to the extent that it may be gratified, will lessen the effectiveness of the other as protector.

The stress of self-confrontation has become too great, and Lorenzo has awakened before recognizing or reconciling the conflicting elements of his complex new relationship with Lisidis: dependence, and desires for both independence and domination. Polémon embodies the first of these tendencies for Lorenzo, and Lucius embodies the latter two. Both Lucius and Polémon serve as psychological defenses for Lorenzo: they take on what seems to him unacceptable feelings, and they satisfy his need for self-punishment. In short, the dream attempts to say: "Lucius, not I, is tempted to be disloyal. Méroé, not Lisidis, is the frightening dominant sorceress. Polémon, not I, died at her hands." Lorenzo's terrified reaction to his dreams elicits a protective maternal response from Lisidis, and she soothes him until he falls asleep. In his new dreams, the whole unresolved cycle of conflicts presumably will be enacted again, and he will remain a permanent victim of the dream.

There remains a need for the implied author, as distinguished from the protagonist, to extricate himself from the dream and to return to waking reality. He does this with a characteristically whimsical *Note sur le rhombus*. There he proudly explains that learned commentators have not identified this magic instrument used by Méroé, although it is mentioned several times by classical authors. It is merely a double German top, which spins with a loud noise and which has returned to favor as a nineteenth-century children's toy "sous le nom de DIABLE." As at the end of *La Fée aux Miettes,* and the beginning of *Jean-François les bas-bleus,* the ending here affirms that rationalistic pedants cannot destroy the pleasure of Nodier's illusions. He knows more than they do, and can beat them at their own game of citation-collecting and source identification. At the same time, to place the final emphasis of the story on a child's toy is modestly to depreciate the seriousness of the tale. Nodier thereby insulates it from criticism through a sort of Romantic irony. But the vested interest of the implied author runs deeper: he wants protection not only from an unsympathetic public, but from himself. The work of art has unleashed intense emotions; it is experienced by him as not entirely controlled. The element of childlike play evoked *within* the play of artistic creativity erects a second barrier of protection between the artist and his fears, the first barrier being the artificial construct which is the work of art itself. This creates a doubly miniaturized universe, where inner conflicts can be safely re-enacted and effectively controlled. (pp. 344-47)

Laurence M. Porter, ''The Forbidden City: A Psychoanalytical Interpretation of Nodier's 'Smarra','' in Symposium, *Vol. XXVI, No. 4, Winter, 1972, pp. 331-48.*

HILDA NELSON (essay date 1972)

[*Nelson focuses on the aim of* L'histoire du Roi de Bohême *and also compares it with the works of François Rabelais and Laurence Sterne.*]

[*L'histoire du roi de Bohême*] may well be nothing more than a long, extended dream, with all the inconsistencies, digressions, absurdities that are inherent in dreams, especially if the dreamer has a vivid imagination.

And what, asks Nodier, is the aim of such a book as this? Nothing, really. What, after all, is the aim of a dream? But Nodier tries to be helpful. "In our age," he says, "the most pressing need for a reasonable man who appreciates the world and life on its own terms, is to know the end of the story of the King of Bohemia and his seven castles." Eventually, after all sorts of detours, which give him the chance to describe places or tell stories, the narrator arrives at his first castle in Koeniggratz, "the saddest of the seven castles of Bohemia."

Loosely stated, the book centers around the narrator Théodore/Nodier, King of Bohemia, who wants to visit his seven castles somewhere near Spain. Only he does not want to go alone—in fact, he cannot go without Don Pic de Fanferluchio and Breloque, for he is too timid and too innocent. And how will he get there? This becomes a pressing question. By horse and carriage? But does he really need them? Does a sheer stretch of the imagination not permit him to travel more easily and without encountering the usual dangers? And this special carriage of the mind, is it not always ready to take him at any time anywhere he wants to go? "All I have to do," says the narrator, "is snap my fingers or click my tongue three times . . . and. . . ." Besides, the trip is even better with the aid of some crushed betel leaves, a glass of wine, or some of that intoxicating powder he has in his pretty little snuff box. But Nodier is helpful once again. In a letter to his friend Jean de Bry dated December 19, 1829, Nodier is quite explicit as to the nature and aim of the book:

> It is a series of reveries, or "*aegrisomnia*," in which I lose myself in three characters, that is to say, in the three main characters that every educated man can discern in that phenomenon, intelligence: imagination, memory, and judgment. In my case, this ill-assorted trinity is composed of a madman, bizarre and capricious, a pedant well oiled in erudition and nomenclatures, and an honest chap who is rather feeble but sensible and whose impressions are always modified by one or the other of the two. This metaphysical idea is certainly the best one, if not the only one, in the book, but it is so poorly presented, so confused and lost in such an irregular canvas, that I hasten to be the first one to say so.

The work is . . . a pastiche of many authors and styles; but above all, it is Rabelais and Sterne who are the guiding lights. The spirit of Rabelais is evident on almost every page; equally prominent is Rabelais' erudition, his love for words, their meanings as well as their sounds. Nodier becomes so imbued with the gigantism and creativeness of Rabelais that he has even become Rabelais. "Rabelais," says Nodier in an essay entitled *Des Types en littérature*, "is the inventor of the most fecund *types* ever created. Every one has gathered what he has reaped. It is brother John, Panurge, Raminagrobis . . . characters . . . whom Rabelais alone has forged." Interestingly enough, Nodier's other guiding light, Laurence Sterne, has, by his own admission, also assumed Rabelais as model. All three do, indeed, have a style that is filled with digressions,

ramblings, parodies, portraits, dialogues, intermingled with the greatest extravagances and absurdities; all three take a mock-serious tone and thus attack all the hallowed institutions man has developed throughout the ages. To these traits are added much wit, irony, humor, and learning. These works resemble the intricacies of a patchwork quilt, made up of individual parts which, nevertheless, have a unity and a totality that become obvious after careful consideration and reading. It is precisely this type of literature, a literature which embodies wit and irony, a fine sensibility and a keen sense of observation and erudition but without being pompous about this erudition, that Nodier greatly admires; furthermore, this type of literature also possesses an innocent earthiness about sex and the natural functions of the body, the ability and courage to digress and be extravagant, and to be moral without forcing morality upon one's readers. Nodier found these traits in Rabelais and Sterne; but he found them lacking in much of French literature. (pp. 109-10)

> *Hilda Nelson, in her* Charles Nodier, *Twayne Publishers, Inc., 1972, 188 p.*

LAURENCE M. PORTER (essay date 1974)

[*Porter examines* Trilby *from a Jungian perspective, noting Nodier's use of folk traditions to weld strains of the personal and collective unconscious. For further commentary by Porter, see excerpt dated 1972.*]

Many pre-nineteenth-century French writers like Montaigne, La Rochefoucauld, Marivaux, and Diderot proved themselves keenly aware of the existence and activity of involuntary, unconscious mental forces. But Charles Nodier's fantastic tales *Smarra, Trilby,* and *La Fée aux Miettes* were the first works of French prose fiction convincingly to simulate dream-structure, and to illustrate, *avant la lettre*, the theories of Freud and Jung. Compared to Nodier, his immediate precursors treat the "états seconds" of consciousness with far less subtlety and penetration. They either "s'abandonnent *passivement* à des extases sans lendemain" (Béguin), or else they identify the source of the perceptions of rational waking consciousness with reality or good, and the sources of perceptions in *états seconds* with illusion or evil, as Cazotte does in *Le Diable amoureux* (a harbinger of *Trilby*). But Nodier's most original *Contes fantastiques* (*Smarra, Trilby, La Fée aux Miettes*), rather than sinking into or condemning the unconscious, consider it as having potential for either good or ill, and attempt to reconcile it with the waking self. It is a Jungian perspective, I believe, which will allow critics most richly to interpret these fantastic tales (Cf. Béguin).

From a Jungian viewpoint, Nodier's *Trilby* employs folk-traditions in such a way as to situate the struggle between a woman's moral sensibility and her instinctive desire in the context of the myths created by the collective unconscious of a rural Scottish community. By thus weaving together the dramas of the personal and of the collective unconscious, Nodier inaugurated in France the mode of psychoanalytic narration which—together with Goethe's *Faust* and German romanticism—helped inspire and reached its culmination in Nerval's *Sylvie* and *Aurélia*.

Nodier's preface to *Trilby*, although it mentions several literary sources, locates the tale's essential origins in folklore: "Comme toutes les traditions populaires, celle-ci a fait le tour du monde et se trouve partout." This tradition, "la plus jolie fantaisie de l'imagination des modernes," relates the love of a superior spiritual being for a human. This situation expresses man's desire for a love more idealistic and perfect than that of which ordinary people are capable, and attempts, as it were, to reach a compromise between the love of creatures and the love of God by choosing an object intermediate between the two. Here the romance of the fairy Trilby and the beautiful fisherman's wife Jeannie follows the same course as do most of Nodier's other stories. Once two beings fall in love, obstacles intensify their passion; the suffering of separation purifies their souls, and leads to a deliverance at first mental (madness) and then physical (death) from the oppressive material order. But *Trilby,* unlike Nodier's other stories, employs three formal ceremonies of exorcism to dramatize the conflicts between a love-ideal and reality. Both in an entire society and in an individual, the exorcisms illustrate the psychic mechanism of repression and its Pyrrhic victory over the subject's libido.

By initially describing the fairies as having "toutes les bonnes qualités et tous les défauts d'un enfant mal élevé," Nodier suggests that they represent the spontaneous child in all of us, half submerged beneath the accretions of adult restraints. The most charming of them, Trilby, dwells in Jeannie's hearth and watches over her house and farmyard while she sleeps. In psychoanalytic terminology, he embodies Jeannie's animus, or soul-image, a constellation of "masculine" personality traits repressed from a woman's ego-consciousness. "Wherever an unconditional, or almost magical, relation exists between the sexes, it is always a question of projection of the soul-image," Jung explained.

More precisely, Trilby represents a projection of what Jungian psychoanalysis identifies as "a particular form of the animus that lures women away from all human relationships and especially from all contacts with real men. He personifies a cocoon of dreamy thoughts . . . which cut a woman off from the reality of life." Jeannie loves Trilby in her daydreams, "cet espace indécis entre le repos et le réveil, où le cœur se rappelle *malgré lui* les impressions qu'il s'est efforcé d'éviter pendant le jour," but her sense of obligation towards her husband Dougal prevents her from summoning Trilby except during "l'erreur *involontair* des songes" (emphasis added). Nodier's language here shows him clearly aware of a universal opposition in human beings, between the moral and social imperatives of rational waking consciousness, and the impulses of instinctive desire (libido), whose objects can reveal themselves only when the vigilance of our public self has relaxed.

"The relation between conscious and unconscious is compensatory. This is one of the best-proven rules of dream interpretation. When we set out to interpret a dream, it is always helpful to ask: What conscious attitude does it compensate?" Here Jeannie is unconsciously discontented with her childless marriage to the loyal, but harsh, insensitive, and inarticulate Dougal. . . . Her need to offer maternal and wifely affection, and to have it returned, finds an outlet in Trilby's timid flirtations with her as she dozes over her spinning-wheel, and in "les rêves innocemment voluptueux" of a loving child which Trilby sends her.

Jeannie's wish-fulfilling fantasies will gradually invade her waking life and acquire hallucinatory force (Cf. Montégut). At first she does not confide her fantasies to Dougal; at length, however, she does complain of Trilby's attentions. Nodier does not explain her motives, but one could speculate that Jeannie feels vaguely guilty of involuntary infidelity toward her husband. She has found Trilby's courtship pleasurable; by describing it to Dougal as if it were a nuisance, Jeannie attempts

to dissociate herself from her secret desires, and to absolve herself in her own eyes. The centenarian monk Ronald, who functions like an instrument of Jeannie's super-ego, arrives fortuitously as soon as she speaks to Dougal. At Dougal's request, Ronald exorcises Trilby from the cottage by reciting the Litanies of the Virgin. As Jung explained, the primitive mind uses the notion of spirits to explain the manifestations of the personal and collective unconscious. (Until the climactic, collective malediction, all Jeannie's society believed in the fairies.) These spirits take upon themselves the individual's guilt and responsibility for his suppressed thoughts. A ceremony of exorcism is ideally intended to give social sanction to a "possessed person's" projections of inadmissible fantasies into the outside world, where they are embodied in imaginary scapegoats. Henceforth Ronald will appear to conduct an exorcism whenever Jeannie's inner conflict between love and marital duty becomes too strong to endure. Her repressed desires do not disappear; once Trilby has been banished, however, they no longer have an acceptable outlet, and thereby become destructive (cf. Jung). The first exorcism serves only to make Jeannie *consciously* dissatisfied with her marriage; the second one drives her insane; and with the third she dies.

Trilby soon reappears in Jeannie's dreams, but as a handsome young Scottish chieftain rather than a child. His sexual maturity and greater size reveal the increasing strength of Jeannie's fantasy, and its now patently erotic character. "En le regardant sous sa nouvelle forme, elle comprenait qu'elle ne pouvait plus prendre à lui qu'un intérêt coupable." Fearing Trilby's return, she still longs for him and jealously imagines that he has found new shelter with women more aristocratic, wealthy, and beautiful than she.

Both husband and wife brood in their unhappiness. For in complaining of Trilby's attentions, Jeannie had made a tacit appeal to which Dougal failed to respond. She was asking him to treat her more affectionately, to demonstrate for her the solicitude she ascribed to Trilby. This implicit, unfavorable comparison between the phantom and himself hurts Dougal's feelings and causes him to withdraw further rather than inspiring him with greater tenderness towards his wife. In effect, his request for the exorcism meant that he refused to acknowledge Jeannie's dissatisfaction. Consciously, however, Dougal's primitive mentality attributes Jeannie's unhappiness to a curse placed on her by evil spirits. He finds it embarrassing openly to acknowledge, even to himself, his jealousy of Trilby, of that part of Jeannie's thoughts from which he is excluded. So he plans once again to resort to religious intervention, in a more radical form; a pilgrimage to the monastery of Balva.

Nodier's account of this pilgrimage attempts to exalt our estimation of Jeannie's love for Trilby by connecting this love with Jeannie's pure, unspoiled Christian faith, and by contrasting her faith with the magical, materialistic concerns of her fellow villagers. All Dougal's village makes this journey for the feast of Saint Columba. Like the crumbling monastery to which they go, their naive Christian faith is falling into ruins at the time of the story. (When the building collapses, says the narrator, Satan shall rule for a time in Scotland.) The pilgrims' self-centered petitions reflect this deterioration. Dougal prays to fish up a box of treasure. He seems to have been corrupted by an ambitious discontent with his life as a simple fisherman. The neighbor ladies want fine clothes so as to outshine Jeannie at the next holiday. They envy her because Trilby's attachment proves her to be the loveliest woman in the village. As for Ronald, he delights in a prideful sense of mastery over both dependent peasantry and fairies, while exhorting the pilgrims to unite in the collective curse expelling all the fairies from Scotland. His very asceticism, advertised to inspire respect, serves as the instrument of self-aggrandizement.

Ronald receives the pilgrims in the refectory, where a gallery of MacFarlane family portraits decorates the wall, and addresses them with the intent of inciting them to enmity against the fairies. As Ronald speaks, Jeannie must decide whether to accept or reject his demand to obey religious authority at the cost of personal feelings. The portrait gallery evokes the total contents of her mind, childhood and present, passed in review during this mental crisis. The earlier generations of Mac-Farlanes, benefactors of the monastery, had paid it tribute out of gratitude to its founder who had driven away the storm-giant Arthur. But more recent generations of MacFarlanes forgot their obligations to the monastery and oppressed it. Their portraits, mysteriously hurled from the wall, have left empty spaces. Nodier's description of these two groups, servants of God and rebels, provides a subtle, indirect commentary on Jeannie's indecisive state. (pp. 97-103)

Ronald, meanwhile, in his harangue, unwittingly admits to spiritual weakness by saying that the monks are forced to use the most uncompromising means to dissociate themselves from the ''sinful'' parts of their personality. Unlike Jeannie, who nourishes her dream, they combat it. . . . What really torments the monks is not ''the evil spirit'' but their own unacknowledged thoughts. The more strongly the unconscious is repressed, as Jung claims, the more destructive it becomes. When long denied an outlet to overt expression, it may eventually erupt as it does here in spectacular apparitions of temptations and devils. Such apparitions then perpetuate a vicious circle by inciting a redoubled effort at repression.

The most recent persecution by the fairies, according to Ronald, occurred during a burial in the crypt, when the torches providing light were extinguished. In a sense, the mutual support of the monastic community was lost to view. Each monk had to confront his own fears and desires alone. . . . What has happened, one may surmise, is that a monk's death has reminded his fellows of their own. Their resulting sense of the transience of life and its opportunities for pleasure temporarily weakens their religious faith, and reactivates their desires for the world they thought they had renounced. Ashamed to admit to these desires in themselves, the monks project them into the outside world, which thus becomes menacing. Their own voices, disavowed by them, are then perceived as the voices of evil spirits.

Two monks die in the darkness. The hand of Saint Duncan's statue (probably a misprint for Dunstan, the tenth-century missionary to the Scots . . .) seizes one. The other is crushed by the statue of the recently canonized Virgin of Lothian ''qui est morte de douleur parce qu'on l'avait séparée de son fiancé.'' This Virgin's odd credentials for sainthood suggest a heterodox morality whose highest values are idealized passion and *sensibilité*. Nodier insinuates this morality behind and around that of Ronald. The deaths which the old monk ascribes to the persecution of spirits, Nodier implicitly presents as a welcome liberation from the cruel frustrations of material existence, and as the doorway to reunion with loved persons in the afterlife. For the narrative implies that the young man crushed by the girl's statue was her fiancé. And later in the story the revelation that Saint Columba is Trilby's brother, as well as the patron saint of unhappy lovers, further glorifies human passion by associating it with the disinterested *caritas* of a saint. But

Ronald, by choosing Columba's feast day to execute his project of vengeance against the fairies, proves himself insensitive to the spiritual order. (pp. 103-05)

When he thus denies love, Jeannie overcomes her fear of Ronald and rejects his authority. While the others curse the fairies, she rushes to the statue of Saint Columba to pray for Trilby's pardon. Her animus-image has erupted autonomously into her consciousness, and the projection changes the world into a replica of this unknown inner face, acquiring hallucinatory force and permanently distorting her perception of reality. . . . By dissociating herself from the exorcism, Jeannie has at least rejected the dangerous self-deception of considering the manifestations of one's own unconscious to be the assaults of an external enemy. But since everyone else in her society has embraced this delusion, Jeannie now has no way to reconcile her private self with social reality.

One day early next spring, Jeannie returns from the Clyde River basin, where she has delivered passengers. Her boat drifts with the tide, as her mind does, given over to the non-rational faculties. The landscape suggests a spiritual transcendence. . . . Jeannie recalls the legend of the giant Arthur, separated from the nymph he loved by the walls of Edinburgh, and then driven from his refuge beside the Clyde by the prayers of Saint Oran. Now she sees this story ''sous un aspect nouveau'': she no longer identifies herself with the society that expelled Arthur. For she has come to belong to the world of the giant and the vanishing heritage of folk traditions which had offered her the consoling image of Trilby.

As night falls, a frail voice calls from across the river. Jeannie rows there to find an aged dwarf, Trilby disguised. Here, as frequently elsewhere, the dwarf manifests the unconscious. His age implies spiritual wisdom. By speaking of his ''son'' Trilby, he will recall to Jeannie's conscious attention the soul-image for which she longs, with both mind and body. The phallic overtones of a small male being evoke the reawakening of Jeannie's frustrated sexual feelings, as the beginning of Jeannie's conversation with the old man reveals. It has to do with hibernating snakes and with catching fish in baskets. Both the spiritual and the sexual meanings of Jeannie's impressions are sustained together till the end of the story. Jeannie's ensuing behavior cannot be exclusively interpreted, either by a diagnosis of hallucinatory madness brought about by an erotic obsession, or by a claim that Jeannie enjoys a superior sensitivity to the spiritual order. For Nodier seeks to create in his reader's mind an equilibrium of material and spiritual principles, of sentiment and reason.

Fantastic lights now flood the scene: aurora borealis, falling stars, and phosphorescence. Apparently Jeannie's perceptions have become deranged, or else she is experiencing a privileged moment of visionary insight. At first the old dwarf says he is Trilby's father; as Jeannie's memories of past love become stronger and more immediate, Trilby doffs his disguise and begins a lyrical outburst of passionate entreaty. His language, in keeping with the rest of Nodier's morally ambiguous narration, combines exalted spirituality with immoderate non-Christian passion: ''Ah! le néant, l'enfer même n'aurait que des tourments imparfaits pour l'*heureux damné* [emphasis added] dont les lèvres auraient effleuré tes lèvres . . .'' When Dougal approaches in his boat, Trilby dives into the water, to be fished up again in the form of the precious casket which Dougal had prayed for on his pilgrimage. Jeannie is told to carry it to their cottage.

The casket, like the dwarf, has an ambivalent meaning. The treasure inside, supernatural wisdom, would be revealed by opening the casket and thus re-establishing contact with the secrets of the unconscious. In terms of the body, to open the box would suggest Jeannie's sexual submission. But the closed box principally contains a repressed past, whose memories, once unlocked, would be released into the present. Trilby speaks from within the box, telling Jeannie he will be freed if she says she loves him. Then they can share a pure spiritual love without violating Jeannie's promises to Dougal "L'amour que j'ai pour toi, ma Jeannie, n'est pas une affection de la terre . . . Tes organes trop faibles encore n'ont pas compris l'amour ineffable d'une âme dégagée de tous les devoirs, et qui peut sans infidélité embrasser toutes les créatures de son choix d'une affection sans limites!"

As in *Atala* or *Le Lys dans La Vallée*, heaven would appear to mean the reconciliation of one's moral sense with one's instinctive desire. Up until now, despite the author's obvious sympathy for him, Trilby might have proved either benevolent, or as wayward as any human lover of someone else's wife. "Our actual knowledge of the unconscious shows that it is a natural phenomenon and that, like Nature herself, it is at least *neutral*. It contains all aspects of human nature—light and dark, beautiful and ugly, good and evil, profound and silly." The ambiguous nature of the animus figure as it first appears is illustrated by Ronald's admission that Trilby belongs to a mysterious race whose destiny is not irreparably determined, and that the secret of his salvation or damnation is still hidden in the mind of God. But from this point on in the story, Trilby as animus figure appears unequivocally in his positive aspect of psychopomp, "a mediator between the conscious and the unconscious [which are to be united through the phenomenon of individuation] and a personification of the latter" (Jung, *Aion*). But Jeannie still hears an invitation to adultery. . . . Repeating to herself her marriage vows, she runs out of her cottage: symbolically, the conflict between libido and super-ego drives her "out of her mind."

At once, Dougal and Ronald return: the super-ego reasserts its dominance. Hearing Ronald say that the last of the evil spirits has been exiled, Jeannie believes Trilby has been found innocent. His seductive speech, she thinks, was a temptation which she had to resist successfully in order to prove herself worthy of eventual reunion with him. Calmer, she goes to the shore to empty Dougal's nets. But she returns to stumble upon Ronald's third and decisive act of exorcism, sealing Trilby for a thousand years into "l'Arbre du Saint," a giant beech tree associated with Saint Columba. (The tree, both tomb and chrysalis, promises rebirth). Running towards Trilby, Jeannie herself falls into a conveniently waiting grave. She must perish when Trilby does; their destinies (as Nodier implies by using that word here to explain her death) are one.

As she dies, a sudden insight allows her to understand the spiritual love Trilby spoke of, a love which can embrace all creatures without disloyalty. She looks at Trilby and her husband in turn. Her conscious and unconscious personalities suddenly being reconciled and integrated, Trilby is no longer her husband's rival. She realizes that she must take the initiative in offering Dougal the tenderness she had yearned for. Now perceiving him as a spiritual child needing guidance and consolation, she addresses him directly, affectionately using his first name, for the first time in the story. With words he surely does not understand, she promises an afterlife together in another world. . . . In death, the dream that never ends, Jeannie's desires shall be innocently fulfilled. And, as the last true believer in Trilby's vanished race, she attains in death the heroic stature of an embodiment of the poetic principle in the human spirit.

Upon Jeannie's individual drama, *Trilby* superimposes the collective tragedy of a society that forfeits an earthly paradise by sinning against the imagination. On this level Ronald represents an ambitious, intolerant institutional church (as distinguished from the communion of true believers) that attempts to supplant popular superstitions with a single set of Christian myths and symbols so as to rule over men's minds unchallenged. At the beginning of the story, the fisherfolk believe in fairies and spirits as much as they believe in the saints. Jeannie, at her spinning wheel, unselfconsciously sings the canticle of Saint Dunstan together with the ballad of the ghost of Aberfoil. But the malediction directed against the fairies . . . expels them from Scotland forever, and destroys the Scottish peasants' once-idyllic communion with nature. Self-exiled from paradise unawares, they must henceforth toil to earn their bread with the sweat of their brow. And the romantically individualistic, self-sufficient life of the rural fishermen whom Nodier portrays will soon be overwhelmed by the urban civilization looming in the background of the story.

The intuitive awareness of a collective unconscious, which Nodier demonstrates in his *Contes fantastiques*, makes him at once an innovator in the literary depiction of human psychology, and a reactionary in terms of literary history. For Nodier "was attempting to reverse literary history and to return the brief narrative to what it once had been: a literature for the people" [see excerpt by George dated 1964]. And this reactionary stance of Nodier the author reflects a generalized distaste, on the part of Nodier the man, for the post-Revolutionary world. In the first preface to *Trilby* he sarcastically explained that the material progress of his day had made it impossible for the sophisticated Parisian public to appreciate folk-literature. As Balzac's *Contes bruns* and many other contemporary accounts suggest, Nodier did come to terms with his milieu: he contributed actively and impressively to the "oral tradition" of the Paris salons. But even towards the end of his career, Nodier could not suppress his intense nostalgia for the lost world of folktales, "ces enchantements de la parole, qui font revivre à la pensée l'heureuse vie des siècles d'ignorance et de vertu." In opposition to commercial modern literature, he steadfastly upheld the folktale as an ideal. . . . (pp. 105-10)

> Laurence M. Porter, "Towards a Prehistory of Depth Psychology in French Romanticism: Temptation and Repression in Nodier's 'Trilby'," in Nineteenth-Century French Studies, Vol. II, Nos. 3-4, Spring-Summer, 1974, pp. 97-110.

GRANT CRICHFIELD (essay date 1978)

[*Crichfield compares Michel in* La fée aux miettes *with other mad heroes in Romantic literature.*]

The romantic madman, while similar to the seer, plays a new role in French literature, becoming a form of the Romantic hero. This lunatic, an outsider *par excellence*, personifies the Romantic's sense of alienation and solitude in a coarse, prosaic world which cannot understand his poetic sensibility. Unlike so many other Romantic characters, however, this madman, precisely because of his lunacy, can resolve the contradictions between his existence and his intuition and actually attains his ideal. He thereby assumes the status of hero and saint, a model for the way to salvation and happiness.

Such Romantic artists as Nodier, Nerval, and Balzac place the madman with poets, geniuses, and seers who are at the summit of beings, indeed on Mount Olympus. Their madness has allowed them to escape earthly existence and to perceive and experience the elemental truths of the universe. For these Romantics, lunatics are no longer pariahs to be feared or jeered at; on the contrary, they are visionaries to whom we must listen and it is ordinary mortals and their lives which are regarded as outside the pale of knowledge, wisdom, and peace. Specifically, in Charles Nodier's *La Fée aux Miettes,* "l'homme purement rationnel" and the positivism he represents are at the bottom of the scale. The narrator of this fairy tale declares, "L'Histoire et les historiens! . . . Malédiction sur elle et sur eux! je prends Urgande à témoin que je trouve mille fois plus de crédibilité aux illusions des lunatiques."

The story is introduced by a man who visits Scotland to prove to his friend, David, the extraordinary truth madmen can possess. Upon visiting an insane asylum near Glasgow, they meet Michel, an inmate, who tells them he is looking for the singing mandrake which he must find before sunset and which will fulfill all his dreams. He then recounts his life story to them. As a child at Granville in Normandy he met an ugly and ancient fairy called La Fée aux Miettes. After a growing fellowship with Michel, the fairy told him that she wanted to become his wife and share her fortune with him, but only on the condition that he find a way for her to return to her home in Scotland. Michel agreed. At this point, the fairy gave to Michel a portrait of herself, yet the likeness was that of a beautiful young woman, Belkiss. Seeing the image, Michel fell in love with the perfect woman it represented. Struck deeply by this love, Michel nevertheless proved his commitment to the Fée aux Miettes by many years and adventures designed by the fairy to test him. Finally, he arrived at Greenock, Scotland, where events became increasingly improbable and illogical, dream increasingly mixed with reality, and Michel judged more and more by the inhabitants as insane. After a series of bizarre events, he again demonstrated his devotion to Belkiss (and thus to the Fée aux Miettes) by refusing Folly Girlfree's offer of marriage, even though it had saved him from execution. Delighted, the Fée aux Miettes took him to her house where they lived blissfully for six months. Then she revealed to him that she would die within the year unless he fulfilled his final mission: to find the singing mandrake and return without having loved another. This singing mandrake would not only unite her and Michel forever, but would enable her to become again the young and beloved Belkiss of the portrait.

In the "conclusion," the narrator learns of Michel's success from a member of the society of the *lunatici* of Sienna: his rescue from incarceration by the Princess Mandrake, his marriage to the Queen of Sheba (synonymous with Belkiss and also the name of a magical boat in the story), and his ascension to the position of Emperor of the Seven Planets.

Although Michel is a lunatic, he is a familiar Romantic character. As René says of himself, "Mon humeur était impétueuse, mon caractère inegal," so Michel has "une âme rêveuse et mobile, quoique soumise et timide." The young and timid Adolphe feels "rempli d'un sentiment d'incertitude sur la destinée, et d'une rêverie vague qui ne m'abandonnait pas" and the melancholic René says, "Il me manquait quelque chose pour remplir l'abîme de mon existence"; one sees in Michel a similar sense of frustration and disillusionment, but which

is perhaps less profound and will be more easily cured than is the case generally for the Romantic character. . . .

The framework of Michel's story resembles as well that of many of his Romantic counterparts because it can be defined as a quest for an aesthetic ideal of spiritual or metaphysical dimensions lacking and unattainable in the material world. The Romantic character is typically at odds with objective reality and is increasingly preoccupied by his subjective reality. The tensions produced by the contradictions between these two worlds or lives usually prove to be impossible to resolve, resulting in a moral paralysis, literal suicide, or languishing death, as for René, Obermann, Chatterton, and Nodier's favorite, Werther. No such end is in store for the lunatic Michel, however. On the contrary, his lunacy enables him actually to find the key to escape from the prison of ordinary reality and to assume new life in the ideal dimension he envisions.

The nature of Michel's family connections reveals the same relationship between him and the traditional Romantic character. As is frequently the case with the Romantic hero or heroine, Michel's ties with his family seem tenuous; his mother's death just after his birth reminds us of the death of René's mother while giving birth to him. Distance or a sense of being cut off from one's father is ever-present among Romantic characters: René was "livre de bonne heure à des mains étrangères," "élevé loin du toit paternel" and feels "timide et contraint devant [son] père"; Adolphe's relationship with his father is plagued by misunderstandings, making them shy and cool toward each other. Michel fits this pattern in that his father leaves him with his uncle to go on a long ocean voyage, and his uncle in turn leaves to find Michel's father and also disappears. However, this parallel is limited because Michel and his father (and uncle) are close and most affectionate. And while Michel's father may be lost to him on earth, his disappearance (and that of his uncle) have to do with his having been initiated into the same visionary life as Michel and thus is only a temporary disappearance. Michel's father and his uncle André, having become "fous" and superintendents of Princess Belkiss's palaces, have become part of the ideal world Michel is striving to attain, thus representing a sort of spiritual union rather than alienation between father, uncle, and son.

Thus, while Michel is in many ways cast in the mold of the conventional Romantic character, a crucial difference exists in him; his madness allows him to resolve the conflict between intuitive knowledge and material reality faced by Romantic characters. Like Louis Lambert, Michel achieves his goal at the end while René and Chatterton do not. Again, as in *Louis Lambert,* this happy ending indicates Nodier's desire to underline the validity of the lunatic's knowledge and the possibility of his attaining it.

Michel's progress toward the ideal is clearly paralleled by his increasing insanity. As his devotion to the Fée aux Miettes and Belkiss becomes stronger, as he consciously rejects worldly values, he is seen as increasingly crazy by the world and the world itself seems more and more crazy to Michel. At first he is immune to the possible ridicule of friends for being in love with the Fée aux Miettes and for believing her stories (and being, therefore, "fou"). A bit later, his friends see him as a "visionnaire" when he refuses to embark on a trip with them because he has given all his money to the Fée aux Miettes. It is especially during the episode at Greenock that Folly Girlfree affirms repeatedly and matter-of-factly, as though no one would dispute it, that Michel is insane, and that others as well, such as Maître Finewood and his co-workers, see him as mad. If the world judges Michel as mad, that world itself is presented as increasingly insane. Again, it is especially during the episode at Greenock that we see this: people laugh for no reason, dogs are married, the judges wear animal masks. There is little difference between Michel's dreams and nightmares and the real world. This underlines the loss of validity of the world for Michel and his loss of validity to the world: it no longer makes any sense to him nor he to it.

Michel's increasing alienation from society worries him very little because he is discovering a new and marvelous dimension of life. While he is constantly confronted with the contradiction between the banality of ordinary existence and the excitement of the world of the Fée aux Miettes, he is never tormented nor paralyzed by the irreconcilability of the two. Michel possesses the ability to shirk the world of Granville and Greenock, to withdraw absolutely from it and to enter a superior plane of thought and deed. This can be called insanity now just as it is in *La Fée aux Miettes,* and it is precisely this insanity that allows Michel not only actively and aggressively to pursue his vision but also to succeed in entering into a life of ecstasy.

While Michel's madness enables him to recognize the true inner beauty of the ancient Fée aux Miettes, he cannot achieve a definite union with her until he finds, specifically, the singing mandrake. A central symbol in the story, the mandrake is rich in association and closely tied to the nature of Michel's powers or madness. According to tradition, the mandrake was born of a marriage between Sky and Earth and thus represents a union of two of the basic elements of our universe. By extension, it has come to represent the idea of the primordial unity of all elements of the universe. The mandrake can represent both Adam, the first man, and Christ, son of God, as well as the mystical relationship between the two because of a resemblance between the form of the root and that of the human body and because of the definition of the mandrake as a union of the essential elements of the universe. The mandrake, like Christ, is interpreted as a kind of *imago dei* and suggests the lost Eden and the promise of regaining it after death. Further, the mandrake, a relative of belladonna, is perhaps most famous for its ability to combat depression, bestow visionary powers, heighten sexual prowess and fecundity, bring serenity of body and mind and even aid against one's enemies. In exploring the connection between Michel's lunacy and the mandrake, it is important to note that, according to legend, the mandrake, upon being uprooted, will issue a scream so terrible that the person killing it must block his ears or the scream will drive him insane or kill him. However, just the contrary is the case for Michel, who is already a lunatic. If he finds the right one, the mandrake will sing a charming song to him:

> C'est moi, c'est moi, c'est moi,
> Je suis la mandragore,
> La fille des beaux jours qui s'éveille à l'aurore,
> Et qui chante pour toi!

With these connotations, it seems even clearer that Michel's lunatic search for the singing mandrake, in which is hidden ''le secret de [ses] dernières illusions,'' represents a search for the primordial unity of the universe, for God, for truth.

Nodier's madman not only bridges the gap between intuition and experience; he also assumes an exemplary status like that of a saint and hero. The lunatic as seer and protector of the truth—even as a sort of conquering hero—is represented on several levels in *La Fée aux Miettes.* Like the virtuous, self-denying saint—and like Jesus, son of a carpenter (or himself a carpenter, depending on the version)—Michel always rejects vanity, pretentiousness, and greed for honest work, material wealth for spiritual fulfillment. As Michel becomes more saintly, the nature of his work becomes more extraordinary: he begins as a simple carpenter, just performing odd jobs at one point, and progresses to a craftsman of such beautiful woods as cedar and cypress on board the mysterious ship, *La Reine de Saba,* which can take people on wonderful voyages via subterranean canals to the land of Solomon.

Michel's sainthood is indicated as well by the numerous allusions to Saint Michael, who, according to tradition, is chief of the Archangels, Special Protector of Good against attacks by Satan, and in this story, ''prince de la lumiére crée et bienaimé du Seigneur souverain de toutes choses.'' Besides the fact of Michel's name, the feast of Saint Michael becomes a kind of reference point for the chronology of the story. For example, the narrator arrives at the asylum in Glasgow to see Michel on Michaelmas Day, this being the day on which Michel recounts his story to the narrator and also finds the singing mandrake, his key to eternal love and wisdom. Moreover, Michaelmas Day is, of course, Michel's birthday and, throughout the story, is a time when Michel makes an annual pilgrimage to the Mont Saint-Michel; it is also the day on which he must remember to return to see the Fée aux Miettes after a year's absence. Like Saint Michael, divine messenger and protector of the truth, Michel proves over and over again himself and the strength of his devotion to the wisdom, purity and goodness that the Fée aux Miettes represents by defending her, saving her, giving her money, swearing his commitment to her.

The nature and truth of Michel's lunatic experiences and his final superior rank are further suggested by the names used in association with them: Belkiss, his idol; the Queen of Sheba, the name of the ship he works on and the name of the woman Michel is reported to have married at the end of the story; the Temples of Solomon, ultimate destination of the Fée aux Miettes, *La Reine de Saba,* and thus Michel. Solomon traditionally represents power and great wisdom. The beautiful and even richer and wiser Queen of Sheba, eventually Solomon's wife, according to tradition, was called Balkis by the Arabians and appears in this tale as the Fée aux Miettes and Belkiss, who are in fact two images of the same being. The ship, *La Reine de Saba,* can make trips in the most unexpected and inexplicable way possible toward the land of Solomon—or wisdom, a major theme of the story—suggesting that truth is found in surprising ways and forms, that is, by faith and commitment to an ideal, and not by imperfect reason, logic, and science.

Nodier's presentation of a madman's visions as the ideal is an example of his use of irony by which, throughout the story, he asserts the seriousness and truth of intuitive, subjective reality, or the life of fantasy, over objective reality, or existence and outer appearances. Nodier seeks to dissolve the barriers and contradictions between the real and the ideal, the objective and the subjective and does so through a constant and progressive destruction of forms we accept and a substitution of new truths: fishing boats that are really magical vehicles to an enchanted land, a grotesque old woman who is really a fairy and finally is a beautiful young queen, the mandrake which normally drives one mad but which will sing a pretty song for the crazy Michel, and, of course, the madman who is a genius and a saint. Even the use of the form of the fairy tale follows suit. A fairy tale may seem to contain pure fantasy and the most unreal and improbable kind of invention, as does *La Fée aux Miettes,* yet at the same time, for Nodier, this contains a message for the way to absolute truth. Thus everywhere in *La Fée aux Miettes* that which seems concrete, reasonable—"real"—is empty and meaningless or contains a hidden meaning, while that which appears impossible, illogical, ugly, and insane turns out to be true and beautiful.

This ironic presentation of an idea of beauty and truth and Nodier's earnestness about their existence can be seen in his own phrase for it: "le fantastique sérieux." If what Michel experiences seems incoherent and bizarre, it is not ridiculous, only wonderful; those who cannot take him seriously are themselves ridiculous and inconsequential, such as the judges at Greenock, or perhaps simply uninteresting and incapable of understanding anything beyond the ordinary, such as Maître Finewood and Folly Girlfree. . . . [We] have reassurances at all levels of reality and of the narration about the seriousness of Michel's experiences, first, from the point of view of ordinary and fairly objective reality, or the narrator, then from that of the inner or subjective reality—Michel—as to his certainty about the truth of his own visions, as well as from the vision itself—the Fairy—representing at once wisdom and the most improbable element of the story. Finally, one finds no narrative ambivalence toward Michel's knowledge and actions as one so often finds in French Romantic literature. He is condemned neither to eternal melancholia and bitterness, nor to sit in silence staring forever at the sunset, nor to suicide. And while René and Adolphe are harshly criticized after recounting their stories, by le Père Souël and Chactas, Adolphe by the *Editeur,* the validity of Michel's story is rather reaffirmed at the end of this tale by a sympathetic narrator.

Like the narrator of Nerval's *Aurélia,* Louis Lambert and, indeed, several of Nodier's other characters, such as Jean-François-les-bas-bleus, the mad Michel is thus really an incarnation of Nodier's perception of the power of the imagination, of the basic unity of the universe, of the belief in the existence of a world more interesting and satisfying than the dull, flat existence most men know. The lunatic perceives another reality through his vision which becomes the only alive, interesting, worthwhile one. The narrator defines it this way:

> Les lunatiques . . . occuperaient selon moi le degré le plus élevé de l'échelle qui sépare notre planète de son satellite, et comme ils communiquent nécessairement de ce degré avec les intelligenes d'un monde qui ne nous est pas connu, il est assez naturel que nous ne les entendions point, et il est absurde d'en conclure que leurs idées manquent de sens et de lucidité, parce qu'elles appartiennent à un ordre de sensations et de raisonnements qui est tout à fait inaccessible à notre éducation et à nos habitudes.

Nodier is never investigating the etiology of madness; indeed, he renders such a discussion impossible. Like other Romantics, he rather insists on the meaning not only of the fact of insanity but also of the content of this state. And this significance is the possibility of integrating the subjective and the objective and thus ending alienation. It is a state of grace.

The madman as seer and prophet is not new. But the representation of the madman and his experiences as totally positive, agreeable, and right, and their use as a vehicle for a thoroughly serious and essentially optimistic view of the universe are new. For the Romantics, the madman is not tragic, nor is he primarily satiric, nor is he humorous. For Nodier, as for Balzac and Nerval, the hero's madness is a metaphor for the serious evocation of an ultimate reality—their most intimate and profound perceptions and feelings about the nature of the universe and

man's place in it. Nodier and other Romantics change the literary use of the insane character and poeticize the nature of his insanity; the Romantic madman becomes, then, a new hero type as well as a new step in the fictional representation of the lunatic. (pp. 835-42)

> *Grant Crichfield, "The Romantic Madman as Hero: Nodier's Michel le Charpentier," in* The French Review, *Vol. LI, No. 6, May, 1978, pp. 835-42.*

R. A. G. PEARSON (essay date 1982)

[*Pearson attempts to determine the significance of the dream sequences in* Smarra *through an analysis of the work's style and structure.*]

Since antiquity all theories of dream have belonged essentially to one of two categories, the categories which are symbolically represented in the *Odyssey* as the gates of ivory and horn. According to the theories of one category, dreams issue from the gates of horn: they are illuminating, ordered and meaningful, communications from another realm and susceptible of interpretation. According to the theories of the other category, dreams issue from the gates of ivory: they are obscure, chaotic and meaningless, mere random products of the cerebral machinery temporarily released from the controlling force of reason. To the first category belong the oneirocriticism of the ancients, the dictionaries of dream symbols of the moderns, and of course the psychoanalytic theories of Freud, Jung and their successors; while to the second belong the theories of eighteenth-century rationalists (epitomized in the article *Songe* in the *Encyclopédie*) and those of their nineteenth-century positivist heirs whose work is summarized in the first chapter of Freud's *Die Traumdeutung* (1900). The dream theories of Romantic writers, it has long been recognized, belong to the first category. For them, in Nerval's phrase, 'le rêve est une seconde vie', permitting the dreamer to experience a world in which the frustrating constrictions of material reality may be transcended, and granting him access to some higher domain of spiritual truth.

While *Die Traumdeutung* may be seen to have constituted the single most substantial contribution in the history of dream theory ('in spite of many thousands of years of effort', asserts Freud, 'the scientific understanding of dreams has made very little advance'), it is clear that in the history of the representation of dream in literature it is the Romantics who introduced the most radical change. Previously, dream experience had tended either to figure merely as an incidental aspect of the life of a character or else to be used as a poetic device—for example, to prepare the reader for a subsequent episode in the plot or to excuse audacity (as in, say, Diderot's *Le Rêve de D'Alembert*). Only with Romanticism does dream become an autonomous literary theme and an area of human experience worthy, as it were, to be the central subject of a literary text.

Of French Romantic writers Nodier was the first to see this potential of dream as a serious literary topic. In his preface to the second edition of *Smarra* he suggests that 'la vie d'un homme organisé poétiquement se divise en deux séries de sensations à peu près égales, même en valeur, l'une qui résulte des illusions de la vie éveillée, l'autre qui se forme des illusions du sommeil', and he expresses his surprise that 'le poète éveillé ait si rarement profité dans ses œuvres des fantaisies du poète endormi', surprise that 'la moitié et la plus forte moitié sans doute des imaginations de l'esprit ne fussent jamais devenues le sujet d'une fable idéale si propre à la poésie'. *Smarra* itself is the first work of literature in the French language to take dream as its central subject.

The question arises as to what critical approach one should adopt in the analysis of a dream narrative. In the words of the classical scholar E. R. Dodds: 'there are two ways of looking at the recorded dream-experience of a past culture: we may try to see it through the eyes of the dreamers themselves, and thus reconstruct as far as may be what it meant to their waking consciousness; or we may attempt, by applying principles derived from modern dream-analysis, to penetrate from its manifest to its latent content'. Dodds goes on to argue that 'the latter procedure is plainly hazardous: it rests on an unproved assumption about the universality of dream-symbols which we cannot control by obtaining the dreamer's associations'. While such a hazard, one might presume, is substantially diminished by the considerably smaller temporal gap between a present-day critic and Nodier than that between Dodds and the Greeks, it is nevertheless proposed to adopt here the first of the two approaches, partly because the second has already been applied to *Smarra* [see excerpt by Porter dated 1972], but more especially in order to suggest a new line of enquiry into the Romantic attitude to dreams. For it is the case that all critical accounts of the role of dream in French Romanticism, from Béguin's *L'Ame romantique et le rêve* onwards, focus on the *function* rather than the *nature* of dream. They investigate what contribution the Romantics saw dream as making to their spiritual, imaginative and artistic lives, but not what the Romantics might have thought about the possible sources, evolution and structure of dream.

It is hoped that the approach proposed here may serve to dispel the critical ambivalence which *Smarra* has provoked since it was first published on 7 September 1821. From the earliest recorded comments to the most recent there has been a tendency to regard it as in some way 'important'—either to an assessment of the *école frénétique* and the more bizarre aspects of French Romanticism or to an understanding of Nodier himself and the development of his interest in the *fantastique*—while at the same time to dismiss it either as incomprehensible or as the elaborate literary patchwork of an eccentric student of Greek and Latin literature. . . . Much of this ambivalence derives from an uncertainty as to what constitutes the true centre of interest in *Smarra*. (pp. 410-12)

Initial reactions to *Smarra* were generally unfavourable, and the disfavour was the result not so much of its disturbing subject-matter (the *école frénétique* had after all been in evidence for a number of years) but of its ill-disguised polemical slant. The nearly anagrammatic pseudonym under which it was published and its supposed Illyrian provenance can have fooled few moderately well-informed contemporaries, particularly as the true identity of the author had already been revealed some three weeks previously in a piece of advance publicity in *La Quotidienne*. Instead it was clear, at least to his reviewers, that the publication of *Smarra* marked a further step in Nodier's campaign in support of the emergent Romantic school of writing. Since 1813, when he himself began as a literary reviewer, Nodier had returned again and again to the familiar argument that 'le genre romantique' was simply the Classicism of the modern era. *Smarra* is an illustration of that argument. The lack of conventional narrative, the often horrifying imagery and especially the references to vampirism place the work squarely in the *école frénétique,* while the wholesale borrowing from *The Golden Ass* and the juxtaposition as epigraphs of apposite quotations from Shakespeare and such 'respectable'

Latin poets as Horace, Virgil and Tibullus affiliate it to an established tradition of oneiric writing. *Smarra* was to be seen as a new development within this tradition and not as a radical departure from it. (pp. 412-13)

[One] can say that the structure of the work is concentric, comprising a story within a story within a story, and a dream within a dream within a dream. In this respect it simulates the multiple perspectives of the dream-world itself as exemplified by Polémon's perception of Méroé. . . . At the centre, and at the furthest remove in time, is Polémon's story, which divides into his waking and sleeping experience. Surrounding this is Lucius's story, which begins with his waking life, continues with his dream of meeting Polémon (the *Récit*) and ends with his dream within a dream (the *Épode*).The structure of the *Récit* mirrors that of the the story itself. At the centre is the encounter with Polémon, which is surrounded by the description of Myrthé, which is surrounded by the description of the 'jeunes filles de Thessalie' and Myrthé's sisters. The singling out of Polémon . . . parallels that of Myrthé. . . . Framing Lucius's account is that of Lorenzo. In the *Prologue,* which, like the *Épisode,* divides into waking and sleeping, Lorenzo addresses the sleeping Lisidis, while in the *Épilogue* Lisidis awakes to converse with a semi-somnolent Lorenzo.

On the grounds of this basic structure alone it is already clear that *Smarra* is neither random nor incoherent. Nor is this tightness of construction gratuitous, for it gives shape to the chain of intentionally repetitive images that comprises the bulk of the narrative, the 'succession de songes bizarres dont la transition n'est souvent déterminée que par un mot'. These images—of light and darkness, the sun and moon, clouds, water, fire, insects, precious stones, mechanical objects, etc.—are so pervasive in *Smarra* that to tabulate them would result in little more than paraphrase. Instead, what is essential to an understanding of the text is an awareness of just how they are linked and repeated. The kind of linking—or 'transition'—to which Nodier refers can be seen on several occasions in the narrative, especially in the *Récit*. The clearest example is the reference to the Cerameicus, where something first envisaged as part of a comparison becomes itself the subject of description. Similarly, the 'sylphides' are seen ascending 'comme la vague apportée par le flux', which immediately gives rise to the question: 'et que m'importent à moi les accidents de la mer?', and the group of spectres to which Polémon belongs are 'comme des figures fantastiques disposées par un mécanicien habile sur une roue qui indique les divisions du temps' which leads on to the description of time itself. These transitions demonstrate how dreams evolve through the free association of ideas. (pp. 415-16)

As for repetition, this lends to the story the tone of incantation. Lucius seeks to conjure from his dreams the 'jeunes filles de Thessalie' or to induce either the reader ('avez-vous jamais vu?', and 'les avez-vous vus?') or Polémon ('veux-tu m'en croire?', which is later echoed by Polémon's own 'le croirais-tu?') to share his vision. The finest example of such incantation occurs in the *Récit* as Lucius calls on Polémon to listen to 'les airs de la harpe de Myrthé', a passage which relies heavily on rhythm and the repetition not only of words but also of particular sounds. . . .

Certainly this repetition is akin to the refrain of a ballad and as such contributes to the incantatory and pseudo-oral quality of *Smarra,* but it is also evidence of the way in which dreams evolve. Nodier does not allude to this in his preface but it constitutes perhaps the most important element in the story.

Quite simply, dream is born of memory. Indeed Lorenzo describes the spirits of dream as 'impatients de renouer la conversation magique des nuits précédentes, et de se raconter des événements inouïs qui se présentent cependant à votre esprit sous l'aspect d'une réminiscence merveilleuse', and Lucius addresses the 'songes séducteurs qui bercez l'âme enivrée dans les souvenirs ineffables du plaisir'. The 'secret de la composition de *Smarra*' is that the dreams of the three protagonists are based on this. The dreamer may remember what he has just dreamt, as in the above case of repeated sentences, what he has just heard, as in the case of Lucius after hearing Polémon's story ('je voyais malgré moi les fantômes de l'imagination de Polémon'), or what he has just read, as in the case of Lorenzo who had been reading *The Golden Ass*. (p. 417)

In venturing some conclusions about *Smarra* one must begin with the question of its style, since this has proved the principal obstacle to its appreciation. It may be that initiation into the 'secret de la composition' does nothing to dispel the impression of over-rich imagery and classical lucubration which *Smarra* immediately provokes, yet it may also be that this impression itself enhances the dream-like atmosphere of the work, and there is evidence that Nodier himself had this in mind. . . . [The mixture] of classical and Romantic elements is not entirely polemical in purpose. This mixture, moreover, contributes to the oneiric atmosphere not only by evoking the contrasts and incongruities of nightmare but also by creating a sense of the timelessness of dream. With its settings which include Greece in the third century B.C. and Italy at some unspecified moment between 1697 and 1821, and its references both to Shakespeare and to Latin authors of the first century B.C. (Horace, Virgil and Catullus) and the second and fourth centuries A.D. (Apuleius and Claudian respectively), the narrative cuts across chronological boundaries with the same ease as its characters ply between Larissa and Corinth. In so doing, of course, *Smarra* adumbrates the erudite handling of time by Nodier's disciple, Gérard de Nerval.

As to the broader question of the status of dream in *Smarra* further conclusions suggest themselves. The idea that dreams consist of the memories of previous experience was not new, and to the modern reader it may seem so self-evident as scarcely to warrant such an intricate literary demonstration. But at the time of *Smarra*'s publication the idea had considerable currency, and one has only to read the various articles in the *Dictionnaire des sciences médicales* on dream, hallucination, delirium and madness to appreciate how prominently it figured in contemporary debate. (pp. 421-22)

Smarra . . . may be regarded as the first, albeit tentative instalment of Nodier's contribution to the study of these phenomena. This contribution was to continue, in the field of literature, with *Trilby* in which dreams figure as an outlet for forbidden desires, and *La Fée aux miettes* in which the dream experience of a solitary is so powerful as to overwhelm his waking perception of reality and to cause his insanity. It continued also, in a more theoretical vein, with the three important essays **"De Quelques Phénomènes du sommeil"**, **"Des Hallucinations et des songes en matière criminelle"**, and **"Piranèse, contes psychologiques, à propos de la monomanie réflective"**. The central and original thesis which Nodier was working towards and which is reflected most clearly in *La Fée aux miettes* and the essay on Piranesi is that dreams may actually cause mental illness: 'toutes les maladies de l'intelligence procèdent des hallucinations du sommeil'. (p. 423)

[It] is evident that the dreams in *Smarra* are not merely a factitious 'excuse' for fantastical narrative and bizarre imagery. Nodier the erudite entomologist, bibliographer, philologist and lexicographer was also a would-be psychologist. This aspiration, as yet implicit and indeed inchoate in *Smarra,* grew into the confidence and conviction with which, eleven years later and some two months after the republication of *Smarra,* Nodier described his aims in writing *La Fée aux miettes.* . . . The 'key' to *La Fée aux miettes* which Nodier invites his reader to find is the same, *mutatis mutandis,* as the 'secret de la composition de *Smarra*', and if anything shows the 'importance' of *Smarra* as a literary experiment, it is the fact that its author thought it an experiment worth repeating. It is not just an experiment in pursuit of new poetic effects. It is an experiment in the literary illustration of psychological theory, and it is in this sense that one must understand Nodier's *caveat* at the end of the second preface: 'quiconque s'est résigné à lire *Smarra* d'un bout à l'autre, sans s'apercevoir qu'il lisait un rêve, a pris une peine inutile'. (p. 424)

> R. A. G. Pearson, *"Poetry or Psychology? The Representation of Dream in Nodier's 'Smarra',"* in French Studies, *Vol. XXXVI, No. 4, October, 1982, pp. 410-26.*

ANNE-MARIE CHRISTIN   (essay date 1985)

[*In this examination of* L'histoire du Roi de Bohême, *Christin focuses on the work's imagery and typography, analyzing also the function of the illustrations for the story, which were done by Tony Johannot.*]

In January of 1830, when *L'Histoire du Roi de Bohême et de ses sept châteaux* was beginning to appear in bookstores, Charles Nodier wrote: "This is a work which does not strike a responsive chord in any mind, and which is not of this era." In point of fact, the book was a commercial failure, and it even bankrupted its publisher, Delangle, who fell victim to the considerable expense of its production. "To the loony bin with the King of Bohemia!" was the refrain with which, in a satire by Scipion Marin two years later, several well-known literary figures attempted to drown out the litany of Nodier's onomatopoeias and quotations assaulting their ears. Champfleury, analyzing the principal illustrated books of the Romantic era—of which Nodier's was the first—confirms the book's misunderstood nature: "By its printing, by the accents of its vignettes, the *Roi de Bohême* continues to be a most singular note in the world of the Romantic book''; but, he adds, ''Nodier wished to be read. . . . He was mistaken.''

Accustomed as they were to more unified works, it was probably inevitable that the public would be put off by the narrative incoherence, visual games, and typographical disorder of this "espèce de rébus." The artists who frequented the Arsenal probably did not share the public's misgivings; however, the diversity of artists' tributes to the book suggests that the author did not find evidence among them, either, of a common accord with his work. According to Balzac, "This book belongs to the school of *disenchantment.* Nodier arrives, casts a glance on our city, our laws, our sciences, and, through his spokesmen Don Pic de Fanferluchio and Breloque, he says to us, with a shout of laughter: 'Science?—Foolishness! What's the use of it? What is it to me?' He sends the Bourbons to die in the stable, in the form of an old aristocratic mare.'' (pp. 462-63)

To be sure, the *Roi de Bohême* is unusual—even within the *oeuvre* of Nodier. Its typographical *tours de force* seem totally inconsistent with the curses Nodier was at the same time heaping on the innovations of the printing industry. Did he not write in 1832 [that] Gutenberg's invention "accelerated civilization in order to hurtle it towards barbarism, just as opium taken in strong doses accelerates life in order to hurtle it towards death"?

In the same way, it is surprising to note that this creation by the triune of author, illustrator, and typographer—which made the *Roi de Bohême* a first not only in the history of French publishing, but also in the history of French literature and art—did not inspire in Nodier a desire to repeat the experiment. He had no doubt undertaken this book as an unpretentious bit of literary dabbling, a "bluette." It was also no doubt very unlikely that any other publisher would have run the risks that ruined Delangle. However, these considerations did not figure in Nodier's decision to return to traditional literary forms immediately after writing *Roi de Bohême*. The effect of this experimental book was to prompt him to go back to telling stories in the old way. That the author of *Smarra* and *Trilby* could forget that the tale-teller in him had been awakened ten years earlier is evidence that the *Roi de Bohême* was certainly the direct cause of such a choice, paradoxical as that might be: "Unfortunately," he explained in December of 1829, "at first I paid no heed to the fantastic tales and fairy stories in which I now delight. I threw myself into one of those rambling plans (the *Roi de Bohême*) where mediocrity is not permitted. Now that the book is done, and what is worse, printed, I am wonderfully aware that it is as bad as it is possible to be."

Of course, these contradictions are not unimportant. They show us that the *Roi de Bohême* is at the center of various undertakings that Nodier may have thought—rightly or wrongly—were no longer worthy of being backed, or that ought to be displaced to a different system.

Indeed, *displacement* is one of the principles of the work. It is remarkable, for example, that the very plurality of authors that gives it originality on the level of its conception as a *book,* reflects, on another level, one of the fundamental givens of the *text.* Nodier confirms that this was his idea—"the best, if not the only one." This story, he tells us, is "a succession of reveries, *'aegri somnia,'* in the midst of which I lose myself in three personae, that is, in the three principal figures that all educated men are able to distinguish in the phenomenon of their intellect—Imagination, Memory and Judgement. In my specialty, this ill-matched trinity is composed of a bizarre and capricious fool, a pedant with a smattering of erudition and nomenclatures, and a weak and sensitive "honnête garçon," whose impressions are each modified by the other."

But Don Pic, Breloque and Théodore were not created by Nodier alone. They too find themselves in a certain way *displaced* outside of the personalities they incarnate. An entire literature animates them, permeating their names, their adventures, their fantasms, and dispersing this multiple "I"—where Imagination was already reckoning itself a zero—in a floating, archaic architecture of memories and quotations. The glitter displayed on the surface of the book disappears in its depths. However, the reader should not conclude from this, as does one of the book's internal critics (guided by the narrator's pen): "Well, sir, I see what this is! Yet another bad pastiche of the countless pastiches of Sterne and Rabelais!" These obvious borrowings, these allusions, are not a sign of weakness, but rather of a new kind of lucidity. They mean to show that, at this outermost limit of the decadence of the society in which the book was conceived, it is necessary, once and for all, to give up belief in the possibility of original thought, even the

most personal thought of its author—indeed, even his own portrait. Nodier imitated Sterne early on—he begins with the little matter of a slipper—but he imitated him as one who mocks antiquated civilizations, who knows that the only thing left to distract his gloominess is to "make puppets dance." "When an order of things dies, there is always some ingenious demon present, smiling all the while, to watch the death-throes and give it the coup de grâce with his jester's scepter." Such is the author of *Tristram Shandy,* "one of those graceful moralists who cheers with a grave smile the agony of moribund peoples, and who scatters rose-petals on their shroud." To imitate Sterne means to borrow not themes or words from him—for these are never more than subordinate indices—but to borrow the *dynamic* which supports them, and to exploit this dynamic to a point that justifies a derision even greater than Sterne's. This entails, for example, breaking into the flow of the stories at the very moment of their beginning or, what amounts to the same thing, *reclosing this beginning on itself,* like a useless treasure, like the beautiful title of a fable that will never be told,—like this "story of the king of Bohemia and his seven castles," which disappeared a first time with Trimm's memory, and which Nodier will not recount any further but will, in homage, have his book engraved with two frontispieces of choice typography instead of one, and upon which he will bestow one of those journalistic condemnations that stigmatizes the completed work, even when that work does not exist.

For it is here that the only possible originality arises: in appearance; in form. "In everything, from now on, nothing will ever be able to be novel except in its form," Nodier will say in the Introduction to his *Notions élémentaires de linguistique,* adding that this form must be simple and manifest: "Of all possible forms, in a civilization breaking down, the simplest is necessarily the most novel."

We lack the documentation to prove that Tony Johannot's vignettes—themselves "novel" for the conception of illustration that they inaugurated in France, and "simple" because the wood-engraving technique used to reproduce them is the most traditional of book-producing techniques—were solicited by Nodier to bring to his text an originality that thought, in his opinion, was no longer capable of proposing. Yet it seems to me that the *Notions élémentaires* allows us to draw out some arguments that confirm this hypothesis. In this text, Nodier examines the origins, first of the spoken word, then of writing. According to him, painting is the intermediary that leads from one to the other. The poetic spoken word of primitive peoples (whose language, unsophisticated by nature, led them almost immediately to invent metaphor, which alone allowed them to express themselves with precision) was naturally to be followed, he explains—when the number of people and the distances that separated them made manifest the insufficiencies of oral transmission—"by a mode of communication that was comprehensible to the eyes, and painting provided it." We know that Nodier imagined no other origin for languages than an imitative one. It is much the same, according to him, for painting: "As the figurative possibilities of language lent themselves admirably to varying the accepted meanings of the spoken word, no one sought any other technique—namely, painting—for varying the accepted meanings of the written word. Man's most abstract perceptions were reclothed in intelligible images, allegory was invented . . . ; from which results the antique use of the emblem, the metaphor of painting. From that time on, as in the time of Horace, painting and poetry were the same."

In this perspective, the image is defined as *the visual equivalent of the spoken word*. Sterne, too, had anticipated this, but in a purely abstract way. In *Tristram Shandy,* a page printed in black faces one announcing the death of "poor Yorick;" another page, of marbled paper, must be interpreted as the "marbled emblem" of the work; while elsewhere wandering curved lines represent imaginary itineraries. Tony Johannot's images have a more complex function. This is no doubt because they are figurative, and because, for this reason, they suggest motifs, a graphic style, that superimposes itself upon the text; but above all it is because insertion of Johannot's images into the very heart of the text, by thus confirming its discontinuities in a spectacular manner, also *displaces its reading,* disturbs it, and renews it by means of parallel commentaries.

In this respect, nothing is more significant than the series of vignettes that gives rhythm to the *Histoire du chien de Brisquet.* At first glance, we find before us an exemplary case of *illustration,* quite as exemplary as—according to Breloque, in any case—this little tale claims to be. Indeed, it is a matter of beautiful images that support and articulate the text with a scrupulous appositeness. In the first place, they are situated at critical moments in the narration: the presentation of the hero (a portrait of the dog, la Bichonne); then, portraits of the other principals in the drama (a family scene in a rustic cottage showing parents, children, and dog, in which it is clear that the father is advising the mother to forbid the children to go out, while the children are begging to be allowed to do so; a dramatic scene (the father strikes down the wolf with an axe-blow, his children are cowering against him and the dead dog is lying on the ground); the epilogue (the dog's tomb). Besides this quality of narrative punctuation, these vignettes also possess a realism—most useful, as we all know, to the comprehension of a story—which, in the second vignette, comes quite close to folkloric minutiae in its excess of authentic detail. (pp. 463-65)

But the reader of the *Roi de Bohême* remains ill at ease. This perfect illustration, of an admirable docility, introduces into the text an excess which contradicts the style of the text and holds it up to ridicule. Conversely, the simplicity of the narration renders derisory and suspect the details of the image that would have seemed quite amusing considered apart from the narration—*Whom to believe?* The popular success of the *Chien de Brisquet* seems to favor Breloque's point of view. But Johannot's images make us understand that such was not, in truth, Nodier's own opinion, and that for him, this story is the same as another later anthology-piece, the *Amours de Gervais et d'Eulalie* (a tale illustrated with the same parodic fidelity, although in a different style: this time the subtle contrast of tones, the intense effect of a beautiful black underlines a "romantic" intention). In these two stories text and image ought to be *read* as one. By itself, the text does not provide the criteria that allow one to appreciate it: these are revealed in its illustrations. Although one might have expected of these illustrations an authentication of the discourse—as they pretend to provide—instead, they demystify its principles and by their proximity give rise to an irony that attacks both when discourse and illustration are paired, but that spares them when each is considered individually.

Thus we see where Nodier's equating of the visual and the word leads: to the provoking of *creative associations*. The image, in essence similar to discourse because it is a "written thought," must work in conjunction with discourse in the metaphorical mode, a process of composition common to both of them, and which constitutes for both a source of innovation. Thus an entire play of diverse complementarities turns the *Roi de Bohême* into a symphonic madness in two registers, each of which brings out the aberrations of the other, underlining them or contradicting them. "Who the devil can tell me what a pale horse is?" asks Nodier.—Never mind, here it is, and it is indeed exceedingly "pale" because the vignette shows it capering about in a skeletal state, guided by a cavalier in a similarly ascetic guise. Further on, the name Venice so inspires the illustrator's zeal that it also overtakes the writer, who finds himself describing, instead of the city itself, the engraving of Venice before him. And when the writer evokes Byron and Delacroix in connection with Venice, Johannot enthusiastically interrupts him to pay homage to them with a medallion uniting Byron's and Delacroix's two profiles. (pp. 466-68)

[The] advantage of this procedure is that it permits author and illustrator alike to enrich the text by adding to it elements exterior to the fiction, determined entirely by the capabilities of their arts, and to make each element in its turn take part in this incongruous dialogue. For his part, Johannot tends to slide from the imaginary towards the real, and to substitute portraits of his friends for the faces called for by the narration. . . . Disorder? Insolence? Such is the essential law of the game that underlies the *Roi de Bohême*: to disturb norms, to upset categories. This is the price of creativity. Split into three persons by his own creation, the author retrieves his physical identity thanks to the image, but this identity is displaced within the interior of a lie. Between the real and the fictional, there is an intense, nurturing cohesion, a fraternal complicity: however, only the image has the power to show this. Though it may be nothing more than ink and paper, it possesses the absolute gift of *presence:* truth recognizes itself in the image, even as mirages endure. The porous narration of the *Roi de Bohême,* while welcoming its spectacular ambiguities, concretizes its own liberty within it.

For his own part, the writer prolongs the visual game with typography. Revealing itself as the much desired innovative "novelty of form," illustration reintroduced a certain state of innocence into the domain of printing, and raised the possibility of using printing in a creative way. "The first written book was itself nothing more than a pastiche of tradition, a plagiarism of the spoken word": *seeing* will replace *writing,* which will have been worn down by this tradition that has never been self-renewing. "Alas! my dear Victor, I have neither your golden pen nor your thousand-colored inks; my dear Tony, I do not have that palette even richer than the rainbow in which you dip your brushes"; but it still remains to try to *paint his thought with letters,* to lead a technique of banal perfection astray by making it *change writing* instead of merely serving to reproduce useless and chatty discourse. The journalistic "Transcription" that flays the *Roi de Bohême* is completely apropos when it vilifies its pages, "black with printer's ink to civilization's shame." The printing in question is in no way trying to be "civilized": it has taken the image as its guide, and seeks in its paradoxes to restore to written expression the poetry that was part of early cultures.

Writing will thus be new through its form—that is, through its typography. (pp. 469-71)

Nodier's expressive typography obeys two principles: those of *motivation* and *debris.* We recognize in the first the basis of the writer's theories concerning language and painting. This is also what grounds his conception of writing. Being "hieroglyphic," writing first appeared as an abstraction of painted expression. "In the sense that it was *real*, that is, that it expressed things themselves, independent of the various appellations that each of them had received from men, . . . it was thus able to be universally intelligible to whoever possessed the key to its emblems." If only the laziness of an overly-advanced civilization had not deformed the system at the very moment of its creation, the alphabet ought to be writing's perfected formula, but identically conceived: "the rational sign that designates itself is what best awakens the idea of sound through a visual analogy, and which one might call its *rebus* and its hieroglyph." The ideal alphabet, which Nodier calls a "grammataire" would be a "purely real" conventional language, "restrained but sufficient; material, if one may put it that way, and nonintellectual, but one that would effortlessly include in its narrow sphere all of the physical dealings of man with man; . . . a cosmopolitan language that would require barely a few days' study by civilized peoples, and that would open to all travelers the route to all countries."

These hypotheses traverse and explain Nodier's games with letters in the **Histoire du Roi de Bohême.** The episode of the hieroglyphic document discovered in the mummy's body manifests this privileged ambivalence of the figure which, besides possessing the power to render fiction real, is also the holder of the initial secrets of writing. However, it also proves that this written representation will remain an image . . . for all those (and they are the most numerous) who have not been initiated into the deciphering of its emblems. The letter has at its disposal the same iconic virtues, but in order to exploit them, it must reanimate in itself a certain emblematic quality. . . . The visual use of the letter implies that in virtue of its own peculiar capabilities (which are in effect different from those of words), it delivers an immediately accessible meaning. It does so in two different ways: with combinations of phonetically imitative syllables as in onomatopoeia, or by participating in a structure that is itself sufficiently hieroglyphic to be able to signify.

Onomatopoeia, of course, is in very special favor with the writer, and the marvelous chapter *Invention* is a truly felicitous piece of sonorous poetry, as audacious as it is ephemeral; conducted to the rhythm of a postchaise, it comes to take the place of the two tales that were denigrated—one by Breloque, the other by the Johannot's parodic illustrations—and it clearly indicates, at the end of the book, that such is the path down which Nodier was then dreaming of steering writing.

But if he hesitates to follow all the way to the end the adventures of a letter abandoned to the abstract hazard of page layout, the writer is on the other hand too frequent a visitor to the print-shop, too initiated into the manipulation of type and forms (in which a historical memory put on alert by the new possibilities of publicity invests itself during his era) not to be attentive, with equal perspicacity, to the visual mimetism inherent in typography, and not to explore its registers in a rather innovative manner. (pp. 473-75)

[In some places, the absence of illustrations] serves to accentuate Nodier's intuition concerning the various functions of graphic expressivity; this intuition, grounded in a comparative reflection of word and image, led him . . . [to use] only the typographical form. The image suggests—or creates—objects and people. Through typography, an *enunciation* concretizes itself. This enunciation can transpose the gift of objectivity it derives from its iconic function into what is the most characteristic of discourse, and create, using only the play of its artifice, a *speaking individual*. The chapter entitled *Distrac-*

tion, printed upside down in relation to its title because the not-yet-awake narrator has no sense of orientation, is a picturesque example of this capability. *Conversation* offers a more subtle example: its five pages organized like any play script—speakers' names in gothic type, stage directions indicated below in smaller-sized roman type than the lines of dialogue—contains a series of mottos (which are the theme of the dialogue), transcribed in tiny capitals to indicate that they are quotations. But are they spoken? Or are they inscribed? Breloque's own motto, which ends the chapter rather like a concluding illustration, is more remarkable still. Indeed, it is reproduced in "ultra-capital letters" and set on three lines, each one more monumental than the last: WHAT IS - THAT - TO ME? . . . It is not immaterial that, in this case as in the one mentioned above, the typographical manifesto was preferred by the author over an illustration that, here as well, would have been perfectly justified. . . . But one necessarily excludes the other. An image gives life to that which discourse could only allusively evoke, but images do not possess the power of speech. Here, the word is the most important, and Nodier knows that he has at his disposal specific and perfectly adequate means of *showing* this.

Thus, the image is the domain of medallions, emblems, and blazons, and typography is the domain of mottos. The image awakens the "luminous secret" of the icons on the surfaces of the book; typography breaks discourse into fragments of truth which are also capable of translating, beneath their expression, the *very voice*, real or fictitious, that articulated them. Only the alphabetical word has this power, for it is at the same time a bearer of meaning and, in its disparate elements, of abstract power—that is, it is capable of transmitting every intentional color, even the most unconscious, linked to a particular individual's taking charge of it.

That is why Nodier tends to slide so spontaneously from the typographical motivation toward *debris*. The pure letter, not having been invented by man according to the "natural" rules of mimology, could be nothing more than decorative. The word in isolation, on the other hand, escaping from conventions both of syntax and of controlled thought, gives access to a sort of *naive fullness* of meaning. Writing, and especially typography, makes the word an assertive unity completely apart, supported by something other than the spoken word, a support richer and more ambiguous because it is of a spatial nature and not simply determined by temporal continuity. (pp. 475-77)

We must still consider why, having thus discovered such new principles of expression, Nodier was later to renounce them, and with so few regrets. I see two reasons for this. The first is that illustration and typographical play are too complementary in the **Histoire du Roi de Bohême,** so much so that the author was thereafter unable to envisage exploiting them separately to the same advantage. These procedures had been evoked jointly, like two techniques that permit the writer visibly to fragment writing, and to carry on Sterne's work by making the effects more explicit and more spectacular. The experiment had a theoretical origin—to be sure, never very clearly formulated—which, beneath its apparent disorder, supported the adventure of the experiment.

On the other hand, as we have seen, Nodier is not dreaming of lettrism or concrete poetry, but rather of literary creation: the difference is important. It means that novelty of forms is only justified in his eyes by the ideas that it brings to light. This is the second reason that must have made him indifferent to his technical discoveries: for him, their value did not derive from their innovative character, but from the *subjective intimacy* that expressed itself through this novelty of forms. By displacing on the surface of the book this fragmentation that was first sought after by way of provocation, by way of a challenge issued both against a past that had become useless and against a chattering modernity, image and typography had served to confirm the effectiveness of procedures that were not exclusive to them, but that allowed for the renewal, not only of the form of a text, but also of its thought and even of its very author. The autonomy of fragments thus set apart or imposed upon the continuity of discourse offered access to equivalents and substitutions of meaning that traditional literature was not able to authorize. The combination of these fragments, produced so naturally in the reading of the *Roi de Bohême* in spite of their heterogeneity, made credible the possibility of a true syntax worked out in discontinuity, whose unity is the doing of the reader, and not of the narrator.

In truth, the *Roi de Bohême* represents the decisive manifestation of a step that *Smara* already allowed us to anticipate, but this time it is more personal—decisive because here it takes on an experimental form which makes it escape from its author. Is this manifestation precisely that of the dream? The *Roi de Bohême* tells us that it is, more essentially, that of *seeing,* of vision considered as a mysterious but absolute mode of thought. (pp. 478-79)

"Dreams are the parody of life": this explains why Nodier placed the *Histoire du Roi de Bohême* under the sign of parody. But the formal diversity of the work and its narrative casualness are also the sign of a more serious and troubling sensitivity to the consequences of this "bizarre play of the dazzling prism of dreams" on the personality of the dreamer. The coach of the imagination, the "pretty carriage, the one that brought us back from Timbuctoo and that will perhaps one day take us to Bohemia," is also a "nautical conveyance"—a *bateau ivre*— or "the spiraling fall of a winged linden seed." But does the carriage offer us a voyage, or a series of metamorphoses? *Who* is thus pulled into these unstable mirages? And also, *who* is the author of this book in which we see the mirages escaping from our grasp? By making a spectacle of writing in the name of visual thought, Nodier displaces the literature of the authoritarian world of discourse toward that of reading and of its willful mishearings—not only because he senses that certain of his readers will "begin the book at the end," but because the very condition of the dream is that it belongs to no one, and delivers the individual from all subjugation, even that of his own consciousness. It is the same for the book that claims to show this. We can say of the book what Nodier says about Punchinello: "What does it matter whose hand makes him dance, and in whose mouth is placed the sharp and strident *articulations* that will give him voice." What does it matter whether the *Roi de Bohême* has one or several authors, and whether each of them has many faces. The truth of a text, if it is a dream—that is, if it is a visible language rather than a spoken language—belongs to each person who follows its pathways. Beneath its fantasies, even the most superficial of them, the *Histoire du Roi de Bohême et de ses sept châteaux* reveals a conception of the book already that of Mallarmé, that of the "book taken from here and there, guessed at like an enigma, whose aspect changes—a book that is almost remade in one's [the reader's] own image": a conception of writing without a master, of the book without an *author.* (pp. 480-81)

> *Anne-Marie Christin, "A Visionary Book: Charles Nodier's 'L'Histoire du Roi de Bohême et de ses sept châteaux'," translated by Janet Solberg, in Visible Language, Vol. XIX, No. 4, Autumn, 1985, pp. 462-83.*

ADDITIONAL BIBLIOGRAPHY

Barton, Francis B. "Laurence Sterne and Charles Nodier." *Modern Philology* XIV, No. 4 (August 1916): 217-28.
  Attempts to determine the degree of Laurence Sterne's influence on Nodier's work.

Bell, Sarah F. "Charles Nodier, Imitator of Dante." *Romance Notes* XI, No. 3 (Spring 1970): 544-48.
  Briefly notes stylistic similarities between Nodier's *Lydie; ou, La résurrection* and Dante's *Divina commedia.*

———. *Charles Nodier: His Life and Works, A Critical Bibliography, 1923-1967.* University of North Carolina Studies in the Romance Languages and Literatures, no. 95. Chapel Hill: University of North Carolina Press, 1971, 188 p.
  Lists and provides summaries of critical studies on Nodier published between 1923 and 1967. This bibliography continues the work of Jean Larat (see entry below).

Brockett, O. G. "Charles Nodier's Estimate of Shakespeare." *Shakespeare Quarterly* XII, No. 3 (Summer 1961): 345-48.
  Discusses Nodier's evaluations of Shakespeare as they relate to eighteenth-century French criticism.

Crichfield, Grant. "The Alchemical *Magnum Opus* in Nodier's *La fée aux miettes.*" *Nineteenth-Century French Studies* 11, Nos. 3, 4 (Spring-Summer 1983): 231-45.
  Highlights allusions to alchemy in *La fée aux miettes.*

———. "Full Circle(s) in Nodier's *La fée aux miettes.*" *French Forum* 9, No. 2 (May 1984): 200-11.
  Examines the seldom-studied symbol of the circle in Nodier's *La fée aux miettes.*

Easton, Malcolm. "The Meditator." In his *Artists and Writers in Paris: The Bohemian Idea, 1803-1867,* pp. 8-19. New York: St Martin's Press, 1964.
  Describes Nodier's affiliations with the Meditators, a society of innovative painters.

Iknayan, Marguerite. *The Idea of the Novel in France: The Critical Reaction, 1815-1848.* Geneva: E. Droz, 1961, 199 p.
  Contains numerous brief references to Nodier.

Kelly, Dorothy. "The Ghost of Meaning: Language in the Fantastic." *Sub-stance,* No. 35 (1982): 46-55.
  Investigates the function of effacement in fantastic literature as revealed in Nodier's story *Inès de las Sierras.*

Knapp, Bettina L. "*La fée aux miettes:* An Alchemical *Hieros Gamos.*" In *Pre-Text, Text, Context: Essays on Nineteenth-Century French Literature,* edited by Robert L. Mitchell, pp. 15-23. Columbus: Ohio State University Press, 1980.
  Examines the male and female cosmic forces operative in *La fée aux miettes.*

Larat, Jean. *Bibliographie critique des oeuvres de Charles Nodier, suivie de documents inédits.* Bibliothèque de la Revue de Littérature Comparée, edited by Baldensperger and Hazard, vol. X. Paris: Champion, 1923, 144 p.
  A comprehensive bibliography of critical studies on Nodier covering the years up to 1923.

Lombard, Charles M. Introduction to *History of the Secret Societies of the Army,* by Charles Nodier, pp. v-xiii. Scholars' Facsimiles and Reprints Series, vol. 318. Delmar, N. Y.: Scholars' Facsimiles & Reprints, 1978.
  Touches on the genesis of those elements of fantasy in *History of the Secret Societies of the Army* that the author developed more fully in his better-known works.

Maples, Robert J. B. "Individuation in Nodier's *La fée aux miettes.*" *Studies in Romanticism* VIII, No. 1 (Autumn 1968): 43-64.

Explores Nodier's portrayal of spiritual truths of the unconscious mind in *La fée aux miettes.*

Morse, J. Mitchell. "Charles Nodier and *Finnegans Wake.*" *Comparative Literature Studies* V, No. 2 (June 1968): 195-201.

Links Nodier's and James Joyce's use of language and dreams through their "independent discovery of an objective literary truth."

Oliver, A. Richard. "Nodier's Criticism of the *Dictionnaire de l'Académie Française.*" *Modern Language Journal* XLI, No. 1 (January 1957): 20-5.

Traces Nodier's several attempts to be admitted into the French Academy as they relate to his fascination with the history of language.

————. "Charles Nodier's Cult of Shakespeare as a Facet of French Romanticism." *Orbis Litterarum* XVII (1962): 154-65.

Examines Nodier's championing of William Shakespeare's dramas and successful introduction of them into the French theater.

————. *Charles Nodier: Pilot of Romanticism.* Syracuse: Syracuse University Press, 1964, 276 p.

A detailed critical biography.

Porter, Laurence M. "The Stylistic Debate of Charles Nodier's *Histoire du Roi de Bohème.*" *Nineteenth-Century French Studies* 1, No. 1 (Fall 1972): 21-32.

Attempts to resolve the critical debate surrounding Nodier's concept of style through an analysis of his *L'histoire du roi de Bohême.*

————. "The Narrative Art of Nodier's *Contes:* Diderot's Contributions to the Quest for Verisimilitude." *The Romanic Review* LXIII, No. 4 (December 1972): 272-83.

Contrasts the objectives and techniques of Nodier and encyclopedist Denis Diderot, whom he admired.

————. "The Quest for Self-Actualization in Nodier's *Fée aux miettes.*" In his *The Literary Dream in French Romanticism: A Psychoanalytic Interpretation,* pp. 125-43. Detroit: Wayne State University Press, 1979.

Traces the emergence of integrated selfhood in *La fée aux miettes.*

Schutz, A. H. "The Nature and Influence of Charles Nodier's Philological Activity." *Studies in Philology* XXIII, No. 4 (October 1926): 464-72.

Delineates, especially within the French Romantic school, Nodier's contributions to the advancement of linguistics.

Storey, Robert. "In Pursuit of Colombine: Charles Nodier and Charles Baudelaire." In his *Pierrots on the Stage of Desire: Nineteenth-Century French Literary Artists and the Comic Pantomime,* pp. 74-104. Princeton: Princeton University Press, 1985.

Closely examines elements of pantomime in *L'histoire du roi de Bohême.*

Switzer, Richard. "Charles Nodier and the Introduction of Illyrian Literature into France." *Mosaic* VI, No. 4 (Summer 1973): 223-35.

Credits Nodier's work, particularly the novel *Jean Sbogar,* with enhancing French interest in Slavic culture.

Ward, Patricia A. "Nodier, Hugo, and the Concept of the Type Character." *The French Review* XLV, No. 5 (April 1972): 944-53.

Compares Nodier's concept of the type character with that of Hugo.

Wilson, N. "Charles Nodier, Victor Hugo, and *Les Feuilles d'Automne.*" *Modern Language Review* LX, No. 1 (January 1965): 21-31.

Examines the influence of Nodier's literary theories on his friend Victor Hugo's *Les Feuilles d'Automne.*

Clara Reeve

1729-1807

English novelist, poet, and critic.

Although primarily a novelist who wrote in the eighteenth-century tradition of sentimental fiction, Reeve is remembered almost exclusively for her Gothic romance *The Old English Baron.* Writing in response to Horace Walpole's *The Castle of Otranto* (1765), which is recognized as the first Gothic novel, Reeve sought to compose a similar story avoiding what she considered Walpole's flawed narrative conception. Whereas Walpole conceived his novel as an entertainment with an abundant display of supernaturalism, Reeve's narrative is distinguished by her didactic theme and moderate use of supernatural elements. Immensely popular during the eighteenth century, *The Old English Baron* remains important for its role in the development of the Gothic genre.

The oldest daughter in a family of eight children, Reeve was born in Ipswich, Suffolk. Her father was a clergyman in the Anglican church, and biographers speculate that his influence on Reeve's early development substantially contributed to the socially conservative, moralistic nature of her works. Educated at home under her father's tutelage, she displayed a special interest in history and biography. After her father died in 1755, Reeve moved to Colchester with her mother and two of her sisters. It was here that she wrote her first book, *Original Poems on Several Occasions,* which was published in 1769. This collection of poetry received little notice, and it was not until the private publication of *The Champion of Virtue: A Gothic Story* in 1777 that her work gained recognition. On the advice of her friend Martha Bridgen, the daughter of novelist Samuel Richardson, Reeve revised this novel and published it in 1778 as *The Old English Baron.* While Walpole himself disparaged the work, remarking in a letter that "any trial for murder at the Old Bailey would make a more interesting story," it was an immediate popular and critical success. Reeve's subsequent attempts at biography, sentimental novels, and a history of English fiction were not as well received as *The Old English Baron,* which appeared in many editions and was widely imitated until the late nineteenth century. Throughout her literary career Reeve's life remained uneventful; she died quietly at Ipswich on 3 December 1807, "admitting," as Sir Walter Scott wrote in his essay on the novelist, "no materials for biography."

Reeve stated in her preface to *The Old English Baron* that the novel was clearly the "literary offspring of *The Castle of Otranto,* written upon the same plan, with a design to unite the most attractive and interesting circumstances of the ancient Romance and modern Novel." While acknowledging her debt to Walpole, she also attacked *The Castle of Otranto* for its over-abundance of supernatural incidents. She noted that Walpole's excessive use of supernatural phenomena, including a ghostly skeleton in a hermit's cowl, a walking picture, and an enormous sword and helmet, "destroys the effect it is intended to excite," contending that the reader's interest quickly flags under such a bombardment of fantastic detail. In order to arouse and maintain interest in her tale, Reeve restricted herself to subtler devices: mysterious sounds, a haunted room, and doors that open by themselves are among the few supernatural manifes-

tations in the novel. Thus, Reeve attempted in *The Old English Baron* to fashion a Gothic story that functioned "within the utmost *verge* of probability." Her cautious approach to writing Gothic fiction anticipated the later, more critically acclaimed novels of Ann Radcliffe, whose characters inhabit a world where realistic detail joins successfully with improbable occurrences. Reeve combined literary Gothicism with the didactic concerns characteristic of sentimental fiction. In *The Old English Baron,* William Lovel murders his brother, Lord Lovel, and cheats the rightful heir, Edmund, of the Lovel fortune and estates. Edmund, unaware of his parentage, is raised by peasants, but his natural nobility brings him to the attention of Baron Fitz-Owen, who, having purchased the Lovel estates from William Lovel, now resides in the murdered lord's castle. Fitz-Owen takes Edmund into his household, where his virtuous character incites the hatred of the Baron's relatives. With the help of ghostly visitations from his true parents, Edmund learns the secret of his birth, triumphs over William Lovel and the Baron's relatives, and is finally restored to his proper station. Throughout this narrative, style, characterization, and structure are determined and limited by the strictures of Reeve's moral concerns.

Reeve's novels written subsequent to *The Old English Baron,* including *The Two Mentors, The Exiles,* and *The School for*

Widows, more obviously belong to the mainstream of the sentimental tradition. Primarily reflecting her concern with morality and the preservation of the social order, these novels are essentially didactic and have attracted little critical interest. Although some recent criticism has focused on *Plans of Education,* an essay on the education of women in society, none of her later works have been as widely acclaimed as *The Old English Baron.* Reeve's novel is often seen as a transitional work bridging the excesses of Walpole and the more realistic novels of Radcliffe. As such, *The Old English Baron* occupies a conspicuous place in the history of Gothic fiction.

(See also *Dictionary of Literary Biography,* Vol. 39: *British Novelists, 1660-1800.*)

PRINCIPAL WORKS

Original Poems on Several Occasions (poetry) 1769
The Champion of Virtue: A Gothic Story (novel) 1777;
     also published in revised form as *The Old English Baron,* 1778
The Two Mentors (novel) 1783
The Progress of Romance, through Times, Countries, and Manners (criticism) 1785
The Exiles; or, Memoirs of the Count de Cronstadt (novel) 1788
The School for Widows (novel) 1791
Plans of Education (epistolary essay) 1792
Memoirs of Sir Roger de Clarendon, the Natural Son of Edward Prince of Wales, Commonly Called the Black Prince (novel) 1793
Destination; or, Memoirs of a Private Family (novel) 1799

CLARA REEVE (essay date 1778)

[*In the following essay, originally published as the preface to the 1778 edition of* The Old English Baron, *Reeve explains her purpose in writing the novel.*]

As this Story is of a species which, though not new, is out of the common track, it has been thought necessary to point out some circumstances to the reader which will elucidate the design, and, it is hoped, will induce him to form a favourable as well as a right judgment of the work before him.

[*The Old English Baron*] is the literary offspring of *The Castle of Otranto,* written upon the same plan, with a design to unite the most attractive and interesting circumstances of the ancient Romance and modern Novel, at the same time it assumes a character and manner of its own that differs from both; it is distinguished by the appellation of a Gothic story, being a picture of Gothic times and manners. Fictitious stories have been the delight of all times and all countries, by oral tradition in barbarous, by writing in more civilized ones; and although some persons of wit and learning have condemned them indiscriminately, I would venture to affirm that even those who so much affect to despise them under one form, will receive and embrace them under another.

Thus, for instance, a man shall admire and almost adore the Epic poems of the Ancients, and yet despise and execrate the ancient romances, which are only Epics in prose.

History represents human nature as it is in real life, alas, too often a melancholy retrospect! Romance displays only the amiable side of the picture; it shows the pleasing features, and throws a veil over the blemishes. Mankind are naturally pleased with what gratifies their vanity; and vanity, like all other passions of the human heart, may be rendered subservient to good and useful purposes.

I confess that it may be abused, and become an instrument to corrupt the manners and morals of mankind; so may poetry, so may plays, so may every kind of composition; but that will prove nothing more than the old saying lately revived by the philosophers, the most in fashion, "that every earthly thing has two handles."

The business of Romance is, first, to excite the attention; and, secondly, to direct it to some useful, or at least innocent, end. Happy the writer who attains both these points, like Richardson; and not unfortunate, or undeserving praise, he who gains only the latter, and furnishes out an entertainment for the reader.

Having in some degree opened my design, I beg leave to conduct my reader back again, till he comes within view of *The Castle of Otranto;* a work which, as already has been observed, is an attempt to unite the various merits and graces of the ancient Romance and modern Novel. To attain this end, there is required a sufficient degree of the marvellous to excite attention; enough of the manners of real life to give an air of probability to the work; and enough of the pathetic to engage the heart in its behalf.

The book we have mentioned is excellent in the two last points, but has a redundancy in the first. The opening excites the attention very strongly; the conduct of the story is artful and judicious; the characters are admirably drawn and supported; the diction polished and elegant; yet with all these brilliant advantages, it palls upon the mind (though it does not upon the ear); and the reason is obvious, the machinery is so violent that it destroys the effect it is intended to excite. Had the story been kept within the utmost *verge* of probability, the effect had been preserved, without losing the least circumstance that excites or detains the attention.

For instance; we can conceive, and allow of, the appearance of a ghost; we can even dispense with an enchanted sword and helmet; but then they must keep within certain limits of credibility. A sword so large as to require a hundred men to lift it; a helmet that by its own weight forces a passage through a courtyard, into an arched vault big enough for a man to go through; a picture that walks out of its frame; a skeleton ghost in a hermit's cowl:—when your expectation is wound up to the highest pitch, these circumstances take it down with a witness, destroy the work of imagination, and instead of attention excite laughter. I was both surprised and vexed to find the enchantment dissolved, which I wished might continue to the end of the book; and several of its readers have confessed the same disappointment to me. The beauties are so numerous that we cannot bear the defects, but want it to be perfect in all respects.

In the course of my observations upon this singular book, it seemed to me that it was possible to compose a work upon the same plan, wherein these defects might be avoided; and the *keeping,* as in *painting,* might be preserved.

But then I began to fear it might happen to me as to certain translators and imitators of Shakespeare; the unities may be preserved, while the spirit is evaporated. However, I ventured to attempt it; I read the beginning to a circle of friends of approved judgment, and by their approbation was encouraged to proceed and to finish it. (pp. 11-14)

> *Clara Reeve, in a preface to her* The Old English Baron: A Gothic Story *and* The Castle of Otranto: A Gothic Story *by Horace Walpole, J.C. Nimmo and Bain, 1883, pp. 11-14.*

THE BRITISH CRITIC   (essay date 1793)

> [*The anonymous reviewer surveys several of Reeve's novels, focusing on* Memoirs of Sir Roger de Clarendon.]

When the **The Old English Baron** made its appearance, every mouth was opened in its praise: every line carried fascination along with it. The younger branch of readers found their attention absolutely rivetted to the story; and, at its conclusion, they have been actually seen to weep, in the spirit of Alexander, because they had not another volume to peruse. A more genuine and unaffected compliment was never paid to any work of fancy.

The **Two Mentors** followed. We hope that no such dismal accident befel the author in the interval, as the poor archbishop of Grenada met with; but, on the perusal of this second work, it was impossible to forbear exclaiming, "Voilà un livre qui sent furieusement l'apoplexie." Tears might again have been shed at the conclusion of the first volume; but they must have been tears of a very different description. For the **Exiles, or the Count de Cronstadt,** it would be unfair to make Mrs. Reeve accountable, because the greater part, if not the whole, of that work, is borrowed from the German. The press still teemed with publications from this lady's prolific pen; but, alas! the name of Clara had lost all its magic, and could no longer attract.

In the tile of the present work [**Memoirs of Sir Roger de Clarendon**], there was something which laid a forcible hold on the mind. The age to which it referred, was the age of heroes. Once more we felt a degree of curiosity, and we prepared for an intellectual banquet.

Alas! all would not do—"No Dolphin came—no Nereid stirr'd." Whether the best of Mrs. Reeve's genius evaporated in her first performance, or whether Ariosto's remark on the sex be too well founded, that they are unfit for works of painful elaboration, we shall not venture to pronounce decisively. Most certain it is, that we found Sir Roger de Clarendon rather dull, and his memoirs little worthy of remembrance. (p. 384)

We shall not enter into a long analysis of the story. The author sets out with acquainting us, that she shall not be able to interest us much in behalf of Sir Roger de Clarendon. Well has she performed her negative promise—and kindly too—for as she brings him to the gallows, if we had loved too well, we had not loved wisely.

Of the three females most prominent on the canvas, Madam Isabel is best drawn; and, if we have a regret on the subject of the work, it is that this character is not a little more expanded. Edith is a miserable piece of still life; and Mabel, a forward, modern boarding-school miss, very ready to run away with papa's footman. In Master Clement Woodville we have a most happy companion for Edith: they were formed for each other; and it would have been an act of barbarity to have parted them.

Sir Roger's assumed silence, and his constant practice of wearing armour to *avoid* impertinent curiosity, seems, in our poor

opinion, an expedient, much of the same kind with that of the bride, in the celebrated Irish Epithalamium, who,

> When she was look'd after, did not appear,
> Till she popp'd out her head, and cry'd *"Faith, I'm not here!"*

The whole episode of the Hermit of Clarendon, is unnatural in the extreme; and the adoption of this anchorite, as tutor in Edward's family, approaches too nearly to the plan of Rousseau's *Eloisa.*

As for the historical extracts, and Master Clement Woodville's register of the Knights of the Garter—gentle ladies—beware of reading them on a winter's evening too near the candle—strong soporifics should be taken in a safer situation.

Such are the **Memoirs of Sir Roger de Clarendon;** concerning whom we have yet to lament, that his biographer has been guilty of the prevailing and fashionable fault of blending truth with fable; a practice which, if it serve to familiarize some general traits of history, is likely at the same time to create in young minds a strange confusion between true and false, which subsequent study may not easily clear away. Were we to condemn, without reserve, the whole class of these performances, the Cyropædia of Xenophon, and the Cyrus of Ramsay, would be included in the proscription; but though we are delighted with the elegant morality of both these works, and in particular should hardly bring ourselves to censure the former author, whose classical excellence mixed delight with the labours of our early studies; yet who does not at this moment feel the inconvenience arising from the total want of distinction between truth and falshood in his pleasing work! What disputes of the learned from this sole cause! What uncertainty in an history which that writer, above all others, had means and opportunities to elucidate! But whatever be pronounced in a case so peculiar as this, it seems clear that forming the modern romance to a deceptive imitation of history, is producing something like Sir Roger de Clarendon himself, more likely to disgrace the better side of its parentage, than to dignify that which is inferior. (pp. 385-86)

We are concerned to see ingenuity at all misapplied, or unsuccessful; but, if in perusing such a work as the present, we miss that charm which should give life to it, the dramatic interest arising from the action and the characters, this defect casts a shade over the whole; and we naturally feel impatient at toiling through what neither informs as history, nor delights as fiction. The morality may be well intended; but morality alone, though in itself among the best things, cannot support a novel: and if even that be in some places defective, the estimate will sink still lower. (p. 388)

> *A review of "Memoirs of Sir Roger de Clarendon," in* The British Critic, *Vol. II, December, 1793, pp. 383-88.*

SIR WALTER SCOTT   (essay date 1827)

> [*Scott was a Scottish novelist, poet, historian, biographer, and critic of the Romantic period who is best known for his novels, which were great popular successes. In the following excerpt, Scott discusses Reeve's ideas on the use of supernatural elements in literature and examines her approach to historical subject matter and narrative realism in* The Old English Baron. *His comments were originally published in 1827 in* The Miscellaneous Prose Works of Sir Walter Scott.]

The various novels of Clara Reeve are all marked by excellent good sense, pure morality, and a competent command of those qualities which constitute a good romance. They were, generally speaking, favourably received at the time, but none of them took the same strong possession of the public mind as *The Old English Baron,* upon which the fame of the authoress may be considered as now exclusively rested. (p. 95)

The authoress has herself informed us that *The Old English Baron* is the "literary offspring of *The Castle of Otranto*" [see excerpt dated 1778]; and she has obliged us by pointing out the different and more limited view which she had adopted, of the supernatural machinery employed by Horace Walpole. She condemns the latter for the extravagance of several of his conceptions; for the gigantic size of his sword and helmet; and for the violent fictions of a walking picture, and a skeleton in a hermit's cowl. A ghost, she contends, to be admitted as an ingredient in romance, must behave himself like ghosts of sober demeanour, and subject himself to the common rules still preserved in grange and hall, as circumscribing beings of his description.

We must, however, notwithstanding her authority, enter our protest against fettering the realm of shadows by the opinions entertained of it in the world of realities. If we are to try ghosts by the ordinary rules of humanity, we bar them of their privileges entirely. For instance, why admit the existence of aerial phantom, and deny it the terrible attribute of magnifying its stature? why admit an enchanted helmet, and not a gigantic one? why allow as an impressive incident the fall of a suit of armour, thrown down, we must suppose, by no mortal hand, and at the same time deny the same supernatural influence the power of producing the illusion (for it is only represented as such) upon Manfred, which gives seeming motion and life to the portrait of his ancestor? It may be said, and it seems to be Miss Reeve's argument, that there is a verge of probability, which even the most violent figment must not transgress; but we reply by the cross question, that if we are once to subject our preternatural agents to the limits of human reason, where are we to stop? We might, under such a rule, demand of ghosts an account of the very circuitous manner in which they are pleased to open their communications with the living world. We might, for example, move a *quo warranto* against the spectre of the murdered Lord Lovel, for lurking about the eastern apartment, when it might have been reasonably expected, that if he did not at once impeach his murderers to the next magistrate, he might at least have put Fitzowen into the secret, and thus obtained the succession of his son more easily than by the dubious and circuitous route of a single combat. It there should be an appeal against this imputation, founded on the universal practice of ghosts, in such circumstances, who always act with singular obliquity in disclosing the guilt of which they complain, the matter becomes a question of precedent; in which view of the case, we may vindicate Horace Walpole for the gigantic exaggeration of his phantom, by the similar expansion of the terrific vision of Fadoun, in Blind Harry's *Life of Wallace;* and we could, were we so disposed, have paralleled his moving picture, by the example of one with which we ourselves had some acquaintance, which was said both to move and to utter groans, to the great alarm of a family of the highest respectability.

Where, then, may the reader ask, is the line to be drawn? or what are the limits to be placed to the reader's credulity, when those of common sense and ordinary nature are once exceeded? The question admits only one answer, namely, that the author himself, being in fact the magician, shall evoke no spirits whom he is not capable of endowing with manners and language

corresponding to their supernatural character. Thus Shakspeare, drawing such characters as Caliban and Ariel, gave them reality, not by appealing to actual opinions, which his audience might entertain respecting the possibility or impossibility of their existence, but by investing them with such attributes as all readers and spectators recognized as those which must have corresponded to such extraordinary beings, had their existence been possible. If he had pleased to put into language the "squeaking and gibbering" of those disembodied phantoms which haunted the streets of Rome, no doubt his wonderful imagination could have filled up the sketch, which, marked by these two emphatic and singularly felicitous expressions, he has left as characteristic of the language of the dead.

In this point of view, our authoress has, with equal judgment and accuracy, confined her flight within those limits on which her pinions could support her; and though we are disposed to contest her general principle, we are willing to admit it as a wise and prudent one, so far as applied to regulate her own composition. In no part of *The Old English Baron,* or of any other of her works, does Miss Reeve show the possession of a rich or powerful imagination. Her dialogue is sensible, easy, and agreeable, but neither marked by high flights of fancy, nor strong bursts of passion. Her apparition is an ordinary fiction, of which popular superstition used to furnish a thousand instances, when nights were long, and a family, assembled round a Christmas log, had little better to do than to listen to such tales. Miss Reeve has been very felicitously cautious in showing us no more of Lord Lovel's ghost than she needs must— he is a silent apparition, palpable to the sight only, and never brought forward into such broad daylight as might have dissolved our reverence. And so far, we repeat, the authoress has used her own power to the utmost advantage, and gained her point by not attempting a step beyond it. But we cannot allow that the rule which, in her own case, has been well and wisely adopted, ought to circumscribe a bolder and a more imaginative writer.

In what may be called the costume, or keeping, of the chivalrous period in which the scene of both is laid, the language and style of Horace Walpole, together with his intimate acquaintance with the manners of the middle ages, form an incalculable difference betwixt *The Castle of Otranto* and *The Old English Baron.* Clara Reeve, probably, was better acquainted with Plutarch and Rapin, than with Froissart or Olivier de la Marche. This is no imputation on the taste of that ingenious lady. In her days, Macbeth was performed in a general's full uniform, and Lord Hastings was dressed like a modern high chamberlain going to court. Or, if she looked to romances for her authority, those of the French school were found introducing, under the reign of Cyrus or of Faramond, or in the early Republic at Rome, the sentiments and manners of the court of Louis XIV. In the present day, more attention to costume is demanded, and authors, as well as players, are obliged to make attempts, however fantastic or grotesque, to imitate the manners, on the one hand, and the dress on the other, of the times in which the scene is laid. Formerly, nothing of this kind was either required or expected; and it is not improbable that the manner in which Walpole circumscribes his dialogue (in most instances) within the stiff and stern precincts prescribed by a strict attention to the manners and language of the times, is the first instance of such restrictions. In *The Old English Baron,* on the contrary, all parties speak and act much in the fashion of the seventeenth century; employ the same phrases of courtesy; and adopt the same tone of conversation. Baron Fitzowen, and the principal characters, talk after the fashion of country squires of that period, and the lower personages like gaffers and gammers of the same era. And "were but the combat in lists left out," or converted into a modern duel, the whole train of incidents might, for any peculiarity to be traced in the dialect or narration, have taken place in the time of Charles II., or in either of the two succeeding reigns. As it is, the story reads as if it had been transcribed into the language, and remodelled according to the ideas, of this latter period. Yet we are uncertain whether, upon the whole, this does not rather add to, than diminish the interest of the work;—at least it gives an interest of a different kind, which, if it cannot compete with that which arises out of a highly exalted and poetical imagination, and a strict attention to the character and manners of the middle ages, has yet this advantage, that it reaches its point more surely, than had a higher, more difficult, and more ambitious line of composition been attempted.

To explain our meaning:—He that would please the modern world, yet present the exact impression of a tale of the middle ages, will repeatedly find that he will be obliged, in despite of his utmost exertions, to sacrifice the last to the first object, and eternally expose himself to the just censure of the rigid antiquary, because he must, to interest the readers of the present time, invest his characters with language and sentiments unknown to the period assigned to his story; and thus his utmost efforts only attain a sort of composition between the true and the fictitious,—just as the dress of Lear, as performed on the stage, is neither that of a modern sovereign, nor the cerulean painting and bear-hide with which the Britons, at the time when that monarch is supposed to have lived, tattooed their persons, and sheltered themselves from cold. All this inconsistency is avoided by adopting the style of our grandfathers and great-grandfathers, sufficiently antiquated to accord with the antiquated character of the narrative, yet copious enough to express all that is necessary to its interest, and to supply that deficiency of colouring which the more ancient times do not afford.

It is not doubt true, that **The Old English Baron,** written in the latter and less ambitious taste, is sometimes tame and tedious, not to say mean and tiresome. The total absence of peculiar character (for every person introduced is rather described as one of a genus that as an original, discriminated, and individual person) may have its effect in producing the tedium which loads the story in some places. This is a general defect in the novels of the period, and it was scarce to be expected that the amiable and accomplished authoress, in her secluded situation, and with acquaintance of events and characters derived from books alone, should have rivalled those authors who gathered their knowledge of the human heart from having, like Fielding and Smollett, become acquainted, by sad experience, with each turn of "many-coloured life." Nor was it to be thought that she should have emulated in this particular her prototype Walpole, who, as a statesman, a poet, and a man of the world, "who knew the world like a man," has given much individual character to his sketch of Manfred. What we here speak of is not the deficiency in the style and costume, but a certain creeping and low line of narrative and sentiment; which may be best illustrated by the grave and minute accounting into which Sir Philip Harclay and the Baron Fitzowen enter,—after an event so unpleasant as the judgment of Heaven upon a murderer, brought about by a judicial combat, and that combat occasioned by the awful and supernatural occurrences in the eastern chamber,—where we find the arrears of the estate gravely set off against the education of the heir, and his early maintenance in the Baron's family. Yet, even these prolix, minute, and un-

necessary details, are precisely such as would occur in a similar story told by a grandsire or grandame to a circle assembled round a winter's fire; and while they take from the dignity of the composition, and would therefore have been rejected by a writer of more exalted imagination, do certainly add in some degree to its reality, and bear in that respect a resemblance to the art with which De Foe impresses on his readers the truth of his fictions, by the insertion of many minute, and immaterial, or unnatural circumstances, which we are led to suppose could only be recorded because they are true. Perhaps, to be circumstantial and abundant in minute detail, and in one word, though an unauthorized one, to be somewhat *prosy,* is a secret mode of securing a certain necessary degree of credulity from the hearers of a ghost-story. It gives a sort of quaint antiquity to the whole, as belonging to the times of "superstitious elde," and those whom we have observed to excel in oral narratives of such a nature, usually study to secure the attention of their audience by employing this art. At least, whether owing to this mode of telling her tale, or to the interest of the story itself, and its appeal to the secret reserve of superstitious feeling which maintains its influence in most bosoms, **The Old English Baron** has always produced as strong an effect as any story of the kind, although liable to the objections which we have freely stated, without meaning to impeach the talents of the amiable authoress. (pp. 96-100)

> *Sir Walter Scott, "Clara Reeve," in* Sir Walter Scott on Novelists and Fiction, *edited by Ioan Williams, Routledge & Kegan Paul, 1968, pp. 94-101.*

CHRISTABEL FORSYTHE FISKE (essay date 1900)

[*In the following excerpt, Fiske compares* The Old English Baron *with* The Castle of Otranto.]

The supernatural element in [*The Castle of Otranto*] is so clumsily palpable that Clara Reeve, who, in 1777, published her **English Baron,** while announcing her book as the offspring of *Otranto,* condemned Walpole's extravagance and declared her intention of keeping his ghostly element within reasonable bounds. Such moderation hints vaguely at Mrs. Radcliffe and becomes Reeve's chief merit. In this she shows advance on Walpole. He strives to excite our fear by *bona fide* ghosts and magical machinery. Where Reeve follows his lead she is not, perhaps, so extravagantly absurd, but she is at least stupid and powerless.

But on occasion she has soared above him to a point he never dreamed of. She touches deftly, at least once, on the human soul quivering beneath the impulse of vague, apprehensive fear. Walpole's sluggish heroes needed a real bogy to stir their nerves. The picture Reeve draws of Edmund wandering at midnight through the apartments of the Old East Wing, through the rafters of which the rain forced its way, and along the passages of which the wind moaned and sighed, reached a high degree of artistic excellence. Compared to it, the ready-made ghosts Walpole sets up seem vulgar and absurd. At this moment, at least, Reeve has touched with successful finger the vast field of Subjective Terror in which Radcliffe was to achieve her fame. It is provoking that this admirable little scene serves merely as prelude to an absurd visitation, in which Edmund's deceased mother administers to him and to the reader several pages of stupid advice. (pp. 47-8)

> *Christabel Forsythe Fiske, "The Tales of Terror," in* The Conservative Review, *Vol. III, No. 1, March, 1900, pp. 37-74.*

JAMES TRAINER   (essay date 1967)

[*In the following excerpt, Trainer analyzes Reeve's use of supernatural devices in* The Old English Baron, *demonstrates the importance of this work in the history of the Gothic novel, and discusses her later novels in terms of their moral themes.*]

In the second volume of her *Progress of Romance* Clara Reeve quotes a passage from *The Trial, or the History of Charles Horton Esq.,* which might well stand as a motto over her own activities as novelist:

> If you wish in a Novel to inculcate some moral truth, to hide a jewel under so thin a veil that its brilliancy may be easily discerned, there should always be a reference to the manners and the time in which it was written; there should be the greatest probability, carried thro' the whole allegory, that your reason may not be shocked, while your imagination is pleased. If Novels were properly regulated with this design always in view, they might become really useful to society. A moral lesson otherwise dry and tedious in itself, might be communicated in a pleasing dress: as a pill has its desired effect, tho' wrapped in a gold or silver leaf.

And if this view—that the primary purpose of the novel is to communicate a moral lesson in a pleasing dress—sounds less than innovatory, it should be recalled that *The Old English Baron* proved to be one of the most successful and influential works of its generation. Its importance in the history of the Gothic novel lay retrospectively in the attempt to temper some of the excesses of Walpole's *Castle of Otranto* and prospectively in the creation of a climate in which Ann Radcliffe's more sophisticated characters could survive.

Horace Walpole's main achievement had been the restoration of the irrational and the supernatural into the novel and his preface to the second edition of *Otranto* announced his intention of "leaving the power of fancy at liberty to expatiate through the boundless realms of invention" while at the same time wishing "to conduct the mortal agents in his drama according to the rules of probability; in short, to make them think, speak and act, as it might be supposed mere men and women would do in extraordinary positions." If the acclaim given to Walpole's novel showed that he correctly diagnosed the malaise of a reading public whose palates had been jaded by the surfeit descriptions of real society to be found in Richardson and Fielding, Clara Reeve believed that his prescribed remedy was too severe. She disapproved of the masculine elements of violence and horror although she accepted fear as something positive, an "agreeable sensation" as Mrs. Barbauld called it, since the reader's fullest pleasure derived from the contemplation of the fear being experienced by the character while knowing all the time that no real evil would befall him. Or, as Devendra Varma has it, the Gothic authors "aimed at awakening the twin emotions of Pity and Fear, but mainly Fear, as being more sublime" [see Additional Bibliography].

In the preface to *The Champion of Virtue,* as the novel was originally called, Clara Reeve conceded the inspiration of *Otranto*, pointed to Walpole's destruction of the very effect he was trying to create, and went on to offer her own formula for satisfactorily compounding the ancient Romance and the modern Novel: "a sufficient degree of the marvellous to excite attention: enough of the manners of real life to give an air of probability to the work: and enough of the pathetic to engage the heart in its behalf" [see excerpt dated 1778]. She is still prepared to admit the supernatural but it has become for her a question of degree, a toning-down process which was to be continued by Ann Radcliffe in the form of the "apparently supernatural" phenomena which in the end could all be attributed to natural causes. As a result many of Mrs. Radcliffe's explanations became absurdly improbable and Clara Reeve's modest and civilized ghosts are the more effective for their almost reluctant participation. Clara had well heeded Fielding's warning in *Tom Jones* that ghosts "are indeed like arsenic, and other dangerous drugs in Physic, to be used with the utmost caution" and certainly not by authors "to whom a horse-laugh in the reader would be any great prejudice or mortification." A little subterranean groaning, some impressive nocturnal thuds, doors which open unaided when the true heir to the castle approaches, this is the sum total of supernatural activity in *The Old English Baron.* It is far outweighed by more tangible reliques of the deceased, armour, necklace, and seal, as well as by the characters' concern with mundane business affairs such as the settling of petty debts, the apportioning of farm stock, the furnishing of apartments, and the quest for general respectability. Her attention to the "manners of real life" leads Clara to dwell upon all her own eighteenth-century social prejudices, the rigid class distinctions in which master and servant have only "the same natural form and endowments" since their difference of birth "had given a conscious superiority to the one, and conscious inferiority to the other." This is a structure which the author warmly approved and indeed it is essential to her story for Edmund radiates to those around him a quality which is taken by them to point to a nobler parentage than a poor peasant couple. Within this stratified society we find a range of almost stock character-types lacking any individual definition but entrusted with a particular function in the advancement of the story—the tyrant-aristocrat Sir Walter Lovel, the faithful family servant Joseph, the envious kinsmen Wenlock and Markham, the upright priest Father Oswald, the persecuted female Edmund's mother, and the desirable but unattainable Lady Emma who has no purpose whatsoever other than to be on hand as a suitable reward for Edmund's assertion of his true lineage.

If this depiction of character is unconvincing it is because here also Clara has been concerned to avoid excesses of temperament and to reduce passions to genteel proportions, so that her narrative is kept within a narrow range of emotions and moments of climax are very rare. It is in this near-elimination of suspense as a unifying factor in the unravelling of her story that she differs most completely from both Walpole and Mrs. Radcliffe. There are admittedly isolated moments of great tension but her inexperience as a novelist (this was after all her first attempt) obtrudes most readily in her persistent habit of premature anticipation of ensuing events, thereby allowing, almost inviting, the reader to prognosticate (usually correctly) upon the outcome of any situation. This is not an intentional device of the modern alienation school but an insurance against our being sceptical when new truths are finally revealed, for she still professes an air of surprise when family relationships ultimately work out to Edmund's absolute advantage. Dreams and visions of a somewhat clumsy kind are the most favoured means of preparing us for what is to come, and in fact Edmund's experiences during his incarceration in the east apartment when he dreams first of a warrior and lady who recognize him as their child, then of a funeral procession, and finally of a wedding feast serve as an outline of the remaining plot. The few dramatic moments of the novel are consistently underplayed. The account of Edmund's bravery in battle in France amounts scarcely to a mention in dispatches and the vital duel between Sir Philip and Sir Walter, after an elaborate selection of judges, seconds, and terrain, is exploited solely for demonstrating the generosity of the victor over the vanquished. The didactic again triumphs over the epic.

This economy, one might almost say parsimony, of means extends into the creation of historical and local atmosphere. Apart from the generalities of the opening sentences which establish the time as the minority of Henry VI in the fifteenth century, there is no regard for historicity just as there is a total absence of the rich and detailed nature descriptions to which Mrs. Radcliffe devoted so many pages. On only one occasion, in the portrayal of the moth-eaten fabrics and decaying furniture of the secret apartments, does she afford herself the luxury of atmospheric description, and that to such good effect that the abandoned wing of the castle with its dilapidated rooms and reputation for mystery became one of the most frequent scenes of incident in later Gothic tales. In thus restricting the marvellous occurrences to a fixed location where strange noises and visions could be associated with the unburied bones of wronged ancestors Clara achieved just the degree of "controlled supernatural" which she felt to be more artistically satisfying.

Much less successful is her perfectionist haste in providing in the final paragraphs brief résumés of the future lives of all her characters. Edmund and Emma produce five children in as many lines before dying peacefully in advanced age, and even the villainous Sir Walter enlists in the army of the Greek Emperor and marries the daughter of one of its chief officers. All of this Clara feels must be cleared away in order to lead more impressively to the final caution of her tale. The moralizing tendency is never far from the surface and at regular intervals it is enunciated for the benefit of the reader. The climax is reached when Lord Graham's priest spells it out at the end: "Let this awful spectacle be a lesson to all present, that though wickedness may triumph for a season, a day of retribution will come!" *The Old English Baron* can in this way be looked upon as a sermon based on an Old Testament text, freshly and fluently delivered, without great pretension in thought or ethics, but full of optimism and cheer for the man whose conscience is clear. That is why Sir Philip is always mindful of his devotions and Edmund quick to appeal to the "higher powers" as proof of his innocence. This religious theme was of course a reflection of the author's own faith and of her background and family traditions. (pp. vii-xii)

[Clara Reeve's] later works reveal a surprising versatility with Gothic, historical, and contemporary novels, but her increasing determination "to support the cause of morality, to reprove vice, and to promote all the social and domestic virtues" detracted from her skill as story-teller and frightened rather than attracted her public.

Her two works dealing with the society of her own time, *The Two Mentors* and *The School for Widows,* exude a sticky wholesomeness which remind one of nothing more strongly than the stories to be found in modern weekly magazines for women. It is neither sentimentality nor melodrama as much as an apparent fear that she might miss an opportunity to improve some needy soul or even influence someone for the worse. This feeling communicates itself most clearly in her preface to *The Exiles, or Memoirs of the Count de Cronstadt:*

> If there are more writers than formerly, there are likewise more readers; especially among the lower classes of people; this consideration should induce every writer to be particularly careful of what he offers to the public, that there be nothing contrary to

religion and virtue; and that through the vehicle of entertainment, moral inferences should be conveyed to the reader.

Unfortunately for Clara, the entertainment became in time obscured to the point of invisibility beneath her moral inferences.

It was in *The Exiles,* however, with its sombre Byronic hero Cronstadt caught between two women, that Clara came nearest again to capturing the spirit of the Gothic romance. Strongly influenced by the Abbé Prévost's *Doyen de Killerine* and Baculard d'Arnaud's *Le comte de Gleichen,* both of which she knew in translation, the novel, which is full of eventful incident and boisterous excitement, in turn provided inspiration for Harriet Lee's *Kruitzner, the German's Tale.*

Her last historical novel was *Memoirs of Sir Roger de Clarendon,* set in the period of Edward III and Richard II but suffering from the very defects which prevented *The Old English Baron* from really coming to life, a lack of authenticity caused by the author's failure to establish sufficiently the milieu in which the events are placed. It had been preceded in 1785 by *The Progress of Romance,* a discussion between Euphrasia, who speaks for Clara, and two imaginary friends, Hortensius and Sophronia, in which she discourses upon the history of English fiction and offers a definition of the ancient Romance ("an heroic fable, which treats of fabulous persons and things") and the modern Novel ("a picture of real life and manners, and of the times in which it was written"). But she remained a reluctant popularizer, alarmed, when she comes to speak of the contemporary novel, at the thought of the potential for evil represented by the growth of the circulating libraries which must, she felt, encourage the publication of inferior writing and in general debase public good taste. No doubt her fear of change and moral decay stemmed from the narrowness and isolation of her own existence for she seems to have travelled but little and to have had few companions. (pp. xii-xiv)

Clara Reeve's name is remembered today only in association with this one novel, and yet without her decisive intervention to make possible supernatural fiction which does not do violence to human reason the new direction taken by Ann Radcliffe would have been unthinkable. The significance of the Gothic novel lay not in its introduction of the machinery of vaults, galleries, and haunted apartments but ultimately in the reader's identification of himself with the characters in their conflict with supernatural powers whose existence he himself darkly recognized. By bringing this other world into the lives of simple men and thereby allowing them a momentary *frisson* which could quickly be banished by appeal to their Christian faith, she was taking a faltering step in the direction of the psychologists concerned to explain today polarities of human feeling towards certain objects or situations. This ambivalence, the simultaneous attraction and repulsion which may be caused by some external phenomenon, is what Clara Reeve was struggling with in her theories to reconcile the marvellous and the probable. (p. xiv)

> *James Trainer, in an introduction to* The Old English Baron: A Gothic Story *by Clara Reeve, edited by James Trainer, Oxford University Press, London, 1967, pp. vii-xviii.*

BETTE B. ROBERTS (essay date 1975)

[*In the following excerpt, originally published in 1975 as part of her doctoral dissertation, Roberts illustrates how Reeve adapted the Gothic elements of* The Castle of Otranto *to serve her mor-*

alistic and socially conservative purposes in writing The Old English Baron.]

[The] central situation in gothic fiction typically involves the pursuit of a young innocent maiden by an older male villain. In *The Castle of Otranto* Manfred, a usurper of his brother's fortune, pursues the beautiful Isabella, fiancée of his dead son. Manfred hopes that by marrying her, he may further accumulate wealth and property. Meanwhile, Isabella meets and falls in love with the handsome peasant Theodore, as he assists her in escaping from Manfred. Theodore, of course, turns out to be the son of the wronged brother of Manfred, whose retributive ghost is active throughout the story. Manfred's pursuit of Isabella involves several direct chase scenes, in which Isabella must use her ingenuity to outwit her aggressor. With the help of the supernatural and benevolent people, Manfred is finally put in his place, and the property is properly restored to Theodore. The masculine pursuit of female innocence is a situation recurrent in gothic fiction, with women writers usually establishing the young victims as the heroines of the novels. Yet Clara Reeve handles this situation quite differently, her alterations reflecting a very proper and moralistic approach to the genre and appealing more overtly to the conservative values of her popular audience.

In *The Old English Baron* there are two major shifts in the central gothic situation which affect everything else, especially the overall tone of fear and anxiety resultant from threatening evil forces. Here the evil character has little power, if any, and the female victim is removed as a protagonist in favor of young Edmund. As the handsome young hero, he is a prized servant-companion of Lord Baron Fitz-Owen and his family, who have purchased some of the Lovel estates. Like Theodore in *Otranto,* Edmund has been cheated out of his inheritance and rank by a scheming uncle, William Lovel, who murdered his brother (Edmund's father) for his own ambitions. Again, the supernatural operates on behalf of the good characters in assisting Edmund to restore his fortune, assume his rank and marry Emma, which he does at the end of the novel. The emphasis upon Edmund and the other moral characters as aggressors seeking out the villainous William Lovel keeps the good forces in control and undercuts the threat and power of evil, and consequently, the gothic tone of fear. Walpole is clearly more interested in his villain Manfred, who plays the major role in *Otranto* and turns out to be remorseful for his crimes; the reader thrills in his machinations and even sympathizes with the personally disastrous results of his excesses.

Despite the importance of **The Old English Baron** as a starting point in adapting the conventions of *Otranto,* the appeal to the reader's fantasies is not as great as it is to the reinforcement of actual social values, which is evident in the author's attempt to incorporate romantic entertainment into the realistic novel, obviously stressing the latter as a mirror of social propriety. The potential for real attraction-repulsion ambivalence is restrained by the virtual incapacitation of the evil figure, and the power afforded to the main action undercuts the repressed escape appeal of the male-female gothic pursuit as a projection of the social tyranny of men over women. This general shift in focus from Walpole's *Otranto* is apparent in the central confrontation of good and evil in the novel and in the stronger reliance upon novelistic techniques rather than those of the romance.

A friend of Edmund's father, Sir Philip Harclay, acts as a benefactor to Edmund and sends a challenge to the usurping uncle, William Lovel. Lovel is virtually forced into accepting the challenge, as the means of deciding whether he or Edmund is the rightful heir to the Lovel fortune, since Harclay has presented all of the evidence on Edmund's behalf to the magistrates. In keeping with the medieval setting, a large tournament is organized with lengthy descriptions of the lists, the clothes, and the contests, which terminates in a joust between Sir Philip Harclay and William Lovel. Seriously wounded in this combat, Lovel lies in bed, surrounded and guarded by Harclay and righteous men who insist that he sign a full confession which will restore Edmund's fortune. The point is that the villain never really has a chance. His crime already in the past, all the reader really confronts is a bed-ridden, cornered figure with little threat to anyone. We should also remember that the physical challenger of Lovel is the older Harclay; the hero Edmund is in no real danger at all. This confrontation contrasts a good deal with Walpole's dramatic scenes of terror in which the evil Manfred comes close to succeeding. Also unlike Walpole's novel is Clara Reeve's inclusion of a domestic situation which serves to de-fuse the gothic plot of usurpation and crime.

In *The Castle of Otranto* Manfred is the source of both Isabella's anxiety and Theodore's outcast position; the villainy is dramatically centered in him. In *The Old English Baron,* however, Edmund's uncle William Lovel is the villain of only the gothic plot, the murder of Edmund's father and usurpation of his fortune. Clara Reeve sets up other antagonists for the hero in the characters of Robert, the eldest son of Lord Baron Fitz-Owen, and Robert's cousins, Richard Wenlock and John Markham. These three young men resent Edmund's virtue and the consequent praise and attention he receives from the Baron. Wenlock has the additional motive of desiring Emma, the Baron's daughter, in whom he sees a preference for Edmund. In a domestic situation very similar to that in Fielding's *Tom Jones,* where Blifil tries to degrade Tom in front of Mr. Allworthy, here the three men plot to undermine Edmund's favor with the Baron.

Clara Reeve thus sets up opportunities not present in *Otranto* for comparison and contrast of family members' behavior and morals, so as to reinforce social morality. Two of the Baron's virtuous children, William and Emma, are drawn to Edmund and act as foils to the Wenlock group, and there are many domestic scenes of quarrel which cause the Baron pain, such as Robert's not sitting down at the table with the rest of the family. Though young Wenlock would surely have assisted William Lovel in ruining Edmund, he is not given the chance, as the plots are kept separate. What unites them are fairly mechanical devices: Edmund's residence with the Fitz-Owens, who own the Lovel estates; Edmund's love of the Baron's daughter Emma, whom he marries after assuming his fortune. This de-fusing of the gothic pursuit in favor of a domestic focus adds familial scenes and social dimensions of characters which are absent in Walpole's fiction, but present in the women writers who follow Clara Reeve in using the gothic genre. Her characters reflect the conventionally one-dimensional moral polarities of Walpole's *Otranto,* along with more novelistic, behavioral details and circumstances. Her treatment of the female characters perhaps best illustrates the mixture of gothic and domestic perspective.

Emma, the young lady beloved by the hero Edmund, is confined to the domestic scenes and seems to have no other function beyond that of bringing out male traits. She is an inspiration and reward for Edmund; near the end of the novel she approaches "With tears on her cheek, sweetly blushing like the damask rose, wet with the dew of morning,'' and indicates her acceptance of Edmund as a husband. Here she indirectly shows the good-nature of the Baron, who wishes that she marry a man of her own choice. When Edmund goes to the chamber shortly thereafter to see that the remains of his parents be given a proper burial, we are told that: ''He committed the Lady Emma to the care of her youngest brother, observing that the scene was too solemn for a Lady to be present at it.'' Clara Reeve, as the first woman to use the gothic mode, clearly does not unify female delicacy with gothic adventure; she keeps them separate appealing more to the reader's security with the patriarchal, middle-class attitudes toward the woman's place. In modifying the whole impact of the gothic experience, however, she suggests the possibility for more adventurous, though never improper, heroines to follow.

While Emma remains an idealized upper-class heroine, reinforcing eighteenth-century etiquette and propriety, Margery Twyford is developed through detail that is especially realistic, as well as domestic. She is Edmund's lower-class foster-mother and the only other female character to consider, excluding Edmund's dead spectre-mother. It is she who reveals the story of Edmund's true noble birth, relating how she was given the baby Edmund to rear as her own. During her narration, she is in constant fear that her husband will return, as she promised him never to reveal the story: '' 'Andrew beat me the last time I spoke to Edmund; and told me he would break every bone in my skin if ever I spoke to him again'.'' In what appears to be extraordinarily realistic conversation from a particularly female sensibility, Margery explains how she lost her ''first born son: I got a hurt by over-reaching myself when I was near my time, and so the poor child died.'' Telling how her husband then brought home the baby Edmund, she continues: '' 'The poor infant was cold, and it cried, and looked up at me so pitifully, that I loved it; beside my milk was troublesome to me, and I was glad to be eased of it, so I gave it the breast, and from that hour I loved the child as if it were my own, and so do I still if I dared to own it'.'' Eventually Margery relates how, in her obedience to her husband, she endured his turning Edmund out of the house.

In Margery's narration we see natural detail that not only goes beyond the tradition of the comically garrulous servant, but reveals female understanding and awareness. Margery Twyford is an everyday novelistic portrait that is unique in romantic stereotypes. Walpole's lower-class figures are used only for comic relief and suspense, as they are either too talkative or too terrified. Margery would not fit in with them at all. In the contrasting treatments of Emma and Margery, we also note the bourgeois reinforcement of eighteenth-century values, as Emma remains the upper-class, idealized heroine; Margery becomes an indelicate, more realistic representative of the lower class. Margery thus appeals not only to the reader's domestic familiarity, but to her complacent acceptance of eighteenth-century social attitudes which aggrandize her own self-importance over those in a lower social class. (pp. 64-71)

The dominant male characters, especially the good ones, receive the same kind of treatment as Emma, in that they basically remain moral stereotypes that reinforce eighteenth-century values; however, they reveal the same kind of novel-romance mixture of characterization. Edmund, for instance, is: ''modest, yet intrepid; gentle and courteous to all; frank and unreserved to those that loved him, discreet and complaisant to those that hated him; generous and compassionate to the distresses of his fellow creatures in general; humble, but not servile, to his patron and superiors.'' Yet, when he is affected by William's demonstration of friendship, he can speak only in ''broken sentences.'' In that Edmund has both the gothic role of asserting his right against the villain and the domestic part of proving himself humble and worthy of the Baron Fitz-Owen's trust, he is in the awkward position of having to keep his ambitions to recover his fortune a secret. So as not to make her hero too aggressive, in accordance with the popular appeal of the passive victim, Clara Reeve has Edmund relying upon the aging chivalric knight, Sir Philip Harclay, whose wisdom and tested valor bring William Lovel to his knees. (pp. 71-2)

[Older] male characters, Harclay and the Baron Fitz-Owen, are venerated primarily as exemplary father-figures. At the end of the novel, the Baron ''died full of years and honours, and his name was never mentioned but with the deepest marks of gratitude, love and veneration. Sweet is the remembrance of the virtuous, and happy are the descendants of such a father! They will think on him and emulate his virtues; they will remember him, and be ashamed to degenerate from their ancestor.'' The dominance of the male characters in the action and the domestic reverence for them as fathers are particularly in accord with reinforcing the patriarchal social positions of men and women, as women not only play the minor role, like Emma here, but are entirely dependent upon the male figure of the family in a husband or father. In Clara Reeve's own case, this

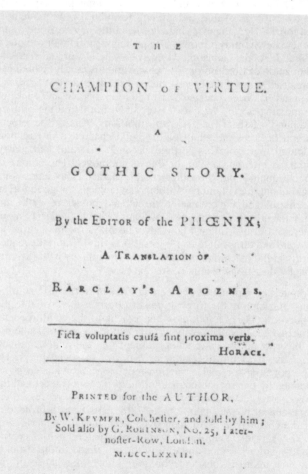

Title page for The Champion of Virtue: A Gothic Story, *later revised as* The Old English Baron.

stress seems appropriate as well to her biography, as we know that she never married and regarded her clergyman-father as an oracle who taught her all she knew. Clearly the dependent relationship upon these good male forces takes precedence over the fantasized escape from the male as evil, as William Lovel is virtually dispensed with as a powerless threat. (pp. 72-3)

As is apparent from this analysis of *The Old English Baron* and its adaptations of gothic conventions from Walpole's *Otranto,* Clara Reeve's novel is weighed more on the side of didactic and domestic morality, rather than gothic romance, which is in accord with her intentions of teaching the reader through entertainment. As such, the novel's appeal to the reader is more one of a parallel reflection and reinforcement of bourgeois values and sex roles, with the imaginative flight occurring only secondarily in the gothic scenes which arouse the emotions momentarily. Since the element of fantasy does play a subordinate role, we must account for the novel's extreme popularity with a predominantly female audience as based upon a more general vicarious pleasure in male-dominated adventure, which is similar to the limitations of her male-dominated experiences, rather than upon wishes and fears which are particularly repressive in nature and applicable to women. To an audience unused to much fantasy in the novel, *The Old English Baron* is an important link between the domestic novel, already familiar to the reader, and the new and unfamiliar gothic romance.

Clara Reeve's *Old English Baron,* in its struggle to reconcile the marvelous and the probable, cannot be underestimated, as it is a forerunner of gothic novels for women readers by women writers who may use the same format or intention to justify a stronger interest in and need for the element of romance, which will exceed entertainment value alone. Clara Reeve prepares for these adaptations by taking the first step herself in including the romance, by bringing a real moral seriousness to Walpole's formula, and by modifying or restraining the indulgent manifestations of the supernatural. The novelty of her work consists in the ways in which the gothic action, character, setting, and supernatural material are domesticized or naturalized by her moral tone and novelistic style, as she writes more *The Champion of Virtue* than *The Old English Baron: A Gothic Story.* (pp. 81-3)

> Bette B. Roberts, "The Old English Baron," in her *The Gothic Romance: Its Appeal to Women Writers and Readers in Late Eighteenth-Century England,* Arno Press, 1980, pp. 60-83.

LEIGH A. EHLERS (essay date 1978)

[*Ehlers argues that* The Old English Baron *is more than just a historical link between early Gothic romance and the works of Ann Radcliffe.*]

When they discuss [them] at all, most critics have treated Clara Reeve's writings as historical curiosities, notable for their sentimental characterizations, but of questionable literary merit. Her *Old English Baron,* for example, has been discussed primarily as a historical link between the somewhat disreputable origins of Gothic romance and the more respectable sublimities of the last great Gothic romancer, Radcliffe. James Trainer, the editor of the Oxford edition of *Old English Baron,* accords it such a transitional status: "Its importance . . . lay retrospectively in the attempt to temper some of the excesses of Walpole's *Castle of Otranto* and prospectively in the creation of a climate in which Ann Radcliffe's more sophisticated characters could survive" [see excerpt dated 1967]. Equating sentiment with an embellishment for characterization, however, fails to account for Reeve's explicit suggestion of the vital connection between sentimentality and Christian morality. Our distance from the eighteenth century may prevent us from perceiving sentimentality in its proper historical context and cause us to see *Old English Baron* as insignificant and its author as incapable of artistic designs. If, however, we put aside any prejudice against the sentimental and grant Reeve her connection between sentiment and morality, we will discover an artistic unity informing her work. In *Old English Baron* we find that sentimentality does not operate for its own sake but rather functions as an integral part of a serious moral purpose.

The reception of Reeve's work by her contemporaries provides a clue to her methodology. The *Monthly Review* recommended *Old English Baron* with one proviso: "The whole is adapted to interest the feelings of the reader,—provided he has either faith, or fancy, enough to be interested in the appearance of ghosts." That is, Reeve's romance appeals to its readers both through its grand sentiments and through its ghosts operating within a Christian context. Robert D. Spector, another of Reeve's editors, acknowledges her interest in sentimentality but faults her "didactic purpose" by calling it "a crutch of respectability." However, the fact remains that *Old English Baron* embodies both the sentimental and the didactic as complementary, not disparate elements. The unifying principle of this Gothic romance is a Christian morality that dictates both structure and characterization. Reeve's manipulation of her narrative structure reflects a Christian providential universe, and her sentimental characterizations, far from providing mere emotional indulgence, depend on and illustrate that same religious worldview.

While Reeve's "didactic purpose" has perhaps alienated modern readers (and apparently her editors), her concern with the moral instruction of her reader fits well into the context of her other writings. As one might expect from the daughter of a curate and the granddaughter of a rector, Reeve the writer bears some similarity to the original title of her Gothic tale—*The Champion of Virtue.* . . . As she argues in a later treatise on English fiction, *The Progress of Romance,* the writer should strive to combine moral instruction and exciting story: "A moral lesson otherwise dry and tedious in itself, might be communicated in a pleasing dress: as a pill has its desired effect, tho' wrapped in a gold or silver leaf." Far from condemning romances as immoral or secular, Reeve admits in her preface to *Old English Baron* that "fictitious Stories have been the delight of all times and all countries." This being the case, the writer of romance should first "excite the attention" of his reader and then "direct it to some useful, or at least innocent, end." The composition of such useful books was the goal to which Reeve dedicated herself, in such works as *The Two Mentors, The School for Widows,* and [*Plans of Education*].

In *Old English Baron,* her best known work, Reeve adopts a three-fold method to construct her didactic fiction: "To attain this end, there is required a sufficient degree of the marvellous, to excite the attention; enough of the manners of real life, to give an air of probability to the work; and enough of the pathetic, to engage the heart in its behalf." The term "marvellous" places *Old English Baron* squarely in the context of popular Gothic fiction, represented by Walpole's notorious *Castle of Otranto.* Reeve, however, prefers to tone down Walpole's emphasis on the supernatural—the walking skeletons, giant helmet, sighing portraits. To do so, she modulates the "marvellous," those elements of plot dealing with supernatural occurrences, by stressing "manners" and "the pathetic," that is, sentimental characterization. Such a balancing of structure and character in **Old English Baron** reveals Reeve's strong belief in providential Christianity and her interest in the emotional responses of individual characters; both elements create the didactic tone dominating throughout the romance and explicitly stated at its closing summary of the events of the story as "a striking lesson to posterity, of the over-ruling hand of Providence, and the certainty of RETRIBUTION."

In structure **Old English Baron** is modeled on what one might term a "providential pattern." An ongoing concern of eighteenth-century writers was to reassert and to assimilate change into the Christian worldview. As Martin C. Battestin points out, "Newton may properly be regarded as the protagonist in the most compelling intellectual drama of the period: the concerted attempt by a host of Christian rationalists to redeem the providential order of creation from those latter-day emmisaries of Antichrist, Descartes and Hobbes" (*The Providence of Wit*). Given the belief in this Christian universe, a writer like Reeve creates a narrative controlled by providence and working, as Aubrey Williams argues, "in and through human choices and natural events, through chance encounters and strange accidents, through improbable mishaps and fantastic coincidences, so that virtuous characters can be *tested* and then rewarded and so that evil can be *proved* and punished" ("Interpositions of Providence and the Design of Fielding's Novels").

The general narrative outline of such providentialist fiction follows a strict sequence of events. The providential pattern takes the hero and/or heroine from a position of initial security to an extended period of insecurity that tests his faith and virtue, and then after reformation and purgation of weakness and sin he is rewarded with a position of restored security and triumph over enemies. Of course, the Edenic parallel is obvious in something like the tri-partite structure of *Tom Jones,* particularly the hero's "fall" from grace when he is ejected from Paradise Hall. Similarly, the characters in **The Old English Baron** replay the Christian history of man; the Lovel family moves in a linear or straightforward fashion through a three-stage progression, with no significant digressions, from "glory" to "ruin" to "restoration" (terms suggested by Williams in "Congreve's *Incognita* and the Contrivances of Providence," in *Imagined Worlds,* ed. Mack and Gregor).

Before considering the specific methods by which Reeve accomplishes her providentially ordered structure, we should note that the emphasis on seeming confusion resolved through divine intervention, on characters revealed primarily in terms of their responses to the providential pattern, and on explicit didactic commentary would seem to place **Old English Baron** within the tradition of eighteenth-century "romance" rather than "novel." While these terms have generated considerable critical debate of late (Henry Knight Miller, for example describes *Tom Jones* as a romance), some evidence can be educed from Reeve's preface to the second edition of **Old English Baron;** she claims to have combined "ancient Romance," which displays "only the amiable side" of life, with the "modern Novel," which concerns itself with "human nature as it is." For Reeve, Richardson is a writer of romance, that is, of a narrative both entertaining and instructive, realistic and didactic, mundane and Christian. As Melvyn New argues, the romances of the eighteenth century are concerned with the conjunction of the world of empirical reality with that of divine order:

> The patterned world of an overarching, if not immediately obvious, order; the dispensation of rewards

and punishments according to an accepted, eternal justice; the surprise discoveries and last-minute rescues which are taken as signs of God's enduring interest and concern in human affairs; the strong sense that the characters are manipulated toward their final reward (or punishment) by forces beyond themselves—these are the essential characteristics of the romance, and they are as well the essential characteristics of a world governed by a providential God. ("'The Grease of God': The Form of Eighteenth-Century English Fiction")

While writers life Defoe, Richardson, Fielding, and Smollett may ultimately displace "the claims of romance . . . from the theoretical center of narrative," nonetheless romance is "the initial structuring principle of eighteenth-century fiction" ("'Grease of God'"). Although Reeve's publications come in the last quarter of the century, her romance reveals little displacement of the religious pattern; instead it explicitly stresses the overall pattern of events, the sequence of glory-ruin-restoration through which its characters move.

The opening pages of **The Old English Baron** establish the mechanics of the providential pattern by telescoping the early life of Sir Philip Harclay. Originally, Sir Philip had possessed a "family-seat in Yorkshire" from which he absents himself for "thirty years travel and warlike service." Upon his return Sir Philip must regain his family estate by proving "the reality of his claim, and the identity of his person . . . after which every thing was *restored* to him" (italics mine). Sir Philip underscores his restoration by creating order and harmony within his household: "He took possession of his own house, established his household, settled the old servants in their former stations, and placed those he brought home in the upper offices of his family." Having settled his domestic arrangements equitably, Sir Philip prevents a potential source of discontent among the servants and at the same time proves his worthiness for restoration. The progress of his life—from estate to war to estate regained—foreshadows the overall structure of *Old English Baron* wherein the Lovel family participates in a similar providential pattern.

Reeve's emphasis (one is tempted to say "typically feminine" emphasis) on the family results in a domestic system of order or a domestic version of the political upheavals in *Otranto* and demonstrates that providence will expose and punish murder even within the private sphere. The Lovel family begins with false harmony in Walter Lovel's possession of the estate after the deaths of his brother and sister-in-law. Eventually his claim is challenged by the ghosts in the haunted apartment and by the suspicions of Joseph and Father Oswald concerning the true identity of the hero Edmund. Once disorder has affected the family, the power to rectify the wrong comes from within the domestic circle, with the ultimate aid of providence. The family trial of Edmund for "gossiping" about Walter's past functions as a paradigm of heavenly judgement: "The Baron was sitting in the great hall on a high chair with a footstep before, with the state and dignity of a judge; before him stood Father Oswald, as pleading the cause for himself and Edmund. Round the Baron's chair stood his eldest son and his kinsmen, with their principal domestics." Edmund is sentenced to two nights in the haunted apartment, during which he providentially receives proof of his true identity and of his father's murder by Walter, the proof being the blood-stained armor plus the family portraits and coat of arms.

A second judgment scene, the duel between Sir Philip as Edmund's champion and Walter, comes explicitly under the guidance of heaven. The dueling field itself is rather like a domestic arena, for it is "enclosed for the lists" and admits only "a limited number of friends and followers." After he has unhorsed and defeated the villain, Sir Philip proclaims the role of providence in the duel, "Heaven, by my hand, has chastised him." Walter is banished, leaving no living descendants behind and losing even his family name—he is now "Walter, commonly called Lord Lovel." The family then restores itself to its proper genealogical structure by installing Edmund as Lord Lovel and solidifies its future by marrying the new Lord to his cousin Emma. Reeve's brief sketch of family history at the close of her romance is more than "perfectionist haste" as Trainer argues. In fact, Reeve's stress on the future happiness of Edmund's family and the births and marriages of his children underscores the final providential restoration. Disorder has been replaced by family order, and those family members who have proved their faith, honor, and virtue are rewarded by the tranquility of their subsequent lives.

To achieve such a narrative structure, Reeve uses four principal means of advancing her providential designs: the supernatural, natural coincidences and discoveries, human agents, and explicitly didactic commentary.

Immediately Reeve uses ghosts to serve her two criteria for a good romance. They engage the reader's attention and then act to restore providential justice to the living—to punish a murderer and to reveal the true heir. As she notes in her preface, the supernatural must be presented "within the utmost *verge* of probability . . . within certain limits of credibility." Therefore, Reeve introduces ghosts, the murdered Lord Lovel and his wife, but confines them mainly to the deserted wing of the castle, an anticipation of Radcliffe's "haunted" chamber in *The Mysteries of Udolpho*. In addition to revealing the proof of Edmund's identity and of the murder, Lovel's ghost provides the only comic relief in the romance when he expells Wenlock and Markham, Edmund's chief enemies, from the haunted apartment by standing "with one hand extended, pointing to the outward door; they took the hint, and crawled away as fast as fear would let them; they staggered along the gallery, and from thence to the Baron's apartment, where Wenlock sunk down in a swoon, and Markham had just strength enough to knock at the door." Through these timely interventions, in addition to Sir Philip's earlier prophetic dream, the ghosts work to Edmund's providential advantage.

In addition, providence arranges a series of natural coincidences and fortuitous discoveries designed to reveal the truth. An example of "seemingly accidental circumstances," which lead the hero "imperceptibly towards the crisis of his fate" can be observed in Fitz-Owen's adoption of Edmund "into his service just in the nick" when the peasant Andrew Twyford wearies of supporting an abandoned child. Similarly fortuitous is Margery Twyford's preservation of the dress, shoes, and signet locket left by Edmund's dying mother. These tokens are accepted later as proof of identity, thus fulfilling Edmund's observation that "Heaven assists us by natural means." Just as natural is the hero's progression from Fitz-Owen's household to the protection of Sir Philip, a transition smoothed by "a happy circumstance"—Sir Philip's servant is providentially available to conduct Edmund to the castle of his master.

Such natural providential coincidences are closely allied to providence's use of human agents to further its ends. While various characters, like Margery and Joseph, provide Edmund with timely aid, the principal human agents are Sir Philip and Oswald. In addition to championing the hero in numerous domestic quarrels, Oswald sends Edmund to Sir Philip with the proofs of identity. Likewise an "instrument of justice in the hand of Heaven," Sir Philip welcomes Edmund as the "child of providence!—the beloved of heaven!" His exemplary morals and benevolence make him a fitting tool for providence: "He spent his time in the service of his Creator, and glorified him in doing good to his creatures." After Sir Philip has vanquished Walter, the corpse of Lord Lovel is exhumed under the direction of Oswald, who underscores this providential discovery: "Behold the day of retribution! of triumph to the innocent, or shame and confusion to the wicked." The active participation of Oswald and Sir Philip must combine with the ghosts and coincidences to overcome the power of evil that is strong in the world. Reeve implies that mere passive knowledge of good (or true identity) is insufficient and that the Christian must wage an active battle against sin.

Finally, Reeve includes numerous explicit reflections that glorify the dispositions of providence. Typical of such verbal appeals to heaven is Edmund's remark that "Providence will in its own time vindicate its ways to man." The hero's humility and piety are models for all Christians, especially when he resigns "himself to the disposal of Heaven" and prays to God as "the only foundation of honour and dignity." Reinforcing Edmund's faith in providence is Sir Philip's speech praising the ways of heaven: "Praise be to God for his wonderful doings towards the children of men! every thing that has befallen thee is by his direction, and he will not leave his work unfinished. . . ." Such didactic speeches, amply scattered throughout the romance, emphasize the interpositions of providence and hence reflect the narrative structure, just as the characters' lives reflect the overriding plans of Heaven.

Reeve's management of the providential pattern ultimately has a twofold focus. The structure affirms the fact that God will eventually right wrongs, punish the wicked and reward the good; in addition, it demonstrates how artful providence is in its manipulation of earthly events. Given Reeve's commitment to a totally Christian worldview, the lack of suspense in her narrative stems not from artistic incompetence but from a conscious moral choice. Contrary to Trainer's accusation that Reeve indulges in a "persistent habit of premature anticipation of ensuing events, thereby allowing, almost inviting the reader to prognosticate (usually correctly) upon the outcome of any situation," the reader *should* be able to prognosticate events precisely because providence guarantees that murder will be punished. Of more immediate importance for the structure of the romance are the methods of heaven, the intricate series of coincidences, discoveries and interventions that effect the providential denouement. Perhaps the clearest indication that Reeve values demonstration over suspense lies in the revelation of Edmund's true identity early in the romance. Even Sir Philip's victory occurs at the two-thirds mark so that the last section of the romance contains only the details of the hero's legal battle to regain his estate. Reeve subordinates mystery and suspense to her glorification of the never-ending manipulations of providence; the structure both embodies and glorifies God's providence, a doubly didactic production by a Christian writer who aims to be morally useful to her readers.

Beyond active assistance in advancing the providential pattern, Reeve's ghosts also are instrumental for her characterizations in that they elicit strong emotions that differentiate individual personality. As Trainer notes, Reeve's characters are reactors "in their conflict with supernatural powers" and experience "simultaneous attraction and repulsion." However, this strategy of observing a character when he is dealing with the super-natural is but part of a more general sentimental approach. Reeve presents a character's passions, revealed mainly through dreams, words, and actions, as an index to his morality. In *Progress of Romance* she argues that "there needs no other proof of a bad and corrupted heart, than its being insensible to the distresses, and incapable to the rewards of virtue.—I should want no other criterion of a *good* or *bad* heart, than the manner in which a young person was affected, by reading *Pamela*." Hence, in *Old English Baron* whatever the omniscient narrator reveals of the feelings, thoughts or dreams of a particular character serves Reeve's abiding didactic interest. Furthermore, her concern with instructive literature dictates the sketchy presentation of the evil characters, Walter Lovel, Wenlock and Markham. Insisting on a rather Platonic approach to the presentation of vice, Reeve treats her villains at great distance, allowing them to show their evil briefly in facial expressions; during his confession Walter's "countenance shewed his inward agitations" as does Wenlock's when he is exiled from Lovel Castle. Arguing that "no harm can possibly arise from the imitation of a perfect character, though the attempt should fall short of the original," Reeve allows Edmund and Sir Philip the fullest and most sentimental development of character in her romance. Beginning with the conjunction of ghosts and dreams, of the supernatural and psychological, these characterizations move outwardly to scenes of public affirmation of emotions revealing the individual's virtue and faith in providence. To put this in Miller's terminology, Reeve's virtuous characters possess a "psycheology," the state of the soul, and only secondarily a "psychology," the state of the mind, both expressed primarily through the outpouring of emotion (*Henry Fielding's "Tom Jones" and the Romance Tradition*). For Reeve, the appeal to sentiment coexists with the appeal to providence.

Consistently throughout *Old English Baron* Sir Philip represents the virtuous knight, "a Christian soldier" whose character, with one exception, reveals itself in action—his war campaigns, his benevolent domestic dispositions, the final duel. The exception to this rather exterior portrait is his dream during which he encounters Lord Lovel's ghost. Here Reeve allows the supernatural to function as a psychological projection of the subconscious mind *and* more importantly (for her) as a manifestation of the Christian's proper faith in providence. Previously surprised that Lovel "should be unknown in his own neighborhood," Sir Philip is overtly disturbed by the information about the death of his old friend under odd circumstances. His unconscious suspicions of murder then express themselves in his dream of Lovel's bloody armor hidden in a "dark and frightful cave" representing the unhallowed grave of the victim. But the second part of the dream emphasizes Sir Philip's Christian faith. He sees a dueling field where "the trumpet sounded, and a voice called out still louder, Forbear! It is not permitted to be revealed till the time is ripe for the event: Wait with patience on the decrees of Heaven." Although he desires to avenge his friend's death, his religious faith acknowledges the supernatural agency of providence in the affairs of men and over the outcome of this particular combat. Sir Philip's waking reaction to the dream stresses faith. Although at first he reasons, "it was natural that the story he had heard should create these ideas, that they should wait on him in his sleep, and that every dream should bear some relation to his deceased friend," he then pays "his devotions to Heaven," tacitly acknowledging that the dream may after all have been providentially designed and that he must wait for further man-ifestations of heaven's will before acting (cf. Hamlet's cautious reaction to his father's ghost). Thus Sir Philip's dream tentatively explores the interior of the human mind but eventually subsumes the psychological into the supernatural providential context of the romance at large.

Given her assumption that sentiment and morality are inexorably linked, Reeve reserves her most sentimental and instructive characterization for the hero Edmund. As the providential pattern exposes the villainy of Walter, Edmund amply illustrates his gentility, virtue, and faith during his rise from peasant to lord. Repeatedly other characters comment on the hero's superiority. Fitz-Owen observes his "uncommon merit, and gentleness of manners," Sir Philip is struck by his "strong resemblance" to the deceased Lord Lovel, and Joseph directly informs him that "I cannot help thinking you were born to a higher station than what you now hold." Edmund's emotional response to these words reveals Christian humility: "The notion and observation of strangers and the affection of individuals, together with that inward consciousness that always attends superiour qualities, would sometimes kindle the flames of ambition in Edmund's heart; but he checked them presently by reflecting upon his low birth and dependent station." A greater testament to the hero's goodness is that his private emotions result in public virtues: "He was modest, yet intrepit; gentle and courteous to all; frank and unreserved to those that loved him, discreet and complaisant to those who hated him; generous and compassionate to the distresses of his fellow-creatures in general; humble, but not servile, to his patrons and superiors." Such consistency between emotions and actions mark Edmund as a model youth, worthy of the rewards of heaven.

While Edmund plays a less active role in the second half of the romance, when Sir Philip becomes his champion, his most important scene, sentimentally and morally, is the two-night stay in the haunted apartment and the subsequent discovery of the actual proofs of his parentage. As she does for Sir Philip's dream, Reeve carefully subordinates the psychological to a demonstration of "the will of Heaven." While the hero's dream, depicting his parents, a funeral and a family feast, fulfills his quest for personal identity, his response to this vision once again reveals Christian humility: "Am I then, said he, not Edmund Twyford, but somebody of consequence in whose fate so many people are interested? Vain thought, that must have arisen from the partial suggestion of my two friends, Mr. William and old Joseph!" The second night in the haunted apartment provides further scope for Edmund's strong religious sensibility: "while he prayed, he felt an enlargement of heart beyond what he had ever experienced before; all idle fears were dispersed, and his heart glowed with divine love and affiance: He seemed raised above the world and all its pursuits." Here Edmund is both sentimental and religious, experiencing what David P. Morris would call the "religious sublime." Similarly, when Oswald and Joseph remark on his resemblance to Lord Lovel, Edmund "changed colour and trembled; he clapped his hand upon his breast, and looked up to Heaven in silence." After listening to Margery Twyford's testimony, the hero expresses himself sentimentally and hence morally: "Edmund's passions, long suppressed, broke out in tears and exclamations; he kneeled down, and, with his hands clasped together, returned thanks to Heaven for the discovery." Thus Christian morality and the emotional intensity attending the discovery of identity are the distinguishing qualities of Edmund's personality. Reeve's omniscient narrative explores the hero both inwardly and outwardly, in his dreams and his actions, all of which demonstrate his reliance on the dispositions of providence.

Although one might accuse Reeve of overly repetitive descriptions of emotions, it must be conceded that she is explicit in making the connection between rapture and righteousness. Her final comment on the virtuous characters sums up her didactic-sentimental approach. The Lovel family resides in "truly a house of joy; not that false kind, in the midst of which there is heaviness, but that of rational creatures grateful to the supreme benefactor, raising their minds by a due enjoyment of earthly blessings to a preparation for a more perfect state here-after." Because for Reeve passion reveals moral character, *Old English Baron* is simply awash with tears, raptures, sighs, transports and the like, all signs invariably associated and arising from a good heart.

While Reeve's examination of the mind may seem shallow by modern standards, *Old English Baron,* both in its structure and its characterization, bears a larger implication for Gothic fiction. By concentrating her romance on the providential pattern and man's reaction to the evidence of divine intervention in everyday life, Reeve partly redeems the somewhat reductive effect of the supernaturalism of *Otranto.* New has argued that Gothic romances "are still replete with the providential language, but . . . find in religious patterns primarily superstition and ghosts" ("'Grease of God'"). While it may be true that Walpole's and especially Lewis' use of the supernatural to a certain extent undercuts religious patterns, Reeve's (like Radcliffe's) restraint in handling her ghosts advances rather than detracts from her providential scheme. All her characters—ghosts, sentimental hero, helpful friends, and calculating villains alike—exist solely within the context of a Christian universe. Within that universe the sentimental and supernatural are natural elements, which she has properly fused here in her didactic demonstration of the power of providence. (pp. 62-76)

Leigh A. Ehlers, "'A Striking Lesson to Posterity': Providence and Character in Clara Reeve's 'The Old English Baron'," in Enlightenment Essays, *Vol. IX, Nos. 1-4, 1978, pp. 62-76.*

ELIZABETH MacANDREW (essay date 1979)

[*MacAndrew examines Reeve's use of symbolism and narrative devices to illuminate the central theme of* The Old English Baron.]

Clara Reeve uses the supernatural more moderately than Walpole because her novel on balance is as much Sentimental as Gothic. In it, for instance, the Good are central to the tale and all ends in an elaborate "comic" resolution with evil conquered, virtue affirmed, and the suitable marriages arranged. *The Castle of Otranto,* on the other hand, ends with the downfall of Manfred. The happy marriage is dealt with in a single sentence, hardly sufficient to constitute a resolution. The difference in tone and emphasis is striking. Clara Reeve presents her unhistorical, sentimentalist view of the Good in a "Gothic tale" to establish the great virtues as timeless and as stemming from the traditional values of Merry England. When she wishes to embody ideas of virtue and honor, vice and the torments of conscience, she uses devices similar to Walpole's. The hero Edmund, for instance, bears his father's face, as Theodore does his grandfather's in *Otranto.* Physical and moral beauty are thus made to correspond, as they do throughout Gothic fiction. The way in which the resemblance is discovered from the

portraits of Edmund's parents is again typically Gothic. The ghost, here as elsewhere, symbolizes the unexpiated guilt that lies so heavily on Sir Walter Lovel's conscience. Thus, when she needs the symbolic, Clara Reeve uses it. When the romance tradition by itself is sufficient, she uses that. (p. 122)

Like *Otranto,* Clara Reeve's *The Old English Baron* is made remote in time by its claim to be a chronicle. But it is set in England, not in "exotic" Italy and at a precise, not a vague time. A true Sentimentalist, she opposes an ideal yet probable good to the manifestation of evil. To do so, she uses her system of narration to set up a closed world within ordinary, if historical, England. The reader is given a sense of a remote world that is discovered with difficulty and exists unknown to the surrounding land.

It was perhaps to enhance this effect that Clara Reeve changed the method of narration in the second edition by suppressing the claim made in the preface to the first that the tale is from an ancient manuscript written in Old English. Because the manuscript is not mentioned until after the first episode, the reader's first experience of the novel is of direct narration of Sir Philip Harclay's journey toward the castle. In the course of this journey, Sir Philip first loses his servant. Then, continuing on alone, he stops several times to ask his way, finding to his surprise that no one knows of Lord Lovel. Even when he reaches the border of the inner world—when he arrives at the cottage—there is a strange ambivalence in Wyatt's information about the deaths of that Lord and his wife. Thus, Sir Philip penetrates step by step into a world which grows more and more alien. This introductory section is in itself a symbolic rendering of the theme that the old values, which have been suppressed by evil doings and are no longer generally known, still lie at the heart of England.

This principal theme is worked out in the story itself when Clara Reeve brings the supernatural to bear. For the hero Edmund to discover his identity and for virtue to be restored, it is necessary for him to undergo the three-day ordeal in the deserted rooms. There, he finds the rooms closed off, empty and cobwebbed, and the portraits of his parents turned to the wall. He maintains his vigil in these sinister surroundings until the ghost finally manifests itself in the room below. Thus, symbolically, evil (the ghost) is exposed when the Good (Edmund's parents), concealed, locked up, and buried is recovered from death through virtue and courage (Edmund). Edmund, like Theodore in *Otranto,* rises from the bottom to the top of baronial society when his spiritual state has been shown to correspond to his noble birth through his display of patience, integrity, and fortitude.

The central theme, having been introduced through the frame and the device of the manuscript, is elaborated in the body of the novel by another narrative device: a cumulative system of narration that creates the impression of a gradual but steady piecing together of the truth. When Sir Philip complete his journey and enters the closed world the sense of the strange is momentarily allayed, but it is quickly apparent that all is not as it appears, that all is not being told. At first there are hints that the servant Joseph Howell knows who Edmund is, and Sir Philip himself is enigmatic about Edmund's resemblance to "a certain dear friend I once had." At this point, the introductory section ends as Sir Philip returns home. The manuscript is mentioned and the story becomes direct "historical" narrative for a few pages. Then follow several breaks in the manuscript, "effaced by time and damp." They are presented as a device to avoid a long account of the French wars, but, in fact, they increase the sense of mystery by reminding us that the narrative is relayed secondhand and we do not have the whole story. On both of these counts, we become aware that the account is not necessarily reliable, so the sense of incompleteness is further enhanced. Then, within this narrative, other voices begin each to contribute what they know, so that all may be fitted together into a whole. Father Oswald tells Edmund about ghosts. Then Joseph tells part of his story. Then Margery tells Edmund's story, which she alone knows.

This cumulative technique is well suited to Clara Reeve's shining, optimistic conclusion in which order is restored, just as the pieces of the puzzle are put together. She apparently was aware of this effect, for her final paragraph draws attention to the method: "Sir Philip Harclay caused the papers relating to his son's history to be collected together. The first part of it was written under his own eye in Yorkshire, the subsequent parts by Father Oswald at the Castle of Lovel. All these, when together, furnish a striking lesson to posterity, of the overruling hand of Providence, and the certainty of RETRIBUTION."

By using the initial journey into the closed world as well as this cumulative technique, however, Clara Reeve gives us a Gothic world of greater immediacy than Walpole's. She may first lay her ghost, then end her novel with marriage and order restored. Nevertheless, in isolating her Gothic events within the ordinary countryside of England, she in effects insists that the terrifying is part of the everyday world, encapsulated within it. The choice of narrative method reveals very directly the novelist's central concern. Clara Reeve wishes to present the stability and lasting power of the ancient virtues. So, through the ancient manuscript and Sir Philip's journey, she evokes a sense of a strange inner world when that world is in the grip of evil. Then, as the testimony of those who know parts of the story (both good and evil parts) accumulates, the evil is recognized and stripped away, leaving Good to reign in its stead. (pp. 127-29)

> Elizabeth MacAndrew, "Setting and Narrative Structure—'Far Other Worlds and Other Seas'," in her The Gothic Tradition in Fiction, *Columbia University Press*, 1979, pp. 109-50.

MARK MADOFF (essay date 1979)

[*Madoff explains that in eighteenth-century England two conflicting views of medieval Gothic culture were maintained: a positive view of a world of chivalry and piety and a negative view that emphasized the tyranny and superstition of the period. Madoff then discusses* The Old English Baron *as representative of the positive conception.*]

Even a quick survey of gothic fiction titles will show that the imaginary gothic world had very generous boundaries. Who were the Goths to hom the term *gothic* referred? Would-be historical answers have ranged from the Germans, Normans, Britons, and Saxons to the Arabs and Moors. Italian Renaissance polemic, following the line of Giorgio Vasari's *Lives of the Painters*, identified them broadly as the barbarian destroyers of Greco-Roman civilization. But the Italians also called *Gothic* the later Germanic invaders who ineptly tried to restore Roman art, law, and custom. As a descriptive or generic label, *gothic* is very confusing. Architectural usage has been only slightly more orderly. Is it possible to determine the meaning of this elusive word? Many etymological accounts have tried

to do so. Reviewing them in relation to the sensibility of gothic fiction, one finds a common meaning for all variants: the gothic is *ancestral*. (p. 338)

[In eighteenth-century England, a] conjunction of aesthetic preferences, political sentiments, and antiquarian fancies produced two conflicting descriptions of gothic ancestors. It did not matter whether they had ever held a place in British history; they still led a vigorous, autonomous existence in the popular imagination. On the one side was an imaginary epoch that surpassed the eighteenth century in elegance of manners, chivalry, chastity, social stability, proper hierarchical relations, vivid pageantry, and faith. On the other side, the material insecurity, tyranny, superstition, and sudden violence of dim ancestral times were potent objects of fear and fascination. (pp. 340-41)

The competing, sometimes converging myths formed the basis of gothic fiction. In the popular novels, the same contradictions between positive and negative meanings of *gothic* applied to characterization and setting. The sure sign of this ambivalence was the transformation of the repulsive, terrifying picture of the Goths into an attractive one. That change yielded the majority of the genre of sensational writing called "gothic." (p. 342)

[The positive and negative myths of gothic ancestry may be represented by] Clara Reeve's *Old English Baron* and M. G. Lewis's *Monk*.... [These particular works illustrate] the connection between early and later gothicism: one is recognizably Utopian in its use of gothic myth, the other anti-Utopian. In addition, the novels occupy the extremes of gothic style and technique. *The Old English Baron* is decorous, unromantic, and rationalistic; *The Monk* is obscene, wildly playful, violent, and psychologically harrowing. Through its own telling of gothic myth, however, each work undertakes an investigation of the origins of the eighteenth-century world, and each tries out an alternative to that world.

In *The Old English Baron* the alternative is idyllic yet dull. Reeve reduces the myth of gothic splendor and superiority until it is insipid.... Nevertheless, *The Old English Baron* reached a large audience, reinforced earlier gothic work, and acquired a school of imitators. Its version of the myth of gothic ancestry, therefore, cannot be dismissed.

Like most others who had been engaged by the the gothic taste, Reeve had a polemical interest in it. In her hands, the positive gothic myth became a means of vindicating bourgeois values. Reeve has adapted the myth so that the imaginary Goths, famous for their pride and independence, are also equipped with modern commercial instincts. She has caused the ethics of a Puritan merchant to walk about in thin romantic garb, with which neither she nor the characters are comfortable. All the usual elements of the laudatory ancestral myth are present in *The Old English Baron*—piety, obedience, loyalty, nobility of sentiment, cooperation—but they are diminished by Reeve's shift in emphasis. Frequent invocations of the "overruling hand of Providence" and the "certainty of Retribution" are deceptive. The central matter of the novel is the restoration of decent, stable family connections and the settlement of competitive claims for wealth and power. Thus, the total effect is more Grandisonian than wild, romantic, or medieval. But Reeve does extrapolate an ideal. For that reason, the total effect of her novel is also Utopian. Reeve implies that the closer one gets to the original gothic state, the closer one approaches a moment of perfect social balance.

It was always a nonhistorical direction that Reeve took, whatever her ostensible subjects and settings, and not only because, as Sir Walter Scott proposed, her imagination was undernourished. J. M. S. Tompkins has explained that Reeve saw in ancient times "the heroic days of pristine morality, and as such she described them, to rebuke her own degenerate age, to stimulate its ideals and to counteract the debilitating influence of pessimists and levellers." That view of the gothic period drew directly on the positive ancestral myth. Like many gothic-myth makers, however, Reeve was more eager to allay her own fears and doubts than to discover what was worth conserving in the authentic past.

Consequently, in *The Old English Baron* Reeve avoided history inasmuch as history revealed exotic, exciting, and forbidden images. Her depiction of gothic life was confined to models of superior conduct. She did not rely on chauvinism (despite the "Old English" of the title), nor on speculative mingling of history with fiction (as in Sophia Lee's *Recess* of 1783-85), nor on exploitation of sex and brutality.

The myth of gothic ancestry was useful to Clara Reeve because it was almost infinitely adaptable. All that had to be retained was its core: the notion that an ideal society had once existed in England, before the onset of urban sophistication and the intrusion of alien free-thinking. The precise outlines of that imaginary society, though based on received patterns, were the work of the dreamer. In the case of *The Old English Baron,* the Goths inhabit a fairly neutral territory where the ethical principles are familiar and congenial.

Unfortunately, the moral excellence of Reeve's putative gothic ancestors did not allow for the action and emotion from which adventure and romance are created. Since Reeve deplored excessive show of emotion, *The Old English Baron* contains more nobility of expression than strength of sentiment. There is courtship by strict rule of negotiation and cash value. There are cautious words of chivalry, occasional allusions to feudal law and custom, and a crucial tournament dispatched in three sentences! (pp. 342-44)

> *Mark Madoff, "The Useful Myth of Gothic Ancestry," in* Studies in Eighteenth-Century Culture, Vol. 8, *edited by Roseann Runte, American Society for Eighteenth-Century Studies, 1979, pp. 337-50.*

ADDITIONAL BIBLIOGRAPHY

Baker, Ernest A. "The Gothic Novel." In his *The History of the English Novel: The Novel of Sentiment and the Gothic Romance,* pp. 175-227. London: H. F. & G. Witherby, 1934.
    Includes a survey of Reeve's works.

Birkhead, Edith. "The Beginnings of Gothic Romance." In her *The Tale of Terror: A Study of the Gothic Romance,* pp. 16-37. New York: E. P. Dutton & Co., 1921.
    Contains a discussion of *The Old English Baron.*

Foster, James R. "D'Arnaud, Clara Reeve, and the Lees." In his *History of the Pre-Romantic Novel in England,* pp. 186-224. New York: Modern Language Association of America, 1949.
    A descriptive survey of Reeve's works.

Frank, Frederick S. *The First Gothics: A Critical Guide to the English Gothic Novel.* Garland Reference Library of the Humanities, vol. 710. New York: Garland Publishing, 1987, 496 p.

Includes critical synopses of Reeve's novels, distinguishing *The Old English Baron* as "Gothified history" and the subsequent novels as "sentimental fiction" with "intermittent Gothic elements." Reeve's influence on other Gothic novels is traced throughout.

Jeaffreson, J. Cordy. "Clara Reeve." In his *Novels and Novelists, from Elizabeth to Victoria,* Vol. I, pp. 269-75. London: Hurst and Blackett, 1858.
    A biographical and critical sketch. Jeaffreson concludes: "Ungifted with imagination, or language, or extensive reading, or good taste, [Clara Reeve] occupies a place amongst *popular* writers of the lowest grade. Her information was scanty, her diction constrained and mean, and the characters which people her pages are no more like men and women, than the cheapest Dutch dolls are like children."

Kievitt, Frank David. "Clara Reeve's *The School for Widows.*" *Mid-Hudson Language Studies* 3 (1980): 73-84.
    Comments that Reeve's *The School for Widows* is "very much in the Richardsonian tradition; as the novel's title implies, Reeve sees the purpose of her novel as primarily one of moral education, offering it to her readers not as a curious story but as a guide to behavior."

Leranbaum, Miriam. "'Mistresses of Orthodoxy': Education in the Lives and Writings of Late Eighteenth-Century English Women Writers." *Proceedings of the American Philosophical Society* 121, No. 4 (12 August 1977): 281-301.
    Relates Reeve's atypical education to her preoccupation with morality and the instruction of society in the later novels.

Lovecraft, Howard Phillips. "The Early Gothic Novel." In his *Supernatural Horror in Literature,* pp. 23-9. New York: Dover Publications, 1973.
    Contains a brief assessment of *The Old English Baron,* which Lovecraft describes as "too definitely insipid for greatness."

McNutt, Dan J. "Clara Reeve (1729-1807)." In his *The Eighteenth-Century Gothic Novel: An Annotated Bibliography of Criticism and Selected Texts,* pp. 166-72. New York: Garland Publishing, 1975.
    An annotated survey of works by and about Reeve.

[Morley, Henry]. Introduction to *The Old English Baron,* by Clara Reeve, pp. 5-9. Cassell's National Library. London: Cassell and Co., 1894.
    A brief survey of Reeve's life and works.

Reeves, John K. "The Mother of *Fatherless Fanny.*" *ELH* 9, No. 3 (September 1942): 224-33.
    An attempt to determine the exact extent of Reeve's contribution to *Fatherless Fanny,* a novel that was published in her name twelve years after she died.

Schnorrenberg, Barbara Brandon. "A Paradise Like Eve's." *Women's Studies* 9, No. 3 (1982): 263-73.
    A description of the utopian characteristics of Reeve's *Plans of Education.*

Summers, Montague. "Historical Gothic." In his *The Gothic Quest: A History of the Gothic Novel,* pp. 153-201. London: Fortune Press, 1938.
    Includes a discussion of *The Old English Baron* with comments on some of Reeve's later novels.

Tompkins, J. M. S. "The Female Novelists." In her *The Popular Novel in England, 1770-1800,* pp. 116-71. 1961. Reprint. Westport, Conn.: Greenwood Press, 1976.
    A general discussion of the works of female novelists in the eighteenth century, including a section on the treatment of marriage in Reeve's *The School for Widows.*

Varma, Devendra P. "Historical-Gothic School: The Heirs of *Otranto.*" In his *The Gothic Flame: Being a History of the Gothic Novel in England, Its Origins, Efflorescence, Disintegration, and Residuary Influences,* pp. 74-84. London: Arthur Barker, 1957.
    Examines Reeve's position in the history of Gothic fiction.

Vaughan, C. E. "Sterne, and the Novel of His Times." In *The Cambridge History of English Literature*. Vol. X, *The Age of Johnson,* edited by Sir A. W. Ward and A. R. Waller, pp. 51-74. New York: G. P. Putnam's Sons, 1913.

    Contains a discussion of *The Old English Baron* and its influence on later historical and romantic novels.

Walpole, Horace. Letter to William Mason. In his *Horace Walpole's Correspondence with William Mason,* Vol. I, edited by W. S. Lewis, Grover Cronin, Jr., and Charles H. Bennett, pp. 378-82. New Haven: Yale University Press, 1955.

    Refers to *The Old English Baron* as a work "professedly written in imitation of *Otranto,* but reduced to reason and probability!"

Catharine Maria Sedgwick

1789-1867

American novelist.

Sedgwick is remembered for her novels depicting New England life from the colonial era through the early nineteenth century. Distinctly American in theme and setting, these works are noted for their realistic description of domestic detail and regional culture. The best known of Sedgwick's novels, *Hope Leslie; or, Early Times in the Massachusetts,* vividly portrays daily life among the Puritans and native Americans in seventeenth-century Massachusetts. While her works are now considered dated, Sedgwick is admired for her attempt to create a uniquely American literature.

Sedgwick was born into a prestigious family in Stockbridge, Massachusetts. Her father, a prominent statesman, was frequently absent, and her mother suffered periodic bouts of mental illness. Consequently, Sedgwick was primarily raised by a servant and her brothers and sisters, to whom she remained deeply attached throughout her life. She attended a local grammar school and later went to boarding schools in Albany and Boston. When her mother died in 1807, Sedgwick went to live with relatives in New York, where she became friends with a number of literary figures, including the poet William Cullen Bryant and the noted theologian and Unitarian minister William Ellery Channing, whose liberal beliefs left a strong impression on her. Sedgwick returned to the family home in Stockbridge after her father's death in 1813. His conversion from Calvinism to Unitarianism shortly before his death, as well as her admiration for Channing, fueled her already strong interest in religion, and in 1821 she too converted to the Unitarian faith. The hostile reaction of conservative friends and relatives inspired Sedgwick's lifelong quest for religious tolerance and also prompted her to begin writing. In 1822, she composed a tract about religious persecution, which, with her brother's encouragement, she eventually developed into her first novel, *A New England Tale.* Sedwick continued to write throughout most of her life, composing moral tracts and didactic tales as well as novels. She divided her time between New York City and the Berkshire Mountains of Massachusetts. In the Berkshires, she became renowned for her tea parties. These gatherings, similar in spirit to European literary salons, brought together some of the leading writers of the period, including Herman Melville, Nathaniel Hawthorne, Ralph Waldo Emerson, and James Fenimore Cooper. Sedgwick also became involved in social causes, promoting improvements in prisons and schools. Yet she avoided controversial stances, and biographers often comment on her ambivalent attitudes: she opposed slavery, but considered abolitionists too extreme in their views; she chose not to marry, but idealized matrimony; and she believed women should not be allowed to vote, but strove to change the laws preventing them from owning property. Sedgwick championed social reform until her late seventies, when she became ill and moved to Boston. There she was cared for by a niece until her death at age seventy-eight.

As a writer, Sedgwick was motivated by a sense of obligation to educate her audience. Thus, all of her works are didactic in tone, stressing the need for religious and racial tolerance and

social and political reform. Her first novel, *A New England Tale,* describes the evils of organized religion. Set in the early nineteenth century, the work tells the story of a noble young woman who is the victim of corrupt church leaders. Because most novels written at this time in America were modeled on the works of English authors, *A New England Tale* gained special recognition for its American setting and characters. Its focus on moral concerns and domestic themes met with immediate acclaim, and Sedgwick soon became one of the country's most popular authors. Her next novel, *Redwood,* was equally well received. As in *A New England Tale,* religious elements figure strongly in the plot, and once again a highly principled heroine serves as the protagonist; since the novel's publication, Debby Lenox has been frequently praised as one of the most captivating and realistically drawn women in early American literature. Sedgwick's third novel, *Hope Leslie,* is a historical romance of colonial New England that describes the customs of the Pequod tribe of native Americans. Considered by many critics to be her best work, *Hope Leslie* is admired for its narrative power and historical accuracy. Following the publication of *Hope Leslie,* Sedgwick was regarded as one of the finest female writers in America. However, her subsequent works, including *Clarence, The Linwoods,* and *Married or Single?,* while widely read by her contemporaries, were not as critically successful as her earlier novels.

At the time of publication, Sedgwick's novels were considered innovative because of their use of local scenery, customs, and characters, and many contemporary critics argued that no previous author had focused on life in America. Although most reviewers concurred that Sedgwick's style was not indicative of any great talent, citing awkward word choice, wooden dialogue, and overbearing didacticism among other flaws, they considered her characters well realized and her plots lively. In addition, most commentators commended the realism of Sedgwick's novels; Hawthorne, in fact, referred to her as "our most truthful novelist." Critical and popular interest in Sedgwick began to diminish, however, after the publication in 1857 of her final novel, *Married or Single?* As other authors began to write novels about American locales, customs, and characters, her works appeared less innovative.

Sedgwick's works continued to inspire little commentary until the mid-twentieth century, when critics began to recognize her historical importance. Modern scholars have argued that she was the first American writer to intentionally feature moral themes and to compose historical romances. Critics have also praised such other aspects of her writings as her terse prose style and courageous, independent female characters. Nonetheless, her works are little read today, largely due to her naive didacticism: the notion that good breeding and manners could cure most social ills has not endured. Yet because she provided one of the first detailed portrayals of American life, recreating the domestic habits, religious beliefs, and moral concerns of early New Englanders, Sedgwick is acknowledged by literary historians for her contribution to the development of a national literature.

(See also *Dictionary of Literary Biography*, Vol. I: *The American Renaissance in New England*.)

PRINCIPAL WORKS

*A New-England Tale; or, Sketches of New-England
     Character and Manners*   (novel)   1822; also published
     in revised form as *A New England Tale, and
     Miscellanies*, 1852
Redwood   (novel)   1824
Hope Leslie; or, Early Times in the Massachusetts   (novel)
     1827
Clarence; or, A Tale of Our Own Times   (novel)   1830
Home   (novel)   1835
The Linwoods; or, "Sixty Years Since" in America   (novel)
     1835
Tales and Sketches. 2 vols.   (short stories)   1835-44
The Poor Rich Man, and the Rich Poor Man   (novel)
     1836
Live and Let Live; or, Domestic Service Illustrated   (novel)
     1837
Letters from Abroad to Kindred at Home   (letters)   1841
Married or Single?   (novel)   1857
Life and Letters of Catharine M. Sedgwick   (unfinished
     autobiography and letters)   1871

THE LITERARY AND SCIENTIFIC REPOSITORY   (essay date
1822)

[*In the following review of* A New England Tale, *the critic admires the novel for its accurate depiction of New England life*.]

Of books that profess to illustrate American society and manners, we have never met with one which so perfectly and agreeably accomplishes the design, to a certain extent, as [*A New-England Tale; or, Sketches of New-England Character and Manners*]. Our political institutions, the state of learning among us, and the influence of religion upon the national character, have been often discussed and displayed; but our domestic manners, the social and the moral influences, which operate in retirement, and in common intercourse, and the multitude of local peculiarities, which form our distinctive features upon the many peopled earth, have very seldom been happily exhibited in our literature. It is true, that Mr. Washington Irving, in his Knickerbocker, "Rip Van Winkle," and the "Legend of Sleepy Hollow," has given, in inimitable burlesque, very natural, just, and picturesque views of one class of people in the land; but they are all ludicrous subjects, and do little towards forming a history of the diversities of passion, sentiment, and behaviour, as they are manifest in any of our little communities, detached, as it were, from the great world. . . . [When we speak of history]—we do not mean to rank the writers of [fiction] among the recorders and statutes, and battles, and party chronicles; but among those true historians which . . . are wanting, to give us just notions of what manner of men the ancient Greeks were, in their domestic affections, and retired deportment; and with whom Fielding classes himself, nearly in these words: 'Those dignified authors who produce what are called true histories, are indeed writers of fictions, while I am a true historian, a describer of society as it exists, and of men as they are.'

An historian of this sort, is the author of the *New-England Tale*, whomsoever *he* or *she* may be; a person of fine feelings, and of fine observation, skilled in interpreting motives of action, well acquainted with that true moral philosophy, which has ascertained much of the natural influences of habit, example, and education upon the formation of character, and with this knowledge, posessing that delicacy of discernment, which produces felicity of manner in literary composition, and is, in fact, a combination of generous sentiments, wide intelligence, and enlightened taste; and which, when applied to literature, communicates whatever it perceives or enjoys with a gracefulness, sensibility, and simplicity, that vanity, mediocrity, and self-assumption, never can attain. The *New-England Tale* is prefaced by a modest declaration that its limited and simple aim is to give a descriptive sketch of some prevailing characteristics of New-England; and this is done in the succeeding pages, so as to afford a continued interest, and a lively pleasure to the reader, and to demand, as an act of justice, (so we think,) sincere commendation from the candid and the rational. Surely no debt which opinion can pay, is rendered with more satisfaction by the debtor, than the honest tribute of praise, accorded by one who has been regaled by a beautiful literary production to him who has bestowed it. (p. 337)

[The story] is original, natural, and beautiful; written with such simplicity, with such 'a soul of goodness,' with such purity of taste, style, and purpose; in such affinity with things lovely, honourable, and of good report, that it must be acceptable to minds in accordance with itself: and they who would correct what is evil, and cherish what is good, in the character of the society which it so truly describes, may be shown in this mirror of just representation, the weeds that are to be rooted out, and the virtues that are to be cultivated, in the fairest and happiest, as well as in the less favoured districts of this our blessed native land. (p. 340)

[We] cannot conclude these remarks upon the *New-England Tale,* without expressing our surprize that it should have been considered a sectarian book, as we have casually heard it called; nor can we imagine what peculiar doctrines should be imputed to the work. It gives illustrations of the Quaker and Methodist sects, highly honourable to them both; and it exposes, very naturally, that frequent abuse of the Christian system, which all of us may hear from pulpits in or land, and of which we often see the practical operation in ordinary life. There are professors and preachers who certainly appear to adopt the partial views of religion taken by Mrs. Wilson. Obedience has no efficacy, according to their representations, and a multiplicity of public and outward services constitute, according to them, the proof of an "inward and spiritual grace." Whether this is true or not, they that hear and see can testify; whether the results of these principles, as they are delineated in the story before us, are probable and natural, reason may infer and experience can show. For our own part, we think the most amiable and charitable liberality pervades the book; and if there are opinions taught and received in society, which produce the consequences described, we know not who can complain or take offence, that the truth should be told. (pp. 368-69)

> *A review of "A New-England Tale; or Sketches of New-England Character and Manners," in* The Literary and Scientific Repository, *Vol. IV, No. 8, May, 1822, pp. 336-70.*

THE MONTHLY REVIEW, LONDON   (essay date 1823)

[*The critic offers praise for* A New England Tale, *especially for its mood of religious tolerance.*]

[*A New-England Tale*] is on the whole a favorable specimen of American talent and feeling. Some objections have been made in America to its religious character, but we do not see any good grounds for such imputations. Every character in the tale, indeed, seems to possess distinct notions on religious subjects: but the author has granted a wise toleration to all of them, except a bigoted Calvinist.—The hero is what is usually called *a wet Quaker;* and the heroine, who is originally, if we mistake not, somewhat of a Methodist, ends by assuming the close cap and sober-colored gown of *a Friend.* Whatever may be thought of admitting such a diversity of faith into the narrative, the practical religion which it contains cannot be censured by any reader.—We have remarked a few *Americanisms* in these pages, but they are generally put into the mouths of the inferior characters, and cannot therefore be justly made objects of criticism.

> *A review of "A New-England Tale," in* The Monthly Review, *London, Vol. CI, May, 1823, p. 105.*

CATHARINE MARIA SEDGWICK   (essay date 1824)

[*In the following excerpt from her preface to* Redwood, *Sedgwick discusses the role of religion in her novel and her desire to accurately depict American life.*]

A few words will be sufficient to indicate the design of [*Redwood*]. We have not composed a tale professedly or chiefly of a religious nature, as if left to the bias of our own inclination, we might possibly have done. We do not think that such attempts have heretofore been eminently successful; or that narrative sermons are of a nature to be particularly interesting. Still we are conscious that the religious principle, with all its attendant doubts, hopes, fears, enthusiasm, and hypocrisy, is a mighty agent in moulding human character, and it may therefore, with propriety, find a place in a work whose object it is to delineate that character. It is a principle of action more permanent and more universal than the affection which unites the sexes; and in the fictious representations of human life, there can be no reason why the greater should be excluded by the less. On these impressions we have acted. We do not anticipate splendid success, but we are sure that we cannot be deprived of the consolation of having intended well. It will be an ample reward if we can believe that we have been able by our trivial labours to co-operate in any degree with the efforts of the good and great, "to give ardour to virtue, and confidence to truth." Our anxiety is only for the great truths of our common religion, not for any of its subdivisions.

The sketch which has been introduced of the society of Shakers was drawn from personal observation. It would have been withheld if we could have supposed that it would have wound the feelings even of a single individual of that obscure sect. But against this there is a sufficient security. The representation is deemed just, and it is hoped would not be thought offensive; and, besides, there is little danger that these light volumes will ever find their way into a sanctuary from whose pale the frivolous amusements and profane literature of the "world's people" are carefully excluded.

Whenever the course of our narrative has thrown opportunities to our way, we have attempted some sketches of the character and manners of the people of this country. We have done this with all faithfulness of purpose. If we have failed, we trust the failure will be ascribed, as it ought—to defect of capacity. We live in a country which is beyond parallel, free, happy, and abundant. As such we would describe it—but no Arcadia, for we have found none. (pp. ix-xi)

> *Catharine Maria Sedgwick, in a preface to her* Redwood: A Tale, *Vol. I, E. Bliss and E. White, 1824, pp. v-xi.*

THE UNITED STATES LITERARY GAZETTE   (essay date 1824)

[*The critic generally commends* Redwood *but faults Sedgwick's tendency to draw caricatures.*]

The literary character of [*Redwood*] is highly respectable, as all would expect it to be who are acquainted with the previous efforts of the author. Common fame attributes these works—*Redwood* and the *New England Tale*—to a lady; if this be so, we can only say we think it surprising,—not that their pages should exhibit much eloquence and bright imagination, but that the style should be so singularly correct, and that its excellence should be so well sustained. Indeed, the literary execution of these volumes, would in no degree discredit an author who had disciplined and fortified his mind by severer studies than ladies are apt to love, and chastened his taste by diligent and profitable study of "the classics"—and acquired all the skill in words which few but practised writers can have. The imagery is sometimes very beautiful and appropriate, and is never offensive to good taste, and there are many passages of true eloquence. As a tale, it is pleasing, and certainly sufficiently interesting to carry the attention along with it, until the whole story is developed, and the persons of the drama finally disposed of. But it exerts nothing of that witchery over the imagination of the reader, which makes him almost mingle his personal identity with that of the prominent characters, and suffer and rejoice with them, and look forward anxiously with them, to learn the destiny which time is bringing. In other words, it is a work of much talent and excellent taste, but not of high and commanding genius. . . .

[The] scene shifts from the banks of Lake Champlain to Lebanon Springs, and the Shaker establishments in their neighbourhood; the list of characters includes a Southern planter, who is a very fine gentleman, his daughter, who is a spoilt child, and altogether weak and wicked, till just at the close of the book, some Yankee yeomen, several heroes and heroines, who are much like others of the same class, an English officer, who is just nothing, an old woman, who is a little bit of a Meg Merrilies, one Indian, and some Shakers. Much beautiful scenery is beautifully described, some striking incidents well told, and some very interesting though not peculiarly original characters well portrayed. The Shaker establishments are visited, and the condition, principles, habits, and, in some measure, the history of this strange sect, are well illustrated. (p. 101)

We think there is one error in this work which should be noticed. Our Yankee ways and fashions are a little caricatured; foreigners might infer that we are rather more loquacious and inquisitive, and prone to "guess" about that which we know, and to "calculate" just where we should expect, than is the fact; and they need no sort of encouragement to fall into this error. (p. 102)

> *A review of "Redwood; a Tale," in* The United States Literary Gazette, *Vol. I, No. 1, April 1, 1824, pp. 101-02.*

[WILLIAM CULLEN BRYANT]   (essay date 1825)

[*Bryant is considered one of the most accomplished American poets of the nineteenth century. His poetic treatment of the themes of nature and mutability identifies him as one of the earliest figures in the Romantic movement in American literature. Bryant, a close friend of Sedgwick, also served as her literary advisor. In the following generally positive review of* Redwood, *he praises its domestic elements, characterization, and subtle didacticism.*]

[*Redwood*] is a story of domestic life, the portraiture of what passes by our firesides and in our streets, in the calm of the country, and amidst a prosperous and well ordered community. The writer, who, we understand, is the same lady to whom the public is already indebted for another beautiful little work of a similar character, has not availed herself of the more obvious and abundant sources of interest, which would naturally suggest themselves to the author of a fictious history, the scene of which should be laid in the United States. She has not gone back to the infancy of our country, to set before us the fearless and hardy men, who made the first lodgement in its vast forests, men in whose characters is to be found the favorite material of the novelist, great virtues mingled with many errors, the strange land to which they had come, and its unknown dangers, and the savage tribes by whom they were surrounded, to whose kindness they owed so much, and from whose enmity they suffered so severely. Nor does the thread of her narrative lead us through those early feuds between the different colonies of North America, who brought with them and kept alive, in their settlements, the animosities of the nations from whom they proceeded, and, in the midst of all their hardships and sufferings, contended about the division of the wilderness, with a fierceness and an obstinacy exasperated by the difference in the characters of those who composed them. Nor has the writer made any use of the incidents of our great national struggle for independence, at once so calamitous

and so glorious, the time of splendid virtues and great sufferings, the war which separated friends, and divided families, and revived the half laid spirit of bloodshed in the uncivilised races about us, and called to our shores so many military adventurers to fight under the standard of Britain, and so many generous volunteers in the cause of humanity and liberty to combat under ours. She has passed by all these periods and situations, so tempting to the writer of fictitious history, so pregnant with interest and teeming with adventure, to make a more hazardous experiment of her powers. She has come down to the very days in which we live, to quiet times and familiar manners, and has laid the scene of her narrative in the most ancient and tranquil parts of the country; presenting us not merely with the picture of what she has imagined, but with the copy of what she has observed. (pp. 245-46)

[The author's] delineations of character are generally striking and happy, and the national peculiarities are hit off with great dexterity and effect, though perhaps, in some instances, they are brought out a little too broadly. There is, however, very little overcharging and exaggeration; the actors in the plot do not come upon the scene in their stage dresses, ready, on every occasion that offers, as in duty bound, to display, resolutely, and with all their might, the supposed peculiarities of the personages they represent, but they are made to look and act like people in the world about us. The characters are not only thus chastely drawn, but they are varied with exceeding art and judgment, and this variety is, for the most part, founded on essential differences. It is not with this, as with some works of the kind, which have fallen in our way, where the parts, which the several personages are made to take in the action, have little connexion with their supposed manners and dispositions, but any part will fit any character, and any character will fit any part, and, bating a few peculiarities in the dialogue, they may be transposed at pleasure without injury to the work, like the words in the famous sentence with which Mons. Jourdain, in the *Bourgeois Gentilhomme*, exercises the ingenuity of his instructor in philosophy. Here, on the contrary, they are made to have a complete and necessary dependence on each other, so complete, that the least change would produce manifest distortion and incongruity. We have some fault to find with the general plan of the story, . . . but the subordinate incidents are invented and managed with great ingenuity and felicity, and a gentle, and sustained, and gradually increasing interest, never growing violent, and never suffered to become feeble, is kept up from the beginning to the end of the work. Parts are written with deep pathos; others display no inconsiderable share of comic power. There is much beautiful and striking description, but it is never so drawn out as to be tiresome, nor introduced so as to interrupt the interest of the story. It is evident, that the author has formed to herself an exalted and severe standard of virtue and morals, but this does not prevent great indulgence to human error, and compassion for human infirmity, and the utmost good nature and allowance to those, whose speculations on abstract subjects have led them to different results from her own. The qualities we have enumerated are all delightfully chastened and regulated, by great good sense and sober practical wisdom, and the whole is given us through the medium of a style perspicuous and elegant. (pp. 256-57)

The least interesting part of the book is that, where we are introduced to the Armstead party, whom Debby and Ellen fall in with on their way to the Shaker village. There is a great deal of conversation here, that does not help forward the progress of the story, and of consequences the interest suffers. There is something, also, not altogether prepossessing in the first appearance of Grace Campbell, with whose character the author has evidently taken great pains. Something like pertness and flippancy, not to say rudeness, is detected in her sallies and repartees in the scene, where we are first made acquainted with her; but all this is more than compensated for, by her spirit, frankness, and warmth of heart, as they are brought out in the further progress of the narrative. Miss Deborah Lenox, however, acquits herself on this, as on all other occasions, to our entire satisfaction. (p. 266)

The moral of *Redwood,* as intimated in the preface, is properly a religious one. We had some apprehensions on seeing this intimation, that the moral would be too anxiously and obtrusively brought forward, and pressed with a wearisome frequency and perseverance. The writer of a novel, the design of which is professedly to instruct, is always in danger of falling into this error. He is himself so full of the importance of the lesson he inculcates, that he is apt to suppose that it cannot be too often nor too earnestly repeated, nor enforced by too much argument and amplification, nor illustrated by too many or too obvious examples. We must say, however, that we see few if any traces of this fault in *Redwood.* The moral is well wrought into the texture of the work, but never officiously presented. It is not enough to say of this novel, that the reader is relieved and refreshed at due intervals, by being let out from the instructions of the author into the great world about him, to amuse himself with what is going on there; and is then gently recalled to the lesson, which the author wishes to teach. It is doing it better justice to say, that the world itself is only then made to the reader, what it ought always to be, the great school and place of discipline, the experience and observation of which should form us to virtue.

We have already spoken of the author's skill in the drawing of characters. Next to the character of Debby, that of Susan is sketched with the greatest spirit and originality. Either of these would of itself suffice to give a reputation to the work. All the others, even the subordinate ones, give ample proofs of a fertile invention, and a wide and close observation. The very persons who seem, at first sight, to be brought forward only for the purpose of exhibiting our national manners, or who are casually introduced, in some single incident of the plot, are, for the most part, distinguished from each other by some striking peculiarity. The Vermont Yeoman, Mr Lenox, and even the Shaker gardener, though but just seen in the course of the narrative, leave a strong individual impression on the mind of the reader, an impression that bears witness to the abundance and variety of the author's resources. The style of the work in that most difficult part, the dialogue, is exceedingly natural, spirited, and appropriate. That of the narrative parts, however, though always flowing and often eloquent, is not in all places equal to that of the dialogue. It may be suggested to the author, whether the anxiety always to express herself pointedly and brilliantly has not, in some instances, taken from the sincerity of her manner, and thus diminished the force and depth of the impression intended to be made. We have also noted some deviations from purity of language, which have doubtless been the more striking in a work written with such apparent care.

The peculiarities in the manners and character of our countrymen, have too long been connected with ideas merely low and ludicrous. We complain of our English neighbors for holding them up as objects simply ridiculous and laughable, but it is by no means certain that we have not encouraged them by our

example. It is time, however, that they were redeemed from these gross and degrading associations. It is time that they should be mentioned, as they deserve to be, with something else than a sneer, and that a feeling of respect should mingle with the smile they occasion. We are happy to see the author of this work connecting them, as we find them connected in real life, with much that is ennobling and elevated, with traits of sagacity, benevolence, moral courage and magnanimity. These are qualities, which by no means impair any comic effect those peculiarities may have; they rather relieve and heighten it. They transform it from mere buffoonery to the finest humor. When this is done, something is done to exalt our national reputation abroad, and to improve our national character at home. It is also a sort of public benefit, to show what copious and valuable materials the private lives and daily habits of our countrymen offer to the writer of genius. It is as if one were to discover to us rich ores and gems lying in the common earth about us. But our readers must by this time be weary of our comments, and we dismiss them, with pleasure, to the perusal of the work itself. (pp. 270-72)

[William Cullen Bryant], in a review of "Redwood, a Tale," in The North American Review, *Vol. XX, No. 47, April, 1825, pp. 245-72.*

MARIA EDGEWORTH   (letter date 1825)

[*Edgeworth is remembered today for her role in the development of the English novel of manners; a number of critics have noted similarities between her works and those of Sedgwick. In the following excerpt from a letter, Edgeworth writes glowingly about* Redwood.]

Redwood has entertained us very much. I am so much flattered by the manner in which my writings are alluded to in this book, that I can hardly suppose I am an unprejudiced judge, but it appears to me a work of superior talent, far greater than even *The New-England Tale* gave me reason to expect. The character of Aunt Deborah is first rate—in Scott's best manner, yet not an imitation of Scott. It is to America what Scott's characters are to Scotland, valuable as original pictures, with enough of individual peculiarity to be interesting, and to give the feeling of reality and life as portraits, with sufficient also of general characteristics to give them the philosophical merit of portraying a class.

Maria Edgeworth, in a letter in May, 1825, in Life and Letters of Catharine M. Sedgwick, *edited by Mary E. Dewey, Harper & Brothers, Publishers, 1871, p. 169.*

THE WESTERN MONTHLY REVIEW   (essay date 1827)

[*The critic offers a mixed response to* Hope Leslie, *terming its writing "handsome," but also noting its stilted characterization.*]

At present, the aim of all, who write for the imagination, is to produce an effect. The author cares not what established rules he violates, in making his book, if, by so doing, he can create a sensation in his readers. This mania does not seem to have touched our authoress. Her story [*Hope Leslie*] presents a regular account of well regulated people, who figure only in still life. We think she has done wisely, in thus treating the single-minded, stern, religious, and noble character of our puritan ancestors. The qualities required to make good rulers and citizens of the new colony 'planted in New-England,' were incompatible with those, which are essential in a modern hero of romance. The puritan character, under other circumstances, has furnished ample materials for fine writing. So many powerful minds have taken up this subject, and exhibited it in all its lights and shadows, that to attempt to say any thing new upon it is a hopeless undertaking. Our authoress was probably aware of this, and has confined herself within the limits allowed by the most rigid, while describing most of the personages; and allowed her fancy to expatiate only in the unexplored regions of the savage mind. (p. 290)

There is in these pages much writing, which, according to the prevailing taste of our country, is handsome. Some of the descriptions are highly wrought. (p. 293)

Master Craddock, the tutor of Hope, is a faint copy of our old favorite, Dominie Sampson. Magawisca is the Rebecca of the piece, or to use an expression of Lord Byron's, 'an incarnation of all the virtues.' From our knowledge of her race, we should have looked in any place for such a character, rather than in an Indian wigwam. This authoress has fallen into the error, so apparent in the works of Cooper and all the American novelists, that have any thing to do with Indians. They dress a figure in the Indian costume; give it a copper skin; make it use extravagantly figurative language; and introduce it with the interjection, ugh! as a natural savage. As a young, brave and heroic warrior, he has thoughts, and performs actions, that can be looked for from those only, who have superadded to the beneficence of nature towards them, the delicacy of feeling, and refinement of civilized life.

The old warrior is this character, mellowed into age. Magawisca is the first genuine Indian angel, that we have met with; and we must give our authoress credit, for having manufactured the savage material into a new shape. This angel, as she stands, is a very pretty fancy; but no more like a squaw, than the croaking of a sand-hill crane is like the sweet, clear and full note of the redbird. Dealers in fiction have privileges; but they ought to have for foundation, some slight resemblance to nature. (pp. 294-95)

There seems to us to be a want of piquancy in this work, which is not entirely atoned for by the good feeling, that pervades it. The parties prosecute their affairs too much, as though they were automata. They have not the free, natural movement of voluntary action. From this air of restraint, we are led to believe, that the authoress thought it her duty to write a novel, and that, governed by this feeling, she set herself to the task; made her outline, and then proceeded to fill it up systematically. The expression of spontaneous feeling, in her characters, is not only repressed, but there is infused into her style an elaborate manner, which, in a measure, destroys, with us, the effect of her many good thoughts. (p. 295)

A review of "Hope Leslie; or, Early Times in the Massachusetts," in The Western Monthly Review, *Vol. I, No. 5, September, 1827, pp. 289-95.*

[F. W. P. GREENWOOD] (essay date 1828)

[*In the following review of* Hope Leslie, *Greenwood assesses the novel as Sedgwick's finest because of its setting and characterization.*]

Hope Leslie is the last of [Catharine Sedgwick's] three larger works, and, in our judgment, the best. It bears the lineaments of the two others, so far as to entitle them to claim a family resemblance to it; but it is written with an easier, freer spirit than the others; its chain of beauty is less frequently interrupted;

it contains a greater number of prominent characters; its style is more matured. In the whole three, however, there is the same purity and delicacy; the same generous, lofty sentiment; the same deep and solemn breathings of religion without parade, and of piety without cant or censoriousness; the same love of the grand and the lovely in nature, together with the same power so to express that love as to waken it up ardently, devotionally in others; the same occasional touches of merry wit and playful satire; the same glowing fancy; and, spread through all, and regulating all, the same good sense, leading to a right apprehension of human life and human motives, restraining genius from extravagance, giving an air of reality to the narrative, and securing our constant respect for the narrator.

There is a natural advantage, if we may use such a phrase, belonging to the last of these tales, which, if the two former had been equal to it in other respects, would yet have clothed it with an interest greatly superior to theirs. This advantage is its date; the times and the scenes in which its plot is laid. At the same time that there is greater danger incurred, and greater care and skill demanded in writing an historical than any other kind of novel, yet when the care and the skill have been successful, and the danger obviously and confessedly escaped, the work makes a stronger appeal to our sympathies, and keeps a more tenacious hold on our memory, than a work of mere imagination from the same hand. (pp. 411-12)

It has been fully demonstrated by many an orator and writer of our country, that the characters of our first settlers, the peculiar features of their age, their troubles, their struggles, their wars, government, manners, opinions, and institutions, all fresh and singular, with the wild scenes amidst which they moved, and the wild men by whom they were surrounded, furnished the most admirable materials for literary fabrics of purely national manufacture, and original patterns, both in poetry and prose. What they said was as true as truth itself. Neither could any fault be found with the recipes which they kindly wrote out; for these were as correct and clearly worded as could reasonably be desired. But the difficulty was to follow them. The article in request was not forthcoming. A few attempts were made, and one or two of them were not entire failures. The authoress of **Hope Leslie,** and hitherto she alone, has been, at least to our satisfaction, completely successful. She has had the industry to study the early history of New England, the costume and carriage, the spirit and temper of the settlers and aboriginal inhabitants, and the talent to combine the results of her researches with the embellishments of her own resources, and present to us the whole, a beautiful work, to verify our theories, to enliven our ancestral attachments, to delight, instruct, and improve us. (p. 412-13)

Magawisca, we must say a word of her, is one of those creations of genius of which it is hard to speak one's impressions in adequate terms, and therefore we shall say of her only a word. Some have questioned her verisimilitude as an Indian. They assert that she is too noble, too delicate, too spiritual for an Indian. This we are disposed to deny. That there were ever many Magawiscas, we indeed doubt ourselves, and therefore we would not propose her as a fair sample of the Indian character; but that the best features of her character have had a real existence in savage life, that she is a possible Indian, we have no doubt whatever; and this is all which is claimed for her in the truly modest preface of our authoress. Possible or impossible, she is a glorious creature, and even if she had no right to her creation, we welcome her to our heart of hearts.

Sir Philip Gardiner we detest. We are sorry that the writer meddled with a rascal of exactly his grain. Nevertheless, if he is necessary to the apprehension, imprisonment, and trial of Magawisca, we cannot spare even him; though we should still think that Rosa might be left out with advantage. (p. 418)

Hope Leslie, the white heroine of the work, is a finely drawn character, full of enthusiasm, affection, truth, and yet sparkling with gaiety and wit. Her friend and rival—yes, both friend and rival—Esther Downing, is lovely too, in her way, which, as was to be expected in those times, was rather a precise one, and her loveliness is as distinct from Hope's as possible. Magawisca too is another friend and rival. . . . Here are three ladies, who seem to love and admire each other as much as they do Everell Fletcher; who, by the way, excellent as he is, hardly deserves such an accumulation of honor. Is this, or is it not, a greater improbability than the character of the Indian heroine? We are afraid to leave the decision of the question to our authoress, who, if the truth must be told, appears to entertain a decided partiality for her own sex. Nor can we blame her for it. We are in no humor, indeed, to find fault with her at all, or for anything. We only hope, that as we have been tardy in noticing the last production of her pen, another will very soon be ready for our inspection. We pray her to go on, in the path in which she must excel, and has excelled, and which she ought consequently to make her peculiar one. We pray her to go on, in the name of her friends, for the public's sake, and for the honor of our youthful literature. (p. 420)

> [*F. W. P. Greenwood*], *in a review of ''Hope Leslie; or, Early Times in Massachusetts,'' in* The North American Review, *Vol. XXVI, No. 59, April, 1828, pp. 403-20.*

[W. HILLARD]   (essay date 1831)

> [*In the following review of* Clarence, *the critic praises the novel for its vitality, for its pronounced moral tone, and, most significantly, for its astute observations. However, the critic also faults the novel's improbable plot.*]

[*Clarence; or, A Tale of Our Own Times*] is perhaps not so finished as *Redwood,* and there is certainly nothing in it which displays so much genius as the character of Aunt Debby in that novel. But we have read it with more interest than any of its predecessors; and the lively and spirited sketches of artificial life and manners in it, will, we think, make it more entertaining to the generality of readers.It has all the fine qualities of head and heart which have so favorably recommended the former works of the fair author; the same pure style, the same elevated tone of morality, the same rare observation and exquisite tact, and the same healthful feeling and warm affections. We have placed the title of this book at the head of our article with the honest purpose of reviewing it, and not of writing an essay upon novels in general. Successful authorship confers a distinction, which must not pass unacknowledged, even in this land of business and politics. It is a duty we owe to ourselves and our literature, to examine the claims of our countrywoman to the high reputation she enjoys; and though our estimate is formed, of course, from a perusal of all her works, yet had she written nothing but *Clarence,* she would amply deserve all our praises.

We know of nothing for which she is more remarkable, than her nice and discriminating habits of observation, and that fine tact, which with the directness of instinct, seizes upon what is important for the description of men and things, and rejects what is superfluous. She has an 'eye practised like a blind man's touch,' and she can distinguish instantly those minute shades which are so imperceptibly blended in nature as to seem but one color to common observers. Her pictures of natural scenery are drawn with the distinct pencil of Cowper, and they rise up and appear to the eye as we read, without any effort of our own to give them shape and presence. Almost every page of *Redwood* and *Hope Leslie* will confirm our remarks, and amidst the multitude of admirable descriptions, we are puzzled to select any one. It is no very easy matter, for instance, to describe a country-seat, though it may seem to be so at first; yet how perfectly has she succeeded in delineating the mansion of Mr. Clarence. We have no confused images of lawns, forest, and shrubbery, but every thing is distinct and defined, and we have no doubt, that if ten or twelve artists were employed each, to make a picture of the scene, their sketches would differ very little. The same remark will apply to her descriptions of artificial life and manners;—such as her account of the Shaker establishment in *Redwood,* and the picture in the second volume of *Clarence,* of the tone, dress, and conversation of the fashionable society of New-York. She is evidently more acquainted with men than books, and has sought truth in the 'light of things,' and not in the 'still air of delightful studies;' and her resources are in the highest degree available, for she has collected their very materials herself. She has kept an observant eye on the masques that make up the world's motley pageant, and drawn thence a living wisdom, far higher than the cold forms of mere learning. She has noted the looks the tones of men, the manner in which they are affected by events, the way in which differing characters display themselves, the things in which all men are alike, and those in which they are most dissimilar. We are disposed to think more highly of this habit of discriminating observation, as a means of intellectual development, than most persons. He who goes about among men with his eyes open, will learn something better than the lore that is hidden in books. This is a thing in which women excel men; it is a merit almost peculiar to female writers. Hence arises the perfect keeping observable in our author's pictures of still life, and the consistency and individuality of her characters, who are always one and the same in their conversation, their letters, and their actions.

She writes English with uncommon elegance and purity; no small merit in these days of extravagance and caricature, when foamy declamation is called strength, and calmness is another name for feebleness. She has the rare merit of never being common-place, and if she has occasion to express a familiar thought, she contrives by some graceful turn or happy allusion, to give it the air and gloss of novelty. She never descends to that vulgar artifice of dressing up little or old ideas in language so ambitious, that we imagine for a moment that we have something very new and fine, till a second glance shews us that all is but varnish and gilding. Her style is perfectly feminine, full of a certain indescribable gracefulness and ease, arising from a fine perception of beauty and an inborn delicacy of taste, which seem always to select the best words, and to put them in their right places. The letters in *Clarence,* we think, are very fine specimens of epistolary style, easy, graceful, and spirited, equally remote from formal stiffness and slipshod carelessness. Almost the only fault of style we have noticed, is an occasional diffuseness, the easily besetting sin of female writers.

We trust that we may be allowed to speak of another winning charm in these novels, arising not so much from the mind as the moral character of the author. We mean the impress everywhere discoverable, of an unaffected goodness of heart, and a warmth of affection which folds in its embrace every thing that lives. As John Paul has somewhere said, she loves God and every little child. Her sympathies are ready and active, and called forth by every shape of distress, and she never turns aside from suffering virtue, however repulsive the garb it may wear. There is a beautiful tenderness and sensibility breathing out from her writings, like the fragrance from a rose. She delights to accumulate images of peace and happiness and sunshine, to describe all that is noble in man and attractive in woman—the virtue that exalts, the struggle that purifies, the trial that calls forth a seraph's energies, and the sweet affections that strew with flowers life's dusty highway. She does not know how to draw a villain; she has no idea of the spasms and convulsions of the mind, around which guilt and remorse have thrown their serpent-folds. Man in the pride of his imperial beauty, full of truth, and honor and grace, with high thoughts and generous affections, with reason sitting on his brow, and the pulse of joy in his veins,—woman, with her veil of gentle loveliness, her lily-like purity, her loving and trusting heart,—the light of friendship, the soul-exchanging glance of love,—these are the themes which call forth her finest powers, and it is in the delineation of these only, that her genius appears in its proper element. Her descriptions of childhood are full of the dewy freshness of life's morning hour. In this respect we know of no one who equals her, no one who draws in colors so speaking the image of a beautiful and happy child, with his heart of gladness and voice of silver-toned glee, his brave spirit, his frolic blood, and his winning tricks. (pp. 73-6)

The love of nature, and a familiar acquaintance with the changeful expressions of the 'mighty mother's' countenance, are among the fine gifts of the author of *Clarence*. Her descriptions of scenery in the western part of Massachusetts in her *New-England Tale*, and in *Redwood*, may challenge a comparison with any in the language. She does not merely draw the features of a landscape, but she gives you the expression, and transfuses into her pages the spirit that hangs over it, like an atmosphere. She looks upon the outward world in the vein of the melancholy Jaques, translating its silence into thoughts and images; but she draws thence the elements of a far more cheerful philosophy. She learns wisdom from the cups of flowers, and the whisper of the pine conveys to her a lesson of truth. Every leaf is pregnant with instruction, and every stream teaches as it brawls. The forms of nature have stamped their own likeness upon the soul of their worshipper, and every mute image without has given birth to a correlative idea within, united by a mysterious affinity, which all may feel, but none can define. In her graphic descriptions of natural scenery, there is no small portion of the fine philosophy of Wordsworth, which regards the fair forms of the outward world as the instruments of a spiritual influence upon the mind of man, as the varied stops through which the myriad tones of a universal harmony are breathed. Woods and mountains are not only enjoyed, but felt and understood,—they are as the face of a long-tried and never-failing friend. This sensibility to natural beauty exerts a most expanding and elevating power upon the spirit of man, and when it is united with that gifted eye, which can read the letters of power and love written all over this goodly universe, nothing short of religion is capable of exerting a more holy ministration.

But more than all the rest, the author of *Clarence* has that high and pure tone of moral and religious feeling, without which genius is a fatal curse, and fine powers are destructive in the exact ratio of their splendor and superiority. She never makes vice interesting or virtue repulsive; but paints each in its true colors, so that the mind obeying its natural instinct is enamored of the one and abhors the other. She draws no beings, half-gods and half-fiends, with a veil of splendid and romantic qualities, covering but not hiding the darkest and foulest traits of character, and constraining us to admire the actor, though we detest the guilt. She never makes merit ludicrous or contemptible, by connecting it with those low or ridiculous qualities, which are offensive to taste; or vice attractive by a graceful garb, which engages our interest, though we feel angry with ourselves for permitting it to do so. She never relates a deed of villainy in that cool way, which makes us feel some doubt, whether the author do not rather admire than otherwise, what he treats so much as a matter of course. She does not look only among the cultivated and the intellectual for fine traits of humanity, nor shrink with sickly fastidiousness from virtue in humble life. . . . Our author . . . has been a keen observer of life and manners, and in accordance with the noble sentiment of Terence, has felt herself interested in whatever relates to humanity, and has learned to contemplate man as one of a species, separate from all adventitious distinctions. We regard her sketches of humble life as among the most felicitious portions of her works; strong, but not coarse, and full of sense, feeling, truth, and the nicest observation, reminding us in this last particular, of the minute accuracy of one of Wilkie's inimitable pictures. She depends for the interest of her stories rather upon the lowly and unobtrusive virtues, which are felt in the hours and minutes of life, gentle firmness, noiseless benevolence, and modest self-respect, than upon the more dazzling qualities, which can seldom be displayed in the common run of events, and if often exerted, give to the character an air of theatrical affectation. This heartiness of moral feeling gives to her works that kind of charm, which an amiable expression gives to a fine countenance, heightening the beauty of every agreeable feature, and making us overlook those which nature has less carefully moulded. We feel that we can cordially admire with a good conscience. No shadow of pity or regret for powers misapplied glides by to break the spell that charms us. We have no sublime free-thinkers, who boldly attack every thing that man holds sacred, no selfish misanthropes, who dare to hate the creatures God has made, no elegant ruffians rewarded with a fortune and a mistress instead of a halter, but the good man is honored and the villain punished. Our author never separates the tie that unites virtue and happiness, vice and misery, which succeed each other as invariably as thunder follows lightning or as spring comes after winter. But she deserves more than the praise which a virtuous heathen might have won; she has told us of the beauty and excellency of religion, and spoken to us in the name of Jesus of Nazareth. We venture to say, that there are few books which make better Sunday reading than hers. Her religion is no stern-eyed Moloch, with brow of gloom and voice of denunciation,—it requires the sacrifice of no natural affections, and frowns upon no innocent pleasures. It is a beautiful and gentle spirit, mingling with the every-day concerns of life, giving new charms to joy, and a touching grace to the wan countenance of sorrow, 'gilding with heavenly alchemy' feelings whose home and birthplace is earth, brightening the golden links of the chain that binds man to his brother man, wafting to our senses the ambrosial airs of Paradise, and scattering gleams from a land of enduring brightness over the dark places of our mortal pilgrimage. The Spirit she worships is a spirit of love, heard in the still small voice as well as in the whirlwind and the thunder, and seen in the rainbow and the dew-drop as well as in the lightning and the cataract, whose temple is nature, for whom the stars burn incense and the sleepless ocean murmurs deep applause, who binds up the wounds of a broken heart, and guides the water-fowl to his reed-sheltered nest. She does not fall into that fatally common fault, of flattering human vanity by representing the mind as able to do every thing of itself, to fight down all opposition, to keep a well-poised equilibrium in all situations by its own unaided energies, and to climb to the highest sphere of virtue alone and unguided. . . . [Among] the champions of the good cause, who are yet true to God and virtue, the author of *Clarence* deserves an elevated rank.

Clarence is a tale of our own times, descriptive of the manners of the present day and of this country. An author who delineates events among which the reader himself might, without any violation of probability, have been an actor, has much to struggle against, and yet something to favor him; and perhaps it would be difficult to say which side of the balance preponderates. (pp. 76-80)

Our objection to [the story] are grounded on the opinion that it is unnatural and improbable, and that the author has attempted to do what the highest genius could not accomplish, to give a highly romantic interest to events occurring is our own prosaic age and country. One thing does not follow another in the natural and easy order in which the real world goes on, but the changes are brought about by means not impossible to be sure, but such as would startle and astonish us in the highest degree, were we to see them really take place. The incidents by which the *denouement* is attained, depend often upon a succession of contingencies, any one of which would seem surprising, but whose coincidence falls hardly short of the miraculous. (p. 84)

Every reader of *Clarence* must have been struck with the violation of [the laws of fiction]. Extraordinary events are continually brought about by extraordinary occurrences, and our surprise is continually called forth by the happening of incidents, which we did not expect even a page or two before. This, as a general rule, is a defect in a novel, though a merit in a drama. It is not impossible, for example, that an old man and a child should be attracted towards each other in the crowd of a populous city, and should form a devoted friendship; that the former should learn that he was the grandfather of his young favorite, and this too from the lips of the faithless wretch, to whom he had many years before intrusted his son and a part of his fortune, and who by successive changes had come to be his fellow-lodger in an obscure boarding-house in New-York: but surely all this is very improbable, and would have been regarded as miraculous, if it had really occurred. The events at Trenton Falls must, we fear, fall under the same censure. (p. 85)

The *denouement* of a novel is the part which most severely tries an author's ingenuity; for it is very possible that a story may have been skilfully constructed to a certain point, and then be wound up in the most hurried and clumsy manner, reminding us of the placid flow of a river till it reaches a cliff, over which it throws itself in foam and thunder. And here we cannot congratulate our author upon her success. A most cumbrous mass of machinery is employed to disengage and bring to a point the tangled threads of her story; plot is set against plot, manœuvre put in opposition to manœuvre, and we are hurried on through so tortuous a maze of policy, that we involuntarily take a long breath by way of relief, when the ladies are finally restored to the arms off the true knights. (p. 87)

The story, with all its faults, is eminently free from the unpardonable sin of dulness. It is, in fact, highly interesting,

perhaps the more so from the romantic coloring thrown over it, and the occasional violations of strict probability. The variety of adventures, the rapid changes of scene, the succession of incidents, never permit the attention to flag for a moment; and though we are conducted to our journey's end by a circuitous route, it is one 'so green and so full of goodly prospects on every side,' that we quite forget our fatigue in the pleasant scenes that open around us. There are some delightful episodes scattered along the narrative . . . whose merit the reader will find out for himself. We were particularly pleased with the description of Abeille and his abode—an oasis of verdure amid a desert of brick pavements and dead walls—his own buoyant temperament proof against that keenest arrow in fortune's quiver, the recollection in poverty of former wealth and splendor. The laughing beauty of his daughter, graceful and merry as one of her own canary-birds, the tempter that enters this Eden of peace, the struggle in the heart of poor Angelique, and her happy deliverance from the snares of the seducer, are sketched with exquisite fidelity; and over all is shed that nameless charm arising from true sensibility and feminine tenderness of feeling, for which all the scenes of our author, in which the workings of the affections are pourtrayed, are so remarkable. The history of Louis Seton (with the exception of, now and then, a little high-flown extravagance) is beautifully told, and the tale of his melancholy fortunes runs like a thread of sable, through the chequered web of the narrative. (p. 88)

If there are any who agree with us in our opinion, that the best part of a novel consists in its sketches of character, they will find a great deal to admire in *Clarence*. The author has gone through the high-ways and bye-ways of life and filled her sketch-book with copies of nature, and by decomposing and combining these anew, she has given us a great variety of characters, each of which has the distinctness of the individuality and the fresh coloring of nature; and yet none of them, (as far as we know) are representatives of any living being. We feel in reading the book, that we have certainly seen this person and been acquainted with that one, but we cannot tell when or where, and in endeavoring to remember, we feel that puzzling sensation attendant upon the effort to recall the effaced images of a dream. In the character of the heroine, (for as in gallantry bound, we assign her the first place,) the author has accomplished what few would have the courage to attempt, and still fewer the talent to execute; namely, the making her principal female character interesting without great personal beauty. We can hardly conceive of a heroine without beauty any more than we can of a star without brightness, or a rose without fragrance, and even Jeanie Deans, universal favorite as she is, is regarded as but a fine exception to a general rule. Miss Clarence is well defined by the author herself, as a 'heroine of the nineteenth century.' She has the strong sense, the quiet energy, the pure-toned feeling, the absence of affectation, extravagance, and mawkish sentimentality, which would secure the highest esteem and admiration in real life, and which enable her to act with decision and success in situations where some young ladies we have read of would only have screamed and fainted away. When we were first introduced to her, we were afraid she was going to be one of those pattern-women, who never do any thing wrong, and who make the worst imaginable heroines, because we know that in whatever circumstances they may be placed, they will do and say exactly what is most proper; but we were refreshed by perceiving, on a little further acquaintance, that she could now and then commit an amiable indiscretion, and be hurried by her warm-hearted impulses out of the pale of rigid prudence. The author has shewn no little skill in suffering her fine traits of character to be developed by circumstances, and in leaving the reader to form his own opinion without continually challenging his admiration, and this makes the lady herself far more interesting; for there is a great charm in those characters that keep something in reserve, and shew new excellencies to meet the call of new emergencies. We regard her as quite superior to the hero, though he is a very fine fellow, spirited, high-minded, self-forgetting, and with 'all good grace to grace a gentleman.' He richly deserves the happiness that falls to his lot, but he has not that charm of individuality which Miss Clarence so eminently possesses. He seems to be merely one of a species, a promising young man about town. We hear rather too much of his white teeth, his flashing eyes, and his noble bearing, and we feel almost afraid that he must himself have participated in the general admiration which his graces and accomplishments excited. But the hero of a modern novel is always the least important personage in it, and all that is required of him is, that he should be young, handsome, and brave, bow gracefully, and speak good English.

Mrs. Layton is the most brilliant and effective character in the book, and the perfect success with which she is conceived and embodied, discovers no inconsiderable portion of genius and inventive power. From the first to the last, she is the same finished piece of art. She wears elegance like a mantle, and to be graceful and *recherchée,* costs her no more effort than to move and breathe. Her conversation and letters are full of that sparkling originality, which arises from the union of wit in conceiving, and taste in expressing thoughts. She has made the art of pleasing a study, and has neglected nothing which may contribute to entire success. She can encourage the diffident, flatter the vain, amuse the grave, instruct the gay, and adapt herself so dexterously to the tastes and opinions of all she talks with, as to make each one imagine himself an object of particular interest to her. She has seen enough of mankind to be able to discover with ease the assailable points in the characters of those whom she wishes to influence, and knows enough of books to quote opportunely and give her opinions confidently; yet to a superficial observer, she might seem to have studied man as profoundly as Bacon or Tacitus, and to possess a mind enriched by tributes from every province in the realms of thought. She is armed cap-a-pie for the encounter of wits, and possesses every weapon requisite for the mimic jousts of a drawing-room, the sparkling repartee, the keen-edged, yet sheathed rebuke, the disguised compliment, the gay *bon mot,* the pensive sentiment. She can employ them all with the happiest effect, wound without seeming to wound, and charm we know not why. Yet with all this, she is deficient in every thing that makes a person truly respectable and praise-worthy. She has not a spark of genuine feeling nor a ray of genuine sense, and has not read one page of the true philosophy of life, that philosophy which feeds the mind with thoughts of beauty, and stamps upon the heart sweet images of love. She fears nothing but ridicule, and worships nothing but opinion. She bows to the golden calf of fashion, and neglecting the unchanging forms of things, watches the shadows of the clouds that pass over them. She is so exquisitely selfish as to sacrifice the affections of others to her own tastes, and she would not hesitate to gratify her slightest whim, though at every step she crushed a human heart. This portrait is drawn with a master hand, and what is peculiarly excellent in it is, that in our admiration of her fine powers, we never cease to lament and pity their perversion. No young lady could ever wish to be like Mrs. Layton, and no one can read her history without learning from it a valuable lesson. We have heard many people express surprise, that the author should have made Gerald Roscoe, a young man of so

much moral purity, (and the young have the least charity for the unprincipled,) so great an admirer of Mrs. Layton, especially as the latter was so little of a hypocrite, and so openly avowed her contempt for things which most people regard as sacred. But no one will object to this, who knows the amount of the influence exerted by a fascinating married woman upon a young imaginative mind, and how possible it is for the strongest and purest natures to be, like Tassos's hero, caught in the toils spread by an artful Armida.

We do not think the character of Pedrillo a very successful effort. He is rather common-place, and has nothing to distinguish him from all the genteel scoundrels that act by 'insinuation and not by bluster.' There is too much of the bragger and bravo about him. He reminds us of a vulgar actor, who rants the louder, and gesticulates the more vehemently as the plot deepens, and the storm grows darker around him. He is a mere tyro in knavery, for the foppery of his dress and the *góut de spectacle* which runs through his air and manners, are the things most calculated to draw the attention of others towards him, and make him an object of suspicion; while the very first effort of a complete knave is to throw people entirely off their guard by an affectation of great plainness and sincerity. He has not the fabled power of the basilisk to slay silently, but his rattles betray him as he moves to his work of death. (pp. 90-3)

There are a number of well-drawn characters besides these, which our limits will hardly permit us to mention. There is Emilie Layton, graceful and lovely as a wood-nymph, pure as a dew-drop, and full of sweetness, feeling and truth: in every thing presenting a most delightful contrast to her artificial and heartless mother. And there is Mr. D. Flint, (whose feelings we will not wound by writing his name at full length,) for whom we have a great deal more respect than we could have supposed possible when we were first acquainted with him. He is a very fair specimen of a Yankee adventurer, and it would be well for New-England if all those of her children who have his bustling perseverence, his impudence, and his self-complacency, had also his honesty, his warmth of heart and his rectitude of principle. Let us not forget that gentle carpet-knight Major Daisy, whose warlike *prænomen* was won, as you may guess, in no desperate fight, and who in all his campaigns never suffered any greater inconvenience, than that of a slight ducking, and never encountered a more dangerous foe than a restive horse. Long may he live, and have no rival near the throne in his judgment of shawls, perfumes, and laces, and may the next lady to whom he offers his illustrious self, have more taste than Gertrude Clarence.

We close our imperfect notice by cordially recommending this novel to the reading public, and we would even beg those who, as a general rule, avoid works of modern fiction, to make an exception in this instance. We are proud of our distinguished countrywoman, and regard her works as an honor to our land; and the reason that we have spoken so much of the faults of **Clarence** and dwelt so sparingly upon its beauties, is, that the latter bear so large a proportion to the former, and are in themselves so striking, that no reader of common apprehension can help finding them out and admiring them for himself. We are grateful to her for the pleasure she has afforded us, and would beg her to continue her labors in the neglected vineyard of American fiction; to paint the glorious scenery of her own native land and the virtues of its children, to tell us of the nobleness of its sons, and the beauty of its daughters, and 'to hold the mirror up to every shape of life and every hue of opinion.' Let her not attempt to give a highly romantic coloring to her plots, for the web of life in our Western world is too coarse to bear the embroidery of romance. Nor let her attempt to give a highly dramatic effect to detached scenes and particular situations, for the power of doing this is a gift bestowed upon very few, and much as we admire the author of *Clarence,* we are constrained to say that she is not one of them. Her excellence consists in her strong sense, her feminine feeling, her powers of description, her vigorous and beautiful English, the touching eloquence with which she pleads the cause of humanity, and above all, the keenness of her observation and her skill in delineating the lights and shadows of character. She has but to look around her to find an ample field for the exercise of her talents;—she may find abundant food for speculation in the Protean forms which society assumes in our wide continent,—in the gay throngs that chase amusement from one watering-place to another, and in the lowly virtues that cluster round our farm-house hearths, and, like flowers that twine around the living rock, give beauty and fragrance to the hardest and coarsest forms of life. To the writer of fiction, whose *forte* is character-drawing, we know of no land like ours, whether we regard the extent of our territory, the variety of the stocks from which we sprung, the youthful and electric vigor with which the veins of our world are filled, and the unchecked freedom with which it is our unvalued privilege to act and think. The face of society has not by long attention been ground down to one uniform level, and vigorous and fantastic shoots of character are not nipped by the frost of hoary convention. The mountain-wind is not more free to blow, than is each man to indulge his wildest whims. And as the harvest is plenty, so are the laborers few;—the materials of romance in the old world are waxing threadbare, but the charm of unworn freshness is here like morning-dew. We would call upon all the sons and daughters of genius to be up and doing, and we would entreat the author of *Clarence* in particular, to persevere in the course she has so successfully entered upon, for her own sake and her country's sake. (pp. 93-5)

> [W. Hillard], in a review of "Clarence; or, A Tale of Our Own Times," in The North American Review, Vol. XXXII, No. 70, January, 1831, pp. 73-95.

[EDGAR ALLAN POE]   (essay date 1835)

[*Considered one of America's most outstanding men of letters, Poe was a distinguished poet, novelist, essayist, journalist, short story writer, editor, and critic. Poe stressed an analytical, rather than emotive, approach to literature and emphasized the specifics of style and construction in a work, instead of concentrating solely on the importance of ideological statement. In the following review of* The Linwoods, *Poe highly recommends the novel, but contends that it is not a masterpiece. For additional commentary by Poe, see excerpt dated 1846.*]

Miss Sedgwick is one among of few American writers who have risen by merely their own intrinsic talents, and without the *a priori* aid of foreign opinion and puffery, to any exalted rank in the estimation of our countrymen. She is at the same time fully deserving of all the popularity she has attained. By those who are most fastidious in matters of literary criticism, the author of *Hope Leslie* is the most ardently admired, and we are acquainted with few persons of sound and accurate discrimination who would hesitate in placing her upon a level with the best of our native novelists. Of American *female* writers we must consider her the first. The character of her pen is essentially feminine. No *man* could have written *Hope*

Leslie; and no man, we are assured, can arise from the perusal of *The Linwoods* without a full conviction that his own abilities would have proved unequal to the delicate yet picturesque handling; the grace, warmth, and radiance; the exquisite and judicious filling in, of the volumes which have so enchanted him. Woman is, after all, the only true painter of that gentle and beautiful mystery, the heart of woman. She is the only proper Scheherazade for the fairy tales of love.

We think *The Linwoods* superior to *Hope Leslie,* and superior to *Redwood.* It is full of deep natural interest, rivetting attention without undue or artificial means for attaining that end. It contains nothing forced, or in any degree exaggerated. Its prevailing features are equability, ease, perfect accuracy and purity of style, a manner never at *outrance* with the subject matter, pathos, and verisimilitude. It cannot, however, be considered as ranking with the master novels of the day. It is neither an *Eugene Aram,* nor a *Contarini Fleming.*

The Linwoods has few—indeed no pretensions to a connected plot of any kind. . . . [In] the creation of Bessie Lee, Miss Sedgwick has given evidence not to be disputed, of a genius far more than common. We do not hesitate to call it a truly beautiful and original conception, evincing imagination of the highest order. It is the old story of a meek and trusting spirit bowed down to the dust by the falsehood of a deceiver. But in the narration of Miss Sedgwick it becomes a magical tale, and bursts upon us with all the freshness of novel emotion. (pp. 57-8)

Jasper Meredith, considered as an actual entity, is . . . a heartless, calculating coxcomb—with merely a spice of what we may call susceptibility to impressions of the beautiful, to redeem him from utter contempt. As a character in a novel, he is admirable—because he is accurately true to nature, and to himself. His perfidy to Bessie (we shall never forget Bessie) meets with poetical justice in a couple of unsuccessful courtships, (in each of which the villain's heart is in some degree concerned,) and in a final marriage with a flirt, Helen Ruthven, who fills him up, with a vengeance, the full measure of his deserts. Mrs. Meredith is a striking picture of the heartless and selfish woman of fashion and aristocracy. Kisel, the servant of Eliot Lee, is original, and is, next to Bessie, the best conception in the book. He is a simple, childish, yet acute and affectionate fool, who follows his master as would a dog, and finally dies at his feet under circumstances of the truest pathos. While Miss Sedgwick can originate such characters as these, she need apprehend few rivals near the throne. . . .

So much real pleasure have we derived from the perusal of *The Linwoods,* that we can hardly find it in our hearts to pick a quarrel with the fair author, for the very few trifling inadvertences into which she has been betrayed. There were, we believe, some points at which we intended to cavil, but not having pencilled them down in the course of perusal, they have now escaped our recollection. Somewhat more energy in occasional passages—somewhat less diffuseness in others—would operate, we think, to the improvement of Miss Sedgwick's generally excellent *style.* Now and then, we meet with a discrepancy between the words and the character of a speaker. For example: "'No more of my contempt for the Yankees, Hal, an' thou lovest me,' replied Jasper; 'you remember Æsop's advice to Crœsus, at the Persian court?' 'No, I am sure I do not. You have the most provoking way of resting the lever by which you bring out your own knowledge, on your friend's ignorance.'" Now all this is very pretty, but it is not the language of school-boys. (p. 58)

There are one or two other trifles with which we have to find fault. Putnam's deficiency in spelling is, perhaps, a little burlesqued; and the imaginary note written to Eliot Lee, is not in accordance with that laconic epistle subsequently introduced, and which was a *bonâ fide* existence. We dislike the death of Kisel—that is we dislike its occuriring so soon—indeed we see no necessity for killing him at all. His end is beautifully managed, but leaves a kind of uneasy and painful impression, which a judicious writer will be chary of exciting. We must quarrel also, with some slight liberties taken with the King's English. Miss Sedgwick has no good authority for the use of such verbs, as "to ray." "They had all heard of Squire Saunders, whose fame rayed through a large circle." Also, "The next morning he called, his kind heart raying out through his jolly face, to present me to General Washington." Nor is she justifiable in making use of the verb "incense," with the meaning attached to it in the following sentence. "Miss Ruthven seemed like an humble worshipper, incensing two divinities." We dislike also, the vulgarity of such a phrase as "I put in my oar"—meaning "I joined in the conversation"—especially in the mouth of so well-bred a lady, as Miss Isabella Linwood.... But we are heartily ashamed of finding fault with such trifles, and should certainly not have done so, had there been a possibility of finding fault with any thing of more consequence. We recommend *The Linwoods* to all persons of taste. But let none others touch it. (pp.58-9)

> [*Edgar Allan Poe*], *"The Linwoods,"* in The Southern Literary Messenger, *Vol. II, No. 8, December, 1835, pp. 57-9.*

THE AMERICAN MONTHLY MAGAZINE   (essay date 1836)

> [*In this excerpt from a survey of Sedgwick's novels, the critic discusses the American spirit of her works and focuses on the instructive elements of* Home *as an example of her attempts to create a national literature.*]

"I should as soon think of galloping through paradise as down one of Miss Sedgwick's pages," was the reply of a reader of [*The Linwoods; or, "Sixty Years Since" in America*], on being accused of making slow progress in the book. And the expression does beautiful justice to that characterstic gracefulness, which, having relations we cannot define with the heart, compels us to linger over the creations of this author. We feel, while under her spell, like the child of the German tale, listening to the story of nature from the little tenant of the woods; we "would hear more and more, and for ever."

It is not Miss Sedgwick's great gift to contrive the incidents of a story. It is, however, true, that she does not give us the old hackneyed routine. But in avoiding this, her drama wants a regular beginning, middle, and end; it is often improbable, and sometimes inconsistent; and we never read one of her stories without smiling at a certain spirit of adventure, which always comes out somewhere in the conduct of her young girls; two or three of whom, in this story of the Linwoods, she sends across a river at midnight, in a thunder-storm, for no better reason than that one of them wants to be with her lover a little while longer; and, although the despatch of the flight, one would think, would be considered the all-important particular of an escape from prison! The reader of her works will recall, in this connexion, Hope Leslie's voyage over the harbor with an Indian boatman; and the midnight walk of Miss Clarence, alone, upon Trenton Falls; and some other adventuresome movements. But let the incidents be granted, and Miss Sedgwick puts such charming people into them, and makes them talk and act so characteristically, and with such *ideal* propriety, that, in our sympathy with their just and natural feelings, we forget they are in improbable situations.

Moreover, this defect, if it is one, is connected with what is to New-Englanders the chief charm of her books. This innocently free action grows out of her complete New-Englandism. She has embodied, as no other of our writers has, the spirit of her native soil; a spirit evolved so inevitably out of the elements of human nature, as it has been peculiarly nurtured and inwardly restrained in this section of our country, that we are sure it could not be seized and expressed—we had almost said it cannot be believed in, by those who live where Custom has laid down her "frosty weight" of conventional etiquette; or where a general laxity of moral principle leaves the passions to flourish, till they seem to be all that is natural in human nature.... And who but a New-Englander could believe in Aunt Debby and her moral influence? or realize that Elliot Lee's manly independence, and persevering enaction of principle, are but a specimen of the early life and general career of almost all our professional men—those who have given the tone to our society? What people but our own are so happy as to know that there is no reason in their political condition, or the prevailing sentiment, to prevent every mechanic in the United States from being such a dignified housekeeper, refined father, and high-toned citizen, as William Barclay; and having even such a paradise as his home? Yet *we* know, that so far as any interference of rules and customs would operate among us, "the course of true love may run smooth," and the farmer's son wed the wealthy and far-descended, and the latter feel honored thereby; that there are Hope Leslies to be found, not merely in our castles in the air, but on our terra firma; that Ellen Bruce is still more common; that almost every town might furnish a Jane Elton; and that where such dreams of beauty are embodied among us as Bessie Lee—and sometimes there are—should they become, like her, the victims of imagination,—just so unharmed might they pass through our land, and find, in Yankee blacksmiths, a refinement which, springing from a deeper source than "high breeding," might put to shame, in the efficiency of its protection, the worn-out mock-chivalry of fashionable Europe. (pp. 15-16)

For the cultivated society . . . is that in which Miss Sedgwick's mind was nurtured. Here her sensibility to the pure and good, her fine powers of observation on character, and her thoughts on social institutions, have been exercised into a vigorous maturity, without her losing, in the cultivation of her taste, the fresh, fearless innocence of thought and feeling which she embodies in her heroines, and which carries them "through the burning ploughshares of this wicked world, unshod and unharmed, like the good Queen Emma" of the English legend. It will be acknowledged that if these fearless actions are necessary to show how essentially pure and harmless is the social atmosphere, they are not, on the whole, to be considered as defects, in works whose principal aim seems to be to describe surrounding society, only so far idealizing it, as to have all that is best within it make its full impression and have its full moral influence.

It was not, however, merely to vindicate the unrulableness in which Miss Sedgwick sometimes indulges her heroines, who are ever "pure in the last recesses of the heart," that these remarks have been made on New England society and its literature. Miss Sedgwick's works begin to claim a higher place than that of elegant literature. She is evidently a republican writer, in a department which has hitherto been devoted to glorifying the spirit of feudalism, and its consequent false views; and which has certainly never before been made a refracting atmosphere to diffuse the light of our institutions over the whole surface of our society, though so admirably adapted to this purpose. (p. 20)

[We] see in all her works, and especially in [*Home*], the marks of a true genius for commencing a literature for the mass of the American people which shall bring up their moral tone to the spirit of their institutions. Her mind appreciates the peculiar dignity of republicanism, and her heart rejoices in its enacted poetry. She perceives how naturally this form of society weds Christianity; and with what self-respecting loyalty it rejoices to obey the sacred oracles of its holy and beautiful bride, ever at hand to be consulted, in the simple temple of Family; that only earthly shrine which God's own hands did ever erect for man to worship in.

This temple of worship she represents also as the school of the homely virtues. Here she would have the courteous bearing of Americans toward each other, whether in or out of Congress halls, to be taught them. Not in the fencing school or the court, but at the humble table, and in the little parlour of the mechanic, grace and urbanity are to be learnt; by more efficient means than the sound of the dancing master's fiddlestick and the prescribed mummeries of a master of court ceremonies—even by the voice of parental affection, making music with the heart—obedience of filial and fraternal love; the forms of politeness being left to sense and nature, governed and restrained as these are by such discipline as William Barclay bestowed upon Wallace, and such motherly hints as his excellent wife gave to her children at table, and to the self-relying Alice, when she would have spoken harshly of the deficiency of working ability in the unfortunate Emily Norton. She would have young men stimulated to the moral glory of patriotic duty, by such mothers as Elliot Lee's, and such sisters as Isabella Linwood, who precede them in sacrifice; restraining their own instinctive impulses by conscientious inquiry into the first principles of action for a man and a citizen, and letting no feminine weakness choke the clear tones of encouragement with which they advise to obey the dictates of moral rectitude, although themselves are to be left, while their sons and brothers are away at the war and the national councils. Here, also, would she have still more private virtues and vices dealt with. The reckless gambler is to be punished as Jane Elton punished Erskine, by plucking out her own heart-cherished fancy, and turning from the semblance of the home offered her by a selfish lover, to the unshared duty of a village school-room, where she could still act according to her own views of right with none to hinder. (How we wish the author had left her there!) Intemperance and all its horrors she would bring more terribly to the heart, because more truly than through visions of demons in the distil-houses and breweries, by pouring the soul-poison down the throat of the skinner Hewson, as the only specific for destroying the last sparks of humanity, and making him the wild beast that could tear her *blind* children from the arms of their mother. And how is all "Liberator"-vituperation put to shame by the genuine argument to the heart and understanding that goes forth from the faithful services of the freed-negro Rose! Even when Miss Sedgwick seems to take the least pains to inculcate a moral, a moral spirit breathes from all her pages: and it is a beautiful, glowing, creative, moral spirit, that not only goes back to repent with Redwood over the past, but with Elliot Lee and William Barclay, goes forward to sanctify the new forms of political and social condition in which it finds itself. What a

morning glow of youth comes from her pages! they ring with the laugh of childhood, whose echoes die away in the softer music of humanity, from the low heart-touched tones of youthful tenderness, and the subdued bass voices of time-chastened sorrows. (pp. 21-2)

In the story *Home* Miss Sedgwick gives herself more scope for direct moral inculation; and we prefer this form, therefore, to that of the more technical novel, for we are sure she never can fall into a bald didactic. Her works are not architectures of stone, and wood, and other dead material; a style of writing adapted to guide other ends. Her productions grow up like the trees and the flowers; and if the forms are not strictly everlasting, yet they live, (the former a long time,) and the most transient of the latter leave a deathless perfume to those who will extract their essence.

We might sustain this remark by references to particular touches of moral sensibility, laying open principles that may be applied to every day's actions, and lend a daily beauty to the most common life, for such abound in these volumes; but we prefer that our readers should seek them for themselves in frequent re-perusals, and shall now bring to a close our desultory hints of our delight in what Miss Sedgwick has already done, and our sense of her fitness for the work she has commenced; for we trust that *Home* is but the commencement of a series. Many subjects there touched upon are not exhausted. The excellent hint for assisting the poor, is but one of many that she would know how to give, adapted to other places than New-York city: for the phases which poverty, and the ignorance which so often produces it, take, vary with the location; in this connexion she could also set forth the precise relation which some necessary public institutions of benevolence ought to hold to the conscience of the people. For Insane Hospitals for the Poor, Blind Asylums, Infirmaries for the Sick, &c., are not only to be supported in this country by private subscription and bequest, but to be administered in a more philosophic and reflective spirit than in those countries where the blind spirit of Catholic almsgiving has moulded all the methods, and pointed out but low ends of charity. Nor could any one, better than herself, illustrate the new relations of master and servant among us, as may be seen from Barclay's management of Martha. And this is unfortunate; for the rich are yet to learn that if they are to be exempted from manual labor, it must be by sharing more equally with those that serve them their wealth;—and those who serve are to learn, at the same time, that, as their privileges rise, and their means of comfort and improvement are enlarged, their sense of duty is to grow more refined, and their service to be more faithful, hearty, and intelligent. Both parties need to have more just views as to what is of essential value, and what is illusion. Perhaps it is but reasonable to believe that what has been called the lower class will prove quite as apt pupils in this new philosophy of life, as those who think themselves the highest. . . . Manufacturing life itself, and the moral dangers and duties it involves, also need illustration. And the New-England school system is yet to be recommended to immense tracts of country that are fast filling up with population, but are making no provision for the cultivation of the judgment of millions of the voters,—and it may be of the legislators and civil officers—of the next generation.

Principles of our institutions, yet deeper than any we have mentioned, occur to us as rich subjects. The abstract perfection of our constitution makes it of itself less affecting to the unreasoning mind than one founded on secondary principles would be. It takes only the sentiment of devotion, which is common enough in human nature to bind the soldier to his banner, the subject of a king to his sense-dazzling master. The lust of his eyes comes in aid of his loyalty. But the sovereign who is to enlist the loyalty of this people is an abstract Existence, to be apprehended only by the better part of our nature. It is law, the law that descends from heaven and abides in the moral region; and which must be clothed by the heart, in order that it may be loved as well as respected; while the lower propensities of our nature must not be allowed to dethrone it, in order to place a blind, headlong, selfish will in its place. It is true, our political writers, from the high-souled, pure-hearted, conscience-clear Quincy, down through all who have written in the various departments of Political Economy and Legislation, even to Webster, . . . have been most truly inspired with an ever-present aim of making political constitution and legislative enactment "coincident with the moral code." But these works are such pure reasonings from first principles, that they are too hard reading to be the popular recreation of our community, who generally take up books only as a pastime. Therefore, although the duties of republicans to the constitution and laws which secure their rights, have been reasoned on and set forth by the framers of our government and their successors in the judicial and legal profession, in lucid arguments, filled with the glowing spirit of a truly humane liberty, the mass of our population is growing up ignorant of the true views which should possess a professedly self-governed nation. Never, therefore, was the feminine genius, whose nature it is to apply principle to domestic and social action, and, like spring and summer, to breathe beauty into and over the sublime but wintry outlines of the political system drawn over by masculine power;—never, we repeat, was feminine genius before called to a work of such far-reaching beneficence as this one,—to accomplish which Miss Sedgwick has given us by her two last works an earnest of her power. To those who think we exaggerate the importance of this work, we would refer to that often repeated saying of a deep thinker—"let me make the ballads of a people, and I care not who makes the laws;" an aphorism whose spirit is more applicable to a government like ours than it can be to any other, since the laws which the people themselves make, will most assuredly flow out of their ballads. And when the writer whom we are calling upon remembers, that each of her "ballads" is to be a whole of itself, and of no very large dimensions, we trust she will perceive that a very great moral object may be attained, with the same ease to herself that has always characterized her efforts hitherto; nor feel her modesty alarmed that she is summoned to the work by the unanimous voice of an admiring public. (pp. 22-5)

> *"The Novels of Miss Sedgwick," in* The American Monthly Magazine, *Vol. VII, January, 1836, pp. 15-25.*

THE NORTH AMERICAN REVIEW   (essay date 1836)

[*In the following review of* The Linwoods, *the critic expresses admiration for its historical setting and moral intent.*]

We think [*The Linwoods*] the most agreeable that Miss Sedgwick has yet published. It is written throughout with the same good taste and quiet unpretending power, which characterize all her productions, and is superior to most of them in the variety of the characters brought into action and the interest of the fable. It also possesses the great additional attraction, that it carries us back to the period of the revolutionary war, the heroic age of our country, which, although only sixty years distant, begins already to wear in the eyes of the degenerate

money-making men of the present times, a poetical, we had almost said fabulous aspect, and consequently offers the finest scenes and materials for romance.

The fair and unaffectedly modest author disclaims in the preface any competition which might seem to be suggested by the title with the "sixty years since" of the great Scottish enchanter; but it is nevertheless certain that the plan has something of the same general character, and the work, though executed with less power, possesses in part the same charm. It spreads before us a map of New York, the young emporium of our western world, now rivalling in wealth, population, splendor and luxury, the proudest capitals of Europe; as she was in her day of small things, a few Dutch-built streets interspersed with gardens and grouped round the battery. We visit the encampment of Washington, nor has our author shrunk from the somewhat hazardous attempt to introduce into her group of characters the grand figure of the hero himself. In this enterprise, she has on the whole acquitted herself with success. There is no attempt at effect in any of the scenes where Washington appears, but the propriety of his character is always well sustained. Miss Sedgwick has also transported us to the interior of one of the quiet villages of New England, and has delineated very happily from the living models around her, the simple virtues, which then as now distinguished their inhabitants, and at that period were heightened into heroism by a universal, all-absorbing devotion to country. Upon this rich canvas of historical fact, our author has embroidered a very ingeniously contrived and pleasantly told story, diversified, as we have said, with rather more than the usual variety of incidents and characters. Of heroes and heroines the supply is ample, there being, independently of Washington, Lafayette and their illustrious companions in arms, not less than three of each class. The work is wound off by three well assorted marriages. The party dissensions of the day afford a very convenient and natural machinery for creating the distress of the story, and keeping the lovers asunder for the necessary length of time. Some of the characters are well drawn. Isabella Linwood is a splendid vision. Bessie, though we suspect, a favorite with the author, is not quite so much so with us; nor has Kizel secured a very high place in our good graces. (pp. 160-61)

We take our leave of Miss Sedgwick, on this as on every former occasion of the same kind, with feelings of unmixed gratitude for the entertainment afforded by her works, and for the favorable moral influence which they exercise upon the community. If her literary power be somewhat less than that of her illustrious English prototype, Miss Edgeworth, the moral strain of her writings is of a yet higher cast. There are some appearances in the present state of learning, which seem to show that the ladies are taking the department of novel-writing into their own hands, and if they would all manage it with the ability, taste and discretion of our author, we cannot say that we should deeply regret the revolution. (p. 194)

> *A review of "The Linwoods; or, Sixty Years Since in America," in* The North American Review, *Vol. XLII, No. 90, January, 1836, pp. 160-95.*

THE SOUTHERN LITERARY MESSENGER   (essay date 1837)

[*In the following laudatory review of* The Poor Rich Man, *and the* Rich Poor Man, *the critic compares Sedgwick to the English novelist Maria Edgeworth, citing their mutual skill at narration and characterization and focusing on the realism that dominates Sedgwick's work.*]

Miss Sedgwick, beyond all question, is the Edgeworth of America. For skill in the art of interweaving the most impressive moral lessons, with trains of incident that rivet the attention and pass irresistibly home to the heart,—for narratives at once natural, simple, touching, and so contrived that no one can rise from the perusal without feeling himself elevated and improved,—and for the truest and happiest exhibitions of character, discriminated exactly according to sex, age, condition, and country,—our country-woman has, in our judgment, no equal on this side of the Atlantic. So just and so captivating are her portraitures of New England manners and character, that if she only had that personal acquaintance and consequent personal standing in the South, which Miss Edgeworth has long enjoyed in England,—so as to make her writings current here,—she might be expected to do as much towards dispelling our ackowledged and indisputable prejudices against the North, as Miss Edgeworth has done towards raising the Irish character, in English eyes. And if she but knew, from familiar personal observation, those good points of *Southern* life, which are either wholly unknown or have been shamefully misrepresented, to the mass of her immediate countrymen,—she might, with her uncommon powers, work a change not less salutary, in *their* feelings towards us of the South. In being the messenger of Truth, between two people whose animosities nearly all arise from ignorance of each other's real merits, she would be the messenger of Peace and Love. . . .

We are disposed to speak . . . [very] strongly in praise of **The Poor Rich Man, and The Rich Poor Man.**

It is a story, mostly, of humble life. Morris Finley, having by sordid means acquired wealth which neither he nor his proud, vain wife,—still less their spoiled and silly daughter—knows how to enjoy rationally or to use beneficently,—and feeling, therefore, more than the curse of poverty,—is justly called "The Poor Rich Man." Harry Aikin, as justly and as quaintly, is called "The Rich Poor Man;" because amid toilsome penury, he and a wife likeminded with himself, not only live happily, rearing up their children to virtue and industry, but contrive to extend helps to the needy around them, which might put many whose incomes are thousands, to the blush. (p. 331)

Not the least merit of the work is, that never once, (to the best of our belief) is *vraisemblance* violated—'the modesty of Nature' overstepped. There is not a fact, which may not well have occurred: not a sentence, which is not appropriate to the person by whom it is uttered. All is probable—life-like—well assorted. Not a particle of *romance* appears. In this respect— simplicity, and *likelihood* of plot—we must own our prime favorite, Miss Edgeworth, to have been here surpassed—though, by the by, we do not agree with the *Edinburgh Review,* that *she* is remarkable for clumsiness in the contrivance of a story. But her heroes and heroines are often so clever and so good; are so wonderfully favored with fine opportunities for heroism; and improve every opportunity so marvellously well;—that poor human nature remains with upturned eyes and folded arms, in mute despair of ever equalling such perfection. Not so in **The Poor Rich Man, and The Rich Poor Man.** Here, no achievement startles, as incredible or strange; no good act, as improbable; no tenor of life, as impracticable; no *speech* even, as unnaturally wise, or eloquent. Any heart, not pitiably depraved—any sound mind, reasonably conversant with the world—will feel and know that all is practicable; will recognize every thing which happens, or is done, or said—as consistent with experience, or with observation. The sagest thoughts appear (and *are*) mere, plain common-sense: the most pathetic

scenes are evident transcripts of every-day life: the most moving and beautiful language comes from people whom it so perfectly suits, that they seem, while uttering it, to stand visible before us, in their work-day clothes. To have been thus, as it were, *common-place,* and yet have made a story of so much good sense and such enchaining interest,—is among the highest triumphs of talent. Perhaps the best praise ever bestowed upon Burns, was unconsciously given by the old housekeeper, who wondered what her mistress could find to admire in the Cotter's Saturday Night: for, said she, "It tells o' just nae mair than I used to see every Saturday, in my father's house." And a good reader-aloud of Shakspeare, will often make a half-attentive listener fancy, that a passage is *spoken, to* or *of* some actually present person or thing: so inevitably (when the Bard *spurns* not the *bounded reign of Existence*) does *presiding Truth confess* the accuracy with which He drew "each change of many-colored life."

The vulgar notion of *criticism* is, that it is synonimous with '*fault-finding.*' We did intend to humor this idea, by exhibiting a list of offences against grammar or rhetoric, which we doubted not we should detect. But on the closest scrutiny, they all (save one) turn out to be *provincialisms,* or other improprieties, entirely in character with the persons who are guilty of them. Such is the clipping of the infinitive mood, thus—"She will be glad to:" a *New Englandism,* against which this journal has heretofore protested, but which is at least appropriate, in the mouth of a poor New England woman. Such are Uncle Phil's "*chores,*"—"*kind of,*"—"*ena most,*"—&c., which stamp his character with stronger verisimilitude and individuality. But there is *one* exception to our general justification of seeming faults. Somewhere in the book, our eye caught the phrase "*was being* executed;" and this, not used by such an ambitious vulgarian as Mrs. Finley, or Mrs. Finley's waiting maid, whose lips it would have well become; but by the authoress, in proper person! Again and again, we aver this to be a violation of English idiom, and countenanced by no respectable precedent, of twenty years' standing. 'Tis pity, that Miss Sedgwick should have lent it the sanction of her authority. She is a writer to establish precedents: and ought therefore to be on her guard.

But how small, how immeasurably small a deduction is this, from what the world owes her for having written **The Poor Rich Man, and The Rich Poor Man**! (p. 334)

> *"Miss Sedgwick," in* The Southern Literary Messenger, *Vol. III, No. 4, April, 1837, pp. 331-34.*

AMERICAN QUARTERLY REVIEW   (essay date 1837)

[*The critic offers a mixed response to* Live and Let Live, *faulting the novel's construction but applauding its message.*]

Miss Sedgwick pursues her design of instructing and entertaining the humbler classes of our citizens, and her aim and execution are both to be commended. . . . [We have] expressed our views in regard to the eminent merit of her works, particularly her later productions addressed to the understanding and feelings of the labouring poor. Nor to them alone is the benefit to be derived from their perusal, confined. While these are taught the advantages of piety, integrity, and industry, the more favoured few are instructed in the equally important lessons of humanity, charity, and economy. High and low, rich and poor, may peruse the sketches of the distinguished authoress with like advantage.

Live and Let Live evinces as much, probably more, talent in the conception, than [*The Poor Rich Man, and the Rich Poor Man*]; while it is far inferior to the latter in polish and finish. We should judge it to be a hasty production. This deduction is rather to be inferred from its abrupt termination—the story, indeed, being defective both in the orderly progress and conclusion which mark her former work. Haste, however, is more apparent in the composition itself; the style being occasionally careless, and defects of grammatical construction not infrequent. This latter is a deficiency which we confess we did not look for in one possessing so deservedly high a repute. We may say, with perfect freedom, of a writer who, like Miss Sedgwick, can endure criticism, that the defect is altogether unpardonable. No publication is permissible where time and leisure are not afforded for the correction of grammatical errors which are so constantly the attendants upon rapid composition. Great injury is done by the sanction of a distinguished name to inaccuracies of this description, particularly where a general looseness upon the point unfortunately prevails.

The mistakes to which we refer occur not merely in the dialogue of persons to whose want of education they might seem appropriate; but they are placed in the mouths of the principal characters, such, for instance, as Mrs. Hyde, who is intended, and most properly, as a specimen of intelligence, education, and refinement. The author, too, herself, when speaking in her own proper person, is equally wanting in her respect for the rules of grammar; a science, which is more cultivated, both in conversation and composition, would have a beneficial influence upon our literature. The phrase "*you was*," is a favourite one. The connection of the two preterites is such instances as these: "I had intended to have done" so and so—is also to be found;—and the selection of the past tense of the verb to form,

The author's father, Theodore Sedgwick.

with the word "having," the past participle; as, for example, "*having drank*," for "*drunk*," may be encountered. It was by no means our purpose to present each individual case of the kind, but merely to indicate some as justifications of our criticism; which, indeed, would have placed such matters to the account of errors of the press, had not their frequency checked this charitable inclination. In any event, the charge of remissness in the correction of the proofs would still have remained.

In the sentiments of the book we in general most cordially concur with the fair author—and admire exceedingly the novelty of their exposition, and the frequent proper boldness which she displays in announcing them. There are occasional remarks however to be found which we cannot acquiesce in—and one which we may be permitted to regret. After giving the observation of the heroine, Lucy, with reference to a little child, Eugene, to whom she was much attached, and whom she was in the habit of carrying in her arms—that "I sometimes felt, when his head lay on my bosom, as if we were worshipping together"—she puts the following sentiments into the mind of Mrs. Hyde; "Oh, how much better is this true worship, than formal prayers and set days." Now we would quarrel with no one's religious belief; but when we reflect that all Christians recognise "set days" as the express appointment of the Almighty—and a very large proportion of them regard "formal prayers" as supported by almost equally high authority—we are disposed to think that it would have been as well if Miss Sedgwick had qualified the expression, or omitted it altogether. The true spirit of prayer all sincere Christians aim at, though they may differ as to the means. (pp. 254-56)

In another point, also, we are unfortunate enough to differ. Miss Sedgwick presses the utility of a servant being qualified for every duty. Learning in turn cookery, waiting, chamber work—in a word, all the details of domestic service with which, of course, a lady is more familiar than ourselves—he or she is to be equal to every emergency. This is all very well in the abstract—but in practice, the Jack of all trades, as the old adage runs, is very apt to be master of none. The theory of the division of labour, experience has shown to be most conducive to perfection in every branch; and we are disposed to think that a proficient in any will never be out of employment in a country where the habits of the people are so adverse to the perfectibility of servants. (p. 256)

> *A review of "Live and Let Live," in* American Quarterly Review, *Vol. XXII, No. XLIII, September, 1837, pp. 254-56.*

[HARRIET MARTINEAU]   (essay date 1837)

[*A British novelist, journalist, and economist, Martineau was a passionate social reformer. In the following excerpt, Martineau offers a survey of Sedgwick's works and praises them as examples of America's developing literature.*]

[Miss Sedgwick] is the most popular writer, we believe, in the United States. Her later works have met the national mind, and warmed the national heart; and, while her education has made her as well acquainted with the literature of the Old World as those of her countrymen who have been able to do nothing better than imitate it, she is thoroughly American in her principles, her intellectual and moral associations, and in her more recent productions. (p. 42)

The *New England Tale,* which appears to be her first work, has for its object the presentation of sketches of life and manners in New England. She explains in her preface that she originally intended it to be a short moral tale of the humblest kind; but that it grew under her hand to be something different. In the preface to the second edition she warns her readers no longer to consider her work as a picture of life and manners in New England, as it would not be fair to her country to suppose her personages average specimens of its inhabitants. This is very true, for most of her characters are far more like the population of an old English novel than of a Massachusetts village in the present century. The Wilsons are all, in their several ways, too bad to be true; and Jane's superhuman patience is unaccounted for. Some of the characters, however, afford a promise of what the author has since attained, especially Mary Hull and Mr Lloyd. Crazy Bet is too palpable an imitation of Madge Wildfire; but we are glad of the sketch, as a contrast with that of Bessie Lee, put forth thirteen years afterwards in [*The Linwoods*]. The sketch of Bessie Lee is exquisite for grace, truth, and pathos; and we could not better illustrate Miss Sedgwick's progress than by pointing to the comparative merits of the two delineations.

The chief object of [*A New England Tale*] appears to be to contrast a pharisaical with a genuine religion. The topic is old, and as difficult as disagreeable in the treatment. (pp. 46-7)

Miss Sedgwick's next production was *Redwood,* which is to us the least pleasing of all her writings. The plot and characters are extravagant, and the exhibition of a faulty religion, here offered in the form of a Shaker community, is as distasteful as that kind of exposure always is. A clandestine marriage, with its mysterious consequences, is the foundation of the story; and the adventures of the personages are too wild, and at the same time commonplace, to be worth detailing at length. The unbelief of Redwood, brought into contrast with the fanaticism of the Shakers, appears to us to be of a kind which exists nowhere but in books; and the angelic and diabolic characters of his two daughters have little life in them. The conversations are strained and pedantic, like those of all the young ladies in Cooper's novels, which have led not a few English readers to imagine that American young ladies talk differently from all other human beings,—an error which Miss Sedgwick is now assisting to rectify in every tale she brings out,

The good parts of *Redwood* are the character of Deborah Lenox, and the sketches of American life, which are, at intervals, hit off with much truth and humour. Deborah is capital—drawn to the life—and absorbing almost all the interest of the reader. She could not have existed anywhere but in New England; she is the true offspring of the place and time; and her conduct and conversation shine out, beside those of the laboured and mawkish young ladies, like a gush of daylight among the lamps of a ballroom. The sentimentalities of the other personages wither before the living pathos of Debby's deeds—including her words; for earnest words are deeds. Miss Debby is the sister of a New England farmer,—a middle-aged, able-bodied, strong-souled woman. She alone, of all the personages in the book, does nothing for effect, or with self-consciousness. She has no patience with what is unreal; but is absolutely gentle with weakness, frailty, and sorrow. She is always doing good, without having any intention of making it her business; and goes her ways, and says her say, as her spirit moves her, dreaming neither of comments nor consequences. There is in her what the pattern women of these novels are deficient in— a deep repose. Busy as she is, bone-setting, driving, shelling

beans, rating hypocrisy, or speculating upon human life, there is that quietude of spirit in her which is the concomitant of true energy. In this character we have the first manifestation of our author's best power. (pp. 49-50)

Hope Leslie followed *Redwood,* at an interval of four years. Its superiority to its predecessor is so great that, but for the touches of domestic interest, the shining out of the spirit of humanity, by which all Miss Sedgwick's writings are distinguished, the two could scarcely be supposed to be by the same hand. The first volume of *Hope Leslie* is, as in all these novels, the best. The story proceeds and closes with a crowd of improbable adventures, not kept in order by any presiding idea; so that they leave the reader's mind in a state of confusion; and still, wherever the author can make the course of her story dependent on precedent, we have the same faults of restlessness in the heroine, pedantry in the conversations, and bad taste in the sentimental reflections. But the tale has many characters of which English fiction affords no precedent; the author has been obliged to draw from observation, or from the history of the first days of the colony; and here she succeeds admirably, as she always does when she relies on her own powers. The characters are no longer daubs. They are naturally composed individually, and well distinguished from each other; not the young ladies and gentlemen, but the Puritans and the Indians. Governor Winthrop is good; and so is the elder Fletcher, except that he reminds the reader of Major Bridgenorth at every turn. Magawisca is a beautiful sketch; and the author has done no small service in preserving such a picture of what the Indians were, in the early colonial days, before they were corrupted and spirit-broken; for they will never be thus seen again. The domestic scenes of this novel, especially in the first volume, before the hair-breadth escapes begin, fix themselves in the memory, avouching their own beauty and truth. (pp. 55-6)

The Linwoods is again an advance upon *Hope Leslie.* It embodies the same faults as the author's former works,—faults which make us wish that she would write no more novels, but as many tales (pictures of the life which passes before her loving eyes) as she can favour us with. Struck as we have been with the spirit of modesty which pervades Miss Sedgwick's writings, we were rather surprised to find Washington and La Fayette moving and speaking among the personages of this novel. They are as well done as they could be by the hand of a quiet-minded woman; but the attempt had better not have been made. There can be no illusion in such a representation of heroes whose living voice has scarcely died away upon the ear of the existing generation; and this part of the work is read with merely a kind of curiosity, unfavourable to the interest of the story. It is only after the lapse of ages, when great historical personages are discerned like gigantic ghosts on the wide plains of Time, that they become fit subjects for fiction; when there are no affections, no associations of reality in readers' minds to be offended by the substitution of an author's conceptions for theirs; but, instead of such associations and affections, a historical curiosity propitious to the author's daring. Centuries must pass before Washington and La Fayette are fit subjects for fiction.

The adventures of this novel are redeemed from some of their improbability by the story being a tale of the Revolutionary war; but they are not on that account the less fatiguing to the reader. There is, however, the exquisite picture of Bessie Lee for him to repose upon. Moving as it is, it is so quiet and so true as to refresh the reader, as a way-side fountain solaces the traveller in busy high-roads.

We refer to the volume of *Tales and Sketches* for the purpose of mentioning that it contains a dialogue, perhaps the most beautiful of the author's single pieces, on "**Old Maids.**" We have never before happened to see the subject expressly treated of in the right spirit, except perhaps in the well-known glorious passage of Jean Paul; and it is remarkable that the first essay on this condition of modern human life should reach us from a country where the condition is supposed to be almost unknown. The fact is, however, that New England contains a large number of unmarried women, and that their position is rendered more unfavourable than it is elsewhere by that very prosperity which is supposed to make marriage a matter of course. In other parts of the country marriage is almost a matter of course; this makes the condition of the single somewhat of a humiliating one; and when the young men of their region wander off to the west, the young women, comparing their prospects with those of all the other girls in the Union, cannot but feel a painful sense of desertion. The prosperity of the country gives rise to a general idea that women are not to work at money-getting employments. Pride and tenderness unite to strengthen the notion, till it becomes an exceedingly difficult thing for women to earn money at any but such mechanical occupations as are very poorly paid. It therefore happens that, between the supposition that every woman is to marry, and the necessity of a large number of women remaining unmarried, while there are no single gentlemen to be seen above the age of five-and-twenty, the condition of old maids in the New England States is one of peculiar depression. The truth of the pictures Miss Sedgwick gives in her Essay is manifest, and the stories themselves are touching; but there is something higher than this—a moral dignity, united with a mournful pathos, which raises this piece above all the many beautiful expressions of individual opinion and feeling which are scattered through her novels. The impression is somewhat injured by the bad taste of one of the speakers, near the opening of the dialogue; but the flippancy of the young lady soon gives way before the seriousness of the subject. On looking it over, though strongly tempted to extract, we perceive that there is no part of this Essay which would not be unjustifiably injured by being separated from the rest.

In her two last and best productions (the last known to the English public) Miss Sedgwick makes her final escape from the atmosphere of conventionalism, and breathes freely amidst nature and truth, as they surround her in her own happy land. She was made for a higher destiny than to tell tales to morbid minds in candle-light retreats; and she has come forth to shed sunshine and kindle sympathy in the homes of New England first, and then in kindred retirements of the Old World. The English will no longer have to turn away from her pages, disappointed to find there faint reflections of a worn-out human life and character. They may learn of her now: she gives them what is fresh, and tells them much that is new. She gives them what no traveller who sees with European eyes can impart: and what not even a personal survey can communicate; she gives them American manners informed and actuated by American life; by thoughts and feelings growing up from birth, with which no stranger can intermeddle. The benefit is communicated unconsciously, and therefore all the more efficaciously. She relies on fact, and on her own American heart and eyes; and it is not for her to know when she instructs, when she surprises us, and what it is in her tales which is to us most valuable. She gives us perhaps the first true insight into American life; and for this we should owe her hearty thanks, if her writings had far less of other kinds of merit than they exhibit.

Such is the service she renders to Europeans. Her own countrymen and women are no less indebted to her. She gives them back a true picture of themselves, and of one another; of their best selves; not as they appear in the flatteries of their public orators, and the contradictions of their newspapers, but as they are in their quiet homes, living in the atmosphere of their best affections. She is no censor, for her trustful and loving nature disqualifies her for such an office. Nor are her tales flatteries; for, much as she loves her neighbours' kind looks and grateful voices, she cares yet more for their permanent welfare. No citizen of the United States is more proud of his country than she,—more satisfied about its destiny; but she sees clearly wherein its greatness lies, and there is no vainglory in her patriotic hope. She wages war with the aristocratic spirit under various forms; and, amidst all her gentleness and easiness, steadily upholds the democratic principles in and by which her country must live peacefully, and flourish greatly and long. It has been and is so much a matter of course for women to lean to aristocratic principles and feelings, their dependent condition makes it so natural for them to repose upon authority and custom, that it is almost a novelty to receive [the democratic sentiments expressed in *Home*] . . . from a meek-spirited and tender-hearted woman. (pp. 57-60)

Home contains two contrasting pictures of the management of domestic influences. They are eminently true; and that of the Barclays is very beautiful. There are no adventures, nor remarkable events. Simple family transactions, a common domestic lot, made up of good and evil, are the material; and through them shines the very spirit of justice and kindliness. The personages belong to what would in England be called the middling class, William Barclay being a printer; and there is much in the little volume which would come home to the hearts of the middling classes in every society. We wish this book was in the house of every mechanic in England. It could not but have some effect upon the next generation. (p. 62)

The other little book, [*The Poor Rich Man, and the Rich Poor Man*], is a tale of contrast too; but it has no formality, and is redeemed by its spirit, truth, and occasional humour, from all resemblance to the common run of religious tracts. It has passages and frequent touches superior to any parts of Miss Sedgwick's former works; and if we finally give the preference to *Home,* it is from our dread of the author's recurrence to the marvellous; of her forsaking her newly-attained simplicity. There is but very slight ground of apprehension of this; but the stories of Mr Barlow, Juliet, and Mrs Smith, hardly accord with the lucid character of the rest of the book, and are its least interesting and pleasing parts. We earnestly hope that the author will henceforth discard all conventional mysteries, and trust, as she can so well afford to do, to the characters of her personages for the interest of her stories. She is well versed in the deepest mysteries of all; in those of the human affections; and among them lies her appropriate range. The simpler the apparatus through which they manifest their workings, the more will the true power of the artist shine out. The story under notice may stand instead of many sermons, and even grave books, on the subject of the vulgarity of an aristocracy graduated upon a scale of wealth. The prevalent vice of English society, and of that of the Eastern cities of the United States, the vulgar aspiration after consequence, by means of ostentation, may feel itself effectually rebuked in the humble tale of the *Poor Rich Man, and the Rich Poor Man.*

It is not, however, for their moral aim, high as it is; nor for their charms of execution, that we most value these little books.

It is because they are the first complete specimens of a higher kind of literature than the United States have hitherto possessed. None would probably be more surprised than the author herself at the importance which we ascribe to what she perhaps considers her humblest works; and a superficial observer may ask why so much is made of two short stories about farmers, children, mechanics, and their wives, and the every-day life of the village and the town. It is because these books are a sign of a new and a better time. The weakness of the American people—a most perilous weakness—has been their want of self-reliance, their proneness to imitate and vie with whatever they could ascertain of the old world. They have resented the fact of their own singularity as an imputation, and wrought hard to keep up a resemblance to the outward and inward life of the mother country. Nothing could come of this but inferiority, insignificance, whether in literature or in anything else. Here we have something better than whole book-stores full of imitative effusions; the vigorous beginning of a national literature; the first distinct utterance of a fresh national mind, telling, not what it ought to see in obedience to old methods of looking, but what it does see of actual life on its own soil. (pp. 64-5)

> [Harriet Martineau], "Miss Sedgwick's Works," in The London and Westminster Review, *Vol. VI, No. I, October, 1837-January, 1838, pp. 42-65.*

THE BOSTON QUARTERLY REVIEW   (essay date 1839)

[*This critic comments on the instructive aspects of* Means and Ends.]

Miss Sedgwick has [in **Means and Ends; or, Self-Training**] given us a very interesting and a very valuable book, which may be read with profit by grown up people as well as by the young. We like the spirit which breathes through Miss Sedgwick's works, and we most heartily thank her in the name of our common countrymen for devoting her fine talents to the noble cause of moral and social progress. Few of our popular writers write with a more truly American feeling. She loves democratic institutions, and sympathizes with the people. We indeed are sometimes unable to adopt all her special views, and often regard her notions as somewhat influenced by that social rank, of which she is one of the brightest ornaments. She is not truly democratic; she seems not to have fully comprehended the real evil of existing society, and does not perceive that the remedies she proposes, can at best but partially mitigate it; but she aims well, and the tendency of her writings is in the right direction.

The subject of education in this little volume is treated with much judiciousness. The views taken are in general pleasing and just. Yet we think we discover a tendency to overrate moral and religious education as distinct from intellectual education. This is the besetting sin, not of the age, but of nearly all late popular writers on education. (p. 389)

> A review of "Means and Ends; or, Self-Training," in The Boston Quarterly Review, *Vol. II, No. III, July, 1839, pp. 389-90.*

THE ECLECTIC REVIEW   (essay date 1841)

[*In this excerpt from a review of* Letters from Abroad to Kindred at Home, *the critic discusses Sedgwick's perceptions of European society as displayed in her letters.*]

[Miss Sedgwick's **Letters from Abroad to Kindred at Home** consists] of letters written during her residence in Europe, to her friends at home. Miss Sedgwick's literary reputation, aided by the numerous letters of introduction which she is understood to have brought to this country, obtained her ready access to the best society in London, which she has described with a fidelity and liveliness that can hardly fail to win the confidence, while it ministers to the pleasure of her readers. Her personal demeanor is reported to have been inartificial and unpretending,—the outward expression of a mind which respected itself too highly to violate truth for the sake of effect, and was too keenly alive to whatever was beautiful or grand, to stoop to any of those exaggerations of phrase by which inferior writers endeavor to supply the absence of real feeling.

The letters are written in an admirable temper, with just such prepossessions as an intelligent American may be expected to entertain. There is no pretension about them, but they nevertheless furnish information which to American readers must be full of interest. 'I forewarn you,' she says to her correspondent in her first letter, 'not to look for any statistics from me—any 'valuable information.' I shall try to tell you truly what I see and hear; to 'chronicle,' as our friend Mr. Dewey says, 'while they are fresh, my sensations." To this rule Miss Sedgwick strictly adheres, and there is in consequence a freshness and individuality about her volumes not frequently met with in the hackneyed ways of authorship. She landed at Portsmouth, July 4, 1839, and was strongly moved by the historical associations which occurred to her memory. (p. 265)

In our author's account of the manners of English society there is much shrewd observation and accurate pencilling. She writes in a spirit perfectly friendly, does full justice to whatever excellencies she noted, yet detects some blemishes to which our self-esteem renders us insensible. One of the chief advantages attending the perusal of such a work as the present is, the impartial view which is given of ourselves,—the un-English aspect under which we are assisted to look at our own habits and manners, the general condition of our society, and the points of attraction and repulsion which our character presents to foreigners. It is doubtless somewhat mortifying to our national vanity to learn that we are not quite perfect; yet it becomes us to be grateful to the instructress, who, by wise counsels conceived in much kindness, puts the means of self-improvement within our reach. (p. 273)

We take leave of Miss Sedgwick with the most hearty goodwill, and with a sincere desire that all our tourists, whether American or English, may imitate the spirit in which she has related to her 'kindred at home' what she saw and heard in the Old World. It is surely time that the mean spirit of detraction in which many have written should be abandoned. Neither the Americans nor ourselves can gain any thing by the reputation of the other being diminished; while each may be benefited by a fair and candid exhibition of the character and habits of its contemporary. (p. 277)

> A review of "Letters from Abroad to Kindred at Home," in The Eclectic Review, *n.s. Vol. X, September, 1841, pp. 265-77.*

EDGAR A. POE   (essay date 1846)

[*In this brief review of Sedgwick's career, Poe focuses on* The Linwoods. *He admires Sedgwick's style but generally considers her overrated as a novelist. For additional commentary by Poe, see excerpt dated 1835.*]

Miss Sedgwick is not only one of our most celebrated and most meritorious writers, but attained reputation at a period when American reputation in letters was regarded as a phenomenon; and thus, like Irving, Cooper, Paulding, Bryant, Halleck, and one or two others, she is indebted, certainly, for *some* portion of the esteem in which she was and is held, to . . . patriotic pride and gratitude. . . , for which we must make reasonable allowance in estimating the absolute merit of our literary pioneers. (p. 130)

Miss Sedgwick has now and then been nick-named "the Miss Edgeworth of America;" but she has done nothing to bring down upon her the vengeance of so equivocal a title. That she has thoroughly studied and profoundly admired Miss Edgeworth may, indeed, be gleaned from her works—but what woman has not? Of imitation there is not the slightest perceptible taint. In both authors we observe the same tone of thoughtful morality, but here all resemblance ceases. In the English-woman there is far more of a certain Scotch prudence, in the American more of warmth, tenderness, sympathy for the weaknesses of her sex. Miss Edgeworth is the more acute, the more inventive and the more rigid. Miss Sedgwick is the more womanly.

All her stories are full of interest. The ***New England Tale*** and ***Hope Leslie*** are especially so, but upon the whole I am best pleased with ***The Linwoods***. Its prevailing features are ease, purity of style, pathos, and verisimilitude. To plot it has little pretension. The scene is in America, and, as the sub-title indicates, "Sixty years since." This, by-the-by, is taken from *Waverly*. The adventures of the family of a Mr. Linwood, a resident of New York, form the principal theme. The character of this gentleman is happily drawn, although there is an antagonism between the initial and concluding touches—the end has forgotten the beginning, like the government of Trinculo. Mr. L. has two children, Herbert and Isabella. Being himself a Tory, the boyish impulses of his son in favor of the revolutionists are watched with anxiety and vexation; and on the breaking out of the war, Herbert, positively refusing to drink the king's health, is expelled from home by his father—an event on which hinges the main interest of the narrative. Isabella is the heroine proper, full of generous impulses, beautiful, intellectual, *spirituelle*—indeed, a most fascinating creature. But the family of a Widow Lee throws quite a charm over all the book—a matronly, pious and devoted mother, yielding up her son to the cause of her country—the son gallant, chivalrous, yet thoughtful; a daughter, gentle, loving, melancholy, and susceptible of light impressions. This daughter, Bessie Lee, is one of the most effective personations to be found in our fictitious literature, and may lay claims to the distinction of originality—no slight distinction where *character* is concerned. It is the old story, to be sure, of a meek and trusting heart broken by treachery and abandonment, but in the narration of Miss Sedgwick it breaks upon us with all the freshness of novel emotion. Deserted by her lover, an accomplished and aristocratical coxcomb, the spirits of the gentle girl sink gradually from trust to simple hope, from hope to anxiety, from anxiety to doubt, from doubt to melancholy, and from melancholy to madness. The gradation is depicted in a masterly manner. She escapes from her home in New England and endeavors to make her way alone to New York, with the object of restoring to him who has abandoned her, some tokens he had given her of his love—an act which her disordered fancy assures her will effect in her own person a disenthralment from passion. Her piety, her madness and her beauty, stand her in stead of the lion of Una, and she reaches the city in safety. In that portion

of the narrative which embodies this journey are some passages which no mind unimbued with the purest spirit of poetry could have conceived, and they have often made me wonder why Miss Sedgwick has never written a poem. (pp. 130-31)

As the author of many *books*—of several absolutely bound volumes in the ordinary "novel" form of auld lang syne, Miss Sedgwick has a certain adventitious hold upon the attention of the public, a species of tenure that has nothing to do with literature proper—a very decided advantage, in short, over her more modern rivals whom fashion and the growing influence *of the want* of an international copyright law have condemned to the external insignificance of the yellow-backed pamphleteering.

We must permit, however, neither this advantage nor the more obvious one of her having been one of our *pioneers,* to bias the critical judgment as it makes estimate of her abilities in comparison with those of her *present* contemporaries. She has neither the vigor of Mrs. Stephens nor the vivacious grace of Miss Chubbuck, nor the pure style of Mrs. Embury, nor the classic imagination of Mrs. Child, nor the naturalness of Mrs. Annan, nor the thoughtful and suggestive originality of Miss Fuller; but in many of the qualities mentioned she excels, and in no one of them is she particularly deficient. She is an author of marked talent, but by no means of such decided genius as would entitle her to that precedence among our female writers which, under the circumstances to which I have alluded, *seems* to be yielded her by the voice of the public. (p. 131)

> *Edgar A. Poe, "Catharine M. Sedgwick," in Godey's Lady's Book, Vol. XXXIII, No. 9, September, 1846, pp. 130-32.*

THE LITERARY WORLD   (essay date 1849)

[*This critic discusses the American settings and themes of Sedgwick's novels and identifies the most outstanding literary qualities of her works.*]

Miss Sedgwick has been aptly instanced as an American writer whose success and popularity have not been the result of transatlantic favor, and whose reputation does not depend upon the *dicta* of foreign critics, inasmuch as it was acquired at the first without their aid. Ever since her first entrance into the world of letters her literary productions have been mainly, in every sense of the word, American. Not only have the scenes and incidents of her works of fiction been drawn from the history of this country or its domestic manners, but her more directly useful and perhaps most praiseworthy efforts have all been in illustration of its social habits and tendencies. Besides this, there are perhaps none of our writers whose works in their spirit and style more completely reflect the prominent characteristics of the American mind. They are marked less by the refinements of highly cultivated taste and imagination than by a rigorous straightforwardness of purpose and a practical energy, of which the principal ingredient is that rare quality in authorship, good common sense.

We do not intend to be understood as limiting our praise of Miss Sedgwick's writings to their indigenous character, any more than we would convey the idea that Americanism by itself is their most satisfactory ingredient. We are not so anxious for the establishment of that "national literature" for which so many ardent appeals are advanced by annual orators and weekly essayists, as to desire its advance at the expense of principles of taste and judgment, which lie far behind the circumstances of locality or nationality. (p. 297)

If, then, Miss Sedgwick's works came to us with no other recommendation than that which she modestly advances in her preface—their American origin, we should hardly recognise their claim. We should not be amongst the readers whom she "hopes to find, who will relish a book for its *home* atmosphere—who will have something of the feelings of him who said he would rather have a single apple from the garden of his father's house than all the fruits of France." This is a proper and a commendable feeling within certain limits; but it would hardly be safe, even for Miss Sedgwick, secure though she be in the friendship and admiration of all American readers, to risk the permanency of her literary reputation upon the slender basis of its nationality.

We think . . . that it has a surer foundation—the foundation of good sense, active and enlightened sympathies, a genial warmth of sentiment, and an earnest energy of thought, ingredients which, while they would give the assurance of success to literary efforts of almost any description which taste or inclination might prompt, receive a higher impulse and a more satisfactory recompense when applied to advance the real and immediate interests of society, and to promote the culture of a *genuine* nationality.

Clarence is, we believe, one of Miss Sedgwick's earlier works. It is a domestic novel; one of a class which the modern improvements in fiction have rather elbowed out of popularity. It is called "A Tale of our own Times," but we outgrow our own recollection so fast in this country that its local descriptions and incidents have entirely lost their contemporary freshness. A description of Broadway some twenty years ago, in the first chapter, would hardly be recognised by a New Yorker; and the author is forced to introduce a note at the end of the chapter, apologizing for the air of antiquity which has unconsciously overgrown her subject. But the story is a good one. We remember reading it with interest, years ago, in a dingy two volume edition, and being very much interested in the fortunes of its characters. It is not one of those books which makes the reader wonder that it could ever have been written by a woman, for Miss Sedgwick, fortunately, has never allied herself to that class of authoresses who studiously ignore in their writings the Providence that has made them women. There is all through *Clarence* a happy feminine grace which adds vastly to its interest and effect. (pp. 297-98)

"Miss Sedgwick's Works," in The Literary World, *No. 140, October 6, 1849, pp. 297-98.*

SISTER MARY MICHAEL WELSH, O.P. (essay date 1937)

[*In this excerpt from her full-length study of Sedgwick, Sister Mary Michael Welsh discusses the social and cultural climate during Sedgwick's era, focusing on the author's attitudes toward religion, penal reform, education, abolition, and the women's movement. In addition, she assesses Sedgwick's role in American literature.*]

During the years (1822-1857) in which Miss Sedgwick was publishing her writings, many important problems, national and sectional, were presenting themselves for solution. The Calvinists of New England were daily losing from their fold members who were out of sympathy with their rigid tenets, men who adopted the more temperate doctrines of the newly established Unitarians. Social problems daily grew more complex. Home conditions and the improvement of the dwellings of the poorer people, especially in the large cities, demanded attention. The public began to realize that the city institutions for the destitute, the orphan, and the insane would bear inspection and investigation. Penal institutions, prisons, jails, and reformatories—all presented interesting problems to the social-minded. Education its means and ends had always been of importance to the colonists, and was still of vital interest to the citizens of the young republic. During the 1830's the crusade against duelling was at its height. The task of securing capable domestic servants was a difficult one in New England; and in conjunction with this was the problem of taking care of the Irish immigrants flocking to our shores.

Miss Sedgwick has wielded her pen in behalf of all these, but the two issues about which she felt most keenly, slavery and secession, she has perhaps mentioned least in her writings. Her contemporary, Mrs. Lydia Frances Child, was most prolific in her anti-slavery propaganda, turning out volume after volume on the horrors of slavery. Miss Sedgwick, however, resisted her example and prudently refrained from putting forth any abolitionist material.

Of all these foregoing problems, the first to effect Miss Sedgwick was the one bearing on religion. Her happy, carefree childhood does not appear to have been subjected to any of the influences likely to disturb its serenity. The first serious thought seems to have been suggested by her doubts relative to the orthodoxy of the Calvinist Church which she had joined at the age of twenty. She followed that stern doctrine for ten years. Apparently she felt that certain heresies had crept in and she recognized that others had existed from the very foundation of the colony. She makes this clear in *Hope Leslie* when Mr. Fletcher is shocked to find that in a religious republic which has been founded on a basis of established truth, heresies are creeping in. He is further dismayed on discovering the lack of religious toleration in those who founded the colony for the express purpose of enjoying undisturbed religious freedom. Of a deeply religious nature, her doubts brought untold anguish. As early as 1810 she wrote to her sister, Mrs. Watson, expressing her anxiety concerning her lack of faith in their professed religion and deploring her utter destitution of the holy affections she desired to possess. (pp. 118-19)

[Miss Sedgwick] was deeply religious, and that not only during emotional conflicts, but in every event of life. She seems always to have sought the spiritual and to have felt the greatness and majesty of the God she wished to serve. She believed that to make His service universal, it should start in the home and that this home should be ideal. Hence in 1835 she published a volume entitled *Home* which had just this object in view.

The picture of home life portrayed in the family of William Barclay, its ideal father, makes clear the joy and pleasure which her own soul experienced in the service and worship of the Heavenly Father. Miss Sedgwick shows, however, that this joy in service cannot endure unless each member of the family is fitted and prepared to be a help to the rest, and not a burden to any other. Miss Sedgwick follows the Barclay family through all the incidents of its daily life, through periods of failure, of struggle, and of success. There is a lesson in these incidents for all. To parents, she points out the proper method of governing a growing family; to children, the necessity of love, respect, and obedience. The unhappy results of a false training, or lack of training, she also makes plain in the turbulent family of Mr. Anthon, for, as is her unalterable custom, she presents both sides of the picture.

This little volume is written with a decidedly moral purpose but at no time is it unpleasantly didactic. She weaves a love theme into the story which makes it entertaining as well as instructive.

To carry out the ideals of home a proper setting is requisite. Miss Sedgwick knew this and was fully aware that the deplorable housing conditions that prevailed even in those days in our large cities, and particularly in New York of which she was writing, were not calculated to lay the basis for an ideal situation. This she makes plain in one of the chapters of *The Poor Rich Man and the Rich Poor Man,* where she brings out the squalor of the impoverished districts. Although Miss Sedgwick wrote purposively of conditions as they existed in 1836, the same problem exists today with no satisfactory solution immediately evident. Not only on this but on many vital issues Miss Sedgwick, it is apparent, was generations ahead of her time.

Busy as the author's life must have been, her charity found time to interest her and her friends in attempts to better social conditions whenever she had an opportunity. As she was one of the first to realize the necessity of improving dwellings, so also was she in the vanguard of those who sought the betterment of public institutions.

Conditions in almshouses were far from satisfactory and she allows the unfortunate Seton in *Clarence* to tell his experience in one of these institutions after he has been taken from the streets through which he has been wandering in delirium brought on by weakness and fever. Unable to give an account of himself, he is taken to the almshouse and shut up there with maniacs. He paints a picture of the neglect, privation, and darkness from which he suffered while there. He wonders that men possessing wealth, and health, and happiness never think of their less fortunate brothers but leave them to wear out wretched lives without lifting a finger to alleviate their sufferings and distress. (pp. 120-21)

During the eighteen-thirties a crusade against duelling was in progress. The people of New England were strongly opposed to this pernicious practice, and in New York there was a growing aversion to it. Nearly every periodical at this time had an article pointing out the folly and sinfulness of such a manner of settling affairs of honor. The history of the new States could furnish a woeful example of this practice.

Miss Sedgwick, along with John Neal, was among the first to make use of this theme in a novel. Her introduction of the duelling scene in *Clarence* gave her an opportunity to present to the public the sane and wholesome aversion that was daily increasing for this mode of setting disputes of honor. Roscoe's reason for refusing to accept the challenge sets forth the author's ideas regarding the lamentable practice. She looks upon life as a precious gift which one must cherish and preserve in order to apply it to the purpose intended by the Giver of Life. She honors the sentiment which originally gave rise to duelling—the principle that honor and truth are to be preferred to life itself—a principle that sustained the martyrs of old—but the duellist sets up false principles as a mistaken code of honor in opposition to truth, and this practice, therefore, is to be deplored.

Another evil, and this an evil common to all times, one that she believed leads frequently to the destruction of happiness, is the tyranny of parents who, for purely mercenary reasons, force their daughters into loveless marriages. Miss Sedgwick also emphasizes this very strongly in *Clarence,* in a letter of

Gerald Roscoe to Mrs. Layton in which he mentions having heard that she has made a grand match for her daughter with the adventurer, Pedrillo. He assures her that he is indignant that such a rumor should be conncted with her name. He is certain that the rumor is without foundation since he knows that Mrs. Layton would never sacrifice her daughter by sponsoring such a marriage. And again in the same volume, the same character says: "An unwilling marriage is the worst slavery—the indulgence of strong and innocent affections beyond all price."

The same subject she also treated in **"Scenes from Life in Town."** Here a designing mother skillfully separates her daughter from her lover and leads her into a loveless marriage with its consequent misery.

Miss Sedgwick is not sentimental on the point of love, however. She believes that a reasonable love is one of the essentials, but that it is not the only one. In **"New Year's Day,"** one of the characters expresses her idea as to the requisites for a happy marriage, one that will endure as long as life lasts and deems it important that both parties be equally endowed in point of culture, capability and taste. Where these qualities are present, the marriage, she believes, will be a happy one. Her severe reprobation is expressed of those who, to escape the stigma of dying old maids, allow themselves to be united for life with persons to whom they might cling to save themselves from shipwreck, but with whom they would not voluntarily elect to pass an evening.

Again and again, the author emphasizes these loveless marriages. In **"Our Village Post Office"** when Mrs. Barnard, who tries to induce Lina to marry a man for whom she does care, but who is considered a good match, tells her that often marry to get a home, Lina replies: "Marry to get a home, Mrs. Barnard, I would wash, iron, sweep, scrub, beg to get a home, sooner than to marry to get one."

In **"Amy Cranstoun"** her aunt reproaches her for refusing Uriah Smith, telling her that she is wicked to refuse such advantageous offer, and this without asking the advice of, or consulting those who have given from her infancy, shelter, food, and raiment. Amy's reply voices the author's philosophy. She implores her aunt not to drive her from the "house of dependence to the house of bondage," into a marriage without love, to spend her life in a service that would be hateful.

As the desire for riches is generally the motive for these marriages, the author tries to impress upon her readers the fact that there is much in life that money cannot buy. That the acquisition of wealth is not the chief end and object of existence, nor the insurer of happiness, Miss Sedgwick is certain. In many passages in her work she plainly shows how little is her regard for earthly riches. In *The Poor Rich Man and the Rich Poor Man* she gives expression to sentiments of a truly evangelical love of poverty. Here, Susan May addressing her father reminds him that the poor should find comfort in the thought that there is nothing low or degrading in poverty, since the "greatest, wisest, and best Being that ever appeared on earth" despised riches, and for our sakes chose a life of poverty.

In *Clarence,* the elder Flint is urged to accept the wealth of his renegade son who has been masquerading under the name of Pedrillo. The old man refuses it, and when advised to reconsider the refusal, replies that he does not want the money. He is near the end of life's journey and the money will not secure for him a greater welcome in the Heavenly Kingdom. It might, on the contrary, prevent his entrance there. Again in the same novel, the author stresses the impotency of wealth to still the anguish of an aching heart. Gerald Roscoe, writing to Mrs. Layton about Mr. Clarence, tells her of the death of his only son just at the moment he acquires his great and unexpected wealth. These riches are powerless to save the life of his son and their very impotence seems to mock him.

The same sentiment occurs again in **"Imelda of Bologna."** The dying woman in reply to Imelda's offer of assistance says: "You cannot bring the dead to life if you fill their graves with gold."

Miss Sedgwick's idea of wealth, however, is a sound and healthy one. It has no relation to the false, socialistic principle of equal wealth for all. She makes clear her valuation of riches and it is but natural that her views of fashionable society, a society that sets itself upon a higher pinnacle than that occupied by its fellow beings, should come under her pen. In *Clarence,* in which life in New York City is so truly and graphically described, Mr. Carroll, or as he really is, Mr. Clarence, gives expression to the author's democratic philosophy regarding class distinctions as they exist in this country. She believes that those who are of, what they choose to consider, the superior class, are there simply because of the possession of greater wealth and not from any acquisition of virtue or intellectual ability. (pp. 123-26)

Society of all grades experienced, in 1837, a cataclysm similar to the one from which the country is now struggling to free itself. Banks failed, the stock market collapsed, and millionaires turned paupers overnight. Miss Sedgwick was fully conscious of the calamity that had befallen the nation. In **"Wilton Harvey"** she pictures the temptations that beset those who become victims of this legalized gamble. The suffering and misery that follows as the aftermath are depicted most graphically. Harvey, honorably and generously, atones for his weakness, but the story emphasizes the fact that there are some evils that can never be repaired. In this volume Miss Sedgwick, at times, comes near to sentimentality. **"New Year's Day"** . . . deals with the fever of speculation that led to the disaster of 1837. That fortune should come as the legitimate result of labor is made plain. (pp. 126-27)

Since it is characteristic of Miss Sedgwick to show a lively interest in all the events of her time whether these result in success or failure, happiness or grief, it is natural to expect that she would have been interested in slavery and its abolition. Both phases of this subject were perhaps the most frequently discussed topics during the years that Miss Sedgwick was at her zenith, yet in her writings she seldom gives any evidence of her deep concern regarding them. She does express her feeling with regard to slavery and secession in her private letters. As early as 1833, writing from Virginia to one of her nieces, she describes the country taverns of this state, which she finds ideal. She seems to attribute this to the great number of well-trained attendants remarking that it is one good resulting from slavery, though, she considers slavery itself far worse than any picture of it she had formed. (pp. 128-29)

In her many novels, the subject of slavery itself is rarely mentioned. In *Redwood,* however, she gives a harrowing description of the separation of a slave from his wife and daughters, and the subsequent harsh treatment of the negro. (pp. 129-30)

Married or Single?, also, has a story of a runaway slave. This time it is a woman, Violet, the wife of a freeman. Violet escapes from her master and comes to her husband who is a butler in a New York family. She is traced to the house by officers who are searching for her and, at the request of one of the relatives of the family, the freedom of Violet and her young son Prince, is bought by Copley, the young lady's betrothed. Violet says that the women of the South feel the curse of slavery as keenly as the slaves themselves and much more than the Abolitionists do, and that some day they may shake it off. Miss Sedgwick implies that the trouble seems to be they do not know where to make a beginning.

In *The Linwoods* Miss Sedgwick voices her sentiments regarding slavery in the incident of Rose. Rose is a slave in Linwood's family. Isabella—age eight—presents her with a silk dress for New Year's, and tells her she should now be as happy as any lady in the land. Rose replies that never for one moment can she be happy while there is nothing to prevent her being bought and sold like cattle,—that she would willingly exchange her life for freedom. (pp. 130-31)

As Miss Sedgwick held herself aloof from the demagogues of Abolition, she also exercised a similar prudence in avoiding any participation in the persecution waged against the followers of the Catholic faith. In no place in her writings can be found anything indicative of sympathy with the bigotry current during this period. That the wanton destruction of property belonging to Catholics was disagreeable to her may be learned from the following quotation from *Letters from Abroad.* She writes:

> We have been out to the Porta del Popolo today to attend service in the English Chapel. It is greatly to the honor of the pope that he permits the public worship of heretics here in the very heart of his dominion. This is better than the burning of the convent in our land of liberty of conscience and universal toleration!

Far different from her forebears, Miss Sedgwick gives an example of admirable tolerance of the religious views of others. In writing from Savoy she remarks that their first resting place was on the pedestal of a crucifix. The cross bore an inscription to the effect that an indulgence of forty days would be granted to all those who should say a Pater Noster or an Ave Maria before the crucifix, after having first made an Act of Contrition. Miss Sedgwick asked a peasant what was meant by an Act of Contrition. The peasant replied that it was a prayer of confession and humiliation, and erroneously added that the indulgence was a deduction of forty days from the time the soul prayed for was sentenced to Purgatory. Miss Sedgwick concluded that this was an easy performance and that the Bishop bartered the Indulgence at a bargain. Her better self eventually governed her, however, for she added:

> . . . the pharisaic feeling was but momentary, my dear C., and I was ashamed when I thought how many weary creatures had paused there and laid down their burdens, while with a simple faith, they performed their act of worship and humiliation, and of love for the departed. When shall we learn to reverence the spirit and disregard the form?

In the light of her tolerance of all religions and religious practices, it is hard to comprehend Miss Sedgwick's failure to understand religious and monastic life, as is evidenced in many of her works. In her *Recollections* she describes a visit, in 1821, to the Maison des Pretres at Montreal. She is surprised to find the clergymen enjoying a day of relaxation in their monastery grounds: a relaxation from what she terms "their slavish service." She believes it is far easier to be good under a "fair sky" than in "the sullen gloom of a cloister." She did not realize that service in the religious life is a voluntary service— that slavish service there does not exist; nor does a sullen gloom

envelop a cloister in which peace and joy always reign. . . .
Twice she had been present at religious professions, which she
describes in *Letters from Abroad* and in an article entitled, **"The
Ladies of the Sacred Heart."**. . . In both cases the description
of the ceremonies is most accurate and her reaction to both the
same. She feels that the seclusion of the nuns cuts them off
entirely from knowledge of the world and unfits them for the
profession of educators. In the article of 1841 she writes: "Female school education here is in the hands of the nuns. You
may imagine how well-fitted to prepare girls to be wives and
mothers, and effective members of society, these poor wretches
must be, who know the world only through their sighs and
unavailing regrets." In the later article, **"The Ladies of the
Sacred Heart,"** her appreciation of the life is no greater. Miss
Sedgwick fails to see the real character of the Nuns' sacrifice,
and believes more good is accomplished by unmarried ladies
who are active in the world. Her misconception of the work
of religious is not due, however, to bigotry; but rather to the
same misunderstanding of the purpose and end of the religious
orders prevalent among a large majority outside the Catholic
Church even in our own day. There were, moreover, but few
nuns in her time in New England, and most of those were
members of semi-enclosed orders. These were probably the
only nuns of whom Miss Sedgwick knew, and she very evidently was not familiar with their work. She was, as her writings on every other subject show, too just to allow her judgments to be perverted or swayed by prejudice of any kind.

The seclusion of women from the world suggests the other
extreme, toward which the women of Miss Sedgwick's day
were tending. Her period saw the beginning of the discussion
concerning "women's rights" which was later to attain such
magnitude. On this point Miss Sedgwick in her writings preserves her usual prudence and moderation. In the last chapter
of *Means and Ends; or, Self-Training,* entitled "Might Makes
Right," she tells the reader very definitely just where she stands
in regard to this subject. She takes the position that if women
would attain their proper intellectual and moral might, their
"rights" would follow as a natural course. She does not believe
that women should enter politics, vote, or enter courts of law.
The woman's duty, she says, is to form character in children,—
be these her sons or pupils—such character as well fit them to
occupy high places in the legislature and courts of the country
and enable them to fulfill their social duties in a praise-worthy
manner.

She does not believe, however, that a woman has no rights,
or that she should occupy only a secondary place. A dialogue
which takes place between two young men in *Married or Single?*
expresses Miss Sedgwick's view of this. One of these young
men, Sidell, remarks: "I am for women using the faculties
Heaven has bestowed on them," and the second responds,
"There's sense in what you say, Sidell, but heaven defend us
from Women's Rights women!" Sidell replies, "Amen and
amen to that."

The injustice of a husband's appropriation and use of his wife's
property to pay his private debts, seemed most unjust to Miss
Sedgwick. (pp. 133-36)

The sketch **"Might versus Right"** was written apparently to
show the injustice of the law that deprives woman of her property rights. Ann Cleveland, the daughter of a wealthy farmer,
marries John Warren, a penniless young man, who, according
to the law at the time, becomes by this union immediately
possessed of his wife's money. This he invests in a dry goods
business, but since he has no qualifications for a mercantile

life, he soon loses all. His wife, as a consequence, sinks lower
and lower in the scale of humanity until she becomes absolutely
destitute.

Miss Sedgwick was confident that a law regulating this would
shortly be enacted for she writes, "It is one of our distinctions,
thank God, in the New World, that we do not rest quietly in
any error; so I have faith that in good time this matter will be
set right." Her prediction was fulfilled about the year 1875,
when, through the instrumentality of one of her brothers, the
law vesting the ownership of a wife's property in the husband
was abrogated.

In 1843 in *Graham's Magazine* her article entitled **"The Post
Office"** was published. The high rate of postage prevailing in
the country inspired its writing. (pp. 136-37)

The injustice of the high rates of postage for the poor and of
free postage for government officials, is made clear from the
speech of one of the by-standers in the post office who voices
Miss Sedgwick's disapproval of this exorbitant rate of postage
for the majority—a majority composed of many who can ill-
afford to meet its excessive demands. She urges upon her
friends the necessity of arousing authorities to action and is
rewarded by seeing these rates reduced.

From the foregoing examples it is reasonable to believe that
Miss Sedgwick was a leader in the thought of her time. In all
her works she had in view the good of humanity, the moral,
physical, and intellectual improvement of her fellow-beings.
She was not a reformer in the strict sense of the word; nor was
she, on the other hand, a mere dreamer. She saw the defects
of the social system of her day and she used rational and
practical methods to correct these defects. Like Dickens at a
later date, she made use of her books and sketches to enlist
the sympathy and cooperation of her readers in endeavoring to
bring about more desirable conditions in all classes of society.
But going beyond the influence that Dickens had, her views
on all the subjects on which she wrote are as applicable to the
present day as they were in her own time. (pp. 137-38)

•　•　•　•　•

It seems strange that the first novelists on American soil should
have been women; and stranger still, that the novels of these
women should have had their origin in New England, since
fiction was so strongly tabooed in this section of the country.
Perhaps this may be explained by the fact that to be acceptable
to the Puritan, a book should have an avowedly moral purpose,
and these novelists wedged a way for their stories through the
permissable tracts and Bible selections that lined the book stalls
and reposed on parlor tables for Sunday perusal, only through
this moral purpose. They represented their stories always as
founded on fact, and usually depicted a beautiful young girl
betrayed by a false lover, or a helpless orphan defrauded of
her inheritance by a wicked relative—all written in imitation
of English models. Poetic justice was never violated; the villain
always met with condign punishment and a miserable end.

This type of sentimental moral tale persisted up to the beginning
of the nineteenth century when these melodramatic productions
began to give way to the romance and realism of Brackenridge,
Brown and Cooper. Romance tinged with realism was the prevailing characteristic of the literary field when Catharine Maria
Sedgwick began to write in 1822. She realized the deficiencies
of her predecessors who, instead of giving their readers real
beings alive and active, peopled their books with characters
that were creations of their own imaginations. Miss Sedgwick,

on the contrary, discounts imagination in the delineation of her characters and draws a living individual, one she has seen and observed, one that is real and true. She was a keen observer, and studied things as well as persons; hence her remarkable descriptions of landscapes and scenes, whether these be invested with the wild beauty of the country, or merely kaleidoscopic views of the city in its many varied phases. Of this power of description as necessary to the writer of romance as it is to the painter, the excellence of which consists in truthful representation, Miss Sedgwick undoubtedly had an abundant share. This special ability in most of her novels is most noteworthy. *The New England Tale* lays the scene in the Berkshires, her own country, where she knows every hill and valley and stream. With crazy Bet she takes the reader through the wilds of the wooded hills to the sacrifice rock of Mononotto to wait for the moon to rise before penetrating further into the denseness of the mighty forest. *Redwood* depicts an electric storm in all its devastating grandeur and paints the beauty of the lakes with their overhanging, flower-laden banks. *Hope Leslie* pictures the wild setting of the pioneer's home, and again, the quieter scenes of the city. Boston, the water front, and the islands of the harbor are in turn introduced. *Clarence* brings the power of description into the very homes of the characters in a more detailed manner than in any other of her works. The life of a country gentleman in its smallest particular is faithfully outlined in the description of Mr. Clarence's country seat. From Trenton Falls at midnight to New York City in every phase, every grade of society is characterized with special emphasis on the fashionable circle. *The Linwoods* pictures New York before and during the Revolution: simple, homely life on a New England farm; camp life with Washington; and a social gathering in General Clinton's drawing room, in which representatives of both armies are brought together. *Married or Single?* has its setting chiefly in New York City with two or three changes to more varied scenes. *The Travelers* is almost entirely descriptive, following a journey up the Hudson, through the Erie Canal in process of construction, along the Great Lakes and the Saint Lawrence to Quebec and Montreal. The descriptions in *Letters from Abroad* present wonderful pictures not only of the many places, churches and other notable structures visited, but no less remarkable pen pictures of celebrities met during the visit.

In addition to a power of description, a good novelist should be able to penetrate the mysteries of the human heart, to divine the motives of the individual conscience, and to anticipate the effects of actions thus motivated. Miss Sedgwick was qualified through her keenness of observation and her native shrewdness of judgment to do just this, and she gives to us in consequence, characters that have both substance and reality. Every one of the novels mentioned furnishes an example of an individual character which towers in strength above anything written by her predecessors. The almost majestic dignity of the faithful Magawisca in *Hope Leslie* is without parallel. The solid, wholesome common sense of Aunt Debby Lenox in *Redwood* is by far the finest portrait of woman's character presented in any novel so far. The hypocritical, canting Mrs. Wilson is an exceedingly strong individual—purely an individual, not to be construed as a type. A score or more with equal claim to strong characterizations could be enumerated, but these will suffice to exemplify Miss Sedgwick's ability to portray intensely human characters.

Miss Sedgwick declares that her purpose in writing is to entertain and to instruct. A study of these novels will show she has succeeded in doing both, for in addition to supplying her readers with an entertaining volume, she has woven into her story the moral lessons she had set her mind on driving home. And she always has a moral—nor is it hidden. It is there without disguise, clear and simple; yet it is never blatant. It does not cry aloud for recognition, rather it seems to accompany or to follow each incident as a natural sequence. Thus it does not interfere with the interest of the tale. (pp. 139-41)

Catharine Sedgwick saw in satire a useful means of setting forth her purpose. She improved on the methods of her predecessors, however, and employed her satire with prudent discrimination. She found a way of injecting it into her situations, or allowed her characters sometimes to indulge in a little gentle sarcasm. She always used it judiciously, however. It was never misplaced, but so cleverly combined with the narrative as to make its presence unobtrusive. (p. 142)

In adapting the language of her dialogue to the speaker's condition, she follows the example of Scott and Maria Edgeworth. In *Live and Let Live*, she does not hesitate to allow Mrs. Simpson to say, when she is trying to induce Lucy Lee to buy her discarded black gown, "it would make quite a *scrumptious* dress."

This and similar expressions suggest a strong tendency to realism, and realism is present in all Miss Sedgwick's longer works. Romanticism predominated the literature of the new country for the first sixty years of its existence. Miss Sedgwick was writing during thirty-five of these sixty years, and while in her novels romanticism prevailed, her realistic tendency is strongly apparent. Her short stories retained more of the romantic spirit many years later than did her novels.

Another prominent trait found not only in her novels but also more especially in her didactic tales is her inclination to idealize. As already seen in *Home* the Barclay family is idealized and their home presented as a model one. In *Live and Let Live* the mutual relations of mistress and servant are ideally portrayed. In the stories where the Indian enters, he is depicted in flattering terms. A perfect character is given an important place in each of her novels. And so, romanticism, realism, and idealism, all have their share in Miss Sedgwick's stories and plainly indicate that she was affected by the transition of the period. Romanticism predominates in all her novels and sketches until after the *Linwoods* in 1835. With the publication of *Home* this same year realism claimed precedence, and as the realistic tendencies became more pronounced, the romantic traits, although they were never wholly discarded, became less and less perceptible. Throughout this transitional era, she continued to introduce ideal characters, the number being equally distributed among the heroes and heroines.

In her realistic portrayal of local conditions of life, Miss Sedgwick may be considered a forerunner of the realism that pervaded the literature of the seventies. It was a genial realism, never harsh or objectionable. Even when she depicts the evil in such characters as Daniel Prime in the sketch of that title, or of Pedrillo in *Clarence*, the aversion one feels for the deeds is tempered by pity for the guilty individual. (pp. 142-43)

As to Miss Sedgwick's place in the literature of her period, she may certainly head the list of women writers, and in the group of novelists she should give place to Cooper and Hawthorne only. She wrote for all ages—children and adults—she belonged to her period, she understood its needs, and she sympathized with its weaknesses. Her love for her fellow-beings was ardent and deep and it was her sincere desire to be of genuine aid to them that influenced her choice of the didactic tale at the very height of her success with the romantic novel. These novels are not read today, not because they have lost interest, but because the flood of literature pouring over our country is so great that it has caused the older literature to be forgotten or set aside. (p. 145)

> *Sister Mary Michael Welsh, O.P., in her* Catharine Maria Sedgwick: Her Position in the Literature and Thought of Her Time Up to 1860, *The Catholic University of America, 1937, 168 p.*

ALEXANDER COWIE   (essay date 1948)

[*A noted authority on American fiction, Cowie is also an esteemed historian, biographer, and critic. In his* The Rise of the American Novel, *from which the following excerpt is drawn, he traces the evolution of the American novel by examining the artistic development of the novelists themselves. Here, Cowie discusses the style of a number of Sedgwick's works and compares them with the novels of James Fenimore Cooper.*]

One of the first of a large number of women writers to win a considerable popularity in the second quarter of the nineteenth century was Catharine Maria Sedgwick. She began to publish in a period when few American novels but Cooper's were deemed worth reading, but before many years she proved that a very good market was available to other native novelists. Finally eschewing the religious themes toward which her nature and training inclined her, as well as the sentimental matter which had been the basis of the most successful books of Hannah Foster and Mrs. Rowson, she cast in her lot with the writers of historical romance who followed in the wake of Cooper. She wisely forbore direct competition with Cooper, however, and mined particularly those veins in which he did not excel. She laid the scene of her most distinguished novel, *Hope Leslie,* in Massachusetts, where, by common consent, Cooper was regarded as relatively unsuccessful. Moreover she merged elements from the novel of manners with the historical romance more successfully than Cooper. She was more adept than most of her contemporaries at recounting domestic detail and the small social transactions of village life. Consequently she elicited the interest of a large public of feminine readers for whom the too steady contemplation of bloody adventure on sea and in forest proved wearisome. She was withal a well-poised, tidy writer, and she focussed her work more rigidly than the blustering romancers. Whereas Cooper's proclivity was for expansiveness and spaciousness, Miss Sedgwick, operating on a smaller radius, proved what may be achieved by greater centripetal force. Yet she was sufficiently identified with the romantic genre to find her reputation sharply reduced when the type passed its peak of popularity. Her other resources, though respectable and even, in the case of her juvenile books, profitable, were not substantial enough from the point of view of belles lettres to create a lasting reputation. Today she is remembered chiefly for *Hope Leslie,* which still receives a measure of critical approval not to be wholly explained on the basis of local pride or patriotism. (pp. 200-01)

Though exciting as a story, *Hope Leslie* is "no romantic fiction," but a compound of controlled invention plus history. A great many authentic sources are behind (sometimes not far enough behind) the march of her narrative. Events, persons, and customs from the pages of history are freely drawn upon—the settlement of Springfield, the Pequod wars, Governor Winthrop's leadership, Thomas Morton's heterodoxy, the blue Laws, the Puritan sabbath, witchcraft, the quarrel over Popish encroachments on Puritan America. Yet the historical material,

if not always perfectly assimilated, is not emphasized to the serious detriment of the narrative, which is everywhere plausible and coherent. The treatment of the Indians is able, especially with respect to the brooding Magawisca, who is torn between loyalty to her race and affection for the Fletcher family, but Miss Sedgwick modestly waives the right to be considered in this respect a competitor of the author of "a recent popular work" (doubtless Cooper's *Last of the Mohicans*). The reader to whom Indian wars are tedious finds plenty of collateral interests, for here, as in (the later) **The Linwoods,** the author centers attention less on the action, however exciting, than on the people: her books are not adventure stories. The characterizations are not always successful—Everell is just a type of an impetuous and attractive young man and Sir Philip is only slightly altered from conventional villains—but the whole story is given vraisemblance by the colloquial speech and natural action of Hope Leslie. Hope's reactions to various situations in which her emotions are deeply involved are indicated with far more plausible psychology than had been evident in the heroines of Charles Brockden Brown or Cooper or any of the lesser novelists who preceded her. Hope shares, moreover, the comic abilities with which some of the minor characters, notably Aunt Grafton, are more fully endowed. Sentiment there is in the story, but Miss Sedgwick's fine common sense keeps it from reaching that saturation point which was one of the abuses of the domestic novel both before and after her time. (pp. 204-05)

Miss Sedgwick's rather obvious use of documentation for the back-ground of **Hope Leslie** (which curiously enough emphasizes the invented characters of the plot as such even while it gives authenticity to the atmosphere) showed her limitations as a writer of historical romance. She herself seems to have felt that she lacked Cooper's power of creating illusion. In **Hope Leslie** she speaks of her difficulty in this respect:

> The mighty master of fiction has but to wave his wand to preserve the past to his readers with all the vividness and distinction of the present; but we, who follow him at an immeasurable distance—we, who have no magician's enchantments, wherewith we can imitate the miracles wrought by the rod of the prophet—we must betake ourselves to the compass and the rule, and set forth our description as minutely and exactly as if we were making out an inventory for a salesman.

Consequently it was perhaps a natural instinct which led her to try her talents in a novel of contemporary life. To this decision she was also urged by the "cheap reprints of popular English novels [which] have reduced the value of copyright productions. . ." In the novel of contemporary manners, moreover, she had the opportunity of exploiting her ability in reporting those details of domestic life which had thus far received relatively little attention at the hands of American novelists. Unfortunately, in her next novel, **Clarence,** she merged her undeniably real episodes from daily life of contemporary New York, where from her youth onward Miss Sedgwick spent a great deal of the year, with a superannuated plot involving mistaken identity, parental tyranny, the perils of an heiress, concealed crime, mysterious manuscripts, overhead conversations, synthetic villains, and other badly worn devices. Her legacy from Miss Edgeworth, whom she refers to both in this novel and elsewhere, included not only a gift for small realism but also antiquated devices for producing action. Miss Edgeworth's wholesome domestic ideals also animate her, as, for example, when Frank Carrol rebukes his wife for setting up for a social star merely because her sister is *haut ton:* "I thank God [says Frank] there is a barrier between us and the fashionable world..." Similarly satire is implied in a woman of fashion's comment on the latest novels: "'No,' said another lady, 'I never read *American* novels, there's no high life in them.'" Miss Sedgwick, who herself moved in good society of the enlightened sort, resolutely supported sound middle-class ideals, and she praised Miss Edgeworth as "the beneficent genius who has made the actual social world better and happier." Miss Sedgwick's own works are provided with a vein of intelligent and inoffensive moralizing, but she had insufficient depth to offer any significant interpretation of urban life. (pp. 206-07)

Clarence appears to have been less read than any of Miss Sedgwick's long stories. Her vivacious transcript of manners was unsuccessfully grafted to an old and devitalized plot structure. In her next novel Miss Sedgwick wisely returned to the species in which she had made her greatest success—the historical romance crossed by the novel of manners.

In this new novel, *The Linwoods,* Miss Sedgwick showed no more inventive genius than before, but she displayed with even greater success her special ability to handle a social milieu. The story is on the surface a tale of Revolutionary days, but the rataplan of military life is heard only from a distance, and the author's main concern is for the personal lives of individual characters whose fortunes are only partially determined by the national crisis.... Miss Sedgwick's interest is focussed on [the] love tangle rather than on the events of the Revolution. She manages to bring in (often with imperfect success) many allusions to the campaigns of the middle years of the war and to celebrate a number of heroes of the American army as well as sympathizers from abroad—Washington, Putnam, Lafayette, Kosciusko, etc. Though allusions to Washington were routine in American historical romances, Miss Sedgwick wrote of him with special authority, for her father had been well acquainted with the President. Her action, moreover, if sometimes too dispersed, is frequently made exciting through siege, capture, and the minor exigencies of warfare. Yet action *per se* is not her forte, and her most advantageous use of the Revolution as a theme lay in her analysis of the critical social relations partially induced by the issue between Tory and Whig.

The characterization is again competent without being profound. The men are on the whole less well drawn than the women. Isabella, the nominal heroine, is sketched in a manner so often employed by later novelists in America that she seems conventional, and yet earlier American novels had provided no complete model for her portrait. Bessie Lee, called by Poe "one of the most effective personalities to be found in our fictitious literature" [see essay dated 1846], undoubtedly has her counterpart among the distressed females of Scott's stories, but her mental decline is recorded with a psychological insight that was probably rare before Miss Sedgwick's time. Even the minor characters, perhaps, less original in type, are sketched with enough individuality (sometimes expressed in humor) to afford entertainment and a sense of reality, especially Herbert's bodyguard, Kisel. Miss Sedgwick was in fact very skilful in the light delineation of character. Her dialogue, too, is exceedingly well-phrased and, despite occasional interludes of language a bit more elaborate than fits the character, very real. Her style here, as in almost all her work, is marked by both fluency and precision. She was, if not a bluestocking, at least a very well-read person and a carefully disciplined writer.

The Linwoods had appeared at about the height of Miss Sedgwick's popularity as a writer of novels. Several editions were called for. It seemed likely that another book in a similar vein would be welcomed, but whether because of a realization that she probably could never surpass *The Linwoods* and *Hope Leslie,* or because she wished to devote herself more definitely to humanitarian projects, Miss Sedgwick never resumed the historical romance. Her prolific writing after this time fell into two classes of books, juveniles and tales with a moral or sociological purpose. The latter concerned themselves largely with the education of girls and with social justice. She devoted herself to doing good to society with much the same zeal that animated the "sweet singer of Hartford," Lydia Huntley Sigourney. *Live and Let Live,* for example, is a story treating of "the manifold trials and discouragements of the mistress of a family in relation to her domestics." The book is more humanitarian than democratic, and to the point of view is always that of the enlightened lady speaking of her "inferiors in position." The author urges American women to instruct their daughters in managing and ministering to a household—for "emergencies constantly occur where a *lady* must perform the primitive offices of women, or her family will be comfortless." Like Enos Hitchcock, author of *Memoirs of the Bloomsgrove Family,* Miss Sedgwick deplores the tendency of the times to confine a young lady's training to "French, Italian, drawing, music, &c." Miss Sedgwick is not radical in her attitude, and most of her discussion of the emancipation of woman is qualified by the implied premise that woman's place is in the home. Yet she dimly discerns a day of something like social equality and of a greater range of intellectual activity for women. In the meantime she argues the need of a housewife's being practical and the justice (as well as wisdom) of treating servants so that there will be a minimum of suffering and discord. If her humanitarian thought does not now seem advanced, it was relatively so in her time, for an anecdote is told of a person who professed to having been improved by reading *Live and Let Live* for previously he "had supposed the Irish were to be treated as you would treat slaves!" As a novel, *Live and Let Live* is ineffective; Miss Sedgwick wrote too early to appreciate fully the possibilities of a story based on the condition of slaves. Nor could she foresee the deluge of tears soon to be wrung from thousands of readers by the plight of governesses who, once the vogue was established by Charlotte Brontë in *Jane Eyre,* became the heroines of many sentimental romances. Hence although she was keenly interested in the improvement of conditions in almshouses and prisons (which she personally visited) and was occasionally in contact with such advanced thinkers as Harriet Martineau, Lucy Stone, Fredrika Bremer, and Margaret Fuller, she confined her analysis of social problems to tracts and her lesser tales. A close liaison between social justice and the novel remained for American writers of a slightly later generation. Moreover Miss Sedgwick always wrote of social improvement with a great awareness of the gulf between classes. The implication is that the lower classes should be aided *as* lower classes rather than encouraged to ascend to a higher class. She was not a crusader for "democracy"; charity interested her more than any radical revision of the social system. She was strongly American, however, and particularly disapproved of imitating the ways of the French, even by the interspersion of too many French phrases in conversation.

As Miss Sedgwick grew older (she lived until 1867), it became clear that writing had become essentially an avocation for her. Indeed as early as 1835 she had expressed the opinion that the art of writing was secondary:

My author existence has always seemed something accidental, extraneous, and independent of my inner self. My books have been a pleasant occupation and excitement in my life. The notice, and friends, or acquaintance, they have procured me, have relieved me from the danger of ennui and blue devils, that are most apt to infest a single person. But they constitute no portion of my happiness—that is, of such as I derive from the dearest relations of life. When I feel that my writings have made any one happier or better, I feel an emotion of gratitude to Him who has made me the medium of any blessing to my fellow-creatures. And I do feel that I am but the instrument.

The emphasis upon utility (perhaps an afterglow of Puritanism in her) explains much in Miss Sedgwick's writing. The passion for writing as such she did not have. She judged not only her own books but the writings of others by the same criteria. (pp. 207-10)

Miss Sedgwick's increasing preoccupation with juvenile and social studies toward the latter part of her career did not detract greatly from the position of eminence she enjoyed in American letters during her lifetime, but it perhaps serves to explain her later loss of fame. She was not a strongly original writer. She was facile, intelligent, and versatile, but she lacked intensity and great power of imagination. (p. 211)

As a follower of Cooper she was exceedingly able and shrewd. She coped valiantly with Indian raids and military campaigns, and she recreated an earlier social atmosphere with more fidelity and finesse than most writers of her period. She was praised by a contemporary critic for "portraits drawn with singular fidelity from life, and incidents so natural that the New Englander can scarcely doubt that they are his village's history." Nevertheless she has suffered somewhat from occupying a position between two eras. Her sobriquet, "the Maria Edgeworth of America," is a reminder not only of her warm humanity, her wit, and her command of phrase, but also of her tendency to fall back on somewhat threadbare narrative devices. Had she come to maturity as a writer a little bit later, she might have capitalized her talents as a social historian more fully, for in her best work she distinctly looks forward to the novel of manners at its best. Moreover in her sharply defined studies of New England manners, she even forecasts dimly the well-balanced social studies of Howells. Like him she possessed a goodly portion of common sense and a style distinguished for naturalness and clarity. She avoided the extremes of both sentiment and melodrama. In her own time she won a vast public—including a larger share of women readers than Cooper or Charles Brockden Brown had been able to win—for her honest, well-proportioned tales compounded of history, light invention, humanitarian sentiment, "cheerful philosophy" and the easy delineation of domestic manners. Good ideals dominated her life and her art. (pp. 211-12)

Alexander Cowie, "Contemporaries and Immediate Followers of Cooper, I," in his The Rise of the American Novel, *American Book Company, 1948, pp. 165-227.*

GLADYS BROOKS   (essay date 1957)

[*Brooks's* Three Wise Virgins, *from which the following excerpt is drawn, details the lives of several nineteenth-century women who sought to improve social conditions. Here, Brooks notes the enduring qualities of* A New England Tale.]

[Involuntarily] and almost by accident, Catharine stumbled upon her career as a writer. . . . Theodore had encouraged his sister to enlarge and print as a tale a tract she had recently composed on the general subject of the religious attitude toward life, on the joys of freedom from Calvinism and the release of the spirit into brighter fields. But she was skeptical as to her own talent. "My brother Theodore makes a most extravagant estimate of my powers. It is one thing to write a spurt of a letter, and another to write a book." However, true to her role as docile and loving sister, she did as she was told and in 1822 *A New England Tale* appeared signed, boldly for those days of sequestered ladies, by *Catharine Maria Sedgwick*. It soon found its way into the loving hands of a public who, trained from infancy in the sharp demarcations between black and white, between good and evil, took pleasure in a story wherein the young heroine emerges triumphantly from beneath the burden of long persecution while those who had sought to injure her are irrevocably routed.

This heroine is, of course, a saintly character, an orphan obedient to the whims of a ruthless aunt, one who nurses the sick, lays out the dead, is patient with the vagaries of the village madwoman, resists the wiles of the wicked villain and ends by marrying a widower much older than herself to live out her life in quiet and blissful companionship: gratifying reward for unalloyed virtue.

Three aspects of *A New England Tale* save it from being no more than the tract it was intended to be in its initial form. First, the authentic quality of the tale's setting within the New England woods and mountains that Miss Sedgwick so well knew as she also knew village customs and the manners born of these. Second, her introduction into the story of the madwoman, a local phenomenon, of whom in her preface to the first edition she says: "The writer has attempted a sketch of a real character under the fictitious appellation of 'Crazy Bet' "—a poetic portrayal done with a touching simplicity. The third saving grace bestowed upon this story, and one that lives in all her writing, springs from the author's sincerity in depicting her heroine, in making her credibly synonymous with things good and true. Sentimentality, and plenty of it, notwithstanding, there is in every one of her books the portrait of a woman who has the courage and intelligence to stand morally on firm ground and, in doing so, to combine her goodness with a kind of feminine charm that does not fail to hold the reader, being derived, obviously from the nature of the author herself. One cannot help falling in love with Jane who moves so genuinely unscathed through the pages of this book. . . . (pp. 180-82)

Gladys Brooks, "Catharine Maria Sedgwick," in her Three Wise Virgins, *E. P. Dutton & Co., Inc., 1957, pp. 157-244.*

MICHAEL DAVITT BELL   (essay date 1970)

[*In this analysis of* Hope Leslie, *Bell contends that the novel is "an invaluable example of the technique of the conventional historical romancer."*]

Few readers today are familiar with the works of Catharine Maria Sedgwick, and most have probably never heard of her. . . . And yet in spite of the obscurity which now envelopes her Catharine Sedgwick was one of the best-known American writers of her day—perhaps the most popular female novelist in America (with the exception of Mrs. Rowson) before 1850. It is not my object, in this article, to attempt to rescue Catharine Sedgwick's reputation. Although *Hope Leslie* is a better book than the few critics who mention it allow, it is no neglected masterpiece. Its interest, rather, is historical. As an extraordinarily conventional book it provides valuable insight into an age which, as David Levin writes, "regarded romantic conventions not as meaningless stereotypes, but as effective ways of communicating a message that all their literate contemporaries would understand." *Hope Leslie* is doubly conventional. For one thing it embodies a conventional 19th century attitude toward history, a belief in "progress"—a belief that history, in the words of Professor Levin, "had been a movement from the 'artificial' toward the 'natural.'" *Hope Leslie* is also conventional in that it expresses this attitude toward history by means of a conventional romantic marriage plot, found again and again in historical romance, in which historical progress becomes identified with the romantic attachment of hero and heroine. As Northrop Frye has written of this "romantic" or "comic" marriage plot, "the device in the plot that brings hero and heroine together causes a new society to crystallize around the hero." In overcoming the obstacles to their marriage, then, the hero and heroine become the primary agents of the new society, of historical progress. Whatever her literary abilities, Miss Sedgwick illuminates the way in which historical and literary conventions were fused in the conventional genre, historical romance. (pp. 213-14)

[Any examination of the plot] should make it clear that Catharine Sedgwick did not stint in her use of material—historical or conventional. We have Indians, pirates, a Catholic villain, a witch trial, a love affair, all set in a scene that ranges from the upper valley of the Housatonic to the inner reaches of Governor Winthrop's domestic establishment. This abundance of material leads to a good deal of confusion.... *Hope Leslie,* in spite of the confusion of its plot, can be quite instructive in showing in detail how, in America in the earlier 19th century, historical *material* became historical *romance.* For one thing, we can see in the book three separate subplots, each having its own historical or conventional basis. These are, in the order of their appearance, the Indian plot involving Mononotto and Magawisca, the seduction plot involving Gardiner, and the drawing-room plot of mistaken love involving Esther Downing.

The Indian plot has two historical sources. The story of the attack seems to have been inspired by the account of the Deerfield Massacre in John Williams' *Redeemed Captive Returning to Zion,* at least as it describes the fate of Williams' family. His wife was killed (on the road, not during the massacre), the captives were taken off to Canada and—suggesting Faith Leslie's marriage to an Indian—Williams' daughter Eunice married an Indian and was never redeemed. The story had special interest for Catharine Sedgwick, since Eunice Williams had been her own grandmother's cousin. Miss Sedgwick alters the incidents to fit her overall story; but she does not very much falsify them. The second source of the Indian plot is not so much historical as legendary (at least by 1827). It is clear that Magawisca's intervention to save Everell from her father is inspired by the story of John Smith and Pocahontas. Miss Sedgwick's principal addition to the tale is the gory detail of the severed arm.

The seduction plot is based on the career of the historical Sir Christopher Gardiner who came to New England before Winthrop to validate a prior claim of Sir Ferdinando Gorges to land which had been awarded to the colony in the 1629 Charter.... But it ought to be noted that in spite of such a minute effort at historical "accuracy" Catharine Sedgwick changes Gardiner's first name, has both Gardiner and his "page" die at the

end, invents his attempt to seduce the heroine and, finally, has Gardiner in New England, not in the early 1630s, but in the middle 1640s. One makes a great mistake to expect literal accuracy in conventional historical romance. Catharine Sedgwick's Sir Philip is not so much based on history as inspired by it.

The inspiration for Esther Downing, finally, is hardly historical at all. There was indeed an historical Emmanuel Downing married to Winthrop's sister Lucy, so that his daughter would have been Winthrop's niece. But none of Downing's numerous daughters was named Esther. In any case, if Esther has no basis in historical fact she has sufficient basis in fictional convention. She is quite clearly an example of the "wrong girl" of the novel of manners—a type exemplified by Harriet Smith in Jane Austen's *Emma.* Because of some sort of misunderstanding this wrong girl always very nearly marries the hero; but the misunderstanding is cleared up at the end and she is either married off elsewhere or otherwise disposed of. In the case of Esther, then, Catharine Sedgwick seems first to have conceived her character in terms of literary convention and then sought out an "historical" personage with whom to identify her.

These more or less historical materials are not brought into the book for their own sake, or simply to create the illusion of historical accuracy. They are, rather, always subordinated to Catharine Sedgwick's view of this particular period of American history. Magawisca, for example, serves several symbolic functions in the romance. She serves as a foil to the intolerance and hypocrisy of the Puritans. After telling Everell how one of her brothers was executed by the English she comments: "You English tell us, Everell, that the book of your law is better than that written on our hearts; for ye say it teaches mercy, compassion, forgiveness: if ye had such a law, and believed it, would ye thus have treated a captive boy?" She also functions as a "dark heroine"—as a rival to the fair heroine, Hope Leslie, for the love of Everell. Magawisca represents the perils of nature. Hope Leslie, as we will see, is also associated with nature, but hers is a tame nature that can be trusted completely. When Everell trusts Magawisca completely at the beginning of the book the result is that his mother and siblings are murdered before his eyes. Magawisca's nature, then, is wild and dangerous; it must be rejected before the final marriage of hero and heroine. Thus at the close, as the lovers stand on the dock, Magawisca leaves Boston forever to disappear in the West.

As Magawisca stands in the romance for the dangers of wild nature, so Sir Philip Gardiner stands for the dangers of European corruption. It is significant, for example, that Mrs. Grafton, the most "artificial" and European of the novel's minor characters, is the most enthusiastic supporter of Sir Philip's suit for Hope's hand. As Magawisca is Hope's rival for Everell's love, Gardiner is Everell's rival for Hope. Gardiner's attempt to marry, seduce or rape the heroine becomes curiously analogous to his effort to divert New England from the Massachusetts Bay Colonists into the hands of his Catholic patron. But as Catharine Sedgwick portrays American history, neither European tyranny nor savage nature seduced America from her destiny. Thus Hope can no more marry Sir Philip than Everell can marry Magawisca.

Esther Downing, finally, very clearly represents narrow Puritan "artificiality" as contrasted with the "natural" (but not wild) Hope Leslie. "A godly, gracious maiden . . . approved by [her] elders," Esther is obviously contrasted with the rebellious Hope.

When Magawisca is jailed Everell asks Esther to help free the prisoner. Esther refuses, saying she lacks "Scripture warrant for interfering between the prisoner and the magistrates." Everell replies, "There must be warrant, as you call it, for sometimes resisting legitimate authority. . . . I should think the sternest conscience would permit you to obey the generous impulses of nature, rather than to render this slavish obedience to the letter of the law." It is Hope, of course, who follows the "generous impulses of nature" by freeing Magawisca. Thus the point of the novel-of-manners plot is clear. In choosing Hope over Esther, Everell is choosing nature over law, the heart over the head, resistance or rebellion over "slavish obedience."

Thus the various elements of Catharine Sedgwick's confusing plot are all related to her book's central, essentially simple, symbolic concern. She is defining American progress, the American "natural," as against wild nature, European tyranny and Puritan artificiality. The trouble with *Hope Leslie* is that the interrelation of the plot elements is often *only* symbolic. For instance, Esther and her novel-of-manners plot are never more than circumstantially related either to the Indians or to Sir Philip. Esther first appears long after the massacre, and— although the readers is told that she visits Magawisca daily in prison—she is never shown in conversation with an Indian. This plot-confusion appears most clearly in a scene that attempts to bring the novel-of-manners and Indian plots together. Hope has arranged to meet Magawisca and Faith on an island in Boston harbor, the home of a former servant of the Fletchers named Digby. Hope visits the island with Sir Philip, Esther and Everell. In Digby's parlor is enacted the climactic scene of the novel-of-manners plot. Digby brings up the subject of marriage between Everell and Hope, Hope corrects him, saying Everell loves Esther, and Everell is thus committed publicly to a profession of love for Esther. But as soon as the characters step outside (Esther remains within) they are in the romantic world of forest, Indians and even pirates. In this new world, Hope is not so much Emma as Florimel; she escapes from the Indians only to run into a pirate camp, jumps into a boat only to discover another of the pirates in it, and makes him take her ashore only by convincing him she is no mortal but rather his patron saint. While one cannot help being impressed with the fertility of Catharine Sedgwick's imagination and with her ingenuity in weaving her plots together circumstantially, the contrast between parlor and forest is simply too great for any true unity to be achieved. The roles of each character in the two worlds are so different as finally to overcome unity of character altogether. In the parlor we are concerned with Hope, Everell and Esther as the *ménage à trois* of the novel of manners. In the forest Esther is forgotten, and Hope and Everell join Magawisca and Sir Philip in forming the essential operatic quartet of romance.

Yet for all the confusion of its plot, the symbolic point of *Hope Leslie* remains manifestly clear. Miss Sedgwick is celebrating the historical movement from artificial to natural or, as romantic historians liked to express it, from "tyranny" to "liberty." This movement is most obviously represented in the contrast between the thwarted romance of William Fletcher and Alice, and the marriage of their children. In England sectarianism and paternal tyranny prevent the marriage of William and Alice. But in the next generation and in America, as Miss Sedgwick reads our history, it is possible for the forces of liberty to defeat the forces of tyranny.

It is a curious feature of Miss Sedgwick's version of New England history that the principal example of Puritan intoler-

ance in *Hope Leslie* is not the suppression of supposed heretics but opposition to the romance of hero and heroine. "Whatever gratified the natural desires of the heart," we are told of Winthrop's views, "was questionable, and almost everything that was difficult and painful assumed the form of a duty." Ludicrously enough, the great governor of Massachusetts spends most of his valuable time suppressing the rebellious high spirits of the hero and heroine. He takes Hope into his own home when he feels that Fletcher has been remiss in her upbringing. And he spends a whole chapter convincing the older Fletcher that Everell and Hope must not be allowed to marry, that Everell should marry the sober Esther Downing. For although Winthrop is generally presented rather favorably, he is nonetheless a representative of Puritan artificiality and must therefore oppose the natural values of the heroine.

And Hope Leslie *is* completely natural. For example, the artificial, fashion-conscious Aunt Grafton writes in a letter to Everell of her (Mrs. Grafton's) refusal to believe the color of a new dress to be *feuille morte*. "Hope," she writes, "thought to convince me I was wrong by matching it with a dead leaf from the forest. Was not that peculiar of Hope?" Even as a physical attribute Hope's naturalness is opposed to tyranny. . . . Hope's natural religion is opposed to the artificial sectarianism of the Puritans. "Like the bird that spreads his wings," Miss Sedgwick writes, "and soars above the limits by which each man fences his own narrow domain, she enjoyed the capacities of her nature, and permitted her mind to expand beyond the contracted boundaries of sectarian faith. Her religion was pure and disinterested." Hope, finally, as Esther notes, follows the dictates of her heart rather than the dictates of her elders. "You do allow yourself," objects Esther, "to much liberty of thought and word: you certainly know that we owe implicit obedience to our elders and superiors; we ought to be guided by their advice, and governed by their authority." "As to authority," Hope relies, "I would not be a machine to be moved at the pleasure of anybody that happened to be a little older than myself." Hope twice defies authority—albeit disinterestedly— by freeing a condemned prisoner from jail.

Hope is self-willed, but we are not to see her as selfish. The ex-servant Digby (whose status is significant) gives the proper reading to her desire to have her own way. "This having one's own way," he says of Hope, "is what everybody likes; it's the privilege we came to this wilderness world for." Hope's rebellious spirit, it would seem, is the spirit of democracy. "Times are changed—," Digby continues, "there is a new spirit in the world—chains are broken—fetters are knocked off—and the liberty set forth in the blessed Word is now felt to be every man's birth right." All this, Digby derives from "this having one's own way." Hope Leslie's "spirit," in short, is the spirit of American history. She *is* liberty; she *is* progress. In her, above all, Catharine Sedgwick embodied her view of the essential movement of American history. Hope's desire for personal liberty—her wish to have her own way— is precisely analogous to the political liberty Catharine Sedgwick saw as the essence of American history. In Catharine Sedgwick's conventional heroine, then, we can see the final example of how literary and historical conventions were fused in American historical romance. For all its shortcomings *Hope Leslie* remains, nonetheless, an invaluable example of the technique of the conventional American historical romancer. (pp. 216-21)

Michael Davitt Bell, "History and Romance Convention in Catharine Sedgwick's 'Hope Leslie'," in

American Quarterly, *Vol. XXII, No. 2, September, 1970, pp. 213-21.*

EDWARD HALSEY FOSTER   (essay date 1974)

[*In the following excerpt from his full-length biographical and critical study of Sedgwick, Foster briefly delineates her role in American literature.*]

To many mid-nineteenth-century critics who sought a thriving American literature, the novels of Catharine Maria Sedgwick seemed to be as significant as works by her distinguished contemporaries, James Fenimore Cooper, William Cullen Bryant, and Washington Irving. It is unlikely today that her didactic tales and her volumes of moral instruction for children will receive any serious consideration in studies of early American literature, but our more recent literary histories of the period should have reconsidered those early Sedgwick novels—notably *Redwood* and *Hope Leslie*—that were so highly praised both in this country and in England. However, surprisingly few modern critics appear to have heard of either novel, and even fewer seem to have read them. (p. v)

[In examining] Miss Sedgwick's works, I find that they deserve more attention from students of American literature than they usually receive. For one thing, Miss Sedgwick was a far more successful stylist than Cooper, the most famous of early American novelists. She also had a greater ability in creating believable women in her fiction than any of her contemporary American authors—a fact which should be of special interest in view of today's studies of women in literature. Indeed, although she could create women as vapid and uninteresting as some of Cooper's females—as, for example, the character of Gertrude Clarence in Miss Sedgwick's *Clarence*—her heroines in *Redwood* and in *Hope Leslie* are fully realized, flesh-and-blood women in an age when most women in fiction seldom seemed quite mortal. Furthermore, although she provided each of her heroines with a suitable husband, she wrote *Married or Single?* to show that marriage was not essential for the happiness of every woman—an opinion which was by no means universally accepted when the novel was published in 1857. (pp. v-vi)

[One can] also demonstrate Miss Sedgwick's importance as a novelist of manners. *Redwood* is in part a study of American manners, and both *Clarence* and *Married or Single?* involve criticism of the manners of aristocrats in New York. Furthermore, . . . much of Miss Sedgwick's fiction—not all of it distinguished as literature—provides important examinations of American civilization from the viewpoint of one who sincerely believed in the Jeffersonian ideal: an agricultural Republic controlled by an aristocracy of talent and virtue. Likewise, she welcomed Jacksonian emphasis on the common man; and *The Linwoods*—published in 1835 while Andrew Jackson was still in office—concludes with the marriage of the son of a poor farmer to the daughter of a New York aristocrat. Miss Sedgwick's Jeffersonian sentiments are at the center of *Clarence,* which contrasts the aristocracy of wealth with the aristocracy of talent and virtue.

In addition, . . . [Miss Sedgwick is important] as a regionalist—her abilities in detailing New England history and landscape as well as manners and customs. Throughout many of her novels and didactic tales, Miss Sedgwick made considerable use of her New England background. . . . [Yet] Miss Sedgwick was much more than a regionalist concerned only with New

England; *Redwood,* for example, introduces Southerners as well as Yankees among the central characters; and *Clarence* is about New York. Although Miss Sedgwick concentrated on New England, she was a writer with national as well as regional interests. (p. vi)

Hope Leslie and *Redwood* have been republished recently. . . , and a handful of studies of Miss Sedgwick's works have appeared during the last dozen or so years, but even her most important novels remain generally unknown to most students of literature. Her historical importance. . . is irrefutable; and at least two of her works, the republished *Redwood* and *Hope Leslie,* demand serious attention as literature. In brief, no American author of her time was more successful in the creation of women in fiction; few were her equals as novelists of manners; and, among her contemporaries, none sketched as credible a picture of Yankee New England. (p. vii)

> *Edward Halsey Foster, in his* Catharine Maria Sedgwick, *Twayne Publishers, Inc., 1974, 171 p.*

ADDITIONAL BIBLIOGRAPHY

Beach, Seth Curtis. "Catharine Maria Sedgwick." In his *Daughters of the Puritans: A Group of Brief Biographies,* pp. 1-39. Boston: American Unitarian Association, 1905.
    A biographical study of Sedgwick.

Birdsall, Richard D. "William Cullen Bryant and Catherine Sedgwick—Their Debt to Berkshire." *The New England Quarterly* XXVIII, No. 3 (September 1955): 349-71.
    Analyzes the influence of the Stockbridge area upon the creative output of Sedgwick and her friend Bryant.

———. *Berkshire County: A Cultural History.* New Haven: Yale University Press, 1959, 401 p.
    A discussion of Berkshire County, Massachusetts, where Sedgwick lived. Birdsall examines Sedgwick's works as an example of the writing inspired by the Berkshires; he also compares the area to the Lake District of England.

Kelley, Mary. "A Woman Alone: Catharine Maria Sedgwick's Spinsterhood in Nineteenth-Century America." *The New England Quarterly* LI, No. 2 (June 1978): 209-25.
    Compares the feminine ideal that Sedgwick professed in her fiction with the realities of her personal life.

Mintz, Steven. "Sister and Brother." In his *A Prison of Expectations: The Family in Victorian Culture,* pp. 147-87. New York: New York University Press, 1983.
    Analyzes Sedgwick's close relationship with her siblings.

Mitchell, Donald G. "Miss Catharine Sedgwick." In his *American Lands and Letters.* Vol. 1, *The Mayflower to Rip-Van-Winkle,* pp. 349-57. New York: Charles Scribner's Sons, 1901.
    Briefly discusses Sedgwick's role in the development of American literature.

Sedgwick, Henry Dwight. "Reminiscences of Literary Berkshire." *The Century Magazine* L, No. 4 (August 1895): 552-68.
    A discussion of the prominent literary figures who resided in or visited Stockbridge, Massachusetts, during Sedgwick's lifetime. The author of the article was her nephew.

Staehelin-Wackernagel, Adelheid. *The Puritan Settler in the American Novel before the Civil War.* The Cooper Monographs on English and American Language and Literature, edited by H. Lüdeke, vol. 7. Bern: Francke Verlag, 1961, 165 p.
    Contains numerous references to Sedgwick's novels as examples of literature about American colonial life.

Sarah Helen Whitman

1803-1878

(Also wrote under pseudonyms of Egeria and Helen) American poet, essayist, and critic.

Whitman is best known as the author of *Edgar Poe and His Critics,* a respected assessment of Poe's character and role in literary history. In this volume Whitman, who had been briefly engaged to Poe, sought to refute posthumous accusations defaming his work and personal life. Though *Edgar Poe and His Critics* did not silence his detractors, most commentators considered Whitman's work a sensitive and insightful defense of Poe. During the last decade of her life, Whitman further contributed to Poe scholarship by supplying critics and biographers with important information concerning the author. Thus, while her two collections of sentimental verse, *Hours of Life, and Other Poems* and *Poems,* are virtually forgotten, her thorough knowledge of Poe's life and works has assured a place for her in American literary history.

Whitman was born in Providence, Rhode Island, to Nicholas Power, a seaman, and his wife, Anna. When she was a young girl, Whitman was sent to live with an aunt on Long Island, where she attended a Quaker school and developed a strong interest in literature. Following graduation, she returned to Providence and began to compose verse. In 1824, she became engaged to John Winslow Whitman, an attorney and editor who encouraged her to publish her first poems in local periodicals. When they were favorably received, Whitman also began to write essays on literary figures for the New York *Tribune* and the Providence *Journal.* In 1828, she married Whitman and settled in Boston, but when her husband died in 1833, she returned to Providence.

After her husband's death, Whitman wrote poetry, published articles on such diverse topics as women's rights, the occult, and progressive education, and became active in the Transcendentalist movement. In 1848, she published an anonymous poem honoring Poe, whose work she had long admired, in the New York *Home Journal.* The two met shortly thereafter and, drawn together by their mutual interest in spiritualism and the supernatural, commenced a tumultuous courtship. When Poe proposed to Whitman—in a cemetery—she accepted, though she was uncertain about her decision. As a premarital condition, therefore, she insisted that he give up alcohol, and she also had legal documents drafted to ensure that Poe could not obtain her money. Whitman ended the engagement a month later when Poe arrived at her home in an inebriated state, but the two remained on friendly terms until his death in 1849. Whitman continued to contribute essays and poems to periodicals, also serving as an adviser to young writers. In 1853, she published *Hours of Life, and Other Poems,* which received praise for its light, sentimental verses and melodic rhyme schemes. A second collection of verse, *Poems,* which appeared posthumously, was similarly received. In reviewing these two works, early critics often cited Poe as an influence and hypothesized that many of the poems were about Whitman's romance with him. Though most modern commentators agree that Whitman's poetry is not particularly original, her technique is considered accomplished.

Whitman made her greatest contribution to literature when, angered by the vilification of Poe by his literary executor, the American critic Rufus Wilmot Griswold, and others, she undertook a defense of Poe's reputation. Griswold had written an obituary of Poe in the New York *Tribune* that depicted him as a bizarre and menacing character possessed of little talent. Shortly thereafter, Griswold also published forged portions of Poe's correspondence in an effort to further defame the author. In response to Griswold's attack, Whitman published *Edgar Poe and His Critics,* an assessment of Poe's life, works, and critical reputation that met with favorable reviews. Typical critical reactions included that of George William Curtis, who in 1860 called *Edgar Poe and His Critics* ''a criticism which is profound by the force of sympathy, and vigorous by its clear comprehension.'' Contemporary reviews also praised Whitman's objectivity, her familiarity with Poe's works, and her thorough knowledge of other biographical and critical studies of Poe. Virtually the only objection voiced was that Poe was too pathetic and strange an individual to merit reappraisal.

Whitman's last years were largely spent answering other scholars' inquiries about Poe. In 1873 John Ingram, an English biographer, contacted Whitman in search of information concerning the author. Their ensuing correspondence, which took place over five years and was later published as *Poe's Helen Remembers,* contains detailed analyses of many of Poe's writings and provides a wealth of material for the student of Poe. These letters also reveal the correspondents' mutual dependence on each other. Though Whitman was capable of being an unbiased critic of Poe, she also needed to prove to others that she had been Poe's great love. Ingram indulged her in this belief in order to obtain as much information as possible but, as he became more familiar with Whitman and knowledgeable about Poe, he adopted an attitude of arrogance and superiority. In a final instance of cruelty, Ingram sent Whitman an article he was about to publish, purportedly for her review, in which he disclosed that another woman had been Poe's "first and last love." Whitman had not known that she had shared Poe's affection and was devastated by this revelation. Despite the harshness of Ingram's actions, Whitman remained gracious and reviewed the article in a purely professional manner. Shortly after this episode, Whitman died at the age of seventy-five. Ironically, Ingram wrote her obituary.

Though Whitman's works are largely overlooked today, her *Edgar Poe and His Critics* is still considered just and insightful. For her unbiased treatment of Poe in this work and for her overall contribution to Poe studies, Whitman remains a minor but significant figure in American literary history.

(See also *Dictionary of Literary Biography*, Vol. I: *The American Renaissance in New England*.)

PRINCIPAL WORKS

Hours of Life, and Other Poems (poetry) 1853
Edgar Poe and His Critics (essay) 1860
Poems (poetry) 1879
Poe's Helen Remembers (letters) 1979

EDGAR ALLAN POE (poem date 1831)

[*The following poem, often considered Poe's greatest lyric, was written to a woman named Helen Stannard. Although it was first published in 1831, Poe later dedicated the verse to Whitman in 1848, saying that fate must have inspired him to write such a work.*]

> Helen thy beauty is to me
>   Like those Nicean barks of yore,
> That gently, o'er a perfumed sea,
>   The weary, wayworn wanderer bore
>   To his own native shore.
>
> On desperate seas long wont to roam,
>   Thy hyacinth hair, thy classic face,
> Thy Naiad airs have brought me home
>   To the glory that was Greece
> And the gradeur that was Rome.
>
> Lo! in you brilliant window-niche
>   How statue-like I see thee stand,
>   The agate lamp within thy hand,
> Ah! Psyche, from the regions which
>   Are Holy Land!

> *Edgar Allan Poe, "To Helen," in his* The Complete Works of Edgar Allan Poe, *edited by Nathan Haskell Dole, 1908. Reprint by Desmond Publishing Company, n.d., p. 60.*

GEORGE WILLIAM CURTIS (essay date 1854)

[*In the following excerpt from an article that first appeared in* Putnam's Monthly *in 1854, Curtis praises the originality of Whitman's poetry, especially her descriptions of nature. For additional commentary by Curtis, see excerpt dated 1860.*]

We have few collections of American verse so strongly individual as [*Hours of Life, and Other Poems*]; so permeated with that sincerity which instantly assures the reader that he is not enjoying the distillation, through the poet, of another's experience, but tastes, at first hand, the honey-dew which has not fallen upon other pages. Such fresh and direct inspiration from nature, compelling the singer to express not only the sentiment inspired by the landscape, but to describe the landscape itself, with a success so remarkable that it is at once song and picture,—such pure and holy and feminine feeling for all changing aspects of nature and the year, as if the singer's heart were a harp so delicate that even chasing sun and shadow swept it into music, and yet a feeling entirely untainted with sentimentality,—such profound and solemnized passion, breathing through every word, as if the poet's life were consecrated to some sublime sorrow, which was, in the truest sense, 'sanctified,'—such affluence of extensive and rare cultivation, everywhere indicated and nowhere obtruded,—are not often discovered in any volume of poems, and never before in those of an American woman.

In keen observation and delicate description of nature Mrs. Whitman resembles Bryant, except that there is a subtlety in her description as if it was derived less from observation of the spectacle and more from sympathy with the spirit. Hence her landscape painting has a glow, a tone, that we do not so deeply recognize in the other poet.

The few translations from the French and German are among the best in English literature, and several of the sonnets addressed to an unknown are only to be matched by the passionate and superb Portuguese sonnets of Mrs. Browning. (pp. ix-xi)

> *George William Curtis, in an extract in* Poems by Sarah Helen Whitman, *Houghton, Osgood and Company, 1879, pp. ix-xi.*

GEORGE RIPLEY (essay date 1854)

[*In the following excerpt from an article that first appeared in the New York* Tribune *in 1854, Ripley expresses admiration for Whitman's talents as a poet, pointing to her "individuality."*]

The principal poem in this volume [*Hours of Life*] is remarkable for the life-like reality with which it weaves the recollections of a profound and intense experience into the natural materials of song. Here are all the usual elements of poetry,—a passionate love of nature, an imagination equally brilliant and plastic, a temperament keenly alive to all beautiful inspirations and influences, a taste ripened and enriched by exquisite culture, and a facility and charm of expression, uniting spontaneous grace and freshness with classical finish. But it is not these qualities that form the peculiar distinction of the volume before us. Rich as it is in characteristics that would establish an enviable poetical fame for any writer, the vein of thought and sentiment which it opens in its leading piece gives it a stamp of individuality, as a revelation of the inner life, which well-nigh eclipses the subordinate felicities of the volume.

Every reader will be struck with the delicacy of touch which Mrs. Whitman brings to the representation of nature. She ha looked on the universe not merely with the artist's eye, but in the spirit of profound communion with its life, and with the passionate longing to wrest from it the solution of the 'eternal mystery.' (pp. xi-xii)

> *George Ripley, in an extract in* Poems *by Sarah Helen Whitman, Houghton, Osgood and Company, 1879, pp. xi-xii.*

THE SOUTHERN LITERARY MESSENGER   (essay date 1860)

[*In the following excerpt, the reviewer commends* Edgar Poe and His Critics *as a sympathetic and sensitive defense of the author.*]

[*Edgar Poe and His Critics*] breathes a spirit of the tenderest sympathy and compassion. It is the plea of a woman in behalf of a poor creature with whom the world dealt hardly, but who, walking, alas, sometimes staggering through the world's market-places without a sixpence in his pocket, though with glorious and regal fancies in his brain, was ever unsparing of his scorn and derision, and sowed a plentiful crop of hatreds and antagonisms which came to an abundant and bitter harvest. Criticism is disarmed by the broad and sunny charity of Mrs. Whitman;—"o'er the waves of a life long benighted and wild," her loving glance comes "like a soft golden calm o'er the sea;" and while she does not meet the special charges which were brought against Poe, she so invests his life and character with a light of her own, that we see him through a glamour it were seemingly cruel to dispel. While we cannot wholly adopt her estimate of the man, we can bear testimony to the earnestness and eloquence of her apology, and it will serve the cause of truth at least, so far, in showing that Edgar Allan Poe was not the worst man of his century.

> *A review of "Edgar Poe and His Critics," in* The Southern Literary Messenger, *n.s. Vol. IX, No. 3, March, 1860, p. 237.*

GEORGE WILLIAM CURTIS   (essay date 1860)

[*Here, Curtis lauds* Edgar Poe and His Critics *as an outstanding work of literary biography. For additional commentary by Curtis, see excerpt dated 1854.*]

In reading [*Edgar Poe and His Critics,* an] exquisitely tender, subtle, sympathetic, and profoundly appreciative sketch of Edgar Poe . . . , it is impossible not to remember the brave woman's arm thrust through the slide to serve as a bolt against the enemy. The praise and the blame which have been cast upon the life and genius of Poe have been almost fierce and frantic. By how many is he not still regarded as a heartless, unprincipled, shiftless vagabond? By how many is he not secretly worshiped and openly extolled as our only great, original poet? And this, at least, is true, that he has exercised more direct influence upon the form of our poetry than any of his contemporaries.

The author of this little book (it has only eighty pages), with an inexpressible grace, reserve, and tender, heroic charity—having a right which no other person has to speak, tells, in a simple, transparent, and quiet strain, what she thinks of his career and genius. She omits nothing; she forces nothing. It is no spotless Prince of fairy she delineates; but a fellow-man of ours, greatly gifted, suffering deeply, often from his own faults—stumbling in the dark ways where we all stumble, but still looking for light—not a model man, by any means, but not the fiend and inhuman being he has been so often represented.

In the delicate reticence of the book—in its tone on inward music, as if the singer were humming a melody beneath the song she sings—there is a perverse and peculiar charm. But it is not a eulogy. It is a criticism which is profound by the force of sympathy, and vigorous by its clear comprehension. Thus, we shall hardly have a finer statement of Poe's intellectual condition than this:

> Wanting in that supreme central force or faculty of the mind whose function is a God-conscious and God-adoring faith, Edgar Poe sought earnestly and conscientiously for such solution of the great problems of thought as were alone attainable to an intellect hurled from its balance by the abnormal preponderance of the analytical and imaginative faculties. It was to this very disproportion that we are indebted for some of those marvelous intellectual creations which, as we shall hope to prove, had an important significance, and an especial adaptation to the time.

It was Poe's mistake and misfortune to wage war upon his fellow-authors. In a series of papers upon the "Literati" he seems like a frenzied East Indian running a muck, with his swift, sharp, glittering crease in hand. But those of us who belong to an epoch just after his—who were not gashed or scored in his wild revels—who have no personal prejudices to appease, and only that charity in our hearts which combined genius and weakness and error must always command—we of the last decade must needs turn these pages with a singular interest and sadness; not without a secret prayer, perhaps, that when our little tasks are ended, and the stains we have left upon so many pages of our books, and our lives are pointed out to public contumely, some hand as firm and gentle as this may pull away the briers to plant rosemary where we lie.

> *George William Curtis, in a review of "Edgar Poe and His Critics," in* Harper's Weekly, *Vol. IV, No. 168, March 17, 1860, p. 163.*

THE KNICKERBOCKER   (essay date 1860)

[*This reviewer contends that* Edgar Poe and His Critics *is unlikely to improve Poe's poor reputation.*]

We were glad to learn that a friend of Poe, and that friend a talented woman, had assumed to defend his character from the accusations with which for ten years it has been associated. We opened [*Edgar Poe and His Critics*] eagerly, and read it at a single sitting. Alas! we were disappointed—sadly disappointed. It is a well-meant effort; but it will not do much more than awaken pity for the infatuated man, in whose behalf pity is thus solicited. It contradicts successfully a few of the more reckless assertions of some of Poe's critics, but it does not wipe out the inconsistencies and dishonorable records in the biography of Dr. Griswold. It magnifies Poe's wonderful genius; exhibits pictures of his singular brilliance in conversation; impresses the reader with a high sense of his exquisite sensitiveness to the beautiful, and his strange magnetic power over minds of kindred tendency; but it does not explain nor satisfactorily account for, his insensibility to moral principle, his utter disregard of truth, his ingratitude to friends, his petty revenges upon literary opponents, his impositions, private and public; in short, it leaves Edgar Allan Poe very much where it found him. After reading it, we turned to Dr. Griswold's memoir, and for the first time were able to peruse it without impatience and a sense of wrong to its subject. Mrs. Whitman's book will not change the public estimate of the singularly gifted man whose memory she desires to honor. We feel sad and disappointed that more cannot be said in vindication of the wayward career of this singular child of genius.

> *A review of "Edgar A. Poe and His Critics," in* The Knickerbocker, *Vol. LV, No. 4, April, 1860, p. 429.*

JOHN H. INGRAM (letter date 1874)

[*In the following excerpt from a letter to Whitman, Ingram offers several critical comments about Whitman's poem "A Pansy from the Grave of Keats." For additional commentary by Ingram, see the excerpt dated 1878.*]

As regards ["**A Pansy from the Grave of Keats**"], I am going to be audacious and make a few critical remarks, not as a critic but to show you how I have read it and appreciate its beauty— it is an amaranthine flower & deserves to be a "joy for ever." . . . If I may dare suggest a change, I would ask why not—in 26th line—have "a fading flush"? The alliterative sound would be improved & would not *flush* be more accordant with "morning gold" than *blush* . . .? *I fancy I should also rather read "The silver blaring* trumpets blow"—the alliteration is as good, & "snarling" seems scarcely so fit an adjective for the representative of a trumpet's sound. The last line but one—the penultimate—is weakened by the inversion—you know how Poe railed against such forms—and even at the risk of identical rhymes, I almost fancy—unless you find another rhyme such as "nought will sever," which is weak—I should read it "Lives the charmed life that lives for ever, A Beauty and a Joy forever." No! I don't like that—so let it remain a beauty and a joy that ne'er will wane to me. (pp. 68-9)

> *John H. Ingram, in a letter to Sarah Helen Whitman on March 11, 1874, in* Poe's Helen Remembers, *edited by John Carl Miller, University Press of Virginia, 1979, pp. 68-71.*

JOHN H. INGRAM (essay date 1878)

[*The following excerpt is from an obituary that appeared in the* London Athenaeum *on 20 July 1878 in which Ingram eulogizes Whitman. For additional commentary by Ingram, see excerpt dated 1874.*]

Information of the death of Mrs. Sarah Helen Whitman, the American author and the heroine of Edgar Poe's lines, "To Helen" [see excerpt dated 1831], has just reached me. She died on the 27th ultimo, at her native city of Providence, wherein the greater portion of her seventy-five years of life had been spent, and where her ancestors, the Powers, had resided for two centuries or more. To the world at large she is merely known as an author of considerable talent and rich and varied reading, but, to those acquainted with the secret of her inner life, she will always be remembered as a brave-hearted woman, who for many years endured unrepiningly a condition of continuous self-sacrifice and anxiety, only paralled by the intermittent martyrdom of Charles Lamb. It could not have failed to comfort her in her last hours to know that the near and dear one for whom she had suffered so much had preceded her by some months in her journey to the grave.

A large portion of Mrs. Whitman's literary labour, consisting chiefly of critical articles and fugitive verse, is unedited, and she steadfastly refused to have republished during her lifetime the two volumes by which she is best known in the world of letters. In 1853 she collected and published at Providence a thick volume of verse, entitled *Hours of Life and Other Poems,*

which not only attracted much attention on account of its melancholy beauty, but because many of the pieces were devoted to the memory of Edgar Poe. In 1860 Mrs. Whitman drew much more marked attention to her admiration for the author of "The Raven" by the publication of *Edgar Poe and His Critics.* This impassioned defence of her celebrated countryman created a profound impression in American coteries. The reputation which her little book so materially helped to clear from slander and misrepresentation was consistently and devotedly cherished by her to the last, and this is no improper moment for me to acknowledge that to Mrs. Whitman's unwearying kindness and cooperation is due a considerable portion of the data upon which my vindicatory *Memoir* of Poe is based.

> *John H. Ingram, "Mrs. Sarah Helen Whitman," in* Poe's Helen Remembers, *edited by John Carl Miller, University Press of Virginia, 1979, p. 506.*

ARTHUR HOBSON QUINN (essay date 1941)

[*An early twentieth-century American critic, editor, and biographer, Quinn was a strong advocate for his native literature before it gained widespread appreciation. In the following excerpt, drawn from Quinn's* Edgar Allan Poe: A Critical Biography, *Quinn offers a sympathetic assessment of* Edgar Poe and His Critics.]

[While *Edgar Poe and His Critics* is] a refutation of Griswold's "remorseless violations of the trust confided in him," Mrs. Whitman did not reply to his charges by detailed examination of them. She proceeded, instead, to paint a portrait of Poe with the brush of spiritual insight, drawn in true perspective through her intimate knowledge of the man, and made vivid by the colors of sympathy of which only a poet-critic could know the values. When she had finished, Edgar Poe in his real nature was there for the eyes of those who wish a true picture, and to such as these, the scandals and half-truths drop, helpless to blind or to confuse.

Mrs. Whitman put her finger at once on the puzzling differences between the various portraits of Poe. They "are valueless as a portrait," she says, "to those who remember the unmatched glory of his face when roused from its habitually introverted and abstracted look by some favorite theme, or profound emotion." This inner light ... shines for us only in his characters, in the lover of Eleanora, of Ulalume, of Annabel Lee.

Mrs. Whitman's tribute to Virginia, and to Poe's devotion to his wife, culminated in her sentence, often paraphrased, "It was to this quiet haven in the beautiful spring of 1846, when the fruit trees were all in bloom and the grass in its freshest verdure, that he brought his Virginia to die." Next comes the sympathetic interpretation of "Ulalume," which identifies the memory that challenges "Astarte's bediamonded crescent" with the spirit of Virginia.

Poe could not have asked for a better interpretation of his poems than Mrs. Whitman offered. Rejecting the criticism, not yet entirely hushed, that his creations were the results of mere artistic skill, and not genuine outgrowths of the inward life of a poet, she said:

> It is not to be questioned that Poe was a consummate master of language—that he had sounded all the secrets of rhythm—that he understood and availed himself of all its resources; the balance and poise of syllables—the alternations of emphasis and cadence—of vowel-sounds and consonants—and all the metrical sweetness of "phrase and metaphrase." Yet this consummate art was in him united with a rare

simplicity. He was the most genuine of enthusiasts, as we think we shall presently show. His genius would follow no leadings but those of his own imperial intellect. With all his vast mental resources he could never write an occasional poem, or adapt himself to the taste of a popular audience. His graver narratives and fantasies are often related with an earnest simplicity, solemnity, and apparent fidelity, attributable, not so much to a deliberate artistic purpose, as to that power of vivid and intense conception that made his dreams realities, and his life a dream. (pp. 688-89)

In several of her critical interpretations, it seems as though the author of "Eleonora" himself were speaking:

> It can hardly have escaped the notice of the most careless reader that certain ideas exercised over him the power of fascination. They return, again and again, in his stories and poems and seem like the utterances of a mind possessed with thoughts, emotions, and images of which the will and the understanding take little cognizance. In the delineation of these, his language often acquires a power and pregnancy eluding all attempts at analysis. It is then that by a few miraculous words he evokes emotional states or commands pictorial effects which live for ever in the memory and form a part of its eternal inheritance. No analysis can dissect—no criticism can disenchant them.

She reprinted the greater "To Helen," which Griswold had omitted, with singular stupidity, from his edition, and analyzed many of his poems with a judgment that still repays the student of Poe. A flash of inspiration, for example, concludes her study of his use of terror as a motive:

> Yet, as out of mighty and terrific discords noblest harmonies are sometimes evolved, so through the purgatorial ministries of awe and terror, and through the haunting Nemesis of doubt, Poe's restless and unappeased soul was urged on to the fulfilment of its appointed work—groping out blindly towards the light, and marking the approach of great spiritual truths by the very depth of the shadow it projected against them.

Mrs. Whitman, like a true critic, is not always in agreement with Poe's own beliefs. A masterly analysis of the growth of scepticism in English and American literature, gives Poe as its climax. It is too elaborate for quotation, and she goes too far in her statement that "the unrest and faithlessness of the age culminated in him." But this survey leads to a brilliant interpretation of the climax of *Eureka*, which was evidently not too much of a puzzle for *her*. The temptation to quote Mrs. Whitman must constantly be resisted, but who has better understood Poe's spiritual domain than the writer of these lines:

> Edgar Poe's dreams were assuredly often presageful and significant, and while he but dimly apprehended through the higher reason the truths which they foreshadowed, he riveted public attention upon them by the strange fascination of his style, the fine analytical temper of his intellect, and, above all, by the weird splendors of his imagination, compelling men to read and to accredit as *possible truths* his most marvellous conceptions. He often spoke of the imageries and incidents of his inner life as more vivid and veritable than those of his outer experience. We find in some pencilled notes appended to a manuscript copy of one of his later poems the words, "all that I have here expressed was actually present to me. Remember the mental condition which gave rise to Ligeia'—recall

A facsimile of the original manuscript of Whitman's poem "Arcturus."

the passage of which I spoke, and observe the coincidence." With all the fine alchymy of his subtle intellect he sought to analyze the character and conditions of this introverted life. "I regard these visions," he says, "even as they arise, with an awe which in some measure moderates or tranquillizes the ecstacy—I so regard them through a conviction that this ecstacy, in itself, is of a character supernal to the human nature—*is a glimpse of the spirit's outer world*."

With such an able defence of Poe in existence, how was it that the myths concerning his character persisted? Unfortunately, the circulation of Mrs. Whitman's volume was limited, although it was reprinted in 1885, and her method of defence, while admirable, did not meet categorically the slanders of Griswold. (pp. 690-91)

> *Arthur Hobson Quinn, "The Recoil of Fate," in his* Edgar Allan Poe: A Critical Biography, *D. Appleton-Century Company, Incorporated, 1941, pp. 642-96.*

ORAL SUMNER COAD   (essay date 1949)

[In the following excerpt from his introduction to Edgar Poe and His Critics, *Coad points to Whitman's work as the first significant defense of Poe's reputation.]*

[In *Edgar Poe and His Critics*, Mrs. Whitman offered] the first authoritative and convincing reply of any length to Griswold and those who took their cue from him. Drawing upon her intimate knowledge of the maligned writer's personality, this high-minded woman chose to disregard for the most part his infirmities of character and to stress instead his devotion to his wife, his courtesy, his rare gifts as a conversationalist, his social charm, and his innate rectitude. And particularly did she invite her readers to attend to that aspect of Poe—the only important aspect of any man of letters—his power of literary creation. Here she emphasized, quite rightly, the fundamental sincerity of his compositions—"genuine outgrowths of the inward life." And with acute insight she saw him, as many later critics have failed to see him, not as a lonely genius wandering forlorn in an alien and uncomprehended world—"out of space, out of time"—but rather as a man in a considerable degree created by his age and in no small measure an expression of it. In general Mrs. Whitman attempted to replace the strange, demonic enigma that Poe had become in the popular fancy, thanks in part to Griswold, by an appealing and understandable human being—a human being who was not without his tragic faults, but who was at the same time a great genius. It is the simple truth to say that Mrs. Whitman wrote the first sound and informed appraisal of this complex personality, and one that still commands respect for its independence, its insight, and its balance, and not less for the generosity of spirit that called it into being. (pp. 18-19)

> *Oral Sumner Coad, in an introduction to* Edgar Poe and His Critics *by Sarah Helen Whitman, edited by Oral Sumner Coad, Rutgers University Press, 1949, pp. 7-25.*

WILLIAM GOLDHURST   (essay date 1980)

[*In the following excerpt from a review of* Poe's Helen Remembers, *Goldhurst analyzes the letters and discusses what they reveal about Whitman's personality.*]

Poe's Helen Remembers is the record, complete and uncut, of the correspondence that ensued between Ingram and Sarah Helen Whitman, a literary lady of Providence, Rhode Island. She who had been Poe's confidante and fiancé in the late 1840s now became one of the English biographer's most enthusiastic allies in his campaign to set the record straight. The letters these two exchanged over a four-year period are lengthy, detailed and sometimes tedious, the editor of the present volume having no alternative (in so highly sensitive an area of American literary history) but to publish every word as written.

Yet there is drama enough for the general reader, and a feast for Poe enthusiasts. Both correspondents are interesting characters who, amid a thicket of reference of dates, names, places and events connected with Poe, reveal their own strengths and weaknesses. Both suffered from severe psychosomatic ailments and were tormented by the mental instability of close relatives. Each felt a need for emotional support from the other, and each, towards the end, flew into a rage over imagined slights from the other. The long-drawn-out exchange of letters is also enlivened by the elegant articulateness both writers employed even when dashing off afterthoughts and postscripts.

The Whitman-Ingram correspondence has an unplanned structure which builds up interest as it progresses. Persistent questions in Poe biography are raised, fussed over, debated and in some cases solved. Whitman tantalizes Ingram with promises to tell the true story of why she and Poe broke off their engagement. Ingram, meanwhile, widens his information network and begins to publish his findings. It becomes clear towards the conclusion that Ingram's devotion to Poe has had the unpleasant side effect of giving him an acute case of conceit. When he began his project the world seemed divided into two camps—those who sympathized with Poe and those who sided with Griswold. Over the years this polarization had shifted its boundaries. Now there were only Ingram on one side and the "worthless scamps" who dared to write anything about Poe on the other.

Throughout the book we tend to admire Poe's Helen as a person and Ingram as a scholar. She emerges as witty, humane, level-headed (except for a weakness for spiritualism and mediums),

and judicious in her advice. She urges Ingram to be more temperate in his reviews and to be more circumspect in accepting as authentic the dubious testimony he received from some of Poe's admirers.

The Whitman-Ingram correspondence concludes on an especially sad note. Ingram sends her an article he has written revealing Poe's passionate interest in another New England woman he was courting during the same period he was engaged to Whitman. In all those intervening years, this was her first inkling that she had had a rival for Poe's affections.

> *William Goldhurst, "Haunted by the Spirit of Edgar Allan Poe," in* Book World—The Washington Post, *April 27, 1980, p. 11.*

JOHN E. REILLY   (essay date 1982)

[*Reilly analyzes Whitman's perception of Poe as detailed in* Edgar Poe and His Critics, *discussing the reasons why her work was occasionally dismissed by students of Poe.*]

Sarah Helen Whitman's reputation has rested principally with students of Poe, especially with his biographers, and we have not served her well. We have made too much of her as "Poe's Helen," as that eccentric Providence widow who, six years older than Poe, came literally within hours of marrying him in December of 1848 and who passed the remainder of her long life cherishing his memory and serving his early biographers both as a living resource and as a kind of research assistant. What we have not made enough of, or perhaps what we have not bothered to discover, is that Mrs. Whitman was much more than just another of those literary ladies who owe their little immortality to having dallied with the author of "The Raven." Mrs. Whitman was a charming, a witty, and a gifted person; she was a talented poet and an unusually perceptive literary critic. . . . [She] was, perhaps, the only contemporary of Poe who recognized some of the larger dimensions of his work, and she was one of only a very few persons in the nineteenth century who managed to achieve a clear understanding of his place within the context of his own age. The best evidence for these claims in her behalf rests in two works she wrote about Poe. One is a [Valentine's Day] poem composed even before she met him. The other is her little book, **Edgar Poe and His Critics**, published ten years after his death. Seen in their proper light, these items should establish Mrs. Whitman as at least a candidate for the most underrated critic of Poe in the nineteenth century.

Mrs. Whitman's interest in Poe's work, her "fascination," as she called it, went back four or five years before she met him for the first time in September of 1848. The events leading up to that meeting were set in motion by an anonymous poetic message she addressed to him earlier in the year. . . . Playfully addressed to Poe in the character of his "grim and ancient Raven," the valentine is, in effect, a fan letter from an unusually impressionable and perceptive reader whose "vagrant fancy" has been haunted by Poe and his work. . . . But the melancholy and gloom in Poe did more than charm Mrs. Whitman's "vagrant fancy." They suggested to her a profound pessimism pervading his work, a pessimism which she saw as a sullen repudiation of the facile and foolish optimism of his contemporaries, especially the optimisim of those celebrants of progress through technology who promoted the absurdity that their Age of Iron could somehow be redeemed, a Golden Age somehow restored, through the alchemy of steam and machinery. Mrs. Whitman makes the point cleverly through the language of her bird metaphor: Poe is our grim and solemn raven among a flock of mere popinjays and parrots. . . . This is a remarkable assessment, especially so when we consider that it was made when most of Poe's contemporaries, even such renowned commentators as Emerson, Walt Whitman, James Russell Lowell, and (later) Henry James, could make little more of him than "the jingle man," an electric light, forty percent fudge, and an index to adolescence. The depths Mrs. Whitman glimpsed in Poe even before she met him in 1848 were not to become widely recognized until well into the following century. (pp. 120-22)

[*Edgar Poe and His Critics*], really no more than an essay of eighty-odd pages, has seldom been taken seriously by students of Poe, presumably for the same reasons that they have seldom taken Mrs. Whitman herself seriously. What probably puts off most readers is the Spiritualism which pervades the book. We tend to dismiss the whole performance as naive and eccentric. Mrs. Whitman, however, took her Spiritualism seriously. She had been interested in the occult for most of her adult life, and when Spiritualism appeared on the scene, coinciding, as it happened, with her romance with Poe, she was swept up in the Movement. Indeed, her interest in Spiritualism and her association with Poe developed together and became so closely intertwined in her mind that she was convinced he was frequently in touch with her even after his death and was personally closer to her then than he had been before "passing over," to use a favorite expression of the Movement. On her part, of the dozen or so poems she devoted to Poe after October of 1849, more than half are addressed to him directly, not as apostrophes but as genuine messages.

It is one of the paradoxes of Mrs. Whitman's mind as well as one of the fascinations about her personality that her eccentricities seem not to have impaired her judgment. Though they may color or even obscure an issue, they tend not to distort or to misrepresent it. And so it is with *Edgar Poe and His Critics*. If we can ignore, discount, penetrate, or outflank its Spiritualism, the reward is well worth the effort. What we will discover is an explanation of what Mrs. Whitman calls "the true point of view from which his genius should be regarded." She recognizes that Poe can be understood not as a detached and alien spirit dwelling somewhere out of Space and out of Time, but that he can be known best only as a product of his own age, as one who shared what she identifies as the "pervading scepticism of the time."

Mrs. Whitman traces the origins of Poe's peculiar genius to a disorder in his personality and to a crisis in his personal life. The disorder was both a deficiency in what she calls "that supreme central force or faculty of the mind, whose function is a God-conscious and God-adoring faith" and an "abnormal preponderance of the analytical and imaginative faculties." Though this may sound like just so much phrenological claptrap, her message unscrambled is that Poe was an intrinsically skeptical soul whose fate it was to have been born into an inherently skeptical age. The personal crisis that Mrs. Whitman singles out is his relationship to Jane Stith Stanard, the young Richmond matron who inspired his first "To Helen" poem [see excerpt dated 1831]. Having been the object of his intense adolescent passion, her premature death precipitated a crisis in the life of young Edgar Poe. Poe himself told the story to Mrs. Whitman during one of his visits with her in Providence. Obviously moved by the impact the experience had had upon him, she retells the story in *Edgar Poe and His Critics,* dwelling heavily upon the significance of young Poem's nocturnal visits

to Mrs. Stanard's grave. "These solitary church-yard vigils, with all their associated memories, present," she concludes, "a key to much that seem strange and abnormal in the poet's after life."

As Mrs. Whitman describes it, Poe's crisis resembles the crisis of youth in Walt Whitman's "Out of the Cradle Endlessly Rocking," where the agony of confronting the loss of a loved one not only thrusts the child into a world of mortality, it transforms him into a poet, into the "outsetting bard." But where Walt Whitman's bard is "a chanter of pains and joys," Poe is a chanter of pain only, and his is a world quite unlike the one Walt Whitman celebrates. Mrs. Whitman describes this painful world and Poe's place in it in the climactic passages of *Edgar Poe and His Critics:*

> When Poe's genius began to unfold itself the age was moving feverously and restlessly through processes of transition and development which seemed about to unsettle all things, yet, gave no clear indication of whither they were leading us.
>
> . . . . .
>
> The negation of Carlyle, and the boundless affirmation of Emerson, served but to stimulate without satisfying the intellect. The liberal ethics of Fourier, with his elaborate social economies and systems of petrified harmony, were leading his disciples through forlorn enterprises to hopeless failures. A "divine dissatisfaction" was everywhere apparent. De Quincey saw something fearful and portentous in the vast accessions to man's physical resources that marked the time, unaccompanied by any improvement in psychal and spiritual knowledge. Goethe had made his great dramatic poem an expression of the soul's craving for a knowledge of spiritual existences—

(pp. 123-24)

Mrs. Whitman recorded her own estimate of *Edgar Poe and His Critics* in a letter she wrote to John H. Ingram in September 1874. Responding to what presumably was a proposal that she revise her book, she protests not only that she is "well satisfied with [it] just as it is" but that she likes "it better & better as the years go by." So far as its reception is concerned, Mrs. Whitman prophesies that "its significance as throwing light on one dominant phase of Poe's genius will be better understood in the near future." Just what she meant by "near future" is not clear. Perhaps she had in mind that the truth about Poe would be revealed at the apocalypse which she and other Spiritualists believed to be at hand. Or being aware of the renewed interest in Poe in the 1870's, especially the sympathy of biographers such as Ingram who sought to challenge Rufus Griswold, perhaps she felt that the world was almost ready to appreciate what she had known all along and recorded in her book. Whatever she meant, Mrs. Whitman was no prophet. Although the book was reprinted in 1885 (seven years after her death), again in 1949, and even now is available through a reprint house, critical appreciation remains what it has been since the earliest reviews—tepid toward the book and patronizing toward Mrs. Whitman. Arthur Hobson Quinn has come closest to giving *Edgar Poe and His Critics* the kind of serious consideration Mrs. Whitman sought, but even Quinn was unwilling to accompany her as far as she seeks to guide us into the labyrinth of Poe's genius [see excerpt dated 1941]. "She goes too far," Quinn protests, but Quinn is mistaken. It is not that Mrs. Whitman goes too far but that she has been far ahead all along. And why not? After all, she did get the jump on the rest of us with her little valentine back in 1848! (pp. 125-26)

John E. Reilly, "Sarah Helen Whitman as a Critic of Poe," in The University of Mississippi Studies in English, *n.s. Vol. III, 1982, pp. 120-27.*

ADDITIONAL BIBLIOGRAPHY

Bruce, Philip Alexander. "Edgar Allan Poe and Mrs. Whitman." *The South Atlantic Quarterly* XII, No. 2 (April 1913): 129-40.
    A detailed discussion of Poe and Whitman's courtship.

Halsband, Robert. Review of *Edgar Poe and His Critics*, by Sarah Helen Whitman. *The Saturday Review* XXXIII, No. 1 (7 January 1950): 25.
    Briefly describes Whitman's approach to her subject in *Edgar Poe and His Critics*.

Poe, Edgar Allan. *The Last Letters of Edgar Allan Poe to Sarah Helen Whitman*. Edited by James A. Harrison. New York: G. P. Putnam's Sons, 1909, 50 p.
    A cumulation of Poe's letters to Whitman.

Ticknor, Caroline. *Poe's Helen*. New York: Charles Scribner's Sons, 1916, 292 p.
    A biography of Whitman based on her correspondence.

Woolf, Virginia. "Poe's Helen." In her *Granite and Rainbow*, pp. 225-28. New York: Harcourt, Brace & World, 1958.
    Analyzes the relationship between Poe and Whitman.

Appendix

The following is a listing of all sources used in Volume 19 of *Nineteenth-Century Literature Criticism*. Included in this list are all copyright and reprint rights and acknowledgments for those essays for which permission was obtained. Every effort has been made to trace copyright, but if omissions have been made, please let us know.

THE EXCERPTS IN NCLC, VOLUME 19, WERE REPRINTED FROM THE FOLLOWING PERIODICALS:

American Literature, v. XXXI, May, 1959. Copyright © 1959, renewed 1987 Duke University Press, Durham, NC. Reprinted by permission of the publisher.

The American Monthly Magazine, v. VII, January, 1836.

American Quarterly, v. XV, Summer, 1963 for "Irving's Headless Hessian: Prosperity and the Inner Life" by Robert A. Bone; v. XXII, September, 1970 for "History and Romance Convention in Catharine Sedgwick's 'Hope Leslie'" by Michael Davitt Bell. Copyright 1963, 1970, American Studies Association. Both reprinted by permission of the publisher and the respective authors.

American Quarterly Review, v. XXII, September, 1837.

The Analectic Magazine, n.s. v. V, March, 1815.

The Athenaeum, n. 737, December 11, 1841; n. 2160, March 20, 1869; v. 108, September 5, 1896.

The Atlas, April 14, 1833.

Augustan Review, v. 2, May, 1816.

Australian Literary Studies, v. 2, June, 1965 for "The Redemptive Theme in 'His Natural Life'" by L. T. Hergenhan. Reprinted by permission of the publisher and the author.

The Australian Quarterly, v. XIV, June, 1942.

Book World—The Washington Post, April 27, 1980. © 1980, *The Washington Post*. Reprinted by permission of the publisher.

The Boston Pilot, February 22, 1890.

The Boston Quarterly Review, v. II, July, 1839.

The British Critic, v. II, December, 1793; v. XIV, July, 1799.

British Lady's Magazine, and Monthly Miscellany, v. 4, September, 1816.

The British Quarterly Review, v. VI, November, 1847.

Bucknell Review, v. XII, May, 1964. Reprinted by permission of the publisher.

Bulletin of The John Rylands Library, v. 23, April, 1939.

Bulletin: National Theatre Conference, v. XII, November, 1950.

The Calcutta Review, v. LXXXIV, January, 1887.

The Canadian-American Review of Hungarian Studies, v. V, Fall, 1978. Copyright © 1978 by the Hungarian Readers' Service Inc. All rights reserved. Reprinted by permission of the publisher.

The Champion, March 31, 1816.

College English, v. 16, December, 1954.

The Conservative Review, v. III, March, 1900.

The Cornhill Magazine, v. CXI, May, 1915.

Critical Quarterly, v. 4, Winter, 1962 for "Jane Austen's 'Emma' " by Malcolm Bradbury. Reprinted by permission of the author.

The Critical Review, Melbourne, n. 9, 1966 for "Jane Austen's Originality: 'Emma' " by T. B. Tomlinson. Reprinted by permission of the author.

The Dublin Review, v. VIII, second quarter, 1840.

The Eclectic Review, n.s. v. X, September, 1841.

The Edinburgh Monthly Review, v. IV, September, 1820.

The Edinburgh Review, v. XIV, April, 1809; v. XXXI, March, 1819.

ELH, v. 21, March, 1954.

The English Review, v. XLVI, June, 1928.

English Studies, Netherlands, v. L, 1969. © 1969 by Swets & Zeitlinger B. V. Reprinted by permission of the publisher.

Enlightenment Essays, v. IX, 1978. Copyright 1978 by *Enlightenment Essays.* Reprinted by permission of the publisher.

Études Slaves et Est-Européenes, v. VI, Spring-Summer, 1961. Copyright 1961. Reprinted by permission of the publisher.

The Explicator, v. IV, February, 1946.

Fortnightly Review, v. LXVII, June, 1887.

The Fortnightly Review, v. LVIII, September 1, 1892.

Fraser's Magazine for Town & Country, v. I, June, 1830; v. XLII, December, 1833.

The French Review, v. XXVIII, January, 1955; v. XXXI, December-January, 1957-58./ v. LI, May, 1978. Copyright 1978 by the American Association of Teachers of French. Reprinted by permission of the publisher.

French Studies, v. XXXVI, October, 1982. Reprinted by permission of the publisher.

Godey's Lady's Book, v.XXXIII, September, 1846.

Harper's Bazar, v. XXXIII, June 30, 1900.

Harper's Weekly, v. IV, March 17, 1860.

Indian Horizons, v. XXXIV, 1985. Reprinted by permission of the publisher.

Interpretations of Poetry and Religion, 1900.

Journal of Commonwealth Literature, v. VII, June, 1972 for "The Pattern of 'His Natural Life': Conflict, Imagery, and Theme as Elements of Structure" by Harold J. Boehm. Copyright by the author. Reprinted by permission of Hans Zell Publishers, an imprint of K. G. Saur Limited.

The Knickerbocker, v. LV, April, 1860.

Lippincott's Magazine of Literature, Science and Education, v. VI, October, 1870.

The Literary Review, Fairleigh Dickinson University, v. 2, Summer, 1959 for "The Humiliation of Emma Woodhouse" by Mark Schorer. Copyright © 1959 by Fairleigh Dickinson University. Reprinted by permission of the publisher and the author.

The Literary and Scientific Repository, v. IV, May, 1822.

The Literary World, n. 140, October 6, 1849.

Littell's Living Age, v. LXV, February 23, 1889.

The Living Age, v. CCXCIV, August 25, 1917.

The London and Westminster Review, v. VI, October, 1837- January, 1838.

Meanjin, v. 5, March, 1946.

The Methodist Review, v. CXIV, January, 1931.

Modern Language Notes, v. LXVII, February, 1952.

The Monthly Review, London, v. XXIX, August, 1799; v. XCIII, October, 1820; v. CI, May, 1823.

The Nation, New York, v. LXII, March 19, 1896; v. CIX, December 6, 1919; v. 155, October 3, 1942; v. 159, July 1, 1944.

Neohelicon, v. X, 1983 for "Of Cockroaches and 'Civilizing' Hungary: Imre Madách as an Aristophanic Satirist" by Dieter P. Lotze. © copyright 1983 by Akademiai Kiado. Reprinted by permission of the Literary Estate of Dieter P. Lotze.

The New Hungarian Quarterly, v. V, Winter, 1964. © *The New Hungarian Quarterly,* 1964. Reprinted by permission of The Hungarian Academy of Sciences.

The New Monthly Magazine, v. LXVI, March, 1836.

The Nineteenth Century, v. XXVIII, July, 1890.

Nineteenth-Century Fiction, v. 21, June, 1966 for "Aesthetic Vision and the World of 'Emma' " by David Lee Minter. © 1966 by The Regents of the University of California. Reprinted by permission of The Regents and author./ v. IV, December, 1949. Copyright 1949, renewed 1977 by The Regents of the University of California. Reprinted by permission of The Regents.

Nineteenth-Century French Studies, v. II, Spring-Summer, 1974. © 1974 by T. H. Goetz. Reprinted by permission of the publisher.

The North American Review, n.s. v. 14, April, 1822; v. XX, April, 1825; v. XXVI, April, 1828; v. XXXII, January, 1831; v. XLII, January, 1836.

The Open Court, v. XXXVIII, January, 1924.

PMLA, v. LXXI, September, 1956.

Proceedings of the Massachusetts Historical Society, December, 1859.

The Quarterly Review, v. I, May, 1809; v. XXV, April, 1821; v. CXLVII, January, 1879; v. CCXVII, 1912; v. CCXXVIII, July, 1917.

Research Studies, v. 36, December, 1968 for "Washington Irving: A Grace Note on 'The Pride of the Village' " by George Monteiro. Reprinted by permission of the author.

The Rice Institute Pamphlet, v. XVII, October, 1931.

The Saturday Review, London, v. 42, August 12, 1876.

Scribner's Monthly, v. XI, April, 1876.

The Sewanee Review, v. XIV, April, 1906.

The Slavonic Review, v. IX, December, 1930.

Southern Folklore Quarterly, v. XIX, September, 1956.

The Southern Literary Messenger, v. II, December, 1835; v. III, April, 1837; v. XVII, April, 1851; n.s. v. IX, March, 1860.

The Southern Quarterly Review, v. VIII, July, 1845.

Southwest Review, v. 72, Autumn, 1987 for "Flaubert's 'L'education sentimentale' and the Problem of Reading 'History': Endless Beginnings" by Jefferson Humphries. © 1987 by the author. Reprinted by permission of the author.

The Speaker, v. I, 1890.

The Spectator, v. VIII, August 15, 1835; v. XLVIII, November 13, 1875; v. 172, June 16, 1944.

Studies in Philology, v. XXXVII, October, 1940.

Studies in Romanticism, v. 10, Winter, 1971. Copyright 1971 by the Trustees of Boston University. Reprinted by permission of the publisher.

Symposium, v. XXVI, Winter, 1972. Copyright © 1972 Helen Dwight Reid Educational Foundation. Reprinted with permission of the Helen Dwight Reid Educational Foundation, published by Heldref Publications, 4000 Albemarle Street, N.W., Washington, DC 20016.

Temple Bar, v. 71, May, 1884.

The Times Literary Supplement, n. 1781, March 21, 1936.

Tinsley's Magazine, v, III, January, 1869.

The United States Literary Gazette, v. I, April 1, 1824; v. I, February 15, 1825.

The University of Mississippi Studies in English, n.s. v III, 1982. Copyright © 1982 The University of Mississippi. Reprinted by permission of the publisher.

University of Toronto, v. XV, January, 1946.

Vanity Fair, v. I, November 28, 1868; v. CLXXX, December 11, 1875.

Victorian Poetry, v. 22, Summer, 1984. Reprinted by permission of the publisher.

Visible Language, v. XIX, Autumn, 1985. © 1985 Visible Language. Reprinted by permission of the publisher.

The Weekly Critical Review, v. II, August 27 and September 3, 1903.

The Western Monthly Review, v. I, September, 1827.

The Westminster Review, n.s. v. IX, January, 1856.

The Wordsworth Circle, v. VII, Autumn, 1976. © 1976 Marilyn Gaull. Reprinted by permission of the editor.

The Yale Review, v. XXXVII, September, 1947. Copyright 1947, by Yale University. Reprinted by permission of the editors.

The Yearbook of English Studies, v. 13, 1983. © Modern Humanities Research Association 1983. All rights reserved. Reprinted by permission of the Editor and the Modern Humanities Research Association.

THE EXCERPTS IN NCLC, VOLUME 19, WERE REPRINTED FROM THE FOLLOWING BOOKS:

Altick, Richard D., and James F. Loucks II. From *Browning's Roman Murder Story: A Reading of "The Ring and the Book."* University of Chicago Press, 1968. © 1968 by The University of Chicago. All rights reserved. Reprinted by permission of the publisher and the authors.

Armstrong, Isobel. From "Browning and the 'Grotesque' Style," in *The Major Victorian Poets: Reconsiderations.* Edited by Isobel Armstrong. Routledge & Kegan Paul, 1969. © Routledge and Kegan Paul Ltd. 1969. Reprinted by permission of Routledge & Kegan Paul PLC.

Austen, Jane. From *Jane Austen's Letters to Her Sister Cassandra and Others.* Edited by R. W. Chapman. Second edition. Oxford University Press, Oxford, 1952.

Austen, Jane. From *The Works of Jane Austen: Minor Works, Vol. VI.* Edited by R. W. Chapman. Revised edition. Oxford University Press, London, 1975. Reprinted by permission of Oxford University Press.

Babb, Howard S. From *Jane Austen's Novels: The Fabric of Dialogue.* Ohio State University Press, 1962. © 1962 by the Ohio State University Press. All rights reserved. Reprinted with permission of the publisher.

Banerjee, Sunil Kumar. From *Bankim Chandra: A Study of His Craft.* Firma K. L. Mukhopadhyay, 1968. © First Edition, 1968 Firma K. L. Mukhopadhyay. Reprinted by permission of the publisher.

Barrett, E. B. From *The Letters of Elizabeth Barrett Browning, Vol. I.* Edited by Frederic G. Kenyon. Smith, Elder, & Co., 1897.

Barrett, Elizabeth Barrett. From a letter in *The Letters of Robert Browning and Elizabeth Barrett Browning: 1845-1846, Vol. I.* Harper & Brothers, Publishers, 1899.

Bart, Benjamin F. From *Flaubert.* Syracuse University Press, 1967. Copyright © 1967 by Syracuse University Press. All rights reserved. Reprinted by permission of the publisher.

Bays, Gwendolyn. From *The Orphic Vision: Seer Poets from Novalis to Rimbaud.* University of Nebraska Press, 1964. Copyright © 1964 by the University of Nebraska Press. All rights reserved. Reprinted by permission of the publisher.

Bloom, Harold. From "Introduction: Reading Browning," in *Robert Browning: A Collection of Critical Essays.* Edited by Harold Bloom and Adrienne Munich. Prentice-Hall, 1979. © 1979 by Prentice-Hall, Inc. All rights reserved. Excerpted by permission of Prentice-Hall, Inc., Englewood Cliffs, NJ.

Bose, S. K. From *Bankim Chandra Chatterji.* Publications Division, Ministry of Information and Broadcasting, 1974. Reprinted by permission of the author.

Bowden, Mary Weatherspoon. From *Washington Irving.* Twayne, 1981. Copyright 1981 by Twayne Publishers. All rights reserved. Reprinted with the permission of Twayne Publishers, a division of G. K. Hall & Co., Boston.

Brandes, Georg. From *Main Currents in Nineteenth Century Literature: Naturalism in England, Vol. IV.* Translated by Mary Morison. William Heinemann, 1905.

Brandes, Georg. From *Main Currents in Nineteenth Century Literature: The Romantic School in France, Vol. V.* Translated by Diana White and Mary Morison. William Heinemann, 1904.

Brombert, Victor. From *The Novels of Flaubert: A Study of Themes and Techniques.* Princeton University Press, 1966. Copyright © 1966 by Princeton University Press. All rights reserved. Reprinted with permission of the publisher.

Brooks, Gladys. From *Three Wise Virgins.* E. P. Dutton & Co., Inc., 1957.

Burrows, J. F. From *Jane Austen's "Emma."* Sydney University Press, 1968. Copyright 1968 Text and Bibliography by J. F. Burrows. Reprinted by permission of the author.

Byrne, Desmond. From *Australian Writers.* Richard Bentley and Son, 1896.

Canby, Henry Seidel. From *The Short Story in English.* Henry Holt and Company, 1909.

Chesterton, G. K. From *Robert Browning.* The Macmillan Company, 1903.

Clark, T. W. From "Bengali Prose Fiction Up to Bankimcandra," in *The Novel in India: Its Birth and Development.* Edited by T. W. Clark. University of California Press, 1970, Allen & Unwin, 1970. © George Allen & Unwin Ltd. 1970. All rights reserved. Reprinted by permission of University of California Press. In Canada by Unwin Hyman Ltd.

Clarke, James Stanier. From a letter in *Jane Austen's Letters to Her Sister Cassandra and Others.* By Jane Austen, edited by R. W. Chapman. Second edition. Oxford University Press, Oxford, 1952.

Coad, Oral Sumner. From an introduction to *Edgar Poe and His Critics.* By Sarah Helen Whitman, edited by Oral Sumner Coad. Rutgers University Press, 1949. Copyright 1949 by the Trustees of Rutgers College. Renewed 1977 by Robert M. Frisch. All rights reserved. Reprinted by permission of the publisher.

Courthope, W. J. From *A History of English Poetry: The Romantic Movement in English Poetry, Effects of the French Revolution, Vol. VI*. Macmillan and Co., Limited, 1910.

Cowie, Alexander. From *The Rise of the American Novel*. American Book Company, 1948.

Crayon, Geoffrey. From *Bracebridge Hall; or, The Humourists*. N.p., 1822.

Curtis, George William. From an extract from *Poems*. By Sarah Helen Whitman. Houghton, Osgood and Company, 1879.

Das Gupta, Jayanta Kumar. From *A Critical Study of the Life and Novels of Bankimcandra*. The Calcutta University, 1937.

Demarest, David P., Jr. From " 'Reductio Ad Absurdum': Jane Austen's Art of Satiric Qualification," in *Six Satirists*. By David P. Demarest, Jr. and others. Carnegie Institute of Technology, 1965. Copyright © 1965 by The Department of English, Carnegie Institute of Technology. Reprinted by permission of the author.

DeVane, William Clyde, Jr. From *Browning's Parleyings: The Autobiography of a Mind*. Yale University Press, 1927.

Dickens, Charles. From a letter in *The Life of Charles Dickens: 1842-1852, Vol. II*. By John Forster. Chapman and Hall, 1873.

Dixon, W. Macneile. From *Thomas Campbell: An Oration*. Jackson, Wylie and Co., 1928.

Dutt, Romesh Chunder. From *The Literature of Bengal*. Revised edition. Thacker Spink & Co., 1895.

Edgeworth, Maria. From a letter in *Life and Letters of Catharine M. Sedgwick*. Edited by Mary E. Dewey. Harper & Brothers, Publishers, 1871.

Edgeworth, Maria. From a letter in *Maria Edgeworth: A Literary Biography*. By Marilyn Butler. Oxford at the Clarendon Press, 1972. © Oxford University Press, 1972. Reprinted by permission of Oxford University Press.

Elliott, Brian. From *Marcus Clarke*. Oxford at the Clarendon Press, 1958.

Faguet, Émile. From *Flaubert*. Translated by Mrs. R. L. Devonshire. Houghton Mifflin Company, 1914.

Ferrier, Susan. From a letter in *Memoir and Correspondence of Susan Ferrier, 1782-1854*. Edited by John A. Doyle. J. Murray, 1898.

Flaubert, Gustave. From *The Letters of Gustave Flaubert: 1857-1880*. Edited and translated by Francis Steegmuller. Cambridge, Mass.: The Belknap Press of Harvard University Press, 1982. Copyright © 1982 by Francis Steegmuller. All rights reserved. Excerpted by permission of the publishers.

Foster, Edward Halsey. From *Catharine Maria Sedgwick*. Twayne, 1974. Copyright 1974 by Twayne Publishers. All rights reserved. Reprinted with the permission of Twayne Publishers, Inc., a division of G. K. Hall & Co., Boston.

Frazer, R. W. From *A Literary History of India*. T. Fisher Unwin, 1898.

George, Albert J. From *Short Fiction in France: 1800-1850*. Syracuse University Press, 1964. Copyright © 1964 by Syracuse University Press. All rights reserved. Reprinted by permission of the publisher.

Ghosh, J. C. From *Bengali Literature*. Oxford University Press, London, 1948.

Gillie, Christopher. From *Character in English Literature*. Barnes & Noble, Inc., 1965. © Christopher Gillie, 1965. Reprinted by permission of the publisher.

Giraud, Raymond. From *The Unheroic Hero in the Novels of Stendhal, Balzac and Flaubert*. Rutgers University Press, 1957.

Goldsmith, Anthony. From an introduction to *Sentimental Education*. By Gustave Flaubert, translated by Anthony Goldsmith. J. M. Dent & Sons Ltd., 1941.

Goncourt, Edmond de, and Jules de Goncourt. From a journal entry in *Paris and the Arts, 1851-1896: From the Goncourt Journal*. Edited and translated by George J. Becker and Edith Philips. Cornell University Press, 1971. Copyright © 1971 by Cornell University. All rights reserved. Used by permission of the publisher, Cornell University Press.

Green, H. M. From *A History of Australian Literature, Pure and Applied, 1789-1923, Vol. I*. Angus and Robertson, 1961. © Dorothy Green, 1962, 1984. Reprinted by permission of Angus and Robertson Publishers.

Groom, Bernard. From *On the Diction of Tennyson, Browning and Arnold*. Oxford at the Clarendon Press, 1939. Reprinted by permission of Oxford University Press.

Harris, Frank. From *Contemporary Portraits*. M. Kennerley, 1915. Copyright 1920 by Frank Harris. Renewed 1943 by Nellie Harris. Reprinted by permission of the author.

Hazlitt, William. From *Lectures on the English Poets*. N.p., 1818.

Hearn, Lafcadio. From *On Poets*. R. Tanabe, T. Ochiai, I. Nishizaki, eds. The Hokuseido Press, 1934.

Hedges, William L. From "Washington Irving: 'The Sketch Book of Geoffrey Crayon, Gent.','' in *Landmarks of American Writing*. Edited by Hennig Cohen. Basic Books, 1969. Copyright © 1969 by Basic Books, Inc., Publishers. Reprinted by permission of the publisher.

Hergenhan, Laurie. From *Unnatural Lives: Studies in Australian Fiction*. University of Queensland Press, 1984. © Laurence Hergenhan, 1983. Reprinted by permission of the publisher.

Hopkins, Gerard Manley, S.J. From *The Correspondence of Gerard Manley Hopkins and Richard Watson Dixon*. Edited by Claude Colleer Abbott. Oxford University Press, London, 1935.

Hunt, Leigh. From *Leigh Hunt's Literary Criticism*. Edited by Lawrence Huston Houtchens and Carolyn Washburn Houtchens. Columbia University Press, 1956.

Ingram, John H. From a letter to Sarah Helen Whitman on March 11, 1874 and "Mrs. Sarah Helen Whitman," in *Poe's Helen Remembers*. Edited by John Carl Miller. University Press of Virginia, 1979. Copyright © 1979 by the Rector and Visitors of the University of Virginia. Reprinted by permission of the publisher.

Isaacs, J. From *An Assessment of Twentieth-Century Literature*. Secker & Warburg, 1951.

James, Henry. From a preface to *A Century of French Romance: Madame Bovary, Vol. X*. Edited by Edmund Gosse. William Heinemann, 1902.

Johnson, E. D. H. From *The Alien Vision of Victorian Poetry*. Princeton University Press, 1952. Copyright 1952, © 1980 renewed by Princeton University Press. Reprinted with permission of the publisher.

Kabir, Humayun. From *The Bengali Novel*. Firma K. L. Mukhopadhyay, 1968. © Humayun Kabir. Reprinted by permission of the publisher.

Kettle, Arnold. From *An Introduction to the English Novel: To George Eliot, Vol. I*. Second edition. Hutchinson University Library, 1967. Reprinted by permission of the publisher.

Kohut, George Alexander. From "Emerich Madách, (1823-1864)," in *Library of the World's Best Literature: Ancient and Modern*. Edited by Charles Dudley Warner and others. R. S. Peale and J. A. Hill, 1896.

Langbaum, Robert. From *The Poetry of Experience: The Dramatic Monologue in Modern Literary Tradition*. Random House, 1957.

Lerner, Laurence. From *The Truthtellers: Jane Austen, George Eliot, D. H. Lawrence*. Chatto & Windus, 1967. Copyright © 1967 by Laurence Lerner. Reprinted by permission of the author.

Levin, Harry. From *The Gates of Horn: A Study of Five French Realists*. Oxford University Press, 1963. Copyright © 1963 by Harry Levin. Reprinted by permission of Oxford University Press, Inc.

Lodge, David. From an introduction to *Emma*. By Jane Austen, edited by David Lodge. Oxford University Press, London, 1971. Introduction © Oxford University Press, 1971. Reprinted by permission of Oxford University Press.

Lotze, Dieter P. From *Imre Madách*. Twayne, 1981. Copyright 1981 by Twayne Publishers. All rights reserved. Reprinted with the permission of Twayne Publishers, a division of G. K. Hall & Co., Boston.

Lukács, Georg. From *The Theory of the Novel: A Historico-Philosophical Essay on the Forms of Great Epic Literature*. Translated by Anna Bostock. The M.I.T. Press, 1971. Translation © The Merlin Press, 1971. Reprinted by permission of the publisher.

MacAndrew, Elizabeth. From *The Gothic Tradition in Fiction*. Columbia University Press, 1979. Copyright © 1979 Columbia University Press. All rights reserved. Used by permission of the publisher.

Macy, John. From *The Spirit of American Literature*. Doubleday, Page & Company, 1913. Copyright 1913 by Doubleday & Company, Inc. Copyright renewed 1940 by William M. Rockwell, as literary executor to the Estate of John Macy. All rights reserved.

Madách, Imre. From a letter in *Imre Madách*. By Dieter P. Lotze. Twayne, 1981. Copyright 1981 by Twayne Publishers. All rights reserved. Reprinted with the permission of Twayne Publishers, a division of G. K. Hall & Co., Boston.

Madoff, Mark. From "The Useful Myth of Gothic Ancestry," in *Studies in Eighteenth-Century Culture, Vol. 8*. Edited by Roseann Runte. American Society for Eighteenth-Century Studies, 1979. Copyright © 1979 American Society for Eighteenth- Century Studies. All rights reserved. Reprinted by permission of the publisher.

Mill, John Stuart. From "Pauline," in *Robert Browning: A Collection of Critical Essays*. Edited by Philip Drew. Methuen & Co. Ltd., 1966. Reprinted by permission of Methuen & Co. Ltd.

Miller, J. Hillis. From *The Disappearance of God: Five Nineteenth-Century Writers*. Cambridge, Mass.: The Belknap Press of Harvard University Press, 1963. Copyright © 1963 by the President and Fellows of Harvard College. All rights reserved. Excerpted by permission of the publishers.

Symons, Arthur. From *The Romantic Movement in English Poetry*. Archibald Constable & Co., Ltd., 1909.

Tagore, Sir Rabindranath. From *My Reminiscences*. Translated by Surendranath Tagore. Macmillan, New York and London, 1917. Copyright, 1916 an 1917 by Macmillan Publishing Company. Renewed 1944 by Subir Tagore. All rights reserved. Reprinted with permission of Macmillan Publishing Company. In Canada by Macmillan, London and Basingstoke.

Thibaudet, Albert. From *French Literature from 1795 to Our Era*. Translated by Charles Lam Markmann. Funk & Wagnalls, 1968. Copyright, 1938 by Librarie Stock, Paris. Translation copyright © 1967 by Harper & Row, Publishers, Inc. All rights reserved. Reprinted by permission of Harper & Row, Publishers, Inc.

Thorlby, Anthony. From *Gustave Flaubert and the Art of Realism*. Bowes & Bowes, 1956.

Trainer, James. From an introduction to *The Old English Baron: A Gothic Story*. By Clara Reeve, edited by James Trainer. Oxford University Press, London, 1967. Introduction © Oxford University Press 1967. Reprinted by permission of Oxford University Press.

Turnell, Martin. From *The Novel in France: Mme de la Fayette, Laclos, Constant, Stendhal, Balzac, Flaubert, Proust*. Hamish Hamilton, 1950.

Wannan, Bill. From an introduction to *A Marcus Clarke Reader*. Edited by Bill Wannan. Lansdowne Press, 1963. Reprinted by permission of the publisher.

Weldon, Fay. From *Letters to Alice on First Reading Jane Austen*. Michael Joseph/Rainbird, 1984. Copyright © 1984 by Fay Weldon. All rights reserved. Reprinted by permission of the publisher.

Welsh, Sister Mary Michael, O.P. From *Catharine Maria Sedgwick: Her Position in the Literature and Thought of Her Time Up to 1860*. The Catholic University of America, 1937.

Wilding, Michael. From "The Short Stories of Marcus Clarke," in *Bards, Bohemians, and Bookmen: Essays in Australian Literature*. Edited by Leon Cantrell. University of Queensland Press, 1976. © University of Queensland Press 1976. Reprinted by permission of the publisher.

Williams, D. A. From "G. Flaubert: 'Sentimental Education' (1869)," in *The Monster in the Mirror: Studies in Nineteenth-Century Realism*. Edited by D. A. Williams. Oxford University Press, 1978. © University of Hull 1978. All rights reserved. Reprinted by permission of University of Hull.

Williams, Orlo, M.C. From *Some Great English Novels: Studies in the Art of Fiction*. Macmillan and Co., Limited, 1926.

Wilson, Edmund. From *The Triple Thinkers: Twelve Essays on Literary Subjects*. Revised edition. Oxford University Press, Inc., 1948. Copyright 1938, 1948 by Edmund Wilson. Copyright renewed 1956, 1971 by Edmund Wilson, and 1976 by Elena Wilson, Executrix of the Estate of Edmund Wilson. Reprinted by permission of Farrar, Straus and Giroux, Inc.

Winegarten, Renee. From *Writers and Revolution: The Fatal Lure of Action*. New Viewpoints, 1974. Copyright © 1974 by Renee Winegarten. Reprinted by permission of the publisher.